STRATEGIC MANAGEMENT
Competitiveness & Globalization
Concepts and Cases
12e

Michael A. Hitt
Texas A&M University
and
Texas Christian University

R. Duane Ireland
Texas A&M University

Robert E. Hoskisson
Rice University

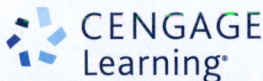

CENGAGE
Learning®

Australia • Brazil • Japan • Korea • Mexico • Singapore • Spain • United Kingdom • United States

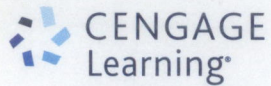
CENGAGE
Learning®

Strategic Management: Competitiveness & Globalization: Concepts and Cases, 12e

Michael A. Hitt, R. Duane Ireland, and Robert E. Hoskisson

Vice President, General Manager, Social Science & Qualitative Business: Erin Joyner

Product Director: Jason Fremder

Senior Product Manager: Scott Person

Content Developer: Tara Singer

Product Assistant: Brian Pierce

Marketing Director: Kristen Hurd

Marketing Manager: Emily Horowitz

Marketing Coordinator: Christopher Walz

Senior Content Project Manager: Kim Kusnerak

Manufacturing Planner: Ron Montgomery

Production Service: Cenveo Publisher Services

Senior Art Director: Linda May

Cover/Internal Designer: Tippy McIntosh

Cover Image: © RomanOkopny/Getty Images

Intellectual Property

    Analyst: Diane Garrity

    Project Manager: Sarah Shainwald

Strategic Focus: © RomanOkopny/Getty Images

Watercolor opener: © BerSonnE/Getty Images

Library of Congress Control Number: 2015955692

ISBN: 978-1-305-50214-7

Cengage Learning
20 Channel Center Street
Boston, MA 02210
USA

Cengage Learning is a leading provider of customized learning solutions with employees residing in nearly 40 different countries and sales in more than 125 countries around the world. Find your local representative at **www.cengage.com.**

Cengage Learning products are represented in Canada by Nelson Education, Ltd.

To learn more about Cengage Learning Solutions, visit **www.cengage.com**

Purchase any of our products at your local college store or at our preferred online store **www.cengagebrain.com**

Printed in Canada
Print Number: 01   Print Year: 2016

To My Family:

I love each and every one of you. Thank you for all of your love and support.

— **MICHAEL, DAD, PAPA**

To Mary Ann:

"Now everyone dreams of a love lasting and true." This was my dream that you have completely fulfilled. Thank you for all of the love, support, and encouragement throughout our life together.

— **R. DUANE IRELAND**

To Kathy:

My love for you is eternal, and I hope that we can be eternally together. Thanks for all the support and love you've given me throughout my life.

— **BOB**

Brief Contents

Contents

7: Merger and Acquisition Strategies 204

Opening Case: Mergers and Acquisitions: Prominent Strategies for Firms Seeking to Enhance Their Performance 205

Part 4: Case Studies C-1

Preface

Our goal in writing each edition of this book is to present a new, up-to-date standard for explaining the strategic management process. To reach this goal with the 12th edition of our market-leading text, we again present you with an intellectually rich yet thoroughly practical analysis of strategic management.

With each new edition, we work hard to achieve the goal of maintaining the standard that we established for presenting strategic management knowledge in a readable style. To prepare for each new edition, we carefully study the most recent academic research to ensure that the content about strategic management that we present to you is up to date and accurate. In addition, we continuously read articles appearing in many different and widely read business publications (e.g., *Wall Street Journal, Bloomberg Businessweek, Fortune, Financial Times, Fast Company,* and *Forbes,* to name a few). We also study postings through social media (such as blogs) given their increasing use as channels of information distribution. By studying a wide array of sources, we are able to identify valuable examples of how companies are using (or not using) the strategic management process. Though many of the hundreds of companies that we discuss in the book will be quite familiar, some will likely be new to you. One reason for this is that we use examples of companies from around the world to demonstrate the globalized nature of business operations. To maximize your opportunities to learn as you read and think about how actual companies use strategic management tools, techniques, and concepts (based on the most current research), we emphasize a lively and user-friendly writing style. To facilitate learning, we use an Analysis-Strategy-Performance framework that is explained in Chapter 1 and referenced throughout the book.

Several *characteristics* of this 12th edition of our book are designed to enhance your learning experience:

- First, we are pleased to note that this book presents you with the most comprehensive and thorough coverage of strategic management that is available in the market.
- The research used in this book is drawn from the "classics" as well as the most recent contributions to the strategic management literature. The historically significant "classic" research provides the foundation for much of what is known about strategic management, while the most recent contributions reveal insights about how to effectively use strategic management in the complex, global business environment in which firms now compete. Our book also presents you with many up-to-date examples of how firms use the strategic management tools, techniques, and concepts that prominent researchers have developed. Indeed, although this book is grounded in the relevant theory and current research, it also is strongly application oriented and presents you, our readers, with a large number of examples and applications of strategic management concepts, techniques, and tools. In this edition, for example, we examine more than 600 companies to describe the use of strategic management. Collectively, no other strategic management book presents you with the *combination* of useful and insightful *research* and *applications* in a wide variety of organizations as does this text.

Company examples you will find in this edition range from large U.S.-based firms such as Apple, Amazon.com, McDonald's, Starbucks, Walmart, Walt Disney, General Electric, Intel, American Express, Coca-Cola, Google, Target, United Technologies, Kellogg, DuPont, Marriott, and Whole Foods. In addition, we examine firms based in countries other than the United States such as Sony, Aldi, Honda, Tata Consultancy, Alibaba, IKEA, Lenova, Luxottica, and Samsung. As these lists suggest, the firms examined in this book compete in a wide range of industries and produce a diverse set of goods and services.

- We use the ideas of many prominent scholars (e.g., Ron Adner, Rajshree Agarwal, Gautam Ahuja, Raffi Amit, Africa Arino, Jay Barney, Paul Beamish, Peter Buckley, Ming-Jer Chen, Russ Coff, Rich D'Aveni, Kathy Eisenhardt, Gerry George, Javier Gimeno, Luis Gomez-Mejia, Melissa Graebner, Ranjay Gulati, Don Hambrick, Connie Helfat, Amy Hillman, Tomas Hult, Dave Ketchen, Dovev Lavie, Yadong Luo, Shige Makino, Costas Markides, Anita McGahan, Danny Miller, Will Mitchell, Margie Peteraf, Michael Porter, Nandini Rajagopalan, Jeff Reuer, Joan Ricart, Richard Rumelt, David Sirmon, Ken Smith, Steve Tallman, David Teece, Michael Tushman, Margarethe Wiersema, Oliver Williamson, Mike Wright, Anthea Zhang, and Ed Zajac) to shape the discussion of *what* strategic management is. We describe the practices of prominent executives and practitioners (e.g., Mary Barra, Jack Ma, Reed Hastings, Howard Schultz, John Mackey, Yang Yuanqing, Angela Ahrendt, Marilyn Hewson, Jeff Immelt, Ellen Kullman, Elon Musk, Paul Pullman, Li Ka-Shing, Karen Patz, and many others) to help us describe *how* strategic management is used in many types of organizations.

The authors of this book are also active scholars. We conduct research on a number of strategic management topics. Our interest in doing so is to contribute to the strategic management literature and to better understand how to effectively apply strategic management tools, techniques, and concepts to increase organizational performance. Thus, our own research is integrated in the appropriate chapters along with the research of numerous other scholars, some of whom are noted above.

In addition to our book's *characteristics,* there are some specific *features* and *revisions* that we have made in this 12th edition that we are pleased to highlight for you:

- **New Opening Cases and Strategic Focus Segments** We continue our tradition of providing all-new Opening Cases and Strategic Focus segments! Many of these deal with companies located outside North America. In addition, all of the company-specific examples included in each chapter are either new or substantially updated. Through all of these venues, we present you with a wealth of examples of how actual organizations, most of which compete internationally as well as in their home markets, use the strategic management process for the purpose of outperforming rivals and increasing their performance.
- **Twenty Cases** are included in this edition. Offering an effective mix of organizations headquartered or based in North America and a number of other countries as well, the cases deal with contemporary and highly important topics. Many of the cases have full financial data (the analyses of which are in the Case Notes that are available to instructors). These timely cases present active learners with opportunities to apply the strategic management process and understand organizational conditions and contexts and to make appropriate recommendations to deal with critical concerns. These cases can also be found in MindTap.
- **New Mini-Cases** have been added that demonstrate how companies deal with major issues highlighted in the text. There are 13 of these cases, one for each chapter, although some of them can overlap with other chapter content. Students will like their conciseness, but they likewise provide rich content that can serve as a catalyst for individual or group analysis and class discussion. Each Mini-Case is followed by a set of questions to guide analysis and discussion.

- **More than 1,200 new references** from 2014 and 2015 are included in the chapters' endnotes. We used the materials associated with these references to support new material added or current strategic management concepts that are included in this edition. In addition to demonstrating the classic and recent research from which we draw our material, the large number of references supporting the book's contents allow us to integrate cutting-edge research and thinking into a presentation of strategic management tools, techniques, and concepts.
- **New content** was added to several chapters. Examples include the strategic ecosystem such as the one used by Apple with its "ecosystem of app producers" (Chapters 1 and 4), sustainable physical environment (Chapter 3), mentoring new CEOs (Chapter 12), strategic leadership in family owned/controlled companies (Chapter 12), and acquisitions and innovation, open innovations, and managing the innovation portfolio (Chapters 4 and 13).
- **Updated information** is provided in several chapters. Examples include the stakeholder host communities (Chapter 1), all new and current demographic data (e.g., ethnic mix, geographic distribution) that describe the economic environment (Chapter 2), the general partner strategies of private equity firms (Chapter 7), information from the *World Economic Forum Competitiveness Report* regarding political risks of international investments (Chapter 8), updates about corporate governance practices being used in different countries (Chapter 10), updated data about the number of internal and external CEO selections occurring in companies today (Chapter 12), a ranking of countries by the amount of their entrepreneurial activities (Chapter 13), and a ranking of companies on their total innovation output (Chapter 13).
- **An Exceptional Balance** between current research and up-to-date applications of that research in actual organizations located throughout the world. The content has not only the best research documentation but also the largest number of effective real-world examples to help active learners understand the different types of strategies organizations use to achieve their vision and mission and to outperform rivals.

Supplements to Accompany This Text

Instructor Website. Access important teaching resources on this companion website. For your convenience, you can download electronic versions of the instructor supplements from the password-protected section of the site, including Instructor's Resource Manual, Comprehensive Case Notes, Cognero Testing, Word Test Bank files, PowerPoint® slides, and Video Segments and Guide. To access these additional course materials and companion resources, please visit www.cengagebrain.com.

- **Instructor's Resource Manual.** The Instructor's Resource Manual, organized around each chapter's knowledge objectives, includes teaching ideas for each chapter and how to reinforce essential principles with extra examples. This support product includes lecture outlines and detailed guides to integrating the MindTap activities into your course with instructions for using each chapter's experiential exercises, branching, and directed cases. Finally, we provide outlines and guidance to help you customize the collaborative work environment and case analysis project to incorporate your approach to case analysis, including creative ideas for using this feature throughout your course for the most powerful learning experience for your class.
- **Case Notes.** These notes include directed assignments, financial analyses, and thorough discussion and exposition of issues in the case. Select cases also have assessment

rubrics tied to National Standards (AACSB outcomes) that can be used for grading each case. The Case Notes provide consistent and thorough support for instructors, following the method espoused by the author team for preparing an effective case analysis.

- **Cognero.** This program is easy-to-use test-creation software that is compatible with Microsoft Windows. Instructors can add or edit questions, instructions, and answers, and select questions by previewing them on the screen, selecting them randomly, or selecting them by number. Instructors can also create and administer quizzes online, whether over the Internet, a local area network (LAN), or a wide area network (WAN).
- **Test Bank.** Thoroughly revised and enhanced, test bank questions are linked to each chapter's knowledge objectives and are ranked by difficulty and question type. We provide an ample number of application questions throughout, and we have also retained scenario-based questions as a means of adding in-depth problem-solving questions. The questions are also tagged to National Standards (AACSB outcomes), Bloom's Taxonomy, and the Dierdorff/Rubin metrics.
- **PowerPoints®.** An all-new PowerPoint presentation, created for the 12th edition, provides support for lectures, emphasizing key concepts, key terms, and instructive graphics.
- **Video Segments.** A collection of 13 BBC videos has been included in the MindTap Learning Path. These new videos are short, compelling, and provide timely illustrations of today's management world. They are available on the DVD and Instructor website. Detailed case write-ups, including questions and suggested answers, appear in the Instructor's Resource Manual and Video Guide.

Cengage Learning Write Experience 3.0. This new technology is the first in higher education to offer students the opportunity to improve their writing and analytical skills without adding to *your* workload. Offered through an exclusive agreement with Vantage Learning, creator of the software used for GMAT essay grading, Write Experience evaluates students' answers to a select set of assignments for writing for voice, style, format, and originality. We have trained new prompts for this edition!

Micromatic Strategic Management Simulation (for bundles only). The Micromatic Business Simulation Game allows students to decide their company's mission, goals, policies, and strategies. Student teams make their decisions on a quarter-by-quarter basis, determining price, sales and promotion budgets, operations decisions, and financing requirements. Each decision round requires students to make approximately 100 decisions. Students can play in teams or play alone, compete against other players or the computer, or use Micromatic for practice, tournaments, or assessment. You can control any business simulation element you wish, leaving the rest alone if you desire. Because of the number and type of decisions the student users must make, Micromatic is classified as a medium to complex business simulation game. This helps students understand how the functional areas of a business fit together without being bogged down in needless detail and provides students with an excellent capstone experience in decision making.

Smartsims (for bundles only). MikesBikes Advanced is a premier strategy simulation providing students with the unique opportunity to evaluate, plan, and implement strategy as they manage their own company while competing online against other students within their course. Students from the management team of a bicycle manufacturing company make all the key functional decisions involving price, marketing, distribution, finance, operations, HR, and R&D. They formulate a comprehensive strategy, starting with their existing product, and then adapt the strategy as they develop new products for emerging markets. Through the Smartsims easy-to-use interface, students are taught the cross-functional disciplines of business and how the development and implementation of strategy involves these disciplines. The competitive nature of MikesBikes encourages involvement and learning in a way that no other teaching methodology can, and your students will have fun in the process!

MindTap. MindTap is the digital learning solution that helps instructors engage students and helps students become tomorrow's strategic leaders. All activities are designed to teach students to problem-solve and think like leaders. Through these activities and real-time course analytics, and an accessible reader, MindTap helps you turn cookie cutter into cutting edge, apathy into engagement, and memorizers into higher-level thinkers.

Customized to the specific needs of this course, activities are built to facilitate mastery of chapter content. We've addressed case analysis from cornerstone to capstone with a functional area diagnostic of prior knowledge, directed cases, branching activities, multimedia presentations of real-world companies facing strategic decisions, and a collaborative environment in which students can complete group case analysis projects together synchronously.

Acknowledgments

We express our appreciation for the excellent support received from our editorial and production team at Cengage Learning. We especially wish to thank Scott Person, our Senior Product Manager, and Tara Singer, our Content Developer. We are grateful for their dedication, commitment, and outstanding contributions to the development and publication of this book and its package of support materials.

We are highly indebted to all of the reviewers of past editions. Their comments have provided a great deal of insight in the preparation of this current edition:

Jay Azriel
York College of Pennsylvania

Lana Belousova
Suffolk University

Ruben Boling
North Georgia University

Matthias Bollmus
Carroll University

Erich Brockmann
University of New Orleans

David Cadden
Quinnipiac University

Ken Chadwick
Nicholls State University

Bruce H. Charnov
Hofstra University

Jay Chok
Keck Graduate Institute, Claremont Colleges

Peter Clement
State University of New York–Delhi

Terry Coalter
Northwest Missouri University

James Cordeiro
SUNY Brockport

Deborah de Lange
Suffolk University

Irem Demirkan
Northeastern University

Dev Dutta
University of New Hampshire

Scott Elston
Iowa State University

Harold Fraser
California State University–Fullerton

Robert Goldberg
Northeastern University

Monica Gordillo
Iowa State University

George Griffin
Spring Arbor University

Susan Hansen
University of Wisconsin–Platteville

Glenn Hoetker
Arizona State University

James Hoyt
Troy University

Miriam Huddleston
Harford Community College

Carol Jacobson
Purdue University

James Katzenstein
California State University, Dominguez Hills

Robert Keidel
Drexel University

Nancy E. Landrum
University of Arkansas at Little Rock

Mina Lee
Xavier University

Patrice Luoma
Quinnipiac University

Mzamo Mangaliso
University of Massachusetts–Amherst

Michele K. Masterfano
Drexel University

James McClain
California State University–Fullerton

Jean McGuire
Louisiana State University

John McIntyre
Georgia Tech

Rick McPherson
University of Washington

Karen Middleton
Texas A&M–Corpus Christi

Raza Mir
William Paterson University

Martina Musteen
San Diego State University

Louise Nemanich
Arizona State University

Frank Novakowski
Davenport University

Consuelo M. Ramirez
University of Texas at San Antonio

Barbara Ribbens
Western Illinois University

Jason Ridge
Clemson University

William Roering
Michigan State University

Manjula S. Salimath
University of North Texas

Deepak Sethi
Old Dominion University

Manisha Singal
Virginia Tech

Warren Stone
University of Arkansas at Little Rock

Elisabeth Teal
University of N. Georgia

Jill Thomas Jorgensen
Lewis and Clark State College

Len J. Trevino
Washington State University

Edward Ward
Saint Cloud State University

Marta Szabo White
Georgia State University

Michael L. Williams
Michigan State University

Diana J. Wong-MingJi
Eastern Michigan University

Patricia A. Worsham
California State Polytechnic University, Pomona

William J. Worthington
Baylor University

Wilson Zehr
Concordia University

Michael A. Hitt
R. Duane Ireland
Robert E. Hoskisson

About the Authors

Michael A. Hitt

Michael Hitt is a University Distinguished Professor Emeritus at Texas A&M University and a Distinguished Research Fellow at Texas Christian University. Dr. Hitt received his Ph.D. from the University of Colorado. He has coauthored or coedited 27 books and authored or coauthored many journal articles. A recent article listed him as one of the 10 most cited authors in management over a 25-year period. The *Times Higher Education 2010* listed him among the top scholars in economics, finance, and management based on the number of highly cited articles he has authored. A recent article in the *Academy of Management Perspectives* lists him as one of the top two management scholars in terms of the combined impact of his work both inside (i.e., citations in scholarly journals) and outside of academia. He has served on the editorial review boards of multiple journals and is a former editor of the *Academy of Management Journal* and a former coeditor of the *Strategic Entrepreneurship Journal*. He received the 1996 Award for Outstanding Academic Contributions to Competitiveness and the 1999 Award for Outstanding Intellectual Contributions to Competitiveness Research from the American Society for Competitiveness. He is a fellow in the Academy of Management and in the Strategic Management Society, a research fellow in the Global Consortium of Entrepreneurship Centers, and received an honorary doctorate from the Universidad Carlos III de Madrid. He is a former president of both the Academy of Management and of the Strategic Management Society and a member of the Academy of Management's Journals' Hall of Fame. He received awards for the best article published in the *Academy of Management Executive* (1999), *Academy of Management Journal* (2000), *Journal of Management* (2006), and *Family Business Review* (2012). In 2001, he received the Irwin Outstanding Educator Award and the Distinguished Service Award from the Academy of Management. In 2004, Dr. Hitt was awarded the Best Paper Prize by the Strategic Management Society. In 2006, he received the Falcone Distinguished Entrepreneurship Scholar Award from Syracuse University. In 2014 and 2015, Dr. Hitt was listed as a Thomson Reuters Highly Cited Researcher (a listing of the world's most influential researchers), and he was also listed as one of The World's Most Influential Scientific Minds (a listing of the top cited researchers in science around the globe).

R. Duane Ireland

R. Duane Ireland is a University Distinguished Professor and holder of the Conn Chair in New Ventures Leadership in the Mays Business School, Texas A&M University. Dr. Ireland teaches strategic management courses at all levels. He has more than 200 publications, including approximately 25 books. His research, which focuses on diversification, innovation, corporate entrepreneurship, strategic entrepreneurship, and the informal economy, has been published in an array of journals. He has served as a member of multiple editorial review boards and is a former editor of the *Academy of Management Journal*. He has been a guest editor for 12 special issues of journals. He is a past president of the Academy of Management. Dr. Ireland is a fellow of the Academy of Management and a fellow of the Strategic Management Society. He is a research fellow in the Global Consortium of Entrepreneurship Centers and received an award in 1999 for Outstanding Intellectual Contributions to Competitiveness Research from the American Society for Competitiveness. He received the Falcone Distinguished Entrepreneurship Scholar Award from Syracuse University in 2005, the USASBE Scholar in Corporate Entrepreneurship Award from USASBE in 2004, and the Riata Distinguished Entrepreneurship Scholar award from Oklahoma State University in 2014. He received awards for the best article published in *Academy of Management Executive* (1999), the *Academy of Management Journal* (2000), and the *Journal of Applied Management and Entrepreneurship* (2010). He received an Association of Former Students Distinguished Achievement Award for Research from Texas A&M University (2012). In 2014 and 2015, Dr. Ireland was listed as a Thomson Reuters Highly Cited Researcher (a listing of the world's most influential researchers), and he was also listed as one of The World's Most Influential Scientific Minds (a listing of the top cited researchers in science around the globe).

Robert E. Hoskisson

Robert E. Hoskisson is the George R. Brown Chair of Strategic Management at the Jesse H. Jones Graduate School of Business, Rice University. Dr. Hoskisson received his Ph.D. from the University of California-Irvine. His research topics focus on corporate governance, acquisitions and divestitures, corporate and international diversification, and cooperative strategy. He teaches courses in corporate and international strategic management, cooperative strategy, and strategy consulting. He has coauthored 26 books, including recent books on business strategy and competitive advantage. Dr. Hoskisson has served on several editorial boards for such publications as the *Strategic Management Journal* (current Associate Editor), *Academy of Management Journal* (Consulting Editor), *Journal of International Business Studies* (Consulting Editor), *Journal of Management* (Associate Editor) and *Organization Science*. His research has appeared in over 130 publications, including the *Strategic Management Journal, Academy of Management Journal, Academy of Management Review, Organization Science, Journal of Management, Academy of Management Perspective, Academy of Management Executive, Journal of Management Studies, Journal of International Business Studies, Journal of Business Venturing, Entrepreneurship Theory and Practice, California Management Review*, and *Journal of World Business*. Dr. Hoskisson is a fellow of the Academy of Management and a charter member of the Academy of Management Journal's Hall of Fame. He is also a fellow of the Strategic Management Society and has received awards from the American Society for Competitiveness and the William G. Dyer Alumni award from the Marriott School of Management, Brigham Young University. He completed three years of service as a Representative-at-Large on the Board of Governors of the Academy of Management. Currently, he serves as Past President of the Strategic Management Society, and thereby serves on the Executive Committee of its Board of Directors.

Case Title	Manu-facturing	Service	Consumer Goods	Food/Retail	High Technology	Internet	Transportation/Communication	International Perspective	Social/Ethical Issues	Industry Perspective
Amazon: Kindle Fire			●		●	●				
American Express		●				●				●
BP in Russia	●							●		●
Carlsberg	●		●					●		●
Fisk Alloy Wire, Inc. and Percon	●								●	
IKEA	●		●	●				●		
Invitrogen					●				●	●
Keurig	●		●							
Kipp Schools		●								
Luck Companies	●								●	●
Martha Stewart		●	●							
Movie Exhibition Industry: 2015		●	●							●
Polaris and Victory Motorcycles	●		●				●			●
Safaricom		●			●	●	●			
Siemens	●				●					
Southwest Airlines		●					●	●		●
Starbucks			●	●		●			●	
Super Selectos			●	●				●		
Tim Hortons				●				●		●
W.L. Gore	●				●		●			

Case Title	Chapters												
	1	2	3	4	5	6	7	8	9	10	11	12	13
Amazon: Kindle Fire				●	●								●
American Express	●			●	●								●
BP in Russia					●			●	●				
Carlsberg		●			●		●	●	●				
Fisk Alloy Wire, Inc. and Percon		●		●			●						
IKEA		●						●	●				
Invitrogen							●					●	●
Keurig				●	●								●
Kipp Schools		●	●									●	●
Luck Companies		●	●	●		●	●			●		●	
Martha Stewart	●				●	●	●			●			
Movie Exhibition Industry: 2015		●	●	●	●								
Polaris and Victory Motorcycles		●	●	●		●	●						●
Safaricom	●	●			●			●				●	
Siemens			●			●					●	●	●
Southwest Airlines		●		●	●		●					●	
Starbucks						●	●	●				●	●
Super Selectos		●			●			●			●		
Tim Hortons				●	●		●		●				
W.L. Gore	●									●	●	●	●

1

Strategic Management and Strategic Competitiveness

Studying this chapter should provide you with the strategic management knowledge needed to:

1-1 Define strategic competitiveness, strategy, competitive advantage, above-average returns, and the strategic management process.

1-2 Describe the competitive landscape and explain how globalization and technological changes shape it.

1-3 Use the industrial organization (I/O) model to explain how firms can earn above-average returns.

1-4 Use the resource-based model to explain how firms can earn above-average returns.

1-5 Describe vision and mission and discuss their value.

1-6 Define stakeholders and describe their ability to influence organizations.

1-7 Describe the work of strategic leaders.

1-8 Explain the strategic management process.

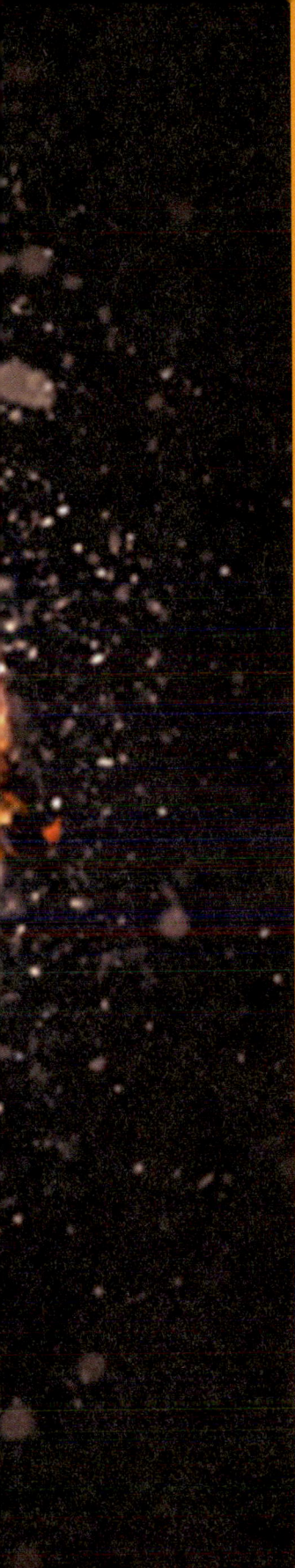

ALIBABA: AN ONLINE COLOSSUS IN CHINA GOES GLOBAL

China now has the world's largest number of internet users and Alibaba is China's largest ecommerce company (23 percent owned by Yahoo and 36 percent owned by Japan's SoftBank). In 2014, when Alibaba completed its initial public offering (IPO) on the New York Stock Exchange, it immediately became worth more than Amazon and eBay combined and has a larger market capitalization than Walmart. Transactions of goods on Alibaba's websites account for more than 2 percent of China's GDP in 2012. Comparatively, Walmart's sales account for 0.03 percent of U.S. GDP in 2012. Alibaba's presence has turned China into the world's second largest ecommerce market after the United States. Chinese consumers purchase products on Tmall, a consumer shopping site on Alibaba analogous to a department store and similar to Amazon. Because of China's vast size and underdeveloped consumer market, it has few national mainland malls or brick and mortar department store chains.

As such, the presence of Alibaba is stimulating consumption that would not otherwise take place in China. Furthermore, Alibaba's presence changed consumer buying habits, especially in third- and fourth-tier (e.g., smaller and more geographically remote) cities because it gives consumers access to items that they could not previously obtain locally.

Alibaba_Crone.PNG

Taobao is another website owned by Alibaba and is comparable to eBay in the United States. On Taobao, Alibaba does not stock or sell its own goods but rather provides platforms where manufacturers, resellers, and other middle-men open online storefronts. Larger consumer branded products prefer Tmall because Alibaba's policies promote this site more heavily and fraudulent brands are less likely to be found on this site. For instance, popular brands such as Prada handbags must provide evidence that they are a licensed distributor before they are allowed to sell on Tmall. Taobao is more focused on small sellers; it has 6 million registered sellers with a vast range in size.

Given these two websites, Alibaba is the easiest way for foreign retailers to enter the Chinese market because it has such reach. Online sales account for 90 percent of marketplace sales in China, compared with 24 percent for the United States in 2014. Accordingly, Alibaba provides the easiest way to enter the Chinese market for foreign retailers due the large access to consumers available through Alibaba's websites. Alibaba's websites also give smaller Chinese manufacturers the opportunity to increase domestic sales because of Alibaba's reach. For example, Weighing Apparatus Group, originally a supplier of household and industrial scales for Bed Bath & Beyond, set up a website on Taobao in 2009. In 2014, one-fifth of its domestic sales now flow through its Taobao online storefront, allowing it to move beyond being only a supplier for other firm's branded products.

Alibaba through its Alipay system is working on a joint venture with Apple to provide back-end services for the Apple Pay payment system allowing iPhone users in China to pay for goods with Apple Pay using their Alipay accounts. This approach is fostering an improved mobile online strategy for Alibaba. It also facilitates better service for online Apple iPhone users who desire to browse and purchase on Alibaba websites.

Fraudulent goods can be an important strategic issue in China because of previous product liability suits from banned or recalled goods sold to U.S. consumers.

As such, Alibaba is collaborating with the United States Consumer Product Safety Commission to improve its credibility among U.S. consumers by helping to ban sale of fake and fraudulently branded or recalled goods. This is also facilitating Alibaba's global access strategy.

Alibaba is also moving into online media content and streaming video services. In 2014, it announced its acquisition of ChinaVision Media, producers or co-producers of films including "Crouching Tiger, Hidden Dragon" and "Breaking the Silence." Just as Amazon and Netflix are producing their own media content, Alibaba is moving in this direction as well, as it competes with other service providers such as Tencent and Baidu in web communications and broadcasting in China. Getting its strategies right in the local domestic Chines market as well as internationally is key to Alibaba's success.

Sources: D. Tsuruoka, 2015, Alibaba blocks sale of unsafe goods to U.S. shoppers, *Investor's Business Daily*, www.investorsbusinessdaily.com, Jan 13; S. Cendrowski, 2014, Alibaba's Maggie Wu and Lucy Peng: The dynamic duo behind the IPO, *Fortune*, www.fortune.com, September 17; R. Flannery, 2014, China media entrepreneur's fortune soars on Alibaba investment, *Forbes*, www.forbes.com, March 12; C. Larson, 2014, In China its meet me at Tmall, *Bloomberg Businessweek*, www.bloombergbusinessweek.com, September 11.

As we see from the Opening Case, Alibaba is highly successful because its strategy in China has allowed it to have a massive impact in regard to online sales in a large emerging economy. It is now seeking to grow globally and gain widespread name/brand recognition through its 2014 IPO in New York. These attributes have enhanced its ability to compete in global online markets. Therefore, we can conclude that Alibaba has achieved *strategic competitiveness*. It clearly has been able to earn *above-average returns*, at least, domestically. Yet Alibaba has received its share of criticism because of its perceived contribution to the sale of fraudulent goods. However, it is addressing this issue through its collaboration with the United States Consumer Product Safety Commission. The top management of Alibaba has used the strategic management process (see Figure 1.1) as the foundation for the commitments, decisions, and actions they took to pursue strategic competitiveness and above-average returns. The strategic management process is fully explained in this book. We introduce you to this process in the next few paragraphs.

Strategic competitiveness is achieved when a firm successfully formulates and implements a value-creating strategy. A **strategy** is an integrated and coordinated set of commitments and actions designed to exploit core competencies and gain a competitive advantage. When choosing a strategy, firms make choices among competing alternatives as the pathway for deciding how they will pursue strategic competitiveness. In this sense, the chosen strategy indicates what the firm *will do* as well as what the firm *will not do*.

As explained in the Opening Case, Alibaba has been a leader in its industry as one of the most successful facilitators of online sales in China and is now seeking to become a successful global business. However, in doing so it must respond to its changing environment. In fact, to adapt to local environments, it sometimes makes major changes. For example, it is coordinating with Apple Pay to improve access for the high number iPhones that Apple is now selling in China.

A firm has a **competitive advantage** "when it implements a strategy that creates superior value for customers and that its competitors are unable to duplicate or find too costly to imitate."[1] An organization can be confident that its strategy has resulted in one or more useful competitive advantages only after competitors' efforts to duplicate its strategy have ceased or failed. In addition, firms must understand that no competitive advantage is permanent.[2] The speed with which competitors are able to acquire the skills

Strategic competitiveness is achieved when a firm successfully formulates and implements a value creating strategy.

A **strategy** is an integrated and coordinated set of commitments and actions designed to exploit core competencies and gain a competitive advantage.

A firm has a **competitive advantage** when it implements a strategy that creates superior value for customers and that competitors are unable to duplicate or find it too costly to try to imitate.

Figure 1.1 The Strategic Management Process

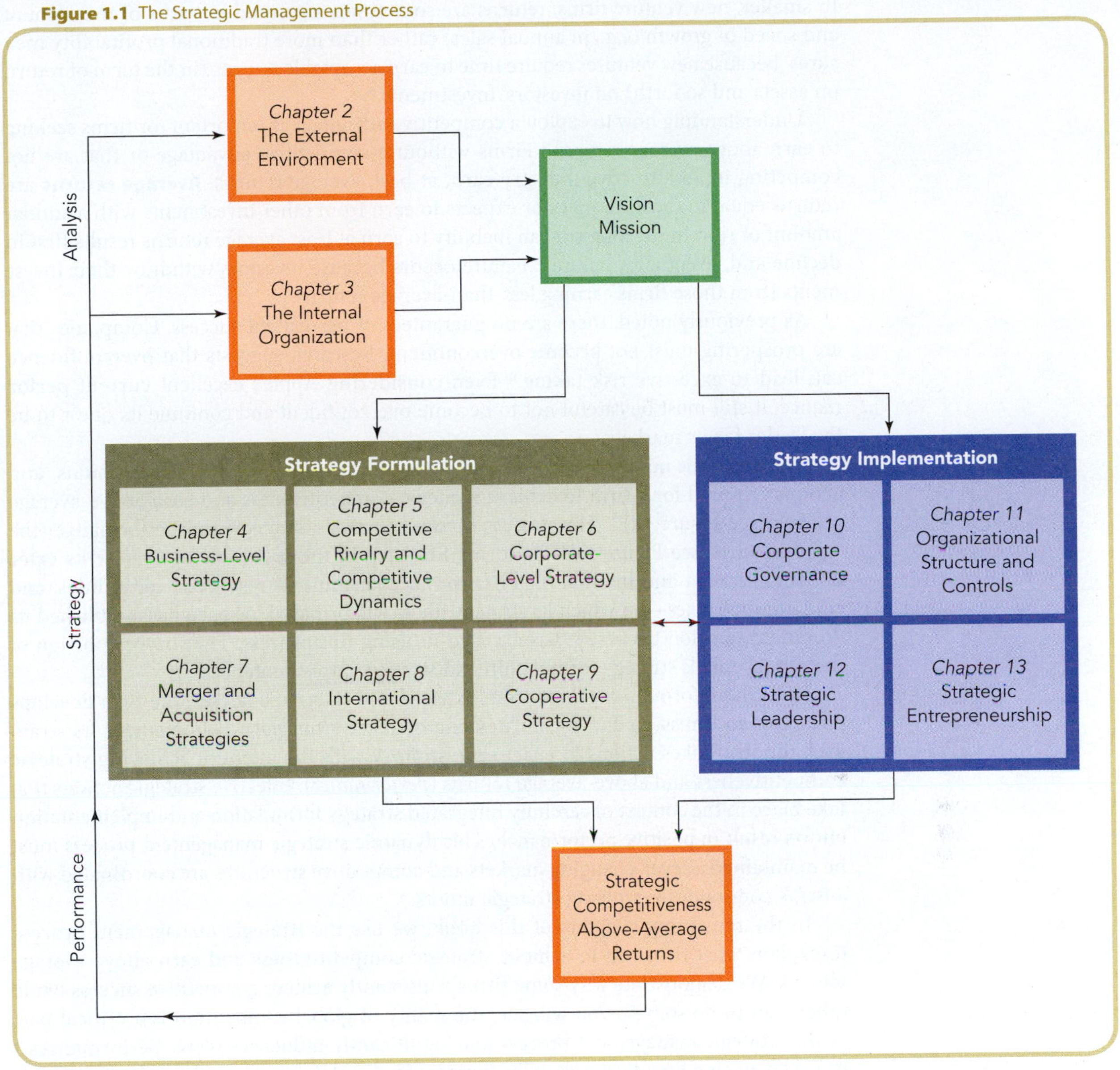

needed to duplicate the benefits of a firm's value-creating strategy determines how long the competitive advantage will last.[3]

Above-average returns are returns in excess of what an investor expects to earn from other investments with a similar amount of risk. **Risk** is an investor's uncertainty about the economic gains or losses that will result from a particular investment. The most successful companies learn how to effectively manage risk.[4] Effectively managing risks reduces investors' uncertainty about the results of their investment.[5] Returns are often measured in terms of accounting figures, such as return on assets, return on equity, or return on sales. Alternatively, returns can be measured on the basis of stock market returns, such as monthly returns (the end-of-the-period stock price minus the beginning stock price divided by the beginning stock price, yielding a percentage return).[6]

Above-average returns are returns in excess of what an investor expects to earn from other investments with a similar amount of risk

Risk is an investor's uncertainty about the economic gains or losses that will result from a particular investment.

In smaller, new venture firms, returns are sometimes measured in terms of the amount and speed of growth (e.g., in annual sales) rather than more traditional profitability measures[7] because new ventures require time to earn acceptable returns (in the form of return on assets and so forth) on investors' investments.[8]

Understanding how to exploit a competitive advantage is important for firms seeking to earn above-average returns.[9] Firms without a competitive advantage or that are not competing in an attractive industry earn, at best, average returns. **Average returns** are returns equal to those an investor expects to earn from other investments with a similar amount of risk. In the long run, an inability to earn at least average returns results first in decline and, eventually, failure.[10] Failure occurs because investors withdraw their investments from those firms earning less-than-average returns.

As previously noted, there are no guarantees of permanent success. Companies that are prospering must not become overconfident. Research suggests that overconfidence can lead to excessive risk taking.[11] Even considering Apple's excellent current performance, it still must be careful not to become overconfident and continue its quest to be the leader for its markets.

The **strategic management process** is the full set of commitments, decisions, and actions required for a firm to achieve strategic competitiveness and earn above-average returns (see Figure 1.1)[12]. The process involves analysis, strategy and performance (the A-S-P model—see Figure 1.1). The firm's first step in the process is to *analyze* its external environment and internal organization to determine its resources, capabilities, and core-competencies—on which its strategy likely will be based. Alibaba has established its dominant position because it has excelled in using this process. The *strategy* portion of the model entails strategy formulation and strategy implementation.

With the information gained from external and internal analyses, the firm develops its vision and mission and formulates one or more *strategies*. To implement its strategies, the firm takes actions to enact each strategy with the intent of achieving strategic competitiveness and above-average returns (*performance*). Effective strategic actions that take place in the context of carefully integrated strategy formulation and implementation efforts result in positive performance. This dynamic strategic management process must be maintained as ever-changing markets and competitive structures are coordinated with a firm's continuously evolving strategic inputs.[13]

In the remaining chapters of this book, we use the strategic management process to explain what firms do to achieve strategic competitiveness and earn above-average returns. We demonstrate why some firms consistently achieve competitive success while others fail to do so.[14] As you will see, the reality of global competition is a critical part of the strategic management process and significantly influences firms' performances.[15] Indeed, learning how to successfully compete in the globalized world is one of the most significant challenges for firms competing in the current century.[16]

Several topics will be discussed in this chapter. First, we describe the current competitive landscape. This challenging landscape is being created primarily by the emergence of a global economy, globalization resulting from that economy, and rapid technological changes. Next, we examine two models that firms use to gather the information and knowledge required to choose and then effectively implement their strategies. The insights gained from these models also serve as the foundation for forming the firm's vision and mission. The first model (industrial organization or I/O) suggests that the external environment is the primary determinant of a firm's strategic actions. According to this model, identifying and then operating effectively in an attractive (i.e., profitable) industry or segment of an industry are the keys to competitive success.[17] The second model (resource-based) suggests that a firm's unique resources and capabilities are the critical link to strategic competitiveness.[18] Thus, the first model is concerned primarily

Average returns are returns equal to those an investor expects to earn from other investments with a similar amount of risk.

The **strategic management process** is the full set of commitments, decisions, and actions required for a firm to achieve strategic competitiveness and earn above-average returns.

with the firm's external environment, while the second model is concerned primarily with the firm's internal organization. After discussing vision and mission, direction-setting statements that influence the choice and use of strategies, we describe the stakeholders that organizations serve. The degree to which stakeholders' needs can be met increases when firms achieve strategic competitiveness and earn above-average returns. Closing the chapter are introductions to strategic leaders and the elements of the strategic management process.

1-1 The Competitive Landscape

The fundamental nature of competition in many of the world's industries is changing. Although financial capital is no longer scarce due to the deep recession, markets are increasingly volatile.[19] Because of this, the pace of change is relentless and ever-increasing. Even determining the boundaries of an industry has become challenging. Consider, for example, how advances in interactive computer networks and telecommunications have blurred the boundaries of the entertainment industry. Today, not only do cable companies and satellite networks compete for entertainment revenue from television, but telecommunication companies are moving into the entertainment business through significant improvements in fiber-optic lines.[20] More recently, internet only streaming services have started to compete with cable, satellite, and telecommunication offerings. "Sling TV is part of a growing wave of offerings expected from tech, telecom and media companies in the coming year, posing a threat to the established television business, which takes in $170 billion a year. Meanwhile, the streaming outlets of Amazon, Hulu and Netflix continue to pour resources into developing more robust offerings. Sony, CBS, HBO and others are starting Internet-only subscription offerings."[21] Interestingly, Netflix and other streaming content providers such as Amazon are producing their own content; Netflix is producing repeat series such as "House of Cards," "Orange Is the New Black," and "Marco Polo".[22] As noted in the opening case, Alibaba intends to enter the entertainment business as Netflix and other content distributors and producers enter international markets.

Other characteristics of the current competitive landscape are noteworthy. Conventional sources of competitive advantage such as economies of scale and huge advertising budgets are not as effective as they once were (e.g., due to social media advertising) in terms of helping firms earn above-average returns. Moreover, the traditional managerial mind-set is unlikely to lead a firm to strategic competitiveness. Managers must adopt a new mind-set that values flexibility, speed, innovation, integration, and the challenges that evolve from constantly changing conditions.[23] The conditions of the competitive landscape result in a perilous business world, one in which the investments that are required to compete on a global scale are enormous and the consequences of failure are severe.[24] Effective use of the strategic management process reduces the likelihood of failure for firms as they encounter the conditions of today's competitive landscape.

Hypercompetition describes competition that is excessive such that it creates inherent instability and necessitates constant disruptive change for firms in the competitive landscape.[25] Hypercompetition results from the dynamics of strategic maneuvering among global and innovative combatants.[26] It is a condition of rapidly escalating competition based on price-quality positioning, competition to create new know-how and establish first-mover advantage, and competition to protect or invade established product or geographic markets.[27] In a hypercompetitive market, firms often aggressively challenge their competitors in the hopes of improving their competitive position and ultimately their performance.[28]

Hypercompetition describes competition that is excessive such that it creates inherent instability and necessitates constant disruptive change for firms in the competitive landscape.

Several factors create hypercompetitive environments and influence the nature of the current competitive landscape. The emergence of a global economy and technology, specifically rapid technological change, are the two primary drivers of hypercompetitive environments and the nature of today's competitive landscape.

1-1a   The Global Economy

A **global economy** is one in which goods, services, people, skills, and ideas move freely across geographic borders. Relatively unfettered by artificial constraints, such as tariffs, the global economy significantly expands and complicates a firm's competitive environment.[29]

Interesting opportunities and challenges are associated with the emergence of the global economy.[30] For example, the European Union (a group of European countries that participates in the world economy as one economic unit and operates under one official currency, the euro) has become one of the world's largest markets, with 700 million potential customers. "In the past, China was generally seen as a low-competition market and a low-cost producer. Today, China is an extremely competitive market in which local market-seeking multinational corporations (MNCs) must fiercely compete against other MNCs and against those local companies that are more cost effective and faster in product development. While China has been viewed as a country from which to source low-cost goods, lately, many MNCs such as Procter & Gamble (P&G), are actually net exporters of local management talent; they have been dispatching more Chinese abroad than bringing foreign expatriates to China."[31] China has become the second-largest economy in the world, surpassing Japan. India, the world's largest democracy, has an economy that also is growing rapidly and now ranks as the fourth largest in the world.[32] Simultaneously, many firms in these emerging economies are moving into international markets and are now regarded as MNCs. This fact is demonstrated by the case of Huawei Technologies Co. Ltd., a Chinese company that has entered the U.S. market. Barriers to entering foreign markets still exist and Huawei has encountered several, such as the inability to gain the U.S. government's approval for acquisition of U.S. firms. Essentially, Huawei must build credibility in the U.S. market, and especially build a positive relationship with stakeholders such as the U.S. government.

The nature of the global economy reflects the realities of a hypercompetitive business environment and challenges individual firms to seriously evaluate the markets in which they will compete. This is reflected in General Motor's actions and outcomes. General Motors sold 3.54 million vehicles in China while selling less in North America, 3.4 million.[33] One result of China being the largest domestic sales market is the increased competition GM now experiences in China from other competitors.

Consider the case of General Electric (GE). Although headquartered in the United States, GE expects that as much as 60 percent of its revenue growth through 2015 will be generated by competing in rapidly developing economies (e.g., China and India). The decision to count on revenue growth in emerging economies instead of in developed countries such as the United States and in Europe seems quite reasonable in the global economy. GE achieved significant growth in 2010 partly because of signing contracts for large infrastructure projects in China and Russia. GE's Chief Executive Officer (CEO), Jeffrey Immelt, argues that we have entered a new economic era in which the global economy will be more volatile and that most of the growth will come from emerging economies such as Brazil, China, and India.[34] Therefore, GE is investing significantly in these emerging economies, in order to improve its competitive position in vital geographic sources of revenue and profitability.

For example, Netflix, a subscription media streaming-video service provider, has seen its growth slow domestically. In the fourth quarter of 2014, Netflix added 1.9 million domestic U.S. streaming subscribers, which was down from 2.3 million in the fourth

A **global economy** is one in which goods, services, people, skills, and ideas move freely across geographic borders.

period a year earlier. However, Netflix was able to add 4.3 streaming customers overall because foreign markets grew faster than expected. When this was announced, its stock price increased 16 percent in after-hours trading. Netflix plans to expand to over 200 countries by 2017, up from its current 50 countries, while likewise seeking to stay profitable. Reed Hastings, Netflix's CEO, was encouraged by profitable results in Canada, Nordic countries, and Latin American countries. This group turned profitable notwithstanding the significant investment necessary to bring streaming services to these countries. In the first part of 2015, the company expects to add Australia and New Zealand and is exploring entering the Chinese market as well. Overall, Netflix added over 2.43 million subscribers outside of the United States, which exceed its expectation of 2.15 million subscribers. Besides international expansion, Netflix is adding a significant number of original shows including "House of Cards," "Orange Is the New Black," and "Marco Polo." It finds that this original content costs less given viewer support compared to licensed content from major studios. This proprietary content as well as its expansion of licensing has lured customers away from cable and satellite TV providers. Its superior technology in providing precisely what consumers want and when they want it provides a domestic advantage which will carry over into its international expansion push (see Chapter 8 Opening Case for an expansion on Netflix's international strategy).[35]

M4OS Photos / Alamy

Along with its international push, Netflix has expanded its ability to allow content to be viewed on many devices (including mobile devices) beside regular TVs, as is shown in the photo.

The March of Globalization

Globalization is the increasing economic interdependence among countries and their organizations as reflected in the flow of goods and services, financial capital, and knowledge across country borders.[36] Globalization is a product of a large number of firms competing against one another in an increasing number of global economies.

In globalized markets and industries, financial capital might be obtained in one national market and used to buy raw materials in another. Manufacturing equipment bought from a third national market can then be used to produce products that are sold in yet a fourth market. Thus, globalization increases the range of opportunities for companies competing in the current competitive landscape.[37]

Firms engaging in globalization of their operations must make culturally sensitive decisions when using the strategic management process, as is the case in Starbucks' operations in European countries. Additionally, highly globalized firms must anticipate ever-increasing complexity in their operations as goods, services, people, and so forth move freely across geographic borders and throughout different economic markets.

Overall, it is important to note that globalization has led to higher performance standards in many competitive dimensions, including those of quality, cost, productivity, product introduction time, and operational efficiency. In addition to firms competing in the global economy, these standards affect firms competing on a domestic-only basis. The reason that customers will purchase from a global competitor rather than a domestic firm is that the global company's good or service is superior. Workers now flow rather freely among global economies, and employees are a key source of competitive advantage.[38]

Thus, managers have to learn how to operate effectively in a "multi-polar" world with many important countries having unique interests and environments.[39] Firms must learn how to deal with the reality that in the competitive landscape of the twenty-first century, only companies capable of meeting, if not exceeding, global standards typically have the capability to earn above-average returns.

Although globalization offers potential benefits to firms, it is not without risks. Collectively, the risks of participating outside of a firm's domestic markets in the global economy are labeled a "liability of foreignness."[40] One risk of entering the global market is the amount of time typically required for firms to learn how to compete in markets that are new to them. A firm's performance can suffer until this knowledge is either developed locally or transferred from the home market to the newly established global location.[41] Additionally, a firm's performance may suffer with substantial amounts of globalization. In this instance, firms may over diversify internationally beyond their ability to manage these extended operations.[42] Over diversification can have strong negative effects on a firm's overall performance.

A major factor in the global economy in recent years has been the growth in the influence of emerging economies. The important emerging economies include not only the BRIC countries (Brazil, Russia, India, and China) but also the VISTA countries (Vietnam, Indonesia, South Africa, Turkey, and Argentina). Mexico and Thailand have also become increasingly important markets.[43] Obviously, as these economies have grown, their markets have become targets for entry by large multinational firms. Emerging economy firms have also began to compete in global markets, some with increasing success.[44] For example, there are now more than 1,000 multinational firms home-based in emerging economies with more than $1 billion in annual sales.[45] In fact, the emergence of emerging-market MNCs in international markets has forced large MNCs based in developed markets to enrich their own capabilities to compete effectively in global markets.[46]

Thus, entry into international markets, even for firms with substantial experience in the global economy, requires effective use of the strategic management process. It is also important to note that even though global markets are an attractive strategic option for some companies, they are not the only source of strategic competitiveness. In fact, for most companies, even for those capable of competing successfully in global markets, it is critical to remain committed to and strategically competitive in both domestic and international markets by staying attuned to technological opportunities and potential competitive disruptions that innovations create.[47] As illustrated in the Strategic Focus, Starbucks has increased its revenue per store through an emphasis on innovation in addition to its international expansion.

1-1b Technology and Technological Changes

Technology-related trends and conditions can be placed into three categories: technology diffusion and disruptive technologies, the information age, and increasing knowledge intensity. These categories are significantly altering the nature of competition and as a result contributing to highly dynamic competitive environments.

Technology Diffusion and Disruptive Technologies

The rate of technology diffusion, which is the speed at which new technologies become available and are used, has increased substantially over the past 15 to 20 years. Consider the following rates of technology diffusion:

It took the telephone 35 years to get into 25 percent of all homes in the United States. It took TV 26 years. It took radio 22 years. It took PCs 16 years. It took the Internet 7 years.[48]

Strategic **Focus**

Starbucks Is "Juicing" Its Earnings per Store through Technological Innovations

An important signal for a company is who is chosen as the new CEO. Howard Schultz of Starbucks has led the company through successful strategic execution over much of its history. In 2015, Kevin Johnson, a former CEO of Juniper Networks and 16 year veteran of Microsoft took over as CEO of Starbucks, succeeding Schultz. Johnson has engaged with the company's digital operations and will supervise information technology and supply chain operations.

Many brick and mortar stores have experienced decreasing sales in the United States as online traffic has increased. Interestingly, 2014 Starbuck sales store operations have risen 5 percent in the fourth quarter; this 5 percent came from increased traffic (2 percent from growth in sales and 3 percent in increased ticket size). The driver of this increase in sales is mainly an increase in technology applications.

To facilitate this increase in sales per store, Starbucks is ramping up its digital tools such as mobile-payment platforms. Furthermore, it has ramped up online sales of gift cards as a way to drive revenue. In December 2014, it allowed customers to place online orders and pick them up in about 150 Starbucks outlets in the Portland, Oregon area. Besides leadership and a focus on technology, Starbucks receives suggestions, ideas, and experimentation from its employees. Starbucks employees, called baristas, are seen as partners who blend, steam, and brew the brand's specialty coffee in over 21,000 stores worldwide. Schultz credits the employees as a dominant force in helping it to build its revenue gains.

To further incentivize employees, Starbucks was one of the first to provide comprehensive health benefits and stock option ownership to part-time employees. Currently, employees have received more than $1 billion worth of financial gain through the stock option program. As an additional perk for U.S. employees, Schultz created a program to pay 100 percent of workers' tuition to finish their degrees through Arizona State University. To date, 1,000 workers have enrolled in this program.

Starbucks is also known for its innovations in new types of stores. For instance, it is testing smaller express stores in New York City that reduce client wait times. As noted earlier, Starbucks has emphasized online payment in its approaches which facilitates the speed of transaction. It now gives Starbucks rewards for mobile payment applications to its 12 million active users. Interestingly, this puts it ahead of iTunes and American Express Serve with its Starbucks mobile payment app in regard to number of users.

To put its innovation on display, Starbucks opened its first "Reserve Roastery and Tasting Room." This is a 15,000 square foot coffee roasting facility and also a consumer retail outlet. According to Schultz, it's a retail theater where "you can watch beans being roasted, talk to master grinders, have your drink brewed in front of you in multiple ways, lounge in a coffee library, order a selection of gourmet brews and locally prepared foods." Schultz calls this store in New York the "Willie Wonka Factory of coffee." Based on this concept, Starbucks will open small "reserve" stores inspired by this flagship roastery concept across New York in 2015.

These technology advances and different store offerings are also taking place internationally. For example, Starbucks is expanding a new store concept in India and it's debuting this new concept store in smaller towns and suburbs. These new outlets are about half the size of existing Starbuck cafes in India.

Kevin Schafer/Getty Images

The photo illustrates the Starbuck's app that allows customers to pre-order and speed service and payment.

Sources: I. Brat & T. Stynes, 2015, Earnings: Starbucks picks a president from technology industry, *Wall Street Journal*, www.wsj.com, January 23; A. Adamczyk, 2014, The next big caffeine craze? Starbucks testing cold-brewed coffee, *Forbes*, www.forbes.com, August 18; R. Foroohr, 2014, Go inside Starbucks' wild new "Willie Wonka Factory of coffee", *Time*, www.time.com, December 8; FRPT-Retail Snapshot, 2014, Starbucks' strategy of expansion with profitability: to debut in towns and suburbs with half the size of the new stores, *FRPT-Retail Snapshot*, September 28, 9–10; L. Lorenzetti, 2014, Fortune's world most admired companies: Starbucks where innovation is always brewing, *Fortune*, www.fortune.com, October 30; P. Wahba, 2014, Starbucks to offer delivery in 2015 in some key markets, *Fortune*, www.fortune.com, November 4; V. Wong, 2014, Your boss will love the new Starbucks delivery service, *Bloomberg Businessweek*, www.businessweek.com, November 3.

The impact of technological changes on individual firms and industries has been broad and significant. For example, in the not-too-distant past, people rented movies on videotapes at retail stores. Now, movie rentals are almost entirely electronic. The publishing industry (books, journals, magazines, newspapers) is moving rapidly from hard copy to electronic format. Many firms in these industries, operating with a more traditional business model, are suffering. These changes are also affecting other industries, from trucking to mail services (public and private).

Perpetual innovation is a term used to describe how rapidly and consistently new, information-intensive technologies replace older ones. The shorter product life cycles resulting from these rapid diffusions of new technologies place a competitive premium on being able to quickly introduce new, innovative goods and services into the marketplace.[49]

In fact, when products become somewhat indistinguishable because of the widespread and rapid diffusion of technologies, speed to market with innovative products may be the primary source of competitive advantage (see Chapter 5).[50] Indeed, some argue that the global economy is increasingly driven by constant innovations. Not surprisingly, such innovations must be derived from an understanding of global standards and expectations of product functionality. Although some argue that large established firms may have trouble innovating, evidence suggests that today these firms are developing radically new technologies that transform old industries or create new ones.[51] Apple is an excellent example of a large established firm capable of radical innovation. Also, in order to diffuse the technology and enhance the value of an innovation, firms need to be innovative in their use of the new technology, building it into their products.[52]

Another indicator of rapid technology diffusion is that it now may take only 12 to 18 months for firms to gather information about their competitors' research and development (R&D) and product decisions.[53] In the global economy, competitors can sometimes imitate a firm's successful competitive actions within a few days. In this sense, the rate of technological diffusion has reduced the competitive benefits of patents.[54] Today, patents may be an effective way of protecting proprietary technology in a small number of industries such as pharmaceuticals. Indeed, many firms competing in the electronics industry often do not apply for patents to prevent competitors from gaining access to the technological knowledge included in the patent application.

Disruptive technologies—technologies that destroy the value of an existing technology and create new markets[55]—surface frequently in today's competitive markets. Think of the new markets created by the technologies underlying the development of products such as iPods, iPads, Wi-Fi, and the web browser. These types of products are thought by some to represent radical or breakthrough innovations (we discuss more about radical innovations in Chapter 13.).[56] A disruptive or radical technology can create what is essentially a new industry or can harm industry incumbents. However, some incumbents are able to adapt based on their superior resources, experience, and ability to gain access to the new technology through multiple sources (e.g., alliances, acquisitions, and ongoing internal research).[57]

Clearly, Apple has developed and introduced "disruptive technologies" such as the iPhone and iPod, and in so doing changed several industries. For example, the iPhone dramatically changed the cell phone industry, and the iPod and its complementary iTunes revolutionized how music is sold to and used by consumers. In conjunction with other complementary and competitive products (e.g., Amazon's Kindle), Apple's iPad is contributing to and speeding major changes in the publishing industry, moving from hard copies to electronic books. Apple's new technologies and products are also contributing to the new "information age." Thus, Apple provides an example of entrepreneurship through technology emergence across multiple industries.[58]

The Information Age

Dramatic changes in information technology (IT) have occurred in recent years. Personal computers, cellular phones, artificial intelligence, virtual reality, massive databases ("big data"), and multiple social networking sites are only a few examples of how information is used differently as a result of technological developments. An important outcome of these changes is that the ability to effectively and efficiently access and use information. IT has become an important source of competitive advantage in virtually all industries. The Internet and IT advances have given small firms more flexibility in competing with large firms, if the technology is used efficiently.[59]

Both the pace of change in IT and its diffusion will continue to increase. For instance, the number of personal computers in use globally is expected to surpass 2.3 billion by 2015. More than 372 million were sold globally in 2011. This number is expected to increase to about 518 million in 2015.[60] The declining costs of IT and the increased accessibility to them are also evident in the current competitive landscape. The global proliferation of relatively inexpensive computing power and its linkage on a global scale via computer networks combine to increase the speed and diffusion of IT. Thus, the competitive potential of IT is now available to companies of all sizes throughout the world, including those in emerging economies.[61]

Increasing Knowledge Intensity

Knowledge (information, intelligence, and expertise) is the basis of technology and its application. In the competitive landscape of the twenty-first century, knowledge is a critical organizational resource and an increasingly valuable source of competitive advantage.[62]

Indeed, starting in the 1980s, the basis of competition shifted from hard assets to intangible resources. For example, "Walmart transformed retailing through its proprietary approach to supply chain management and its information-rich relationships with customers and suppliers."[63] Relationships with customers and suppliers are an example of an intangible resource which needs to be managed.[64]

Knowledge is gained through experience, observation, and inference and is an intangible resource (tangible and intangible resources are fully described in Chapter 3). The value of intangible resources, including knowledge, is growing as a proportion of total shareholder value in today's competitive landscape.[65] In fact, the Brookings Institution estimates that intangible resources contribute approximately 85 percent of total shareholder value.[66] The probability of achieving strategic competitiveness is enhanced for the firm that develops the ability to capture intelligence, transform it into usable knowledge, and diffuse it rapidly throughout the company.[67] Therefore, firms must develop (e.g., through training programs) and acquire (e.g., by hiring educated and experienced employees) knowledge, integrate it into the organization to create capabilities, and then apply it to gain a competitive advantage.[68]

A strong knowledge-base is necessary to create innovations. In fact, firms lacking the appropriate internal knowledge resources are less likely to invest money in R&D.[69] Firms must continue to learn (building their knowledge-base) because knowledge spillovers to competitors are common. There are several ways in which knowledge spillovers occur, including the hiring of professional staff and managers by competitors.[70] Because of the potential for spillovers, firms must move quickly to use their knowledge in productive ways. In addition, firms must build routines that facilitate the diffusion of local knowledge throughout the organization for use everywhere that it has value.[71] Firms are better able to do these things when they have strategic flexibility.

Strategic flexibility is a set of capabilities used to respond to various demands and opportunities existing in a dynamic and uncertain competitive environment. Thus, strategic flexibility involves coping with uncertainty and its accompanying risks.[72]

Strategic flexibility is a set of capabilities used to respond to various demands and opportunities existing in a dynamic and uncertain competitive environment.

Firms should try to develop strategic flexibility in all areas of their operations. However, those working within firms to develop strategic flexibility should understand that the task is not easy, largely because of inertia that can build up over time. A firm's focus and past core competencies may actually slow change and strategic flexibility.[73]

To be strategically flexible on a continuing basis and to gain the competitive benefits of such flexibility, a firm has to develop the capacity to learn. Continuous learning provides the firm with new and up-to-date skill sets, which allow it to adapt to its environment as it encounters changes.[74] Firms capable of rapidly and broadly applying what they have learned exhibit the strategic flexibility and the capacity to change in ways that will increase the probability of successfully dealing with uncertain, hypercompetitive environments.

1-2 The I/O Model of Above-Average Returns

From the 1960s through the 1980s, the external environment was thought to be the primary determinant of strategies that firms selected to be successful.[75] The industrial organization (I/O) model of above-average returns explains the external environment's dominant influence on a firm's strategic actions. The model specifies that the industry or segment of an industry in which a company chooses to compete has a stronger influence on performance than do the choices managers make inside their organizations.[76] The firm's performance is believed to be determined primarily by a range of industry properties, including economies of scale, barriers to market entry, diversification, product differentiation, the degree of concentration of firms in the industry, and market frictions.[77] We examine these industry characteristics in Chapter 2.

Grounded in economics, the I/O model has four underlying assumptions. First, the external environment is assumed to impose pressures and constraints that determine the strategies that would result in above-average returns. Second, most firms competing within an industry or within a segment of that industry are assumed to control similar strategically relevant resources and to pursue similar strategies in light of those resources. Third, resources used to implement strategies are assumed to be highly mobile across firms, so any resource differences that might develop between firms will be short-lived. Fourth, organizational decision makers are assumed to be rational and committed to acting in the firm's best interests, as shown by their profit-maximizing behaviors.[78] The I/O model challenges firms to find the most attractive industry in which to compete. Because most firms are assumed to have similar valuable resources that are mobile across companies, their performance generally can be increased only when they operate in the industry with the highest profit potential and learn how to use their resources to implement the strategy required by the industry's structural characteristics. To do so, they must imitate each other.[79]

The five forces model of competition is an analytical tool used to help firms find the industry that is the most attractive for them. The model (explained in Chapter 2) encompasses several variables and tries to capture the complexity of competition. The five forces model suggests that an industry's profitability (i.e., its rate of return on invested capital relative to its cost of capital) is a function of interactions among five forces: suppliers, buyers, competitive rivalry among firms currently in the industry, product substitutes, and potential entrants to the industry.[80]

Firms use the five forces model to identify the attractiveness of an industry (as measured by its profitability potential) as well as the most advantageous position for the firm to take in that industry, given the industry's structural characteristics.[81]

Figure 1.2 The I/O Model of Above-Average Returns

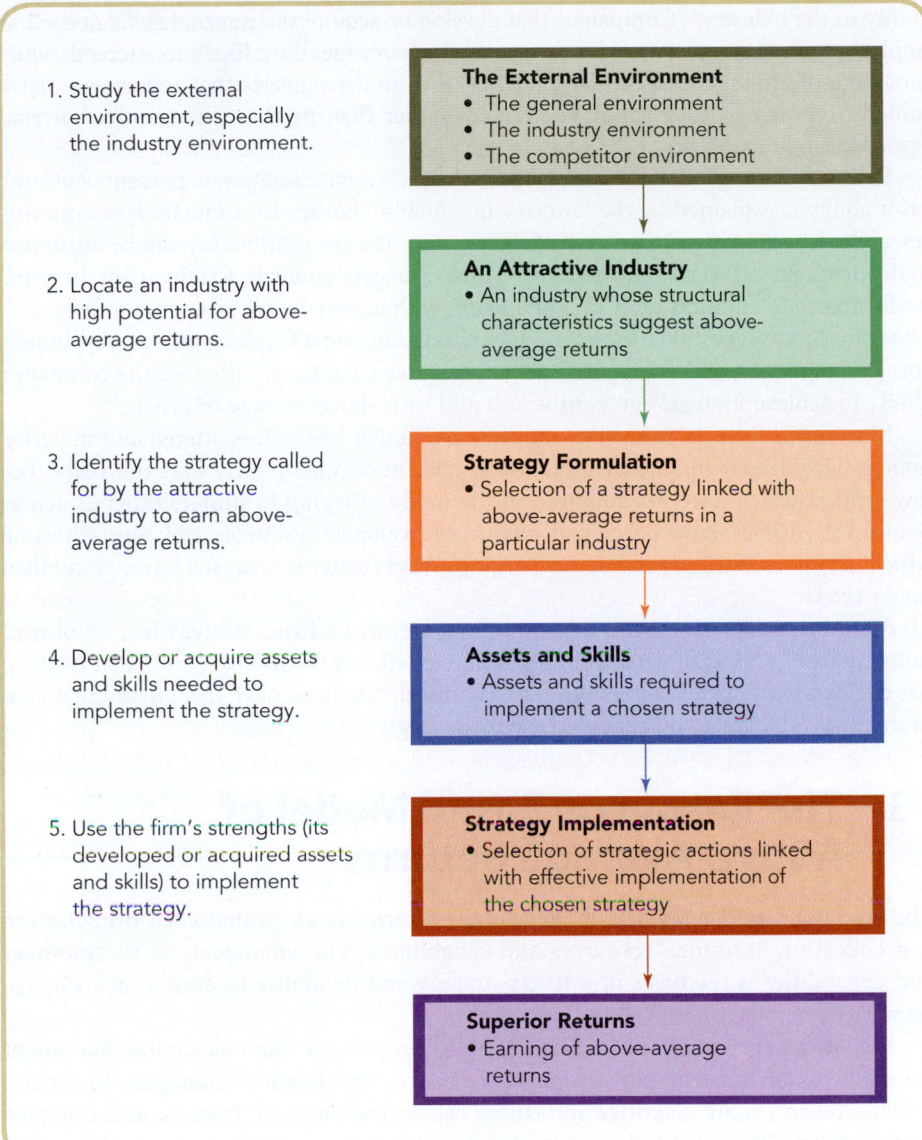

1. Study the external environment, especially the industry environment.

The External Environment
- The general environment
- The industry environment
- The competitor environment

2. Locate an industry with high potential for above-average returns.

An Attractive Industry
- An industry whose structural characteristics suggest above-average returns

3. Identify the strategy called for by the attractive industry to earn above-average returns.

Strategy Formulation
- Selection of a strategy linked with above-average returns in a particular industry

4. Develop or acquire assets and skills needed to implement the strategy.

Assets and Skills
- Assets and skills required to implement a chosen strategy

5. Use the firm's strengths (its developed or acquired assets and skills) to implement the strategy.

Strategy Implementation
- Selection of strategic actions linked with effective implementation of the chosen strategy

Superior Returns
- Earning of above-average returns

Typically, the model suggests that firms can earn above-average returns by producing either standardized goods or services at costs below those of competitors (a cost leadership strategy) or by producing differentiated goods or services for which customers are willing to pay a price premium (a differentiation strategy). The cost leadership and product differentiation strategies are discussed more fully in Chapter 4. The fact that the fast food industry faces "higher commodity costs, fiercer competition, a restaurant industry showing little to no growth, and a strapped lower-income consumer,"[82] suggests that fast food giant McDonald's is competing in a relatively unattractive industry.

As shown in Figure 1.2, the I/O model suggests that above-average returns are earned when firms are able to effectively study the external environment as the foundation for identifying an attractive industry and implementing the appropriate strategy. For example, in some industries, firms can reduce competitive rivalry and erect barriers to entry by forming joint ventures. Because of these outcomes, the joint ventures increase profitability in the industry.[83] Companies that develop or acquire the internal skills needed to implement strategies required by the external environment are likely to succeed, while those that do not are likely to fail.[84] Hence, this model suggests that returns are determined primarily by external characteristics rather than by the firm's unique internal resources and capabilities.

Research findings support the I/O model because approximately 20 percent of a firm's profitability is explained by the industry in which it chooses to compete. However, this research also shows that 36 percent of the variance in firm profitability can be attributed to the firm's characteristics and actions.[85] Thus, managers' strategic actions affect the firm's performance in addition to or in conjunction with external environmental influences.[86] These findings suggest that the external environment and a firm's resources, capabilities, core competencies, and competitive advantages (see Chapter 3) influence the company's ability to achieve strategic competitiveness and earn above-average returns.

Most of the firms in the airline industry are similar in services offered and in performance. They largely imitate each other and have performed poorly over the years. The few airlines which have not followed in the mode of trying to imitate others, such as Southwest Airlines, have developed unique and valuable resources and capabilities on which they have relied to provide a superior product (better service at a lower price) than major rivals.

As shown in Figure 1.2, the I/O model assumes that a firm's strategy is a set of commitments and actions flowing from the characteristics of the industry in which the firm has decided to compete. The resource-based model, discussed next, takes a different view of the major influences on a firm's choice of strategy.

1-3 The Resource-Based Model of Above-Average Returns

The resource-based model of above-average returns assumes that each organization is a collection of unique resources and capabilities. The *uniqueness* of its resources and capabilities is the basis of a firm's strategy and its ability to earn above-average returns.[87]

Resources are inputs into a firm's production process, such as capital equipment, the skills of individual employees, patents, finances, and talented managers. In general, a firm's resources are classified into three categories: physical, human, and organizational capital. Described fully in Chapter 3, resources are either tangible or intangible in nature.

Individual resources alone may not yield a competitive advantage.[88] In fact, resources have a greater likelihood of being a source of competitive advantage when they are formed into a capability. A **capability** is the capacity for a set of resources to perform a task or an activity in an integrative manner.[89] **Core competencies** are capabilities that serve as a source of competitive advantage for a firm over its rivals.[90] Core competencies are often visible in the form of organizational functions. For example, Apple's R&D function is one of its core competencies, as its ability to produce innovative new products that are perceived as valuable in the marketplace, is a critical reason for Apple's success.

According to the resource-based model, differences in firms' performances across time are due primarily to their unique resources and capabilities rather than the industry's structural characteristics. This model also assumes that firms acquire different resources and develop unique capabilities based on how they combine and use the resources; that resources and certainly capabilities are not highly mobile across firms; and that the

Resources are inputs into a firm's production process, such as capital equipment, the skills of individual employees, patents, finances, and talented managers.

A **capability** is the capacity for a set of resources to perform a task or an activity in an integrative manner.

Core competencies are capabilities that serve as a source of competitive advantage for a firm over its rivals.

differences in resources and capabilities are the basis of competitive advantage.[91] Through continued use, capabilities become stronger and more difficult for competitors to understand and imitate. As a source of competitive advantage, a capability must not be easily imitated but also not too complex to understand and manage.[92]

The resource-based model of superior returns is shown in Figure 1.3. This model suggests that the strategy the firm chooses should allow it to use its competitive advantages in an attractive industry (the I/O model is used to identify an attractive industry).

Not all of a firm's resources and capabilities have the potential to be the foundation for a competitive advantage. This potential is realized when resources and capabilities are valuable, rare, costly to imitate, and non-substitutable.[93] Resources are *valuable* when they allow a firm to take advantage of opportunities or neutralize threats in its external environment. They are *rare* when possessed by few, if any, current and potential competitors. Resources are *costly to imitate* when other firms either cannot obtain them or are at a

Figure 1.3 The Resource-Based Model of Above-Average Returns

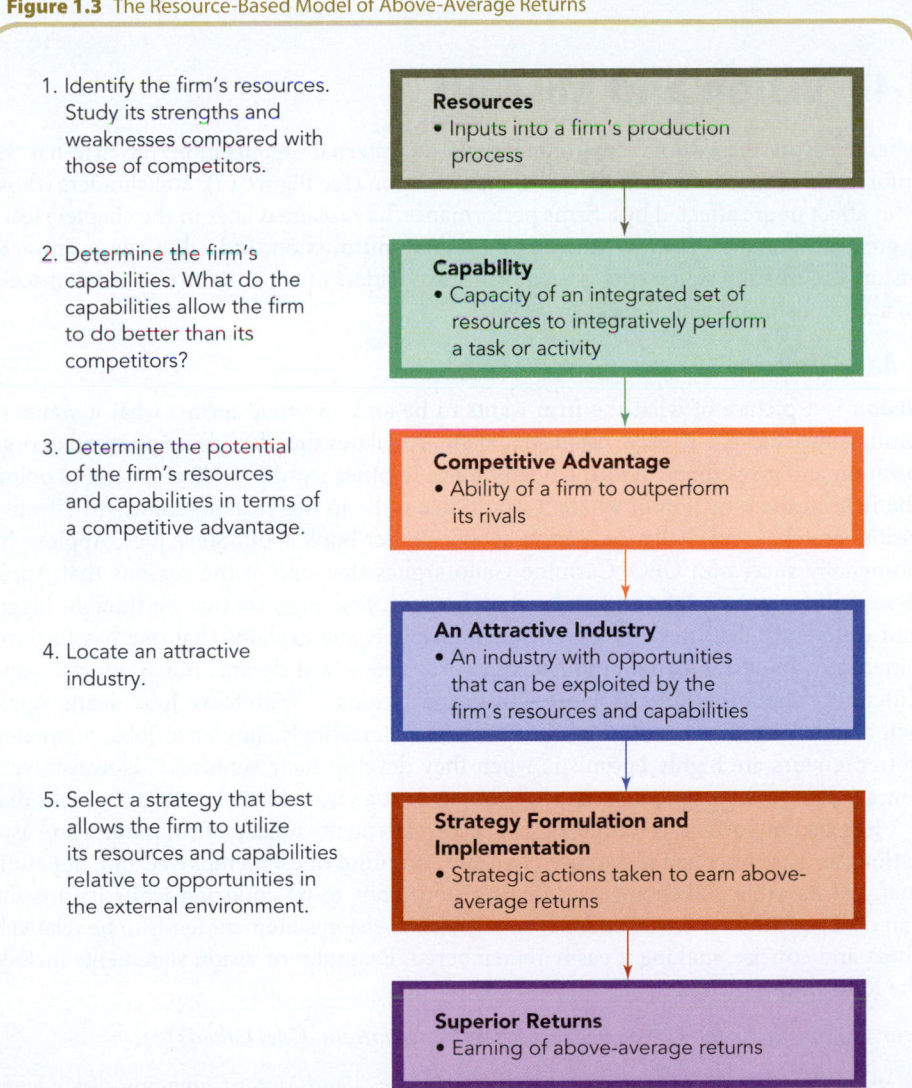

1. Identify the firm's resources. Study its strengths and weaknesses compared with those of competitors.

Resources
- Inputs into a firm's production process

2. Determine the firm's capabilities. What do the capabilities allow the firm to do better than its competitors?

Capability
- Capacity of an integrated set of resources to integratively perform a task or activity

3. Determine the potential of the firm's resources and capabilities in terms of a competitive advantage.

Competitive Advantage
- Ability of a firm to outperform its rivals

4. Locate an attractive industry.

An Attractive Industry
- An industry with opportunities that can be exploited by the firm's resources and capabilities

5. Select a strategy that best allows the firm to utilize its resources and capabilities relative to opportunities in the external environment.

Strategy Formulation and Implementation
- Strategic actions taken to earn above-average returns

Superior Returns
- Earning of above-average returns

cost disadvantage in obtaining them compared with the firm that already possesses them. And they are *non-substitutable* when they have no structural equivalents. Many resources can either be imitated or substituted over time. Therefore, it is difficult to achieve and sustain a competitive advantage based on resources alone. Individual resources are often integrated to produce configurations in order to build capabilities. These capabilities are more likely to have these four attributes.[94] When these four criteria are met, however, resources and capabilities become core competencies.

As noted previously, research shows that both the industry environment and a firm's internal assets affect that firm's performance over time.[95] Thus, to form a vision and mission, and subsequently to select one or more strategies and determine how to implement them, firms use both the I/O and resource-based models.[96] In fact, these models complement each other in that one (I/O) focuses outside the firm while the other (resource-based) focuses inside the firm. Next, we discuss the formation of a firm's vision and mission—actions taken after the firm understands the realities of its external environment (Chapter 2) and internal organization (Chapter 3).

1-4 Vision and Mission

After studying the external environment and the internal organization, the firm has the information it needs to form its vision and a mission (see Figure 1.1). Stakeholders (those who affect or are affected by a firm's performance, as explained later in the chapter) learn a great deal about a firm by studying its vision and mission. Indeed, a key purpose of vision and mission statements is to inform stakeholders of what the firm is, what it seeks to accomplish, and who it seeks to serve.

1-4a Vision

Vision is a picture of what the firm wants to be and, in broad terms, what it wants to ultimately achieve.[97] Thus, a vision statement articulates the ideal description of an organization and gives shape to its intended future. In other words, a vision statement points the firm in the direction of where it would like to be in the years to come. An effective vision stretches and challenges people as well. In her book about Steve Jobs, Apple's phenomenally successful CEO, Carmine Gallo argues that one of the reasons that Apple is so innovative was Jobs' vision for the company. She suggests that he thought bigger and differently than most people. To be innovative, she explains that one has to think differently about the firm's products and customers—"sell dreams not products"—and differently about the story to "create great expectations."[98] With Steve Jobs' death, Apple will be challenged to remain highly innovative. Interestingly, similar to Jobs, many new entrepreneurs are highly optimistic when they develop their ventures.[99] However, very few are able to develop and successfully implement a vision in the manner that Jobs did.

It is also important to recognize that vision statements reflect a firm's values and aspirations and are intended to capture the heart and mind of each employee and, hopefully, many of its other stakeholders. A firm's vision tends to be enduring while its mission can change with new environmental conditions. A vision statement tends to be relatively short and concise, making it easily remembered. Examples of vision statements include the following:

Our vision is to be the world's best quick service restaurant. (McDonald's)

To make the automobile accessible to every American. (Ford Motor Company's vision when established by Henry Ford)

Vision is a picture of what the firm wants to be and, in broad terms, what it wants to ultimately achieve.

As a firm's most important and prominent strategic leader, the CEO is responsible for working with others to form the firm's vision. Experience shows that the most effective vision statement results when the CEO involves a host of stakeholders (e.g., other top-level managers, employees working in different parts of the organization, suppliers, and customers) to develop it. In short, they need to develop a clear and shared vision for it to be successful.[100] In addition, to help the firm reach its desired future state, a vision statement should be clearly tied to the conditions in the firm's external environment and internal organization. Moreover, the decisions and actions of those involved with developing the vision, especially the CEO and the other top-level managers, must be consistent with that vision.

1-4b Mission

The vision is the foundation for the firm's mission. A **mission** specifies the businesses in which the film intends to compete and the customers it intends to serve.[101] The firm's mission is more concrete than its vision. However, similar to the vision, a mission should establish a firm's individuality and should be inspiring and relevant to all stakeholders.[102] Together, the vision and mission provide the foundation that the firm needs to choose and implement one or more strategies. The probability of forming an effective mission increases when employees have a strong sense of the ethical standards that guide their behaviors as they work to help the firm reach its vision.[103] Thus, business ethics are a vital part of the firm's discussions to decide what it wants to become (its vision) as well as who it intends to serve and how it desires to serve those individuals and groups (its mission).[104]

Even though the final responsibility for forming the firm's mission rests with the CEO, the CEO and other top-level managers often involve more people in developing the mission. The main reason for this is that the mission deals more directly with product markets and customers, and middle- and first-level managers and other employees have more direct contact with customers and the markets in which they serve. Examples of mission statements include the following:

Be the best employer for our people in each community around the world and deliver operational excellence to our customers in each of our restaurants. (McDonald's)

Our mission is to be recognized by our customers as the leader in applications engineering. We always focus on the activities customers' desire; we are highly motivated and strive to advance our technical knowledge in the areas of material, part design and fabrication technology. (LNP, a GE Plastics Company)

McDonald's mission statement flows from its vision of being the world's best quick-service restaurant. LNP's mission statement describes the business areas (material, part design, and fabrication technology) in which the firm intends to compete.

Clearly, vision and mission statements that are poorly developed do not provide the direction a firm needs to take appropriate strategic actions. Still, as shown in Figure 1.1, a firm's vision and mission are critical aspects of the *analysis* and the base required to engage in *strategic actions* that help to achieve strategic competitiveness and earn above-average returns. Therefore, firms must accept the challenge of forming effective vision and mission statements.

1-5 Stakeholders

Every organization involves a system of primary stakeholder groups with whom it establishes and manages relationships.[105] **Stakeholders** are the individuals, groups,

A **mission** specifies the businesses in which the firm intends to compete and the customers it intends to serve.

Stakeholders are the individuals, groups, and organizations that can affect the firm's vision and mission, are affected by the strategic outcomes achieved, and have enforceable claims on the firm's performance.

The Failure of BlackBerry to Develop an Ecosystem of Stakeholders

In 2007 the Apple iPhone was introduced as a consumer product which became known as the smartphone. At the time, the dominant player in this category was Research in Motion (RIM) and later known as BlackBerry. As late as 2010, BlackBerry held 43 percent of the commercial and government communication sectors. As consumers, including the business and government segments, found the smartphone to be superior as far as utility, BlackBerry's market share began to decrease precipitously. Although BlackBerry's technology allowed it to be a superior communication device for email and phone, the iPhone was superior as a handheld computer device, including communication and messaging, with much more versatility.

BlackBerry's demise provides an informed example of how the competitive landscape has changed in regard to successful business model implementation. Previously, having a good product or service and well run cost-effective company with sound capital structure was sufficient. With newer business models, having an effective strategy to manage the ecosystem or network of suppliers and customers has become more salient. Because BlackBerry had remarkably loyal customers and a strong product it failed to recognize the importance of Apple's ecosystem innovation, which allowed it to expand and diversify its range of applications for its handheld computer (smartphone). In particular, complementors to the industry (a concept explored in Chapter 2) were key; the innovation for Apple was its ecosystem of app developers. Apple not only focused on the value chain of making the iPhone and iPad, but it also focused on managing the ecosystem of creating valuable apps. As a result, an army of software developers were committed to producing iPhone applications, was behind the development of Apple's device for the general consumer and for business professionals. They created a network of stakeholders and facilitated a way to make it easy to install apps on the phone. App developers responded in huge numbers. When the app store launched in 2008, there were 500 apps. Within a year there were 55,000 apps and over a billion downloads. This was the significant difference between the small development community focused on BlackBerry and the massive development community that arose around applications for the iPhone. The "open" system strategy approach used by Google in fostering the Android system allowed a competitive ecosystem to develop that rivaled that of the iPhone.

Even now BlackBerry has not been able to create the type of stakeholder ecosystem comparable to those of Apple and Google.

Since 2010 BlackBerry has had two new CEOs and, although there are improvements, the firm has never recovered. Although BlackBerry has tried to focus on the business and government sectors using its classic look with physical keyboard, it still had a 34 percent drop in revenue in fourth quarter of 2014. The reviews of its latest product, the BlackBerry Classic, note that although consumers are likely to appreciate the retro feel of the device because of the perfected physical keyboard and mouse-like track pad, preloaded apps are slow and poorly designed. The app situation is problematic because BlackBerry doesn't have the number of app developers of the Apple or Google ecosystems. Many of the apps that you do find are difficult to download and often do not resize to fit the Classics' square screen well. As such you get a real physical keyboard to help with emails, manage your calendar, and browse the web, but few other good software

Both the iPhone and Android systems have more fully developed app ecosystems than Blackberry, which has limited Blackberry's success.

© Bloomua/Shutterstock.com

applications. Although this is the Classic is the best model ever released, it is expected that BlackBerry will continue to decline due to the lack of quality apps such as the ones found in its competitors' ecosystems.

Apple was able to outsource innovation to more developers than it could afford to employ thereby ensuring a steady stream of desirable new applications and content.

Transparent revenue sharing for these developers and a few early app millionaires created incentive at negligible expense. On the other hand, BlackBerry restricted its development community and could not hope to innovate fast enough to compete with the iPhone's positive feedback loop accruing value to customers, innovators, and content providers, resulting in profitable market share which drew capital market players as well.

In summary, BlackBerry's big failure was that it did not pay attention to the complementary software that became available on other ecosystems. A big lesson here is that managing supplier and stakeholder value creation also creates strong support from customers because it creates value for the all stakeholders and likewise draws financial capital and an associated increasing stock price.

Sources: S. Cojocaru & C. Cojocaru, 2014, New trends in mobile technology leadership, *Manager*, 19(1): 79–89; M. Cording, J. S. Harrison, R. E. Hoskisson, & K. Jonsen, 2014, "Walking the talk": A multi-stakeholder exploration of organizational authenticity, employee productivity and post-merger performance, *Academy of Management Perspectives*, 28(1): 38–56; B. Dummit, 2014, BlackBerry's revenue falls 34%; decline underscores challenges smartphone maker faces, even as it cuts costs, *Wall Street Journal*, www.wsj.com, Dec 20; M. Freer, 2014, Four success strategies from failed business models, *Forbes*, www.forbes.com, Jul 21; D. Gallagher, 2014, BlackBerry's new plan could bear fruit; attempt at revival is showing signs of life, *Wall Street Journal*, www.wsj.com, Nov 16; D. Reisinger, 2014, Why BlackBerry is showing signs of stability under CEO John Chin, *eWeek*, www.eweek.com, Dec 22; M. G. Jacobides, 2013, BlackBerry forgot to manage the ecosystem, *Business Strategy Review*, 24(4), 8; B. Matichuk, 2013, BlackBerry's business model led to its failure, *Troy Media*, www.troymedia.com, Oct 1.

and organizations that can affect the firm's vision and mission, are affected by the strategic outcomes achieved, and have enforceable claims on the firm's performance.[106] Claims on a firm's performance are enforced through the stakeholders' ability to withhold participation essential to the organization's survival, competitiveness, and profitability.[107] Stakeholders continue to support an organization when its performance meets or exceeds their expectations.[108] Also, research suggests that firms that effectively manage stakeholder relationships outperform those that do not. Stakeholder relationships and the firm's overall reputation among stakeholders can therefore be a source of competitive advantage.[109] This can be illustrated through the application of a strong stakeholder strategy in the comparison between BlackBerry's and Apple's ecosystem of stakeholders in the strategic focus. BlackBerry was unable to develop a strong set of application suppliers compared to the Apple ecosystem of app supplier stakeholders.[110]

Although organizations have dependency relationships with their stakeholders, they are not equally dependent on all stakeholders at all times. As a consequence, not every stakeholder has the same level of influence.[111] The more critical and valued a stakeholder's participation, the greater a firm's dependency on it. Greater dependence, in turn, gives the stakeholder more potential influence over a firm's commitments, decisions, and actions. Managers must find ways to either accommodate or insulate the organization from the demands of stakeholders controlling critical resources.[112]

1-5a   Classifications of Stakeholders

The parties involved with a firm's operations can be separated into at least three groups.[113] As shown in Figure 1.4, these groups are the capital market stakeholders (shareholders and the major suppliers of a firm's capital), the product market stakeholders (the firm's primary customers, suppliers, host communities, and unions representing the workforce), and the organizational stakeholders (all of a firm's employees, including both non-managerial and managerial personnel).

Each stakeholder group expects those making strategic decisions in a firm to provide the leadership through which its valued objectives will be reached.[114] The objectives of the various stakeholder groups often differ from one another, sometimes placing

Figure 1.4 The Three Stakeholder Groups

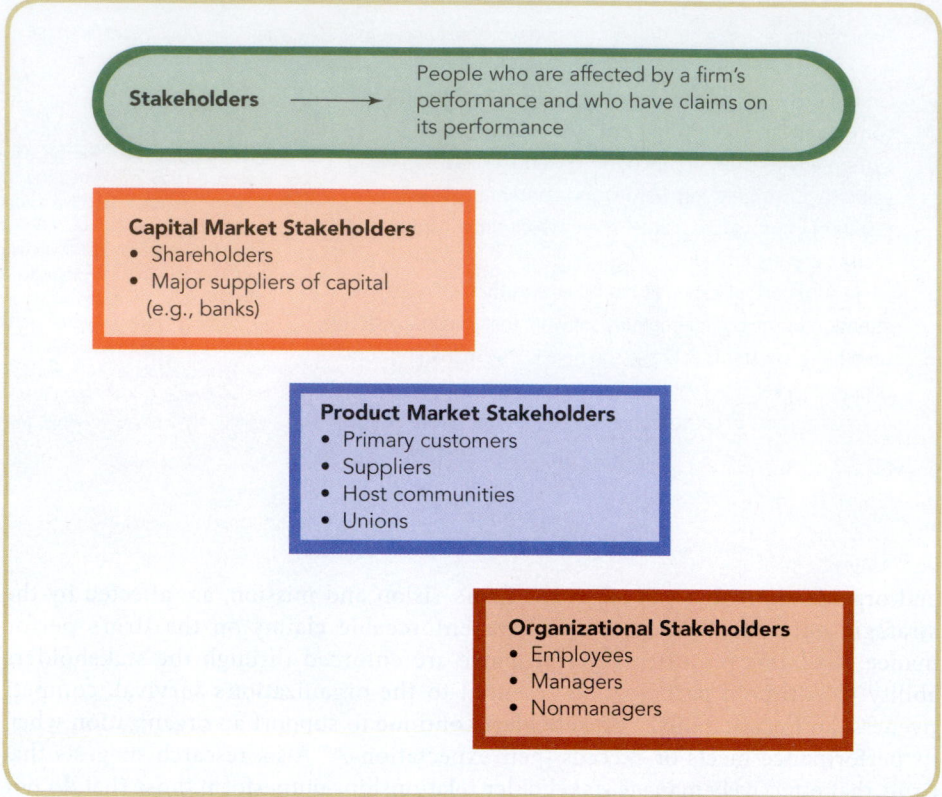

those involved with a firm's strategic management process in situations where trade-offs have to be made. The most obvious stakeholders, at least in U.S. organizations, are *shareholders*—individuals and groups who have invested capital in a firm in the expectation of earning a positive return on their investments. These stakeholders' rights are grounded in laws governing private property and private enterprise.

In contrast to shareholders, another group of stakeholders—the firm's customers—prefers that investors receive a minimum return on their investments. Customers could have their interests maximized when the quality and reliability of a firm's products are improved, but without high prices. High returns to customers, therefore, might come at the expense of lower returns for capital market stakeholders.

Because of potential conflicts, each firm must carefully manage its stakeholders. First, a firm must thoroughly identify and understand all important stakeholders. Second, it must prioritize them in case it cannot satisfy all of them. Power is the most critical criterion in prioritizing stakeholders. Other criteria might include the urgency of satisfying each particular stakeholder group and the degree of importance of each to the firm.[115]

When the firm earns above-average returns, the challenge of effectively managing stakeholder relationships is lessened substantially. With the capability and flexibility provided by above-average returns, a firm can more easily satisfy multiple stakeholders. When the firm earns only average returns, it is unable to maximize the interests of all stakeholders. The objective then becomes one of at least minimally satisfying each stakeholder.

Trade-off decisions are made in light of how important the support of each stakeholder group is to the firm. For example, environmental groups may be very important to firms in the energy industry but less important to professional service firms. A firm earning below-average returns does not have the capacity to minimally satisfy all stakeholders. The managerial challenge in this case is to make trade-offs that minimize the amount of support lost from stakeholders. Societal values also influence the general weightings allocated among the three stakeholder groups shown in Figure 1.4. Although all three groups are served by and, in turn, influence firms decisions in the major industrialized nations, the priorities in their service and influence vary because of cultural and institutional differences. Next, we present additional details about each of the three major stakeholder groups.

© Africa Studio/Shutterstock.com

As a firm formulates its strategy, it must consider all of its primary stakeholders in the product and capital markets as well as organizational shareholders.

Capital Market Stakeholders

Shareholders and lenders both expect a firm to preserve and enhance the wealth they have entrusted to it. The returns they expect are commensurate with the degree of risk they accept with those investments (i.e., lower returns are expected with low-risk investments, while higher returns are expected with high-risk investments). Dissatisfied lenders may impose stricter covenants on subsequent borrowing of capital. Dissatisfied shareholders may reflect their concerns through several means, including selling their stock. Institutional investors (e.g., pension funds, mutual funds) often are willing to sell their stock if the returns are not what they desire, or they may take actions to improve the firm's performance such as pressuring top managers and members of boards of directors to improve the strategic decisions and governance oversight.[116] Some institutions owning major shares of a firm's stock may have conflicting views of the actions needed, which can be challenging for managers. This is because some may want an increase in returns in the short-term while the others desire a focus on building long-term competitiveness.[117] Managers may have to balance their desires with those of other shareholders or prioritize the importance of the institutional owners with different goals. Clearly shareholders who hold a large share of stock (sometimes referred to as blockholders, see Chapter 10) are influential, especially in the determination of the firm's capital structure (i.e., the amount of equity versus the amount of debt used). Large shareholders often prefer that the firm minimize its use of debt because of the risk of debt, its cost, and the possibility that debt holders have first call on the firm's assets over the shareholders in case of default.[118]

When a firm is aware of potential or actual dissatisfactions among capital market stakeholders, it may respond to their concerns. The firm's response to stakeholders who are dissatisfied is affected by the nature of its dependence on them (which, as noted earlier, is also influenced by a society's values). The greater and more significant the dependency is, the more likely the firm is to provide a significant response. Sometimes firms are unable to satisfy key stakeholders such as creditors and have to file for bankruptcy.

Product Market Stakeholders

Some might think that product market stakeholders (customers, suppliers, host communities, and unions) share few common interests. However, all four groups can benefit as firms engage in competitive battles. For example, depending on product and industry characteristics, marketplace competition may result in lower product prices being charged to a firm's customers and higher prices being paid to its suppliers (the firm might be willing to pay higher supplier prices to ensure delivery of the types of goods and services that are linked with its competitive success).[119]

Customers, as stakeholders, demand reliable products at the lowest possible prices. Suppliers seek loyal customers who are willing to pay the highest sustainable prices for the goods and services they receive. Although all product market stakeholders are important, without customers, the other product market stakeholders are of little value. Therefore, the firm must try to learn about and understand current and potential customers.[120]

Host communities are represented by national (home and abroad), state/province, and local government entities with which the firm must deal. Governments want companies willing to be long-term employers and providers of tax revenue without placing excessive demands on public support services. These stakeholders also influence the firm through laws and regulations. In fact, firms must deal with laws and regulations developed and enforced at the national, state, and local levels (the influence is polycentric—multiple levels of power and influence).[121]

Union officials are interested in secure jobs, under highly desirable working conditions, for employees they represent. Thus, product market stakeholders are generally satisfied when a firm's profit margin reflects at least a balance between the returns to capital market stakeholders (i.e., the returns lenders and shareholders will accept and still retain their interests in the firm) and the returns in which they share.

Organizational Stakeholders

Employees—the firm's organizational stakeholders—expect the firm to provide a dynamic, stimulating, and rewarding work environment. Employees generally prefer to work for a company that is growing and in which the employee can develop their skills, especially those skills required to be effective team members and to meet or exceed global work standards. Workers who learn how to use new knowledge productively are critical to organizational success. In a collective sense, the education and skills of a firm's workforce are competitive weapons affecting strategy implementation and firm performance.[122] Strategic leaders are ultimately responsible for serving the needs of organizational stakeholders on a day-to-day basis. In fact, to be successful, strategic leaders must effectively use the firm's human capital.[123] The importance of human capital to their success is probably why outside directors are more likely to propose layoffs compared to inside strategic leaders, while such insiders are likely to use preventative cost-cutting measures and seek to protect incumbent employees.[124] A highly important means of building employee skills for the global competitive landscape is through international assignments. The process of managing expatriate employees and helping them build knowledge can have significant effects over time on the firm's ability to compete in global markets.[125]

1-6 Strategic Leaders

Strategic leaders are people located in different areas and levels of the firm using the strategic management process to select strategic actions that help the firm achieve its vision and fulfill its mission. Regardless of their location in the firm, successful strategic leaders are decisive, committed to nurturing those around them, and committed to helping the firm create value for all stakeholder groups.[126] In this vein, research evidence suggests that employees who perceive that their CEO is a visionary leader also believe that the CEO leads the firm to operate in ways that are consistent with the values of all stakeholder groups rather than emphasizing only maximizing profits for shareholders. In turn, visionary leadership motivates employees to expend extra effort, thereby helping to increase firm performance.

Thomas SAMSON/Getty Images

Tony Hsieh, CEO of Zappos.com, an online shoe and clothing retailer, has been helpful in shaping Zappos's entrepreneurial culture.

When identifying strategic leaders, most of us tend to think of CEOs and other top-level managers. Clearly, these people are strategic leaders. In the final analysis, CEOs are responsible for making certain their firm effectively uses the strategic management process. Indeed, the pressure on CEOs to manage strategically is stronger than ever.[127] However, many other people help choose a firm's strategy and then determine the actions for successfully implementing it.[128] The main reason is that the realities of twenty-first century competition that we discussed earlier in this chapter (e.g., the global economy, globalization, rapid technological change, and the increasing importance of knowledge and people as sources of competitive advantage) are creating a need for those "closest to the action" to be making decisions and determining the actions to be taken. In fact, all managers (as strategic leaders) must think globally and act locally.[129] Thus, the most effective CEOs and top-level managers understand how to delegate strategic responsibilities to people throughout the firm who influence the use of organizational resources. Delegation also helps to avoid too much managerial hubris at the top and the problems it causes, especially in situations allowing significant managerial discretion.[130]

Organizational culture also affects strategic leaders and their work. In turn, strategic leaders' decisions and actions shape a firm's culture. **Organizational culture** refers to the complex set of ideologies, symbols, and core values that are shared throughout the firm and that influence how the firm conducts business. It is the social energy that drives—or fails to drive—the organization.[131] For example, Southwest Airlines is known for having a unique and valuable culture. Its culture encourages employees to work hard but also to have fun while doing so. Moreover, its culture entails respect for others—employees and customers alike. The firm also places a premium on service, as suggested by its commitment to provide POS (Positively Outrageous Service) to each customer.

1-6a The Work of Effective Strategic Leaders

Perhaps not surprisingly, hard work, thorough analyses, a willingness to be brutally honest, a penchant for wanting the firm and its people to accomplish more, and tenacity are prerequisites to an individual's success as a strategic leader. The top strategic

Strategic leaders are people located in different areas and levels of the firm using the strategic management process to select strategic actions that help the firm achieve its vision and fulfill its mission.

Organizational culture refers to the complex set of ideologies, symbols, and core values that are shared throughout the firm and that influence how the firm conducts business.

leaders are chosen on the basis of their capabilities (their accumulation of human capital and skills over time). Effective top management teams (those with better human capital, management skills, and cognitive abilities) make better strategic decisions.[132] In addition, strategic leaders must have a strong strategic orientation while simultaneously embracing change in the dynamic competitive landscape we have discussed.[133] In order to deal with this change effectively, strategic leaders must be innovative thinkers and promote innovation in their organization.[134] Promoting innovation is facilitated by a diverse top management team representing different types of expertise and leveraging relationships with external parties.[135] Strategic leaders can best leverage partnerships with external parties and organizations when their organizations are ambidextrous, both innovative and good at execution.[136] In addition, strategic leaders need to have a global mind-set, or sometimes referred to as an ambicultural approach to management.[137]

Strategic leaders, regardless of their location in the organization, often work long hours, and their work is filled with ambiguous decision situations. However, the opportunities afforded by this work are appealing and offer exciting chances to dream and to act. The following words, given as advice to the late Time Warner chair and co-CEO Steven J. Ross by his father, describe the opportunities in a strategic leader's work:

There are three categories of people—the person who goes into the office, puts his feet up on his desk, and dreams for 12 hours; the person who arrives at 5 A.M. and works for 16 hours, never once stopping to dream; and the person who puts his feet up, dreams for one hour, then does something about those dreams.[138]

The operational term used for a dream that challenges and energizes a company is vision. The most effective strategic leaders provide a vision as the foundation for the firm's mission and subsequent choice and use of one or more strategies.[139]

1-7   The Strategic Management Process

As suggested by Figure 1.1, the strategic management process is a rational approach firms use to achieve strategic competitiveness and earn above-average returns. Figure 1.1 also features the topics we examine in this book to present the strategic management process.

This book is divided into three parts aligned with the A-S-P process explained in the beginning of the chapter. In Part 1, we describe the *analyses* (A) necessary for developing strategies. Specifically, we explain what firms do to analyze their external environment (Chapter 2) and internal organization (Chapter 3). These analyses are completed to identify marketplace opportunities and threats in the external environment (Chapter 2) and to decide how to use the resources, capabilities, core competencies, and competitive advantages in the firm's internal organization to pursue opportunities and overcome threats (Chapter 3). The analyses explained in Chapters 2 and 3 are the well-known SWOT analyses (strengths, weaknesses, opportunities, threats).[140] Firms use knowledge about its external environment and internal organization, then formulates its strategy taking into account its vision and mission.

The firm's analyses (see Figure 1.1) provide the foundation for choosing one or more *strategies* (S) and deciding which one(s) to implement. As suggested in Figure 1.1 by the horizontal arrow linking the two types of strategic actions, formulation and implementation must be simultaneously integrated for a successful strategic management process. Integration occurs as decision makers review implementation issues when choosing strategies and consider possible changes to the firm's strategies while implementing a current strategy.

In Part 2 of this book, we discuss the different strategies firms may choose to use. First, we examine business-level strategies (Chapter 4). A business-level strategy describes the actions a firm takes to exploit its competitive advantage over rivals. A company competing in a single product market (e.g., a locally owned grocery store operating in only one location) has but one business-level strategy, while a diversified firm competing in multiple product markets (e.g., General Electric) forms a business-level strategy for each of its businesses. In Chapter 5, we describe the actions and reactions that occur among firms in marketplace competition. Competitors typically respond to and try to anticipate each other's actions. The dynamics of competition affect the strategies firms choose as well as how they try to implement the chosen strategies.[141]

For the diversified firm, corporate-level strategy (Chapter 6) is concerned with determining the businesses in which the company intends to compete as well as how to manage its different businesses. Other topics vital to strategy formulation, particularly in the diversified company, include acquiring other businesses and, as appropriate, restructuring the firm's portfolio of businesses (Chapter 7) and selecting an international strategy (Chapter 8). With cooperative strategies (Chapter 9), firms form a partnership to share their resources and capabilities in order to develop a competitive advantage. Cooperative strategies are becoming increasingly important as firms seek ways to compete in the global economy's array of different markets.[142]

To examine actions taken to implement strategies, we consider several topics in Part 3 of the book. First, we examine the different mechanisms used to govern firms (Chapter 10). With demands for improved corporate governance being voiced by many stakeholders in the current business environment, organizations are challenged to learn how to simultaneously satisfy their stakeholders' different interests.[143] Finally, the organizational structure and actions needed to control a firm's operations (Chapter 11), the patterns of strategic leadership appropriate for today's firms and competitive environments (Chapter 12), and strategic entrepreneurship (Chapter 13) as a path to continuous innovation are addressed.

It is important to emphasize that primarily because they are related to how a firm interacts with its stakeholders, almost all strategic management process decisions have ethical dimensions.[144] Organizational ethics are revealed by an organization's culture; that is to say, a firm's decisions are a product of the core values that are shared by most or all of a company's managers and employees. Especially in the turbulent and often ambiguous competitive landscape in the global economy, those making decisions as a part of the strategic management process must understand how their decisions affect capital market, product market, and organizational stakeholders differently and regularly evaluate the ethical implications of their decisions.[145] Decision makers failing to recognize these realities accept the risk of placing their firm at a competitive disadvantage.[146]

As you will discover, the strategic management process examined in this book calls for disciplined approaches to serve as the foundation for developing a competitive advantage. Therefore, it has a major effect on the *performance* (P) of the firm.[147] Performance is reflected in the firm's ability to achieve strategic competitiveness and earn above-average returns. Mastery of this strategic management process will effectively serve you, our readers, and the organizations for which you will choose to work.

SUMMARY

- Firms use the strategic management process to achieve strategic competitiveness and earn above-average returns. Firms *analyze* the external environment and their internal organization, then formulate and implement a *strategy* to achieve a desired level of *performance* (A-S-P). Performance is reflected by the firm's level of strategic competitiveness and the extent to which it earns above-average returns. Strategic competitiveness is achieved when a firm develops and implements a value-creating strategy. Above-average returns (in excess of what investors expect to earn from other investments with similar levels of risk) provide the foundation needed to simultaneously satisfy all of a firm's stakeholders.

- The fundamental nature of competition is different in the current competitive landscape. As a result, those making strategic decisions must adopt a different mind-set, one that allows them to learn how to compete in highly turbulent and chaotic environments that produce a great deal of uncertainty. The globalization of industries and their markets along with rapid and significant technological changes are the two primary factors contributing to the turbulence of the competitive landscape.

- Firms use two major models to help develop their vision and mission when choosing one or more strategies in pursuit of strategic competitiveness and above-average returns. The core assumption of the I/O model is that the firm's external environment has a large influence on the choice of strategies more than do the firm's internal resources, capabilities, and core competencies. Thus, the I/O model is used to understand the effects an industry's characteristics can have on a firm when deciding what strategy or strategies to use in competing against rivals. The logic supporting the I/O model suggests that above-average returns are earned when the firm locates an attractive industry or part of an industry and successfully implements the strategy dictated by that industry's characteristics. The core assumption of the resource-based model is that the firm's unique resources, capabilities, and core competencies have more of an influence on selecting and using strategies than does the firm's external environment. Above-average returns are earned when the firm uses its valuable, rare, costly-to-imitate, and non-substitutable resources and capabilities to compete against its rivals in one or more industries. Evidence indicates that both models yield insights that are linked to successfully selecting and using strategies. Thus, firms want to use their unique resources, capabilities, and core competencies as the foundation to engage in one or more strategies that allow them to effectively compete against rivals in their industry.

- Vision and mission are formed to guide the selection of strategies based on the information from the analyses of the firm's internal organization and external environment. Vision is a picture of what the firm wants to be and, in broad terms, what it wants to ultimately achieve. Flowing from the vision, the mission specifies the business or businesses in which the firm intends to compete and the customers it intends to serve. Vision and mission provide direction to the firm and signal important descriptive information to stakeholders.

- Stakeholders are those who can affect, and are affected by, a firm's performance. Because a firm is dependent on the continuing support of stakeholders (shareholders, customers, suppliers, employees, host communities, etc.), they have enforceable claims on the company's performance. When earning above-average returns, a firm generally has the resources it needs to satisfy the interests of all stakeholders. However, when earning only average returns, the firm must carefully manage its stakeholders in order to retain their support. A firm earning below-average returns must minimize the amount of support it loses from unsatisfied stakeholders.

- Strategic leaders are people located in different areas and levels of the firm using the strategic management process to help the firm achieve its vision and fulfill its mission. In general, CEOs are responsible for making certain that their firms properly use the strategic management process. The effectiveness of the strategic management process is increased when it is grounded in ethical intentions and behaviors. The strategic leader's work demands decision trade-offs, often among attractive alternatives. It is important for all strategic leaders, especially the CEO and other members of the top-management team, to conduct thorough analyses of conditions facing the firm, be brutally and consistently honest, and work jointly to select and implement the correct strategies.

KEY TERMS

above-average returns 5
average returns 6
capability 16
competitive advantage 4
core competencies 16

global economy 8
hypercompetition 7
mission 19
organizational culture 25
resources 16

REVIEW QUESTIONS

1. What are strategic competitiveness, strategy, competitive advantage, above-average returns, and the strategic management process?

2. What are the characteristics of the current competitive landscape? What two factors are the primary drivers of this landscape?

3. According to the I/O model, what should a firm do to earn above-average returns?

4. What does the resource-based model suggest a firm should do to earn above-average returns?

5. What are vision and mission? What is their value for the strategic management process?

6. What are stakeholders? How do the three primary stakeholder groups influence organizations?

7. How would you describe the work of strategic leaders?

8. What are the elements of the strategic management process? How are they interrelated?

Mini-Case

Competition in the Airlines Industry

For many years, the airline industry was highly regulated which resulted in most airlines acting like each other by definition. However, the similarities among the large airline companies remained after the industry was partially deregulated more than 30 years ago. These similarities–in services, routes, and performance–have persisted even to the present time. For example, airlines often offer a new service (e.g., Wi-Fi availability on flights), but these services are easily imitated, therefore, any differentiation in offerings is only temporary.

In recent times, consolidation has occurred in both European and U.S. airline industries. In particular, poor performance led U.S. Air and America West to merge. Additionally, much for the same reasons, Northwest Airlines and Delta Airlines merged. Likewise United Airlines and Continental merged to create the largest airline in the industry. More recently, American Airlines and U.S. Air have been approved to merge. Much of the consolidation was approved because several of the airlines went through bankruptcy proceedings (e.g., Continental and United both went through bankruptcy before their merger). All of these mergers, however, have not created highly differentiated services (or prices). All of airlines largely provide the same type of services, and prices do not differ greatly among the large "full-service" carriers.

In fact, it seems that the primary competition is in trying to make fewer mistakes. In fact, industry statistics that report positive accounts, announce such outcomes as a reduction in lost bags, fewer cancellations of flights, and fewer delays. What this suggests is that all of these areas still likely represent major problem areas. It seems pretty bad when the most positive statement one can make is that fewer bags have been lost in recent times. Although profits have been up more recently, this is primarily due to lower fuel costs and stronger demand because the economy is growing, something that is not controlled by those in charge of the strategy.

Obviously, there are differences between airlines across time. United, the largest airline, merged with Continental to create more financial efficiencies and to offer greater travel options to customers.

However, it has had significant problems making the merger of the two systems work effectively. In fact, it announced a major net loss for 2012 because of its problems. For example, in November 2012, a computer malfunction (software problem) caused the delay of 250 of United's flights globally for almost two hours. Its reservation system failed twice during 2012, which shut down its website, stranding passengers as flights were then delayed or cancelled. United's on time performance suffered and was once of the worst in the industry for 2012. The number of customer complaints for United was much higher than in the past. In short, it is relatively easy to determine why the airline suffered a serious net loss in 2012. Yet, Delta, which performed very poorly a few years earlier, performed better in 2014. It made a net profit for the third year in a row. Its on-time performance was about 10 percentage points higher than United's. And, while United is eliminating flights and furloughing employees to cuts costs (trying to make a profit), in 2012 Delta purchased a 49 percent share of Virgin Atlantic to gain access to the highly valuable New York–London routes and gates in both locations. Delta was also one of the first airlines to introduce Wi-Fi to passengers during flights, although most other airlines have duplicated this service. Interestingly, the one program most airlines have used to establish some differentiation is their loyalty programs. However, benefits of these loyalty programs have been decreasing over time with less availability and more miles deducted.

Furthermore, research shows that airlines attrack brand switching customers who tend to move to the brand with the most perks for them at the time.

Certainly, some reduced-service airlines have fared much better in most of the categories noted above (e.g., profits, on-time flights, customer complaints). Among these is Southwest Airlines. Interestingly, while it started as a low-price airline (and has maintained this feature), it also has generally offered superior service compared to the full-service airlines. The large airlines tried, but were unable, to imitate Southwest. In effect, Southwest developed its resources and capabilities which over time allowed it to provide service much more effectively and at a lower price than its full-service rivals. However, JetBlue has duplicated much of Southwest's strategy, although it is focused on business travelers.

Sources: E. Glusac, 2015, What price loyalty?, *Entrepreneur*, May, 16; S. Sharf, 2015, American Airlines reports lower revenue, higher profit, *Forbes*, www.forbes.com, April 24; S. Schaefer, 2015, Cleared for takeoff. *Forbes Asia*, May, 18; C. M. Voorhees, R. C. White, M. McCall, & P. Randhawa, 2015, Fool's gold? Assessing the impact of the value of airline loyalty programs on brand equity perceptions and share of wallet, *Cornell Hospitality Quarterly*, 56(2): 202–212; 2013, Anatomy of 99.5%, Delta Airlines Website, blog.delta.com, February 15; S. McCartney, 2013, Believe it or not, flying is improving, *Wall Street Journal*, www.wsj.com, January 9; J. Freed, 2012, Delta grabs bigger share of key NY–London route, *Bloomberg Businessweek*, www.businessweek.com, December 11; D. Benoit, 2012, Delta lands London space with Virgin joint venture, *Wall Street Journal*, blogs.wsj.com/deals, December 11; J. Mouawad, 2012, For United, big problems at biggest airline, *New York Times*, www.nytimes.com, November 28; C. Negroni, 2012, Good airlines news: Losing fewer bags, *New York Times*, www.nytimes.com, August 6.

Case Discussion Questions

1. How important is the environment to the performance of airlines in the airline industry? What does this suggest regarding the industrial organization (I/O) model to explain how firms can earn above-average returns?

2. Why is there a lot of imitation in the airlines industry, and how does this affect firm performance?

3. How important is the resource-based model to explain how well firms perform in the airlines industry?

4. How can strategic leaders be successful in an industry like the airlines industry?

NOTES

1.   D. J. Teece, 2014, The foundations of enterprise performance: Dynamic and ordinary capabilities in an (economic) theory of firms. *Academy of Management Perspectives*, 28: 328–352; D. G. Sirmon, M. A. Hitt, R. D. Ireland, & B. A. Gilbert, 2011, Resource orchestration to create competitive advantage: Breadth, depth and life cycle effects, *Journal of Management*,

37: 1390–1412; D. G. Sirmon, M. A. Hitt, & R. D. Ireland, 2007, Managing firm resources in dynamic environments to create value: Looking inside the black box, *Academy of Management Review*, 32: 273–292.

2.   J. Denrell, C. Fang, & Z. Zhao, 2013, Inferring superior capabilities from sustained superior performance: A Bayesian analysis, *Strategic Management*

Journal, 34: 182–196; R. D'Aveni, G. B. Dagnino, & K. G. Smith, 2010, The age of temporary advantage, *Strategic Management Journal*, 31: 1371–1385; R. D. Ireland & J. W. Webb, 2009, Crossing the great divide of strategic entrepreneurship: Transitioning between exploration and exploitation, *Business Horizons*, 52: 469–479.

3.   G. Pacheco-de-Almeida, A. Hawk, & B. Yeung, 2015, The right speed and its value, *Strategic Management Journal*, 36: 159–176; G. Pacheco-de-Almeida & P. Zemsky, 2007, The timing of resource development and sustainable competitive advantage, *Management Science*, 53: 651–666.

4.   D. Gaddis Ross, 2014, Taking a chance: A formal model of how firms use risk in strategic interaction with other firms, *Academy of Management Review*, 39: 202–226.

5.   A. Nair, E. Rustambekov, M. McShane, & S. Fainshmidt, 2014, Enterprise risk management as a dynamic capability: A test of its effectiveness during a crisis, *Managerial & Decision Economics*, 35: 555–566; K. D. Miller, 2007, Risk and rationality in entrepreneurial processes, *Strategic Entrepreneurship Journal*, 1: 57–74.

6.   C. C. Miller, N. T. Washburn, & W. H. Glick, 2013, The myth of firm performance, *Organization Science*, 24: 948–964.

7.   P. Steffens, P. Davidsson, & J. Fitzsimmons, 2009, Performance configurations over time: Implications for growth- and profit-oriented strategies, *Entrepreneurship Theory and Practice*, 33: 125–148.

8.   E. Karniouchina, S. J. Carson, J. C. Short, & D. J. Ketchen, 2013, Extending the firm vs. industry debate: Does industry life cycle stage matter? *Strategic Management Journal*, 34: 1010–1018; J. C. Short, A. McKelvie, D. J. Ketchen, Jr., & G. N. Chandler, 2009, Firm and industry effects on firm performance: A generalization and extension for new ventures, *Strategic Entrepreneurship Journal*, 3: 47–65.

9.   R. Mudambi & T. Swift, 2014, Knowing when to leap: Transitioning between exploitative and explorative R&D, *Strategic Management Journal*, 35: 126–145; D. G. Sirmon, M. A. Hitt, J.-L. Arregle, & J. T. Campbell, 2010, The dynamic interplay of capability strengths and weaknesses: Investigating the bases of temporary competitive advantage, *Strategic Management Journal*, 31: 1386–1409.

10. D. Ucbasaran, D. A. Shepherd, A. Lockett, & S. J. Lyon, 2013, Life after business failure: The process and consequences of business failure for entrepreneurs, *Journal of Management*, 39: 163–202.

11. P. M. Picone, G. B. Dagnino, G., & A. Minà, 2014, The origin of failure: A multidisciplinary appraisal of the hubris hypothesis and proposed research agenda, *Academy of Management Perspectives*, 28: 447–468.

12. J. Hansen, R. McDonald, & R. Mitchell, 2013, Competence resource specialization, causal ambiguity, and the creation and decay of competitiveness: The role of marketing strategy in new product performance and shareholder value, *Journal of the Academy of Marketing Science*, 41: 300–319; Y. Zhang & J. Gimeno, 2010, Earnings pressure and competitive behavior: Evidence from the U.S. electronics industry, *Academy of Management Journal*, 53: 743–768.

13. J. Garcia-Sanchez, L. F. Mesquita, & R. S. Vassolo, 2014, What doesn't kill you makes you stronger: The evolution of competition and entry-order advantages in economically turbulent contexts, *Strategic Management Journal*, 35: 1972–1992; J. Bock, T. Opsahl, G. George, & D. M. Gann, 2012, The effects of culture and structure on strategic flexibility during business model innovation, *Journal of Management Studies*, 49: 275–305.

14. Garcia-Sanchez, Mesquita, & Vassolo, What doesn't kill you makes you stronger; J. T. Li, 2008, Asymmetric interactions between foreign and domestic banks: Effects on market entry, *Strategic Management Journal*, 29: 873–893.

15. N. Hashai & P. J. Buckley, 2014, Is competitive advantage a necessary condition for the emergence of the multinational enterprise?. *Global Strategy Journal*, 4: 35–48; R. G. Bell, I. Filatotchev, & A. A. Rasheed, 2012, The liability of foreignness in capital markets: Sources and remedies, *Journal of International Business Studies*, 43: 107–122.

16. A. Kuznetsova & O. Kuznetsova, 2014, Building professional discourse in emerging markets: Language, context and the challenge of sensemaking, *Journal of International Business Studies*, 45: 583–599; J. H. Fisch, 2012, Information costs and internationalization performance, *Global Strategy Journal*, 2: 296–312.

17. R. Makadok & D. G. Ross, 2013, Taking industry structuring seriously: A strategic perspective on product differentiation, *Strategic Management Journal*, 34: 509–532; Karniouchina, Carson, Short, & Ketchen, Extending the firm vs. industry debate; M. A. Delmas, & M. W. Toffel, 2008, Organizational responses to environmental demands: Opening the black box, *Strategic Management Journal*, 29: 1027–1055.

18. A. V. Sakhartov & T. B. Folta, 2014, Resource relatedness, redeployability, and firm value, *Strategic Management Journal*, 35: 1781–1797; J. Barney, D. J. Ketchen, & M. Wright, 2011, The future of resource-based theory: Revitalization or decline? *Journal of Management*, 37: 37: 1299–1315.

19. R. Scaggs, 2014, Markets take wild ride on ruble, oil, *Wall Street Journal*, www.wsj.com, December 17; M. Statman, 2011, Calm investment behavior in turbulent investment times, in *What's Next 2011*, New York: McGraw-Hill Professional, E-Book; E. Thornton, 2009, The new rules, *Businessweek*, January 19, 30–34; T. Friedman, 2005, *The World Is Flat: A Brief History of the 21st Century*, New York: Farrar, Strauss and Giroux.

20. D. Searcey, 2006, Beyond cable. Beyond DSL. *Wall Street Journal*, July 24, R9.

21. E. Steel, 2015, Dish Network unveils Sling TV, a streaming service to rival cable (and it has ESPN), *New York Times*, www.nytimes.com, January 5.

22. V. Luckerson, 2014, Netflix wants new original content every three weeks, *Time*, www.time.com, December 9.

23. B. Agypt & B. A. Rubin, 2012, Time in the new economy: The impact of the interaction of individual and structural temporalities and job satisfaction, *Journal of Management*, 49: 403–428; J. A. Lamberg, H. Tikkanen, T. Nokelainen, & H. Suur-Inkeroinen, 2009, Competitive dynamics, strategic consistency, and organizational survival, *Strategic Management Journal*, 30: 45–60.

24. A. Hawk, G. Pacheco-De-Almeida, & B. Yeung, 2013, Fast-mover advantages: Speed capabilities and entry into the emerging submarket of Atlantic basin LNG, *Strategic Management Journal*, 34: 1531–1550; J. Hagel, III, J. S. Brown, & L. Davison, 2008, Shaping strategy in a world of constant disruption, *Harvard Business Review*, 86(10): 81–89.

25. B. L. King, 2013, Succeeding in a hypercompetitive world: VC advice for smaller companies *Journal of Business Strategy*, 34(4): 22–30; D'Aveni, Dagnino, & Smith, The age of temporary advantage; A. V. Izosimov, 2008, Managing hypergrowth, *Harvard Business Review*, 86(4): 121–127; J. W. Selsky, J. Goes, & O. N. Babüroglu, 2007, Contrasting perspectives of strategy making: Applications in "Hyper" environments, *Organization Studies*, 28: 71–94.

26. S. Greengard, 2015, Disruption Is the New Normal. *CIO Insight*, January 5, 2; D'Aveni, Dagnino, & Smith, The age of temporary advantage.

27. D'Aveni, Dagnino, & Smith, The age of temporary advantage.

28. A. Kriz, R. Voola, & U. Yuksel, 2014, The dynamic capability of ambidexterity in hypercompetition: Qualitative insights, *Journal of Strategic Marketing*, 22: 287–299; D. J. Bryce & J. H. Dyer, 2007, Strategies to crack well-guarded markets, *Harvard Business Review* 85(5): 84–92.

29. P. Regnér & U. Zander, 2014, International strategy and knowledge creation: The advantage of foreignness and liability of concentration, *British Journal of Management*, 25: 551–569; S. H. Lee & M. Makhija, 2009, Flexibility in internationalization: Is it valuable during an economic crisis? *Strategic Management Journal*, 30: 537–555.

30. K. E. Meyer & Y. Su, 2015, Integration and responsiveness in subsidiaries in emerging economies. *Journal of World Business*, 50: 149–158; Y. Luo & S. L. Wang, 2012, foreign direct investment strategies by developing country multinationals: A diagnostic model for home country effects, *Global Strategy Journal*, 2: 244–261.

31. Y. Luo, 2007, From foreign investors to strategic insiders: Shifting parameters, prescriptions and paradigms for MNCs in China, *Journal of World Business*, 42: 14–34.

32. S. Awate, M. M. Larsen, & R. Mudambi, 2015, Accessing vs sourcing knowledge: A comparative study of R&D internationalization between emerging and advanced economy firms, *Journal of International Business Studies*, 46: 63–86; M. A. Hitt & X. He, 2008, Firm strategies in a changing global competitive landscape, *Business Horizons*, 51: 363–369.

33. M. Rhodan, 2015, GM sold a record number of vehicles in 2014. *Time*, www.time.com, January 16.

34. A. Ritesh, 2014, Jeffrey Immelt on General Electric's exposure in Russia, growth in emerging markets, *Benzinga*, www.benzinga.com, December 17; J.-F. Hennart, 2012, Emerging market multinationals and the theory of the multinational enterprise, *Global Strategy Journal*, 2: 168–187; S. Malone, 2011, GE's Immelt sees new economic era for globe, *Financial Post*, www.financialpost.com, March 13.

35. S. Ramachandran & T. Stynes, 2015, Netflix steps up foreign expansion: Subscriber editions top streaming service's forecast, helped by growth in markets abroad, *Wall Street Journal*, www.wsj.com, January 21.

36. R. M. Holmes, T. Miller, M. A. Hitt, & M. P. Salmador, 2013, The interrelationships among informal institutions, formal institutions, and inward foreign direct investment, *Journal of Management*, 39: 531–566; K. D. Brouthers, 2013, A retrospective on: Institutions, cultural and transaction cost influences on entry mode choice and performance, *Journal of International Business Studies*, 44: 14–22.

37. U. Andersson, P. J. Buckley, & H. Dellestrand, 2015. In the right place at the right time!: The influence of knowledge governance tools on knowledge transfer and utilization in MNEs, *Global Strategy Journal*, 5: 27–47; H. Kirca, G. T. Hult, S. Deligonul, M. Z. Perry, & S. T. Cavusgil, 2012, A multilevel examination of the drivers of firm multinationality: A meta-analysis, *Journal of Management*, 38: 502–530.

38. D. G. Collings, 2014. Integrating global mobility and global talent management: Exploring the challenges and strategic opportunities, *Journal of World Business*, 49: 253–261; Y.-Y. Chang, Y. Gong, & M. W. Peng, 2012, Expatriate knowledge transfer, subsidiary absorptive capacity, and subsidiary performance, *Academy of Management Journal*, 55: 927–948.

39. J. P. Quinlan, 2011, Speeding towards a messy, multi-polar world, in *What's Next 2011*, New York: McGraw-Hill Professional, E-Book.

40. H. Kim & M. Jensen, 2014, Audience heterogeneity and the effectiveness of market signals: How to overcome liabilities of foreignness in film exports? *Academy of Management Journal*, 57: 1360–1384; B. Elango, 2009, Minimizing effects of "liability of foreignness": Response strategies of foreign firms in the United States, *Journal of World Business*, 44: 51–62.

41. F. Jiang, L. Liu, & B W. Stening, 2014, Do foreign firms in China incur a liability of foreignness? The local Chinese firms' perspective, *Thunderbird International Business Review*, 56: 501–518; J. Mata & E. Freitas, 2012, Foreignness and exit over the life cycle of firms, *Journal of International Business Studies*, 43: 615–630.

42. T. Chi & Z. J. Zhao, 2014, Equity Structure of MNE affiliates and scope of their activities: distinguishing the incentive and control effects of ownership, *Global Strategy Journal*, 4: 257–279; M. A. Hitt, R. E. Hoskisson, & H. Kim, 1997, International diversification: Effects on innovation and firm performance in product-diversified firms, *Academy of Management Journal*, 40: 767–798.

43. S. Keukeleire & B. Hooijmaaijers, 2014, The BRICS and other emerging power alliances and multilateral organizations in the Asia- Pacific and the Global South: Challenges for the European Union and its view on multilateralism, *Journal of Common Market Studies*, 52: 582–599.

44. K. Kalasin, P. Dussauge, & M. Rivera-Santos, 2014, The expansion of emerging economy firms into advanced markets: The influence of intentional path-breaking change, *Global Strategy Journal*, 4: 75–103; R. Ramamurti, 2012, What is really different about emerging market multinationals? *Global Strategy Journal*, 2: 41–47.

45. M. Naim, 2013, Power outage, *Bloomberg Businessweek*, March 3: 4–5.

46. H. Kim, R. E. Hoskisson, & S.-H. Lee, 2015. Why strategic factor markets matter: 'New' multinationals' geographic diversification and firm profitability, *Strategic Management Journal*, Forthcoming; G. McDermott, R. Mudambi, & R. Parente, 2013, Strategic modularity and the architecture of the multinational firm, *Global Strategy Journal*, 3: 1–7.

47. R. D. Ireland & J. W. Webb, 2007, Strategic entrepreneurship: Creating competitive advantage through streams of innovation, *Business Horizons*, 50(1): 49–59; G. Hamel, 2001, Revolution vs. evolution: You need both, *Harvard Business Review*, 79(5): 150–156.

48. K. H. Hammonds, 2001, What is the state of the new economy? *Fast Company*, September, 101–104.

49. M. E. Schramm & M. Y. Hu, 2013, Perspective: The evolution of R&D conduct in the pharmaceutical industry, *Journal of Product Innovation Management*, 30: 203–213; S. W. Bradley, J. S. McMullen, K. W. Artz, & E. M. Simiyu, 2012, Capital is not enough: Innovation in developing economies, *Journal of Management Studies*, 49: 684–717; D. Dunlap-Hinkler, M. Kotabe, & R. Mudambi, 2010, A story of breakthrough versus incremental innovation: Corporate entrepreneurship in the global pharmaceutical industry, *Strategic Entrepreneurship Journal*, 4: 106–127.

50. G. Pacheco-de-Almeida, A. Hawk, & B. Yeung, B. 2015, The right speed and its value, *Strategic Management Journal*, 36: 159–176; A. Hawk, G. Pacheco-De-Almeida, & B. Yeung, B. 2013, Fast-mover advantages: Speed capabilities and entry into the emerging submarket of Atlantic basin LNG, *Strategic Management Journal*, 34: 1531–1550.

51. P. C. Patel, S. A. Fernhaber, P. P. McDougall-Covin, & R. P. van der Have, 2014, Beating competitors to international markets: The value of geographically balanced networks for innovation, *Strategic Management Journal*, 35: 691–711; N. Furr, F. Cavarretta, & S. Garg, 2012, Who changes course? The role of domain knowledge and novel framing in making technological changes, *Strategic Entrepreneurship Journal*, 6: 236–256; L. Jiang, J. Tan, & M. Thursby, 2011, Incumbent firm invention in emerging fields: Evidence from the semiconductor industry, *Strategic Management Journal*, 32: 55–75.

52. M. G. Jacobides, 2013, BlackBerry forgot to manage the ecosystem, *Business Strategy Review*, 24(4): 8; R. Adner & R. Kapoor, 2010, Value creation in innovation ecosystems: How the structure of technological interdependence affects firm performance in new technology generations, *Strategic Management Journal*, 31: 306–333.

53. C. M. Christensen, 1997, *The Innovator's Dilemma*, Boston: Harvard Business School Press.

54. K Bilir, 2014, Patent laws, product life-cycle lengths, and multinational activity, 2014, *American Economic Review*, 104: 1979–2013.

55. C. Christensen, 2015, Disruptive innovation is a strategy, not just the technology, *Business Today*, 23(26): 150–158; A. Kaul, 2012, Technology and corporate scope: Firm and rival innovation as antecedents of corporate transactions, *Strategic Management Journal*, 33: 347–367.

56. J. Henkel, T. Rønde, & M. Wagner, 2015, And the winner is—acquired. Entrepreneurship as a contest yielding radical innovations. *Research Policy*, 44: 295–310; C M. Christensen, 2006, The ongoing process of building a theory of disruption, *Journal of Product Innovation Management*, 23: 39–55.

57. U. Stettner & D. Lavie, 2014, Ambidexterity under scrutiny: Exploration and exploitation via internal organization,

alliances, and acquisitions, *Strategic Management Journal*, 35: 1903–1929; L. Capron & O. Bertrand, 2014, Going abroad in search of higher productivity at home, *Harvard Business Review*, 92(6): 26; L Capron, 2013, Cisco's corporate development portfolio: A blend of building, borrowing and buying, *Strategy & Leadership*, 41: 27–30.

58. R. Kapoor & J. M. Lee, 2013, Coordinating and competing in ecosystems: How organizational forms shape new technology investments, *Strategic Management Journal*, 34: 274–296; J. Woolley, 2010, Technology emergence through entrepreneurship across multiple industries, *Strategic Entrepreneurship Journal*, 4: 1–21.

59. P. Chen & S. Wu, 2013, The impact and implications of on-demand services on market structure, *Information Systems Research*, 24: 750–767; K. Celuch, G. B. Murphy, & S. K. Callaway, 2007, More bang for your buck: Small firms and the importance of aligned information technology capabilities and strategic flexibility, *Journal of High Technology Management Research*, 17: 187–197.

60. 2013, Worldwide PC Market, eTForecasts, www.etforecasts.com, accessed on March 10, 2013.

61. F. De Beule, S. Elia, & L. Piscitello, 2014, Entry and access to competencies abroad: Emerging market firms versus advanced market firms. *Journal of International Management*, 20: 137–152; M. S. Giarratana & S. Torrisi, 2010, Foreign entry and survival in a knowledge-intensive market: Emerging economy countries' international linkages, technology competences and firm experience, *Strategic Entrepreneurship Journal*, 4: 85–104.

62. C. Phelps, R. Heidl, & A., Wadhwa, 2012, Knowledge, networks, and knowledge networks: A review and research agenda, *Journal of Management*, 38: 1115–1166; R. Agarwal, D. Audretsch, & M. B. Sarkar, 2010, Knowledge spillovers and strategic entrepreneurship, *Strategic Entrepreneurship Journal*, 4: 271–283.

63. M. Gottfredson, R. Puryear, & S. Phillips, 2005, Strategic sourcing: From periphery to the core, *Harvard Business Review*, 83(2): 132–139.

64. R.-J. Jean, R. R. Sinkovics, & T. P. Hiebaum, 2014, The effects of supplier involvement and knowledge protection on product innovation in customer-supplier relationships: A study of global automotive suppliers in China. *Journal of Product Innovation Management*, 31: 98–113.

65. M. J. Donate & J. D. Sánchez de Pablo, 2015, The role of knowledge-oriented leadership in knowledge management practices and innovation, *Journal of Business Research*, 68: 360–370;

J. T. Macher & C. Boerner, 2012, Technological development at the boundary of the firm: A knowledge-based examination in drug development, *Strategic Management Journal*, 33: 1016–1036.

66. E. Sherman, 2010, Climbing the corporate ladder, *Continental Magazine*, November, 54–56.

67. K. Srikanth & P. Puranam, 2014, The Firm as a coordination system: Evidence from software services offshoring, *Organization Science*, 25: 1253–1271; K. Z. Zhou & C. B. Li, 2012, How knowledge affects radical innovation: Knowledge base, market knowledge acquisition, and internal knowledge sharing, *Strategic Management Journal*, 33: 1090–1102.

68. D. Laureiro-Martínez, S. Brusoni, N. Canessa, & M. Zollo, 2015, Understanding the exploration-exploitation dilemma: An fMRI study of attention control and decision-making performance, *Strategic Management Journal*, 36, 319–338; C. A. Siren, M. Kohtamaki, & A. Kuckertz, 2012, Exploration and exploitation strategies, profit performance and the mediating role of strategic learning: Escaping the exploitation trap, *Strategic Entrepreneurship Journal*, 6: 18–41.

69. A. Cuervo-Cazurra & C. A. Un, 2010, Why some firms never invest in formal R&D, *Strategic Management Journal*, 31: 759–779.

70. S. Carnahan & D. Somaya, 2013, Alumni effects and relational advantage: The impact on outsourcing when a buyer hires employees from a supplier's competitors, *Academy of Management Journal*, 56: 1578–1600; H. Yang, C. Phelps, & H. K. Steensma, 2010, Learning from what others have learned from you: The effects of knowledge spillovers on originating firms, *Academy of Management Journal*, 53: 371–389.

71. R. Aalbers, W. Dolfsma, & O. Koppius, 2014, Rich ties and innovative knowledge transfer within a firm, *British Journal of Management*, 25: 833–848; A. Jain, 2013, Learning by doing and the locus of innovative capability in biotechnology research, *Organization Science*, 24: 1683–1700.

72. D. Herhausen, R. E. Morgan, & H. W. Volberda, 2014, A meta analysis of the antecedents and consequences of strategic flexibility, *Academy of Management Annual Meeting Proceedings*, 1051–1057; S. Kortmann, C. Gelhard, C. Zimmermann, & F. T. Piller, 2014, Linking strategic flexibility and operational efficiency: The mediating role of ambidextrous operational capabilities, *Journal of Operations Management*, 32(7/8): 475–490.

73. Garcia-Sanchez, Mesquita, & Vassolo, What doesn't kill you makes you; R. G. McGrath, 2013, *The end of competitive advantage*, Boston: Harvard Business School Press.

74. E. G. Anderson Jr. & K. Lewis, 2014, A dynamic model of individual and collective learning amid disruption, *Organization Science*, 25: 356–376; M. L. Santos-Vijande, J. A. Lopez-Sanchez, & J. A. Trespalacios, 2011, How organizational learning affects a firm's flexibility, competitive strategy, and performance, *Journal of Business Research*, 65: 1079–1089; A. C. Edmondson, 2008, The competitive imperative of learning, *Harvard Business Review*, 86(7/8): 60–67.

75. R. E. Hoskisson, M. A. Hitt, W. P. Wan, & D. Yiu, 1999, Swings of a pendulum: Theory and research in strategic management, *Journal of Management*, 25: 417–456.

76. Karniouchina, Carson, Short, & Ketchen, Extending the firm vs. industry debate: Does industry life cycle stage matter; E. H. Bowman & C. E. Helfat, 2001, Does corporate strategy matter? *Strategic Management Journal*, 22: 1–23.

77. S. F. Karabag & C. Berggren, 2014, Antecedents of firm performance in emerging economies: Business groups, strategy, industry structure, and state support, *Journal of Business Research*, 67: 2212–2223; J. T. Mahoney & L. Qian, 2013, Market frictions as building blocks of an organizational economics approach to strategic management, *Strategic Management Journal*, 34: 1019–1041.

78. Schramm & Hu, Perspective: The evolution of R&D conduct in the pharmaceutical; J. Galbreath & P. Galvin, 2008, Firm factors, industry structure and performance variation: New empirical evidence to a classic debate, *Journal of Business Research*, 61: 109–117.

79. R. Casadesus-Masanell & F. Zhu, 2013, Business model innovation and competitive imitation: The case of sponsor-based business models, *Strategic Management Journal*, 34: 464–482; H. E. Posen, J. Lee, & S. Yi, 2013, The power of imperfect imitation, *Strategic Management Journal*, 34: 149–164; M. B. Lieberman & S. Asaba, 2006, Why do firms imitate each other? *Academy of Management Journal*, 31: 366–385.

80. M. E. Porter, 1985, *Competitive Advantage*, New York: Free Press; M. E. Porter, 1980, *Competitive Strategy*, New York: Free Press.

81. F. J. Mas-Ruiz, F. J., Ruiz-Moreno, & A. Ladrón de Guevara Martínez, 2014, Asymmetric rivalry within and between strategic groups, *Strategic Management Journal*, 35: 419–439; J. C. Short, D. J. Ketchen, Jr., T. B. Palmer, & G. T. M. Hult, 2007, Firm, strategic group, and industry influences on performance, *Strategic Management Journal*, 28: 147–167.

82. B. Kowitt, 2014, Fallen arches, *Fortune*, December 1, 106–116.

83. S. D. Pathak, Z. Wu, & D. Johnston, D. 2014, Toward a structural view of co-opetition in supply networks, *Journal of Operations Management*, 32: 254–267; T. W. Tong &

J. J. Reuer, 2010, Competitive consequences of interfirm collaboration: How joint ventures shape industry profitability, *Journal of International Business Studies*, 41: 1056–1073.

84. P. Brody & V. Pureswaran, 2015, The next digital gold rush: How the internet of things will create liquid, transparent markets, *Strategy & Leadership*, 43(1): 36–41; C. Moschieri, 2011, The implementation and structuring of divestitures: The unit's perspective, *Strategic Management Journal*, 32: 368–401.

85. A. M. McGahan & M. E. Porter, 2003, The emergence and sustainability of abnormal profits, *Strategic Organization*, 1: 79–108; M. McGahan, 1999, Competition, strategy and business performance, *California Management Review*, 41(3): 74–101.

86. N. J. Foss & P. G. Klein, 2014, Why managers still matter, *MIT Sloan Management Review*, 56(1): 73–80; J. W. Upson, D. J. Ketchen, B. L. Connelly, & A. L. Ranft, 2012, Competitor analysis and foothold moves, *Academy of Management Journal*, 55: 93–110; A. Zavyalova, M. D. Pfarrer, R. K. Reger, & D. K. Shapiro, 2012, Managing the message: The effects of firm actions and industry spillovers on media coverage following wrongdoing, *Academy of Management Journal*, 55: 1079–1101.

87. L. A., Costa, K. Cool, & I. Dierickx, 2013, The competitive implications of the deployment of unique resources, *Strategic Management Journal*, 34: 445–463; M. G. Jacobides, S. G. Winter, & S. M. Kassberger, 2012, The dynamics of wealth, profit and sustainable advantage, *Strategic Management Journal*, 33: 1384–1410; J. Kraaijenbrink, J.-C. Spender, & A. J. Groen, 2010, The resource-based view: A review and assessment of its critiques, *Journal of Management*, 38: 349–372.

88. M. Naor, J. S. Jones, E. S. Bernardes, S. M. Goldstein, & R. Schroeder, 2014, The culture-effectiveness link in a manufacturing context: A resource-based perspective, *Journal of World Business*, 49, 321–331; A. Arora & A. Nandkumar, 2012, Insecure advantage? Markets for technology and the value of resources for entrepreneurial ventures, *Strategic Management Journal*, 33: 231–251.

89. O. Schilke, 2014, On the contingent value of dynamic capabilities for competitive advantage: The nonlinear moderating effect of environmental dynamism, *Strategic Management Journal*, 35: 179–203; Teece, The foundations of enterprise performance: Dynamic and ordinary capabilities in an (economic) theory of firms.

90. P. J. Holahan, Z. Z. Sullivan, & S. K. Markham, 2014, Product development as core competence: How formal product development practices differ for radical,

more innovative, and incremental product innovations, *Journal of Product Innovation Management*, 31: 329–345.

91. J. R. Lecuona & M. Reitzig, 2014, Knowledge worth having in 'excess': The value of tacit and firm-specific human resource slack, *Strategic Management Journal*, 35: 954–973; H. Wang & K. F. E. Wong, 2012, The effect of managerial bias on employees' specific human capital investments, *Journal of Management Studies*, 49: 1435–1458.

92. Y. Lin & L. Wu, 2014, Exploring the role of dynamic capabilities in firm performance under the resource-based view framework, *Journal of Business Research*, 67: 407–413; C. Weigelt, 2013, Leveraging supplier capabilities: The role of locus of capability development, *Strategic Management Journal*, 34: 1–21; S. L. Newbert, 2007, Empirical research on the resource-based view of the firm: An assessment and suggestions for future research, *Strategic Management Journal*, 28: 121–146.

93. R. Nag & D. A. Gioia, 2012, From common to uncommon knowledge: Foundations of firm-specific use of knowledge as a resource, *Academy of Management Journal*, 55: 421–455; D. M. DeCarolis, 2003, Competencies and imitability in the pharmaceutical industry: An analysis of their relationship with firm performance, *Journal of Management*, 29: 27–50.

94. Y. Y. Kor & A. Mesko, 2013, Dynamic managerial capabilities: Configuration and orchestration of top executives' capabilities and the firm's dominant logic, *Strategic Management Journal*, 34: 233–244; M. Gruber, F. Heinemann, & M. Brettel, 2010, Configurations of resources and capabilities and their performance implications: An exploratory study on technology ventures, *Strategic Management Journal*, 31: 1337–1356.

95. R. Kapoor & N. R. Furr, 2015, Complementarities and competition: Unpacking the drivers of entrants' technology choices in the solar photovoltaic industry, *Strategic Management Journal*, 36: 416–436; E. Levitas & H. A. Ndofor, 2006, What to do with the resource-based view: A few suggestions for what ails the RBV that supporters and opponents might accept, *Journal of Management Inquiry*, 15: 135–144.

96. B. Larrañeta, S. A. Zahra, & J. L. Galán González, 2014, Strategic repertoire variety and new venture growth: The moderating effects of origin and industry dynamism, *Strategic Management Journal*, 35: 761–772; M. Makhija, 2003, Comparing the source-based and market-based views of the firm: Empirical evidence from Czech privatization, *Strategic Management Journal*, 24: 433–451.

97. S. E. Reid & U. Brentani, 2015, Building a measurement model for market

visioning competence and its proposed antecedents: organizational encouragement of divergent thinking, divergent thinking attitudes, and ideational behavior, *Journal of Product Innovation Management*, 32: 243–262.

98. C. Gallo, 2010, *The Innovation Secrets of Steve Jobs*, NY: McGraw-Hill.

99. G. Christ, 2014, Leadership & strategy: Life after Steve Jobs: CEO succession. *Industry Week*, April, 28.

100. A. M. Carton, C. Murphy, & J. R. Clark, 2014, A (blurry) vision of the future: How leader rhetoric about ultimate goals influences performance, *Academy of Management Journal*, 57: 1544–1570; Foss & Klein, Why managers still matter.

101. P. Bolton, M. K. Brunnermeier, & L Veldkamp, L. 2013, Leadership, coordination, and corporate culture, *Review of Economic Studies*, 80: 512–537; R. D. Ireland & M. A. Hitt, 1992, Mission statements: Importance, challenge, and recommendations for development, *Business Horizons*, 35: 34–42.

102. B. E. Perrott, 2015, Building the sustainable organization: An integrated approach, *Journal of Business Strategy*, 36(1): 41–51; S. Khalifa, 2012, Mission, purpose, and ambition: Redefining the mission statement, *Journal of Business and Strategy*, 5: 236–251.

103. R. Srinivasan, 2014, Visioning: The method and process, *OD Practitioner*, 46(1): 34–41; J. H. Davis, J. A. Ruhe, M. Lee, & U. Rajadhyaksha, 2007, Mission possible: Do school mission statements work? *Journal of Business Ethics*, 70: 99–110.

104. A. Ebrahim & V. K. Rangan, V. K. 2014, What Impact?, *California Management Review*, 56(3): 118–141; L. W. Fry & J. W. Slocum, Jr., 2008, Maximizing the triple bottom line through spiritual leadership, *Organizational Dynamics*, 37: 86–96; A. J. Ward, M. J. Lankau, A. C. Amason, J. A. Sonnenfeld, & B. A. Agle, 2007, Improving the performance of top management teams, *MIT Sloan Management Review*, 48(3): 85–90.

105. M. Cording, J. S. Harrison, R. E. Hoskisson, & K. Jonsen, 2014, "Walking the talk": A multi-stakeholder exploration of organizational authenticity, employee productivity and post-merger performance, *Academy of Management Perspectives*, 28: 38–56; K. Basu & G. Palazzo, 2008, Corporate social responsibility: A process model of sensemaking, *Academy of Management Review*, 33: 122–136.

106. R. Garcia-Castro & R. Aguilera, 2015, Incremental value creation and appropriation in a world with multiple stakeholders, *Strategic Management Journal*, forthcoming; G. Kenny, 2012, From a stakeholder viewpoint: Designing measurable objectives, *Journal of Business Strategy*, 33(6): 40–46;

D. A. Bosse, R. A. Phillips, & J. S. Harrison, 2009, Stakeholders, reciprocity, and firm performance, *Strategic Management Journal*, 30: 447–456.

107. N. Darnell, I. Henrique, & P. Sadorsky, 2010, Adopting proactive environmental strategy: The influence of stakeholders and firm size, *Journal of Management Studies*, 47: 1072–1122; G. Donaldson & J. W. Lorsch, 1983, *Decision Making at the Top: The Shaping of Strategic Direction*, New York: Basic Books, 37–40.

108. S. Sharma & I. Henriques, 2005, Stakeholder influences on sustainability practices in the Canadian forest products industry, *Strategic Management Journal*, 26: 159–180.

109. Y. Mishina, E. S. Block, & M. J. Mannor, 2015, The path dependence of organizational reputation: How social judgment influences assessments of capability and character, *Strategic Management Journal*, forthcoming; D. Crilly & P. Sloan, 2012, Enterprise logic: Explaining corporate attention to stakeholders from the 'inside-out', *Strategic Management Journal*, 33: 1174–1193.

110. Jacobides, BlackBerry forgot to manage the ecosystem.

111. K. Chang, I. Kim, & Y. Li, 2014, The heterogeneous impact of corporate social responsibility activities that target different stakeholders, *Journal of Business Ethics*, 125: 211–234.

112. J. Wolf, J. 2014, The relationship between sustainable supply chain management, stakeholder pressure and corporate sustainability performance, *Journal of Business Ethics*, 119: 317–328; A. Soleimani, W. D. Schneper, & W. Newburry, 2014, The impact of stakeholder power on corporate reputation: A cross-country corporate governance perspective, *Organization Science*, 25: 991–1008; G. Pandher & R. Currie, 2013, CEO compensation: A resource advantage and stakeholder-bargaining perspective, *Strategic Management Journal*, 34: 22–41.

113. A. H. Reilly & K. A. Hynan, 2014, Corporate communication, sustainability, and social media: It's not easy (really) being green, *Business Horizons*, 57: 747–758; D. Bush & B. D. Gelb, 2012, Antitrust enforcement: An inflection point? *Journal of Business Strategy*, 33(6): 15–21; J. L. Murrillo-Luna, C. Garces-Ayerbe, & P. Rivera-Torres, 2008, Why do patterns of environmental response differ? A stakeholders' pressure approach, Strategic *Management Journal*, 29: 1225–1240.

114. J. P. Doh & N. R. Quigley, 2014, Responsible leadership and stakeholder management: Influence pathways and organizational outcomes, *Academy of Management Perspectives*, 28: 255–274; R. Boutilier, 2009, *Stakeholder Politics: Social Capital, Sustainable Development, and the*

Corporation, Sheffield, U.K.: Greenleaf Publishing.

115. W. J. Henisz, S. Dorobantu, & L. J. Nartey, 2014, Spinning gold: The financial returns to stakeholder engagement, *Strategic Management Journal*, 35: 1727–1748; F. G. A. de Bakker & F. den Hond, 2008, Introducing the politics of stakeholder influence, *Business & Society*, 47: 8–20.

116. M. Goranova & L. V. Ryan, 2014, Shareholder activism: A multidisciplinary review, *Journal of Management*, 40: 1230–1268.

117. I. Filatotchev & O. Dotsenko, 2015, Shareholder activism in the UK: Types of activists, forms of activism, and their impact on a target's performance, *Journal of Management & Governance*, 19: 5–24; B. L. Connelly, L. Tihanyi, S. T. Certo, & M. A. Hitt, 2010, Marching to the beat of different drummers: The influence of institutional owners on competitive actions, *Academy of Management Journal*, 53: 723–742.

118. L. Jiang & Y. Zhu, 2014, Effects of foreign institutional ownership on foreign bank lending: Some evidence for emerging markets, *International Review of Finance*, 14: 263–293.

119. S. Wilkins & J. Huisman, 2014, Corporate images' impact on consumers' product choices: The case of multinational foreign subsidiaries, *Journal of Business Research*, 67: 2224–2230; L. Pierce, 2009, Big losses in ecosystems niches: How core firm decisions drive complementary product shakeouts, *Strategic Management Journal*, 30: 323–347.

120. M. Bertini & O. Koenigsberg, 2014, When customers help set prices, *MIT Sloan Management Review*, 55(4): 57–64; O. D. Fjeldstad & A. Sasson, 2010, Membership matters: On the value of being embedded in customer networks, *Journal of Management Studies*, 47: 944–966.

121. B. Batjargal, M. A. Hitt, A. S. Tsui, J.-L. Arregle, J. Webb, & T. Miller, 2013, Institutional polycentrism, entrepreneurs' social networks and new venture growth, *Academy of Management Journal*, in press.

122. H. Su, 2014, Business ethics and the development of intellectual capital, *Journal of Business Ethics*, 119: 87–98; D. A. Ready, L. A. Hill, & J. A. Conger, 2008, Winning the race for talent in emerging markets, *Harvard Business* Review, 86(11): 62–70.

123. S. E. Jackson, R. S. Schuler, & K. Jiang, 2014, An aspirational framework for strategic human resource management, *Academy of Management Annals*, 8: 1–56; T. R. Crook, S. Y. Todd, J. G. Combs, D. J. Woehr, & D. J. Ketchen, 2011, Does human capital matter? A meta-analysis of the relationship between human capital and firm performance, *Journal of Applied Psychology*, 96: 443–456.

124. R. Eckardt, B. C. Skaggs, & M. Youndt, 2014, Turnover and knowledge loss: An examination of the differential impact of production manager and worker turnover in service and manufacturing firm, *Journal of Management Studies*, 51: 1025–1057; J. I. Hancock, D. G. Allen, F. A. Bosco, K. R. McDaniel, & C. A. Pierce, 2013, Meta-analytic review of employee turnover as a predictor of firm performance, *Journal of Management*, 39: 573–603.

125. W. A. Schiemann, 2014, From talent management to talent optimization, *Journal of World Business*, 49: 281–288; R. Takeuchi, 2010, A critical review of expatriate adjustment research through a multiple stakeholder view: Progress, emerging trends and prospects, *Journal of Management*, 36: 1040–1064.

126. S. E. Reid & U. Brentani, 2015, Building a measurement model for market visioning competence and its proposed antecedents: organizational encouragement of divergent thinking, divergent thinking attitudes, and ideational behavior, *Journal of Product Innovation Management*, 32: 243–262; M. A. Hitt, K. T. Haynes, & R. Serpa, 2010, Strategic leadership for the 21st century, *Business Horizons*, 53: 437–444.

127. S. Gunz & L. Thorne, 2015, Introduction to the special issue on tone at the top, *Journal of Business Ethics*, 126: 1–2; C. Crossland, J. Zyung, N. Hiller, & D. Hambrick, 2014. CEO career variety: Effects on firm–level strategic and social novelty. *Academy of Management Journal*, 57: 652–674; D. C. Hambrick, 2007, Upper echelons theory: An update, *Academy of Management Review*, 32: 334–339.

128. G. Bhalla, 2014, How to plan and manage a project to co-create value with stakeholders, *Strategy & Leadership*, 42: 19–25; J. C. Camillus, 2008, Strategy as a wicked problem, *Harvard Business Review* 86(5): 99–106; A. Priestland & T. R. Hanig, 2005, Developing first-level managers, *Harvard Business Review*, 83(6): 113–120.

129. M. Voronov, D. De Clercq, & C. R. Hinings, 2013, Conformity and distinctiveness in a global institutional framework: The legitimation of Ontario fine wine, *Journal of Management Studies*, 50: 607–645; B. Gutierrez, S. M. Spencer, & G. Zhu, 2012, Thinking globally, leading locally: Chinese, Indian, and Western leadership, *Cross Cultural Management*, 19: 67–89.

130. D. B. Wangrow, D. J. Schepker, & V. L. Barker, 2014, Managerial discretion: An empirical review and focus on future research directions, *Journal of Management*, 41: 99–135; J. Li & Y. Tang, 2010, CEO hubris and firm risk taking in China: The moderating role of managerial discretion, *Academy of Management Journal*, 53: 45–68.

131. C. A. O'Reilly, D. F. Caldwell, J A. Chatman, & B. Doerr, B. 2014, The promise and

problems of organizational culture: CEO personality, culture, and firm performance, *Group & Organization Management*, 39: 595–625.

132. D. C. Hambrick, S. E. Humphrey, & A. Gupta, 2015, Structural interdependence within top management teams: A key moderator of upper echelons predictions, *Strategic Management Journal*, 36: 449–461; K. D. Clark & P. G. Maggitti, 2012, TMT potency and strategic decision making in high technology firms, *Journal of Management Studies*, 49: 1168–1193.

133. M. M. Heyden, S. van Doorn, M. Reimer, F. J. Van Den Bosch, & H. W. Volberda, 2013, Perceived environmental dynamism, relative competitive performance, and top management team heterogeneity: Examining correlates of upper echelons' advice-seeking, *Organization Studies:* 34: 1327–1356; R. Shambaugh, 2011, Leading in today's economy: The transformational leadership model, in *What's Next 2011*, NY: McGraw-Hill.

134. S. Khavul & G. D. Bruton, 2013, Harnessing innovation for change: Sustainability and poverty in developing countries, *Journal of Management Studies*, 50: 285–306; A. Leiponen & C. E. Helfat, 2010, Innovation objectives, knowledge sources and the benefits of breadth, *Strategic Management Journal*, 31: 224–236.

135. L Wei & L. Wu, 2013, What a diverse top management team means: Testing an integrated model, *Journal of Management Studies*, 50: 389–412; T. Buyl, C. Boone, W. Hendriks, & P. Matthyssens, 2011, Top management team functional diversity and firm performance: The moderating role of CEO characteristics, *Journal of Management Studies*, 48: 151–177.

136. Stettner & Lavie, Ambidexterity under scrutiny: Exploration and exploitation via internal organization, alliances, and acquisitions; Q. Cao, Z. Simsek, & H. Zhang, 2010, Modelling the joint impact of the CEO and the TMT on organizational ambidexterity, *Journal of Management Studies*, 47: 1272–1296.

137. N. Gaffney, D. Cooper, B. Kedia, & J. Clampit, 2014, Institutional transitions, global mindset, and EMNE internationalization, *European Management Journal*, 32: 383–391; M.-J. Chen & D. Miller, 2010, West meets east: Toward an ambicultural approach to management, *Academy of Management Perspectives*, 24: 17–37.

138. M. Loeb, 1993, Steven J. Ross, 1927–1992, *Fortune*, January 25, 4.

139. F. Jing, G. Avery, & H. Bergsteiner, 2014, Enhancing performance in small professional firms through vision communication and sharing, *Asia Pacific Journal of Management*, 31: 599–620.

140. R. F. Everett, 2014, A crack in the foundation: Why SWOT might be less than effective in market sensing analysis, *Journal of Marketing & Management*, 1: 58–78; M. M. Helms & J. Nixon, 2010, Exploring SWOT analysis—where are we now? A review of the academic research from the last decade, *Journal of Strategy and Management*, 3: 215–251.

141. T. Keil, T. Laamanen, & R. G. McGrath, 2013, Is a counterattack the best defense? Competitive dynamics through acquisitions, *Long Range Planning*, 46: 195–215; T. Yu, M. Subramaniam, & A. A. Cannella, Jr., 2009, Rivalry deterrence in international markets: Contingencies governing the mutual forbearance hypothesis, *Academy of Management Journal*, 52: 127–147.

142. O. Schilke & K. S. Cook, 2015, Sources of alliance partner trustworthiness: Integrating calculative and relational perspectives, *Strategic Management Journal*, 36: 276–297; K. H. Heimeriks, C. B. Bingham, & T. Laamanen, 2015, Unveiling the temporally contingent role of codification in alliance success, *Strategic Management Journal*, 36: 462–473.

143. L. A. Cunningham, 2015, The secret sauce of corporate leadership, *Wall Street Journal*, www.wsj.com, January 26; S. D. Julian, J. C. Ofori-Dankwa, & R. T. Justis, 2008, Understanding strategic responses to interest group pressures, *Strategic Management Journal*, 29: 963–984; C. Eesley & M. J. Lenox, 2006, Firm responses to secondary stakeholder action, *Strategic Management Journal*, 27: 765–781.

144. Y. Luo, Y. Liu, Q. Yang, V. Maksimov, & J. Hou, 2015, Improving performance and reducing cost in buyer–supplier relationships: The role of justice in curtailing opportunism, *Journal of Business Research*, 68: 607–615; Y. Luo, 2008, Procedural fairness and interfirm cooperation in strategic alliances, *Strategic Management Journal*, 29: 27–46.

145. H. S. James, D. Ng, & P. J. Klein, 2015, Complexity, novelty, and ethical judgment by entrepreneurs, *International Journal of Entrepreneurial Venturing*, forthcoming; B. A. Scott, A. S. Garza, D. E. Conlon, & K. You Jin, 2014, Why do managers act fairly in the first place? A daily investigation of "hot" and "cold" motives and discretion, *Academy of Management Journal*, 57: 1571–1591.

146. M. Sharif & T. Scandura, T. 2014, Do perceptions of ethical conduct matter during organizational change? Ethical leadership and employee involvement, *Journal of Business Ethics*, 124: 185–196; B. W. Heineman Jr., 2007, Avoiding integrity land mines, *Harvard Business Review*, 85(4): 100–108.

147. D. C. Hambrick & T. J. Quigley, 2014, Toward more accurate contextualization of the CEO effect on firm performance, *Strategic Management Journal*, 35: 473–491; P. Klarner & S. Raisch, 2013, Move to the beat—Rhythms of change and firm performance, *Academy of Management Journal*, 56: 160–184.

2

The External Environment: Opportunities, Threats, Industry Competition, and Competitor Analysis

Studying this chapter should provide you with the strategic management knowledge needed to:

2-1 Explain the importance of analyzing and understanding the firm's external environment.

2-2 Define and describe the general environment and the industry environment.

2-3 Discuss the four parts of the external environmental analysis process.

2-4 Name and describe the general environment's seven segments.

2-5 Identify the five competitive forces and explain how they determine an industry's profitability potential.

2-6 Define strategic groups and describe their influence on firms.

2-7 Describe what firms need to know about their competitors and different methods (including ethical standards) used to collect intelligence about them.

ARE THERE CRACKS IN THE GOLDEN ARCHES?

McDonald's is the largest restaurant chain in the world. It has 14,350 restaurants in the United States, with the largest market share of any such chain (7.3 percent). In total, it has more than 36,000 restaurants worldwide. Over the years, McDonald's was a leader, not only in market share, but also with the introduction of new menu items to the fast food market. For example, it first introduced breakfast items to this market, and its breakfast menu now accounts for about 25 percent of its sales. It successfully introduced Chicken McNuggets to this market, and currently, McDonald's is the single largest restaurant customer of Tyson Foods, the largest distributor of chicken products. In more recent years, McDonald's successfully introduced gourmet coffee products and began to compete against Starbucks. With all of this success, what is the problem?

The problems revolve around competition and changing consumer tastes. Consumers have become more health-conscious, and competitors have been more attuned to customer desires. As a result, McDonald's suffered a decline in its total sales revenue of 2.4 percent and a drop in net income of 15 percent in 2014. This was the first decline in both figures in 33 years. It seems that McDonald's did a poor job of analyzing its environment and especially its customers and competitors. During this same time, some of McDonald's competitors flourished. For example, Sonic enjoyed a 7 percent increase in its sales, and Chipotle recorded a large

Ruaridh Stewart/ZUMA Press/Newscom

20 percent increase. Other specialty burger restaurants, such as Smashburger, have stolen business from McDonald's even though their burgers are priced a little higher than McDonald's burgers. The quality of these competitors' products is perceived to be higher and many are "made to order" and thus customized to the customer's desires. And, partly because the volume and complexity of the McDonald's menu items have grown, the time required for service has also increased. This change has been most evident in the drive-through lanes in which the wait time has grown by approximately 20 percent in recent years.

Because of the lack of understanding the changing market and competitive landscape, McDonald's was unable to be proactive and now is in a reactive mode. For example, in 2013, it decided to add chicken wings to its menu. Wings were sold successfully at McDonald's in Hong Kong, and it imported its "cayenne-and-chili-pepper coating" used there. The market test for the wings in Atlanta was successful, so the firm implemented a major campaign to sell them at its restaurants throughout the United States. The eight-week campaign was a miserable failure (some referred to it as the "mighty wings debacle"). Perhaps they were too spicy for the broad market, but some believe that they were also too expensive at $1.00 per wing, with a box of five wings costing $1.00 more than a similar number at KFC. Because of these problems, McDonald's hired a new CEO in 2015, hoping to overcome its woes.

The new CEO must act quickly. McDonald's has recently announced that it is changing to use only chickens raised without antibiotics to be sensitive to human health concerns. It has also market tested custom hamburgers in Australia with success. In fact, Australia is one of

McDonald's bright spots around the world. Sales have increased in Australia when they have fallen in the United States, Europe, and Asia. Making major changes to the McDonald's menu is challenging partly because of its scale and supply chain. It orders hundreds of millions of pounds of chicken each year, so it will take a few years to fully implement the change to antibiotic-free chicken. Changing vegetables in Happy Meals (e.g., adding baby carrots) and implementing new wraps which require additional (new) vegetables (such as cucumbers) will take time because they require obtaining large scale suppliers that can provide the necessary quantity and quality at the right price and in the right location(s).

McDonald's was once a leader, and now it is fighting from behind, trying to stem its downturn. It has to respond quickly and effectively to its external environment, especially its customers and competitors.

Sources: A. Gasparro, 2015, For McDonald's, a minor menu change takes planning, MSN, www.msn.com/en-us/money, March 5; A. Gasparro, 2015, McDonald's new chief plots counter attack, *Wall Street Journal*, www.wsj.com, March 1; M. Hefferman, 2015, It's still a happy meal in Australia for McDonald's, *Sidney Times Herald*, www.smh.com.au, March 10; J. Kell, 2015, McDonald's sales still down as a new CEO takes the helm, *Fortune*, www.Fortune.com, March 9; D. Shanker, 2015, Dear McDonald's new CEO: Happy first day. Here's some (unsolicited) advice, *Fortune*, www.Fortune.com, March 2; S. Strom, 2015, McDonald's seeks its fast-food soul, *New York Times*, www.nytimes.com, March 7; S. Strom, 2015, McDonald's tests custom burgers and other new concepts as sales drop, *New York Times*, www.nytimes.com, January 23; B. Kowitt, 2014, Fallen Arches, *Fortune*, December, 106–116.

As suggested in the Opening Case and by research, the external environment (which includes the industry in which a firm competes as well as those against whom it competes) affects the competitive actions and responses firms take to outperform competitors and earn above-average returns.[1] For example, McDonald's has been experiencing a reduction in returns in recent times because of changing consumer tastes and enhanced competition. McDonald's is attempting to respond to the threats from its environment by changing its menu and types of supplies purchased. The sociocultural segment of the general environment (discussed in this chapter) is the source of some of the changing values in society placing a great emphasis on healthy food choices. The Opening Case also describes some of the ways McDonald's is responding to the specific concerns for health by purchasing only chicken that has not received antibiotics.

As noted in Chapter 1, the characteristics of today's external environment differ from historical conditions. For example, technological changes and the continuing growth of information gathering and processing capabilities increase the need for firms to develop effective competitive actions and responses on a timely basis.[2] (We fully discuss competitive actions and responses in Chapter 5.) Additionally, the rapid sociological changes occurring in many countries affect labor practices and the nature of products that increasingly diverse consumers demand. Governmental policies and laws also affect where and how firms choose to compete.[3] And, changes to a number of nations' financial regulatory systems that have been enacted since 2010 are expected to increase the complexity of organizations' financial transactions.[4]

Firms understand the external environment by acquiring information about competitors, customers, and other stakeholders to build their own base of knowledge and capabilities.[5] On the basis of the new information, firms take actions, such as building new capabilities and core competencies, in hopes of buffering themselves from any negative environmental effects and to pursue opportunities as the basis for better serving their stakeholders' needs.[6]

In summary, a firm's competitive actions and responses are influenced by the conditions in the three parts (the general, industry, and competitor) of its external environment (see Figure 2.1) and its understanding of those conditions. Next, we fully describe each part of the firm's external environment.

Figure 2.1 The External Environment

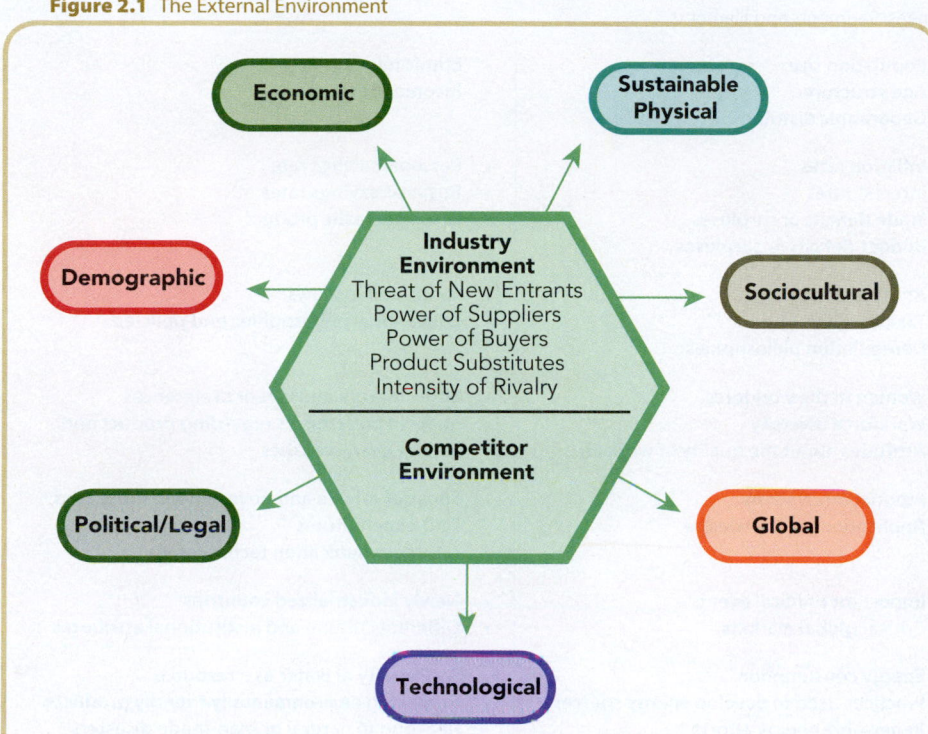

2-1 The General, Industry, and Competitor Environments

The **general environment** is composed of dimensions in the broader society that influence an industry and the firms within it.[7] We group these dimensions into seven environmental *segments:* demographic, economic, political/legal, sociocultural, technological, global, and sustainable physical. Examples of *elements* analyzed in each of these segments are shown in Table 2.1.

Firms cannot directly control the general environment's segments. Accordingly, what a company seeks to do is recognize trends in each segment of the general environment and then *predict* each trend's effect on it. For example, it has been predicted that over the next 10 to 20 years, millions of people living in emerging market countries will join the middle class. In fact, by 2030, it is predicted that two-thirds of the global middle class, about 525 million people, will live in the Asia-Pacific region of the world. Of course no firm, including large multinationals, is able to control where growth in potential customers may take place in the next decade or two. Nonetheless, firms must study this anticipated trend as a foundation for predicting its effects on their ability to identify strategies to use that will allow them to remain successful as market conditions change.[8]

The **industry environment** is the set of factors that directly influences a firm and its competitive actions and responses: the threat of new entrants, the power of suppliers, the power of buyers, the threat of product substitutes, and the intensity of rivalry among competing firms.[9] In total, the interactions among these five factors

The **general environment** is composed of dimensions in the broader society that influence an industry and the firms within it.

The **industry environment** is the set of factors that directly influences a firm and its competitive actions and responses: the threat of new entrants, the power of suppliers, the power of buyers, the threat of product substitutes, and the intensity of rivalry among competing firms.

Table 2.1 The General Environment: Segments and Elements

Demographic segment	• Population size • Age structure • Geographic distribution	• Ethnic mix • Income distribution
Economic segment	• Inflation rates • Interest rates • Trade deficits or surpluses • Budget deficits or surpluses	• Personal savings rate • Business savings rates • Gross domestic product
Political/Legal segment	• Antitrust laws • Taxation laws • Deregulation philosophies	• Labor training laws • Educational philosophies and policies
Sociocultural segment	• Women in the workforce • Workforce diversity • Attitudes about the quality of work life	• Shifts in work and career preferences • Shifts in preferences regarding product and service characteristics
Technological segment	• Product innovations • Applications of knowledge	• Focus of private and government-supported R&D expenditures • New communication technologies
Global segment	• Important political events • Critical global markets	• Newly industrialized countries • Different cultural and institutional attributes
Sustainable physical environment segment	• Energy consumption • Practices used to develop energy sources • Renewable energy efforts • Minimizing a firm's environmental footprint	• Availability of water as a resource • Producing environmentally friendly products • Reacting to natural or man-made disasters

determine an industry's profitability potential; in turn, the industry's profitability potential influences the choices each firm makes about its competitive actions and responses. The challenge for a firm is to locate a position within an industry where it can favorably influence the five factors or where it can successfully defend itself against their influence. The greater a firm's capacity to favorably influence its industry environment, the greater the likelihood it will earn above-average returns.

How companies gather and interpret information about their competitors is called **competitor analysis**. Understanding the firm's competitor environment complements the insights provided by studying the general and industry environments.[10] This means, for example, that McDonald's needs to do a better job of analyzing and understanding its general and industry environments.

An analysis of the general environment focuses on environmental trends and their implications, an analysis of the industry environment focuses on the factors and conditions influencing an industry's profitability potential, and an analysis of competitors is focused on predicting competitors' actions, responses, and intentions. In combination, the results of these three analyses influence the firm's vision, mission, choice of strategies, and the competitive actions and responses it will take to implement those strategies. Although we discuss each analysis separately, the firm can develop and implement a more effective strategy when it effectively integrates the insights provided by analyses of the general environment, the industry environment, and the competitor environment.

How companies gather and interpret information about their competitors is called **competitor analysis**.

2-2   External Environmental Analysis

Most firms face external environments that are turbulent, complex, and global—conditions that make interpreting those environments difficult.[11] To cope with often ambiguous and incomplete environmental data and to increase understanding of the general environment, firms complete an *external environmental analysis*. This analysis has four parts: scanning, monitoring, forecasting, and assessing (see Table 2.2).

Identifying opportunities and threats is an important objective of studying the general environment. An **opportunity** is a condition in the general environment that, if exploited effectively, helps a company reach strategic competitiveness. Most companies—and certainly large ones—continuously encounter multiple opportunities as well as threats.

In terms of possible opportunities, a combination of cultural, political, and economic factors is resulting in rapid retail growth in parts of Africa, Asia, and Latin America. Accordingly, Walmart, the world's largest retailer, and the next three largest global giants (France's Carrefour, U.K.–based Tesco, and Germany's Metro) are expanding in these regions. Walmart is expanding its number of retail units in Chile (404 units), India (20 units), and South Africa (360 units). Interestingly, Carrefour exited India after four years and in the same year (2014) that Tesco opened stores in India. While Metro closed its operations in Egypt, it has stores in China, Russia, Japan, Vietnam, and India in addition to many eastern European countries.[12]

A **threat** is a condition in the general environment that may hinder a company's efforts to achieve strategic competitiveness.[13] Finnish-based Nokia Corp. is dealing with threats including one regarding its intellectual property rights. In mid-2013, the company filed two complaints against competitor HTC Corp. alleging that the Taiwanese smartphone manufacturer had infringed on nine of Nokia's patents. However, the patent dispute ended in 2014 when the two companies signed a collaboration agreement.[14] This threat obviously deals with the political/legal segment.

Firms use multiple sources to analyze the general environment through scanning, monitoring, forecasting, and assessing. Examples of these sources include a wide variety of printed materials (such as trade publications, newspapers, business publications, and the results of academic research and public polls), trade shows, and suppliers, customers, and employees of public-sector organizations. Of course, the information available from Internet sources is of increasing importance to a firm's efforts to study the general environment.

2-2a   Scanning

Scanning entails the study of all segments in the general environment. Although challenging, scanning is critically important to the firms' efforts to understand trends in the general environment and to predict their implications. This is particularly the case for companies competing in highly volatile environments.[15]

Table 2.2 Parts of the External Environment Analysis

Scanning	• Identifying early signals of environmental changes and trends
Monitoring	• Detecting meaning through ongoing observations of environmental changes and trends
Forecasting	• Developing projections of anticipated outcomes based on monitored changes and trends
Assessing	• Determining the timing and importance of environmental changes and trends for firms' strategies and their management

An **opportunity** is a condition in the general environment that, if exploited effectively, helps a company reach strategic competitiveness.

A **threat** is a condition in the general environment that may hinder a company's efforts to achieve strategic competitiveness.

Through scanning, firms identify early signals of potential changes in the general environment and detect changes that are already under way.[16] Scanning activities must be aligned with the organizational context; a scanning system designed for a volatile environment is inappropriate for a firm in a stable environment.[17] Scanning often reveals ambiguous, incomplete, or unconnected data and information that require careful analysis.

Many firms use special software to help them identify events that are taking place in the environment and that are announced in public sources. For example, news event detection uses information-based systems to categorize text and reduce the trade-off between an important missed event and false alarm rates. Increasingly, these systems are used to study social media outlets as sources of information.[18]

Broadly speaking, the Internet provides a wealth of opportunities for scanning. Amazon.com, for example, records information about individuals visiting its website, particularly if a purchase is made. Amazon then welcomes these customers by name when they visit the website again. The firm sends messages to customers about specials and new products similar to those they purchased in previous visits. A number of other companies, such as Netflix, also collect demographic data about their customers in an attempt to identify their unique preferences (demographics is one of the segments in the general environment). More than 2.4 billion people use the Internet in some way including about 78.6 percent of the population in North America and 63.2 percent in Europe. So the Internet represents a healthy opportunity to gather information on users.[19]

2-2b Monitoring

When *monitoring*, analysts observe environmental changes to see if an important trend is emerging from among those spotted through scanning.[20] Critical to successful monitoring is the firm's ability to detect meaning in environmental events and trends. For example, those monitoring retirement trends in the United States learned in 2013 that 57 percent of U.S. workers surveyed reported that excluding the value of their home, they have only $25,000 or less in savings and investments set aside for their retirement. This particular survey also discovered "that 28 percent of Americans have no confidence they will have enough money to retire comfortably—the highest level in the (survey's) 23-year history."[21] Partly because of the major economic recessions and low wage growth, 67 percent of respondents to a more recent survey suggested that they had savings that would cover only six months or less of their expenses. And, approximately 28 percent of the respondents said that they had no savings.[22] Firms seeking to serve retirees' financial needs will continue monitoring this change in workers' savings and investment patterns to see if a trend is developing. Once they identify that saving less for retirement (or other needs) is indeed a trend, these firms will seek to understand its competitive implications.

Effective monitoring requires the firm to identify important stakeholders and understand its reputation among these stakeholders as the foundation for serving their unique needs.[23] (Stakeholders' unique needs are described in Chapter 1.) One means of monitoring major stakeholders is by using directors that serve on other boards of directors (referred to as interlocking directorates). They facilitate information and knowledge transfer from external sources.[24] Scanning and monitoring are particularly important when a firm competes in an industry with high technological uncertainty.[25] Scanning and monitoring can provide the firm with information. These activities also serve as a means of importing knowledge about markets and about how to successfully commercialize the new technologies the firm has developed.[26]

2-2c Forecasting

Scanning and monitoring are concerned with events and trends in the general environment at a point in time. When *forecasting*, analysts develop feasible projections of what might happen, and how quickly, as a result of the events and trends detected through scanning and monitoring.[27] For example, analysts might forecast the time that will be required for a new technology to reach the marketplace, the length of time before different corporate training procedures are required to deal with anticipated changes in the composition of the workforce, or how much time will elapse before changes in governmental taxation policies affect consumers' purchasing patterns.

Forecasting events and outcomes accurately is challenging. Forecasting demand for new technological products is difficult because technology trends are continually driving product life cycles shorter. This is particularly difficult for a firm such as Intel, whose products go into many customers' technological products, which are consistently updated. Increasing the difficulty, each new wafer fabrication or silicon chip technology production plant in which Intel invests becomes significantly more expensive for each generation of chip products. In this instance, having access to tools that allow better forecasting of electronic product demand is of value to Intel as the firm studies conditions in its external environment.[28]

2-2d Assessing

When *assessing*, the objective is to determine the timing and significance of the effects of environmental changes and trends that have been identified.[29] Through scanning, monitoring, and forecasting, analysts are able to understand the general environment. Additionally, the intent of assessment is to specify the implications of that understanding. Without assessment, the firm has data that may be interesting but of unknown competitive relevance. Even if formal assessment is inadequate, the appropriate interpretation of that information is important.

Accurately assessing the trends expected to take place in the segments of a firm's general environment is important. However, accurately interpreting the meaning of those trends is even more important. In slightly different words, although gathering and organizing information is important, appropriately interpreting the intelligence the collected information provides to determine if an identified trend in the general environment is an opportunity or threat is critical.[30]

2-3 Segments of the General Environment

The general environment is composed of segments that are external to the firm (see Table 2.1). Although the degree of impact varies, these environmental segments affect all industries and the firms competing in them. The challenge to each firm is to scan, monitor, forecast, and assess the elements in each segment to predict their effects on it. Effective scanning, monitoring, forecasting, and assessing are vital to the firm's efforts to recognize and evaluate opportunities and threats.

2-3a The Demographic Segment

The **demographic segment** is concerned with a population's size, age structure, geographic distribution, ethnic mix, and income distribution.[31] Demographic segments are commonly analyzed on a global basis because of their potential effects across countries' borders and because many firms compete in global markets.

Population Size

The world's population doubled (from 3 billion to 6 billion) between 1959 and 1999. Current projections suggest that population growth will continue in the twenty-first century, but at a slower pace. In 2015, the world's population was 7.3 billion, and it is projected to be 9 billion by 2042 and roughly 9.25 billion by 2050.[32] In 2015, China was the world's

The **demographic segment** is concerned with a population's size, age structure, geographic distribution, ethnic mix, and income distribution.

largest country by population with approximately 1.4 billion people. By 2050, however, India is expected to be the most populous nation in the world (approximately 1.69 billion). China (1.4 billion), the United States (439 million), Indonesia (313 million), and Pakistan (276 million) are expected to be the next four most populous countries in 2050.[33] Firms seeking to find growing markets in which to sell their goods and services want to recognize the market potential that may exist for them in these five nations.

Firms also want to study changes occurring within the populations of different nations and regions of the world to assess their strategic implications. For example, 23 percent of Japan's citizens are 65 or older, while the United States and China will not reach this level until 2036.[34] Aging populations are a significant problem for countries because of the need for workers and the burden of supporting retirement programs. In Japan and some other countries, employees are urged to work longer to overcome these problems.

Age Structure

The most noteworthy aspect of this element of the demographic segment is that the world's population is rapidly aging. For example, predictions are that "by 2050, over one-fifth of the U.S. population will be 65 or older up from the current figure (in 2012) of one-seventh. The number of centenarians worldwide will double by 2023 and double again by 2035. Projections suggest life expectancy will surpass 100 in some industrialized countries by the second half of this century—roughly triple the lifespan that prevailed worldwide throughout most of human history."[35] In China, the 65 and over population is expected to reach roughly 330 million by 2050, which will be close to one-fourth of the nation's total population.[36] In the 1950s, Japan's population was one of the youngest in the world. However, 45 is now the median age in Japan, with the projection that it will be 55 by 2040. With a fertility rate that is below replacement value, another prediction is that by 2040 there will be almost as many Japanese people 100 years old or older as there are newborns.[37] By 2050, almost 25 percent of the world's population will be aged 65 or older. These changes in the age of the population have significant implications for availability of qualified labor, healthcare retirement policies, and business opportunities among others.[38]

In Japan, an expectation that the working age population will shrink from 81 million to about 57 million by 2040 threatens companies with an inadequate workforce. On the other hand, there may be an opportunity for Japanese firms to increase the productivity of their workers and/or to establish additional operations in other nations. A potential opportunity is represented by delayed retirements of baby boomers (those born between 1947 and 1965) expected in the United States (and perhaps other countries). Delayed retirements may help companies "avoid or defer the baby-boomer brain drain that has been looming for so long." In this sense, "organizations now have a fresh opportunity to address the talent gap created by a shortage of critical skills in the marketplace as well as the experience gap created by multiple waves of downsizing over the past decade."[39] Firms can also use their older more experienced workers to transfer their knowledge to younger employees, helping them to quickly gain valuable skills. There is also an opportunity for firms to more effectively use the talent available in the workforce. For example, moving women into higher level professional and managerial jobs could offset the challenges created by decline in overall talent availability. And, based on research, it may even enhance overall outcomes.[40]

Geographic Distribution

How a population is distributed within countries and regions is subject to change over time. For example, over the last few decades the U.S. population has shifted from states in the Northeast and Great Lakes region to states in the west (California), south (Florida), and southwest (Texas). California's population has grown by approximately 5 million since 2000, while Texas's population has grown by 6.1 million, and Florida's by 3.9 million in the same time period.[41] These changes are characterized as moving from the "Frost Belt" to the "Sun Belt." Outcomes from these shifts include the facts that the gross domestic product (GDP) of California in 2011 was just under $2 trillion, an amount that makes California the ninth-largest economy in the world. In this same year, at a value of $1.3 trillion, Texas' GDP was second to that of California.[42]

The least popular states, based on people leaving in recent years, are Illinois, New Jersey New York, Michigan, Maine, Connecticut, and Wisconsin. In a shift in the pattern witnessed for the first decade-plus of the twenty-first century, Washington, D.C., has become one of the most popular destination for relocation along with Oregon. Washington, D.C., seemed to be popular because of its somewhat recession-proof economic opportunities generated by a maturing high-tech sector and federal government jobs. Additionally, the city of Portland, Oregon, is attractive for its mix of economic growth, effective urban planning, and scenic landscapes.[43]

Firms want to carefully study the patterns of population distributions in countries and regions to identify opportunities and threats. Thus, in the United States, current patterns suggest the possibility of opportunities in Washington, D.C., as well as in states on the West Coast, including Oregon, and those in the South and Southwest. In contrast, firms competing in the Northeast and Great Lakes areas may concentrate on identifying threats to their ability to operate profitably in those areas.

Of course, geographic distribution patterns differ throughout the world. For example, in China, the majority of the population still lives in rural areas; however, growth patterns are shifting to urban communities such as Shanghai and Beijing.[44] Recent shifts in Europe show small population gains for countries such as France, Germany, and the United Kingdom, while Greece experienced a small population decline. Overall, the geographic distribution patterns in Europe have been reasonably stable.[45]

Ethnic Mix

The ethnic mix of countries' populations continues to change, creating opportunities and threats for many companies as a result. For example, Hispanics have become the largest ethnic minority in the United States.[46] In fact, the U.S. Hispanic market is the third largest "Latin American" economy behind Brazil and Mexico. Spanish is now the dominant language in parts of the United States such as in Texas, California, Florida, and New Mexico. Given these facts, some firms might want to assess how their goods or services could be adapted to serve the unique needs of Hispanic consumers. Interestingly, by 2020, more than 50 percent of children in the United States will be a member of a minority ethnic group, and the population in the United States is projected to have a majority of minority ethnic members by 2044.[47] The ethnic diversity of the population is important not only because of consumer needs but also because of the labor force composition. Interestingly, research has shown that firms with greater ethnic diversity in their managerial team are likely to enjoy higher performance.[48]

Additional evidence is of interest to firms when examining this segment. For example, African countries are the most ethnically diverse in the world, with Uganda having the highest ethnic diversity rating and Liberia having the second highest. In contrast, Japan and the Koreas are the least ethnically diversified in their populations. European countries are largely ethnically homogeneous while the Americas are more diverse. "From the United States through Central America down to Brazil, the 'new world' countries, maybe in part because of their histories of relatively open immigration (and, in some cases, intermingling between natives and new arrivals) tend to be pretty diverse."[49]

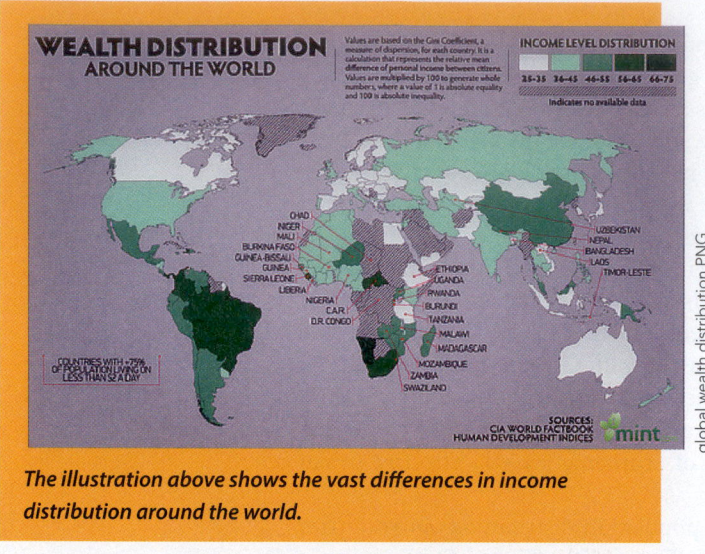

The illustration above shows the vast differences in income distribution around the world.

Income Distribution

Understanding how income is distributed within and across populations informs firms of different groups' purchasing power and discretionary income. Of particular interest to firms are the average incomes of households and individuals. For instance, the increase in dual-career couples has had a notable effect on average incomes. Although real income has been declining in general in some nations, the household income of dual-career couples has increased, especially in the United States. These figures yield strategically relevant information for firms. For instance, research indicates that whether an employee is part of a dual-career couple can strongly influence the willingness of the employee to accept an international assignment. However, because of recent global economic conditions, many companies were still pursuing international assignments but changing them to avoid some of the additional costs of funding expatriates abroad.[50]

The growth of the economy in China has drawn many firms, not only for the low-cost production, but also because of the large potential demand for products, given its large population base. However, in recent times, the amount of China's gross domestic product that makes up domestic consumption is the lowest of any major economy at less than one-third. In comparison, India's domestic consumption of consumer goods accounts for two-thirds of its economy, or twice China's level. As such, many western multinationals are interested in India as a consumption market as its middle class grows extensively. Although India has poor infrastructure, its consumers are in a better position to spend. Because of situations such as this, paying attention to the differences between markets based on income distribution can be very important.[51] These differences across nations suggest it is important for most firms to identify the economic systems that are most likely to produce the most income growth and market opportunities.[52] Thus, the economic segment is a critically important focus of firms' environmental analysis.

2-3b The Economic Segment

The **economic environment** refers to the nature and direction of the economy in which a firm competes or may compete.[53] In general, firms seek to compete in relatively stable economies with strong growth potential. Because nations are interconnected as a result of the global economy, firms must scan, monitor, forecast, and assess the health of their host nation as well as the health of the economies outside it.

It is challenging for firms studying the economic environment to predict economic trends that may occur and their effects on them. There are at least two reasons for this. First, the global recession of 2008 and 2009 created numerous problems for companies throughout the world, including problems of reduced consumer demand, increases in firms' inventory levels, development of additional governmental regulations, and a tightening of access to financial resources. Second, the global recovery from the economic shock in 2008 and 2009 continues to be persistently slow and relatively weak compared to previous recoveries. Firms have to adjust not only to the economic shock and try to recover from it, they have to respond to what appears to be an unpredictable recovery.

The **economic environment** refers to the nature and direction of the economy in which a firm competes or may compete.

For example, the economies in a number of European countries are still suffering from the major recession (e.g., Greece, Spain). Of likely concern to firms is the fact that historically, high degrees of economic uncertainty coincide with periods of lower growth. And again, according to some research, "it is clear that (economic) uncertainty has increased in recent times."[54] This current degree of economic uncertainty suggests the possibility of slower growth for the foreseeable future.

When facing economic uncertainty, firms want to be certain to study the economic environment in multiple regions and countries throughout the world. Although economic growth remains relatively weak and economic uncertainty has been strong in Europe, the economic growth has been better in the United States in recent times. For example, the projected average annual economic growth in Europe for 2015–2017 is 1.4 percent and in the United States it is 2.9 percent. Alternatively, the projected average annual economic growth for 2015–2017 is 7.0 percent in China, 6.8 percent in India, 2.6 percent in Brazil, and 3.6 percent in Mexico. These estimates highlight the anticipation of the continuing development of emerging economies.[55] Ideally, firms will be able to pursue growth opportunities in regions and nations where they exist while avoiding the threats of slow growth periods in other settings.

Christopher Polk/ACMA2010/Getty Images

To date, most legalized gambling has been provided in resorts such as MGM Resorts. However, recent changes in regulations within the state of Nevada in the United States allows online gambling which is now being evaluated as an opportunity for these resorts.

2-3c The Political/Legal Segment

The **political/legal segment** is the arena in which organizations and interest groups compete for attention, resources, and a voice in overseeing the body of laws and regulations guiding interactions among nations as well as between firms and various local governmental agencies.[56] Essentially, this segment is concerned with how organizations try to influence governments and how they try to understand the influences (current and projected) of those governments on their competitive actions and responses. Commonly, firms develop a political strategy to specify how they will study the political/legal segment as well as approaches they might take (such as lobbying efforts) in order to successfully deal with opportunities and threats that surface within this segment at different points in time.[57]

Regulations formed in response to new national, regional, state, and/or local laws that are legislated often influence a firm's competitive actions and responses.[58] For example, the state of Nevada in the United States recently legalized the business of online poker/gambling. New Jersey and Delaware quickly took the same action. In response to Nevada's regulatory change, firms such as MGM Resorts International were trying to decide the degree to which these decisions represented a viable opportunity. According to a MGM official, the immediate concern with respect to Nevada is that "the state may be too small to provide a lucrative online market on a stand-alone basis."[59]

At a regional level, changes in the laws regarding the appropriate regulation of European banks are still being actively debated.[60] For interactive, technology-based firms

The **political/legal segment** is the arena in which organizations and interest groups compete for attention, resources, and a voice in overseeing the body of laws and regulations guiding interactions among nations as well as between firms and various local governmental agencies.

such as Facebook, Google, and Amazon, among others, "the effort in Europe to adopt the world's strongest data protection law has drawn the attention of dozens of lobbyists from U.S. technology and advertising companies."[61] Highly restrictive laws about consumer privacy could threaten how these firms conduct business in the European Union. Finally, in a comprehensive sense, recent transformations from state-owned to private firms occurring in multiple nations have substantial implications for the competitive landscapes in a number of countries and across multiple industries.[62]

2-3d   The Sociocultural Segment

The **sociocultural segment** is concerned with a society's attitudes and cultural values. Because attitudes and values form the cornerstone of a society, they often drive demographic, economic, political/legal, and technological conditions and changes.

Individual societies' attitudes and cultural orientations are anything but stable, meaning that firms must carefully scan, monitor, forecast, and assess them to recognize and study associated opportunities and threats. Successful firms must also have an awareness of changes taking place in the societies and their associated cultures in which they are competing. Indeed, societal and culture changes challenge firms to find ways to "adapt to stay ahead of their competitors and stay relevant in the minds of their consumers."[63] Research has shown that sociocultural factors influence the entry into new markets and the development of new firms in a country.[64]

Attitudes about and approaches to health care are being evaluated in nations and regions throughout the world. For Europe, the European Commission has developed a health care strategy for all of Europe that is oriented to preventing diseases while tackling lifestyle factors influencing health such as nutrition, working conditions, and physical activity. This Commission argues that promoting attitudes to take care of one's health is especially important in the context of an aging Europe as shown by the projection that the proportion of people over 65 living in Europe will increase from 17 percent in 2010 to almost 30 percent by 2060.[65] At issue for business firms is that attitudes and values about health care can affect them; accordingly, they must carefully examine trends regarding health care in order to anticipate the effects on their operations.

The **sociocultural segment** is concerned with a society's attitudes and cultural values.

As the U.S. labor force has grown in size, it has become more diverse, with significantly more women and minorities from a variety of cultures entering the workplace. In 1993, the total U.S. workforce was slightly less than 130 million; in 2005, it was slightly greater than 148 million. It is predicted to grow to more than 192 million by 2050.

However, the rate of growth in the U.S. labor force has declined over the past two decades largely as a result of slower growth of the nation's population and because of a downward trend in the labor force participation rate. More specifically, data show that "after nearly five decades of steady growth, the overall participation rate—defined as the proportion of the civilian non-institutional population in the labor force—peaked at an annual average of 67.1 percent for each year from 1997 to 2000.

Healthcare is becoming increasingly important as the proportion of people older than 65 is growing larger in many nations throughout the world.

© Alexander Raths/Shutterstock.com

By September 2012, the rate had dropped to 63.6 percent"[66] and is expected to fall to 58.5 percent by 2050. Other changes in the U.S. labor force between 2010 and 2050 are expected. During this time period, the growth in Asian members of the labor force is projected to more than double in size, while the growth in Caucasian members of the labor force is predicted to be much slower compared to other racial groups. In contrast, people of Hispanic origin are expected to account for roughly 80 percent of the total growth in the labor force. Finally, "it is projected that the higher growth rate of the female labor force relative to that of men will end by 2020, and the growth rates for men and women will be similar for the 2020–2050 period."[67]

Greater diversity in the workforce creates challenges and opportunities, including combining the best of both men's and women's traditional leadership styles. Although diversity in the workforce has the potential to improve performance, research indicates that diversity initiatives must be successfully managed in order to reap these organizational benefits.

Although the lifestyle and workforce changes referenced previously reflect the attitudes and values of the U.S. population, each country is unique with respect to these sociocultural indicators. National cultural values affect behavior in organizations and thus also influence organizational outcomes such as differences in CEO compensation.[68] Likewise, the national culture influences to a large extent the internationalization strategy that firms pursue relative to one's home country.[69] Knowledge sharing is important for dispersing new knowledge in organizations and increasing the speed in implementing innovations. Personal relationships are especially important in China as *guanxi* (personal relationships or good connections) has become a way of doing business within the country and for individuals to advance their careers in what is becoming a more open market society. Understanding the importance of guanxi is critical for foreign firms doing business in China.[70]

2-3e   The Technological Segment

Pervasive and diversified in scope, technological changes affect many parts of societies. These effects occur primarily through new products, processes, and materials. The **technological segment** includes the institutions and activities involved in creating new knowledge and translating that knowledge into new outputs, products, processes, and materials.

Given the rapid pace of technological change and risk of disruption, it is vital for firms to thoroughly study the technological segment.[71] The importance of these efforts is suggested by the finding that early adopters of new technology often achieve higher market shares and earn higher returns. Thus, both large and small firms should continuously scan the general environment to identify potential substitutes for technologies that are in current use, as well as to identify newly emerging technologies from which their firm could derive competitive advantage.[72]

As a significant technological development, the Internet offers firms a remarkable capability in terms of their efforts to scan, monitor, forecast, and assess conditions in their general environment. Companies continue to study the Internet's capabilities to anticipate how it allows them to create more value for customers and to anticipate future trends.

Additionally, the Internet generates a significant number of opportunities and threats for firms across the world. Predictions about Internet usage in the years to come are one reason for this. By 2016, the estimate is that there will be 3 billion Internet users globally. Overall, firms can expect that in the future the Internet "will have more users (especially in developing markets), more mobile users, more users accessing it with various devices

The **technological segment** includes the institutions and activities involved in creating new knowledge and translating that knowledge into new outputs, products, processes, and materials.

throughout the day, and many more people engaged in an increasingly participatory medium."[73] Considering that about 144 billion e-mails are currently sent each day, and there has been an explosive growth in the demand for mobile Internet access, the effect of this increase in users has significant implications for businesses.[74]

In spite of the Internet's far-reaching effects and the opportunities and threats associated with its potential, wireless communication technology is becoming a significant technological opportunity for companies to pursue. Handheld devices and other wireless communications equipment are used to access a variety of network-based services. The use of handheld computers with wireless network connectivity, Web-enabled mobile phone handsets, and other emerging platforms (e.g., consumer Internet-access devices such as the iPhone, iPad, Apple Watch, and Kindle) has increased substantially and may soon become the dominant form of communication and commerce. In fact, with each new version of these products, additional functionalities and software applications are generating multiple opportunities—and potential threats—for companies of all types.

2-3f   The Global Segment

The **global segment** includes relevant new global markets, existing markets that are changing, important international political events, and critical cultural and institutional characteristics of global markets.[75] For example, firms competing in the automobile industry must study the global segment. The fact that consumers in multiple nations are willing to buy cars and trucks "from whatever area of the world"[76] supports this position.

When studying the global segment, firms should recognize that globalization of business markets may create opportunities to enter new markets as well as threats that new competitors from other economies may also enter their market.[77] In terms of an opportunity for automobile manufacturers, the possibility for these firms to sell their products outside of their home market would seem attractive. But what markets might firms choose to enter? Currently, automobile and truck sales are expected to increase in Brazil, Russia, India, China, and to a lesser extent, Indonesia, and Malaysia. In contrast, sales are expected to decline, at least in the near term, in Europe and Japan. These markets, then, are the most and least attractive ones for automobile manufacturers desiring to sell outside their domestic market. At the same time, from the perspective of a threat, Japan, Germany, Korea, Spain, France, and the United States appear to have excess production capacity in the automobile manufacturing industry. In turn, overcapacity signals the possibility that companies based in markets where this is the case will simultaneously attempt to increase their exports as well as sales in their domestic market.[78] Thus, global automobile manufacturers should carefully examine the global segment in order to precisely identify all opportunities and threats.

In light of threats associated with participating in international markets, some firms choose to take a more cautious approach to globalization. For example, family business firms, even the larger ones, often take a conservative approach to entering international markets. These firms participate in what some refer to as *globalfocusing*. Globalfocusing often is used by firms with moderate levels of international operations who increase their internationalization by focusing on global niche markets.[79] This approach allows firms to build on to and use their core competencies while limiting their risks within the niche market. Another way in which firms limit their risks in international markets is to focus their operations and sales in one region of the world.[80] Success with these efforts finds a firm building relationships in and knowledge of its markets. As the firm builds these strengths, rivals find it more difficult to enter its markets and compete successfully.

The **global segment** includes relevant new global markets, existing markets that are changing, important international political events, and critical cultural and institutional characteristics of global markets.

Firms competing in global markets should recognize each market's sociocultural and institutional attributes. For example, Korean ideology emphasizes communitarianism, a characteristic of many Asian countries. Alternatively, the ideology in China calls for an emphasis on *guanxi*—personal connections—while in Japan, the focus is on *wa*—group harmony and social cohesion.[81] The institutional context of China suggests a major emphasis on centralized planning by the government. The Chinese government provides incentives to firms to develop alliances with foreign firms having sophisticated technology in hopes of building knowledge and introducing new technologies to the Chinese markets over time.[82] As such, it is important to analyze the strategic intent of foreign firms when pursuing alliances and joint ventures abroad, especially where the local partners are receiving technology which may in the long run reduce the foreign firms' advantages.[83]

Increasingly, the *informal economy* as it exists throughout the world is another aspect of the global segment requiring analysis. Growing in size, this economy has implications for firms' competitive actions and responses in that increasingly firms competing in the formal economy will find that they are competing against informal economy companies as well.

2-3g   The Sustainable Physical Environment Segment

The **sustainable physical environment segment** refers to potential and actual changes in the physical environment and business practices that are intended to positively respond to those changes with the intent of creating a sustainable environment.[84] Concerned with trends oriented to sustaining the world's physical environment, firms recognize that ecological, social, and economic systems interactively influence what happens in this particular segment and that they are part of an interconnected global society.[85]

Companies across the globe are concerned about the physical environment, and many record the actions they are taking in reports with names such as "Sustainability" and "Corporate Social Responsibility." Moreover and in a comprehensive sense, an increasing number of companies are interested in sustainable development, which is "the development that meets the needs of the present without compromising the ability of future generations to meet their own needs."[86]

There are many parts or attributes of the physical environment that firms consider as they try to identify trends in the physical environment segment.[87] Because of the importance to firms of becoming sustainable, certification programs have been developed to help them understand how to be sustainable organizations.[88] As the world's largest retailer, Walmart's environmental footprint is huge, meaning that trends in the physical environment can significantly affect this firm and how it chooses to operate. Perhaps in light of trends occurring in the physical environment, Walmart has announced that its goal is to produce zero waste and to use 100 percent renewable energy to power its operations.[89]

As our discussion of the general environment shows, identifying anticipated changes and trends among segments and their elements is a key objective of analyzing this environment. With a focus on the future, the analysis of the general environment allows firms to identify opportunities and threats. It is necessary to have a top management team with the experience, knowledge, and sensitivity required to effectively analyze the conditions in a firm's general environment and other parts such as the industry environment and competitors.[90] In fact, it seems that the prior CEO of Target may not have been committed to analyzing the environment in depth (See Strategic Focus on Target). But the new CEO, Brian Cornell, demonstrated his commitment by locating his office close to the center of the data collection unit and checking in with the staff in this unit each morning to gain the latest information.

The **sustainable physical environment segment** refers to potential and actual changes in the physical environment and business practices that are intended to positively respond to those changes with the intent of creating a sustainable environment.

Target Lost Its Sway Because Tar-zhey No Longer Drew the Customers

Target became known by consumers as Tar-zhey, the retailer of cheaper but 'chic' products. The firm offered a step up in quality goods at a slightly higher price than discount retailers such as Walmart, but was targeted below major, first line retailers such as Macy's and Nordstrom. Additionally, it promoted its stores to offer one-stop shopping with clothing, toys, health products, and food goods, among other products. For many years, Tar-zhey "hit the bullseye" and performed well serving this large niche in the market. But the company took its eye off the target and began losing market share (along with other poor strategic actions).

The first major crack in the ship appeared with the announcement of a massive cyberattack on Target's computer system that netted customers' personal information. The attack exposed customers (data on 70 million customers) to potentially substantial losses due to credit card fraud. Not only was this a public relations disaster, it drew a focus on Target that identified other problems. The "light" on Target showed that the strategic decision to enter the Canadian market in a major way (133 stores across multiple geographic areas) was failing. Finally, the careful analysis showed that Target was losing customers to established competitors and new rivals, especially Internet retailers (e.g., Amazon.com).

Target's marketing chief stated that "it's not that we became insular. We were insular." This suggests that the firm was not analyzing its environment. By allowing rivals, and especially newer Internet competitors, to woo the company's customers, it lost sales, market share, and profits. It obviously did not predict and prepare for the significant competition from Internet rivals. Competitors were offering better value to customers (perhaps more variety and convenience through online sales). When combined with the loss of consumer confidence because of the massive hack of personal customer data, Target's reputation and market share were simultaneously harmed.

The unparalleled failure of the Canadian operations within a very short time (two years) also showed a lack of market understanding likely stemming from the failure to analyze the market. It is probable that all of the problems Target was experiencing were transferred to its Canadian operations as well. In addition, it failed to attract customers from its major Canadian retailers, such as Loblaw Companies, Canada's largest grocer that recently introduced low-cost clothing boutiques. Costco and Walmart were also well-established in the Canadian market. Target was unable to differentiate the value it provided from the established retailers in Canada. It also experienced problems in its Canadian supply chain suggesting again that it did not fully understand the business markets in Canada before entering the market.

Because of all of the problems experienced, Target's CEO resigned in May 2014. A new CEO, Brian Cornell, was hired

three months later. He was a top executive at PepsiCo and had experience heading Sam's Warehouse for Walmart as well. Cornell is the first CEO to be hired from outside the company, and most of his experience is from outside the industry as well. Since arriving on the job in August of 2014, Cornell has started making changes. For example, he is trying to regain Target's "chic" image by focusing on fashion, infant's, children's, and health departments to increase customer traffic and sales. The focus in foods is more upscale, more organic food, specialty granola, coffee and tea, wine, and beer. Sales exceeded the forecast in the fourth quarter of 2014 with the highest growth in three years. In January 2015, Cornell also closed all Canadian stores and thereby laid off 17,600 employees, a painful but necessary move. Finally, he announced another layoff of close to 2,000 employees in March 2015. Most of these employees will come from the main office with the intent to make Target more nimble and agile.

Target Lily Pulitzer Line.PNG

Lily Pulitzer has been providing bold fashions for resort wear for more than 50 years.

Interestingly, Cornell did not take the large corner suite accorded to the former CEOs but instead chose a smaller office near the company's market data collection site. There a staff of ten employees gather information from social media sites such as Pinterest, Facebook, and Twitter and from television news from nine large TV screens. The CEO stops by every morning to learn the latest information. These actions alone suggest the importance he places on gathering and analyzing data on the market and competitors' actions.

Sources: 2015, What your new CEO is reading: Smell ya later; targets new CEO, *CIO Journal/Wall Street Journal*, www.wsj.com/cio, March 6; I. Austen & H. Tabuchi, 2015, Target's red ink runs out in Canada, *New York Times*, www.ntimes.com, January 15; H. Tabuchi, 2015, Target plans to cut jobs to help save $2 billion, *New York Times*, www.ntimes.com, March 3; P. Ziobro & C. Delaney, 2015, Target sales grow at fastest rate in three years, *Wall Street Journal*, www.wsj.com, February 25; J. Reingold, 2014, Can Target's new CEO get the struggling retailer back on target? *Fortune*, www.fortune.com, July 31; G. Smith, 2014, Target turns to PepsiCo's Brian Cornell to restore its fortunes, *Fortune*, www.fortune.com, July 31; P. Ziobro, M. Langley, & J. S. Lublin, 2014, Target's problem: Tar-zhey isn't working. *Wall Street Journal*, www.wsj.com, May 5.

As described in the Strategic Focus, Target failed to maintain a good understanding of its industry; hence, the loss of market share to new Internet company rivals and other more established competitors. It did not understand its markets, competitors, and suppliers in Canada, and thus its entry into the Canadian market failed miserably. We conclude that critical to a firm's choices of strategies and their associated competitive actions and responses is an understanding of its industry environment and its competitors. And, the country's general environment influences the industry and competitive environments.[91] Next, we discuss the analyses firms complete to gain such an understanding.

2-4 Industry Environment Analysis

An **industry** is a group of firms producing products that are close substitutes. In the course of competition, these firms influence one another. Typically, companies use a rich mix of different competitive strategies to pursue above-average returns when competing in a particular industry. An industry's structural characteristics influence a firm's choice of strategies.[92]

Compared with the general environment, the industry environment (measured primarily in the form of its characteristics) has a more direct effect on the competitive actions and responses a firm takes to succeed.[93] To study an industry, the firm examines five forces that affect the ability of all firms to operate profitably within a given industry. Shown in Figure 2.2, the five forces are: the threats posed by new entrants, the power of suppliers, the power of buyers, product substitutes, and the intensity of rivalry among competitors.

The five forces of competition model depicted in Figure 2.2 expands the scope of a firm's competitive analysis. Historically, when studying the competitive environment, firms concentrated on companies with which they directly competed. However, firms must search more broadly to recognize current and potential competitors by identifying

Figure 2.2 The Five Forces of Competition Model

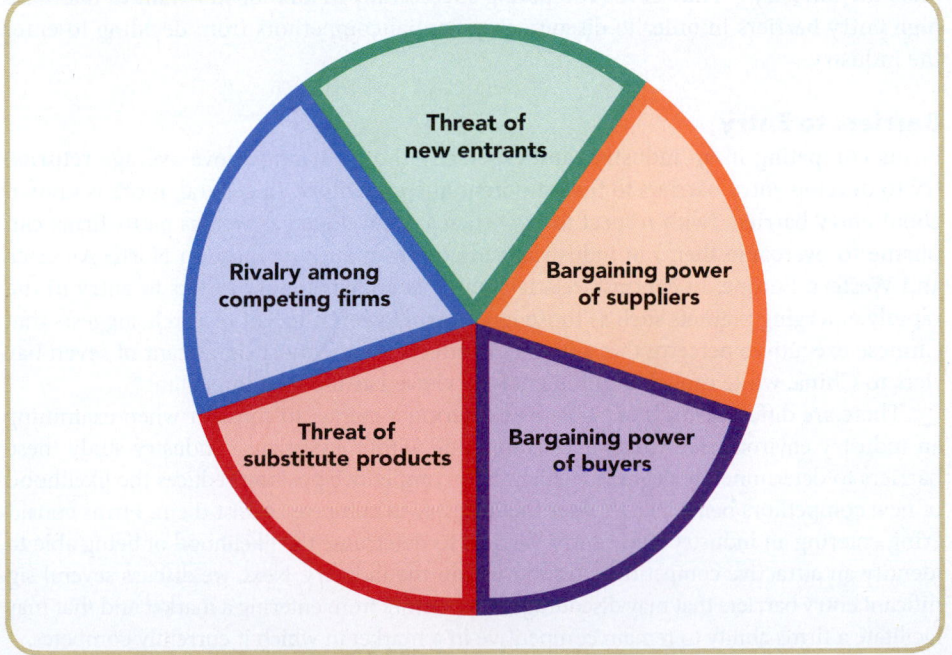

An **industry** is a group of firms producing products that are close substitutes.

potential customers as well as the firms serving them. For example, the communications industry is now broadly defined as encompassing media companies, telecoms, entertainment companies, and companies producing devices such as smartphones.[94] In such an environment, firms must study many other industries to identify companies with capabilities (especially technology-based capabilities) that might be the foundation for producing a good or a service that can compete against what they are producing.

When studying the industry environment, firms must also recognize that suppliers can become a firm's competitors (by integrating forward) as can buyers (by integrating backward). For example, several firms have integrated forward in the pharmaceutical industry by acquiring distributors or wholesalers. In addition, firms choosing to enter a new market and those producing products that are adequate substitutes for existing products can become a company's competitors.

Next, we examine the five forces the firm needs to analyze in order to understand the profitability potential within an industry (or a segment of an industry) in which it competes or may choose to compete.

2-4a   Threat of New Entrants

Identifying new entrants is important because they can threaten the market share of existing competitors.[95] One reason new entrants pose such a threat is that they bring additional production capacity. Unless the demand for a good or service is increasing, additional capacity holds consumers' costs down, resulting in less revenue and lower returns for competing firms. Often, new entrants have a keen interest in gaining a large market share. As a result, new competitors may force existing firms to be more efficient and to learn how to compete in new dimensions (e.g., using an Internet-based distribution channel).

The likelihood that firms will enter an industry is a function of two factors: barriers to entry and the retaliation expected from current industry participants. Entry barriers make it difficult for new firms to enter an industry and often place them at a competitive disadvantage even when they are able to enter. As such, high entry barriers tend to increase the returns for existing firms in the industry and may allow some firms to dominate the industry.[96] Thus, firms competing successfully in an industry want to maintain high entry barriers in order to discourage potential competitors from deciding to enter the industry.

Barriers to Entry

Firms competing in an industry (and especially those earning above-average returns) try to develop entry barriers to thwart potential competitors. In general, more is known about entry barriers (with respect to how they are developed as well as paths firms can pursue to overcome them) in industrialized countries such as those in North America and Western Europe. In contrast, relatively little is known about barriers to entry in the rapidly emerging markets such as those in China. However, recent research suggests that Chinese executives perceive that advertising effects are the most significant of seven barriers to China, while capital requirements are viewed as the least important.[97]

There are different kinds of barriers to entering a market to consider when examining an industry environment. Companies competing within a particular industry study these barriers to determine the degree to which their competitive position reduces the likelihood of new competitors being able to enter the industry to compete against them. Firms considering entering an industry study entry barriers to determine the likelihood of being able to identify an attractive competitive position within the industry. Next, we discuss several significant entry barriers that may discourage competitors from entering a market and that may facilitate a firm's ability to remain competitive in a market in which it currently competes.

Economies of Scale *Economies of scale* are derived from incremental efficiency improvements through experience as a firm grows larger. Therefore, the cost of producing each unit declines as the quantity of a product produced during a given period increases. A new entrant is unlikely to quickly generate the level of demand for its product that in turn would allow it to develop economies of scale.

Economies of scale can be developed in most business functions, such as marketing, manufacturing, research and development, and purchasing.[98] Firms sometimes form strategic alliances or joint ventures to gain scale economies. This is the case for Mitsubishi Heavy Industries Ltd. and Hitachi Ltd., as these companies "merged their operations for fossil-fuel-based power systems into a joint venture aimed at gaining scale to compete against global rivals."[99]

Becoming more flexible in terms of being able to meet shifts in customer demand is another benefit for an industry incumbent and a possible entry barrier for the firms considering entering the industry. For example, a firm may choose to reduce its price with the intention of capturing a larger share of the market. Alternatively, it may keep its price constant to increase profits. In so doing, it likely will increase its free cash flow, which is very helpful during financially challenging times.

Some competitive conditions reduce the ability of economies of scale to create an entry barrier such as the use of scale free resources.[100] Also, many companies now customize their products for large numbers of small customer groups. In these cases, customized products are not manufactured in the volumes necessary to achieve economies of scale. Customization is made possible by several factors including flexible manufacturing systems. In fact, the new manufacturing technology facilitated by advanced information systems has allowed the development of mass customization in an increasing number of industries. Online ordering has enhanced customers' ability to buy customized products. Companies manufacturing customized products can respond quickly to customers' needs in lieu of developing scale economies.

Product Differentiation Over time, customers may come to believe that a firm's product is unique. This belief can result from the firm's service to the customer, effective advertising campaigns, or being the first to market a good or service.[101] Greater levels of perceived product uniqueness create customers who consistently purchase a firm's products. To combat the perception of uniqueness, new entrants frequently offer products at lower prices. This decision, however, may result in lower profits or even losses.

The Coca-Cola Company and PepsiCo have established strong brands in the markets in which they compete, and these companies compete against each other in countries throughout the world. Because each of these competitors has allocated a significant amount of resources over many decades to build its brands, customer loyalty is strong for each firm. When considering entry into the soft drink market, a potential entrant would be well advised to pause to determine actions it would take for the purpose of trying to overcome the brand image and consumer loyalty each of these giants possess.

Capital Requirements Competing in a new industry requires a firm to have resources to invest. In addition to physical facilities, capital is needed for inventories, marketing activities, and other critical business functions. Even when a new industry is attractive, the capital required for successful market entry may not be available to pursue the market opportunity.[102] For example, defense industries are difficult to enter because of the substantial resource investments required to be competitive. In addition, because of the high knowledge requirements of the defense industry, a firm might acquire an existing company as a means of entering this industry, but it must have access to the capital necessary to do this.

Switching Costs *Switching costs* are the one-time costs customers incur when they buy from a different supplier. The costs of buying new ancillary equipment and of retraining employees, and even the psychological costs of ending a relationship, may be incurred in switching to a new supplier. In some cases, switching costs are low, such as when the consumer switches to a different brand of soft drink. Switching costs can vary as a function of time, as shown by the fact that in terms of credit hours toward graduation, the cost to a student to transfer from one university to another as a freshman is much lower than it is when the student is entering the senior year.

Occasionally, a decision made by manufacturers to produce a new, innovative product creates high switching costs for customers. Customer loyalty programs, such as airlines' frequent flyer miles, are intended to increase the customer's switching costs. If switching costs are high, a new entrant must offer either a substantially lower price or a much better product to attract buyers. Usually, the more established the relationships between parties, the greater the switching costs.

Access to Distribution Channels Over time, industry participants commonly learn how to effectively distribute their products. After building a relationship with its distributors, a firm will nurture it, thus creating switching costs for the distributors. Access to distribution channels can be a strong entry barrier for new entrants, particularly in consumer nondurable goods industries (e.g., in grocery stores where shelf space is limited) and in international markets.[103] New entrants have to persuade distributors to carry their products, either in addition to or in place of those currently distributed. Price breaks and cooperative advertising allowances may be used for this purpose; however, those practices reduce the new entrant's profit potential. Interestingly, access to distribution is less of a barrier for products that can be sold on the Internet.

Cost Disadvantages Independent of Scale Sometimes, established competitors have cost advantages that new entrants cannot duplicate. Proprietary product technology, favorable access to raw materials, desirable locations, and government subsidies are examples. Successful competition requires new entrants to reduce the strategic relevance of these factors. For example, delivering purchases directly to the buyer can counter the advantage of a desirable location; new food establishments in an undesirable location often follow this practice. Zara is owned by Inditex, the largest fashion clothing retailer in the world.[104] From the time of its launching, Spanish clothing company Zara relied on classy, well-tailored, and relatively inexpensive items that were produced and sold by adhering to ethical practices to successfully enter the highly competitive global clothing market and overcome that market's entry barriers.[105]

Government Policy Through their decisions about issues such as the granting of licenses and permits, governments can also control entry into an industry. Liquor retailing, radio and TV broadcasting, banking, and trucking are examples of industries in which government decisions and actions affect entry possibilities. Also, governments often restrict entry into some industries because of the need to provide quality service or the desire to protect jobs. Alternatively, deregulating industries, such as the airline and utilities industries in the United States, generally results in additional firms choosing to enter and compete within an industry.[106] It is not uncommon for governments to attempt to regulate the entry of foreign firms, especially in industries considered critical to the country's economy or important markets within it.[107] Governmental decisions and policies regarding antitrust issues also affect entry barriers. For example, in the United States, the Antitrust Division of the Justice Department or the Federal Trade Commission will sometimes disallow a proposed merger because officials conclude that approving it would create a firm that is too dominant in an industry and would thus create unfair competition.[108] Such a negative ruling would obviously be an entry barrier for an acquiring firm.

Expected Retaliation

Companies seeking to enter an industry also anticipate the reactions of firms in the industry. An expectation of swift and vigorous competitive responses reduces the likelihood of entry. Vigorous retaliation can be expected when the existing firm has a major stake in the industry (e.g., it has fixed assets with few, if any, alternative uses), when it has substantial resources, and when industry growth is slow or constrained.[109] For example, any firm attempting to enter the airline industry can expect significant retaliation from existing competitors due to overcapacity.

Locating market niches not being served by incumbents allows the new entrant to avoid entry barriers. Small entrepreneurial firms are generally best suited for identifying and serving neglected market segments. When Honda first entered the U.S. motorcycle market, it concentrated on small-engine motorcycles, a market that firms such as Harley-Davidson ignored. By targeting this neglected niche, Honda initially avoided a significant amount of head-to-head competition with well-established competitors. After consolidating its position, Honda used its strength to attack rivals by introducing larger motorcycles and competing in the broader market.

2-4b Bargaining Power of Suppliers

Increasing prices and reducing the quality of their products are potential means suppliers use to exert power over firms competing within an industry. If a firm is unable to recover cost increases by its suppliers through its own pricing structure, its profitability is reduced by its suppliers' actions.[110] A supplier group is powerful when:

Apple's Watch was a highly anticipated entry into the smartwatch market. However, Google has formed a partnership with TAG Heuer and Intel to develop a smartwatch to respond to Apple.

© Hadrian/Shutterstock.com

- It is dominated by a few large companies and is more concentrated than the industry to which it sells.
- Satisfactory substitute products are not available to industry firms.
- Industry firms are not a significant customer for the supplier group.
- Suppliers' goods are critical to buyers' marketplace success.
- The effectiveness of suppliers' products has created high switching costs for industry firms.
- It poses a credible threat to integrate forward into the buyers' industry. Credibility is enhanced when suppliers have substantial resources and provide a highly differentiated product.[111]

Some buyers attempt to manage or reduce suppliers' power by developing a long-term relationship with them. Although long-term arrangements reduce buyer power, they also increase the suppliers' incentive to be helpful and cooperative in appreciation of the longer-term relationship (guaranteed sales). This is especially true when the partners develop trust in one another.[112]

The airline industry is one in which suppliers' bargaining power is changing. Though the number of suppliers is low, the demand for major aircraft is also relatively low. Boeing and Airbus aggressively compete for orders of major aircraft, creating more power for buyers in the process. When a large airline signals that it might place a "significant" order for wide-body airliners that either Airbus or Boeing might produce, both companies are likely to battle for the business and include a financing arrangement, highlighting the buyer's power in the potential transaction. And, with China's expected entry into the large commercial airliner industry, buyer power is likely to increase in the future.

2-4c   Bargaining Power of Buyers

Firms seek to maximize the return on their invested capital. Alternatively, buyers (customers of an industry or a firm) want to buy products at the lowest possible price—the point at which the industry earns the lowest acceptable rate of return on its invested capital. To reduce their costs, buyers bargain for higher quality, greater levels of service, and lower prices.[113] These outcomes are achieved by encouraging competitive battles among the industry's firms. Customers (buyer groups) are powerful when:

- They purchase a large portion of an industry's total output.
- The sales of the product being purchased account for a significant portion of the seller's annual revenues.
- They could switch to another product at little, if any, cost.
- The industry's products are undifferentiated or standardized, and the buyers pose a credible threat if they were to integrate backward into the sellers' industry.

Consumers armed with greater amounts of information about the manufacturer's costs and the power of the Internet as a shopping and distribution alternative have increased bargaining power in many industries.

2-4d   Threat of Substitute Products

Substitute products are goods or services from outside a given industry that perform similar or the same functions as a product that the industry produces. For example, as a sugar substitute, NutraSweet (and other sugar substitutes) places an upper limit on sugar manufacturers' prices—NutraSweet and sugar perform the same function, though with different characteristics. Other product substitutes include e-mail and fax machines instead of overnight deliveries, plastic containers rather than glass jars, and tea instead of coffee.

Newspaper firms have experienced significant circulation declines over the past 15 years. The declines are a result of the ready availability of substitute outlets for news including Internet sources, cable television news channels, along with e-mail and cell phone alerts. Likewise, satellite TV and cable and telecommunication companies provide substitute services for basic media services such as television, Internet, and phone. Tablets such as the iPad are reducing the number of PCs sold as suggested by the fact that worldwide shipments of PCs been declining each year since 2010.[114]

In general, product substitutes present a strong threat to a firm when customers face few if any switching costs and when the substitute product's price is lower or its quality and performance capabilities are equal to or greater than those of the competing product. Differentiating a product along dimensions that are valuable to customers (such as quality, service after the sale, and location) reduces a substitute's attractiveness.

2-4e   Intensity of Rivalry among Competitors

Because an industry's firms are mutually dependent, actions taken by one company usually invite responses. Competitive rivalry intensifies when a firm is challenged by a competitor's actions or when a company recognizes an opportunity to improve its market position.[115]

Firms within industries are rarely homogeneous; they differ in resources and capabilities and seek to differentiate themselves from competitors. Typically, firms seek to differentiate their products from competitors' offerings in ways that customers value and in which the firms have a competitive advantage. Common dimensions on which rivalry is based include price, service after the sale, and innovation. More recently, firms have begun to act quickly (speed a new product to the market) in order to gain a competitive advantage.[116]

Next, we discuss the most prominent factors that experience shows affect the intensity of rivalries among firms.

Apple Commercial.PNG

Firms making PCs try to differentiate their products in order to gain a competitive advantage. For example, Apple visually shows and verbally explains the differences between its Mac and the typical PC.

Numerous or Equally Balanced Competitors

Intense rivalries are common in industries with many companies. With multiple competitors, it is common for a few firms to believe they can act without eliciting a response. However, evidence suggests that other firms generally are aware of competitors' actions, often choosing to respond to them. At the other extreme, industries with only a few firms of equivalent size and power also tend to have strong rivalries. The large and often similar-sized resource bases of these firms permit vigorous actions and responses. The competitive battles between Airbus and Boeing and between Coca-Cola and PepsiCo exemplify intense rivalry between relatively equal competitors.

Slow Industry Growth

When a market is growing, firms try to effectively use resources to serve an expanding customer base. Markets increasing in size reduce the pressure to take customers from competitors. However, rivalry in no-growth or slow-growth markets becomes more intense as firms battle to increase their market shares by attracting competitors' customers. Certainly, this has been the case in the fast-food industry as explained in the Opening Case about McDonald's. McDonald's, Wendy's, and Burger King use their resources, capabilities, and core competencies to try to win each other's customers. The instability in the market that results from these competitive engagements may reduce the profitability for all firms engaging in such battles. As noted in the Opening Case, McDonald's has suffered from this competitive rivalry.

High Fixed Costs or High Storage Costs

When fixed costs account for a large part of total costs, companies try to maximize the use of their productive capacity. Doing so allows the firm to spread costs across a larger volume of output. However, when many firms attempt to maximize their productive capacity, excess capacity is created on an industry-wide basis. To then reduce inventories, individual companies typically cut the price of their product and offer rebates and other special discounts to customers. However, doing this often intensifies competition. The pattern of excess capacity at the industry level followed by intense rivalry at the firm level is frequently observed in industries with high storage costs. Perishable products, for example, lose their value rapidly with the passage of time.

As their inventories grow, producers of perishable goods often use pricing strategies to sell products quickly.

Lack of Differentiation or Low Switching Costs

When buyers find a differentiated product that satisfies their needs, they frequently purchase the product loyally over time. Industries with many companies that have successfully differentiated their products have less rivalry, resulting in lower competition for individual firms. Firms that develop and sustain a differentiated product that cannot be easily imitated by competitors often earn higher returns. However, when buyers view products as commodities (i.e., as products with few differentiated features or capabilities), rivalry intensifies. In these instances, buyers' purchasing decisions are based primarily on price and, to a lesser degree, service. Personal computers are a commodity product and the cost to switch from a computer manufactured by one firm to another is low. Thus, the rivalry among Dell, Hewlett-Packard, Lenovo, and other computer manufacturers is strong as these companies consistently seek to find ways to differentiate their offerings.

High Strategic Stakes

Competitive rivalry is likely to be high when it is important for several of the competitors to perform well in the market. Competing in diverse businesses (such as semiconductors, petrochemicals, fashion, medicine, and skyscraper and plant construction, among others), Samsung is a formidable foe for Apple in the global smartphone market. Samsung has committed a significant amount of resources to develop innovative products as the foundation for its efforts to try to outperform Apple in selling this particular product. Only a few years ago, Samsung held a sizable lead in market share (33 percent to 18 percent), but in the fourth quarter of 2014, the two firms' market share was virtually equal. It seems that apple received a significant boost with the release of the iPhone 6.[117] However, this market is extremely important to both firms, suggesting that the smartphone rivalry between them (and others) will remain quite intense.

High strategic stakes can also exist in terms of geographic locations. For example, a number of automobile manufacturers have established manufacturing facilities in China, which has been the world's largest car market since 2009.[118] Because of the high stakes involved in China for General Motors and other firms (including domestic Chinese automobile manufacturers) producing luxury cars (including Audi, BMW, and Mercedes-Benz), rivalry among them in this market is quite intense.

High Exit Barriers

Sometimes companies continue competing in an industry even though the returns on their invested capital are low or even negative. Firms making this choice likely face high exit barriers, which include economic, strategic, and emotional factors causing them to remain in an industry when the profitability of doing so is questionable.

Exit barriers are especially high in the airline industry. Profitability in this industry has been very difficult to achieve in recent years partly because of the latest global financial crisis. However, profits in the airline industry increased in 2013 and 2014. Industry consolidation and efficiency enhancements to how airline alliances integrate their activities helped reduce airline companies' costs while improving economic conditions in a number of countries. This resulted in a greater demand for travel. These are positive signs, at least in the short run, for these firms given that they do indeed face very high barriers if they were to contemplate leaving the airline travel industry.[119] Common exit barriers that firms face include the following:

- Specialized assets (assets with values linked to a particular business or location)
- Fixed costs of exit (such as labor agreements)

- Strategic interrelationships (relationships of mutual dependence, such as those between one business and other parts of a company's operations, including shared facilities and access to financial markets)
- Emotional barriers (aversion to economically justified business decisions because of fear for one's own career, loyalty to employees, and so forth)
- Government and social restrictions (often based on government concerns for job losses and regional economic effects; more common outside the United States)

2-5 Interpreting Industry Analyses

Effective industry analyses are products of careful study and interpretation of data and information from multiple sources. A wealth of industry-specific data is available for firms to analyze for the purpose of better understanding an industry's competitive realities. Because of globalization, international markets and rivalries must be included in the firm's analyses. And, because of the development of global markets, a country's borders no longer restrict industry structures. In fact, in general, entering international markets enhances the chances of success for new ventures as well as more established firms.[120]

Analysis of the five forces within a given industry allows the firm to determine the industry's attractiveness in terms of the potential to earn average or above-average returns. In general, the stronger the competitive forces, the lower the potential for firms to generate profits by implementing their strategies. An unattractive industry has low entry barriers, suppliers and buyers with strong bargaining positions, strong competitive threats from product substitutes, and intense rivalry among competitors. These industry characteristics make it difficult for firms to achieve strategic competitiveness and earn above-average returns. Alternatively, an attractive industry has high entry barriers, suppliers and buyers with little bargaining power, few competitive threats from product substitutes, and relatively moderate rivalry.[121] Next, we explain strategic groups as an aspect of industry competition.

2-6 Strategic Groups

A set of firms emphasizing similar strategic dimensions and using a similar strategy is called a **strategic group**.[122] The competition between firms within a strategic group is greater than the competition between a member of a strategic group and companies outside that strategic group. Therefore, intra-strategic group competition is more intense than is inter-strategic group competition. In fact, more heterogeneity is evident in the performance of firms within strategic groups than across the groups. The performance leaders within groups are able to follow strategies similar to those of other firms in the group and yet maintain strategic distinctiveness as a foundation for earning above-average returns.[123]

The extent of technological leadership, product quality, pricing policies, distribution channels, and customer service are examples of strategic dimensions that firms in a strategic group may treat similarly. Thus, membership in a particular strategic group defines the essential characteristics of the firm's strategy.

The notion of strategic groups can be useful for analyzing an industry's competitive structure. Such analyses can be helpful in diagnosing competition, positioning, and the profitability of firms competing within an industry. High mobility barriers, high rivalry, and low resources among the firms within an industry limit the formation of strategic groups.[124] However, after strategic groups are formed, their membership remains

A **strategic group** is a set of firms emphasizing similar strategic dimensions and using a similar strategy.

Strategic Focus

Watch Out All Retailers, Here Comes Amazon; Watch Out Amazon, Here Comes Jet.com

Amazon's sales in 2014 were $88.99 billion, an increase of 19.4 percent over 2013. In fact, its sales in 2014 were a whopping 160 percent more than its sales in 2010, only four years prior. Amazon has been able to achieve remarkable gains in sales by providing high quality, rapid, and relatively inexpensive (relative to competitors) service. Amazon has taken on such formidable competitors as Walmart, Google, and Barnes & Noble, among others and has come out of it as a winner, particularly in the last 4–5 years.

Walmart has been making progress in its online sales. In 2014, it grew its online sales by about $3 billion, for a 30 percent increase. That is, until one compares it to Amazon's sales increase in 2014 of about $14.5 billion. Much opportunity remains for both to improve as total 2014 online sales were $300 billion.

Google is clearly the giant search engine with 88 percent of the information search market. However, when consumers are shopping to purchase goods, Amazon is the leader. In the third quarter of 2014, 39 percent of online shoppers in the United States began their search on Amazon, compared to 11 percent for Google. Interestingly, in 2009 the figures were 18 percent for Amazon and 24 percent for Google. So, Amazon appears to be winning this competitive battle with Google.

Barnes & Noble lost out to Google before by ignoring it as a threat. Today, B&N has re-established itself in market niches trying not to compete with Google. For example, its college division largely sells through college bookstores, which have a 'monopoly' location granted by the university. However, Amazon is now targeting the college market by developing agreements with universities to operate co-branded websites to sell textbooks, university t-shirts, etc. Most of the students already shop on Amazon, making the promotion easier to market to universities and to sell to students.

A few years ago, Amazon was referred to as the Walmart of the Internet. But, Amazon has diversified its product/service line much further than Walmart. For example, Amazon now competes against Netflix and other services providing video entertainment. In fact, Amazon won two Golden Globe Awards in 2015 for programs it produced. Amazon recently began to market high fashion clothing for men and women. Founder and CEO of Amazon, Jeff Bezos, stated that Amazon's goal is to become a $200 billion company, and to do that, the firm must learn how to sell clothes and food.

It appears that Amazon is beating all competitors, even formidable ones such as Google and Walmart. But, Amazon still needs to carefully watch its competition. A new company, Jet.com, is targeting Amazon. Jet.com was founded by Marc Lore, who founded the highly successful Diaper.com and a former competitor of Amazon, Quidsi. Amazon hurt Quidsi in a major price war and eventually acquired the company for $550 million. Lore worked for Amazon for two years thereafter but eventually quit to found Jet.com. Jet.com plans to market 10 million products and guarantee the lowest price. Its annual membership will be $50 compared to Amazon Prime's cost of $99. Competing with Amazon represents a major challenge. However, Jet.com has raised about $240 million in venture funding with capital from such players as Bain Capital Ventures, Google Ventures, Goldman Sachs, and Norwest Venture partners. Its current market value is estimated to be $600 million. The future competition between the two companies should be interesting.

Sources: G. Bensiger, 2015, Amazon makes a push on college campuses, *Wall Street Journal*, www.wsj.com, February 1; K. Bhasin & L. Sherman, 2015, Amazon Coutre: Jeff Bezos wants to sell fancy clothes, *Bloomberg*, www.bloomberg.com, February 18; L. Dormehl, 2015, Amazon and Netflix score big at the Golden Globe, *Fast Company*, www.fastcomany.com, January 12; S. Soper, 2015, Amazon.com rival Jet.com raises $140 million in new funding, *Bloomberg*, www.bloomberg.com, February 11; B. Stone, 2015, Amazon bought this man's company. Now he is coming for him, *Bloomberg*, www.bloomberg.com, January 7; M. Kwatinetz, 2014, In online sales, could Walmart ever top Amazon? *Fortune*, www.fortune.com, October 23; R. Winkler & A. Barr, 2014, Google shopping to counter Amazon, *Wall Street Journal*, www.wsj.com, December 15.

relatively stable over time. Using strategic groups to understand an industry's competitive structure requires the firm to plot companies' competitive actions and responses along strategic dimensions such as pricing decisions, product quality, distribution channels, and so forth. This type of analysis shows the firm how certain companies are competing similarly in terms of how they use similar strategic dimensions.

Strategic groups have several implications. First, because firms within a group offer similar products to the same customers, the competitive rivalry among them can be intense. The more intense the rivalry, the greater the threat to each firm's profitability. Second, the strengths of the five forces differ across strategic groups. Third, the closer the strategic groups are in terms of their strategies, the greater is the likelihood of rivalry between the groups.

As explained in the Strategic Focus, Amazon appears to be winning competitive battles against formidable rivals such as Google and Walmart. It must be diligent, however, because a new competitor, Jet.com, is coming after Amazon's market. Thus, even such successful firms as Amazon must continuously analyze and understand their competitors if they are to maintain their current market leading positions.

2-7 Competitor Analysis

The competitor environment is the final part of the external environment requiring study. Competitor analysis focuses on each company against which a firm competes directly. The Coca-Cola Company and PepsiCo, Home Depot and Lowe's, Carrefour SA and Tesco PLC, and Amazon and Google are examples of competitors that are keenly interested in understanding each other's objectives, strategies, assumptions, and capabilities. Indeed, intense rivalry creates a strong need to understand competitors.[125] In a competitor analysis, the firm seeks to understand the following:

- What drives the competitor, as shown by its *future objectives*.
- What the competitor is doing and can do, as revealed by its *current strategy*.
- What the competitor believes about the industry, as shown by its *assumptions*.
- What the competitor's capabilities are, as shown by its *strengths* and *weaknesses*.[126]

Knowledge about these four dimensions helps the firm prepare an anticipated response profile for each competitor (see Figure 2.3). The results of an effective competitor analysis help a firm understand, interpret, and predict its competitors' actions and responses. Understanding competitors' actions and responses clearly contributes to the firm's ability to compete successfully within the industry.[127] Interestingly, research suggests that executives often fail to analyze competitors' possible reactions to competitive actions their firm takes,[128] placing their firm at a potential competitive disadvantage as a result.

Critical to an effective competitor analysis is gathering data and information that can help the firm understand its competitors' intentions and the strategic implications resulting from them.[129] Useful data and information combine to form **competitor intelligence** which is the set of data and information the firm gathers to better understand and anticipate competitors' objectives, strategies, assumptions, and capabilities. In competitor analysis, the firm gathers intelligence not only about its competitors, but also regarding public policies in countries around the world. Such intelligence facilitates an understanding of the strategic posture of foreign competitors. Through effective competitive and public policy intelligence, the firm gains the insights needed to make effective strategic decisions regarding how to compete against rivals.

When asked to describe competitive intelligence, phrases such as "competitive spying" and "corporate espionage" come to my mind for some. These phrases denote the fact that competitive intelligence is an activity that appears to involve trade-offs.[130] The reason for this is that "what is ethical in one country is different from what is ethical in other countries." This position implies that the rules of engagement to follow when gathering competitive intelligence change in different contexts.[131] However, firms avoid the possibility of legal entanglements and ethical quandaries only when their competitive intelligence

Competitor intelligence is the set of data and information the firm gathers to better understand and anticipate competitors' objectives, strategies, assumptions, and capabilities.

Figure 2.3 Competitor Analysis Components

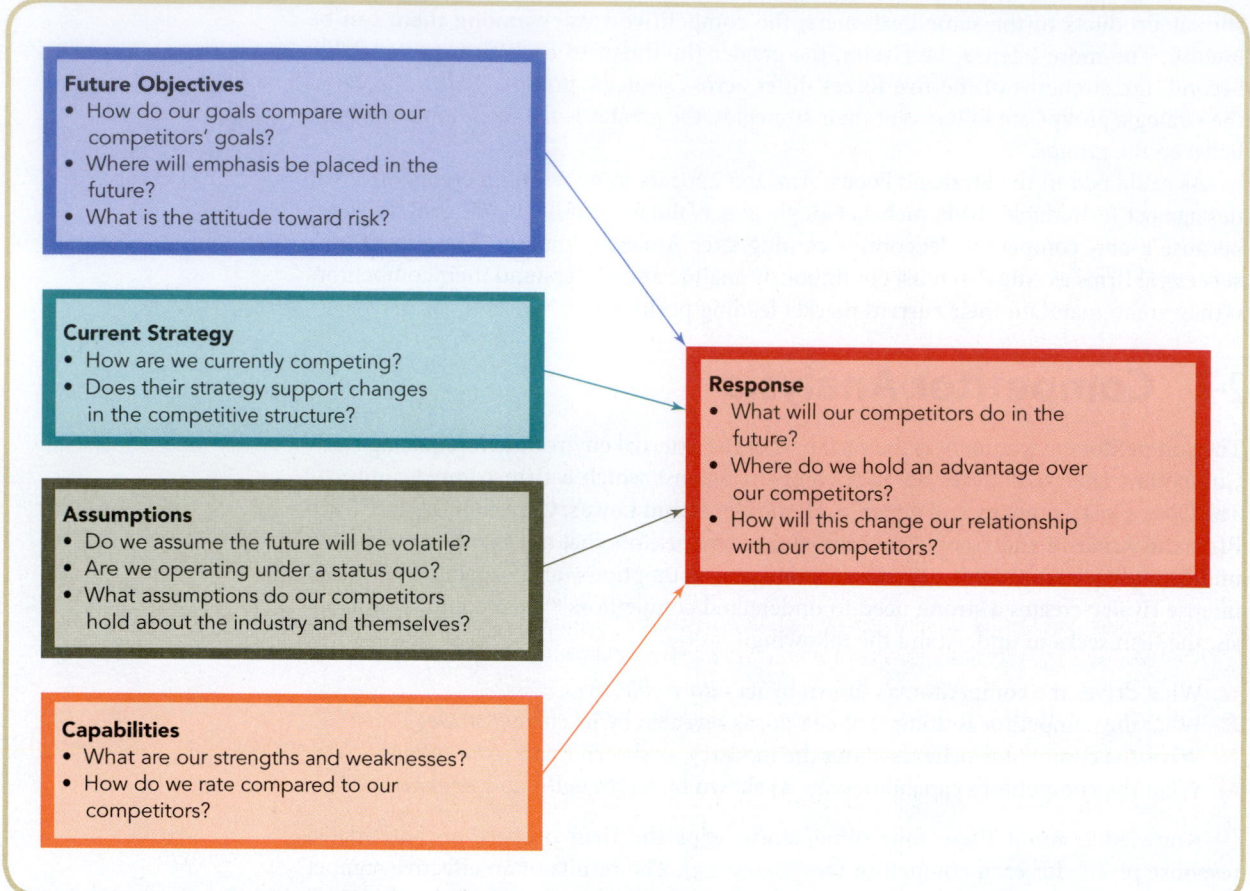

gathering methods are governed by a strict set of legal and ethical guidelines.[132] This means that ethical behavior and actions, as well as the mandates of relevant laws and regulations, should be the foundation on which a firm's competitive intelligence-gathering process is formed.

When gathering competitive intelligence, firms must also pay attention to the complementors of its products and strategy.[133] **Complementors** are companies or networks of companies that sell complementary goods or services that are compatible with the focal firm's good or service. When a complementor's good or service contributes to the functionality of a focal firm's good or service, it in turn creates additional value for that firm.

There are many examples of firms whose good or service complements other companies' offerings. For example, firms manufacturing affordable home photo printers complement other companies' efforts to sell digital cameras. Intel and Microsoft are perhaps the most widely recognized complementors. The Microsoft slogan "Intel Inside" demonstrates the relationship between two firms that do not directly buy from or sell to each other but their products are highly complementary.

Alliances among airline companies such as Oneworld and Star find member companies sharing their route structures and customer loyalty programs as a means of complementing each other's operations. (Alliances and other cooperative strategies are described

Complementors are companies or networks of companies that sell complementary goods or services that are compatible with the focal firm's good or service.

in Chapter 9.) In the example we are considering here, each of the two alliances is a network of complementors. American Airlines, British Airways, Finnair, Japan Airlines, and Royal Jordanian are among the airlines forming the Oneworld alliance. Air Canada, Brussels Airlines, Croatia Airlines, Lufthansa, and United Airlines are five of the members forming the Star alliance. Both of these alliances constantly adjust their members and services offered to better meet customers' needs.

As our discussion shows, complementors expand the set of competitors that firms must evaluate when completing a competitor analysis. In this sense, American Airlines and United Airlines examine each other both as direct competitors on multiple routes but also as complementors that are members of different alliances (Oneworld for American and Star for United). In all cases though, ethical commitments and actions should be the foundation on which competitor analyses are developed.

2-8   Ethical Considerations

Firms must follow relevant laws and regulations as well as carefully articulated ethical guidelines when gathering competitor intelligence. Industry associations often develop lists of these practices that firms can adopt. Practices considered both legal and ethical include:

1. Obtaining publicly available information (e.g., court records, competitors' help-wanted advertisements, annual reports, financial reports of publicly held corporations, and Uniform Commercial Code filings)
2. Attending trade fairs and shows to obtain competitors' brochures, view their exhibits, and listen to discussions about their products.

In contrast, certain practices (including blackmail, trespassing, eavesdropping, and stealing drawings, samples, or documents) are widely viewed as unethical and often are illegal as well.

Some competitive intelligence practices may be legal, but a firm must decide whether they are also ethical, given the image it desires as a corporate citizen. Especially with electronic transmissions, the line between legal and ethical practices can be difficult to determine. For example, a firm may develop website addresses that are similar to those of its competitors and thus occasionally receive e-mail transmissions that were intended for those competitors. The practice is an example of the challenges companies face in deciding how to gather intelligence about competitors while simultaneously determining how to prevent competitors from learning too much about them. To deal with these challenges, firms should establish principles and take actions that are consistent with them.

Professional associations are available to firms as sources of information regarding competitive intelligence practices. For example, while pursuing its mission to help firms make "better decisions through competitive intelligence," the Strategy and Competitive Intelligence Professionals association offers codes of professional practice and ethics to firms for their possible use when deciding how to gather competitive intelligence.[134]

Open discussions of intelligence-gathering techniques can help a firm ensure that employees, customers, suppliers, and even potential competitors understand its convictions to follow ethical practices when gathering intelligence about its competitors. An appropriate guideline for competitor intelligence practices is to respect the principles of common morality and the right of competitors not to reveal certain information about their products, operations, and intentions.

SUMMARY

- The firm's external environment is challenging and complex. Because of its effect on performance, the firm must develop the skills required to identify opportunities and threats that are a part of its external environment.

- The external environment has three major parts:

  1. The general environment (segments and elements in the broader society that affect industries and the firms competing in them)

  2. The industry environment (factors that influence a firm, its competitive actions and responses, and the industry's profitability potential)

  3. The competitor environment (in which the firm analyzes each major competitor's future objectives, current strategies, assumptions, and capabilities).

- Scanning, monitoring, forecasting, and assessing are the four parts of the external environmental analysis process. Effectively using this process helps the firm in its efforts to identify opportunities and threats.

- The general environment has seven segments: demographic, economic, political/legal, sociocultural, technological, global, and sustainable physical. For each segment, the firm has to determine the strategic relevance of environmental changes and trends.

- Compared with the general environment, the industry environment has a more direct effect on the firm's competitive actions and responses. The five forces model of competition includes the threat of entry, the power of suppliers, the power of buyers, product substitutes, and the intensity of rivalry among competitors. By studying these forces, the firm finds a position in an industry where it can influence the forces in its favor or where it can buffer itself from the power of the forces to achieve strategic competitiveness and earn above-average returns.

- Industries are populated with different strategic groups. A strategic group is a collection of firms following similar strategies along similar dimensions. Competitive rivalry is greater within a strategic group than between strategic groups.

- Competitor analysis informs the firm about the future objectives, current strategies, assumptions, and capabilities of the companies with which it competes directly. A thorough competitor analysis examines complementors that support forming and implementing rivals' strategies.

- Different techniques are used to create competitor intelligence: the set of data, information, and knowledge that allow the firm to better understand its competitors and thereby predict their likely competitive actions and responses. Firms absolutely should use only legal and ethical practices to gather intelligence. The Internet enhances firms' ability to gather insights about competitors and their strategic intentions.

KEY TERMS

competitor analysis 42
competitor intelligence 65
complementors 66
demographic segment 45
economic environment 48
general environment 41
global segment 52
industry environment 41

industry 55
opportunity 43
political/legal segment 49
sociocultural segment 50
sustainable physical environment segment 53
strategic group 63
threat 43
technological segment 51

REVIEW QUESTIONS

1. Why is it important for a firm to study and understand the external environment?

2. What are the differences between the general environment and the industry environment? Why are these differences important?

3. What is the external environmental analysis process (four parts)? What does the firm want to learn when using this process?

4. What are the seven segments of the general environment? Explain the differences among them.

5. How do the five forces of competition in an industry affect its profitability potential? Explain.

6. What is a strategic group? Of what value is knowledge of the firm's strategic group in formulating that firm's strategy?

7. What is the importance of collecting and interpreting data and information about competitors? What practices should a firm use to gather competitor intelligence and why?

Mini-Case

The Informal Economy: What It Is and Why It Is Important?

The informal economy refers to commercial activities that occur at least partly outside a governing body's observation, taxation, and regulation. In slightly different words, sociologists Manuel Castells and Alejandro Portes suggest that the "informal economy is characterized by one central feature: it is unregulated by the institutions of society in a legal and social environment in which similar activities are regulated." Firms located in the informal economy are typically thought of as businesses that are unregistered but that are producing and selling *legal* products (that is, they sell many of the same products you might buy in legal businesses but perhaps cheaper because they do not pay government fees and taxes). In contrast to the informal economy, the formal economy is comprised of commercial activities that a governing body taxes and monitors for society's benefit and whose outputs are included in a country's gross domestic product.

For some, working in the informal economy is a choice, such as is the case when individuals decide to supplement the income they are earning through employment in the formal economy with a second job in the informal economy. However, for most people working in the informal economy is a necessity rather than a choice—a reality that contributes to the informal economy's size and significance. Although generalizing about the quality of informal employment is difficult, evidence suggests that it typically means poor employment conditions and greater poverty for workers.

Estimates of the informal economy's size across countries and regions vary. In developing countries, the informal economy accounts for as much as three-quarters of all nonagricultural employment, and perhaps as much as 90 percent in some countries in South Asia and sub-Saharan Africa. But the informal economy is also prominent in developed countries such as Finland, Germany, and France (where the informal economy is estimated to account for 18.3 percent, 16.3 percent, and 15.3 percent, respectively, of these nations' total economic activity). In the United States, recent estimates are that the informal economy is now generating as much as $2 trillion in economic activity on an annual basis. This is double the size of the U.S. informal economy in 2009. In terms of the number of people working in an informal economy, it is suggested that "India's informal economy ... (includes) hundreds of millions of shopkeepers, farmers, construction workers, taxi drivers, street vendors, rag pickers, tailors, repairmen, middlemen, black marketers, and more."

There are various causes of the informal economy's growth, including an inability of a nation's economic environment to create a significant number of jobs relative to available workers. This has been a particularly acute problem during the recent global recession. In the words of a person living in Spain: "Without the underground (informal) economy, we would be in a situation of probably violent social unrest." Governments' inability to facilitate growth efforts in their nation's economic environment is another issue. In this regard, another Spanish citizen suggests that "what the government should focus on is reforming the formal economy to make it more efficient and competitive."

In a general sense, the informal economy yields threats and opportunities for formal economy firms. One threat is that informal businesses may have a cost advantage when competing against formal economy firms because they do not pay taxes or incur the costs of regulations. But the informal economy surfaces opportunities as well. For example, formal-economy firms can try to understand the needs of customers that informal-economy firms are satisfying and then find ways to better meet their needs. Another valuable opportunity is to attract some of the informal economy's talented human capital to accept positions of employment in formal economy firms.

Sources: A. Picchi, 2013, A shadow economy may be keeping the U.S. afloat, *MSN Money*, www.msn.com, May 3; 2013, Meeting on informal economy statistics: Country experience, international recommendations, and application, *United Nations Economic Commission for Africa*, www.uneca.org, April; 2013, About the informal economy, Women in informal employment: Globalizing and organizing, www.wiego.org, May;

G. Bruton, R. D. Ireland, & D. J. Ketchen, Jr., 2012, Toward a research agenda on the informal economy, *Academy of Management Perspectives*, 26(3): 1–11; R. D. Ireland, 2012, 2012 program theme: The informal economy, *Academy of Management*, www.meeting.aomonline.org, March; R. Minder, 2012, In Spain, jobless find a refuge off the books, *New York Times*, www.nytimes.com, May 18.

Case Discussion Questions

1. What are the implications of the informal economy for firms that operate only in the formal economy?

2. When firms consider analyzing their competition, should they include firms in the informal economy? Please explain why or why not.

3. What opportunities does the informal economy present to firms operating in the formal economy?

4. What threats does the informal economy present to firms operating in the formal economy?

5. How do firms operating in the formal economy identify and analyze the parts of the informal economy relevant to their strategies?

NOTES

1. R. Krause, M. Semadeni & A. A. Cannella, 2013, External COO/presidents as expert directors: A new look at the service of role of boards, *Strategic Management Journal*, 34: 1628–1641; Y. Y. Kor & A. Mesko, 2013, Dynamic managerial capabilities: Configuration and orchestration of top executives' capabilities and the firm's dominant logic, *Strategic Management Journal*, 34: 233–234.

2. K.-Y. Hsieh, W. Tsai, & M.-J. Chen, 2015, If they can do it, why not us? Competitors as reference points for justifying escalation of commitment, *Academy of Management Journal*, 58: 38–58; R. Kapoor & J. M. Lee, 2013, Coordinating and competing in ecosystems: How organizational forms shape new technology investments, *Strategic Management Journal*, 34: 274–296.

3. C. E. Stevens, E. Xie, & M. W. Peng, 2015, Toward a legitimacy-based view of political risk: The case of Google and Yahoo in China, *Strategic Management Journal*, 36: in press; E.-H. Kim, 2013, Deregulation and differentiation: Incumbent investment in green technologies, *Strategic Management Journal*, 34: 1162–1185.

4. R. J. Sawant, 2012, Asset specificity and corporate political activity in regulated industries, *Academy of Management Review*, 37: 194–210; S. Hanson, A. Kashyap, & J. Stein, 2011, A macroprudential approach to financial regulation. *Journal of Economic Perspectives*, 25: 3–28.

5. S. Garg, 2013, Venture boards: Distinctive monitoring and implications for firm performance, *Academy of Management Review*, 38: 90–108; J. Harrison, D. Bosse, & R. Phillips, 2010, Managing for stakeholders, stakeholder utility functions, and competitive advantage, *Strategic Management Journal*, 31: 58–74.

6. S. C. Schleimer & T. Pedersen, 2013, The driving forces of subsidiary absorptive capacity, *Journal of Management Studies*, 50: 646–672; M. T. Lucas & O. M. Kirillova, 2011, Reconciling the resource-based and competitive positioning perspectives on manufacturing flexibility, *Journal of Manufacturing Technology Management*, 22: 189–203.

7. M. Taissig & A. Delios, 2015, Unbundling the effects of institutions on firm resources: The contingent value of being local in emerging economy private equity, *Strategic Management Journal*, 36: in press; C. Qian, Q. Cao, & R. Takeuchi, 2013, Top management team functional diversity and organizational innovation in China: The moderating effects of environment, *Strategic Management Journal*, 34: 110–120.

8. EY, 2015, Middle class growth in emerging markets entering the global middle class, www.ey.com, March 6; EY, 2015 Middle class growth in emerging markets hitting the sweet spot, www.ey.com, March 6.

9. E. V. Karniouchina, S. J. Carson, J. C. Short, & D. J. Ketchen, 2013, Extending the firm vs. industry debate: Does industry life cycle stage matter? *Strategic Management Journal*, 34: 1010–1018.

10. R. B. MacKay & R. Chia, 2013, Choice, chance, and unintended consequences in strategic change: A process understanding of the rise and fall of NorthCo Automotive, *Academy of Management Journal*, 56: 208–230; J. P. Murmann, 2013, The coevolution of industries and important features of their environments, *Organization Science*, 24: 58–78; G. J. Kilduff, H. A. Elfenbein, & B. M. Staw, 2010, The psychology of rivalry: A relationally dependent analysis of competition, *Academy of Management Journal*, 53: 943–969.

11. R. E. Hoskisson, M. Wright, I. Filatotchev, & M. W. Peng, 2013, Emerging multinationals from mid-range economies: The influence of institutions and factor markets, *Journal of Management Studies*, 50: 127–153; A. Hecker & A. Ganter, 2013, The influence of product market competition on technological and management innovation: Firm-level evidence from a large-scale survey, *European Management Review*, 10: 17–33.

12. Walmart, 2015, Our locations. www.corporate.walmart.com, March 6; Metro Cash and Carry, 2015, International Operations, en.wikipedia.org, February 1; BBC news, 2014, Carrefour to exit India business, www.bbc.com, July 8; BBC news, 2014, Tesco signs deal to enter India's supermarket sector, www.bbc.com, March 21.

13. F. Bridoux & J. W. Stoelhorst, 2014, Microfoundations for stakeholder theory: Managing stakeholders with heterogeneous motives, *Strategic Management Journal*, 35: 107–125; B. Gilad, 2011, The power of blindspots. What companies don't know, surprises them. What they don't want to know, kills them, *Strategic Direction*, 27(4): 3–4.

14. B. Bradlee, 2014, Patent battle between Nokia and HTC ends with the signing of a patent and technology collaboration agreement, Capital Technologies, www.captees.com, February 9; A. Poon & J. Rossi, 2013, Patent battle between Nokia, HTC heats up, *Wall Street Journal*, www.wsj.com, May 24.

15. D. Li, 2013, Multilateral R&D alliances by new ventures, *Journal of Business Venturing*, 28: 241–260; A. Graefe, S. Luckner, & C. Weinhardt, 2010, Prediction markets for foresight, *Futures*, 42: 394–404.

16. J. Tang, K. M. Kacmar, & L. Busenitz, 2012, Entrepreneurial alertness in the pursuit of new opportunities, *Journal of Business Venturing*, 27: 77–94; D. Chrusciel, 2011, Environmental scan: Influence on strategic direction, *Journal of Facilities Management*, 9(1): 7–15.

17. D. E. Hughes, J. Le Bon, & A. Rapp, 2013, Gaining and leveraging customer-based competitive intelligence: The pivotal role of social capital and salesperson adaptive selling skills, *Journal of the Academy of Marketing Science*, 41: 91–110; J. R. Hough & M. A. White, 2004, Scanning actions and environmental dynamism: Gathering information for strategic decision making, *Management Decision*, 42: 781–793; V. K. Garg, B. A. Walters, & R. L. Priem, 2003, Chief executive scanning emphases, environmental dynamism, and manufacturing firm performance, *Strategic Management Journal*, 24: 725–744.

18. C.-H. Lee & T. F. Chien, 2013, Leveraging microblogging big data with a modified density-based clustering approach for event awareness and topic ranking, *Journal of Information Science*, 39: 523–543.

19. The Culturist, 2013, More than 2 billion people use the Internet, here's what they're up to, www.theculturist.com, May 9.

20. S. Garg, 2013, Venture boards: Distinctive monitoring and implications for firm performance, *Academy of Management Review*, 38: 90–108; L. Fahey, 1999, *Competitors*, New York: John Wiley & Sons, 71–73.

21. K. Greene & V. Monga, 2013, Workers saving too little to retire, *Wall Street Journal*, www.wsj.com, March 19.

22. M. Hadley, 2014, Americans still don't have enough savings, *USA Today*, www.usatoday.com, June 23.

23. B. L. Connelly & E. J. Van Slyke, 2012, The power and peril of board interlocks, *Business Horizons*, 55: 403–408; C. Dellarocas, 2010, Online reputation systems: How to design one that does what you need, *MIT Sloan Management Review*, 51: 33–37.

24. G. Martin, R. Gozubuyuk, & M. Becerra, 2015, Interlocks and firm performance: The role of uncertainty in the directorate interlock-performance relationship, *Strategic Management Journal*, 36: 235–253.

25. K. L. Turner & M. V. Makhija, 2012, The role of individuals in the information processing perspective, *Strategic Management Journal*, 33: 661–680; X. Zhang, S. Majid, & S. Foo, 2010, Environmental scanning: An application of information literacy skills at the workplace, *Journal of Information Science*, 36: 719–732.

26. L. Sleuwaegen, 2013, Scanning for profitable (international) growth, *Journal of Strategy and Management*, 6: 96–110; J. Calof & J. Smith, 2010, The integrative domain of foresight and competitive intelligence and its impact on R&D management, *R & D Management*, 40(1): 31–39.

27. S. Phandis, C. Caplice, Y. Sheffi, & M. Singh, 2015, Effect of scenario planning on field experts judgment of long-range investment decisions, *Strategic Management Journal*, in press; A. Chwolka & M. G. Raith, 2012, The value of business planning before start-up—A decision-theoretical perspective, *Journal of Business Venturing*, 27: 385–399.

28. S. D. Wu, K. G. Kempf, M. O. Atan, B. Aytac, S. A. Shirodkar, & A. Mishra, 2010, Improving new-product forecasting at Intel Corporation, *Interfaces*, 40: 385–396.

29. K. D. Miller & S.-J. Lin, 2015, Analogical reasoning for diagnosing strategic issues in dynamic and complex environments, *Strategic Management Journal*, in press; R. Klingebiel, 2012, Options in the implementation plan of entrepreneurial initiatives: Examining firms' attainment of flexibility benefit, *Strategic Entrepreneurship Journal*, 6: 307–334; T. Sueyoshi & M. Goto, 2011, Methodological comparison between two unified (operational and environmental) efficiency measurements for environmental assessment, *European Journal of Operational Research*, 210: 684–693.

30. P. Jarzabkowski & S. Kaplan, 2015, Strategy tools-in-use: A framework for understanding "technologies of rationality" in practice, *Strategic Management Journal*, 36: 537–558; N. J. Foss, J. Lyngsie, & S. A. Zahra, 2013, The role of external knowledge sources and organizational design in the process of opportunity exploitation, *Strategic Management Journal*, 34: 1453–1471.

31. D. Grewal, A. Roggeveen, & R. C. Runyan, 2013, Retailing in a connected world, *Journal of Marketing Management*, 29: 263–270; R. King, 2010, Consumer demographics: Use demographic resources to target specific audiences, *Journal of Financial Planning*, 23(12): S4–S6.

32. 2015, World, population clock: 7 billion people (2015), www.worldometers.info/world-population, March 6; 2013, U.S. Census Bureau, International Programs World Population, www.census.gov/population/international/data/worldpop/, May 21.

33. World population clock; 2013, The world population and the top ten countries with the highest population, *Internet World Stats*, www.internetworldstats.com, May 21.

34. T. Kambayashi, 2011, Brief: Aging Japan sees slowest population growth yet, *McClatchy-Tribune Business News*, www.mcclatchy.com, February 25; S. Moffett, 2005, Fast-aging Japan keeps its elders on the job longer, *Wall Street Journal*, June 15, A1, A8.

35. D. Bloom & D. Canning, 2012, How companies must adapt for an aging workforce, *HBR Blog Network*, www.hbr.org, December 3.

36. 2012, Humanity's aging, *National Institute on Aging*, www.nia.nih.gov, March 27.

37. M. B. Dougherty, 2012, Stunning facts about Japan's demographic implosion, *Business Insider*, www.businessinsider.com, April 24.

38. M. Chand & R. L. Tung, 2014, The aging of the world's population and its effects on global business, *Academy of Management Perspectives*, 28: 409–429.

39. 2013, The aging workforce: Finding the silver lining in the talent gap, *Deloitte*, www.deloitte.com, February.

40. D. Cumming, T. Leung, & O. Rui, 2015, Gender diversity and securities fraud, *Academy of Management Journal*, in press; A. Joshi, J. Son, & H. Roh, 2015, When can women close the gap? A meta-analytic test of sex differences in performance and rewards, *Academy of Management Journal*, in press.

41. 2015, List of U.S. states and territories by population, *Wikipedia*, en.wikipedia.org, March 9.

42. 2013, 2013 Cal Facts, Legislative Analysts' Office, www.lao.ca.gov, January 2.

43. J. Goudreau, 2013, The states people are fleeing in 2013, *Forbes*, www.forbes.com, February 7.

44. R. Dobbs, S. Smit, J. Remes, J. Manyika, C. Roxburgh & A. Restrepo, 2011, *Urban world: Mapping the economic power of cities*, Chicago: McKinsey Global Institute, March.

45. 2012, Population and population change statistics, *European Commission*, www.epp.eurostat.ec.europa.eu, October.

46. S. Reddy, 2011, U.S. News: Latinos fuel growth in decade, *Wall Street Journal*, March 25, A2.

47. 2015, New census bureau report analyzes U.S. population projects, www.census.gov, March 3.

48. G. Andrrevski, O. C. Richard, J.D. Shaw, & W. J. Ferrier, 2014, Racial diversity and firm performance: The mediating role of competitive intensity, *Journal of Management*, 40: 820–844.

49. M. Fisher, 2013, A revealing map of the world's most and least ethnically diverse countries, *The Washington Post*, www.washingtonpost.com, May 16.

50. A. Hain-Cole, 2010, Companies juggle cost cutting with competitive benefits for international assignments, *Benefits & Compensation International: A Magazine for Global Companies*, 40: 26.

51. J. Lee, 2010, Don't underestimate India's consumers, *Bloomberg Businessweek*, www.businessweek.com, January 21.

52. W. Q. Judge, A. Fainschmidt, & J. L. Brown, 2014, Which model of capitalism best delivers both wealth and equality? *Journal of International Business Studies*, 45: 363–386.

53. G. A. Shinkle & B. T. McCann, 2013, New product deployment: The moderating influence of economic institutional context, *Strategic Management Journal*, 35: 1090–1101; L. Fahey & V. K. Narayanan, 1986, *Macroenvironmental Analysis for Strategic Management (The West Series in Strategic Management)*, St. Paul, Minnesota: West Publishing Company, 105.

54. A. Chakrabarti, 2015, Organizational adaptation in an economic shock: The role of growth reconfiguration, *Strategic Management Journal*, in press; N. Bloom, M. A. Kose, & M. E. Terrones, 2013, Held back by uncertainty, *Finance & Development*, 50: 38–41, March.

55. 2015, Global economic prospects: Having physical space and using it, The World bank, www.worldbank.org, January.

56. J. K. Ault & A. Spicer, 2014, The institutional context of poverty: State fragility as a predictor of cross-national variation in commercial microfinance lending, *Strategic Management Journal*, 36; R. J. Sawant, 2012, Asset specificity and corporate political activity in regulated industries, *Academy of Management Review*, 37: 194–210.

57. T. A. Khoury, M. Junkunc, & S. Mingo, 2015, Navigating political hazard risks and legal system quality: Venture capital investments in Latin America, *Journal of Management*, 41: 808–840; M. R. King, 2015, Political bargaining and multinational bailouts, *Journal of International Business Studies*, 46: 206–222; N. Jia, 2014, Are collective political actions and private political actions substitutes or complements? Empirical evidence from China's private sector, *Strategic Management Journal*, 35: 292–315.

58. S. G. Lazzarini, 2015, Strategizing by the government: Can industrial policy create firm-level competitive advantage, *Strategic Management Journal*, 36: 97–112.

59. S. Zeidler, 2013, MGM assessing costs of operating online poker in Nevada, *Reuters*, www.mobile,reuters.com, May 2.

60. R. Ayadi, E. Arbak, W. P. de Goren, & D. T. Llewellyn, 2013, *Regulation of European Banks and Business Models: Towards a New Paradigm?* Brookings Institution Press, Washington, D.C.

61. K. J. O'Brien, 2013, Firms brace for new European data privacy law, *New York Times*, www.nytimes.com, May 13.

62. C. Jiang, S. Yao, & G. Feng, 2013, Bank ownership, privatization, and performance: Evidence from a transition country, *Journal of Banking & Finance*, 37: 3364–3372; N. Boubakri & L. Bouslimi, 2010, Analysts following of privatized firms around the world: The role of institutions and

ownership structure, *International Journal of Accounting*, 45: 413–442.

63. L. Richards, 2013, The effects of socio-culture on business, *The Houston Chronicle*, www.chron.com, May 26.

64. J. G. York & M. J. Lennox, 2014, Exploring the sociocultural determinants of de novo and de alio entry into emerging industries, *Strategic Management Journal*, 35: 1930–1951.

65. 2013, Health strategy, *European Commission Public Health*, www.europa.eu, May 23.

66. M. Toosi, 2012, Projections of the labor force to 2050: A visual essay, *Monthly Labor Review*, October.

67. Ibid., 13.

68. T. Grenness, 2011, The impact of national culture on CEO compensation and salary gaps between CEOs and manufacturing workers, *Compensation & Benefits Review*, 43: 100–108.

69. G. Lucke, T. Kostova, & K. Roth, 2014, Multiculturalism from a cognitive perspective: Patterns and implications, *Journal of International Business Studies*, 45:169–190; Y. Zeng, O. Shenkar, S.-H. Lee, & S. Song, 2013, Cultural differences, MNE learning abilities, and the effect of experience on subsidiary mortality in a dissimilar culture: Evidence from Korean MNEs, *Journal of International Business Studies*, 44: 42–65.

70. J. Liu, C. Hui, C. Lee, & Z. X. Chen, 2013, Why do I feel valued and why do I contribute? A relational approach to employee's organization-based self-esteem and job performance, *Journal of Management Studies*, 50: 1018–1040; C. M. Chan, S. Makino, & T. Isobe, 2010, Does subnational region matter? Foreign affiliate performance in the United States and China, *Strategic Management Journal*, 31: 1226–1243; P. J. Buckley, J. Clegg, & H. Tan, 2006, Cultural awareness in knowledge transfer to China—The role of guanxi and mianzi, *Journal of World Business*, 41: 275–288.

71. S. Grodal, 2015, The co-evolution of technologies and categories during industry emergence, *Academy of Management Review*, in press; N. R. Furr & D. C. Snow, Intergenerational hybrids: Spillbacks, spillforwards and adapting to technological discontinuities, *Organization Science*, in press; J. P. Eggers, 2014, Competing technologies and industry evolution: The benefits of making mistakes in the flat panel display industry, *Strategic Management Journal*, 35: 159–178.

72. L. Fuentelsaz, E. Garrido, & J. P. Maicas, 2015, Incumbents, technological change and institutions: How the value of complementary resources varies across markets, *Strategic Management Journal*, in press; A. Furlan, A. Cabigiosu, & A. Camuffo, 2014, When the mirror gets misted up: Modularity and technological change, *Strategic Management Journal*, 35: 789–807.

73. 2013, Consumers (everywhere) know a good deal when they see it, *bcg.perspectives*, www.bcgperspectives.com, January 11.

74. W. Bock, D. Field, P. Zwillenberg, & K. Rogers, 2015, The growth of the global mobile Internet economy, *bcg.perspectives, www.bcgperspectives.com*; The Culturist, 2013.

75. P. Buckley & R. Strange, 2015, The governance of the global factory: Location and control of world economic activity, *Academy of Management Perspectives*, in press; J.-E. Vahlne & I. Ivarsson, 2014, The globalization of Swedish MNEs: Empirical evidence and theoretical explanations, *Journal of International Business Studies*, 45: 227–247; E. R. Banalieva & C. Dhanaraj, 2013, Home-region orientation in international expansion strategies, *Journal of International Business Studies*, 44: 89–116.

76. K. Kyung-Tae, R. Seung-Kyu, & O. Joongsan, 2011, The strategic role evolution of foreign automotive parts subsidiaries in China, *International Journal of Operations & Production Management*, 31: 31–55.

77. S. T. Cavusgil & G. Knight, 2015, The born global firm: An entrepreneurial and capabilities perspective on early and rapid internationalization, *Journal of International Business Studies*, 46: 3–16; S. Sui & M. Baum, 2014, Internationalization strategy, firm resources and the survival of SMEs in the export market, *Journal of International Business Studies*, 45: 821–841.

78. 2013, Growth and globalization: Keeping a lid on capacity, KPMG, Automotive executive survey, www.kpmb.com, January 15.

79. T.J. Pukall & A. Calabro, 2014, The internationalization of family firms: A critical review and integrative model, *Family Business Review*, 27: 103–125; K. E. Meyer, 2006, Globalfocusing: From domestic conglomerates to global specialists, *Journal of Management Studies*, 43: 1110–1144.

80. R. G. Flores, R. V. Aguilera, A. Mahdian, & P. M. Vaaler, 2013, How well do supra-national regional grouping schemes fit international business research models? *Journal of International Business Studies*, 44: 451–474; Hoskisson, Wright, Filatotchev, & Peng, Emerging multinationals.

81. F. J. Froese, 2013, Work values of the next generation of business leaders in Shanghai, Tokyo, and Seoul, *Asia Pacific Journal of Management*, 30: 297–315; M. Muethel & M. H. Bond, 2013, National context and individual employees' trust of the out-group: The role of societal trust, *Journal of International Business Studies*, 4: 312–333; M. A. Hitt, M. T. Dacin, B. B. Tyler, & D. Park, 1997, Understanding the differences in Korean and U.S. executives' strategic orientations, *Strategic Management Journal*, 18: 159–167.

82. D. Ahlstrom, E. Levitas, M. A. Hitt, T. Dacin, & H. Zhu, 2014, The three faces of China: Strategic alliance partner selection in three Chinese economies," *Journal of World Business*, 49: 572–585; X. Li, 2012, Behind the recent surge of Chinese patenting: An institutional view, *Research Policy*, 41: 236–249.

83. T. Yu, M. Subramaniam, & A. A. Cannella, Jr., 2013, Competing globally, allying locally: Alliances between global rivals and host-country factors, *Journal of International Business Studies*, 44: 117–137; T. K. Das & R. Kumar, 2011, Regulatory focus and opportunism in the alliance development process, *Journal of Management*, 37: 682–708.

84. B. Perrott, 2014, The sustainable organization: Blueprint for an integrated model, *Journal of Business Strategy*, 35: 26–37; A. G. Scherer, G. Palazzo, & D. Seidl, 2013, Managing legitimacy in complex and heterogeneous environments: Sustainable development in a globalized world, *Journal of Management Studies*, 50: 259–284; J. Harris, 2011, Going green to stay in the black: Transnational capitalism and renewable energy, *Perspectives on Global Development & Technology*, 10: 41–59.

85. B. W. Lewis, J. L. Walls, & G. W. S. Dowell, 2014, Difference in degrees: CEO characteristics and firm environmental disclosure, *Strategic Management Journal*, 35: 712–722; P. Berrone, A. Fosfuri, L. Gelabert, & L. R. Gomez-Mejia, 2013, Necessity as the mother of 'green' inventions: Institutional pressures and environmental innovations, *Strategic Management Journal*, 34: 891–909; M. Delmas, V. H. Hoffmann, & M. Kuss, 2011, Under the tip of the iceberg: Absorptive capacity, environmental strategy, and competitive advantage, *Business & Society*, 50: 116–154.

86. 2013, What is sustainable development? International institute for sustainable development, www.iisd.org, May 5.

87. J. K. Hall, G. A. Daneke, & M. J. Lenox, 2010, Sustainable development and entrepreneurship: Past contributions and future directions, *Journal of Business Venturing*, 25: 439–448.

88. M. A. Delmas & O. Gergaud, 2014, Sustainable certification for future generations: The case of family firms, *Family Business Review*, 27: 228–243.

89. D. Ferris, 2012, Will economic growth destroy the environment—or save it? *Forbes*, www.forbes.com, October 17.

90. S. M. Ben-Menahern, Z. Kwee, H. W. Volberda, & F. A. J. Van Den Bosch, 2013, Strategic renewal over time: The enabling role of potential absorptive capacity in aligning internal and external rates of change, *Long Range Planning*, 46: 216–235; V. Souitaris & B. Maestro, 2010, Polychronicity in top management teams: The impact on strategic decision processes and performance of new technology ventures, *Strategic Management Journal*, 31: 652–678.

91. S.-J. Chang & B. Wu, 2014, Institutional barriers and industry dynamics, *Strategic Management Journal*, 35: 1103–1121.

92. M. Schimmer & M. Brauer, 2012, Firm performance and aspiration levels as determinants of a firm's strategic repositioning within strategic group structures, *Strategic Organization*, 10: 406–435; J. Galbreath & P. Galvin, 2008, Firm factors, industry structure and performance variation: New empirical evidence to a classic debate, *Journal of Business Research*, 61: 109–117.

93. J. J. Tarzijan & C. C. Ramirez, 2011, Firm, industry and corporation effects revisited: A mixed multilevel analysis for Chilean companies, *Applied Economics Letters*, 18: 95–100; V. F. Misangyl, H. Elms, T. Greckhamer, & J. A. Lepine, 2006, A new perspective on a fundamental debate: A multilevel approach to industry, corporate, and business unit effects, *Strategic Management Journal*, 27: 571–590.

94. E. T. Fukui, A. B. Hammer, & L. Z. Jones, 2013, Are U.S. exports influenced by stronger IPR protection measures in recipient markets? *Business Horizons*, 56: 179–188; D. Sullivan & J. Yuening, 2010, Media convergence and the impact of the Internet on the M&A activity of large media companies, *Journal of Media Business Studies*, 7(4): 21–40.

95. G. D. Markman & T. L. Waldron, 2014, Small entrants and large incumbents: A framework of micro entry, *Academy of Management Perspectives*, 28: 179–197; K. Muller, K. Huschelrath, & V. Bilotkach, 2012, The construction of a low-cost airline network—facing competition and exploring new markets, *Managerial and Decision Economics*, 33: 485–499.

96. F. Karakaya & S. Parayitam, 2013, Barriers to entry and firm performance: A proposed model and curvilinear relationships, *Journal of Strategic Marketing*, 21: 25–47; B. F. Schivardi & E. Viviano, 2011, Entry barriers in retail trade, *Economic Journal*, 121: 145–170; A. V. Mainkar, M. Lubatkin, & W. S. Schulze, 2006, Toward a product-proliferation theory of entry barriers, *Academy of Management Review*, 31: 1062–1075.

97. V. Niu, L. C. Dong, & R. Chen, 2012, Market entry barriers in China, *Journal of Business Research*, 65: 68–76.

98. R. Vandaie & A. Zaheer, 2014, Surviving bear hugs: Firm capability, large partner alliances and growth, *Strategic Management Journal*, 35: 566–577; V. K. Garg, R. L. Priem, & A. A. Rasheed, 2013, A theoretical explanation of the cost advantages of multi-unit franchising, *Journal of Marketing Channels*, 20: 52–72.

99. P. Jackson & M. Iwata, 2012, Global deal: Mitsubishi Heavy, Hitachi to merge businesses, *Wall Street Journal*, www.wsj.com, November 30.

100. C. G. Asmussen, 2015, Strategic factor markets, scale free resources and economic performance: The impact of product market rivalry, *Strategic Management Journal*, in press.

101. G. A. Shinkle & B. T. McCann, 2014, New produce deployment: The moderating influence of economic institutional context, *Strategic Management Journal*, 35: 1090–1101.

102. J. J. Ebbers & N. M. Wijnberg, 2013, Nascent ventures competing for start-up capital: Matching reputations and investors, *Journal of Business Venturing*, 27: 372–384; T. Rice & P. E. Strahan, 2010, Does credit competition affect small-firm finance? *Journal of Finance*, 65: 861–889.

103. Z. Khan, Y. K. Lew, & R. R. Sinkovics, 2015, International joint ventures as boundary spanners: Technological knowledge transfer in an emerging economy, *Global Strategy Journal*, 5: 48–68.

104. 2013, Zara-owned Inditex's profits rise by 22%, *BBC News Business*, www.bbc.co.uk, March 13.

105. M. Hume, 2011, The secrets of Zara's success, *Telegraph.co.uk*, www.telegraph.co.uk, June 22.

106. Y. Pan, L. Teng, A. B. Supapol, X. Lu, D. Huang, & Z. Wang, 2014, Firms; FDI ownership: The influence of government ownership and legislative connections, *Journal of International Business*, 45: 1029–1043; 2011, Airline deregulation, revisited, *Bloomberg Businessweek*, www.businessweek.com, January 21.

107. S. H. Ang, M. H. Benischke, & J. P. Doh, 2015, The interactions of institutions on foreign market entry mode, *Strategic Management Journal*, in press.

108. J. Jaeger, 2010, Anti-trust reviews: Suddenly, they're a worry, *Compliance Week*, 7(80): 48–59.

109. N. Argyes, L. Bigelow, & J. A. Nickerson, 2015, Dominant designs, innovation shocks and the follower's dilemma, *Strategic Management Journal*, 36: 216–234.

110. J. B. Heide, A. Kumar, & K. H. Wathne, 2014, Concurrent sourcing, governance mechanisms and performance outcomes in industrial value chains, *Strategic Management Journal*, 35: 1164–1185; L. Poppo & K. Z. Zhou, 2014, Managing contracts for fairness in buyer-supplier exchanges, *Strategic Management Journal*, 35: 1508–1527.

111. M. J. Mol & C. Brewster, 2014, The outsourcing strategy of local and multinational firms: A supply base perspective, *Global Strategy Journal*, 4: 20–34.

112. J. Roloff, M. S. ABländer, & D. Z. Nayir, 2015, The supplier perspective: Forging strong partnerships with buyers; *Journal of Business Strategy*, 36(1): 25–32; L. Poppo, K. Z. Zhou, & J. J. Li, 2015, When can you trust "trust?" Calculative trust, relational trust and supplier performance, *Strategic Management Journal*, in press.

113. F. H. Liu, 2014, OEM supplier impact on buyer competence development, *Journal of Strategy and Management*, 7: 2–18; S. Bhattacharyya & A. Nain, 2011, Horizontal acquisitions and buying power: A product market analysis, *Journal of Financial Economics*, 99: 97–115.

114. 2015, Computer sales statistics, *Statistic Brain*, www.statisticbrain.com, January 14; I. Sherr & S. Ovide, 2013, Computer sales in free fall, *Wall Street Journal*, www.wsj.com, April 11.

115. C. Giachetti & G. B. Dagnino, 2014, Detecting the relationship between competitive intensity and firm product line length: Evidence from the worldwide mobile phone industry, *Strategic Management Journal*, 35: 138–1409.

116. G. Pacheco-de-Almeida, A. Hawk, & B. Yeung, 2015, The right speed and its value, *Strategic Management Journal*, 36: 159–176.

117. M.-J. Lee & J. Cheng, 2015, Samsung vs. Apple: who was no. 1? *Wall Street Journal Digits*, blog.wsj.com, January 29; P. Cohan, 2013, Samsung trouncing Apple, *Forbes*, www.forbes.com, April 26.

118. K. Bradsher, 2014, China's embrace of foreign cars, *New York Times*, www.nytimes.com, April 8; K. Bradsher, 2013, Chinese auto buyers grow hungry for larger cars, *New York Times*, www.nytimes.com, April 21.

119. H. Martin, 2014, Global airline industry expects record profits in 2014, *Los Angeles Times*, articles.latimes.com, February 9; R. Wall, 2013, Airline profits to top $10 billion on improving sales outlook, *Bloomberg*, www.bloomberg.com, March 20.

120. M. A. Hitt, D. Li, & K Xu, 2015, International Strategy: From local to global and beyond, *Journal of World Business*, in press; A. Goerzen, C. G. Asmussen, & B. B. Nielsen, 2013, Global cities and multinational enterprise location strategy, *Journal of International Business Studies*, 44: 427–450.

121. M. E. Porter, 1980, *Competitive Strategy*, New York: Free Press.

122. F. J. Mas-Ruiz, F. Ruiz-Moreno, & A. L. de Guevara Martinez, 2013, Asymmetric rivalry within and between strategic groups, *Strategic Management Journal*, in press; M. S. Hunt, 1972, Competition in the major home appliance industry, 1960–1970 (doctoral dissertation, Harvard University); Porter, *Competitive Strategy*, 129.

123. D. Miller, I. Le Breton-Miller, & R. H. Lester, 2013, Family firm governance, strategic conformity, and performance: Institutional vs. strategic perspectives,

Organization Science, 24: 189–209; S. Cheng & H. Chang, 2009, Performance implications of cognitive complexity: An empirical study of cognitive strategic groups in semiconductor industry, *Journal of Business Research*, 62: 1311–1320; G. McNamara, D. L. Deephouse, & R. A. Luce, 2003, Competitive positioning within and across a strategic group structure: The performance of core, secondary, and solitary firms, *Strategic Management Journal*, 24: 161–181.

124. B. P. S. Murthi, A. A. Rasheed, & I. Goll, 2013, An empirical analysis of strategic groups in the airline industry using latent class regressions, *Managerial and Decision Economics*, 34(2): 59–73; J. Lee, K. Lee, & S. Rho, 2002, An evolutionary perspective on strategic group emergence: A genetic algorithm-based model, *Strategic Management Journal*, 23: 727–746.

125. K.-Y. Hsieh, W. Tsai, & M.-J. Chen, 2015, If they can do it, why not us? Competitors as reference points in justifying escalation of commitment, *Academy of management Journal, 58: 38–58;* T. Keil, T. Laarmanen, & R. G. McGrath, 2013, Is a counterattack the best defense? Competitive dynamics through acquisitions, *Long Range Planning*, 46: 195–215.

126. Porter, *Competitive Strategy*, 49.

127. R. L. Priem, S. Li, & J. C. Carr, 2012, Insights and new directions from demand-side approaches to technology innovation, entrepreneurship, and strategic management research, *Journal of Management*, 38: 346–374; J. E. Prescott & R. Herko, 2010, TOWS: The role of competitive intelligence, *Competitive Intelligence Magazine*, 13(3): 8–17.

128. D. E. Hughes, J. Le Bon, & A. Rapp, 2013. Gaining and leveraging customer-based competitive intelligence: The pivotal role of social capital and salesperson adaptive selling skills, *Journal of the Academy of Marketing Science*, 41: 91–110; D. B. Montgomery, M. C. Moore, & J. E. Urbany,

2005, Reasoning about competitive reactions: Evidence from executives, *Marketing Science*, 24: 138–149.

129. H. Akbar & N. Tzokas, 2012, An exploration of new product development's front-end knowledge conceptualization process in discontinuous innovations, *British Journal of Management*, 24: 245–263; K. Xu, S. Liao, J. Li, & Y. Song, 2011, Mining comparative opinions from customer reviews for competitive intelligence, *Decision Support Systems*, 50: 743–754; S. Jain, 2008, Digital piracy: A competitive analysis, *Marketing Science*, 27: 610–626.

130. S. Wright, 2013, Converting input to insight: Organising for intelligence-based competitive advantage. In S. Wright (ed.), *Competitive Intelligence, Analysis and Strategy: Creating Organisational Agility*. Abingdon: Routledge, 1–35; J. G. York, 2009, Pragmatic sustainability: Translating environmental ethics into competitive advantage, *Journal of Business Ethics*, 85: 97–109.

131. R. Huggins, 2010, Regional competitive intelligence: Benchmarking and policy-making. *Regional Studies*, 44: 639–658.

132. L. T. Tuan, 2013, Leading to learning and competitive intelligence, *The Learning Organization*, 20: 216–239; K. A. Sawka, 2008, The ethics of competitive intelligence, *Kiplinger Business Resource Center Online*, www.kiplinger.com, March.

133. R. B. Bouncken & S. Kraus, 2013, Innovation in knowledge-intensive industries: The double-edged sword of coopetition, *Journal of Business Research*, 66: 2060–2070; T. Mazzarol & S. Reboud, 2008, The role of complementary actors in the development of innovation in small firms, *International Journal of Innovation Management*, 12: 223–253; A. Brandenburger & B. Nalebuff, 1996, *Co-opetition*, New York: Currency Doubleday.

134. 2015, SCIP Code of ethics for CI professionals, www.scip.org, March 25.

3

The Internal Organization: Resources, Capabilities, Core Competencies, and Competitive Advantages

Studying this chapter should provide you with the strategic management knowledge needed to:

3-1 Explain why firms need to study and understand their internal organization.

3-2 Define value and discuss its importance.

3-3 Describe the differences between tangible and intangible resources.

3-4 Define capabilities and discuss their development.

3-5 Describe four criteria used to determine if resources and capabilities are core competencies.

3-6 Explain how firms analyze their value chain for the purpose of determining where they are able to create value when using their resources, capabilities, and core competencies.

3-7 Define outsourcing and discuss reasons for its use.

3-8 Discuss the importance of identifying internal strengths and weaknesses.

3-9 Discuss the importance of avoiding core rigidities.

DATA ANALYTICS, LARGE PHARMACEUTICAL COMPANIES, AND CORE COMPETENCIES: A BRAVE NEW WORLD

To date, and perhaps surprisingly, the idea of using data strategically remains somewhat novel in some organizations. However, the reality of "big data" and "big data analytics" (which is "the process of examining big data to uncover hidden patterns, unknown correlations, and other useful information that can be used to make better decisions") is quickly changing this situation. Indeed, some suggest that, today, an organization wishing to be innovative will, at a minimum, commit to quickly learning how to comprehensively use big data analytics (BDA) across all customer channels (mobile, Web, e-mail and physical stores) as well as throughout its supply chain.

This is the situation for large pharmaceutical companies (these firms are often called "big pharma") in that many are considering the possibility of developing a core competence in terms of BDA. (We define and discuss core competencies in this chapter.) But why are these firms evaluating this possibility? There are several reasons. In addition to the vast increases in the amounts of data that must be studied and interpreted for competitive purposes, "health care reform and the changing landscape of health care delivery" systems throughout the world are influencing these firms to think about developing BDA as a core competence.

© Creativa Images/Shutterstock.com

Many benefits can accrue to big pharma firms capable of forming BDA as a core competence. For example, having BDA as a core competence is expected to help a firm quickly identify trial candidates and accelerate their recruitment, develop improved inclusion and exclusion criteria to use in clinical trials, and uncover unintended uses and indications for products. In terms of customer functionality, superior products can be provided at a faster pace as a foundation for helping patients live better and healthy lives.

Big pharma firms could try to develop BDA as a core competence themselves or collaborate with companies specializing in helping others do so. Currently, venture capitalists are funding an increasing number of entrepreneurial start-ups that specialize in the data analytics field. Regardless of the approach used, changes to an organization's culture often are required if the BDA process is to be appropriately supported. This is the case at Ford Motor Company where the firm is using BDA to establish the view that it is a mobility company rather than an automotive company. This perspective finds Ford using BDA and research on autonomous vehicles and mobile technologies to support its work on a number of functionalities for customers including, for example, being able to use their Ford product to "communicate with home thermostats so a person's heat might be automatically lowered as he or she drives away from the house."

As we discuss in this chapter, capabilities are the foundation for developing core competencies. There are several capabilities big pharma companies could form and emphasize in order for BDA to be a core competence. Supportive architecture, the proper mix of data scientists, and "technology that integrates and manages new types and sources of data flexibly and scalably while maintaining the highest standards of data governance, data quality, and data security" are examples of capabilities that big pharma firms may seek to possess if they wish to develop BDA as a core competence.

As with most companies, big pharma firms may encounter difficulty in the short run when seeking to develop BDA as a core competence. A recent survey suggests that insufficient skills by senior-level managers to permit a full operational understanding of the BDA process, the difficulty associated with determining the data that are the most strategically relevant, and an inability to consistently and quickly gain access to complete and fully accurate data are challenges requiring attention. Of course, not all big pharma firms will be successful in their efforts to develop the BDA process as a core competence.

Sources: Big data analytics: What it is & why it matters, 2015, SAS, www.sas.com, April 2; Big data for the pharmaceutical industry, *Informatica*, www.informatica.com, March 17; B. Atkins, 2015, Big data and the board, *Wall Street Journal Online*, www.wsj.com, April 16; D. Gage, 2015, Zetta Venture Partners closes $60M fund to back data-analytics startups, *Wall Street Journal Online*, www.wsj.com, February 11; R. King, 2015, Ford wants to sharpen big data skills at its Silicon Valley innovation center, *Wall Street Journal Online*, www.wsj.com, January 22; Are you prepared to make the decisions that matter most? *PcW's Global Data & Analytics Survey 2014*, www.pwc.com, November 12; S. F. DeAngelis, 2014, Pharmaceutical big data analytics promises a healthier future, *Enterrasolutions.com*, www.enterrasolutions.com, June 5; T. Wolfram, 2014, Data analytics has big pharma rethinking its core competencies, *Forbes Online*, www.forbes.com, December 22.

As discussed in the first two chapters, several factors in the global economy, including the rapid development of the Internet's capabilities and globalization in general, are making it difficult for firms to find ways to develop competitive advantages.[1] Increasingly, innovation appears to be a vital path to efforts to develop competitive advantages, particularly sustainable ones.[2] Fashion retailer Zara's ability to produce new clothing designs quickly is a core competence and also a competitive advantage for the firm. This ability is a product of innovations the firm established in terms of sophisticated information technologies that are used to track inventories and relying on groups of creative designers rather than individuals to quickly develop new fashions. The continual appearance of fresh designs the firm consistently produces through its innovations results in 17 visits per customer per year in its stores compared to the average of three visits per year in competitors stores.[3] You will learn more about Zara given that this firm is the subject of the Mini-Case appearing at the end of this chapter. Innovative actions will be required by big pharma companies seeking to develop capabilities that can be the foundation on which the process of big data analytics can become a core competence (see the Opening Case).

As is the case for Zara and big pharma companies, innovation is critical to firm success. This means that many firms seek to develop innovation as a core competence. We define and discuss core competencies in this chapter and explain how firms use their resources and capabilities to form them. As a core competence, innovation has long been critical to Boeing's success, too. Today however, the firm is focusing on incremental innovations as well as developing new technologies that are linked to major innovations and the projects they spawn, such as the 787 Dreamliner. The incremental innovations are ones Boeing believes enable the firm to more quickly deliver reliable products to customers at a lower cost.[4] Innovation is also becoming more vital to U.S. medical schools. Efforts are underway for the purpose of identifying methods to use to produce "young doctors who are better prepared to meet the demands of the nation's changing health-care system."[5] As we discuss in this chapter, firms and organizations such as those we mention here, achieve strategic competitiveness and earn above-average returns by acquiring, bundling, and leveraging their resources for the purpose of taking advantage of opportunities in the external environment in ways that create value for customers.[6]

Even if the firm develops and manages resources in ways that create core competencies and competitive advantages, competitors will eventually learn how to duplicate the benefits of any firm's value-creating strategy; thus, all competitive advantages have a limited life.[7] Because of this, the question of duplication of a competitive advantage is not if it will happen, but when. In general, a competitive advantage's sustainability is a function of three factors:

1. The rate of core competence obsolescence because of environmental changes.
2. The availability of substitutes for the core competence.
3. The imitability of the core competence.[8]

For all firms, the challenge is to effectively manage current core competencies while simultaneously developing new ones.[9] Only when firms are able to do this can they expect to achieve strategic competitiveness, earn above-average returns, and remain ahead of competitors in both the short and long term.

We studied the general, industry, and competitor environments in Chapter 2. Armed with knowledge about the realities and conditions of their external environment, firms have a better understanding of marketplace opportunities and the characteristics of the competitive environment in which those opportunities exist. In this chapter, we focus on the firm itself. By analyzing its internal organization, a firm determines what it can do. Matching what a firm *can do* (a function of its resources, capabilities, and core competencies in the internal organization) with what it *might do* (a function of opportunities and threats in the external environment) is a process that yields insights that the firm requires to select strategies from among those we discuss in Chapters 4 through 9.

We begin this chapter by briefly describing conditions associated with analyzing the firm's internal organization. We then discuss the roles of resources and capabilities in developing core competencies, which are the sources of the firm's competitive advantages. Included in this discussion are the techniques firms use to identify and evaluate resources and capabilities and the criteria for identifying core competencies from among them. Resources by themselves typically are not competitive advantages. In fact, resources create value when the firm uses them to form capabilities, some of which become core competencies, and hopefully competitive advantages. Because of the relationship among resources, capabilities, and core competencies, we also discuss the value chain and examine four criteria that firms use to determine if their capabilities are core competencies and, as such, sources of competitive advantage.[10] The chapter closes with comments about outsourcing as well as the need for firms to prevent their core competencies from becoming core rigidities. The existence of core rigidities indicates that the firm is too anchored to its past, a situation that prevents it from continuously developing new capabilities and core competencies.

3-1 Analyzing the Internal Organization

3-1a The Context of Internal Analysis

One of the conditions associated with analyzing a firm's internal organization is the reality that in today's global economy, some of the resources that were traditionally critical to firms' efforts to produce, sell, and distribute their goods or services, such as labor costs, access to financial resources and raw materials, and protected or regulated markets, although still important, are now less likely to be the source of competitive advantages.[11] An important reason for this is that an increasing number of firms are using their resources to form core competencies through which they successfully implement an international strategy (discussed in Chapter 8) as a means of overcoming the advantages created by these more traditional resources.

Upscale retailer Neiman Marcus Group, for example, is taking actions to enable it to cater to wealthy shoppers across the world. These actions demonstrate CEO Karen Katz's international ambitions for Neiman Marcus, a retailer that historically has operated store fronts in the United States only. To quickly gain access to international markets, one of the actions the firm is taking is to acquire e-commerce sites located outside the United States.

Munich-based Mytheresa.com is a recent and significant acquisition and provides Neiman Marcus with a strong foothold in Europe and a developing foothold in Asia. Establishing effective distribution channels is critical to Neiman Marcus' efforts to develop new competencies as a foundation for serving affluent customers throughout the world.[12]

Given the increasing importance of the global economy, those analyzing their firm's internal organization should use a global mind-set to do so. A **global mind-set** is the ability to analyze, understand, and manage an internal organization in ways that are not dependent on the assumptions of a single country, culture, or context.[13] Because they are able to span artificial boundaries, those with a global mind-set recognize that their firms must possess resources and capabilities that allow understanding of and appropriate responses to competitive situations that are influenced by country-specific factors and unique cultures. Using a global mind-set to analyze the internal organization has the potential to significantly help the firm in its efforts to outperform rivals.[14] A global mind-set is influencing Neiman Marcus' decisions to find ways to serve wealthy customers in countries throughout the world rather than in the United States only.

Finally, analyzing the firm's internal organization requires that evaluators examine the firm's entire portfolio of resources and capabilities. This perspective suggests that individual firms possess at least some resources and capabilities that other companies do not—at least not in the same combination. Resources are the source of capabilities, some of which lead to the development of core competencies; in turn, some core competencies may lead to a competitive advantage for the firm.[15] Understanding how to leverage the firm's unique bundle of resources and capabilities is a key outcome decision makers seek when analyzing the internal organization.[16] Figure 3.1 illustrates the relationships among resources, capabilities, core competencies, and competitive advantages and shows how their integrated use can lead to strategic competitiveness. As we discuss next, firms use the resources in their internal organization to create value for customers.

A **global mind-set** is the ability to analyze, understand, and manage an internal organization in ways that are not dependent on the assumptions of a single country, culture, or context.

Figure 3.1 Components of an Internal Analysis

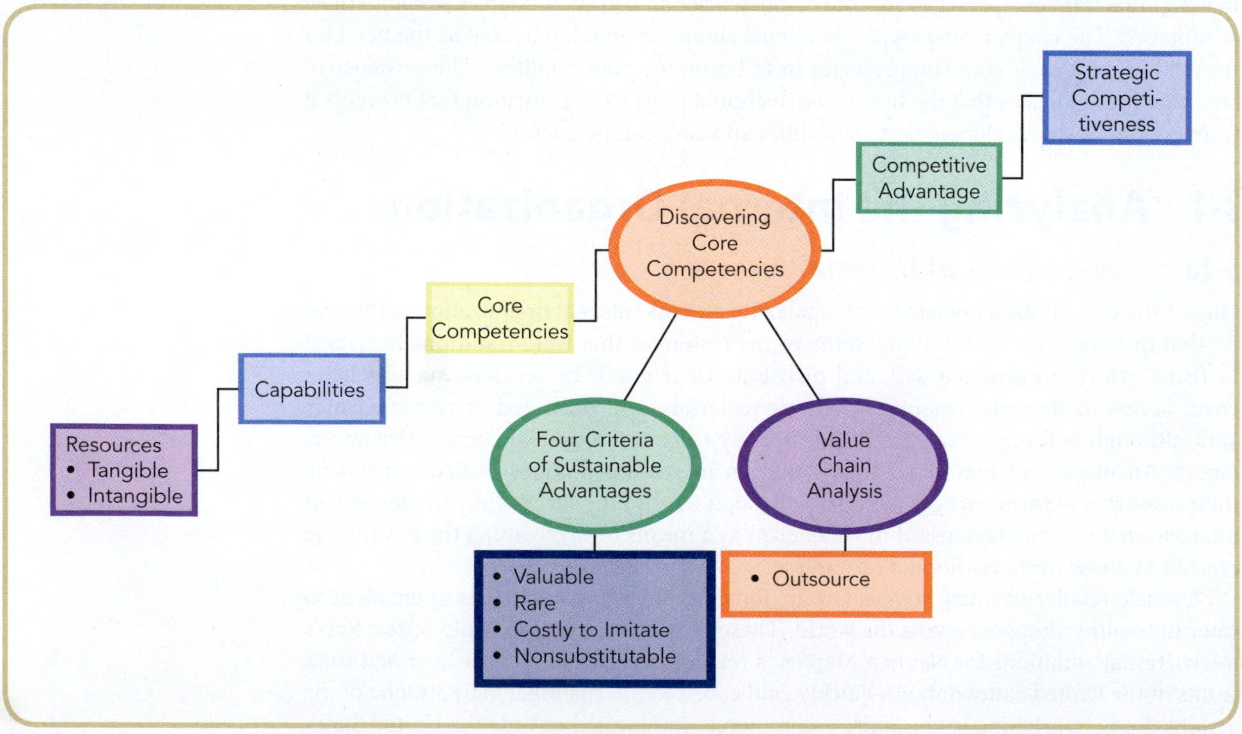

3-1b   Creating Value

Firms use their resources as the foundation for producing goods or services that will create value for customers.[17] **Value** is measured by a product's performance characteristics and by its attributes for which customers are willing to pay. Firms create value by innovatively bundling and leveraging their resources to form capabilities and core competencies.[18] Firms with a competitive advantage create more value for customers than do competitors.[19] Walmart uses its "every day low price" approach to doing business (an approach that is grounded in the firm's core competencies, such as information technology and distribution channels) to create value for those seeking to buy products at a low price compared to competitors' prices for those products. The stronger these firms' core competencies, the greater the amount of value they're able to create for their customers.[20]

Ultimately, creating value for customers is the source of above-average returns for a firm. What the firm intends regarding value creation affects its choice of business-level strategy (see Chapter 4) and its organizational structure (see Chapter 11).[21] In Chapter 4's discussion of business-level strategies, we note that value is created by a product's low cost, by its highly differentiated features, or by a combination of low cost and high differentiation compared to competitors' offerings. A business-level strategy is effective only when it is grounded in exploiting the firm's capabilities and core competencies. Thus, the successful firm continuously examines the effectiveness of current capabilities and core competencies while thinking about the capabilities and competencies it will require for future success.[22]

At one time, firms' efforts to create value were largely oriented toward understanding the characteristics of their industry in which they competed and, in light of those characteristics, determining how they should be positioned relative to competitors. This emphasis on industry characteristics and competitive strategy underestimated the role of the firm's resources and capabilities in developing core competencies as the source of competitive advantages. In fact, core competencies, in combination with product-market positions, are the firm's most important sources of competitive advantage.[23] A firm's core competencies, integrated with an understanding of the results of studying the conditions in the external environment, should drive the selection of strategies.[24] As Clayton Christensen noted, "successful strategists need to cultivate a deep understanding of the processes of competition and progress and of the factors that undergird each advantage. Only thus will they be able to see when old advantages are poised to disappear and how new advantages can be built in their stead."[25] By emphasizing core competencies when selecting and implementing strategies, companies learn to compete primarily on the basis of firm-specific differences. However, while doing so they must be simultaneously aware of changes in the firm's external environment.[26]

3-1c   The Challenge of Analyzing the Internal Organization

The strategic decisions managers make about the internal organization are nonroutine,[27] have ethical implications,[28] and significantly influence the firm's ability to earn above-average returns.[29] These decisions involve choices about the resources the firm needs to collect and how to best manage and leverage them.

Making decisions involving the firm's assets—identifying, developing, deploying, and protecting resources, capabilities, and core competencies—may appear to be relatively easy. However, this task is as challenging and difficult as any other with which managers are involved; moreover, the task is increasingly internationalized.[30] Some believe that the pressure on managers to pursue only decisions that help the firm meet anticipated quarterly earnings makes it difficult to accurately examine the firm's internal organization.[31]

Value is measured by a product's performance characteristics and by its attributes for which customers are willing to pay.

Gene Blevins/Polaris/Newscom

At one time, Polaroid's cameras created a significant amount of value for customers. Poor decisions may have contributed to the firm's subsequent inability to create value and its initial filing for bankruptcy in 2001.

The challenge and difficulty of making effective decisions are implied by preliminary evidence suggesting that one-half of organizational decisions fail.[32] Sometimes, mistakes are made as the firm analyzes conditions in its internal organization.[33] Managers might, for example, think a capability is a core competence when it is not. This may have been the case at Polaroid Corporation as decision makers continued to believe that the capabilities it used to build its instant film cameras were highly relevant at the time its competitors were developing and using the capabilities required to introduce digital cameras. In this instance, Polaroid's decision makers may have concluded that superior manufacturing was a core competence, as was the firm's ability to innovate in terms of creating value-adding features for its instant cameras. If a mistake is made when analyzing and managing a firm's resources, such as appears to have been the case some years ago at Polaroid, decision makers must have the confidence to admit it and take corrective actions.[34]

A firm can improve by studying its mistakes; in fact, the learning generated by making and correcting mistakes can be important to efforts to create new capabilities and core competencies.[35] One capability that can be learned from failure is when to quit. Polaroid should have obviously changed its strategy earlier than it did, and by doing so it may have been able to avoid more serious failure. Another potential example concerns News Corp.'s Amplify unit. As of mid-2015, the firm had invested over $1 billion in the unit that makes tablets, sells online curricula, and offers testing services. In 2014, Amplify generated a $193 million dollar loss as it seeks to change the way children are taught. Facing competition from well-established textbook publishers that are enhancing their ability to sell digital products such as those Amplify sells, News Corp. may want to carefully evaluate its previous decisions to see if mistakes were made and if so, how future decisions might be error free.[36]

As we discuss next, three conditions—uncertainty, complexity, and intraorganizational conflict—affect managers as they analyze the internal organization and make decisions about resources (see Figure 3.2).

Figure 3.2 Conditions Affecting Managerial Decisions about Resources, Capabilities, and Core Competencies

Conditions	**Uncertainty**	**Uncertainty exists about the characteristics of the firm's general and industry environments and customers' needs.**
	Complexity	**Complexity results from the interrelationships among conditions shaping a firm.**
	Intraorganizational Conflicts	**Intraorganizational conflicts may exist among managers making decisions as well as among those affected by the decisions.**

When studying the internal organization, managers face uncertainty because of a number of issues, including those of new proprietary technologies, rapidly changing economic and political trends, transformations in societal values, and shifts in customers' demands.[37] Environmental uncertainty increases the complexity and range of issues to examine when studying the internal environment.[38] Consider how uncertainty affects how to use resources at coal companies such as Peabody Energy Corp. and Murray Energy Corp.

Peabody is the world's largest private coal sector producer. The firm's coal products fuel approximately 10 percent of all U.S. electricity generation and 2 percent of worldwide electricity. But this firm and others competing in its industry face a great deal of uncertainty, particularly political uncertainty. As a result, there are questions about how Peabody and its competitors might best allocate their resources *today* to prepare for success *tomorrow*. Viewing coal as a "dirty fuel" and its production as environmental unfriendly, the U.S. Environmental Protection Agency (EPA) announced in 2014 and described in greater detail in 2015 new regulations. Focusing on carbon emissions, the EPA's carbon regulations "call for a 30 percent cut in power-plant carbon emissions by 2030 based on emissions levels in 2005." Coal producers such as Peabody, Arch Coal, and Murray Energy to name only a few, believe that the regulations are too strict and that moreover, the EPA misinterpreted the Clean Air Act when developing them. Time is required for the parties to sort through all of these issues, some of which will be decided by various courts given lawsuits filed by states (such as West Virginia) and firms (such as Murray Energy Corp.).[39] The issue though is that the decision makers in these energy firms face a great deal of uncertainty as they examine the resources, capabilities, and core competencies that form their firms' internal organization.[40]

Biases regarding how to cope with uncertainty affect decisions made about how to manage the firm's resources and capabilities to form core competencies.[41] Additionally, intraorganizational conflict may surface when decisions are made about the core competencies a firm should develop and nurture. Conflict might surface in the energy companies mentioned above about the degree to which resources and capabilities should be used to form new core competencies to support newer "clean technologies."

In making decisions affected by these three conditions, judgment is required. *Judgment* is the capability of making successful decisions when no obviously correct model or rule is available or when relevant data are unreliable or incomplete. In such situations, decision makers must be aware of possible cognitive biases, such as overconfidence. Individuals who are too confident in the decisions they make about how to use the firm's resources may fail to fully evaluate contingencies that could affect those decisions.[42]

When exercising judgment, decision makers often take intelligent risks. In the current competitive landscape, executive judgment can become a valuable capability. One reason is that, over time, effective judgment that decision makers demonstrate allows a firm to build a strong reputation and retain the loyalty of stakeholders whose support is linked to above-average returns.[43]

Finding individuals who can make the most successful decisions about using the organization's resources is challenging. Being able to do this is important because the quality of leaders' decisions regarding resources and their management affect a firm's ability to achieve strategic competitiveness. Individuals holding these key decision-making positions are called *strategic leaders*. Discussed fully in Chapter 12, for our purposes in this chapter we can think of strategic leaders as individuals with an ability to make effective decisions when examining the firm's resources, capabilities, and core competencies for the purpose of making choices about their use.

Next, we consider the relationships among a firm's resources, capabilities, and core competencies. While reading these sections, keep in mind that organizations have more resources than capabilities and more capabilities than core competencies.

3-2 Resources, Capabilities, and Core Competencies

Resources, capabilities, and core competencies are the foundation of competitive advantage. Resources are bundled to create organizational capabilities. In turn, capabilities are the source of a firm's core competencies, which are the basis of establishing competitive advantages.[44] We show these relationships in Figure 3.1 and discuss them next.

3-2a Resources

Broad in scope, resources cover a spectrum of individual, social, and organizational phenomena. By themselves, resources do not allow firms to create value for customers as the foundation for earning above-average returns. Indeed, resources are combined to form capabilities.[45] For example, Subway links its fresh ingredients with several other resources including the continuous training it provides to those running the firm's fast food restaurants as the foundation for customer service as a capability; customer service is also a core competence for Subway.

As its sole distribution channel, the Internet is a resource for Amazon.com. The firm uses the Internet to sell goods at prices that typically are lower than those offered by competitors selling the same goods through more costly brick-and-mortar storefronts. By combining other resources (such as access to a wide product inventory), Amazon has developed a reputation for excellent customer service. Amazon's capability in terms of customer service is a core competence as well in that the firm creates unique value for customers through the services it provides to them. Amazon also uses its technological core competence to offer AWS (Amazon Web Services), services through which businesses can rent computing power from Amazon at a cost of pennies per hour. Much smaller than AWS, Rackspace seeks to leverage its core competence of "economies of expertise" as it competes against its larger rival.[46]

Some of a firm's resources (defined in Chapter 1 as inputs to the firm's production process) are tangible while others are intangible. **Tangible resources** are assets that can be observed and quantified. Production equipment, manufacturing facilities, distribution centers, and formal reporting structures are examples of tangible resources. Its stock of oil and gas pipelines are a key tangible resource for energy giant Kinder Morgan. **Intangible resources** are assets that are rooted deeply in the firm's history, accumulate over time, and are relatively difficult for competitors to analyze and imitate. Because they are embedded in unique patterns of routines, intangible resources are difficult for competitors to analyze and imitate. Knowledge, trust between managers and employees, managerial capabilities, organizational routines (the unique ways people work together), scientific capabilities, the capacity for innovation, brand name, the firm's reputation for its goods or services and how it interacts with people (such as employees, customers, and suppliers), and organizational culture are intangible resources.[47]

Intangible resources require nurturing to maintain their ability to help firms engage in competitive battles. This is the case for brand as an intangible. Brand has long been a valuable intangible resource for Coca-Cola Company. The same is true for "logo-laden British brand Superdry." Recently though, SuperGroup PLC, the owner of Superdry, has encountered problems in efforts to maintain and hopefully enhance the value of the Superdry brand. We discuss these issues in the Strategic Focus.

Tangible resources are assets that can be observed and quantified.

Intangible resources are assets that are rooted deeply in the firm's history, accumulate over time, and are relatively difficult for competitors to analyze and imitate.

Strategic **Focus**

Strengthening the Superdry Brand as a Foundation to Strategic Success

British-based SuperGroup, owner of Superdry and its carefully banded product lines, is taking actions to deal with recent performance problems. These problems manifested themselves in various ways, including the need for the firm to issue three profit warnings in one six-month period and a 34 percent decline in the price of its stock in 2014 compared to 2013.

Founded in 1985, the firm is recognized as a distinctive, branded fashion retailer selling quality clothing and accessories. In fact, the firm says that "the Superdry brand is at the heart of the business." The brand is targeted to discerning customers who seek to purchase "stylish clothing that is uniquely designed and well made." In this sense, the company believes that its men's and women's products have "wide appeal, capturing elements of 'urban' and 'streetwear' designs with subtle combinations of vintage Americana, Japanese imagery, and British tailoring, all with strong attention to detail." Thus, the firm's brand is critical to the image it conveys with its historical target customer—teens and those in their early twenties. Those leading SuperGroup believe that customers love the Superdry products as well as the "theatre and personality" of the stores in which they are sold. These outcomes are important given the company's intention of providing customers with "personalized shopping experiences that enhance the brand rather than just selling clothes."

As noted above, problems have affected the firm's performance. What the firm wants to do, of course, is correct the problems before the Superdry brand is damaged. Management turmoil is one of the firm's problems. In January of 2015, the CEO abruptly left. Almost simultaneously, the CFO was suspended for filing for personal bankruptcy, and the Chief Operating Officer left to explore other options. Some analysts believe that the firm's growth had been ill-conceived, signaling the possibility of ineffective strategic decisions on the part of the firm's upper-level leaders. As one analyst said: "The issue with SuperGroup is that they've expanded too quickly, without the supporting infrastructure."

Efforts are now underway to address these problems. In particular, those now leading SuperGroup intend to better control the firm as a means of protecting the value of its brand. A new CEO has been appointed who believes that "the business is very much more in control" today than has been the case recently. A well-regarded interim CFO has been appointed, and the firm's board has been strengthened by added experienced individuals. Commenting about these changes, an observer

Bloomberg/Getty Images

Products are displayed in this Superdry store in ways that will personalize customers' shopping experiences.

said that SuperGroup has "moved from an owner-entrepreneurial style of management to a more professional and experienced type of management. The key thing is, it is much better now than it was."

Direct actions are also being taken to enhance the Superdry brand. The appointment of Idris Elba, *The Wire* actor, is seen as a major attempt to reignite the brand's image. In fact, SuperGroup says that Elba epitomizes what the Superdry brand is—British, grounded, and cool. The thinking here, too, is that Elba, who at the time of his selection was 42, would appeal to the customer who was "growing up" with the Superdry brand. For these customers, who are 25 and older, SuperGroup is developing Superdry products with less dramatic presentations of the brand's well-known large logos. Additional lines of clothing, for skiing and rugby for example, are being developed for the more mature Superdry customer. After correcting the recently encountered problems, SuperGroup intends to expand into additional markets, including China. In every instance though, the firm will protect the brand when entering new competitive arenas and will rely on it as the foundation for intended success.

Sources: About SuperGroup, 2015, SuperGroupPLC.com, www.supergroup.co.uk, April 5; S. Chaudhuri, 2015, Superdry brand works to iron out problems, *Wall Street Journal Online*, www.wsj.com, April 15; S. Chaudhuri, 2015, Superdry looks to U.S. to drive growth, *Wall Street Journal Online*, www.wsj.com, March 26; H. Mann, 2015, SuperGroup strategy oozes Hollywood glamour, *Interactive Investor*, www.iii.co.uk, March 26; A. Monaghan & S. Butler, 2015, Superdry signs up Idris Elba, *The Guardian Online*, www.theguardian.com, March 26; A. Petroff, 2015, Is this the worst CFO ever? *CNNMoney*, www.money.cnn.com, February 25.

For each analysis, tangible and intangible are grouped into categories. The four primary categories of tangible resources are financial, organizational, physical, and technological (see Table 3.1). The three primary categories of intangible resources are human, innovation, and reputational (see Table 3.2).

Table 3.1 Tangible Resources

Financial Resources	• The firm's capacity to borrow • The firm's ability to generate funds through internal operations
Organizational Resources	• Formal reporting structures
Physical Resources	• The sophistication of a firm's plant and equipment and the attractiveness of its location • Distribution facilities • Product inventory
Technological Resources	• Availability of technology-related resources such as copyrights, patents, trademarks, and trade secrets

Sources: Adapted from J. B. Barney, 1991, Firm resources and sustained competitive advantage, *Journal of Management*, 17: 101; R. M. Grant, 1991, *Contemporary Strategy Analysis*, Cambridge: U.K.: Blackwell Business, 100–102.

Table 3.2 Intangible Resources

Human Resources	• Knowledge • Trust • Skills • Abilities to collaborate with others
Innovation Resources	• Ideas • Scientific capabilities • Capacity to innovate
Reputational Resources	• Brand name • Perceptions of product quality, durability, and reliability • Positive reputation with stakeholders such as suppliers and customers

Sources: Adapted from R. Hall, 1992, The strategic analysis of intangible resources, *Strategic Management Journal*, 13: 136–139: R. M. Grant, 1991, *Contemporary Strategy Analysis*, Cambridge: U.K.: Blackwell Business, 101–104.

Tangible Resources

As tangible resources, a firm's borrowing capacity and the status of its physical facilities are visible. The value of many tangible resources can be established through financial statements, but these statements do not account for the value of all of the firm's assets because they disregard some intangible resources.[48] The value of tangible resources is also constrained because they are hard to leverage—it is difficult to derive additional business or value from a tangible resource. For example, an airplane is a tangible resource, but "you can't use the same airplane on five different routes at the same time. You can't put the same crew on five different routes at the same time. And the same goes for the financial investment you've made in the airplane."[49]

Although production assets are tangible, many of the processes necessary to use them are intangible. Thus, the learning and potential proprietary processes associated with a tangible resource, such as manufacturing facilities, can have unique intangible attributes, such as quality control processes, unique manufacturing processes, and technologies that develop over time.[50]

Intangible Resources

Compared to tangible resources, intangible resources are a superior source of capabilities and subsequently, core competencies.[51] In fact, in the global economy, a firm's intellectual capital often plays a more critical role in corporate success than do physical assets.[52] Because of this, being able to effectively manage intellectual capital is an increasingly important skill for today's leaders to develop.[53]

Because intangible resources are less visible and more difficult for competitors to understand, purchase, imitate, or substitute for, firms prefer to rely on them rather than on tangible resources as the foundation for their capabilities. In fact, the more unobservable (i.e., intangible) a resource is, the more valuable that resource is to create capabilities.[54] Another benefit of intangible resources is that, unlike most tangible resources, their use can be leveraged. For instance, sharing knowledge among employees does not diminish its value for any one person. To the contrary, two people sharing their individualized knowledge sets often can be leveraged to create additional knowledge that, although new to each individual, contributes potentially to performance improvements for the firm.

Reputational resources (see Table 3.2) are important sources of a firm's capabilities and core competencies. Indeed, some argue that a positive reputation can even be a source of competitive advantage.[55] Earned through the firm's actions as well as its words, a value-creating reputation is a product of years of superior marketplace competence as perceived by stakeholders.[56] A reputation indicates the level of awareness a firm has been able to develop among stakeholders and the degree to which they hold the firm in high esteem.[57]

A well-known and highly valued brand name is a specific reputational resource.[58] A continuing commitment to innovation and aggressive advertising facilitates firms' efforts to take advantage of the reputation associated with their brands.[59] Harley-Davidson has a reputation for producing and servicing high-quality motorcycles with unique designs. Because of the desirability of its reputation, the company also produces a wide range of accessory items that it sells on the basis of its reputation for offering unique products with high quality. Sunglasses, jewelry, belts, wallets, shirts, slacks, belts, and hats are just a few of the large variety of accessories customers can purchase from a Harley-Davidson dealer or from its online store.[60]

Taking advantage of today's technologies, some firms are using social media as a means of influencing their reputation. Comcast for example is "adding more social media representatives as it tries to work on its reputation for inefficient, unresponsive or just plain rude customer service."[61] Similarly, General Motors is using social media to respond to customer concerns about product recalls the firm has experienced over the past few years. A key purpose of GM's efforts with its social media campaign is to "fundamentally redefine (itself) as an open, transparent, listening organization."[62] Recognizing that thousands of conversations occur daily throughout the world and that what is being said can affect its reputation,

© StockPhoto.com/Courtney Keating

Developing capabilities in specific functional areas can give companies a competitive edge. The effective use of social media to direct advertising to specific market segments has given some firms an advantage over their rivals.

Coca-Cola company encourages its employees to be a part of these social-media based discussion as a means of positively influencing the company's reputation. Driving the nature of these conversations is a set of social media "commitments" that Coca-Cola employees use as a foundation for how they will engage with various social media. Being transparent and protecting consumers' privacy are examples of the commitments the firm established.[63]

3-2b Capabilities

The firm combines individual tangible and intangible resources to create capabilities. In turn, capabilities are used to complete the organizational tasks required to produce, distribute, and service the goods or services the firm provides to customers for the purpose of creating value for them. As a foundation for building core competencies and hopefully competitive advantages, capabilities are often based on developing, carrying, and exchanging information and knowledge through the firm's human capital.[64] Hence, the value of human capital in developing and using capabilities and, ultimately, core competencies cannot be overstated.[65] In fact, it seems to be "well known that human capital makes or breaks companies."[66] At pizza-maker Domino's, human capital is critical to the firm's efforts to change how it competes. Describing this, CEO Patrick Doyle says that, in many ways, Domino's is becoming "a technology company … that has adapted the art of pizza-making to the digital age."[67]

As illustrated in Table 3.3, capabilities are often developed in specific functional areas (such as manufacturing, R&D, and marketing) or in a part of a functional area (e.g., advertising). Table 3.3 shows a grouping of organizational functions and the capabilities that some companies are thought to possess in terms of all or parts of those functions.

Table 3.3 Example of Firms' Capabilities

Functional Areas	Capabilities	Examples of Firms
Distribution	• Effective use of logistics management techniques	• Walmart
Human Resources	• Motivating, empowering, and retaining employees	• Microsoft
Management Information Systems	• Effective and efficient control of inventories through point-of-purchase data collection methods	• Walmart
Marketing	• Effective promotion of brand-name products • Effective customer service • Innovative merchandising	• Procter & Gamble • Ralph Lauren Corp. • McKinsey & Co. • Nordstrom Inc. • Crate & Barrel
Management	• Ability to envision the future of clothing	• Hugo Boss • Zara
Manufacturing	• Design and production skills yielding reliable products • Product and design quality • Miniaturization of components and products	• Komatsu • Witt Gas Technology • Sony
Research & Development	• Innovative technology • Development of sophisticated elevator control solutions • Rapid transformation of technology into new products and processes • Digital technology	• Caterpillar • Otis Elevator Co. • Chaparral Steel • Thomson Consumer Electronics

3-2c   Core Competencies

Defined in Chapter 1, core competencies are capabilities that serve as a source of competitive advantage for a firm over its rivals. Core competencies distinguish a company competitively and reflect its personality. Core competencies emerge over time through an organizational process of accumulating and learning how to deploy different resources and capabilities.[68] As the capacity to take action, core competencies are the "crown jewels of a company," the activities the company performs especially well compared to competitors and through which the firm adds unique value to the goods or services it sells to customers.[69] Thus, if a big pharma company (such as Pfizer) developed big data analytics as a core competence, one could conclude that the firm had formed capabilities through which it was able to analyze and effectively use huge amounts of data in a competitively-superior manner.

Innovation is thought to be a core competence at Apple. As a capability, R&D activities are the source of this core competence. More specifically, the way Apple has combined some of its tangible (e.g., financial resources and research laboratories) and intangible (e.g., scientists and engineers and organizational routines) resources to complete research and development tasks creates a capability in R&D. By emphasizing its R&D capability, Apple is able to innovate in ways that create unique value for customers in the form of the products it sells, such as the iWatch, suggesting that innovation is a core competence for Apple.

Excellent customer service in its retail stores is another of Apple's core competencies. In this instance, unique and contemporary store designs (a tangible resource) are combined with knowledgeable and skilled employees (an intangible resource) to provide superior service to customers. A number of carefully developed training and development procedures are capabilities on which Apple's core competence of excellent customer service is based. The procedures that are capabilities include specification of how employees are to interact with customers, carefully written training manuals to describe on-site tech support that is to be provided to customers, and deep thinking about every aspect of the store's design including music that is played.[70]

3-3   Building Core Competencies

Two tools help firms identify their core competencies. The first consists of four specific criteria of sustainable competitive advantage that can be used to determine which capabilities are core competencies. Because the capabilities shown in Table 3.3 have satisfied these four criteria, they are core competencies. The second tool is the value chain analysis. Firms use this tool to select the value-creating competencies that should be maintained, upgraded, or developed and those that should be outsourced.

3-3a   The Four Criteria of Sustainable Competitive Advantage

Capabilities that are valuable, rare, costly to imitate, and nonsubstitutable are core competencies (see Table 3.4). In turn, core competencies can lead to competitive advantages for the firm over its rivals. Capabilities failing to satisfy the four criteria are not core competencies, meaning that although every core competence is a capability, not every capability is a core competence. In slightly different words, for a capability to be a core competence, it must be valuable and unique from a customer's point of view. For a core competence to be a potential source of competitive advantage, it must be inimitable and nonsubstitutable by competitors.[71]

Table 3.4 The Four Criteria of Sustainable Competitive Advantage

Valuable Capabilities	• Help a firm neutralize threats or exploit opportunities
Rare Capabilities	• Are not possessed by many others
Costly-to-Imitate Capabilities	• Historical: A unique and a valuable organizational culture or brand name • Ambiguous cause: The causes and uses of a competence are unclear • Social complexity: Interpersonal relationships, trust, and friendship among managers, suppliers, and customers
Nonsubstitutable Capabilities	• No strategic equivalent

A sustainable competitive advantage exists only when competitors are unable to duplicate the benefits of a firm's strategy or when they lack the resources to attempt imitation. For some period of time, the firm may have a core competence by using capabilities that are valuable and rare, but imitable. For example, some firms are trying to develop a core competence and potentially a competitive advantage by out-greening their competitors.[72] (Interestingly, developing a "green" core competence can contribute to the firm's efforts to earn above-average returns while benefitting the broader society.) For many years, Walmart has been committed to using its resources in ways that support environmental sustainability while pursuing a competitive advantage in the process. To facilitate these efforts, Walmart recently labeled over 10,000 products on its e-commerce site as products that are "Made by a Sustainability Leader." Initially, these items were batched into roughly 80 product categories. In addition to seeking a competitive advantage through these actions, Walmart hoped to make it easier for customers to make "sustainable choices" when purchasing products. Walmart is also working to supply 100 percent of its needs from renewable energy sources, to create zero waste from its operations, and to lead the industry in deploying clean technologies as a means of reducing fuel consumption and air pollution.[73] Of course, Walmart competitors such as Target are engaging in similar actions. Time will reveal the degree to which Walmart's green practices can be imitated.

The length of time a firm can expect to create value by using its core competencies is a function of how quickly competitors can successfully imitate a good, service, or process. Value-creating core competencies may last for a relatively long period of time only when all four of the criteria we discuss next are satisfied. Thus, Walmart would know that it has a core competence and possibly a competitive advantage in terms of green practices if the ways the firm uses its resources to complete these practices satisfy the four criteria.

Valuable

Valuable capabilities allow the firm to exploit opportunities or neutralize threats in its external environment. By effectively using capabilities to exploit opportunities or neutralize threats, a firm creates value for customers.[74] For example, Groupon created the "daily deal" marketing space; the firm reached $1 billion in revenue faster than any other company in history. In essence, the opportunity Groupon's founders pursued when launching the firm in 2008 was to create a marketplace through which businesses could introduce their goods or services to customers who would be able to experience them at a discounted price. Restaurants, hair and nail salons, and hotels are examples of the types of companies making frequent use of Groupon's services.

Valuable capabilities allow the firm to exploit opportunities or neutralize threats in its external environment.

Young, urban professionals desiring to affordably experience the cities in which they live are the firm's target customers.[75] However, competing daily-deal websites such as LivingSocial and Blackboard Eats quickly surfaced and are offering similar and often less expensive deals. Groupon may succeed but shorter development cycles, especially for such online firms, makes it harder for successful startups to create enduring competitive advantage. "In other words, they are increasingly vulnerable to the same capital-market pressures that plague big companies—but before they've developed lasting corporate assets."[76]

Rare

Rare capabilities are capabilities that few, if any, competitors possess. A key question to be answered when evaluating this criterion is "how many rival firms possess these valuable capabilities?" Capabilities possessed by many rivals are unlikely to become core competencies for any of the involved firms. Instead, valuable but common (i.e., not rare) capabilities are sources of competitive parity.[77] Competitive advantage results only when firms develop and exploit valuable capabilities that become core competencies and that differ from those shared with competitors. The central problem for Groupon is that its capabilities to produce the "daily deal" reached competitive parity quickly. Similarly, Walmart has developed valuable capabilities that it uses to engage in green practices; but, as mentioned previously, Target seeks to develop sustainability capabilities[78] through which it can duplicate Walmart's green practices. Target's success in doing so, if this happens, would suggest that Walmart's green practices are valuable but not rare.

Costly to Imitate

Costly-to-imitate capabilities are capabilities that other firms cannot easily develop. Capabilities that are costly to imitate are created because of one reason or a combination of three reasons (see Table 3.4). First, a firm sometimes is able to develop capabilities because of *unique historical conditions*. As firms evolve, they often acquire or develop capabilities that are unique to them.[79]

A firm with a unique and valuable *organizational culture* that emerged in the early stages of the company's history "may have an imperfectly imitable advantage over firms founded in another historical period;"[80] one in which less valuable or less competitively useful values and beliefs strongly influenced the development of the firm's culture. Briefly discussed in Chapter 1, organizational culture is a set of values that are shared by members in the organization. An organizational culture is a source of advantage when employees are held together tightly by their belief in it and the leaders who helped to create it.[81] Historically, emphasizing cleanliness, consistency, and service and the training that reinforces the value of these characteristics created a culture at McDonald's that some thought was a core competence and a competitive advantage for the firm. However, as explained in Chapter 2's Opening Case, McDonald's recent performance is worrying investors. One of the actions the firm is taking to address this matter is to change its organizational structure in its U.S. operations, largely for the purpose of giving "leaders in its 22 U.S. regions more autonomy in making local menu and marketing decisions."[82] Hopefully, a different organizational structure will facilitate McDonald's efforts to reinvigorate its historically unique culture as a core competence.

A second condition of being costly to imitate occurs when the link between the firm's core competencies and its competitive advantage is *causally ambiguous*.[83] In these instances, competitors aren't able to clearly understand how a firm uses its capabilities that are core competencies as the foundation for competitive advantage. As a result, firms are uncertain about the capabilities they should develop to duplicate the benefits of a

Rare capabilities are capabilities that few, if any, competitors possess.

Costly-to-imitate capabilities are capabilities that other firms cannot easily develop.

Although it has close to 150 stores and over 22,000 employees, CarMax has developed a small-company culture that is difficult for competitors to imitate.

Augusta Chronicle/ZUMA Press, Inc./Alamy

competitor's value-creating strategy. For years, firms tried to imitate Southwest Airlines' low-cost strategy, but most have been unable to do so, primarily because they can't duplicate this firm's unique culture.

Social complexity is the third reason that capabilities can be costly to imitate. Social complexity means that at least some, and frequently many, of the firm's capabilities are the product of complex social phenomena. Interpersonal relationships, trust, friendships among managers and between managers and employees, and a firm's reputation with suppliers and customers are examples of socially complex capabilities. Southwest Airlines is careful to hire people who fit with its culture. This complex interrelationship between the culture and human capital adds value in ways that other airlines cannot, such as jokes on flights by the flight attendants or the cooperation between gate personnel and pilots.

Nonsubstitutable

Nonsubstitutable capabilities are capabilities that do not have strategic equivalents. This final criterion "is that there must be no strategically equivalent valuable resources that are themselves either not rare or imitable. Two valuable firm resources (or two bundles of firm resources) are strategically equivalent when they each can be separately exploited to implement the same strategies."[84] In general, the strategic value of capabilities increases as they become more difficult to substitute. The more intangible, and hence invisible, capabilities are, the more difficult it is for firms to find substitutes and the greater the challenge is to competitors trying to imitate a firm's value-creating strategy. Firm-specific knowledge and trust-based working relationships between managers and nonmanagerial personnel, such as has existed for years at Southwest Airlines, are examples of capabilities that are difficult to identify and for which finding a substitute is challenging. However, causal ambiguity may make it difficult for the firm to learn and may stifle progress because the firm may not know how to improve processes that are not easily codified and thus are ambiguous.[85]

In summary, only using valuable, rare, costly-to-imitate, and nonsubstitutable capabilities has the potential for the firm to create sustainable competitive advantages. Table 3.5 shows the competitive consequences and performance implications resulting from combinations of the four criteria of sustainability. The analysis suggested by the table helps managers determine the strategic value of a firm's capabilities. The firm should not emphasize capabilities that fit the criteria described in the first row in the table (i.e., resources and capabilities that are neither valuable nor rare and that are imitable and for which strategic substitutes exist). Capabilities yielding competitive parity and either temporary or sustainable competitive advantage, however, should be supported. Some competitors such as Coca-Cola and PepsiCo and Boeing and Airbus may have capabilities that result in competitive parity. In such cases, the firms will nurture these capabilities while simultaneously trying to develop capabilities that can yield either a temporary or sustainable competitive advantage.

Nonsubstitutable capabilities are capabilities that do not have strategic equivalents.

Table 3.5 Outcomes from Combinations of the Criteria for Sustainable Competitive Advantage

Is the Capability Valuable?	Is the Capability Rare?	Is the Capability Costly to Imitate?	Is the Capability Nonsubstitutable?	Competitive Consequences	Performance Implications
No	No	No	No	• Competitive disadvantage	• Below-average returns
Yes	No	No	Yes/no	• Competitive parity	• Average returns
Yes	Yes	No	Yes/no	• Temporary competitive advantage	• Average returns to above-average returns
Yes	Yes	Yes	Yes/no	• Sustainable competitive advantage	• Above-average returns

3-3b   Value Chain Analysis

Value chain analysis allows the firm to understand the parts of its operations that create value and those that do not.[86] Understanding these issues is important because the firm earns above-average returns only when the value it creates is greater than the costs incurred to create that value.[87]

The value chain is a template that firms use to analyze their cost position and to identify the multiple means that can be used to facilitate implementation of a chosen strategy.[88] Today's competitive landscape demands that firms examine their value chains in a global rather than a domestic-only context.[89] In particular, activities associated with supply chains should be studied within a global context.[90]

We show a model of the value chain in Figure 3.3. As depicted in the model, a firm's value chain is segmented into value chain activities and support functions. **Value chain activities** are activities or tasks the firm completes in order to produce products and

Value chain activities are activities or tasks the firm completes in order to produce products and then sell, distribute, and service those products in ways that create value for customers.

Figure 3.3 A Model of the Value Chain

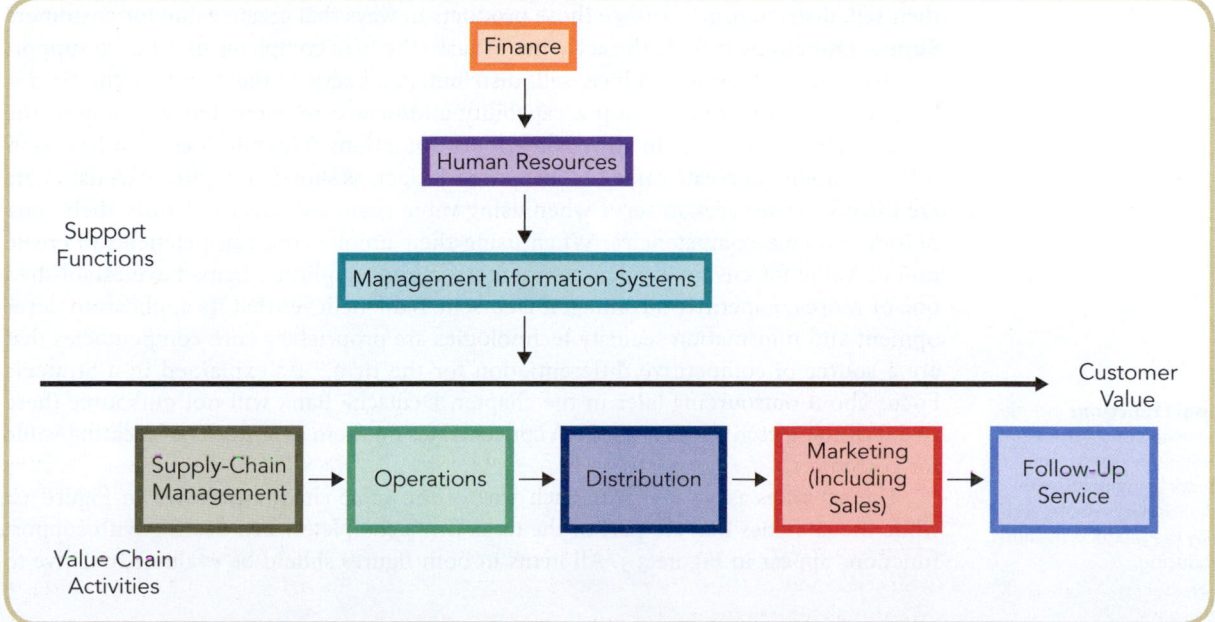

Figure 3.4 Creating Value through Value Chain Activities

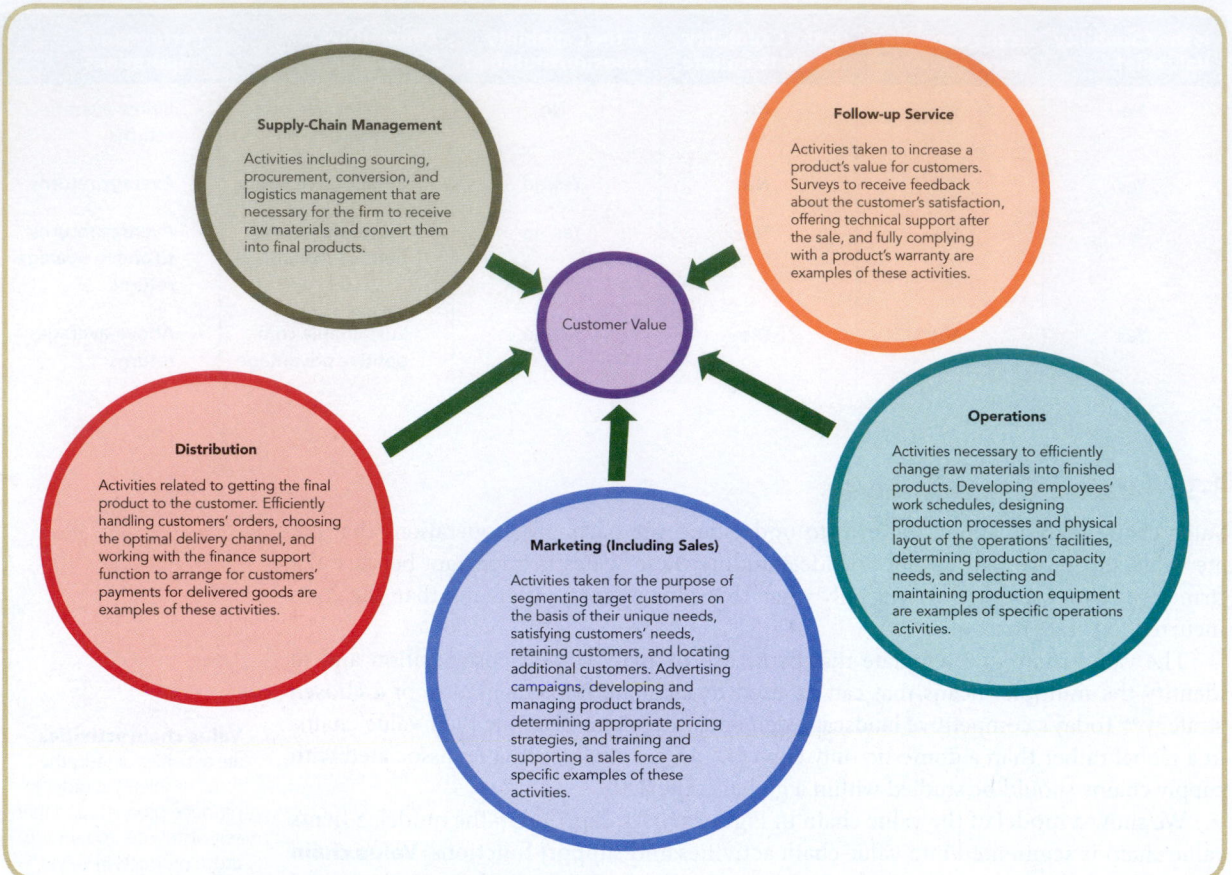

then sell, distribute, and service those products in ways that create value for customers. **Support functions** include the activities or tasks the firm completes in order to support the work being done to produce, sell, distribute, and service the products the firm is producing. A firm can develop a capability and/or a core competence in any of the value chain activities and in any of the support functions. When it does so, it has established an ability to create value for customers. In fact, as shown in Figure 3.3, customers are the ones firms seek to serve when using value chain analysis to identify their capabilities and core competencies. When using their unique core competencies to create unique value for customers that competitors cannot duplicate, firms have established one or more competitive advantages. Deutsche Bank believes that its application development and information security technologies are proprietary core competencies that are a source of competitive differentiation for the firm.[91] As explained in a Strategic Focus about outsourcing later in the chapter, Deutsche Bank will not outsource these two technologies given that the firm concentrates on them as a means of creating value for customers.

The activities associated with each part of the value chain are shown in Figure 3.4, while the activities that are part of the tasks firms complete when dealing with support functions appear in Figure 3.5. All items in both figures should be evaluated relative to

Support functions include the activities or tasks the firm completes in order to support the work being done to produce, sell, distribute, and service the products the firm is producing.

Figure 3.5 Creating Value through Support Functions

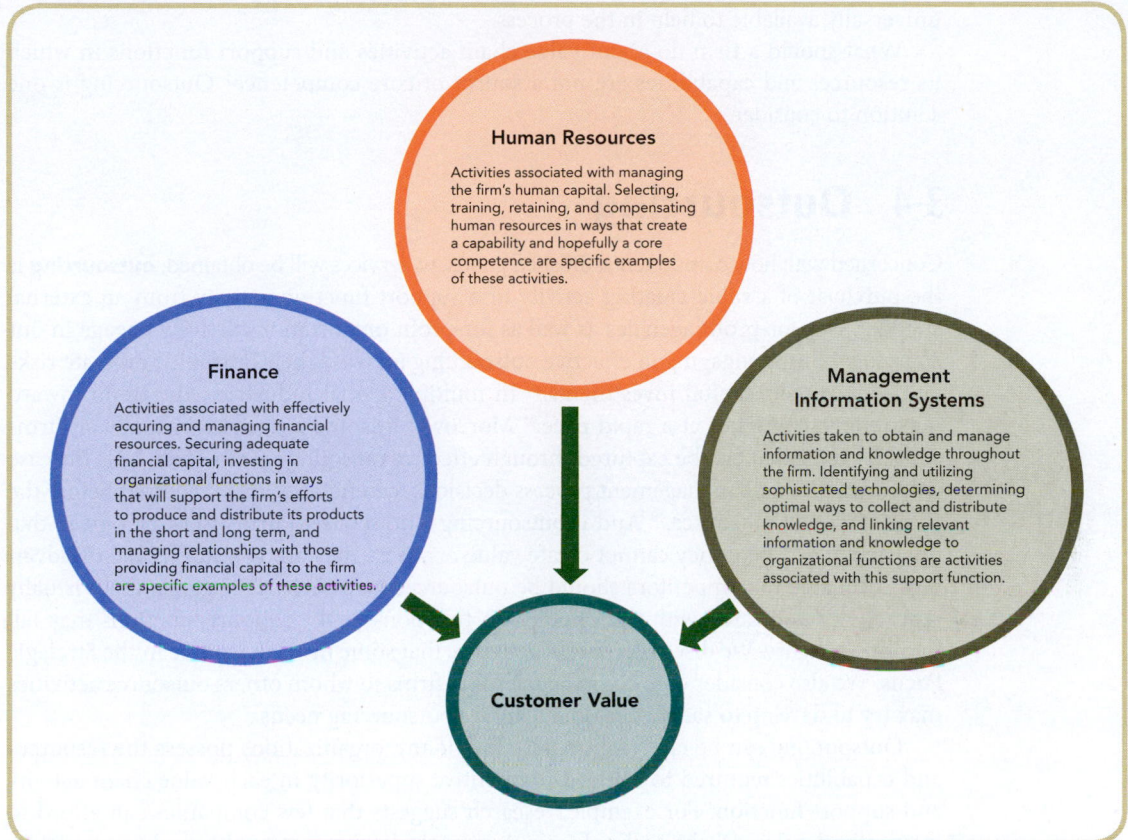

competitors' capabilities and core competencies. To become a core competence and a source of competitive advantage, a capability must allow the firm to either

1. Perform an activity in a manner that provides value superior to that provided by competitors.
2. Perform a value-creating activity that competitors cannot perform.

Only under these conditions does a firm create value for customers and have opportunities to capture that value.

Creating value for customers by completing activities that are part of the value chain often requires building effective alliances with suppliers (and sometimes others to which the firm outsources activities, as discussed in the next section) and developing strong positive relationships with customers. When firms have strong positive relationships with suppliers and customers, they are said to have social capital.[92] The relationships themselves have value because they lead to transfers of knowledge as well as to access to resources that a firm many not hold internally.[93] To build social capital whereby resources such as knowledge are transferred across organizations requires trust between partners. Indeed, partners must trust each other in order to allow their resources to be used in such a way that both parties will benefit over time while neither party will take advantage of the other.[94]

Evaluating a firm's capability to execute its value chain activities and support functions is challenging. Earlier in the chapter, we noted that identifying and assessing the value of a firm's resources and capabilities requires judgment. Judgment is equally necessary when using value chain analysis because no obviously correct model or rule is universally available to help in the process.

What should a firm do about value chain activities and support functions in which its resources and capabilities are not a source of core competence? Outsourcing is one solution to consider.

3-4 Outsourcing

Concerned with how components, finished goods, or services will be obtained, **outsourcing** is the purchase of a value-creating activity or a support function activity from an external supplier. Not-for-profit agencies as well as for-profit organizations actively engage in outsourcing.[95] Firms engaging in effective outsourcing increase their flexibility, mitigate risks, and reduce their capital investments.[96] In multiple global industries, the trend toward outsourcing continues at a rapid pace.[97] Moreover, in some industries virtually all firms seek the value that can be captured through effective outsourcing. However, as is the case with other strategic management process decisions, careful analysis is required before the firm decides to outsource.[98] And if outsourcing is to be used, firms must recognize that only activities where they cannot create value or where they are at a substantial disadvantage compared to competitors should be outsourced.[99] Experience suggests that virtually any activity associated with the value chain functions or the support functions may fall into this category. We discuss different activities that some firms outsource in the Strategic Focus. We also consider core competencies that firms to whom others outsource activities may try to develop to satisfy customers' future outsourcing needs.

Outsourcing can be effective because few, if any, organizations possess the resources and capabilities required to achieve competitive superiority in each value chain activity and support function. For example, research suggests that few companies can afford to internally develop all the technologies that might lead to competitive advantage.[100] By nurturing a smaller number of capabilities, a firm increases the probability of developing core competencies and achieving a competitive advantage because it does not become overextended. In addition, by outsourcing activities in which it lacks competence, the firm can fully concentrate on those areas in which it has the potential to create value.

There are concerns associated with outsourcing.[101] Two significant ones are the potential loss in a firm's ability to innovate and the loss of jobs within the focal firm. When evaluating the possibility of outsourcing, firms should anticipate possible effects on their ability to innovate in the future as well as the impact of losing some of their human capital. On the other hand, firms are sometimes able to enhance their own innovation capabilities by studying how the companies to which they've outsourced complete those activities.[102] Because a focal firm likely knows less about a foreign company to which it chooses to outsource, concerns about potential negative outsourcing effects in these cases may be particularly acute, requiring careful study and analysis as a result.[103] Deciding to outsource to a foreign supplier is commonly called *offshoring*.

3-5 Competencies, Strengths, Weaknesses, and Strategic Decisions

By analyzing the internal organization, firms identify their strengths and weaknesses as reflected by their resources, capabilities, and core competencies. If a firm has weak capabilities or does not have core competencies in areas required to achieve a competitive advantage, it must acquire those resources and build the needed capabilities and competencies.

Outsourcing is the purchase of a value-creating activity or a support function activity from an external supplier.

Strategic **Focus**

"We're Outsourcing that Activity but Not That One? I'm Surprised!"

Clearly, firms do not want to outsource activities through which they are able to create value. Moreover, they want to concentrate on those activities in the value chain functions and the support functions where they are able to create the greatest amount of value. Recognizing the activities in these two categories is a critical responsibility of those studying a firm's internal organization.

As we discussed in the Opening Case, big pharma companies are considering the possibility that they may use some of their resources and capabilities to try to develop "big data analytics" as a core competence given the increasing value that is thought to accrue to companies in this industry that are able to do so. In contrast, these same firms are outsourcing drug safety processes and procedures to firms, many of which are located in India or have offices located there. In fact, monitoring drug safety is "one of outsourcing's newest frontiers and the now $2 billion business is booming as regulators require closer tracking of rare side effects and interactions between medicines." Accenture, Cognizant, and Tata Consultancy Services Ltd. are some of the firms to which big pharma companies AstraZeneca PLC, Novartis AG, and Bristol-Myers Squibb Co. are outsourcing the monitoring of drug safety. Thus, the big pharma firms have decided that data analytics processes are an activity in which they can capture value while monitoring drug safety is not.

Similar examples exist within firms competing in other industries. As mentioned above, Deutsche Bank has outsourced some data center services to Hewlett-Packard; however, it is retaining control over certain technology application areas it believes are proprietary and, as such, are core competencies through which the firm creates value. United Airlines is outsourcing U.S. airport jobs that employ "workers in areas including check-in, baggage-handling, and customer service." This outsourcing decision suggests that United believes that it cannot create value by completing these tasks in house or that it is too expensive to attempt to do so.

Based in India, Wipro and Infosys are two companies that have historically been successful as firms to whom others outsource activities. However, this success has been largely a product of being able to employ relatively inexpensive programmers to complete tasks lacking significant amounts of complexity. This is no longer the case today as customers are asking outsourcing firms to help them analyze large amounts of data and engage the cloud for computing purposes. Stated

more directly, some believe that "Bangalore's outsourcing industry—which grew at breakneck speeds for years and changed the way the world of IT works—has matured. While it will continue to find ways to peddle the talents of India's inexpensive programmers and engineers, it needs to find new businesses if it wants to thrive."

Stuart Forster/Alamy

These individuals are working in a firm to which other companies have outsourced certain activities for completion.

This reality means that these outsourcing firms must find ways to produce their own software that can be used to create different types of value for customers rather than remaining focused on their initial core competencies in terms of integrating and maintaining their customers' software. It seems that firms such as Wipro and Infosys are challenged to develop competencies in terms of their own software niches and to learn how to competitively price their new products to compete against the likes of SAP. To do this, these outsourcing firms are hiring specialized code writers, data scientists, and statisticians for the purpose of creating their own proprietary software through which they can generate value by how they uniquely scrub and crunch customers' data.

Sources: Deutsche Bank, H-P divide IT responsibility in cloud deal, *Wall Street Journal Online*, www.wsj.com, February 25; D. A. Thoppil, 2015, Indian outsourcers struggle to evolve as growth slows, *Wall Street Journal Online*, www.wsj.com, February 22; S McLain, 2015, Big Pharma farms out drug safety to India, *Wall Street Journal Online*, www.wsj.com, February 2; S. McLain, 2015, New outsourcing frontier in India: Monitoring drug safety, *Wall Street Journal Online*, www.wsj.com, February 1; D. A. Thoppil, 2015, Wipro profit rises 8.8%, *Wall Street Journal Online*, www.wsj.com, January 16; S. Carey, 2015, United studies outsourcing up to 2,000 airport jobs, *Wall Street Journal Online*, www.wsj.com, January 13; D. A. Thoppil, 2015, Infosys profit rises 13%, *Wall Street Journal Online*, www.wsj.com, January 9.

Alternatively, the firm could decide to outsource a function or activity where it is weak in order to improve its ability to use its remaining resources to create value.[104]

In considering the results of examining the firm's internal organization, managers should understand that having a significant quantity of resources is not the same as having the "right" resources. The "right" resources are those with the potential to be formed into core competencies as the foundation for creating value for customers and developing competitive advantages as a result of doing so. Interestingly, decision makers sometimes become more focused and productive when seeking to find the right resources when the firm's total set of resources is constrained.[105]

Tools such as outsourcing help the firm focus on its core competencies as the source of its competitive advantages. However, evidence shows that the value-creating ability of core competencies should never be taken for granted. Moreover, the ability of a core competence to be a permanent competitive advantage can't be assumed. The reason for these cautions is that all core competencies have the potential to become *core rigidities*.[106] Typically, events occurring in the firm's external environment create conditions through which core competencies can become core rigidities, generate inertia, and stifle innovation. "Often the flip side, the dark side, of core capabilities is revealed due to external events when new competitors figure out a better way to serve the firm's customers, when new technologies emerge, or when political or social events shift the ground underneath."[107]

Historically, Borders Group Inc. relied on its large storefronts that were conveniently located for customers to visit and browse through books and magazines in a pleasant atmosphere as sources of its competitive success. Over the past two decades or so, though, digital technologies (part of the firm's external environment) rapidly changed customers' shopping patterns for reading materials. Amazon.com's use of the Internet significantly changed the competitive landscape for Borders and similar competitors such as Barnes & Noble. It is possible that Borders' core competencies of store locations and a desirable physical environment for customers became core rigidities for this firm, eventually leading to its filing of bankruptcy in early 2011 and subsequent liquidation.[108] Managers studying the firm's internal organization are responsible for making certain that core competencies do not become core rigidities.

After studying its external environment to determine what it *might choose to do* (as explained in Chapter 2) and its internal organization to understand what it *can do* (as explained in this chapter), the firm has the information required to select a business-level strategy that it will use to compete against rivals. We describe different business-level strategies in the next chapter.

SUMMARY

- In the current competitive landscape, the most effective organizations recognize that strategic competitiveness and above-average returns result only when core competencies (identified by studying the firm's internal organization) are matched with opportunities (determined by studying the firm's external environment).

- No competitive advantage lasts forever. Over time, rivals use their own unique resources, capabilities, and core competencies to form different value-creating propositions that duplicate the focal firm's ability to create value for customers.

- Because competitive advantages are not permanently sustainable, firms must exploit their current advantages while simultaneously using their resources and capabilities to form new advantages that can lead to future competitive success.

- Effectively managing core competencies requires careful analysis of the firm's resources (inputs to the production process) and capabilities (resources that have been purposely integrated to achieve a specific task or set of tasks). The knowledge the firm's human capital possesses is among the most significant of an organization's capabilities and ultimately provides the base for most competitive advantages. The firm must create an organizational culture that allows people to integrate their individual knowledge with that held by others so that, collectively, the firm has a significant amount of value-creating organizational knowledge.

■ Capabilities are a more likely source of core competence and subsequently of competitive advantages than are individual resources. How a firm nurtures and supports its capabilities so they can become core competencies is less visible to rivals, making efforts to understand and imitate the focal firm's capabilities difficult.

■ Only when a capability is valuable, rare, costly to imitate, and nonsubstitutable is it a core competence and a source of competitive advantage. Over time, core competencies must be supported, but they cannot be allowed to become core rigidities. Core competencies are a source of competitive advantage only when they allow the firm to create value by exploiting opportunities in its external environment. When this is no longer possible, the company shifts its attention to forming other capabilities that satisfy the four criteria of sustainable competitive advantage.

■ Value chain analysis is used to identify and evaluate the competitive potential of resources and capabilities. By studying their skills relative to those associated with value chain activities and support functions, firms can understand their cost structure and identify the activities through which they are able to create value.

■ When the firm cannot create value in either a value chain activity or a support function, outsourcing is considered. Used commonly in the global economy, outsourcing is the purchase of a value-creating activity from an external supplier. The firm should outsource only to companies possessing a competitive advantage in terms of the particular value chain activity or support function under consideration. In addition, the firm must continuously verify that it is not outsourcing activities through which it could create value.

KEY TERMS

costly-to-imitate capabilities 91
global mind-set 80
intangible resources 84
nonsubstitutable capabilities 92
outsourcing 96
rare capabilities 91

support functions 94
tangible resources 84
value 81
valuable capabilities 90
value chain activities 93

REVIEW QUESTIONS

1. Why is it important for a firm to study and understand its internal organization?

2. What is value? Why is it critical for the firm to create value? How does it do so?

3. What are the differences between tangible and intangible resources? Why is it important for decision makers to understand these differences? Are tangible resources more valuable for creating capabilities than are intangible resources, or is the reverse true? Why?

4. What are capabilities? How do firms create capabilities?

5. What four criteria must capabilities satisfy for them to become core competencies? Why is it important for firms to use these criteria to evaluate their capabilities' value-creating potential?

6. What is value chain analysis? What does the firm gain by successfully using this tool?

7. What is outsourcing? Why do firms outsource? Will outsourcing's importance grow in the future? If so, why?

8. How do firms identify internal strengths and weaknesses? Why is it vital that managers have a clear understanding of their firm's strengths and weaknesses?

9. What are core rigidities? What does it mean to say that each core competence could become a core rigidity?

Mini-Case

Zara: The Capabilities behind the Spanish "Fast Fashion" Retail Giant

Amancio Ortega built the world's largest fashion empire through his Zara branded products and company-owned stores. Through his management approach, Ortega became quite wealthy. In fact, in 2015 he was the fourth wealthiest person in the world (with a worth of $64.5 billion). This placed him behind only Bill Gates (the wealthiest of all), Carlos "Slim" Helu and family, and Warren Buffett.

Headquartered in La Coruña, in Spain's Galicia region, Ortega founded the Inditex Group with Zara as its flagship brand. Despite Spain's 24 percent unemployment rate and crippling debt, in 2012 Zara increased its revenue 17 percent. Also in 2012, Zara averaged a new store opening every day, including its six thousandth store launched on London's Oxford Street. Although the influence of the economic environment (an influence from the external environment that we examined in Chapter 2) affects Zara's success, the way Zara uses its resources and capabilities as the foundation for core competencies (core competencies are capabilities that serve as a potential source of competitive advantage for a firm over its rivals) demonstrates the value of understanding a firm's internal organization.

Ortega built this successful business based on two critical goals: Give customers what they want, and get it to them faster than anyone else. To do "fast fashion," as it is called, there are several critical capabilities that must be in place. The first critical capability is the ability to design quickly; the design pace at Zara has been described as "frantic." The designers create about three items of new clothing a day, and pattern makers cut one sample for each. The second critical capability is the commercial sales specialists from each region where Zara has stores. They provide input on customers' tastes and buying habits which are reported through store managers. Each specialist is trained to keep an eye on what people are wearing, which Ortega, as well, does personally since founding Zara. As such, Zara has a team approach to match quick and creative design with information coming in from the sales staff through regional specialists and sector specialists to operationalize new fashion ideas.

Zara's supply chain is also managed much more efficiently than those of other companies. The logistics department is the essence of the company. Rather than waiting for cloth to come in after designing, Zara already has a large supply of basic cloth and owns its own dyeing operation to maintain control and speed. Zara's objective is to deliver customized orders to every store in its empire with a 24-hour turnaround for Europe, the Mideast, and much of the United States, and a 48 hour turnaround for Asia and Latin America. The frequent shipments keep product inventories fresh but also scarce since they send out very few items in each shipment. This approach compels customers to visit stores frequently in search of what they want and, because of the scarcity, creates an incentive for them to buy on the spot because it will likely not be in stock tomorrow. Accordingly, Zara's global store average of 17 visits per customer per year is considerably higher than the average of three visits per year for its competitors.

Until 2010 Zara did not have an online strategy. Unlike most retailers it has used very little advertising because it has focused on a rather cheap but fashionable approach. The fashion draws the interest of customers and, thereby, created a huge following on Facebook, with approximately 10 million followers. This compares favorably to other competitors such as Gap. The rarity of the individual pieces of clothing gives customers a sense of individuality. This creates a stronger potential for Zara to pursue an online strategy relative to its competitors.

Most Zara stores are owned by the parent company, and many of its suppliers, although not owned by the company, are considered long-time, relationship-oriented partners. As such, these partners identify with the company and, therefore, are loyal. This approach also sets Zara apart and makes its strategy difficult to duplicate because all of the various facets and capabilities of the company fit together through a unified culture. As noted above, Zara also operates its own dyeing plant for cloth, giving it significant control over its products. Likewise, it sews many of these garments in its own factories and, thus, maintains a high level of quality control and an ability to make quick changes. Overall, the company has a unique set of capabilities that fit together well as it manages activities to produce "fast fashion," which creates demand from their customers and loyalty from their partner suppliers.

Sources: E. Carlyle, 2013, The year's biggest winner: Zara billionaire Amancio Ortega, *Forbes*, www.forbes.com, March 4; R. Dudley, A. Devnath, & M. Townsend, 2013, The hidden cost of fast fashion, *Bloomberg Businessweek*, February 11, 15–17; V. Walt, 2013, Meet the third-richest man in the world, *Fortune*, January 14, 74–79; 2012, Inditex, Asos post double-digit sales gains, *Women's Wear Daily*, September 20, 6; B. Borzykowski, 2012, Zara eludes the pain in Spain, *Canadian Business*, September 17, 67; K. Willems, W. Janssens, G. Swinnen, M. Brengman, S. Streukens, & N. Vancauteren, 2012, From Armani to Zara: Impression formation based on fashion store patronage, *Journal of Business Research*, 65: 1487–1494.

Case Discussion Questions

1. What influences from the external environment over the next several years do you think might affect the way Zara competes?

2. How easy or difficult do you think it would be for competitors to imitate Zara's supply chain as a capability?

3. Is getting products to customers as quickly as possible an outcome that you believe would create value in industries in addition to clothing? If so, which industries and why?

4. What value does Zara create for its customers?

5. As you study how Zara competes and the capabilities it uses to do so, are there areas of the firm's operations you believe might be candidates for outsourcing? If so, what areas and why might those be outsourced in the future?

NOTES

1. A. Gambardella, C. Panico, & G. Valentini, 2015, Strategic incentives to human capital, *Strategic Management Journal*, 36: 37–52; C. Gilbert, M. Eyring, & R. N. Foster, 2012, Two routes to resilience. *Harvard Business Review*, 90(12): 65–73; H. A. Ndofor, D. G. Sirmon, & X. He, 2011, Firm resources, competitive actions and performance: Investigating a mediated model with evidence from the in-vitro diagnostics industry, *Strategic Management Journal*, 32: 640–657.

2. R. Khanna, I. Guler, & A. Nerkar, 2015, Fail often, fail big, and fail fast: Learning from small failures and R&D performance in the pharmaceutical industry, *Academy of Management Journal*, in press; C. Engel & M. Kleine, 2015, Who is afraid of pirates? An experiment on the deterrence of innovation by imitation, *Research Policy*, 44: 20–33; K. Wilson & Y. L. Doz, 2012, 10 rules for managing global innovation, *Harvard Business Review*, 90(10): 84–90.

3. S. Denning, 2015, How Agile and Zara are transforming the U.S. fashion industry, *Forbes Online*, www.forbes.com, March 13; M. Schoultz, 2015, Is Zara the most innovative fashion retailer? *Digital Spark Marketing*, www.digitalsparkmarketing.com, April 10.

4. J. Ostrower, 2015, At Boeing, innovation means small steps, not giant leaps, *Wall Street Journal Online*, www.wsj.com, April 2.

5. M. Beck, 2015, Innovation is sweeping through U.S. medical schools, *Wall Street Journal Online*, www.wsj.com, February 16.

6. M. Keyhani, M. Levesque, & A. Madhok, 2015, Toward a theory of entrepreneurial rents: A simulation of the market process, *Strategic Management Journal*, 36: 76–96; L. Ngo & A. O'Cass, 2012, In search of innovation and customer-related performance superiority: The role of market orientation, marketing capability, and innovation capability interactions, *Journal of Product Innovation Management*, 29: 861–877; D. G. Sirmon, M. A. Hitt, & R. D. Ireland, 2007, Managing firm resources in dynamic markets to create value: Looking inside the black box, *Academy of Management Review*, 32: 273–292.

7. M.-J. Chen & D. Miller, 2015, Reconceptualizing competitive dynamics: A multidimensional framework, *Strategic Management Journal*, 36: 758–775; F. Polidoro, Jr. & P. K. Toh, 2011, Letting rivals come close or warding them off? The effects of substitution threat on imitation deterrence, *Academy of Management Journal*, 54: 369–392; A. W. King, 2007, Disentangling interfirm and intrafirm causal ambiguity: A conceptual model of causal ambiguity and sustainable competitive advantage, *Academy of Management Review*, 32: 156–178.

8. I. Le Breton-Miller & D. Miller, 2015, The paradox of resource vulnerability: Considerations for organizational curatorship, *Strategic Management Journal*, 36: 397–415; M. Semadeni & B. S. Anderson, 2010, The follower's dilemma: Innovation and imitation in the professional services industry, *Academy of Management Journal*, 53: 1175–1193.

9. U. Stettner & D. Lavie, 2014, Ambidexterity under scrutiny: Exploration and exploitation via internal organization, alliances, and acquisitions, *Strategic Management Journal*, 35: 1903–1929; M. G. Jacobides, S. G. Winter, & S. M. Kassberger, 2012, The dynamics of wealth, profit, and sustainable advantage, *Strategic Management Journal*, 33: 1384–1410.

10. S. Nadkarni, T. Chen, & J. Chen, 2015, The clock is ticking: Executive temporal depth, industry velocity and competitive aggressiveness, *Strategic Management Journal*, in press; L. A. Costa, K. Cool, & I. Dierickx, 2013, The competitive implications of the deployment of unique resources, *Strategic Management Journal*, 34: 445–463; M. A. Peteraf & J. B. Barney, 2003, Unraveling the resource-based tangle, *Managerial and Decision Economics*, 24: 309–323; J. B. Barney, 2001, Is the resource-based "view" a useful perspective for strategic management research? Yes, *Academy of Management Review*, 26: 41–56.

11. R. Roy & M. B. Sarkar, 2015, Knowledge, firm boundaries, and innovation: Mitigating the incumbent's curse during radical technological change, *Strategic Management Journal*: in press; G. Zied & J. McGuire, 2011, Multimarket competition, mobility barriers, and firm performance, *Journal of Management Studies*, 48: 857–890.

12. P. Wahba, 2014, Neiman Marcus goes after international luxury with e-commerce deal, *Fortune Online*, www.fortune.com, September 15.

13. D. Piaskowska & G. Trojanowski, 2014, Twice as smart: The importance of managers' formative-years' international experience for their international orientation and foreign acquisition decisions, *British Journal of Management*, 25: 40–57; M. Javidan, R. M. Steers, & M. A. Hitt (eds.), 2007, *The Global Mindset:* Amsterdam: Elsevier Ltd.

14. H. Liang, B. Ren, & S. Li Sun, 2015, An anatomy of state control in the globalization of state-owned enterprises, *Journal of International Business Studies*, 46: 223–240; A. Diaz, M. Magni, & F. Poh, 2012, From oxcart to Wal-Mart: Four keys to reaching emerging-market consumers, *McKinsey Quarterly*, October, 58–67; O. Levy, S. Taylor, & N. A. Boyacigiller, 2010, On the rocky road to strong global culture, *MIT Sloan Management Review*, 51: 20–22.

15. J. J. Ebbers, 2014, Networking behavior and contracting relationships among entrepreneurs in business incubators, *Entrepreneurship Theory and Practice*, 38: 1159–1181; R. A. D'Aveni, G. B. Dagnino, & K. G. Smith, 2010, The age of temporary advantage, *Strategic Management Journal*, 31: 1371–1385; E. Danneels, 2008, Organizational antecedents of second-order competences, *Strategic Management Journal*, 29: 519–543.

16. R. Vandaie & A. Zaheer, 2015, Alliance partners and firm capability: Evidence from the motion picture industry, *Organization Science*, in press; S. A. Zahra & S. Nambisan, 2012, Entrepreneurship and strategic thinking in business ecosystems, *Business Horizons*, 55: 219–229.

17. A. Waeraas & H. L. Sataoen, 2015, Being all things to all customers: Building reputation in an institutionalized field, *British Journal of Management*, 26: 310–326; D. G. Sirmon, M. A. Hitt, R. D. Ireland, & B. A. Gilbert, 2011, Resource orchestration to create competitive advantage: Breadth, depth, and life cycle effects, *Journal of Management*, 37: 1390–1412; R. Adner & R. Kapoor, 2010, Value creation in innovation ecosystems: How the structure of technological interdependence affects firm performance in new technology generations, *Strategic Management Journal*, 31: 306–333.

18. C. Grimpe & K. Hussinger, 2014, Resource complementarity and value capture in firm acquisitions: The role of intellectual property rights, *Strategic Management Journal*, 35: 1762–1780; M. A. Hitt, R. D. Ireland, D. G. Sirmon, & C. A. Trahms, 2011, Strategic entrepreneurship: Creating value for individuals, organizations, and society, *Academy of Management Perspectives*, 25: 57–75; D. G. Sirmon, S. Gove, & M. A. Hitt, 2008, Resource management in dyadic competitive rivalry: The effects of resource bundling and deployment, *Academy of Management Journal*, 51: 919–935.

19. B. Clarysse, M. Wright, J. Bruneel, & A. Mahajan, 2014, Creating value in ecosystems: Crossing the chasm between knowledge and business ecosystems, *Research Policy*, 43: 1164–1176; J. S. Harrison, D. A. Bosse, & R. A. Phillips, 2010, Managing for stakeholders, stakeholder utility functions, and competitive advantage, *Strategic Management Journal*, 31: 58–74; J. L. Morrow, Jr., D. G. Sirmon, M. A. Hitt, & T. R. Holcomb, 2007, Creating value in the face of declining performance: Firm strategies and organizational recovery, *Strategic Management Journal*, 28: 271–283.

20. P. Bromiley & D. Rau, 2014, Towards a practice-based view of strategy, *Strategic Management Journal*, 35: 1249–1256; V. Rindova, W. J. Ferrier, & R. Wiltbank, 2010, Value from gestalt: How sequences of competitive actions create advantage for firms in nascent markets, *Strategic Management Journal*, 31: 1474–1497.

21. C. Tantalo & R. L. Priem, 2015, Value creation through stakeholder synergy, *Strategic Management Journal*, in press; E. R. Brenes, D. Montoya, & L. Ciravegna, 2014, Differentiation strategies in emerging markets: The case of Latin American agribusinesses, *Journal of Business Research*, 67: 847–855; D. G. Sirmon, M. A. Hitt, J.-L. Arregle, & J. T. Campbell, 2010, The dynamic interplay of capability strengths and weaknesses: Investigating the bases of temporary competitive advantage, *Strategic Management Journal*, 31: 1386–1409.

22. S. Nadkarni & J. Chen, 2015, Bridging yesterday, today, and tomorrow: CEO temporal focus, environmental dynamism, and rate of new product introduction, *Academy of Management Journal*, in press; S. Nadkarni, T. Chen, & J. Chen, 2014, The clock is ticking: Executive temporal depth, industry velocity, and competitive aggressiveness, *Strategic Management Journal*, in press; F. Aime, S. Johnson, J. W. Ridge, & A. D. Hill, 2010, The routine may be stable but the advantage is not: Competitive implications of key employee mobility, *Strategic Management Journal*, 31: 75–87.

23. M. Arrfelt, R. M. Wiseman, G. McNamara, & G. T. M. Hult, 2015, Examining a key corporate role: The influence of capital allocation competency on business unit performance, *Strategic Management Journal*, in press; D. Li & J. Liu, 2014, Dynamic capabilities, environmental dynamism, and competitive advantage: Evidence from China, *Journal of Business Research*, 67: 2793–2799; D. J. Teece, 2012, Dynamic capabilities: Routines versus entrepreneurial action, *Journal of Management Studies*, 49: 1395–1401.

24. A. M. Kleinbaum & T. E. Stuart, 2015, Network responsiveness: The social structural microfoundations of dynamic capabilities, *Academy of Management*

Perspectives*, in press; M. H. Kunc & J. D. W. Morecroft, 2010, Managerial decision making and firm performance under a resource-based paradigm, *Strategic Management Journal*, 31: 1164–1182.

25. C. M. Christensen, 2001, The past and future of competitive advantage, *Sloan Management Review*, 42(2): 105–109.

26. J. Gomez, R. Orcos, & S. Palomas, 2015, Competitors' strategic heterogeneity and firm performance, *Long Range Planning*, in press; S. K. Parker & C. G. Collins, 2010, Taking stock: Integrating and differentiating multiple proactive behaviors, *Journal of Management*, 36: 633–662.

27. M. G. Butler & C. M. Callahan, 2014, Human resource outsourcing: Market and operating performance effects of administrative HR functions, *Journal of Business Research*, 67: 218–224; Y. Y. Kor & A. Mesko, 2013, Dynamic managerial capabilities: Configuration and orchestration of top executives' capabilities and the firm's dominant logic, *Strategic Management Journal*, 34: 233–244; D. P. Forbes, 2007, Reconsidering the strategic implications of decision comprehensiveness, *Academy of Management Review*, 32: 361–376.

28. E. Maitland & A. Sammartino, 2015, Decision making and uncertainty: The role of heuristics and experience in assessing a politically hazardous environment, *Strategic Management Journal*, in press; L. B. Mulder, J. Jordan, & F. Rink, 2015, The effect of specific and general rules on ethical decisions, *Organizational Behavior and Human Decision Processes*, 126: 115–129; T. M. Jones, W. Felps, & G. A. Bigley, 2007, Ethical theory and stakeholder-related decisions: The role of stakeholder culture, *Academy of Management Review*, 32: 137–155.

29. D. C. Hambrick & T. J. Quigley, 2014, Toward a more accurate contextualization of the CEO effect on firm performance, *Strategic Management Journal*, 35: 473–491; M. S. Gary & R. E. Wood, 2011, Mental models, decision rules, and performance heterogeneity, *Strategic Management Journal*, 32: 569–594.

30. T. W. Tong, J. J. Reuer, B. B. Tyler, & S. Zhang, 2015, Host country executives' assessments of international joint ventures and divestitures: An experimental approach, *Strategic Management Journal*, 36: 254–275; A. Arrighetti, F. Landini, & A. Lasagni, 2014, Intangible assets and firm heterogeneity: Evidence from Italy, *Research Policy*, 43: 202–213; C. B. Bingham & K. M. Eisenhardt, 2011, Rational heuristics: The 'simple rules' that strategists learn from process experience, *Strategic Management Journal*, 32: 1437–1464.

31. R. Mudambi & T. Swift, 2014, Knowing when to leap: Transitioning between exploitative and explorative R&D, *Strategic Management Journal*, 35: 126–145; Y. Zhang & J. Gimeno, 2010, Earnings pressure and

competitive behavior: Evidence from the U.S. electricity industry, *Academy of Management Journal*, 53: 743–768; L. M. Lodish & C. F. Mela, 2007, If brands are built over years, why are they managed over quarters? *Harvard Business Review*, 85(7/8): 104–112.

32. M. Jenkins, 2014, Innovate or imitate? The role of collective beliefs in competences in competing firms, *Long Range Planning*, 47: 173–185; P. Madsen & V. Desai, 2010, Failing to learn? The effects of failure and success on organizational learning in the global orbital launch vehicle industry, *Academy of Management Journal*, 53: 451–476; P. C. Nutt, 2002, *Why Decisions Fail*, San Francisco, Barrett-Koehler Publishers.

33. A. O. Laplume & P. Dass, 2015, Outstreaming for ambidexterity: Evolving a firm's core business from components to systems by serving internal and external customers, *Long Range Planning*, in press; D. Maslach, 2015, Change and persistence with failed technological innovation, *Strategic Management Journal*, in press; J. P. Eggers, 2012, All experience is not created equal: Learning, adapting and focusing in product portfolio management, *Strategic Management Journal*, 33: 315–335.

34. S. Singh, P. D. Corner, & K. Pavlovich, 2015, Failed, not finished: A narrative approach to understanding venture failure stigmatization, *Journal of Business Venturing*, 30: 150–166; S. Mousavi & G. Gigerenzer, 2014, Risk, uncertainty, and heuristics, *Journal of Business Research*, 67: 1671–1678; J. D. Ford & L. W. Ford, 2010, Stop blaming resistance to change and start using it, *Organizational Dynamics*, 39: 24–36.

35. V. Desai, 2015, Learning through the distribution of failures within an organization: Evidence from heart bypass surgery performance, *Academy of Management Journal*, in press; J. P. Eggers & L. Song, 2015, Dealing with failure: Serial entrepreneurs and the costs of changing industries between ventures, *Academy of Management Journal*, in press; K. Muehlfeld, P. Rao Sahib, & A. Van Witteloostuijn, 2012, A contextual theory of organizational learning from failures and successes: A study of acquisition completion in the global newspaper industry, 1981–2008, *Strategic Management Journal*, 33: 938–964.

36. L. Colby, 2015, News Corp.'s $1 billion plan to overhaul education is riddled with failures, *Bloomberg Online*, www. bloomberg.com, April 7.

37. W. Smith, 2015, Dynamic decision making: A model of senior leaders managing strategic paradoxes, *Academy of Management Journal*, in press; 2013, Strategy in a world of "biblical change": Our era of uncertainty calls for business leaders with vision, foresight and a global

perspective, *Strategic Direction*, 29(3): 19–22; G. S. Dowell, M. B. Shackell & N. V. Stuart, 2011, Boards, CEOs, and surviving a financial crisis: Evidence from the internet shakeout, *Strategic Management Journal*, 32: 1025–1045.

38. S. R. Hiatt & W. D. Sine, 2014, Clear and present danger: Planning and new venture survival amid political and civil violence, *Strategic Management Journal*, 35: 773–785; A. Arora & A. Nandkumar, 2012, Insecure advantage? Markets for technology and the value of resources for entrepreneurial ventures, *Strategic Management Journal*, 33: 231–251; S. S. K. Lam & J. C. K. Young, 2010, Staff localization and environmental uncertainty on firm performance in China, *Asia Pacific Journal of Management*, 27: 677–695.

39. B. Kendall & A. Harder, 2015, Litigation awaits new EPA emissions rules, *Wall Street Journal Online*, www.wsj.com, March 22.

40. C. Dulaney, 2015, Peabody Energy names new CEO, *Wall Street Journal Online*, www. wsj.com, January 22.

41. J. Winkler, C. P. Jian-Wej Kuklinski, & R. Moser, 2015, Decision making in emerging markets: The Delphi approach's contribution to coping with uncertainty and equivocality, *Journal of Business Research*, 68: 1118–1126; O. H. Azar, 2014, The default heuristic in strategic decision making: When is it optimal to choose the default without investing in information search? *Journal of Business Research*, 67: 1744–1748.

42. D. M. Cain, D. A. Moore, & U. Haran, 2015, Making sense of overconfidence in market entry, *Strategic Management Journal*, 36: 1–18; M. Gary, R. E. Wood, & T. Pillinger, 2012, Enhancing mental models, analogical transfer, and performance in strategic decision making, *Strategic Management Journal*, 33: 1229–1246; J. R. Mitchell, D. A. Shepherd, & M. P. Sharfman, 2011, Erratic strategic decisions: When and why managers are inconsistent in strategic decision making, *Strategic Management Journal*, 32: 683–704.

43. D. Laureiro-Martinez, 2014, Cognitive control capabilities, routinization propensity, and decision-making performance, *Organization Science*, 25: 1111–1133; P. D. Windschitl, A. M. Scherer, A. R. Smith, & J. P. Rose, 2013, Why so confident? The influence of outcome desirability on selective exposure and likelihood judgment, *Organizational Behavior & Human Decision Processes*, 120: 73–86.

44. D. Albert, M. Kreutzer, & C. Lechner, 2015, Resolving the paradox of interdependency and strategic renewal in activity systems, *Academy of Management Review*, 40: 210–234; L. Alexander & D. van Knippenberg, 2014, Teams in pursuit of

radical innovation: A goal orientation perspective, *Academy of Management Review*, 39: 423–438; C. Weigelt, 2013, Leveraging supplier capabilities: The role of locus of capability deployment, *Strategic Management Journal*, 34: 1–21.

45. A. Lipparini, G. Lorenzoni, & S. Ferriani, 2014, From core to periphery and back: A study on the deliberate shaping of knowledge flows in interfirm dyads and networks, *Strategic Management Journal*, 35: 578–595; J. M. Shaver, 2011, The benefits of geographic sales diversification: How exporting facilitates capital investment, *Strategic Management Journal*, 32: 1046–1060.

46. J. Bloomberg, 2015, Is Rackspace the Nordstrom of cloud? *Forbes Online*, www. forbes.com, January 21.

47. S. Raithel & M. Schwaiger, 2015, The effects of corporate reputation perceptions of the general public on shareholder value, *Strategic Management Journal*: in press; B. S. Anderson & Y. Eshima, 2013, The influence of firm age and intangible resources on the relationship between entrepreneurial orientation and firm growth among Japanese SMEs, *Journal of Business Venturing*, 28: 413–429.

48. A. Vomberg, C. Homburg, & T. Bornemann, 2015, Talented people and strong brands: The contribution of human capital and brand equity to firm value, *Strategic Management Journal*, 36: in press; J. Choi, G. W. Hecht, & W. B. Tayler, 2012, Lost in translation: The effects of incentive compensation on strategy surrogation, *Accounting Review*, 87: 1135–1163.

49. A. M. Webber, 2000, New math for a new economy, *Fast Company*, January/ February, 214–224.

50. R. Sydler, S. Haefliger, & R. Pruksa, 2014, Measuring intellectual capital with financial figures: Can we predict firm profitability? *European Management Journal*, 32: 244–259; F. Neffke & M. Henning, 2013, Skill relatedness and firm diversification, *Strategic Management Journal*, 34: 297–316; E. Danneels, 2011, Trying to become a different type of company: Dynamic capability at Smith Corona, *Strategic Management Journal*, 32: 1–31.

51. F. Honore, F. Munari, & B. van Pottelsberghe de La Potterie, 2015, corporate governance practices and companies' R&D intensity: Evidence from European countries, *Research Policy*, 44: 533–543; J. Gómez & P. Vargas, 2012, Intangible resources and technology adoption in manufacturing firms, *Research Policy*, 41: 1607–1619; K. E. Meyer, R. Mudambi, & R. Narula, 2011, Multinational enterprises and local contexts: The opportunities and challenges of multiple embeddedness, *Journal of Management Studies*, 48: 235–252.

52. J.-Y. Lee, D. G. Bachrach, & D. M. Rousseau, 2015, Internal labor markets, firm-specific human capital, and heterogeneity antecedents of employee idiosyncratic deal requests, *Organization Science*, in press.

53. J. Raffiee & R. Coff, 2015, Micro-foundations of firm-specific human capital: When do employees perceive their skills to be firm-specific? *Academy of Management Journal*, in press.

54. A. Jain & R.-A. Thietart, 2014, Capabilities as shift parameters for the outsourcing decision, *Strategic Management Journal*, 35: 1881–1890; R. E. Ployhart, C. H. Van Iddekinge, & W. I. MacKenzie, Jr., 2011, Acquiring and developing human capital in service contexts: The interconnectedness of human capital resources, *Academy of Management Journal*, 54: 353–368.

55. S. Raithel & M. Schwaiger, 2015, The effects of corporate reputation perceptions of the general public on shareholder value, *Strategic Management Journal*, in press; K. Kim, B. Jeon, H. Jung, W. Lu, & J. Jones, 2012, Effective employment brand equity through sustainable competitive advantage, marketing strategy, and corporate image, *Journal of Business Research*, 65: 1612–1617; L. Diestre & N. Rajagopalan, 2011, An environmental perspective on diversification: The effects of chemical relatedness and regulatory sanctions, *Academy of Management Journal*, 54: 97–115.

56. W.-Y. Hun, H. Kim, & J. Woo, 2014, How CSR leads to corporate brand equity: Mediating mechanisms of corporate brand credibility and reputation, *Journal of Business Ethics*, 125: 75–86; G. Dowling & P. Moran, 2012, Corporate reputations: Built in or bolted on? *California Management Review*, 54(2): 25–42; M. D. Pfarrer, T. G. Pollock, & V. P. Rindova, 2010, A tale of two assets: The effects of firm reputation and celebrity on earnings surprises and investors' reactions, *Academy of Management Journal*, 53: 1131–1152; T. G. Pollock, G. Chen, & E. M. Jackson, 2010, How much prestige is enough? Assessing the value of multiple types of high-status affiliates for young firms, *Journal of Business Venturing*, 25: 6–23.

57. A. P. Petkova, A. Wadhwa, X. Yao, & S. Jain, 2014, Reputation and decision making under ambiguity: A study of U.S. venture capital firms' investments in the emerging clean energy sector, *Academy of Management Journal*, 57: 422–448; Y. Wang, G. Berens, & C. van Riel, 2012, Competing in the capital market with a good reputation, *Corporate Reputation Review*, 15: 198–221; J. J. Ebbers & N. M. Wijnberg, 2012, Nascent ventures competing for start-up capital: Matching reputations and investors, *Journal of Business Venturing*, 27: 372–384.

58. P. Foroudi, T.C. Melewar, & S. Gupta, 2014, Linking corporate logo, corporate image, and reputation: An examination of consumer perceptions in the financial setting, *Journal of Business Research*, 67: 2269–2281; S. Tischer & L. Hildebrandt, 2014, Linking corporate reputation and shareholder value using the publication of reputation rankings, *Journal of Business Research*, 67: 1007–1017.

59. C. A. Roster, 2014, Cultural influences on global firms' decisions to cut the strategic brand ties that bind: A commentary essay, *Journal of Business Research*, 67: 486–488; N. Rosenbusch & J. Brinckmann, 2011, Is innovation always beneficial? A meta-analysis of the relationship between innovation and performance in SMEs, *Journal of Business Venturing*, 26: 441–457.

60. 2015, Harley-Davidson Motor Apparel, www.harley-davidson.com, April 5.

61. T. Arbel, 2015, Comcast gets social to shake bad customer-service reputation, Yahoo.com, www.yahoo.com, March 24.

62. V. Goel, 2014, G.M. uses social media to manage customers and its reputation, *New York Times Online*, www.nytimes.com, March 23.

63. Social media principles, 2015, Coca-Cola Company Home page, www.coca-colacompany.com, April 6.

64. Y. Lin & L.-Y. Wu, 2014, Exploring the role of dynamic capabilities in firm performance under the resource-based view framework, *Journal of Business Research*, 67: 407–413; R. W. Coff, 2010, The coevolution of rent appropriation and capability development, *Strategic Management Journal*, 31: 711–733; J. Bitar & T. Hafsi, 2007, Strategizing through the capability lens: Sources and outcomes of integration, *Management Decision*, 45: 403–419.

65. S. Chowdhury, E. Schulz, M. Milner, & D. Van De Voort, 2014, Core employee based human capital and revenue productivity in small firms: An empirical investigation, *Journal of Business Research*, 67: 2473–2479; A. M. Subramanian, 2012, A longitudinal study of the influence of intellectual human capital on firm exploratory innovation, *IEEE Transactions on Engineering Management*, 59: 540–550; T. Dalziel, R. J. Gentry, & M. Bowerman, 2011, An integrated agency-resource dependence view of the influence of directors' human and relational capital on firms' R&D spending, *Journal of Management Studies*, 48: 1217–1242.

66. K. Freeman, 2015, CEOs must prioritize human capital, *Wall Street Journal Online*, www.wsj.com, February 27.

67. S. Moore, 2015, How pizza became a growth stock, *Wall Street Journal Online*, www.wsj.com, March 13.

68. D. J. Teece, 2014, The foundations of enterprise performance: Dynamic and ordinary capabilities in an (economic)

theory of firms, *Academy of Management Perspectives*, 28: 328–352; K. M. Heimeriks, M. Schijven, & S. Gates, 2012, Manifestations of higher-order routines: The underlying mechanisms of deliberate learning in the context of postacquisition integration, *Academy of Management Journal*, 55: 703–726; C. Zott, 2003, Dynamic capabilities and the emergence of intraindustry differential firm performance: Insights from a simulation study, *Strategic Management Journal*, 24: 97–125.

69. Y. Zhao, E. Cavusgil, & S. T. Cavusgil, 2014, An investigation of the black-box supplier integration in new product development, *Journal of Business Research*, 67: 1058–1064; H. R. Greve, 2009, Bigger and safer: The diffusion of competitive advantage, *Strategic Management Journal*, 30: 1–23; C. K. Prahalad & G. Hamel, 1990, The core competence of the corporation, *Harvard Business Review*, 68(3): 79–93.

70. D. Reisinger, 2015, Apple's genius bar to get smarter with 'concierge'—report, *CNET*.com, www.cnet.com, February 24; Y. I. Kane & I. Sherr, 2011, Secrets from Apple's genius bar: Full loyalty, no negativity, *Wall Street Journal*, www.wsj.com, June 15.

71. J. Schmidt, R. Makadok, & T. Keil, 2015, Customer-specific synergies and market convergence, *Strategic Management Journal*, in press; M. Makri, M. A. Hitt, & P. J. Lane, 2010, Complementary technologies, knowledge relatedness, and invention outcomes in high technology mergers and acquisitions, *Strategic Management Journal*, 31: 602–628; S. Newbert, 2008, Value, rareness, competitive advantage, and performance: A conceptual-level empirical investigation of the resource-based view of the firm, *Strategic Management Journal*, 29: 745–768.

72. J. Boynton, 2015, Walmart unveils virtual sustainability shop, *Triple Pundit.com*, www.triplepundit.com, February 24.

73. Walmart environmental sustainability, 2015, *Wall-Mart Homepage*, www.walmart.com, March 30; A. Winston, 2015, Can Walmart get us to buy sustainable products? *Harvard Business Review blog*, www.hbr.org, February 24.

74. A. Kaul & Z (Brian) Wu, 2015, A capabilities-based perspective on target selection in acquisitions, *Strategic Management Journal*: in press; D. S. K. Lim, N. Celly, E. A. Morse, & W. G. Rowe, 2013, Rethinking the effectiveness of asset and cost retrenchment: The contingency effects of a firm's rent creation mechanism, *Strategic Management Journal*, 34: 42–61.

75. D. Roos, 2011, How does Groupon work? *Howstuffworks.com*, www.howstuffworks.com, June 12.

76. S. D. Anthony, 2012, The new corporate garage, *Harvard Business Review*, 90(9): 44–53.

77. H. A. Ndofor, D. G. Sirmon, & X. He, 2015, Utilizing the firm's resources: How TMT heterogeneity and resulting faultlines affect TMT tasks, *Strategic Management Journal*: in press; Q. Gu & J. W. Lu, 2011, Effects of inward investment on outward investment: The venture capital industry worldwide—1985–2007, *Journal of International Business Studies*, 42: 263–284.

78. Sustainability, 2015, Target Home Page, www.target.com, April 10.

79. S. G. Lazzarini, 2015, Strategizing by the government: Can industrial policy create firm-level competitive advantage? *Strategic Management Journal*, 36: 97–112; H. Rahmandad, 2012, Impact of growth opportunities and competition on firm-level capability development trade-offs, *Organization Science*, 23: 138–154; C. A. Coen & C. A. Maritan, 2011, Investing in capabilities: The dynamics of resource allocation, *Organization Science*, 22: 199–217.

80. J. B. Barney, 1991, Firm resources and sustained competitive advantage, *Journal of Management*, 17: 99–120.

81. M. E. B. Herrera, 2015, Creating competitive advantage by institutionalizing corporate social innovation, *Journal of Business Research*: in press; C. M. Wilderom, P. T. van den Berg & U. J. Wiersma, 2012, A longitudinal study of the effects of charismatic leadership and organizational culture on objective and perceived corporate performance, *Leadership Quarterly*, 23: 835–848; C. C. Maurer, P. Bansal, & M. M. Crossan, 2011, Creating economic value through social values: Introducing a culturally informed resource-based view, *Organization Science*, 22: 432–448.

82. J. Jargon, 2014, McDonald's plans to change U.S. structure, *Wall Street Journal Online*, www.wsj.com, October 30.

83. T. Alnuaimi & G. George, 2015, Appropriability and the retrieval of knowledge after spillovers, *Strategic Management Journal*: in press; L. Mulotte, P. Dussauge, & W. Mitchell, 2013, Does pre-entry licensing undermine the performance of subsequent independent activities? Evidence from the global aerospace industry, 1944–2000, *Strategic Management Journal*, 34: 358–372; A. W. King & C. P. Zeithaml, 2001, Competencies and firm performance: Examining the causal ambiguity paradox, *Strategic Management Journal*, 22: 75–99.

84. Barney, Firm resources, 111.

85. Z. Erden, D. Klang, R. Sydler, & G. von Krogh, 2014, Knowledge-flows and firm performance, *Journal of Business Research*, 67: 2777–2785; E. Beleska-Spasova & K. W. Glaister, 2013, Intrafirm causal ambiguity in an international context, *International Business Review*, 22: 32–46; K. Srikanth & P. Puranam, 2011, Integrating distributed work: Comparing task design, communication, and tacit coordination mechanisms, *Strategic Management Journal*, 32: 849–875.

86. M. G. Jacobides & C. J. Tae, 2015, Kingpins, bottlenecks, and value dynamics along a sector, *Organization Science:* in press; J. B. Heide, A. Kumar, & K. H. Wathne, 2014, Concurrent sourcing, governance mechanisms, and performance outcomes in industrial value chains, *Strategic Management Journal*, 35: 1164–1185; G. K. Acharyulu & B. Shekhar, 2012, Role of value chain strategy in healthcare supply chain management: An empirical study in India, *International Journal of Management*, 29: 91–97.

87. M. E. Porter, 1985, *Competitive Advantage*, New York: Free Press, 33–61.

88. P. Frow, S. Nenonen, A. Payne, & K. Storbacka, 2015, Managing co-creation design: A strategic approach to innovation, *British Journal of Management*: in press; R. Garcia-Castro & C. Francoeur, 2015, When more is not better: Complementarities, costs and contingencies in stakeholder management, *Strategic Management Journal*, in press; J. Alcacer, 2006, Location choices across the value chain: How activity and capability influence co-location, *Management Science*, 52: 1457–1471.

89. Y. M. Zhou, 2015, Supervising across borders: The case of multinational hierarchies, *Organization Science*, in press; S. T. Cavusgil & G. Knight, 2014, The born global firm: An entrepreneurial and capabilities perspective on early and rapid internationalization, *Journal of International Business Studies*, 46: 3–16; N. Haworth, 2013, Compressed development: Global value chains, multinational enterprises and human resource development in 21st century Asia, *Journal of World Business*, 48: 251–259.

90. R. Garcia-Castro & R. V. Aguilera, 2015, Incremental value creation and appropriation in a world with multiple stakeholders, *Strategic Management Journal*, 36: 137–147; S. Manning, M. M. Larsen, & P. Bharati, 2015, Global delivery models: The role of talent, speed and time zones in the global outsourcing industry, *Journal of International Business Studies*, in press; A. Jara & H. Escaith, 2012, Global value chains, international trade statistics and policymaking in a flattening world, *World Economics*, 13(4): 5–18.

91. C. Boulton & S. Norton, 2015, Deutsche Bank, H-P divide IT responsibility in cloud deal, *Wall Street Journal Online*, www.wsj.com, February 26.

92. R. Lungeanu & E. Zajac, 2015, Venture capital ownership as a contingent resource: How owner/firm fit influences IPO outcomes, *Academy of Management Journal*, in press; J.-Y. Lee, D. G. Bachrach, & K. Lewis, 2014, Social network ties, transactive memory, and performance in groups, *Organization Science*, 25: 951–967.

93. S. G. Lazzarini, 2015, Strategizing by the government: Can industrial policy create firm-level competitive advantage? *Strategic Management Journal*, 36: 97–112; H. Yang, Y. Zheng, & X. Zhao, 2014, Exploration or exploitation: Small firms' alliance strategies with large firms, *Strategic Management Journal*, 35: 146–157.

94. C. Lioukas & J. Reuer, 2015, Isolating trust outcomes from exchange relationships: Social exchange and learning benefits of prior ties in alliances, *Academy of Management Journal*, in press; J. Song, 2014, Subsidiary absorptive capacity and knowledge transfer within multinational corporations, *Journal of International Business Studies*, 45: 73–84.

95. G. E. Mitchell, 2014, Collaborative propensities among transnational NGOs registered in the United States, *The American Review of Public Administration*, 44: 575–599.

96. S. M. Handley & C. M. Angst, 2015, The impact of culture on the relationship between governance and opportunism in outsourcing relationships, *Strategic Management Journal*, in press; D. J. Teece, 2014, A dynamic capabilities-based entrepreneurial theory of the multinational enterprise, *Journal of International Business Studies*, 45: 8–37.

97. C. Peeters, C. Dehon, & P. Garcia-Prieto, 2015, The attention stimulus of cultural differences in global services sourcing, *Journal of International Business Studies*, 46: 241–251; D. O. Kazmer, 2014, Manufacturing outsourcing, onshoring, and global equilibrium, *Business Horizons*, 57: 463–472; A. J. Mauri & J. Neiva de Figueiredo, 2012, Strategic patterns of internationalization and performance variability: Effects of US-based MNC cross-border dispersion, integration, and outsourcing, *Journal of International Management*, 18: 38–51.

98. A. Gunasekaran, Z. Irani, K.-L. Choy, L. Filippi, & T. Papadopoulos, 2015, Performance measures and metrics in outsourcing decisions: A review for research and applications, *International Journal of Production Economics*, 161: 153–166; W. L. Tate, L. M. Ellram, T. Schoenherr, & K. J. Petersen, 2014, Global competitive conditions driving the manufacturing location decision, *Business Horizons*, 57: 381–390; C. Weigelt & M. B. Sarkar, 2012, Performance implications of outsourcing for technological innovations: Managing the efficiency and adaptability trade-off, *Strategic Management Journal*, 33: 189–216.

99. A. Jain & R.-A. Thietart, 2014, Capabilities as shift parameters for the outsourcing decision, *Strategic Management Journal*, 35: 1881–1890; J. Li, 2012, The alignment between organizational control mechanisms and outsourcing strategies: A commentary essay, *Journal of Business Research*, 65: 1384–1386.

100. R. Kapoor & N. R. Furr, 2015, Complementarities and competition: Unpacking the drivers of entrants' technology choices in the solar photovoltaic industry, *Strategic Management Journal*, 36: 416–436; N. Raassens, S. Wuyts, & I. Geyskens, 2012, The market valuation of outsourcing new product development, *Journal of Marketing Research*, 49: 682–695.

101. S. Holloway & A. Parmigiani, 2015, Friends and profits don't mix: The performance implications of repeated partnerships, *Academy of Management Journal*, in press; A. Arino, J. J. Reuer, K. J. Mayer, & J. Jane, 2014, Contracts, negotiation, and learning: An examination of termination provisions, *Journal of Management Studies*, 51: 379–405; A. Martinez-Noya, E. Garcia-Canal, & M. F. Guillen, 2013, R&D outsourcing and the effectiveness of intangible investments: Is proprietary core knowledge walking out of the door? *Journal of Management Studies*, 50: 67–91.

102. J. Alcacer & J. Oxley, 2014, Learning by supplying, *Strategic Management Journal*, 35: 204–223; S. Sonenshein, 2013, How organizations foster the creative use of resources, *Academy of Management Journal*, 57: 814–848; C. Grimpe & U. Kaiser, 2010, Balancing internal and external knowledge acquisition: The gains and pains from R&D outsourcing, *Journal of Management Studies*, 47: 1483–1509.

103. T. Obloj & P. Zemsky, 2015, Value creation and value capture under moral hazard: Exploring the micro-foundations of buyer-supplier relationships, *Strategic Management Journal*, in press; S. M. Handley, 2012, The perilous effects of capability loss on outsourcing management and performance, *Journal of Operations Management*, 30: 152–165; P. D. O. Jensen & T. Pederson, 2011, The economic geography of offshoring: The fit between activities and local context, *Journal of Management Studies*, 48: 352–372.

104. S. M. Handley & C. M. Angst, 2015, The impact of culture on the relationship between governance and opportunism in outsourcing relationships, *Strategic Management Journal*, in press; M. Kang, X. Wu, P. Hong, & Y. Park, 2012, Aligning organizational control practices with competitive outsourcing performance, *Journal of Business Research*, 65: 1195–1201.

105. M. Taussig & A. Delios, 2015, Unbundling the effects of institutions on firm resources: The contingent value of being local in emerging economy private equity, *Strategic Management Journal*, in press; O. Baumann & N. Stieglitz, 2014, Rewarding value-creating ideas in organizations: The power of low-powered incentives, *Strategic Management Journal*, 35: 358–375.

106. U. Stettner & D. Lavie, 2014, Ambidexterity under scrutiny: Exploration and exploitation via internal organization, alliances, and acquisitions, *Strategic Management Journal*, 35: 1903–1929; E. Rawley, 2010, Diversification, coordination costs, and organizational rigidity: Evidence from microdata, *Strategic Management Journal*, 31: 873–891.

107. D. L. Barton, 1995, *Wellsprings of Knowledge: Building and Sustaining the Sources of Innovation*, Boston: Harvard Business School Press, 30–31.

108. J. Linkner, 2014, Book highlight— Disrupt or be disrupted, *Global Business and Organizational Excellence*, 34: 78–87; J. Milliot, 2013, As e-books grow, so does Amazon, *Publishers Weekly*, February 11, 4.

4

Business-Level Strategy

Studying this chapter should provide you with the strategic management knowledge needed to:

4-1   Define business-level strategy.

4-2   Discuss the relationship between customers and business-level strategies in terms of *who, what,* and *how.*

4-3   Explain the differences among business-level strategies.

4-4   Use the five forces of competition model to explain how above-average returns can be earned through each business-level strategy.

4-5   Describe the risks of using each of the business-level strategies.

HAIN CELESTIAL GROUP: A FIRM FOCUSED ON "ORGANIC" DIFFERENTIATION

This chapter is about a firm's business-level strategy, and what it takes to be successful in creating a strategy that allows a firm to compete successfully in a particular industry or industry segment. Hain Celestial Group is an example of a differentiation strategy at the business level. Differentiation is a business-level strategy that will be defined more clearly in this chapter. Briefly, it allows a firm to be differentiated from its competitors and allows it to build a loyal following of customers. As indicated in Chapter 2, consumers often follow social trends. Hain Celestial Group has built strong capabilities in producing natural and organic foods, and it has built its strategy to take advantage of this changing consumer trend in the food business across a number of related industries: consumer food producers, grocery stores, and restaurants.

Hain Celestial's CEO, Irwin Simon, founded the company in 1983 and it went public in 1993. The company grew through a series of acquisitions of small organic and natural foods producers.

Bob Kresse/Alamy

These acquisitions, as Simon's puts it, are "not GE or Heinz or Campbells' …. Growth is coming from companies like Ell's and BluePrint—entrepreneurial start-ups." The largest acquisition to date was Celestial Seasonings which is a supplier of teas and juices. The effect of these acquisitions has allowed Hain Celestial to become the largest supplier to natural food retailer Whole Foods Markets. BluePrint, the company noted above, is focused on natural juices marketed to consumers to 'clean' their bodies. Brands like Terra vegetable chips, Dream nondairy milk, and Celestial Seasonings tea are household names for the health-oriented shopper and these brands have made Hain Celestial the largest natural foods company in the world.

The natural food trend has allowed Hain Celestial to sell their branded products to traditional grocery store chains, which account for about 60 percent of its U.S. sales. Its brands are also having an impact on sales outside of the United States, representing approximately 40 percent of total revenues in 2014. Their successful acquisition strategy has focused on "buying brands started by someone else" and then "figure out how to grow them from there."

Meanwhile, large branded food firms that have not focused as intensely on this natural segment have experienced earning "indigestion." Branded packaged food producers such as Kellogg's Company (maker of breakfast cereals and foods including Frosted Flakes and Pop-Tarts), Kraft Foods Group (maker of Oscar Meyer deli meats, Maxwell House coffee, and Velveeta cheese), Campbell Soup Company (Campbell's Soup, Pepperidge Farm, and Goldfish snacks), ConAgra Foods, Inc. (maker of Chef Boyardee ravioli, Hunt's ketchup, Marie Callender's pies and snacks, Orville Redenbacher's popcorn, PAM nonstick cooking spray, and Peter Pan peanut butter), J.M. Smucker Company (makers of Smucker's jams and jellies, Pillsbury baking mixes, Crisco shortening, Jif peanut butter, and Folgers coffee), and Mondelēz International, Inc. (maker of Oreo cookies and Cadbury chocolate) only have a peripheral focus on this segment. Their earnings have stalled in part because their brands are not focused on the natural and organic trend desired by consumers as much as Hain Celestial, whose earnings and stock price has climbed much higher on a relative basis. Of course, U.S. main-line brand firms such as those mentioned above have experienced a downturn in earning from the increased value of the dollar, but Hain Celestial also has substantial foreign exposure, as noted above.

To deal with the slump, different strategic approaches have been taken. Smucker's, for example, has moved into pet food through its acquisition of Big Heart Pet Foods (maker of Milk-Bone dog treats and Meow Mix cat food). Others, such as Nestlé (maker of Crunch and Butterfinger candy bars and other chocolates), are removing artificial ingredients such as colors and dyes from candy and chocolate. Hershey Company and Mars, Incorporated, who make up 65 percent of the global markets share in packaged candy, are reducing high fructose corn syrup and increasing the sugar content. Mondelēz is seeking to reduce saturated fats and sodium in its snacks by 10 percent. However, these changes do not allow these firms to overcome the problem of rapidly changing consumer tastes toward nature food.

Grocery stores are also seeking to enter in this natural segment. To compete with Trader Joe's, Whole Foods, and the trend among other supermarkets (such as Kroger and Safeway) who are moving into in this segment, Walmart is introducing a line of low-priced organic foods. Walmart is joining Wild Oats Marketplace (an independent producer in the natural food segment) "to place about 100 organic products into its store" and the "Wild Oats line will be priced 25 percent lower than competing national organic brands." However, Hain Celestial has the more direct strategy and image to take advantage of this trend and sell to those outlets seeking to distribute more natural and organic food products.

This same trend is occurring in restaurants. Chipotle Mexican Grill, Inc. has successfully taken advantage of the trend towards natural foods, while McDonald's is struggling to take advantage of the same trend.

Sources: J. Bacon, 2015, Brands capitalise on health-driven resolutions, *Marketing Week*, www.marketingweek.com, January 29; A. Chen & A. Gasparro, 2015, Smucker's latest food firm hurt by changing tastes, *Wall Street Journal*, February 14–15, B4; A. Gasparro, 2015, Indigestion hits food giants, *Wall Street Journal*, February 13, B1; A. Gasparro, 2015, Nestlé bars artificial color, flavors, *Wall Street Journal*, February 18, B6; M. Esterl, 2015, PepsiCo earnings, revenue drop on foreign-exchange impact. *Wall Street Journal*, www.wsj.com, February 12; L. Light, 2015, How to revive McDonald's, *Wall Street Journal*, www.wsj.com, February 11; M. Alva, 2014, Organic growth comes naturally to Hain Celestial Group, *Investor's Business Daily*, July 24, A5; A. Kingston, 2014, Juice junkies, *Maclean's*, June 30, 64–66; SCTWeek, 2014, Walmart to sell low-price organic food, 2014, *SCTWeek*, April 11, 4.

Increasingly important to firm success, strategy is concerned with making choices among two or more alternatives.[1] As noted in Chapter 1, when choosing a strategy, the firm decides to pursue one course of action instead of others. The choices are influenced by opportunities and threats in the firm's external environment[2] (see Chapter 2) as well as the nature and quality of the resources, capabilities, and core competencies in its internal organization[3] (see Chapter 3). As shown in the Opening Case, Hain Celestial Group has the right capabilities (strong producer of natural and organic food products) matched to an opportunity in the industry environment (strong consumer demand for natural and organic food products) which has made it a formidable competitor producing above-average returns. However, other branded food producers have struggled to meet changing consumer tastes and have realized poorer performance as a result.[4]

In previous chapters, analysis of the external environment and of internal firm resources and capabilities, which is the first step in the strategic management process, was discussed. This chapter is the first on strategy, which is the second part of the strategic management process explained in Chapter 1. The fundamental objective of using any type of strategy (see Figure 1.1) is to gain strategic competitiveness and earn above-average returns.[5] Strategies are purposeful, precede the taking of actions to which they apply, and demonstrate a shared understanding of the firm's vision and mission.[6] An effectively formulated strategy marshals, integrates, and allocates the firm's resources, capabilities, and competencies so that it will be properly aligned with its external environment.[7] A properly developed strategy also rationalizes the firm's vision and mission along with the actions taken to achieve them. Information about a host of variables including markets, customers, technology, worldwide finance, and the changing world economy must be collected and analyzed to properly form and use strategies. In the final analysis, sound strategic choices that reduce uncertainty regarding outcomes are the foundation for building successful strategies.[8]

Business-level strategy, this chapter's focus, indicates the choices the firm has made about how it intends to compete in individual product markets. **Business-level strategy** is an integrated and coordinated set of commitments and actions the firm uses to gain a competitive advantage by exploiting core competencies in specific product markets.[9] The choices are important because long-term performance is linked to a firm's strategies. Given the complexity of successfully competing in the global economy, the choices about how the firm will compete can be difficult.[10] For example, King Digital Entertainment, a video game developer, has done well recently through its "Candy Crush" franchise. The simple concepts of this game series has made it popular among players not typically drawn to traditional video games. It has focused on casual game players rather than on a more dedicated base of gamers. Electronic Arts, Inc. (EA) has focused on the more dedicated game consumers and has developed franchises such as "Call of Duty" and "Madden NFL" and not only has developed this digitally but also into mobile devices. However, Zynga focused on the casual game market and has faced severe declines of its Facebook-based games "FarmVille" and "CityVille." These games also focused on the casual market, and these consumers, as Zynga has discovered, can be fickle. As such, King Digital Entertainment has been seeking to expand beyond the casual game segment for mobile devices and create stronger franchises across many platforms. However, it may be difficult to break into and maintain the loyalty of more dedicated customers as EA has done through its ever more graphic and sophisticated game software.[11]

Every firm must develop and implement a business-level strategy. However, some firms may not use all the strategies—corporate-level, merger and acquisition, international, and cooperative—we examine in Chapters 6 through 9. A firm competing in a single-product market in a single geographic location does not need a corporate-level strategy regarding product diversity or an international strategy to deal with geographic diversity. In contrast, a diversified firm will use one of the corporate-level strategies as well as a separate business-level strategy for each product market in which it competes. Every firm—ranging from the local dry cleaner to the multinational corporation—must develop and use at least one business-level strategy. Thus business-level strategy is the *core* strategy—the strategy that the firm forms to describe how it intends to compete in a product market.[12]

We discuss several topics to examine business-level strategies. Because customers are the foundation of successful business-level strategies and should never be taken for granted,[13] we present information about customers that is relevant to business-level strategies. In terms of customers, when selecting a business-level strategy the firm determines

1. *who* will be served,
2. *what* needs those target customers have that it will satisfy, and
3. *how* those needs will be satisfied.

Selecting customers and deciding which of their needs the firm will try to satisfy, as well as how it will do so, are challenging tasks. Global competition has created many attractive options for customers, thus making it difficult to determine the strategy to best serve them.[14] Effective global competitors have become adept at identifying the needs of customers in different cultures and geographic regions as well as learning how to quickly and successfully adapt the functionality of a firm's good or service to meet those needs.

A **business-level strategy** is an integrated and coordinated set of commitments and actions the firm uses to gain a competitive advantage by exploiting core competencies in specific product markets.

Descriptions of the purpose of business-level strategies—and of the five business-level strategies—follow the discussion of customers. The five strategies we examine are called *generic* because they can be used in any organization competing in any industry.[15] Our analysis describes how effective use of each strategy allows the firm to favorably position itself relative to the five competitive forces in the industry (see Chapter 2). In addition, we use the value chain (see Chapter 3) to show examples of the primary and support activities necessary to implement specific business-level strategies. Because no strategy is risk-free,[16] we also describe the different risks the firm may encounter when using these strategies. In Chapter 11, we explain the organizational structures and controls linked with the successful use of each business-level strategy.

4-1   Customers: Their Relationship with Business-Level Strategies

Strategic competitiveness results only when the firm satisfies a group of customers by using its competitive advantages as the basis for competing in individual product markets.[17] A key reason firms must satisfy customers with their business-level strategy is that returns earned from relationships with customers are the lifeblood of all organizations.[18]

The most successful companies try to find new ways to satisfy current customers and/or to meet the needs of new customers. Being able to do this can be even more difficult when firms and consumers face challenging economic conditions. During such times, firms may decide to reduce their workforce to control costs. This can lead to problems, however, because having fewer employees makes it more difficult for companies to meet individual customers' needs and expectations. In these instances, firms can follow several possible courses of action, including paying extra attention to their best customers and developing a flexible workforce by cross-training employees so they can undertake a variety of responsibilities on their jobs.

4-1a   Effectively Managing Relationships with Customers

The firm's relationships with its customers are strengthened when it delivers superior value to them. Strong interactive relationships with customers often provide the foundation for the firm's efforts to profitably serve customers' unique needs.

Importantly, delivering superior value often results in increased customer satisfaction. In turn, customer satisfaction has a positive relationship with profitability because satisfied customers are most likely to be repeat customers. However, more choices and easily accessible information about the functionality of the firms' products are creating increasingly sophisticated and knowledgeable customers, making it difficult to earn their loyalty. As such, many firms are working with customers to co-create value through working closely together to ensure customer satisfaction.[19]

A number of companies have become skilled at the art of *managing* all aspects of their relationship with their customers.[20] For example, Amazon.com, Inc. is widely

Customers standing in a grocery store checkout line. Successful business strategies satisfy customers' needs.

Rubberball/Mike Kemp/Getty Images

recognized for the quality of information it maintains about its customers, the services it renders, and its ability to anticipate customers' needs. Using the information it has, Amazon tries to serve what it believes are the unique needs of each customer; and it has a strong reputation for being able to do this successfully.[21]

As we discuss next, firms' relationships with customers are characterized by three dimensions. Companies such as Acer Inc. and Amazon understand these dimensions and manage their relationships with customers in light of them.

4-1b Reach, Richness, and Affiliation

The *reach* dimension of relationships with customers is concerned with the firm's access and connection to customers. In general, firms seek to extend their reach, adding customers in the process of doing so.

Reach is an especially critical dimension for social networking sites such as Facebook and MySpace in that the value these firms create for users is to connect them with others. Traffic to MySpace has been declining in recent years; at the same time, the number of Facebook users has been dramatically increasing in the United States and abroad. Reach is also important to Netflix, Inc. Although its user base is still growing in the United States, its growth rate has slowed. However, streaming video customers in foreign markets grew faster than expected. When this was announced, their stock price increased 16 percent in after-hours trading. Netflix plans to expand to over 200 countries by 2017, up from its 50 in 2014.[22]

Richness, the second dimension of firms' relationships with customers, is concerned with the depth and detail of the two-way flow of information between the firm and the customer. The potential of the richness dimension to help the firm establish a competitive advantage in its relationship with customers leads many firms to offer online services in order to better manage information exchanges with their customers. Broader and deeper information-based exchanges allow firms to better understand their customers and their needs. Such exchanges also enable customers to become more knowledgeable about how the firm can satisfy them. Internet technology and e-commerce transactions have substantially reduced the costs of meaningful information exchanges with current and potential customers. As we have noted, Amazon is a leader in using the Internet to build relationships with customers. In fact, it bills itself as the most "customer-centric company" on earth. Amazon and other firms use rich information from customers to help them develop innovative new products that better satisfy customers' needs.[23]

Affiliation, the third dimension, is concerned with facilitating useful interactions with customers. Viewing the world through the customer's eyes and constantly seeking ways to create more value for the customer have positive effects in terms of affiliation.[24] This approach enhances customer satisfaction and produces fewer customer complaints. In fact, for services, customers often do not complain when dissatisfied; instead they simply go to competitors for their service needs, although a firm's strong brand can mitigate the switching.[25] Tesco, the largest retail grocer in the United Kingdom, as well as other firms have changed the title of its lead marketing officer to "Chief Customer Officer." This suggests the importance of the customer to most businesses, especially those focused on consumers. Likewise, because of data available through digitization, firms have a tremendous amount of individual customer data, and this data-gathering trend is growing, allowing firms to customize their products and services.[26]

As we discuss next, effectively managing customer relationships (along the dimensions of reach, richness, and affiliation) helps the firm answer questions related to the issues of *who, what,* and *how.*

4-1c Who: Determining the Customers to Serve

Deciding *who* the target customer is that the firm intends to serve with its business-level strategy is an important decision.[27] Companies divide customers into groups based on differences in the customers' needs (needs are discussed further in the next section) to make this decision. Dividing customers into groups based on their needs is called **market segmentation**. Market segmentation is a process used to cluster people with similar needs into individual and identifiable groups.[28] In the animal food products business, for example, the food-product needs of owners of companion pets (e.g., dogs and cats) differ from the needs for food and health-related products of those owning production animals (e.g., livestock). A subsidiary of Colgate-Palmolive Company, Hill's Pet Nutrition, sells food products for pets. In fact, the company's mission is "to help enrich and lengthen the special relationship between people and their pets."[29] Thus, Hill's Pet Nutrition targets the needs of different segments of customers with the food products it sells for animals.

Almost any identifiable human or organizational characteristic can be used to subdivide a market into segments that differ from one another on a given characteristic. Common characteristics on which customers' needs vary are illustrated in Table 4.1.

4-1d What: Determining Which Customer Needs to Satisfy

After the firm decides *who* it will serve, it must identify the targeted customer group's needs that its goods or services can satisfy. In a general sense, *needs (what)* are related to a product's benefits and features. Successful firms learn how to deliver to customers what they want, when they want it. Having close and frequent interactions with both current and potential customers helps the firm identify those individuals' and groups' current and future needs. Target, a retail store and online marketer, has been successful with analyzing its many sources of data and customizing its information for in store and online "guests." It has available data, through online sources, of many customer demographics (age, marital status, income category, etc.) as well as shopping frequency, products purchased, and geographic distance from local stores. It utilizes this information to develop is promotion and marketing strategies.[30]

From a strategic perspective, a basic need of all customers is to buy products that create value for them. The generalized forms of value that goods or services provide are either low cost with acceptable features or highly differentiated features with acceptable cost. The most effective firms continuously strive to anticipate changes in customers' needs. The firm that fails to anticipate and certainly to recognize changes in its customers' needs

Market segmentation is a process used to cluster people with similar needs into individual and identifiable groups.

Table 4.1 Basis for Customer Segmentation

Consumer Markets
1. Demographic factors (age, income, sex, etc.)
2. Socioeconomic factors (social class, stage in the family life cycle)
3. Geographic factors (cultural, regional, and national differences)
4. Psychological factors (lifestyle, personality traits)
5. Consumption patterns (heavy, moderate, and light users)
6. Perceptual factors (benefit segmentation, perceptual mapping)

Industrial Markets
1. End-use segments (identified by Standard Industrial Classification [SIC] code)
2. Product segments (based on technological differences or production economics)
3. Geographic segments (defined by boundaries between countries or by regional differences within them)
4. Common buying factor segments (cut across product market and geographic segments)
5. Customer size segments

Source: Based on information in S. C. Jain, 2009, *Marketing Planning and Strategy*, Mason, OH: South-Western Cengage Custom Publishing.

may lose its customers to competitors whose products can provide more value to the focal firm's customers. It is also recognized that consumer needs and desires have been changing in recent years. For example, more consumers desire to have an experience rather than to simply purchase a good or service. As a result, one of Starbucks' goals has been to provide an experience, not just a cup of coffee. Customers also prefer to receive customized goods and services. Again, Starbucks has been doing this for some time, allowing customers to design their own drinks, within their menus (which have become rather extensive over time).

Customers also demand fast service. Chipotle Mexican Grill, as noted in the Opening Case, is a leader in the fast-casual dining segment catering to the millennial generation. This fast-casual segment, including Chipotle, Panera Bread, Five Guys Burgers and Fries, Panda Express, and others, has been increasing their presence, as well as growth per outlet, compared to McDonald's who has had a difficult time maintaining a level playing field against the fast-casual service speed and per outlet growth. Also, one observer noted: "A decade ago, there were 9,000 fast-casual restaurants in the U.S., versus nearly 14,000 McDonald's. Now, fast-casual restaurants number more than 21,000 … while McDonald's U.S. restaurant count has risen only slightly."[31] Unhappy consumers lead to lost sales—both theirs and those of others who learn of their dissatisfaction. Therefore, it is important to maintain customer satisfaction by meeting and satisfying their needs.[32]

4-1e How: Determining Core Competencies Necessary to Satisfy Customer Needs

After deciding *who* the firm will serve and the specific *needs* of those customers, the firm is prepared to determine how to use its capabilities and competencies to develop products that can satisfy the needs of its target customers. As explained in Chapters 1 and 3, *core competencies* are resources and capabilities that serve as a source of competitive advantage for the firm over its rivals. Firms use core competencies (*how*) to implement value-creating strategies, thereby satisfying customers' needs. Only those firms with the capacity to continuously improve, innovate, and upgrade their competencies can expect to meet and hopefully exceed customers' expectations across time.[33] Firms must continuously upgrade their capabilities to ensure that they maintain the advantage over their rivals by providing customers with a superior product.[34] Often these capabilities are difficult for competitors to imitate, partly because they are constantly being upgraded, but also because they are integrated and used as configurations of capabilities to perform an important activity (e.g., R&D).[35]

Companies draw from a wide range of core competencies to produce goods or services that can satisfy customers' needs. For example, Merck & Co., Inc. is a large pharmaceutical firm well-known for its research and development (R&D) capabilities. In recent times, Merck has been building on these capabilities by investing heavily in R&D. The new drugs Merck intends to produce are directed at meeting the needs of consumers and to sustain Merck's competitive advantage in the industry.[36]

SAS Institute Inc. is the world's largest, privately owned software company and is the leader in business intelligence and analytics. Customers use SAS programs for data warehousing, data mining, and decision support purposes. SAS serves 60,000 sites in 139 countries and serves 93 percent of the top *Fortune* 100 firms. Allocating approximately 23 percent of revenues to R&D in 2014, a percentage exceeding those allocated by its competitors, SAS relies on its core competence in R&D to satisfy the data-related needs of such customers as the U.S. Census Bureau and a host of consumer goods firms (e.g., hotels, banks, and catalog companies).[37]

Many types of firms now emphasize innovation, not only those in high technology industries. This innovation appears to be driven by customers, along with providing a product or service that satisfies their customers' needs in a manner superior to that of rivals' products or services to gain or sustain a competitive advantage. For example, L'Oréal has gained competitive advantages due to their innovations in cosmetic and beauty products. The Executive Vice President of L'Oréal in the United States, Frédéric Rozé, noted: "At the end of the day, our success comes from our capacity to transform ourselves, to metamorphose ourselves,"[38]

Our discussion about customers shows that all organizations must use their capabilities and core competencies (the *how*) to satisfy the needs (the *what*) of the target group of customers (the *who*) the firm has chosen to serve. Next, we describe the different business-level strategies that are available to firms to use to satisfy customers as the foundation for earning above-average returns.

4-2   The Purpose of a Business-Level Strategy

The purpose of a business-level strategy is to create differences between the firm's position and those of its competitors.[39] To position itself differently from competitors, a firm must decide whether it intends to *perform activities differently* or to *perform different activities*. Strategy defines the path which provides the direction of actions to be taken by leaders of the organization.[40] In fact, "choosing to perform activities differently or to perform different activities than rivals" is the essence of business-level strategy.[41] Thus, the firm's business-level strategy is a deliberate choice about how it will perform the value chain's primary and support activities to create unique value. Indeed, in the current complex competitive landscape, successful use of a business-level strategy results from the firm learning how to integrate the activities it performs in ways that create superior value for customers.

The manner in which Southwest Airlines Co. has integrated its activities is the foundation for the successful use of its primary cost leadership strategy (this strategy is discussed later in the chapter) but also includes differentiation through the unique services provided to customers. The tight integration among Southwest's activities is a key source of the firm's ability, historically, to operate more profitably than its competitors.

Southwest Airlines has configured the activities it performs into six areas of strategic intent—limited passenger service; frequent, reliable departures; lean, highly productive ground and gate crews; high aircraft utilization with few aircraft models; very low ticket prices; and short-haul, point-to-point routes between mid-sized cities and secondary airports. Individual clusters of tightly linked activities make it possible to achieve its strategic intent. For example, no meals, no seat assignments, and no baggage transfers form a cluster of individual activities that support the strategic intent to offer limited passenger service.

Southwest's tightly integrated activities make it difficult for competitors to imitate the firm's cost leadership strategy. The firm's unique culture and customer service are sources of competitive advantage that rivals have been unable to imitate, although some have tried and largely failed (e.g., US Airways' MetroJet subsidiary, United Airlines' Shuttle by United, Delta's Song, and Continental Airlines' Continental Lite). Hindsight shows that these competitors offered low prices to customers, but weren't able to operate at costs close to those of Southwest or to provide customers with any notable sources of differentiation, such as a unique experience while in the air. The key to Southwest's success has been its ability to continuously maintain low costs while providing customers with *acceptable* levels of differentiation such as an engaging culture. Firms using the cost leadership strategy must understand that in terms of sources of differentiation accompanying the cost leader's product, the customer defines *acceptable*. Fit among activities is a key to the sustainability of competitive advantage for all firms, including Southwest Airlines. Strategic fit among the many activities is critical for competitive advantage. It is more difficult for a competitor to match a configuration of integrated activities than to imitate a particular activity such as sales promotion, or a process technology.[42]

4-3 Types of Business-Level Strategies

Firms choose between five business-level strategies to establish and defend their desired strategic position against competitors: *cost leadership, differentiation, focused cost leadership, focused differentiation*, and *integrated cost leadership/differentiation* (see Figure 4.1). Each business-level strategy can help the firm to establish and exploit a particular *competitive advantage* within a particular *competitive scope*. How firms integrate the activities they perform within each different business-level strategy demonstrates how they differ from one another.[43] For example, firms have different activity maps, and thus, a Southwest Airlines activity map differs from those of competitors JetBlue, United Airlines, American Airlines, and so forth. Superior integration of activities increases the likelihood of being able to gain an advantage over competitors and to earn above-average returns.

When selecting a business-level strategy, firms evaluate two types of potential competitive advantages: "lower cost than rivals or the ability to differentiate and command a premium price that exceeds the extra cost of doing so."[44] Having lower costs results from the firm's ability to perform activities differently than rivals; being able to differentiate indicates the firm's capacity to perform different (and valuable) activities. Thus, based on the nature and quality of its internal resources, capabilities, and core competencies, a firm seeks to form either a cost competitive advantage or a distinctiveness competitive advantage as the basis for implementing its business-level strategy.[45]

Figure 4.1 Five Business-Level Strategies

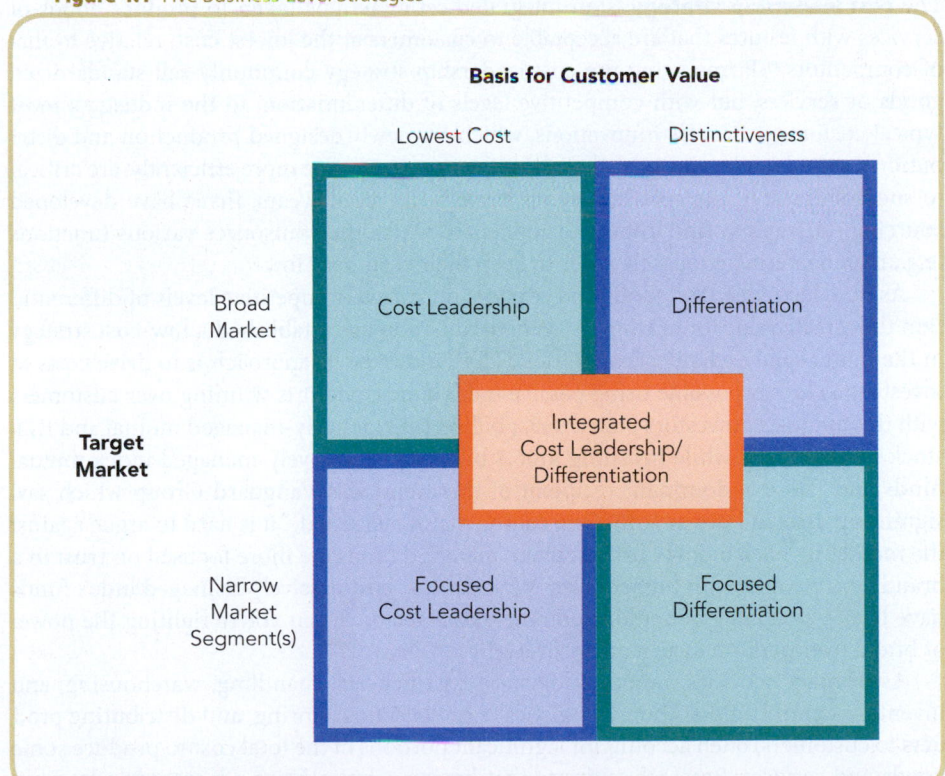

Source: Based on M. E. Porter, 1998, *Competitive Advantage: Creating and Sustaining Superior Performance*, New York: The Free Press; D. G. Sirmon, M. A. Hitt, & R. D. Ireland, 2007, Managing firm resources in dynamic environments to create value: Looking inside the black box, *Academy of Management Review*, 32: 273–292; D. G. Sirmon, M. A. Hitt, R. D. Ireland, & B. A. Gilbert, 2011, Resource orchestration to create competitive advantage: Breadth, depth and life cycles effects, *Journal of Management*, 37: 1390–1412.

Two types of target markets are broad market and narrow market segment(s) (see Figure 4.1). Firms serving a broad market seek to use their capabilities to create value for customers on an industry-wide basis. A narrow market segment means that the firm intends to serve the needs of a narrow customer group. With focus strategies, the firm "selects a segment or group of segments in the industry and tailors its strategy to serving them to the exclusion of others."[46] Buyers with special needs and buyers located in specific geographic regions are examples of narrow customer groups. As shown in Figure 4.1, a firm could also strive to develop a combined low cost/ distinctiveness value creation approach as the foundation for serving a target customer group that is larger than a narrow market segment but not as comprehensive as a broad (or industry-wide) customer group. In this instance, the firm uses the integrated cost leadership/differentiation strategy.

None of the five business-level strategies shown in Figure 4.1 is inherently or universally superior to the others.[47] The effectiveness of each strategy is contingent both on the opportunities and threats in a firm's external environment and on the strengths and weaknesses derived from the firm's resource portfolio. It is critical, therefore, for the firm to select a business-level strategy that represents an effective match between the opportunities and threats in its external environment and the strengths of its internal organization based on its core competencies.[48] After the firm chooses its strategy, it should consistently emphasize actions that are required to successfully use it.

4-3a   Cost Leadership Strategy

The **cost leadership strategy** is an integrated set of actions taken to produce goods or services with features that are acceptable to customers at the lowest cost, relative to that of competitors.[49] Firms using the cost leadership strategy commonly sell standardized goods or services, but with competitive levels of differentiation, to the industry's most typical customers. Process innovations, which are newly designed production and distribution methods and techniques that allow the firm to operate more efficiently, are critical to successful use of the cost leadership strategy. In recent years, firms have developed sourcing strategies to find low-cost suppliers to which they outsource various functions (e.g., manufacturing goods) in order to keep their costs very low.[50]

As noted, cost leaders' goods and services must have competitive levels of differentiation that create value for customers. Vanguard Group has established a low-cost strategy in the mutual and exchange traded fund (ETF) industry. Its approach is to drive costs to investors as low as possible using passive index funds, and it is winning over customers with this approach. Investors pulled $98.4 billion from actively-managed mutual and ETF stock funds in 2014 while investing $166.8 billion into passively-managed index mutual funds and ETFs. A dominant recipient of this trend was Vanguard Group which saw significant asset inflows in 2014. One commentator suggested, "it is hard to argue against the marketing pitch of low-cost." Actively-managed funds are more focused on trust in a brand which comes with higher costs. Whereas low-cost passively-managed index funds have been performing better, one commentator noted, "when you're fighting the power of brand over performance, it's a hard slog."[51]

As primary activities, inbound logistics (e.g., materials handling, warehousing, and inventory control) and outbound logistics (e.g., collecting, storing, and distributing products to customers) often account for significant portions of the total cost to produce some goods and services. Research suggests that having a competitive advantage in logistics creates more value with a cost leadership strategy than with a differentiation strategy.[52] Thus, cost leaders seeking competitively valuable ways to reduce costs may want to concentrate on the primary activities of inbound logistics and outbound logistics. In so doing, many firms choose to outsource their manufacturing operations to low-cost firms with

The **cost leadership strategy** is an integrated set of actions taken to produce goods or services with features that are acceptable to customers at the lowest cost, relative to that of competitors.

low-wage employees (e.g., China).[53] However, care must be taken because outsourcing also makes the firm more dependent on supplier firms over which they have little control. Outsourcing creates interdependencies between the outsourcing firm and the suppliers. If dependencies become too great, it gives the supplier more power with which the supplier may increase prices of the goods and services provided. Such actions could harm the firm's ability to maintain a low-cost competitive advantage.[54]

Cost leaders also carefully examine all support activities to find additional potential cost reductions. Developing new systems for finding the optimal combination of low cost and acceptable levels of differentiation in the raw materials required to produce the firm's goods or services is an example of how the procurement support activity can facilitate successful use of the cost leadership strategy.

Big Lots, Inc. uses the cost leadership strategy. With its vision of being "The World's Best Bargain Place," Big Lots is the largest closeout retailer in the United States with annual sales approaching $5 billion from more than 1,400 stores. For Big Lots, closeout goods are brand-name products from 3,000 manufacturers provided for sale at substantially lower prices than sold by other retailers.[55]

As described in Chapter 3, firms use value-chain analysis to identify the parts of the company's operations that create value and those that do not. Figure 4.2 demonstrates

Figure 4.2 Examples of Value-Creating Activities Associated with the Cost Leadership Strategy

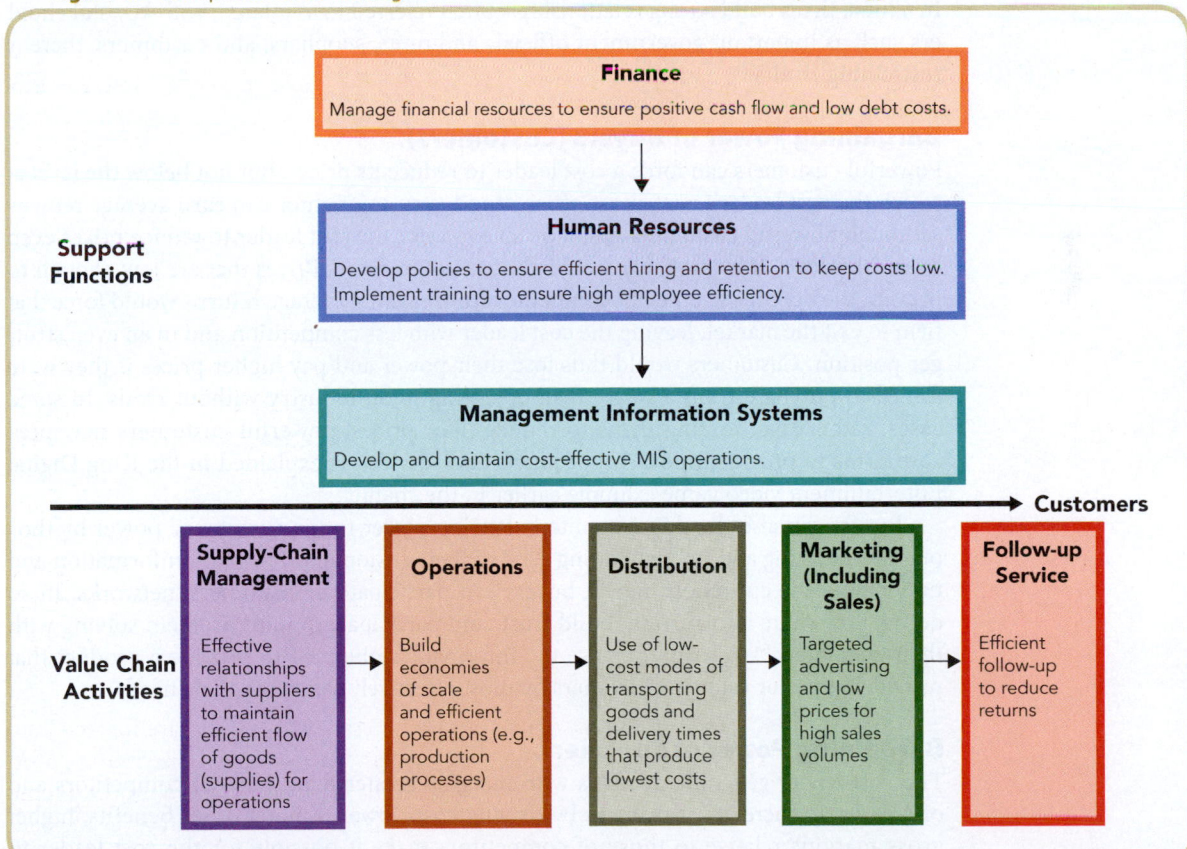

Source: Based on M. E. Porter, 1998, *Competitive Advantage: Creating and Sustaining Superior Performance*, New York: The Free Press; D. G. Sirmon, M. A. Hitt, & R. D. Ireland, 2007, Managing firm resources in dynamic environments to create value: Looking inside the black box, *Academy of Management Review*, 32: 273–292; D. G. Sirmon, M. A. Hitt, R. D. Ireland, & B. A. Gilbert, 2011, Resource orchestration to create competitive advantage: Breadth, depth and life cycles effects, *Journal of Management*, 37: 1390–1412.

the value-chain activities and support functions that allow a firm to create value through the cost leadership strategy. Companies unable to effectively integrate the activities and functions shown in this figure typically lack the core competencies needed to successfully use the cost leadership strategy.

Effective use of the cost leadership strategy allows a firm to earn above-average returns in spite of the presence of strong competitive forces (see Chapter 2). The next sections (one for each of the five forces) explain how firms implement a cost leadership strategy.

Rivalry with Existing Competitors

Having the low-cost position is valuable when dealing with rivals. Because of the cost leader's advantageous position, rivals hesitate to compete on the basis of price, especially before evaluating the potential outcomes of such competition.[56] The changes Walmart made to attract upscale customers created vulnerability in its low-cost position to rivals. Amazon, Family Dollar, and others took advantage of the opportunity. Amazon appears to have become a low-cost leader, and the Family Dollar stores provide low costs and easy access for customers. Both of these rivals have siphoned off some of Walmart's customers.

The degree of rivalry present is based on a number of different factors such as size and resources of rivals, their dependence on the particular market, and location and prior competitive interactions, among others.[57] Firms may also take actions to reduce the amount of rivalry that they face. For example, firms sometimes form joint ventures to reduce rivalry and increase the amount of profitability enjoyed by firms in the industry.[58] In China, firms build strong relationships, often referred to as guanxi, with key stakeholders such as important government officials and units, suppliers, and customers, thereby restraining rivalry.[59]

Bargaining Power of Buyers (Customers)

Powerful customers can force a cost leader to reduce its prices, but not below the level at which the cost leader's next-most-efficient industry competitor can earn average returns. Although powerful customers might be able to force the cost leader to reduce prices even below this level, they probably would choose not to do so. Prices that are low enough to prevent the next-most-efficient competitor from earning average returns would force that firm to exit the market, leaving the cost leader with less competition and in an even stronger position. Customers would thus lose their power and pay higher prices if they were forced to purchase from a single firm operating in an industry without rivals. In some cases, rather than forcing firms to reduce their prices, powerful customers may pressure firms to provide innovative products and services as explained in the King Digital Entertainment video game example earlier in the chapter.

Buyers can also develop a counterbalancing power to the customers' power by thoroughly analyzing and understanding each of their customers. To obtain information and understand the customers' needs, buyers can participate in customers' networks. In so doing, they share information, build trust, and participate in joint problem solving with their customers.[60] In turn, they use the information obtained to provide a product that provides superior value to customers by most effectively satisfying their needs.

Bargaining Power of Suppliers

The cost leader generally operates with margins greater than those of competitors and often tries to increase its margins by driving costs lower. Among other benefits, higher gross margins relative to those of competitors make it possible for the cost leader to absorb its suppliers' price increases. When an industry faces substantial increases in the cost of its supplies, only the cost leader may be able to pay the higher prices and continue to earn either average or above-average returns. Alternatively, a powerful cost leader may be able to force its suppliers to hold down their prices, which would reduce the suppliers' margins in the process. Walmart lost its way in this regard. By reducing the number and type of products sold in Walmart stores, it reduced its bargaining power with several suppliers. In so doing, it was unable to gain the best (lowest) prices on goods relative to its competitors. Thus, Amazon and the Dollar Stores began winning market share from Walmart by offering lower prices.

The fact remains that Walmart is the largest retailer in North America, thus giving the firm a great deal of power with its suppliers. Walmart is the largest supermarket operator in the United States, and its Sam's Club division is the second largest warehouse club in the United States. Collectively, its sales volume of approximately $485.7 billion in fiscal 2014 and the market penetration (more than 200 million people visit one of Walmart's 11,000 stores each week) still allow Walmart to obtain low prices from its suppliers.[61]

Some firms create dependencies on suppliers by outsourcing whole functions. They do so to reduce their overall costs.[62] They may outsource these activities to reduce their costs because of earnings pressures from stakeholders (e.g., institutional investors who own a major stock holding in the company) in the industry.[63] However, "outsourcing can create new costs, as suppliers and partners demand a larger share of the value created."[64] Often when there is such earnings pressure, the firm may see foreign suppliers whose costs are also lower, providing them the capability to offer the goods at lower prices.[65] Yet, when firms outsource, particularly to a foreign supplier, they also need to invest time and effort into building a good relationship, hopefully developing trust between the firms. Such efforts facilitate the integration of the supplier into the firm's value chain.[66]

Potential Entrants

Through continuous efforts to reduce costs to levels that are lower than competitors, a cost leader becomes highly efficient. Because increasing levels of efficiency (e.g., economies of scale) enhance profit margins, they serve as a significant entry barrier to potential competitors.[67] New entrants must be willing to accept less than average returns until they gain the experience required to approach the cost leader's efficiency. To earn even average returns, new entrants must have the competencies required to match the cost levels of competitors other than the cost leader. The low profit margins (relative to margins earned by firms implementing the differentiation strategy) make it necessary for the cost leader to sell large volumes of its product to earn above-average returns. However, firms striving to be the cost leader must avoid pricing their products so low that they cannot operate profitably, even though volume increases.

Product Substitutes

Compared with its industry rivals, the cost leader also holds an attractive position relative to product substitutes. A product substitute becomes a concern for the cost leader when its features and characteristics, in terms of cost and differentiation, are potentially attractive to the firm's customers. When faced with possible substitutes, the cost leader has more flexibility than its competitors. To retain customers, it often can reduce the price of its good or service. With still lower prices and competitive levels of differentiation, the cost leader increases the probability that customers prefer its product rather than a substitute.

Competitive Risks of the Cost Leadership Strategy

The cost leadership strategy is not risk free. One risk is that the processes used by the cost leader to produce and distribute its good or service could become obsolete because of competitors' innovations.[68] These innovations may allow rivals to produce goods or services at costs lower than those of the original cost leader, or to provide additional differentiated features without increasing the product's price to customers.

A second risk is that too much focus by the cost leader on cost reductions may occur at the expense of trying to understand customers' perceptions of "competitive levels of differentiation." Walmart, for example, has been criticized for having too few salespeople available to help customers and too few individuals at checkout registers. These complaints suggest that there might be a discrepancy between how Walmart's customers define "minimal acceptable levels of service" and the firm's attempts to drive its costs increasingly lower.

Imitation is a final risk of the cost leadership strategy. Using their own core competencies, competitors sometimes learn how to successfully imitate the cost leader's strategy. When this happens, the cost leader must increase the value its good or service provides to customers. Commonly, value is increased by selling the current product at an even lower price or by adding differentiated features that create value for customers while maintaining price.

4-3b Differentiation Strategy

The **differentiation strategy** is an integrated set of actions taken to produce goods or services (at an acceptable cost) that customers perceive as being different in ways that are important to them.[69] While cost leaders serve a typical customer in an industry, differentiators target customers for whom value is created by the manner in which the firm's products differ from those produced and marketed by competitors. Product innovation, which is "the result of bringing to life a new way to solve the customer's problem—through a new product or service development—that benefits both the customer and the sponsoring company,"[70] is critical to successful use of the differentiation strategy.[71]

Firms must be able to produce differentiated products at competitive costs to reduce upward pressure on the price that customers pay. When a product's differentiated features are produced at noncompetitive costs, the price for the product may exceed what the firm's target customers are willing to pay. If the firm has a thorough understanding of what its target customers value, the relative importance they attach to the satisfaction of different needs and for what they are willing to pay a premium, the differentiation strategy can be effective in helping it earn above-average returns. Of course, to achieve these returns, the firm must apply its knowledge capital (knowledge held by its employees and managers) to provide customers with a differentiated product that provides them with superior value.[72]

Through the differentiation strategy, the firm produces distinctive products for customers who value differentiated features more than they value low cost. For example, superior product reliability, durability and high-performance sound systems are among the differentiated features of Toyota Motor Corporation's Lexus products. However, Lexus offers its vehicles to customers at a competitive purchase price relative to other luxury automobiles. As with Lexus products, a product's unique attributes, rather than its purchase price, provide the value for which customers are willing to pay.

To maintain success with the differentiation strategy results, the firm must consistently upgrade differentiated features that customers value and/or create new valuable features (i.e., innovate) without significant cost increases.[73] This approach requires firms to constantly change their product lines.[74] These firms may also offer a portfolio of products that complement each other, thereby enriching the differentiation for the customer and perhaps satisfying a portfolio of consumer needs.[75] Because a differentiated product satisfies customers' unique needs, firms following the differentiation strategy are able to charge premium prices. The ability to sell a good or service at a price that substantially exceeds the cost of creating its differentiated features allows the firm to outperform rivals and earn above-average returns. Rather than costs, a firm using the differentiation strategy primarily concentrates on investing in and developing features that differentiate a product in ways that create

The **differentiation strategy** is an integrated set of actions taken to produce goods or services (at an acceptable cost) that customers perceive as being different in ways that are important to them.

value for customers.[76] Overall, a firm using the differentiation strategy seeks to be different from its competitors on as many dimensions as possible. The less similarity between a firm's goods or services and those of its competitors, the more buffered it is from rivals' actions. Commonly recognized differentiated goods include Toyota's Lexus, Ralph Lauren's wide array of product lines, Caterpillar's heavy-duty earth-moving equipment, and McKinsey & Co.'s differentiated consulting services.

Under Armour, Inc. is a fitness apparel company which concentrates on high-tech exercise gear for both on consumer and professional markets. It recently surpassed Adidas to become the number two sportswear apparel brand in the United States by retail sales. Although it remains far behind Nike, which has long held the lead, Under Armour has continued its strong growth by pursuing

Bernhard Lang/fortune.com

Under Armour, a company in fitness apparel, has specialized in the strong knowledge of its base customer. To re-enforce this focus it has been purchasing fitness apps such as MyFitnessPal.

a differentiation strategy. It has built an even stronger knowledge of its consumer base by purchasing the nutrition and exercise tracking platforms MyFitnessPal and Endomondo. MyFitnessPal has 120 million users (mostly in the United States), while Endomondo has 80 million users (mostly in Europe). In the 2015 Consumer Electronics Show in Las Vegas, Under Armour unveiled UA Record, "a dashboard under which it hopes to unite its digital resources." Although the acquisitions will continue to be operated separately, they will help Under Armour in "developing a digital ecosystem which provides unparalleled data" on potential customers. Through this information, it can further customize products for those who are drawn to its brand.[77]

A good or service can be differentiated in many ways. Unusual features, responsive customer service, rapid product innovations and technological leadership, perceived prestige and status, different tastes, and engineering design and performance are examples of approaches to differentiation.[78] While the number of ways to reduce costs may be finite, virtually anything a firm can do to create real or perceived value is a basis for differentiation. Consider product design as a case in point. Because it can create a positive experience for customers, design is an important source of differentiation (even for cost leaders seeking to find ways to add functionalities to their low-cost products as a way of differentiating their products from competitors) and, hopefully, for firms emphasizing it, of competitive advantage.[79] Apple is often cited as the firm that sets the standard in design, with the iPod, iPhone, and iPad demonstrating Apple's product design capabilities. Apple's extremely successful new product launches and market share captured with them has invited competition, the most significant of which is Samsung. As described in Chapter 3, Samsung has some strong capabilities and thus has become a formidable competitor. Although it largely imitates Apple's products, it also improves on them by adding features attractive to customers (i.e., imperfect imitation).[80] Therefore, Samsung is partially differentiating from Apple's unique (differentiated) products.

The value chain can be analyzed to determine if a firm is able to link the activities required to create value by using the differentiation strategy. Examples of value chain activities and support functions that are commonly used to differentiate a good or service are shown in Figure 4.3. Companies without the skills needed to link these activities

Figure 4.3 Examples of Value-Creating Activities Associated with the Differentiation Strategy

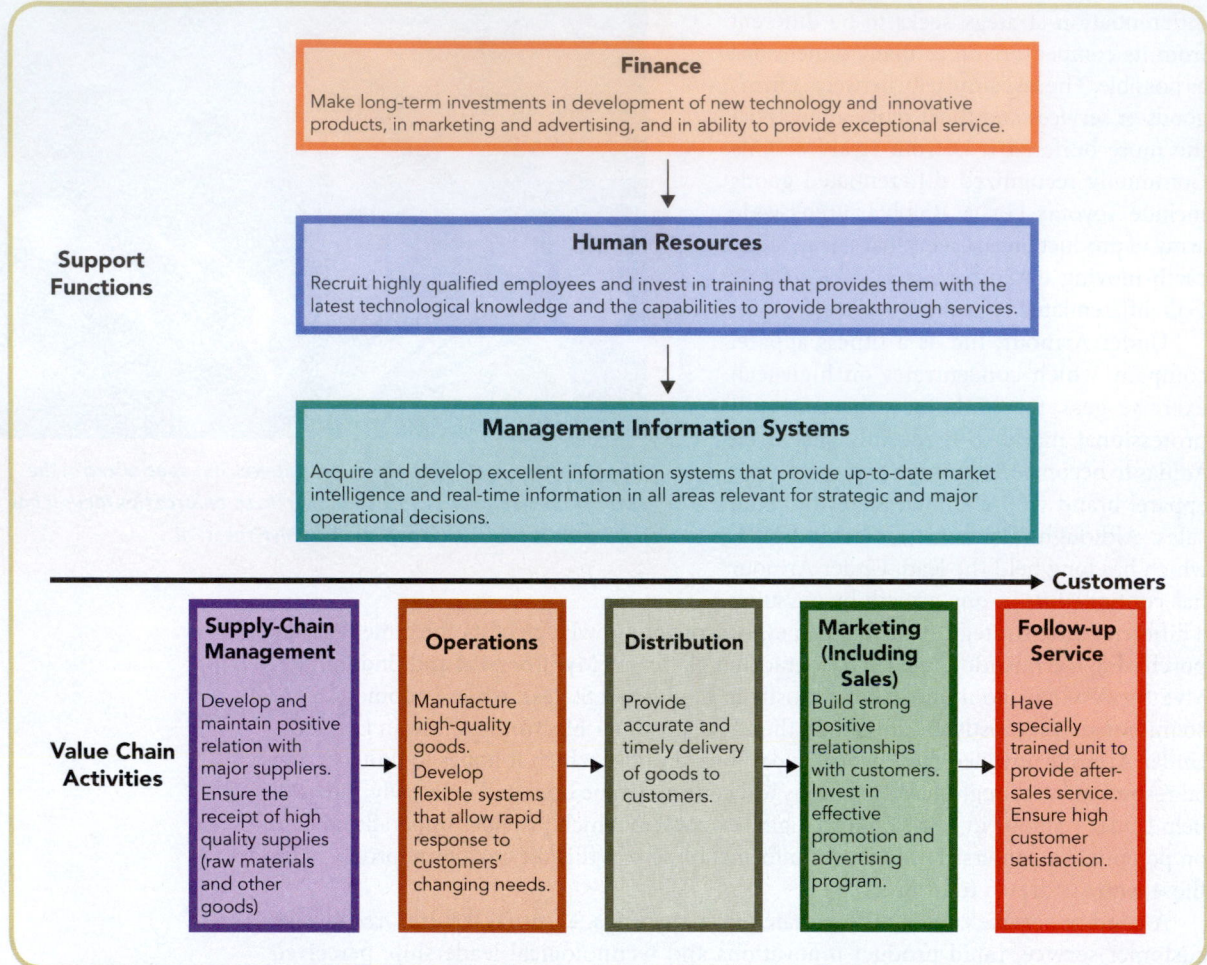

Source: Based on information from M. E. Porter, 1998, *Competitive Advantage: Creating and Sustaining Superior Performance*, New York: The Free Press; D. G. Sirmon, M. A. Hitt, & R. D. Ireland, 2007, Managing firm resources in dynamic environments to create value: Looking inside the black box, *Academy of Management Review*, 32: 273–292; D. G. Sirmon, M. A. Hitt, R. D. Ireland, & B. A. Gilbert, 2011, Resource orchestration to create competitive advantage: Breadth, depth and life cycles effects, *Journal of Management*, 37: 1390–1412.

cannot expect to successfully use the differentiation strategy. Next, we explain how firms using the differentiation strategy can successfully position themselves in terms of the five forces of competition (see Chapter 2) to earn above-average returns.

Rivalry with Existing Competitors

Customers tend to be loyal purchasers of products differentiated in ways that are meaningful to them. As their loyalty to a brand increases, customers' sensitivity to price increases is reduced. The relationship between brand loyalty and price sensitivity insulates a firm from competitive rivalry. Thus, reputations can sustain the competitive advantage of firms following a differentiation strategy.[81] Alternatively, when highly capable rivals such as Samsung practice imperfect imitation by imitating and improving on products, companies such as Apple must pay attention. Thus, Apple must try to incrementally improve its iPhone and iPad products to exploit its investments. However, it must also invest in exploring highly novel and valuable products to establish new markets to remain ahead of Samsung.[82]

Bargaining Power of Buyers (Customers)

The distinctiveness of differentiated goods or services reduces customers' sensitivity to price increases. Customers are willing to accept a price increase when a product still satisfies their unique needs better than a competitor's offering. Thus, the golfer whose needs are specifically satisfied by Callaway golf clubs will likely continue buying those products even if the price increases. Purchasers of brand-name food items (e.g., Heinz ketchup and Kleenex tissues) accept price increases in those products as long as they continue to perceive that the product satisfies their distinctive needs at an acceptable cost. In all of these instances the customers are relatively insensitive to price increases because they do not think an acceptable product alternative exists.

Bargaining Power of Suppliers

Because the firm using the differentiation strategy charges a premium price for its products, suppliers must provide high-quality components, driving up the firm's costs. However, the high margins the firm earns in these cases partially insulate it from the influence of suppliers in that higher supplier costs can be paid through these margins.[83] Alternatively, because of buyers' relative insensitivity to price increases, the differentiated firm might choose to pass the additional cost of supplies on to the customer by increasing the price of its unique product. However, when buyer firms outsource the total function or large portions of it to a supplier, especially R&D for a firm following a differentiation strategy, they can become dependent on and thus vulnerable to that supplier.[84]

Potential Entrants

Customer loyalty and the need to overcome the uniqueness of a differentiated product create substantial barriers to potential entrants. Entering an industry under these conditions typically demands significant investments of resources and patience while seeking customers' loyalty. In these cases, some potential entrants decide to make smaller investments to see if they can gain a "foothold" in the market. If it does not work they will not lose major resources, but if it works they can then invest greater resources to enhance their competitive position.[85]

Product Substitutes

Firms selling brand-name goods and services to loyal customers are positioned effectively against product substitutes. In contrast, companies without brand loyalty face a higher probability of their customers switching either to products which offer differentiated features that serve the same function (particularly if the substitute has a lower price) or to products that offer more features and perform more attractive functions. As such, they may be vulnerable to innovations from outside the industry that better satisfy customers' needs (e.g., Apple's iPod in the music industry).[86]

Competitive Risks of the Differentiation Strategy

One risk of the differentiation strategy is that customers might decide that the price differential between the differentiator's product and the cost leader's product is too large. In this instance, a firm may be offering differentiated features that exceed target customers' needs. The firm then becomes vulnerable to competitors that are able to offer customers a combination of features and price that is more consistent with their needs.

Another risk of the differentiation strategy is that a firm's means of differentiation may cease to provide value for which customers are willing to pay. A differentiated product becomes less valuable if imitation by rivals causes customers to perceive that competitors offer essentially the same goods or services, but at a lower price. This is the case, as illustrated

Strategic Focus

Apple vs. Samsung: Apple Differentiates and Samsung Imperfectly Imitates

In recent history Apple has been a product innovator and dominates the tech industry by creating new markets through first-mover advantage. This has been done with new concept products such the iPod, iPhone, and iPad products. Almost none of its high-tech rivals, such as Samsung, Nokia, BlackBerry, Google, Dell, and now Lenovo, have created whole new mobile product categories. However, more recently, Samsung has been a successful challenger of Apple's products. In fact, it has been so successful that Apple took Samsung to court with a lawsuit for patent infringement. Apple won the lawsuit with a nearly $1 billion judgment against Samsung. Samsung with its Android (created by Google) operating system appears to be a quick follower or imitator of Apple's differentiation strategy. Although Samsung's Galaxy S4 smartphone with a larger screen was a great success, the Galaxy S5 fell flat and allowed Apple iPhone 6 products to overtake the market share lead from Samsung.

However, Samsung itself has been challenged by low-end imitators of the smartphone product. One of these competitors is Xiaomi Inc., a privately owned smartphone producer in Beijing, China. Xiaomi's smartphone product has been wildly successful and popular in China because of its "fan base" network and online approach for selling low-end smartphones. A competitor of Xiaomi is Lenovo which recently purchased the Motorola mobility assets from Google. Xiaomi has been more successful than Lenovo. Lenovo CEO, Yang Yuanqing, has suggested, "the online model is disrupting the traditional model … we definitely need to address this." Xiaomi's fan club approach and online distribution channel has resulted in lower overhead and a pricing edge compared to traditional retail vendors. Although Apple outsold Xiaomi in the fourth quarter of 2014, Xiaomi was not too far behind. While Apple is seen as a differentiated "luxury product," there is enough quality in the Xiaomi product to challenge the market share of Apple. However, because the Galaxy S5 product was relatively less well received by consumers, Xiaomi has surpassed the sales of Samsung. Similarly, Micromax, a low-end smartphone producer in India, has overtaken Samsung in India by following Xiaomi's "copycat" strategy. As such, these low-end producers have provided relatively high quality products often sold through nontraditional channels (e.g., Xiaomi's fan club and online sales channel). They are also rapid second followers of Apple and have created a dilemma for Samsung.

In response to the very significant success of iPhone 6, as well as the significant success of low-end phones in large emerging economies, Samsung has recently introduced its Galaxy S6 products. Given the competition, Samsung Galaxy S6

phones have copied many of the features of the iPhone 6: high grade aluminum back and glass screen (Galaxy S5 had a plastic back) with smooth curved edges, embedded battery, and better finger print scanning. Samsung also focused on high quality apps, even reducing some of their own proprietary apps that were perceived to be of lower quality. They have also tried to

The Xiaomi Note smartphone device picture here has help the company challenge Apple and Samsung products in China and other emerging markets due to its quality at a low price.

improve on the battery life compared to the iPhone 6 and have added wireless charging as an upgrade. The initial showing of these products suggests a strong upgrade and a fast response to the iPhone 6 success. It remains to be seen whether these products will allow it to regain its preeminence in the luxury market behind Apple. Samsung obviously has a lot riding on the success of these new products.

Additionally, it has also has come out with the Samsung Pay system similar to Apple Pay. However it has upped the ante on Apple Pay by being compatible with the equipment currently

©D8nn/Shutterstock.com

used by most stores. Apple Pay has been slow to be adopted by retailers because they need to pay switching costs for new equipment to process transactions through Apple Pay. It remains to be seen whether Samsung will be able to maintain its differentiation relative to Apple's luxury branded products and the challengers on the low end such as Xiaomi, Lenovo, and Micromax.

Sources: J. Cheng, 2015, Samsung unveils Galaxy S6 to answer iPhone 6, *Wall Street Journal*, www.wsj.com, March 1; E. Dou, 2015, Lenovo's smartphone challenge: Battling Apple, Xiaomi in China with Motorola, *Wall Street Journal*, www.wsj.com, February 4; A. Fitzpatrick, 2015, Apple might finally be beating Samsung in smartphone sales, *Time*, www.time.com, February 3; R. Flannery, 2015, China's smartphone sensation Xiaomi says sells triple in '14: Eyes int'l growth, *Forbes*, www.forbes.com, January 3; V. Govindarajan & G. Bagla, 2015, Can Indians innovate in India?, *Business Today*, 24(4): 120–121; S. Grobart, 2015, Samsung's fancy new Galaxy S6 Edge phones, *Bloomberg BusinessWeek*, www.bloomberg.com, March 1; S. Y. Lee & H. T. Wolde, 2015, Samsung unveils sleek new Galaxy phones to battle Apple, *Reuters*, www.reuters.com, March 2; P. Olson, 2015, Apple's U.S. iPhone sells surpass Android for first time in years, *Forbes*, www.forbes.com, February 4; M. Reardon, 2015, Samsung answers Apple with curvy Galaxy S6 phones, Samsung Pay, *CNET*, www.cnet.com, March 1; T. Bajarin, 2014, How tiny tech firms are disrupting the giants, *PC Magazine*, December, 36–38. B. Einhorn, B. Shrivastava, & J. Lee, 2014, Samsung's China problems come to India, *Bloomberg BusinessWeek*, October 27, 44–45; D. Reisinger, 2014, Xiaomi sours while Samsung sinks in Gartner smartphone market study, *eWeek*, www.eweek.com, December 16.

in the Strategic Focus, where low-end smartphone producers, Xiaomi and Micromax in China and India, respectively, are having success competing against Samsung smartphones.[87] A third risk of the differentiation strategy is that experience can narrow customers' perceptions of the value of a product's differentiated features. For example, customers having positive experiences with generic tissues may decide that the differentiated features of the Kleenex product are not worth the extra cost. To counter this risk, firms must continue to meaningfully differentiate their product (e.g., through innovation) for customers at a price they are willing to pay.[88]

Counterfeiting is the differentiation strategy's fourth risk. Counterfeits are products which are labeled with a trademark or logo that is identical to or indistinguishable from a legal logo owned by another party, thus infringing the rights of the legal owner. When a consumer purchases such a product and discovers the deception, regret creates distrust of the branded product and reduces differentiation.[89] Companies such as Dell must take actions to deal with the problems counterfeit goods create for them when their rights are infringed upon.

4-3c Focus Strategies

The **focus strategy** is an integrated set of actions taken to produce goods or services that serve the needs of a particular competitive segment. Thus, firms use a focus strategy when they utilize their core competencies to serve the needs of a particular industry segment or niche to the exclusion of others. Examples of specific market segments that can be targeted by a focus strategy include

1. a particular buyer group (e.g., youths or senior citizens),
2. a different segment of a product line (e.g., products for professional painters or the do-it-yourself group), or
3. a different geographic market (e.g., northern or southern Italy by using a foreign subsidiary).[90]

There are many specific customer needs firms can serve by using a focus strategy. For example, Goya Foods, Inc. is the largest Hispanic-owned food company in the United States. Segmenting the Hispanic market into unique groups, Goya offers more than 2,200 products to consumers. The firm is a leading authority on Hispanic food and seeks "to be the premier source for authentic Latin cuisine."[91] By successfully using a focus strategy, firms such as Goya gain a competitive advantage in specific market niches or segments, even though they do not possess an industry-wide competitive advantage.

The **focus strategy** is an integrated set of actions taken to produce goods or services that serve the needs of a particular competitive segment.

Although the breadth of a target is clearly a matter of degree, the essence of the focus strategy "is the exploitation of a narrow target's differences from the balance of the industry."[92] Firms using the focus strategy intend to serve a particular segment of an industry more effectively than can industry-wide competitors. In fact, entrepreneurial firms commonly serve a specific market niche or segment, partly because they do not have the knowledge or resources to serve the broader market. In fact, they generally prefer to operate "below the radar" of larger and more resource rich firms that serve the broader market. They succeed when they effectively serve a segment whose unique needs are so specialized that broad-based competitors choose not to serve that segment or when they satisfy the needs of a segment being served poorly by industry-wide competitors.

Firms can create value for customers in specific and unique market segments by using the focused cost leadership strategy or the focused differentiation strategy.

Focused Cost Leadership Strategy

Based in Sweden, IKEA, a global furniture retailer with locations in 35 countries and territories and sales revenue of 28.7 billion euros in 2014, uses the focused cost leadership strategy. Young buyers desiring style at a low cost are IKEA's target customers.[93] For these customers, the firm offers home furnishings that combine good design, function, and acceptable quality with low prices. According to the firm, it seeks "to offer a wide range of well-designed, functional home furnishing products at prices so low that as many people as possible will be able to afford them."[94]

IKEA emphasizes several activities to keep its costs low. For example, instead of relying primarily on third-party manufacturers, the firm's engineers design low-cost, modular furniture ready for assembly by customers. To eliminate the need for sales associates or decorators, IKEA positions the products in its stores so that customers can view different living combinations (complete with sofas, chairs, tables, etc.) in a single room-like setting, which helps the customer imagine how furniture will look in their home. A third practice that helps keep IKEA's costs low traditionally has been to require customers to transport their own purchases rather than providing delivery service. However, for competitive reason, they have recently started to offer a low cost delivery service as an option.

Although it is a cost leader, IKEA also offers some differentiated features that appeal to its target customers, including its unique furniture designs, in-store playrooms for children, wheelchairs for customer use, and extended hours. Thus, IKEA's focused cost leadership strategy also includes some differentiated features with its low-cost products.

Focused Differentiation Strategy

Other firms implement the focused differentiation strategy. As noted earlier, there are many dimensions on which firms can differentiate their goods or services. For example, the new generation of food trucks populating cities such as Los Angeles use the focused differentiation strategy. They serve organic food crafted by highly trained chefs and well-known restaurateurs who own and operate many of these trucks. In fact, the Green Truck, headquartered in Los Angeles, demonstrates these characteristics. Moreover, the owners of these trucks often use Twitter and Facebook to inform customers of their locations as they move from point to point in their focal city.[95]

With a focus strategy, firms must be able to complete various primary value-chain activities and support functions in a competitively superior manner to develop and sustain a competitive advantage and earn above-average returns. The activities required to use the focused cost leadership strategy are virtually identical to those of the industry-wide cost leadership strategy (see Figure 4.2), and activities required to use the focused differentiation strategy are largely identical to those of the industry-wide differentiation strategy (see Figure 4.3). Similarly, the manner in which each of the two focus strategies allows a firm to deal successfully with the five competitive forces parallels those of the two broad strategies. The only difference is in the firm's competitive scope; the firm focuses on a narrow industry segment. Thus, Figures 4.2 and 4.3 and the text describing the five competitive forces also explain the relationship between each of the two focus strategies and competitive advantage. However, the competitive forces in a given industry often favor either a cost leadership or a differentiation strategy.[96]

Competitive Risks of Focus Strategies

With either focus strategy, the firm faces the same general risks as does the company using the cost leadership or the differentiation strategy on an industry-wide basis. However, focus strategies have three additional risks.

First, a competitor may be able to focus on a more narrowly defined competitive segment and thereby "out-focus" the focuser. This would happen to IKEA if another firm found a way to offer IKEA's customers (young buyers interested in stylish furniture at a low cost) additional sources of differentiation while charging the same price or to provide the same service with the same sources of differentiation at a lower price. Second, a company competing on an industry-wide basis may decide that the market segment served by the firm using a focus strategy is attractive and worthy of competitive pursuit.[97] For example, as noted in the Opening Case, Krogers, Safeway, and Walmart are seeking to compete with focused organic grocers Whole Foods and Trader Joe's. As a result, Whole Food's has lowered its prices on many items, increased its advertising, introduced more private brands, and is testing a loyalty program in order to compete more effectively. Co-CEO and founder, John Mackey, said, "Whole Foods Market is a very competitive company, and when we are challenged, when competition rears its head, we respond."[98] Its strategy has resulted in more customers coming to its stores, although in earlier stages of its response, it profit margins were eroding.

The third risk involved with a focus strategy is that the needs of customers within a narrow competitive segment may become more similar to those of industry-wide customers as a whole over time. As a result, the advantages of a focus strategy are either reduced or eliminated. As illustrated in the example in the Strategic Focus, the unique demand of do-it-yourself electronic dabblers that RadioShack traditionally focused on dissipated over time. RadioShack executives struggled over many years to find the right focus and made too many strategic changes over time, which ultimately lead to bankruptcy.

4-3d Integrated Cost Leadership/Differentiation Strategy

Most consumers have high expectations when purchasing goods or services. In general, it seems that most consumers want to pay a low price for products with somewhat highly differentiated features. Because of these customer expectations, a number of firms engage in primary value-chain activities and support functions that allow them to simultaneously pursue low cost and differentiation.[99] Firms seeking to do this use the **integrated cost leadership/differentiation strategy** which involves engaging in primary value-chain activities and support functions that allow a firm to simultaneously pursue low cost and differentiation. The objective of using this strategy is to efficiently produce products with some differentiated features. Efficient production is the source of maintaining low costs, while differentiation is the source of creating unique value. Firms that successfully use the integrated cost leadership/differentiation strategy usually adapt quickly to new technologies and rapid changes in their external environments. Simultaneously concentrating on developing two sources of competitive advantage (cost and differentiation) increases the number of primary value-chain activities and support functions in which the firm must become competent. Such firms often have strong networks with external parties that perform some of the value-chain activities and/or support functions.[100] In turn, having skills in a larger number of activities and functions makes a firm more flexible.

The **integrated cost leadership/differentiation strategy** involves engaging in primary value-chain activities and support functions that allow a firm to simultaneously pursue low cost and differentiation.

Strategic Focus

RadioShack's Failed Focus Strategy: Strategic Flip-Flopping

RadioShack filed for bankruptcy in February 2015 after nearly a century of being a mainstay in American malls and on "Main Street" throughout the United States. Of course, one reason is that the business of selling electronic components products has been degraded by online sellers such as Amazon. RadioShack tried to avert bankruptcy by closing stores, but its finances deteriorated faster than expected. Because of the financial distress, it had turned to private equity for capital as it tried to turn around its poor performance, but the demands by these creditors increased the decline.

The real strategy difficulties, however, pertain to its efforts to pursue many different trends without a consistent underlying strategic approach. RadioShack was founded in Boston in 1921, 94 years prior to its bankruptcy. It flourished in the 1970s and 1980s by focusing on "electronic gadgetry." At first their strategy focused on ham radio enthusiasts. When Charles Tandy took over as CEO in 1963, the chain had been well established for decades with a focus on hobbyist and do-it-yourselfers. At the time, RadioShack eschewed national brands and sold private RadioShack brands including accessories, batteries, and a wide range of transistors and capacitors. All of these items could be heavily marked up. One could describe this as a focus differentiation strategy with an emphasis on electronic gadgets that the customers could improve through modifications and accessorizing. "The target audience was people who needed one piece of equipment every week," focusing on technologically oriented people with enthusiasm for RadioShack's products.

They also had a 100+ page catalogs filled with stuff like stylus', tape head demagnetizers, Realistic (RadioShack private brand) receivers and speakers, intercoms, and boomboxes. CB radios became another trend the RadioShack consumers followed, which became popular during the oil crisis in the early 1970s. When this trend slowed, they focused on personal computers. The TRS 80, one of the first mass-market personal computers, helped to replace the CB radio boom. This computer, with 16K of memory, used software designed by a "little known start-up named Microsoft." However as the computer business became commoditized and profit-margins decreased, RadioShack needed a new "anchor" product. They found it in cell phones.

In the 1990s, Radio-Shack opened a number of big box electronic stores, including Incredible Universe, Famous Brand Electronics, and Computer City. These were essentially "anti-RadioShacks." These RadioShack-owned brands were ultimately pillaged by large online sellers of electronic products and became an albatross for RadioShack even though the large volume of products sold allowed them to reach the peak revenue in 1996 ($6.3B). RadioShack was a specialty store. These large stores failed because, as CEO Leonard Roberts looking back lamented, "I don't think we knew how to operate those stores."

However, RadioShack was good at selling cell phones when they became popular. Their customers were intrigued but intimidated with this new product, and the salespeople could spend time helping them to pick the right product. However, signing someone up for a mobile phone contract took 45 minutes, and many stores were staffed for long stretches by a single employee. Their regular customers in search of the right small electronic component or accessory often left in frustration because they couldn't get the help needed because RadioShack employees were focused on selling cell phones. Likewise, RadioShack lost in e-commerce. They tried a ship-to-store model with RadioShack Unlimited, but RadioShack's executives never truly committed to e-commerce. In essence, because its differentiation focus

Paul Hawthorne/WireImage/Getty Images

It it early stages (this photo is from 2003), Radio Shack was very successful but it lost its focus as it tried too many different strategic approaches.

strategy on the hobbyist and electronic enthusiast was compromised by trying to focus on different trends and achieve growth, seemingly required by capital markets, RadioShack was never able to recover its focus and apply a consistent strategic approach.

Ultimately its technologically-oriented mainstay customers were offended and found other sources for their product purchases, mostly through online sources. In the end, RadioShack just wasn't getting the traffic needed to drive revenues, and its differentiation strategy failed.

Sources: J. Brustein, 2015, Inside RadioShack's collapse: How did the electronics retailer go broke? Gradually, then all at once, *Bloomberg Business*

Week, Feb 9–15, 54–59; L. Chen, 2015, Next RadioShack? Here are the most troubled retail stores. *Forbes*, February 10, 13; D. Fitzgerald & M. Jarzemsky, 2015, Beseiged RadioShack spirals into bankruptcy, *Wall Street Journal*, Feb 6, A1–A2; S. Grossman, 2015, John Oliver wants you to remember that one day we'll all be like RadioShack, *Time*, www.time.com, February 12; C. Mims, 2015, RadioShack suffers as free time evaporated, *Wall Street Journal*, Feb 9, B1, B6; P. Wahba, 2015, RadioShack pulls the plug and files for bankruptcy, *Fortune*, www.fortune.com, February 9.

Concentrating on the needs of its core customer group (e.g., higher-income, fashion-conscious discount shoppers), Target stores uses an integrated cost leadership/differentiation strategy as shown by its "Expect More. Pay Less." brand promise in its mission statement. It does this by seeking to provide convenience by a faster checkout, increased savings for quality products, and a dedicated team providing more personalized service.[101]

Often firms are "caught in the middle" because they do not differentiate effectively or provide the lowest-cost goods. JCPenney is a prime example of this failure. It attempted to integrate low cost (reducing pricing on most goods in the store) with differentiation (creating specialized stores for name-brand goods within each store). This strategy is very difficult to implement effectively. It could not compete with the low-cost leaders such as Walmart and Family Dollar stores, nor could it compete effectively with the more upscale and differentiated department stores, such as Target and Macy's. RadioShack (see the Strategic Focus) provides another example of a firm "caught in the middle" between maintain differentiation on electronic dabblers and seeking new growth trends such as selling cellphones to achieve low cost through volume.

Interestingly, most emerging market firms have competed using the cost leadership strategy. Their labor and other supply costs tend to be considerably lower than multinational firms based in developed countries. However, in recent years some of the emerging market firms are building their capabilities to produce innovation. Coupled with their capabilities to produce lower cost goods, they may be able to gain an advantage on large multinational firms. As such, some of the emerging market firms are beginning to use an integrated low cost and differentiation strategy.[102]

Flexibility is required for firms to complete primary value-chain activities and support functions in ways that allow them to use the integrated cost leadership/differentiation strategy in order to produce somewhat differentiated products at relatively low costs. Chinese auto manufacturers have developed a means of product design that provides a flexible architecture that allows low-cost manufacturing but also car designs that are differentiated from competitors.[103] Flexible manufacturing systems, information networks, and total quality management systems are three sources of flexibility that are particularly useful for firms trying to balance the objectives of continuous cost reductions and continuous enhancements to sources of differentiation as called for by the integrated strategy.

Flexible Manufacturing Systems

Using a flexible manufacturing system (FMS), the firm integrates human, physical, and information resources to create relatively differentiated products at relatively low costs. A significant technological advance, the FMS is a computer-controlled process used to produce a variety of products in moderate, flexible quantities with a minimum of manual intervention.[104] Automobile manufacturing in the Ford-Changan alliance in Chongqing

FMS car system.PNG

This photo illustrates the flexibility of computer aided manufacturing lines as two different vehicle bodies are pieced together on the same line.

shows the clear benefits of flexible production. As Yuan Fleng Xin, manufacturing engineering manager for the Changan Ford partnership, notes: "We can introduce new models within hours, simply by configuring the line for production of the next model, while still being able to produce the existing models during the introduction of new models … This allows the phasing-in of new models, and the phasing-out of old models, directly driven by market demand and not by production capacity, lead time nor a need to wait for infrastructure build-up."[105] Often the flexibility is derived from modularization of the manufacturing process (and sometimes other value-chain activities as well).[106]

The goal of a FMS is to eliminate the "low cost versus product variety" trade-off that is inherent in traditional manufacturing technologies. Firms use a FMS to change quickly and easily from making one product to making another. Used properly, a FMS allows the firm to respond more effectively to changes in its customers' needs, while retaining low-cost advantages and consistent product quality. Because a FMS also enables the firm to reduce the lot size needed to manufacture a product efficiently, the firm's capacity to serve the unique needs of a narrow competitive scope is higher. In industries of all types, effective combinations of the firm's tangible assets (e.g., machines) and intangible assets (e.g., employee skills) facilitate implementation of complex competitive strategies, especially the integrated cost leadership/differentiation strategy.

Information Networks

By linking companies with their suppliers, distributors, and customers information networks provide another source of flexibility. These networks, when used effectively, help the firm satisfy customer expectations in terms of product quality and delivery speed.[107]

Earlier, we discussed the importance of managing the firm's relationships with its customers in order to understand their needs. Customer relationship management (CRM) is one form of an information-based network process that firms use for this purpose.[108] An effective CRM system provides a 360-degree view of the company's relationship with customers, encompassing all contact points, business processes, and communication media and sales channels. Salesforce.com is the largest provider of online customer relationship management, and it is moving to the cloud, allowing large database storage and access from multiple devices including smartphones.[109] The firm can use this information to determine the trade-offs its customers are willing to make between differentiated features and low cost—an assessment that is vital for companies using the integrated cost leadership/differentiation strategy. Managing supply chains through sophisticated information networks is also prominent in today's information-based society.[110] Such systems help firms to monitor their markets and stakeholders and allow them to better predict future scenarios. This capability helps firms to adjust their strategies to be better prepared for the future. Thus, to make comprehensive strategic decisions with effective knowledge of the organization's context, good information flow is essential. Better quality managerial decisions require accurate information on the firm's environment.

Total Quality Management Systems

Total quality management (TQM) is a managerial process that emphasizes an organization's commitment to the customer and to continuous improvement of all processes through problem-solving approaches based on empowerment of employees.[111] Firms develop and use TQM systems to

1. increase customer satisfaction,
2. cut costs, and
3. reduce the amount of time required to introduce innovative products to the marketplace.[112]

Firms able to simultaneously reduce costs while enhancing their ability to develop innovative products increase their flexibility, an outcome that is particularly helpful to firms implementing the integrated cost leadership/differentiation strategy. Exceeding customers' expectations regarding quality is a differentiating feature and eliminating process inefficiencies to cut costs allows the firm to offer that quality to customers at a relatively low price. Thus, an effective TQM system helps the firm develop the flexibility needed to identify opportunities to simultaneously increase differentiation and reduce costs. Research has found that TQM systems facilitate cost leadership strategies more effectively than they do differentiating strategies when the strategy is implemented alone.[113] However, it facilitates the potential synergy between the two strategies when they are integrated into one. TQM systems are available to all competitors so they may help firms maintain competitive parity, but alone they rarely lead to a competitive advantage.[114]

Competitive Risks of the Integrated Cost Leadership/Differentiation Strategy

The potential to earn above-average returns by successfully using the integrated cost leadership/differentiation strategy is appealing. However, it is a risky strategy because firms find it difficult to perform primary value-chain activities and support functions in ways that allow them to produce relatively inexpensive products with levels of differentiation that create value for the target customer. Moreover, to properly use this strategy across time, firms must be able to simultaneously reduce costs incurred to produce products (as required by the cost leadership strategy) while increasing product differentiation (as required by the differentiation strategy).

Firms that fail to perform the value-chain activities and support functions in an optimum manner become "stuck in the middle."[115] Being stuck in the middle means that the firm's cost structure is not low enough to allow it to attractively price its products and that its products are not sufficiently differentiated to create value for the target customer. This appears to be the problem experienced by JCPenney, at least as perceived by the customers. Its prices were not low enough and the differentiation not great enough to attract the customers needed. In fact, its declining sales suggest that it lost many of its current customers without attracting others to offset the loss. These firms will not earn above-average returns and will earn average returns only when the structure of the industry in which it competes is highly favorable.[116] Thus, companies implementing the integrated cost leadership/differentiation strategy must be able to produce (or offer) products that provide the target customer some differentiated features at a relatively low cost/price.

Firms can also become stuck in the middle when they fail to successfully implement *either* the cost leadership *or* the differentiation strategy. In other words, industry-wide competitors too can become stuck in the middle. Trying to use the integrated strategy is costly in that firms must pursue both low costs and differentiation.

Firms may need to form alliances with other companies to achieve differentiation, yet alliance partners may extract prices for the use of their resources that make it difficult

Total quality management (TQM) is a managerial process that emphasizes an organization's commitment to the customer and to continuous improvement of all processes through problem-solving approaches based on empowerment of employees.

to meaningfully reduce costs.[117] Firms may be motivated to make acquisitions to maintain their differentiation through innovation or to add products to their portfolio not offered by competitors.[118] Research suggests that firms using "pure strategies," either cost leadership or differentiation, often outperform firms attempting to use a "hybrid strategy" (i.e., integrated cost leadership/differentiation strategy). This research suggests the risky nature of using an integrated strategy.[119] However, the integrated strategy is becoming more common and perhaps necessary in many industries because of technological advances and global competition. This strategy often necessitates a long-term perspective to make it work effectively, and therefore requires dedicated owners that allow the implementation of a long-term strategy that can require several years to produce positive returns.[120]

SUMMARY

- A business-level strategy is an integrated and coordinated set of commitments and actions the firm uses to gain a competitive advantage by exploiting core competencies in specific product markets. Five business-level strategies (cost leadership, differentiation, focused cost leadership, focused differentiation, and integrated cost leadership/differentiation) are examined in the chapter.

- Customers are the foundation of successful business-level strategies. When considering customers, a firm simultaneously examines three issues: *who*, *what*, and *how*. These issues, respectively, refer to the customer groups to be served, the needs those customers have that the firm seeks to satisfy, and the core competencies the firm will use to satisfy customers' needs. Increasing segmentation of markets throughout the global economy creates opportunities for firms to identify more distinctive customer needs that they can serve with one of the business-level strategies.

- Firms seeking competitive advantage through the cost leadership strategy produce no-frills, standardized products for an industry's typical customer. However, these low-cost products must be offered with competitive levels of differentiation. Above-average returns are earned when firms continuously emphasize efficiency such that their costs are lower than those of their competitors, while providing customers with products that have acceptable levels of differentiated features.

- Competitive risks associated with the cost leadership strategy include (1) a loss of competitive advantage to newer technologies, (2) a failure to detect changes in customers' needs, and (3) the ability of competitors to imitate the cost leader's competitive advantage through their own distinct strategic actions.

- Through the differentiation strategy, firms provide customers with products that have different (and valued) features. Differentiated products must be sold at a cost that customers believe is competitive relative to the product's features as compared to the cost/feature combinations available from competitors' goods. Because of their distinctiveness,

- differentiated goods or services are sold at a premium price. Products can be differentiated on any dimension that some customer group values. Firms using this strategy seek to differentiate their products from competitors' goods or services on as many dimensions as possible. The less similarity to competitors' products, the more buffered a firm is from competition with its rivals.

- Risks associated with the differentiation strategy include (1) a customer group's decision that the unique features provided by the differentiated product over the cost leader's goods or services are no longer worth a premium price, (2) the inability of a differentiated product to create the type of value for which customers are willing to pay a premium price, (3) the ability of competitors to provide customers with products that have features similar to those of the differentiated product, but at a lower cost, and (4) the threat of counterfeiting, whereby firms produce a cheap imitation of a differentiated good or service.

- Through the cost leadership and the differentiated focus strategies, firms serve the needs of a narrow market segment (e.g., a buyer group, product segment, or geographic area). This strategy is successful when firms have the core competencies required to provide value to a specialized market segment that exceeds the value available from firms serving customers across the total market (industry).

- The competitive risks of focus strategies include (1) a competitor's ability to use its core competencies to "out focus" the focuser by serving an even more narrowly defined market segment, (2) decisions by industry-wide competitors to focus on a customer group's specialized needs, and (3) a reduction in differences of the needs between customers in a narrow market segment and the industry-wide market.

- Firms using the integrated cost leadership/differentiation strategy strive to provide customers with relatively low-cost products that also have valued differentiated features. Flexibility is required for firms to learn how to use primary value-chain activities and support functions in ways that allow them to produce differentiated products at relatively low costs. This flexibility is facilitated by flexible manufacturing systems and improvements and interconnectedness in information systems within and between firms (buyers and suppliers). The primary risk of this strategy is that a firm might produce products that do not offer sufficient value in terms of either low cost or differentiation. In such cases, the company becomes "stuck in the middle." Firms stuck in the middle compete at a disadvantage and are unable to earn more than average returns.

KEY TERMS

business-level strategy 111
cost leadership strategy 118
differentiation strategy 122
focus strategy 127

integrated cost leadership/differentiation strategy 129
market segmentation 114
total quality management (TQM) 133

REVIEW QUESTIONS

1. What is a business-level strategy?

2. What is the relationship between a firm's customers and its business-level strategy in terms of *who*, *what*, and *how*? Why is this relationship important?

3. What are the differences among the cost leadership, differentiation, focused cost leadership, focused differentiation, and integrated cost leadership/differentiation business-level strategies?

4. How can each of the business-level strategies be used to position the firm relative to the five forces of competition in a way that helps the firm earn above-average returns?

5. What are the specific risks associated with using each business-level strategy?

Mini-Case

Is JCPenney Killing Itself with a Failed Strategy?

A few years ago, JCPenney was a traditional, low-end department store that appeared to be in a slow decline. Bill Ackman of Pershing Square Capital Management, a hedge fund investor, bought a large stake in the company and pushed to hire a new CEO, Ron Johnson. Johnson, who had successfully created the Apple retail store concept, was tasked with turning around the company's fortunes.

In January 2012, Johnson announced the new strategy for the company and rebranding of JCPenny. The strategy announced by Johnson entailed a remake of the JCPenny retail stores to create shops focused on specific brands such as Levi's, IZOD, and Liz Claiborne and types of goods such as home goods featuring Martha Stewart products within each store. Simultaneously, Johnson announced a new pricing system.

The old approach of offering special discounts throughout the year was eliminated in favor of a new customer-value pricing approach that reduced prices on goods across the board by as much as 40 percent. So, the price listed was the price to be paid without further discounts. The intent was to offer customers a "better deal" on all products as opposed to providing special, high discounts on selected products.

The intent was to build JCPenny into a higher-end (a little more upscale) retailer that provided good prices on branded merchandise (mostly clothes and home goods). These changes overlooked the firm's current customers; JCPenny began competing for customers who normally shopped at Target, Macy's, and Nordstrom, to name a few of its competitors. Unfortunately, the first year of this new strategy appeared it to be a failure. Total sales in 2012 were $4.28 billion less than in 2011, and the firm's stock price declined by 55 percent. Interestingly, its Internet sales declined by 34 percent compared to an increase of 48 percent for its new rival, Macy's. All of this translated into a net loss for the year of slightly less than $1 billion for JCPenny.

It seems that the new executive team at JCPenny thought that they could retain their current customer base (perhaps with the value pricing across the board), while attracting new customers with the new "store-within-a-store" concept. According to Roger Martin, a former executive, strategy expert, and current Dean at the University of Toronto, "… the new JCPenney is competing against and absolutely slaughtering an important competitor, and it's called the old J.C. Penney." Only about one-third of the stores had been converted to the new approach when the company began to heavily promote the concept. Its new store sales produced increases in sales per square foot, but the old stores' sales per square foot markedly declined. It appears that Penney was not attracting customers from its rivals but rather cannibalizing customers from its old stores. According to Martin the new CEO likely understands a lot about capital markets but does not know how to satisfy customers and gain a competitive advantage. Additionally, the former CEO of JCPenney, Allen Questrom, described Johnson as having several capabilities (e.g., intelligent, strong communicator) but believes that he and his executive team made a major strategic error and was especially insensitive to the JCPenny customer base.

The question now is whether the company can survive such a major decline in sales and stock price. In 2013, it announced the layoff of approximately 2,200 employees to reduce costs. In addition, CEO Johnson announced that he was reinstituting selected discounts in pricing and offering comparative pricing on products (relative prices with rivals). The good news is that transformed stores are obtaining sales of $269 per square foot, whereas the older stores are producing $134 per square foot. Will Johnson's strategy survive long enough for all of the stores to be converted and save the company? The answer is probably not, because Johnson was fired by the JCPenny board of directors on April 8, 2013, about 1.5 years after he assumed the CEO position.

Sources: P. Wahba, 2015, J.C. Penney still blaming Ron Johnson-era for slow profit growth *Fortune*, www.fortune.com, March; N. Tichy, 2014, J.C. Penney and the terrible costs of hiring an outsider CEO, *Fortune*, www.fortune.com, November 13; J. Reingold, A. Sloan, & D. Burke, 2013, When Wall Street wears the pants, *Fortune*, April 8, 74–81; S. Schaefer, 2013, Ron Johnson out as JCPenney chief, *Forbes*, www.forbes.com, April 8; M. Nisen, 2013, Former JC Penney CEO says Ron Johnson is 'a very nice man' who will probably fail, *Yahoo! Finance*, finance.yahoo.com, accessed April 6; B. Byrnes, 2013, How J.C. Penney is killing itself, *The Motley Fool*, www.fool.com, March 31; B. Jopson, 2013, JC Penney cuts 2,200 jobs as retailer struggles, *Financial Times*, www.ft.com, March 8; J. Macke, 2013, J.C. Penney's last shot at survival, *Yahoo! Finance*, finance.yahoo.com, accessed March 1; S. Clifford, 2013, Chief talks of mistakes and big loss at JC Penney, *New York Times*, www.nytimes.com, February 27; M. Halkias, 2013, J.C. Penney CEO Ron Johnson says changes will return retailer to growth, *Dallas Morning news*, www.dallasnews.com, February 9; They're back: JCPenney adds sales, 2013, *USA Today*, www.usatoday.com, January 28; A. R. Sorkin, 2012, A dose of realism for the chief of J.C. Penney, *New York Times DealB%k*, dealbook.nytimes.com, November 12.

Case Discussion Questions

1. What strategy was the new CEO at JCPenney seeking to implement given the generic strategies found in Chapter 4?

2. What was the result of change in strategy implemented?

3. Why was this strategy a disaster for JCPenney?

4. What does it mean to be "stuck in the middle" between two strategies (i.e., between low cost and differentiation strategies)?

NOTES

1. J. Garcia-Sanchez, L. F. Mesquita, & R. S. Vassolo, 2014, What doesn't kill you makes you stronger: The evolution of competition and entry-order advantages in economically turbulent contexts, *Strategic Management Journal*, 35: 1972–1992; H. Greve, 2009, Bigger and safer: The diffusion of competitive advantage, *Strategic Management Journal*, 30: 1–23.

2. O. Schilke, 2014, On the contingent value of dynamic capabilities for competitive advantage: The nonlinear moderating effect of environmental dynamism, *Strategic Management Journal*, 35: 179–203; M. A. Delmas & M. W. Toffel, 2008, Organizational responses to environmental demands: Opening the black box, *Strategic Management Journal*, 29: 1027–1055.

3. M. E. Porter & J. E. Heppelmann, 2014, How smart, connected products are transforming competition, *Harvard Business Review*, 92(11): 64–88; M. G. Jacobides, S. G. Winter, & S. M. Kassberger, 2012, The dynamics of wealth, profit, and sustainable advantage, *Strategic Management Journal*, 33: 1384–1410.

4. A. Gasparro, 2015, Indigestion hits food giants, *Wall Street Journal*, February 13, B1.

5. F. F. Suarez, S. Grodal, & A. Gotsopoulos, 2015, Perfect timing? Dominant category, dominant design, and the window of opportunity for firm entry, *Strategic Management Journal*, 36: 437–448; J. Schmidt & T. Keil, 2013, What makes a resource valuable? Identifying the drivers of firm-idiosyncratic resource value, *Academy of Management Review*, 38: 208–228; C. Zott & R. Amit, 2008, The fit between product market strategy and business model: Implications for firm performance, *Strategic Management Journal*, 29: 1–26.

6. S. E. Reid & U. Brentani, 2015, Building a measurement model for market visioning competence and its proposed antecedents: Organizational encouragement of divergent thinking, divergent thinking attitudes, and ideational behavior, *Journal of Product Innovation Management*, 32: 243–262; S. Kaplan, 2008, Framing contests: Strategy making under uncertainty, *Organization Science*, 19: 729–752.

7. J. R. Lecuona & M. Reitzig, 2014, Knowledge worth having in 'excess': The value of tacit and firm-specific human resource slack. *Strategic Management Journal*, 35: 954–973; L. A. Costa, K. Cool, & I. Dierickx, 2013, The competitive implications of the deployment of unique resources, *Strategic Management Journal*, 34: 445–463; K. Shimizu & M. A. Hitt, 2004, Strategic flexibility: Organizational preparedness to reverse ineffective strategic decisions, *Academy of Management Executive*, 18: 44–59.

8. C. Eesley, D. H. Hsu, & E. B. Roberts, 2014, The contingent effects of top management teams on venture performance: Aligning founding team composition and innovation strategy and commercialization environment, *Strategic Management Journal*, 35: 1798–1817; J. A. Lamberg, H. Tikkanen, T. Nokelainen, & H. Suur-Inkeroinen, 2009, Competitive dynamics, strategic consistency, and organizational survival, *Strategic Management Journal*, 30: 45–60.

9. R. Kapoor & N. R. Furr, 2015, Complementarities and competition: Unpacking the drivers of entrants' technology choices in the solar photovoltaic industry, *Strategic Management Journal*, 36: 416–436; I. Goll, N. B. Johnson, & A. A. Rasheed, 2008, Top management team demographic characteristics, business strategy, and firm performance in the U.S. airline industry: The role of managerial discretion, *Management Decision*, 46: 201–222.

10. S. L. Fourné, J. P. Jansen, & T. M. Mom, 2014, Strategic agility in MNEs: Managing tensions to capture opportunities across emerging and established markets, *California Management Review*, 56(3): 13–38; J. W. Spencer, 2008, The impact of multinational enterprise strategy on indigenous enterprises: Horizontal spillovers and crowding out in developing countries, *Academy of Management Review*, 33: 341–361.

11. D. Gallagher, 2015, King not yet fit to wear a crown, *Wall Street Journal*, Feb 14–15, B14.

12. R. E. Hoskisson, M. A. Hitt, R. D. Ireland, & J. S. Harrison, 2013, *Competing for Advantage*, Mason, OH: Cengage Learning.

13. M. Subramony & S. D. Pugh, 2015, Services management research: Review, integration, and future directions, *Journal of Management*, 41: 349–373; R. J. Harrington & A. K. Tjan, 2008, Transforming strategy one customer at a time, *Harvard Business Review*, 86(3): 62–72.

14. M. J. Mol & C. Brewster, 2014, The outsourcing strategy of local and multinational firms: A supply base perspective, *Global Strategy Journal*, 4: 20–34; K. R. Fabrizio & L. G. Thomas, 2012, The impact of local demand on innovation in a global industry, *Strategic Management Journal*, 33: 42–64.

15. M. E. Porter, 1980, *Competitive Strategy*, New York: Free Press.

16. J. Calandro Jr., 2015, A leader's guide to strategic risk management, *Strategy & Leadership*, 43: 26–35; M. Baghai, S. Smit, & P. Viguerie, 2009, Is your growth strategy flying blind?, *Harvard Business Review*, 87(5): 86–96.

17. I. Le Breton-Miller & D. Miller, 2015, The paradox of resource vulnerability: Considerations for organizational curatorship, *Strategic Management Journal*, 36(3): 397–415; D. G. Sirmon, S. Gove, & M. A. Hitt, 2008, Resource management in dyadic competitive rivalry: The effects of resource bundling and deployment, *Academy of Management Journal*, 51: 919–935.

18. L. A. Bettencourt, R. F. Lusch, & S. L. Vargo, 2014, A service lens on value creation: Marketing's role in achieving strategic advantage, *California Management Review*, 57(1): 44–66.

19. F. J. Gouillart, 2014, The race to implement co-creation of value with stakeholders: Five approaches to competitive advantage, *Strategy & Leadership*, 42: 2–8.

20. L. A. Bettencourt, C. P. Blocker, M. B. Houston, & D. J. Flint, 2015, Rethinking customer relationships, *Business Horizons*, 58: 99–108; P. E. Frown & A. F. Payne, 2009, Customer relationship management: A strategic perspective, *Journal of Business Market Management*, 3: 7–27.

21. M. Ritson, 2014, Amazon has seen the future of predictability, *Marketing Week*, January 23, 10; H. Green, 2009, How Amazon aims to keep you clicking, *BusinessWeek*, March 2: 34–35.

22. S. Ramachandran & T. Stynes, 2015, Netflix steps up foreign expansion: Subscriber editions top streaming service's forecast, helped by growth in markets abroad, *Wall Street Journal*, www.wsj.com, January 21.

23. R. Parmar, I. Mackenzie, D. Cohn, & D. Gann, 2014, The new patterns of innovation, *Harvard Business Review*, 92(1/2): 86–95; M. Bogers, A. Afuah, & B. Bastian, 2010, Users as innovators: A review, critique and future research directions, *Journal of Management*, 36: 857–875.

24. D. Yagil & H. Medler-Liraz, 2013, Moments of truth: Examining transient authenticity and identity in service encounters. *Academy of Management Journal*, 56: 473–497.

25. A. S. Balaji & B. C. Krishnan, 2015, How customers cope with service failure? A study of brand reputation and customer satisfaction, *Journal of Business Research*, 68: 665–674; L-Y Jin, 2010, Determinants of customers' complaint intention, *Nankai Business Review International*, 1: 87–99.

26. R. Mortimer, 2014, The creation of a chief customer officer role at Tesco signals a quiet revolution in marketing thinking, *Marketing Week*, June 6, 3.

27. P. Skålén, J. Gummerus, C. Koskull, & P. Magnusson, 2015, Exploring value propositions and service innovation: A service-dominant logic study, *Journal of the Academy of Marketing Science*, 43: 137–158; M. Dixon, E. V. Karniouchina, B. D. Rhee, R. Verma, & L. Victorino, 2014, The role of coordinated marketing-operations strategy in services: Implications for managerial decisions and execution, *Journal of Service Management*, 25: 275–294; S. F. Slater, E. M. Olson, & G. T. Hult, 2010, Worried about strategy implementation? Don't overlook marketing's role, *Business Horizons*, 53: 469–479.

28. S. Han, Y. Ye, X. Fu, & Z. Chen, 2014, Category role aided market segmentation approach to convenience store chain category management, *Decision Support Systems*, 57: 296–308; P. Riefler, A. Diamantopoulos, & J. A. Siguaw, 2012, Cosmopolitan consumers as a target group for segmentation, *Journal of International Business Studies*, 43: 285–305.

29. 2015, About Hill's pet nutrition, Hill's Pet Nutrition, www.hillspet.com, February 23.

30. H. B. Corrigan, G. Craciun, & A. M. Powell, 2014, How does Target know so much about its customers? Utilizing customer analytics to make marketing decisions, *Marketing Education Review*, 24(2): 159–166.

31. J. Jargon, 2014, Millennials lose taste for McDonald's, *Wall Street Journal*, August 25, B1.

32. A. S. Sengupta, M. Balaji, & B. C. Krishnan, 2015, How customers cope with service failure? A study of brand reputation and customer satisfaction, *Journal of Business Research*, 68: 665–674; C. A. Funk, J. D. Arthurs, L. J. Trevino, & J. Joireman, 2010, Consumer animosity in the global value chain: The effect of international shifts on willingness to purchase hybrid products. *Journal of International Business Studies*, 41: 639–651.

33. Schilke, On the contingent value of dynamic capabilities for competitive advantage; P. J. Holahan, Z. Z. Sullivan, & S. K. Markham, 2014, Product development as core competence: How formal product

development practices differ for radical, more innovative, and incremental product innovations, *Journal of Product Innovation Management*, 31: 329–345.

34. D. J. Teece, 2014, The foundations of enterprise performance: Dynamic and ordinary capabilities in an (economic) theory of firms, *Academy of Management Perspectives*, 28: 328–352; D. J. Teece, 2012, Dynamic capabilities: Routines versus entrepreneurial action, *Journal of Management Studies*, 49: 1395–1401; P. L. Drnevich & A. P. Kriauciunas, 2011, Clarifying the conditions and limits of the contributions of ordinary and dynamic capabilities to relative firm performance, *Strategic Management Journal*, 32: 254–279.

35. R. Mudambi & T. Swift, 2014, Knowing when to leap: Transitioning between exploitative and explorative R&D, *Strategic Management Journal*, 35: 126–145; M. Gruber, F. Heinimann, M. Brietel, & S. Hungeling, 2010, Configurations of resources and capabilities and their performance implications: An exploratory study on technology ventures, *Strategic Management Journal*, 31: 1337–1356.

36. J. Haas, 2014, Focus on the core: Merck claims R&D restructuring poised to produce results, *In Vivo*, 32: 6–8.

37. 2015, About SAS, www.sas.com, February 24.

38. WWD: Women's Wear Daily, 2014, Change agents set the agenda, *WWD: Women's Wear Daily*, May 23, 8–10.

39. M. E. Porter, 1985, *Competitive Advantage*, New York: Free Press, 26.

40. R. Rumelt, 2011, *Good Strategy/Bad Strategy*, New York: Crown Business.

41. M. E. Porter, 1996, What is strategy?, *Harvard Business Review*, 74(6): 61–78.

42. Porter, What is strategy?

43. A. Agnihotri, 2014, The role of the upper echelon in the value chain management, *Competitiveness Review*, 24: 240–255; J. S. Srai & L. S. Alinaghian, 2013, Value chain reconfiguration in highly disaggregated industrial systems: Examining the emergence of health care diagnostics, *Global Strategy Journal*, 3: 88–108.

44. M. E. Porter, 1994, Toward a dynamic theory of strategy. In R. P. Rumelt, D. E. Schendel, & D. J. Teece (eds.), *Fundamental Issues in Strategy*. Boston: Harvard Business School Press: 423–461.

45. Porter, What is strategy?, 62.

46. Porter, *Competitive Advantage*, 15.

47. J. Block, J. Kohn, D. Miller, & K. Ullrich, 2015, Necessity entrepreneurship and competitive strategy, *Small Business Economics*, 44: 37–54; J. Gonzales-Benito & I. Suarez-Gonzalez, 2010, A study of the role played by manufacturing strategic objectives and capabilities in understanding the relationship between Porter's generic strategies and business performance, *British Journal of Management*, 21: 1027–1043.

48. Schilke, On the contingent value of dynamic capabilities for competitive advantage: The nonlinear moderating effect of environmental dynamism; Hoskisson, Ireland, Hitt, & Harrison, *Competing for Advantage*.

49. Porter, *Competitive Strategy*, 35–40.

50. B. Berman, 2015, How to compete effectively against low-cost competitors, *Business Horizons*, 58: 87–97; P. D. Orberg Jensen & B. Petersen, 2013, Global sourcing of services: Risk, process, and collaborative architecture, *Global Strategy Journal*, 3: 67–87; C. Weigelt, 2013, Leveraging supplier capabilities: The role of locus of capability deployment, *Strategic Management Journal*, 34: 1–21.

51. K. Grind, 2015, Vanguard problem riddles Fidelity, *Wall Street Journal*, Feb 13, C2.

52. J.-K. Park & Y. K. Ro, 2013, Product architectures and sourcing decisions: Their impact on performance, *Journal of Management*, 39: 814–846; M. Kotabe & R. Mudambi, 2009, Global sourcing and value creation: Opportunities and challenges, *Journal of International Management*, 15: 121–125.

53. S. Carnahan & D. Somaya, 2013, Alumni effects and relational advantage: The impact on outsourcing when a buyer hires employees from a supplier's competitors, *Academy of Management Journal*, 56: 1578–1600; R. Liu, D. J. Feils, & B. Scholnick, 2011, Why are different services outsources to different countries?, *Journal of International Business Studies*, 42: 558–571.

54. M. J. Lennox, S. F. Rockart, & A. Y. Lewin, 2010, Does interdependency affect firm and industry profitability? An empirical test, *Strategic Management Journal*, 31: 121–139.

55. 2015, Company overview, Big Lots, www.biglots.com, February 25.

56. A. Hinterhuber & S. M. Liozu, 2014, Is innovation in pricing your next source of competitive advantage?, *Business Horizons*, 57: 413–423; J. Morehouse, B. O'Mera, C. Hagen, & T. Huseby, 2008, Hitting back: Strategic responses to low-cost rivals, *Strategy & Leadership*, 36: 4–13.

57. J. Alcácer, C. L. Dezső, & M. Zhao, 2013, Firm rivalry, knowledge accumulation, and MNE location choices, *Journal of International Business Studies*, 44: 504–520; G. J. Kilduff, H. A. Elfenbein, & B. W. Staw, 2010, The psychology of rivalry: A relationally dependent analysis of competition, *Academy of Management Journal*, 53: 943–969.

58. S. D. Pathak, Z. Wu, & D, Johnston, D. 2014, Toward a structural view of co-opetition in supply networks, *Journal of Operations Management*, 32: 254–267; T. W. Tong & J. J. Reuer, 2010, Competitive consequences of interfirm collaboration: How joint ventures shape industry profitability, *Journal of International Business Studies*, 41: 1056–1073.

59. Y. Luo, Y. Huang, & S. L. Wang, 2011, Guanxi and organizational performance: A meta-analysis, *Management and Organization Review*, 8: 139–172.

60. G. Bhalla, 2014, How to plan and manage a project to co-create value with stakeholders, *Strategy & Leadership*, 42: 19–25; O. D. Fjeldstad & A. Sasson, 2010, Membership matters: On the value of being embedded in customer networks, *Journal of Management Studies*, 47: 944–966.

61. 2015, Our story, http://corporate.walmart.com, accessed February 25.

62. F. J. Contractor, V. Kumar, S. K. Kundu, & T. Pedersen, 2010, Reconceptualizing the firm in a world of outsourcing and offshoring: The organizational and geographical relocation of high-value company functions. *Journal of Management Studies*, 47: 1417–1433.

63. Y. Zhang & J. Gimeno, 2010, Earnings pressure and competitive behavior: Evidence from the U.S. electricity industry, *Academy of Management Journal*, 53: 743–768.

64. Heppelmann & Porter, How smart, connected products are transforming competition.

65. M. M. Larsen, S. Manning, & T. Pedersen, 2013, Uncovering the hidden costs of offshoring: The interplay of complexity, organizational design, and experience, *Strategic Management Journal*, 34: 533–552.

66. S. Chang & B. Wu, 2014, Institutional barriers and industry dynamics, *Strategic Management Journal*, 35: 1103–1123; Heppelmann & Porter, How smart, connected products are transforming competition; T. J. Kull, S. C. Ellis, & R. Narasimhan, 2013, Reducing behavioral constraints to supplier integration: A socio-technical systems perspective, *Journal of Supply Chain Management*, 49: 64–86; J. Dyer & W. Chu, 2011, The determinants of trust in supplier-automaker relations in the U.S., Japan and Korea: A retrospective, *Journal of International Business Studies*, 42: 28–34.

67. Heppelmann & Porter, How smart, connected products are transforming competition; O. Ormanidhi & O. Stringa, 2008, Porter's model of generic competitive strategies, *Business Economics*, 43: 55–64; J. Bercovitz & W. Mitchell, 2007, When is more better? The impact of business scale and scope on long-term business survival, while controlling for profitability, *Strategic Management Journal*, 28: 61–79.

68. Heppelmann & Porter, How smart, connected products are transforming competition; A. Kaul, 2012, Technology and corporate scope: Firm and rival innovation as antecedents of corporate transactions, *Strategic Management Journal*, 33: 347–367; K. Z. Zhou & F. Wu, 2010, Technological capability, strategic flexibility and product innovation, *Strategic Management Journal*, 31: 547–561.

69. Porter, *Competitive Strategy*, 35–40.

70. 2015, Product innovation, www.1000ventures.com, March 5.

71. H. Ryu, J. Lee, & B. Choi, 2015, Alignment between service innovation strategy and business strategy and its effect on firm performance: An empirical investigation, *IEEE Transactions on Engineering Management*, 62: 100–113; C. A. Siren, M. Kohtamaki, & A. Kuckertz, 2012, Exploration and exploitation strategies, profit performance and the mediating role of strategic learning: Escaping the exploitation trap, *Strategic Entrepreneurship Journal*, 6: 18–41.

72. M. Terpstra & F. H. Verbeeten, 2014, Customer satisfaction: Cost driver or value driver? Empirical evidence from the financial services industry, *European Management Journal*, 32: 499–508; U. Lichtenthaler & H. Ernst, 2012, Integrated knowledge exploitation: The complementarity of product development and technology licensing, *Strategic Management Journal*, 33: 513–534.

73. K. Rahman & C. S. Areni, 2014, Generic, genuine, or completely new? Branding strategies to leverage new products. *Journal of Strategic Marketing*, 22: 3–15; R. Kotha, Y. Zheng, & G. George, 2011, Entry into new niches: The effects of firm age and the expansion of technological capabilities on innovative output and impact, *Strategic Management Journal*, 32: 1011–1024.

74. M. J. Donate, & J. D. Sánchez de Pablo, 2015, The role of knowledge-oriented leadership in knowledge management practices and innovation, *Journal of Business Research*, 68: 360–370; J. T. Macher & C. Boerner, 2012, Technological development at the boundaries of the firm: A knowledge-based examination in drug development, *Strategic Management Journal*, 33: 1016–1036.

75. R. Kapoor & J. M. Lee, 2013, Coordinating and competing in ecosystems: How organizational forms shape new technology investments, *Strategic Management Journal*, 34: 274–296; F. T. Rothaermel, M. A. Hitt, & L. A. Jobe, 2006, Balancing vertical integration and strategic outsourcing: Effects on product portfolio, product success and firm performance, *Strategic Management Journal*, 27: 1033–1056.

76. Kapoor & Furr, 2015, Complementarities and competition: Unpacking the drivers of entrants' technology choices in the solar photovoltaic industry; D. Somaya, 2012, Patent strategy and management: An integrative review and research agenda, *Journal of Management*, 38: 1084–1114.

77. S. Germano, 2015, UnderArmour grows online, *Wall Street Journal*, Feb 5, B3.

78. Bettencourt, Lusch, & Vargo, A service lens on value creation; N. E. Levitas & T. Chi, 2010, A look at the value creation effects of patenting and capital investment through a real-option lens: The moderation role of uncertainty, *Strategic Entrepreneurship Journal*, 4: 212–233; L. A. Bettencourt & A. W. Ulwick, 2008, The customer-centered innovation map, *Harvard Business Review*, 86(5): 109–114.

79. R. Simons, 2014, Choosing the right customer. *Harvard Business Review*, 92(3): 48–55; M. Abbott, R. Holland, J. Giacomin, & J. Shackleton, 2009, Changing affective content in brand and product attributes, *Journal of Product & Brand Management*, 18: 17–26.

80. H. E. Posen, J. Lee, & S. Yi, 2013, The power of imperfect imitation, *Strategic Management Journal*, 34: 149–164.

81. Y. Mishina, E. S. Block, & M. J. Mannor, 2015, The path dependence of organizational reputation: How social judgment influences assessments of capability and character, *Strategic Management Journal*, forthcoming; B. K. Boyd, D. D. Bergh, & D. J. Ketchen, 2010, Reconsidering the reputation-performance relationship: A resource-based view, *Journal of Management*, 36: 588–609.

82. D. Laureiro-Martínez, S. Brusoni, N. Canessa, & M. Zollo, 2015, Understanding the exploration-exploitation dilemma: An fMRI study of attention control and decision-making performance, *Strategic Management Journal*, 36, 319–338; R. Mudambi & T. Swift, 2013, Knowing when to leap: Transitioning between exploitative and explorative R&R, *Strategic Management Journal*, in press.

83. S. Wilkins & J. Huisman, 2014, Corporate images' impact on consumers' product choices: The case of multinational foreign subsidiaries, *Journal of Business Research*, 67: 2224–2230; O. Chatain, 2011, Value creation, competition and performance in buyer-supplier relationships, *Strategic Management Journal*, 32: 76–102.

84. A. Marinez-Noya, E. Garcia-Canal, & M. F. Guillen, 2013, R&D outsourcing and the effectiveness of intangible investments: Is proprietary core knowledge walking out the door?, *Journal of Management Studies*, 5: 67–91.

85. Heppelmann & Porter, How smart, connected products are transforming competition; J. W. Upson, S. J. Ketchen, B. L. Connelly, & A. L. Ranft, 2012, Competitor analysis and foothold moves, *Academy of Management Journal*, 55: 93–110.

86. J. Harvey, P. Cohendet, L Simon, & S. Borzillo, 2015, Knowing communities in the front end of innovation, *Research Technology Management*, 58: 46–54; S. Anokhin & J. Wincent, 2012, Start-up rates and innovation: A cross-country examination, *Journal of International Business Studies*, 43: 41–60.

87. T. Bajarin, 2014, How tiny tech firms are disrupting the giants, *PC Magazine*, December, 36–38. B. Einhorn, B. Shrivastava, & J. Lee, 2014, Samsung's China problems come to India, *Bloomberg BusinessWeek*, October 27, 44–45.

88. J. West & M. Bogers, 2014, Leveraging external sources of innovation: A review of research on open innovation, *Journal of Product Innovation Management*, 31: 814–831; M. M. Crossan & M. Apaydin, 2010, A multi-dimensional framework of organizational innovation: A systematic review of the literature, *Journal of Management Studies*, 47: 1154–1180.

89. J. Chen, L. Teng, L., S. Liu, & H. Zhu, 2015, Anticipating regret and consumers' preferences for counterfeit luxury products, *Journal of Business Research*, 68: 507–515; X. Bian & L. Moutinho, 2009, An investigation of determinants of counterfeit purchase consideration, *Journal of Business Research*, 62: 368–378.

90. Porter, *Competitive Strategy*; M. Selove, 2014, How do firms become different? A dynamic model, *Management Science*, 60: 980–989.

91. 2015, About Goya foods, www.goyafoods.com, March 3.

92. Porter, *Competitive Advantage*, 15.

93. J. Mcintosh, 2015, IKEA profits flat in fiscal 2014. *Furniture/Today*, February 2, 47; K. Kling & I. Goteman, 2003, IKEA CEO Andres Dahlvig on international growth and IKEA's unique corporate culture and brand identity, *Academy of Management Executive*, 17: 31–37.

94. 2015, About IKEA, IKEA, www.ikea.com, March 3.

95. 2015, about Green Truck, www.greentruckonthego.com; March 3; A. Kadet, 2015, City news–metro money: Wheelin' and dealin' from a truck, *Wall Street Journal*, www.wsj.com, February 28. K. McLaughlin, 2009, Food truck nation, *Wall Street Journal*, www.wsj.com, June 5.

96. A. Barroso & M. S. Giarratana, 2013, Product proliferation strategies and firm performance: The moderating role of product space complexity, *Strategic Management Journal*, 34: 1435–1452.

97. C. E. Armstrong, 2012, Small retailer strategies for battling the big boxes: A "Goliath" victory?, *Journal of Strategy and Management*, 5: 41–56.

98. A. Gasparro & T. Stynes, 2015, Whole Foods benefits from increase in customers, *Wall Street Journal*, February 12, B4.

99. R. D. Banker, R. Mashruwala, & A. Tripathy, 2014, Does a differentiation strategy lead to more sustainable financial performance than a cost leadership strategy?, *Management Decision*, 56: 872–896; C. L. Hill, 1988, Differentiation versus low cost or differentiation and low cost: A contingency framework, *Academy of Management Review*, 13: 401–412.

100. C. Cennamo & J. Santalo, 2013, Platform competition: Strategic trade-offs in platform markets, *Strategic Management Journal*, 34: 1331–1350; H. A. Ndofor, D. G. Sirmon, & X. He, 2011, Firm resources, competitive actions and performance: Investigating a mediated model with evidence from the in-vitro diagnostics

industry, *Strategic Management Journal*, 32: 640–657; R. A. D'Aveni, G. B. Dagnino, & K. G. Smith, 2010, The age of temporary advantage, *Strategic Management Journal*, 31: 1371–1385.

101. 2015, Mission and Value, www.target.com, March 5.

102. S. Awate, M. M. Larsen, & R. Mudambi, 2015, Accessing vs sourcing knowledge: A comparative study of R&D internationalization between emerging and advanced economy firms, *Journal of International Business Studies*, 46: 63–86; E. R. Brenes, D. Montoya, & L. Ciravegna, 2014, Differentiation strategies in emerging markets: The case of Latin American agribusinesses, *Journal of Business Research*, 67: 847–855; G. A. Shinkle, A. P. Kriauciunas, & G. Hundley, 2013, Why pure strategies may be wrong for transition economy firms, *Strategic Management Journal*, 34: 1244–1254.

103. C. Eckel, L. Iacovone, B. Javorcik, & J. P. Neary, 2015, Multi-product firms at home and away: Cost-versus quality-based competence, *Journal of International Economics*, 95: 216–232; H. Wang & C. Kimble, 2010, Low-cost strategy through product architecture: Lessons from China, *Journal of Business Strategy*, 31(3): 12–20.

104. M. I. M. Wahab, D. Wu, and C.-G. Lee, 2008, A generic approach to measuring the machine flexibility of manufacturing systems, *European Journal of Operational Research*, 186: 137–149.

105. 2014, Rethinking car assembly, *Automotive Manufacturing Solutions*, November, 2–3.

106. A. Furlan, A. Cabigiosu, & A. Camuffo, 2014, When the mirror gets misted up: Modularity and technological change, *Strategic Management Journal*, 35, 789–807; M. Kotabe, R. Parente, & J. Y. Murray, 2007, Antecedents and outcomes of modular production in the Brazilian automobile industry: A grounded theory approach, *Journal of International Business Studies*, 38: 84–106.

107. P. Theodorou & G. Florou, 2008, Manufacturing strategies and financial performance—the effect of advanced information technology: CAD/CAM systems, *Omega*, 36: 107–121.

108. N. A. Morgan & L. L. Rego, 2009, Brand portfolio strategy and firm performance, *Journal of Marketing*, 73: 59–74.

109. P. Barlas, 2015, Salesforce.com large deals boom, fueling growth, *Investors Business Daily*, www.investors.com, February 26; D. Elmuti, H. Jia, & D. Gray, 2009, Customer relationship management strategic application and organizational effectiveness: An empirical investigation, *Journal of Strategic Marketing*, 17: 75–96.

110. D. J. Ketchen, T. R. Crook, & C. W. Craighead, 2014, From Supply chains to supply ecosystems: Implications for strategic sourcing research and practice, *Journal of Business Logistics*, 35: 165–171; B. Huo, Y. Qi, Z. Wang, & X. Zhao, 2014, The impact of supply chain integration on firm performance: The moderating role of competitive strategy, *Supply Chain Management*, 19: 369–384.

111. J. D. Westphal, R. Gulati, & S. M. Shortell, 1997, Customization or conformity: An institutional and network perspective on the content and consequences of TQM adoption, *Administrative Science Quarterly*, 42: 366–394.

112. H. Su, K. Linderman, R. G. Schroeder, & A. H. Van de Ven, 2014, A comparative case study of sustaining quality as a competitive advantage, *Journal of Operations Management*, 32: 429–445; S. Modell, 2009, Bundling management control innovations: A field study of organisational experimenting with total quality management and the balanced scorecard, *Accounting, Auditing & Accountability Journal*, 22: 59–90.

113. C. D. Zatzick, T. P. Moliterno, & T. Fang, 2012, Strategic (mis)fit: The implementation of TQM in manufacturing organizations, *Strategic Management Journal*, 33: 1321–1330.

114. J. Singh & H. Singh, 2015, Continuous improvement philosophy—literature review and directions, *Benchmarking: An International Journal*, 22: 75–119; A. Keramati & A. Albadvi, 2009, Exploring the relationship between use of information technology in total quality management and SMEs performance using canonical correlation analysis: A survey on Swedish car part supplier sector, *International Journal of Information Technology and Management*, 8: 442–462; R. J. David & S. Strang, 2006, When fashion is fleeting: Transitory collective beliefs and the dynamics of TQM consulting, *Academy of Management Journal*, 49: 215–233.

115. Porter, *Competitive Advantage*, 16.

116. Ibid., 17.

117. Y. Wang & N. Rajagopalan, 2014, Alliance capabilities: Review and research agenda, *Journal of Management*, 41: 236–260; M. A. Hitt, L. Bierman, K. Uhlenbruck, & K. Shimizu, 2006, The importance of resources in the internationalization of professional service firms: The good, the bad, and the ugly, *Academy of Management Journal*, 49: 1137–1157.

118. C. Christensen, 2015, Disruptive innovation is a strategy, not just the technology, *Business Today*, 23: 150–158; P. Puranam, H. Singh, & M. Zollo, 2006, Organizing for innovation: Managing the coordination-autonomy dilemma in technology acquisitions, *Academy of Management Journal*, 49: 263–280.

119. S. Thornhill & R. E. White, 2007, Strategic purity: A multi-industry evaluation of pure vs. hybrid business strategies, *Strategic Management Journal*, 28: 553–561.

120. A. Faelten, M. Gietzmann, & V. Vitkova, 2015, Learning from your investors: Can the geographical composition of institutional investors affect the chance of success in international M&A deals?, *Journal of Management & Governance*, 19: 47–69; B. Connelly, L. Tihanyi, S. T. Certo, & M. A. Hitt, 2010, Marching to the beat of different drummers: The influence of institutional owners on competitive actions, *Academy of Management Journal*, 53: 723–742.

5

Competitive Rivalry and Competitive Dynamics

Studying this chapter should provide you with the strategic management knowledge needed to:

5-1 Define competitors, competitive rivalry, competitive behavior, and competitive dynamics.

5-2 Describe market commonality and resource similarity as the building blocks of a competitor analysis.

5-3 Explain awareness, motivation, and ability as drivers of competitive behavior.

5-4 Discuss factors affecting the likelihood a competitor will take competitive actions.

5-5 Describe factors affecting the likelihood a competitor will respond to actions taken by its competitors.

5-6 Explain competitive dynamics in slow-cycle, in fast-cycle, and in standard-cycle markets.

DOES GOOGLE HAVE COMPETITION?
DYNAMICS OF THE HIGH TECHNOLOGY MARKETS

Google is especially known for its search business. In fact, many people now say they "googled it" when explaining that they searched the Internet for information on a particular subject. Google's market share of the search markets is estimated to be about 75 percent in the United States and an even higher 90 percent in Europe. In fact, many argue that this level of market share gives Google an effective monopoly in these markets. Of course, this level of market share has given Google significant power with advertisers and customers, power which the firm can use against its competitors. For example, the Federal Trade Commission (FTC) in the United States has stated that Google has pressured sites such as Yelp, TripAdvisor, and even Amazon to allow it to obtain information on users of their sites. Additionally, the FTC argued that Google has prevented advertisers from placing advertisements on other search engines. But, the FTC also stated that Google had violated no laws. Google's two largest rivals in the search business are Bing and Yahoo, both of which have about 12+ percent of the market. Yet, with continuing changes at other Internet-based companies, firms such as Amazon and Facebook may become important search market rivals in the near future by changing the focus of online shoppers. These companies now compete for advertisers in a number of markets.

Google is much more than a search business. It has entered many markets and is doing research on and/or preparing to enter many more markets. For example, Google recently opened its first Google retail shop in London and plans to open several more. The intent is to compete, at least partially, with Apple's successful retail stores. In another service market, Google recently introduced Android Pay as a competitive response to Apple Pay and Samsung Pay (also in response to Apple's service product). Google has introduced a new flight search tool, Google Flights, that helps customers find the best (including cheapest) airplane flights. This new service competes with several such services but especially with its large rival Expedia (originally started by Microsoft) which acquired Travelocity and Orbitz (two major competitors) in 2015.

Google has also recently entered several other new markets, such as the insurance search market (e.g., for the best auto insurance), and is offering wireless connection to the Internet competing with large telecommunications providers AT&T and Verizon. It is also planning entries in the smartphone and smartwatch markets. The smartwatch product is being developed in an alliance with TAG Heuer and Intel. The Google prototype smartphone will operate with a core product and multiple components. It will be similar to a Lego product where a customer can change screens such as adding a large screen to watch a major sporting event (e.g., the Super Bowl). Of course, these smartphone and smartwatch products will compete directly with Apple products and other companies as well.

Thus, Google competes in many markets and with multiple rivals. In some markets, Google dominates such as information search. But in other markets, it is a new entrant with a small market share competing against established and major companies (e.g., airline flight search and wireless Internet services). In some markets, Google is a primary actor (e.g., search) offering major new services, and in other markets, it is a responder (e.g., Android Pay). As a result, Google's competitive actions are exceedingly complex with competitive dynamics across multiple markets and competitors.

Sources: K. Benner, 2015, Don't be afraid of the big, bad Google, *The New Zealand Herald*, www.nzherald.co.nz, March 28; S. Buckley, 2015, Google Fiber's presence pressures AT&T to adjust 1 gig pricing plans, *FierceTelecom*, www.fiercetelecom.com, April 1; A. Chowdhry, 2015, Google's new flight search tool helps you find the best price, *Forbes*, www.forbes.com, February 27; C. Dougherty, 2015, Google and Intel to team up with TAG Heuer on a luxury smartwatch, *New York Times*, bits.blog.nytimes.com, March 19; 2015, Google high street riposte to Apple, *Yahoo*, uk.news.yahoo.com, March 11; 2015, Google opens its first retail store, *RTE News*, www.rte.ie, March 11; D. Lumb, 2015, Google answers Apple Pay with (surprise) Android Pay, *Fast Company*, www.fastcompany.com, March 2; V. Kotsev, 2015, Google shows off the smartphone of the future, and it's basically a Lego set, *Fast Company*, www.fastcompany.com, January 14; D. Lyons, 2015, Five myths about Google, *The Washington Post*, www.washingtonpost.com, March 20; 2015, Zuckerberg downplays Facebook/Google rivalry, *SeekingAlpha*, www.seekingalpha.com, March 26; 2014, Google plans to test high-speed wireless Internet, *Fortune*, fortune.com, October 15.

Firms operating in the same market, offering similar products, and targeting similar customers are **competitors**.[1] Google has many competitors because it competes in a number of markets. For example, Google competes against Bing and Yahoo in the general search market and against AT&T and Verizon in the wireless Internet market. Its planned entry into the smartphone market will compete against Apple and Samsung, among others. Thus, Google engages in a significant amount of competitive behavior (defined fully below, competitive behavior is essentially the set of actions and responses a firm takes as it competes against its rivals).

Firms interact with their competitors as part of the broad context within which they operate while attempting to earn above-average returns.[2] Another way to consider this is to note that no firm competes in a vacuum; rather, each firm's actions are part of a mosaic of competitive actions and responses taking place among a host of companies seeking the same objective—superior performance. And evidence shows that the decisions firms make about their interactions with competitors significantly affect their ability to earn above-average returns.[3] Because of this, firms seek to reach optimal decisions when considering how to compete against their rivals.[4]

Competitive rivalry is the ongoing set of competitive actions and competitive responses that occur among firms as they maneuver for an advantageous market position.[5] Especially in highly competitive industries, firms constantly jockey for advantage as they launch strategic actions and respond or react to rivals' moves.[6] It is important for those leading organizations to understand competitive rivalry because the reality is that some firms learn how to outperform their competitors, meaning that competitive rivalry influences an individual firm's ability to gain and sustain competitive advantages.[7] Rivalry results from firms initiating their own competitive actions and then responding to actions taken by competitors.[8]

Competitive behavior is the set of competitive actions and responses a firm takes to build or defend its competitive advantages and to improve its market position.[9] As explained in the Opening Case, Google takes many major actions to compete but also responds to rival's strategic action as exemplified by its Android Pay in response to similar services offered by Apple and Samsung. Through competitive behavior, Google seeks to successfully position itself relative to the five forces of competition (see Chapter 2) and to defend its current competitive advantages while building advantages for the future (see Chapter 3).

Increasingly, competitors engage in competitive actions and responses in more than one market which can be observed with Google and Apple and with Google and Amazon, for example.[10] Firms competing against each other in several product or geographic markets are engaged in **multimarket competition**.[11] All competitive behavior—that is, the total set of actions and responses taken by all firms competing within a market—is called **competitive dynamics**. The relationships among all of these key concepts are shown in Figure 5.1.

Competitors are firms operating in the same market, offering similar products, and targeting similar customers.

Competitive rivalry is the ongoing set of competitive actions and competitive responses that occur among firms as they maneuver for an advantageous market position.

Competitive behavior is the set of competitive actions and responses a firm takes to build or defend its competitive advantages and to improve its market position.

Multimarket competition occurs when firms compete against each other in several product or geographic markets.

Competitive dynamics refer to all competitive behaviors—that is, the total set of actions and responses taken by all firms competing within a market.

Figure 5.1 From Competition to Competitive Dynamics

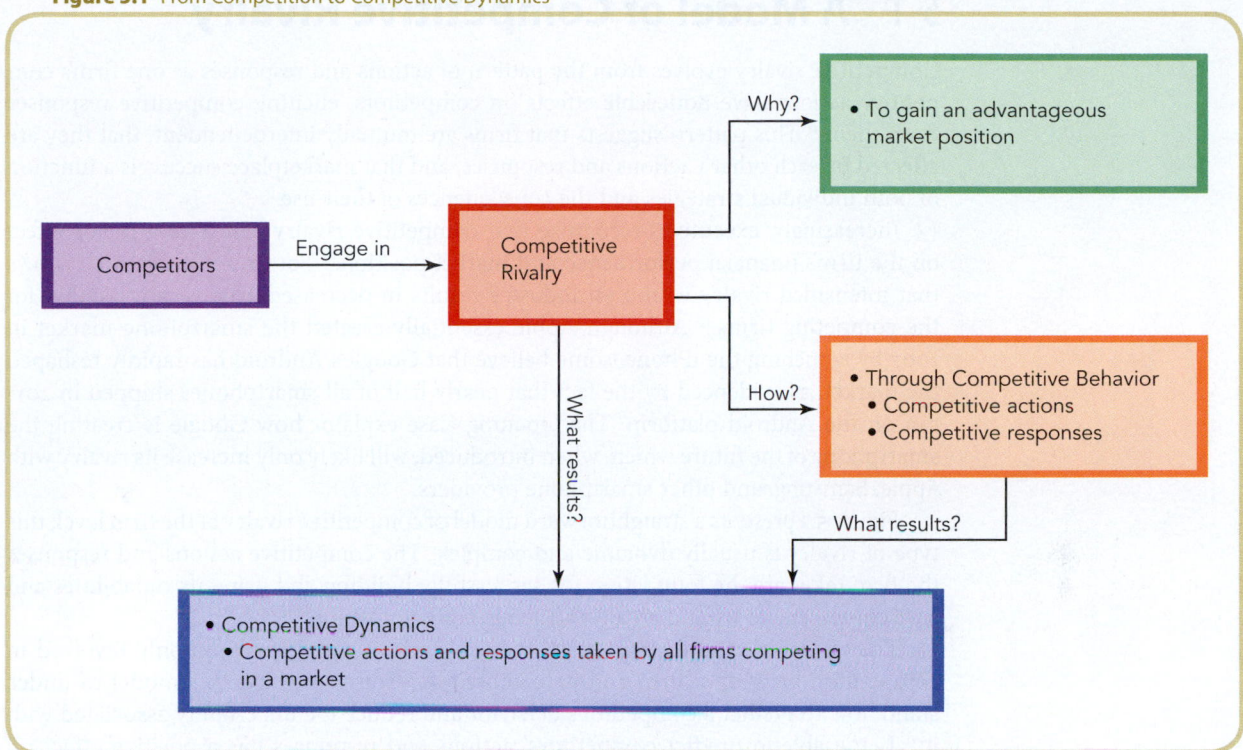

Source: Adapted from M. J. Chen, 1996, Competitor analysis and inferfirm rivalry: Toward a theoretical integration, *Academy of Management Review*, 21: 100-134.

This chapter focuses on competitive rivalry and competitive dynamics. A firm's strategies are dynamic in nature because actions taken by one firm elicit responses from competitors that, in turn, typically result in responses from the firm that took the initial action.[12] For example, in recent years, cigarette manufacturers took actions to introduce electronic cigarettes as a new product. Commonly called e-cigarettes, and with their health benefits still unknown, this product is a battery-powered device that converts heated, nicotine-laced liquid into vapor. The more prominent position in this market has been held by Lorillard, Inc., which is now merging with Reynolds American to become an even more formidable competitor in this market and other tobacco product markets. The other large tobacco product firm, Altria Group, introduced its MarkTen e-cigarette to compete with the other major firms in this market. Additional competitive actions and responses among these firms and with international cigarette manufacturers can be expected in the foreseeable future.[13]

Competitive rivalries affect a firm's strategies, as a strategy's success is determined not only by the firm's initial competitive actions but also by how well it anticipates competitors' responses to them *and* by how well the firm anticipates and responds to its competitors' initial actions (also called attacks).[14] Although competitive rivalry affects all types of strategies (e.g., corporate-level, merger and acquisition, and international), its dominant influence is on the firm's business-level strategy or strategies. Indeed, firms' actions and responses to those of their rivals are part of the basic building blocks of business-level strategies.[15]

Recall from Chapter 4 that business-level strategy is concerned with what the firm does to successfully use its core competencies in specific product markets. In the global economy, competitive rivalry is intensifying, meaning that its effect on firms' strategies is increasing. However, firms that develop and use effective business-level strategies tend to outperform competitors in individual product markets, even when experiencing intense competitive rivalry.

5-1   A Model of Competitive Rivalry

Competitive rivalry evolves from the pattern of actions and responses as one firm's competitive actions have noticeable effects on competitors, eliciting competitive responses from them.[16] This pattern suggests that firms are mutually interdependent, that they are affected by each other's actions and responses, and that marketplace success is a function of both individual strategies and the consequences of their use.[17]

Increasingly, executives recognize that competitive rivalry can have a major effect on the firm's financial performance and market position.[18] For example, research shows that intensified rivalry within an industry results in decreased average profitability for the competing firms.[19] Although Apple essentially created the smartphone market in 2007 by launching the iPhone, some believe that Google's Android has rapidly reshaped the market, as evidenced by the fact that nearly half of all smartphones shipped in 2012 ran on the Android platform. The Opening Case explains how Google is creating the smartphone of the future which, when introduced, will likely only increase its rivalry with Apple, Samsung, and other smartphone providers.

Figure 5.2 presents a straightforward model of competitive rivalry at the firm level; this type of rivalry is usually dynamic and complex. The competitive actions and responses the firm takes are the foundation for successfully building and using its capabilities and core competencies to gain an advantageous market position.[20]

The model in Figure 5.2 presents the sequence of activities commonly involved in competition between a firm and its competitors. Companies use this model to understand how to predict a competitor's behavior and reduce the uncertainty associated with it.[21] Being able to predict competitors' actions and responses has a positive effect on the firm's market position and its subsequent financial performance.[22] The total of all the individual rivalries modeled in Figure 5.2 that occur in a particular market reflect the competitive dynamics in that market.

The remainder of the chapter explains components of the model shown in Figure 5.2. We first describe market commonality and resource similarity as the building blocks of a competitor analysis. Next, we discuss the effects of three organizational characteristics—awareness, motivation, and ability—on the firm's competitive behavior. We then examine competitive rivalry between firms (interfirm rivalry). To do this, we explain the factors

Figure 5.2 A Model of Competitive Reality

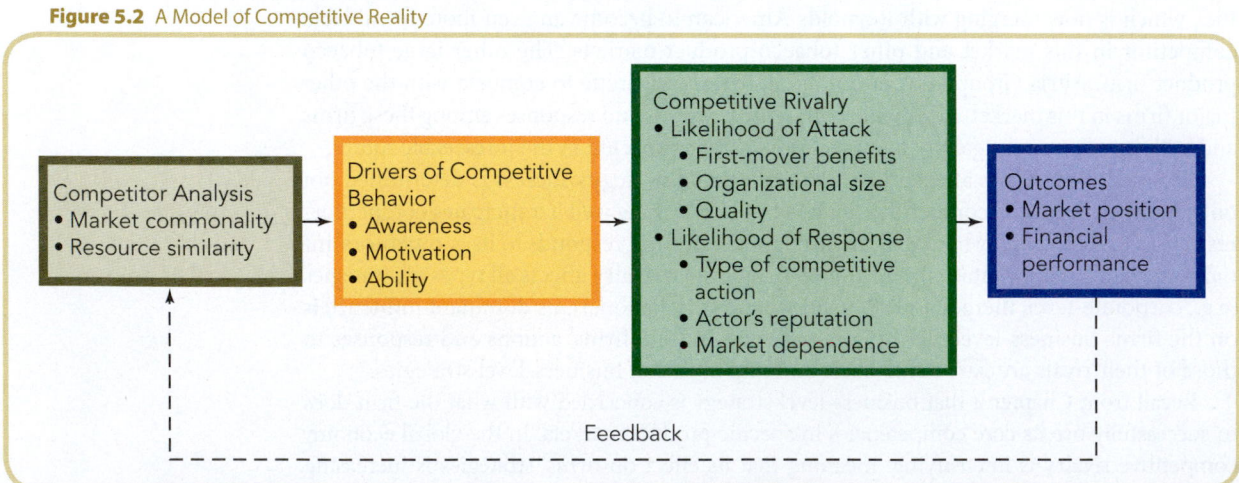

Source: Adapted from M. J. Chen, 1996, Competitor analysis and inferfirm rivalry: Toward a theoretical integration, *Academy of Management Review*, 21: 100–134.

that affect the likelihood a firm will take a competitive action and the factors that affect the likelihood a firm will respond to a competitor's action. In the chapter's final section, we turn our attention to competitive dynamics to describe how market characteristics affect competitive rivalry in slow-cycle, fast-cycle, and standard-cycle markets.

5-2 Competitor Analysis

As previously noted, a competitor analysis is the first step the firm takes to be able to predict the extent and nature of its rivalry with each competitor. Competitor analyses are especially important when entering a foreign market because firms doing so need to understand the local competition and foreign competitors currently operating in that market.[23] Without such analyses, they are less likely to be successful.

The number of markets in which firms compete against each other is called market commonality while the similarity in their resources is called resource similarity (both terms will be discussed later). These two dimensions of competition determine the extent to which firms are competitors. Firms with high market commonality and highly similar resources are direct and mutually acknowledged competitors. The drivers of competitive behavior—as well as factors influencing the likelihood that a competitor will initiate competitive actions and will respond to its competitors' actions—influence the intensity of rivalry.[24]

In Chapter 2, we discussed competitor analysis as a technique firms use to understand their competitive environment. Together, the general, industry, and competitive environments comprise the firm's external environment. We also described how competitor analysis is used to help the firm *understand* its competitors. This understanding results from studying competitors' future objectives, current strategies, assumptions, and capabilities (see Figure 2.3 in Chapter 2). In this chapter, the discussion of competitor analysis is extended to describe what firms study to be able to *predict* competitors' behavior in the form of their competitive actions and responses. The discussions of competitor analysis in Chapter 2 and in this chapter are complementary in that firms must first *understand* competitors (Chapter 2) before their competitive actions and responses can be *predicted* (this chapter).

Being able to accurately predict rivals' likely competitive actions and responses helps a firm avoid situations in which it is unaware of competitors' objectives, strategies, assumptions, and capabilities. Lacking the information needed to predict these conditions for competitors creates *competitive blind spots*. Typically, competitive blind spots find a firm being surprised by a competitor's actions, potentially resulting in negative outcomes.[25] Increasingly, members of a firm's board of directors are expected to use their knowledge and expertise about other businesses and industry environments to help a firm avoid competitive blind spots.[26]

5-2a Market Commonality

Every industry is composed of various markets. The financial services industry has markets for insurance, brokerage services, banks, and so forth. To concentrate on the needs of different, unique customer groups, markets can be further subdivided. The insurance market could be broken into market segments (such as commercial and consumer), product segments (such as health insurance and life insurance), and geographic markets (such as Southeast Asia and Western Europe). In general, the capabilities that Internet technologies generate help to shape the nature of industries' markets along with patterns of competition within those industries. For example, according to a Procter and Gamble (P&G) official: "Facebook is both a marketing and a distribution channel, as P&G has worked to develop 'f-commerce' capabilities on its fan pages, fulfilled by Amazon, which has become a top 10 retail account for Pampers," a disposable diaper product.[27]

Competitors tend to agree about the different characteristics of individual markets that form an industry. For example, in the transportation industry, the commercial air travel market differs from the ground transportation market, which is served by such firms as YRC Worldwide (one of the largest, less-than-truckload—LTL—carriers in North America and selected as Walmart's LTL Carrier of the Year) and its major competitors Arkansas Best, Con-way, Inc., and FedEx Freight.[28] Although differences exist, many industries' markets are partially related in terms of technologies used or core competencies needed to develop a competitive advantage. For example, although railroads and truck ground transport compete in a different segment and can be substitutes, different types of transportation companies need to provide reliable and timely service. Commercial air carriers such as Southwest, United, and Jet Blue must therefore develop service competencies to satisfy their passengers, while ground transport companies such as YRC, railroads, and their major competitors must develop such competencies to satisfy the needs of those using their services to ship goods.

Firms sometimes compete against each other in several markets, a condition called market commonality. More formally, **market commonality** is concerned with the number of markets with which the firm and a competitor are jointly involved and the degree of importance of the individual markets to each.[29] Firms competing against one another in several or many markets are said to be engaging in multimarket competition.[30] Coca-Cola and PepsiCo compete across a number of product markets (e.g., soft drinks, bottled water) as well as geographic markets (throughout North America and in many other countries throughout the world). Airlines, chemicals, pharmaceuticals, and consumer foods are examples of other industries with firms often competing against each other in multiple markets.

Firms competing in several of the same markets have the potential to respond to a competitor's actions not only within the market in which a given set of actions are taken, but also in other markets where they compete with the rival. This potential creates a complicated mosaic in which the competitive actions or responses a firm takes in one market may be designed to affect the outcome of its rivalry with a particular competitor in a second market.[31] This potential complicates the rivalry between competitors. In fact, research suggests that a firm with greater multimarket contact is less likely to initiate an attack, but more likely to move (respond) aggressively when attacked. For instance, research in the computer industry found that "firms respond to competitive attacks by introducing new products but do not use price as a retaliatory weapon."[32] Thus in general, multimarket competition reduces competitive rivalry, but some firms will still compete when the potential rewards (e.g., potential market share gain) are high.[33]

5-2b Resource Similarity

Resource similarity is the extent to which the firm's tangible and intangible resources are comparable to a competitor's in terms of both type and amount.[34] Firms with similar types and amounts of resources are likely to have similar strengths and weaknesses and use similar strategies on the basis of their strengths to pursue what may be similar opportunities in the external environment.

"Resource similarity" describes part of the relationship between FedEx and United Parcel Service (UPS). These companies compete in many of the same markets, and thus are also accurately described as having market commonality. For example, these firms have similar types of truck and airplane fleets, similar levels of financial capital, and rely on equally talented reservoirs of human capital along with sophisticated information

Market commonality is concerned with the number of markets with which the firm and a competitor are jointly involved and the degree of importance of the individual markets to each.

Resource similarity is the extent to which the firm's tangible and intangible resources are comparable to a competitor's in terms of both type and amount.

technology systems (resources). In addition to competing aggressively against each other in North America, the firms share many other country markets in common. Thus, the rivalry between these two firms is intense.

When performing a competitor analysis, a firm analyzes each of its competitors with respect to market commonality and resource similarity. The results of these analyses can be mapped for visual comparisons. In Figure 5.3, we show different hypothetical intersections between the firm and individual competitors in terms of market commonality and resource similarity. These intersections indicate the extent to which the firm and those with which it compares itself are competitors. For example, the firm and its competitor displayed in quadrant I have similar types and amounts of resources (i.e., the two firms have a similar portfolio of resources). The firm and its competitor in quadrant I would use their similar resource portfolios to compete against each other in many markets that are important to each. These conditions lead to the conclusion that the firms modeled in quadrant I are direct and mutually acknowledged competitors.

In contrast, the firm and its competitor shown in quadrant III share few markets and have little similarity in their resources, indicating that they aren't direct and mutually acknowledged competitors. Thus a small, local, family-owned restaurant concentrating on selling "gourmet" hamburgers does not compete directly against McDonald's. The mapping of competitive relationships is fluid as companies enter and exit markets and as rivals' resources change in type and amount, meaning that the companies with which a given firm is a direct competitor change over time.

Kellogg has held a dominant market position in cold cereal sales for a long time but its sales of cereals have begun to decline as explained in the Strategic Focus. Its major competitors are responding better to the changes in the market than Kellogg. Kellogg seems to be trying to force its products on the market rather than changing its product lines to satisfy consumer needs. General Mills' purchase of Yoplait is positioning that firm to advance in the newer breakfast food market. Kellogg's response appears to be weak and is likely to be ineffective. Without major changes, Kellogg is likely to suffer additional decline.

Figure 5.3 A Framework of Competitor Analysis

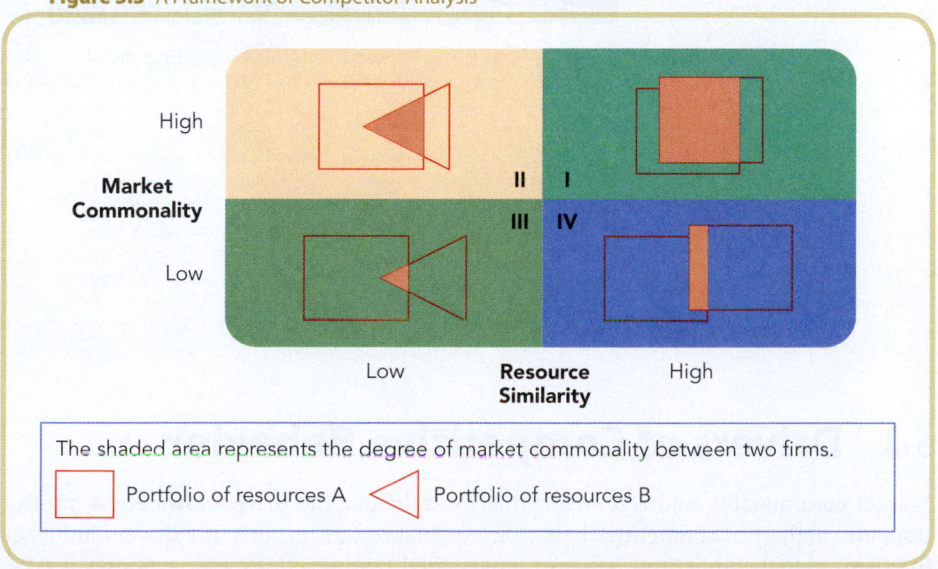

Source: Adapted from M. J. Chen, 1996, Competitor analysis and interfirm rivalry: Toward a theoretical integration, *Academy of Management Review*, 21: 100–134.

Strategic Focus

Does Kellogg Have the Tiger by the Tail or Is It the Reverse?

Kellogg Company has been the leading and largest cereal maker in the U.S. market for some time. It once had 45 percent of the U. S. cereal market. Thus, for a number of years, Kellogg was flying high with its "Tony the Tiger" advertisements and its leading cereals of Frosted Flakes, Frosted Mini-Wheats, and Special K cereals, among others. That is no longer the case, especially with the changes in the breakfast food market. In fact, cereal, which at one time comprised approximately 38 percent of the breakfast foods in the United States, currently accounts for about 28 percent of the breakfast food sales. United States consumers are moving away from processed foods and carbohydrates to fruit, yogurt, and protein such as eggs for breakfast meals. As a result, Kellogg's sales of its cereals are slumping, profits are slipping, and its stock price is declining. A recent survey of analysts found that 90 percent recommended selling or putting a hold on Kellogg stock, with only 10 percent recommending that investors buy it.

In 2014, sales for 19 of Kellogg's top 25 cereals declined. While other major cereal makers also struggled, General Mills' (e.g., Cheerios, Lucky Charms) sales were 50 percent better than Kellogg's. And, Post's sales in 2014 even net a two percent increase. So, Kellogg's competitors seem to be weathering the crisis better than it is able to do. To deal with the declining sales, Kellogg acquired Pringles for $2.7 billion. Yet, Pringles clearly represents processed foods which the consumer is beginning to resist. Alternatively, General Mills acquired a controlling ownership position in Yoplait, the second-largest manufacturer of yogurt in the world. This acquisition strengthened General Mill's market position with the increasing demand for yogurt. Kellogg is also trying to revive its Special K and Kashi sales by adding fruit and other items. Some believe that these actions will generate few positive returns. In addition, Kellogg invests heavily in advertising with outlays of more than $1 billion annually.

Obviously, Kellogg is losing market share to its major rivals in the cereal market, but it is also losing to other firms that are providing different breakfast foods increasingly desired by the United States consumer. Kellogg's breakfast cereal sales declined by 6 percent in 2014, and their outlook is not good. Yet, Kellogg is investing in special advertising campaigns to encourage consumers to eat more cereal for breakfast. At one time, Kellogg had an advantage because of its size; it could invest more resources in advertising and marketing in general, thereby building relations with retailers (and consumers). Today, its large size appears to be hurting the firm. Kellogg seems unable to make the major changes required to respond to the new demands in the breakfast food market. Its competitors are responding more effectively, suggesting a dark future for Kellogg.

Perhaps Kellogg would do well to promote a healthy breakfast that includes cereal (e.g., along with fruit, milk, juice and egg).

ElinaManninen/Getty Images

Sources: J. Kell, 2014, Decline in cereal sales bites into Kellogg's results, *Fortune*, www.fortune.com, October 30; A. A. Newman, 2014, With a night campaign, Kellogg's aims for snappier sales, *New York Times*, www.nytimes.com, December 17; S. Danshkhu and S. Neville, 2015, Food companies give frosty reception to labour sugar clamp, *Financial Times*, www.ft.com, January 15; M. Badkar, 2015, Kellogg loses ground after forecasts cut, *Financial Times*, www.ft.com, February 12; S. A. Gasparro, 2015, Kellogg posts loss, cautions on outlook, *Wall Street Journal*, www.wsj.com, February 12; S. Strom, 2015, A sharp loss for Kellogg as sales of cereal falter, *New York Times*, www.nytimes.com, February 12; 2015, Kellogg cuts long-term outlook on sluggish cereal, snack sales, *Fortune*, www.fortune.com, February 12; D. Leonard, 2015, Bad news in cereal city, *Bloomberg Business*, March 2–6, pp. 42–47.

5-3 Drivers of Competitive Behavior

Market commonality and resource similarity influence the drivers (awareness, motivation, and ability) of competitive behavior (see Figure 5.2). In turn, the drivers influence the firm's actual competitive behavior, as revealed by the actions and responses it takes while engaged in competitive rivalry.[35]

Awareness, which is a prerequisite to any competitive action or response taken by a firm, refers to the extent to which competitors recognize the degree of their mutual interdependence that results from market commonality and resource similarity.[36] Awareness affects the extent to which the firm understands the consequences of its competitive actions and responses. A lack of awareness can lead to excessive competition, resulting in a negative effect on all competitors' performance.[37]

Awareness tends to be greatest when firms have highly similar resources (in terms of types and amounts) to use while competing against each other in multiple markets. Komatsu Ltd., Japan's top construction machinery maker, and U.S.-based Caterpillar Inc. have similar resources and are aware of each other's actions given that they compete against each other in markets throughout the world. Founded in 1925, Caterpillar is the world's leading manufacturer of construction and mining equipment, diesel and natural gas engines, and industrial gas turbines, while Komatsu is the world's second largest seller of construction and mining machinery behind Caterpillar. Recently, differences in the exchange rates for the U. S. dollar and the Japanese yen have favored Komatsu. Komatsu has used this advantage to aggressively seek new customers and sales through its product pricing strategies.[38] Over the years, these firms have competed aggressively against each other for market share in multiple countries and regions.

Motivation, which concerns the firm's incentive to take action or to respond to a competitor's attack, relates to perceived gains and losses. Thus, a firm may be aware of competitors but may not be motivated to engage in rivalry with them if it perceives that its position will not improve or that its market position won't be damaged if it doesn't respond.[39] A benefit of not having the motivation to engage in rivalry at a point in time with a competitor is that the firm that lacks motivation to compete against another firm retains resources that can be used for other purposes including competing against a different rival.

Market commonality affects the firm's perceptions and resulting motivation. For example, a firm is generally more likely to attack the rival with whom it has low market commonality than the one with whom it competes in multiple markets. The primary reason for this is the high stakes involved in trying to gain a more advantageous position over a rival with whom the firm shares many markets. As mentioned earlier, multimarket competition can result in a competitor responding to the firm's action in a market different from the one in which that action was taken. Actions and responses of this type can cause both firms to lose focus on core markets and to battle each other with resources that had been allocated for other purposes. Because of the high competitive stakes under the condition of market commonality, the probability is high that the attacked firm will respond to its competitor's action in an effort to protect its position in one or more markets.[40]

In some instances, the firm may be aware of the markets it shares with a competitor and be motivated to respond to an attack by that competitor, but lack the ability to do so. *Ability* relates to each firm's resources and the flexibility they provide. Without available resources (such as financial capital and people), the firm is not able to attack a competitor or respond to its actions. For example, smaller and newer firms tend to be more innovative but generally have fewer resources to attack larger and established competitors. Likewise, foreign firms often are at a disadvantage against local firms because of the local firms' social capital (relationships) with consumers, suppliers, and government officials.[41] However, similar resources suggest similar abilities to attack and respond. When a firm faces a competitor with similar resources, careful study of a possible attack before initiating it is essential because the similarly resourced competitor is likely to respond to that action.[42]

Resource *dissimilarity* also influences competitive actions and responses between firms in that the more significant the difference between resources owned by the acting firm and those against whom it has taken action, the longer is the delay by the firm

Small competitors, such as A&T Grocery, find it difficult to respond to the competitive threat that exists with Walmart. Yet, they must find a way to respond, perhaps by offering personalized services, in order to survive such a threat.

David Grossman/Alamy

with a resource disadvantage.[43] For example, Walmart initially used a focused cost leadership strategy to compete only in small communities (those with a population of 25,000 or less). Using sophisticated logistics systems and efficient purchasing practices, among other methods, to gain competitive advantages, Walmart created a new type of value (primarily in the form of wide selections of products at the lowest competitive prices) for customers in small retail markets. Local competitors lacked the ability to marshal needed resources at the pace required to respond to Walmart's actions quickly and effectively. However, even when facing competitors with greater resources (greater ability) or more attractive market positions, firms should eventually respond, no matter how daunting the task seems. Choosing not to respond can ultimately result in failure, as happened with at least some local retailers who didn't respond to Walmart's competitive actions. Today, with Walmart as the world's largest retailer, it is indeed difficult for smaller competitors to have the resources required to effectively respond to its competitive actions or competitive responses.[44]

5-4 Competitive Rivalry

The ongoing competitive action/response sequence between a firm and a competitor affects the performance of both firms. Because of this, it is important for companies to carefully analyze and understand the competitive rivalry present in the markets in which they compete.[45]

As we described earlier, the predictions drawn from studying competitors in terms of awareness, motivation, and ability are grounded in market commonality and resource similarity. These predictions are fairly general. The value of the final set of predictions the firm develops about each of its competitors' competitive actions and responses is enhanced by studying the "Likelihood of Attack" factors (such as first-mover benefits and organizational size) and the "Likelihood of Response" factors (such as the actor's reputation) that are shown in Figure 5.2. Evaluating and understanding these factors allow the firm to refine the predictions it makes about its competitors' actions and responses.

5-4a Strategic and Tactical Actions

Firms use both strategic and tactical actions when forming their competitive actions and competitive responses in the course of engaging in competitive rivalry.[46] A **competitive action** is a strategic or tactical action the firm takes to build or defend its competitive advantages or improve its market position. A **competitive response** is a strategic or tactical action the firm takes to counter the effects of a competitor's competitive action. A **strategic action** or a **strategic response** is a market-based move that involves a significant commitment of organizational resources and is difficult to implement and reverse. A **tactical action** or a **tactical response** is a market-based move that is taken to fine-tune

A **competitive action** is a strategic or tactical action the firm takes to build or defend its competitive advantages or improve its market position.

A **competitive response** is a strategic or tactical action the firm takes to counter the effects of a competitor's competitive action.

A **strategic action** or a **strategic response** is a market-based move that involves a significant commitment of organizational resources and is difficult to implement and reverse.

A **tactical action** or a **tactical response** is a market-based move that is taken to fine-tune a strategy; it involves fewer resources and is relatively easy to implement and reverse.

a strategy; it involves fewer resources and is relatively easy to implement and reverse. When engaging rivals in competition, firms must recognize the differences between strategic and tactical actions and responses and develop an effective balance between the two types of competitive actions and responses.

A few years ago, Nokia Corporation, implemented an important strategic action by partnering with Microsoft "to deliver an ecosystem with unrivalled global reach and scale" in its smartphone business. This relationship was, in part, a strategic response to Apple's success. However, in 2013, Microsoft acquired Nokia's cellphone business as a critical part of Microsoft's mobile device strategy.[47] This represented a strategic action by Microsoft.

Walmart prices aggressively as a means of increasing revenues and gaining market share at the expense of competitors. In this regard, the firm engages in a continuous stream of tactical actions to attack rivals by changing some of its products' prices and tactical responses to respond to price changes taken by competitors such as Costco and Target.

5-5 Likelihood of Attack

In addition to market commonality; resource similarity; and the drivers of awareness, motivation, and ability, other factors affect the likelihood a competitor will use strategic actions and tactical actions to attack its competitors. Three of these factors—first-mover benefits, organizational size, and quality—are discussed next. Second and late movers are considered as part of the discussion of first-mover benefits.

5-5a First-Mover Benefits

A **first mover** is a firm that takes an initial competitive action in order to build or defend its competitive advantages or to improve its market position. The first-mover concept has been influenced by the work of the famous economist Joseph Schumpeter, who argued that firms achieve competitive advantage by taking innovative actions[48] (innovation is defined and discussed in Chapter 13). In general, first movers emphasize research and development (R&D) as a path to develop innovative goods and services that customers will value.[49]

The benefits of being a successful first mover can be substantial.[50] This is especially true in fast-cycle markets (discussed later in the chapter) where changes occur rapidly, and where it is virtually impossible to sustain a competitive advantage for any length of time. A first mover in a fast-cycle market can experience many times the valuation and revenue of a second mover.[51] This evidence suggests that although first-mover benefits are never absolute, they are often critical to a firm's success in industries experiencing rapid technological developments and relatively short product life cycles.[52] In addition to earning above-average returns until its competitors respond to its successful competitive action, the first mover can gain

- the loyalty of customers who may become committed to the goods or services of the firm that first made them available.
- market share that can be difficult for competitors to take during future competitive rivalry[53]

The general evidence that first movers have greater survival rates than later market entrants is perhaps the culmination of first-mover benefits.[54]

The firm trying to predict its rivals' competitive actions might conclude that they will take aggressive strategic actions to gain first movers' benefits. However, even though a firm's competitors might be motivated to be first movers, they may lack the ability to do so.

A **first mover** is a firm that takes an initial competitive action in order to build or defend its competitive advantages or to improve its market position.

First movers tend to be aggressive and willing to experiment with innovation and take higher yet reasonable levels of risk, and their long-term success depends on retaining the ability to do so.[55]

To be a first mover, the firm must have the readily available resources to significantly invest in R&D as well as to rapidly and successfully produce and market a stream of innovative products.[56] Organizational slack makes it possible for firms to have the ability (as measured by available resources) to be first movers. *Slack* is the buffer or cushion provided by actual or obtainable resources that aren't currently in use and are in excess of the minimum resources needed to produce a given level of organizational output.[57] As a liquid resource, slack can quickly be allocated to support competitive actions, such as R&D investments and aggressive marketing campaigns that lead to first-mover advantages. This relationship between slack and the ability to be a first mover allows the firm to predict that a first-mover competitor likely has available slack and will probably take aggressive competitive actions to continuously introduce innovative products. Furthermore, the firm can predict that, as a first mover, a competitor will try to rapidly gain market share and customer loyalty in order to earn above-average returns until its competitors are able to effectively respond to its first move.

Firms evaluating their competitors should realize that being a first mover carries risk. For example, it is difficult to accurately estimate the returns that will be earned from introducing product innovations to the marketplace.[58] Additionally, the first mover's cost to develop a product innovation can be substantial, reducing the slack available to support further innovation. Thus, the firm should carefully study the results a competitor achieves as a first mover. Continuous success by the competitor suggests additional product innovations, while lack of product acceptance over the course of the competitor's innovations may indicate less willingness in the future to accept the risks of being a first mover.[59]

A **second mover** is a firm that responds to the first mover's competitive action, typically through imitation. More cautious than the first mover, the second mover studies customers' reactions to product innovations. In the course of doing so, the second mover also tries to find any mistakes the first mover made so that it can avoid them and the problems they created. Often, successful imitation of the first mover's innovations allows the second mover to avoid the mistakes and the major investments required of the pioneering first movers.[60]

Second movers have the time to develop processes and technologies that are more efficient than those used by the first mover or that create additional value for consumers.[61] The most successful second movers rarely act too fast (so they can fully analyze the first mover's actions) nor too slow (so they do not give the first mover time to correct its mistakes and "lock in" customer loyalty). Overall, the outcomes of the first mover's competitive actions may provide a blueprint for second and even late movers as they determine the nature and timing of their competitive responses.[62]

Determining whether a competitor is an effective second mover (based on its past actions) allows a first-mover firm to predict when or if the competitor will respond quickly to successful, innovation-based market entries. The first mover can expect a successful second-mover competitor to study its market entries and to respond with a new entry into the market within a short time period. As a second mover, the competitor will try to respond with a product that provides greater customer value than does the first mover's product. The most successful second movers are able to rapidly and meaningfully interpret market feedback to respond quickly yet successfully to the first mover's successful innovations.

Home-improvement rating site Angie's List was founded roughly two decades ago. More than two million U.S. households have been using the service to gain information about the quality of 700-plus services (plumbing, electrical work, and so forth) provided

A **second mover** is a firm that responds to the first mover's competitive action, typically through imitation.

by local companies. Angie's List members submit reviews at the rate of over 60,000 per month. Although the firm enjoyed success for several years, it suffered net losses during the of 2009–2014. And, because of this, its stock price has tumbled almost 50 percent from its highest values. The firm has suffered a number of problems in recent years, but perhaps the largest challenge has come from its competition. Its primary competitor is Consumer Reports. But, it also has suffered from competitors that offer free lists and/or search services such as Yelp, Porch.com, home improvement network, and Google Local.[63] Second movers have clearly responded to the initial success of Angie's List. Each of the second movers offers a slightly different service to customers, trying to improve on the quality, breath, and/or depth of what Angie's List offers. Thus, being successful requires substantial and continuous efforts because competitors are likely to erode or eliminate existing competitive advantages.

Daniel Acker/Bloomberg/Getty Images

The Angie's List website is displayed on a computer screen. The consumer-review website has spawned a number of second movers that attempt to improve on Angie's List features and target narrow market segments.

A **late mover** is a firm that responds to a competitive action a significant amount of time after the first mover's action and the second mover's response. Typically, a late response is better than no response at all, although any success achieved from the late competitive response tends to be considerably less than that achieved by first and second movers. However, on occasion, late movers can be successful if they develop a unique way to enter the market and compete. For firms from emerging economies, this often means a niche strategy with lower-cost production and manufacturing. It can also mean that they need to learn from the competitors or others in the market in order to market products that allow them to compete.[64]

The firm competing against a late mover can predict that the competitor will likely enter a particular market only after both the first and second movers have achieved success in that market. Moreover, on a relative basis, the firm can predict that the late mover's competitive action will allow it to earn average returns only after the considerable time required for it to understand how to create at least as much customer value as that offered by the first and second movers' products.

5-5b Organizational Size

An organization's size affects the likelihood it will take competitive actions as well as the types and timing of those actions.[65] In general, small firms are more likely than large companies to launch competitive actions and tend to do it more quickly. Smaller firms are thus perceived as nimble and flexible competitors who rely on speed and surprise to defend their competitive advantages or develop new ones while engaged in competitive rivalry, especially with large companies, to gain an advantageous market position.[66] Small firms' flexibility and nimbleness allow them to develop variety in their competitive actions; large firms tend to limit the types of competitive actions used.[67]

Large firms, however, are likely to initiate more competitive actions along with more strategic actions during a given period.[68] Thus, when studying its competitors in terms of organizational size, the firm should use a measurement such as total sales revenue or total number of employees. The competitive actions the firm likely will encounter from

A **late mover** is a firm that responds to a competitive action a significant amount of time after the first mover's action and the second mover's response.

competitors larger than it is will be different from the competitive actions it will encounter from smaller competitors.

The organizational size factor adds another layer of complexity. When engaging in competitive rivalry, firms prefer to be able to have the capabilities required to take a large number of unique competitive actions. For this to be the case, a firm needs to have the amount of slack resources that a large, successful company typically holds if it is to be able to launch a greater *number* of competitive actions. Simultaneously though, the firm needs to be flexible when considering competitive actions and responses it might take if it is to be able to launch a greater *variety* of competitive actions. Collectively then, firms are best served competitively when their size permits them to take an appropriate number of unique or diverse competitive actions and responses.

5-5c Quality

Quality has many definitions, including well-established ones relating it to the production of goods or services with zero defects and as a cycle of continuous improvement.[69] From a strategic perspective, we consider quality to be the outcome of how a firm competes through its value chain activities and support functions (see Chapter 3). Thus, **quality** exists when the firm's goods or services meet or exceed customers' expectations. Some evidence suggests that quality may be the most critical component in satisfying the firm's customers.[70]

In the eyes of customers, quality is about doing the right things relative to performance measures that are important to them.[71] Customers may be interested in measuring the quality of a firm's goods and services against a broad range of dimensions. Sample quality dimensions in which customers commonly express an interest are shown in Table 5.1.

Table 5.1 Quality Dimensions of Products and Services

Product Quality Dimensions
1. *Performance*—Operating characteristics
2. *Features*—Important special characteristics
3. *Flexibility*—Meeting operating specifications over some period of time
4. *Durability*—Amount of use before performance deteriorates
5. *Conformance*—Match with pre-established standards
6. *Serviceability*—Ease and speed of repair
7. *Aesthetics*—How a product looks and feels
8. *Perceived quality*—Subjective assessment of characteristics (product image)

Service Quality Dimensions
1. *Timeliness*—Performed in the promised period of time
2. *Courtesy*—Performed cheerfully
3. *Consistency*—Giving all customers similar experiences each time
4. *Convenience*—Accessibility to customers
5. *Completeness*—Fully serviced, as required
6. *Accuracy*—Performed correctly each time

Source: Adapted from J. Evans, 2008, *Managing for Quality and Performance*, 7th Ed., Mason, OH: Thomson Publishing.

Quality exists when the firm's goods or services meet or exceed customers' expectations.

Quality is possible only when top-level managers support it and when its importance is institutionalized throughout the entire organization and its value chain.[72] When quality is institutionalized and valued by all, employees and managers alike become vigilant about continuously finding ways to improve it.[73]

Quality is a universal theme in the global economy and is a necessary but insufficient condition for competitive success.[74] Without quality, a firm's products lack credibility, meaning that customers don't think of them as viable options. Indeed, customers won't consider buying a product or using a service until they believe that it can satisfy at least their base-level expectations in terms of quality dimensions that are important to them.[75]

Quality affects competitive rivalry. The firm evaluating a competitor whose products suffer from poor quality can predict declines in the competitor's sales revenue until the quality issues are resolved. In addition, the firm can predict that the competitor likely won't be aggressive in its competitive actions until the quality problems are corrected in order to gain credibility with customers.[76] However, after the problems are corrected, that competitor is likely to take more aggressive competitive actions.

5-6 Likelihood of Response

The success of a firm's competitive action is affected by the likelihood that a competitor will respond to it as well as by the type (strategic or tactical) and effectiveness of that response. As noted earlier, a competitive response is a strategic or tactical action the firm takes to counter the effects of a competitor's competitive action. In general, a firm is likely to respond to a competitor's action when either

- the action leads to better use of the competitor's capabilities to develop a stronger competitive advantage or an improvement in its market position,
- the action damages the firm's ability to use its core competencies to create or maintain an advantage or
- the firm's market position becomes harder to defend.[77]

In addition to market commonality and resource similarity, and awareness, motivation, and ability, firms evaluate three other factors—type of competitive action, actor's reputation, and market dependence—to predict how a competitor is likely to respond to competitive actions (see Figure 5.2).

5-6a Type of Competitive Action

Competitive responses to strategic actions differ from responses to tactical actions. These differences allow the firm to predict a competitor's likely response to a competitive action that has been launched against it. Strategic actions commonly receive strategic responses and tactical actions receive tactical responses. In general, strategic actions elicit fewer total competitive responses because strategic responses, such as market-based moves, involve a significant commitment of resources and are difficult to implement and reverse.[78]

Another reason that strategic actions elicit fewer responses than do tactical actions is that the time needed to implement a strategic action and to assess its effectiveness can delay the competitor's response to that action.[79] In contrast, a competitor likely will respond quickly to a tactical action, such as when an airline company almost immediately matches a competitor's tactical action of reducing prices in certain markets. Either strategic actions or tactical actions that target a large number of a rival's customers are likely to elicit strong responses.[80] In fact, if the effects of a competitor's strategic action on the focal firm are significant (e.g., loss of market share, loss of major resources such as critical employees), a response is likely to be swift and strong.[81]

The IBM brand has had a very strong positive reputation for many years.

5-6b   Actor's Reputation

In the context of competitive rivalry, an *actor* is the firm taking an action or a response, while *reputation* is "the positive or negative attribute ascribed by one rival to another based on past competitive behavior."[82] A positive reputation may be a source of above-average returns, especially for consumer goods producers.[83] Thus, a positive corporate reputation is of strategic value[84] and affects competitive rivalry. To predict the likelihood of a competitor's response to a current or planned action, firms evaluate the responses that the competitor has taken previously when attacked—past behavior is assumed to be a predictor of future behavior.

Competitors are more likely to respond to strategic or tactical actions when they are taken by a market leader.[85] In particular, evidence suggests that commonly successful actions, especially strategic actions, will be quickly imitated. For example, although a second mover, IBM committed significant resources to enter the information service market. Competitors such as Hewlett-Packard (HP), Dell Inc., and others responded with strategic actions to enter this market as well.[86] IBM has invested heavily to build its capabilities in service related software as well. And, the investments appear to be paying off as IBM recently reported that a study of 800 firms using its Software-as-a-Service (SaaS) had achieved a competitive advantage in their markets.[87]

In contrast to a firm with a strong reputation, competitors are less likely to respond to actions taken by a company with a reputation for risky, complex, and unpredictable competitive behavior. For example, the firm with a reputation as a price predator (an actor that frequently reduces prices to gain or maintain market share) generates few responses to its pricing tactical actions because price predators, which typically increase prices once their market share objective is reached, lack credibility with their competitors.[88]

5-6c   Market Dependence

Market dependence denotes the extent to which a firm's revenues or profits are derived from a particular market.[89] In general, competitors with high market dependence are likely to respond strongly to attacks threatening their market position.[90] Interestingly, the threatened firm in these instances may not always respond quickly, even though an effective response to an attack on the firm's position in a critical market is important.

At an annual compound growth rate of 11 percent, recent predictions are that e-commerce sales will grow more than any other segment of the retail industry through at least 2017. Obviously, this growth rate is attractive to firms of all kinds including, as it turns out, Walmart. Established in 2000 as part of the world's largest firm by sales volume (with revenue of roughly $469 billion in 2012), Walmart.com is the giant retailer's attempt to become extremely successful in the e-commerce space. Today, over 1 million products are available through Walmart.com, with additional ones being regularly added to the site. Of course, competing in e-commerce pits Walmart.com squarely in competition with Amazon.com the largest online store on the planet.[91]

Although important, Walmart currently has very little dependence for its success on the e-commerce market. Of course, Walmart is taking actions such as trying to better integrate its physical stores with its technological and logistics skills[92] and is searching for ways to deliver purchases to online buyers in a fast and efficient (e.g., low cost) manner hoping to better compete with Amazon.com.

In contrast to Walmart, Amazon.com currently derives a strong majority of its sales volume from the e-commerce market, meaning that it has a high degree of market dependence. With approximately $89 billion in revenue in 2014, the firm is substantially smaller than Walmart's sales revenue of slightly more than $476 billion, although its total e-commerce sales revenue dwarfs that of Walmart.com's.[93] Given its dominant market position in e-commerce and in light of its dependence on the e-commerce market, it is virtually guaranteed that Amazon.com will continue responding to Walmart.com's competitive actions and responses.

5-7 Competitive Dynamics

Whereas competitive rivalry concerns the ongoing actions and responses between a firm and its direct competitors for an advantageous market position, *competitive dynamics* concerns the ongoing actions and responses among *all* firms competing within a market for advantageous positions.

To explain competitive dynamics, we explore the effects of varying rates of competitive speed in different markets (called slow-cycle, fast-cycle, and standard-cycle markets) on the behavior (actions and responses) of all competitors within a given market. Competitive behaviors, as well as the reasons for taking them, are similar within each market type, but differ across types of markets. Thus, competitive dynamics differ in slow-cycle, fast-cycle, and standard-cycle markets.

As noted in Chapter 1, firms want to sustain their competitive advantages for as long as possible, although no advantage is permanently sustainable. However, as we discuss next, the sustainability of the firm's competitive advantages differs by market type. The degree of sustainability is primarily affected by how quickly competitors can imitate a rival's competitive advantages and how costly it is to do so.

5-7a Slow-Cycle Markets

Slow-cycle markets are markets in which the firm's competitive advantages are shielded from imitation, commonly for long periods of time, and where imitation is costly.[94] Thus, competitive advantages are sustainable over longer periods of time in slow-cycle markets.

Building a unique and proprietary capability produces a competitive advantage and success in a slow-cycle market. This type of advantage is difficult for competitors to understand. As discussed in Chapter 3, a difficult-to-understand and costly-to-imitate capability usually results from unique historical conditions, causal ambiguity, and/or social complexity. Copyrights and patents are examples of these types of capabilities. After a proprietary advantage is developed on the basis of using its capabilities, the competitive actions and responses a firm takes in a slow-cycle market are oriented to protecting, maintaining, and extending that advantage. Major strategic actions in these markets, such as acquisitions, usually carry less risk than in faster-cycle markets.[95] Clearly, firms that gain an advantage can grow more and earn higher returns than those who simply track with the industry, especially in mature and declining industries.[96] However, as shown by the example of Kellogg, executives must be careful not to become overconfident in their success as competitors and markets change.[97]

Slow-cycle markets are markets in which the firm's competitive advantages are shielded from imitation, commonly for long periods of time, and where imitation is costly.

The Walt Disney Company continues to extend its proprietary characters, such as Mickey Mouse, Minnie Mouse, and Goofy. These characters have a unique historical development as a result of Walt and Roy Disney's creativity and vision for entertaining people. Products based on the characters seen in Disney's animated films are sold through Disney's theme park shops as well as freestanding retail outlets called Disney Stores. Because copyrights shield it, the proprietary nature of Disney's advantage in terms of animated character trademarks protects the firm from imitation by competitors.

Consistent with another attribute of competition in a slow-cycle market, Disney protects its exclusive rights to its characters and their use. As with all firms competing in slow-cycle markets, Disney's competitive actions (such as building theme parks in France, Japan, and China) and responses (such as lawsuits to protect its right to fully control use of its animated characters) maintain and extend its proprietary competitive advantage while protecting it.

Patent laws and regulatory requirements in the United States requiring FDA (Food and Drug Administration) approval to launch new products shield pharmaceutical companies' positions. Competitors in this market try to extend patents on their drugs to maintain advantageous positions that patents provide. However, after a patent expires, the firm is no longer shielded from competition, allowing generic imitations and usually leading to a loss of sales and profits. This was the case for Pfizer when Lipitor (which is the best-selling drug in history) went off patent in the fall of 2011. The firm's profits declined 19 percent in the first quarter after that event.

The competitive dynamics generated by firms competing in slow-cycle markets are shown in Figure 5.4. In slow-cycle markets, firms launch a product (e.g., a new drug) that has been developed through a proprietary advantage (e.g., R&D) and then exploit it for as long as possible while the product is shielded from competition. Eventually, competitors respond to the action with a counterattack. In markets for drugs, this counterattack commonly occurs as patents expire or are broken through legal means, creating the need for another product launch by the firm seeking a protected market position.

Figure 5.4 Gradual Erosion of a Sustained Competitive Advantage

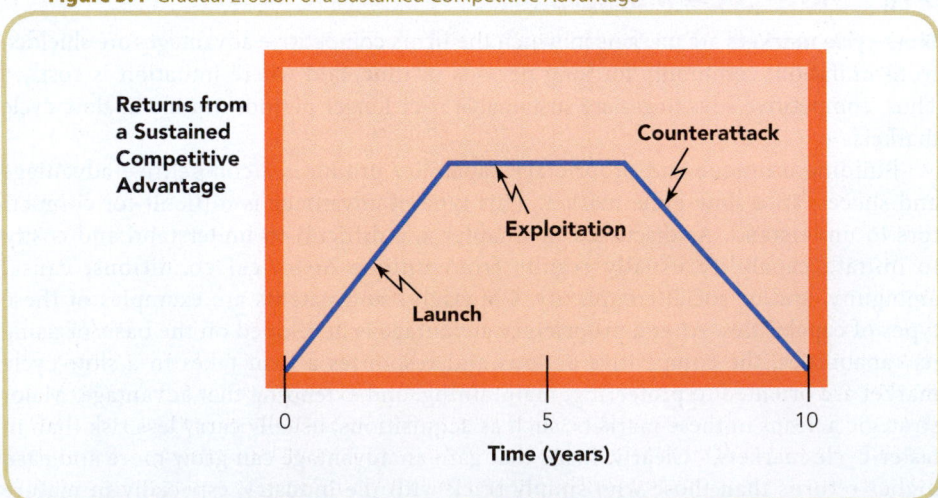

Source: Adapted from I. C. MacMillan, 1988, Controlling competitive dynamics by taking strategic initiative, *Academy of Management Executive*, II(2): 111–118.

5-7b Fast-Cycle Markets

Fast-cycle markets are markets in which the firm's capabilities that contribute to competitive advantages aren't shielded from imitation and where imitation is often rapid and inexpensive.[98] Thus, competitive advantages aren't sustainable in fast-cycle markets. Firms competing in fast-cycle markets recognize the importance of speed; these companies appreciate that "time is as precious a business resource as money or head count—and that the costs of hesitation and delay are just as steep as going over budget or missing a financial forecast."[99] Such high-velocity environments place considerable pressures on top managers to quickly make strategic decisions that are also effective. The often substantial competition and technology-based strategic focus make the strategic decision complex, increasing the need for a comprehensive approach integrated with decision speed, two often-conflicting characteristics of the strategic decision process.[100]

Reverse engineering and the rate of technology diffusion facilitate the rapid imitation that takes place in fast-cycle markets. A competitor uses reverse engineering to quickly gain the knowledge required to imitate or improve the firm's products. Technology is diffused rapidly in fast-cycle markets, making it available to competitors in a short period. The technology often used by fast-cycle competitors isn't proprietary, nor is it protected by patents as is the technology used by firms competing in slow-cycle markets. For example, only a few hundred parts, which are readily available on the open market, are required to build a PC. Patents protect only a few of these parts, such as microprocessor chips. Interestingly, research also demonstrates that showing what an incumbent firm knows and its research capability can be a deterrent to other firms to enter a market, even a fast-cycle market.[101]

Fast-cycle markets are more volatile than slow-cycle and standard-cycle markets. Indeed, the pace of competition in fast-cycle markets is almost frenzied, as companies rely on innovations as the engines of their growth. Because prices often decline quickly in these markets, companies need to profit rapidly from their product innovations.

Recognizing this reality, firms avoid "loyalty" to any of their products, preferring to cannibalize their own products before competitors learn how to do so through successful imitation. This emphasis creates competitive dynamics that differ substantially from those found in slow-cycle markets. Instead of concentrating on protecting, maintaining, and extending competitive advantages, as in slow-cycle markets, companies competing in fast-cycle markets focus on learning how to rapidly and continuously develop new competitive advantages that are superior to those they replace. They commonly search for fast and effective means of developing new products. For example, it is common in some industries with fast-cycle markets for firms to use strategic alliances to gain access to new technologies and thereby develop and introduce more new products into the market.[102] In recent years, many of these alliances have been offshore (with partners in foreign countries) in order to access appropriate skills while maintaining lower costs. However, finding the balance between sharing knowledge and skills with a foreign partner and preventing that partner from appropriating value from the focal firm's contributions to the alliance is challenging.[103]

The competitive behavior of firms competing in fast-cycle markets is shown in Figure 5.5. Competitive dynamics in this market type entail actions and responses that are oriented to rapid and continuous product introductions and the development of a stream of ever-changing competitive advantages. The firm launches a product to achieve a competitive advantage and then exploits the advantage for as long as possible. However, the firm also tries to develop another temporary competitive advantage before competitors can respond to the first one. Thus, competitive dynamics in fast-cycle markets often result in rapid product upgrades as well as quick product innovations.[104]

Fast-cycle markets are markets in which the firm's capabilities that contribute to competitive advantages aren't shielded from imitation and where imitation is often rapid and inexpensive.

Figure 5.5 Developing Temporary Advantages to Create Sustained Advantage

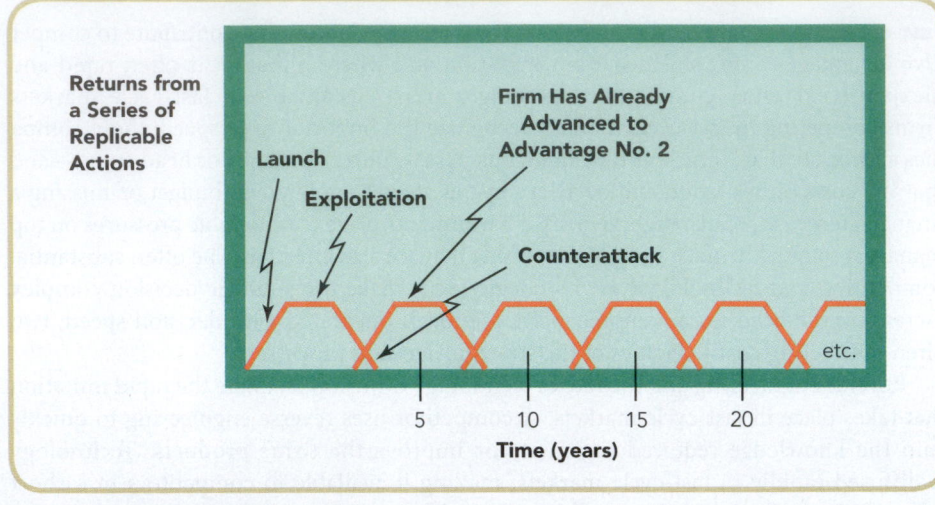

Source: Adapted from I. C. MacMillan, 1988, Controlling competitive dynamics by taking strategic initiative, *Academy of Management Executive*, II(2): 111–118.

Apple largely competes in fast-cycle markets; with the introduction of the new apple watch, Apple and its rivals are changing a typical standard cycle market to a fast-cycle market with 'smart' watches. Some analysts suggested that Apple had orders for at least a million watches before the official launch date. But, Apple's watch enters a market in which the product not only serves functional purposes but often is used as a 'fashion statement' for the owner. Apple's entry is inviting significant competition. As noted in the Opening Case, Google has partnered with TAG Heuer and Intel to develop a prestigious 'smart watch'. Apple may also experience some difficulties with its pricing for the watch. The base price for the watch is $349 with an aluminum case and elastic wrist band. The high-end price is $17,000 that comes with an 18-caret gold case, leather wrist band, and a brass buckle. Apple's watch is reported to continue its tradition of technological excellence which is difficult for competitors to match or beat. This new product market will have significantly interesting competitive dynamics.[105]

As our discussion suggests, innovation plays a critical role in the competitive dynamics in fast-cycle markets. For individual firms then, innovation is a key source of competitive advantage. Through innovation, the firm can cannibalize its own products before competitors successfully imitate them and still maintain an advantage through next-generation products.

As explained in the Strategic Focus, Aldi is having a major effect in the retail food markets across countries, especially in the United Kingdom, United States, and Australia. Aldi's extreme emphasis on low cost is hurting many of the major supermarket chains in each of those countries, and Aldi is gaining market share and expanding in all of them. The competitive rivalry is gaining strength. The retail food industry has largely operated as a standard-cycle market and sold products with small margins. With Aldi's growing power in the markets, firms are forced to operate with even smaller margins and reduced profits or cut their costs in order to compete on prices. It will be interesting to observe the winners and losers in this "war" in each country.

5-7c   Standard-Cycle Markets

Standard-cycle markets are markets in which the firm's competitive advantages are partially shielded from imitation, and imitation is moderately costly. Competitive advantages are partially sustainable in standard-cycle markets, but only when the firm is able to continuously

Standard-cycle markets are markets in which the firm's competitive advantages are partially shielded from imitation and imitation is moderately costly.

Strategic **Focus**

The Ripple Effect of Supermarket Wars: Aldi Is Changing the Markets in Many Countries

Aldi was started as a small, family-owned grocery store by Mrs. Albrecht located in Essen, Germany in 1913. Two sons, Karl and Theo, took over the store in 1946 and soon began expansion. They emphasized low costs from the very beginning and thereby, provided very low prices for customers relative to competitors. Over time, Aldi expanded to other European countries, and it entered the United States market in 1976. Currently, Aldi has 8,500 stores with 1,400 of those in the United States. It operates stores in 18 countries, and it has stores in 36 states in the United States. Its annual sales revenues in the United States are approximately $70 million.

Aldi holds its costs down in a variety of ways. It largely sells its own brand-label products in "no frill" stores. The company limits the number of external brands it sells (usually one or two per product), and it has low packaging, transportation, and employee costs. The products are sold in stores similar to warehouse stores—on pallets and boxed in cut-a-way cardboard boxes. In Germany, Aldi advertises very little, but it does advertise in the United States. It produces its own ads in-house (no external agency) and advertises mostly through newspaper inserts and a few television commercials.

Aldi and another discount store, Lidl, have hurt the largest four supermarkets in the U.K. market—Tesco, Walmart's Asda, J Sainsbury, and Wm. Morrison Supermarkets. Aldi and Lidl have stolen market share from these retailers, especially Tesco and Morrison, and now have about 8.6 percent of the market. And, they are targeting growth to about 17 percent share of the market within the next five years. Tesco has controlled about 30 percent of the discount supermarket market, but it has been declining. Morrison's recent poor performance has precipitated turnover in most of the top executives at the firm. In addition, the new CEO, David Potts, has been making major changes—largely cutting costs in order to compete on prices. As a result of reduced costs, Morrison cut its prices on 130 staple items such as milk and eggs. Likewise, Tesco reduced prices of 380 of its brand products by about 25 percent. Yet, Aldi is emboldened by its gain in market share and plans to invest about $900 million to open 550 new stores in Britain by 2022.

Aldi is having similar effects on the Australian market. It has gained market share from the two largest supermarkets in Australia—Coles and Woolworths. Woolworths has signaled its plans to reduce its prices to avoid being perceived as the "expensive option." This action does not seem to concern Aldi which has announced plans for a $700 million expansion of 120–130 new stores by 2020 to add to its current number of 300 stores in Australia.

Aldi appears to be harming some competition in the United States as well. For example, a rival discount food retailer, Bottom

Dollar owned by Delhaize from Belgium, closed all of its stores (New Jersey, Pennsylvania, and Ohio) and sold the locations and leases to Aldi. Aldi does have stiffer competition in the United States from Walmart, Sam's (Walmart's warehouse stores), and Costco, among other discount food retailers. Yet, Aldi is still, not only surviving, but flourishing and growing in the U.S. market as well.

These supermarket wars caused by Aldi in the various markets are not only causing a ripple effect across country borders. The effects are also rippling to wholesalers and other suppliers. For example, wholesale prices have been declining, and some of the major supermarket chains, such as Tesco and Morrison, have been reducing the number of brands on their shelves. Interestingly, manufacturers of popular products, such as Mr. Kipling cakes and Bistro gravy, stand to gain shelf space and increase sales as a result to rivals' products being taken off the shelves. Of course, the suppliers whose products are eliminated will suffer.

The bottom line is that Aldi is having a major effect on rivals in multiple countries and on many other companies that supply products to the industry.

Aldi Organic Product.PNG

Aldi's low cost technique for displaying and selling goods with cutout boxes of goods stacked on pallets.

Sources: 2014, Aldi targets doubling of UK stores with 600 million pound investment, *New York Times*, www.nytimes.com, November 10; T. Hua, 2015, Tesco's overhaul points to a price war, *Wall Street Journal*, www.wsj.com, January 5; L. Northrup, 2015, Bottom dollar food to close stores, sell chain to Aldi, *Consumerist*, www.consumerist.com, January 5; 2015, Mr. Kipling Maker Premier Foods sees positives in supermarket wars, *New York Times*, www.nytimes.com, January 23; 2015, Morrisons cuts prices on 130 grocery staples like milk, eggs, *New York Times*, www.nytimes.com, February 15; 2015, British shop price decline steepens in February—BRC, *New York Times*, www.nytimes.com, March 3; K. Ross, 2015, Supermarket wars: Aldi takes on market share as Woolworths drops prices, Smart Company, www.smartcompany.com, March 9; A. Felsted, 2015, Morrison chiefs take express checkout from struggling supermarket, *Financial Times*, www.ft.com, March 24; 2015, Aldi Foods, www.grocery.com, accessed March 25.

upgrade the quality of its capabilities as a foundation for being able to stay ahead of competitors. The competitive actions and responses in standard-cycle markets are designed to seek large market shares, to gain customer loyalty through brand names, and to carefully control a firm's operations in order to consistently provide the same positive experience for customers.[106] This is how the retail food industry operated for many years. But, it is changing with discount competitors such as Aldi gaining strength in the market.

Companies competing in standard-cycle markets tend to serve many customers in what are typically highly competitive markets. Because the capabilities and core competencies on which their competitive advantages are based are less specialized, imitation is faster and less costly for standard-cycle firms than for those competing in slow-cycle markets. However, imitation is slower and more expensive in these markets than in fast-cycle markets. Thus, competitive dynamics in standard-cycle markets rest midway between the characteristics of dynamics in slow-cycle and fast-cycle markets. Imitation comes less quickly and is more expensive for standard-cycle competitors when a firm is able to develop economies of scale by combining coordinated and integrated design and manufacturing processes with a large sales volume for its products.

Because of large volumes, the size of mass markets, and the need to develop scale economies, the competition for market share is intense in standard-cycle markets. This form of competition is readily evident in the battles among consumer foods' producers, such as candy makers and major competitors Hershey Co.; Nestlé, SA; Mondelēz International, Inc. (the name for the former Kraft Foods Inc.); and Mars. (Of the firms, Hershey is far more dependent on candy sales than are the others.) Taste and the ingredients used to develop it, advertising campaigns, package designs, and availability through additional distribution channels are some of the many dimensions on which these competitors aggressively compete for the purpose of increasing their share of the candy market, as broadly defined.[107] In recent years, candy manufacturers have also had to contend with criticism from health professionals about the sugar, saturated fats, and calories their products provide, in terms of how all of these attributes can have negative effects on personal health.[108]

Innovation can also drive competitive actions and responses in standard-cycle markets, especially when rivalry is intense. Some innovations in standard-cycle markets are incremental rather than radical in nature (incremental and radical innovations are discussed in Chapter 13). For example, consumer foods producers are innovating within their lines of healthy products (as discussed in the Strategic Focus on Kellogg). Today, many firms are relying on innovation as a means of competing in standard-cycle markets and earning above-average returns.

Overall, innovation has a substantial influence on competitive dynamics as it affects the actions and responses of all companies competing within a slow-cycle, fast-cycle, or standard-cycle market. We have emphasized the importance of innovation to the firm's strategic competitiveness in earlier chapters and do so again in Chapter 13. These discussions highlight the importance of innovation for firms regardless of the type of competitive dynamics they encounter while competing.

SUMMARY

- Competitors are firms competing in the same market, offering similar products, and targeting similar customers. Competitive rivalry is the ongoing set of competitive actions and responses occurring between competitors as they compete against each other for an advantageous market position. The outcomes of competitive rivalry influence the firm's ability to sustain its competitive advantages as well as the level (average, below average, or above average) of its financial returns.

■ Competitive behavior is the set of competitive actions and responses an individual firm takes while engaged in competitive rivalry. Competitive dynamics is the set of actions and responses taken by all firms that are competitors within a particular market.

■ Firms study competitive rivalry in order to predict the competitive actions and responses each of their competitors are likely to take. Competitive actions are either strategic or tactical in nature. The firm takes competitive actions to defend or build its competitive advantages or to improve its market position. Competitive responses are taken to counter the effects of a competitor's competitive action. A strategic action or a strategic response requires a significant commitment of organizational resources, is difficult to successfully implement, and is difficult to reverse. In contrast, a tactical action or a tactical response requires fewer organizational resources and is easier to implement and reverse. For example, for an airline company, entering major new markets is an example of a strategic action or a strategic response; changing its prices in a particular market is an example of a tactical action or a tactical response.

■ A competitor analysis is the first step the firm takes to be able to predict its competitors' actions and responses. In Chapter 2, we discussed what firms do to *understand* competitors. This discussion was extended in this chapter to describe what the firm does to *predict* competitors' market-based actions. Thus, understanding precedes prediction. Market commonality (the number of markets with which competitors are jointly involved and their importance to each) and resource similarity (how comparable competitors' resources are in terms of type and amount) are studied to complete a competitor analysis. In general, the greater the market commonality and resource similarity, the more firms acknowledge that they are direct competitors.

■ Market commonality and resource similarity shape the firm's awareness (the degree to which it and its competitors understand their mutual interdependence), motivation (the firm's incentive to attack or respond), and ability (the quality of the resources available to the firm to attack and respond). Having knowledge of these characteristics of a competitor increases the quality of the firm's predictions about that competitor's actions and responses.

■ In addition to market commonality, resource similarity, awareness, motivation, and ability, three more specific factors affect the likelihood a competitor will take competitive actions. The first of these is first-mover benefits. First movers, those taking an initial competitive action, often gain loyal customers and earn above-average returns until competitors can successfully respond to their action. Not all firms can be first movers because they may lack the awareness, motivation, or ability required to engage in this type of competitive behavior. Moreover, some firms prefer to be a second mover (the firm responding to the first mover's action). One reason for this is that second movers, especially those acting quickly, often can successfully compete against the first mover. By evaluating the first mover's product, customers' reactions to it, and the responses of other competitors to the first mover, the second mover may be able to avoid the early entrant's mistakes and find ways to improve upon the value created for customers by the first mover's goods or services. Late movers (those that respond a long time after the original action was taken) commonly are lower performers and are much less competitive.

■ Organizational size tends to reduce the variety of competitive actions that large firms launch, while it increases the variety of actions undertaken by smaller competitors. Ideally, a firm prefers to initiate a large number of diverse actions when engaged in competitive rivalry. Another factor, quality, is a base denominator for competing successfully in the global economy. It is a necessary prerequisite to achieving competitive parity. However, it is a necessary but insufficient condition for establishing an advantage.

■ The type of action (strategic or tactical) the firm took, the competitor's reputation for the nature of its competitor behavior, and that competitor's dependence on the market in which the action was taken are analyzed to predict a competitor's response to the firm's action. In general, the number of tactical responses taken exceeds the number of strategic responses. Competitors respond more frequently to the actions taken by the firm with a reputation for predictable and understandable competitive behavior, especially if that firm is a market leader. In general, the firm can predict that when its competitor is highly dependent on its revenue and profitability in the market in which the firm took a competitive action, that competitor is likely to launch a strong response. However, firms that are more diversified across markets are less likely to respond to a particular action that affects only one of the markets in which they compete.

■ In slow-cycle markets, competitive advantages generally can be maintained for at least a period of time, and competitive dynamics often include actions and responses intended to protect, maintain, and extend the firm's proprietary advantages. In fast-cycle markets, competition is substantial as firms concentrate on developing a series of temporary competitive advantages. This emphasis is necessary because firms' advantages in fast-cycle markets aren't proprietary and, as such, are subject to rapid and relatively inexpensive imitation. Standard-cycle markets have a level of competition between that in slow-cycle and fast-cycle markets; firms often (but not always) are moderately shielded from competition in these markets as they use capabilities that produce competitive advantages that are moderately sustainable. Competitors in standard-cycle markets serve mass markets and try to develop economies of scale to enhance their profitability. Innovation is vital to competitive success in each of the three types of markets. Companies should recognize that the set of competitive actions and responses taken by all firms differs by type of market.

KEY TERMS

competitors 144
competitive rivalry 144
competitive behavior 144
competitive dynamics 144
competitive action 152
competitive response 152
first mover 153
fast-cycle markets 161
late mover 155
multimarket competition 144

market commonality 148
quality 156
resource similarity 148
strategic action 152
strategic response 152
second mover 154
slow-cycle markets 159
standard-cycle markets 162
tactical action 152
tactical response 152

REVIEW QUESTIONS

1. Who are competitors? How are competitive rivalry, competitive behavior, and competitive dynamics defined in the chapter?

2. What is market commonality? What is resource similarity? In what way are these concepts the building blocks for a competitor analysis?

3. How do awareness, motivation, and ability affect the firm's competitive behavior?

4. What factors affect the likelihood a firm will take a competitive action?

5. What factors affect the likelihood a firm will initiate a competitive response to a competitor's action(s)?

6. What competitive dynamics can be expected among firms competing in slow-cycle markets? In fast-cycle markets? In standard-cycle markets?

Mini-Case

FedEx and United Parcel Service (UPS): Maintaining Success while Competing Aggressively

Identified recently as one of the 50 greatest or most intense competitive rivalries of all time, FedEx and UPS are similar in many ways, including their resources, the markets they serve, and the competitive dimensions that they emphasize to implement similar strategies. These similarities mean that the firms are direct competitors and that they are keenly aware of each other and have the motivation and ability to respond to the competitive actions they take against each other. The two firms are the largest global courier delivery companies in what is a highly competitive industry on a global basis.

FedEx and UPS compete in many of the same product markets, including next day delivery, cheaper ground delivery, time-guaranteed delivery (both domestically and internationally), and freight services. However, the firms concentrate on different segments in attempting to create superior stakeholder value and to avoid direct, head-to-head competition in a host of product segments and markets. In this regard, FedEx "intends to leverage and extend the FedEx brand and to provide customers with seamless access to its entire portfolio of integrated transportation services," while UPS "seeks to position itself as the primary coordinator of the flow of goods, information, and funds throughout the entire supply chain (the movement from the raw materials and parts stage through final consumption of the finished product)."

Thus, while these firms are similar, they also seek to differentiate themselves in ways that enhance the possibility of being able to gain strategic competitiveness and earn above-average returns. In broad-stroke terms, FedEx concentrates more on transportation services and international markets. (Recently, FedEx was generating 48 percent of revenue internationally, while UPS was earning 22 percent of its revenue from international markets.) Meanwhile, UPS concentrates more on the entire value chain while competing domestically. FedEx is the world's largest international air shipping firm, while UPS is the world's largest package delivery company.

There are many actions the firms have recently taken to sharpen their ability to outcompete their primary competitor. In mid-2013, FedEx learned that its contract to fly domestic mail for the U.S. Postal Service had been selected for renewal. UPS also bid on the contract, and thus it lost this competitive battle to its rival. To support its strength in logistics as part of the entire supply chain, UPS recently agreed to buy "Hungary-based pharmaceutical-logistics company Cemelog Zrt for an undisclosed amount in a deal to strengthen its health-care business in Europe, giving it access to the increasingly important markets of Central and Eastern Europe." UPS is also emphasizing trans-border European Union services as a

growth engine for the foreseeable future. To enhance its ability to compete against UPS and other rivals as well, FedEx is restructuring some of its operations to increase efficiency. Similarly, the firm is increasing its emphasis on finding ways for its independent express, ground, and freight networks to work together more synergistically.

Although the rivalry between FedEx and UPS is intense and aggressive, it is also likely that this rivalry makes each firm stronger and more agile because each has to be at its best in order to outperform the other. Thus in many ways, each of these firms is a "good competitor" for the other one.

Sources: 2013, FedEx Corp., *Standard & Poor's Stock Report*, www.standardandpoors.com, May 25; 2013; United Parcel Service, Inc., *Standard & Poor's Stock Report*, www.standardandpoors.com, May 25; L. Eaton, 2013, FedEx CEO: Truck fleets to shift to natural gas from diesel, *Wall Street Journal*, www.wsj.com, March 8; V. Mock, 2013, UPS to appeal EU's block of TNT merger, *Wall Street Journal*, www.wsj.com, April 7; B. Morris & B. Sechler, 2013, FedEx customers like slower and cheaper, *Wall Street Journal*, www.wsj.com, March 20; B. Sechler, 2013, Online shopping boosts profit for UPS, *Wall Street Journal*, www.wsj.com, April 25; B. Sechler, 2013, FedEx fends off rivals for U.S. Postal, *Wall Street Journal*, www.wsj.com, April 23.

Case Discussion Questions

1. FedEx and UPS have many similar resources and compete across many of the same markets. How are they different? Stated differently, how do they differentiate themselves?

2. What are some of the major and unique strategic actions taken by each firm? Have these actions been successful?

3. Based on information in the case and from your research, which of these firms do you predict will be the most successful in the future? Please explain your reasons.

NOTES

1. S. Carnahan & D. Somaya, 2013, Alumni effects and relational advantage: The impact of outsourcing when your buyer hires employees from your competitors, *Academy of Management Journal*, 56: 1578–1600; M.-J. Chen & D. Miller, 2012, Competitive dynamics: Themes, trends, and a prospective research platform, *Academy of Management Annals*, 6: 135–210; M.-J. Chen, 1996, Competitor analysis and interfirm rivalry: Toward a theoretical integration, *Academy of Management Review*, 21: 100–134.

2. M. G. Jacobides & C. J. Tae, 2015, Kingpins, bottlenecks, and value dynamics along a sector, *Organization Science*, in press; P. C. Patel, S. A. Fernhaber, P. P. McDougall-Covin, & R. P. van der Have, 2014, Beating competitors to international markets: The value of geographically balanced networks

for innovation, *Strategic Management Journal*, 35: 691–711.

3. S. B. Choi & C. Williams, 2014, The impact of innovation intensity, scope and spillovers on sales growth in Chinese firms, *Asia Pacific Journal of Management*, 31: 25–46; T. Zahavi & D. Lavie, 2013, Intra-industry diversification and firm performance, *Strategic Management Journal*, 34: 978–998.

4. K. M. Park, K. Jung, & K. C. Noh, 2014, Strategic actions and customer mobility: Antecedents and consequences of strategic actions in the Korean mobile telecommunications service industry, *Asia Pacific Journal of Management*, 31: 171–193; P. T. M. Ingenbleek & I. A. van der Lans, 2013, Relating price strategies and price-setting practices, *European Journal of Marketing*, 47: 27–48.

5. F. J. Mas-Ruiz, F. Ruiz-Moreno, & A. L. de Guevara Martinez, 2014, Asymmetric rivalry within and between strategic groups, *Strategic Management Journal*, 35: 419–439; P. J. Derfus, P. G. Maggitti, C. M. Grimm, & K. G. Smith, 2008, The red queen effect: Competitive actions and firm performance, *Academy of Management Journal*, 51: 61–80; C. M. Grimm, H. Lee, & K. G. Smith, 2006, *Strategy as Action: Competitive Dynamics and Competitive Advantage*, New York: Oxford University Press.

6. C. Giachetti & G. B. Dagnino, 2014, Detecting the relationship between competitive intensity and firm product line length: Evidence from the worldwide mobile phone industry, *Strategic Management Journal*, 35: 1398–1409; R. B. Mackay & R. Chia, 2012, Choice, chance,

and unintended consequences in strategic change: A process understanding of the rise and fall of NorthCo Automotive, *Academy of Management Journal*, 56: 1–13.

7. M. Srivastava, A. Frankly, & L. Martinette, 2013, Building a sustainable competitive advantage, *Journal of Technology Management & Innovation*, 8: 47–60; G. J. Kilduff, H. A. Elfenbein, & B. M. Staw, 2010, The psychology of rivalry: A relationally dependent analysis of competition, *Academy of Management Journal*, 53: 943–969; D. G. Sirmon, S. Gove, & M. A. Hitt, 2008, Resource management in dyadic competitive rivalry: The effects of resource bundling and deployment, *Academy of Management Journal*, 51: 919–935.

8. R. Kapoor & N. R. Furr, 2015, Complementarities and competition: Unpacking the drivers of entrants' technology choices in the solar photovoltaic industry, *Strategic Management Journal*, 6: 416–436; S.-J. Chang & S. H. Park, 2012, Winning strategies in China: Competitive dynamics between MNCs and local firms, *Long Range Planning*, 45: 1–15.

9. A. Nair & D. D. Selover, 2012, A study of competitive dynamics, *Journal of Business Research*, 65: 355–361; Grimm, Lee, & Smith, *Strategy as Action*.

10. R. Chellappa, V. Sambamurthy, & N. Saraf, 2010, Competing in crowded markets: Multimarket contact and the nature of competition in the enterprise systems software industry, *Information Systems Research: Special Issue on Digital Systems and Competition*, 21: 614–630.

11. T. Yu, M. Subramaniam, & A. A. Cannella, 2009, Rivalry deterrence in international markets: Contingencies governing the mutual forbearance hypothesis, *Academy of Management Journal*, 52: 127–147; K. G. Smith, W. J. Ferrier, & H. Ndofor, 2001, Competitive dynamics research: Critique and future directions. In M. A. Hitt, R. E. Freeman, & J. S. Harrison (eds.), *Handbook of Strategic Management*, Oxford, U.K.: Blackwell Publishers, 326.

12. F. Bridoux, K. G. Smith, & C. M. Grimm, 2011, The management of resources: Temporal effects of different types of actions on performance, *Journal of Management*, 33: 1281–1310; G. Young, K. G. Smith, & C. M. Grimm, 1996, "Austrian" and industrial organization perspectives on firm-level competitive activity and performance, *Organization Science*, 73: 243–254.

13. R. Duprey, 2015, Giant tobacco merger finds itself at the mercy of a tiny rival, *Motley Fool*, www.motleyfool.com, March 23; 2014, Altria set to pose a stiff challenge to existing e-cigarette leaders, *Forbes*, www.forbes.com, June 3; M. Esteri, 2013, Big tobacco is about to dive into e-cigarettes, *Wall Street Journal*, www.wsj.com, May 29.

14. R. Katila, E. L. Chen, & H. Piezunka, 2012, All the right moves: How entrepreneurial firms compete effectively, *Strategic Entrepreneurship Journal*, 6: 116–132; J. Marcel, P. Barr, & I. Duhaime, 2011, The influence of executive cognition on competitive dynamics, *Strategic Management Journal*, 32: 115–138.

15. R. Casadesus-Masanell & F. Zhu, 2013, Business model innovation and competitive imitation: The case of sponsor-based business models, *Strategic Management Journal*, 34: 464–482; M.-J. Chen & D. C. Hambrick, 1995, Speed, stealth, and selective attack: How small firms differ from large firms in competitive behavior, *Academy of Management Journal*, 38: 453–482.

16. M. A. Abebe & A. Angriawan, 2014, Organizational and competitive influences of exploration and exploitation activities in small firms, *Journal of Business Research*, 67: 339–345; V. Rindova, W. Ferrier, & R. Wiltbank, 2010, Value from gestalt: How sequences of competitive actions create advantage for firms in nascent markets, *Strategic Management Journal*, 31: 1474–1497; T. Yu & A. A. Cannella, Jr., Rivalry between multinational enterprises: An event history approach, *Academy of Management Journal*, 50: 665–686.

17. A. E. Bass & S. Chakrabarti, 2014, Resource security: Competition for global resources, strategic intent and governments as owners, *Journal of International Business Studies*, 45: 961–979; J. Villanueva, A. H. Van de Ven, & H. Sapienza, 2012, Resource mobilization in entrepreneurial firms, *Journal of Business Venturing*, 27: 19–30; Smith, Ferrier, & Ndofor, Competitive dynamics research, 319.

18. C. Boone, F. C. Wezel, & A. van Witteloostuijn, 2013, Joining the pack or going solo? A dynamic theory of new firm positioning, *Journal of Business Venturing*, 28: 511–527; H. Ndofor, D. G. Sirmon, & X. He, 2011, Firm resources, competitive actions and performance: Investigating a mediated model with evidence from the in-vitro diagnostics industry, *Strategic Management Journal*, 32: 640–657.

19. S.-J. Chang & B. Wu, 2014, Institutional barriers and industry dynamics, *Strategic Management Journal*, 35: 1103–1123; L. M. Ellram, W. L. Tate, & E. G. Feitzinger, 2013, Factor-market rivalry and competition for supply chain resources, *Journal of Supply Chain Management*, 49: 29–46; D. G. Sirmon, M. A. Hitt, J. Arregle, & J. Campbell, 2010, The dynamic interplay of capability strengths and weaknesses: Investigating the bases of temporary competitive advantage, *Strategic Management Journal*, 31: 1386–1409.

20. H. Rahmandad, 2012, Impact of growth opportunities and competition on firm-level capability development trade-offs, *Organization Science*, 34: 138–154; Y. Y. Kor & J. T. Mahoney, 2005, How dynamics, management, and governance of resource deployments influence firm-level performance, *Strategic Management Journal*, 26: 489–496.

21. Y. Zhang, Y. Li, & H. Li, 2014, FDI Spillovers over time in an emerging market: The roles of entry tenure and barriers to imitation, *Academy of Management Journal*, 57: 698–722; L. Mulotte, P. Dussauge, & W. Mitchell, 2013, Does pre-entry licensing undermine the performance of subsequent independent activities? Evidence from the global aerospace industry, 1944–2000, *Strategic Management Journal*, 34: 358–372.

22. L. K. S. Lim, 2013, Mapping competitive prediction capability: Construct conceptualization and performance payoffs, *Journal of Business Research*, 66: 1576–1586; J. C. Baum & A. Satorra, 2007, The persistence of abnormal returns at industry and firm levels: Evidence from Spain, *Strategic Management Journal*, 28: 707–722.

23. M. A. Hitt & K. Xu, 2015, The transformation of China: Effects of the institutional environment on business actions, *Long Range Planning*, in press; J.-L. Arregle, T. L. Miller, M. A. Hitt, & P. W. Beamish, 2013, Do regions matter? An integrated institutional and semiglobalization perspective on the internationalization of MNEs, *Strategic Management Journal*, 34: 910–934.

24. R. M. Holmes, H. Li, M. A. Hitt, & K. DeGetto, 2015, The effects of China's location advantages and location disadvantages on MNCs' establishment of China R&D centers, *Long Range Planning*, in press; O. Alexy, G. George, & A. Salter, 2013, Cui Bono? The selective revealing of knowledge and its implications for innovative activity, *Academy of Management Review*, 38: 270–291; Chen, Competitor analysis, 109.

25. T. Lawton, T. Rajwani, & P. Reinmoeller, 2012, Do you have a survival instinct? Leveraging genetic codes to achieve fit in hostile business environments, *Business Horizons*, 55: 81–91; 2011, The power of blindspots. What companies don't know, surprises them. What they don't want to know, kills them, *Strategic Direction*, 27(4): 3–4; D. Ng, R. Westgren, & S. Sonka, 2009, Competitive blind spots in an institutional field, *Strategic Management Journal*, 30: 349–369.

26. E. Metayer, 2013, How intelligent is your company? *Competia*, www.competia.com, March.

27. J. Neff, 2011, P&G e-commerce chief sees blurring of sales, marketing, *Advertising Age*, April 11, 8.

28. 2015, About YRC, YRC homepage, www.yrc.com, April 13.

29. J. W. Upson, D. J. Ketchen, Jr., B. L. Connelly, & A. L. Ranft, 2012, Competitor analysis and foothold moves, *Academy of Management Journal*, 55: 93–110; Chen, Competitor analysis, 106.

30. T. Yu & A. A. Cannella, Jr., 2013, A comprehensive review of multimarket competition research, *Journal of*

Management, 39: 76–109; J. Anand, L. F. Mesquita, & R. S. Vassolo, 2009, The dynamics of multimarket competition in exploration and exploitation activities, *Academy of Management Journal*, 52: 802–821.

31. S. P. L. Fourne, J. J. P. Jansen, & T. J. M. Mom, 2014, Strategic agility in MNEs: Managing tensions to capture opportunities across emerging and established markets, *California Management Review*, 56(3): 1–26.

32. W. Kang, B. Bayus, & S. Balasubramanian, 2010, The strategic effects of multimarket contact: Mutual forbearance and competitive response in the personal computer industry, *Journal of Marketing Research*, 47: 415–427.

33. V. Bilotkach, 2011, Multimarket contact and intensity of competition: Evidence from an airline merger, *Review of Industrial Organization*, 38: 95–115; H. R. Greve, 2008, Multimarket contact and sales growth: Evidence from insurance, *Strategic Management Journal*, 29: 229–249; J. Gimeno, 1999, Reciprocal threats in multimarket rivalry: Staking out "spheres of influence" in the U.S. airline industry, *Strategic Management Journal*, 20: 101–128.

34. M. Liu, 2015, Davids against goliaths? Collective identities and the market success of peripheral organizations during resource partitioning, *Organization Science*, in press; L. A. Costa, K. Cool, & I. Dierickx, 2013, The competitive implications of the deployment of unique resources, *Strategic Management Journal*, 34: 445–463; Chen, Competitor analysis, 107.

35. P. J. Patel, S. A. Fernhaber, P. P. McDougal-Covin, & R. P. Van Der Have, 2014, Beating competitors to international markets: The value of geographically balanced networks for innovation, *Strategic Management Journal*, 35: 691–711; J. Haleblian, G. McNamara, K. Kolev, & B. J. Dykes, 2012, Exploring firm characteristics that differentiate leaders from followers in industry merger waves: A competitive dynamics perspective, *Strategic Management Journal*, 33: 1037–1052; Chen, Competitor analysis, 110.

36. K.-Y. Hsieh, W. Tsai, & M.-J. Chen, 2015, If they can do it, why not us? Competitors reference points for justifying escalation of commitment, *Academy of Management Journal*, 58: 38–58; C. Flammer, 2013, Corporate social responsibility and shareholder reaction: The environmental awareness of investors, *Academy of Management Journal*, 56: 758–781.

37. B. Larraneta, S. A. Zahra, & J. L. Galan, 2014, Strategic repertoire variety and new venture growth: The moderating effects of origin and industry dynamism, *Strategic Management Journal*, 35: 761–772; J. Tang & B. S.-C. Liu, 2012, Strategic alignment and foreign entry performance: A holistic approach of the impact of entry timing, mode and location, *Business and Systems Research*, 6: 456–478; R. S. Livengood & R. K. Reger, 2010, That's our turf! Identity domains and competitive dynamics, *Academy of Management Review*, 35: 48–66.

38. S. D. Singh, 2015, Caterpillar faces 'aggressive' Komatsu fueled by yen, *Yahoo*, finance.yahoo.com, March 23; B. Tita, 2013, Caterpillar expected to cut 2013 forecasts, *Wall Street Journal*, www.wsj.com, April 21.

39. A. Compagni, V. Mele, & D. Ravasi, 2015, How early implementations influence later adoptions of innovation: Social positioning and skill reproduction in the diffusion of robotic surgery, *Academy of Management Journal*, 58: 242–278; S. H. Park & D. Zhou, 2005, Firm heterogeneity and competitive dynamics in alliance formation, *Academy of Management Review*, 30: 531–554.

40. T.-J. A. Peng, S. Pike, J. C.-H. Yang, & G. Roos, 2012, Is cooperation with competitors a good idea? An example in practice, *British Journal of Management*, 23: 532–560; Chen, Competitor analysis, 113.

41. L.-H. Lin, 2014, Subsidiary performance: The contingency of the multinational corporation's strategy, *European Management Journal*, 32: 928–937; C. Williams & S. Lee, 2011, Entrepreneurial contexts and knowledge coordination within the multinational corporation, *Journal of World Business*, 46: 253–264; M. Leiblein & T. Madsen, 2009, Unbundling competitive heterogeneity: Incentive structures and capability influences on technological innovation, *Strategic Management Journal*, 30: 711–735.

42. R. Makadok, 2010, The interaction effect of rivalry restraint and competitive advantage on profit: Why the whole is less than the sum of the parts, *Management Science*, 56: 356–372.

43. C. M. Grimm & K. G. Smith, 1997, *Strategy as Action: Industry Rivalry and Coordination*, Cincinnati: South-Western Publishing Co., 125.

44. H. Brea-Solis, R. Casadesus-Masanell, & E. Grifell-Tatje, 2015, Business model evaluation: Quantifying Walmart's sources of advantage, *Strategic Entrepreneurship Journal*, 9: 12–33.

45. M. A. Cusumano, S. J. Kahl, & F. F. Suarez, 2015, Services, industry evolution and the competitive strategies of product firms, *Strategic Management Journal*, 36: 559–575; J. Alcacer, C. L. Dezso, & M. Zhao, 2013, Firm rivalry, knowledge accumulation, and MNE location choices, *Journal of International Business Studies*, 44: 504–520.

46. G. Gavetti, 2012, Perspective—Toward a behavioral theory of strategy, *Organization Science*, 23: 267–285; B. L. Connelly, L. Tihanyi, S. T. Certo, & M. A. Hitt, 2010, Marching to the beat of different drummers: The influence of institutional owners on competitive actions, *Academy of Management Journal*, 53: 723–742.

47. T. B. Lee, 2013, Here's why Microsoft is buying Nokia's phone business, *Washington Post*, www.washingtonpost.com, September 3; 2011, Nokia and Microsoft announce plans for a broad strategic partnership to build a new global mobile ecosystem, Microsoft Home Page, www.microsoft.com, February 10.

48. J. Schumpeter, 1934, *The Theory of Economic Development*, Cambridge, MA: Harvard University Press.

49. N. Argyres, L. Bigelow, & J. A. Nickersoon, 2015, Dominant designs, innovation schocks and the follower's dilemma, *Strategic Management Journal*, 36: 216–234; S. Bakker, H. van Lente, & M. T. H. Meeus, 2012, Dominance in the prototyping phase—The case of hydrogen passenger cars, *Research Policy*, 41: 871–883.

50. C. B. Bingham, N. R. Furr, & K. M. Eisenhardt, 2014, The opportunity paradox, *MIT Sloan Management Review*, 56(1): 29–39; L. Sleuwaegen & J. Onkelinx, 2014, International commitment, post-entry growth and survival of international new ventures, *Journal of Business Venturing*, 29: 106–120; F. F. Suarez & G. Lanzolla, 2007, The role of environmental dynamics in building a first mover advantage theory, *Academy of Management Review*, 32: 377–392.

51. G. M. McNamara, J. Haleblian, & B. J. Dykes, 2008, The performance implications of participating in an acquisition wave: Early mover advantages, bandwagon effects, and the moderating influence of industry characteristics and acquirer tactics, *Academy of Management Journal*, 51, 113–130.

52. R. K. Sinha & C. H. Noble, 2008, The adoption of radical manufacturing technologies and firm survival, *Strategic Management Journal*, 29: 943–962; D. P. Forbes, 2005, Managerial determinants of decision speed in new ventures, *Strategic Management Journal*, 26: 355–366.

53. H. R. Greve, 2009, Bigger and safer: The diffusion of competitive advantage, *Strategic Management Journal*, 30: 1–23; W. T. Robinson & S. Min, 2002, Is the first to market the first to fail? Empirical evidence for industrial goods businesses, *Journal of Marketing Research*, 39: 120–128.

54. J. C. Short & G. T. Payne, 2008, First-movers and performance: Timing is everything, *Academy of Management Review*, 33: 267–270.

55. E. de Oliveira & W. B. Werther, Jr., 2013, Resilience: Continuous renewal of competitive advantages, *Business Horizons*, 56: 333–342.

56. A. Hawk, G. Pacheco-De-Almeida, & B. Yeung, 2013, Fast-mover advantages: Speed capabilities and entry into the emerging submarket of Atlantic basin LNG, *Strategic Management Journal*, 34: 1531–1550; N. M. Jakopin & A. Klein, 2012, First-mover and incumbency advantages in mobile telecommunications, *Journal of Business Research*, 65: 362–370.

57. E. R. Banalieva, 2014, Embracing the second best? Synchronization of reform speeds, excess high discretion slack and performance of transition economy firms, *Global Strategy Journal*, 4: 104–126; K. Mellahi & A. Wilkinson, 2010, A study of the association between level of slack reduction following downsizing and innovation output, *Journal of Management Studies*, 47: 483–508.

58. R. Mudambi & T. Swift, 2014, Knowing when to leap: Transitioning between exploitative and explorative R&D, *Strategic Management Journal*, 35: 126–145; M. B. Lieberman & D. B. Montgomery, 1988, First-mover advantages, *Strategic Management Journal*, 9: 41–58.

59. H. R. Greve & M.-D. L. Seidel, 2015, The thin red line between success and failure: Path dependence in the diffusion of innovative production technologies, *Strategic Management Journal*, 36: 475–496; G. Pacheco-De-Almeida, 2010, Erosion, time compression, and self-displacement of leaders in hypercompetitive environments, *Strategic Management Journal*, 31: 1498–1526.

60. J. Y. Yang, J. Li, & A. Delios, 2015, Will a second mouse get the cheese? Learning from early entrant's failures in a foreign market, *Organization Science*, in press; F. Zhu & M. Iansiti, 2012, Entry into platform-based markets, *Strategic Management Journal*, 33: 88–106.

61. M. A. Stanko & J. D. Bohlmann, 2013, Demand-side inertia factors and their benefits for innovativeness, *Journal of the Academy of Marketing Science*, 41: 649–668; M. Poletti, B. Engelland, & H. Ling, 2011, An empirical study of declining lead times: Potential ramifications on the performance of early market entrants, *Journal of Marketing Theory and Practice*, 19: 27–38.

62. S. Bin, 2011, First-mover advantages: Flexible or not?, *Journal of Management & Marketing Research*, 7: 1–13; J. Gimeno, R. E. Hoskisson, B. B. Beal, & W. P. Wan, 2005, Explaining the clustering of international expansion moves: A critical test in the U.S. telecommunications industry, *Academy of Management Journal*, 48: 297–319; K. G. Smith, C. M. Grimm, & M. J. Gannon, 1992, *Dynamics of Competitive Strategy*, Newberry Park, CA: Sage Publications.

63. A. Picchi, 2014, Why Angie's list is getting a rash of bad reviews, CBS News, www.cbsnews.com, January 16.

64. N. K. Park, J. M. Mezias, J Lee, & J.-H. Han, 2014, Reverse knowledge diffusion: competitive dynamics and the knowledge seeking behavior of Korean high-tech firms, *Asia Pacific Journal of Management*, 31: 355–37; A. Fleury & M. Fleury, 2009, Understanding the strategies of late-movers in international manufacturing, *International Journal of Production Economics*, 122: 340–350; J. Li & R. K. Kozhikode, 2008, Knowledge management and innovation strategy:

The challenge for latecomers in emerging economies, *Asia Pacific Journal of Management*, 25: 429–450.

65. E. Golovko & G. Valentini, 2014, Selective learning-by-exporting: Firm size and product versus process innovation, *Global Strategy Journal*, 4: 161–180; F. Karakaya & P. Yannopoulos, 2011, Impact of market entrant characteristics on incumbent reactions to market entry, *Journal of Strategic Marketing*, 19: 171–185; S. D. Dobrev & G. R. Carroll, 2003, Size (and competition) among organizations: Modeling scale-based selection among automobile producers in four major countries, 1885–1981, *Strategic Management Journal*, 24: 541–558.

66. W. Stam, S. Arzianian, & T. Elfring, 2014, Social capital of entrepreneurs and small firm performance: A meta-analysis of contextual and methodological moderators, *Journal of Business Venturing*, 29: 152–173; L. F. Mesquita & S. G. Lazzarini, 2008, Horizontal and vertical relationships in developing economies: Implications for SMEs access to global markets, *Academy of Management Journal*, 51: 359–380.

67. G. D. Markman & T. L. Waldron, 2014, Small entrants and large incumbents: A framework of micro entry, *Academy of Management Perspectives*, 28: 178–197; C. Zhou & A. Van Witteloostuijn, 2010, Institutional constraints and ecological processes: Evolution of foreign-invested enterprises in the Chinese construction industry, 1993–2006, *Journal of International Business Studies*, 41: 539–556; M. A. Hitt, L. Bierman, & J. D. Collins, 2007, The strategic evolution of U.S. law firms, *Business Horizons*, 50: 17–28.

68. Young, Smith, & Grimm, "Austrian" and industrial organization perspectives.

69. P. B. Crosby, 1980, *Quality Is Free*, New York: Penguin; W. E. Deming, 1986, *Out of the Crisis*, Cambridge, MA: MIT Press.

70. X. Luo, V. K. Kanuri, & M. Andrews, 2014, How does CEO tenure matter? The mediating role of firm-employee and firm-customer relationships, *Strategic Management Journal*, 35: 492–511; R. C. Ford & D. R. Dickson, 2012, Enhancing customer self-efficacy in co-producing service experiences, *Business Horizons*, 55: 179–188.

71. B. G. King & E. T. Walker, 2014, Winning hearts and minds: Field theory and the three dimensions of strategy, *Strategic Organization*, 12: 134–141; L. A. Bettencourt & S. W. Brown, 2013, From goods to great: Service innovation in a product-dominated company, *Business Horizons*, 56: 277–283.

72. F. Pakdil, 2010, The effects of TQM on corporate performance. *The Business Review*, 15: 242–248; A. Azadegan, K. J. Dooley, P. L. Carter, & J. R. Carter, 2008, Supplier innovativeness and the role of interorganizational learning in enhancing manufacturing capabilities, *Journal of Supply Chain Management*, 44(4): 14–35.

73. M. Terziovski & P. Hermel, 2011, The role of quality management practice in the performance of integrated supply chains: A multiple cross-case analysis, *The Quality Management Journal*, 18(2): 10–25; K. E. Weick & K. M. Sutcliffe, 2001, *Managing the Unexpected*, San Francisco: Jossey-Bass, 81–82.

74. D. P. McIntyre, 2011, In a network industry, does product quality matter? *Journal of Product Innovation Management*, 28: 99–108; G. Macintosh, 2007, Customer orientation, relationship quality, and relational benefits to the firm, *Journal of Services Marketing*, 21: 150–159.

75. K. R. Sarangee & R. Echambadi, 2014, Firm-specific determinants of product line technology strategies in high technology markets, *Strategic Entrepreneurship Journal*, 8: 149–166; S. Thirumalai & K. K. Sinha, 2011, Product recalls in the medical device industry: An empirical exploration of the sources and financial consequences, *Management Science*, 57: 376–392.

76. M. Su & V. R. Rao, 2011, Timing decisions of new product preannouncement and launch with competition, *International Journal of Production Economics*, 129: 51–64.

77. M. L. Sosa, 2013, Decoupling market incumbency from organizational prehistory: Locating the real sources of competitive advantage in R&D for radical innovation, *Strategic Management Journal*, 34: 245–255; T. R. Crook, D. J. Ketchen, J. G. Combs, & S. Y. Todd, 2008, Strategic resources and performance: A meta-analysis, *Strategic Management Journal*, 29: 1141–1154.

78. S. W. Smith, 2014, Follow me to the innovation frontier? Leaders, laggards and the differential effects of imports and exports on technological innovation, *Journal of International Business Studies*, 45: 248–274; C. Lutz, R. Kemp, & S. Gerhard Dijkstra, 2010, Perceptions regarding strategic and structural entry barriers, *Small Business Economics*, 35: 19–33; M. J. Chen & I. C. MacMillan, 1992, Nonresponse and delayed response to competitive moves, *Academy of Management Journal*, 35: 539–570.

79. S. Awate, M. M. Larsen, & R. Mudambi, 2015, Accessing vs sourcing knowledge: A comparative study of R&D internationalization between emerging and advanced economy firms, *Journal of International Business Studies*, 46: 63–86; S. M. Ben-Menahern, Z. Kwee, H. W. Volberda, & F. A. J. Van Den Bosch, 2013, Strategic renewal over time: The enabling role of potential absorptive capacity in aligning internal and external rates of change, *Long Range Planning*, 46: 216–235; M. J. Chen, K. G. Smith, & C. M. Grimm, 1992, Action characteristics as predictors of competitive responses, *Management Science*, 38: 439–455.

80. S. Ansari & P. Krop, 2012, Incumbent performance in the face of a radical innovation: Towards a framework for incumbent challenger dynamics, *Research Policy*, 41: 1357–1374; M. J. Chen & D. Miller, 1994, Competitive attack, retaliation and performance: An expectancy-valence framework, *Strategic Management Journal*, 15: 85–102.

81. K. Muller, K. Huschelrath, & V. Bilotkach, 2012, The construction of a low-cost airline network—facing competition and exploring new markets, *Managerial and Decision Economics*, 33: 485–499; N. Huyghebaert & L. M. van de Gucht, 2004, Incumbent strategic behavior in financial markets and the exit of entrepreneurial start-ups, *Strategic Management Journal*, 25: 669–688.

82. O. Sorenson, 2014, Status and reputation: Synonyms or separate concepts? *Strategic Organization*, 12: 62–69; Smith, Ferrier, & Ndofor, Competitive dynamics research, 333.

83. E. Fauchart & R. Cowan, 2014, Weak links and the management of reputational interdependencies, *Strategic Management Journal*, 35: 532–549; V. Babic-Hodovic, M. Arlsanagic, & E. Mehic, 2013, Importance of internal marketing for service companies corporate reputation and customer satisfaction, *Journal of Business Administration Research*, 2: 49–57; T. Obloj & L. Capron, 2011, Role of resource gap and value appropriation: Effect of reputation gap on price premium in online auctions, *Strategic Management Journal*, 32: 447–456.

84. Q. Gu & X. Lu, 2014, Unraveling the mechanisms of reputation and alliance formation: A study of venture capital syndication in China, *Strategic Management Journal*, 35: 739–750; I Stern, J. M. Dukerich, & E. Zajac, 2014, Unmixed signals: How reputation and status affect alliance formation, *Strategic Management Journal*, 35: 512–531; P. W. Roberts & G. R. Dowling, 2003, Corporate reputation and sustained superior financial performance, *Strategic Management Journal*, 24: 1077–1093.

85. B. Larraneta, S. A. Zahra, & J. L. G. Gonzalez, 2014, Strategic repertoire variety and new venture growth: The moderating effects of origin and industry dynamism, *Strategic Management Journal*, 35: 761–772; W. J. Ferrier, K. G. Smith, & C. M. Grimm, 1999, The role of competitive actions in market share erosion and industry dethronement: A study of industry leaders and challengers, *Academy of Management Journal*, 42: 372–388.

86. R. Karlgaard, 2011, Transitions: Michael reinvents Dell, *Forbes*, www.forbes.com, May 9.

87. 2014, While many companies try SaaS for cost savings, top performers discover competitive advantage according to IBM study, IBM News Release, www-03.ibm.com, January 28.

88. M. Fassnacht & S. El Husseini, 2013, EDLP versus Hi-Lo pricing strategies in retailing—a state of the art article, *Journal of Business Economics*, 83: 259–289; Smith, Grimm, & Gannon, *Dynamics of Competitive Strategy*.

89. J. Xia & S. Li, 2013, The divestiture of acquired subunits: A resource dependence approach, *Strategic Management Journal*, 34: 131–148; A. Karnani & B. Wernerfelt, 1985, Multiple point competition, *Strategic Management Journal*, 6: 87–97.

90. G. Ahrne, P. Aspers, & N. Brusson, 2014, The organization of markets, *Organization Studies*, 36: 7–27; Smith, Ferrier, & Ndofor, Competitive dynamics research, 330.

91. C. O'Connor, 2013, Wal-Mart vs. Amazon: World's biggest e-commerce battle could boil down to vegetables, *Forbes*, www.forbes.com, April 23.

92. J. Wohl & A. Barr, 2013, Wal-Mart steps up its online game with help from stores, Reuters, www.reuters.com, March 26.

93. 2015, Walmart Stores, Inc., MarketWatch, www.marketwatch.com, April 15; 2015, Amazon.com's investor relations, Amazon.com, www.amazon.com, January 29.

94. C. Boone, F. C. Wezel, & A. van Witleloostuijn, 2013, Joining the pack or going solo? A dynamic theory of new firm positioning, *Journal of Business Venturing*, 28: 511–527; J. R. Williams, 1992, How sustainable is your competitive advantage? *California Management Review*, 34(3): 29–51.

95. R. A. D'Aveni, G. Dagnino, & K. G. Smith, 2010, The age of temporary advantage, *Strategic Management Journal*, 31: 1371–1385; N. Pangarkar & J. R. Lie, 2004, The impact of market cycle on the performance of Singapore acquirers, *Strategic Management Journal*, 25: 1209–1216.

96. G. N. Chandler, J. C. Broberg, & T. H. Allison, 2014, Customer value propositions in declining industries: Differences between industry representative and high-growth firms, *Strategic Entrepreneurship Journal*, 8: 234–253.

97. D. M. Cain, D. A. Moore, & U. Haran, 2015, Making sense of overconfidence in market entry, *Strategic Management Journal*, 36: 1–18.

98. M. A. Schilling, 2015, Technology shocks, technological collaboration and innovation outcomes, *Organization Science*, in press; L.-C. Hsu & C.-H. Wang, 2012, Clarifying the effect of intellectual capital on performance: The mediating role of dynamic capability, *British Journal of Management*, 23: 179–205.

99. 2003, How fast is your company? *Fast Company*, June, 18.

100. N. R. Furr & D. C. Snow, 2015, Intergenerational hybrids: Spillbacks, spillforwards and adapting to technological discontinuities, *Organization Science*, in press; R. Klingebiel & A. De Meyer, 2013, Becoming aware of the unknown: Decision making during the implementation of a strategic initiative, *Organization Science*, 24: 133–153; C. Hall & D. Lundberg, 2010, Competitive knowledge and strategy in high velocity environments, *IUP Journal of Knowledge Management*, 8(1/2): 7–17.

101. C. B. Dobni, M. Klassen, & W. T. Nelson, 2015, Innovation strategy in the U.S.: Top executives offer their views, *Journal of Business Strategy*, 36(1): 3–13; G. Clarkson & P. Toh, 2010, 'Keep out' signs: The role of deterrence in the competition for resources, *Strategic Management Journal*, 31: 1202–1225.

102. A. K. Chatterji & K. R. Fabrizio, 2014, Using users: When does external knowledge enhance corporate product innovation? *Strategic Management Journal*, 35: 1427–1445; M. Kumar, 2011, Are joint ventures positive sum games? The relative effects of cooperative and noncooperative behavior, *Strategic Management Journal*, 32: 32–54; D. Li, L. Eden, M. A. Hitt, & R. D. Ireland, 2008, Friends, acquaintances or strangers? Partner selection in R&D alliances, *Academy of Management Journal*, 51: 315–334.

103. M. M. Larsen, S. Manning, & T. Pedersen, 2013, Uncovering the hidden costs of offshoring: The interplay of complexity, organizational design, and experience, *Strategic Management Journal*, 34: 533–552; F. Zirpoli & M. C. Becker, 2011, What happens when you outsource too much?, *MIT Sloan Management Review*, 52(2): 59–64.

104. B. Wu, Z. Wan, & D. A. Levinthal, 2014, Complementary assets as pipes and prisms: Innovation incentives and trajectory choices, *Strategic Management Journal*, 35: 1257–1278; D. Desai, 2013, The competitive advantage of adaptive networks: An extension of the dynamic capability view, *International Journal of Business Environment*, 5: 379–397.

105. R. Mohammed, 2015, The Apple watch's big pricing problem, *Harvard Business Review*, hbr.org, April 10.

106. S. P. Gudergan, T. Devinney, N. F. Richter, & R. S. Ellis, 2012, Strategic implications for (non-equity) alliance performance, *Long Range Planning*, 45: 451–476; V. Kumar, F. Jones, R. Venkatesan, & R. Leone, 2011, Is market orientation a source of sustainable competitive advantage or simply the cost of competing?, *Journal of Marketing*, 75: 16–30.

107. L. Josephs, 2011, Candy lovers face bitter Easter, *Wall Street Journal*, February 18, C10.

108. M. Kulas, 2015, Why is candy bad for your health? Livestrong.com, www.livestrong.com, January 28.

6

Corporate-Level Strategy

Studying this chapter should provide you with the strategic management knowledge needed to:

6-1   Define corporate-level strategy and discuss its purpose.

6-2   Describe different levels of diversification achieved using different corporate-level strategies.

6-3   Explain three primary reasons firms diversify.

6-4   Describe how firms can create value by using a related diversification strategy.

6-5   Explain the two ways value can be created with an unrelated diversification strategy.

6-6   Discuss the incentives and resources that encourage diversification.

6-7   Describe motives that can encourage managers to over diversify a firm.

DISNEY ADDS VALUE USING A RELATED DIVERSIFICATION STRATEGY

The Walt Disney Company has pursued a related diversification strategy by using its movies to create franchises and platforms around its popular cartoon and action movie figures. It is the second largest mass media producer after Comcast. While other more focused content providers such as Discover Communications, CBS, and Viacom have seen decreasing revenues because of lower ratings and TV ad weakness, Disney was strengthened through its other businesses based on its diversification strategy. These other businesses include consumer products, interactive consumer products, interactive parks and resorts, and studio entertainment parks. It also has strong cable and TV franchises through ESPN and ABC. Although its ad revenues have decreased like other more focused content producers and distributors, its other businesses are growing and allow it to maintain higher earnings compared to other rival media producing firms.

Disney's strategy is successful because its corporate strategy, compared to its business-level strategy, adds value across its set of businesses above what the individual businesses could create individually. In the literature this is often known as synergy, or in the more academic literature it is known as economies of scope (which will be defined more formally later in the chapter). First, Disney has a related set of businesses in its studio entertainment, consumer products and interactive media, media network outlets, parks and resorts, and studio entertainment parks.

CriEnglish.com

Within its studio entertainment businesses, Disney can share activities across its different production firms: Touchstone Pictures, Hollywood Pictures, Dimension Films, Pixar Films, and Marvel Entertainment (a fairly recent acquisition). By sharing activities among these semi-independent studios, it can learn faster and gain success by the knowledge sharing and efficiencies associated with each studio's expertise. The corporation also has broad and deep knowledge about its customers which is a corporate-level capability in terms advertising and marketing. This capability allows Disney to cross sell products highlighted in its movies through its media distribution outlets, parks and resorts, as well as consumer product businesses.

Recently, Disney, for example, has been moving from its historical central focus on animation in movies such as *Cinderella*, *The Jungle Book*, and *Beauty and the Beast*, into the same titles or stories using a live action approach. The recent release of *Cinderella*, a live action version of the original 1950 animated classic, stays particularly close to the "fairy tale version of the script." This approach comes from its understanding of its customers and what they prefer. Other approaches such as this can be found in *Alice in Wonderland* with Johnny Depp and *Maleficent*, which was a slight twist on the original *Sleeping Beauty*, starring Angelina Jolie as the wicked queen. The action versions of these two movies grossed $1.3 billion and $813 million globally, respectively. Although Disney has had some relatively unsuccessful pictures, *John Carter*, *The Lone Ranger*, and *The Sorcerer's Apprentice*, its action movies based on its animated fairy tales have been relatively more successful. Disney will be promoting *Cinderella* products in its stores and in other focused retail outlets and will be advertising its products along with the direct connections to *Alice*, *Maleficent*, and *Frozen*. All of these have been consumer product successes, and *Cinderella* is likely to have the same appeal. Disney is also seeking to produce action movies such as *Beauty and the Beast*, *The Jungle Book*, and others in the near future. All of these feed products into its Disney stores and Disney themed sections in department stores, such as J. C. Penney, as well as promote resort themes and thus drive interrelated revenue through cross selling.

One of the downside problems for these fairy tale themes is that the stories are in the public domain. As such, other competitors are seeking to follow Disney's successful approach. For example, Time Warner Inc.'s Warner Bros. Studio will release *Pan*, which seems to be beating Disney to the punch on its former *Peter Pan* movie success. Likewise, Time Warner will release *Jungle Book* in 2017 and has another script based on *Beauty and the Beast*. Comcast's Universal Pictures is developing the *Little Mermaid*. However, neither of these studios has the marketing power nor the franchising capability of Disney and its interrelated business and corporate skills. Although they are seeking to build these skills, they cannot duplicate Disney's corporate strategy and parent added value because they are more primarily focused on content and distribution as well as advertising. As such, Disney has a current corporate parental advantage over its more focused movie and content producing and distribution competitors. Disney's corporate strategy has put it in the list of top 10 most admired firms in *Fortune* magazine.

Sources: B. Fritz, 2015, Disney recycles fairy tales, minus cartoons, *Wall Street Journal*, March 11, B1, B6; M. Gottfried, 2015, Walt Disney has built a better mousetrap, *Wall Street Journal*, Feb 5, C8; M. Lev-Ram, 2015, Empire of tech, *Fortune*, January 1, 48–58; C. Palmeri & A. Sakoui, 2015, Disney's princesses' give a little live action, *Bloomberg BusinessWeek*, March 9, 30–31; C. Tkaczyk, 2015, The world's most admired companies, *Fortune*, March 1, 97–104; D. Leonard, 2014, The master of Marvel universe, *Bloomberg BusinessWeek*, April 7, 62–68; C. Palmeri & B. Faries, 2014, Big Mickey is watching, *Bloomberg BusinessWeek*, March 10, 22–23.

Our discussions of business-level strategies (Chapter 4) and the competitive rivalry and competitive dynamics associated with them (Chapter 5) have concentrated on firms competing in a single industry or product market.[1] In this chapter, we introduce you to corporate-level strategies, which are strategies firms use to *diversify* their operations from a single business competing in a single market into several product markets—most commonly, into several businesses. Thus, a **corporate-level strategy** specifies actions a firm takes to gain a competitive advantage by selecting and managing a group of different businesses competing in different product markets. Corporate-level strategies help companies to select new strategic positions—positions that are expected to increase the firm's value.[2] As explained in the Opening Case, Disney competes in a number of related entertainment and distribution industries.[3]

As is the case with Disney, firms use corporate-level strategies as a means to grow revenues and profits, but there can be additional strategic intents to growth. Firms can pursue defensive or offensive strategies that realize growth but have different strategic intents. Firms can also pursue market development by entering different geographic markets (this approach is discussed in Chapter 8). Firms can acquire competitors (horizontal integration) or buy a supplier or customer (vertical integration). As we see in the Opening Case, Disney has acquired Pixar and Marvel movie production studios, thereby increasing its horizontal integration in the movie product and distribution business. Such acquisition strategies are discussed in Chapter 7. The basic corporate strategy, the topic of this chapter, focuses on diversification.

The decision to pursue growth is not a risk-free choice for firms. Indeed, General Electric (GE) experienced difficulty in its media businesses, especially with NBC, which it eventually sold to Comcast. GE also suffered significant revenue declines in its financial services businesses and thus reduced its assets in that area, choosing to seek growth in other businesses such as equipment for the oil industry and equipment for industrial firms to better utilize the Internet. Effective firms carefully evaluate their growth options (including the different corporate-level strategies) before committing firm resources to any of them.

A **corporate-level strategy** specifies actions a firm takes to gain a competitive advantage by selecting and managing a group of different businesses competing in different product markets.

Because the diversified firm operates in several different and unique product markets and likely in several businesses, it forms two types of strategies: corporate-level (company-wide) and business-level (competitive).[4] Corporate-level strategy is concerned with two key issues: in what product markets and businesses the firm should compete and how corporate headquarters should manage those businesses.[5] For the diversified company, a business-level strategy (see Chapter 4) must be selected for each of the businesses in which the firm has decided to compete. In this regard, each of GE's product divisions uses different business-level strategies; while most focus on differentiation, its consumer electronics business has products that compete in market niches which include some that are intended to serve the average income consumer. Thus, cost must also be an issue along with some level of quality.

As is the case with a business-level strategy, a corporate-level strategy is expected to help the firm earn above-average returns by creating value.[6] Some suggest that few corporate-level strategies actually create value.[7] As the Opening Case indicates, realizing value through a corporate strategy can be achieved, but it is challenging to do so. In fact, Disney is one of the few large, widely diversified firms that has been successful over time.

Evidence suggests that a corporate-level strategy's value is ultimately determined by the degree to which "the businesses in the portfolio are worth more under the management of the company than they would be under any other ownership."[8] Thus, an effective corporate-level strategy creates, across all of a firm's businesses, aggregate returns that exceed what those returns would be without the strategy[9] and contributes to the firm's strategic competitiveness and its ability to earn above-average returns.[10]

Product diversification, a primary form of corporate-level strategies, concerns the scope of the markets and industries in which the firm competes as well as "how managers buy, create, and sell different businesses to match skills and strengths with opportunities presented to the firm."[11] Successful diversification is expected to reduce variability in the firm's profitability as earnings are generated from different businesses.[12] Diversification can also provide firms with the flexibility to shift their investments to markets where the greatest returns are possible rather than being dependent on only one or a few markets.[13] Because firms incur development and monitoring costs when diversifying, the ideal portfolio of businesses balances diversification's costs and benefits. CEOs and their top-management teams are responsible for determining the best portfolio for their company.[14]

We begin this chapter by examining different levels of diversification (from low to high). After describing the different reasons firms diversify their operations, we focus on two types of related diversification (related diversification signifies a moderate to high level of diversification for the firm). When properly used, these strategies help create value in the diversified firm, either through the sharing of resources (the related constrained strategy) or the transferring of core competencies across the firm's different businesses (the related linked strategy). We then examine unrelated diversification, which is another corporate-level strategy that can create value. Thereafter, the chapter shifts to the incentives and resources that can stimulate diversification which is value neutral. However, managerial motives to diversify, the final topic in the chapter, can actually destroy some of the firm's value.

6-1 Levels of Diversification

Diversified firms vary according to their level of diversification and the connections between and among their businesses. Figure 6.1 lists and defines five categories of businesses according to increasing levels of diversification. The single and dominant business categories denote no or relatively low levels of diversification; more fully diversified

Figure 6.1 Levels and Types of Diversification

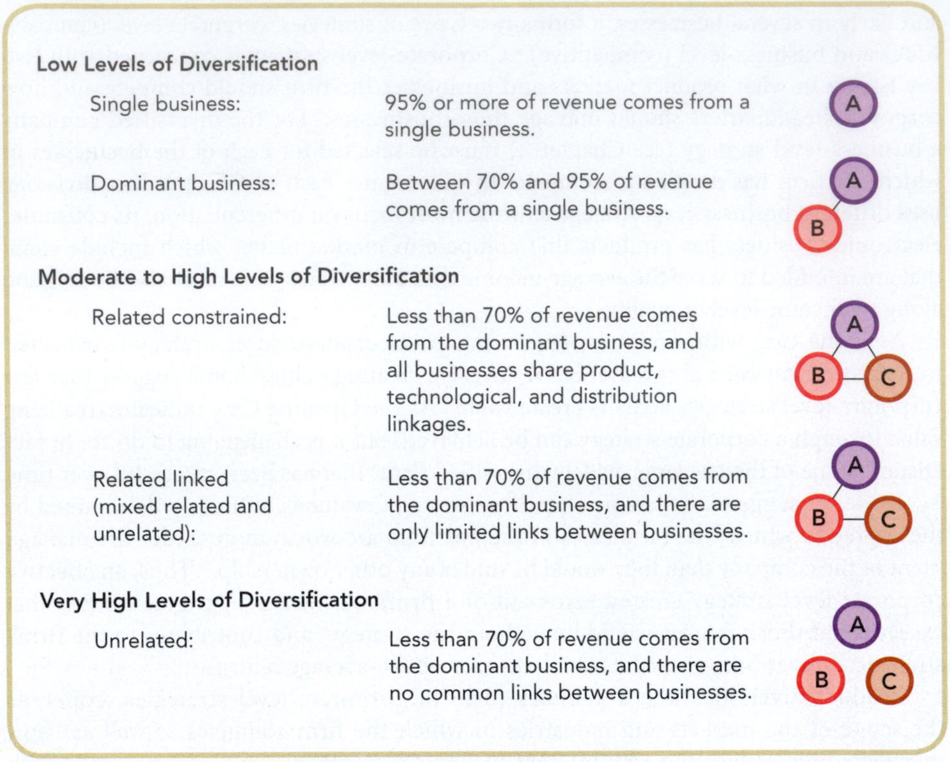

Low Levels of Diversification

Single business: 95% or more of revenue comes from a
                                single business.

Dominant business: Between 70% and 95% of revenue
                                comes from a single business.

Moderate to High Levels of Diversification

Related constrained: Less than 70% of revenue comes
                                from the dominant business, and
                                all businesses share product,
                                technological, and distribution
                                linkages.

Related linked   Less than 70% of revenue comes from
(mixed related and   the dominant business, and there are
unrelated):   only limited links between businesses.

Very High Levels of Diversification

Unrelated: Less than 70% of revenue comes from
                                the dominant business, and there are
                                no common links between businesses.

Source: Adapted from R. P. Rumelt, 1974, *Strategy, Structure and Economic Performance*, Boston: Harvard Business School.

firms are classified into related and unrelated categories. A firm is related through its diversification when its businesses share several links. For example, businesses may share product markets (goods or services), technologies, or distribution channels. The more links among businesses, the more "constrained" is the level of diversification. "Unrelated" refers to the absence of direct links between businesses.

6-1a   Low Levels of Diversification

A firm pursuing a low level of diversification uses either a single- or a dominant-business, corporate-level diversification strategy. A *single-business diversification strategy* is a corporate-level strategy wherein the firm generates 95 percent or more of its sales revenue from its core business area.[15] For example, McIlhenny Company, headquartered on Avery Island in Louisiana and producer of Tabasco brand, has maintained is focus on its family's hot sauce products for seven generations. On its website, the following quote is provided about its products: "Back in 1868, Edmund McIlhenny experimented with pepper seeds from Mexico (or somewhere in Central America) to create his own style of Louisiana hot sauce—our Original Red Sauce. Since then we've continued this tradition of exploration and experimentation, and today McIlhenny Company crafts seven unique and distinct flavors of sauce, each with its own variety of deliciousness. From mild to wild, there's something for everyone!"[16] Historically McIlhenny has used a single-business strategy while operating in relatively few product markets. Recently, it has begun to partner with other firms so that the Tabasco taste can be found in jelly bean candies (Jelly Belly brand), Hot & Spicy Cheez-It snack crackers (Sunshine brand), jerky (Slim Jim brand), and even Tabasco flavored canned meat (Spam brand).

With the *dominant-business diversification strategy*, the firm generates between 70 and 95 percent of its total revenue within a single business area. United Parcel Service (UPS) uses this strategy. Recently UPS generated 61 percent of its revenue from its U.S. package delivery business and 22 percent from its international package business, with the remaining 17 percent coming from the firm's nonpackage business.[17] Though the U.S. package delivery business currently generates the largest percentage of UPS's sales revenue, the firm anticipates that in the future its other two businesses will account for the majority of revenue growth. This expectation suggests that UPS may become more diversified, both in terms of its goods and services and in the number of countries in which those goods and services are offered.

Firms that focus on one or very few businesses and markets can earn positive returns, because they develop capabilities useful for these markets and can provide superior service to their customers. Additionally, there are fewer challenges in managing one or a very small set of businesses, allowing them to gain economies of scale and efficiently use their resources.[18] Family-owned and controlled businesses, such as McIlhenny Company's Tabasco sauce business, are commonly less diversified. They prefer the narrower focus because the family's reputation is related closely to that of the business. Thus, family members prefer to provide quality goods and services which a focused strategy better allows.[19]

Sany Heavy Industry Co., Ltd is China's largest producer of heavy equipment. In fact, it is the fifth largest producer of this type of equipment globally. Sany has seven core businesses including: concrete machinery, excavators, hoisting machinery, pile driving machinery, road construction machinery, port machinery, and wind turbine.[20] While each is distinct, some similar technologies are used in the production and equipment. Furthermore, related technologies allow similarities in production processes and equipment for certain parts allowing a transfer of knowledge across these businesses. In addition, customers and markets share some similarities because most relate to some form of construction. Although Sany might be evaluated by some to be using a single-business corporate strategy because of its focus on heavy equipment manufacturing. If this is the case, it has a series of differentiated products and is likely following a product proliferation strategy. A product proliferation strategy represents a form of intra-industry diversification.[21] Yet, as noted, Sany also has seven business divisions, one for each type of heavy equipment it manufactures. Thus, it might also be considered by some to engage in moderate diversification in the form of highly related constrained diversification, which is discussed next.

6-1b Moderate and High Levels of Diversification

A firm generating more than 30 percent of its revenue outside a dominant business and whose businesses are related to each other in some manner uses a related diversification corporate-level strategy. When the links between the diversified firm's businesses are rather direct, meaning they use similar sourcing, throughput and outbound processes, it is a *related constrained diversification strategy*. Campbell Soup, Procter & Gamble, and Merck & Co. use a related constrained strategy. A firm shares resources and activities across its businesses with a related constrained strategy.

For example, the Publicis Groupe uses a related constrained strategy, deriving value from the potential synergy across its various groups (mobile and interactive online communication, television, magazines and newspapers, cinema and radio, and outdoor signage), especially the digital capabilities in its advertising business. Given its recent performance, the related constrained strategy has created value for Publicis customers and its shareholders by helping target particular audiences through appropriate media and digital strategies.[22]

The diversified company with a portfolio of businesses that have only a few links between them is called a mixed related and unrelated firm and is using the *related linked diversification strategy* (see Figure 6.1). GE uses a related-linked corporate-level diversification strategy. Compared with related constrained firms, related linked firms share fewer resources and assets between their businesses, concentrating instead on transferring knowledge and core competencies between the businesses. GE has four strategic business units (see Chapter 11 for a definition of SBUs) it calls "divisions," each composed of related businesses. There are few relationships across the strategic business units, but many among the subsidiaries or divisions within them. As with firms using each type of diversification strategy, companies implementing the related linked strategy constantly adjust the mix in their portfolio of businesses as well as make decisions about how to manage these businesses.[23] Managing a diversified firm such as GE is highly challenging, but GE appears to have been well managed over the years given its success.

A highly diversified firm that has no relationships between its businesses follows an *unrelated diversification strategy*. United Technologies Corporation, Textron, Samsung, and Hutchison Whampoa Limited (HWL) are examples of firms using this type of corporate-level strategy. Commonly, firms using this strategy are called *conglomerates*. HWL is a leading international corporation with five core businesses: ports and related services; property and hotels; retail; energy, infrastructure, investments and others; and telecommunications. These businesses are not related to each other, and the firm makes no efforts to share activities or to transfer core competencies between or among them. Each of these five businesses is quite large as exemplified by the retailing arm of the retail and manufacturing business which has more than 9,300 stores in 33 countries. Groceries, cosmetics, electronics, wine, and airline tickets are some of the product categories featured in these stores. This firm's size and diversity suggest the challenge of successfully managing the unrelated diversification strategy. However, Hutchison's past CEO and Board Chair, Li Ka-shing, has been successful at not only making smart acquisitions, but also at divesting businesses with good timing.[24] Another form of unrelated diversification strategy is pursued by private equity firms such Carlyle Group, Blackstone, and KKR.[25] They often have an unrelated set of portfolio firms.

6-2 Reasons for Diversification

A firm uses a corporate-level diversification strategy for a variety of reasons (see Table 6.1). Typically, a diversification strategy is used to increase the firm's value by improving its overall performance. Value is created either through related diversification or through unrelated diversification when the strategy allows a company's businesses to increase revenues or reduce costs while implementing their business-level strategies.[26]

Other reasons for using a diversification strategy may have nothing to do with increasing the firm's value; in fact, diversification can have neutral effects or even reduce a firm's value. Value-neutral reasons for diversification include a desire to match and thereby neutralize a competitor's market power (e.g., to neutralize another firm's advantage by acquiring a similar distribution outlet). Decisions to expand a firm's portfolio of businesses to reduce managerial risk or increase top managers pay can have a negative effect on the firm's value. Greater amounts of diversification reduce managerial risk in that if one of the businesses in a diversified firm fails, the top executive of that business does not risk total failure by the corporation. As such, this reduces the top executives' employment risk. In addition, because diversification can increase a firm's size and thus managerial compensation, managers have motives to diversify a firm to a level that reduces its value.[27] Diversification rationales that may have a neutral or negative effect on the firm's value are discussed later in the chapter.

Table 6.1 Reasons for Diversification

Value-Creating Diversification
• Economies of scope (related diversification)
• Sharing activities
• Transferring core competencies
• Market power (related diversification)
• Blocking competitors through multipoint competition
• Vertical integration
• Financial economies (unrelated diversification)
• Efficient internal capital allocation
• Business restructuring
Value-Neutral Diversification
• Antitrust regulation
• Tax laws
• Low performance
• Uncertain future cash flows
• Risk reduction for firm
• Tangible resources
• Intangible resources
Value-Reducing Diversification
• Diversifying managerial employment risk
• Increasing managerial compensation

Operational relatedness and corporate relatedness are two ways diversification strategies that can create value (see Figure 6.2). Studies of these independent relatedness dimensions show the importance of resources and key competencies.[28] The figure's vertical dimension depicts opportunities to share operational activities between businesses (operational relatedness) while the horizontal dimension suggests opportunities for transferring corporate-level core competencies (corporate relatedness). The firm with a strong capability in managing operational synergy, especially in sharing assets between its businesses, falls in the upper left quadrant, which also represents vertical sharing of assets through vertical integration. The lower right quadrant represents a highly developed corporate capability for transferring one or more core competencies across businesses.

This capability is located primarily in the corporate headquarters office. Unrelated diversification is also illustrated in Figure 6.2 in the lower left quadrant. Financial economies (discussed later), rather than either operational or corporate relatedness, are the source of value creation for firms using the unrelated diversification strategy.

6-3 Value-Creating Diversification: Related Constrained and Related Linked Diversification

With the related diversification corporate-level strategy, the firm builds upon or extends its resources and capabilities to build a competitive advantage by creating value for customers.[29] The company using the related diversification strategy wants to develop and exploit economies of scope between its businesses.[30] In fact, even nonprofit organizations have found that carefully planned and implemented related diversification can create value.[31]

Figure 6.2 Value-Creating Diversification Strategies: Operational and Corporate Relatedness

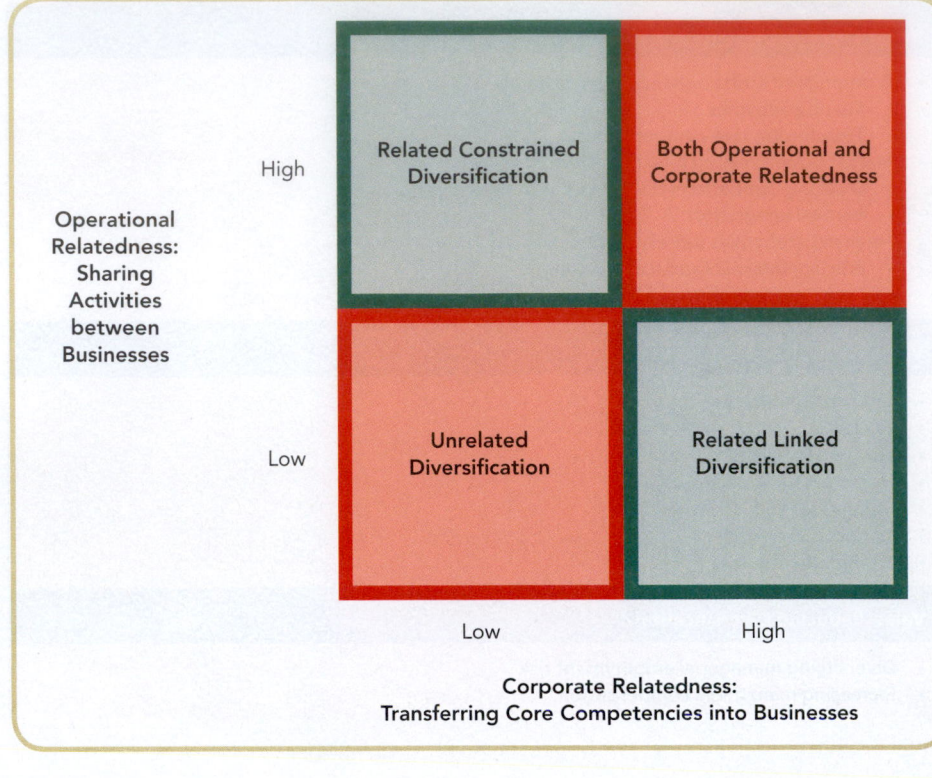

Economies of scope are cost savings a firm creates by successfully sharing resources and capabilities or transferring one or more corporate-level core competencies that were developed in one of its businesses to another of its businesses.[32]

As illustrated in Figure 6.2, firms seek to create value from economies of scope through two basic kinds of operational economies: sharing activities (operational relatedness) and transferring corporate-level core competencies (corporate relatedness). The difference between sharing activities and transferring competencies is based on how separate resources are jointly used to create economies of scope. To create economies of scope, tangible resources such as plant and equipment or other business-unit physical assets often must be shared. Less tangible resources such as manufacturing know-how and technological capabilities can also be shared.[33] However, know-how transferred between separate activities with no physical or tangible resource involved is a transfer of a corporate-level core competence, not an operational sharing of activities.[34]

6-3a Operational Relatedness: Sharing Activities

Firms can create operational relatedness by sharing either a primary activity (e.g., inventory delivery systems) or a support activity (e.g., purchasing practices)—see Chapter 3's discussion of the value chain. Firms using the related constrained diversification strategy share activities in order to create value. Procter & Gamble uses this corporate-level strategy. Sany, described in an example above, also shares activities. For example, Sany's various businesses share marketing activities because all of their equipment is sold to firms in the construction industry. This is evidenced by the sponsorship of a NASCAR racecar in an attempt to reach executives in the construction industry. (see more on Sany in the Mini-case at the end of the Chapter)

Economies of scope are cost savings a firm creates by successfully sharing resources and capabilities or transferring one or more corporate-level core competencies that were developed in one of its businesses to another of its businesses.

Activity sharing is also risky because ties among a firm's businesses create links between outcomes. For instance, if demand for one business's product is reduced, it may not generate sufficient revenues to cover the fixed costs required to operate the shared facilities. These types of organizational difficulties can reduce activity-sharing success. Additionally, activity sharing requires careful coordination between the businesses involved. The coordination challenges must be managed effectively for the appropriate sharing of activities (see Chapter 11 for further discussion).[35]

Although activity sharing across businesses is not risk-free, research shows that it can create value. For example, studies of acquisitions of firms in the same industry (horizontal acquisitions), such as the banking and software industries, found that sharing resources and activities and thereby creating economies of scope contributed to post-acquisition increases in performance and higher returns to shareholders.[36] Additionally, firms that sold off related units in which resource sharing was a possible source of economies of scope have been found to produce lower returns than those that sold off businesses unrelated to the firm's core business.[37] Still other research discovered that firms with closely related businesses have lower risk.[38] These results suggest that gaining economies of scope by sharing activities across a firm's businesses may be important in reducing risk and in creating value. More attractive results are obtained through activity sharing when a strong corporate headquarters office facilitates it.[39]

Procter & Gamble (P&G) is a consumer products firm that shares a lot of activities among its divisions; for example, most of its products are sold through retail outlets and those sales activities can be shared among its divisions.

Charles Pertwee/Corbis News/Corbis

6-3b Corporate Relatedness: Transferring of Core Competencies

Over time, the firm's intangible resources, such as its know-how, become the foundation of core competencies. **Corporate-level core competencies** are complex sets of resources and capabilities that link different businesses, primarily through managerial and technological knowledge, experience, and expertise.[40] Firms seeking to create value through corporate relatedness use the related linked diversification strategy as exemplified by GE.

In at least two ways, the related linked diversification strategy helps firms to create value. First, because the expense of developing a core competence has already been incurred in one of the firm's businesses, transferring this competence to a second business eliminates the need for that business to allocate resources to develop it. Resource intangibility is a second source of value creation through corporate relatedness. Intangible resources are difficult for competitors to understand and imitate. Because of this difficulty, the unit receiving a transferred corporate-level competence often gains an immediate competitive advantage over its rivals.[41]

A number of firms have successfully transferred one or more corporate-level core competencies across their businesses. Virgin Group Ltd. transfers its marketing core competence across airlines, cosmetics, music, drinks, mobile phones, health clubs, and a number of other businesses.[42] Honda has developed and transferred its competence in engine design and manufacturing among its businesses making products such as motorcycles,

Corporate-level core competencies are complex sets of resources and capabilities that link different businesses, primarily through managerial and technological knowledge, experience, and expertise.

Virgin Group, known for its airline, has also transferred its brand through its marketing competence to other product areas such as cosmetics, music, drinks, mobile phones, health clubs, and a number of other businesses.

lawnmowers, and cars and trucks. Company officials state that Honda is a major manufacturer of engines focused on providing products for all forms of human mobility.[43]

One way managers facilitate the transfer of corporate-level core competencies is by moving key people into new management positions.[44] However, the manager of an older business may be reluctant to transfer key people who have accumulated knowledge and experience critical to the business's success. Thus, managers with the ability to facilitate the transfer of a core competence may come at a premium, or the key people involved may not want to transfer. Additionally, the top-level managers from the transferring business may not want the competencies transferred to a new business to fulfill the firm's diversification objectives.[45] Research suggests that the nature of the top management team can influence the success of the knowledge and skill transfer process.[46] Research also suggests too much dependence on outsourcing can lower the usefulness of core competencies thereby, reducing their useful transferability to other business units in the diversified firm.[47]

6-3c   Market Power

Firms using a related diversification strategy may gain market power when successfully using a related constrained or related linked strategy. **Market power** exists when a firm is able to sell its products above the existing competitive level or to reduce the costs of its primary and support activities below the competitive level, or both.[48] Heinz was bought by a private equity firm in Brazil called 3G Capital Partners LP that is currently approaching Kraft Foods Group to combine these two firms. This deal is supported by Warren Buffet's Berkshire Hathaway & Co. who teamed up with 3G to buy Heinz's well established ketchup and frozen food brands businesses for $23 billion. In a similar deal to build market power, 3G took private food restaurant Burger King Worldwide, Inc., and also bought Tim Hortons Inc. (a Canadian coffee and donut fast-food restaurant) through its Burger King holdings. Warren Buffet also contributed $11 million to help finance the latter deal. These deals obvious build market power for the combining firms in branded consumer foods and fast food restaurants.[49]

Ericsson has the largest share of the global market in telecommunications equipment, and for many years its leadership position has afforded the company considerable market power. That market power and its leadership position in research helped it garner major contracts in telecommunications equipment; "About 40 percent of the world's wireless calls and data move through Ericsson's network hardware."[50] As communication firms move to the "cloud" it is seeking acquisitions and contracts to maintain that market power.

In addition to efforts to gain scale as a means of increasing market power, firms can foster increased market power through multipoint competition and vertical integration. **Multipoint competition** exists when two or more diversified firms simultaneously compete in the same product areas or geographical markets.[51] Through multi-point competition, rival firms often experience pressure to diversify because other firms in their dominant industry segment have made acquisitions to compete in a different market segment.

Market power exists when a firm is able to sell its products above the existing competitive level or to reduce the costs of its primary and support activities below the competitive level, or both.

Multipoint competition exists when two or more diversified firms simultaneously compete in the same product areas or geographical markets.

The actions taken by UPS and FedEx in two markets, overnight delivery and ground shipping, illustrate multipoint competition. UPS moved into overnight delivery, FedEx's stronghold; in turn, FedEx bought trucking and ground shipping assets to move into ground shipping, UPS's stronghold. Similarly, J.M. Smucker Company, a snack food producer, recently bought Big Heart Pet Brands which specializes in snacks such as Milk-Bone dog biscuits, treats and chews and has over $2.2 billion in annual revenue. Smucker's competitor, Mars, had acquired a significant portion of Proctor & Gamble's dog and cat food division in 2014. Apparently Smucker's was seeking to keep up its size and cross-industry positions relative to Mars by also diversifying into snacks for pets.[52]

© Oleksiy Mark/Shutterstock.com

When firm pursue vertical integration more information is processed at headquarters and thus more knowledge processing is needed as illustrated by these servers. External relations with suppliers are also supported by such information networks.

Some firms using a related diversification strategy engage in vertical integration to gain market power. **Vertical integration** exists when a company produces its own inputs (backward integration) or owns its own source of output distribution (forward integration). In some instances, firms partially integrate their operations, producing and selling their products by using company-owned businesses as well as outside sources.[53]

Vertical integration is commonly used in the firm's core business to gain market power over rivals. Market power is gained as the firm develops the ability to save on its operations, avoid sourcing and market costs, improve product quality, possibly protect its technology from imitation by rivals, and potentially exploit underlying capabilities in the marketplace. Vertically integrated firms are better able to improve product quality and improve or create new technologies than specialized firms because they have access to more information and knowledge that are complementary.[54] Market power also is created when firms have strong ties between their productive assets for which no market prices exist. Establishing a market price would result in high search and transaction costs, so firms seek to vertically integrate rather than remain separate businesses.[55]

Vertical integration has its limitations. For example, an outside supplier may produce the product at a lower cost. As a result, internal transactions from vertical integration may be expensive and reduce profitability relative to competitors.[56] Also, bureaucratic costs can be present with vertical integration.[57] Because vertical integration can require substantial investments in specific technologies, it may reduce the firm's flexibility, especially when technology changes quickly. Finally, changes in demand create capacity balance and coordination problems. If one business is building a part for another internal business but achieving economies of scale requires the first division to manufacture quantities that are beyond the capacity of the internal buyer to absorb, it would be necessary to sell the parts outside the firm as well as to the internal business. Thus, although vertical integration can create value, especially through market power over competitors, it is not without risks and costs.[58]

Around the turn of the twenty-first century, manufacturing firms such as Intel and Dell began to reduce vertical integration by reducing ownership of self-manufactured parts and component. This trend also occurred in some large auto companies, such

Vertical integration exists when a company produces its own inputs (backward integration) or owns its own source of output distribution (forward integration).

as Ford and General Motors, as they developed independent supplier networks.[59] Flextronics, an electronics contract manufacturer, is a large contract manufacturer that helps to support this approach to supply-chain management.[60] Such firms often manage their customers' entire product lines and offer services ranging from inventory management to delivery and after-sales service. Interestingly, however, some firms are beginning to reintegrate in order to gain better control over the quality and timing of their supplies.[61] Samsung has maintained control of its operations through a vertical integration strategy, while being a manufacturer for competitors such as Apple in consumer electronics.

6-3d   Simultaneous Operational Relatedness and Corporate Relatedness

As Figure 6.2 suggests, some firms simultaneously seek operational and corporate relatedness to create economies of scope.[62] The ability to simultaneously create economies of scope by sharing activities (operational relatedness) and transferring core competencies (corporate relatedness) is difficult for competitors to understand and learn how to imitate. However, if the cost of realizing both types of relatedness is not offset by the benefits created, the result is diseconomies because the cost of organization and incentive structure is very expensive.[63]

As noted in the Opening Case, The Walt Disney Company uses a related diversification strategy to simultaneously create economies of scope through operational and corporate relatedness. Disney has five separate but related businesses: media networks, parks and resorts, studio entertainment, consumer products, and interactive media. Within the firm's Studio Entertainment business, for example, Disney can gain economies of scope by sharing activities among its different movie distribution companies, such as Touchstone Pictures, Hollywood Pictures, and Dimension Films. Broad and deep knowledge about its customers is a capability on which Disney relies to develop corporate-level core competencies in terms of advertising and marketing. With these competencies, Disney is able to create economies of scope through corporate relatedness as it cross-sells products that are highlighted in its movies through the distribution channels that are part of its parks and resorts and consumer products businesses. Thus, characters created in movies become figures that are marketed through Disney's retail stores (which are part of the consumer products business). In addition, themes established in movies become the source of new rides in the firm's theme parks, which are part of the parks and resorts business, and provide themes for clothing and other retail business products.[64]

Although The Walt Disney Company has been able to successfully use related diversification as a corporate-level strategy through which it creates economies of scope by sharing some activities and by transferring core competencies, it can be difficult for investors to identify the value created by a firm (e.g., The Walt Disney Company) as it shares activities and transfers core competencies. For this reason, the value of the assets of a firm using a diversification strategy to create economies of scope often is discounted by investors.[65]

Disney sells many products related to its movies in its own stores as well as more broadly through other retail outlets.

RICHARD B. LEVINE/Newscom

6-4 Unrelated Diversification

Firms do not seek either operational relatedness or corporate relatedness when using the unrelated diversification corporate-level strategy. An unrelated diversification strategy (see Figure 6.2) can create value through two types of financial economies. **Financial economies** are cost savings realized through improved allocations of financial resources based on investments inside or outside the firm.[66]

Efficient internal capital allocations can lead to financial economies. Efficient internal capital allocations reduce risk among the firm's businesses—for example, by leading to the development of a portfolio of businesses with different risk profiles. The second type of financial economy concerns the restructuring of acquired assets. Here, the diversified firm buys another company, restructures that company's assets in ways that allow it to operate more profitably, and then sells the company for a profit in the external market.[67] Next, we discuss the two types of financial economies in greater detail.

6-4a Efficient Internal Capital Market Allocation

In a market economy, capital markets are believed to efficiently allocate capital. Efficiency results as investors take equity positions (ownership) with high expected future cash-flow values. Capital is also allocated through debt as shareholders and debt holders try to improve the value of their investments by taking stakes in businesses with high growth and profitability prospects.

In large diversified firms, the corporate headquarters office distributes capital to its businesses to create value for the overall corporation. As exampled in the Strategic Focus, GE has used this approach to internal capital allocation among its unrelated business units. The nature of these distributions can generate gains from internal capital market allocations that exceed the gains that would accrue to shareholders as a result of capital being allocated by the external capital market.[68] Because those in a firm's corporate headquarters generally have access to detailed and accurate information regarding the actual and potential future performance of the company's portfolio of businesses, they have the best information to make capital distribution decisions.[69]

Compared with corporate office personnel, external investors have relatively limited access to internal information and can only estimate the performances of individual businesses as well as their future prospects. Moreover, although businesses seeking capital must provide information to potential suppliers (e.g., banks or insurance companies), firms with internal capital markets can have at least two informational advantages. First, information provided to capital markets through annual reports and other sources emphasize positive prospects and outcomes. External sources of capital have a limited ability to understand the operational dynamics within large organizations. Even external shareholders who have access to information are unlikely to receive full and complete disclosure.[70] Second, although a firm must disseminate information, that information also becomes simultaneously available to the firm's current and potential competitors. Competitors might attempt to duplicate a firm's value-creating strategy with insights gained by studying such information. Thus, the ability to efficiently allocate capital through an internal market helps the firm protect the competitive advantages it develops while using its corporate-level strategy as well as its various business-unit–level strategies.

If intervention from outside the firm is required to make corrections to capital allocations, only significant changes are possible because the power to make changes by outsiders is often indirect (e.g., through members of the board of directors). External parties can try to make changes by forcing the firm into bankruptcy or changing the top management team. Alternatively, in an internal capital market, the corporate headquarters office can fine-tune its corrections, such as choosing to adjust managerial incentives

Financial economies are cost savings realized through improved allocations of financial resources based on investments inside or outside the firm.

GE and United Technology Are Firms that Have Pursued Internal Capital Allocation and Restructuring Strategies

GE competes in many different industries ranging from appliances, aviation, and consumer electronics to energy, financial services, health care, oil, and wind turbines. Historically, GE has done an exceptionally good job of allocating capital across its many businesses, although it has suffered a discount to other diversified competitors of late. Even though GE is a related linked firm, it differentially allocates capital across its major strategic business units. Even though GE Capital (GE's financial services business unit) produced high returns for GE over the last few decades, it received a healthy amount of capital from internal allocations. However, GE has been balancing its financial services portfolio over the last few years.

In particular, GE committed to shrinking its financial operation because Jeff Immelt, GE's CEO, has been under pressure by investors to make GE a more focused industrial company, primarily because its stock price has stayed below $30 since the financial crisis. Ultimately, the goal is to scale back GE Capital from 42 percent of the profit in 2014 to 25 percent of GE's profit in 2016. Before the financial crisis, almost 50 percent of profits were derived from GE Capital. Regulation has forced GE to keep more capital in its financial arm, and thus it can no longer pull as much cash out "to help pay dividends, buy back shares, and help finance GE's industrial operations." It also prevents other restructuring efforts. For example, GE wanted to sell its appliance business, but had to hold on to it for several years during the crisis because the price it could get would be too low. Immelt added, "make no mistake, the ultimate size of GE Capital will be based on competitiveness, returns, and the impact of regulation on the entire company." However, since the financial crisis, GE realized the risks of have so much capital invested in GE Capital which almost toppled GE.

GE is also under pressure because it had built up its oil and gas service operations through acquisitions. However, since the drop in oil prices, this unit has come under pressure. When these assets were purchased, crude oil was selling for $100 per barrel, but crude oil has been recently selling for near $50 per barrel.

Also, United Technologies, an unrelated firm, has allocated resources internally according to their best and most efficient use. Similar to GE, it often bought, restructured, and operated the businesses until it made sense to sell them. United Technologies owns Otis Elevator, building fires and security system brands Chubb and Kidde, Pratt & Whitney jet engines, Carrier air conditioners, and Sikorsky Aircraft. Sikorsky is best known for its Black Hawk helicopters, and it is one of the largest helicopter makers in the world. United Technologies' new CEO,

Gregory J. Hayes, told analysts that it was evaluating its portfolio. The Sikorsky division has come under pressure amidst softer military spending and weakness in demand for oil services companies which utilize helicopters to fly employees to platforms offshore as well as onshore. Although Hayes had considered a tax free spinoff, he ultimately contracted to sell the Sikorsky business unit to Lockheed Martin, a big defense contractor. Interestingly, he is also hunting for a large acquisition to purchase, restructure, and include in United Technologies portfolio.

Both GE and United Technology have used internal capital allocate resources among their diversified business units efficiently. Also, both businesses have used the restructuring strategy to make their operations more efficient and, when appropriate, sold them on the open market, either through selloff to another acquirer or through spinoffs where two stock prices are created, one for the legacy business and one for the spinoff firm (the variety of restructuring strategies will be developed and compared more fully in Chapter 7).

Although GE is seeking to pare back its financial business, GE Capital, with the downturn in oil and gas commodity prices, its Oil and Gas service unit has also experienced difficulties.

Simon Dawson/Bloomberg/Getty Images

Sources: D. Cameron, 2015, Lockheed Martin to buy Sikorsky for $9 billion, *Wall Street Journal*, www.wsj.com, July 21; R. Clough, 2015, A crude awakening for GE, *Bloomberg Businessweek*, March 16, 19; C. Dillow, 2015, What happens if United Technologies unloads Sikorsky?, *Fortune*, www.fortune.com, March 23; C. Grant, 2015, GE's capital control isn't a cure; selling its Asian lending unit won't be enough to revive its stock, *Wall Street Journal*, www.wsj.com, March 16; T. Mann, 2015, GE weighs deeper cuts in bank unit, *Wall Street Journal*, March 12, B1, B2; D. Mattioli & D. Cimilluca, 2015, Sikorsky spin-off considered, *Wall Street Journal*, March 12, B3; G. Smith, 2015, Siemens' long-feared slimdown isn't as drastic as feared, *Fortune*, www.fortune,com, February 23; J. Bogaisky, 2014, Is Bouygues crying uncle on Alstom?, GE said in talks for $13b acquisition. *Forbes*, April 23, 19; T. Mann, 2014, United Technologies CEO hunting for major acquisition, *Wall Street Journal*, www.wsj.com, December 12.

or encouraging strategic changes in one of the firm's businesses.[71] Thus, capital can be allocated according to more specific criteria than is possible with external market allocations. Because it has less accurate information, the external capital market may fail to allocate resources adequately to high-potential investments. The corporate headquarters office of a diversified company can more effectively perform such tasks as disciplining underperforming management teams through resource allocations.[72]

In spite of the challenges associated with it, a number of corporations continue to use the unrelated diversification strategy, especially in Europe and in emerging markets. As an example, Siemens is a large diversified German conglomerate that engages in substantial diversification in order to balance its economic risk. In economic downturns, diversification can help some companies improve future performance.[73]

The Achilles' heel for firms using the unrelated diversification strategy in a developed economy is that competitors can imitate financial economies more easily than they can replicate the value gained from the economies of scope developed through operational relatedness and corporate relatedness. This issue is less of a problem in emerging economies, in which the absence of a "soft infrastructure" (including effective financial intermediaries, sound regulations, and contract laws) supports and encourages use of the unrelated diversification strategy.[74] In fact, in emerging economies such as those in Korea, India, and Chile, research has shown that diversification increases the performance of firms affiliated with large diversified business groups.[75]

6-4b Restructuring of Assets

Financial economies can also be created when firms learn how to create value by buying, restructuring, and then selling the restructured companies' assets in the external market.[76] As in the real estate business, buying assets at low prices, restructuring them, and selling them at a price that exceeds their cost generates a positive return on the firm's invested capital. This is a strategy that has been taken up by private equity firms, who buy, restructure and then sell, often within a four or five year period.[77]

Unrelated diversified companies that pursue this strategy try to create financial economies by acquiring and restructuring other companies' assets, but it involves significant trade-offs. For example, United Technologies as illustrated in the Strategic Focus has used this strategy. Likewise, Danaher Corp.'s success requires a focus on mature manufacturing businesses because of the uncertainty of demand for high-technology products. It has acquired 400 businesses since 1984 and applied the Danaher Business System to reduce costs and create a lean organization.[78] In high-technology businesses, resource allocation decisions are highly complex, often creating information-processing overload on the small corporate headquarters offices that are common in unrelated diversified firms. High-technology and service businesses are often human-resource dependent; these people can leave or demand higher pay and thus appropriate or deplete the value of an acquired firm.[79]

Buying and then restructuring service-based assets so they can be profitably sold in the external market is also difficult. Thus, for both high-technology firms and service-based companies, relatively few tangible assets can be restructured to create value and sell profitably. It is difficult to restructure intangible assets such as human capital and effective relationships that have evolved over time between buyers (customers) and sellers (firm personnel). Ideally, executives will follow a strategy of buying businesses when prices are lower, such as in the midst of a recession, and selling them at late stages in an expansion.[80] Because of the increases in global economic activity, including more cross-border acquisitions, there is also a growing number of foreign divestitures and restructuring in internal markets (e.g., partial or full privatization of state-owned enterprises). Foreign divestitures are even more complex than domestic ones and must be managed carefully.[81]

6-5 Value-Neutral Diversification: Incentives and Resources

The objectives firms seek when using related diversification and unrelated diversification strategies all have the potential to help the firm create value through the corporate-level strategy. However, these strategies, as well as single- and dominant-business diversification strategies, are sometimes used with objectives that are value-neutral. Different incentives to diversify sometimes exist, and the quality of the firm's resources may permit only diversification that is value neutral rather than value creating.

6-5a Incentives to Diversify

Incentives to diversify come from both the external environment and a firm's internal environment. External incentives include antitrust regulations and tax laws. Internal incentives include low performance, uncertain future cash flows, and the pursuit of synergy, and reduction of risk for the firm.

Antitrust Regulation and Tax Laws

Government antitrust policies and tax laws provided incentives for U.S. firms to diversify in the 1960s and 1970s.[82] Antitrust laws prohibiting mergers that created increased market power (via either vertical or horizontal integration) were stringently enforced during that period.[83] Merger activity that produced conglomerate diversification was encouraged primarily by the Celler-Kefauver Antimerger Act (1950), which discouraged horizontal and vertical mergers. As a result, many of the mergers during the 1960s and 1970s were "conglomerate" in character, involving companies pursuing different lines of business. Between 1973 and 1977, 79.1 percent of all mergers were conglomerate in nature.[84]

During the 1980s, antitrust enforcement lessened, resulting in more and larger horizontal mergers (acquisitions of target firms in the same line of business, such as a merger between two oil companies).[85] In addition, investment bankers became more open to the kinds of mergers facilitated by regulation changes; as a consequence, takeovers increased to unprecedented numbers.[86] The conglomerates, or highly diversified firms, of the 1960s and 1970s became more "focused" in the 1980s and early 1990s as merger constraints were relaxed and restructuring was implemented.[87]

In the beginning of the twenty-first century, antitrust concerns emerged again with the large volume of mergers and acquisitions (see Chapter 7).[88] Mergers are now receiving more scrutiny than they did in the 1980s, 1990s, and the first decade of the 2000s.[89]

The tax effects of diversification stem not only from corporate tax changes, but also from individual tax rates. Some companies (especially mature ones) generate more cash from their operations than they can reinvest profitably. Some argue that *free cash flows* (liquid financial assets for which investments in current businesses are no longer economically viable) should be redistributed to shareholders as dividends.[90] However, in the 1960s and 1970s, dividends were taxed more heavily than were capital gains. As a result, before 1980, shareholders preferred that firms use free cash flows to buy and build companies in high-performance industries. If the firm's stock value appreciated over the long term, shareholders might receive a better return on those funds than if the funds had been redistributed as dividends because returns from stock sales would be taxed more lightly than would dividends.

Under the 1986 Tax Reform Act, however, the top individual ordinary income tax rate was reduced from 50 to 28 percent, and the special capital gains tax was changed to treat capital gains as ordinary income. These changes created an incentive for shareholders to stop encouraging firms to retain funds for purposes of diversification. These tax law changes also influenced an increase in divestitures of unrelated business units after 1984. Thus, while individual tax rates for capital gains and dividends created a shareholder incentive to increase diversification before 1986, they encouraged lower diversification after 1986, unless the diversification was funded by tax-deductible debt. Yet, there have been changes in the maximum individual tax rates since the 1980s. The top individual tax rate has varied from 31 percent in 1992 to 39.6 percent in 2013. There have also been some changes in the capital gains tax rates.

Corporate tax laws also affect diversification. Acquisitions typically increase a firm's depreciable asset allowances. Increased depreciation (a non-cash-flow expense) produces lower taxable income, thereby providing an additional incentive for acquisitions. At one time, acquisitions were an attractive means for securing tax benefits, but changes recommended by the Financial Accounting Standards Board (FASB) eliminated the "pooling of interests" method to account for the acquired firm's assets. It also eliminated the write-off for research and development in process, and thus reduced some of the incentives to make acquisitions, especially acquisitions in related high-technology industries (these changes are discussed further in Chapter 7).[91]

Thus, regulatory changes such as the ones we have described create incentives or disincentives for diversification. Interestingly, European antitrust laws have historically been stricter regarding horizontal mergers than those in the United States, but recently have become more similar.[92]

Low Performance

Some research shows that low returns are related to greater levels of diversification.[93] If high performance eliminates the need for greater diversification, then low performance may provide an incentive for diversification. In the Strategic Focus, Coca-Cola has not met its growth and profit targets in its dominant business of soft drinks in recent years. As such, it has sought to diversify into higher growth areas such as bottled water, tea, and fruit juices.

Firms such as Coca-Cola, which has an incentive to diversify, need to be careful because often there are brand risks to moving into areas that are new and where the company lacks operational expertise. There can be negative synergy (where potential synergy between acquiring and target firms is illusory) and problems between leaders and cultural fit difficulties with recent acquisitions.[94] Research evidence and the experience of a number of firms suggest that an overall curvilinear relationship, as illustrated in Figure 6.3,

Figure 6.3 The Curvilinear Relationship between Diversification and Performance

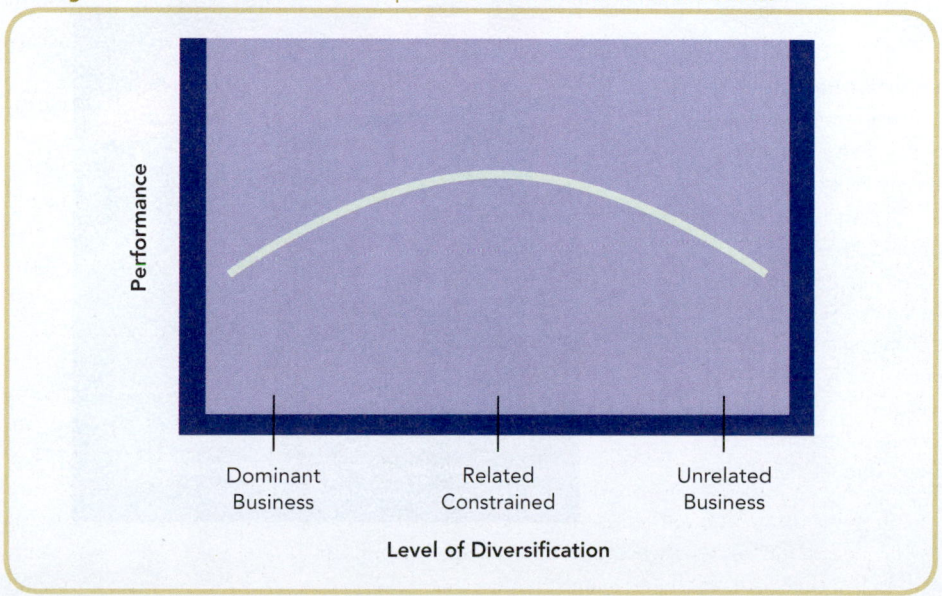

Strategic Focus

Coca-Cola's Diversification to Deal with Its Reduced Growth in Soft Drinks

Many package good and food distribution companies have been facing difficulties with the changing tastes among consumers. As indicated in an earlier chapter, McDonald's has been facing healthy fast-food competitors like Chipotle Mexican Grill. Likewise, companies such as Campbell's Soup and General Mills have also been experiencing more health conscious consumers both from millennials and baby boomers. Coca-Cola also has experienced a drop in demand for its dominant soft drink business. Coca-Cola had promised a 3–4 percent annual growth volume to investors for 2014 and that "this would be the year of execution" declared CEO Muhtar Kent. However, by 2015 Coca-Cola had fallen short of this volume goal. Its revenue slipped 2 percent to $46 billion, and profits fell 17 percent to $7.1 billion from the prior year (2013). Because consumers' tastes are changing, Coca-Cola has chosen to "polish the diamond" by improving its marketing and execution in soft drinks. However, its efforts through advertising and execution to realize its revenue and profit goals were not sufficient.

Seeing this decline over time, Coca-Cola has been diversifying, as well as trying to improve execution, to deal with depressed volumes in its dominant soft drink business. Sixty-three percent of Americans told a Gallop poll in 2014 that they were avoiding soft drinks. In fact, soft drink sales have been falling for 10 straight years and, as a result, Coca-Cola sales are slowing or shrinking around the world. In fact, supermarket firm Whole Foods will not carry the product. It seems that today's consumers want "healthier, tastier, more unique, and less mass market" products. This trend has impacted Kellogg Company, Kraft Foods Group, McDonald's, and others that have focused on general consumers. In fact, Heinz was taken private by 3G Capital Partners LP and was recently combined with Kraft Foods Group to form the Kraft Heinz Company. This deal is supported by Warren Buffet's Berkshire Hathaway & Co. because these are high cash flow businesses that fit the Berkshire Hathaway unrelated diversification approach of investing. Businesses which are still independent, such as Coca-Cola, have been pursuing diversification to deal with the future risks of consumers' changing tastes.

In 2007, Coca-Cola commissioned a study focused on nonalcoholic drink concepts. It launched its "Venture & Emerging Brands" (VEB) unit to cultivate relationships and to ultimately purchase small start-ups. Through this process, it now owns Fuze Tea, Zico coconut water, and the organic brand Honest Tea. In fact, soft drinks have decreased in consumption almost 90 percent between 2003 and 2013, while sports drinks and bottled water have increased nearly 40 percent during the same period. Coca-Cola partnered with Monster, the leader in energy drinks, which have become very popular, and in 2015 Coca-Cola took ownership of Monster's non-energy drink business. In the "water" market, Coca-Cola owns Glacéau and Fruitwater, which it launched in 2013. In "juices," it owns Odwalla, Simply, and Fuze, in addition to its long standing brand, Minute Maid. Finally, Coca-Cola is trying to adjust its marketing strategy and advertise new products along with its standard, more-healthy products such as Caffeine-free Coke, Coke Zero, and others. However, no one wants to repeat the "new Coke" marketing disaster that occurred previously, so they are very cautious about product proliferation where there could be potential for a huge mistake that damages the brand.

Coca-Cola has also tinkered with other approaches such as its Freestyle soda fountain machine "that offers more than 100 different drink choices; some, such as Orange Coke, aren't available in cans." It now has these drink machines in fast food chains such as Five Guys and Burger King. This approach has consistently raised drink sales by double-digits every year, mostly because the volume for these drink machines is higher; "the largest fountain drink is 40 ounces versus 16 ounces for a standard Coca-Cola can product."

Freestyle Soda Fountain.PNG

©DisneyFoodBlog.com

The photo illustrates a Freestyle soda machine that Coca-Cola and other firms have been using to dispense and mix their various drink products.

Even with some of these new approaches, health critics are challenging some of the advertising for "healthy products" which have a lot of sugar but are classified as "juices." Often these products have as much sugar as standard soft drinks. As such, diversification away from falling sales is not an easy approach because you have to build up growth in new areas that are more risky but also, when mistakes are made, can damage the overall company brand equity. Nonetheless, the diversification approach is often taken when there are risks and uncertainty around the future success of your main product line.

Sources: M. Chahal, 2015, Coca-Cola's strategy: Heritage with 'digital backbone', *Marketing Week*, www.marketingweek.com, March 11; D. Cimilluca, D. Mattioli, & A. Gasparro, 2015, Brazil's 3G in serious talks for Kraft, *Wall Street Journal*, www.wsj.com, March 25, A1, A6; M. Esterl, 2015, Soft drinks hit 10th year of decline, *Wall Street Journal*, www.wsj.com, March 27; M. Esterl, 2015, What is Coke CEO's solution for lost fizz? More soda: Despite changing consumer taste, Muhtar Kent pushes strategy to sell more cola, *Wall Street Journal*, www.wsj.com, March 19; B. Geier, 2015, Coke's plan to save Coke is to sell more Coke, *Fortune*, www.fortune.com, March 19; A. Brones, 2014, Americans are drinking less soda, but we're still addicted to sugar, *Care2*, www.care2.com, April 15; S. Sharf, 2014, Coca-Cola profit declines 14%, future growth plan fails to impress, *Forbes*, www.forbes.com, October 21; C. Suddath & D. Stanford, 2014, Coke confronts its big fat problem, *Bloomberg BusinessWeek*, www.bloombergbusinessweek.com, July 31.

may exist between diversification and performance.[95] Although low performance can be an incentive to diversify, firms that are more broadly diversified compared to their competitors may have overall lower performance.

Uncertain Future Cash Flows

As a firm's product line matures or is threatened, diversification may be an important defensive strategy.[96] Small firms and companies in mature or maturing industries sometimes find it necessary to diversify for long-term survival.[97]

Diversifying into other product markets or into other businesses can reduce the uncertainty about a firm's future cash flows. Alcoa, the largest U.S. aluminum producer, has been pursuing a "multi-material" diversification strategy driven by the highly competitive nature of its basic commodity business.[98] Alcoa has been diversifying into other metals beside aluminum while simultaneously moving into a variety of end product industries. In 2015, for example, it announced that it would acquire RTI International Metals, Inc., which is one of the largest titanium producers for the aerospace industry. Alcoa's CEO, Klaus Kleinfield, noted that the deal "increases our position substantially in titanium and high-tech machinery" with "almost no overlap" with Alcoa's current business.[99] In 2014, it bought Firth Rixson Limited and Germany's TITAL, which make titanium and aluminum casting for jet engines and airframes. However, 40 percent of its revenue still comes from mining and smelting raw aluminum, the price of which has suffered because of lower demand and associated excess capacity and foreign competition, especially from Chinese producers.

Synergy and Firm Risk Reduction

Diversified firms pursuing economies of scope often have investments that are too inflexible to realize synergy among business units. As a result, a number of problems may arise. **Synergy** exists when the value created by business units working together exceeds the value that those same units create working independently. However, as a firm increases its relatedness among business units, it also increases its risk of corporate failure because synergy produces joint interdependence among businesses that constrains the firm's flexibility to respond. This threat may force two basic decisions.

Synergy exists when the value created by business units working together exceeds the value that those same units create working independently.

First, the firm may reduce its level of technological change by operating in environments that are more certain. This behavior may make the firm risk averse and thus uninterested in pursuing new product lines that have potential but are not proven. Alternatively, the firm may constrain its level of activity sharing and forgo potential benefits of synergy. Either or both decisions may lead to further diversification.[100] Operating in environments that are more certain will likely lead to related diversification into industries which lack less potential[101], while constraining the level of activity sharing may produce additional, but unrelated, diversification, where the firm lacks expertise. Research suggests that a firm using a related diversification strategy is more careful in bidding for new businesses, whereas a firm pursuing an unrelated diversification strategy may be more likely to overbid because it is less likely to have full information about the firm it wants to acquire.[102] However, firms using either a related or an unrelated diversification strategy must understand the consequences of paying large premiums.[103] These problems often cause managers to become more risk averse and focus on achieving short-term returns. When this occurs, managers are less likely to be concerned about social problems and in making long-term investments (e.g., developing innovation). Alternatively, diversified firms (related and unrelated) can be innovative if the firm pursues these strategies appropriately.[104]

6-5b Resources and Diversification

As already discussed, firms may have several value-neutral incentives as well as value-creating incentives (e.g., the ability to create economies of scope) to diversify. However, even when incentives to diversify exist, a firm must have the types and levels of resources and capabilities needed to successfully use a corporate-level diversification strategy.[105] Although both tangible and intangible resources facilitate diversification, they vary in their ability to create value. Indeed, the degree to which resources are valuable, rare, difficult to imitate, and nonsubstitutable (see Chapter 3) influences a firm's ability to create value through diversification. For instance, free cash flows are a tangible financial resource that may be used to diversify the firm. However, compared with diversification that is grounded in intangible resources, diversification based on financial resources only is more visible to competitors and thus more imitable and less likely to create value on a long-term basis.[106] Tangible resources usually include the plant and equipment necessary to produce a product and tend to be less-flexible assets. Any excess capacity often can be used only for closely related products, especially those requiring highly similar manufacturing technologies. For example, large computer makers such as Dell and Hewlett-Packard have underestimated the demand for tablet computers. Apple developed a tablet computer, the iPad, and many expect such tablets to eventually replace the personal computer (PC). In fact, Dell's and HP's sales of their PCs have been declining since the introduction of the iPad. Apple sold 42.4 million iPads in in the last quarter of 2012 and the first quarter of 2013. While Samsung and other competitors have developed tablets to rival Apple's iPad and are selling a considerable number; Dell, HP, Lenovo, and others have responded by making cheaper tablet-like laptops and iPad like tablets and have stayed in the game without having to diversify too much.[107]

Excess capacity of other tangible resources, such as a sales force, can be used to diversify more easily. Again, excess capacity in a sales force is more effective with related diversification because it may be utilized to sell products in similar markets (e.g., same customers). The sales force would be more knowledgeable about related product characteristics, customers, and distribution channels.[108] Tangible resources may create resource interrelationships in production, marketing, procurement, and technology, defined earlier as activity sharing. Interestingly, Dyson, which produces vacuum cleaners, has invested in battery technology. Dyson's CEO, James Dyson, has indicated that the company, besides producing a battery operated vacuum, "will launch 100 products in four categories that are new to the company" using the new more efficient battery technology.[109]

Intangible resources are more flexible than tangible physical assets in facilitating diversification. Although the sharing of tangible resources may induce diversification, intangible resources such as tacit knowledge could encourage even more diversification.[110] Service firms also pursue diversification strategies especially through greenfield ventures (opening a new business for the firm without acquiring a previous established brand-name business). Alvarez & Marsal, a professional service firm that has focused on helping to restructure firms that experience financial distress, has diversified into several additional service businesses. It has a reputation (an intangible asset) in New York financial circles for its ability to do interim management for firms that are experiencing financial distress and often gone into bankruptcy. Alvarez & Marsal managed the largest U.S. bankruptcy in history, the wind down of Lehman Bros. after it folded. As part of this massive wind down, it needed to manage the treasury and cash assets of the company in a way to realize the best returns possible for the remaining stakeholders and creditors who held right to debt secured assets. Through its experience over a number of bankruptcies, but in particular the Lehman Bros. bankruptcy, Alvarez & Marsal has gained a reputation and ability in investment management especially for short-term treasury deposits. These capabilities have lead the firm to open a new business to manage treasury and cash assets for other companies, but also for endowments and local and state government entities. It also serves as a consultant for private equity firms which are closely associated with firms in financial distress and restructuring strategies. From its interim management business, it has moved into performance improvement consulting. Through its reputation and skills in serving private equity clients, Alvarez and Marsal also gained knowledge about investing in private equity businesses and have likewise started a private equity fund.[111] This approach to diversification is not unfamiliar to other professional service firms such as Bain Strategy Consulting, which also started Bain Capital, a private equity fund through the support of Bain partners (owners) in their consulting business.

Sometimes, however, the benefits expected from using resources to diversify the firm for either value-creating or value-neutral reasons are not gained. Research suggests that picking the right target firm partner is critical to acquisition success.[112] For example, Sara Lee Corporation executives found that they could not realize synergy between elements of their company's diversified portfolio, and subsequently shed businesses accounting for 40 percent of company revenue to focus on food and food-related products and more readily achieve synergy. Ultimately, Sara Lee split into two companies: Hillshire Brands which focuses on meat and food products, and D.E. Master Blenders 1753, a beverage and bakery company. Incidentally, Hillshire Brands was purchased by Tyson Foods in 2014 and Sara Lee no longer exists as a separate company, although the brand is part of Tyson Foods.[113]

6-6 Value-Reducing Diversification: Managerial Motives to Diversify

Managerial motives to diversify can exist independent of value-neutral reasons (i.e., incentives and resources) and value-creating reasons (e.g., economies of scope).

The desire for increased compensation and reduced managerial risk are two motives for top-level executives to diversify their firm beyond value-creating and value-neutral levels.[114] In slightly different words, top-level executives may diversify a firm in order to spread their own employment risk, as long as profitability does not suffer excessively.[115]

Diversification provides additional benefits to top-level managers that shareholders do not enjoy. Research evidence shows that diversification and firm size are highly correlated, and as firm size increases, so does executive compensation.[116] Because large firms are complex, difficult-to-manage organizations, top-level managers commonly receive substantial levels of compensation to lead them, but the amounts vary across countries.[117] Greater levels of diversification can increase a firm's complexity, resulting in still more compensation for executives to lead an increasingly diversified organization. Governance mechanisms, such as the board of directors, monitoring by owners, executive compensation practices, and the market for corporate control, may limit managerial tendencies to over diversify.[118] These mechanisms are discussed in more detail in Chapter 10.

In some instances, though, a firm's governance mechanisms may not be strong, allowing executives to diversify the firm to the point that it fails to earn even average returns.[119] The loss of adequate internal governance may result in relatively poor performance, thereby triggering a threat of takeover. Although takeovers may improve efficiency by replacing ineffective managerial teams, managers may avoid takeovers through defensive tactics, such as "poison pills," or may reduce their own exposure with "golden parachute" agreements.[120] Therefore, an external governance threat, although restraining managers, does not flawlessly control managerial motives for diversification.[121]

Most large publicly held firms are profitable because the managers leading them are positive stewards of firm resources, and many of their strategic actions, including those related to selecting a corporate-level diversification strategy, contribute to the firm's success.[122] As mentioned, governance mechanisms should be designed to deal with exceptions to the managerial norms of making decisions and taking actions that increase the firm's ability to earn above-average returns. Thus, it is overly pessimistic to assume that managers usually act in their own self-interest as opposed to their firm's interest.[123]

Top-level executives' diversification decisions may also be held in check by concerns for their reputation. If a positive reputation facilitates development and use of managerial power, a poor reputation can reduce it. Likewise, a strong external market for managerial talent may deter managers from pursuing inappropriate diversification.[124] In addition, a diversified firm may acquire other firms that are poorly managed in order to restructure its own asset base. Knowing that their firms could be acquired if they are not managed successfully encourages executives to use value-creating diversification strategies.

As shown in Figure 6.4, the level of diversification with the greatest potential positive effect on performance is based partly on the effects of the interaction of resources, managerial motives, and incentives on the adoption of particular diversification strategies. As indicated earlier, the greater the incentives and the more flexible the resources, the higher the level of expected diversification. Financial resources (the most flexible) should have a stronger relationship to the extent of diversification than either tangible or intangible resources. Tangible resources (the most inflexible) are useful primarily for related diversification.

As discussed in this chapter, firms can create more value by effectively using diversification strategies. However, diversification must be kept in check by corporate governance

Figure 6.4 Summary Model of the Relationship between Diversification and Firm Performance

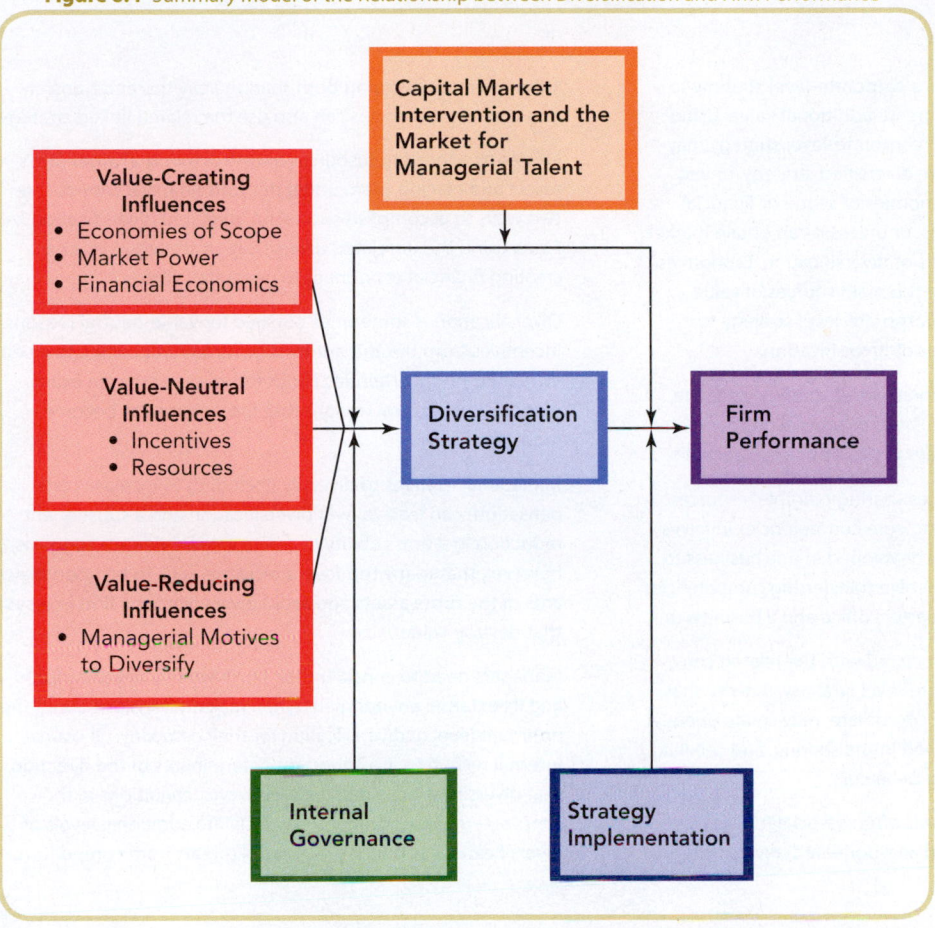

Source: Adapted from R. E. Hoskisson & M. A. Hitt, 1990, Antecedents and performace outcomes of diversification: A review and critique of theoretical perspectives, *Journal of Management*, 16: 498.

(see Chapter 10). Appropriate strategy implementation tools, such as organizational structures, are also important for the strategies to be successful (see Chapter 11).

We have described corporate-level strategies in this chapter. In the next chapter, we discuss mergers and acquisitions as prominent means for firms to diversify and to grow profitably. These trends toward more diversification through acquisitions, which have been partially reversed due to restructuring (see Chapter 7), indicate that learning has taken place regarding corporate-level diversification strategies.[125] Accordingly, firms that diversify should do so cautiously, choosing to focus on relatively few, rather than many, businesses. In fact, research suggests that although unrelated diversification has decreased, related diversification has increased, possibly due to the restructuring that continued into the 1990s through the early twenty-first century. This sequence of diversification followed by restructuring has occurred in Europe and in countries such as Korea, following actions of firms in the United States and the United Kingdom.[126] Firms can improve their strategic competitiveness when they pursue a level of diversification that is appropriate for their resources (especially financial resources) and core competencies and the opportunities and threats in their country's institutional and competitive environments.[127]

SUMMARY

- The primary reason a firm uses a corporate-level strategy to become more diversified is to create additional value. Using a single- or dominant-business corporate-level strategy may be preferable to seeking a more diversified strategy, unless a corporation can develop economies of scope or financial economies between businesses, or unless it can obtain market power through additional levels of diversification. Economies of scope and market power are the main sources of value creation when the firm uses a corporate-level strategy to achieve moderate to high levels of diversification.

- The related diversification corporate-level strategy helps the firm create value by sharing activities or transferring competencies between different businesses in the company's portfolio.

- Sharing activities usually involves sharing tangible resources between businesses. Transferring core competencies involves transferring core competencies developed in one business to another business. It also may involve transferring competencies between the corporate headquarters office and a business unit.

- Sharing activities is usually associated with the related constrained diversification corporate-level strategy. Activity sharing is costly to implement and coordinate, may create unequal benefits for the divisions involved in the sharing, and can lead to fewer managerial risk-taking behaviors.

- Transferring core competencies is often associated with related linked (or mixed related and unrelated) diversification,

although firms pursuing both sharing activities and transferring core competencies can also use the related linked strategy.

- Efficiently allocating resources or restructuring a target firm's assets and placing them under rigorous financial controls are two ways to accomplish successful unrelated diversification. Firms using the unrelated diversification strategy focus on creating financial economies to generate value.

- Diversification is sometimes pursued for value-neutral reasons. Incentives from tax and antitrust government policies, low performance, or uncertainties about future cash flow are examples of value-neutral reasons that firms choose to become more diversified.

- Managerial motives to diversify (including to increase compensation) can lead to over diversification and a subsequent reduction in a firm's ability to create value. Evidence suggests, however, that many top-level executives seek to be good stewards of the firm's assets and avoid diversifying the firm in ways that destroy value.

- Managers need to consider their firm's internal organization and its external environment when making decisions about the optimum level of diversification for their company. Of course, internal resources are important determinants of the direction that diversification should take. However, conditions in the firm's external environment may facilitate additional levels of diversification, as might unexpected threats from competitors.

KEY TERMS

corporate-level strategy 174
economies of scope 180
corporate-level core competencies 181
market power 182

multipoint competition 182
vertical integration 183
financial economies 185
synergy 191

REVIEW QUESTIONS

1. What is corporate-level strategy and why is it important?

2. What are the different levels of diversification firms can pursue by using different corporate-level strategies?

3. What are three reasons firms choose to diversify their operations?

4. How do firms create value when using a related diversification strategy?

5. What are the two ways to obtain financial economies when using an unrelated diversification strategy?

6. What incentives and resources encourage diversification?

7. What motives might encourage managers to over diversify their firm?

Mini-Case

Sany Heavy Industry Co., Ltd

The Sany Heavy Industry Co., Ltd is China's largest producer of heavy equipment. In fact, it is the fifth largest producer of this type of equipment globally. In 2014, its revenue was decreasing because of the downturn of overall GNP in China. Sany's total sales revenue in 2012 was $12.9 billion, well behind industry leader Caterpillar at $65.9 billion. However, Sany has a goal of eventually unseating Caterpillar as the industry leader. Sany plans to achieve $47 billion in annual sales within 10 years. Sany has already surpassed Caterpillar as a leader in its Chinese domestic markets.

Sany has four core businesses: (1) cranes, (2) road construction machinery, (3) port machinery, and (4) pumpover machinery. While each is distinct, some similar technologies are used in the production and equipment. Furthermore, similar technologies allow similarities in production processes and equipment for certain parts. Therefore, there is a transfer of knowledge across these businesses. In addition, customers and markets share some similarities because all relate to some form of construction. For this reason, in the United States, Sany has become a major sponsor of a Chevrolet on the NASCAR auto racing circuit. Sany America's marketing director, Joe Hanneman, said that research showed NASCAR racing events to be the primary recreation event for people in the U.S. construction industry.

Sany invests 5 percent of its annual sales in R&D to continuously improve the quality of existing products, identify new technologies, and develop new products. Through the end of 2012, Sany held 3,303 patents as a result of its R&D efforts. Indicative of its intent to be a technological leader in its industry, Sany has developed new postdoctoral research centers to attract top research scientists. In 2013, the company was awarded China's National Technology Invention Prize for its "super-length-boom" technology.

Although it has been pursuing technological innovations, Sany was recently accused of patent violations by Manitowoc, a diversified producer of equipment including large cranes. In 2014, a judgement went against Sany concluding "one Sany crane product infringed one of Manitowoc's patents and that six trade secrets of Manitowoc were both protectable as trade secrets and misappropriated." This is a negative signal for Sany as it seeks to pursue more diversified growth outside of China.

Sany continues to grow organically and through acquisitions. For example, in 2012, it acquired Putzmeister, a well-known concrete pump manufacturer. In addition, it has established subsidiaries in many countries, including the United States, Germany, and Brazil, to enhance its international equipment sales and broaden its market reach. Largely because of its major goal of internationalization, it is moving its corporate headquarters from Changsha to Beijing for enriched international connections.

Sources: 2015, Sany Heavy Industry Co. Ltd., www.sanygroup.com, accessed on June 12; 2015, www.manitowoc.com, press release, The Manitowoc Company receives favorable final determination in Sany patent infringement lawsuit, April 17; R. Flannery, 2014, Profit drops by 48% at Chinese billionaire's equipment flagship Sany Heavy, *Forbes*, www.forbes.com, August 31; 2015, www.manitowoc.com, 2013, Yellow Table Survey: Sany ranks no. 5 among construction machinery manufacturers in 2013, China Construction Machinery Online, www.cmbol.com, April 15; M. Barris, 2013, Sany turns to NASCAR to fuel sales, *China Daily*, www.chinadaily.com, April 4; 2013, Awarded National Technology Invention Prize, *Get to Know Sany*, 15th issue, February 15; L. Hooks, P. J. Davis, & N. Munshi, 2013, Caterpillar digs into trouble in China, *Financial Times*, www.ft.com, February 12; J. R. Hagerty & C. Murphy, 2013, Sany tries to gain traction in the U.S., *Wall Street Journal*, www.wsj.com, January 28; 2013, Sany Heavy Industry Co. Ltd: Sany Group's top 10 events in 2012, *$-traders*, www.4-traders.com, January 22; Z. Yangpeng & F. Zhiwei, 2012, Sany to move HQ to Beijing from Changsha, *China Daily*, www.usa.chinadaily.com, November 11.

Case Discussion Questions

1. What corporate diversification strategy is being pursued by Sany? What evidence do you have that supports your position?

2. How does the level of change in gross domestic product (indicator of country economic health) influence a firm like Sany?

3. Why does a firm such as Sany (in the heavy equipment industry) spend so much of its revenue on R&D and innovation?

4. Given that it is now seeking international expansion, how do you expect the judgement against it (patent and trade secret infringement case) to affect its growth prospects outside of China?

NOTES

1. M. E. Porter, 1980, *Competitive Strategy*, New York: The Free Press, xvi.

2. J. P. O'Brien, P. David, T. Yoshikawa, & A. Delios, 2014, How capital structure influences diversification performance: A transaction cost perspective, *Strategic Management Journal*, 35: 1013–1031; M. D. R. Chari, S. Devaraj, & P. David, 2008, The impact of information technology investments and diversification strategies on firm performance, *Management Science*, 54: 224–234.

3. M. Gottfried, 2015, Walt Disney has built a better mousetrap, *Wall Street Journal*, Feb 5, C8.

4. M. E. Porter, 1987, From competitive advantage to corporate strategy, *Harvard Business Review*, 65(3): 43–59.

5. P. C. Nell & B. Ambos, 2013, Parenting advantage in the MNC: An embeddedness perspective on the value added by headquarters, *Strategic Management Journal*, 34: 1086–1103; M. E. Raynor, 2007, What is corporate strategy, really? *Ivey Business Journal*, 71: 1–3.

6. Queen, P. 2015, Enlightened shareholder maximization: Is this strategy achievable?, *Journal of Business Ethics*, 127: 683–694; W. P. Wan, R. E. Hoskisson, J. C. Short, & D. W. Yiu, 2011, Resource-based theory and corporate diversification: Accomplishments and opportunities, *Journal of Management*, 37: 1335–1368.

7. C. Custódio, 2014, Mergers and acquisitions accounting and the diversification discount, *Journal of Finance*, 69: 219–240; K. Lee, M. W. Peng, & K. Lee, 2008, From diversification premium to diversification discount during institutional transitions, *Journal of World Business*, 43: 47–65.

8. Campbell, M. Goold, & M. Alexander, 1995, Corporate strategy: The question for parenting advantage, *Harvard Business Review*, 73(2): 120–132.

9. W. Su & E. W. K. Tsang, 2015, Product diversification and financial performance: The moderating role of secondary stakeholders, *Academy of Management Journal*, forthcoming; K. Favaro, 2013, We're from corporate and we are here to help: Understanding the real value of corporate strategy and the head office, *Strategy+Business Online*, www.strategy-business.com, April 8; D. Collis, D. Young, & M. Goold, 2007, The size, structure, and performance of corporate headquarters, *Strategic Management Journal*, 28: 283–405.

10. M. Kleinbaum & T. E. Stuart, 2014, Inside the black box of the corporate staff: Social networks and the implementation of corporate strategy, *Strategic Management Journal*, 35: 24–47; G. Kenny, 2012, Diversification: Best practices of the leading companies, *Journal of*

Business Strategy, 33(1): 12–20; D. Miller, 2006, Technological diversity, related diversification performance, *Strategic Management Journal*, 27: 601–619.

11. D. D. Bergh, 2001, Diversification strategy research at a crossroads: Established, emerging and anticipated paths. In M. A. Hitt, R. E. Freeman, & J. S. Harrison (eds.), *Handbook of Strategic Management*, Oxford, U.K.: Blackwell Publishers, 363–383.

12. S. F. Matusik & M. A. Fitza, 2012, Diversification in the venture capital industry: Leveraging knowledge under uncertainty, *Strategic Management Journal*, 33: 407–426.

13. J. R. Lecuona & M. Reitzig, 2014, Knowledge worth having in 'excess': The value of tacit and firm-specific human resource slack, *Strategic Management Journal*, 35: 954–973; G. Ray, X. Ling, & J. B. Barney, 2013, Impact of information technology capital on firm scope and performance: The role of asset characteristics, *Academy of Management Journal*, 56: 1125–1147.

14. D. H. Zhu & G. Chen, 2015, CEO narcissism and the impact of prior board experience on corporate strategy, *Administrative Science Quarterly*, 60: 31–65; J. J. Marcel, 2009, Why top management team characteristics matter when employing a chief operating officer: A strategic contingency perspective, *Strategic Management Journal*, 30: 647–658.

15. R. P. Rumelt, 1974, *Strategy, Structure, and Economic Performance*, Boston: Harvard Business School; L. Wrigley, 1970, *Divisional Autonomy and Diversification* (Ph.D. dissertation), Harvard Business School.

16. 2015, Tabasco Products, www.tabasco.com, March 24.

17. 2015, United Parcel Service 2014 Annual Report, www.ups.com, March 24.

18. R. Rumelt, 2011, *Good Strategy/Bad Strategy: The Difference and Why It Matters*, New York: Crown Business Publishing.

19. L. R. Gomez-Mejia, J. T. Campbell, G. Martin, R. E. Hoskisson, M. Makri, & D. G. Sirmon, 2014, Socioemotional wealth as a mixed gamble: Revisiting family firm R&D investments with the behavioral agency model, *Entrepreneurship: Theory & Practice*, 38: 1351–1374; L. R. Gomez-Mejia, M. Makri, & M. L. Kintana, 2010, Diversification decisions in family controlled firms, *Journal of Management Studies*, 47: 223–252.

20. 2015, About SANY, www.sanygroup.com, accessed on March 27.

21. A. Barroso & M. S. Giarratana, 2013, Product proliferation strategies and firm performance: The moderating role of product space complexity, *Strategic Management Journal*, 34: 1435–1452.

22. 2015, Publicis Groupe, Wikipedia, http://en.wikipedia.org/wiki/Publicis, March 24.

23. J.-H. Lee & A. S. Gaur, 2013, Managing multi-business firms: A comparison between Korean chaebols and diversified U.S. firms, *Journal of World Business*, 48: 443–454; J. L. Stimpert, I. M. Duhaime, & J. Chesney, 2010, Learning to manage a large diversified firm, *Journal of Leadership and Organizational Studies*, 17: 411–425.

24. G. Smith, 2015, Hutchison Whampoa close to buying UK's o2 for $15 billion, *Fortune*, www.fortune.com, February 3; 2015, Hutchison Whampoa Limited 2014 Annual Report, www.hutchison-whampoa.com, accessed March 25, 2015.

25. R. E. Hoskisson, W, Shi, X. Yi, & J. Jing, 2013, The evolution and strategic positioning of private equity firms, *Academy of Management Perspectives*, 27: 22–38.

26. T. M. Alessandri & A. Seth, 2014, The effects of managerial ownership on international and business diversification: Balancing incentives and risks, *Strategic Management Journal*, 35: 2064–2075; C.-N. Chen & W. Chu, 2012, Diversification, resource concentration and business group performance: Evidence from Taiwan, *Asia Pacific Journal of Management*, 29: 1045–1061.

27. S. Pathak, R. E. Hoskisson, & R. A. Johnson, 2014, Settling up in CEO compensation: The impact of divestiture intensity and contextual factors in refocusing firms, *Strategic Management Journal*, 35: 1124–1143; D. H. Ming Chng, M. S. Rodgers, E. Shih, & X.-B. Song, 2012, When does incentive compensation motivate managerial behavior? An experimental investigation of the fit between incentive compensation, executive core self-evaluation and firm performance, *Strategic Management Journal*, 33: 1343–1362; J. E. Core & W. R. Guay, 2010, Is CEO pay too high and are incentives too low? A wealth-based contracting framework, *Academy of Management Perspectives*, 24: 5–19.

28. C. Chadwick, J. F. Super, & K. Kwon, 2015, Resource orchestration in practice: CEO emphasis on SHRM, commitment-based HR systems, and firm performance, *Strategic Management Journal*, 36, 360–376; D. G. Sirmon, M. A. Hitt, R. D. Ireland, & B. A. Gilbert, 2011, Resource orchestration to create competitive advantage: Breadth, depth and life cycle effects, *Journal of Management*, 37: 1390–1412.

29. T. Zahavi & D. Lavie, 2013, Intra-industry diversification and firm performance, *Strategic Management Journal*, 34: 978–998; H. Tanriverdi & C.-H. Lee, 2008, Within-industry diversification and firm performance in the presence of network externalities: Evidence from the software industry, *Academy of Management Journal*, 51: 381–397.

30. F. Bauer & K. Matzler, 2014, Antecedents of M&A success: The role of strategic complementarity, cultural fit, and degree and speed of integration, *Strategic Management Journal*, 35: 269–291; M. E. Graebner, K. M. Eisenhardt, & P. T. Roundy, 2010, Success and failure of technology acquisitions: Lessons for buyers and sellers, *Academy of Management Perspectives*, 24: 73–92.

31. G. M. Kistruck, I. Qureshi, & P. W. Beamish, 2013, Geographic and product diversification in charitable organizations, *Journal of Management*, 39: 496–530.

32. A. Arora, S. Belenzon, & L. A. Rios, 2014, Make, buy, organize: The interplay between research, external knowledge, and firm structure, *Strategic Management Journal*, 35: 317–337; F. Neffke & M. Henning, 2013, Skill relatedness and firm diversification, *Strategic Management Journal*, 34: 297–316.

33. Y. Chen, Y. Jiang, C. Wang, & W. C. Hsu, 2014, How do resources and diversification strategy explain the performance consequences of internationalization?, *Management Decision*, 52, 897–915; M. Makri, M. A. Hitt, & P. J. Lane, 2010, Complementary technologies, knowledge relatedness and invention outcomes in high technology mergers and acquisitions, *Strategic Management Journal*, 31: 602–628.

34. A. V. Sakhartov & T. B. Folta, 2014, Resource relatedness, redeployability, and firm value, *Strategic Management Journal*, 35: 1781–1797; D. Miller, 2006, Technological diversity, related diversification, and firm performance, *Strategic Management Journal*, 27: 601–619.

35. M. V. S. Kumar, 2013, The costs of related diversification: The impact of core business on the productivity of related segments, *Organization Science*, 24: 1827–1846.

36. M. A. Hitt, D. King, H. Krishnan, M. Makri, M. Schijven, K. Shimizu, & H. Zhu, 2012, Creating value through mergers and acquisitions: Challenges and opportunities. In D. Faulkner, S. Teerikangas, & R. Joseph (eds.), *Oxford Handbook of Mergers and Acquisitions*, Oxford, U.K.: Oxford University Press, 2012, 71–113; P. Puranam & K. Srikanth, 2007, What they know vs. what they do: How acquirers leverage technology acquisitions, *Strategic Management Journal*, 28: 805–825.

37. E. R. Feldman, 2014, Legacy divestitures: Motives and implications, *Organization Science*, 25: 815–832; L. B. Lien, 2013, Can the survivor principle survive diversification? *Organization Science*, in press; D. D. Bergh, 1995, Size and relatedness of units sold: An agency theory and resource-based perspective, *Strategic Management Journal*, 16: 221–239.

38. M. Lubatkin & S. Chatterjee, 1994, Extending modern portfolio theory into the domain of corporate diversification: Does it apply? *Academy of Management Journal*, 37: 109–136.

39. M. Menz, S. Kunisch, & D. J. Collis, 2015, The corporate headquarters in the contemporary corporation: Advancing a multimarket firm perspective, *Academy of Management Annals*, forthcoming; T. Kono, 1999, A strong head office makes a strong company, *Long Range Planning*, 32: 225–236.

40. A. Caimo & A. Lomi, 2015, Knowledge sharing in organizations: A Bayesian analysis of the role of reciprocity and formal structure. *Journal of Management*, 41: 665–691; Puranam & Srikanth, What they know vs. what they do; F. T. Rothaermel, M. A. Hitt, & L. A. Jobe, 2006, Balancing vertical integration and strategic outsourcing: Effects on product portfolio, product success, and firm performance, *Strategic Management Journal*, 27: 1033–1056.

41. M. Cui & S. L. Pan, 2015, Developing focal capabilities for e-commerce adoption: A resource orchestration perspective, *Information & Management*, 52: 200–209.

42. C. Huston, 2013, The value of a good name, *Wall Street Journal*, July 18, B5; J. Thottam, 2008, Branson's flight plan, *Time*, April 28, 40.

43. 2015, Operations overview, Honda Motor Company, www.honda.com, Accessed March 29.

44. N. D. Nguyen & A, Aoyama, A. 2014, Achieving efficient technology transfer through a specific corporate culture facilitated by management practices, *Journal of High Technology Management Research*, 25: 108–122; L. C. Thang, C. Rowley, T. Quang, & M. Warner, 2007, To what extent can management practices be transferred between countries?: The case of human resource management in Vietnam, *Journal of World Business*, 42: 113–127; G. Stalk Jr., 2005, Rotate the core, *Harvard Business Review*, 83(3): 18–19.

45. U. Andersson, P. J. Buckley, & H. Dellestrand, 2015, In the right place at the right time!: The influence of knowledge governance tools on knowledge transfer and utilization in MNEs, *Global Strategy Journal*, 5: 27–47; J. A. Martin & K. M. Eisenhardt, 2010, Rewiring: Cross-business unit collaborations in multibusiness organizations, *Academy of Management Journal*, 53: 265–301.

46. T. Hutzschenreuter & J. Horstkotte, 2013, Performance effects of top management team demographic faultlines in the process of product diversification, *Strategic Management Journal*, 34: 704–726.

47. E. Linares-Navarro, T. Pedersen, & J. Pla-Barber, 2014, Fine slicing of the value chain and offshoring of essential activities: Empirical evidence from European multinationals, *Journal of Business Economics & Management*, 15: 111–134; S. Gupta, A. Woodside, C. Dubelaar, & D. Bradmore, 2009, Diffusing knowledge-based core competencies for leveraging innovation strategies: Modeling outsourcing to knowledge process organizations (KPOs) in pharmaceutical networks, *Industrial Marketing Management*, 38: 219–227.

48. A. Pehrsson, 2010, Business-relatedness and the strategy of moderations: Impacts on foreign subsidiary performance, *Journal of Strategy and Management*, 3: 110–133; S. Chatterjee & J. Singh, 1999, Are trade-offs inherent in diversification moves? A simultaneous model for type of diversification and mode of expansion decisions, *Management Science*, 45: 25–41.

49. D. Cimilluca, D. Mattioli, & A. Gasparro, 2015, Brazil's 3G in serious talks for Kraft, *Wall Street Journal*, www.wsj.com, March 25.

50. A. Ewing, 2014, Ericsson looks for a home in the cloud, *Bloomberg Businessweek*, November 17, 36–37.

51. H. Kai-Yu & F. Vermeulen, 2014, The structure of competition: How competition between one's rivals influences imitative market entry, *Organization Science*, 25: 299–319; L. Fuentelsaz & J. Gomez, 2006, Multipoint competition, strategic similarity and entry into geographic markets, *Strategic Management Journal*, 27: 477–499; J. Gimeno & C. Y. Woo, 1999, Multimarket contact, economies of scope, and firm performance, *Academy of Management Journal*, 42: 239–259.

52. M. J. De La Merced, 2015, Smucker to buy Big Heart Pet Brands for $5.8 billion, *New York Times*, www.nyt.com, February 3.

53. F. Brahm & J. Tarziján, 2014, Transactional hazards, institutional change, and capabilities: Integrating the theories of the firm, *Strategic Management Journal*, 35: 224–245; T. A. Shervani, G. Frazier, & G. Challagalla, 2007, The moderating influence of firm market power on the transaction cost economics model: An empirical test in a forward channel integration context, *Strategic Management Journal*, 28: 635–652.

54. N. Lahiri & S. Narayanan, 2013, Vertical integration, innovation and alliance portfolio size: Implications for firm performance, *Strategic Management Journal*, 34: 1042–1064; D. J. Teece, 2012, *Strategy, Innovation and the Theory of the Firm*, Northampton, MA: Edward Elgar Publishing Ltd.

55. R. Kapoor & J. M. Lee, 2013, Coordinating and competing in ecosystems: How organizational forms shape new technology investments, *Strategic Management Journal*, 34: 274–296; R. Carter & G. M. Hodgson, 2006, The impact of empirical tests of transaction cost economics on the debate on the nature of the firm, *Strategic Management Journal*, 27: 461–476; O. E. Williamson, 1996, Economics and organization: A primer, *California Management Review*, 38(2): 131–146.

56. R. Kapoor, 2013, Persistence of integration in the face of specialization: How firms navigated the winds of disintegration

and shaped the architecture of the semiconductor industry, *Organization Science*, 24: 1195–1213; S. Novak & S. Stern, 2008, How does outsourcing affect performance dynamics? Evidence from the automobile industry, *Management Science*, 54: 1963–1979.

57. C. Weigelt & D. J. Miller, 2013, Implications of internal organization structure for firm boundaries *Strategic Management Journal*, 34: 1411–1434; E. Rawley, 2010, Diversification, coordination costs and organizational rigidity: Evidence from microdata, *Strategic Management Journal*, 31: 873–891.

58. M. Bucheli & M. Kim, 2015, Attacked from both sides: A dynamic model of multinational corporations' strategies for protection of their property rights, *Global Strategy Journal*, 5: 1–26; C. Wolter & F. M. Veloso, 2008, The effects of innovation on vertical structure: Perspectives on transaction costs and competences, *Academy of Management Review*, 33: 586–605.

59. W. L. Tate, L. M. Ellram, T. Schoenherr, & K. L. Petersen, 2014, Global competitive conditions driving the manufacturing location decision, *Business Horizons*, 57: 381–390; T. Hutzschenreuter & F. Grone, 2009, Changing vertical integration strategies under pressure from foreign competition: The case of U.S. and German multinationals, *Journal of Management Studies*, 46: 269–307.

60. 2015, Flextronics International Ltd., www. flextronics.com, March 28.

61. S. Cabral, B. Quelin, & W. Maia, 2014, Outsourcing failure and reintegration: The influence of contractual and external factors, *Long Range Planning*, 47: 365–378.

62. J. Sears & G. Hoetker, 2014, Technological overlap, technological capabilities, and resource recombination in technological acquisitions, *Strategic Management Journal*, 35: 48–67; K. M. Eisenhardt & D. C. Galunic, 2000, Coevolving: At last, a way to make synergies work, *Harvard Business Review*, 78(1): 91–111.

63. O. Schilke, 2014, On the contingent value of dynamic capabilities for competitive advantage: The nonlinear moderating effect of environmental dynamism, *Strategic Management Journal*, 35: 179–203; P. David, J. P. O'Brien, T. Yoshikawa, & A. Delios, 2010, Do shareholders or stakeholders appropriate the rents from corporate diversification? The influence of ownership structure, *Academy of Management Journal*, 53: 636–654; J. A. Nickerson & T. R. Zenger, 2008, Envy, comparison costs, and the economic theory of the firm, *Strategic Management Journal*, 13: 1429–1449.

64. M. Gottfried, 2015, Walt Disney has built a better mousetrap, *Wall Street Journal*, Feb 5, C8.

65. T. Zenger, 2013, Strategy: The uniqueness challenge, *Harvard Business Review*, 91(11): 52–58.

66. F. Anjos & C. Fracassi, 2015, Shopping for Information? Diversification and the Network of Industries, *Management Science*, 61: 161–183; C. Rudolph & B. Schwetzler, 2013, Conglomerates on the rise again? A cross-regional study on the impact of the 2008–2009 financial crisis on the diversification discount, *Journal of Corporate Finance*, 22: 153–165; D. W. Ng, 2007, A modern resource-based approach to unrelated diversification. *Journal of Management Studies*, 44: 1481–1502.

67. Porter, *Competitive Advantage*.

68. G. Matvos & A. Seru, 2014, Resource allocation within firms and financial market dislocation: Evidence from diversified conglomerates, *Review of Financial Studies*, 27: 1143–1189; D. Collis, D. Young, & M. Goold, 2007, The size, structure, and performance of corporate headquarters, *Strategic Management Journal*, 28: 283–405; O. E. Williamson, 1975, *Markets and Hierarchies: Analysis and Antitrust Implications*, NY: Macmillan Free Press.

69. A. Ataullah, I. Davidson, H. Le, & G. Wood, 2014, Corporate diversification, information asymmetry and insider trading, *British Journal of Management*, 25: 228–251.

70. B. N. Cline, J. L. Garner, & S. A. Yore, 2014, Exploitation of the internal capital market and the avoidance of outside monitoring, *Journal of Corporate Finance*, 25: 234–250; R. Aggarwal & N. A. Kyaw, 2009, International variations in transparency and capital structure: Evidence from European firms. *Journal of International Financial Management & Accounting*, 20: 1–34.

71. D. Buchuk, B. Larrain, F. Muñoz, & I. F. Urzúa, 2014, The internal capital markets of business groups: Evidence from intra-group loans, *Journal of Financial Economics*, 112: 190–212.

72. M. Sengul & J. Gimeno, 2013, Constrained delegation: Limiting subsidiaries' decision rights and resources in firms that compete across multiple industries, *Administrative Science Quarterly*, 58: 420–471; E. Dooms & A. A. Van Oijen, 2008, The balance between tailoring and standardizing control, *European Management Review*, 5: 245–252; M. E. Raynor & J. L. Bower, 2001, Lead from the center: How to manage divisions dynamically, *Harvard Business Review*, 79(5): 92–100.

73. G. Smith, 2015, Siemens' long-feared slimdown isn't as drastic as feared, *Fortune*, www.fortune.com; B. Quint. 2009, Companies deal with tough times through diversification, *Information Today*, 26: 7–8.

74. H. Zhu & C. Chung, 2014, Portfolios of political ties and business group strategy in emerging economies: Evidence from Taiwan, *Administrative Science Quarterly*, 59: 599–638; S. L. Sun, X. Zhoa, & H. Yang, 2010, Executive compensation in Asia: A critical

review, *Asia Pacific Journal of Management*, 27: 775–802; A. Delios, D. Xu, & P. W. Beamish, 2008, Within-country product diversification and foreign subsidiary performance, *Journal of International Business Studies*, 39: 706–724.

75. S. F. Karabag & C. Berggren, 2014, Antecedents of firm performance in emerging economies: Business groups, strategy, industry structure, and state support, *Journal of Business Research*, 67: 2212–2223; Lee, Park, Shin, Disappearing internal capital markets: Evidence from diversified business groups in Korea; A. Chakrabarti, K. Singh, & I. Mahmood, 2006, Diversification and performance: Evidence from East Asian firms, *Strategic Management Journal*, 28: 101–120.

76. S. Schönhaar, U. Pidun, & M. Nippa, M. 2014, Transforming the business portfolio: How multinationals reinvent themselves, *Journal of Business Strategy*, 35(3): 4–17; D. D. Bergh, R. A. Johnson, & R. L. Dewitt, 2008, Restructuring through spin-off or sell-off: Transforming information asymmetries into financial gain, *Strategic Management Journal*, 29: 133–148; C. Decker & M. Mellewigt, 2007, Thirty years after Michael E. Porter: What do we know about business exit? *Academy of Management Perspectives*, 2: 41–55; S. J. Chang & H. Singh, 1999, The impact of entry and resource fit on modes of exit by multibusiness firms, *Strategic Management Journal*, 20: 1019–135.

77. Hoskisson, Wei, Yi, Jing, The evolution and strategic positioning of private equity firms.

78. 2015, About us, Danaher, www.danaher. com, March 30; S. Ward, 2014, Danaher's best recent deal: Its shares, *Barron's*, June 9, 21.

79. D. H. Frank & T. Obloj, 2014, Firm-specific human capital, organizational incentives, and agency costs: Evidence from retail banking, *Strategic Management Journal*, 35: 1279–1301; R. Coff, 2003, Bidding wars over R&D-intensive firms: Knowledge, opportunism, and the market for corporate control, *Academy of Management Journal*, 46: 74–85.

80. I. Ioannou, 2014, When do spinouts enhance parent firm performance? Evidence from the U.S. automobile industry, 1890–1986, *Organization Science*, 25: 529–551; J. Xia & S. Li, 2013, The divestiture of acquired subunits: A resource-dependence approach, *Strategic Management Journal*, 34: 131–148; C. Moschieri & J. Mair, 2012, Managing divestitures through time— Expanding current knowledge, *Academy of Management Perspectives*, 26: 35–50.

81. T. W. Tong, J. J. Reuer, B. B. Tyler, & S. Zhang, 2015, Host country executives' assessments of international joint ventures and divestitures: An experimental approach, *Strategic Management Journal*, 36: 254–275; H. Berry, 2013, When do firms divest foreign operations? *Organization Science*, 24: 246–261; D. Ma, 2012, A relational view

82. P. Pautler, 2015, A brief history of the FTC's Bureau of Economics: Reports, mergers, and information regulation. *Review of Industrial Organization*, 46: 59–94; M. Lubatkin, H. Merchant, & M. Srinivasan, 1997, Merger strategies and shareholder value during times of relaxed antitrust enforcement: The case of large mergers during the 1980s, *Journal of Management*, 23: 61–81.

83. D. P. Champlin & J. T. Knoedler, 1999, Restructuring by design? Government's complicity in corporate restructuring, *Journal of Economic Issues*, 33: 41–57.

84. R. M. Scherer & D. Ross, 1990, *Industrial Market Structure and Economic Performance*, Boston: Houghton Mifflin.

85. A. Shleifer & R. W. Vishny, 1994, Takeovers in the 1960s and 1980s: Evidence and implications. In R. P. Rumelt, D. E. Schendel, & D. J. Teece (eds.), *Fundamental Issues in Strategy*, Boston: Harvard Business School Press, 403–422.

86. S. Chatterjee, J. S. Harrison, & D. D. Bergh, 2003, Failed takeover attempts, corporate governance and refocusing, *Strategic Management Journal*, 24: 87–96; Lubatkin, Merchant, & Srinivasan, Merger strategies and shareholder value; D. J. Ravenscraft, & R. M. Scherer, 1987, *Mergers, Sell-Offs and Economic Efficiency*, Washington, DC: Brookings Institution, 22.

87. D. A. Zalewski, 2001, Corporate takeovers, fairness, and public policy, *Journal of Economic Issues*, 35: 431–437; P. L. Zweig, J. P. Kline, S. A. Forest, & K. Gudridge, 1995, The case against mergers, *BusinessWeek*, October 30, 122–130.

88. E. J. Lopez, 2001, New anti-merger theories: A critique, *Cato Journal*, 20: 359–378; 1998, The trustbusters' new tools, *The Economist*, May 2, 62–64.

89. D. Bush & B. D. Gelb, 2012 Anti-trust enforcement: An inflection point? *Journal of Business Strategy*, 33(6): 15–21.

90. M. C. Jensen, 1986, Agency costs of free cash flow, corporate finance, and takeovers, *American Economic Review*, 76: 323–329.

91. M. A. Hitt, J. S. Harrison, & R. D. Ireland, 2001, *Mergers and Acquisitions: A Guide to Creating Value for Stakeholders*, NY: Oxford University Press.

92. M. T. Brouwer, 2008, Horizontal mergers and efficiencies; theory and antitrust practice, *European Journal of Law and Economics*, 26: 11–26.

93. T. Afza, C. Slahudin, & M. S. Nazir, 2008, Diversification and corporate performance: An evaluation of Pakistani firms, *South Asian Journal of Management*, 15: 7–18; J. M. Shaver, 2006, A paradox of synergy: Contagion and capacity effects in mergers and acquisitions, *Academy of Management Journal*, 31: 962–976.

94. C. Sundaramurthy, K. Pukthuanthong, & Y. Kor, 2014, Positive and negative synergies between the CEO's and the corporate board's human and social capital: A study of biotechnology firms, *Strategic Management Journal*, 35: 845–868; Bauer & Matzler, Antecedents of M&A success: The role of strategic complementarity, cultural fit, and degree and speed of integration;

95. L. E. Palich, L. B. Cardinal, & C. C. Miller, 2000, Curvilinearity in the diversification-performance linkage: An examination of over three decades of research, *Strategic Management Journal*, 21: 155–174.

96. J. P. O'Brien, P. David, T. Yoshikawa, & A. Delios, 2014, How capital structure influences diversification performance: A transaction cost perspective, *Strategic Management Journal*, 35: 1013–1031; Sirmon, Hitt, Ireland, & Gilbert, Resource orchestration to create competitive advantage; A. E. Bernardo & B. Chowdhry, 2002, Resources, real options, and corporate strategy, *Journal of Financial Economics*, 63: 211–234.

97. T. B. Mackey & J. B. Barney, 2013, Incorporating opportunity costs in strategic management research: The value of diversification and payout as opportunities forgone when reinvesting in the firm, *Strategic Organization*, 11: 347–363; W. H. Tsai, Y. C. Kuo, J.-H. Hung, 2009, Corporate diversification and CEO turnover in family businesses: Self-entrenchment or risk reduction? *Small Business Economics*, 32: 57–76; N. W. C. Harper & S. P. Viguerie, 2002, Are you too focused? *McKinsey Quarterly*, Mid-Summer, 29–38.

98. J. W. Miller, 2015, Alcoa looks to shed more capacity, *Wall Street Journal*, March 10, B3.

99. J. W. Miller, 2015, Alcoa makes deal to broaden reach in aircraft industry, *Wall Street Journal*, March 10, B3.

100. Sakhartov & Folta, Resource relatedness, redeployability, and firm value; T. B. Folta & J. P. O'Brien, 2008, Determinants of firm-specific thresholds in acquisition decisions, *Managerial and Decision Economics*, 29: 209–225.

101. N. M. Kay & A. Diamantopoulos, 1987, Uncertainty and synergy: Towards a formal model of corporate strategy, *Managerial and Decision Economics*, 8: 121–130.

102. R. W. Coff, 1999, How buyers cope with uncertainty when acquiring firms in knowledge-intensive industries: Caveat emptor, *Organization Science*, 10: 144–161.

103. P. B. Carroll & C. Muim 2008, 7 ways to fail big, *Harvard Business Review*, 86(9): 82–91.

104. Y. R. Choi, S. A. Zahra, T. Yoshikawa, & B. H. Han, 2015, Family ownership and R&D investment: The role of growth opportunities and business group membership, *Journal of Business Research*, 68: 1053–1061; S. K. Kim, J. D. Arthurs, A. Sahaym, & J. B. Cullen, 2013, Search behavior of the diversified firm: The impact of fit on innovation,

Strategic Management Journal, 34: 999–1009; J. Kang, 2013, The relationship between corporate diversification and corporate social performance, *Strategic Management Journal*, 34: 94–109.

105. Sears & Hoetker, Technological overlap, technological capabilities, and resource recombination in technological acquisitions; D. G. Sirmon, S. Gove, & M. A. Hitt, 2008, Resource management in dyadic competitive rivalry: The effects of resource bundling and deployment, *Academy of Management Journal*, 51: 919–935; S. J. Chatterjee & B. Wernerfelt, 1991, The link between resources and type of diversification: Theory and evidence, *Strategic Management Journal*, 12: 33–48.

106. G. Ertug & F. Castellucci, 2015, Who shall get more? How intangible assets and aspiration levels affect the valuation of resource providers, *Strategic Organization*, 13: 6–31; O'Brien, David, Yoshikawa, & Delios, How capital structure influences diversification performance; E. N. K. Lim, S. S. Das, & A. Das, 2009, Diversification strategy, capital structure, and the Asian financial crisis (1997–1998): Evidence from Singapore firms, *Strategic Management Journal*, 30: 577–594; W. Keuslein, 2003, The Ebitda folly, *Forbes*, March 17, 165–167.

107. C. Zillman, 2014, Michael Dell: Long live the PC, *Fortune*, www.fortune.com, May 23;

108. L. Capron & J. Hull 1999, Redeployment of brands, sales forces, and general marketing management expertise following horizontal acquisitions: A resource-based view, *Journal of Marketing*, 63: 41–54.

109. C. Mims, 2015, In battery revolution, a clean leap forward, *Wall Street Journal*, March 16, B4.

110. M. V. S. Kumar, 2009, The relationship between product and international diversification: The effects of short-run constraints and endogeneity. *Strategic Management Journal*, 30: 99–116; C. B. Malone & L. C. Rose, 2006. Intangible assets and firm diversification, *International Journal of Managerial Finance*, 2: 136–153.

111. J. Chekler, 2015, Alvarez & Marsal to launch investment arm, *Wall Street Journal*, www.wsj.com, March 25.

112. M. Rogan & O. Sorenson, 2014, Picking a (poor) partner: A relational perspective on acquisitions, *Administrative Science Quarterly*, 59: 301–329; C. Moschieri, 2011, The implementation and structuring of divestitures: The unit's perspective, *Strategic Management Journal*, 32: 368–401; K. Shimizu & M. A. Hitt, 2005, What constrains or facilitates divestitures of formerly acquired firms? The effects of organizational inertia, *Journal of Management*, 31: 50–72.

113. J. Bunge & L. Hoffman, 2014, Tables turn for Hillshire CEO as an acquirer becomes prey, *Wall Street Journal*, June 2, B1; D. Cimilluca & R. Van Daalen, 2013,. A year after its creation, Sara Lee coffee spinoff fetches

$9.8 billion. *Wall Street Journal*, April 13, B3; D. Cimilluca & J. Jargon, 2009, Corporate news: Sara Lee weighs sale of European business, *Wall Street Journal*, March 13, B3.

114. M. van Essen, J. Otten, & E. J. Carberry, 2015, Assessing managerial power theory: A meta-analytic approach to understanding the determinants of CEO compensation, *Journal of Management*, 41: 164–202; A. J. Nyberg, I. S. Fulmer, B. Gerhart, & M. A. Carpenter, 2010, Agency theory revisited: CEO return, and shareholder interest alignment, *Academy of Management Journal*, 53: 1029–1049.

115. X. Castañer & N. Kavadis, 2013, Does good governance prevent bad strategy? A study of corporate governance, financial diversification, and value creation by French corporations, 2000–2006, *Strategic Management Journal*, 34: 863–876; D. Souder, Z. Simsek, & S. G. Johnson, 2012, The differing effects of agent and founder CEOs on the firm's market expansion, *Strategic Management Journal*, 33: 23–41; R. E. Hoskisson, M. W. Castleton, & M. C. Withers, 2009, Complementarity in monitoring and bonding: More intense monitoring leads to higher executive compensation, *Academy of Management Perspectives*, 23: 57–74.

116. D. E. Black, S. S. Dikolli, & S. D. Dyreng, 2014, CEO pay-for-complexity and the risk of managerial diversion from multinational diversification, *Contemporary Accounting Research*, 31: 103–135; Pathak, Hoskisson, & Johnson, 2014.

117. E. M. Fich, L. T. Starks, & A. S. Yore, 2014, CEO deal-making activities and compensation, *Journal of Financial Economics*, 114: 471–492; M. van Essen, P. P. Heugens, J. Otto, & J. van Oosterhout, 2012, An institution-based view of executive compensation: A multilevel meta-analytic test, *Journal of International Business Studies*, 43: 396–423; Y. Deutsch, T. Keil, & T. Laamanen, 2011, A dual agency view of board compensation: The joint effects of outside director and CEO options on firm risk, *Strategic Management Journal*, 32: 212–227.

118. R. Krause, K. A. Whitler, & M. Semadeni, 2014, Power to the principals! An experimental look at shareholder say-on-pay voting, *Academy of Management Journal*, 57: 94–115.

119. Zhu & Chen, CEO narcissism and the impact of prior board experience on corporate strategy; A. J. Wowak & D. C. Hambrick, 2010, A model of person-pay interaction: How executives vary in their responses to compensation arrangements, *Strategic Management Journal*, 31: 803–821; J. Bogle, 2008, Reflections on CEO compensation, *Academy of Management Perspectives*, 22: 21–25.

120. E. Y. Rhee & P. C. Fiss, 2014, Framing controversial actions: Regulatory focus, source credibility, and stock market reaction to poison pill adoption, *Academy of Management Journal*, 57: 1734–1758; M. Kahan & E. B. Rock, 2002, How I learned to stop worrying and love the pill: Adaptive responses to takeover law, *University of Chicago Law Review*, 69: 871–915.

121. B. W. Benson, W. N. Davidson, T. R. Davidson, & H. Wang, 2015, Do busy directors and CEOs shirk their responsibilities? Evidence from mergers and acquisitions, *Quarterly Review of Economics & Finance*, 55: 1–19; R. C. Anderson, T. W. Bates, J. M. Bizjak, & M. L. Lemmon, 2000, Corporate governance and firm diversification, *Financial Management*, 29: 5–22; J. D. Westphal, 1998, Board games: How CEOs adapt to increases in structural board independence from management, *Administrative Science Quarterly*, 43: 511–537.

122. C. E. Devers, G. Mcnamara, J. Haleblian, & M. E. Yoder, 2013, Do they walk the talk? Gauging acquiring CEO and director confidence in the value creation potential of announced acquisitions, *Academy of Management Journal*, 56: 1679–1702; S. M. Campbell, A. J. Ward, J. A. Sonnenfeld, & B. R. Agle, 2008, Relational ties that bind: Leader-follower relationship dimensions and charismatic attribution, *Leadership Quarterly*, 19: 556–568; M. Wiersema, 2002, Holes at the top: Why CEO firings backfire, *Harvard Business Review*, 80(12): 70–77.

123. R. E. Hoskisson, J. D. Arthurs, R. E. White, & C. M. Wyatt, 2013. Multiple agency theory: An emerging perspective on corporate governance. In M. Wright, D. S. Siegel, K. Keasey, & I. Filatotchev (eds.), *The Oxford Handbook of Corporate Governance*, Oxford: Oxford University Press; D. Allcock & I. Filatotchev, 2010, Executive incentive schemes in initial public offerings: The effects of multiple-agency conflicts and corporate governance, *Journal of Management*, 36: 663–686; N. Wasserman, 2006, Stewards, agents, and the founder discount: Executive compensation in new ventures, *Academy of Management Journal*, 49: 960–976.

124. E. F. Fama, 1980, Agency problems and the theory of the firm, *Journal of Political Economy*, 88: 288–307.

125. H. Kim, R. E. Hoskisson, & S. Lee, 2015, Why strategic factor markets matter: 'New' multinationals' geographic diversification and firm profitability, *Strategic Management Journal*, 36: 518–536; M. Y. Brannen & M. F. Peterson, 2009, Merging without alienating: Interventions promoting cross-cultural organizational integration and their limitations, *Journal of International Business Studies*, 40: 468–489; M. L. A. Hayward, 2002, When do firms learn from their acquisition experience? Evidence from 1990–1995, *Strategic Management Journal*, 23: 21–39.

126. R. E. Hoskisson, R. A. Johnson, L. Tihanyi, & R. E. White, 2005, Diversified business groups and corporate refocusing in emerging economies, *Journal of Management*, 31: 941–965.

127. R. Chittoor, P. Kale, & P. Puranam, 2015. Business groups in developing capital markets: Towards a complementarity perspective, *Strategic Management Journal*, forthcoming; C. N. Chung & X. Luo, 2008, Institutional logics or agency costs: The influence of corporate governance models on business group restructuring in emerging economies, *Organization Science*, 19: 766–784; W. P. Wan & R. E. Hoskisson, 2003, Home country environments, corporate diversification strategies, and firm performance, *Academy of Management Journal*, 46: 27–45.

7

Merger and Acquisition Strategies

Studying this chapter should provide you with the strategic management knowledge needed to:

7-1   Explain the popularity of merger and acquisition strategies in firms competing in the global economy.

7-2   Discuss reasons why firms use an acquisition strategy to achieve strategic competitiveness.

7-3   Describe seven problems that work against achieving success when using an acquisition strategy.

7-4   Name and describe the attributes of effective acquisitions.

7-5   Define the restructuring strategy and distinguish among its common forms.

7-6   Explain the short- and long-term outcomes of the different types of restructuring strategies.

MERGERS AND ACQUISITIONS: PROMINENT STRATEGIES FOR FIRMS SEEKING TO ENHANCE THEIR PERFORMANCE

"Companies are turning to the capital markets at a record pace to fund acquisitions" read the headlines in mid-2015. At that point in time, U.S. firms had already raised roughly $206.3 billion to support their intended merger and acquisition activity. On a world-wide scale, announced and completed mergers and acquisitions (M&A) by mid-2015 totaled $1.47 trillion. This total was a 30 percent increase from the same time in 2014 and was the highest amount allocated to implement merger and acquisition strategies since 2007. If this pace continued through the end of 2015, the total global value of M&A transactions would exceed $3.7 trillion. At the time, many executives anticipated that this robust amount of M&A activity would likely continue and perhaps become even stronger in the next few years. But why? What causes firms to use strategies that call for them to either merge with another or acquire another firm? (As we explain later, a merger finds firms combining themselves as coequals, while acquisitions find the target firm being purchased by the acquiring firm.)

As we discuss next, the influences on firms' decisions to use mergers and acquisitions' strategies are varied and interesting. The discussion of these influences in the Opening Case reinforces the discussion in the chapter about specific reasons why firms choose to implement these strategies.

The need to create value for stakeholders is a primary influence on firms' decisions to engage in M&A activity. Firms create value in multiple ways, including through the successful implementation of their business-level, diversification, international and cooperative strategies. Sometimes though, firms can create additional value by merging with another company or acquiring a firm. This is the case for life sciences companies today where weak R&D pipelines are yielding too few products, increasing the difficulty of creating sufficient amounts of value for stakeholders as a result. An analyst of this industry recently suggested that "this pressure to create value is driving M&A, divestitures, and restructurings at unprecedented levels throughout the industry." (We discuss restructuring strategies, including those involving divestitures, later in the chapter.) For firms in this industry, specific influences resulting in decisions to engage in M&A activity include patent expirations, pricing pressures, and growth opportunities in foreign and emerging markets.

BhFoton/Shutterstock.com

Increasing confidence in a firm's domestic economy, and perhaps in global economies as well, is another influence on M&A activity. Observers of business conditions in the world are now concluding that the after effects of the 2007/2008 global crisis on companies have largely faded, resulting in boards of directors becoming more confident that their company should pursue all feasible strategies with the potential to increase firm value. This is particularly the case when growth in a firm's domestic market is stagnant or declining. This appears to be the situation facing a number of Japanese firms today in that although a number of them have significant amounts of cash on hand, their domestic markets are shrinking in size. Accordingly, these firms are examining what they believe are attractive merger and acquisition opportunities outside of Japan. These firms do indeed seem eager to engage in M&A activity as indicated by the fact that they paid an average premium of 46 percent for the acquisitions they completed during 2015's first quarter.

But companies interested in implementing M&A strategies sometimes face hurdles in their attempts to do so. Firms seeking to merge with or acquire Chinese firms often face complicated trade barriers and other rules, procedures, and laws that are in place to protect domestic firms. Honeywell International, Inc., for example, is frustrated with the pace of the acquisitions it has been able to finalize recently in China. The firm seeks to complete $10 billion in M&A activity in China by the end of 2018, although it is not confident that this goal will be reached. The U.K. government is looking more carefully at companies' attempts to acquire British firms. Mainly, government officials believe that at least some and potentially many of these transactions are against the public's interest and may pose a risk to the continuing employment of local/native workers. Thus, while certain factors influence a firm's decision to use M&A strategies, the reality is that some conditions may prevent them from being able to do so, at least in certain situations.

Sources: 2015, M&A trends report 2015, Deloitte, www2.deloitte.com, April 21; 2015, For life sciences CFOs: Using M&A to drive shareholder value, Deloitte, www2.deloitte.com, April 21; D. Cimilluca, D. Mattioli, & S. Raice, 2015, Rising optimism fuels deal rebound, *Wall Street Journal Online*, www.wsj.com, April 8; A. Fukase, 2015, Japanese M&A overseas takes off, *Wall Street Journal Online*, www.wsj.com, April 28; W. Ma, 2015, China's lower growth goal doesn't spook foreign companies, *Wall Street Journal Online*, www.wsj.com, March 5; L Wei & B. Spegele, 2015, China considering mergers among its big state oil companies, *Wall Street Journal Online*, www.wsj.com, February 17.

We examined corporate-level strategy in Chapter 6, focusing on types and levels of product diversification strategies firms use to create value for stakeholders and competitive advantages for the firms. As noted in that chapter, diversification allows a firm to create value by productively using excess resources to exploit new opportunities.[1] In this chapter, we explore merger and acquisition strategies. Firms throughout the world use these strategies, often in concert with diversification strategies, to become more diversified. In other words, firms often become more diversified by completing mergers and/or acquisitions. As we discuss in this chapter, although a popular strategy for small corporations[2] as well as large ones, using these strategies does not always lead to the success firms seek.[3] And as described in the Opening Case, certain conditions may preclude a firm from engaging in merger and acquisition activity, even though various factors are influencing it to try to do so.

A key objective of this chapter is to explain how firms can successfully use merger and acquisition strategies to create stakeholder value and competitive advantages.[4] To reach this objective, we first explain the continuing popularity of merger and acquisition strategies. As part of this explanation, we describe the differences between mergers, acquisitions, and takeovers. We next discuss specific reasons why firms choose to use merger and acquisition strategies and some of the problems organizations may encounter when doing so. We then describe the characteristics associated with effective acquisitions (we focus on acquisition strategies in the chapter) before closing the chapter with a discussion of different types of restructuring strategies. Restructuring strategies are commonly used to correct or deal with the results of ineffective mergers and acquisitions.

7-1 The Popularity of Merger and Acquisition Strategies

Merger and acquisition (M&A) strategies have been popular among U.S. firms for many years. Some believe that these strategies played a central role in the restructuring of U.S. businesses during the 1980s and 1990s and that they continue generating these types of benefits in the twenty-first century.[5] As discussed in other parts of this chapter, mergers and acquisitions are also occurring with greater frequency in many regions of the world.[6]

In the final analysis, firms use these strategies for the purpose of trying to create more value for all stakeholders.

Although popular as a way of creating value and earning above-average returns, it is challenging to effectively implement merger and acquisition strategies. This is particularly true for the acquiring firms in that some research results indicate that shareholders of the acquired firms often earn above-average returns from acquisitions, while shareholders of the acquiring firms typically earn returns that are close to zero.[7] Moreover, in approximately two-thirds of all acquisitions, the acquiring firm's stock price falls immediately after the intended transaction is announced. This negative response reflects investors' skepticism about the likelihood that the acquirer will be able to achieve the synergies required to justify the premium to purchase the target firm.[8]

Discussed more fully later in the chapter, paying excessive premiums to acquire firms can negatively influence the results a firm achieves through an acquisition strategy. Determining the worth of a target firm is difficult; this difficulty increases the likelihood a firm will pay a premium to acquire a target. Premiums are paid when those leading an acquiring firm conclude that the target firm would be worth more under its ownership than it would be as part of any other ownership arrangement or if it were to remain as an independent company. Recently, for example, Alexion Pharmaceuticals, Inc. paid a 124 percent premium to buy Synageva BioPharma Corp. Although Synageva did not have a product on the market at the time of the transaction, it was in late-stage development of a promising treatment for a rare genetic disease. Alexion placed high value on both this product and Synageva's overall innovation capabilities, factors that influenced the decision to pay a premium. The following comment from Alexion's CEO shows why the firm paid a premium to acquire a particular company:

> A **merger** is a strategy through which two firms agree to integrate their operations on a relatively coequal basis.

"We think the valuation is appropriate because we think Synageva is so much more valuable in our hand than anyone else's hands."[9]

This may in fact be the case. Overall though, paying a premium that exceeds the value of a target once integrated with the acquiring firm can result in negative outcomes.[10]

7-1a Mergers, Acquisitions, and Takeovers: What Are the Differences?

A **merger** is a strategy through which two firms agree to integrate their operations on a relatively coequal basis. A proposed merger of equals between two Canadian mining firms—Alamos Gold Inc. and AuRico Gold Inc.—was announced in mid-2015. This merger between two smaller miners was being considered so the combined firms could generate synergies through cost savings and a joint focus on low-risk mining operations. Openly stating that the merger was viewed by both firms as a merger of equals, Alamos' CEO stated that "the combination of diversified production from three mines and a pipeline of low-cost growth projects in safe

Hand-out/AURICO GOLD INC./Newscom

Pictured here are individual employees from two companies—Alamos Gold Inc. and AuRico Gold Inc.—who will now work together in the same company as a result of a merger.

jurisdictions equate to a leading gold intermediate and a significant re-rate opportunity for our collective shareholders."[11]

Even though the transaction that was proposed to take place between Alamos and AuRico was to be a merger of equals, evidence suggests that finalizing a proposal for firms to merge on an equal or a relatively equal basis is difficult. In an analyst's words:

"A merger of equals: It's how executives love to present big corporate tie-ups. The reality is that it isn't easy working out how to share control of multibillion-dollar businesses among strong-willed executives and reassure shareholders, wary of how management infighting can destroy value in meagdeals."[12]

On a practical basis, deciding who will lead the merged firm, how to fuse what are often disparate corporate cultures, and how to reach an agreement about the value of each company prior to the merger are issues that commonly affect firms' efforts to merge on a coequal basis.

To more fully consider issues such as these and others that surface when firms propose to merge as equals, we discuss the merger between Swiss-based Holcim Ltd. and French-based Lafarge SA in the Strategic Focus. Prior to deciding to merge, Holcim and Lafarge were long-time competitors. As we discuss, the route to finalizing this merger was not without challenges.

An **acquisition** is a strategy through which one firm buys a controlling, or 100 percent, interest in another firm with the intent of making the acquired firm a subsidiary business within its portfolio. After the acquisition is completed, the management of the acquired firm reports to the management of the acquiring firm.

Although most mergers that are completed are friendly in nature, acquisitions can be friendly or unfriendly. A **takeover** is a special type of acquisition where the target firm does not solicit the acquiring firm's bid; thus, takeovers are unfriendly acquisitions. As explained in Chapter 10, firms have developed defenses (mostly corporate governance devices) that can be used to prevent an unrequested and undesired takeover bid from being successful.[13]

Commonly, firms think of unsolicited bids as "hostile" takeovers. When such a bid is received, the takeover target may try to determine the highest amount the acquiring firm is willing to pay, even while simultaneously using defense mechanisms to prevent a takeover attempt from succeeding. Multiple exchanges may take place between a potential acquirer and its target before a resolution to the unsolicited bid is reached; and these exchanges can become quite complicated. The exchanges among Teva Pharmaceutical, Mylan N.V., and Perrigo Company that were initiated in the spring of 2015 demonstrate this complexity. Mylan made a hostile bid for Perrigo before receiving a hostile bid itself from Teva. The following comment captures the complexity of this situation:

"But Teva says it doesn't want Mylan if Mylan buys Perrigo, Perrigo rebuffed Mylan's offer, and earlier, Mylan said it wasn't thrilled with Teva's takeover interest."[14]

As the three firms worked to sort out the matter, some felt that the price firms would ultimately be willing to pay to complete an intended transaction would decide the fate of the hostile takeover bids involving the three firms.

On a comparative basis, acquisitions are more common than mergers and takeovers. Accordingly, we focus the remainder of this chapter's discussion on acquisitions.

7-2   Reasons for Acquisitions

In this section, we discuss reasons why firms decide to acquire another company. As this discussion shows, there are many unique reasons that firms choose to use an acquisition strategy.

An **acquisition** is a strategy through which one firm buys a controlling, or 100 percent, interest in another firm with the intent of making the acquired firm a subsidiary business within its portfolio.

A **takeover** is a special type of acquisition where the target firm does not solicit the acquiring firm's bid; thus, takeovers are unfriendly acquisitions.

Strategic **Focus**

A Merger of Equals: Making It Happen Isn't Easy!

Founded in France in 1833, Lafarge became a successful global industrial company specializing in three product areas—cement, construction aggregates, and concrete. The other party in a "merger of equals," that required well over a year to design and bring to the conclusion the firms intended, is Holcim, a materials and aggregates company that was founded in Switzerland in 1912. Holcim's global ambitions were obvious early when the firm expanded into France and throughout Europe and the Middle East during the 1920s. This expansion resulted in long-term and active competitions between Lafarge and Holcim.

In April of 2014, Lafarge and Holcim announced that they had settled on terms that would result in a merger of equals and that, accordingly, they were prepared to seek regulatory approval of the proposed transaction. Obtaining such approvals was anticipated to be challenging given that the diversity of the independent firms' global operations meant that 15 or so different jurisdictions could potentially object to a merger between the firms.

What influenced Lafarge and Holcim to want to merge as coequals given the difficulties of doing so? The prevailing thought is that mergers of equals are always more fragile to bring about in light of the need to effectively meld what are commonly two different cultures and specify the leadership structure that will be used to operate the newly-created firm. These issues are in addition to a core one of identifying the financial aspects of the transactions that will appeal to each firm's shareholders.

In spite of challenges such as these, Lafarge and Holcim thought that merging as equals would create a firm with enhanced and significant competitive abilities. Leaders of the two firms concluded that together LafargeHolcim, the agreed upon name for the combined firm, would have the most balanced and diversified portfolio in the building materials industry. The firms anticipated that integrating their operations would generate approximately $1.5 billion in annual cost savings. In an overall sense, company leaders thought that the anticipated positive benefits of merging would come about primarily as a result of being able to meld Holcim's marketing strengths with Lafarge's innovation capabilities.

Perhaps not unexpectedly, the transaction proposed between Lafarge and Holcim almost fell apart. This happened in March of 2015 when Holcim's board, "after first agreeing to a $44 billion merger with Lafarge, rejected the deal's terms as undervaluing Holcim. Corporate leadership also was a concern." This objection surfaced after the firms had received regulatory approvals from key jurisdictions, including the European Union, India, and the United States, regarding the number of divestitures of units they would make to prevent them from having highly concentrated positions in different global markets. At the core of the dispute was the conviction among Holcim's

board members that the financial terms should be more attractive for their shareholders and that Lafarge's CEO should not be appointed as CEO of the newly-created firm. One reason for these convictions was that in the nearly one year since terms of the initial merger were agreed upon, Holcim's "operating performance and share price had outperformed those of Lafarge." After restructuring the financing of the transaction and agreeing that a different CEO would be appointed for the new firm, 94 percent of Holcim's shareholders approved the transaction's terms.

After dealing with challenges, LafargeHolcim became a firm that was a merger of equals in July 2015. Speaking to the future, one board member said that "this isn't just another merger. It is an opportunity to create a new Number One in our industry." Assuming that this merger of equals achieves the potential some anticipate, all of the work required to bring it about will be validated. Going forward though, implementation challenges may come into play, at least in the short term, given the potential

FRANCK FIFE/AFP/Getty Images

Shown here left to right shaking hands during an announcement of their firms' intention to merge are Rolf Soiron, the chair of Holcim's board of directors and Bruno Lafont, CEO of Lafarge SA. Later, Eric Olsen was selected as the CEO of the newly formed firm, called LafargeHolcim.

incompatibility of Holcim's decentralized management approach with the more centralized approach that characterized Lafarge when it competed as an independent firm. Those leading the integration processes associated with the details of combining the two firms will need to pay close attention to this issue.

Sources: 2015, Holcim and Lafarge obtain merger clearances in the United States and Canada paving the way to closing their merger, *Holcim Home Page*, www.holcim.com, May 4; 2015, Lafarge to cut 380 jobs ahead of merger with Holcim, *Global Cement*, www.globalcement.com, May 19; M. Curtin, 2015, Holcim-Lafarge shows 'merger of equals' doesn't equal smooth sailing, *Wall Street Journal Online*, www.wsj.com, March 16; M. Curtin, 2015, A 'merger of equals' is more fragile, *Wall Street Journal Online*, www.wsj.com, March 16; J. Franklin, 2015, Holcim and Lafarge name post-merger board candidates, *Reuters*, www.reuters.com, April 14; J. Revill, 2015, Holcim moves step closer to Lafarge merger, *Wall Street Journal Online*, www.wsj.com, May 8.

7-2a Increased Market Power

Achieving greater market power is a primary reason for acquisitions.[15] Defined in Chapter 6, *market power* exists when a firm is able to sell its goods or services above competitive levels or when the costs of its primary or support activities are lower than those of its competitors. Market power usually is derived from the size of the firm, the quality of the resources it uses to compete, and its share of the market(s) in which it competes.[16] Therefore, most acquisitions that are designed to achieve greater market power entail buying a competitor, a supplier, a distributor, or a business in a highly related industry so a core competence can be used to gain competitive advantage in the acquiring firm's primary market.

Next, we discuss how firms use horizontal, vertical, and related types of acquisitions to increase their market power. Active acquirers simultaneously pursue two or all three types of acquisitions in order to do this. Evidence suggests, for example, that Amazon "for years has been expanding the scale and scope of its operation, both horizontally and vertically."[17] These three types of acquisitions, and proposed mergers as well, are subject to regulatory review by various governmental entities. Sometimes these reviews bring about the dissolution of proposed transactions. In 2015 for example, Comcast abandoned its effort to acquire Time Warner for $45.2 billion in light of opposition to the transaction, primarily from the U.S. Department of Justice.[18]

Horizontal Acquisitions

The acquisition of a company competing in the same industry as the acquiring firm is a *horizontal acquisition*. Horizontal acquisitions increase a firm's market power by exploiting cost-based and revenue-based synergies.[19] Horizontal acquisitions occur frequently in the pharmaceutical industry. An indication of this is the fact that, in the first few months of 2015, intended or completed horizontal acquisitions reached a combined value of roughly $180 billion. With respect to a specific firm, Mylan N.V. became the second largest generic drug seller in the United States by acquiring a number of firms in its industry over the past few years.[20] Research suggests that horizontal acquisitions result in higher performance when the firms have similar characteristics,[21] such as strategy, managerial styles, and resource allocation patterns. Similarities in these characteristics, as well as previous alliance management experience, support efforts to integrate the acquiring and the acquired firm. Horizontal acquisitions are often most effective when the acquiring firm effectively integrates the acquired firm's assets with its own, but only after evaluating and divesting excess capacity and assets that do not complement the newly combined firm's core competencies.[22]

Vertical Acquisitions

A *vertical acquisition* refers to a firm acquiring a supplier or distributor of one or more of its products. Through a vertical acquisition, the newly formed firm controls additional parts of the value chain (see Chapter 3),[23] which is how vertical acquisitions lead to increased market power.

Through vertical integration, a firm has an opportunity to appropriate value being generated in a part of the value chain in which it does not currently compete and to better control its own destiny in terms of costs and access. These factors influenced Delta Air Lines' decision in 2012 to purchase a refinery.[24] Owning access to a source of what could become jet fuel reduces the likelihood that a raw material critical to the firm's operations would become unavailable to it or that Delta would be subjected to market forces in terms of having access to the raw material. Identical logic explains Italian confectionary giant Ferrero's purchase of Oltan Gida, Turkey's largest hazelnut company, because having ready access to a steady flow of a key ingredient at an attractive price has the potential to positively affect the firm's efforts to earn above-returns.[25]

Related Acquisitions

Acquiring a firm in a highly related industry is called a *related acquisition*. Through a related acquisition, firms seek to create value through the synergy that can be generated by integrating some of their resources and capabilities.

Cisco Systems designs, manufacturers, and sells networking equipment. Over time though, the firm has engaged in related acquisitions, primarily as a foundation for being able to compete aggressively in other product markets. For example, as software becomes a more integral aspect of all networking products, the firm is making plans to acquire small- and medium-sized software companies. Such purchases appear to support the belief that Cisco is committed to competing successfully in the SDN (software-defined networking) space. Over the past few years, Cisco acquired Insieme Metworks, Tail-F, and Cariden to elaborate its SDN plans. Acquiring companies in related industries is a common practice for Cisco, and it is a practice that, in some analysts' eyes, has "opened up market opportunities on many occasions throughout the firm's history."[26]

7-2b   Overcoming Entry Barriers

Barriers to entry (introduced in Chapter 2) are factors associated with a market, or the firms currently operating in it, that increase the expense and difficulty new firms encounter when trying to enter that particular market. For example, well-established competitors may have economies of scale in manufacturing or servicing their products. In addition, enduring relationships with customers often create loyalties that are difficult for new entrants to overcome. When facing differentiated products, new entrants typically must spend considerable resources to advertise their products and may find it necessary to sell below competitors' prices to entice new customers.

Facing the entry barriers that economies of scale and differentiated products create, a new entrant may find that acquiring an established company is more effective than entering the market as a competitor offering a product that is unfamiliar to current buyers. In fact, the higher the barriers to market entry, the greater the probability that a firm will acquire an existing firm to overcome them. For example, Scripps Networks Interactive, Inc., the niched lifestyle-cable-channel with a portfolio including the Food Network, HGTV, and Travel Channel, wants to expand internationally, given the growth potential of markets outside the United States. Rather than establish its own operations in multiple international markets, Scripps is acquiring existing firms to overcome entry barriers that exist for various reasons, such as product loyalty. Recently, Scripps took a controlling stake in Polish TV operator TVN with the possibility of purchasing the remaining part of the firm in the future.[27] In light of TVN's "incredible portfolio of channels and services," Scripps' executives saw this transaction as "an important milestone in the ongoing strategic development of the firm's international business."[28]

As this discussion suggests, a key advantage of using an acquisition strategy to overcome entry barriers is that the acquiring firm gains immediate access to a market that is attractive to it. This can be especially important for firms seeking to enter international markets, as is the case for Scripps Networks Interactive. We further discuss cross-border acquisitions next.

Cross-Border Acquisitions

Acquisitions made between companies with headquarters in different countries are called *cross-border acquisitions*.[29] Historically, North American and European companies were the most active acquirers of companies outside their domestic markets. However, today's global competitive landscape is one in which firms from economies throughout the world are engaging in cross-border acquisitions, and for a host of reasons. In the Strategic Focus, we discuss different cross-border acquisitions that are being pursued or have been completed recently and are products of different strategic rationales.

Strategic **Focus**

Different Strategic Rationales Driving Cross-Border Acquisitions

As is true for acquisitions between firms headquartered in the same nation, a clear strategic rationale should be the foundation for all cross-border acquisitions. The decision to acquire a company should be carefully identified, examined, and agreed upon by key decision makers throughout the firm prior to finalizing an acquisition decision. The most successful acquisitions, including cross-border ones, are products of a rational decision process that is grounded in careful analysis of a proposed transaction with its strategic rationale as a guiding force.

The strategic rationale sometimes finds firms deciding to acquire ownership percentages of target firms to see if a full acquisition is warranted at a later date. This seems to be the situation with Alibaba Group Holding Limited, the Chinese-based company that is the world's largest e-commerce platform as measured by volume of transactions. Today though, China remains the firm's primary focus. Saying that the firm "must absolutely globalize and it must be a successful effort," Alibaba's CEO has committed the firm to thinking globally and taking actions accordingly. With the strategic rationale of "becoming more global" as a driver, the firm is acquiring parts of firms outside its home market, including its 9 percent purchase of U.S. online retailer Zulily, Inc. and its investments in mobile messaging app-maker Tango, also a U.S. firm. The following statement describes the rationale or logic driving Alibaba's acquisitions:

"We have made, and intend to continue to make, strategic investments and acquisitions to expand our user base, enhance our cloud computing business, add complementary products and technologies and further strengthen our ecosystem."

While some of Alibaba's strategic acquisitions will take place in China, a host of others will be cross-border transactions.

In other cases, altering a firm's competitive scope provides a strategic rationale for cross-border acquisitions. For example, based in Oxford, England, Circassia Pharmaceuticals PLC recently acquired Swedish-listed Aerocrine AB. Historically, Circassia competed with a laser-like focus on a single technology platform used to produce allergy vaccines. Aerocrine is an asthma-diagnostic company. Thus, the acquisition finds Circassia moving into the asthma market. According to Circassia's CEO, this transactions moves the firm closer to its goal of becoming "a self-sustaining specialty biopharmaceutical company focused on allergy and asthma."

Based in Spain, Banco Popular Español S.A. is pursuing acquisitions outside its home market. The bank's CEO noted that the rationale for this action is to prevent the firm from being too dependent on a single economy when that economy suffers from an economic downturn. In his words:

"In future crises, we would like the bank to be more diversified so we don't have the same level of dependence on a single economy that we have now. This will be a limited diversification, mainly in Latin America and done in a very gradual way over time without rushing."

Thus, it seems that the bank is committed to carefully examine each target before concluding that it should be acquired.

Zulily.PNG

Alibaba has taken an ownership position in U.S.-based Zulily (an e-commerce company) for the purpose of becoming a more global firm.

In mid-2015, Altice SA, a Luxembourg-based cable-and-telecom company controlled by French cable investor Patrick Drahi, was in advanced talks to buy U.S. firm Suddenlink in a transaction valued at between $8 and $10 billion. Already possessing communications companies from France to the Caribbean, many of which were acquired, adding Suddenlink to the fold would result in Altice being one of the world's largest cable and broadband market companies. An analyst captures Drahi's rationale for the string of cross-border acquisitions Altice has completed and intends to complete in the future in the following manner:

"Mr. Drahi has been betting that the future of the telecom industry lies in combining cable and broadband operators with mobile companies to offer clients higher-priced bundles combining television, broadband, fixed telephony, and mobile services."

The high degree of fragmentation in the global telecommunications market seems to yield opportunities for aggressive investors, such as Drahi, to gain value by consolidated firms on a global basis, using cross-border acquisitions in part to do so.

Thus, multiple reasons drive the decision to complete cross-border acquisitions. As we've noted, we can expect the most successful of these transactions, including the ones described here, to be based on a strong strategic rationale.

Sources: R. Bender, S. Ramachandran, & S. Raice, 2015, Altice in advanced talks to buy cable company Suddenlink, *Wall Street Journal Online*, www.wsj.com, May 19; J. Neumann, 2015, Spain's Banco Popular seeking acquisitions abroad, *Wall Street Journal Online*, www.wsj.com, May 18; D. Roland, 2015, U.K. biotech Circassia moves into asthma with two acquisitions, *Wall Street Journal Online*, www.wsj.com, May 15; C. Tejada, 2015, Alibaba to focus on expansion abroad, CEO says, *Wall Street Journal Online*, www.wsj.com, May 14; M. J. de la Merced, 2014, Alibaba's acquisition strategy focused: Focused largely on China and mobile, *New York Times*, www.nytimes.com, May 7.

Firms should recognize that cross-border acquisitions such as the ones discussed in the Strategic Focus are not risk free, even when a strong strategic rationale undergirds the completed transactions. China, for example, is a country with political and legal obstacles that increase acquisition risk.[30] Being able to conduct an effective due-diligence process when acquiring a company in China can be difficult where the target firm's financial data and corporate governance practices may lack complete transparency.[31] For instance, believing that the firm was going to be "its Chinese business card," Caterpillar, an earthmoving equipment company, acquired Chinese manufacturing company Siwei. After completing the purchase however, Caterpillar said it discovered "deliberate, multiyear, coordinated accounting misconduct at Siwei." Following complicated efforts to sort through everything, Caterpillar had to write down 86 percent of its $677 million purchase of Siwei.[32] Thus, firms must carefully study the risks as well as the potential benefits when contemplating cross-border acquisitions.

7-2c Cost of New Product Development and Increased Speed to Market

Developing new products internally and successfully introducing them into the marketplace often requires significant investment of a firm's resources, including time, making it difficult to quickly earn a profitable return.[33] Because an estimated 88 percent of innovations fail to achieve adequate returns, concerns exist in firms about their ability to achieve adequate returns from the capital they invest to develop and commercialize new products. Potentially contributing to these less-than-desirable rates of return is the successful imitation of approximately 60 percent of innovations within four years after the patents are obtained. These types of outcomes may lead managers to perceive internal product development as a high-risk activity.[34]

An acquisition strategy is another course of action a firm can take to gain access to new products and to current products that are new to it. Compared with internal product development processes, acquisitions provide more predictable returns as well as faster market entry. Returns are more predictable because the performance of the acquired firm's products can be assessed prior to completing the acquisition.[35]

WelchAllyn is a leading global manufacturer of medical diagnostic equipment. With a desire to provide diagnostic tools to doctors and nurses through which they can provide better healthcare to patients, WelchAllyn is completing a number of acquisitions to adapt to the rapidly changing health care environment. Rather than relying on internal innovation to produce all the new products it wants to sell, this firm has chosen to acquire solid companies through which it can quickly gain access to products that are related to its own and that target the same customers. Recently, for example, WelchAllyn acquired Scale-Tronix, a small firm that manufacturers "medical scales and patient weighing systems for hospitals, clinics, and extended-care facilities."[36] Scale-Tronix's specialization in a complete line of scales for use in the health care field allows WelchAllyn to immediately expand the scope of its product offerings to its customers.

7-2d Lower Risk Compared to Developing New Products

The outcomes of an acquisition can be estimated more easily and accurately than the outcomes of an internal product development process; as such, managers may view acquisitions as less risky.[37] However, firms should be cautious when using acquisitions to reduce risk relative to the risk incurred when developing new products internally. Indeed, even though research suggests acquisition strategies are a common means of avoiding risky internal ventures (and therefore risky R&D investments), acquisitions may also become a substitute for internal innovation.

Over time, being dependent on others for innovation leaves a firm vulnerable and less capable of mastering its own destiny when it comes to using innovation as a driver of wealth creation. Thus, a clear strategic rationale, such as the ones influencing the cross-border acquisitions described in a Strategic Focus in this chapter, should drive each acquisition a firm chooses to complete. If a firm is being acquired to gain access to a specific innovation or to a target's innovation-related capabilities, the acquiring firm should be able to specify how the innovation is or the innovation-based skills are to be integrated with its operations for strategic purposes.

7-2e Increased Diversification

Acquisitions are also used to diversify firms. Based on experience and the insights resulting from it, firms typically find it easier to develop and introduce new products in markets they are currently serving. In contrast, it is difficult for companies to develop products that differ from their current lines for markets in which they lack experience. Thus, it is relatively uncommon for a firm to develop new products internally to diversify its product lines.[38]

Acquisition strategies can be used to support the use of both related and unrelated diversification strategies. As we mentioned in Chapter 6, Campbell Soup uses a related constrained strategy. This global food company generates annual revenue in excess of $8 billion. In addition to the iconic soups, the firm's brands include Pepperidge Farm cookies, Arnott's Kjeldsens and Royal Dansk biscuits, and Pace Mexican sauce, among many others. Campbell recently restructured around product categories rather than geographies and brand groups. Americas Simple Meals and Beverages, Global Biscuits and Snacks, and Packaged Fresh are the three new business units. The firm's new structure is thought to be one that "will align the organization of the company's businesses with its core growth strategies."[39] One outcome from this reorganization is that Campbell feels it is better positioned to acquire "brands that are more popular and present greater growth opportunities."[40] Of course, given the firm's related constrained diversification strategy, brands that are acquired will share some similarities with those in one of the firm's newly-developed product categories.

Pictured here are some of the products from Campbell Soup Co.'s new business unit called Packaged Fresh.

Campbell Soup Company

In contrast to Campbell Soup, Samsung Group, a huge conglomerate, uses an unrelated diversification strategy to further diversify its operations. Headquartered in Suwon, South Korean, Samsung's portfolio recently included almost 70 companies competing in unrelated areas such as electronics, construction, life insurance, and fashion. It is South Korea's largest chaebol, or business conglomerate. Samsung Electronics, one of the firm's three core units, features three businesses that are well known to consumers throughout the world—mobile devices such as smartphones, consumer electronics (televisions and home appliances), and electronics components such as semiconductors and display panels. With roughly $56 billion in cash in mid-2015, Samsung intended to use some of this cash to complete what one observer called a "string of seemingly unrelated M&A deals." A printing-solutions company, a mobile payments start-up firm, and a battery-making affiliate are three recent acquisitions that appear to have the potential to increase the firm's level of diversification as it enters new competitive arenas.[41]

Firms using acquisition strategies should be aware that, in general, the more related the acquired firm is to the acquiring firm, the greater is the probability that the acquisition will be successful.[42] Thus, horizontal acquisitions and related acquisitions tend to contribute more to the firm's strategic competitiveness than do acquisitions of companies operating in product markets that differ from those in which the acquiring firm competes. Nonetheless, the unrelated diversification strategy, such as the one Samsung is implementing, can also lead to success when used in ways that enhance firm value.

7-2f   Reshaping the Firm's Competitive Scope

As discussed in Chapter 2, the intensity of competitive rivalry is an industry characteristic that affects a firm's profitability.[43] To reduce the negative effect of an intense rivalry on financial performance, firms may use acquisitions to lessen their product and/or market dependencies. Reducing a company's dependence on specific products or markets shapes the firm's competitive scope. For example, Campbell Soup's intention to increase its position in organic foods in its new Packaged Fresh unit reduces its dependence on traditional and nongrowth areas such as soups. If Campbell continues to emphasize its Packaged Fresh units, perhaps through internal growth as well as acquisitions, the firm's competitive scope will change.

7-2g   Learning and Developing New Capabilities

Firms sometimes complete acquisitions to gain access to capabilities they lack. Research shows that firms can broaden their knowledge base and reduce inertia through acquisitions[44] and that they increase the potential of their capabilities when they acquire diverse talent through cross-border acquisitions.[45] Of course, firms are better able to learn these acquired capabilities if they share some similar properties with the firm's current capabilities. Thus, firms should seek to acquire companies with different but related and complementary capabilities as a path to building their own knowledge base.

CenturyLink is a U.S.-based, multinational, communications corporation. The firm provides communications and data services to businesses, governmental agencies, and residential homes. With a focus on developing its capabilities to serve customers' needs for large-scale big data analytics, CenturyLink recently acquired Orchestrate, a firm that "offers a fully managed database service for rapid application development." The acquisition strengthened CenturyLink's cloud platform capabilities, primarily by integrating Orchestrate's experienced data services team with CenturyLink's own product development and technology organization.[46] By integrating their capabilities, the firms hope that they are enhancing their learning capabilities as a path to better serving customers dealing with big data analytics.

7-3 Problems in Achieving Acquisition Success

Effective and appropriate use of the acquisition strategies discussed in this chapter can facilitate firms' efforts to earn above-average returns. However, even when pursued for value-creating reasons, acquisition strategies are not problem-free. Reasons for the use of acquisition strategies and potential problems with such strategies are shown in Figure 7.1.

Figure 7.1 Reasons for Acquisitions and Problems in Achieving Success

Reasons for Acquisitions	Problems in Achieving Success
Increased market power	Integration difficulties
Overcoming entry barriers	Inadequate evaluation of target
Cost of new product development and increased speed to market	Large or extraordinary debt
Lower risk compared to developing new products	Inability to achieve synergy
Increased diversification	Too much diversification
Reshaping the firm's competitive scope	Managers overly focused on acquisitions
Learning and developing new capabilities	Too large

Table 7.1 Attributes of Successful Acquisitions

Attributes	Results
1. Acquired firm has assets or resources that are complementary to the acquiring firm's core business	1. High probability of synergy and competitive advantage by maintaining strengths
2. Acquisition is friendly	2. Faster and more effective integration and possibly lower premiums
3. Acquiring firm conducts effective due diligence to select target firms and evaluate the target firm's health (financial, cultural, and human resources)	3. Firms with strongest complementarities are acquired and overpayment is avoided
4. Acquiring firm has financial slack (cash or a favorable debt position)	4. Financing (debt or equity) is easier and less costly to obtain
5. Merged firm maintains low to moderate debt position	5. Lower financing cost, lower risk (e.g., of bankruptcy), and avoidance of trade-offs that are associated with high debt
6. Acquiring firm has a sustained and consistent emphasis on R&D and innovation	6. Maintain long-term competitive advantage in markets
7. Acquiring firm manages change well and is flexible and adaptable	7. Faster and more effective integration facilitates achievement of synergy

Research suggests that perhaps 20 percent of mergers and acquisitions are successful, approximately 60 percent produce disappointing results, and the remaining 20 percent are clear failures; and evidence suggests that technology acquisitions have even higher failure rates.[47] In general, though, companies appear to be increasing their ability to achieve success with acquisition strategies. Later, we discuss a number of attributes that are associated with successful acquisitions (the attributes appear in Table 7.1). In spite of this increasing success, firms using acquisition strategies should be aware of problems that tend to affect acquisition success when problems do surface. We show these problems in Figure 7.1 and discuss them next.

7-3a   Integration Difficulties

The importance of a successful integration should not be underestimated.[48] Indeed, some believe that the integration process is the strongest determinant of whether either a merger or an acquisition will be successful. This belief highlights the fact that post-acquisition integration is often a complex set of organizational processes that is difficult and challenging. The processes tend to generate uncertainty and often resistance because of cultural clashes and organizational politics.[49] How people are treated during the integration process relative to perceptions of fairness is an important issue to consider when trying to integrate the acquiring and acquired firms. Among the challenges associated with integration processes are the need to:

- meld two or more unique corporate cultures
- link different financial and control systems
- build effective working relationships (particularly when management styles differ)
- determine the leadership structure and those who will fill it for the integrated firm.[50]

These types of challenges, and others as well, may affect Nokia's proposed acquisition of Alcatel-Lucent.

In mid-2015, Finnish telecommunications company Nokia was in advanced talks to acquire its French Rival Alcatel-Lucent. If completed, the transaction would create the second largest mobile equipment manufacturer in the world. Benefits sought through this acquisition included those of giving Nokia a stronger position in the United States, creating synergy through cost reductions achieved by eliminating duplicative processes and operations, and increasing the newly-formed firm's pricing power, partly as a result of its size. The reaction to the proposed transaction was generally positive, with one analyst suggesting that being left to fend for themselves as independent firms and "as subscale players in a fiercely competitive market (was), arguably, a worse alternative" compared to completing the acquisition.[51]

In spite of the overall positive reaction to the proposed transaction, concerns were simultaneously raised about how effectively Nokia and Alcatel-Lucent would be able to complete the integration process. Highlighting this matter, one analyst said that the implementation of the acquisition would be much "messier" than would structuring the deal's finances. Among the issues associated with integration were those related to the fact that telecommunications' firms are "notoriously difficult to integrate" and the need to carefully involve customers with the combined firm's efforts to integrate the two firms' different operating platforms. Given that both firms had been independently trying to restructure prior to the announced acquisition, others wondered if the anticipated cost savings were overly optimistic.[52] Thus, those involved with integrating Nokia and Alcatel-Lucent seem to be facing integration-related challenges.

7-3b   Inadequate Evaluation of Target

Due diligence is a process through which a potential acquirer evaluates a target firm for acquisition. In an effective due-diligence process, hundreds of items are examined in areas as diverse as the financing for the intended transaction, differences in cultures between the acquiring and target firm, tax consequences of the transaction, and actions that would be necessary to successfully meld the two workforces. Due diligence is commonly performed by investment bankers such as Deutsche Bank, Goldman Sachs, and Morgan Stanley, as well as accountants, lawyers, and management consultants specializing in that activity, although firms actively pursuing acquisitions may form their own internal due-diligence team. Even in instances when a company does its own due diligence, companies almost always work with intermediaries such as large investment banks to facilitate their due-diligence efforts. Interestingly, research suggests that acquisition performance increases with the number of due-diligence–related transactions facilitated by an investment bank, but decreases when the relationship with a particular investment bank becomes exclusive.[53] Thus, using investment banks as part of the due-diligence process a firm completes to examine a proposed merger or acquisition is a complex matter requiring careful managerial attention.

As noted earlier in the chapter, the due diligence Caterpillar performed prior to acquiring Chinese firm Siwei was inadequate and ineffective. Although due diligence often focuses on evaluating the accuracy of the financial position and accounting standards used (a financial audit), due diligence also needs to examine the quality of the strategic fit and the ability of the acquiring firm to effectively integrate the target to realize the potential gains from the deal.[54] A comprehensive due-diligence process reduces the likelihood an acquiring firm will have the experience Caterpillar did as a result of acquiring Siwei.

Early evidence suggests that French IT services company Cap Gemini S.A. completed an effective due-diligence process prior to deciding to spend $4.04 billion to acquire U.S.-based iGate Corporation. At the time, this was the 10th largest acquisition of a U.S.-based technology firm by a European company. Noting that the deal made sense for both parties largely because of complementarities in their businesses and the positive nature of the transaction from a financial perspective, analysts felt that there was a strong fit between the firms and that the acquisition had a strong strategic rationale for Cap Gemini.

In this respect, one observer said that "the added huge bonus for Cap Gemini is that it gives them, in one move, a great presence and foothold in the U.S. market, which has always been a challenge for them as a Europe-centric provider. This boosts their presence and revenue in the largest market for global sourcing and gives them a credible offering for the U.S. market."[55] Even with these positives, the firms will have to work diligently to avoid problems during the integration process.

Commonly, firms are willing to pay a premium to acquire a company they believe will increase their ability to earn above-average returns. Determining the precise premium that is appropriate to pay is challenging. While the acquirer can estimate the value of anticipated synergies, it is just that—an estimate. Only after working to integrate the firms and then engaging in competitive actions in the marketplace will the absolute value of synergies be known.

When firms overestimate the value of synergies or the value of future growth potential associated with an acquisition, the premium they pay may prove to be too large. Excessive premiums can have dilutive effects on the newly formed firm's short- and long-term earning potential. In November 2011, for example, Gilead Sciences paid an 89 percent premium to acquire Pharmasset.[56] At first glance, this premium seems excessive. However, since the acquisition was completed, Gilead's stock price has soared. Moreover, the firm's hepatitis C drug franchise, to which Gilead obtain access by acquiring Pharmasset, reached sales of $12.4 billion in 2014 and was seen as a huge success. In this instance then, it seems that the premium Gilead paid to acquire Pharmasset was not excessive. The managerial challenge is to effectively examine each acquisition target for the purpose of determining the amount of premium that is appropriate for the acquiring firm to pay.

7-3c Large or Extraordinary Debt

To finance a number of acquisitions completed during the 1980s and 1990s, some companies significantly increased their debt levels. Although firms today are more prudent about the amount of debt they'll accept to complete an acquisition, those evaluating the possibility of an acquisition for their company need to be aware of the problem that taking on too much debt can create. In this sense, firms using an acquisition strategy want to verify that their purchases do not create a debt load that overpowers their ability to remain solvent and vibrant as a competitor.

A financial innovation called junk bonds supported firms' earlier efforts to take on large amounts of debt when completing acquisitions. *Junk bonds*, which are used less frequently today and are now more commonly called high-yield bonds, are a financing option through which risky acquisitions are financed with money (debt) that provides a large potential return to lenders (bondholders). Because junk bonds are unsecured obligations that are not tied to specific assets for collateral, interest rates for these high-risk debt instruments sometimes reached between 18 and 20 percent during the 1980s.[57] Additionally, interest rates for these types of bonds tend to be quite volatile, a condition that potentially exposes companies to greater financial risk.[58] Some prominent financial economists viewed debt as a means to discipline managers, causing the managers to act in the shareholders' best interests.[59] Managers adopting this perspective are less concerned about the amount of debt their firm assumes when acquiring other companies. However, the perspective that debt disciplines managers is not as widely supported today as was the case in the past.[60]

Bidding wars, through which an acquiring firm overcommits to the decision to acquire a target, can result in large or extraordinary debt. While finance theory suggests that managers will make rational decisions when seeking to complete an acquisition, other research suggests that rationality may not always drive the acquisition decision. Hubris, escalation of commitment to complete a particular transaction, and self-interest sometimes influence executives to pay a large premium which, in turn, may result in taking on too much debt to acquire a target. Executives need to be aware of these possibilities and challenge themselves to engage in rational decision making only when dealing with an acquisition strategy.

7-3d   Inability to Achieve Synergy

Derived from *synergos*, a Greek word that means "working together," *synergy* exists when the value created by units working together exceeds the value that those units could create working independently (see Chapter 6). That is, synergy exists when assets are worth more when used in conjunction with each other than when they are used separately. For shareholders, synergy generates gains in their wealth that they could not duplicate or exceed through their own portfolio diversification decisions.[61] Synergy is created by the efficiencies derived from economies of scale and economies of scope and by sharing resources (e.g., human capital and knowledge) across the businesses in the newly created firm's portfolio.[62]

A firm develops a competitive advantage through an acquisition strategy only when a transaction generates private synergy. *Private synergy* is created when combining and integrating the acquiring and acquired firms' assets yield capabilities and core competencies that could not be developed by combining and integrating either firm's assets with another company. Private synergy is possible when firms' assets are complementary in unique ways; that is, the unique type of asset complementarity is not always possible simply by combining two companies' sets of assets with each other.[63] Although difficult to create, the attractiveness of private synergy is that because of its uniqueness, it is difficult for competitors to understand and imitate, meaning that a competitive advantage results for the firms able to create it.

It is possible that Southwest Airlines' acquisition of AirTran has created private synergy. Among other outcomes, this acquisition added 21 cities to Southwest's network; 7 of these are international locations. Previous to the acquisition, Southwest serviced only U.S. cities. In commenting about the results of this transaction, an observer said that "Southwest has done a commendable job integrating AirTran. Southwest smoothly absorbed AirTran's Atlanta operations, making them similar to the rest of its focus cities, rather than remaining a hub."[64] Very importantly, as a firm using the cost leadership strategy, Southwest's integrated cost structure still allows it to have lower costs than its rivals, including JetBlue. The lowest cost position is the firm's competitive advantage. Early financial results are also impressive in that, following the acquisition, Southwest's profit grew from $178 million in 2011 to $421 million in 2012, $754 million in 2013, and $946 million in 2014. Thus, the evidence suggests that the acquiring firm, Southwest, and the acquired firm, AirTran, were able to create private synergy by combing the two firms.

A firm's ability to account for costs that are necessary to create anticipated revenue and cost-based synergies affects its efforts to create private synergy. Firms experience several expenses when seeking to create private synergy through acquisitions. Called transaction costs, these expenses are incurred when firms use acquisition strategies to create synergy.[65] Transaction costs may be direct or indirect. Direct costs include legal fees and charges from investment bankers who complete due diligence for the acquiring firm. Indirect costs include managerial time to evaluate target firms and then to complete negotiations, as well as the loss of key managers and employees following an acquisition.[66] After acquiring Canadian-based Wheels Group Inc., Radiant Logistics' earnings were affected by short-term, nonrecurring transaction costs associated with the acquisition. As a mid-size freight forwarder based in the United States, Radiant acquired Wheels in order to extend its "geographic reach and customer bases by consolidating operators in a fragmented market."[67] Company officials expected the newly formed firm to quickly return to profitability following payment of the nonrecurring acquisition costs. Firms tend to underestimate the sum of indirect costs when specifying the value of the synergy that may be created by integrating the acquired firm's assets with the acquiring firm's assets.

7-3e   Too Much Diversification

As explained in Chapter 6, diversification strategies, when used effectively, can help a firm earn above-average returns. In general, firms using related diversification strategies outperform those employing unrelated diversification strategies. However, conglomerates formed by using an unrelated diversification strategy also can be successful.

At some point, however, firms can become overdiversified. The level at which this happens varies across companies because each firm has different capabilities to manage diversification. Recall from Chapter 6 that related diversification requires more information processing than does unrelated diversification. Because of this need to process additional amounts of information, related diversified firms become overdiversified with a smaller number of business units than do firms using an unrelated diversification strategy.[68] Regardless of the type of diversification strategy implemented, however, the firm that becomes overdiversified will experience a decline in its performance and likely a decision to divest some of its units.[69] Commonly, such divestments, which tend to reshape a firm's competitive scope, are part of a firm's restructuring strategy. (Restructuring is discussed in greater detail later in the chapter.)

Even when a firm is not overdiversified, a high level of diversification can have a negative effect on its long-term performance. For example, the scope created by additional amounts of diversification often causes managers to rely on financial rather than strategic controls to evaluate business units' performance (financial and strategic controls are discussed in Chapters 11 and 12). Top-level executives often rely on financial controls to assess the performance of business units when they do not have a rich understanding of business units' objectives and strategies. Using financial controls, such as return on investment (ROI), causes individual business-unit managers to focus on short-term outcomes at the expense of long-term investments. Reducing long-term investments to generate short-term profits can negatively affect a firm's overall performance ability.[70]

Another problem resulting from overdiversification is the tendency for acquisitions to become substitutes for innovation. Typically, managers have no interest in acquisitions substituting for internal R&D efforts; however, a reinforcing cycle evolves. Costs associated with acquisitions may result in fewer allocations to activities, such as R&D, that are linked to innovation. Without adequate support, a firm's innovation skills begin to atrophy. Without internal innovation skills, a key option available to a firm to gain access to innovation is to complete additional acquisitions. Evidence suggests that a firm using acquisitions as a substitute for internal innovations eventually encounters performance problems.[71]

7-3f   Managers Overly Focused on Acquisitions

Typically, a considerable amount of managerial time and energy is required for acquisition strategies to be used successfully. Activities with which managers become involved include:

- searching for viable acquisition candidates
- completing effective due-diligence processes
- preparing for negotiations
- managing the integration process after completing the acquisition

Top-level managers do not personally gather all of the information and data required to make acquisitions. However, these executives do make critical decisions regarding the firms to be targeted, the nature of the negotiations, and so forth. Company experiences show that participating in and overseeing the activities required for making acquisitions can divert managerial attention from other matters that are necessary for long-term competitive success, such as identifying and taking advantage of other opportunities and interacting with important external stakeholders.[72]

Both theory and research suggest that managers can become overly involved in the process of making acquisitions.[73] One observer suggested, "some executives can become preoccupied with making deals—and the thrill of selecting, chasing, and seizing a target."[74] The over-involvement can be surmounted by learning from mistakes and by not having too much agreement in the boardroom. Dissent is helpful to make sure that all sides of a question are considered. For example, research suggests that there may be group bias in the decision making of boards of directors regarding acquisitions. The research suggests that possible group polarization leads to either higher premiums paid or lower premiums paid after group discussions about potential premiums for target firms.[75] When failure does occur, leaders may be tempted to blame the failure on others and on unforeseen circumstances rather than on their excessive involvement in the acquisition process. Finding the appropriate degree of involvement with the firm's acquisition strategy is a challenging, yet important, task for top-level managers.

7-3g   Too Large

Most acquisitions result in a larger firm, which should create or enhance economies of scale. In turn, scale economies can lead to more efficient operations—for example, two sales organizations can be integrated using fewer sales representatives because the combined sales force can sell the products of both firms (particularly if the products of the acquiring and target firms are highly related).[76] However, size can also increase the complexity of the managerial challenge and create diseconomies of scope; that is, not enough economic benefit to outweigh the costs of managing the more complex organization created through acquisitions.

Thus, while many firms seek increases in size because of the potential economies of scale and enhanced market power size creates, at some level, the additional costs required to manage the larger firm will exceed the benefits of the economies of scale and additional market power. The complexities generated by the larger size often lead managers to implement more bureaucratic controls to manage the combined firm's operations. *Bureaucratic controls* are formalized supervisory and behavioral rules and policies designed to ensure consistency of decisions and actions across a firm's units. However, across time, formalized controls often lead to relatively rigid and standardized managerial behavior.[77] Certainly, in the long run, the diminished flexibility that accompanies rigid and standardized managerial behavior may produce less innovation. Because of innovation's importance to competitive success, the bureaucratic controls resulting from a large organization that might be built at least in part by using an acquisition strategy can negatively affect a firm's performance. Thus, managers may decide their firm should complete acquisitions in the pursuit of increased size as a path to profitable growth. At the same time, managers should avoid allowing their firm to get to a point where acquisitions are creating a degree of size that increases its inefficiency and ineffectiveness.

7-4   Effective Acquisitions

As we've noted, acquisition strategies do not always lead to above-average returns for the acquiring firm's shareholders.[78] Nonetheless, some companies are able to create value when using an acquisition strategy.[79] Research evidence suggests that the probability of being able to create value through acquisitions increases when the nature of the acquisition and the processes used to complete it are consistent with the "attributes of successful acquisitions" shown in Table 7.1.[80] For example, when the target firm's assets are complementary to the acquired firm's assets, an acquisition is more successful. With complementary assets, the integration of two firms' operations has a higher probability of creating synergy. In fact, integrating two firms with complementary assets frequently produces unique capabilities and core competencies. With complementary assets, the acquiring firm can maintain its focus on core businesses and leverage the complementary assets and capabilities from the acquired firm. In effective acquisitions, targets are often selected and "groomed" by establishing a working relationship prior to the acquisition.[81] As discussed in Chapter 9, firms sometimes form strategic alliances to test the feasibility of a future merger or acquisition between them, an experience that can also contribute to acquisition success.

Research evidence also shows that friendly acquisitions facilitate integration of the acquiring and acquired firms. Of course, a target firm's positive reaction to a bid from the acquiring firm increases the likelihood that a friendly transaction will take place. For example, AdvancedCath responded positively to being acquired by TE Connectivity, a world leader in designing and managing highly-engineered connectors, sensors, and electronic components that are sold to manufacturers who integrate them into their products. AdvancedCath is a leading source of catheter systems, products that complement those included in TE's Medical business unit. Commenting about the value the acquisition creates for his firm, AdvancedCath's CEO said that "with TE's global footprint, we can provide better support to our global customers as they progress through development, clinical trials, and volume manufacturing."[82] After completing a friendly acquisition, firms collaborate to create synergy while integration their operations.[83] This is in contrast to hostile takeovers, situations in which common disagreements, such as those concerned with the combined firm's leadership structure and operational methods that will be used in the newly created firm, strongly increase the difficulty associated with attempts to create synergy through the integration process.

Additionally, effective due-diligence processes involving the deliberate and careful selection of target firms and an evaluation of the relative health of those firms (financial health, cultural fit, and the value of human resources) contribute to successful acquisitions.[84] Financial slack in the form of debt equity or cash, in both the acquiring and acquired firms, also frequently contributes to acquisition success. Even though financial slack provides access to financing for the acquisition, it is still important to maintain a low or moderate level of debt after the acquisition to keep debt costs low. When substantial debt is used to finance acquisitions, companies with successful acquisitions reduce the debt quickly, partly by selling off assets from the acquired firm, especially noncomplementary or poorly performing assets. For these firms, debt costs do not preclude long-term investments in areas such as R&D, and managerial discretion in the use of cash flow is relatively flexible.

Another attribute of successful acquisition strategies is an emphasis on innovation, as demonstrated by continuing investments in R&D activities.[85] Innovation is critical to the anticipated success of Nokia's proposed acquisition of Alcatel-Lucent. According to Nokia officials, "the combined company will have unparalleled innovation capabilities, with Alcatel-Lucent's Bell Labs and Nokia's FutureWorks as well as Nokia Technologies." The initial combination of the two firms would create a R&D staff in excess of 40,000 with an allocation of EUR 4.7 billion in R&D in the first year.[86] Thus, this acquisition appears to satisfy the criterion of emphasizing innovation in a newly created firm.

Flexibility and adaptability are the final two attributes of successful acquisitions. When executives of both the acquiring and the target firms have experience in managing change and learning from acquisitions, they are more skilled at adapting their capabilities to new environments.[87] As a result, they are more adept at integrating the two organizations, which is particularly important when firms have different organizational cultures.

As we have explained, firms using an acquisition strategy seek to create wealth and earn above-average returns. Sometimes, though, the results of an acquisition strategy fall short of expectations. When this happens, firms consider using restructuring strategies.

7-5   Restructuring

Restructuring is a strategy through which a firm changes its set of businesses or its financial structure.[88] Restructuring is a global phenomenon.[89] Historically, divesting businesses from company portfolios and downsizing have accounted for a large percentage of firms' restructuring strategies. Commonly, firms focus on fewer products and markets following restructuring.

Although restructuring strategies are generally used to deal with acquisitions that are not reaching expectations, firms sometimes use restructuring strategies because of changes they have detected in their external environment. For example, opportunities sometimes surface in a firm's external environment that a diversified firm can pursue because of the capabilities it has formed by integrating firms' operations. In such cases, restructuring may be appropriate to position the firm to create more value for stakeholders, given environmental changes and the opportunities associated with them.[90]

As discussed next, firms use three types of restructuring strategies: downsizing, downscoping, and leveraged buyouts.

7-5a   Downsizing

Downsizing is a reduction in the number of a firm's employees and, sometimes, in the number of its operating units; but, the composition of businesses in the company's portfolio may not change through downsizing. Thus, downsizing is an intentional managerial strategy that is used for the purpose of improving firm performance. In contrast, organizational decline, which too often results in a reduction of a firm's resources including the number of its employees and potentially in the number of its units, is an unintentional outcome of what turned out to be a firm's ineffective competitive actions.[91] When downsizing, firms make intentional decisions about resources to retain and resources to eliminate. Organizational decline however, finds firms losing access to an array of resources, many of which are critical to current and future performance. Thus, downsizing is a legitimate strategy and is not necessarily a sign of organizational decline.[92]

Downsizing can be an appropriate strategy to use after completing an acquisition, particularly when there are significant operational and/or strategic relationships between the acquiring and the acquired firm. In these instances, the newly formed firm may have excess capacity in functional areas such as sales, manufacturing, distribution, human resource management, and so forth. In turn, excess capacity may prevent the combined firm from realizing anticipated synergies and the reduced costs associated with them.[93] Managers should remember that, as a strategy, downsizing will be far more effective when they consistently use human resource practices that ensure procedural justice and fairness in downsizing decisions.[94]

7-5b   Downscoping

Downscoping refers to divestiture, spin-off, or some other means of eliminating businesses that are unrelated to a firm's core businesses. Downscoping has a more positive effect on firm performance than does downsizing[95] because firms commonly find that

Restructuring is a strategy through which a firm changes its set of businesses or its financial structure.

downscoping causes them to refocus on their core business.[96] Managerial effectiveness increases because the firm has become less diversified, allowing the top management team to better understand and manage the remaining businesses.[97]

Firms often use the downscoping and downsizing strategies simultaneously. When doing this, firms need to avoid layoffs of key employees, as such layoffs might lead to a loss of one or more core competencies. Instead, a firm that chooses to simultaneously engage in downscoping and downsizing should intentionally become smaller as a result of decisions made to reduce the diversity of businesses in its portfolio, allowing it to focus on its core areas as a result.[98]

In general, U.S. firms use downscoping as a restructuring strategy more frequently than do European companies—in fact, the trend not too long ago in Europe, Latin America, and Asia was to build conglomerates. In Latin America, these conglomerates are called *grupos*. More recently though, many Asian and Latin American conglomerates have chosen to downscope their operations as a path to refocusing on their core businesses. This recent downscoping trend has occurred simultaneously with increasing globalization and with more open markets that have greatly enhanced competition.[99]

7-5c   Leveraged Buyouts

A *leveraged buyout* (LBO) is a restructuring strategy whereby a party (typically a private equity firm) buys all of a firm's assets in order to take the firm private.[100] Once a private equity firm completes this type of transaction, the target firm's company stock is no longer traded publicly.

Traditionally, leveraged buyouts were used as a restructuring strategy to correct for managerial mistakes or because the firm's managers were making decisions that primarily served their own interests rather than those of shareholders.[101] However, some firms complete leveraged buyouts for the purpose of building firm resources and expanding their operations rather than simply to restructure a distressed firm's assets.

Significant amounts of debt are commonly incurred to finance a buyout; hence, the term *leveraged* buyout. To support debt payments and to downscope the company to concentrate on the firm's core businesses, the new owners may quickly sell a number of assets. Indeed, it is not uncommon for those buying a firm through an LBO to restructure the firm to the point that it can be sold at a profit within a five- to eight-year period.

Management buyouts (MBOs), employee buyouts (EBOs), and whole-firm buyouts, in which one company or partnership purchases an entire company instead of a part of it, are the three types of LBOs. In part because of managerial incentives, MBOs, more so than EBOs and whole-firm buyouts, have been found to lead to downscoping, increased strategic focus, and improved performance.[102] Research shows that management buyouts can lead to greater entrepreneurial activity and growth.[103] As such, buyouts can represent a form of firm rebirth to facilitate entrepreneurial efforts and stimulate strategic growth and productivity.[104]

7-5d   Restructuring Outcomes

The short- and long-term outcomes that result from use of the three restructuring strategies are shown in Figure 7.2. As indicated, downsizing typically does not lead to higher firm performance.[105] In fact, some research results show that downsizing contributes to lower returns for both U.S. and Japanese firms. The stock markets in the firms' respective nations evaluate downsizing negatively, believing that it has long-term negative effects on the firms' efforts to achieve strategic competitiveness. Investors also seem to conclude that downsizing occurs as a consequence of other problems in a company.[106] This assumption may be caused by a firm's diminished corporate reputation when a major downsizing is announced.[107]

Figure 7.2 Restructuring and Outcomes

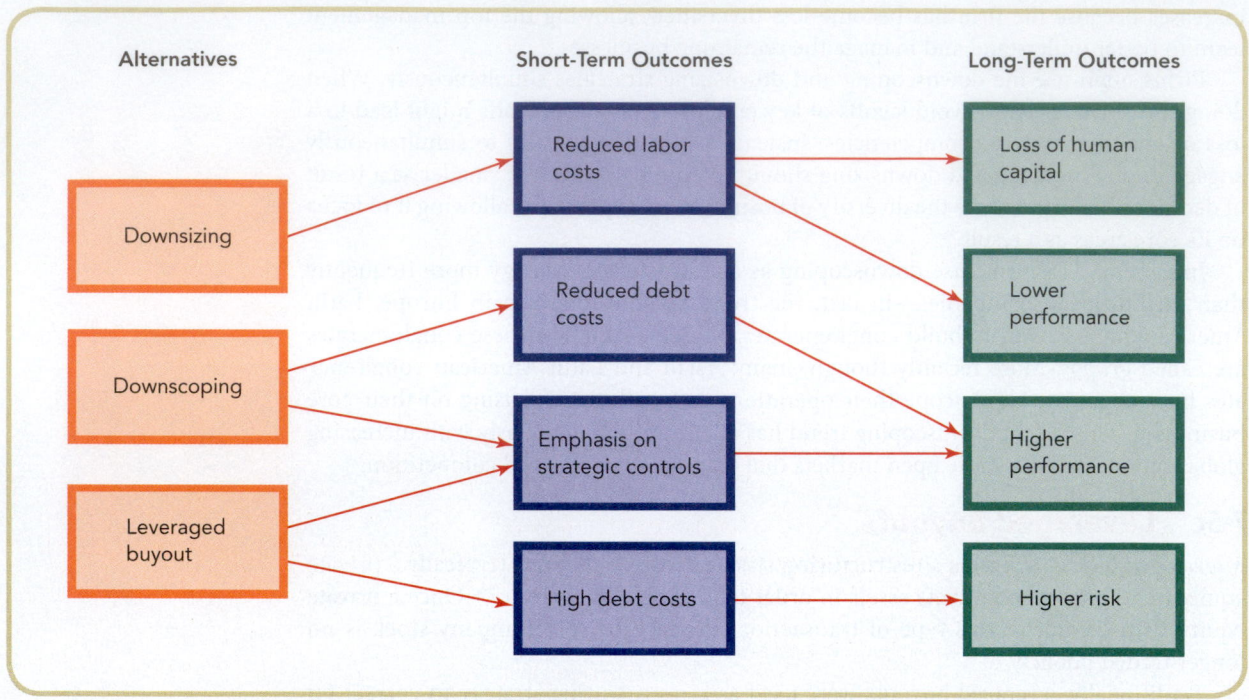

The loss of human capital is another potential problem of downsizing (see Figure 7.2). Losing employees with many years of experience with the firm represents a major loss of knowledge. As noted in Chapter 3, knowledge is vital to competitive success in the global economy. Research also suggests that a loss of valuable human capital can also spill over into dissatisfaction of customers.[108] Thus, in general, downsizing may be of more tactical (or short-term) value than strategic (or long-term) value, meaning that firms should exercise caution when restructuring through downsizing.

Compared to downsizing and leveraged buyouts, downscoping generally leads to more positive outcomes in both the short and long term. Downscoping's desirable long-term outcome of higher performance is a product of reduced debt costs and the emphasis on strategic controls derived from concentrating on the firm's core businesses. In so doing, the refocused firm should be able to increase its ability to compete.[109]

Whole-firm LBOs have been hailed as a significant innovation in the financial restructuring of firms. However, this type of restructuring can be complicated, especially when cross-border transactions are involved[110]; moreover, they can involve negative trade-offs.[111] First, the resulting large debt increases the firm's financial risk, as is evidenced by the number of companies that filed for bankruptcy in the 1990s after executing a whole-firm LBO. Sometimes, the intent of the owners to increase the efficiency of the acquired firm and then sell it within five to eight years creates a short-term and risk-averse managerial focus.[112] As a result, these firms may fail to invest adequately in R&D or take other major actions designed to maintain or improve the company's ability to compete successfully against rivals.[113] Because buyouts more often result in significant debt, most LBOs have been completed in mature industries where stable cash flows are the norm. Stable cash flows support the purchaser's efforts to service the debt obligations assumed as a result of taking a firm private.

SUMMARY

◼ Mergers and acquisitions as a strategy are popular for companies based in countries throughout the world. Through this strategy, firms seek to create value and outperform rivals. Globalization and deregulation of multiple industries in many of the world's economies are two of the reasons for this popularity among both large and small firms.

◼ Firms use acquisition strategies to

  ◼ increase market power

  ◼ overcome entry barriers to new markets or regions

  ◼ avoid the costs of developing new products and increase the speed of new market entries

  ◼ reduce the risk of entering a new business

  ◼ become more diversified

  ◼ reshape their competitive scope by developing a different portfolio of businesses

  ◼ enhance their learning as the foundation for developing new capabilities

◼ Among the problems associated with using an acquisition strategy are

  ◼ the difficulty of effectively integrating the firms involved

  ◼ incorrectly evaluating the target firm's value

  ◼ creating debt loads that preclude adequate long-term investments (e.g., R&D)

  ◼ overestimating the potential for synergy

  ◼ creating a firm that is too diversified

  ◼ creating an internal environment in which managers devote increasing amounts of their time and energy to analyzing and completing the acquisition

  ◼ developing a combined firm that is too large, necessitating extensive use of bureaucratic, rather than strategic, controls

◼ Effective acquisitions have the following characteristics:

  ◼ the acquiring and target firms have complementary resources that are the foundation for developing new capabilities

  ◼ the acquisition is friendly, thereby facilitating integration of the firms' resources

  ◼ the target firm is selected and purchased on the basis of completing a thorough due-diligence process

  ◼ the acquiring and target firms have considerable slack in the form of cash or debt capacity

  ◼ the newly formed firm maintains a low or moderate level of debt by selling off portions of the acquired firm or some of the acquiring firm's poorly performing units

  ◼ the acquiring and acquired firms have experience in terms of adapting to change

  ◼ R&D and innovation are emphasized in the new firm

◼ Restructuring is used to improve a firm's performance by correcting for problems created by ineffective management. Restructuring by downsizing involves reducing the number of employees and hierarchical levels in the firm. Although it can lead to short-term cost reductions, the reductions may be realized at the expense of long-term success because of the loss of valuable human resources (and knowledge) and overall corporate reputation.

◼ The goal of restructuring through downscoping is to reduce the firm's level of diversification. Often, the firm divests unrelated businesses to achieve this goal. Eliminating unrelated businesses makes it easier for the firm and its top-level managers to refocus on the core businesses.

◼ Through a leveraged buyout (an LBO), a firm is purchased so that it can become a private entity. LBOs usually are financed largely through debt, although limited partners (institutional investors) are becoming more prominent. General partners have a variety of strategies, and some emphasize equity versus debt when limited partners have a longer time horizon. Management buyouts (MBOs), employee buyouts (EBOs), and whole-firm LBOs are the three types of LBOs. Because they provide clear managerial incentives, MBOs have been the most successful of the three. Often, the intent of a buyout is to improve efficiency and performance to the point where the firm can be sold successfully within five to eight years.

◼ Commonly, restructuring's primary goal is gaining or reestablishing effective strategic control of the firm. Of the three restructuring strategies, downscoping is aligned most closely with establishing and using strategic controls and usually improves performance more on a comparative basis.

KEY TERMS

acquisition 208
merger 207

restructuring 224
takeover 208

REVIEW QUESTIONS

1. Why are merger and acquisition strategies popular in many firms competing in the global economy?

2. What reasons account for firms' decisions to use acquisition strategies as a means to achieving strategic competitiveness?

3. What are the seven primary problems that affect a firm's efforts to successfully use an acquisition strategy?

4. What are the attributes associated with a successful acquisition strategy?

5. What is the restructuring strategy, and what are its common forms?

6. What are the short- and long-term outcomes associated with the different restructuring strategies?

Mini-Case

Strategic Acquisitions and Accelerated Integration of Those Acquisitions are a Vital Capability of Cisco Systems

Cisco Systems is in the business of building the infrastructure that allows the Internet to work. As the Internet evolved, however, Cisco's business was required to change with this evolution. As part of its advancement, Cisco Systems has used an acquisition strategy to build network products and extend its reach into new areas, both related and unrelated. In the beginning, digital connectivity was important through e-mail and Web browsing and searches. This evolved into a network economy facilitating e-commerce, digital supply chains, and digital collaboration. Subsequently, the digital interaction phase moved Cisco into developing infrastructure for social media, mobile and cloud computing, and digital video. The next stage seems to be "the Internet of everything" connecting people, processes, and data. This will require the basic core in routing, switching, and services, as well as large data centers to facilitate visualization through cloud computing. Video and collaboration as well as basic architecture of the business will be transforming to become the base strategic business blocks. Furthermore, the need to have strong digital security will be paramount.

Cisco has entered many aspects of the business in which it competes through acquisitions. For instance, in 2012, Cisco acquired TV software developer NDS for $5 billion. NDS Group develops software for television networks. In particular, its solutions allow pay-TV providers to deliver digital content to TVs, DVRs, PCs, and other multimedia devices. It provides solutions that protect digital content so that only paid subscribers can access it. Because of Cisco's customer-driven focus, it has sought to help its customers capture these market transitions and meet their particular needs. Of course, Cisco also builds the routers that allow video data and e-mail communications to come together through their blade servers (individual and modular servers that cut down on cabling). These routers and servers support cloud computing for the mobile devices that deliver the video that NDS software enables on desktop and mobile devices.

Also in 2012, Cisco purchased Meraki for $1.2 billion. Meraki provides solutions that optimize services in the cloud. For instance, it offers mid-sized customers Wi-Fi, switching, security, and mobile device management centrally from a set of cloud servers. For instance, if you are a guest at a university or other company campus it supports, you can bring your own personal device into the network, which allows guest networking and facilitates application controls. It manages the firewall and other advanced networking services to protect security as well.

John Chambers, Cisco CEO, has helped the firm move through the many transitions noted earlier. In the IT sector, 90 percent of acquisitions fail. However, as Chambers notes, "although Cisco does better than anyone else, we know that a third of our acquisitions won't work." Chambers worked for companies that did not successfully make transitions. Wang Laboratories missed a transition, and after experiencing this as an executive, Chambers learned to have a "healthy paranoia." He adds, "more than anything, I've tried to make Cisco a company that can see big transitions and move." One way they do this is to "listen to the customers very closely" to understand the necessary changes.

As Cisco makes the transition into the all-everything network, not only must it manage the cloud, but it also must provide service to the mobile devices that work in cellular networks. Accordingly, Cisco also acquired Intucell, a self-optimizing network software developer, for $475 million. It likewise acquired Truviso, Inc., a provider of network data analysis and reporting software, for an undisclosed price (Truviso was partly owned by venture capital firms and was headquartered in Israel). Most recently, Cisco acquired Ubiquisys, which cuts cellular carriers' costs "by shifting traffic from congested towers to more targeted locations inside an office, home or public space, which also boosts the service's reliability." This shifting-traffic approach is especially efficient when seeking to improve "coverage in crowded areas such as stadiums, convention centers and subway stations." These acquisitions help cellular network customers manage their products in the network more efficiently in the delivery of data, e-mail, and video services. As you can see, for this series of acquisitions, Cisco has used acquisitions strategically to move into new areas as its environment changes, to learn about new technologies, and to gain knowledge on new technologies as it experiences these transitions.

In the process of this rapid change, Cisco has developed a distinct ability to integrate acquisitions. When Cisco contemplates an acquisition, along with financial due diligence to make sure that it is paying the right price, it develops a detailed plan for possible post-merger integration. It begins communicating early with stakeholders about integration plans and conducts rigorous post-mortems to identify ways "to make subsequent integrations more efficient and effective." Once a deal is completed, this allows the company to hit the ground running when the deal becomes public. Cisco is ready "from Day 1 to explain how the two companies are going to come together and provide unique value and how the integration effort itself will be structured to realize value." The firm does not "want the [acquired] organization to go in limbo," which can happen if the integration process is not well thought out. Also, during the integration process, it is important to know how far the integration should go. Sometimes integration is too deep, and value that was being sought in the acquisition is destroyed. Sometimes it may even pay to keep the business separate from Cisco's other operations to allow the business to function without integration until the necessary learning is complete. "Cisco learned the hard way that complex deals require you to know at a high level of detail how you're going to drive value."

Sources: L. Capron, 2013, Cisco's corporate development portfolio: A blend of building, borrowing, and buying, *Strategy & Leadership*, 41(2): 27–30; D. FitzGerald & S. Chaudhuri, 2013, Corporate news: Cisco doubles down on small-cell transmitters with Ubiquisys, *Wall Street Journal*, April 4, B7; T. Geron, 2012, Meraki-Cisco deal a boost for Sequoia, Google-connected VCs, *Forbes*, November 19, 18; R. Karlgaard, 2012, Cisco's Chambers: Driving change, *Forbes*, February 22, 68; A. Moscaritolo, 2012, Cisco to acquire TV software developer NDS for $5 billion, *PC Magazine*, March 1; B. Worthern, D. Cimilluca, & A. Das, 2012, Cisco hedges bet on video delivery, *Wall Street Journal*, March 16, B1; R. Myers, 2011, Integration acceleration, *CFO*, 27: 52–57.

Case Discussion Questions

1. Of the "Reasons for Acquisitions" section in the chapter, which reasons are the primary drivers of Cisco's acquisition strategy?

2. Of the acquisitions Cisco has completed, which ones are horizontal acquisitions and which ones are vertical acquisitions? Which of these acquisitions do you believe have the strongest likelihood of being successful and why?

3. Explain John Chambers' views about acquisitions. How have his views affected the nature of Cisco's acquisition strategy?

4. Describe the core plan Cisco has in place to guide the integration of an acquired firm into its operations. What are the strengths of this plan, and what are its potential weaknesses?

NOTES

1. M. Menz, S. Kunisch, & D. J. Collis, 2015, The corporate headquarters in the contemporary corporation: Advancing a multimarket firm perspective, *Academy of Management Annals*, 9: 633–714; M. Gruber, I. C. MacMillan, & J. D. Thompson, 2012, From minds to markets: How human capital endowments shape market opportunity identification of technology start-ups, *Journal of Management*, 38: 1421–1449; D. J. Teece, 2010, Alfred Chandler and "capabilities" theories of strategy and management, *Industrial and Corporate Change*, 19: 297–316.

2. R. Ragozzino & D. P. Blevins, 2015, Venture-backed firms: How does venture capital involvement affect their likelihood of going public or being acquired? *Entrepreneurship Theory and Practice*, in press; H. R. Greve, 2011, Positional rigidity: Low performance and resource acquisition in large and small firms, *Strategic Management Journal*, 32: 103–114; R. Ragozzino & J. J. Reuer, 2010, The opportunities and challenges of entrepreneurial acquisitions, *European Management Review*, 70: 80–90.

3. P.-X. Meschi & E. Metais, 2015, Too big to learn: The effects of major acquisition failures on subsequent acquisition divestment, *British Journal of Management*, in press; K. Muehlfeld, P. Rao Sahib, & A. Van Witteloostuijn, 2012, A contextual theory of organizational learning from failures and successes: A study of acquisition completion in the global newspaper industry, 1981–2008, *Strategic Management Journal*, 33: 938–964; M. A. Hitt, D. King, H. Krishnan, M. Makri, M. Schijven, K. Shimizu, & H. Zhu, 2009, Mergers and acquisitions: Overcoming pitfalls, building synergy and creating value, *Business Horizons*, 52: 523–529.

4. D. A. Basuil & D. K. Datta, 2015, Effects of industry- and region-specific acquisition experience on value creation in cross-border acquisitions: The moderating role of cultural similarity, *Journal of Management Studies*, in press; A. S. Gaur, S. Malhotra, & P. Zhu, 2013, Acquisition announcements and stock market valuations of acquiring firms' rivals: A test of the growth probability hypothesis in China, *Strategic Management Journal*, 34: 215–232; G. M. McNamara, J. Haleblian, & B. J. Dykes, 2008, The performance implications of participating in an acquisition wave: Early mover advantages, bandwagon effects, and the moderating influence of industry characteristics and acquirer tactics, *Academy of Management Journal*, 51: 113–130.

5. C. Moschieri & J. M. Campa, 2014, New trends in mergers and acquisitions: Idiosyncrasies of the European market, *Journal of Business Research*, 67: 1478–1485; J. J. Reuer, T. W. Tong, & C. Wu, 2012, A signaling theory of acquisition premiums: Evidence from IPO targets, *Academy of Management Journal*, 55: 667–683.

6. J. B. Edwards, 2015, M&A deal-makers are dealing in 2014: A commentary, *Journal of Corporate Accounting & Finance*, 26: 19–24.

7. J. S. Ang & A. K. Ismail, 2015, What premiums do target shareholders expect? Explaining negative returns upon offer announcement, *Journal of Corporate Finance*, 30: 245–256; M. Cornett, B. Tanyeri, & H. Tehranian, 2011, The effect of merger anticipation on bidder and target firm announcement period returns, *Journal of Corporate Finance*, 17: 595–611.

8. A. Kaul & X. (Brian) Wu, 2015, A capabilities-based perspective on target selection in acquisitions, *Strategic Management Journal*, in press; J. Cicon, J. Clarke, S. P. Ferris, & N. Jayaraman, 2014, Managerial expectations of synergy and the performance of acquiring firms: The contribution of soft data, *Journal of Behavioral Finance*, 15: 161–175; J. Sears & G. Hoetker, 2014, Technological overlap, technological capabilities, and resource recombination in technological acquisitions, *Strategic Management Journal*, 35: 48–67.

9. P. Loftus, J. D. Rockoff, & M. Farrell, 2015, Alexion-Synageva deal shows lure of rare-disease drugs, *Wall Street Journal Online*, www.wsj.com, May 6.

10. J.-Y. (Jay) Kim, S. Finkelstein, & J. Haleblian, 2015, All aspirations are not created equal: The differential effects of historical and social aspirations on acquisition behavior, *Academy of Management Journal*, in press; V. Ambrosini, C. Bowman, & R. Schoenberg, 2011, Should acquiring firms pursue more than one value creation strategy? An empirical test of acquisition performance, *British Journal of Management*, 22: 173–185; K. J. Martijn Cremers, V. B. Nair, & K. John, 2009, Takeovers and the cross-section of returns, *Review of Financial Studies*, 22: 1409–1445.

11. J. McKinnon, 2015, Canada's Alamos Gold and AuRico Gold to merge, *Wall Street Journal Online*, www.wsj.com, April 13.

12. M. Curtin, 2015, A 'merger of equals' is more fragile, *Wall Street Journal Online*, www.wsj.com, March 16.

13. N. Aktas, E. Croci, & S. A. Simsir, 2015, Corporate governance and takeover outcomes, *Corporate Governance: An International Review*, in press; M. Humphery-Jenner, 2014, Takeover defenses as drivers of innovation and value-creation, *Strategic Management Journal*, 35: 668–690.

14. R. Barusch, 2015, Dealpolitik: Three ways to look at the three-way pharma scrum, *Wall Street Journal Online*, www.wsj.com, April 23.

15. K. Huschelrath & K. Muller, 2015, Market power, efficiencies, and entry evidence from an airline merger, *Managerial and Decision Economics*, 36: 239–255; J. Garcia-Quevedo, G. Pellegrino, & M. Vivarelli, 2014, R&D drivers and age: Are young firms different? *Research Policy*, 43: 1544–1556.

16. V. Bilotkach & P. A. Lakew, 2014, On sources of market power in the airline industry: Panel data evidence from the US airports, *Transportation Research Part A: Policy and Practice*, 59: 288–305; M. A. Hitt, D. King, H. Krishnan, M. Makri, M. Schijven, K. Shimizu, & H. Zhu, 2012, Creating value through mergers and acquisitions: Challenges and opportunities, in D. Faulkner, S. Teerikangas, & R. Joseph (eds.), *Oxford Handbook of Mergers and Acquisitions*, Oxford, U.K.: Oxford University Press, 71–113; J. Haleblian, C. E. Devers, G. McNamara, M. A. Carpenter, & R. B. Davison, 2009, Taking stock of what we know about mergers and acquisitions: A review and research agenda, *Journal of Management*, 35: 469–502.

17. P. Mourdoukoutas, 2014, Amazon's big problem, *Forbes*, www.forbes.com, May 7.

18. H. Furchtgott-Roth, 2015, Comcast and Time Warner Cable: Autopsy of a failed merger, *Forbes*, www.forbes.com, April 24.

19. D. Burghardt & M. Helm, 2015, Firm growth in the course of mergers and acquisitions, *Small Business Economicx*, 44: 889–904; D. K. Oler, J. S. Harrison, & M. R. Allen, 2008, The danger of misinterpreting short-window event study findings in strategic management research: An empirical illustration using horizontal acquisitions, *Strategic Organization*, 6: 151–184.

20. J. D. Rockoff & J. Walker, 2015, Meet pharma's newest movers and shakers, *Wall Street Journal Online*, www.wsj.com, April 22.

21. W. Moatti, C. R. Ren, J. Anand, & P. Dussauge, 2015, Disentangling the performance effects of efficiency and bargaining power in horizontal growth strategies: An empirical investigation in the global retail industry, *Strategic Management Journal*, 36: 745–757; C. E. Fee & S. Thomas, 2004, Sources of gains in horizontal mergers: Evidence from customer, supplier, and rival firms, *Journal of Financial Economics*, 74: 423–460.

22. T. H. Reus, B. T. Lamont, & K. M. Ellis, 2015, A darker side of knowledge transfer following international acquisitions, *Strategic Management Journal*, in press; G. E. Halkos & N. G. Tzeremes, 2013, Estimating the degree of operational efficiency gains from a potential bank merger and acquisition: A DEA bootstrapped approach, *Journal of*

Banking & Finance, 37: 1658–1668; L. Capron, W. Mitchell, & A. Swaminathan, 2001, Asset divestiture following horizontal acquisitions: A dynamic view, *Strategic Management Journal*, 22: 817–844.

23. C.-H. Chou, 2014, Strategic delegation and vertical integration, *Managerial and Decision Economics*, 35: 580–586; J. Shenoy, 2012, An examination of the efficiency, foreclosure, and collusion rationales for vertical takeovers, *Management Science*, 58: 1482–1501.

24. K. Favaro, 2015, Vertical integration 2.0: An old strategy makes a comeback, *Strategy & Business*, www.strategy-business. com, May 6.

25. N. Wilson, 2014, Nutella maker Ferrero buys Turkey's biggest Hazelnut company, *International Business Times*, www.ibtimes. co/uk, July 7.

26. P. Burrows, 2015, Cisco CEO says company remains in hunt for software makers, *Bloomberg*, www.bloomberg.com, February 19; C. Talbot, 2015, Cisco targets software companies for acquisition, *FierceEnterpriseCommunications*, www. fierceenterprisecommunications.com, February 23.

27. L. Beilfuss, 2015, Scripps Networks profit falls on acquisitions, restructuring costs, *Wall Street Journal Online*, www.wsj.com, May 7.

28. 2015, Scripps Networks Interactive to acquire controlling interest in Polish TV operator TVN, Scripps Networks Interactive Home Page, www. scrippsnetworksinteractive.com, March 16.

29. B. B. Fancis, I. Hasan, X. Sun, & M. Waisman, 2014, Can firms learn by observing? Evidence from cross-border M&As, *Journal of Corporate Finance*, 25: 202–215; I. Erel, R. C. Liao, & M. S. Weisbach, 2012, Determinants of cross-border mergers and acquisitions, *Journal of Finance*, 67: 1045–1082; K. Boeh, 2011, Contracting costs and information asymmetry reduction in cross-border M&A, *Journal of Management Studies*, 48: 568–590; R. Chakrabarti, N. Jayaraman, & S. Mukherjee, 2009, Mars-Venus marriages: Culture and cross-border M&A, *Journal of International Business Studies*, 40: 216–237.

30. Y. Chen, W. Li, & K. J. Lin, 2015, Cumulative voting: Investor protection or antitakeover? Evidence from family firms in China, *Corporate Governance: An International Review*, 23: 234–238; J. Lahart, 2012, Emerging risk for multinationals, *Wall Street Journal*, November 15, C12; Y. W. Chin, 2011, M&A under China's Anti-Monopoly Law, *Business Law Today*, 19: 1–5.

31. 2015, China 2015 regulatory transparency scorecard, *The US-China Business Council*, www.uschina.org, March; L. Burkitt, 2015, Nine out of 10 Chinese charities fail transparency text, report finds, *Wall Street Journal Online*, www.wsj.com, April 1.

32. 2014, Special report—How Caterpillar got bulldozed in China, *Reuters Industries*, www. reteurs.com, January 22; S. Montlake, 2013, Cat scammed, *Forbes*, March 4, 36–38.

33. H. Liu, X.-H. Ding, H. Guo, & J.-H. Luo, 2014, How does slack affect product innovation in high-tech Chinese firms: The contingent value of entrepreneurial orientation, *Asia Pacific Journal of Management*, 31: 47–68; L. Capron & W. Mitchell, 2012, *Build, Borrow or Buy: Solving the Growth Dilemma*, Cambridge: Harvard Business Review Press; G. K. Lee & M. B. Lieberman, 2010, Acquisition vs. internal development as modes of market entry, *Strategic Management Journal*, 31: 140–158.

34. H. Berends, M. Jelinek, I. Reymen, & R. Stultiens, 2014, Product innovation processes in small firms: Combining entrepreneurial effectuation and managerial causation, *Journal of Product Innovation Management*, 31: 616–635; H. Evanschitzky, M. Eisend, R. J. Calantone, & Y. Jiang, 2012, Success factors of product innovation: An updated meta-analysis, *Journal of Product Innovation Management*, 29: 21–37; H. K. Ellonen, P. Wilstrom, & A. Jantunen, 2009, Linking dynamic-capability portfolios and innovation outcomes, *Technovation*, 29: 753–762.

35. U. Stettner & D. Lavie, 2014, Ambidexterity under scrutiny: Exploration and exploitation via internal organization, alliances, and acquisitions, *Strategic Management Journal*, 35: 1903–1929; M. Makri, M. A. Hitt, & P. J. Lane, 2010, Complementary technologies, knowledge relatedness, and invention outcomes in high technology M&As, *Strategic Management Journal*, 31: 602–628; M. A. Hitt, R. E. Hoskisson, R. A. Johnson, & D. D. Moesel, 1996, The market for corporate control and firm innovation, *Academy of Management Journal*, 39: 1084–1119.

36. 2015, Welch Allyn continues acquisitions, buys scale maker, *Wall Street Journal Online*, www.wsj.com, May 6.

37. C. Grimpe & K. Hussinger, 2014, Resource complementarity and value capture in firm acquisitions: The role of intellectual property rights, *Strategic Management Journal*, 35: 1762–1780; W. P. Wan & D. W. Yiu, 2009, From crisis to opportunity: Environmental jolt, corporate acquisitions, and firm performance, *Strategic Management Journal*, 30: 791–801; G. Ahuja & R. Katila, 2001, Technological acquisitions and the innovation performance of acquiring firms: A longitudinal study, *Strategic Management Journal*, 22: 197–220.

38. O. Koryak, K. F. Mole, A. Lockett, J. C. Hayton, D. Ucbasaran, & G. P. Hodgkinson, 2015, Entrepreneurial leadership, capabilities and firm growth, *International Small Business Journal*, 33: 89–105; N. Zhou & A. Delios, 2012, Diversification and diffusion: A social networks and institutional perspective, *Asia Pacific Journal of Management*, 29: 773–798; M. A. Hitt, R. E. Hoskisson, R. D. Ireland, & J. S. Harrison, 1991, Effects of acquisitions on R&D inputs and outputs, *Academy of Management Journal*, 34: 693–706.

39. 2015, Campbell announces plans for a reorganization of its business operations and appoints the presidents of its three new business divisions, Campbell Soup Home Page, www.campbellsoupcompany. com, January 29.

40. J. Kell, 2015, Campbell Soup is still searching for its recipe for success, *Fortune*, www. fortune, February 25.

41. M.-J. Lee, 2015, Samsung's latest acquisition: Utah-based Yesco Electronics, *Wall Street Journal Online*, www.wsj.com, March 5.

42. A. Chakrabarti & W. Mitchell, 2015, The role of geographic distance in completing related acquisitions: Evidence from U.S. chemical manufacturers, *Strategic Management Journal*, in press; F. Bauer & K. Matzler, 2014, Antecedents of M&A success: The role of strategic complementarity, cultural fit, and degree and speed of integration, *Strategic Management Journal*, 35: 269–291; T. Laamanen & T. Keil, 2008, Performance of serial acquirers: Toward an acquisition program perspective, *Strategic Management Journal*, 29: 663–672.

43. T. J. Hannigan, R. D. Hamilton, III, & R. Mudambi, 2015, Competition and competitiveness in the US airline industry, *Competitiveness Review*, 25: 134–155; D. G. Sirmon, S. Gove, & M. A. Hitt, 2008, Resource management in dyadic competitive rivalry: The effects of resource bundling and deployment, *Academy of Management Journal*, 51: 919–933.

44. S. Banerjee, J. C. Prabhu, & R. K. Chandy, 2015, Indirect learning: How emerging-market firms grow in developed markets, *Journal of Marketing*, 79: 10–28; A. Kaul, 2012, Technology and corporate scope: Firm and rival innovation as antecedents of corporate transactions, *Strategic Management Journal*, 33: 347–367; M. Zollo & J. J. Reuer, 2010, Experience spillovers across corporate development activities, *Organization Science*, 21: 1195–1212.

45. A. Hajro, 2015, Cultural influences and the mediating role of socio-cultural integration processes on the performance of cross-border mergers and acquisitions, *International Journal of Human Resource Management*, 26: 192–215; A. Ataullahm, H. Le, & A. S. Sahota, 2014, Employee productivity, employment growth, and the cross-border acquisitions by emerging market firms, *Human Resource Management*, 53: 987–1004; T. Gantumur & A. Stephan, 2012, Mergers & acquisitions and innovation performance in the telecommunications equipment industry, *Industrial & Corporate Change*, 21: 277–314.

46. 2015, CenturyLink acquires Orchestrate to enhance cloud platform with new database capabilities, CenturyLink Home Page, www.centurylink.com, April 20.

47. M. G. Colombo & L. Rabbiosi, 2014, Technological similarity, post-acquisition R&D reorganization, and innovation performance in horizontal acquisitions, *Research Policy*, 2014, 43: 1039–1054; M. E. Graebner, K. M. Eisenhardt, & P. T. Roundy, 2010, Success and failure in technology acquisitions: Lessons for buyers and sellers, *Academy of Management Perspectives*, 24, 73–92; J. A. Schmidt, 2002, Business perspective on mergers and acquisitions, in J. A. Schmidt (ed.), *Making Mergers Work*, Alexandria, VA: Society for Human Resource Management, 23–46.

48. A. Trichterborn, D. Z. Knyphausen-Aufseb, & L. Schweizer, 2015, How to improve acquisition performance: The role of a dedicated M&A function, M&A learning process, and M&A capability, *Strategic Management Journal*, in press; A. Zaheer, X. Castañer, & D. Souder, 2013, Synergy sources, target autonomy, and integration in acquisitions, *Journal of Management*, 39: 604–632; K. M. Ellis, T. H. Reus, & B. T. Lamont, 2009, The effects of procedural and informational justice in the integration of related acquisitions, *Strategic Management Journal*, 30: 137–161.

49. R. Shen, Y. Tang, & G. Chen, 2014, When the role fits: How firm status differentials affect corporate takeovers, *Strategic Management Journal*, 35: 2012–2030; T. H. Reus, 2012, Culture's consequences for emotional attending during cross-border acquisition implementation, *Journal of World Business*, 47: 342–351.

50. H. Zhu, J. Xia, & S. Makino, 2015, How do high-technology firms create value in international M&A? Integration, autonomy and cross-border contingencies, *Journal of World Business*, in press; J. Q. Barden, 2012, The influences of being acquired on subsidiary innovation adoption, *Strategic Management Journal*, 33: 1269–1285; H. G. Barkema & M. Schijven, 2008, Toward unlocking the full potential of acquisitions: The role of organizational restructuring, *Academy of Management Journal*, 51: 696–722.

51. T. Hua, 2015, Nokia can't cut its way to success with Alcatel, *Wall Street Journal Online*, wsj.com, April 14.

52. T. Hua, 2015, Nokia's ambitions could crack under integration pressure, *Wall Street Journal Online*, www.wsj.com, April 15.

53. S. F. Rockart & N. Dutt, 2015, The rate and potential of capability development trajectories, *Strategic Management Journal*, 36: 53–75; A. Sleptsov, J. Anand, & G. Vasudeva, 2013, Relationship configurations with information intermediaries: The effect of firm-investment bank ties on expected acquisition performance, *Strategic Management Journal*, 34: 957–977.

54. J. B. Edwards, 2014, The urge to merge, *Journal of Corporate Accounting & Finance*, 25: 51–55; R. Duchin & B. Schmidt, 2013, Riding the merger wave: Uncertainty, reduced monitoring, and bad acquisitions, *Journal of Financial Economics*, 107: 69–88; J. DiPietro, 2010, Responsible acquisitions yield growth, *Financial Executive*, 26: 16–19.

55. 2015, Capgemini to acquire iGate for $4 billion, *livemint*, www.livemint.com, April 28.

56. J. Wieczner, 2015, Fat pharma: Pfizer-Hospira and the top 10 overpriced drug deals ever, *Fortune*, www.fortune.com, February 6.

57. B. Becker & V. Ivashiina, 2015, Reaching for yield in the bond market, *Journal of Finance*, in press; G. Yago, 1991, *Junk Bonds: How High Yield Securities Restructured Corporate America*, NY: Oxford University Press, 146–148.

58. D. H. Kim & D. Stock, 2014, The effect of interest rate volatility and equity volatility on corporate bond yield spreads: A comparison of noncallables and callables, *Journal of Corporate Finance*, 26: 20–35.

59. M. C. Jensen, 1986, Agency costs of free cash flow, corporate finance, and takeovers, *American Economic Review*, 76: 323–329.

60. I. M. Pandey & V. Ongpipattanakul, 2015, Agency behavior and corporate restructuring choices during performance decline in an emerging economy, *International Journal of Managerial Finance*, 11: 244–267; S. Guo, E. S. Hotchkiss, & W. Song, 2011, Do buyouts (still) create value? *Journal of Finance*, 66: 479–517.

61. K. Craninckx & N. Huyghebaert, 2015, Large shareholders and value creation through corporate acquisitions in Europe: The identity of the controlling shareholder matters, *European Management Journal*, 33: 116–131; M. Rahman & M. Lambkin, 2015, Creating or destroying value through mergers and acquisitions: A marketing perspective, *Industrial Marketing Management*, 46: 24–35; S. W. Bauguess, S. B. Moeller, F. P. Schlingemann, & C. J. Zutter, 2009, Ownership structure and target returns, *Journal of Corporate Finance*, 15: 48–65; H. Donker & S. Zahir, 2008, Takeovers, corporate control, and return to target shareholders, *International Journal of Corporate Governance*, 1: 106–134.

62. J. Jaffe, J. Jindra, D. Pedersen, & T. Voetmann, 2015, Returns to acquirers of public and subsidiary targets, *Journal of Corporate Finance*, 31: 246–270; C. Tantalo & R. L. Priem, 2015, Value creation through stakeholder synergy, *Strategic Management Journal*, in press; Y. M. Zhou, 2011, Synergy, coordination costs, and diversification choices, *Strategic Management Journal*, 32: 624–639.

63. G. Speckbacher, K. Neumann, & W. H. Hoffmann, 2015, Resource relatedness and the mode of entry into new businesses: Internal resource accumulation vs. access

by collaborative arrangement, *Strategic Management Journal*, in press; J. B. Barney, 1988, Returns to bidding firms in mergers and acquisitions: Reconsidering the relatedness hypothesis, *Strategic Management Journal*, 9 (Special Issue): 71–78.

64. Trefis team, 2014, What has AirTran done for Southwest Airlines? *Forbes*, www.forbes.com, December 11.

65. A. Chakrabarti, 2015, Organizational adaptation in an economic shock: The role of growth reconfiguration, *Strategic Management Journal*, in press; O. E. Williamson, 1999, Strategy research: Governance and competence perspectives, *Strategic Management Journal*, 20: 1087–1108.

66. R. Stunda, 2014, The market impact of mergers and acquisitions on firms in the U.S., *Journal of Accounting and Taxation*, 6: 30–37; S. Snow, 2013, How to avoid a post-acquisition idea slump, *Fast Company*, February, 50; M. Cleary, K. Hartnett, & K. Dubuque, 2011, Road map to efficient merger integration, *American Banker*, March 22, 9; S. Chatterjee, 2007, Why is synergy so difficult in mergers of related businesses? *Strategy & Leadership*, 35: 46–52.

67. P. Page, 2015, Canada acquisition weighs on Radiant's earnings in recent quarter, *Wall Street Journal Online*, www.wsj.com, May 18.

68. P.-X. Meschi & E. Metais, 2015, Too big to learn: The effects of major acquisition failures on subsequent acquisition divestment, *British Journal of Management*, in press; W. P. Wan, R. E. Hoskisson, J. C. Short, & D. W. Yiu, 2011, Resource-based theory and corporate diversification: Accomplishments and opportunities, *Journal of Management*, 37: 1335–1368; E. Rawley, 2010, Diversification, coordination costs and organizational rigidity: Evidence from microdata, *Strategic Management Journal*, 31: 873–891.

69. S. Schonhaar, U. Pidun, & M. Nippa, 2014, Transforming the business portfolio: How multinational reinvent themselves, *Journal of Business Strategy*, 35: 4–17; S. Pathak, R. E. Hoskisson, & R. A. Johnson, 2014, Settling up in CEO compensation: The impact of divestiture intensity and contextual factors in refocusing firms, *Strategic Management Journal*, 35: 1124–1143; M. L. A. Hayward & K. Shimizu, 2006, De-commitment to losing strategic action: Evidence from the divestiture of poorly performing acquisitions, *Strategic Management Journal*, 27: 541–557.

70. J. B. Edwards, 2015, M&A deal-makers are dealing in 2014: A commentary, *Journal of Corporate Accounting & Finance*, 26: 19–24; J. Hagedoorn & N. Wang, 2012, Is there complementarity or substitutability between internal and external R&D strategies? *Research Policy*, 41: 1072–1083; P. David, J. P. O'Brien, T. Yoshikawa, & A. Delios, 2010, Do shareholders or

stakeholders appropriate the rents from corporate diversification? The influence of ownership structure, *Academy of Management Journal*, 53: 636–654; R. E. Hoskisson & R. A. Johnson, 1992, Corporate restructuring and strategic change: The effect on diversification strategy and R&D intensity, *Strategic Management Journal*, 13: 625–634.

71. F. Szucs, 2014, M&A and R&D: Asymmetric effects on acquirers and targets? *Research Policy*, 43: 1264–1273; R. D. Banker, S. Wattal, & J. M. Plehn-Dujowich, 2011, R&D versus acquisitions: Role of diversification in the choice of innovation strategy by information technology firms, *Journal of Management Information Systems*, 28: 109–144; J. L. Stimpert, I. M. Duhaime, & J. Chesney, 2010, Learning to manage a large diversified firm, *Journal of Leadership and Organizational Studies*, 17: 411–425; T. Keil, M. V. J. Maula, H. Schildt, & S. A. Zahra, 2008, The effect of governance modes and relatedness of external business development activities on innovative performance, *Strategic Management Journal*, 29: 895–907.

72. B. E. Perrott, 2015, Building the sustainable organization: An integrated approach, *Journal of Business Strategy*, 36: 41–51; A. Kacperczyk, 2009, With greater power comes greater responsibility? Takeover protection and corporate attention to stakeholders, *Strategic Management Journal*, 30: 261–285; M. L. Barnett, 2008, An attention-based view of real options reasoning, *Academy of Management Review*, 33: 606–628.

73. M. V. S. Kumar, J. Dixit, & B. Francis, 2015, The impact of prior stock market reactions on risk taking in acquisitions, *Strategic Management Journal*, in press; J. A. Martin & K. J. Davis, 2010, Learning or hubris? Why CEOs create less value in successive acquisitions, *Academy of Management Perspectives*, 24: 79–81; M. L. A. Hayward & D. C. Hambrick, 1997, Explaining the premiums paid for large acquisitions: Evidence of CEO hubris, *Administrative Science Quarterly*, 42: 103–127; R. Roll, 1986, The hubris hypothesis of corporate takeovers, *Journal of Business*, 59: 197–216.

74. F. Vermeulen, 2007, Business insight (a special report): Bad deals: Eight warning signs that an acquisition may not pay off, *Wall Street Journal*, April 28, R10.

75. D. H. Zhu, 2013, Group polarization on corporate boards: Theory and evidence on board decisions about acquisition premiums, *Strategic Management Journal*, 34: 800–822.

76. G. Kling, A. Ghobadian, M. A. Hitt, U. Weitzel, & N. O'Regan, 2014, The effects of cross-border and cross-industry mergers and acquisitions on home-region and global multinational enterprises, *British Journal of Management*, 25: S116–S132; V. Swaminathan, F. Murshed, & J. Hulland,

2008, Value creation following merger and acquisition announcements: The role of strategic emphasis alignment, *Journal of Marketing Research*, 45: 33–47.

77. O.-P. Kauppila, 2014, So, what am I supposed to do? A multilevel examination of role clarity, *Journal of Management Studies*, 51: 737–763; M. Wagner, 2011, To explore or to exploit? An empirical investigation of acquisitions by large incumbents, *Research Policy*, 40: 1217–1225; H. Greve, 2011, Positional rigidity: Low performance and resource acquisition in large and small firms, *Strategic Management Journal*, 32: 103–114.

78. D. N. Angwin, S. Paroutis, & R. Connell, 2015, Why good things don't happen: The micro-foundations of routines in the M&A process, *Journal of Business Research*, 68: 1367–1381; E. Gomes, D. N. Angwin, Y. Weber, & S. Tarba, 2013, Critical success factors through the mergers and acquisitions process: Revealing pre- and post-M&A connections for improved performance, *Thunderbird International Business Review*, 55: 13–35; M. Cording, P. Christmann, & C. Weigelt, 2010, Measuring theoretically complex constructs: The case of acquisition performance, *Strategic Organization*, 8: 11–41.

79. D. Gamache, G. McNamara, M. Mannor, & R. Johnson, 2015, Motivated to acquire? The impact of CEO regulatory focus on firm acquisitions, *Academy of Management Journal*, inn press; A. Riviezzo, 2013, Acquisitions in knowledge-intensive industries: Exploring the distinctive characteristics of the effective acquirer, *Management Research Review*, 36: 183–212; S. Chatterjee, 2009, The keys to successful acquisition programmes, *Long Range Planning*, 42: 137–163.

80. O. Ahlers, A. Hack, & F. W. Kellermanns, 2014, Stepping into the buyers' shoes: Looking at the value of family firms through the eyes of private equity investors, *Journal of Family Business Strategy*, 6: 384–396; M. A. Hitt, R. D. Ireland, J. S. Harrison, & A. Best, 1998, Attributes of successful and unsuccessful acquisitions of U.S. firms, *British Journal of Management*, 9: 91–114.

81. S. R. Jory & T. N. Nog, 2014, Cross-border acquisitions of state-owned enterprises, *Journal of International Business Studies*, 45: 1096–1114; K. Uhlenbruck, M. A. Hitt, & M. Semadeni, 2006, Market value effects of acquisitions involving Internet firms: A resource-based analysis, *Strategic Management Journal*, 27: 899–913.

82. 2015, TE Connectivity to acquire AdvancedCath, *Pr NewsWire*, www.prnewswire.com, March 4.

83. M. Humphery-Jenner, 2014, Takeover defenses, innovation, and value creation: Evidence from acquisition decisions, *Strategic Management Journal*, 35: 668–690; A. Rouzies & H. L. Colman, 2012,

Identification processes in post-acquisition integration: The role of social interactions, *Corporate Reputation Review*, 15: 143–157; D. K. Ellis, T. Reus, & B. Lamont, 2009, The effects of procedural and informational justice in the integration of related acquisitions, *Strategic Management Journal*, 30: 137–161.

84. S. Graffin, J. Haleblian, & J. T. Kiley, 2015, Ready, AIM, acquire: Impression offsetting and acquisitions, *Academy of Management Journal*, in press; R. Agarwal, J. Anand, J. Bercovitz, & R. Croson, 2012, Spillovers across organizational architectures: The role of prior resource allocation and communication in post-acquisition coordination outcomes, *Strategic Management Journal*, 33: 710–733; M. E. Graebner, 2009, Caveat venditor: Trust asymmetries in acquisitions of entrepreneurial firms, *Academy of Management Journal*, 52: 435–472.

85. F. Szucs, 2014, M&A and R&D: Asymmetric effects on acquirers and targets? *Research Policy*, 43: 1264–1273; Y. Suh, J. You, & P. Kim, 2013, The effect of innovation capabilities and experience on cross-border acquisition performance, *Global Journal of Business Research*, 7: 59–74; J. Jwu-Rong, H. Chen-Jui, & L. Hsieh-Lung, 2010, A matching approach to M&A, R&D, and patents: Evidence from Taiwan's listed companies, *International Journal of Electronic Business Management*, 8: 273–280.

86. 2015, Nokia and Alcatel-Lucent to combine to create an innovation leader in next generation technology and services for an IP connected world, Nokia Home Page, www.nokia.com, April 15.

87. D. N. Angwin & M. Meadows, 2015, New integration strategies for post-acquisition management, *Long Range Planning*, in press; K. H. Heimeriks, M. Schijven, & S. Gates, 2013, Manifestations of higher-order routines: The underlying mechanisms of deliberate learning in the context of postacquisition integration, *Academy of Management Journal*, 55: 703–726; M. L. McDonald, J. D. Westphal, & M. E. Graebner, 2008, What do they know? The effects of outside director acquisition experience on firm acquisition performance, *Strategic Management Journal*, 29: 1155–1177.

88. M. McCann & R. Ackrill, 2015, Managerial and disciplinary responses to abandoned acquisitions in bidding firms: A new perspective, *Corporate Governance: An International Review*, in press; C. Moschieri & J. Mair, 2012, Managing divestitures through time—Expanding current knowledge, *Academy of Management Perspectives*, 26: 35–50; D. Lee & R. Madhaven, 2010, Divestiture and firm performance: A meta-analysis, *Journal of Management*, 36: 1345–1371.

89. N. Kavadis & X. Castaner, 2015, Who drives corporate restructuring? Co-existing

owners in French firms, *Corporate Governance: An International Review*, in press; Y. G. Suh & E. Howard, 2009, Restructuring retailing in Korea: The case of Samsung-Tesco, *Asia Pacific Business Review*, 15: 29–40; Z. Wu & A. Delios, 2009, The emergence of portfolio restructuring in Japan, *Management International Review*, 49: 313–335.

90. E. R. Feldman, 2015, Corporate spinoffs and analysts' coverage decisions: The implications for diversified firms, *Strategic Management Journal*, in press; A. Fortune & W. Mitchell, 2012, Unpacking firm exit at the firm and industry levels: The adaptation and selection of firm capabilities, *Strategic Management Journal*, 33: 794–819; J. L. Morrow, Jr., D. G. Sirmon, M. A. Hitt, & T. R. Holcomb, 2007, Creating value in the face of declining performance: Firm strategies and organizational recovery, *Strategic Management Journal*, 28: 271–283.

91. W. McKinley, S. Latham, & M. Braun, 2014, Organizational decline and innovation: Turnarounds and downward spirals, *Academy of Management Review*, 39: 88–110.

92. C. Tangpong, M. Agebe, & Z. Li, 2015, A temporal approach to retrenchment and successful turnaround in declining firms, *Journal of Management Studies*, in press; H. A. Krishnan, M. A. Hitt, & D. Park, 2007, Acquisition premiums, subsequent workforce reductions and post-acquisition performance, *Journal of Management*, 44: 709–732.

93. I. Paeleman & T. Vanacker, 2015, Less is more, or not? On the interplay between bundles of slack resources, firm performance and firm survival, *Journal of Management Studies*, in press; D. K. Lim, N. Celly, E. A. Morse, & W. Rowe, 2013, Rethinking the effectiveness of asset and cost retrenchment: The contingency effects of a firm's rent creation mechanism, *Strategic Management Journal*, 34: 42–61.

94. L. S. Alberet, D. G. Allen, J. E. Biggane, & Q. (Kathy) Ma, 2015, Attachment and responses to employment dissolution, *Human Resource Management*, 25: 94–106; R. Iverson & C. Zatzick, 2011, The effects of downsizing on labor productivity: The value of showing consideration for employees' morale and welfare in high-performance work systems, *Human Resource Management*, 50: 29–43; C. O. Trevor & A. J. Nyberg, 2008, Keeping your headcount when all about you are losing theirs: Downsizing, voluntary turnover rates, and the moderating role of HR practices, *Academy of Management Journal*, 51: 259–276.

95. T. J. Chemmanur, K. Krishnan, & D. K. Nandy, 2014, The effects of corporate spin-offs on productivity, *Journal of Corporate Finance*, 27: 72–98; R. E. Hoskisson & M. A. Hitt, 1994, *Downscoping: How to Tame the Diversified Firm*, NY: Oxford University Press.

96. E. R. Feldman, R. (Raffi) Amit, & B. Villalonga, 2015, Corporate divestitures and family control, *Strategic Management Journal*, in press; A. T. Nicolai, A. Schulz, & T. W. Thomas, 2010, What Wall Street wants—Exploring the role of security analysts in the evolution and spread of management concepts, *Journal of Management Studies*, 47: 162–189; L. Dranikoff, T. Koller, & A. Schneider, 2002, Divestiture: Strategy's missing link, *Harvard Business Review*, 80(5): 74–83.

97. A. Nadolska & H. G. Barkema, 2014, Good learners: How top management teams affect the success and frequency of acquisitions, *Strategic Management Journal*, 35: 1483–1507; R. E. Hoskisson & M. A. Hitt, 1990, Antecedents and performance outcomes of diversification: A review and critique of theoretical perspectives, *Journal of Management*, 16: 461–509.

98. E. Vidal & W. Mitchell, 2015, Adding by subtracting: The relationship between performance feedback and resource reconfiguration through divestitures, *Organization Science*, in press; S. Schonhaar, U. Pidun, & M. Nippa, 2014, Transforming the business portfolio: How multinationals reinvent themselves, *Journal of Business Strategy*, 35: 4–17.

99. W. G. Xavier, R. Bandeira-de-Mello, & R. Marcon, 2014, Institutional environment and business groups' resilience in Brazil, *Journal of Business Research*, 67: 900–907; H. Berry, 2013, When do firms divest foreign operations? *Organization Science*, 24: 246–261; C. Chi-Nien & L. Xiaowei, 2008, Institutional logics or agency costs: The influence of corporate governance models on business group restructuring in emerging economies, *Organization Science*, 19: 766–784; R. E. Hoskisson, R. A. Johnson, L. Tihanyi, & R. E. White, 2005, Diversified business groups and corporate refocusing in emerging economies, *Journal of Management*, 31: 941–965.

100. H. D. Park & P. C. Patel, 2015, How does ambiguity influence IPO underpricing? The role of the signaling environment, *Journal of Management Studies*, in press.

101. A. N. Link, C. J. Ruhm, & D. S. Siegel, 2014, Private equity and the innovation strategies of entrepreneurial firms: Empirical evidence form the small business innovation research program, *Managerial and Decision Economics*, 35: 103–113; S. N. Kaplan & P. Stromberg, 2009, Leveraged buyouts and private equity, *Journal of Economic Perspectives*, 23: 121–146.

102. S. Pathak, R. E. Hoskisson, & R. A. Johnson, 2014, Settling up in CEO compensation: The impact of divestiture intensity and contextual factors in refocusing firms, *Strategic Management Journal*, 35: 1124–1143; N. Wilson, M. Wright, D. S. Siegel, & L. Scholes, 2012, Private equity portfolio company performance during the global recession, *Journal of Corporate Finance*, 18:

193–205; R. Harris, D. S. Siegel, & M. Wright, 2005, Assessing the impact of management buyouts on economic efficiency: Plant-level evidence from the United Kingdom, *Review of Economics and Statistics*, 87: 148–153.

103. E. Autio, M. Kenney, P. Mustar, D. Siegel, & M. Wright, 2014, Entrepreneurial innovation: The importance of context, *Research Policy*, 43: 1097–1108; H. Bruining, E. Verwaal, & M. Wright, 2013, Private equity and entrepreneurial management in management buy-outs, *Small Business Economics*, 40: 591–605; M. Meuleman, K. Amess, M. Wright, & L. Scholes, 2009, Agency, strategic entrepreneurship, and the performance of private equity-backed buyouts, *Entrepreneurship Theory and Practice*, 33: 213–239.

104. F. Castellaneta & O. Gottschalg, 2015, Does ownership matter in private equity? The sources of variance in buyouts' performance, *Strategic Management Journal*, in press; W. Kiechel III, 2007, Private equity's long view, *Harvard Business Review*, 85(4): 18–20; M. Wright, R. E. Hoskisson, & L. W. Busenitz, 2001, Firm rebirth: Buyouts as facilitators of strategic growth and entrepreneurship, *Academy of Management Executive*, 15: 111–125.

105. Y.-Y. Ji, J. P. Guthrie, & J. G. Messersmith, 2014, The tortoise and the hare: The impact of employment instability on firm performance, *Human Resource Management Journal*, 24: 355–373; E. G. Love & M. Kraatz, 2009, Character, conformity, or the bottom line? How and why downsizing affected corporate reputation, *Academy of Management Journal*, 52: 314–335; J. P. Guthrie & D. K. Datta, 2008, Dumb and dumber: The impact of downsizing on firm performance as moderated by industry conditions, *Organization Science*, 19: 108–123.

106. M. Brauer & T. Laamanen, 2014, Workforce downsizing and firm performance: An organizational routine perspective, *Journal of Management Studies*, 51: 1311–1333; H. A. Krishnan & D. Park, 2002, The impact of work force reduction on subsequent performance in major mergers and acquisitions: An exploratory study, *Journal of Business Research*, 55: 285–292; P. M. Lee, 1997, A comparative analysis of layoff announcements and stock price reactions in the United States and Japan, *Strategic Management Journal*, 18: 879–894.

107. S. Mariconda & F. Lurati, 2015, Ambivalence and reputation stability: An experimental investigation on the effects of new information, *Corporate Reputation Review*, 18: 87–98; D. J. Flanagan & K. C. O'Shaughnessy, 2005, The effect of layoffs on firm reputation, *Journal of Management*, 31: 445–463.

108. J. Habel & M. Klarmann, 2015, Customer reactions to downsizing: When and how is satisfaction affected? *Journal of the*

Academy of Marketing Science, in press;
P. Williams, K. M. Sajid, & N. Earl, 2011,
Customer dissatisfaction and defection:
The hidden costs of downsizing, *Industrial
Marketing Management*, 40: 405–413.

109. F. Bertoni & A. P. Groh, 2014, Cross-border
investments and venture capital exits
in Europe, *Corporate Governance: An
International Review*, 22: 84–99;
C. Moschieri & J. Mair, 2011, Adapting for
innovation: Including divestitures in the
debate, *Long Range Planning*, 44: 4–25;
K. Shimizu & M. A. Hitt, 2005, What constrains
or facilitates divestitures of formerly
acquired firms? The effects of organizational
inertia, *Journal of Management*, 31: 50–72.

110. J X. Cao, D. Cumming, M. Qian, & X. Wang,
2015, Cross-border LBOs, *Journal of Banking
and Finance*, 50: 69–80.

111. K. Cao, J. Coy, & T. Nguyen, 2015, The
likelihood of management involvement, offer
premiums, and target shareholder wealth
effects: Evidence from the 2002–2007 LBO
wave, *Research in International Business and
Finance*, in press; P. G. Klein, J. L. Chapman, &
M. P. Mondelli, 2013, Private equity and
entrepreneurial governance: Time for a
balanced view, *Academy of Management
Perspectives*, 27: 39–51; D. T. Brown, C. E. Fee, &
S. E. Thomas, 2009, Financial leverage and
bargaining power with suppliers: Evidence
from leveraged buyouts, *Journal of Corporate
Finance*, 15: 196–211.

112. H.-C. Huang, Y.-C. Su, & Y.-H. Chang,
2014, Dynamic return-order imbalance
relationship response to leveraged buyout
announcements, *Global Journal of Business
Research*, 8: 55–63; S. B. Rodrigues &

J. Child, 2010, Private equity, the
minimalist organization and the quality of
employment relations, *Human Relations*,
63: 1321–1342; G. Wood & M. Wright, 2009,
Private equity: A review and synthesis,
*International Journal of Management
Reviews*, 11: 361–380.

113. L. Bouvier & T. M. Misar, 2015, Design and
impacts of securitized leveraged buyouts,
Cogent Economics & Finance, 3: http://
dx.doi.org/10.1080/23322039.2015.1009307;
M. Goergen, N. O'Sullivan, & G. Wood, 2011,
Private equity takeovers and employment
in the UK: Some empirical evidence,
*Corporate Governance: An International
Review*, 19: 259–275; W. F. Long &
D. J. Ravenscraft, 1993, LBOs, debt, and
R&D intensity, *Strategic Management
Journal*, 14 (Special Issue): 119–135.

8

International Strategy

Studying this chapter should provide you with the strategic management knowledge needed to:

8-1 Explain incentives that can influence firms to use an international strategy.

8-2 Identify three basic benefits firms achieve by successfully implementing an international strategy.

8-3 Explore the determinants of national advantage as the basis for international business-level strategies.

8-4 Describe the three international corporate-level strategies.

8-5 Discuss environmental trends affecting the choice of international strategies, particularly international corporate-level strategies.

8-6 Explain the five modes firms use to enter international markets.

8-7 Discuss the two major risks of using international strategies.

8-8 Discuss the strategic competitiveness outcomes associated with international strategies, particularly with an international diversification strategy.

8-9 Explain two important issues firms should have knowledge about when using international strategies.

NETFLIX IGNITES GROWTH THROUGH INTERNATIONAL EXPANSION, BUT SUCH GROWTH ALSO FIRES UP THE COMPETITION

Netflix has been pursuing a typical international strategy by developing strong capabilities in technological innovation domestically and then using that base technology to expand abroad. Its technology is focused on understanding customer viewing patterns and providing content that matches that pattern as well as having a broad selection of content produced by network television and movie studios in addition to its own original content, which has become a strong force in the market (see examples in Chapter 1 and Chapter 4).

However, Netflix has reached a near saturation point in the domestic U.S. market. As an obvious extension, it has begun to extend its services abroad in countries that are close culturally and geographically to its U.S. customer base, such as Canada, Nordic, and Latin American countries. Although it is trying to foster more growth by partnering with firms such as Marriott for access to its hotel entertainment systems, Netflix's primary growth is coming from its international expansion efforts which allow it to share its cost across a broader range of countries and a larger subscriber base. In the fourth quarter of 2014, Netflix added 1.9 million U.S. streaming subscribers, but this was down from 2.4 million in the period a year earlier. However, overall in 2014 it added 4.3 million streaming customers, exceeding its 4 million forecast, primarily driven because foreign markets grew faster than expected. Netflix already has some services in approximately 50 countries. In the first quarter of 2015, it expanded into Australia and New Zealand. It is also exploring the opportunity of obtaining a government license to offer its streaming services in China.

Getty Images

Netflix's international growth strategy has some confounding complexities. First, Netflix must seek global licenses with its contract video and movie content providers. However, the content providers want to distribute their content in international markets as well, and thus Netflix will have to pay more for the content to get a global license, in addition to the costs of initial start-up and licensing in new foreign countries. This drives up the costs of pursuing its global strategy, at least in the short term.

Second, as it pursues its global streaming strategy, there are both increased domestic competition for subscriber growth as well as new entrants into foreign markets as they see the opportunity that Netflix is trying to realize. For example, Alibaba, whose home country is China, recently indicated that it would start up its own video streaming service and even contracted to produce original content, copying Netflix's strategy (see the opening case in Chapter 1). Interestingly, there is some speculation that Alibaba, given its huge size and recent cash from an initial public offering (IPO), would seek to purchase Netflix as a way of fostering its entry push into the U.S. In addition, Netflix has many other domestic streaming competitors, including Amazon and Hulu.

For example, in the United States, Hulu has been increasing its subscriber base substantially by partnering with television networks to get their best content. Netflix had been cherry-picking this content with lower contractual pricing, but it is having to pay more, and as such, Netflix is not choosing as much prime content. Meanwhile, Hulu has a better relationship with the television networks because it was originally founded and partly owned by the networks. As such, Hulu is willing to pay a higher price for the premium television network video content. This strategy has helped increase its subscriber base from 6 million in 2014 to potentially 9 million in 2015. Furthermore, the television network producers see Netflix as a competitor because it is now producing its own video television content for its subscriber base. A positive for Netflix, though, is that it can use its propriety video content globally without the contractual complexities noted earlier.

In summary, although the international expansion strategy has facilitated growth and profits for Netflix through sharing costs and expenses across a large subscriber base, it has also increased the complexity of its management structure. Additionally, the difficulty in global contracting for top-level domestic U.S. content has increased both international and domestic competition as it has pursued its international strategy.

Sources: M. Armenta & S. Ramachandran, 2015, Business news: Netflix builds steam abroad—International operations spilled red ink but growth in number of subscribers propels the stock higher, *Wall Street Journal*, April 16, B3; B. Darrow, 2015, Alibaba to opening streaming video service in China, *Fortune*, www.fortune.com, June 15; K. Hagey & S. Ramachandran, 2015, Hulu courts TV networks in bid to catch up with Netflix, *Wall Street Journal*, A1, A2; J. Lansing, 2015, TV everywhere: The thundering head, *Broadcasting & Cable*, May 11, 19; S. Ramachandran, 2015, Netflix steps up foreign expansion, subscriber additions top streaming service's forecast, helped by growth in markets abroad, *Wall Street Journal*, www.wsj.com, January 21; A. Tracy, 2015, Marriott and Netflix have partnered up, *Forbes*, June 10, 22; F. Video, 2015, Netflix eyes China for continued global expansion, *Fortune*, www.fortune.com, June 11; S. Saghoee, 2014, Who could buy Netflix?, *Fortune*, www.fortune.com, November 18.

Our description of Netflix's competitive actions in this chapter's Opening Case (e.g., international expansion strategy) highlights the importance of international markets for this firm. Netflix is using its growth in international markets to overcome weakening subscriber growth in its U.S. market. Being able to effectively compete in countries and regions outside a firm's domestic market is increasingly important to firms of all types, as exemplified by Netflix. One reason for this is that the effects of globalization continue to reduce the number of industrial and consumer markets in which only domestic firms can compete successfully. In place of what historically were relatively stable and predictable domestic markets, firms across the globe find they are now competing in globally oriented industries—industries in which firms must compete in all world markets where a consumer or commercial good or service is sold in order to be competitive.[1] Unlike domestic markets, global markets are relatively unstable and much less predictable.

The purpose of this chapter is to discuss how international strategies can be a source of strategic competitiveness for firms competing in global markets. To do this, we examine a number of topics (see Figure 8.1). After describing incentives that influence firms to identify international opportunities, we discuss three basic benefits that can accrue to firms that successfully use international strategies. We then turn our attention to the international strategies available to firms. Specifically, we examine both international business-level strategies and international corporate-level strategies. The five modes of entry firms can use to enter international markets for implementing their international strategies are then examined. Firms encounter economic and political risks when using international strategies. Some refer to these as economic and political institutions.[2] These risks must be effectively managed if the firm is to achieve the desired outcomes of higher performance and enhanced innovation. After discussing the outcomes firms seek when using international strategies, the chapter closes with mention of two cautions about international strategy that should be kept in mind.

Figure 8.1 Opportunities and Outcomes of International Strategy

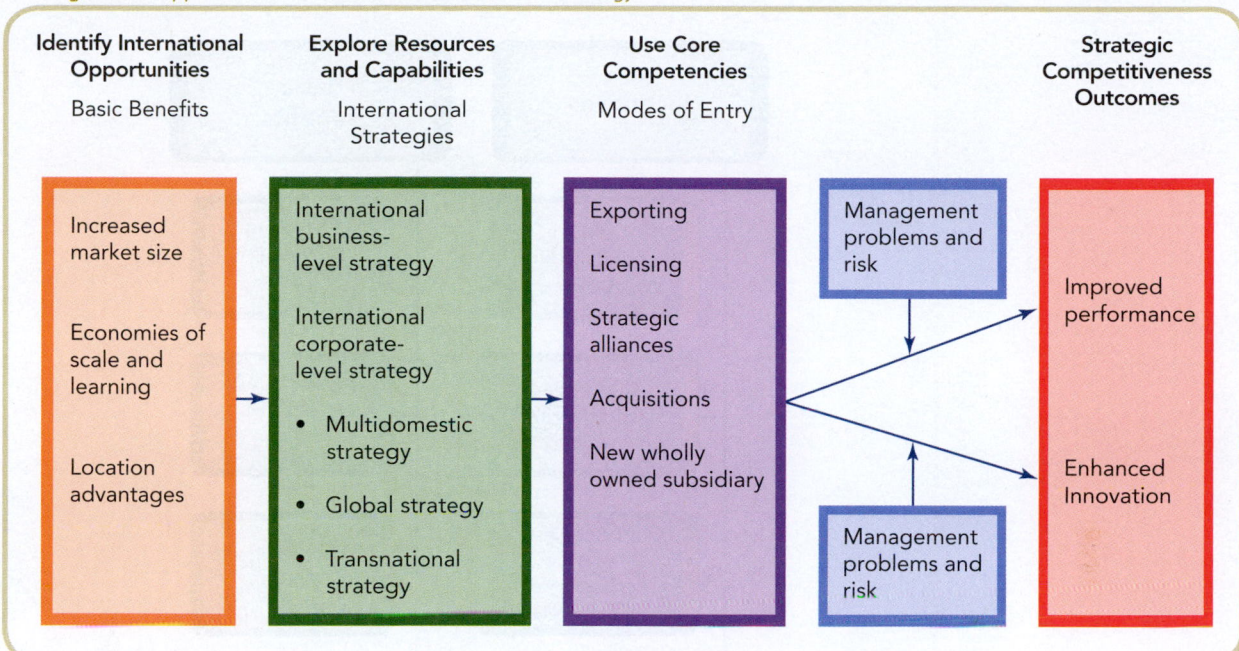

8-1   Identifying International Opportunities

An **international strategy** is a strategy through which the firm sells its goods or services outside its domestic market.[3] In some instances, firms using an international strategy become quite diversified geographically as they compete in numerous countries or regions outside their domestic market. This is the case for Netflix in that it competes in about 50 countries. In other cases, firms engage in less international diversification because they compete in a smaller number of markets outside their "home" market.

There are incentives for firms to use an international strategy and to diversify their operations geographically, and they can gain three basic benefits when they successfully do so.[4] We show international strategy's incentives and benefits in Figure 8.2.

8-1a   Incentives to Use International Strategy

Raymond Vernon expressed the classic rationale for an international strategy.[5] He suggested that typically a firm discovers an innovation in its home-country market, especially in advanced economies such as those in Germany, France, Japan, Sweden, Canada, and the United States. Often demand for the product then develops in other countries, causing a firm to export products from its domestic operations to fulfil demand. Continuing increases in demand can subsequently justify a firm's decision to establish operations outside of its domestic base, as illustrated in the Opening Case on Netflix. As Vernon noted, engaging in an international strategy has the potential to help a firm extend the life cycle of its product(s).

Gaining access to needed and potentially scarce resources is another reason firms use an international strategy. Key supplies of raw material—especially minerals and energy— are critical to firms' efforts in some industries to manufacture their products. Energy and mining companies have access to the raw materials, through their worldwide operations, which they in turn sell to manufacturers requiring those resources. Rio Tinto Group is

An **international strategy** is a strategy through which the firm sells its goods or services outside its domestic market.

Figure 8.2 Incentives and Basic Benefits of International Strategy

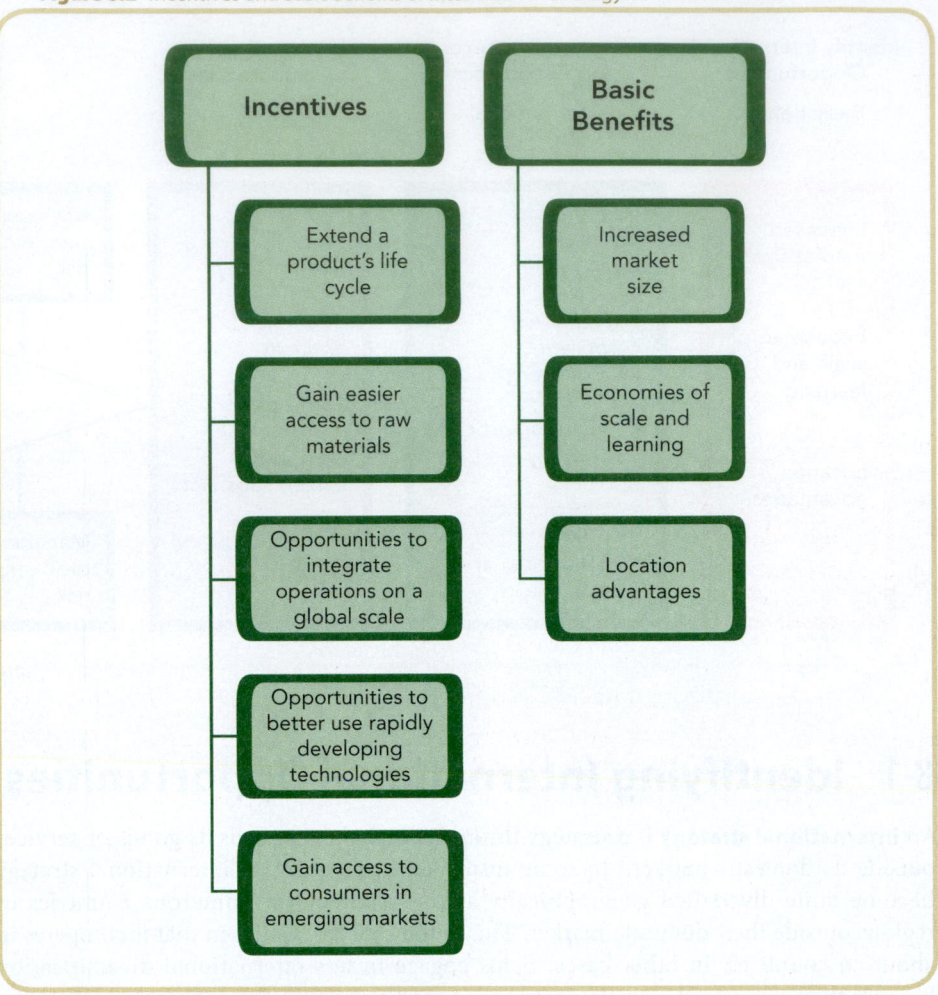

a leading international mining corporation. Operating as a global organization, the firm has 71,000 employees across six continents to include Australia, North America, South America, Europe, Asia, and Africa. Rio Tinto uses its capabilities of technology and innovation (see first incentive noted above), exploration, marketing, and operational processes to identify, extract, and market mineral resources throughout the world.[6] In other industries where labor costs account for a significant portion of a company's expenses, firms may choose to establish facilities in other countries to gain access to less expensive labor. Clothing and electronics manufacturers are examples of firms pursuing an international strategy for this reason.

Increased pressure to integrate operations on a global scale is another factor influencing firms to pursue an international strategy. As nations industrialize, the demand for some products and commodities appears to become more similar. This borderless demand for globally branded products may be due to growing similarities in lifestyle in developed nations. Increases in global communications also facilitate the ability of people in different countries to visualize and model lifestyles in other cultures. In an increasing number of industries, technology drives globalization because the economies of scale necessary to reduce costs to the lowest level often require an investment greater than that needed to meet domestic market demand. Moreover, in emerging markets, the increasingly rapid adoption of technologies such as the Internet and mobile applications permits greater integration of trade, capital, culture, and labor. For instance, Vietnam is experiencing a "mobile revolution." In 2015, over 40 percent of the population has smartphones and access to the Internet, compared to 12 percent ten years ago. This is driving $4 billion in e-commerce business in 2015 versus $700 million in 2012.[7] In this sense, technologies are the foundation for efforts to bind together disparate markets and operations across the world. International strategy also makes it possible for firms to use technologies to organize their operations into a seamless whole.[8]

The potential of large demand for goods and services from people in emerging markets such as China and India is another strong incentive for firms to use an international strategy.[9] This is the case for French-based Carrefour S.A. This firm is the world's second-largest retailer (behind only Walmart) and the largest retailer in Europe. Carrefour operates five main grocery store formats—hypermarkets, supermarkets, cash & carry, hypercash stores, and convenience stores. The firm also sells products online.[10] In some areas of the world, Carrefour performed poorly and in 2014. For example, it withdrew from India as did another large U.K. retailer, Tesco. One observer concluded that "both Carrefour and Tesco have been withdrawing from non-core international markets where they cannot see long-term returns. Both had neglected their core domestic operations and saw sales at home suffer."[11] Both companies have been attempting to fine tune their business models in both domestic and international locations.

Even though India differs from Western countries in many respects, such as culture, politics, and the precepts of its economic system, it offers a huge potential market, and the government is becoming more supportive of foreign direct investment.[12] Differences among Chinese, Indian, and Western-style economics and cultures make the successful use of an international strategy challenging. As such, firms seeking to meet customer demands in emerging markets must learn how to manage an array of political and economic risks, which we discuss later in the chapter.[13]

We've now discussed incentives that influence firms to use international strategies. Firms derive three basic benefits by successfully using international strategies:

1. increased market size
2. increased economies of scale and learning
3. development of a competitive advantage through location (e.g., access to low-cost labor, critical resources, or customers).

These benefits will be examined here in terms of both their costs (e.g., higher coordination expenses and limited access to knowledge about host country political influences)[14] and their challenges.

8-1b Three Basic Benefits of International Strategy

As noted, effectively using one or more international strategies can result in three basic benefits for the firm. These benefits facilitate the firm's effort to achieve strategic competitiveness (see Figure 8.1) when using an international strategy.

Increased Market Size

Firms can expand the size of their potential market—sometimes dramatically—by using an international strategy to establish stronger positions in markets outside their domestic market. As noted, access to additional consumers is a key reason Carrefour sees international markets such as China as a major source of growth.

China's WH Group (formerly known as Shuanghui International) acquired the U.S. based, Smithfield Foods, Inc., a large pork producer in the U.S. Pork consumption accounts for more than 60 percent of the total meat consumption in China creating an opportunity for foreign pork producers to export more pork to China and overcome potential trade barriers in doing so. The acquisition also helps WH Group to upgrade its global image, while providing the resources that Smithfield needed. It allows both firms to expand their market size as well.[15]

Firms such as Netflix, Carrefour, and WH Group understand that effectively managing different consumer tastes and practices linked to cultural values or traditions in different markets is challenging. Nonetheless, they accept this challenge because of the potential to enhance the firms' size and performance. Other firms accept the challenge of successfully implementing an international strategy largely because of limited growth opportunities in their domestic market. This appears to be at least partly the case for major competitors Coca-Cola and PepsiCo, firms that have not been able to generate significant growth in their U.S. domestic and North American markets for some time. Indeed, most of these firms' growth is occurring in international markets. An international market's overall size also has the potential to affect the degree of benefit a firm can accrue as a result of using an international strategy. In general, larger international markets offer higher potential returns and pose less risk for the firm choosing to invest in those markets. Also related is the strength of the science base of the international markets in which a firm may compete. This is important because scientific knowledge and human capital are needed to facilitate efforts to more effectively sell and/or produce products that create value for customers.[16]

Economies of Scale and Learning

By expanding the number of markets in which they compete, firms may be able to enjoy economies of scale, particularly in manufacturing operations. More broadly, firms able to make continual process improvements enhance their ability to reduce costs while, hopefully, increasing the value their products create for customers. For example, rivals Airbus SAS and Boeing have multiple manufacturing facilities and outsource some activities to firms located throughout the world, partly for the purpose of developing economies of scale as a source of being able to create value for customers.

Economies of scale are critical in a number of settings in addition to the airline manufacturing industry. Automobile manufacturers certainly seek economies of scale as a benefit of their international strategies. Ford Motor Company employs 224,000 people worldwide and operates in six global regions: North America, Central and South America, Europe, Middle East, Africa, and Asia Pacific. Ford is planning on increasing sales in each region, especially in Asia.[17] Overall, Ford seeks to increase the annual number of products it sells outside of North America, for example, it increased its market share in Europe in 2014. Demonstrating the use of this international strategy is the fact that Ford is now run as a single global business developing cars and trucks that can be built and sold throughout the world.[18] Firms may also be able to exploit core competencies in international markets through resource and knowledge sharing between units and network partners across country borders.[19] By sharing resources and knowledge in this manner, firms can learn how to create synergy, which in turn can help each firm learn how to produce higher quality products at a lower cost.

Operating in multiple international markets also provides firms with new learning opportunities,[20] perhaps even in terms of research and development (R&D) activities. Increasing the firm's R&D ability can contribute to its efforts to enhance innovation, which is critical to both short- and long-term success. However, research results suggest that to take advantage of international R&D investments, firms need to already have a strong R&D system in place to absorb knowledge resulting from effective R&D activities.[21]

Location Advantages

Locating facilities outside their domestic market can sometimes help firms reduce costs. This benefit of an international strategy accrues to the firm when its facilities in international locations provide easier access to lower cost labor, energy, and other natural resources. Other location advantages include access to critical supplies and to customers. Once positioned in an attractive location, firms must manage their facilities effectively to gain the full benefit of a location advantage.[22]

A firm's costs, particularly those dealing with manufacturing and distribution, as well as the nature of international customers' needs affect the degree of benefit it can capture through a location advantage.[23] Cultural influences may also affect location advantages and disadvantages. International business transactions are easier for a firm to complete when there is a strong cultural match with which the firm is involved while implementing its international strategy.[24] Finally, physical distances influence a firms' location choices as well as how it manages facilities in the chosen locations.[25]

8-2 International Strategies

Firms choose to use one or both basic types of international strategy: business-level international strategy and corporate-level international strategy. At the business-level, firms select from among the generic strategies of cost leadership, differentiation, focused cost leadership, focused differentiation, and integrated cost leadership/differentiation. At the corporate level, multidomestic, global, and transnational international strategies (the transnational is a combination of the multidomestic and global strategies) are considered. To contribute to the firm's efforts to achieve strategic competitiveness in the form of improved performance and enhanced innovation (see Figure 8.1), each international strategy the firm uses must be based on one or more core competencies.[26]

8-2a International Business-Level Strategy

Firms considering the use of any international strategy first develop domestic-market strategies (at the business level and at the corporate level if the firm has diversified at the product level). This is important because the firm may be able to use some of the capabilities and core competencies it has developed in its domestic market as the foundation for competitive success in international markets, as illustrated in the Opening Case on Netflix. However, research results indicate that the value created by relying on capabilities and core competencies developed in domestic markets as a source of success in international markets diminishes as a firm's geographic diversity increases.[27]

As we know from our discussion of competitive dynamics in Chapter 5, firms do not select and then use strategies in isolation of market realities. In the case of international strategies, conditions in a firm's domestic market affect the degree to which the firm can build on capabilities and core competencies it established to create capabilities and core competencies in international markets. The reason is grounded in Michael Porter's analysis of why some nations are more competitive than other nations and why and how some industries within nations are more competitive relative to those industries in other nations. Porter's core argument is that conditions or factors in a firm's home base—that is, in its domestic market—either hinder or support the firm's efforts to use an international business-level strategy for the purpose of establishing a competitive advantage in international markets. Porter identifies four factors as determinants of a national advantage that some countries possess (see Figure 8.3).[28] Interactions among these four factors influence a firm's choice of international business-level strategy.

Figure 8.3 Determinants of National Advantage

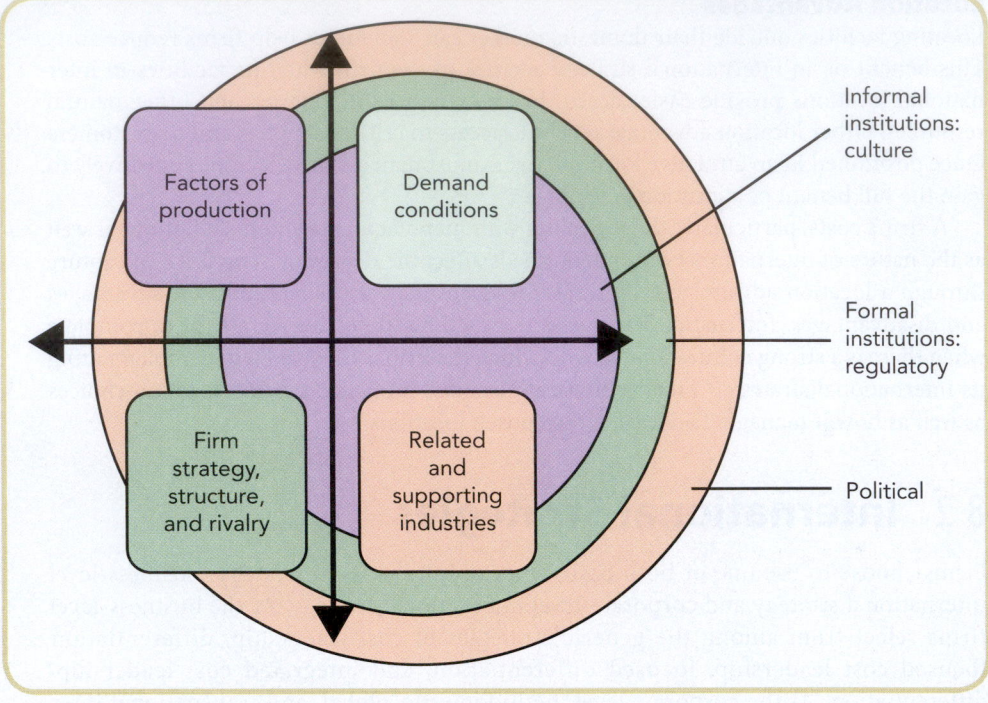

The first determinant of national advantage is factors of production. This determinant refers to the inputs necessary for a firm to compete in any industry. Labor, land, natural resources, capital, and infrastructure (transportation, delivery, and communication systems) represent such inputs. There are basic factors (natural and labor resources) and advanced factors (digital communication systems and a highly educated workforce). Other factors of production are generalized (highway systems and the supply of debt capital) and specialized (skilled personnel in a specific industry, such as the workers in a port that specialize in handling bulk chemicals). If a country possesses advanced and specialized production factors, it is likely to serve an industry well by spawning strong home-country competitors that also can be successful global competitors.

Ironically, countries often develop advanced and specialized factors because they lack critical basic resources. For example, South Korea lacks abundant natural resources but has a workforce with a strong work ethic, a large number of engineers, and systems of large firms to create an expertise in manufacturing. Similarly, Germany developed a strong chemical industry, partly because Hoechst and BASF spent years creating a synthetic indigo dye to reduce their dependence on imports, unlike the United Kingdom, whose colonies provided large supplies of natural indigo.[29]

The second factor or determinant of national advantage, demand conditions, is characterized by the nature and size of customers' needs in the home market for the products firms competing in an industry produce. Meeting the demand generated by a large number of customers creates conditions through which a firm can develop scale-efficient facilities and enhance the capabilities, and perhaps core competencies, required to use those facilities. Once enhancements are in place, the probability that the capabilities and core competencies will benefit the firm as it diversifies geographically increases.

This is the case for Chiquita Brands International, which spent years building its businesses and developing economies of scale and scale efficient facilities, however, it diversified into too many different product lines. In recent years it has refocused the firm on its bananas and packaged salad product lines. Now, Chiquita produces almost one-third of the bananas it sells on its own farms in Latin America. It is the market leader in bananas in Europe and is number two in the market in North America. Chiquita is using its capabilities and core competencies in growing and distributing its brand bananas in its international markets. However, in 2015 it was purchased by Brazil's Cutrale Group which added Chiquita brand bananas and fresh packaged salads to its fruit business in oranges, apples, and peaches.[30]

The third factor in Porter's model of the determinants of national advantage is related and supporting industries. Italy has become the leader in the shoe industry because of related and supporting industries. For example, a well-established leather-processing industry provides the leather needed to construct shoes and related products. Also, many people travel to Italy to purchase leather goods, providing support in distribution. Supporting industries in leather-working machinery and design services also contribute to the success of the shoe industry. In fact, the design services industry supports its own related industries, such as ski boots, fashion apparel, and furniture. In Japan, cameras and copiers are related industries. Similarly, Germany is known for the quality of its machine tools and Belgium is known for skilled manufacturing (supporting and related industries are important in these two settings also).

Firm strategy, structure, and rivalry make up the final determinant of national advantage and also foster the growth of certain industries. The types of strategy, structure, and rivalry among firms vary greatly from nation to nation. The excellent technical training system in Germany fosters a strong emphasis on continuous product and process improvements. In Italy, the national pride of the country's designers spawns strong industries not only in shoes but also sports cars, fashion apparel, and furniture. In the United States, competition among computer manufacturers and software producers contributes to further development of these industries.

The four determinants of national advantage (see Figure 8.3) emphasize the structural characteristics of a specific economy that contribute to some degree to national advantage and influence the firm's selection of an international business-level strategy. Policies of individual governments also affect the nature of the determinants as well as how firms compete within the boundaries governing bodies establish and enforce within a particular economy.[31] While studying their external environment (see Chapter 2), firms considering the possibility of using an international strategy need to gather information and data that will allow them to understand the effects of governmental policies and their enforcement on the nation's ability to establish advantages relative to other nations. Likewise, firms need to understand the relative degree of increased competitiveness the entering firm might receive by examining the country resources necessary to help the firm compete on a global basis in a focal industry.

Leading companies should recognize that a firm based in a country with a national competitive advantage is not guaranteed success as it implements its chosen international business-level strategy. The actual strategic choices managers make may be the most compelling reasons for success or failure as firms diversify geographically. Accordingly, the factors illustrated in Figure 8.3 are likely to produce the foundation for a firm's competitive advantages only when it develops and implements an appropriate international business-level strategy that takes advantage of distinct country factors. Thus, these distinct country factors should be thoroughly considered when making a decision about which international business-level strategy to use. The firm will then make continuous adjustments to its international business-level strategy in light of the nature of competition it encounters in different international markets and in light of customers' needs. Lexus, for example, does not have the share of the luxury car market in China that it desires. Accordingly, Toyota (Lexus' manufacturer) is adjusting how it implements its international differentiation business-level strategy in China to better serve customers. However, it is still far behind other luxury brands such as BMW, Audi, and Cadillac which are growing faster than Lexus. Several analysts noted that it was not getting the traction desired in part because Toyota decided not to put a production facility in China, thus having to pay a 25 percent tariff for each vehicle sold.[32]

8-2b International Corporate-Level Strategy

A firm's international business-level strategy is also based, at least partially, on its international corporate-level strategy. Some international corporate-level strategies give individual country units the authority to develop their own business-level strategies, while others dictate the business-level strategies in order to standardize the firm's products and sharing of resources across countries.[33]

International corporate-level strategy focuses on the scope of a firm's operations through geographic diversification.[34] International corporate-level strategy is required when the firm operates in multiple industries that are located in multiple countries or regions (e.g., Southeast Asia or the European Union) and in which it sells multiple products. The headquarters unit guides the strategy, although as noted, business- or country-level managers can have substantial strategic input depending on the type of international corporate-level strategy the firm uses. The three international corporate-level strategies are shown in Figure 8.4; the international corporate-level strategies vary in terms of two dimensions—the need for global integration and the need for local responsiveness.

Multidomestic Strategy

A **multidomestic strategy** is an international strategy in which strategic and operating decisions are decentralized to the strategic business units in individual countries or

A **multidomestic strategy** is an international strategy in which strategic and operating decisions are decentralized to the strategic business units in individual countries or regions for the purpose of allowing each unit the opportunity to tailor products to the local market.

Figure 8.4 International Corporate-Level Strategies

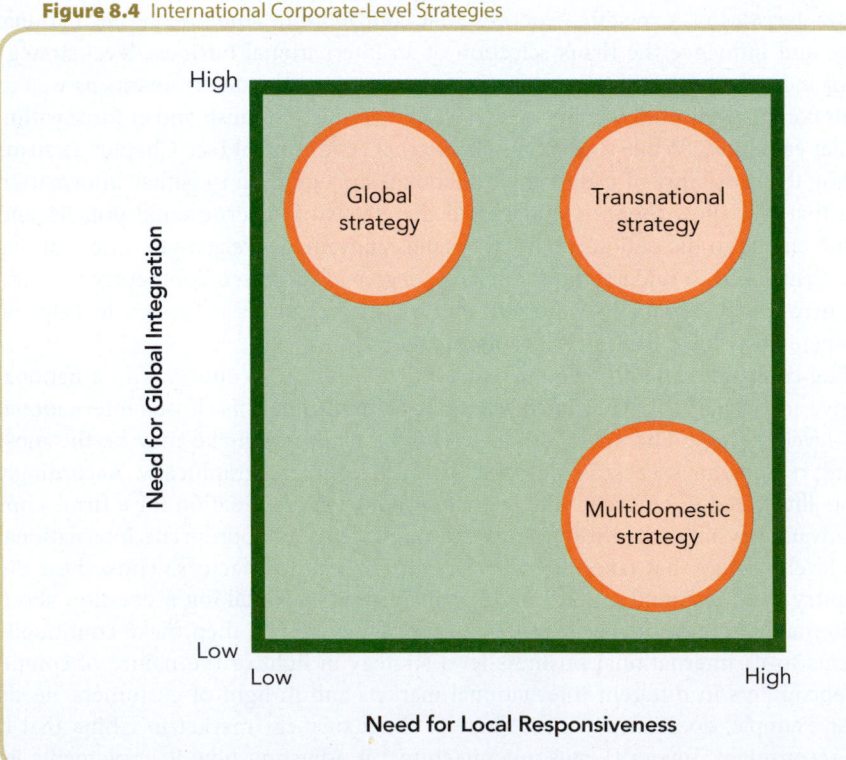

regions for the purpose of allowing each unit the opportunity to tailor products to the local market.[35] With this strategy, the firm's need for local responsiveness is high while its need for global integration is low. Influencing these needs is the firm's belief that consumer needs and desires, industry conditions (e.g., the number and type of competitors), political and legal structures, and social norms vary by country. Thus, a multidomestic strategy focuses on competition within each country because market needs are thought to be segmented by country boundaries. To meet the specific needs and preferences of local customers, country or regional managers have the autonomy to customize the firm's products. Therefore, these strategies should maximize a firm's competitive response to the idiosyncratic requirements of each market.[36] The multidomestic strategy is most appropriate for use when the differences between the markets a firm serves and the customers in them are significant.

The use of multidomestic strategies usually expands the firm's local market share because the firm can pay attention to the local clientele's needs. However, using a multidomestic strategy results in less knowledge sharing for the corporation as a whole because of the differences across markets, decentralization, and the different international business-level strategies employed by local units.[37] Moreover, multidomestic strategies do not allow the development of economies of scale and thus can be more costly.

Unilever is a large European consumer products company selling products in over 180 countries. The firm has more than 400 global brands that are grouped into three business units—foods, home care, and personal care. Historically, Unilever has used a highly decentralized approach for the purpose of managing its global brands. This approach allows regional managers considerable autonomy to adapt the characteristics of specific products to satisfy the unique needs of customers in different markets. More recently however, Unilever has sought to increase the coordination between its independent subsidiaries in order to establish an even stronger global brand presence. One way coordination is achieved is by having the presidents of each of the five global regions serve as members of the top management team.[38] As such, Unilever may be transitioning from a multidomestic strategy to a transnational strategy.

Global Strategy

A **global strategy** is an international strategy in which a firm's home office determines the strategies that business units are to use in each country or region.[39] This strategy indicates that the firm has a high need for global integration and a low need for local responsiveness. These needs indicate that, compared to a multidomestic strategy, a global strategy seeks greater levels of standardization of products across country markets. The firm using a global strategy seeks to develop economies of scale as it produces the same, or virtually the same, products for distribution to customers throughout the world who are assumed to have similar needs. The global strategy offers greater opportunities to take innovations developed at the corporate-level, or in one market, and apply them in other markets.[40] Improvements in global accounting and financial reporting standards facilitate use of this strategy.[41] A global strategy is most effective when the differences between markets and the customers the firm is serving are insignificant.

Efficient operations are required to successfully implement a global strategy. Increasing the efficiency of a firm's international operations mandates resource sharing and greater coordination and cooperation across market boundaries. Centralized decision making as designed by headquarters details how resources are to be shared and coordinated across markets. Research results suggest that the outcomes a firm achieves by using a global strategy become more desirable when the strategy is used in areas in which regional integration among countries is occurring.[42]

A **global strategy** is an international strategy in which a firm's home office determines the strategies that business units are to use in each country or region.

As illustrated in the following Strategic Focus, IKEA has implemented the global strategy. IKEA has centralized a number of its activities, including design and packaging. Accordingly, it integrates and centralizes some support functions from the firm's value chain (see Chapter 3). This integration and centralization brings about the types of benefits sought by firms when using a global strategy. Significant cost savings increases the productivity of the involved support functions, which foster economies of scale benefiting IKEA.

Strategic Focus

Furniture Giant IKEA's Global Strategy

Founded in Sweden, IKEA has pursued a global strategy in developing its well-designed, inexpensive retail furniture strategy. As with most companies pursuing a global strategy, it emphasizes global efficiencies.

One particular approach that IKEA has used is to reduce shipping weight by efficient packaging. Efficient packaging and the associated benefit of lower transportation costs "is at the heart of IKEA's ability to stay affordable." For example, in 2011 the company cut the price of its Bjursta label dining table to €199 from €279 by making the table legs hollow thus reducing weight and raw material costs. "Instead of changing products once they have hit shelves, IKEA is increasingly designing things with packaging and manufacturing in mind from the start." A tradeoff they have experienced is that packaging can become too efficient at the expense of consumer frustration at the complexity of assembly once the product is in the home. So, simple assembly is also an important criteria.

In 2015, IKEA plans to open 13 new stores adding to its current total of 315. It is seeking to buy land in India to open its first locations. Furthermore, the firm is ramping up its focus on online shopping, currently available only in 13 of 27 country locations. It saw 1.5 billion online visits in 2014, up from 200 million in the prior year, which also exceeds its visits to physical stores. Ikea is expanding this strategy by increasing its "click-and-collect merchandising approach where people order online and pick-up the merchandise at a physical location."

IKEA is also focusing on developing city-center stores with a smaller range of products compared to its majority of suburban store locations. However, the suburban stores will likely be maintained as its central focus. Even when in a suburban location, IKEA seeks to be within walking distance of transportation hubs such as subway stations.

Although, IKEA is focused on efficiency, it also takes a long time to study each new country market entry. It focuses on where a growing middle-class is developing. It has entered China,

is planning on a strong entry into India, and is considering Brazil as well. All of these economies have a growing middle-class. Even in these countries, IKEA is focusing on "flat packing, transporting, and reassembling its quirky Swedish-styling all across the planet."

One of IKEA's latest strategies to improve its image is to develop a sounder approach to sustainability. Accordingly, its store roofs are outfitted with solar panels, and it will operate 314 wind turbines in 9 countries, putting the company on tract to be energy independent by 2020. IKEA recycles left over wood scraps from their furniture as well as the soft plastic film used in packaging to make the Skrutt desk pads it sells. It's also starting to phase out non-LED light bulbs in its stores and has begun selling solar panels. With this strategy, IKEA expects to be seen as a company that takes its social and environmental responsibility seriously as it expands internationally. But in the process, it also expects to lower its costs.

Face to Face/UPPA/Photoshot

The founding CEO of IKEA, Ingvar Kamprad, in front of one of IKEA's store fronts.

Sources: S. Chaudhury, 2015, IKEA's favorite design idea: Shrink the box, *Wall Street Journal*, June 18, B10; B. Kowitt, 2015, How IKEA took over the world, *Fortune*, www.fortune.com, March 13; M. Locker, 2015, IKEA is getting into the wedding business, *Time*, www.time.com, April 20; A. Molin, 2015, IKEA builds momentum in Europe, *Wall Street Journal*, www.wsj.com, January 29; J. Sanburn, F. Trianni, & D. Tsai, 2015, Find out why you overshop in IKEA, *Time*, www.time.com, March 17; C. Zillman, 2015, Here's how IKEA is fighting climate change, *Fortune*, www.fortune.com, June 11.

Because of increasing global competition and the need to simultaneously be cost efficient and produce differentiated products, the number of firms using a transnational international corporate-level strategy is increasing.

Transnational Strategy

A **transnational strategy** is an international strategy through which the firm seeks to achieve both global efficiency and local responsiveness. Realizing the twin goals of global integration and local responsiveness is difficult because global integration requires close global coordination while local responsiveness requires local flexibility. "Flexible coordination"—building a shared vision and individual commitment through an integrated network—is required to implement the transnational strategy. Such integrated networks allow a firm to manage its connections with customers, suppliers, partners, and other parties more efficiently rather than using arm's-length transactions.[43] The transnational strategy is difficult to use because of its conflicting goals (see Chapter 11 for more on the implementation of this and other corporate-level international strategies). On the positive side, effectively implementing a transnational strategy can produce higher performance than implementing either the multidomestic or global strategies if the circumstances are right.[44]

Transnational strategies are becoming increasingly necessary to successfully compete in international markets. Reasons for this include the fact that continuing increases in the number of viable global competitors challenge firms to reduce their costs. Simultaneously, the increasing sophistication of markets with greater information flows, made possible largely by the diffusion of the Internet and the desire for specialized products to meet consumers' unique needs, pressures firms to differentiate their products in local markets. Differences in culture and institutional environments also require firms to adapt their products and approaches to local environments. However, some argue that transnational strategies are not required to successfully compete in international markets. Those holding this view suggest that most multinational firms try to compete at the regional level (e.g., the European Union) rather than at the country level. To the degree this is the case, the need for the firm to simultaneously offer relatively unique products that are adapted to local markets and to produce those products at lower costs permitted by developing scale economies is reduced.[45]

The complexities of competing in global markets increase the need for the use of a transnational strategy. Mondelēz International was created as a spinoff company from Kraft, which separated its domestic grocery products in order to focus on its high-growth snack foods business, in which it has 80 percent of sales come from foreign markets. Mondelēz had $34 billion in revenue in 2014 and has power brands (brands that are globally known and respected) and local brands.[46] So, because it globally integrates its operations to standardize and maintain its power brands while simultaneously developing and marketing local brands that are specialized to meet the needs of local customers, Mondelēz pursues the transnational strategy. It is the global market leader in biscuits, chocolate, candy, and powdered beverages, and it holds the number two position in the global markets for chewing gum and coffee. About 45 percent of its sales come from fast-growing, emerging markets and with the variety of brands offered, it must adjust its strategy accordingly. For instance, besides having recently signed a global agreement

A **transnational strategy** is an international strategy through which the firm seeks to achieve both global efficiency and local responsiveness.

Pictured above are many of the international brands that Mondelez manages globally while implementing the transnational strategy.

with Google for online and social media advertising, Mondelēz has to decide "if a brand is a local, regional, or global priority and adjust spend accordingly."[47]

Next we discuss trends in the global environment that are affecting the choices firms make when deciding which international corporate-level strategies to use and in which international markets to compete.

8-3   Environmental Trends

Although the transnational strategy is difficult to implement, an emphasis on global efficiency is increasing as more industries, and the companies competing within them, encounter intensified global competition. Magnifying the scope of this issue is the fact that, simultaneously, firms are experiencing demands for local adaptations of their products. These demands can be from customers (for products to satisfy their tastes and preferences) and from governing bodies (for products to satisfy a country's regulations). In addition, most multinational firms desire coordination and sharing of resources across country markets to hold down costs, as demonstrated in the Opening Case on Netflix.[48]

Because of these conditions, some large multinational firms with diverse products use a multidomestic strategy with certain product lines and a global strategy with others when diversifying geographically. Many multinational firms may require this type of flexibility if they are to be strategically competitive, in part due to trends that change over time.

Liability of foreignness and regionalization are two important trends influencing a firm's choice and use of international strategies, particularly international corporate-level strategies. We discuss these trends next.

8-3a   Liability of Foreignness

The dramatic success of Japanese firms such as Toyota and Sony in the United States and other international markets in the 1980s was a powerful jolt to U.S. managers. This success awakened U.S. managers to the importance of international competition and the fact that many markets were rapidly becoming globalized. In the twenty-first century, Brazil, Russia, India, and China (BRIC) represent major international market opportunities for firms from many countries, including the United States, Japan, Korea, and members of the European Union. In addition, emerging economies such as Indonesia, Malaysia, Mexico, Colombia, Kenya, and Poland have shown rapid growth, internet penetration, and improving rule of law.[49] However, even if foreign markets seem attractive, as appears to be the case with the BRIC countries and other growing economies, there are legitimate concerns for firms considering entering these markets. This is the *liability of foreignness*,[50] a set of costs associated with various issues firms face when entering foreign markets, including unfamiliar operating environments; economic, administrative, and cultural differences; and the challenges of coordination over distances.[51] Four types of distances commonly associated with liability of foreignness are cultural, administrative, geographic, and economic.[52]

Walt Disney Company's experience while opening theme parks in foreign countries demonstrates the liability of foreignness. For example, Disney suffered "lawsuits in France, at Disneyland Paris, because of the lack of fit between its transferred personnel policies and the French employees charged to enact them."[53] Disney executives learned from this experience and from building the firm's theme park in Hong Kong, and the company "went out of its way to tailor the park to local tastes."[54] Thus, as with Walt Disney Company, firms thinking about using an international strategy to enter foreign markets must be aware of the four types of distances they'll encounter when doing so and determine actions to take to reduce the potentially negative effects associated with those distances.

8-3b Regionalization

Regionalization is a second global environmental trend influencing a firm's choice and use of international strategies. This trend is becoming prominent largely because *where* a firm chooses to compete can affect its strategic competitiveness.[55] As a result, the firm considering using international strategies must decide if it should enter individual country markets or if it would be better served by competing in one or more regional markets.

Currently, the global strategy is used less frequently. It remains difficult to successfully implement even when the firm uses Internet-based strategies, although country borders matter less when e-commerce matters more.[56] In addition, the amount of competition vying for a limited amount of resources and customers can limit a firm's focus to a specific region rather than on country-specific markets that are located in multiple parts of the world. A regional focus allows a firm to marshal its resources to compete effectively rather than spreading their limited resources across multiple country-specific international markets.[57]

However, a firm that competes in industries where the international markets differ greatly (in which it must employ a multidomestic strategy) may wish to narrow its focus to a particular region of the world. In so doing, it can better understand the cultures, legal and social norms, and other factors that are important for effective competition in those markets. For example, a firm may focus on Asian markets only, rather than competing simultaneously in the Middle East, Europe, and Asia or the firm may choose a region of the world where the markets are more similar and coordination and sharing of resources would be possible. In this way, the firm may be able to better understand the markets in which it competes, as well as achieve some economies, even though it may have to employ a multidomestic strategy. Research suggests that most large retailers are better at focusing on a particular region rather than being truly global.[58] Firms commonly focus much of their international market entries on countries adjacent to their home country, which might be referred to as their home region.[59]

Countries that develop trade agreements to increase the economic power of their regions may promote regional strategies. The European Union and South America's Organization of American States (OAS) are country associations that developed trade agreements to promote the flow of trade across country boundaries within their respective regions.[60] Many European firms acquire and integrate their businesses in Europe to better coordinate pan-European brands as the European Union tries to create unity across the European markets. This process is likely to continue as new countries are added to the agreement, some international firms may prefer to focus on regions rather than multiple country markets when entering international markets.

The North American Free Trade Agreement (NAFTA), signed by the United States, Canada, and Mexico in 1993, facilitates free trade across country borders in North America. NAFTA loosens restrictions on international strategies within this region and provides greater opportunity for regional international strategies.[61]

Most firms enter regional markets sequentially, beginning in markets with which they are more familiar. They also introduce their largest and strongest lines of business into these markets first, followed by other product lines once the initial efforts are deemed successful. The additional product lines typically are introduced in the original investment location.[62] However, research also suggests that the size of the market and industry characteristics can influence this decision.[63]

Regionalization is important to most multinational firms, even those competing in many regions across the globe. For example, most large multinational firms have organizational structures that group operations within the same region (across countries) for managing and coordination purposes. Managing businesses by regions helps multinational enterprises (MNEs) deal with the complexities and challenges of operating in multiple international markets. As the Opening Case on Netflix suggests, managing across regions creates more costs, notwithstanding the benefits.

After selecting its business- and corporate-level international strategies, the firm determines how it will enter the international markets in which it has chosen to compete. We turn to this topic next.

8-4 Choice of International Entry Mode

Five modes of entry into international markets are available to firms. We show these entry modes and their characteristics in Figure 8.5. Each means of market entry has its advantages and disadvantages, suggesting that the choice of entry mode can affect the degree of success the firm achieves by implementing an international strategy.[64] Many firms competing in multiple markets may use one or more or all five entry modes.[65]

Figure 8.5 Modes of Entry and their Characteristics

Type of Entry	Characteristics
Exporting	High cost, low control
Licensing	Low cost, low risk, little control, low returns
Strategic alliances	Shared costs, shared resources, shared risks, problems of integration (e.g., two corporate cultures)
Acquisitions	Quick access to new markets, high costs, complex negotiations, problems of merging with domestic operations
New wholly owned subsidiary	Complex, often costly, time consuming, high risk, maximum control, potential above-average returns

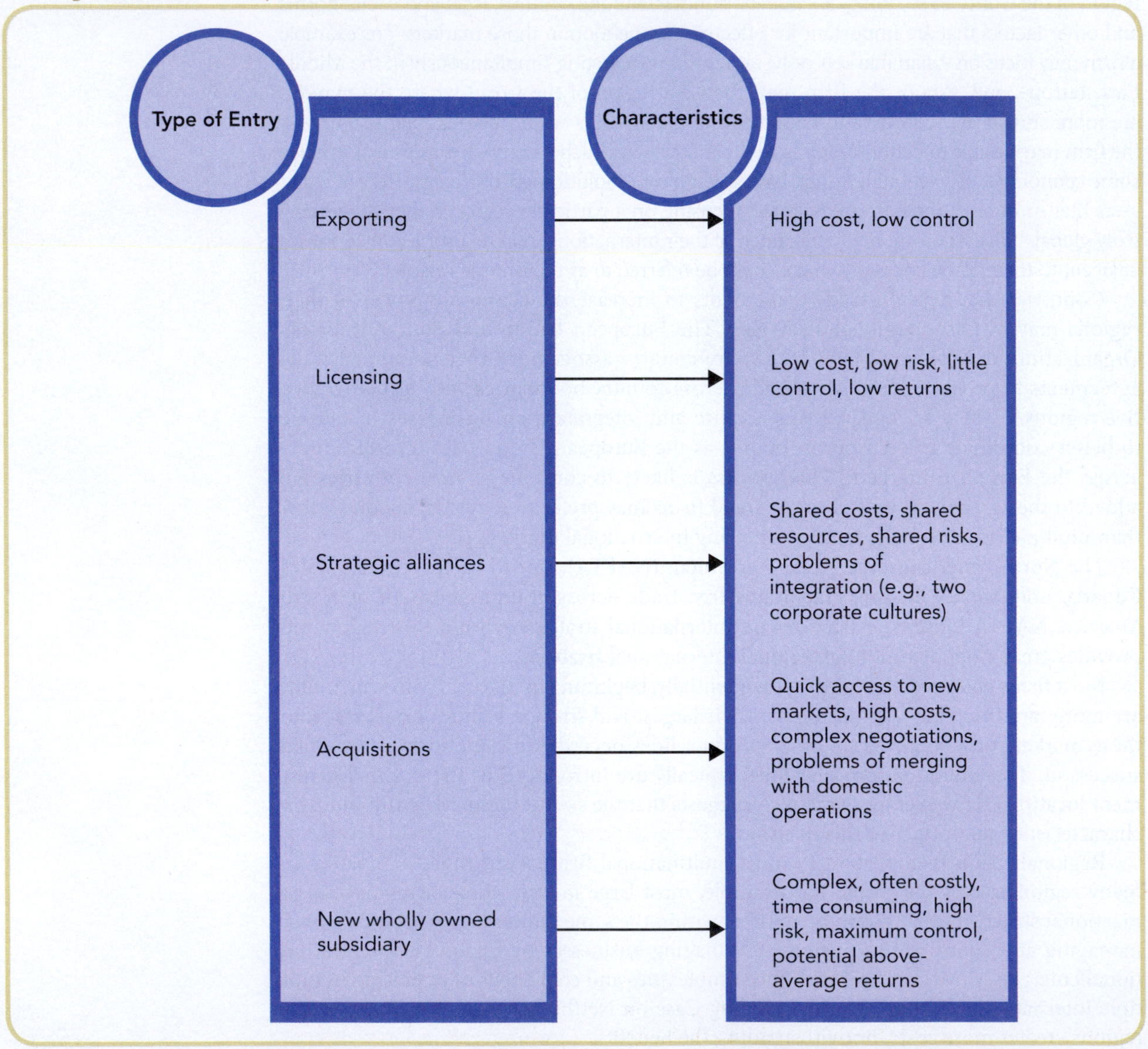

8-4a   Exporting

For many firms, exporting is the initial mode of entry used.[66] *Exporting* is an entry mode through which the firm sends products it produces in its domestic market to international markets. Exporting is a popular entry mode choice for small businesses to initiate an international strategy.[67]

The number of small U.S. firms using an international strategy is increasing, with some predicting that up to 50 percent of small U.S. firms will be involved in international trade by 2018, most of them through export.[68] By exporting, firms avoid the expense of establishing operations in host countries (e.g., in countries outside their home country) in which they have chosen to compete. However, firms must establish some means of marketing and distributing their products when exporting. Usually, contracts are formed with host-country firms to handle these activities. Potentially high transportation costs to export products to international markets and the expense of tariffs placed on the firm's products as a result of host countries' policies are examples of exporting costs. The loss of some control when the firm contracts with local companies in host countries for marketing and distribution purposes can be expensive, making it harder for the exporting firm to earn profits.[69] Evidence suggests that, in general, using an international cost leadership strategy when exporting to developed countries has the most positive effect on firm performance, while using an international differentiation strategy with larger scale when exporting to emerging economies leads to the greatest amount of success. In either case, younger firms with a strong management team and market orientation capabilities are more successful.[70]

Firms export mostly to countries that are closest to their facilities because usually transportation costs are lower and there is greater similarity between geographic neighbors. For example, the United States' NAFTA partners, Mexico and Canada, account for more than half of the goods exported from the state of Texas. The Internet has also made exporting easier. Firms of any size can use the Internet to access critical information about foreign markets, examine a target market, research the competition, and find lists of potential customers.[71] Governments also use the Internet to support the efforts of those applying for export and import licenses, facilitating international trade among countries while doing so.

8-4b   Licensing

Licensing is an entry mode in which an agreement is formed that allows a foreign company to purchase the right to manufacture and sell a firm's products within a host country's market or a set of host countries' markets.[72] The licensor is normally paid a royalty on each unit produced and sold. The licensee takes the risks and makes the monetary investments in facilities for manufacturing, marketing, and distributing products. As a result, licensing is possibly the least costly form of international diversification. As with exporting, licensing is an attractive entry mode option for smaller firms, and potentially for newer firms as well.[73]

China, a country accounting for almost one-third of all cigarettes smoked worldwide, is obviously a huge market for this product. U.S. cigarette firms want to have a strong presence in China but have had trouble entering this market, largely because of successful lobbying by state-owned tobacco firms against such entry. Because of these conditions, cigarette manufacturer Philip Morris International (PMI) had an incentive to form a deal with these state-owned firms. Accordingly, PMI and the China National Tobacco Corporation (CNTC) completed a licensing agreement at the end of 2005. This agreement provides CNTC access to the most famous brand in the world, Marlboro.[74] Because it is a licensing agreement rather than a foreign direct investment by PMI, China maintains control of distribution. The Marlboro brand was launched at two Chinese manufacturing plants in 2008. The Chinese state-owned tobacco monopoly, as part of the agreement, also receives PMI's help through a joint venture in distributing its own brands in select foreign markets. The Chinese cigarettes have also been distributed in other countries such as the Czech Republic and Poland.[75]

Another potential benefit of licensing as an entry mode is the possibility of earning greater returns from product innovations by selling the firm's innovations in international markets as well as in the domestic market.[76] Firms can obtain a larger market for their innovative new products, which helps them to pay off the R&D costs to develop them and to earn a faster return on the innovations than if they only sell them in domestic markets. This is done with little risk and without additional investment costs.

Licensing also has disadvantages. For example, after a firm licenses its product or brand to another party, it has little control over selling and distribution. Developing licensing agreements that protect the interests of both parties, while supporting the relationship embedded within an agreement, helps prevent this potential disadvantage.[77] In addition, licensing provides the least potential returns because returns must be shared between the licensor and the licensee. Another disadvantage is that the international firm may learn the technology of the party with whom it formed an agreement and then produce and sell a similar competitive product after the licensing agreement expires. In a classic example, Komatsu first licensed much of its technology from International Harvester, Bucyrus-Erie, and Cummins Engine to compete against Caterpillar in the earthmoving equipment business. Komatsu then dropped these licenses and developed its own products using the technology it gained from the U.S. companies.[78] Because of potential disadvantages, the parties to a licensing arrangement should finalize an agreement only after they are convinced that both parties' best interests are protected.

8-4c Strategic Alliances

Increasingly popular as an entry mode among firms using international strategies,[79] a *strategic alliance* finds a firm collaborating with another company in a different setting in order to enter one or more international markets.[80] Firms share the risks and the resources required to enter international markets when using strategic alliances.[81] Moreover, because partners bring their unique resources together for the purpose of working collaboratively, strategic alliances can facilitate developing new capabilities and possibly core competencies that may contribute to the firm's strategic competitiveness.[82] Indeed, developing and learning how to use new capabilities and/or competencies (particularly those related to technology) is often a key purpose for which firms use strategic alliances as an entry mode.[83] Firms should be aware that establishing trust between partners is critical for developing and managing technology-based capabilities while using strategic alliances.[84]

French-based Limagrain is the fourth largest seed company in the world through its subsidiary Vilmorin & Cie. An international agricultural cooperative group specializing in field seeds, vegetable seeds, and cereal products, part of Limagrain's strategy calls for it to continue to enter and compete in additional international markets. Limagrain is using strategic alliances as an entry mode. In 2011, the firm formed a strategic alliance with the Brazilian seed company Sementes Guerra in Brazil. The joint venture is named Limagrain Guerra do Brasil. Corn is the focus of the joint venture between these companies. Guerra is a family-owned company engaged in seed research; the production of corn, wheat, and soybeans; and the distribution of those products to farmers in Brazil and neighboring countries. Limagrain also had an earlier, successful joint venture with KWS in the United States. This venture, called AgReliant Genetics, focused primarily on corn and soybeans.[85]

Not all alliances formed for the purpose of entering international markets are successful.[86] Incompatible partners and conflict between the partners are primary reasons for failure when firms use strategic alliances as an entry mode. Another issue is that international strategic alliances are especially difficult to manage. Trust is an important aspect of alliances and must be carefully managed. The degree of trust between partners strongly influences alliance success. The probability of alliance success increases as the amount of trust between partners expands. Efforts to build trust are affected by at least four fundamental issues: the initial condition of the relationship, the negotiation process to arrive at an agreement, partner interactions, and external events.[87] Trust is also influenced by the country cultures involved and the relationships between the countries' governments (e.g., degree of political differences) where the firms in the alliance are home based.[88] Firms should be aware of these issues when trying to appropriately manage trust.

Research has shown that equity-based alliances, over which a firm has more control, are more likely to produce positive returns.[89] (We discuss equity-based and other types of strategic alliances in Chapter 9.) However, if trust is required to develop new capabilities through an alliance, equity positions can serve as a barrier to the necessary relationship building. Trust can be an especially important issue when firms have multiple partners supplying raw materials and/or services in their value chain (often referred to as outsourcing).[90] If conflict in a strategic alliance formed as an entry mode is not manageable, using acquisitions to enter international markets may be a better option.[91]

8-4d Acquisitions

When a firm acquires another company to enter an international market, it has completed a cross-border acquisition. Specifically, a *cross-border acquisition* is an entry mode through which a firm from one country acquires a stake in or purchases all of a firm located in another country.[92]

As free trade expands in global markets, firms throughout the world are completing a larger number of cross-border acquisitions. The ability of cross-border acquisitions to provide rapid access to new markets is a key reason for their growth. In fact, of the five entry modes, acquisitions often are the quickest means for firms to enter international markets.[93]

For example, two European supermarket chains have been seeking a merger which will have significant effects in the U.S. market. The proposed $29 billion merger between Ahold, the Dutch owner of the Stop and Shop and Giant chains in the United States, with Delhaize, the Belgian operator of American chains Food Lion and Hannaford, would give the merged Ahold-Delhaize combination a 4.6 percent share of the U.S. grocery market, making it the fourth-largest player by revenue. This would give the combined European-based firms a major footprint on the East Coast and over 2,000 stores in the United States. Ahold also owns Peapod, a large online grocer in the United States thus strengthening its stake in United States markets. Ahold owns the leading grocery chain in the Netherlands, Heijn, and has stores in Belgium and the Czech Republic. Delhaize owns its namesake store in Belgium, Alpha Beta chains in Greece, and other stores in Eastern Europe.[94]

LAURIE DIEFFEMBACQ/Getty Images

The CEOs of Ahold, Dick Boer (left), and Belgian rival Delhaize, Frans Mullerand Delhaize, shake hands prior to announcing the merger of these giant food distribution chains in a significant cross-border merger.

Interestingly, firms use cross-border acquisitions less frequently to enter markets where corruption affects business transactions and, hence, the use of international strategies. A firm's preference is to use joint ventures to enter markets in which corruption is an issue, rather than using acquisitions. (Discussed fully in Chapter 9, a joint venture is a type of strategic alliance in which two or more firms create a legally independent company and share their resources and capabilities to operate it.) However, these ventures fail more often, although this is less frequently the case for firms experienced with entering "corrupt" markets. When acquisitions are made in such countries, acquirers commonly pay smaller premiums to purchase firms.[95]

Although increasingly popular, acquisitions as an entry mode are not without costs, nor are they easy to successfully complete and operate. Cross-border acquisitions have some of the disadvantages of domestic acquisitions (see Chapter 7). In addition, they often require debt financing to complete, which carries an extra cost. Another issue for firms to consider is that negotiations for cross-border acquisitions can be exceedingly complex and are generally more complicated than are the negotiations associated with domestic acquisitions. Dealing with the legal and regulatory requirements in the target firm's country and obtaining appropriate information to negotiate an agreement are also frequent problems. Finally, the merging of the new firm into the acquiring firm is often more complex than is the case with domestic acquisitions. The firm completing the cross-border acquisition must deal not only with different corporate cultures, but also with potentially different social cultures and practices.[96] These differences make integrating the two firms after the acquisition more challenging because it is difficult to capture the potential synergy when integration is slowed or stymied because of cultural differences.[97] Therefore, while cross-border acquisitions are popular as an entry mode primarily because they provide rapid access to new markets, firms considering this option should be fully aware of the costs and risks associated with using it.

8-4e New Wholly Owned Subsidiary

A **greenfield venture** is an entry mode through which a firm invests directly in another country or market by establishing a new wholly owned subsidiary. The process of creating a greenfield venture is often complex and potentially costly, but this entry mode affords maximum control to the firm and has the greatest amount of potential to contribute to the firm's strategic competitiveness as it implements international strategies. This potential is especially true for firms with strong intangible capabilities that might be leveraged through a greenfield venture.[98] Moreover, having additional control over its operations in a foreign market is especially advantageous when the firm has proprietary technology.

Research also suggests that "wholly owned subsidiaries and expatriate staff are preferred" in service industries where "close contacts with end customers" and "high levels of professional skills, specialized know-how, and customization" are required.[99] Other research suggests that, as investments, greenfield ventures are used more prominently when the firm's business relies significantly on the quality of its capital-intensive manufacturing facilities. In contrast, cross-border acquisitions are more likely to be used as an entry mode when a firm's operations are human-capital intensive—for example, if a strong local union and high cultural distance (between the countries involved) would cause difficulty in transferring knowledge to a host nation through a greenfield venture.[100]

The risks associated with greenfield ventures are significant in that the costs of establishing a new business operation in a new country or market can be substantial. To support the operations of a newly established operation in a foreign country, the firm may have to acquire knowledge and expertise about the new market by hiring either host-country nationals, possibly from competitors, or through consultants, which can be costly.

A **greenfield venture** is an entry mode through which a firm invests directly in another country or market by establishing a new wholly owned subsidiary.

This new knowledge and expertise often is necessary to facilitate the building of new facilities, establishing distribution networks, and learning how to implement marketing strategies that can lead to competitive success in the new market.[101] Importantly, while taking these actions, the firm seeks to maintain control over the technology, marketing, and distribution of its products. Research also suggests that when the country risk is high, firms prefer to enter with joint ventures instead of greenfield investments. However, if firms have previous experience in a country, they prefer to use a wholly owned greenfield venture rather than a joint venture.[102]

China has been an attractive market for foreign retailers (e.g., Walmart) because of its large population, the growing economic capabilities of Chinese citizens, and the opening of the Chinese market to foreign firms. For example, by 2005 more than 300 foreign retailers had entered China, many of them using greenfield ventures. Of course, China is a unique environment, partly because of its culture, but more so because of the government control and intervention. Good relationships with local and national government officials are quite important to foreign firms' success in China. Because of these complexities and the challenges they present, foreign retailers' success in this market has been mixed despite the substantial opportunities that exist there. Expansion, however, is going to be more difficult, given how popular the online retailer Alibaba and its affiliates and competitors have become. Thus great care should be exercised when selecting the best mode for entering particular markets, as we discuss next.[103]

8-4f Dynamics of Mode of Entry

Several factors affect the firm's choice about how to enter international markets. Market entry is often achieved initially through exporting, which requires no foreign manufacturing expertise and investment only in distribution. Licensing can facilitate the product improvements necessary to enter foreign markets, as in the Komatsu example. Strategic alliances are a popular entry mode because they allow a firm to connect with an experienced partner already in the market. Partly because of this, geographically diversifying firms often use alliances in uncertain situations, such as an emerging economy where there is significant risk (e.g., Venezuela). However, if intellectual property rights in the emerging economy are not well protected, the number of firms in the industry is growing fast, and the need for global integration is high, other entry modes such as a joint venture (see Chapter 9) or a wholly owned subsidiary are preferred.[104] In the final analysis though, all three modes—export, licensing, and strategic alliance—can be effective means of initially entering new markets and for developing a presence in those markets.

Acquisitions, greenfield ventures, and sometimes joint ventures are used when firms want to establish a strong presence in an international market. Aerospace firms Airbus and Boeing have used joint ventures, especially in large markets, to facilitate entry, while military equipment firms such as Thales SA have used acquisitions to build a global presence. Japanese auto manufacturer Toyota has established a presence in the United States through both greenfield ventures and joint ventures. Because of Toyota's highly efficient manufacturing processes, the firm wants to maintain control over manufacturing when possible. As such, it is opening a new regional center to bring together supplier coordination and regional North American research in Michigan as well as opening a new North American headquarters facility in Texas.[105] Both acquisitions and greenfield ventures are likely to come at later stages in the development of a firm's international strategies.

Thus, to enter a global market, a firm selects the entry mode that is best suited to its situation. In some instances, the various options will be followed sequentially, beginning with exporting and eventually leading to greenfield ventures. In other cases, the firm may use several, but not all, of the different entry modes, each in different markets. The decision regarding which entry mode to use is primarily a result of the industry's competitive conditions; the country's situation and government policies; and the firm's unique set of resources, capabilities, and core competencies.

FEMSA, the large multibusiness Mexican firm, has been expanding its operations into multiple countries in recent years. Most of its expansion has been into other Latin American countries (where it better understands the culture and markets). A recent acquisition in Brazil has capped a series of acquisitions to become a powerhouse in bottling and distribution. In fact, FEMSA is Coca-Cola's largest bottler worldwide, including some operations in Asia. Its most common mode of entry has been acquisitions. It has considerable experience with acquisitions given that a large amount of its domestic growth has also come from acquisitions.[106]

8-5 Risks in an International Environment

International strategies are risky, particularly those that would cause a firm to become substantially more diversified in terms of geographic markets served. Firms entering markets in new countries encounter a number of complex institutional risks.[107] Political and economic risks cannot be ignored by firms using international strategies (see specific examples of political and economic risks in Figure 8.6).

8-5a Political Risks

Political risks "denote the probability of disruption of the operations of multinational enterprises by political forces or events whether they occur in host countries, home country, or result from changes in the international environment."[108] Possible disruptions to a firm's operations when seeking to implement its international strategy create numerous problems, including uncertainty created by government regulation; the existence of many, possibly conflicting, legal authorities or corruption; and the potential nationalization of private assets.[109] Firms investing in other countries, when implementing their

Figure 8.6 Risks in the International Environment

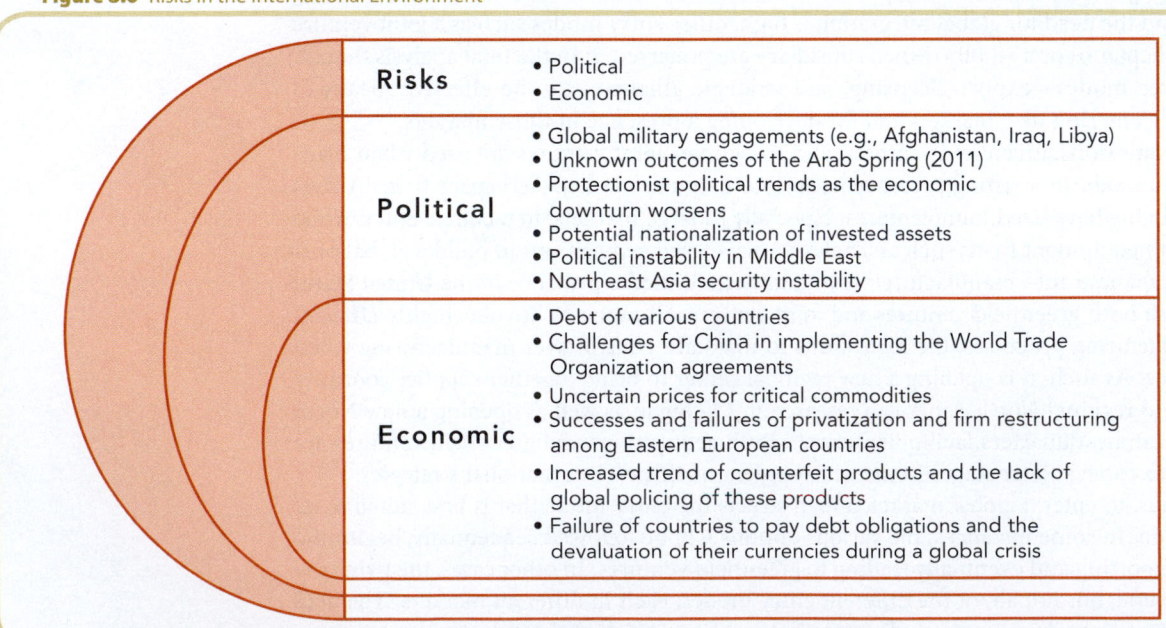

Risks	• Political • Economic
Political	• Global military engagements (e.g., Afghanistan, Iraq, Libya) • Unknown outcomes of the Arab Spring (2011) • Protectionist political trends as the economic downturn worsens • Potential nationalization of invested assets • Political instability in Middle East • Northeast Asia security instability
Economic	• Debt of various countries • Challenges for China in implementing the World Trade Organization agreements • Uncertain prices for critical commodities • Successes and failures of privatization and firm restructuring among Eastern European countries • Increased trend of counterfeit products and the lack of global policing of these products • Failure of countries to pay debt obligations and the devaluation of their currencies during a global crisis

international strategy, may have concerns about the stability of the national government and the effects of unrest and government instability on their investments or assets.[110] A recent study also suggests that political risk in one country often spreads to others, as in the Arab Spring revolutions among many mid-eastern countries.[111] To deal with these concerns, firms should conduct a political risk analysis of the countries or regions they may enter using one of the five entry modes. Through political risk analysis, the firm examines potential sources and factors of noncommercial disruptions of their foreign investments and the operations flowing from them.[112] However, occasionally firms might use political (institutional) weaknesses as an opportunity to transfer activities or practices that stakeholders see as undesirable for their operations in the home country to a new market so they can continue earning returns on these questionable practices.[113]

FIFA, the international soccer federation which sponsors world cup soccer matches along with its regional and country affiliates, have come under heavy scrutiny for possible corrupt practices, as illustrated in the Strategic Focus. Much of the alleged corruption that has taken place has been indirectly supported by the nature of the governments and institutions in which soccer is popular, especially in less developed countries. Bribes were alleged to have been paid for Africa to receive the World Cup and the recent decisions by FIFA to host the games in Russian and Qatar in 2018 and 2022 have come under question.[114] Many of the countries, for example Brazil and Paraguay, are seeking to overhaul their country soccer regulating bodies because of the scandal.[115]

Russia has experienced a relatively high level of institutional instability in the years following its revolutionary transition to a more democratic government. In an effort to regain more central control and reduce the decentralized chaos, Russian leaders took actions such as prosecuting powerful private firm executives, seeking to gain state control of firm assets, and not approving some foreign acquisitions of Russian businesses. The initial institutional instability, followed by the actions of the central government, caused some firms to delay or avoid significant foreign direct investment in Russia. The riskiness of the situation has worsened as Russia has taken the Crimea from Ukraine and used proxy rebels to fight in Eastern Ukraine. "The resulting U.S. and European Union sanctions, in conjunction with falling oil prices, sent the Russian economy into a tailspin. The ruble lost half its value, and, despite a muted recovery in oil and a boost to industry from the devaluation, Russia's economy is set to shrink by 2.7 percent this year [2015], according to a World Bank report."[116]

8-5b Economic Risks

Economic risks include fundamental weaknesses in a country or region's economy with the potential to cause adverse effects on firms' efforts to successfully implement their international strategies. As illustrated in the example of Russian institutional instability and property rights, political risks and economic risks are interdependent. If firms cannot protect their intellectual property, they are highly unlikely to use a means of entering a foreign market that involves significant and direct investments. Therefore, countries need to create, sustain, and enforce strong intellectual property rights in order to attract foreign direct investment.[117]

In emerging economies, one of the significant economic risks is the availability of important infrastructure to allow large industry players, such as miners, to have sufficient electrical power in national grids to meet their power usage requirements. Often, inefficient, state-owned electric power producers are forced to run intermittent blackouts, which is devastating for continuous process manufacturing and refining such as found in the mining industry. South Africa used to have a reliable electrical power grid. However the state-owned electrical utility, Eskom Holdings Ltd., has neglected to build new power plants and sufficiently maintain current operating generating plants.

Strategic **Focus**

The Global Soccer Industry and the Effect of the FIFA Scandal

The Fédération Internationale de Football Association (FIFA) was founded in Paris in 1904 and was initially comprised of only European nations. By World War II, FIFA had added a few South American members. Newly independent states in Africa, Asia, and the Caribbean joined later. However it continued to be governed "as though it was an exclusive European club"—until 1974 when João Havelange, a Brazilian, won election as FIFA's president. Havelange was able to transform the organization and expand the World Cup competition to teams from nations outside Europe and South America and made the tournament a major money making enterprise. With the amount of exposure and money involved, companies desire sponsorship rights because of the advertising potential. Adidas AG and Coca-Cola were original sponsors. Havelange also oversaw significant increases in revenue from television rights. In the process, Havelange was alleged to have participated in much corruption and eventually was suspected of amassing $50 million in bribes.

Havelange facilitated the election of Sepp Blatter who became FIFA president in 1998 and continued to follow Havelange's approach to politics. After FIFA became a worldwide organization, especially in developing countries in Latin America, Africa, and the Caribbean, more allegations of corruption surfaced. One analyst suggested that "FIFA could not have developed soccer in poorer countries without corrupt practices." Of course, there has also been corruption in more developed countries in the United Kingdom and other places, including the United States, although normally not through blatant bribery as has been discovered over time by FIFA officials. On May 27, 2015, the United States Department of Justice and the FBI announced a long list of indictments and simultaneous arrests of FIFA officials were made at the Zurich FIFA meetings in Switzerland. Several days after the indictment, though he was not officially indicted, Blatter stepped down from his long presidency.

In order to understand the amount of exposure and money involved, an estimated one billion people watched at least some of the 2010 World Cup Final. In the same year the National Football League's Super Bowl accumulated only 114.4 million worldwide viewers. Given the massive exposure, it is no wonder that sponsors as well as television and media outlets want to be involved. However, sponsors do not want to be associated with a large scandal. Coca-Cola, Adidas, Nike, McDonald's, and Hyundai Motor were all said to be "deeply concerned" about the FBI allegations and the indictments brought recently by the United States Department of Justice against a growing list of regional and country level

FIFA-affiliated executives who were identified as having participated in the alleged corruption.

Many of the sponsors are cautious about supporting an organization that has been as tainted politically as has FIFA. Apparently, the way the corruption has been pursued is through intermediaries who are paid exorbitant amounts for contracts that they helped to establish; then these intermediaries funnel the bribes to the leaders of the regional and country FIFA related associations. For example, in order for Nike to get a contract in the soccer-crazed country of Brazil, it paid a sports marketing agency, Traffic Brazil, $30 million between 1996 and 1999 which Traffic Brazil used, in part, for bribes and kick-backs. This allowed Nike to sign a 10-year, $160 million agreement to become a co-sponsor of the CBF, the Brazilian soccer confederation. Nike's strategic intent for the deal was to better compete with its chief overseas rival, Adidas. In 2014, the World Cup was held in Brazil, and Nike had $2.3 billion in sales of soccer products, an annual increase of 21 percent, compared with $2.29 billion in sales for Adidas, which was up 20 percent over its previous year. These figures illustrate how strong the incentives are for sponsors as well as for media outlets to participate; the advertising potential and selling opportunities are enormous for those involved.

VALERIANO DI DOMENICO/Getty Images

Former FIFA President, Sepp Blatter, speaking during a press conference at the headquarters of the world's football governing body in Zurich shortly before stepping down from his FIFA leadership position.

However, because of the weak institutional infrastructure in many countries around the world where the game of soccer is played, there is opportunity for corruption. Apparently, many involved in the FIFA infrastructure globally, regionally, and within specific countries have taken advantage of this opportunity. For example, Paraguay has been the headquarters for the Latin American regional confederation known as CONMEBOL. CONMEBOL has been centered in Paraguay since 1998 when Nicolás Leoz, a Paraguayan business man and president of the Latin American Confederation, negotiated to have the confederation headquartered there by having the Paraguay parliament secure prosecutorial immunity for the organization. In essence, this gave the federation license to act in ways that would protect it against local law enforcement officials, just as a local embassy would have exemption from prosecution in a particular foreign country. As such, this allowed the local confederation to pursue deals under the table. Leoz was charged in the FIFA indictments by the U.S. Department of Justice, along with 13 other FIFA officials, of bribery and money laundering schemes related to funds he received from sports marketing firms during his tenure at CONMEBOL. Interestingly, following the indictment, Paraguay's congress moved quickly to repeal the prosecutorial immunity for the CONMEBOL federation.

Likewise, many other legal and investigative organizations in Switzerland, Latin America, and around the world, including INTERPOL, an international investigation organization, have begun to initiate their own enquiries. Many fans in the soccer world have been excited about these indictments because many have felt that the corruption was hurting the game. People were profiting in illegal ways that created corruption throughout many organizations associated with the game of soccer. This Strategic Focus outlines a main danger of working in countries where many participate in corrupt practices which are indirectly sponsored by the government. This is not to say officials in more developed governments are not also corrupt, but the rule of law is not as strong in many developing countries.

Sources: 2015, A timeline of the FIFA scandal, *LA Times*, www.latimes.com, June 2; P. Blake, 2015, FIFA scandal: Why the US is policing a global game, *BBC News*, www.bbc.com, May 28; M. Futterman, A. Viswanatha, & C. M. Matthews, 2015, Soccer's geyser of cash, *Wall Street Journal*, May 28, A1, A10; S. Germano, 2015, Nike is cooperating with investigators, *Wall Street Journal*, May 28, A11; P. Keirnan, R. Jelmayer, & L. Magalhaes, 2015, Soccer boss learned ropes from his Brazilian mentor, *Wall Street Journal*, May 30–31, A4; K. Malic, 2015, The corruption rhetoric of the FIFA scandal, *New York Times*, www.nytimes.com, June 16; S. S. Munoz, 2015, FIFA pro shows soccer state within a state, *Wall Street Journal*, June 20–21, A7, S. Varinca, T. Micklel, & J. Robinson, 2015, Scandal pressures soccer's sponsors, *Wall Street Journal*, May 29, A1, A8; A. Viswanatha, S. Germano, & P. Kowsmann, 2015, U.S. probes Nike Brazil money, *Wall Street Journal*, June 13–14, B1, B4; M. Yglesias & J. Stromberg, 2015, FIFA's huge corruption and bribery scandal, explained, *VOX*, www.vox.com, June 3; C. Zillman, 2015, Here's how major FIFA sponsors are reacting to the scandal, *Fortune*, www.fortune.com, May 28.

As such, power outages have been intermittent and lasting up to 12 hours. This has caused a significant decrease in productivity for the dominant industry, mining, which produces 60 percent of South Africa's exports. The mining industry uses 15 percent of the country's electricity, and, as such, Eskom negotiates with each large commercial customer to reduce its power input at peak times. ArcelorMittal S.A., a large steel firm, has been losing $130,000 an hour because it has had to dial back its power usage "almost daily." DRDGOLD's gold production dropped 3 percent in the last 3 months of 2014 because of power outages. As this example suggests, infrastructure can be a significant economic risk in emerging or partially developed economies such as South Africa.[118]

Another economic risk is the perceived security risk of a foreign firm acquiring firms that have key natural resources or firms that may be considered strategic in regard to intellectual property. For instance, many Chinese firms have been buying natural resource firms in Australia and Latin America. as well as manufacturing assets in the United States.

Bloomberg/Getty Images

Darkness surrounding residential homes due to blackout by Eskom Holdings SOC Ltd. in the Troyeville suburb of Johannesburg, South Africa, in 2014.

This has made the governments of the key resource firms nervous about such strategic assets falling under the control of state-owned Chinese firms.[119] Terrorism has also been of concern. Indonesia has difficulty competing for investment against China and India, countries that are viewed as having fewer security risks.

As noted earlier, the differences and fluctuations in the value of currencies is among the foremost economic risks of using an international strategy.[120] This is especially true as the level of the firm's geographic diversification increases to the point where the firm is trading in a large number of currencies. The value of the dollar relative to other currencies can affect the value of the international assets and earnings of U.S. firms. For example, an increase in the value of the U.S. dollar can reduce the value of U.S. multinational firms' international assets and earnings in other countries. Furthermore, the value of different currencies can, at times, dramatically affect a firm's competitiveness in global markets because of its effect on the prices of goods manufactured in different countries. An increase in the value of the dollar can harm U.S. firms' exports to international markets because of the price differential of the products. For example, Johnson & Johnson recently reported that the firm's international results were impacted negatively by the increased value of the dollar, while Unilever's results were positive due to the decreased value of the euro relative to the dollar.[121] Thus, government oversight and control of economic and financial capital, as well as corporate governance rules in a country, affect not only local economic activity, but also foreign investments in the country.[122]

8-6 Strategic Competitiveness Outcomes

As previously discussed, international strategies can result in three basic benefits (increased market size; economies of scale and learning; and location advantages) for firms. These basic benefits are gained when the firm successfully manages political, economic, and other institutional risks while implementing its international strategies. In turn, these benefits are critical to the firm's efforts to achieve strategic competitiveness (as measured by improved performance and enhanced innovation—see Figure 8.1).

Overall, the degree to which firms achieve strategic competitiveness through international strategies is expanded or increased when they successfully implement an international diversification strategy. As an extension or elaboration of international strategy, an **international diversification strategy** is a strategy through which a firm expands the sales of its goods or services across the borders of global regions and countries into a potentially large number of geographic locations or markets. Instead of entering one or just a few markets, the international diversification strategy finds firms using international business-level and international corporate-level strategies for the purpose of entering multiple regions and markets in order to sell their products.

8-6a International Diversification and Returns

Evidence suggests numerous reasons for firms to use an international diversification strategy,[123] meaning that international diversification should be related positively to a firm's performance as measured by the returns it earns on its investments. Research has shown that as international diversification increases, a firm's returns decrease initially but then increase quickly as it learns how to manage the increased geographic diversification it has created.[124] In fact, the stock market is particularly sensitive to investments in international markets. Firms that are broadly diversified into multiple international markets usually achieve the most positive stock returns, especially when they diversify geographically into core business areas.[125]

An **international diversification strategy** is a strategy through which a firm expands the sales of its goods or services across the borders of global regions and countries into a potentially large number of geographic locations or markets.

Many factors contribute to the positive effects of international diversification, such as private versus government ownership, potential economies of scale and experience, location advantages, increased market size, and the opportunity to stabilize returns. The stabilization of returns through international diversification helps reduce a firm's overall risk.[126] Large, well-established firms and entrepreneurial ventures can both achieve these positive outcomes by successfully implementing an international diversification strategy. As described in an earlier example, FEMSA was using an acquisition strategy to increase its international diversification. FEMSA's financial results suggest that it has achieved positive returns from this strategy.

8-6b Enhanced Innovation

In Chapter 1, we indicated that developing new technology is at the heart of strategic competitiveness. As noted in our discussion of the determinants of national advantage (see Figure 8.3), a nation's competitiveness depends, in part, on the capacity of its industries to innovate. Eventually and inevitably, competitors outperform firms that fail to innovate. Therefore, the only way for individual nations and individual firms to sustain a competitive advantage is to upgrade it continually through innovation.[127]

An international diversification strategy creates the potential for firms to achieve greater returns on their innovations (through larger or more numerous markets) while reducing the often substantial risks of R&D investments. Additionally, international diversification may be necessary to generate the resources required to sustain a large-scale R&D operation. An environment of rapid technological obsolescence makes it difficult to invest in new technology and the capital-intensive operations necessary to compete in such an environment. Firms operating solely in domestic markets may find such investments difficult because of the length of time required to recoup the original investment. However, diversifying into a number of international markets improves a firm's ability to appropriate additional returns from innovation before domestic competitors can overcome the initial competitive advantage created by the innovation.[128] In addition, firms moving into international markets are exposed to new products and processes. If they learn about those products and processes and integrate this knowledge into their operations, further innovation can be developed. To incorporate the learning into their own R&D processes, firms must manage those processes effectively in order to absorb and use the new knowledge to create further innovations.[129] For a number of reasons then, international strategies and certainly an international diversification strategy provide incentives for firms to innovate.[130]

The relationship among international geographic diversification, innovation, and returns is complex. Some level of performance is necessary to provide the resources the firm needs to diversify geographically; in turn, geographic diversification provides incentives and resources to invest in R&D. Effective R&D should enhance the firm's returns, which then provide more resources for continued geographic diversification and investment in R&D.[131] Of course, the returns generated from these relationships increase through effective managerial practices. Evidence suggests that more culturally diverse top management teams often have a greater knowledge of international markets and their idiosyncrasies, but their orientation to expand internationally can be affected by the nature of their incentives.[132] Moreover, managing the business units of a geographically diverse multinational firm requires skill, not only in managing a decentralized set of businesses, but also coordinating diverse points of view emerging from businesses located in different countries and regions. Firms able to do this increase the likelihood of outperforming their rivals.[133]

8-7   The Challenge of International Strategies

Effectively using international strategies creates basic benefits and contributes to the firm's strategic competitiveness. However, for several reasons, attaining these positive outcomes is difficult.

8-7a   Complexity of Managing International Strategies

Pursuing international strategies, particularly an international diversification strategy, typically leads to growth in a firm's size and the complexity of its operations. In turn, larger size and greater operational complexity make a firm more difficult to manage. At some point, size and complexity either cause the firm to become virtually unmanageable or increase the cost of its management beyond the value created using international strategies. Different cultures and institutional practices (e.g., those associated with governmental agencies) that are part of the countries in which a firm competes when using an international strategy also can create difficulties.[134]

Firms have to build on their capabilities and other advantages to overcome the challenges encountered in international markets. For example, some firms from emerging economies that hold monopolies in their home markets can invest the resources gained there to enhance their competitiveness in international markets (because they don't have to be concerned about competitors in home markets).[135] The key is for firms to overcome the various liabilities of foreignness regardless of their source.

8-7b   Limits to International Expansion

Learning how to effectively manage an international strategy improves the likelihood of achieving positive outcomes such as enhanced performance. However, at some point, the degree of geographic and possibly product diversification the firm's international strategies bring about causes the returns from using the strategies to level off and eventually become negative.[136]

There are several reasons for the limits to the positive effects of the diversification associated with international strategies. First, greater geographic dispersion across country borders increases the costs of coordination between units and the distribution of products. This is especially true when firms have multiple locations in countries that have diverse subnational institutions. Second, trade barriers, logistical costs, cultural diversity, and other differences by country (e.g., access to raw materials and different employee skill levels) greatly complicate the implementation of an international strategy.[137]

Institutional and cultural factors can be strong barriers to the transfer of a firm's core competencies from one market to another.[138] Marketing programs often have to be redesigned and new distribution networks established when firms expand into new markets. In addition, firms may encounter different labor costs and capital expenses. In general, it becomes increasingly difficult to effectively implement, manage, and control a firm's international operations with increases in geographic diversity.[139]

The amount of diversification in a firm's international operations that can be managed varies from company to company and is affected by managers' abilities to deal with ambiguity and complexity. The problems of central coordination and integration are mitigated if the firm's international operations compete in friendly countries that are geographically close and have cultures similar to its own country's culture. In that case, the firm is likely to encounter fewer trade barriers, the laws and customs are better understood, and the product is easier to adapt to local markets.[140] For example, U.S. firms may find it less difficult to expand their operations into Mexico, Canada, and Western European countries than into Asian countries.

The relationships between the firm using an international strategy and the governments in the countries in which the firm is competing can also be constraining.[141] The reason for this is that the differences in host countries' governmental policies and practices can be substantial, creating a need for the focal firm to learn how to manage what can be a large set of different enforcement policies and practices. At some point, the differences create too many problems for the firm to be successful. Using strategic alliances is another way firms can deal with this limiting factor. Partnering with companies in different countries allows the foreign-entering firm to rely on its partner to help deal with local laws, rules, regulations, and customs. But these partnerships are not risk free and managing them tends to be difficult.[142]

SUMMARY

- The use of international strategies is increasing. Multiple factors and conditions are influencing the increasing use of these strategies, including opportunities to

  - extend a product's life cycle

  - gain access to critical raw materials, sometimes including relatively inexpensive labor

  - integrate a firm's operations on a global scale to better serve customers in different countries

  - better serve customers whose needs appear to be more alike today as a result of global communications media and the Internet's capabilities to inform

  - meet increasing demand for goods and services that is surfacing in emerging markets

- When used effectively, international strategies yield three basic benefits: increased market size, economies of scale and learning, and location advantages. Firms use international business-level and international corporate-level strategies to geographically diversify their operations.

- International business-level strategies are usually grounded in one or more home-country advantages. Research suggests that there are four determinants of national advantage: factors of production; demand conditions; related and supporting industries; and patterns of firm strategy, structure, and rivalry.

- There are three types of international corporate-level strategies. A multidomestic strategy focuses on competition within each country in which the firm competes. Firms using a multidomestic strategy decentralize strategic and operating decisions to the business units operating in each country, so that each unit can tailor its products to local conditions. A global strategy assumes more standardization of products across country boundaries; therefore, a competitive strategy is centralized and controlled by the home office. Commonly, large multinational firms, particularly those with multiple diverse products being sold in many different markets, use a

multidomestic strategy with some product lines and a global strategy with others.

- A transnational strategy seeks to integrate characteristics of both multidomestic and global strategies for the purpose of being able to simultaneously emphasize local responsiveness and global integration.

- Two global environmental trends—liability of foreignness and regionalization—are influencing firms' choices of international strategies as well as their implementation. Liability of foreignness challenges firms to recognize that distance between their domestic market and international markets affects how they compete. Some firms choose to concentrate their international strategies on regions (e.g., the EU and NAFTA) rather than on individual country markets.

- Firms can use one or more of five entry modes to enter international markets. Exporting, licensing, strategic alliances, acquisitions, and new wholly owned subsidiaries, often referred to as greenfield ventures, are the five entry modes. Most firms begin with exporting or licensing because of their lower costs and risks. Later they often use strategic alliances and acquisitions as well. The most expensive and risky means of entering a new international market is establishing a new wholly owned subsidiary (greenfield venture). On the other hand, such subsidiaries provide the advantages of maximum control by the firm and, if successful, the greatest returns. Large, geographically diversified firms often use most or all five entry modes across different markets when implementing international strategies.

- Firms encounter a number of risks when implementing international strategies. The two major categories of risks firms need to understand and address when diversifying geographically through international strategies are political risks (risks concerned with the probability that a firm's operations will be disrupted by political forces or events, whether they occur in the firm's domestic market or in the markets the firm has entered to implement its international strategies) and economic risks (risks resulting from fundamental weaknesses in a country's or a region's economy with the potential to adversely affect a firm's ability to implement its international strategies).

■ Successful use of international strategies (especially an international diversification strategy) contributes to a firm's strategic competitiveness in the form of improved performance and enhanced innovation. International diversification facilitates innovation in a firm because it provides a larger market to gain greater and faster returns from investments in innovation. In addition, international diversification can generate the resources necessary to sustain a large-scale R&D program.

■ In general, international diversification helps to achieve above-average returns, but this assumes that the

diversification is effectively implemented and that the firm's international operations are well managed. International diversification provides greater economies of scope and learning which, along with greater innovation, help produce above-average returns.

■ A firm using international strategies to pursue strategic competitiveness often experiences complex challenges that must be overcome. Some limits also constrain the ability to manage international expansion effectively. International diversification increases coordination and distribution costs, and management problems are exacerbated by trade barriers, logistical costs, and cultural diversity, among other factors.

KEY TERMS

global strategy 247
greenfield venture 256
international strategy 239

international diversification strategy 262
multidomestic strategy 246
transnational strategy 248

REVIEW QUESTIONS

1. What incentives influence firms to use international strategies?

2. What are the three basic benefits firms can achieve by successfully using an international strategy?

3. What four factors are determinants of national advantage and serve as a basis for international business-level strategies?

4. What are the three international corporate-level strategies? What are the advantages and disadvantages associated with these individual strategies?

5. What are some global environmental trends affecting the choice of international strategies, particularly international corporate-level strategies?

6. What five entry modes do firms consider as paths to use to enter international markets? What is the typical sequence in which firms use these entry modes?

7. What are political risks and what are economic risks? How should firms approach dealing with these risks?

8. What are the strategic competitiveness outcomes firms can reach through international strategies, and particularly through an international diversification strategy?

9. What are two important issues that can potentially affect a firm's ability to successfully use international strategies?

Mini-Case

An International Strategy Powers ABB's Future

ABB, headquartered in Zurich, Switzerland, is a major competitor in the power and automation technologies industries across the major markets globally. It has 140,000 employees operating in almost 100 countries. In fact, it has five major businesses—power products, power systems, discrete automation, low voltage products, and process

automation. It operates in eight major regions: (1) Northern Europe, (2) Central Europe, (3) the Mediterranean, (4) North America, (5) South America, (6) India, the Middle East, and Africa, (7) North Asia, and (8) South Asia. Over time, ABB has been a successful company using its geographic diversification across the globe to its advantage.

It also exemplifies the difficulty of managing an international strategy and operations. For example, its power systems business has experienced performance problems in recent years due to poor performance in some countries due primarily to the economy downturn. Notwithstanding the difficulty of managing in emerging economies, much of its growth is focused on improving country infrastructure such as power systems and grids. In 2014, the firm announced that the Asia, Middle East, and Africa (AMEA) region currently contributes about 37 percent of ABB's total revenue, or about $15.3 billion, and "emerging markets were planned to contribute to two-thirds of the forecast growth between 2015 and 2020."

In recent years, most of ABB's entries to new markets and expansions in existing markets have come from acquisitions of existing businesses in those markets. Recently, it acquired Siemens' solar energy business, Power-One, and U.S.-based Los Gatos Research, a manufacturer of gas analyzers used in environmental monitoring and research. The purchase of Power-One represents a major risk as the solar power industry is in a downturn. Yet some analysts predict a brighter future for the industry over the long term. ABB also uses other modes of entry and expansion, exemplified by the 2013 joint venture with China's Jiangsu Jinke Smart Electric Company to design, manufacture, and provide follow-up service on high voltage instrument transformers. It also recently procured major contracts for business in Brazil and South Africa.

Partly due to the global economic recession that began in 2008, recent weak economic performance, and some poor expansion decisions, ABB's performance has been weaker than expected. As a result, the CEO and chief technology officer announced their resignations in 2013. Despite these changes, ABB is a highly respected global brand, and, after its recent changes (e.g., closing some country operations), its revenues and earnings have started to rise. These positive changes have been largely attributed to the success of its North American businesses. Its acquisitions of Baldor (maker of industrial motors) in 2010 and Thomas & Betts in 2012 greatly enhanced its North American operations and revenues. It has also had success in manufacturing equipment and robots with its robotics business headquartered in the United States. It is even moving to help small companies, such as ones in the beer industry, to automate their production processes. Therefore, even in turbulent times, ABB's future looks bright.

Sources: 2015, About ABB, www.abb.com, accessed on June 18; J. R. Hagerty, 2015, Meet the new robots, *Wall Street Journal*, June 3, R1–R2; 2104, Emerging markets key to ABB's growth strategy, *MEED: Middle East Economic Digest*, September 12, 14; J. Revill, 2014, Robots keep the beer flowing. *Wall Street* Journal, December 27, B4; 2013, ABB procures contract in Brazil, *Zacks Equity Research*, www.zacks.com, May 14; 2013, ABB's South African project, *Zacks Equity Research*, www.zacks.com, May 13; P. Winters, 2013, ABB loses Banerjee after Hogan's decision to step down, *Bloomberg Businessweek*, www.businessweek.com, May 13; J. Revill & A. Morse, 2013, ABB CEO to resign, *Wall Street Journal*, www.wsj.com, May 10; 2013, ABB strengthens footprints in China, *Zacks Equity Research*, www.zacks.com, May 10; J. Revill, 2013, ABB buys US gas analyzer company Los Gatos Research, *Wall Street Journal*, www.wsj.com, May 3; 2013, ABB/Power-One: Shining example, *Financial Times*, www.ft.com, April 22; W. Pentland, 2013, ABB gambles big on solar power, *Forbes*, www.forbes.com, April 22; M. Scott, 2013, ABB to buy Power-One for $1 billion, *New York Times Dealbook*, http://dealbook.nytimes.com, April 22; J. Shotter, 2013, ABB boosted by US ventures, *Financial Times*, www.ft.com, February 14; J. Shotter, 2012, ABB overhauls power systems division, *Financial Times*, www.ft.com, December 14.

Case Discussion Questions

1. What are the dominant reason's for ABB to enter into international markets?

2. Which corporate international strategy would you classify ABB as using? Explain your answer.

3. Why has ABB used acquisitions and joint ventures as dominant entry modes in international markets?

4. What are the main political and economic risks that ABB must deal with given that it has a strong focus on entering emerging economies?

5. What are the significant organizational complexities that ABB encounters as it tries to manage its international strategy?

NOTES

1. C. G. Asmussen & N. J. Foss, 2014, Competitive advantage and the existence of the multinational corporation: Earlier research and the role of frictions, *Global Strategy Journal*, 4: 49–54; C. N. Pitellis & D. J. Teece, 2012, Cross-border market co-creation, dynamic capabilities and the entrepreneurial theory of the multinational enterprise. In D. J. Teece (ed.), *Strategy, Innovation and the Theory of the Firm*, Cheltenham, U.K.: Edward Elgar, 341–364; M. J. Nieto & A. Rodriguez, 2011, Offshoring of R&D: Looking abroad to improve innovation performance, *Journal of International Business Studies*, 42: 345–361.

2. S. K. Majumdar & A. Bhattacharjee, 2014, Firms, markets, and the state: Institutional change and manufacturing sector profitability variances in India, *Organization Science*, 25: 509–528; R. M. Holmes, T. Miller, M. A. Hitt, & M. P. Salmador, 2013, The interrelationship among informal institutions, formal institutions and inward foreign direct investment, *Journal of Management*, 39: 531–566.

3. A. Gaur & A. Delios, 2015, International diversification of emerging market firms: The role of ownership structure and group affiliation, *Management International Review*, 55: 235–253; J.-L. Arregle, L. Naldi, M. Nordqvist, & M. A. Hitt, 2012, Internationalization of family-controlled firms: A study of the effects of external involvement in governance, *Entrepreneurship Theory and Practice*, 36: 1115–1143; M. A. Hitt, L. Tihanyi, T. Miller, & B. Connelly, 2006, International diversification: Antecedents, outcomes and moderators, *Journal of Management*, 32: 831–867.

4. H. Kim, R. E. Hoskisson, & S. Lee, 2015, Why strategic factor markets matter: 'New' multinationals' geographic diversification and firm profitability, *Strategic Management Journal*, 36: 518–536; M. F. Wiersema & H. P. Bowen, 2011, The relationship between international diversification and firm performance: Why it remains a puzzle, *Global Strategy Journal*, 1: 152–170.

5. R. Vernon, 1996, International investment and international trade in the product cycle, *Quarterly Journal of Economics*, 80: 190–207.

6. 2015, Our strategy, Rio Tinto homepage, www.riotinto.com, accessed on June 16.

7. J. Hookway, Vietnam's mobile revolution, *Wall Street Journal*, June 15, B4.

8. M. J. Mol & C. Brewster, 2014, The outsourcing strategy of local and multinational firms: A supply base perspective, *Global Strategy Journal*, 4: 20–34; J. Li, Y. Li, & D. Shapiro, 2012, Knowledge seeking and outward FDI of emerging market firms: The moderating effect of inward FDI, *Global Strategy Journal*, 2: 277–295.

9. J. P. Murmann, S. Z. Ozdemir, & D. Sardana, 2015, The role of home country demand in the internationalization of new ventures, *Research Policy*, 44: 1207–1225; K. E. Meyer, R. Mudambi, & R. Nanula, 2011, Multinational enterprises and local contexts: The opportunities and challenges of multiple embeddedness, *Journal of Management Studies*, 48: 235–252.

10. 2015, Our stores, Carrefour Group homepage, www.carrefour.com, June 18.

11. D. Gray, 2014, What Tesco can learn from Carrefour, *Stores Magazine*, September, 66.

12. V. Mallet, 2014, Narendra Modi prepares to raise India's FDI limits, *Financial Times*, www.ft.com, May 30; T. R. Annamalai & A. Deshmukh, 2011, Venture capital and private equity in India: An analysis of investments and exits, *Journal of Indian Business Research*, 3: 6–21.

13. S. L. Fourné, J. P. Jansen, & T. M. Mom, 2014, Strategic agility in MNEs: Managing tensions to capture opportunities across emerging and established markets, *California Management Review*, 56(3): 13–38; R. Ramamurti, 2012, What is really different about emerging market multinationals? *Global Strategy Journal*, 2: 41–47.

14. P. Regnér & J. Edman, 2014, MNE institutional advantage: How subunits shape, transpose and evade host country institutions, *Journal of International Business Studies*, 45: 275–302; M. Carney, E. R. Gedajlovic, P. M. A. R. Heugens, M. van Essen, & J. van Oosterhout, 2011, Business group affiliation, performance, context, and strategy: A meta-analysis, *Academy of Management Journal*, 54: 437–460; B. Elango, 2009, Minimizing effects of "liability of foreignness": Response strategies of foreign firm in the United States, *Journal of World Business*, 44: 51–62.

15. 2013, Midrange growth strategy starting from fiscal year 2013, News Release, www.takeda.com, May 9; K. Inagaki & J. Osawa, 2011, Takeda, Toshiba make $16 billion M&A push, *Wall Street Journal*, www.wsj.com, May 20; K. Iagaki, 2011, Takeda buys Nycomed for $14 billion, *Wall Street Journal*, www.wsj.com, May 20.

16. K. Kalasin, P. Dussauge, & M. Rivera-Santos, 2014, the expansion of emerging economy firms into advanced markets: The influence of intentional path-breaking change, *Global Strategy Journal*, 4: 75–103; A. Verbeke & W. Yuan, 2013, The drivers of multinational enterprise subsidiary entrepreneurship in China: A resource-based view perspective, *Journal of Management Studies*, 50: 236–258; S. B. Choi, S. H. Lee, & C. Williams, 2011, Ownership and firm innovation in transition economy: Evidence from China, *Research Policy*, 40: 441–452.

17. 2015, Corporate, Ford Motor Company, www.ford.com, accessed June 19; N. E. Boudette, 2011, Ford forecasts sharp gains from Asian sales, *Wall Street Journal*, www.wsj.com, June 8.

18. D. McCann, 2014, One Ford, One Finance. *CFO*, July, 16–17.

19. R. Erkelens, B. Hooff, M. Huysman, & P. Vlaar, 2015, Learning from locally embedded knowledge: Facilitating organizational learning in geographically dispersed settings, *Global Strategy Journal*, 5: 177–197; A. H. Kirka, G. T. Hult, S. Deligonul, M. Z. Perry, & S. T. Cavusgil, 2012, A multilevel examination of the drivers of firm multinationality: A meta-analysis, *Journal of Management*, 38: 502–530; L. Nachum & S. Song, 2011, The MNE as a portfolio: Interdependencies in MNE growth trajectory, *Journal of International Business Studies*, 42: 381–405.

20. M. Kim, 2015, Geographic scope, isolating mechanisms, and value appropriation, *Strategic Management Journal*, in press; G. Qian, T. A. Khoury, M. W. Peng, & Z. Qian, 2010, The performance implications of intra- and inter-regional geographic diversification, *Strategic Management Journal*, 31: 1018–1030; H. Zou & P. N. Ghauri, 2009, Learning through international acquisitions: The process of knowledge acquisition in China, *Management International Review*, 48: 207–226.

21. R. Sambharya & J. Lee, 2014, Renewing dynamic capabilities globally: An empirical study of the world's largest MNCs, *Management International Review*, 54: 137–169; Y. Zhang, H. Li, Y. Li, & L.-A. Zhou, 2010, FDI spillovers in an emerging market: The role of foreign firms' country origin diversity and domestic firms' absorptive capacity, *Strategic Management Journal*, 31: 969–989; J. Song & J. Shin, 2008, The paradox of technological capabilities: A study of knowledge sourcing from host countries of overseas R&D operations, *Journal of International Business Studies*, 39: 291–303.

22. N. Hashai & P. J. Buckley, 2014, Is competitive advantage a necessary condition for the emergence of the multinational enterprise? *Global Strategy Journal*, 4: 35–48; F. J. Froese, 2013, Work values of the next generation of business leaders in Shanghai, Tokyo and Seoul, *Asia Pacific Journal of Management*, 30: 297–315.

23. F. Lo & F. Lin, 2015, Advantage transfer on location choice and subsidiary performance, *Journal of Business Research*, 68: 1527–1531; A. Gambardella & M. S. Giarratana, 2010, Localized knowledge

spillovers and skill-based performance, *Strategic Entrepreneurship Journal*, 4: 323–339; A. M. Rugman & A. Verbeke, 2009, A new perspective on the regional and global strategies of multinational services firms, *Management International Review*, 48: 397–411.

24. C. Peeters, C. Dehon, & P. Garcia-Prieto, 2015, The attention stimulus of cultural differences in global services sourcing, *Journal of International Business Studies*, 46: 241–251; O. Shenkar, 2012, Cultural distance revisited: Towards a more rigorous conceptualization and measurement of cultural differences, *Journal of International Business Studies*, 43: 1–11; R. Chakrabarti, Gupta-Mukherjee, & N. Jayaraman, 2009, Mars-Venus marriages: Culture and cross-border M&A, *Journal of International Business Studies*, 40: 216–236.

25. S. L. Sun, M. W. Peng, R. P. Lee, & W. Tan, 2015, Institutional open access at home and outward internationalization, *Journal of World Business*, 50: 234–246; B. T. McCann & G. Vroom, 2010, Pricing response to entry and agglomeration effects, *Strategic Management Journal*, 31: 284–305.

26. Sambharya & Lee, Renewing dynamic capabilities globally: An empirical study of the world's largest MNCs; Y. Y. Chang, Y. Gong, & M. Peng, 2012, Expatriate knowledge transfer, subsidiary absorptive capacity and subsidiary performance, *Academy of Management Journal*, 55: 927–948; P. Kappen, 2011, Competence-creating overlaps and subsidiary technological evolution in the multinational corporation, *Research Policy*, 40: 673–686.

27. H. Liang, B. Ren, & S. L. Sun, 2015, An anatomy of state control in the globalization of state-owned enterprises, *Journal of International Business Studies*, 46: 223–240; Y. Fang, M. Wade, A. Delios, & P. W. Beamish, 2013, An exploration of multinational enterprise knowledge resources and foreign subsidiary performance, *Journal of World Business*, 48: 30–38; A. Arino, 2011, Building the global enterprise: Strategic assembly, *Global Strategy Journal*, 1: 47–49.

28. M. E. Porter, 1990, *The Competitive Advantage of Nations*, NY: The Free Press.

29. Ibid., 84.

30. D. Dulaney, 2014, Chiquita agrees to $742 million buyout, *Wall Street Journal*, www.wsj.com, October 28; D. Englander, 2013, Chiquita Brands—Stocks with appeal, *Wall Street Journal*, www.wsj.com, April 28.

31. M. Bucheli & M. Kim, M. 2015, Attacked from both sides: A dynamic model of multinational corporations' strategies for protection of their property rights, *Global Strategy Journal*, 5: 1–26; C. Wang, J. Hong, M. Kafouros, & M. Wright, 2012, Exploring the role of government involvement in outward FDI from emerging economies, *Journal of International Business Studies*, 43: 655–676; J. Nishimura & H. Okamuro,

2011, Subsidy and networking: The effects of direct and indirect support programs of the cluster policy, *Research Policy*, 40: 714–727.

32. C. Trundell & Y Hagiwara, 2015, Lexus flag China ambitions with new ES's Shanghai debut, *Bloomberg Business*, www.bloombergbusiness.com, April 9.

33. S. Song, M. Makhija, & S. Lee, 2014, Within-country growth options versus across-country switching options in foreign direct investment, *Global Strategy Journal*, 4: 127–142.

34. Kim, Hoskisson, & Lee, Why strategic factor markets matter: 'New multinationals' geographic diversification and firm profitability; M. Musteen, D. K. Datta, & J. Francis, 2014, Early internationalization by firms in transition economies into developed markets: The role of international networks, *Global Strategy Journal*, 4: 221–237.

35. R. Qu & Z. Zhang, 2015, Market orientation and business performance in MNC foreign subsidiaries—moderating effects of integration and responsiveness, *Journal of Business Research*, 68: 919–924.

36. W. Aghina, A. De Smet, & S Heywood, 2014, The past and future of global organizations, *McKinsey Quarterly*, March, 97–106; S. Zaheer & L. Nachum, 2011, Sense of place: From location resources to MNE locational capital, *Global Strategy Journal*, 1: 96–108; N. Guimaraes-Costs & M. P. E. Cunha, 2009, Foreign locals: A liminal perspective of international managers, *Organizational Dynamics*, 38: 158–166.

37. S. C. Schleimer & T. Pedersen, T. 2014, The effects of MNC parent effort and social structure on subsidiary absorptive capacity, *Journal of International Business Studies*, 45: 303–320; J.-S. Chen & A. S. Lovvorn, 2011, The speed of knowledge transfer within multinational enterprises: The role of social capital, *International Journal of Commerce and Management*, 21: 46–62; H. Kasper, M. Lehrer, J. Muhlbacher, & B. Muller, 2009, Integration-responsiveness and knowledge-management perspectives on the MNC: A typology and field study of cross-site knowledge-sharing practices, *Journal of Leadership & Organizational Studies*, 15: 287–303.

38. 2015, Introduction to Unilever global, Unilever homepage, www.unilever.com, accessed on June 19; J. Neff, 2008, Unilever's CMO finally gets down to business, *Advertising Age*, July 11.

39. K. E. Meyer & S. Estrin, 2014, Local context and global strategy: Extending the integration responsiveness framework to subsidiary strategy, *Global Strategy Journal*, 4: 1–19; M. P. Koza, S. Tallman, & A. Ataay, 2011, The strategic assembly of global firms: A microstructural analysis of local learning and global adaptation, *Global Strategy Journal*, 1: 27–46; P. J. Buckley, 2009, The impact of the global factory on economic

development, *Journal of World Business*, 44: 131–143.

40. H. Berry, 2014, Global integration and innovation: Multicountry knowledge generation within MNCs, *Strategic Management Journal*, 35: 869–890; A. Zaheer & E. Hernandez, 2011, The geographic scope of the MNC and its alliance portfolio: Resolving the paradox of distance, *Global Strategy Journal*, 1: 109–126.

41. C. Wang, 2014, Accounting standards harmonization and financial statement comparability: Evidence from transnational information transfer, *Journal of Accounting Research*, 52: 955–992; L. Hail, C. Leuz, & P. Wysocki, 2010, Global accounting convergence and the potential adoption of IFRS by the U.S. (part II): Political factors and future scenarios for U.S. accounting standards, *Accounting Horizons*, 24: 567–581; R. G. Barker, 2003, Trend: Global accounting is coming, *Harvard Business Review*, 81(4): 24–25.

42. J. U. Kim & R. V. Aguilera, 2015, The world is spiky: An internationalization framework for a semi-globalized world, *Global Strategy Journal*, 5: 113–132; J.-L. Arregle, T. Miller, M. A. Hitt, & P. W. Beamish, 2013, Do regions matter? An integrated institutional and semiglobalization perspective on the internationalization of MNEs, *Strategic Management Journal*, 34: 910–934; L. H. Shi, C. White, S. Zou, & S. T. Cavusgil, 2010, Global account management strategies: Drivers and outcomes, *Journal of International Business Studies*, 41: 620–638.

43. S. Morris, R. Hammond, & S. Snell, 2014, A microfoundations approach to transnational capabilities: The role of knowledge search in an ever-changing world, *Journal of International Business Studies*, 45: 405–427; R. Greenwood, S. Fairclough, T. Morris, & M. Boussebaa, 2010, The organizational design of transnational professional service firms, *Organizational Dynamics*, 39: 173–183.

44. K. J. Breunig, R. Kvålshaugen, & K. M. Hydle, 2014, Knowing your boundaries: Integration opportunities in international professional service firms, *Journal of World Business*, 49: 502–511; C. Stehr, 2010, Globalisation strategy for small and medium-sized enterprises, *International Journal of Entrepreneurship and Innovation Management*, 12: 375–391; A. M. Rugman & A. Verbeke, 2008, A regional solution to the strategy and structure of multinationals, *European Management Journal*, 26: 305–313.

45. X. Zhang, W. Zhong, & S. Makino, 2015, Customer involvement and service firm internationalization performance: An integrative framework, *Journal of International Business Studies*, 46: 355–380; 2010, Regional resilience: Theoretical and empirical perspectives, *Cambridge Journal of Regions, Economy and Society*, 3–10; Rugman & Verbeke, A regional

solution to the strategy and structure of multinationals.

46. 2015, Unleashing a global snacking powerhouse, Mondelez International, www.mondelezinternational.com, accessed on June 22.

47. A. Millington, 2015, Mondelez splashes £10m to grow savoury snacks business as it looks to balance its portfolio, *Marketing Week*, www.marketingweek.com, April 10.

48. M. W. Peng & Y. Jiang, 2010, Institutions behind family ownership and control in large firms, *Journal of Management Studies*, 47: 253–273; A. M. Rugman & A. Verbeke, 2003, Extending the theory of the multinational enterprise: Internationalization and strategic management perspectives, *Journal of International Business Studies*, 34: 125–137.

49. I. Bremmer, E. Fry, & D. Shanker, 2015 The new world of business, *Fortune*, February 1, 86–92; D. Klonowski, 2011, Private equity in emerging markets: Stacking up the BRICs, *Journal of Private Equity*, 14: 24–37.

50. F. Jiang, L. Liu, & B. W. Stening, 2014, Do Foreign Firms in China Incur a Liability of Foreignness? The Local Chinese Firms' Perspective, *Thunderbird International Business Review*, 56: 501–518; J. Mata & E. Freitas, 2012, Foreignness and exit over the life cycle of firms, *Journal of International Business Studies*, 43: 615–630. R. G. Bell, I. Filatotchev, & A. A. Rasheed, 2012, The liability of foreignness, in capital markets: Sources and remedies, *Journal of International Business Studies*, 43: 107–122.

51. J. Aguilera-Caracuel, E. M. Fedriani, & B. L. Delgado-Márquez, 2014, Institutional distance among country influences and environmental performance standardization in multinational enterprises, *Journal of Business Research*, 67: 2385–2392; R. Salomon & Z. Wu, 2012, Institutional distance and local isomorphism strategy, *Journal of International Business Studies*, 43: 347–367.

52. T. Hutzschenreuter, I. Kleindienst, & S. Lange, 2014, Added psychic distance stimuli and MNE performance: Performance effects of added cultural, governance, geographic, and economic distance in MNEs' international expansion, *Journal of International Management*, 20: 38–54; J. T. Campbell, L. Eden, & S. R. Miller, 2012, Multinationals and corporate social responsibility in host countries: Does distance matter? *Journal of International Business Studies*, 43: 84–106; P. Ghemawat, 2001, Distance still matters, *Harvard Business Review*, 79(8): 137–145.

53. N. Y. Brannen, 2004, When Mickey loses face: Recontextualization, semantic fit and semiotics of foreignness, *Academy of Management Review*, 29: 593–616.

54. M. Schuman, 2006, Disney's Hong Kong headache, *Time*, www.time.com, May 8.

55. G. Suder, P. W. Liesch, S. Inomata, I. Mihailova, & B. Meng, 2015, The evolving geography of production hubs and regional value chains across East Asia: Trade in value-added, *Journal of World Business*, 50: 404–416; Arregle, Miller, Hitt, & Beamish, Do regions matter?; J. Cantwell & Y. Zhang, 2011, Innovation and location in the multinational firm, *International Journal of Technology Management*, 54: 116–132.

56. L. Stevens, 2015, Borders matter less and less in e-commerce, *Wall Street Journal*, June 24, B8; K. Ito & E. L. Rose, 2010, The implicit return on domestic and international sales: An empirical analysis of U.S. and Japanese firms, *Journal of International Business Studies*, 41: 1074–1089; A. M. Rugman & A. Verbeke, 2007, Liabilities of foreignness and the use of firm-level versus country level data: A response to Dunning et al. (2007), *Journal of International Business Studies*, 38: 200–205.

57. A. Ghobadian, A. M. Rugman, & R. L. Tung, 2014, Strategies for firm globalization and regionalization, *British Journal of Management*, 25: S1–S5; Arregle, Miller, Hitt, & Beamish, Do regions matter?; E. R. Banalieva, M. D. Santoro, & R. J. Jiang, 2012, Home region focus and technical efficiency of multinational enterprises: The moderating role of regional integration, *Management International Review*, 52: 493–518.

58. B. V. Dimitrova, B. Rosenbloom, & T. L. Andras, 2014, Does the degree of retailer international involvement affect retailer performance? *International Review of Retail, Distribution & Consumer Research*, 24: 243–277; A. M. Rugman & S. Girod, 2003, Retail multinationals and globalization: The evidence is regional, *European Management Journal*, 21: 24–37.

59. D. E. Westney, 2006, Review of the regional multinationals: MNEs and global strategic management (book review), *Journal of International Business Studies*, 37: 445–449.

60. S. Arita & K. Tanaka, 2014, Heterogeneous multinational firms and productivity gains from falling FDI barriers, *Review of World Economics*, 150: 83–113; R. D. Ludema, 2002, Increasing returns, multinationals and geography of preferential trade agreements, *Journal of International Economics*, 56: 329–358.

61. L Caliendo & F. Parro, 2015, Estimates of the trade and welfare effects of NAFTA, *Review of Economic Studies*, 82: 1–44; M. Aspinwall, 2009, NAFTA-ization: Regionalization and domestic political adjustment in the North American economic area, *Journal of Common Market Studies*, 47: 1–24.

62. N. Åkerman, 2015, Knowledge-acquisition strategies and the effects on market knowledge—profiling the internationalizing firm, *European Management Journal*, 33: 79–88; D. Zu & O. Shenar, 2002, Institutional distance and the multinational enterprise, *Academy of Management Review*, 27: 608–618.

63. P. J. Buckley & N. Hashai, 2014, The role of technological catch up and domestic market growth in the genesis of emerging country based multinationals, *Research Policy*, 43: 423–437; A. Ojala, 2008, Entry in a psychically distant market: Finnish small and medium-sized software firms in Japan, *European Management Journal*, 26: 135–144.

64. V. Hernández & M. J. Nieto, 2015, The effect of the magnitude and direction of institutional distance on the choice of international entry modes, *Journal of World Business*, 50: 122–132; K. D. Brouthers, 2013, Institutional, cultural and transaction cost influences on entry mode choice and performance, *Journal of International Business Studies*, 44: 1–13.

65. J.-F. Hennart & A. H. L. Slangen, A. 2015, Yes, we really do need more entry mode studies! A commentary on Shaver, *Journal of International Business Studies*, 46: 114–122; B. Maekelburger, C. Schwens, & R. Kabst, 2012, Asset specificity and foreign market entry mode choice of small and medium-sized enterprises: The moderating influence of knowledge safeguards and institutional safeguards, *Journal of International Business Studies*, 43: 458–476.

66. S. Gerschewski, E. L. Rose, & V. J. Lindsay, 2015, Understanding the drivers of international performance for born global firms: An integrated perspective, *Journal of World Business*, 50: 558–575; C. A. Cinquetti, 2009, Multinationals and exports in a large and protected developing country, *Review of International Economics*, 16: 904–918.

67. S. T. Cavusgil & G. Knight, 2015, The born global firm: An entrepreneurial and capabilities perspective on early and rapid internationalization, *Journal of International Business Studies*, 46: 3–16; P. Ganotakis & J. H. Love, 2012, Export propensity, export intensity and firm performance: The role of the entrepreneurial founding team, *Journal of International Business Studies*, 43: 693–718.

68. I. Zander, P. McDougall-Covin, & E. L. Rose, 2015, Born globals and international business: Evolution of a field of research, *Journal of International Business Studies*, 46: 27–35; M. Bandyk, 2008, Now even small firms can go global, *U.S. News & World Report*, March 10, 52.

69. S. Sui & M. Baum, 2014, Internationalization strategy, firm resources and the survival of SMEs in the export market, *Journal of International Business Studies*, 45: 821–841; B. Cassiman & E. Golovko, 2010, Innovation and internationalization through exports, *Journal of International Business Studies*, 42: 56–75.

70. E. Golovko & G. Valentini, 2014, Selective learning-by-exporting: Firm size and product versus process innovation, *Global Strategy Journal*, 4: 161–180; X. He, K. D. Brouthers, & I. Filatotchev, 2013, Resource-based and institutional perspectives on export channel selection and export performance, *Journal of*

Management, 39: 27–47; M. Hughes, S. L. Martin, R. E. Morgan, & M. J. Robson, 2010, Realizing product-market advantage in high-technology international new ventures: The mediating role of ambidextrous innovation, *Journal of International Marketing*, 18: 1–21.

71. A. Troianovski, 2014, German seeds web shopping in the developing world, *Wall Street Journal*, January 14, A1, A12; P. Ganotakis & J. H. Love, 2011, R&D, product innovation, and exporting: Evidence from UK new technology-based firms, *Oxford Economic Papers*, 63: 279–306; M. Gabrielsson & P. Gabrielsson, 2011, Internet-based sales channel strategies of born global firms, *International Business Review*, 20: 88–99.

72. B. Bozeman, H. Rimes, & J. Youtie, J. 2015, The evolving state-of-the-art in technology transfer research: Revisiting the contingent effectiveness model, *Research Policy*, 44: 34–49; P. S. Aulakh, M. Jiang, & Y. Pan, 2010, International technology licensing: Monopoly rents transaction costs and exclusive rights, *Journal of International Business Studies*, 41: 587–605; R. Bird & D. R. Cahoy, 2008, The impact of compulsory licensing on foreign direct investment: A collective bargaining approach, *American Business Law Journal*, 45: 283–330.

73. M. Bianchi, M. Frattini, J. Lejarraga, & A. Di Minin, 2014, Technology exploitation paths: combining technological and complementary resources in new product development and licensing, *Journal of Product Innovation Management*, 31: 146–169; M. S. Giarratana, & S. Torrisi, 2010, Foreign entry and survival in a knowledge-intensive market: Emerging economy countries' international linkages, technology competences, and firm experience, *Strategic Entrepreneurship Journal*, 4: 85–104; U. Lichtenthaler, 2008, Externally commercializing technology assets: An examination of different process stages, *Journal of Business Venturing*, 23: 445–464.

74. N. Byrnes & F. Balfour, 2009, Philip Morris unbound, *BusinessWeek*, May 4, 38–42.

75. 2015, PMI around the world, Philip Morris International homepage, www.pmi.com, accessed on June 23.

76. J. Li-Ying & Y. Wang, 2015, Find them home or abroad? The relative contribution of international technology in-licensing to "indigenous innovation" in China, *Long Range Planning*, 48: 123–134; E. Dechenaux, J. Thursby, & M. Thursby, 2011, Inventor moral hazard in university licensing: The role of contracts, *Research Policy*, 40: 94–104; S. Hagaoka, 2009, Does strong patent protection facilitate international technology transfer? Some evidence from licensing contrasts of Japanese firms, *Journal of Technology Transfer*, 34: 128–144.

77. A. Agarwal, I. Cockburn, & I. Zhang, L. Deals not done: Sources of failure in the market for ideas, *Strategic Management Journal*, 36: 976–986; U. Lichtenthaler, 2011, The evolution of technology licensing management: Identifying five strategic approaches, *R&D Management*, 41: 173–189; M. Fiedler & I. M. Welpe, 2010, Antecedents of cooperative commercialisation strategies of nanotechnology firms, *Research Policy*, 39: 400–410.

78. C. A. Barlett & S. Rangan, 1992, Komatsu Limited. In C. A. Bartlett & S. Ghoshal (eds.), *Transnational Management: Text, Cases and Readings in Cross-Border Management*, Homewood, IL: Irwin, 311–326.

79. F. J. Contractor & J. J. Reuer, 2014, Structuring and governing alliances: New directions for research, *Global Strategy Journal*, 4: 241–256; S. Veilleux, N. Haskell, & F. Pons, 2012, Going global: How smaller enterprises benefit from strategic alliances, *Journal of Business Strategy*, 33(5): 22–31; C. Schwens, J. J. Eiche, & R. Kabst, 2011, The moderating impact of informal institutional distance and formal institutional risk on SME entry mode choice, *Journal of Management Studies*, 48: 330–351.

80. J. J. Reuer & R. Ragozzino, 2014, Signals and international alliance formation: The roles of affiliations and international activities, *Journal of International Business Studies*, 45: 321–337; T. Barnes, S. Raynor, & J. Bacchus, 2012, A new typology of forms of international collaboration, *Journal of Business and Strategy*, 5: 81–102; S. Prashantham & S. Young, 2011, Post-entry speed of international new ventures, *Entrepreneurship Theory and Practice*, 35: 275–292.

81. F. J. Contractor & J. A. Woodley, 2015, How the alliance pie is split: Value appropriation by each partner in cross-border technology transfer alliances, *Journal of World Business*, 50: 535–547; Z. Bhanji & J. E. Oxley, 2013, Overcoming the dual liability of foreignness and privateness in international corporate citizenship partnerships, *Journal of International Business Studies*, 44: 290–311; J. S. Harrison, M. A. Hitt, R. E. Hoskisson, & R. D. Ireland, 2001, Resource complementarity in business combinations: Extending the logic to organization alliances, *Journal of Management*, 27: 679–690.

82. W. Shi, S. L. Sun, B. C. Pinkham, & M. W. Peng, 2014, Domestic alliance network to attract foreign partners: Evidence from international joint ventures in China, *Journal of International Business Studies*, 45: 338–362; R. A. D'Aveni, G. B. Dagnino, & K. G. Smith, 2010, The age of temporary advantage, *Strategic Management Journal*, 31: 1371–1385; M. A. Hitt, D. Ahlstrom, M. T. Dacin, E. Levitas, & L. Svobodina, 2004, The institutional effects on strategic alliance

partner selection in transition economies: China versus Russia, *Organization Science*, 15: 173–185.

83. Z. Khan, R. R. Sinkovics, & Y. K. Lew, 2015, International joint ventures as boundary spanners: Technological knowledge transfer in an emerging economy, *Global Strategy Journal*, 5: 48–68; G. Vasudeva, J. W. Spencer, & H. J. Teegen, 2013, Bringing the institutional context back in: A cross-national comparison of alliance partner selection and knowledge acquisition, *Organization Science*, 24: 319–338; R. A. Corredoira & L. Rosenkopf, 2010, Should auld acquaintance be forgot? The reverse transfer of knowledge through mobility ties, *Strategic Management Journal*, 31: 159–181.

84. X. Jiang, F. Jiang, X. Cai, & H. Liu, 2015, How does trust affect alliance performance? The mediating role of resource sharing, *Industrial Marketing Management*, 45: 128–138; J-P. Roy, 2012, IJV partner trustworthy behavior: The role of host country governance and partner selection criteria, *Journal of Management Studies*, 49: 332–355; M. J. Robson, C. S. Katsikeas, & D. C. Bello, 2008, Drivers and performance outcomes of trust in international strategic alliances: The role of organizational complexity, *Organization Science*, 19: 647–668.

85. 2015, A culture of partnership in favor of collective intelligence, Limagrain, www. limagrain.com, accessed on June 23; 2011, Limagrain signs strategic alliance to enter Brazilian corn market, *Great Lakes Hybrids*, www.greatlakeshybrids.com, February 14.

86. M. del Mar Benavides-Espinosa & D. Ribeiro-Soriano, 2014, Cooperative learning in creating and managing joint ventures, *Journal of Business Research*, 67: 648–655; S. Kotha & K. Srikanth, 2013, Managing a global partnership model: Lessons from the Boeing 787 'dreamliner' program, *Global Strategy Journal*, 3: 41–66; C. Schwens, J. Eiche, & R. Kabst, 2011, The moderating impact of informal institutional distance and formal institutional risk on SME entry mode choice, *Journal of Management Studies*, 48: 330–351.

87. R. Kumar, 2014, Managing ambiguity in strategic alliances, *California Management Review*, 56(4): 82–102; Y. Luo, O. Shenkar, & H. Gurnani, 2008, Control-cooperation interfaces in global strategic alliances: A situational typology and strategic responses, *Journal of International Business Studies*, 39: 428–453.

88. I. Arikan & O. Shenkar, 2013, National animosity and cross-border alliances, *Academy of Management Journal*, 56:516–1544; T. K. Das, 2010, Interpartner sensemaking in strategic alliances: Managing cultural differences and internal tensions, *Management Decision*, 48: 17–36.

89. A. Iriyama & R. Madhavan, 2014, Post-formation inter-partner equity transfers in international joint ventures: the role

of experience, *Global Strategy Journal*, 4:
331–348; B. B. Nielsen, 2010, Strategic fit,
contractual, and procedural governance in
alliances, *Journal of Business Research*, 63:
682–689; D. Li, L. Eden, M. A. Hitt, &
R. D. Ireland, 2008, Friends, acquaintances
and stranger? Partner selection in R&D
alliances, *Academy of Management Journal*,
51: 315–334.

90. A. M. Joshi & N. Lahiri, 2015, Language
friction and partner selection in cross-
border R&D alliance formation, *Journal of
International Business Studies*, 46: 123–152;
P. D. O. Jensen & B. Petersen, 2013, Global
sourcing of services: Risk, process and
collaborative architecture, *Global Strategy
Journal*, 3: 67–87.

91. T. W. Tong, J. J. Reuer, B. B. Tyler, & S. Zhang,
2015, Host country executives' assessments
of international joint ventures and
divestitures: An experimental approach,
Strategic Management Journal, 36: 254–275;
S.-F. S. Chen, 2010, A general TCE model
of international business institutions;
market failure and reciprocity, *Journal of
International Business Studies*, 41: 935–959;
J. Wiklund & D. A. Shepherd, 2009, The
effectiveness of alliances and acquisitions:
The role of resource combination activities,
Entrepreneurship Theory and Practice,
33:193–212.

92. G. Kling, A. Ghobadian, M. A. Hitt,
U. Weitzel, & N. O'Regan, 2014, The effects
of cross-border and cross-industry mergers
and acquisitions on home-region and
global multinational enterprises, *British
Journal of Management*, 25: S116–S132.

93. A. Arslan & Y. Wang, Y. 2015, Acquisition
entry strategy of Nordic multinational
enterprises in China: An analysis of key
determinants, *Journal of Global Marketing*,
28: 32–51; A. Guar, S. Malhotra, & P. Zhu,
2013, Acquisition announcements and
stock market valuations of acquiring firms'
rivals: A test of the growth probability
hypothesis in China, *Strategic Management
Journal*, 34: 215–232; M. A. Hitt & V. Pisano,
2003, The cross-border merger and
acquisition strategy, *Management Research*,
1: 133–144.

94. I. Walker & A. Gasparro, 2015, Merge unites
major supermarket players, *Wall Street
Journal*, June 25, B1

95. P. C. Narayan & M. Thenmozhi, 2014, Do
cross-border acquisitions involving
emerging market firms create value:
Impact of deal characteristics, *Management
Decision*, 52: 1–23; S. Malhotra, P.-C. Zhu, &
W. Locander, 2010, Impact of host-
country corruption on U.S. and Chinese
cross-border acquisitions, *Thunderbird
International Business Review*, 52: 491–507;
P. X. Meschi, 2009, Government corruption
and foreign stakes in international joint
ventures in emerging economies, *Asia
Pacific Journal of Management*, 26: 241–261.

96. F. J. Contractor, S. Lahiri, B. Elango, &
S. K. Kundu, Institutional, cultural

and industry related determinants of
ownership choices in emerging market
FDI acquisitions, *International Business
Review*, 23: 931–941; J. Li & C. Qian, 2013,
Principal-principal conflicts under weak
institutions: A study of corporate takeovers
in China, *Strategic Management Journal*,
34: 498–508; A. Madhok & M. Keyhani,
2012, Acquisitions as entrepreneurship:
Asymmetries, opportunities, and the
internationalization of multinationals
from emerging economies, *Global Strategy
Journal*, 2: 26–40.

97. S. Lee, J. Kim, & B. I. Park, 2015, Culture
clashes in cross-border mergers and
acquisitions: A case study of Sweden's
Volvo and South Korea's Samsung,
International Business Review, 24: 580–593;
E. Vaara, R. Sarala, G. K. Stahl, & I. Bjorkman,
2012, *Journal of Management Studies*, 49:
1–27; D. R. Denison, B. Adkins, & A. Guidroz,
2011, Managing cultural integration in
cross-border mergers and acquisitions.
In W. H. Mobley, M. Li, & Y. Wang (eds.),
Advances in Global Leadership, vol. 6,
Bingley, U.K.: Emerald Publishing Group,
95–115.

98. U. Stettner & D. Lavie, 2014, Ambidexterity
under scrutiny: Exploration and
exploitation via internal organization,
alliances, and acquisitions, *Strategic
Management Journal*, 35: 1903–1929;
S.-J. Chang, J. Chung, & J. J. Moon, 2013,
When do wholly owned subsidiaries
perform better than joint ventures?
Strategic Management Journal, 34: 317–337;
Y. Fang, G.-L. F. Jiang, S. Makino, &
P. W. Beamish, 2010, Multinational firm
knowledge, use of expatriates, and
foreign subsidiary performance, *Journal of
Management Studies*, 47: 27–54.

99. S. Lahiri, B. Elango, & S. K. Kundu, 2014,
Cross-border acquisition in services:
Comparing ownership choice of developed
and emerging economy MNEs in India,
Journal of World Business, 49: 409–420;
C. Bouquet, L. Hebert, & A. Delios, 2004,
Foreign expansion in service industries:
Separability and human capital intensity,
Journal of Business Research, 57: 35–46.

100. O. Bertrand & L. Capron, L. 2015,
Productivity enhancement at home via
cross-border acquisitions: The roles of
learning and contemporaneous domestic
investments, *Strategic Management Journal*,
36: 640–658; C. Schwens, J. Eiche, &
R. Kabst, 2011, The moderating impact of
informal institutional distance and formal
institutional risk on SME entry mode
choice, *Journal of Management Studies*, 48:
330–351; K. F. Meyer, S. Estrin,
S. K. Bhaumik, & M. W. Peng, 2009,
Institutions, resources, and entry strategies
in emerging economies, *Strategic
Management Journal*, 30: 61–80.

101. G. O. White, T. A. Hemphill, J. R. Joplin, &
L. A. Marsh, 2014, Wholly owned foreign
subsidiary relation-based strategies

in volatile environments, *International
Business Review*, 23: 303–312; Chang,
Chung & Moon, When do wholly owned
subsidiaries perform better than joint
ventures?; K. D. Brouthers & D. Dikova,
2010, Acquisitions and real options:
The greenfield alternative, *Journal of
Management Studies*, 47: 1048–1071.

102. 2015. Walmart's China expansion won't be
easy, *Fortune*, www.fortune.com, May 6;
Y. Parke & B. Sternquist, 2008, The global
retailer's strategic proposition and choice
of entry mode, *International Journal of
Retail & Distribution Management*; 36:
281–299.

103. X. He, J. Zhang, & J. Wang, 2015, Market
seeking orientation and performance
in China: The impact of institutional
environment, subsidiary ownership
structure and experience. *Management
International Review*, 55: 389–419;
L. Q. Siebers, 2012, Foreign retailers in
China: The first ten years, *Journal of
Business Strategy*, 33(1): 27–38.

104. White, Hemphill, Joplin, & Marsh, Wholly
owned foreign subsidiary relation-based
strategies in volatile environments;
A. M. Rugman, 2010, Reconciling
internalization theory and the eclectic
paradigm, *Multinational Business Review*,
18: 1–12; J. Che & G. Facchini, 2009, Cultural
differences, insecure property rights and
the mode of entry decision, *Economic
Theory*, 38: 465–484.

105. J. Muller, 2015, Toyota is laying down
deeper roots in Michigan. *Forbes*,
June 11, 24.

106. 2014, Corporate with the best regional
strategy, *LatinFinance*, July–August, 31.

107. A. Cuervo-Cazurra, A. Inkpen, A. Musacchio, &
K. Ramaswamy, 2014, Governments as
owners: State-owned multinational
companies, *Journal of International Business
Studies*, 45: 919–942; B. Batjargal, M. Hitt,
A. S. Tsui, J.-L. Arregle, J. Webb, &
T. Miller, 2013, Institutional polycentrism,
entrepreneurs' social networks and new
venture growth, *Academy of Management
Journal*, 56: 1024–1049.

108. C. Giersch, 2011, Political risk and political
due diligence, *Global Risk Affairs*, www.
globalriskaffairs.com, March 4.

109. G. G. Goswami & S. Haider, 2014, Does
political risk deter FDI inflow? An analytical
approach using panel data and factor
analysis, *Journal of Economic Studies*,
41: 233–252; J. Li & Y. Tang, 2010, CEO
hubris and firm risk taking in China: The
moderating role of managerial discretion,
Academy of Management Journal, 53: 45–68;
I. Alon & T. T. Herbert, 2009, A stranger in
a strange land: Micro political risk and the
multinational firm, *Business Horizons*, 52:
127–137; P. Rodriguez, K. Uhlenbruck, &
L. Eden, 2003, Government corruption
and the entry strategies of multinationals,
Academy of Management Review, 30:
383–396.

110. A. Jiménez, I. Luis-Rico, & D. Benito-Osorio, 2014, The influence of political risk on the scope of internationalization of regulated companies: Insights from a Spanish sample, *Journal of World Business*, 49: 301–311; D. Quer, E. Claver, & L. Rienda, 2012, Political risk, cultural distance, and outward foreign direct investment: Empirical evidence from large Chinese firms, *Asia Pacific Journal of Management*, 29: 1089–1104; O. Branzei & S. Abdelnour, 2010, Another day, another dollar: Enterprise resilience under terrorism in developing countries, *Journal of International Business Studies*, 41: 804–825.

111. G. Bekaert, C. R. Harvey, C. T. Lundblad, & S. Siegel, 2014, Political risk spreads, *Journal of International Business Studies*, 45: 471–493.

112. C. L. Brown, S. T. Cavusgil, & A. W. Lord, 2015, Country-risk measurement and analysis: A new conceptualization and managerial tool, *International Business Review*, 24: 246–265; Giersch, Political risk and political due diligence.

113. D. L. Keig, L. E. Brouthers, & V. B. Marshall, 2015, Formal and informal corruption environments and multinational enterprise social irresponsibility, *Journal of Management Studies*, 52: 89–116; J. Surroca, J. A. Tribo, & S. A. Zahra, 2013, Stakeholder pressure on MNEs and the transfer of socially irresponsible practices to subsidiaries, *Academy of Management Journal*, 56: 549–572.

114. A. Flynn, 2015, Questions re-emerge on World Cup venues, *Wall Street Journal*, May 28, A10.

115. R. Johnson, R. Jelmaye, & L. Magalhaes, Scandal spurs overhaul of Brazil's soccer body, *Wall Street Journal*, June 12, A9.

116. O. Matthews, 2015, Russia retreats. *Newsweek Global*, June 19, 12–16.

117. C. Grimpe & K. Hussinger, 2014, Resource complementarity and value capture in firm acquisitions: The role of intellectual property rights, *Strategic Management Journal*, 35: 1762–1780.

118. A. Wexler, 2015, Power outages mar South Africa's economic expansion, *Wall Street Journal*, www.wsj.com, May 8.

119. P. Kiernan & P. Trevisani, 2015, China seeks to keep its ties tight with South America, *Wall Street Journal*, May 20, A14; G. Fornes & A. Butt-Philip, 2011, Chinese MNEs and Latin America: A review, *International Journal of Emerging Markets*, 6: 98–117; S. Globerman & D. Shapiro, 2009, Economic and strategic considerations surrounding Chinese FDI in the United States, *Asia Pacific Journal of Management*, 26: 163–183.

120. E. Beckmann & H. Stix, 2015, Foreign currency borrowing and knowledge about exchange rate risk, *Journal of Economic Behavior & Organization*, 11: 21–16; C. R. Goddard, 2011, Risky business: Financial-sector liberalization and China, *Thunderbird International Business Review*, 53: 469–482; I. G. Kawaller, 2009, Hedging

currency exposures by multinationals: Things to consider, *Journal of Applied Finance*, 18: 92–98.

121. P. Loftus & T. Stynes, 2015, J&J'S weak results tied to U.S. Dollar, device revenues, *Wall Street Journal*, April 15, B6; P. Evans, 2015, Unilever gets boost from Euro's weakness, *Wall Street Journal*, April 17, B6.

122. R. G. Bell, I. Filatotchev, & R. Aguilera, 2014, Corporate governance and investors' perceptions of foreign IPO value: An institutional perspective, *Academy of Management Journal*, 57: 301–320.

123. M. Alessandri & A. Seth, 2014, The effects of managerial ownership on international and business diversification: Balancing incentives and risks, *Strategic Management Journal*, 35: 2064–2075; F. J. Contractor, 2012, Why do multinational firms exist? A theory note about the effect of multinational expansion on performance and recent methodological critiques, *Global Strategy Journal*, 2: 318–331; P. David, J. P. O'Brien, T. Yoshikawa, & A. Delios, 2010, Do shareholders or stakeholders appropriate the rents from corporate diversification? The influence of ownership structure, *Academy of Management Journal*, 53: 636–654.

124. L. Zhou & A. Wu, A. 2014, Earliness of internationalization and performance outcomes: Exploring the moderating effects of venture age and international commitment, *Journal of World Business*, 49: 132–142; L. Li, 2007, Multinationality and performance: A synthetic review and research agenda, *International Journal of Management Reviews*, 9: 117–139; J. A.Doukas & O. B. Kan, 2006, Does global diversification destroy firm value? *Journal of International Business Studies*, 37: 352–371

125. H. Tan & J. A. Mathews, 2015, Accelerated internationalization and resource leverage strategizing: The case of Chinese wind turbine manufacturers, *Journal of World Business*, 50: 417–427; J. H. Fisch, 2012, Information costs and internationalization performance, *Global Strategy Journal*, 2: 296–312; S. E. Christophe & H. Lee, 2005, What matters about internationalization: A market-based assessment, *Journal of Business Research*, 58: 636–643.

126. S. Kraus, T. C. Ambos, F. Eggers, & B. Cesinger, 2015, Distance and perceptions of risk in internationalization decisions, *Journal of Business Research*, 68: 1501–1505; H. Berry, 2013, When do firms divest foreign operations? *Organization Science*, 24: 246–261; T. J. Andersen, 2011, The risk implications of multinational enterprise, *International Journal of Organizational Analysis*, 19: 49–70.

127. Berry, Global integration and innovation: Multi-country knowledge generation within MNCs; A. Y. Lewin, S. Massini, & C. Peeters, 2011, Microfoundations of internal and external absorptive capacity routines, *Organization Science*, 22: 81–98.

128. P. C. Patel, S. A. Fernhaber, P. P. McDougal-Covin, & R. P. van der Have, 2014, Beating competitors to international markets: The value of geographically balanced networks for innovation, *Strategic Management Journal*, 35: 691–711.

129. S. Awate, M. M. Larsen, & R. Mudambi, 2015, Accessing vs sourcing knowledge: A comparative study of R&D internationalization between emerging and advanced economy firms, *Journal of International Business Studies*, 46: 63–86; O. Bertrand & M. J. Mol, 2013, The antecedents and innovation effects of domestic and offshore R&D outsourcing: The contingent impact of cognitive distance and absorptive capacity, *Strategic Management Journal*, 34: 751–760; B. S. Reiche, 2012, Knowledge benefits of social capital upon repatriation: A longitudinal study of international assignees, *Journal of Management Studies*, 49: 1052–1072.

130. J. Alcacer & J. Oxley, 2014, Learning by supplying, *Strategic Management Journal*, 35: 204–223; G. R. G. Benito, R. Lunnan & S. Tomassen, 2011, Distant encounters of the third kind: Multinational companies locating divisional headquarters abroad, *Journal of Management Studies*, 48: 373–394; M. A. Hitt, L. Tihanyi, T. Miller, & B. Connelly, 2006, International diversification: Antecedents, outcomes, and moderators, *Journal of Management*, 32: 831–867.

131. R. Belderbos, B. Lokshin, & B. Sadowski, 2015, The returns to foreign R&D, *Journal of International Business Studies*, 46, 491–504; I. Guler & A. Nerkar, 2012, The impact of global and local cohesion on innovation in the pharmaceutical industry, *Strategic Management Journal*, 33: 535–549.

132. M. Alessandri & A. Seth, 2014, The effects of managerial ownership on international and business diversification: Balancing incentives and risks, *Strategic Management Journal*, 35: 2064–2075; X. Fu, 2012, Foreign direct investment and managerial knowledge spillovers through diffusion of management practices, *Journal of Management Studies*, 49: 970–999; D. Holtbrugge & A. T. Mohr, 2011, Subsidiary interdependencies and international human resource management practices in German MNCs, *Management International Review*, 51: 93–115.

133. B. B. Nielsen & S. Nielsen, S. 2013, Top management team nationality diversity and firm performance: A multilevel study. *Strategic Management Journal*, 34, 373–382; M. Halme, S. Lindeman, & P. Linna, 2012, Innovation for inclusive business: Intrapreneurial bricolage in multinational corporations, *Journal of Management Studies*, 49: 743–784; I. Filatotchev & M. Wright, 2010, Agency perspectives on corporate governance of multinational enterprises, *Journal of Management Studies*, 47: 471–486.

134. C. Hsu, Y. Lien, & H. Chen, H. 2015, R&D internationalization and innovation performance, *International Business Review*, 24: 187–195; J. I. Siegel & S. H. Schwartz, 2013, Egalitarianism, cultural distance and foreign direct investment: A new approach, *Organization Science*, 24: 1174–1194; G. A. Shinkle & A. P. Kriauciunas, 2012, The impact of current and founding institutions on strength of competitive aspirations in transition economies, *Strategic Management Journal*, 33: 448–458.

135. R. Chittoor, P. S. Aulakh, & S. Ray, 2015, Accumulative and assimilative learning, institutional infrastructure, and innovation orientation of developing economy firms, *Global Strategy Journal*, 5: 133–153; P. C. Nell & B. Ambos, 2013, Parenting advantage in the MNC: An embeddedness perspective on the value added by headquarters, *Strategic Management Journal*, 34: 1086–1103; J.-F. Hennart, 2012, Emerging market multinationals and the theory of the multinational enterprise, *Global Strategy Journal*, 2: 168–187.

136. S. Schmid & T. Dauth, 2014, Does internationalization make a difference? Stock market reaction to announcements of international top executive appointments, *Journal of World Business*, 49: 63–77; Wiersema & Bowen, The relationship between international diversification and firm performance; C.-F. Wang, L.-Y. Chen, & S.-C. Change, 2011, International diversification and the market value of new product introduction, *Journal of International Management*, 17: 333–347.

137. J. U. Kim & R. V. Aguilera, 2015, The world is spiky: An internationalization framework for a semi-globalized world, *Global Strategy Journal*, 5: 113–132; R. Belderbos, T. W. Tong, & S. Wu, 2013, Multinationality and downside risk: The roles of option portfolio and organization, *Strategic Management Journal*, in press; W. Shi, S. L. Sun, & M. W. Peng, 2012, Sub-national institutional contingencies, network positions and IJV partner selection, *Journal of Management Studies*, 49: 1221–1245.

138. P. Regnér & J. Edman, J. 2014, MNE institutional advantage: How subunits shape, transpose and evade host country institutions, *Journal of International Business Studies*, 45: 275–302; B. Baik, J.-K. Kang, J.-M. Kim, & J. Lee, 2013, The liability of foreignness in international equity investments: Evidence from the U.S. stock market, *Journal of International Business Studies*, 44: 391–411.

139. S. Song, 2014, Entry mode irreversibility, host market uncertainty, and foreign subsidiary exits, *Asia Pacific Journal of Management*, 31: 455–471; S.-H. Lee & S. Song, 2012, Host country uncertainty, intra-MNC production shifts, and subsidiary performance, *Strategic Management Journal*, 33: 1331–1340.

140. D. W. Williams & D. A. Grégoire, 2015, Seeking commonalities or avoiding differences? Re-conceptualizing distance and its effects on internationalization decisions, *Journal of International Business Studies*, 46: 253–284; L. Berchicci, A. King, & C. L. Tucci, 2011, Does the apple always fall close to the tree? The geographical proximity choice of spin-outs, *Strategic Entrepreneurship Journal*, 5: 120–136; A. Ojala, 2008, Entry in a psychically distant market: Finnish small and medium-sized software firms in Japan, *European Management Journal*, 26: 135–144.

141. W. Shi, R. E. Hoskisson, & Y. Zhang, 2015. A geopolitical perspective into the opposition to globalizing state-owned enterprises in target states. *Global Strategy Journal*, in press; M. L. L. Lam, 2009, Beyond credibility of doing business in China: Strategies for improving corporate citizenship of foreign multinational enterprises in China, *Journal of Business Ethics*, 87: 137–146.

142. M. H. Ho & F. Wang, 2015, Unpacking knowledge transfer and learning paradoxes in international strategic alliances: Contextual differences matter, *International Business Review*, 24: 287–297; E. Fang & S. Zou, 2010, The effects of absorptive capacity and joint learning on the instability of international joint ventures in emerging economies, *Journal of International Business Studies*, 41: 906–924; D. Lavie & S. Miller, 2009, Alliance portfolio internationalization and firm performance, *Organization Science*, 19: 623–646.

9

Cooperative Strategy

Studying this chapter should provide you with the strategic management knowledge needed to:

9-1   Define cooperative strategies and explain why firms use them.

9-2   Define and discuss the three major types of strategic alliances.

9-3   Name the business-level cooperative strategies and describe their use.

9-4   Discuss the use of corporate-level cooperative strategies.

9-5   Understand the importance of cross-border strategic alliances as an international cooperative strategy.

9-6   Explain cooperative strategies' risks.

9-7   Describe two approaches used to manage cooperative strategies.

GOOGLE, INTEL, AND TAG HEUER: COLLABORATING TO PRODUCE A SMARTWATCH

When using different types of cooperative strategies, firms commit to sharing some of their unique resources in order to reach an objective that is important to all participants. A key reason cooperative strategies are used is that individual firms sometimes identify opportunities they can't pursue because they lack the type and/or quantity of resources needed to do so.

Some partnerships are formed between similar firms who desire to develop scale economies to enhance their competitiveness. For years, automobile manufacturers have formed large numbers of partnerships for this reason. In other instances, firms competing in different industries uniquely combine their unique resources to pursue what they believe is a value-creating shared objective. This reason describes the rationale driving the partnership Google, Intel and TAG Heuer have formed to design and produce a smartwatch. A number of observers of the partnership among these three firms viewed it positively given their conclusion that TAG Heuer lacked the technology skills to build a competitive smartwatch while the Silicon Valley firms lacked the design skills to do so successfully.

In part, the decision Google, Intel and TAG Heuer made to collaborate is a strategic action taken in response to Apple's introduction of the iWatch. A common opinion among those leading Swiss watch manufacturing companies is that the worst decision that could be made would be for the companies to fail to respond to the iWatch. Google, Intel and TAG Heuer believe they are uniquely qualified to respond to the iWatch

FABRICE COFFRINI/AFP/Getty Images

given the technology used to produce it and in light of Apple's decision to offer "upscale" luxury versions of the product, priced initially between $10,000 and $17,000. Recognizing the threat of smartwatches, other Swiss watchmakers, in addition to TAG Heuer, are taking action. "Swatch, Breitling, Montblanc, and Frederique Constant are among those that have entered the fray, with products ranging from a messaging device that clips to a watch strap to a gold-plated watch containing a fitness tracker." Supporting the decision among all of these firms to be involved with smartwatches is the size of the market for this product. In 2014, 4.6 million smartwatches were sold globally. Analysts thought the market for this product might jump to as many as 30 million units in 2015. In contrast, the number of Swiss watches sold in 2015 was expected to decline by 6.3 percent from the number sold a year earlier.

TAG Heuer CEO Jean-Claude Biver describes the nature of the alliance his firm has formed with Google and Intel as follows: "Swiss watchmaking and Silicon Valley is a marriage of technological innovation with watchmaking credibility. Our collaboration provides a rich host of synergies, forming a win-win partnership, and the potential for our three companies is enormous." In essence then, he believes that Google and Intel bring unique technological innovation to the partnership while his firm brings its reputation and skills as a successful manufacturer of luxury Swiss watches. Part of the reason TAG Heuer's watches are thought of as a luxury good is that the firm is a unit of French luxury giant LVMH Moet Hennessy Louis Vuitton SA. Influencing the formation of this alliance is Google's desire to demonstrate that its software can effectively power wearables, Intel's desire to show how its chips can be used in wearables, and TAG Heuer's desire to design and produce more technologically sophisticated watches that meet the needs of today's tech-savvy consumers. To expand their footprint in luxury goods, both Google and Intel have established additional alliances. Intel is collaborating with Luxottica Group SpA to produce smart eyewear and Google is partnering with the same firm to create new designs of Google Glass.

As is the case with all strategies, alliances such as the one among Google, Intel and TAG Heuer are not risk free. The degree to which the cultures of technology firms that are strongly oriented to producing innovation after innovation with the precision-oriented culture of a luxury Swiss watchmaker can be successfully integrated is an important concern. Another risk is that the significant amount of coordination that will be required to integrate the firms' operations that are based in different countries along with all of the companies that are involved with the international electronics supply chain may not be achieved efficiently. In spite of these potential risks, the opportunity to innovate in a rapidly expanding global market seems to be more than sufficient to support the decision among Google, Intel and TAG Heuer to collaboratively design and produce a novel smartwatch.

Sources: A. Chen, 2015, Google, Intel, TAG Heuer to collaborate on Swiss smartwatch, *Wall Street Journal Online*, //www.wsj.com, March 19; M. Clerizol, 2015, There's something in the way they move, *Wall Street Journal Online*, www.wsj.com, March 18; L. Dignan, 2015, Can TAG Heuer, Intel, Google collaborate and create a smart enough watch? *ZDNET Online*, www.zdnet.com, March 19; S. Kessler, 2015, Intel, Google, and TAG Heuer announce a Swiss smartwatch, *Fast Company Online*, www.fastcompany.com, March, 19; J. Newman, 2015, TAG Heuer, Google, and Intel get together to announce a conceptual smartwatch, *PCWorld Online*, www.pcworld.com, March 19; J. Revill, 2015, Swiss watchmakers rise to the smartwatch challenge, *Wall Street Journal Online*, www.wsj.com, March 19; K. Sintumuang, 2015, Will the Apple watch eclipse the classic Swiss watch? *Wall Street Journal Online*, www.wsj.com, April 17.

In describing the multiple arenas in which Google competes in Chapter 5's Opening Case, we mentioned the firm's plans to enter the smartwatch market. In this chapter's Opening Case, we describe in detail the actions Google is taking to do this. More specifically, we describe the cooperative strategy Google, Intel, and TAG Heuer have formed in order to apply technological innovations to compete in the world of luxury fashion. None of these firms could produce the particular type of smartwatch the collaborators plan to develop without the other two partners. This collaboration is one through which each company is using some of its unique resources (as well as the capabilities and core competencies that flow from them) in order to design, produce, and then launch a product into a specific market. It is the specific combination of each firm's unique resources through which a particular smartwatch is to be developed. Thus, as is the case for all companies implementing cooperative strategies, these three firms intend to use their resources in ways that will create the greatest amount of value for stakeholders.[1]

Forming a cooperative strategy like the one among Google, Intel, and TAG Heuer has the potential to help companies reach an objective that is important to all of them, such as firm growth. Specifically, a **cooperative strategy** is a means by which firms collaborate to achieve a shared objective.[2] Cooperating with others is a strategy firms use to create value for a customer that it likely could not create by itself. As noted above, this is the situation for Google, Intel, and TAG Heuer in that none of these firms could create the specific smartwatch the firms intended to develop without the combination of the three companies' resources. (Throughout this chapter, the term "resources" is used comprehensively and refers to a firm's capabilities as well as its resources.)

Firms also try to create competitive advantages when using a cooperative strategy.[3] A competitive advantage developed through a cooperative strategy often is called a *collaborative* or *relational* advantage,[4] indicating that the relationship that develops among collaborating partners is commonly the basis on which to build a competitive advantage. Importantly, successfully using cooperative strategies finds a firm outperforming its rivals in terms of strategic competitiveness and above-average returns,[5] often because they've been able to form a competitive advantage.

A **cooperative strategy** is a means by which firms collaborate to achieve a shared objective.

We examine several topics in this chapter. First, we define and offer examples of different strategic alliances as primary types of cooperative strategies. We focus on strategic alliances because firms use them more frequently than other types of cooperative relationships. In succession, we describe business-level, corporate-level, international, and network cooperative strategies. The chapter closes with a discussion of the risks of using cooperative strategies as well as how effectively managing the strategies can reduce these risks.

9-1 Strategic Alliances as a Primary Type of Cooperative Strategy

A **strategic alliance** is a cooperative strategy in which firms combine some of their resources to create a competitive advantage. Strategic alliances involve firms with some degree of exchange and sharing of resources to jointly develop, sell, and service goods or services.[6] In addition, firms use strategic alliances to leverage their existing resources while working with partners to develop additional resources as the foundation for new competitive advantages.[7] To be certain, the reality today is that strategic alliances are a vital strategy that firms use as a means to try to outperform rivals.[8]

An alliance involving Juniper and Aruba Networks is an example of a partnership that has been formed to combine individual firms' unique resources in order to create competitive advantages as a path to outperforming rivals. To enhance their ability to innovate as a way to solve complex enterprise problems, Juniper and Aruba formed an alliance through which they are collaborating at both the product development stage and the sales stage by leveraging their client relationships and reseller networks. Commenting about this alliance, one analyst indicated that Juniper will contribute "its expertise in wired infrastructure (enterprise switches and routers) (while) Aruba provides its wireless mobility solutions."[9]

Before describing three types of major strategic alliances and reasons for their use, we need to note that, for all cooperative strategies, success is more likely when partners behave cooperatively. Actively solving problems, being trustworthy, and consistently pursuing ways to combine partners' resources to create value are examples of cooperative behavior known to contribute to alliance success.[10]

9-1a Types of Major Strategic Alliances

Joint ventures, equity strategic alliances, and nonequity strategic alliances are the three major types of strategic alliances that firms use. The ownership arrangement is a key difference among these alliances.

A **joint venture** is a strategic alliance in which two or more firms create a legally independent company to share some of their resources to create a competitive advantage. Typically, partners in a joint venture own equal percentages and contribute equally to the venture's operations. Often formed to improve a firm's ability to compete in uncertain competitive environments, joint ventures can be effective in establishing long-term relationships and in transferring tacit knowledge between partners.

GM and China-based SAIC Motor Corp., China's largest automobile manufacturer by sales volume, recently formed a joint venture to develop new cars that cater specifically to Chinese tastes. Called Shanghai GM Co., each partner owns 50 percent of this cooperative strategy. The partners intend to invest a total of 100 billion yuan, or approximately $16.4 billion, between 2016 and 2020 for the purpose of developing at least "10 all-new or face-lift" models during each of the five years included within the investment time horizon. Part of the investment is to be allocated to bring green technologies to China. Using some green technologies to produce automobiles is a key way the joint venture's products are to be differentiated from those produced by competitors.[11] Demonstrating the complexities

A **strategic alliance** is a cooperative strategy in which firms combine some of their resources to create a competitive advantage.

A **joint venture** is a strategic alliance in which two or more firms create a legally independent company to share some of their resources to create a competitive advantage.

This is a photo of the Shanghai GM facility where the work of the firms' joint venture takes place.

Shanghai GM.PNG

associated with being a successful competitor in today's business environment is the fact that SAIC also has a joint venture with Volkswagen AG. Among other products, the SAIC-VW joint venture manufacturers the Tiguan sport-utility model, which is the number one foreign-brand SUV being sold in China.[12]

Because it can't be codified, tacit knowledge, which is increasingly critical to firms' efforts to develop competitive advantages, is learned through experiences such as those taking place when people from partner firms work together in a joint venture.[13] Overall, a joint venture may be the optimal type of cooperative arrangement when firms need to combine their resources to create a competitive advantage that is substantially different from any they possess individually and when the partners intend to compete in highly uncertain environments.

An **equity strategic alliance** is an alliance in which two or more firms own different percentages of a company that they have formed by combining some of their resources to create a competitive advantage. Many foreign direct investments in China by multinational corporations are completed through equity strategic alliances. For example, Boston Scientific has formed an alliance with Frankenman Medical Equipment Company, a firm with headquarters in Suzhou, China. Boston Scientific will become a shareholder of Frankenman and will also provide "services and expertise to Frankenman to support its continued growth, development pipeline, and manufacturing capabilities." This alliance will combine Boston Scientific's capabilities related to less invasive endoscopic technologies with Frankenman's local market expertise.[14] Likewise, many Chinese firms, particularly those that are state owned, use equity alliances to engage in outward foreign direct investment.[15]

Firms sometimes form equity alliances in order to refocus their strategy as a means of creating a competitive advantage. This appears to be the case with the alliance Johnson Controls recently developed with Yanfeng Automotive Trim Systems Co., Ltd. Called Yanfeng Automotive Interiors, the alliance will produce and sell cockpit systems, floor consoles, and instrument panels in India, Japan, China, Europe, and the United States. Johnson has a 30 percent stake in the partnership, while Yanfeng holds a 70 percent interest. This relationship finds Johnson spinning off its automotive-interiors business to the alliance. Analysts viewed the forming of this partnership as a move by Johnson to focus on its higher-margin, non-auto businesses such as "York heating and air-conditioning equipment for commercial buildings."[16]

A **nonequity strategic alliance** is an alliance in which two or more firms develop a contractual relationship to share some of their resources to create a competitive advantage.[17] In this type of alliance, firms do not establish a separate independent company and therefore do not take equity positions. For this reason, nonequity strategic alliances are less formal, demand fewer partner commitments than do joint ventures and equity strategic alliances, and generally do not foster an intimate relationship between partners; nonetheless, research evidence indicates that they can create value for the involved firms.[18] The relative informality and lower commitment levels characterizing nonequity strategic alliances make them unsuitable for complex projects where success requires partners to be able to effectively transfer tacit knowledge to each other.[19] Licensing agreements, distribution agreements, and supply contracts are examples of nonequity strategic alliances.

An **equity strategic alliance** is an alliance in which two or more firms own different percentages of the company they have formed by combining some of their resources to create a competitive advantage.

A **nonequity strategic alliance** is an alliance in which two or more firms develop a contractual relationship to share some of their resources to create a competitive advantage.

Commonly, outsourcing arrangements are organized in the form of a nonequity strategic alliance. (Discussed in Chapter 3, *outsourcing* is the purchase of a value-chain activity or a support-function activity from another firm.) Apple Inc. and most other companies involved with selling computers, tablets, and smartphones use nonequity strategic alliances to outsource most or all of the activities required to manufacture their products. Apple, for example, has traditionally outsourced most of its manufacturing to Foxconn Technology Group. Recently, Foxconn, with most of its production facilities located in China, was manufacturing 70 percent of all iPhone 6 phones.[20] Firms often choose to use nonequity strategic alliances to outsource manufacturing activities to Chinese companies because of the cost efficiencies those firms generate through scale economies.[21] This collaborative pattern between a product designer such as Apple and

Courtesy of ZDnet

This is a Foxconn employee who is working to produce iPhone 6s for Apple.

a manufacturer such as Foxconn is likely to continue. One reason for this is that Foxconn, for example, works within an ecosystem of firms that supply it with the component parts it requires to manufacture products for its customers. Effective ecosystems, such as the one in which Foxconn operates, create value that is difficult for competitors to imitate.[22]

9-1b Reasons Firms Develop Strategic Alliances

Cooperative strategies are an integral part of the competitive landscape and are quite important to many companies. The fact that alliances can account for up to 25 percent or more of a typical firm's sales revenue demonstrates their importance. In addition to partnerships among for-profit organizations, alliances are also formed between educational institutions and individual companies for the purpose of commercializing ideas flowing from basic research projects that are completed at universities.[23] Moreover, in addition to dyadic partnerships where two firms form a collaborative relationship for competitive purposes, competition now occurs between large alliances themselves in some industries. This pattern of competition exists in the global airline industry where individual airlines compete against each other but simultaneously join alliances (such as Star, OneWorld and SkyTeam) which in turn compete against each other.[24] The array of alliances with which firms are involved highlight the various options available to companies seeking to increase their competitiveness by cooperating with others.

Overall, there are many reasons firms choose to participate in strategic alliances. We mention two key reasons here and discuss additional ones below by explaining how strategic alliances may help firms improve their competitiveness while competing in either slow-, fast-, or standard-cycle markets.

Making it possible for firms to create value they couldn't generate by acting independently and entering markets more rapidly combine to form the first important reason firms form strategic alliances.[25] The partnership formed among online news publishers *The Guardian*, *CNN International*, *Financial Times*, and *The Economist* for the purpose of making it possible for advertisers to reach online audiences with scale demonstrates this reason. Called Pangea, those forming this alliance concluded that the collaboration would help the firms efficiently expand on a global basis. In commenting about this, one firm's executive said that "we've come together to ensure the quality that's represented by these publisher brands is now available at scale."[26]

A second major reason firms form strategic alliances is that most (if not all) companies lack the full set of resources needed to pursue all identified opportunities and reach their objectives in the process of doing so, a reality indicating that partnering with others will increase the probability of reaching firm-specific performance objectives. Given constrained resources, firms can collaborate for a number of purposes, including those of reaching new customers and broadening both the product offerings and the distribution of their products without adding significantly to their cost structures.

Through the partnership between Expedia and Latin American online travel leader Decolar.com, which operates the Portuguese Decolar.com and Spanish Despegar.com websites, both firms are deriving important benefits that neither could access acting independently. In this sense, the partnership "...offers Expedia better exposure to the Latin American travelers (while) Decolar benefits by expanding its portfolio of international hotel supply through Expedia."[27]

As we discussed in Chapter 5, when considering competitive rivalry and competitive dynamics, unique competitive conditions characterize slow-, fast-, and standard-cycle markets.[28] As shown in Figure 9.1, these unique market types create different reasons for firms to use strategic alliances.

In short, *slow-cycle markets* are markets where the firm's competitive advantages are shielded from imitation for relatively long periods of time and where imitation is costly. Railroads and, historically, telecommunications, utilities, and financial services are

Figure 9.1 Reasons for Strategic Alliances by Market Type

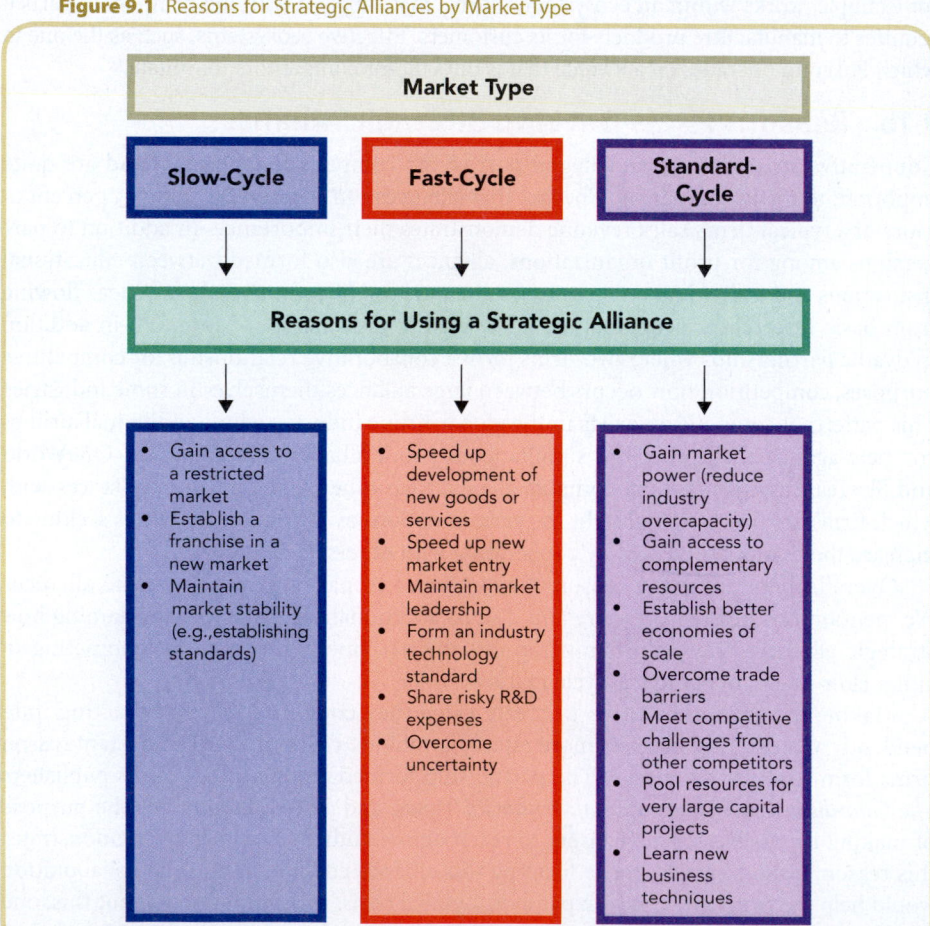

industries characterized as slow-cycle markets. In *fast-cycle markets*, the firm's competitive advantages are not shielded from imitation, preventing their long-term sustainability. Competitive advantages are moderately shielded from imitation in *standard-cycle markets*, typically allowing them to be sustained for a longer period of time than in fast-cycle market situations, but for a shorter period of time than in slow-cycle markets.

Slow-Cycle Markets

Firms in slow-cycle markets often use strategic alliances to enter restricted markets or to establish a franchise in a new market. For example, Carnival Corporation, owner and operator of Carnival Cruise Line, recently formed two joint ventures with state-owned China Merchants Group, which is a conglomerate with businesses in financial investments and property development as well as transportation. One venture between the two firms focuses on shipbuilding while the second concentrates on developing new ports and travel destinations in and around China. The launching of China's first domestic cruise brand that will target Chinese customers is one outcome associated with the collaborations between the two companies. Carnival's interest with these joint ventures is to quickly scale up its operations in China where the cruise industry is beginning to grow rapidly. Similarly, China Merchants Group wants to partner with a major competitor in the cruise industry to better position itself for future growth.[29]

Slow-cycle markets are becoming rare in the twenty-first century competitive landscape for several reasons, including the privatization of industries and economies, the rapid expansion of the Internet's capabilities for quick dissemination of information, and the speed with which advancing technologies make quickly imitating even complex products possible.[30] Firms competing in slow-cycle markets should recognize the likelihood that in the future, they will encounter situations in which their competitive advantages become partially sustainable (in the instance of a standard-cycle market) or unsustainable (in the case of a fast-cycle market). Cooperative strategies can help firms transition from relatively sheltered markets, such as the travel cruise market in which Carnival Corporation competes, to more competitive ones.[31]

Fast-Cycle Markets

Fast-cycle markets are unstable, unpredictable, and complex; in a word, hypercompetitive.[32] Combined, these conditions virtually preclude establishing sustainable competitive advantages, forcing firms to constantly seek sources of new competitive advantages while creating value by using current ones. Alliances between firms with current excess resources and those with promising resources help companies competing in fast-cycle markets effectively transition from the present to the future and gain rapid entry into new markets. As such, a "collaboration mindset" is of paramount importance for firms competing in fast-cycle markets.[33]

Micron Technology, Inc. and Seagate Technology LLC are competitors in manufacturing storage solutions, a competitive arena in which establishing sustainable competitive advantages is all but impossible. Because of this, innovation is critical to their success as well as for

think4photop/Shutterstock.com

Shown here is a Carnival Cruise Line ship that may soon transport Chinese customers through the firm's joint venture with China Merchants Group.

others operating in this industry given the fast-cycle nature of the storage-solution market. Micron and Seagate recently formed a strategic alliance for the purpose of combining the firms' innovation and expertise. Resulting from this collaboration, the partners believe, will be an ability to provide customers with "industry-leading" storage solutions. In turn, Micron and Seagate believe that customers buying the products that will flow from the collaboration will themselves be able to innovate faster while producing their goods and services. As reflected by the following comment from a customer, those anticipating buying products from the firms' strategic alliance seem to believe that novel products will be available to them to purchase: "The strategic agreement between Micron and Seagate promises to deliver new and innovative flash-based storage solutions."[34]

Standard-Cycle Markets

In standard-cycle markets, alliances are more likely to be made by partners that have complementary resources. The alliances formed by airline companies are an example of standard-cycle market alliances.

When initially established, airline alliances were intended to allow firms to share their complementary resources to make it easier for passengers to fly between secondary cities in the United States and Europe. Today, airline alliances are mostly global in nature and are formed primarily so members can gain marketing clout, have opportunities to reduce costs, and have access to additional international routes.[35] Of these reasons, international expansion by having access to more international routes is the most important because these routes are the path to increased revenues and potential profits. To support efforts to control costs, alliance members jointly purchase some items and share facilities such as passenger gates, customer service centers, and airport passenger lounges when possible. For passengers, airline alliances create benefits such as less complicated ticket buying processes, easier connections for international flights, and the earning of frequent flyer miles.

There are three major airline alliances operating today. Star Alliance is the largest with 27 members. With 16 members, Oneworld Alliance is the smallest, while the 20-member SkyTeam Alliance is in between the other two alliances in terms of total number of members. All three alliances continue to add members to expand their geographic coverage and to respond to market trends, such as the increasing amount of travel from regions throughout the world to Asia. In general, most airline alliances, such as the three we mention here, are formed to help firms gain economies of scale and meet competitive challenges (see Figure 9.1). Code sharing agreements and the ability to reduce costs associated with operations, maintenance, and purchases are examples of how airline alliances help members gain economies of scale as a path to increasing their competitiveness.[36]

9-2   Business-Level Cooperative Strategy

A **business-level cooperative strategy** is a strategy through which firms combine some of their resources to create a competitive advantage by competing in one or more product markets. As discussed in Chapter 4, business-level strategy details what the firm intends to do to gain a competitive advantage in specific product markets. Thus, the firm forms a business-level cooperative strategy when it believes that combining some of its resources with those of one or more partners will create competitive advantages that it can't create by itself and will lead to success in a specific product market. We present the four business-level cooperative strategies in Figure 9.2.

9-2a   Complementary Strategic Alliances

Complementary strategic alliances are business-level alliances in which firms share some of their resources in complementary ways to create a competitive advantage.[37] Vertical and horizontal are the two dominant types of complementary strategic alliances (see Figure 9.2).

A **business-level cooperative strategy** is a strategy through which firms combine some of their resources to create a competitive advantage by competing in one or more product markets.

Complementary strategic alliances are business-level alliances in which firms share some of their resources in complementary ways to create a competitive advantage.

Figure 9.2 Business-Level Cooperative Strategies

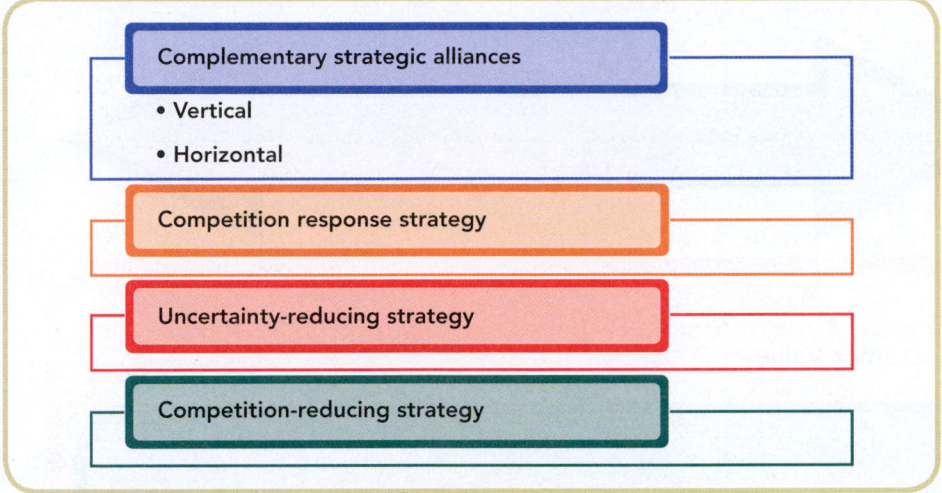

> **Complementary strategic alliances**
> - Vertical
> - Horizontal
>
> **Competition response strategy**
>
> **Uncertainty-reducing strategy**
>
> **Competition-reducing strategy**

Vertical Complementary Strategic Alliance

In a *vertical complementary strategic alliance*, firms share some of their resources from different stages of the value chain for the purpose of creating a competitive advantage (see Figure 9.3).[38] Oftentimes, vertical complementary alliances are formed to adapt to environmental changes;[39] sometimes the changes represent an opportunity for partnering firms to innovate while adapting.[40]

Companies recognize that today's consumers are more connected than ever as they use various devices such as smartphone applications, GPS systems, and the wireless Internet. GE Lighting and Qualcomm Atheros, Inc. (a subsidiary of Qualcomm Incorporated) formed a vertical complementary alliance to bring another functionality to "tech savvy" shoppers. By combining Qualcomm's wireless technologies, which yield positioning information, with GE's LED bulbs that are used to light retail stores, these two firms are making it possible for retailers to "talk" to customers while they shop. The real-time connection this configuration creates allows "retailers to combine contextual information with location to create revolutionary new tools such as indoor navigation, infinite aisle, suggested items, product information, and special offers or coupons to those who opt in and download the retailer's app."[41]

Horizontal Complementary Strategic Alliance

A *horizontal complementary strategic alliance* is an alliance in which firms share some of their resources from the same stage (or stages) of the value chain for the purpose of creating a competitive advantage. Automobile manufacturers make frequent use of this type of alliance, as do pharmaceutical companies. In this regard, Sorrento Therapeutics, Inc. is collaborating with NantWorks LLC to develop "next generation immunotherapies

Ringo Chiu/ZUMA Press, Inc./Alamy

Mr. Patrick Soon-Shiong, pictured here, is the CEO of Nantworks LLC. This firm is collaborating with Sorrento Therapeutics to develop innovative drugs for the purpose of combating serious diseases such as cancer.

Figure 9.3 Vertical and Horizontal Complementary Strategic Alliances

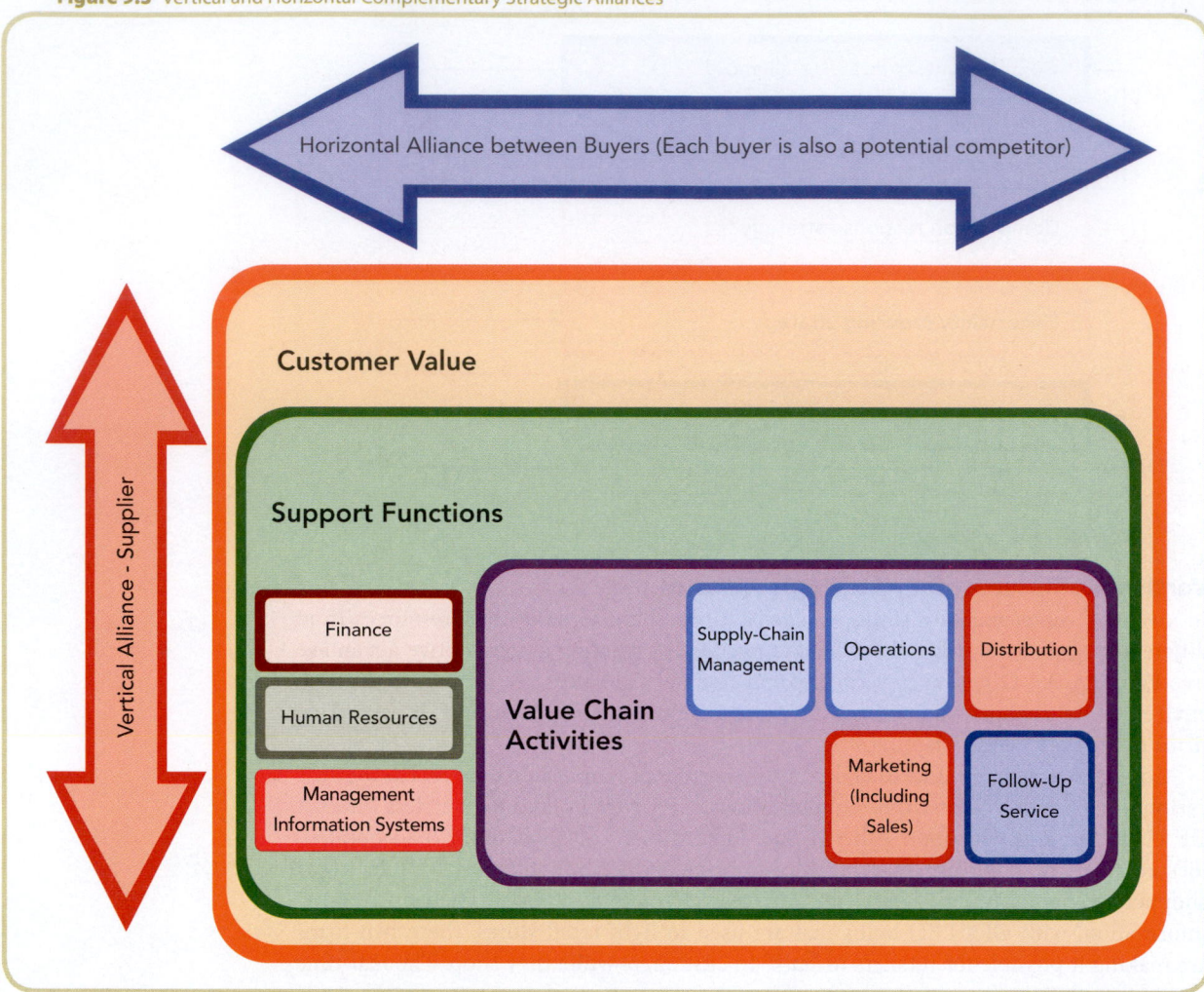

for cancer and autoimmune diseases."[42] More comprehensively, some of the world's largest pharmaceutical firms, including Pfizer, Bristol-Myers Squibb, GlaxoSmithKline and Eli Lilly, are sharing some of their proprietary assets through a collaboration organized by the U.S.-based National Institutes of Health. The primary purpose of this five-year partnership is to more quickly discover and produce drugs that cure challenging and, what historically have been, intractable diseases.[43]

Commonly, firms use complementary strategic alliances to focus on joint long-term product development and distribution opportunities.[44] For example, Boeing Company and Lockheed Martin Corporation recently formed a partnership "to defend their profitable Pentagon space rocket business with an all-new rocket equipped with reusable engines that could slash satellite-launch costs and provide a steppingstone to various commercial space ventures."[45] Thus, the essence of this collaboration is pursuing opportunities to find ways to monetize operations in space.

9-2b Competition Response Strategy

As discussed in Chapter 5, competitors initiate competitive actions (strategic and tactical) to attack rivals and launch competitive responses (strategic and tactical) to their competitors' actions. Strategic alliances can be used at the business level to respond to competitors' attacks. The alliance among Google, Intel, and TAG Heuer that is discussed in the Opening Case is a strategic response to Apple's strategic action of introducing the iWatch. Because they can be difficult to reverse and expensive to operate, strategic alliances are primarily formed to take strategic rather than tactical actions and to respond to competitors' actions in a like manner.

In October of 2007, SABMiller and Molson Coors Brewing Company formed a partnership. At the time, these firms held the second and third largest shares of the U.S. brew market. When formed, MillerCoors LLC, the name of the partnership, commanded roughly 29 percent of the U.S. brew market. However, Anheuser-Busch held 49 percent of the market. Indeed, the MillerCoors collaboration was a response to the size and scale of Anheuser-Busch's operations. (Anheuser-Busch itself was acquired by InBev in 2008, an acquisition that created the world's largest brewer.) Indicating that the collaboration would result in significant cost reductions and an ability to generate economies of scale through the firms' combined operations, a company official said that "Miller and Coors will be a stronger, more competitive U.S. brewer than either company can be on its own." Analysts agreed with this assessment, with one person noting that the partnership would give the two companies "substantially more scale, which helps them with their retailers and their distributors and helps erode Anheuser Busch's No. 1 competitive advantage, which is their (market) share."[46] A successful collaboration in response to competitors for many years, MillerCoors today is struggling as it tries to compete against consumers' emerging preference for craft brews and cocktails instead of domestic lagers.[47] Thus, finding ways to effectively manage this alliance going forward is critical to its future.

9-2c Uncertainty-Reducing Strategy

Firms sometimes use business-level strategic alliances to hedge against risk and uncertainty, especially in fast-cycle markets.[48] These strategies are also used where uncertainty exists, such as in entering new product markets, especially those within emerging economies.

The relationship between hybrid vehicles and batteries that are needed to power them create a situation for which alliances are being formed to reduce uncertainty. More specifically, there is insufficient industry capacity among battery manufacturers to meet the demand for the type of batteries used in hybrids. This lack of a sufficient supply of electric batteries creates uncertainty for automobile manufacturers. To reduce this uncertainty, auto manufacturers are forming alliances. For example, Daimler AG formed a partnership with Tesla through which it buys Tesla batteries to use in its "smart" minicar as well as its Freightliner trucks. This collaboration continues even though Daimler recently sold its 4 percent ownership stake in Tesla.[49] Knowing that it has access to quality batteries through Tesla reduces Daimler's uncertainty with respect to a component part that is critical to building some of its products.

We further discuss Tesla in the Strategic Focus. As you will see, alliances are critical to this firm's current operations and will no doubt affect its ability to achieve success in the long term.

9-2d Competition-Reducing Strategy

Used to reduce competition, collusive strategies differ from strategic alliances in that collusive strategies are often an illegal cooperative strategy. Explicit collusion and tacit collusion are the two types of collusive strategies.

Explicit collusion exists when two or more firms negotiate directly to jointly agree about the amount to produce as well as the prices for what is produced.[50] Explicit collusion

Strategic **Focus**

Strategic Alliances as the Foundation for Tesla Motors' Operations

Founded in 2003, Tesla Motors, the manufacturer of electric vehicles, has formed many alliances as a means of competing during the early years of its life. For example, the company created a R&D partnership with Dana Holding Corporation initially for the purpose of jointly designing and producing a system capable of controlling the build-up of heat in its car batteries. Overall, Tesla has partnered with many companies working in the value chain that is used to produce its products. In this sense, alliances have been formed with suppliers, R&D experts, as well as original equipment manufacturers such as Daimler. One of the projects on which Daimler and Tesla are collaborating is the B-Class Electric Drive, an all-electric vehicle from Mercedes-Benz. Other partnerships that have been formed over the years include Tesla's nonequity strategic alliance with Sotira, a French company, and an equity alliance with Panasonic, a Japanese-based firm. The purpose of the partnership with Sotira is to manufacturer the carbon fiber bodies for its cars, while battery cells for the Tesla battery pack are produced through the collaboration with Panasonic.

Interestingly, its on-going work with batteries and recent hints from founder and CEO Elon Musk suggest that Tesla may, at is core, become a battery company rather than an automobile manufacturer. Appearing to support this possibility were comments indicating that Tesla intends to make and sell mega-batteries for homes and electric utility companies. The firm's decision to build and operate a 10-million-square-foot facility (dubbed the Gigafactory) to build batteries seems to reflect Tesla's capacity to build an array of batteries with different functionalities. With an initial investment of $5 billion, this factory was to be the largest lithium-ion-battery plant in the world. One goal of the Gigafactory is to "make batteries so cheap that electric cars can compete with conventional gasoline engines." Interestingly, the Gigafactory's size and scale allow Tesla to produce a quantity of batteries exceeding the firm's needs for its cars. In turn, analysts suggested that the company may seek additional partnerships as a way of continuing to develop innovative batteries and to sell some of the outputs from its plant.

In early 2015, Apple announced an internal project that was aimed at developing an Apple-branded electric vehicle. With a code-name "Titan," the initial work was oriented to designing a vehicle that resembles a minivan. Early assessments were that Apple intended to compete directly against Tesla if it decided to enter the electric vehicle market space. At the same time, the seriousness with which Apple is approaching this initial

design work is unknown, especially given the company's pattern of going so far as developing product prototypes before deciding to abandon a potential innovation. Additionally, the complexity of designing and producing an electric vehicle is such that several years would be required for Apple to introduce its product to the market, even if it chose to do so. Still, Apple's large investable assets and its innovative successes suggest that Tesla executives would be well served to carefully observe the firm's progress with respect to the Titan project.

Doug Cheeseman/Getty Images

Shown here is a Telsa Roadster and the electric battery pack that powers the car.

Other recent speculation regarding Tesla and Apple centered on the possibility of Apple acquiring Tesla, at a rumored cost of roughly $75 billion. In contrast, some analysts were suggesting that "some sort of joint venture or collaboration remains the smartest bet for both companies" (Apple and Tesla). As Tesla looks to its future, might the possibility of collaborating with another innovative firm, but one with significant financial resources, be a viable option? And from a broad perspective, might "a collaboration between the two tech giants, each with enormous clout and credibility, go a long way to converting the electric car from niche curiosity to mass consumer good?"

Sources: K. Finley, 2015, Tesla isn't an automaker. It's a battery company, *Wired*, www.wired.com, April 22; N. Gordon-Bloomfield, Move over Tesla: LG Chem now largest manufacturer of electric car battery packs thanks to Daimler deal, *Transport Evolved*, www.transportevolved.com, April 2; T. Lee, 2015, Apple, Tesla alliance still makes most sense for electric car, *San Francisco Chronicle Online*, www.sfchronicle.com, February 17; D. Wakabayashi & M. Ramsey, 2015, Apple gears up to challenge Tesla in electric cars, *Wall Street Journal Online*, www.wsj.com, February 13; C. Trudell & A. Ohnsman, 2014, Why the Tesla-Toyota partnership short-circuited, *Bloomberg News Online*, www.bloomberg.com, August. 7.

strategies are illegal in the United States and most developed economies (except in regulated industries). Accordingly, companies choosing to explicitly collude with other firms should recognize that competitors and regulatory bodies likely will challenge the acceptability of their competitive actions.

Tacit collusion exists when several firms in an industry indirectly coordinate their production and pricing decisions by observing each other's competitive actions and responses.[51] Tacit collusion tends to take place in industries dominated by a few large firms. "With tacit collusion, competitors don't agree to pricing, but since there are so few of them they all understand very well how their competition will behave, and are able to prevent dramatic prices slides by using this understanding."[52] Tacit collusion results in production output that is below fully competitive levels and above fully competitive prices. In addition to the effects on competition within a particular market, research suggests that tacit collusion between two firms can lead to less competition in other markets in which both firms operate.[53]

As suggested above, tacit collusion tends to be used as a competition-reducing, business-level strategy in industries with a high degree of concentration, such as the airline and breakfast cereal industries. Research in the airline industry suggests that tacit collusion reduces service quality and on-time performance.[54] Firms in these industries recognize their interdependence, which means that their competitive actions and responses significantly affect competitors' behavior toward them. Understanding this interdependence and carefully observing competitors can lead to tacit collusion.

Over time, four firms—Kellogg Company (producers of Kellogg's Corn Flakes, Fruit Loops, etc.), General Mills, Inc. (Cheerios, Lucky Charms, etc.), Ralcorp Holdings, now owned by ConAgra Foods (producing mostly private store brands), and Quaker Foods North America, a part of PepsiCo (Quaker Oatmeal, Cap'n Crunch, etc.)—have accounted for as much as 80 percent of sales volume in the ready-to-eat segment of the U.S. cereal market.[55] The global breakfast cereals market is expected to grow at roughly 4 percent annually for the next few years, reaching a total of $43.2 billion by 2019.[56] Some believe that the high degree of concentration in the global breakfast cereals industry results in prices to consumers that substantially exceed the costs companies incur to produce and sell their products. If prices are above the competitive level in this industry, it may be a possibility that the dominant firms use a tacit collusion cooperative strategy.

Mutual forbearance is a form of tacit collusion in which firms do not take competitive actions against rivals they meet in multiple markets. Rivals learn a great deal about each other when engaging in multimarket competition, including how to deter the effects of their rivals' competitive attacks and responses. Given what they know about each other as competitors, firms choose not to engage in what could be destructive competition in multiple product markets.[57]

In general, governments in free-market economies seek to determine how rivals can form cooperative strategies for the purpose of increasing their competitiveness without violating established regulations about competition.[58] However, this task is challenging when evaluating collusive strategies, particularly tacit ones. For example, the regulation of securities analysts through Regulation Fair Disclosure (Reg-FD) as established in the United States promoted more potential competition through competitive parity by eliminating privileged access to proprietary firm information as a critical source of competitive advantage. In doing so, research suggests that it led to more mutual forbearance among competing firms because they had more awareness of information possessed by their competitors, thus leading to more tacit collusion.[59] In the final analysis, individual companies must analyze the effect of a competition-reducing strategy on their performance and competitiveness and decide if pursuing such a strategy facilitates or inhibits their competitive success.

9-2e   Assessing Business-Level Cooperative Strategies

Firms use business-level cooperative strategies to develop competitive advantages that can contribute to successful positions in individual product markets. Evidence suggests that complementary business-level strategic alliances, especially vertical ones, have the greatest probability of creating a competitive advantage and possibly even a sustainable one.[60] Horizontal complementary alliances are sometimes difficult to maintain because often they are formed between firms that compete against each other at the same time they are cooperating. Airline companies, for example, want to compete aggressively against others serving their markets and customers. However, the need to develop scale economies and to share resources (such as scheduling systems) dictates that alliances be formed so the companies can compete by using cooperative actions and responses while they simultaneously compete against one another through competitive actions and responses. The challenge in these instances is for each firm to find ways to create the greatest amount of value from their simultaneous competitive and cooperative actions.

Although strategic alliances designed to respond to competition and to reduce uncertainty can also create competitive advantages, these advantages often are more temporary than those developed through complementary (both vertical and horizontal) alliances. The primary reason for this is that complementary alliances have a stronger focus on creating value than do competition-reducing and uncertainty-reducing alliances, which are formed to respond to competitors' actions or reduce uncertainty rather than to attack competitors.

9-3   Corporate-Level Cooperative Strategy

A **corporate-level cooperative strategy** is a strategy through which a firm collaborates with one or more companies to expand its operations. Diversifying alliances, synergistic alliances, and franchising are the most commonly used corporate-level cooperative strategies (see Figure 9.4).

Firms use diversifying and synergistic alliances to improve their performance by diversifying their operations through a means other than or in addition to internal organic growth or a merger or acquisition.[61] When a firm seeks to diversify into markets in which the host nation's government prevents mergers and acquisitions, alliances become an especially appropriate option. Corporate-level strategic alliances are also attractive compared with mergers, and particularly acquisitions, because they require fewer resource commitments[62] and permit greater flexibility in terms of efforts to diversify partners'

A **corporate-level cooperative strategy** is a strategy through which a firm collaborates with one or more companies to expand its operations.

Figure 9.4 Corporate-Level Cooperative Strategies

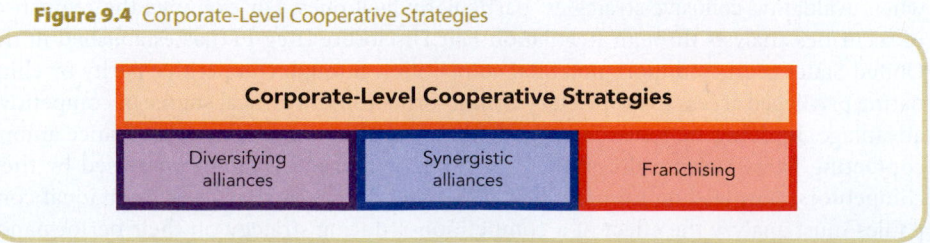

operations.[63] An alliance can be used as a way to determine whether the partners might benefit from a future merger or acquisition between them. This "testing" process often characterizes alliances formed to combine firms' unique technological resources and capabilities.[64]

9-3a Diversifying Strategic Alliance

A **diversifying strategic alliance** is a strategy in which firms share some of their resources to engage in product and/or geographic diversification. Companies using this strategy typically seek to enter new markets (either domestic or outside of their home setting) with existing products or with newly developed products. Sikorsky Aircraft Corporation, a subsidiary of United Technologies Corporation, formed an alliance with Tata Advanced Systems partially to diversify where some of its products are produced. Through this partnership, Sikorsky's S-92 helicopter cabins are manufactured in India, as are more than 5,000 detailed aerospace components. This alliance allows Sikorsky to diversify the global supply chain that is critical to producing its products.[65]

9-3b Synergistic Strategic Alliance

A **synergistic strategic alliance** is a strategy in which firms share some of their resources to create economies of scope. Similar to the business-level horizontal complementary strategic alliance, synergistic strategic alliances create synergy across multiple functions or multiple businesses between partner firms. The partnership between French-based Renault SA and Japan-based Nissan Motor Company that was formed in 1999 is a synergistic strategic alliance because, among other outcomes, the firms seek to create economies of scope by sharing their resources to develop manufacturing platforms that can be used to produce cars that will carry either the Renault or the Nissan brand. BMW relies on its collaboration with Chinese auto maker Brilliance (BBA is the name of this partnership) to produce engines in China as well as models including "BMW's 3-series and 5-series vehicles as well as the small X1 SUV."[66] This relationship is critical to BMW's efforts to maintain strong sales in China, a market in which roughly one-fifth of its total output is sold.

9-3c Franchising

Franchising is a strategy in which a firm (the franchisor) uses a franchise as a contractual relationship to describe and control the sharing of its resources with its partners (the franchisees).[67] A *franchise* is a "form of business organization in which a firm that already has a successful product or service (the franchisor) licenses its trademark and method of doing business to other businesses (the franchisees) in exchange for an initial franchise fee and an ongoing royalty rate."[68] Often, the effectiveness of these strategic alliances is a product of how well the franchisor can replicate its success across multiple partners in a cost-effective way.[69] As with diversifying and synergistic strategic alliances, franchising is an alternative to pursuing growth through mergers and acquisitions. McDonald's, Choice Hotels International, Hilton International, Marriott International, Mrs. Fields Cookies, Subway, and Ace Hardware are well-known firms using the franchising corporate-level cooperative strategy.

Franchising is a particularly attractive strategy to use in fragmented industries, such as retailing, hotels and motels, and commercial printing. In fragmented industries, a large number of small and medium-sized firms compete as rivals; however, no firm or small set of firms has a dominant share, making it possible for a company to gain a large market share by consolidating independent companies through the contractual relationships that are a part of a franchise agreement.

A **diversifying strategic alliance** is a strategy in which firms share some of their resources to engage in product and/or geographic diversification.

A **synergistic strategic alliance** is a strategy in which firms share some of their resources to create economies of scope.

Franchising is a strategy in which a firm (the franchisor) uses a franchise as a contractual relationship to describe and control the sharing of its resources with its partners (the franchisees).

In the most successful franchising strategy, the partners (the franchisor and the franchisees) work closely together.[70] A primary responsibility of the franchisor is to develop programs to transfer to the franchisees the knowledge and skills that are needed to successfully compete at the local level.[71] In return, franchisees should provide feedback to the franchisor regarding how their units could become more effective and efficient.[72] Working cooperatively, the franchisor and its franchisees find ways to strengthen the core company's brand name, which is often the most important competitive advantage for franchisees operating in their local markets.[73]

9-3d Assessing Corporate-Level Cooperative Strategies

Costs are incurred to implement each type of cooperative strategy.[74] Compared with their business-level counterparts, corporate-level cooperative strategies commonly are broader in scope and more complex, making them relatively more challenging and costly to use.

In spite of these costs, firms can create competitive advantages and value for customers by effectively using corporate-level cooperative strategies.[75] Internalizing successful alliance experiences makes it more likely that the strategy will attain the desired advantages. In other words, those involved with forming and using corporate-level cooperative strategies can also use them to develop useful knowledge about how to succeed in the future. To gain maximum value from this knowledge, firms should organize it and verify that it is always properly distributed to those involved with forming and using alliances.

We explained in Chapter 6 that firms answer two questions when dealing with corporate-level strategy: in which businesses and product markets will the firm choose to compete and how will those businesses be managed? These questions are also answered as firms form corporate-level cooperative strategies. Thus, firms able to develop corporate-level cooperative strategies and manage them in ways that are valuable, rare, imperfectly imitable, and nonsubstitutable (see Chapter 3) develop a competitive advantage that is in addition to advantages gained through the activities completed to implement business-level cooperative strategies. (Later in the chapter, we further describe alliance management as another potential competitive advantage.)

9-4 International Cooperative Strategy

The new competitive landscape finds firms using cross-border transactions for several purposes. In Chapter 7, we discussed cross-border acquisitions—actions through which a company located in one country acquires a firm located in a different country. In Chapter 8, we described how firms use cross-border acquisitions as a way of entering international markets. Here in Chapter 9, we examine cross-border strategic alliances as a type of international cooperative strategy. Thus, as the discussions in Chapters 7, 8 and 9 show, firms engage in cross-border activities to achieve several related objectives.

A **cross-border strategic alliance** is a strategy in which firms with headquarters in different countries decide to combine some of their resources to create a competitive advantage. Taking place in virtually all industries, the number of cross-border alliances firms are completing continues to increase.[76] These alliances are sometimes formed instead of mergers and acquisitions, which can be riskier. Even though cross-border alliances can themselves be complex and hard to manage,[77] they have the potential to help firms use some of their resources to create value in locations outside their home market. The cross-border alliance between Renault and Nissan that we mentioned earlier is thought to be one of "the auto-industry's most successful cross-border alliances."[78] Through this collaboration, the partners cooperate in terms of development, procurement, and production processes partly in order to be able to create value in markets throughout the world that neither firm could create operating independently.

A **cross-border strategic alliance** is a strategy in which firms with headquarters in different countries decide to combine some of their resources to create a competitive advantage.

Limited domestic growth opportunities and foreign government economic policies are key reasons firms use cross-border alliances. As discussed in Chapter 8, local ownership is an important national policy objective in some nations. In India and China, for example, governmental policies reflect a strong preference to license local companies. Thus, in some countries, the full range of entry mode choices we described in Chapter 8 may not be available to firms seeking to geographically diversify. Indeed, investment by foreign firms in these instances may be allowed only through a partnership with a local firm, such as in a cross-border alliance. Important too is the fact that strategic alliances with local partners can help firms overcome certain liabilities of moving into a foreign country, including those related to a lack of knowledge of the local culture or institutional norms.[79] A cross-border strategic alliance can also help foreign partners from an operational perspective because the local partner has significantly more information about factors contributing to competitive success such as local markets, sources of capital, legal procedures, and politics.[80] Interestingly, research results suggest that firms with foreign operations have longer survival rates than domestic-only firms, although this is reduced if there are competition problems between foreign subsidiaries.[81]

In general, cross-border strategic alliances are more complex and risky than domestic strategic alliances. Complexity and, perhaps, risk may be factors associated with the alliance recently completed between Airbus Group NV and Korea Aerospace Industries Ltd. These firms are partnering to build at least 300 military and civilian helicopters in South Korea.[82] Complexity is suggested by the fact that the partners are committed to designing and producing "next-generation light civilian and military helicopters" that will satisfy South Korean customers. Risks include those of relying on unique, firm-specific cultures and practices as the foundation for designing next generation products in an acceptable time period and producing those products at acceptable costs. In spite of the risks, firms, such as Airbus and Korea Aerospace, choose to form and operate cross-border strategic alliances partly because companies competing internationally tend to outperform domestic-only competitors.

9-5 Network Cooperative Strategy

In addition to forming their own alliances with individual companies, an increasing number of firms are collaborating in multiple alliances called networks.[83] A **network cooperative strategy** is a strategy where several firms agree to form multiple partnerships to achieve shared objectives.

Through its Global Partner Network, Cisco has formed alliances with a host of companies including IBM, Emerson, Hitachi, CA Technologies Fujitsu, Intel, Nokia, and Wipro. Cisco uses alliances to drive its growth, differentiate itself from competitors, enter new businesses areas, and create competitive advantages. Recently, Cisco's annual revenues earned from its alliances exceeded $5 billion. Sometimes, several of the firms with which Cisco has formed individual alliances partner together to form a network to achieve shared objectives.[84]

Demonstrating the complexity of network cooperative strategies is the fact that Cisco also competes against a number of the firms with whom it has formed cooperative agreements, including network strategies. For example, Cisco is competing against IBM when selling and servicing its servers. At the same time, Cisco and IBM's alliance is very active as the two firms help organizations "find better ways to connect people, share critical data, and create analytic insights to improve"[85] their ability to earn above-average returns. Overall, the example of the simultaneous "cooperative and competitive" relationships between Cisco and IBM demonstrates how firms use network cooperative strategies

A **network cooperative strategy** is a strategy where several firms agree to form multiple partnerships to achieve shared objectives.

more extensively as a way of creating value for customers by offering many goods and services in many geographic (domestic and international) markets.

A network cooperative strategy is particularly effective when it is formed by geographically clustered firms,[86] as in California's Silicon Valley and Rome, Italy's aerospace cluster. Effective social relationships and interactions among partners while sharing their resources make it more likely that a network cooperative strategy will be successful,[87] as does having a productive *strategic center firm* (we discuss strategic center firms in detail in Chapter 11). Firms involved in networks gain information and knowledge from multiple sources. They can use these heterogeneous knowledge sets to produce more and better innovation. As a result, firms involved in networks of alliances tend to be more innovative.[88] However, there are disadvantages to participating in networks as a firm can be locked into its partnerships, precluding the development of alliances with others. In certain network configurations, such as Japanese *keiretsus*, firms in a network are expected to help other firms in that network whenever support is required. Such expectations can become a burden and negatively affect the focal firm's performance over time.[89]

9-5a Alliance Network Types

An important advantage of a network cooperative strategy is that firms gain access to their partners' other partners. Having access to multiple collaborations increases the likelihood that additional competitive advantages will be formed as the set of shared resources expands.[90] In turn, being able to develop new resources further stimulates product innovations that are critical to strategic competitiveness in the global economy.

The set of strategic alliance partnerships that firms develop when using a network cooperative strategy is called an *alliance network*. Companies' alliance networks vary by industry characteristics. A *stable alliance network* is formed in mature industries where demand is relatively constant and predictable. Through a stable alliance network, firms try to extend their competitive advantages to other settings while continuing to profit from operations in their core, relatively mature industry. Thus, stable networks are built primarily to *exploit* the economies (scale and/or scope) that exist between the partners, such as in the airline and automobile industries.[91]

Dynamic alliance networks are used in industries characterized by frequent product innovations and short product life cycles.[92] The industries in which Apple and IBM compete are examples of this situation. Partly in response, these two firms recently formed a partnership through which they collaborate on business services. The purpose of the partnership is to "get more iPhones and iPads into corporate hands and more IBM services such as analytics, data storage, and supply-chain management onto mobile devices."[93] Of course, Apple and IBM each partner with a host of other firms to develop component parts that are critical to producing the products that are central to the success of their recently-formed partnership. Thus, a network of relationships

Mathias Rosenthal/Shutterstock.com

Shown in the middle here is representation of a strategic center firm with links to other firms in an alliance network.

among multiple companies is foundational to achieving the objectives Apple and IBM seek through their partnership.

In dynamic alliance networks, partners typically *explore* new ideas and possibilities with the potential to lead to product innovations, entries to new markets, and the development of new markets. These are outcomes sought by Apple and IBM through the collaboration described above. Research suggests that firms that help to broker relationships between companies remain important network participants as these networks change.[94] Often, large firms in industries such as software and pharmaceuticals create networks of relationships with smaller entrepreneurial startup firms in their search for innovation-based outcomes.[95] An important outcome for small firms successfully partnering with larger firms in an alliance network is the credibility they build by being associated with their larger collaborators.[96]

9-6 Competitive Risks with Cooperative Strategies

Stated simply, many cooperative strategies fail. In fact, evidence shows that two-thirds of cooperative strategies have serious problems in their first two years and that as many as 50 percent of them fail. This failure rate suggests that even when the partnership has potential complementarities and synergies, alliance success is elusive.[97] Although failure is undesirable, it can be a valuable learning experience, meaning that firms should carefully study a cooperative strategy's failure to gain insights with respect to how to form and manage future cooperative arrangements.[98] We show prominent cooperative strategy risks in Figure 9.5. We discuss a few cooperative strategies that have failed and possible reasons for those failures in the Strategic Focus.

One cooperative strategy risk is that a firm may act in a way that its partner thinks is opportunistic. BP plc and OAO Rosneft developed a joint venture to explore Russia's Arctic Ocean in search of oil. However, the investment by minority partners of this joint venture was driven down in value at one point by 50 percent over concern that the Russian government, Rosneft's dominant owner, would expropriate value from the deal.[99] In general, opportunistic behaviors surface either when formal contracts fail to prevent them or when an alliance is based on a false perception of

Figure 9.5 Managing Competitive Risks in Cooperative Strategies

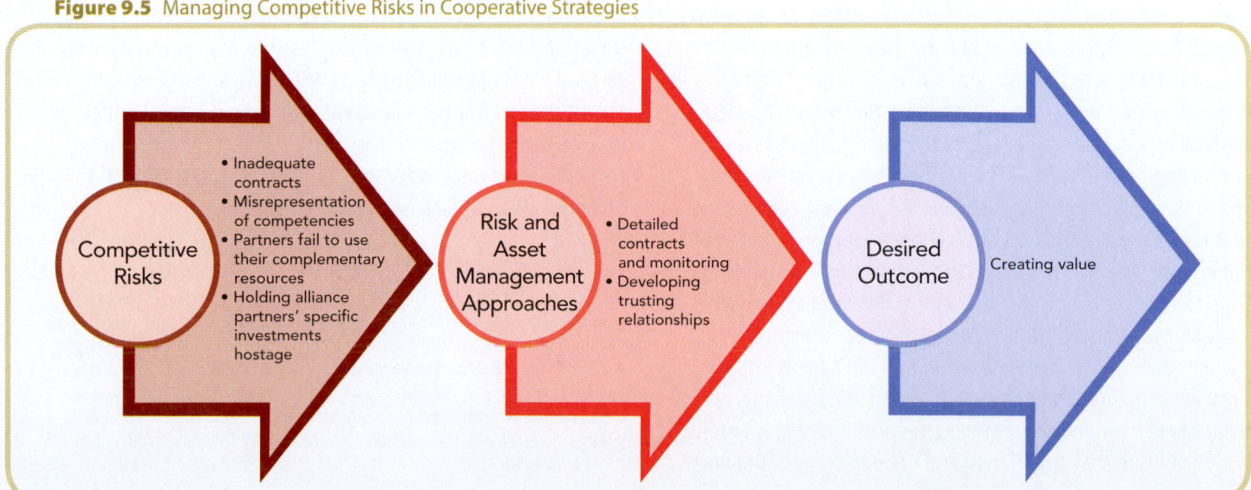

Strategic **Focus**

Failing to Obtain Desired Levels of Success with Cooperative Strategies

The complexity associated with most cooperative strategies increases the difficulty of successfully using them. One complexity is the fact that often, firms collaborating to complete certain projects are simultaneously competing with each other as well. As explained earlier, this reality describes the relationship between Cisco and IBM as well as those existing with airline companies that have joined one of the three major alliance networks (Star, Oneworld, and SkyTeam). Another complication is that firms sometimes form a partnership with a company that is itself a collaboration between other companies. Recently, for example, Ford Motor Company formed a joint venture with carbon manufacturer DowAksa, a firm that is itself a joint venture organized by Dow Chemical Company and Istanbul-based Aksa Akrilik Kimya Sanayii A.S. The purpose of the Ford/DowAksa collaboration is to find ways to develop cheaper grades of carbon fiber components that can be integrated into Ford's automobiles and trucks. Because it is much lighter than steel, carbon fiber helps auto manufacturers reduce the weight of their products which in turn facilitates their efforts to increase products' gas mileage. We see then that, for multiple reasons, the complexities of cooperative strategies increase the challenge of effectively implementing them and may contribute to alliance failure.

Redbox and Verizon terminated their relationship that was organized to become the streaming subscription components of Redbox's rental business after only two years. (Outerwall founded Redbox in partnership with McDonald's Ventures, LLC. McDonald's interest was to distribute DVDs through rental kiosks at its restaurants as a means of attracting customers and providing them with a unique service.) Competing against the likes of Netflix and Hulu Plus, Redbox's streaming service failed to attract a sufficient number of customers, perhaps in part because it was able to stream to customers only items that its competitors were also streaming. Unlike Netflix and Hulu Plus, Redbox was not developing its own original content as a means of creating unique value for customers. Because the service made available through the Redbox and Verizon collaboration was losing money and was not gaining a sufficient number of subscribers, the partners chose to terminate their relationship.

Carefully executing the operational details of a planned cooperative strategy is foundational to its performance and influences if it will succeed or fail. In mid-2015 for example, First Solar, Inc. and SunPower Corporation, the two largest U.S. solar-panel manufacturers were in the planning stages to form a joint venture that would own and operate some of the firms' projects. The proposed partners believed that the collaboration would create value by combining "SunPower's polysilicon technology with First Solar's thin-film panels." However, SunPower recorded a loss in the first quarter of 2015, partly because of costs it was incurring to structure the proposed relationship with First Solar. This demonstrates the importance of identifying efficient as well as effective ways to structure a proposed collaboration between companies as a means of increasing the likelihood of operational success.

Who is Danny/Shutterstock.com

The handshake between partners suggests the cooperation that is needed between parties for business collaborations to succeed.

Earlier, we noted that MillerCoors, the joint venture formed between Molson Coors and SABMiller, is encountering difficulties. Some analysts believe that a reason for this is that, while the partnership had been very successful during its first six years in terms of substantially reducing costs by creating economies of scale, it had failed to increase the market shares held by two of its important products, Miller Lite and Coors Light. The situation with the MillerCoors partnership suggests that long-term cooperative strategy success results when partners find unique ways to create value for customers in addition to finding ways to reduce operating costs.

Sources: M. Armental, 2015, SunPower swings to loss on costs related to planned joint venture, *Wall Street Journal Online*, www.wsj.com, April 30; D. Harris, 2015, China joint ventures: How not to get burned, Above the Law, www.abovethelaw.com, February 9; Molson Coors, U.S. joint venture MillerCoors facing stiff challenges, *Wall Street Journal Online*, www.wsj.com, May 7; J. D. Stoll, 2015, Ford to develop carbon-fiber material for cars, *Wall Street Journal Online*, www.wsj.com, April 17; P. E. Farrell, 2014, The 7 deadly sins of joint ventures, *Entrepreneur*, www.entrepreneur.com, September 2; Q. Plummer, 2014, Redbox instant will be killed Oct. 7: A failed joint venture, Tech Times, www.techtimes.com, October 6.

partner trustworthiness. Typically, an opportunistic firm wants to acquire as much of its partner's tacit knowledge as it can.[100] Full awareness of what a partner wants in a cooperative strategy reduces the likelihood that a firm will suffer from another's opportunistic actions.[101]

Some cooperative strategies fail when it is discovered that a firm has misrepresented the resources it can bring to the partnership. This risk is more common when the partner's contribution is based on some of its intangible assets. Superior knowledge of local conditions is an example of an intangible asset that partners often fail to deliver. An effective way to deal with this risk may be to ask the partner to provide evidence that it does, in fact, possess the resources (even when they are largely intangible) it will share in the cooperative strategy.[102]

The cooperative relationships in the form of nonequity strategic alliances that are being created between some large pharmaceutical companies and outsourcing firms is potentially an example of the "misrepresentation of available resources" risk. As discussed in Chapter 3, pharmaceutical companies are outsourcing the monitoring of drug safety to firms claiming to have the requisite human capital skills needed to successfully complete various monitoring tasks. But is this the case? Not everyone is convinced. In fact, "critics of the (outsourcing) practice say drug monitoring is difficult, requiring deep experience and a knack for detective work in addition to knowledge of biochemistry and pharmacology, and that the shift toward outsourcing carries risks that deadly side effects will go unnoticed."[103] Thus, pharmaceutical companies may need to carefully monitor the quality of the human capital resource their partners provide for the purpose of completing what appears to be complicated monitoring work.

A firm's failure to make available to its partners the resources (such as the most sophisticated technologies) that it committed to the cooperative strategy is a third risk. This particular risk surfaces most commonly when firms form an international cooperative strategy, especially in emerging economies.[104] In these instances, different cultures and languages can cause misinterpretations of contractual terms or trust-based expectations.

A final risk is that one firm may make investments that are specific to the alliance while its partner does not. For example, the firm might commit resources to develop manufacturing equipment that can be used only to produce products associated with the alliance. If the partner isn't also making alliance-specific investments, the firm is at a relative disadvantage in terms of returns earned from the alliance compared with investments made to earn the returns.

9-7 Managing Cooperative Strategies

Although they are difficult to manage, cooperative strategies are an important means of growth and enhanced firm performance. Because the ability to effectively manage cooperative strategies is unevenly distributed across organizations in general, assigning managerial responsibility for a firm's cooperative strategies to a high-level executive or to a team improves the likelihood that the strategies will be well managed. In turn, being able to successfully manage cooperative strategies can itself be a competitive advantage.[105]

Those responsible for managing the firm's cooperative strategies should take the actions necessary to coordinate activities, categorize knowledge learned from previous experiences, and make certain that what the firm knows about how to effectively form and use cooperative strategies is in the hands of the right people at the right time. Firms must also learn how to manage both the tangible and intangible assets (such as knowledge) that are involved with a cooperative arrangement. Too often, partners concentrate on managing tangible assets at the expense of taking action to also manage a cooperative relationship's intangible assets.[106]

Cost minimization and opportunity maximization are the two primary approaches firms use to manage cooperative strategies[107] (see Figure 9.5). In the *cost-minimization* approach, the firm develops formal contracts with its partners. These contracts specify how the cooperative strategy is to be monitored and how partner behavior is to be controlled. The joint venture between GM China and SAIC Motor Corp. that we discussed earlier is being managed largely through formal contractual relationships. The goal of the cost-minimization approach is to minimize the cooperative strategy's cost and to prevent opportunistic behavior by a partner.

Maximizing a partnership's value-creating opportunities is the focus of the *opportunity-maximization* approach. In this case, partners are prepared to take advantage of unexpected opportunities to learn from each other and to explore additional marketplace possibilities. Less formal contracts, with fewer constraints on partners' behaviors, make it possible for partners to explore how their resources can be shared in multiple value-creating ways. This appears to be the approach being used to manage the Pangea partnership we discussed earlier that has been formed among online news publishers since for the beta-testing phrase, a central team with "commercial leadership and operational resources from all the member publishers" was organized.[108] Finding additional ways to collaborate was one of the objectives associated with the decision to organize this team.

Firms can successfully use both approaches to manage cooperative strategies. However, the costs to monitor the cooperative strategy are greater with cost minimization because writing detailed contracts and using extensive monitoring mechanisms is expensive, even though the approach is intended to reduce alliance costs. Although monitoring systems may prevent partners from acting in their own self-interests, they also often preclude positive responses to new opportunities that surface to productively use each alliance partner's unique resources. Thus, formal contracts and extensive monitoring systems tend to stifle partners' efforts to gain maximum value from their participation in a cooperative strategy and require significant resources to be put into place and used.[109]

The relative lack of detail and formality that is a part of the contract developed when using the opportunity-maximization approach means that firms need to trust that each party will act in the partnership's best interests. The psychological state of *trust* in the context of cooperative arrangements is the belief that a firm will not do anything to exploit its partner's vulnerabilities, even if it has an opportunity to do so. When partners trust each other, there is less need to write detailed formal contracts to specify each firm's alliance behaviors,[110] and the cooperative relationship tends to be more stable.[111] On a relative basis, trust tends to be more difficult to establish in international cooperative strategies than domestic ones. Differences in trade policies, cultures, laws, and politics that are part of cross-border alliances account for the increased difficulty.

Research showing that trust between partners increases the likelihood of success when using alliances highlights the benefits of the opportunity-maximization approach to managing cooperative strategies. Trust may also be the most efficient way to influence and control alliance partners' behaviors. Research indicates that trust can be a capability that is valuable, rare, imperfectly imitable, and often nonsubstitutable.[112] Thus, firms known to be trustworthy can have a competitive advantage in terms of how they develop and use cooperative strategies. Increasing the importance of trust in alliances is the fact that it is not possible to specify all operational details of a cooperative strategy in a formal contract. As such, being confident that its partner can be trusted reduces the firm's concern about its inability to contractually control all alliance details.

SUMMARY

■ A cooperative strategy is one through which firms work together to achieve a shared objective. Strategic alliances, where firms combine some of their resources for the purpose of creating a competitive advantage, are the primary form of cooperative strategies. Joint ventures (where firms create and own equal shares of a new venture), equity strategic alliances (where firms own different shares of a newly created venture), and nonequity strategic alliances (where firms cooperate through a contractual relationship) are the three major types of strategic alliances. Outsourcing, discussed in Chapter 3, commonly occurs as firms form nonequity strategic alliances.

■ Collusive strategies are the second type of cooperative strategies (with strategic alliances being the other). In many economies, explicit collusive strategies are illegal unless sanctioned by government policies. Increasing globalization has led to fewer government-sanctioned situations of explicit collusion. Tacit collusion, also called mutual forbearance, is a cooperative strategy through which firms tacitly cooperate to reduce industry output below the potential competitive output level, thereby raising prices above the competitive level.

■ The reasons firms use strategic alliances vary by slow-cycle, fast-cycle, and standard-cycle market conditions. To enter restricted markets (slow cycle), to move quickly from one competitive advantage to another (fast cycle), and to gain market power (standard cycle) are among the reasons firms choose to use strategic alliances.

■ Four business-level cooperative strategies are used to help the firm improve its performance in individual product markets:

  ■ Through vertical and horizontal complementary alliances, companies combine some of their resources to create value in different parts (vertical) or the same parts (horizontal) of the value chain

  ■ Competition response strategies are formed to respond to competitors' actions, especially strategic actions

  ■ Uncertainty-reducing strategies are used to hedge against the risks created by the conditions of uncertain competitive environments (such as new product markets)

  ■ Competition-reducing strategies are used to avoid excessive competition while the firm marshals its resources to improve its strategic competitiveness

Complementary alliances have the highest probability of helping a firm form a competitive advantage; competition-reducing alliances have the lowest probability.

■ Firms use corporate-level cooperative strategies to engage in product and/or geographic diversification. Through diversifying strategic alliances, firms agree to share some of their resources to enter new markets or produce new products. Synergistic alliances are ones where firms share some of their resources to develop economies of scope. Synergistic alliances are similar to business-level horizontal complementary alliances where firms try to develop operational synergy, except that synergistic alliances are used to develop synergy at the corporate level. Franchising is a corporate-level cooperative strategy where the franchisor uses a franchise as a contractual relationship to specify how resources will be shared with franchisees.

■ As an international cooperative strategy, a cross-border strategic alliance is used for several reasons, including the performance superiority of firms competing in markets outside their domestic market and governmental restrictions on a firm's efforts to grow through mergers and acquisitions. Commonly, cross-border strategic alliances are riskier than their domestic counterparts, particularly when partners aren't fully aware of each other's reason for participating in the partnership.

■ In a network cooperative strategy, several firms agree to form multiple partnerships to achieve shared objectives. A firm's opportunity to gain access "to its partner's other partnerships" is a primary benefit of a network cooperative strategy. Network cooperative strategies are used to form either a stable alliance network or a dynamic alliance network. In mature industries, stable networks are used to extend competitive advantages into new areas. In rapidly changing environments where frequent product innovations occur, dynamic networks are used primarily as a tool of innovation.

■ Cooperative strategies aren't risk free. If a contract is not developed appropriately, or if a partner misrepresents its resources or fails to make them available, failure is likely. Furthermore, a firm may be held hostage through asset-specific investments made in conjunction with a partner, which may be exploited.

■ Trust is an increasingly important aspect of successful cooperative strategies. Firms place high value on opportunities to partner with companies known for their trustworthiness. When trust exists, a cooperative strategy is managed to maximize the pursuit of opportunities between partners. Without trust, formal contracts and extensive monitoring systems are used to manage cooperative strategies. In this case, the interest is "cost minimization" rather than "opportunity maximization."

KEY TERMS

business-level cooperative strategy 284
complementary strategic alliances 284
cooperative strategy 278
corporate-level cooperative strategy 290
cross-border strategic alliance 292
diversifying strategic alliance 291
equity strategic alliance 280

franchising 291
joint venture 279
network cooperative strategy 293
nonequity strategic alliance 280
strategic alliance 279
synergistic strategic alliance 291

REVIEW QUESTIONS

1. What is the definition of cooperative strategy, and why is this strategy important to firms competing in the twenty-first century competitive landscape?

2. What is a strategic alliance? What are the three major types of strategic alliances that firms form for the purpose of developing a competitive advantage?

3. What are the four business-level cooperative strategies? What are the key differences among them?

4. What are the three corporate-level cooperative strategies? How do firms use each of these strategies for the purpose of creating a competitive advantage?

5. Why do firms use cross-border strategic alliances?

6. What risks are firms likely to experience as they use cooperative strategies?

7. What are the differences between the cost-minimization approach and the opportunity-maximization approach to managing cooperative strategies?

Mini-Case

Alliance Formation, Both Globally and Locally, in the Global Automobile Industry

The academic literature on alliances has some interesting recent findings, one of which is the rationale that because firms are often located in the same country, and often in the same region of the country, it is easier for them to collaborate on major projects. As such, they compete globally, but may cooperate locally. Historically, firms have learned to collaborate by establishing strategic alliances and forming cooperative strategies when there is intensive competition. This interesting paradox is due to several reasons. First, when there is intense rivalry, it is difficult to maintain market power. As such, using a cooperative strategy can reduce market power through better norms of competition; this pertains to the idea of "*mutual forbearance*". Another rationale that has emerged is based on the resource-based view of the firm (see Chapter 3).

To compete, firms often need resources that they don't have but may be found in other firms in or outside of the focal firm's home industry. As such, these "complementary resources" are another rationale for why large firms form joint ventures and strategic alliances within the same industry or in vertically related industries.

Because firms are co-located and have similar needs, it's easier for them to jointly work together, for example, to produce engines and transmissions as part of the powertrain. This is evident in the European alliance between Peugeot-Citroën and Opel-Vauxhall (owned by General Motors). It is also the reason for a recent U.S. alliance between Ford and General Motors in developing upgraded nine- and ten-speed transmissions. Furthermore, Ford and GM are looking to develop, together, eleven- and twelve-speed automatic transmissions to improve fuel efficiency and help the firms meet new federal guidelines regarding such efficiency.

In regard to resource complementarity, a very successful alliance was formed in 1999 by French-based Renault and Japan-based Nissan. Each of these firms lacked the necessary size to develop economies of scale and economies of scope that were critical to succeed in the 1990s and beyond in the global automobile industry. When the alliance was formed, each firm took an ownership stake in the other. The larger of the two companies, Renault, holds a 43.3 percent stake in Nissan, while Nissan has a 15 percent stake in Renault. It is interesting to note that Carlos Ghosn serves as the CEO of both companies. Over time, this corporate-level synergistic alliance has developed three values to guide the relationship between the two firms:

1. *trust* (work fairly, impartially, and professionally)
2. *respect* (honor commitments, liabilities, and responsibilities)
3. *transparency* (be open, frank, and clear)

Largely due to these established principles, the Renault-Nissan alliance is a recognized success. One could argue that the main reason for the success of this alliance is the complementary assets that the firms bring to the alliance; Nissan is strong in Asia, while Renault is strong in Europe. Together they have been able to establish other production locations, such as those in Latin America, which they may not have obtained independently.

Some firms enter alliances because they are "squeezed in the middle;" that is, they have moderate volumes, mostly for the mass market, but need to collaborate to establish viable economies of scale. For example, Fiat-Chrysler needs to boost its annual sales from $4.3 billion to something like $6 billion, and likewise needs to strengthen its presence in the booming Asian market to have enough global market power. As such, it is entering joint ventures with two undersized Japanese carmakers, Mazda and Suzuki. However, the past history of Mazda and Suzuki with alliances may be a reason for their not being overly enthusiastic about the prospects of the current alliances. Fiat broke up with GM, Chrysler with Daimler, and Mazda with Ford.

This is also the situation in Europe locally for Peugeot-Citroën of France, which is struggling for survival along with the GM European subsidiary, Opel-Vauxhall. More specifically, Peugeot-Citroën and Opel-Vauxhall have struck a tentative agreement to share platforms and engines to get the capital necessary for investment in future models. As such, in all these examples, the firms need additional market share, but also enough capital to make the investment necessary to realize more market power to compete.

In summary, there are a number of rationales why competitors not only compete but also cooperate in establishing strategic alliances and joint ventures in order to meet strategic needs for increased market power, take advantage of complementary assets, and cooperate with close neighbors, often in the same region of a country.

Sources: 2013, Markets and makers: Running harder, *Economist*, April 20, ss4–ss7; J. Boxell, 2013, Peugeot reaffirms push into BRICs, *Financial Times*, www.ft.com, February 7; D. Pearson & J. Bennett, 2013, Corporate news: GM, Peugeot pledge to deepen car alliance – Tough market in Europe has slowed progress, but automakers now see opportunities to cooperate outside the region, *Wall Street Journal Online*, www.wsj.com, January 10; J. B. White, 2013, Mazda uses alliances to boost sales, *Wall Street Journal Online*, www.wsj.com, January 27; T. Yu, M. Subramaniam, & A. A. Cannella, Jr., 2013, Competing globally, allying locally: Alliances between global rivals and host-country factors, *Journal of International Business Studies*, 44: 117-137; W. Kim, 2012, The voyage of the Renault-Nissan alliance: A successful venture, *Advances in Management*, 5(9): 25–29.

Case Discussion Questions

1. How can the resource-based view of the firm (see Chapters 1 and 3) help us understand why firms develop and use cooperative strategies such as strategic alliances and joint ventures?

2. What is the relationship between the core competencies a firm possesses, the core competencies the firm feels it needs, and decisions to form cooperative strategies?

3. What does it mean to say that the partners of an alliance have "complementary assets"? What complementary assets do Renault and Nissan share?

4. What are the risks associated with the corporate-level strategic alliance between Renault and Nissan? What have these firms done to mitigate these risks?

5. Is it possible that some of the firms mentioned in this Mini-Case (e.g., Renault, Nissan, Mazda, Peugot-Citroen, Opel-Vauxhall) might form a network cooperative strategy? If so, what conditions might influence a decision by these firms to form this particular type of strategy?

NOTES

1. B. B. Tyler & T. Caner, 2015, New product
    introductions below aspirations, slack and
    R&D alliances: A behavioral perspective,
    Strategic Management Journal, in press;
    O. Schilke, 2014, Second-order dynamic
    capabilities: How do they matter? *Academy
    of Management Perspectives*, 28: 368–380;
    U. Wassmer & P. Dussauge, 2012, Network
    resource stocks and flows: How do alliance
    portfolios affect the value of new alliance
    formations? *Strategic Management Journal*,
    33: 871–883.

2. A. L. Brito, E. P. Z. Brito, & L. H. Hashiba,
    2014, What type of cooperation with
    suppliers and customers leads to superior
    performance? *Journal of Business Research*,
    67: 952–959; R. A. Heidl, H. K. Steensma, &
    C. Phelps, 2014, Divisive faultlines and the
    unplanned dissolutions of multipartner
    alliances, *Organization Science*, 25: 1351–
    1371; D. Lavie, P. R. Haunschild, & P. Khanna,
    2012, Organizational differences, relational
    mechanisms, and alliance performance,
    Strategic Management Journal, 33:
    1453–1479.

3. Z. Khan, O. Shenkar, & Y. K. Lew, 2015,
    Knowledge transfer from international
    joint ventures to local suppliers in
    a developing economy, *Journal of
    International Business Studies*, in press.

4. S. J. D. Schillebeeckx, S. Chaturvedi,
    G. George, & Z. King, 2015, What do I want?
    The effects of individual aspiration and
    relational capability on collaboration
    preferences, *Strategic Management Journal*,
    in press; R. J. Arend, P. C. Patel, &
    H. D. Park, 2014, Explaining post-IPO venture
    performance through a knowledge-based
    view typology, *Strategic Management
    Journal*, 35: 376–397; J. H. Dyer & H. Singh,
    1998, The relational view: Cooperative
    strategy and sources of interorganizational
    competitive advantage, *Academy of
    Management Review*, 23: 660–679.

5. R. R. Kehoe & D. Tzabbar, 2015,
    Lighting the way or stealing the shine?
    An examination of the duality in star
    scientists' effects on firm innovative
    performance, *Strategic Management
    Journal*, 36: 709–727; R. Vandaie &
    A. Zaheer, 2014, Surviving bear hugs:
    Firm capability, large partner alliances, and
    growth, *Strategic Management Journal*,
    35: 566–577; J. Walter, F. W. Kellermanns, &
    C. Lechner, 2012, Decision making within
    and between organizations: Rationality,
    politics, and alliance performance, *Journal
    of Management*, 38: 1582–1610.

6. C. Lioukas & J. Reuer, 2015, Isolating trust
    outcomes from exchange relationships:
    Social exchange and learning benefits
    of prior ties in alliances, *Academy of
    Management Journal*, in press;
    J. Charterina & J. Landeta, 2013, Effects of

knowledge-sharing routines and dyad-
based investments on company innovation
and performance: An empirical study
of Spanish manufacturing companies,
International Journal of Management,
30: 197–216.

7. J. Wu & P. Olk, 2014, Technological
    advantage, alliances with customers, local
    knowledge and competitor identification,
    Journal of Business Research, 67: 2106–2114;
    J. L. Cummings & S. R. Holmberg, 2012,
    Best-fit alliance partners: The use of critical
    success factors in a comprehensive partner
    selection process, *Long Range Planning*,
    45: 136–159.

8. N. Rahman & H. J. Korn, 2014, Alliance
    longevity: Examining relational and
    operational antecedents, *Long Range
    Planning*, 47: 245–261; S. Xu, A. P. Fenik, &
    M. B. Shaner, 2014, Multilateral alliances
    and innovation output: The importance of
    equity and technological scope, *Journal of
    Business Research*, 67: 2403–2410.

9. Treflis team, 2014, Juniper collaborates with
    Aruba to expand converged networking
    solutions portfolio, *Forbes Online*, www.
    forbes.com, June 13.

10. Y. Liu & T. Ravichandran, 2015, Alliance
    experience, IT-enabled knowledge
    integration, and ex-ante value gains,
    Organization Science, 26: 511–530; J. Roy,
    2012, IJV partner trustworthy behaviour:
    The role of host country governance
    and partner selection criteria, *Journal of
    Management Studies*, 49: 332–355.

11. C. Murphy, 2015, GM China venture to
    spend $16 billion to develop new products,
    Wall Street Journal Online, www.wsj.com,
    April 19.

12. R. Yu, 2015, SAIC Motor's tie-ups with
    Volkswagen, GM rev up 2014 profit, *Wall
    Street Journal Online*, www.wsj.com, April 2.

13. J. H. Love, S. Roper, & P. Vahter, 2014,
    Learning from openness: The dynamics of
    breadth in external innovation linkages,
    Strategic Management Journal, 35:
    1703–1716; E. Chrysostome, R. Nigam, &
    C. Jarilowski, 2013, Revisiting strategic
    learning in international joint ventures:
    A knowledge creation perspective,
    International Journal of Management, 30(1):
    88–98; D. Tan & K. E. Meyer, 2011, Country-
    of-origin and industry FDI agglomeration
    of foreign investors in an emerging
    economy, *Journal of International Business
    Studies*, 42: 504–520.

14. 2015, Boston Scientific signs strategic
    alliance with Frankenman Medical
    Equipment Company, Boston
    Scientific Company Home Page, www.
    bostonscientific.com, April 14.

15. W. (Stone) Shi, S. L. Sun, B. C. Pinkham, &
    M. W. Peng, 2014, Domestic alliance
    network to attract foreign partners:

Evidence from international joint ventures
in China, *Journal of International Business
Studies*, 45: 338–362; L. Cui & F. Jiang, 2012,
State ownership effect on firms' FDI
ownership decisions under institutional
pressure: A study of Chinese outward-
investing firms, *Journal of International
Business Studies*, 43: 264–284; J. Xia,
J. Tan, & D. Tan, 2008, Mimetic entry and
bandwagon effect: The rise and decline of
international equity joint venture in China,
Strategic Management Journal, 29: 195–217.

16. C. Dulaney, 2015, Johnson Controls
    auto-interiors spinoff expected to begin
    operations in July, *Wall Street Journal Online*,
    www.wsj.com, April 14.

17. J. Reuer & S. Devarakonda, 2015,
    Mechanisms of hybrid governance:
    Administrative committees in non-equity
    alliances, *Academy of Management Journal*,
    in press; A. Majocchi, U. Mayrhofer, &
    J. Camps, 2013, Joint ventures or non-equity
    alliances? Evidence from Italian firms,
    Management Decision, 51: 380–395.

18. B. T. McCann, J. J. Reuer, & N. Lahiri,
    2015, Agglomeration and the choice
    between acquisitions and alliances:
    An information economics perspective,
    Strategic Management Journal, in press;
    S. P. Gudergan, T. Devinney, N. Richter, &
    R. Ellis, 2012, Strategic implications for
    (non-equity) alliance performance, *Long
    Range Planning*, 45: 451–476.

19. F. J. Contractor & J. J. Reuer, 2014,
    Structuring and governing alliances: New
    directions for research, *Global Strategy
    Journal*, 4: 241–256; J. J. Reuer, E. Klijn, &
    C. S. Lioukas, 2014, Board involvement
    in international joint ventures, *Strategic
    Management Journal*, 35: 1626–1644;
    J. Schweitzer & S. P. Gudergan, 2011,
    Contractual complexity, governance
    and organisational form in alliances,
    *International Journal of Strategic Business
    Alliances*, 2: 26–40.

20. 2015, Will Tim Cook stop outsourcing
    the manufacture of Apple products to
    homophobic China? *Ricochet*, www.
    ricochet.com, March 31.

21. B. Shobert, 2015, Will Apple's business
    model work on pharmaceuticals? *Forbes
    Online*, www.forbes, March 11.

22. J. Righetti, 2014, 5 reasons why China will
    remain the world's factory, www.linkedin.
    com/pulse, August 21.

23. D. Aristie, M. Vecchi, & F. Venturini,
    2015, University and inter-firm R&D
    collaborations: Propensity and intensity
    of cooperation in Europe, *Journal of
    Technology Transfer*, in press; D. Mindruta,
    2013, Value creation in university-firm
    research collaborations: A matching
    approach, *Strategic Management Journal*,
    34: 644–665.

24. K. Lange, M. Geppert, A. Saka-Helmhout, & F. Becker-Ritterspach, 2015, Changing business models and employee representation in the airline industry: A comparison of British Airways and Deutsche Lufthansa, *British Journal of Management*, in press; X. Hu, R. Caldentey, & G. Vulcano, 2013, Revenue sharing in airline alliances, *Management Science*, 59: 1177–1195; U. Wassmer, 2010, Alliance portfolios: A review and research agenda, *Journal of Management*, 36: 141–171.

25. W. Yang & K. E. Meyer, 2015, Competitive dynamics in an emerging economy: Competitive pressures, resources, and the speed of action, *Journal of Business Research*, 68: 1176–1185; T. de Leeuw, B. Lokshin, & G. Duysters, 2014, Returns to alliance portfolio diversity: The relative effects of partner diversity on firm's innovative performance and productivity, *Journal of Business Research*, 67: 1839–1849.

26. J. Marshall, 2015, News publishers for programmatic advertising alliance, *CMO Today*, www.blogs.wsj.com/cmo, March 18.

27. Treflis team, 2015, Expedia seeks Latin American dominance: Strengthens partnership with Decolar.com, *Forbes Online*, www.forbes.com, March 12.

28. D. J. Teece, 2014, A dynamic capabilities-based entrepreneurial theory of the multinational enterprise, *Journal of International Business Studies*, 45: 8–37; J. R. Williams, 1998, *Renewable Advantage: Crafting Strategy Through Economic Time*, New York: Free Press.

29. L. Burkitt, 2015, Carnival in talks with China Merchants on cruise ports, ships, *Wall Street Journal Online*, www.wsj.com, January 26.

30. S. Artinger & T. C. Powell, 2015, Entrepreneurial failure: Statistical and psychological explanations, *Strategic Management Journal*, in press; H. Rahmandad & N. Repenning, 2015, Capability erosion dynamics, *Strategic Management Journal*, in press; A. Tafti, S. Mithas, & M. S. Krishnan, 2013, The effect of information technology-enabled flexibility on formation and market value of alliances, *Management Science*, 59: 207–225.

31. J. J. Reuer & R. Ragozzino, 2014, Signals and international alliance formation: The roles of affiliations and international activities, *Journal of International Business Studies*, 45: 321–337; H. K. Steensma, J. Q. Barden, C. Dhanaraj, M. Lyles, & L. Tihanyi, 2008, The evolution and internalization of international joint ventures in a transitioning economy, *Journal of International Business Studies*, 39: 491–507.

32. C. B. Bingham, K. H. Heimeriks, M. Schijven, & S. Gates, 2015, Concurrent learning: How firms develop multiple dynamic capabilities in parallel, *Strategic Management Journal*, in press; S. T. Cavusgil & G. Knight, 2014, The born global firm: An entrepreneurial and

capabilities perspective on early and rapid internationalization, *Journal of International Business Studies*, 46: 3–16; H. E. Posen & D. A. Levinthal, 2012, Chasing a moving target: Exploitation and exploration in dynamic environments, *Management Science*, 58: 587–601.

33. H. Milanov & S. A. Fernhaber, 2014, When do domestic alliances help ventures abroad? Direct and moderating effects from a learning perspective, *Journal of Business Venturing*, 29: 377–391; X. Yin, J. Wu, & W. Tsai, 2012, When unconnected others connect: Does degree of brokerage persist after the formation of a multipartner alliance? *Organization Science*, 23: 1682–1699.

34. 2015, Micron, Seagate announce strategic alliance, Micron Home Page, www.micron.com, February 12.

35. H. M. Khameseh & M. Nasiriyar, 2014, Avoiding alliance myopia: Forging learning outcomes for long-term success, *Journal of Business Strategy*, 35: 37–44; A.-P. de Man, N. Roijakkers, & H. de Graauw, 2010, Managing dynamics through robust alliance governance structures: The case of KLM and Northwest Airlines, *European Management Journal*, 28: 171–181.

36. Airline alliances, 2015, *Maps of the World*, www.mapsoftheworld.com, April 22.

37. Q. Gu & X. Lu, 2014, Unraveling the mechanisms of reputation and alliance formation: A study of venture capital syndication in China, *Strategic Management Journal*, 35: 739–750; G. Vasudeva, J. W. Spencer, & H. J. Teegen, 2013, Bringing the institutional context back in: A cross-national comparison of alliance partner selection and knowledge acquisition, *Organization Science*, 24: 319–338; W. Shi & J. E. Prescott, 2011, Sequence patterns of firms' acquisition and alliance behavior and their performance implications, *Journal of Management Studies*, 48: 1044–1070.

38. U. Stettner & D. Lavie, 2014, Ambidexterity under scrutiny: Exploration and exploitation via internal organization, alliances, and acquisitions, *Strategic Management Journal*, 35: 1903–1929; N. Lahiri & S. Narayanan, 2013, Vertical integration, innovation and alliance portfolio size: Implications for firm performance, *Strategic Management Journal*, 34: 1042–1064; S. M. Mudambi & S. Tallman, 2010, Make, buy or ally? Theoretical perspectives on knowledge process outsourcing through alliances, *Journal of Management Studies*, 47: 1434–1456.

39. R. Kapoor & P. J. McGrath, 2014, Unmasking the interplay between technology evolution and R&D collaboration: Evidence from the global semiconductor manufacturing industry, 1990–2010, *Research Policy*, 43: 555–569; J. Hagedoorn & N. Wang, 2012, Is there complementarity or substitutability between internal and

external R&D strategies? *Research Policy*, 41: 1072–1083; M. Meuleman, A. Lockett, S. Manigart, & M. Wright, 2010, Partner selection decisions in interfirm collaborations: The paradox of relational embeddedness, *Journal of Management Studies*, 47: 995–1019.

40. E. Revilla, M. Sáenz, & D. Knoppen, 2013, Towards an empirical typology of buyer–supplier relationships based on absorptive capacity, *International Journal of Production Research*, 51: 2935–2951; J. Zhang & C. Baden-Fuller, 2010, The influence of technological knowledge base and organizational structure on technology collaboration, *Journal of Management Studies*, 47: 679–704; J. Wiklund & D. A. Shepherd, 2009, The effectiveness of alliances and acquisitions: The role of resource combination activities, *Entrepreneurship Theory and Practice*, 33: 193–212.

41. 2015, GE intelligent lighting to transform retail experience through Qualcomm collaboration, GE Home Page, www.ge.com, May 4.

42. T. Stynes, 2015, Sorrento reaches collaboration deal valued at $110 million, *Wall Street Journal Online*, www.wsj.com, March 16.

43. J. Wieczner, 2014, Can drugmakers find profit in collaboration? *Fortune Online*, www.fortune.com, February 11.

44. H. Parker & Z. Brey, 2015, Collaboration costs and new product development performance, *Journal of Business Research*, 68: 1653–1656; C. Häeussler, H. Patzelt, & S. A. Zahra, 2012, Strategic alliances and product development in high technology new firms: The moderating effect of technological capabilities, *Journal of Business Venturing*, 27: 217–233; M. Makri, M. A. Hitt, & P. J. Lane, 2010, Complementary technologies, knowledge relatedness, and invention outcomes in high technology mergers and acquisitions, *Strategic Management Journal*, 31: 602–628.

45. D. Cameron, 2015, Boeing-Lockheed venture plans new rocket with reusable engine, *Wall Street Journal Online*, www.wsj.com, April 13.

46. A. Martin, 2007, Merger for SABMiller and Molson Coors, *New York Times Online*, www.nytimes.com, October 10.

47. T. Mickle, 2015, Molson Coors, U.S. joint venture MillerCoors facing stiff challenges, *Wall Street Journal Online*, www.wsj.com, May 7.

48. H. Yang & H. K. Steensma, 2014, When do firms rely on their knowledge spillover recipients for guidance in exploring unfamiliar knowledge? *Research Policy*, 43: 1496–1507; N. Mouri, M. B. Sarkar, & M. Frye, 2012, Alliance portfolios and shareholder value in post-IPO firms: The moderating roles of portfolio structure and firm-level uncertainty, *Journal of Business Venturing*, 27: 355–371; J. J. Reuer & T. W. Tong, 2005, Real options in international joint ventures, *Journal of Management*, 31: 403–423.

49. 2014, Tesla Motors in talks with BMW, possible alliance in batteries, carbon fiber body parts, Tesla Home Page, www.myteslamotors.com, November 23.

50. H.-T. Normann, J. Rosch, & L. M. Schultz, 2015, Do buyer groups facilitate collusion? *Journal of Economic Behavior & Organization*, 109: 72–84; M. A. Fonseca & H. Normann, 2012, Explicit vs. tacit collusion—The impact of communication in oligopoly experiments, *European Economic Review*, 56: 1759–1772; M. Escrihuela-Villar & J. Guillén, 2011, On collusion and industry size, *Annals of Economics and Finance*, 12: 31–40.

51. J. Boone & K. Zigic, 2015, Trade policy in markets with collusion: The case of North-South R&D spillovers, *Research in Economics*, in press; M. Van Essen & W. B. Hankins, 2013, Tacit collusion in price-setting oligopoly: A puzzle redux, *Southern Economic Journal*, 79: 703–726; Y. Lu & J. Wright, 2010, Tacit collusion with price-matching punishments, *International Journal of Industrial Organization*, 28: 298–306.

52. J. Handy, 2014, Can a DRAM oligopoly really work? *Forbes Online*, www.forbes.com, May 30.

53. F. J. Mas-Ruiz, F. Ruiz-Moreno, & A. L. de Guevara Martinez, 2014, Asymmetric rivalry within and between strategic groups, *Strategic Management Journal*, 35: 419–439; R. W. Cooper & T. W. Ross, 2009, Sustaining cooperation with joint ventures, *Journal of Law, Economics, and Organization*, 25: 31–54.

54. M. T. Gustafson, I. T. Ivanov, & J. Ritter, 2015, Financial condition and product market cooperation, *Journal of Corporate Finance*, 31: 1–16; L. Zou, C. Yu, & M. Dresner, 2012, Multimarket contact, alliance membership, and prices in international airline markets, *Transportation Research Part E: Logistics and Transportation Review*, 48: 555–565; J. T. Prince & D. H. Simon, 2009, Multi-market contact and service quality: Evidence from on-time performance in the U.S. airline industry, *Academy of Management Journal*, 52: 336–354.

55. B. Chidmi, 2012, Vertical relationships in the ready-to-eat breakfast cereal industry in Boston, *Agribusiness*, 28: 241–259; N. Panteva, 2011, IBISWorld Industry Report 31123: Cereal production in the U.S., January.

56. E. Shroeder, 2014, Global breakfast cereal market to reach $43.2 billion by 2019, *Food Business News Online*, www.foodbusinessnews.com, February 14.

57. P. F. Skilton & E. Bernardes, 2015, Competition network structure and product market entry, *Strategic Management Journal*, in press; R. M. Bakker & J. Knoben, 2014, Built to last or meant to end: Intertemporal choice in strategic alliance portfolios, *Organization Science*, 26: 256–276; Z. Guedri & J. McGuire, 2011, Multimarket competition, mobility barriers, and firm performance, *Journal of Management Studies*, 48: 857–890.

58. I. K. Wang, H.-S. Yang, & D. J. Miller, 2015, Collaboration in the shadow of the technology frontier: Evidence from the flat panel display industry, *Managerial and Decision Economics*, in press; P. Massey & M. McDowell, 2010, Joint dominance and tacit collusion: Some implications for competition and regulatory policy, *European Competition Journal*, 6: 427–444.

59. A.H. Bowers, H. R. Greve, H. Mitsuhashi, & J. A. C. Baum, 2014, Competitive parity, status disparity, and mutual forbearance: Securities analysts' competition for investor attention, *Academy of Management Journal*, 57: 38–62.

60. Y. Liu & T. Ravichandran, 2015, Alliance experience, IT-enabled knowledge integration, and ex-ante value gains, *Organization Science*, 26: 511–530; P. Dussauge, B. Garrette, & W. Mitchell, 2004, Asymmetric performances: The market share impact of scale and link alliances in the global auto industry, *Strategic Management Journal*, 25: 701–711.

61. M. Rogan & H. R. Greve, 2014, Resource dependence dynamics: Partner reactions to mergers, *Organization Science*, 26: 239–255; L. Capron & W. Mitchell, 2012, *Build, Borrow or Buy: Solving the Growth Dilemma*, Cambridge: Harvard Business Review Press; C. Häussler, 2011, The determinants of commercialization strategy: Idiosyncrasies in British and German biotechnology, *Entrepreneurship Theory and Practice*, 35: 653–681.

62. F. Castellaneta & M. Zollo, 2014, The dimensions of experiential learning in the management of activity load, *Organization Science*, 26: 140–157; Y. Lew & R. R. Sinkovics, 2013, Crossing borders and industry sectors: Behavioral governance in strategic alliances and product innovation for competitive advantage, *Long Range Planning*, 46: 13–38; P. Ritala & H.-K. Ellonen, 2010, Competitive advantage in interfirm cooperation: Old and new explanations, *Competitiveness Review*, 20: 367–383.

63. H. M. Khamesh & M. Nasiriyar, 2014, Avoiding alliance myopia: Forging learning outcomes for long-term success, *Journal of Business Strategy*, 35(4): 37–44; H. Liu, X. Jiang, J. Zhang, & X. Zhao, 2013, Strategic flexibility and international venturing by emerging market firms: The moderating effects of institutional and relational factors, *Journal of International Marketing*, 21: 79–98; J. Anand, R. Oriani, & R. S. Vassolo, 2010, Alliance activity as a dynamic capability in the face of a discontinuous technological change, *Organization Science*, 21: 1213–1232.

64. B. T. McCann, J. J. Reuer, & N. Lahiri, 2015, Agglomeration and the choice between acquisitions and alliances: An information economics perspective, *Strategic Management Journal*, in press; S. Chang & M. Tsai, 2013, The effect of prior alliance experience on acquisition performance, *Applied Economics*, 45: 765–773.

65. 2013, TATA Sikorsky JV delivers first fully indigenous S-92 helicopter cabin, United Technologies Home Page, www.utc.com, October 24.

66. 2014, BMW expands joint venture with Chinese carmaker Brilliance, *DW*, www.dw.de, December 14.

67. I. Ater & O. Rigbi, 2015, Price control and advertising in franchising chains, *Strategic Management Journal*, in press; V. K. Garg, R. L. Priem, & A. A. Rasheed, 2013, A theoretical explanation of the cost advantages of multi-unit franchising, *Journal of Marketing Channels*, 20: 52–72; J. G. Combs, D. J. Ketchen, Jr., C. L. Shook, & J. C. Short, 2011, Antecedents and consequences of franchising: Past accomplishments and future challenges, *Journal of Management*, 37: 99–126.

68. B. R. Barringer & R. D. Ireland, 2016, *Entrepreneurship: Successfully Launching New Ventures*, 5th ed., Prentice-Hall, 510.

69. C.-W. Wu, 2015, Antecedents of franchise strategy and performance, *Journal of Business Research*, 68: 1581–1588; W. E. Gillis, J. G. Combs, & D. J. Ketchen, Jr., 2014, Using resource-based theory to help explain plural form franchising, *Entrepreneurship Theory and Practice*, 38: 449–472; D. Grewal, G. R. Iyer, R. G. Javalgi, & L. Radulovich, 2011, Franchise partnership and international expansion: A conceptual framework and research propositions, *Entrepreneurship Theory and Practice*, 35: 533–557.

70. J.-S. Chiou & C. Droge, 2015, The effects of standardization and trust on franchisee's performance and satisfaction: A study on franchise systems in the growth stage, *Journal of Small Business Management*, 53: 129–144; N. Mumdziev & J. Windsperger, 2013, An extended transaction cost model of decision rights allocation in franchising: The moderating role of trust, *Managerial and Decision Economics*, 34: 170–182; J. McDonnell, A. Beatson & C.-H. Huang, 2011, Investigating relationships between relationship quality, customer loyalty and cooperation: An empirical study of convenience stores' franchise chain systems, *Asia Pacific Journal of Marketing and Logistics*, 23: 367–385.

71. A. El Akremi, R. Perrigot, & I. Piot-Lepetit, 2015, Examining the drivers for franchised chains performance through the lens of the dynamic capabilities approach, *Journal of Small Business Management*, 53: 145–165; B. Merrilees & L. Frazer, 2013, Internal branding: Franchisor leadership as a critical determinant, *Journal of Business Research*, 66: 158–164; T. M. Nisar, 2011, Intellectual property securitization and growth capital in retail franchising, *Journal of Retailing*, 87: 393–405.

72. I. Alon, M. Boulanger, E. Misati, & M. Madanoglu, 2015, Are the parents to blame? Predicting franchisee failure, *Competitiveness Review*, 25: 205–217; D. Grace, S. Weaven, L. Frazer, & J. Giddings, 2013,

Examining the role of franchisee normative expectations in relationship evaluation, *Journal of Retailing*, 89: 219–230; W. R. Meek, B. Davis-Sramek, M. S. Baucus, & R. N. Germain, 2011, Commitment in franchising: The role of collaborative communication and a franchisee's propensity to leave, *Entrepreneurship Theory and Practice*, 35: 559–581.

73. M. W. Nyadzayo, M. J. Matanda, & M. T. Ewing, 2015, The impact of franchisor support, brand commitment, brand citizenship behavior, and franchisee experience on franchisee-perceived brand image, *Journal of Business Research*, in press; N. Gorovaia & J. Windsperger, 2013, Real options, intangible resources and performance of franchise networks, *Managerial and Decision Economics*, 34: 183–194; T. W. K. Leslie & L. S. McNeill, 2010, Towards a conceptual model for franchise perceptual equity, *Journal of Brand Management*, 18: 21–33.

74. H. Parker & Z. Brey, 2015, Collaboration costs and new product development performance, *Journal of Business Research*, 68: 1653–1656; S. Demirkan & I. Demirkan, 2014, Implications of strategic alliances for earnings quality and capital market investors, *Journal of Business Research*, 67: 1806–1816; M. Onal Vural, L. Dahlander, & G. George, 2013, Collaborative benefits and coordination costs: Learning and capability development in science, *Strategic Entrepreneurship Journal*, 7: 122–137.

75. C. E. Eesley, D. H. Hsu, & E. B. Roberts, 2014, The contingent effects of top management teams on venture performance: Aligning founding team composition with innovation strategy and commercialization environment, *Strategic Management Journal*, 35: 1798–1817; G. Ahuja, C. M. Lampert, & E. Novelli, 2013, The second face of appropriability: Generative appropriability and its determinants, *Academy of Management Review*, 38: 248–269; C. Choi & P. Beamish, 2013, Resource complementarity and international joint venture performance in Korea, *Asia Pacific Journal of Management*, 30: 561–576.

76. Z. Khan, O. Shenkar, & Y. K. Lew, 2015, Knowledge transfer from international joint ventures to local suppliers in a developing economy, *Journal of International Business Studies*, in press; R. Belderbos, T. W. Tong, & S. Wu, 2014, Multinationality and downside risk: The roles of option portfolio and organization, *Strategic Management Journal*, 35: 88–106; S. Veilleux, N. Haskell, & F. Pons, 2012, Going global: How smaller enterprises benefit from strategic alliances, *Journal of Business Strategy*, 33(5): 22–31;

77. A. Dechezlepretre, E. Neumayer, & R. Perekins, 2015, Environmental regulation and the cross-border diffusion of new technology: Evidence from automobile patents, *Research Policy*, 44: 244–257;

I. Arikan & O. Shenkar, 2013, National animosity and cross-border alliances, *Academy of Management Journal*, 56: 1516–1544.

78. Y. Kubota & J. Chow, 2015, French clout at Renault roils Nissan deal, *Wall Street Journal Online*, www.wsj.com, April 20.

79. Q. Gu & X. Lu, 2014, Unraveling the mechanisms of reputation and alliance formation: A study of venture capital syndication in China, *Strategic Management Journal*, 35: 739–750; L. Li, G. Qian, & Z. Qian, 2013, Do partners in international strategic alliances share resources, costs, and risks? *Journal of Business Research*, 66: 489–498; A. Zaheer & E. Hernandez, 2011, The geographic scope of the MNC and its alliance portfolio: Resolving the paradox of distance, *Global Strategy Journal*, 1: 109–126.

80. Z. Khan, Y. K. Lew, & R. R. Sinkovics, 2015, International joint ventures as boundary spanners: Technological knowledge transfer in an emerging economy, *Global Strategy Journal*, 5: 48–68; M. Meuleman & M. Wright, 2011, Cross-border private equity syndication: Institutional context and learning, *Journal of Business Venturing*, 26: 35–48.

81. J. J. Hotho, M. A. Lyles, & M. Easterby-Smith, 2015, The mutual impact of global strategy and organizational learning: Current themes and future directions, *Global Strategy Journal*, 5: 85–112; B. B. Nielsen & S. Gudergan, 2012, Exploration and exploitation fit and performance in international strategic alliances, *International Business Review*, 21: 558–574; D. Kronborg & S. Thomsen, 2009, Foreign ownership and long-term survival, *Strategic Management Journal*, 30: 207–219.

82. I.-S. Nam & R. Wall, 2015, Airbus, Korea Aerospace sign helicopter deal, *Wall Street Journal Online*, www.wsj.com, March 16.

83. S. Xu, A. P. Fenik, & M. B. Shaner, 2014, Multilateral alliances and innovation output: The importance of equity and technological scope, *Journal of Business Research*, 67: 2403–2410; D. Lavie, C. Lechner, & H. Singh, 2007, The performance implications of timing of entry and involvement in multipartner alliances, *Academy of Management Journal*, 50: 578–604.

84. 2015, Cisco Partner Summit, Cisco homepage, www.cisco.com, May 7.

85. 2015, Strategic alliances—IBM, Cisco Home Page, www.cisco.com, May 7.

86. C. Geldes, C. Felzensztein, E. Turkina, & A. Durand, 2015, How does proximity affect interfirm marketing cooperation? A study of an agribusiness cluster, *Journal of Business Research*, 68: 263–272; W. Fu, J. Revilla Diez, & D. Schiller, 2013, Interactive learning, informal networks and innovation: Evidence from electronics firm survey in the Pearl River Delta, China, *Research Policy*, 42: 635–646; A. T. Ankan & M. A. Schilling, 2011,

Structure and governance in industrial districts: Implications for competitive advantage, *Journal of Management Studies*, 48: 772–803.

87. A. Phene & S. Tallman, 2014, Knowledge spillovers and alliance formation, *Journal of Management Studies*, 51: 1058–1090; C. Casanueva, I. Castro, & J. L. Galán, 2013, Informational networks and innovation in mature industrial clusters, *Journal of Business Research*, 66: 603–613; J. Wincent, S. Anokhin, D. Örtqvist, & E. Autio, 2010, Quality meets structure: Generalized reciprocity and firm-level advantage in strategic networks, *Journal of Management Studies*, 47: 597–624; D. Lavie, 2007, Alliance portfolios and firm performance: A study of value creation and appropriation in the U.S. software industry, *Strategic Management Journal*, 28: 1187–1212.

88. Y. Zheng & H. Yang, 2015, Does familiarity foster innovation? The impact of alliance partner repeatedness on breakthrough innovations, *Journal of Management Studies*, 52: 213–230; L. Dobusch & E. Schübler, 2013, Theorizing path dependence: A review of positive feedback mechanisms in technology markets, regional clusters, and organizations, *Industrial & Corporate Change*, 22: 617–647; A. M. Joshi & A. Nerkar, 2011, When do strategic alliances inhibit innovation by firms? Evidence from patent pools in the global optical disc industry, *Strategic Management Journal*, 32: 1139–1160.

89. S. Perkins, R. Morck, & B. Yeung, 2014, Innocents abroad: The hazards of international joint ventures with pyramidal group firms, *Global Strategy Journal*, 4: 310–330; J. P. MacDuffie, 2011, Inter-organizational trust and the dynamics of distrust, *Journal of International Business Studies*, 42: 35–47; H. Kim, R. E. Hoskisson, & W. P. Wan, 2004, Power, dependence, diversification strategy and performance in keiretsu member firms, *Strategic Management Journal*, 25: 613–636.

90. B. Kang & K. Motohashi, 2015, Essential intellectual property rights and inventors' involvement in standardization, *Research Policy*, 44: 483–492; V. Van de Vrande, 2013, Balancing your technology-sourcing portfolio: How sourcing mode diversity enhances innovative performance, *Strategic Management Journal*, 34: 610–621; A. V. Shipilov, 2009, Firm scope experience, historic multimarket contact with partners, centrality, and the relationship between structural holes and performance, *Organization Science*, 20: 85–106.

91. K.-H. Huarng & A. Mas-Tur, 2015, Sprit of strategy (S.O.S.): The new S.O.S. for competitive business, *Journal of Business Research*, 68: 1383–1387; S. Gupta & M. Polonsky, 2014, Inter-firm learning and knowledge-sharing in multinational networks: An outsourced organization's perspective, *Journal of Business Research*,

67: 615–622; A. S. Cui & G. O'Connor, 2012, Alliance portfolio resource diversity and firm innovation, *Journal of Marketing*, 76: 24–43.

92. F. Collet & D. Philippe, 2014, From hot cakes to cold feet: A contingent perspective on the relationship between market uncertainty and status homophily in the formation of alliances, *Journal of Management Studies*, 51: 406–432; G. Cuevas-Rodriguez, C. Cabello-Medina, & A. Carmona-Lavado, 2014, Internal and external social capital for radical product innovation: Do they always work well together? *British Journal of Management*, 25: 266–284; G. Soda, 2011, The management of firms' alliance network positioning: Implications for innovation, *European Management Journal*, 29: 377–388.

93. E. Lam & C. Pellegrini, 2014, Apple-IBM deal snaps Blackberry rally on turnaround doubt, *BloombergBusiness*, www.bloomberg.com, July 17.

94. I. Castro & J. L. Roldan, 2015, Alliance portfolio management: Dimensions and performance, *European Management Review*, in press; C. Martin-Rios, 2014, Why do firms seek to share human resource management knowledge? The importance of inter-firm networks, *Journal of Business Research*, 67: 190–199.

95. A. Gambardella, C. Panico, & G. Valentini, 2015, Strategic incentives to human capital, *Strategic Management Journal*, 36: 37–52; A. G. Karamanos, 2012, Leveraging micro- and macro-structures of embeddedness in alliance networks for exploratory innovation in biotechnology, *R&D Management*, 42: 71–89; D. Somaya, Y. Kim, & N. S. Vonortas, 2011, Exclusivity in licensing alliances: Using hostages to support technology commercialization, *Strategic Management Journal*, 32: 159–186.

96. U. Ozmel & I. Guler, 2015, Small fish, big fish: The performance effects of the relative standing in partners' affiliate portfolios, *Strategic Management Journal*, in press; M. J. Nieto & L. Santamaría, 2010, Technological collaboration: Bridging the innovation gap between small and large firms, *Journal of Small Business Management*, 48: 44–69; P. Ozcan & K. M. Eisenhardt, 2009, Origin of alliance portfolios: Entrepreneurs, network strategies, and firm performance, *Academy of Management Journal*, 52: 246–279.

97. L.-Y. Wu, P.-Y. Chen, & K.-Y. Chen, 2015, Why does loyalty-cooperation behavior vary over buyer-seller relationship? *Journal of Business Research*, in press; H. R. Greve, H. Mitsuhashi, & J. A. C. Baum, 2013, Greener pastures: Outside options and strategic alliance withdrawal, *Organization Science*, 24: 79–98; H. R. Greve, J. A. C. Baum, H. Mitsuhashi, & T. J. Rowley, 2010, Built to last but falling apart: Cohesion, friction, and withdrawal from interfirm alliances,

Academy of Management Journal, 53: 302–322.

98. S. Dasi-Rodriguez & M. Pardo-del-Val, 2015, Seeking partners in international alliances: The influence of cultural factors, *Journal of Business Research*, 68: 1522–1526; G. Vasudeva & J. Anand, 2011, Unpacking absorptive capacity: A study of knowledge utilization from alliance portfolios, *Academy of Management Journal*, 54: 611–623; J.-Y. Kim & A. S. Miner, 2007, Vicarious learning from the failures and near-failures of others: Evidence from the U.S. commercial banking industry, *Academy of Management Journal*, 50: 687–714.

99. J. Marson, 2013, TNK-BP investors appeal to Rosneft's chief over shares, *Wall Street Journal Online*, www.wsj.com, April 17.

100. B. Kang & R. P. Jindal, 2015, Opportunism in buyer-seller relationships: Some unexplored antecedents, *Journal of Business Research*, 68: 735–742; L.-Y. Wu, P.-Y. Chen, & K.-Y. Chen, 2015, Why does loyalty-cooperation behavior vary over buyer-seller relationship? *Journal of Business Research*, in press; K. Zhou & D. Xu, 2012, How foreign firms curtail local supplier opportunism in China: Detailed contracts, centralized control, and relational governance, *Journal of International Business Studies*, 43: 677–692.

101. A. Spithoven & P. Teirlinck, 2015, Internal capabilities, network resources and appropriate mechanisms as determinants of R&D outsourcing, *Research Policy*, 44: 711–725; A. V. Werder, 2011, Corporate governance and stakeholder opportunism, *Organization Science*, 22: 1345–1358; T. K. Das & R. Kumar, 2011, Regulatory focus and opportunism in the alliance development process, *Journal of Management*, 37: 682–708.

102. I. Stern, J. M. Dukerich, & E. Zajac, 2014, Unmixed signals: How reputation and status affect alliance formation, *Strategic Management Journal*, 35: 512–531; A. S. Cui, 2013, Portfolio dynamics and alliance termination: The contingent role of resource dissimilarity, *Journal of Marketing*, 77: 15–32; M. B. Sarkar, P. S. Aulakh, & A. Madhok, 2009, Process capabilities and value generation in alliance portfolios, *Organization Science*, 20: 583–600.

103. S. McLain, 2015, New outsourcing frontier in India: Monitoring drug safety, *Wall Street Journal Online*, www.wsj.com, February 1.

104. M. Kafouros, C. Wang, P. Piiperopoulos, & M. Zhang, 2015, Academic collaborations and firm innovation performance in China: The role of region-specific institutions, *Research Policy*, 44: 803–817; S. Kraus, T. C. Ambos, F. Eggers, & B. Cesinger, 2015, Distance and perceptions of risk in internationalization decisions, *Journal of Business Research*, 68: 1501–1505; M. Nippa & S. Beechler, 2013, What do we know about the success and failure of international joint ventures? In search of relevance and

holism, in T. M. Devinney, T. Pedersen, & L. Tihanyi (eds.), *Philosophy of Science and Meta-knowledge in International Business and Management*, 26: 363–396

105. M. Menz & C. Scheef, 2014, Chief strategy officers: Contingency analysis of their presence in top management teams, *Strategic Management Journal*, 35: 461–471; I. Neyens & D. Faems, 2013, Exploring the impact of alliance portfolio management design on alliance portfolio performance, *Managerial & Decision Economics*, 34: 347–361; D. G. Sirmon, M. A. Hitt, R. D. Ireland, & B. A. Gilbert, 2011, Resource orchestration to create competitive advantage: Breadth, depth, and life cycle effects, *Journal of Management*, 37: 1390–1412; M. H. Hansen, R. E. Hoskisson, & J. B. Barney, 2008, Competitive advantage in alliance governance: Resolving the opportunism minimization-gain maximization paradox, *Managerial and Decision Economics*, 29: 191–208.

106. G. Speckbacher, K. Neumann, & W. H. Hoffmann, 2015, Resource relatedness and the mode of entry into new businesses: Internal resource accumulation vs. access by collaborative arrangement, *Strategic Management Journal*, in press; C. C. Chung & P. W. Beamish, 2010, The trap of continual ownership change in international equity joint ventures, *Organization Science*, 21: 995–1015.

107. D. J. Harmon, P. H. Kim, & K. J. Mayer, 2015, Breaking the letter vs. spirit of the law: How the interpretation of contract violations affects trust and the management of relationships, *Strategic Management Journal*, 36: 497–517; M. H. Hansen, R. E. Hoskisson, & J. B. Barney, 2008, Competitive advantage in alliance governance: Resolving the opportunism minimization-gain maximization paradox, *Managerial and Decision Economics*, 29: 191–208.

108. J. Marshall, 2015, News publishers for programmatic advertising alliance, *Wall Street Journal Online*, ww.wsj.com, March 18.

109. T. Felin & T. R. Zenger, 2014, Closed or open innovation? Problem solving and the governance choice, *Research Policy*, 43: 914–925; N. N. Arranz & J. C. F. de Arroyabe, 2012, Effect of formal contracts, relational norms and trust on performance of joint research and development projects, *British Journal of Management*, 23: 575–588.

110. B. S. Vanneste, P. Puranam, & T. Kretschmer, 2014, Trust over time in exchange relationships: Meta-analysis and theory, *Strategic Management Journal*, 35: 1891–1902; G. Ertug, I. Cuypers, N. Noorderhaven, & B. Bensaou, 2013, Trust between interna-tional joint venture partners: Effects of home countries, *Journal of International Business Studies*, 44: 263–282; J. J. Li, L. Poppo, & K. Z. Zhou, 2010, Relational mechanisms, formal contracts, and local knowledge acquisition by international subsidiaries, *Strategic Management Journal*, 31: 349–370.

111. H. Yang, Y. Zheng, & X. Zhao, 2014, Exploration or exploitation? Small firms' alliance strategies with large firms, *Strategic Management Journal*, 35: 146–157; S. E. Fawcett, S. L. Jones, & A. M. Fawcett, 2012, Supply chain trust: The catalyst for collaborative innovation, *Business Horizons*, 55: 163–178; H. C. Dekker & A. Van den Abbeele, 2010, Organizational learning and interfirm control: The effects of partner search and prior exchange experience, *Organization Science*, 21: 1233–1250.

112. A. Shipilov, R. Gulati, M. Kilduff, S. Li, & W. Tsai, 2014, Relational pluralism within and between organizations, *Academy of Management Journal*, 57: 449–459; R. Kumar & A. Nathwani, 2012, Business alliances: Why managerial thinking and biases determine success, *Journal of Business Strategy*, 33(5): 44–50; C. C. Phelps, 2010, A longitudinal study of the influence of alliance network structure and composition on firm exploratory innovation, *Academy of Management Journal*, 53: 890–913.

10

Corporate Governance

THE CORPORATE RAIDERS OF THE 1980S HAVE BECOME THE ACTIVIST SHAREHOLDERS OF TODAY

In the 1980s, large activist shareholders would buy significant stakes in companies and often seek to increase the debt load, sell off business units reducing diversification, and downsize by laying off many workers. If the firms did not respond as the activist shareholders required, they would make the company pay a premium on the shares they bought, often called "greenmail." Today activist investors are doing many of the same things, but it seems that they are being supported by institutional investors who often follow the activist investors' lead or support them in their activities. Interestingly, the number of activist funds have grown from just 76 in 2010 to 203 in 2014. Their activities have increased as well with 136 firms targeted in 2010 rising to 344 in 2014. One Citigroup analyst, Tobias Levkovich, suggested that "we suspect there is a limited universe for the activists, and eventually the arbitrage opportunity will be exhausted."

One of the strategies these activist investors pursue is to pressure firms to allow representatives to stand for election to the targeted company's board. Another strategy gaining momentum is the access to the proxy process to include shareholder resolutions for shareholder votes. This access has been allowed by the courts and the U.S. Securities and Exchange Commission's (SEC) efforts to require more proxy voting action opportunities to shareholders. However, the U.S. Chamber of Commerce and Society of Corporate Secretaries & Governance Professionals are worried that "the proliferation of the proxy access will lead to the nomination of 'special interest' directors harming long-term shareholders." Nonetheless, regulators'

Heidi Gutman/CNBC/NBCU Photo Bank/Getty Images

decisions have seemed to open the flood gates to firms allowing more proxy access. As such, firm shareholders will be able to vote on strategic issues presented by activist shareholders as well as lead activist shareholders by directly nominating board members who represent their interests.

Some of these firms are quite large and visible, such as DuPont, Vivendi, and QUALCOMM. For example, DuPont's CEO Ellen Kullman has fought a proxy battle in media outlets. Trian Fund Management L.P. representatives, headed by CEO Nelson Peltz, have criss-crossed the country as has CEO Kullman's team, seeking to persuade shareholders about their opposing positions regarding access to board seats. Trian wants four board seats, most importantly for Mr. Peltz, and is "seeking to oust the heads of several key board committees." Kullman has responded, "Mr. Peltz wants to establish a 'shadow management' team dedicated to pushing a short-term agenda." She argues that DuPont has cut $1 billion in cost and pursued other efficiencies and that Trian wants to nominate directors that lack the expertise and patience needed to steer an agricultural and chemical company that often requires decades to create innovation and launch products. Kullman argues, "can you cut costs and create a bump short-term? Yes, but where are you going to be in 2 years, in 5 years? Do you exist in 10?" Often these activist investors seek stock buybacks and increases in dividends as well as selling off "non-performing businesses." Over time, in part due to such activism, objections to corporate governance arrangements have become more strident and monitoring of top executives more intense.

However, there are risks to activist approaches, as evidenced in the Herbalife conflict. William Ackman's Pershing Square Capital Management L.P. has been alleging that nutritional-products company Herbalife is "an illegal pyramid scheme." Although typically activist investors push companies to improve short-term value through leadership changes, stock buybacks, and break-ups, others want the opposite to happen; they "short" the stock and make arguments that create turmoil and perceived weakness that result in the lowering of the company share price increasing the value of a short position. Such negative commentary has brought Herbalife under investigation by the SEC and the Federal Trade Commission (FTC). Of course, Herbalife's stock price has come down. Most short-sellers don't broadcast their position because it might cause a government backlash and investigation focused on them. Nonetheless, some such as Mr. Ackman's attacks on Herbalife, have brought this controversy into focus.

Although all of this activism has caused some chaos in the board room, it has made for overall better, albeit more intense, governance and has given more voice for shareholders into strategy issues which are pertinent to the topic of our book. As you go through this chapter, these issues will become clearer as the various governance devices are defined and their purpose explained to foster better understanding.

Sources: A. Ackerman & J. S. Lublin, 2015, Activists win ground in major boardrooms, *Wall Street Journal*, March 17, 215 B1, B2; R. Bender, 2015, Shareholder presses Vivendi further, *Wall Street Journal*, March 15, B3; D. Benoit, 2015, Herbalife fracas puts activist risk right in the spotlight, *Wall Street Journal*, March 17, C3; D. Benoit & D. Clark, 2015, Activists puts pressure on Qualcomm, *Wall Street Journal*, April 13, B1, B2; J. Bunge & C. Dulaney, 2015, DuPont posts declines ahead of vote, *Wall Street Journal*, April 22, b4; S. Gandel, 2015, In DuPont fight, Nelson Peltz pushes for open proxy, *Fortune*, www.fortune.com, March 13; A. Gara, 2015, DuPont spinoff fans flames in Trian Management's scorched earth fight. *Forbes*, www.forbes.com, March 30; L. Hoffman & D. Benoit, 2015, Activist investors ramp up, and boardroom rifts ensue, *Wall Street Journal*, April 17, C1, C2; B. Levisohn, 2015, Activism's Dark Side, *Barron's*, March 2, 11; A. VanderMey, 2015, Actively mediocre: Activist investors scold CEOs over stock prices, but their returns are just so-so, *Fortune*, May 1, 12.

As the Opening Case suggests, corporate governance is complex and designed to provide oversight of how firms operate. At a broader level, it reflects the type of infrastructure provided by individual nations as the framework within which companies compete. Given that we are concerned with the strategic management process firms use, our focus in this chapter is on corporate governance in companies (although we do also address governance at the level of nations). The complexity and the potential problems with corporate governance, such as having true checks and balances in the system of governance, are shown by the example of activist shareholders in the Opening Case.

Comprehensive in scope and complex in nature, corporate governance is a responsibility that challenges firms and their leaders. Evidence suggests that corporate governance is critical to firms' success and dealing appropriately with this challenge is important. Because of this, governance is an increasingly important part of the strategic management process.[1] For example, if the board makes the wrong decisions in selecting, governing, and compensating the firm's CEO as its strategic leader, the shareholders and the firm suffer. When CEOs are motivated to act in the best interests of the firm—in particular, the shareholders—the company's value is more likely to increase. Additionally, effective leadership succession plans and appropriate monitoring and direction-setting efforts by the board of directors contribute positively to a firm's performance.

Corporate governance is the set of mechanisms used to manage the relationships among stakeholders and to determine and control the strategic direction and performance of organizations.[2] At its core, corporate governance is concerned with identifying ways to ensure that decisions (especially strategic decisions) are made effectively and that they facilitate a firm's efforts to achieve strategic competitiveness.[3] Governance can also be thought of as a means to establish and maintain harmony between parties (the firm's owners and its top-level managers) whose interests may conflict.

In modern corporations—especially those in nations with "Westernized" infrastructures and business practices such as in the United States and the United Kingdom—ensuring that top-level managers' interests are aligned with other stakeholders' interests,

Corporate governance is the set of mechanisms used to manage the relationships among stakeholders and to determine and control the strategic direction and performance of organizations.

particularly those of shareholders, is a primary objective of corporate governance. Thus, corporate governance involves oversight in areas where owners, managers, and members of boards of directors may have conflicts of interest. Processes used to elect members of the firm's board of directors, the general management of CEO pay and more focused supervision of director pay, and the corporation's overall strategic direction are examples of areas in which oversight is sought.[4] Because corporate governance is an ongoing process concerned with how a firm is to be managed, its nature evolves in light of the types of never-ending changes in a firm's external environment that we discussed in Chapter 2.

The recent global emphasis on corporate governance stems mainly from the apparent failure of corporate governance mechanisms to adequately monitor and control top-level managers' decisions (as exemplified by the growing focus on governance issues among activist investors in the Opening Case). In turn, undesired or unacceptable consequences resulting from using corporate governance mechanisms cause changes such as electing new members to the board of directors with the hope of providing more effective governance. A second and more positive reason for this interest comes from evidence that a well-functioning corporate governance system can create a competitive advantage for an individual firm.[5]

As noted earlier, corporate governance is of concern to nations as well as to individual firms.[6] Although corporate governance reflects company standards, it also collectively reflects the societal standards of nations.[7] For example, the independence of board members and practices a board should follow to exercise effective oversight of a firm's internal control efforts are changes to governance standards that have been fostered in Singapore.[8] Efforts such as these are important because research shows that firms seek to invest in nations with national governance standards that are acceptable to them.[9] This is particularly the case when firms consider the possibility of expanding geographically into emerging markets.

In the chapter's first section, we describe the relationship on which the modern corporation is built—namely, the relationship between owners and managers. We use the majority of the chapter to explain various mechanisms owners use to govern managers and to ensure that they comply with their responsibility to satisfy stakeholders' needs, especially those of shareholders.

Three internal governance mechanisms and a single external one are used in the modern corporation. The three internal governance mechanisms described in this chapter are

1. ownership concentration, represented by types of shareholders and their different incentives to monitor managers;
2. the board of directors; and
3. executive compensation.

We then consider the market for corporate control, an external corporate governance mechanism. Essentially, this market is a set of potential owners seeking to acquire undervalued firms and earn above-average returns on their investments by replacing ineffective top-level management teams.[10] The chapter's focus then shifts to the issue of international corporate governance. We briefly describe governance approaches used in several countries outside of the United States and United Kingdom. In part, this discussion suggests that the structures used to govern global companies competing in both developed and emerging economies are becoming more, rather than less, similar. Closing our analysis of corporate governance is a consideration of the need for these control mechanisms to encourage and support ethical and socially responsible behavior in organizations.

10-1 Separation of Ownership and Managerial Control

Historically, U.S. firms were managed by founder-owners and their descendants. In these cases, corporate ownership and control resided with the same group of people. As firms grew larger, "the managerial revolution led to a separation of ownership and control in most large corporations, where control of the firm shifted from entrepreneurs to professional managers while ownership became dispersed among thousands of unorganized stockholders who were removed from the day-to-day management of the firm."[11] These changes created the modern public corporation, which is based on the efficient separation of ownership and managerial control. Supporting the separation is a basic legal premise suggesting that the primary objective of a firm's activities is to increase the corporation's profit and, thereby, the owners' (shareholders') financial gains.[12]

The separation of ownership and managerial control allows shareholders to purchase stock, which entitles them to income (residual returns) from the firm's operations after paying expenses. This right, however, requires that shareholders take a risk that the firm's expenses may exceed its revenues. To manage this investment risk, shareholders maintain a diversified portfolio by investing in several companies to reduce their overall risk.[13] The poor performance or failure of any one firm in which they invest has less overall effect on the value of the entire portfolio of investments. Thus, shareholders specialize in managing their investment risk.

Commonly, those managing small firms also own a significant percentage of the firm. In such instances, there is less separation between ownership and managerial control. Moreover, in a large number of family-owned firms, ownership and managerial control are not separated to any significant extent. Research shows that family-owned firms perform better when a member of the family is the CEO rather than when the CEO is an outsider.[14]

In many regions outside the United States, such as in Latin America, Asia, and some European countries, family-owned firms dominate the competitive landscape.[15] The primary purpose of most of these firms is to increase the family's wealth, which explains why a family CEO often is better than an outside CEO. Family ownership is also significant in U.S. companies in that at least one-third of the S&P 500 firms have substantial family ownership, holding on average about 18 percent of a firm's equity.[16]

Family-controlled firms face at least two critical issues related to corporate governance. First, as they grow, they may not have access to all of the skills needed to effectively manage the firm and maximize returns for the family. Thus, outsiders may be required to facilitate growth. Second, as they grow, they may need to seek outside capital and thus give up some of the ownership. In these cases, protecting the minority owners' rights becomes important.[17] To avoid these potential problems, when family firms grow and become more complex, their owner-managers may contract with managerial specialists. These managers make major decisions in the owners' firm and are compensated on the basis of their decision-making skills. Research suggests that firms in which families own enough equity to have influence without major control tend to make the best strategic decisions.[18]

Without owner (shareholder) specialization in risk bearing and management specialization in decision making, a firm may be limited by its owners' abilities to simultaneously manage it and make effective strategic decisions relative to risk. Thus, the separation and specialization of ownership (risk bearing) and managerial control (decision making) should produce the highest returns for the firm's owners.

10-1a Agency Relationships

The separation between owners and managers creates an agency relationship. An agency relationship exists when one or more persons (the principal or principals) hire another person or persons (the agent or agents) as decision-making specialists to perform a service.[19] Thus, an **agency relationship** exists when one party delegates decision-making responsibility to a second party for compensation (see Figure 10.1).

In addition to shareholders and top-level managers, other examples of agency relationships are top managers who hire subsidiary managers, client firms engaging consultants and the insured contracting with an insurer. Moreover, within organizations, an agency relationship exists between managers and their employees, as well as between top-level managers and the firm's owners.[20] However, in this chapter we focus on the agency relationship between the firm's owners (the principals) and top-level managers (the principals' agents) because these managers are responsible for formulating and implementing the firm's strategies, which have major effects on firm performance.[21]

The separation between ownership and managerial control can be problematic. Research evidence documents a variety of agency problems in the modern corporation.[22] Problems can surface because the principal and the agent have different interests and goals or because shareholders lack direct control of large publicly traded corporations. Problems also surface when an agent makes decisions that result in pursuing goals that conflict with those of the principals. Thus, the separation of ownership and control potentially allows divergent interests (between principals and agents) to occur, which can lead to managerial opportunism.

An **agency relationship** exists when one party delegates decision-making responsibility to a second party for compensation.

Figure 10.1 An Agency Relationship

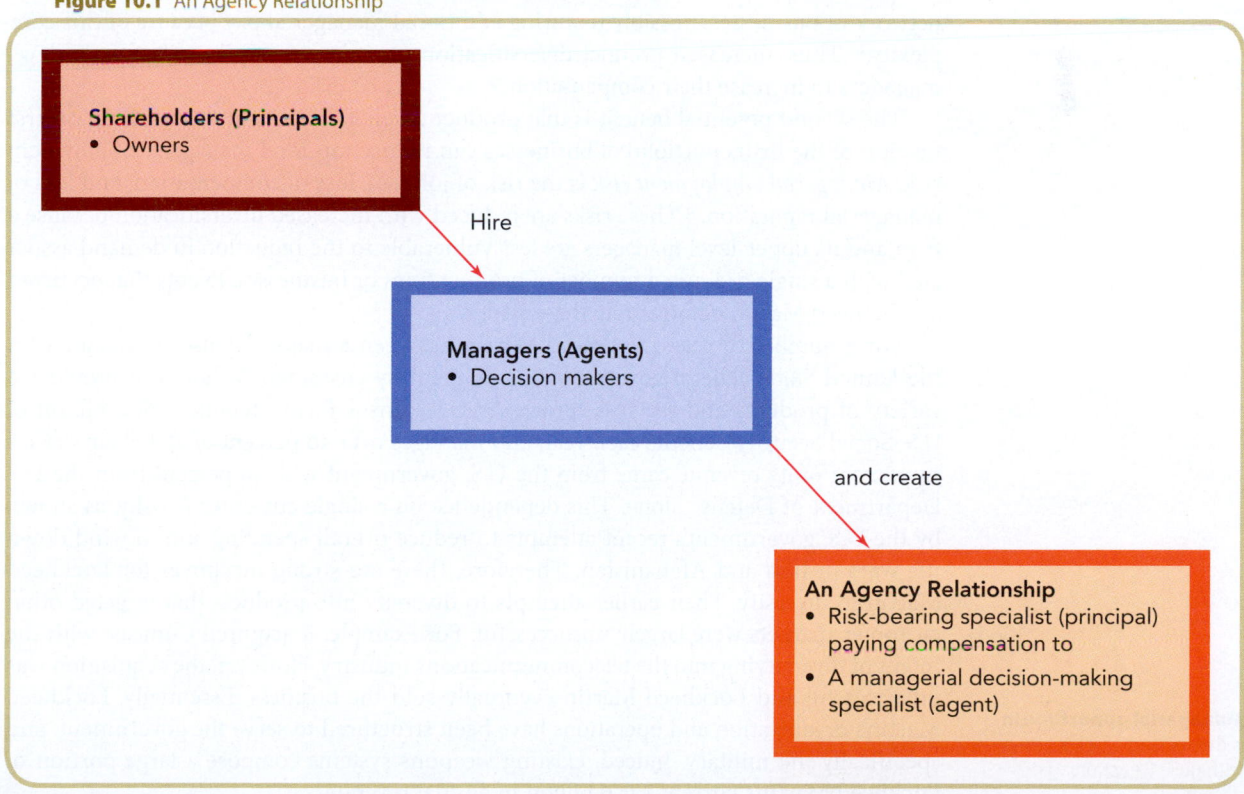

Managerial opportunism is the seeking of self-interest with guile (i.e., cunning or deceit).[23] Opportunism is both an attitude (i.e., an inclination) and a set of behaviors (i.e., specific acts of self-interest).[24] Principals do not know beforehand which agents will or will not act opportunistically. A top-level manager's reputation is an imperfect predictor; moreover, opportunistic behavior cannot be observed until it has occurred. Thus, principals establish governance and control mechanisms to prevent agents from acting opportunistically, even though only a few are likely to do so. Interestingly, research suggests that when CEOs feel constrained by governance mechanisms, they are more likely to seek external advice that, in turn, helps them make better strategic decisions.[25]

The agency relationship suggests that any time principals delegate decision-making responsibilities to agents, the opportunity for conflicts of interest exists. Top-level managers, for example, may make strategic decisions that maximize their personal welfare and minimize their personal risk.[26] Decisions such as these prevent maximizing shareholder wealth. Decisions regarding product diversification demonstrate this situation.

10-1b Product Diversification as an Example of an Agency Problem

As explained in Chapter 6, a corporate-level strategy to diversify the firm's product lines can enhance a firm's strategic competitiveness and increase its returns, both of which serve the interests of all stakeholders and certainly shareholders and top-level managers. However, product diversification can create two benefits for top-level managers that shareholders do not enjoy, meaning that they may prefer product diversification more than shareholders do.[27]

One reason managers prefer more diversification compared to shareholders is the fact that it usually increases the size of a firm and size is positively related to executive compensation. Diversification also increases the complexity of managing a firm and its network of businesses, possibly requiring additional managerial pay because of this complexity.[28] Thus, increased product diversification provides an opportunity for top-level managers to increase their compensation.[29]

The second potential benefit is that product diversification and the resulting diversification of the firm's portfolio of businesses can reduce top-level managers' employment risk. *Managerial employment risk* is the risk of job loss, loss of compensation, and loss of managerial reputation.[30] These risks are reduced with increased diversification because a firm and its upper-level managers are less vulnerable to the reduction in demand associated with a single or limited number of product lines or businesses. Events that occurred at Lockheed Martin demonstrate these issues.

For a number of years, Lockheed Martin has been a major defense contractor with the United States federal government as its primary customer. Although it provides a variety of products and services (processes U.S. census forms, handles $600 billion of U.S. Social Security benefits each year, and manages over 50 percent of global air traffic), 79 percent of its revenue came from the U.S. government with 59 percent from the U.S. Department of Defense alone. This dependence on a single customer is risky, as shown by the U.S. government's recent attempts to reduce overall spending and to wind down the wars in Iraq and Afghanistan. Therefore, there are strong incentives for Lockheed Martin to diversify. Their earlier attempts to diversify into products that targeted other customer markets were largely unsuccessful. For example, it acquired Comcast with the intent of diversifying into the telecommunications industry. However, the acquisition was unsuccessful and Lockheed Martin eventually sold the business. Essentially, Lockheed Martin's organization and operations have been structured to serve the government, and specifically the military. Indeed, existing weapons systems compose a large portion of Lockheed Martin's current $45.6 billion in annual revenue.

Managerial opportunism is the seeking of self-interest with guile (i.e., cunning or deceit).

Lockheed Martin's new CEO in 2013, Marillyn Hewson, is tasked with charting a future for the company that likely includes diversification. The firm's Center for Innovation is working on several potential products and services in the health care and cybersecurity industries. So, it appears that it will try to diversify organically by developing innovations internally (using its current capabilities) rather than acquiring other firms as it did in the past. In fact, Hewson describes Lockheed Martin as a global security enterprise, suggesting its new focus and vision. While previous diversification efforts were unsuccessful, Lockheed Martin is trying again with a new CEO and emphasis on internal innovation and international expansion.[31]

Free cash flow is the source of another potential agency problem. Calculated as operating cash flow minus capital expenditures, free cash flow represents the cash remaining after the firm has invested in all projects that have positive net present value within its current businesses.[32] Top-level managers may decide to invest free cash flow in product lines that are not associated with the firm's current lines of business to increase the firm's degree of diversification (as is currently being done at Lockheed Martin). However, when managers use free cash flow to diversify the firm in ways that do not have a strong possibility of creating additional value for stakeholders and certainly for shareholders, the firm is overdiversified. Overdiversification is an example of self-serving and opportunistic managerial behavior. In contrast to managers, shareholders may prefer that free cash flow be distributed to them as dividends, so they can control how the cash is invested.[33]

In Figure 10.2, Curve S shows shareholders' optimal level of diversification. As the firm's owners, shareholders seek the level of diversification that reduces the risk of the firm's total failure while simultaneously increasing its value by developing economies of scale and scope (see Chapter 6). Of the four corporate-level diversification strategies shown in Figure 10.2, shareholders likely prefer the diversified position noted by point A on Curve S—a position that is located between the dominant business and related-constrained diversification strategies. Of course, the optimum level of diversification

Figure 10.2 Manager and Shareholder Risk and Diversification

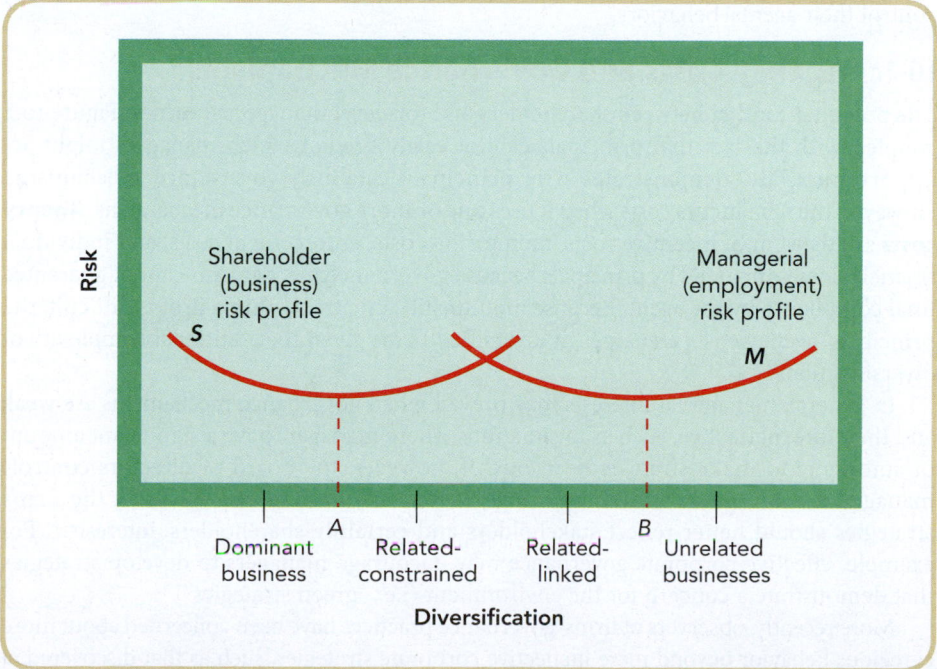

owners seek varies from firm to firm.[34] Factors that affect shareholders' preferences include the firm's primary industry, the intensity of rivalry among competitors in that industry, the top management team's experience with implementing diversification strategies, and the firm's perceived expertise in the new business and its effects on other firm strategies, such as its entry into international markets.[35]

As is the case for principals, top-level managers—as agents—also seek an optimal level of diversification. Declining performance resulting from too much diversification increases the probability that external investors (representing the market for corporate control) will purchase a substantial percentage of or the entire firm for the purpose of controlling it. If a firm is acquired, the employment risk for its top-level managers increases significantly. Furthermore, these managers' employment opportunities in the external managerial labor market (discussed in Chapter 12) are affected negatively by a firm's poor performance. Therefore, top-level managers prefer that the firms they lead be diversified. However, their preference is that the firm's diversification falls short of the point at which it increases their employment risk and reduces their employment opportunities.[36] Curve M in Figure 10.2 shows that top-level managers prefer higher levels of product diversification than do shareholders. Top-level managers might find the optimal level of diversification as shown by point B on Curve M.

In general, shareholders prefer riskier strategies and more focused diversification. Shareholders reduce their risk by holding a diversified portfolio of investments. Alternatively, managers cannot balance their employment risk by working for a diverse portfolio of firms; therefore, managers may prefer a level of diversification that maximizes firm size and their compensation while also reducing their employment risk. Finding the appropriate level of diversification is difficult for managers. Research has shown that too much diversification can have negative effects on the firm's ability to create innovation (managers' unwillingness to take on higher risks). Alternatively, diversification that strategically fits the firm's capabilities can enhance its innovation output.[37] However, too much or inappropriate diversification can also divert managerial attention from other important firm activities such as corporate social responsibility.[38] Product diversification, therefore, is a potential agency problem that could result in principals incurring costs to control their agents' behaviors.

10-1c Agency Costs and Governance Mechanisms

The potential conflict between shareholders and top-level managers shown in Figure 10.2, coupled with the fact that principals cannot easily predict which managers might act opportunistically, demonstrates why principals establish governance mechanisms. However, the firm incurs costs when it uses one or more governance mechanisms. **Agency costs** are the sum of incentive costs, monitoring costs, enforcement costs, and individual financial losses incurred by principals because governance mechanisms cannot guarantee total compliance by the agent. Because monitoring activities within a firm is difficult, the principals' agency costs are larger in diversified firms given the additional complexity of diversification.[39]

In general, managerial interests may prevail when governance mechanisms are weak and therefore ineffective, such as in situations where managers have a significant amount of autonomy to make strategic decisions. If, however, the board of directors controls managerial autonomy, or if other strong governance mechanisms are used, the firm's strategies should better reflect stakeholders and certainly shareholders' interests.[40] For example, effective corporate governance may encourage managers to develop strategies that demonstrate a concern for the environment (i.e., "green strategies").[41]

More recently, observers of firms' governance practices have been concerned about more egregious behavior beyond mere ineffective corporate strategies, such as that discovered at

Agency costs are the sum of incentive costs, monitoring costs, enforcement costs, and individual financial losses incurred by principals because governance mechanisms cannot guarantee total compliance by the agent.

Enron and WorldCom, and the more recent actions by major financial institutions. Partly in response to these behaviors, the U.S. Congress enacted the Sarbanes-Oxley Act (SOX) in 2002 and passed the Dodd-Frank Wall Street Reform and Consumer Protection Act (Dodd-Frank) in mid-2010.

Because of these two acts, corporate governance mechanisms should receive greater scrutiny.[42] While the implementation of SOX has been controversial to some, most believe that its use has led to generally positive outcomes in terms of protecting stakeholders and certainly shareholders' interests. For example, Section 404 of SOX, which prescribes significant transparency improvement on internal controls associated with accounting and auditing, has arguably improved the internal auditing scrutiny (and thereby trust) in firms' financial reporting. Moreover, research suggests that internal controls associated with Section 404 increase shareholder value.[43] Nonetheless, some argue that the Act, especially Section 404, creates excessive costs for firms. In addition, a decrease in foreign firms listing on U.S. stock exchanges occurred at the same time as listing on foreign exchanges increased. In part, this shift may be because of the costs SOX generates for firms seeking to list on U.S. exchanges.

Dodd-Frank is recognized as the most sweeping set of financial regulatory reforms in the United States since the Great Depression. The Act is intended to align financial institutions' actions with society's interests. Dodd-Frank includes provisions related to the categories of consumer protection, systemic risk oversight, executive compensation, and capital requirements for banks. Some legal analysts offer the following description of the Act's provisions: "(Dodd-Frank) creates a Financial Stability Oversight Council headed by the Treasury Secretary, establishes a new system for liquidation of certain financial companies, provides for a new framework to regulate derivatives, establishes new corporate governance requirements, and regulates credit rating agencies and securitizations. The Act also establishes a new consumer protection bureau and provides for extensive consumer protection in financial services."[44]

More intensive application of governance mechanisms as mandated by legislation such as SOX and Dodd-Frank affects firms' choice of strategies. For example, more intense governance might find firms choosing to pursue fewer risky projects, possibly decreasing shareholder wealth as a result. In considering how some provisions associated with Dodd-Frank dealing with banks might be put into practice, a U.S. federal regulator said, "To put it plainly, my view is that we are in danger of trying to squeeze too much risk and complexity out of banking."[45] As this comment suggests, determining governance practices that strike an appropriate balance between protecting stakeholders' interests and allowing firms to implement strategies with some degree of risk is difficult.

Next, we explain the effects of the three internal governance mechanisms on managerial decisions regarding the firm's strategies.

10-2 Ownership Concentration

Ownership concentration is defined by the number of large-block shareholders and the total percentage of the firm's shares they own. **Large-block shareholders** typically own at least 5 percent of a company's issued shares. Ownership concentration as a governance mechanism has received considerable interest because large-block shareholders are increasingly active in their demands that firms adopt effective governance mechanisms to control managerial decisions so that they will best represent owners' interests.[46] In recent years, the number of individuals who are large-block shareholders has declined. Institutional owners have replaced individuals as large-block shareholders.

Ownership concentration is defined by the number of large-block shareholders and the total percentage of the firm's shares they own.

Large-block shareholders typically own at least 5 percent of a company's issued shares.

In general, diffuse ownership (a large number of shareholders with small holdings and few, if any, large-block shareholders) produces weak monitoring of managers' decisions. One reason for this is that diffuse ownership makes it difficult for owners to effectively coordinate their actions. As noted earlier, diversification beyond the shareholders' optimum level can result from ineffective monitoring of managers' decisions. Higher levels of monitoring could encourage managers to avoid strategic decisions that harm shareholder value, such as too much diversification. Research evidence suggests that ownership concentration is associated with lower levels of firm product diversification.[47] Thus, with high degrees of ownership concentration, the probability is greater that managers' decisions will be designed to maximize shareholder value.[48] However, the influence of large-block shareholders is mitigated to a degree in Europe by strong labor representation on boards of directors.[49]

As noted, ownership concentration influences decisions made about the strategies a firm will use and the value created by their use. In general, ownership concentration's influence on strategies and firm performance is positive. For example, when large-block shareholders have a high degree of wealth, they have power relative to minority shareholders to appropriate the firm's wealth; this is particularly the case when they are in managerial positions. Excessive appropriation at the expense of minority shareholders is somewhat common in emerging economy countries where minority shareholder rights often are not as protected as they are in the United States. In fact, in some of these countries, state ownership of an equity stake (even minority ownership) can be used to control these potential problems.[50] The importance of boards of directors to mitigate excessive appropriation of minority shareholder value has been found in firms with strong family ownership where family members have incentives to appropriate shareholder wealth, especially in the second generation after the founder has departed.[51] In general, family-controlled businesses will outperform nonfamily controlled businesses, especially smaller and private firms because of the importance of enhancing the family's wealth and maintaining the family business.[52] However, families often try to balance the pursuit of economic and noneconomic objectives such that they sometimes may be moderately risk averse (thereby influencing their innovative output).[53]

10-2a The Increasing Influence of Institutional Owners

A classic work published in the 1930s argued that a separation of ownership and control had come to characterize the "modern" corporation.[54] This change occurred primarily because growth prevented founders-owners from maintaining their dual positions in what were increasingly complex companies. More recently, another shift has occurred: Ownership of many modern corporations is now concentrated in the hands of institutional investors rather than individual shareholders.[55]

Institutional owners are financial institutions, such as mutual funds and pension funds, that control large-block shareholder positions. Because of their prominent ownership positions, institutional owners, as large-block shareholders, have the potential to be a powerful governance mechanism. Estimates of the amount of equity in U.S. firms held by institutional owners range from 60 to 75 percent. Recent commentary suggests the importance of pension funds to an entire economy: "Pension funds are critical drivers of growth and economic activity in the United States because they are one of the only significant sources of long-term, patient capital."[56]

These percentages suggest that as investors, institutional owners have both the size and the incentive to discipline ineffective top-level managers and that they can significantly influence a firm's choice of strategies and strategic decisions.[57] As the Opening Case indicates, institutional and other large-block shareholders are becoming more active in their efforts to influence a corporation's strategic decisions, unless they have a

Institutional owners are financial institutions, such as mutual funds and pension funds, that control large-block shareholder positions.

business relationship with the firm. Initially, these shareholder activists and institutional investors concentrated on the performance and accountability of CEOs and contributed to the dismissal of a number of them. More recently, activists target the actions of boards more directly via proxy vote proposals that are intended to give shareholders more decision rights because they believe board processes have been ineffective.[58] A rule approved by the SEC allowing large shareholders (owning 1 to 5 percent of a company's stock) to nominate up to 25 percent of a company's board of directors enhances shareholders' decision rights.[59]

The institutional investor BlackRock, Inc., is the largest manager of financial assets in the world, with just under $4 trillion invested and holdings in most of the largest global corporations. Interestingly, it was once described as a "silent giant" because it did not engage in activism. However, recently the silent giant has been awakened, as it has begun asking more questions of the firms in which it holds significant investments. Most of its actions are "behind the scenes," only voting against a director or a company proposal when its unobtrusive actions have failed to change the firm's behavior. BlackRock has become more "confrontational" in order to ensure the value of its investments, and some wish that it would become even more active because of the power of its large equity holdings.[60] BlackRock's CEO, Larry Fink, recently sent a letter to S&P 500 listed firms suggesting that they focus on the long-term: "It is critical … to understand that corporate leaders' duty of care and loyalty is not to every investor or trader who owns their companies' shares at any moment in time, but to the company and its long-term owners,"[61] To date, research suggests that institutional activism may not have a strong direct effect on firm performance, but it may indirectly influence a targeted firm's strategic decisions, including those concerned with international diversification and innovation. Thus, to some degree at least, institutional activism has the potential to discipline managers and to enhance the likelihood of a firm taking future actions that are in shareholders' best interests such as investing in human capital.[62]

Board of directors is a group of elected individuals whose primary responsibility is to act in the owners' best interests by formally monitoring and controlling the firm's top level managers.

10-3 Board of Directors

Shareholders elect the members of a firm's board of directors. The **board of directors** is a group of elected individuals whose primary responsibility is to act in the owners' best interests by formally monitoring and controlling the firm's top-level managers.[63] Those elected to a firm's board of directors are expected to oversee managers and to ensure that the corporation operates in ways that will best serve stakeholders' interests, and particularly the owners' interests. Helping board members reach their expected objectives are their powers to direct the affairs of the organization and reward and discipline top-level managers.

Though important to all shareholders, a firm's individual shareholders with small ownership percentages are very dependent on the board of directors to represent their interests. Unfortunately, evidence suggests that boards have not been highly effective

Bloomberg/Getty Images

Larry Fink, CEO of BlackRock, the largest mutual fund provider, has suggested that managers need to focus on long-term strategy rather than responding to short-term trader proposals.

in monitoring and controlling top-level managers' decisions and subsequent actions.[64] Because of their relatively ineffective performance and in light of the recent financial crisis, boards are experiencing increasing pressure from shareholders, lawmakers, and regulators to become more forceful in their oversight role to prevent top-level managers from acting in their own best interests. Moreover, in addition to their monitoring role, board members increasingly are expected to provide resources to the firms they serve. These resources include their personal knowledge and expertise and their relationships with a wide variety of organizations.[65]

Generally, board members (often called directors) are classified into one of three groups (see Table 10.1). *Insiders* are active top-level managers in the company who are elected to the board because they are a source of information about the firm's day-to-day operations.[66] *Related outsiders* have some relationship with the firm, contractual or otherwise, that may create questions about their independence, but these individuals are not involved with the corporation's day-to-day activities. *Outsiders* provide independent counsel to the firm and may hold top-level managerial positions in other companies or may have been elected to the board prior to the beginning of the current CEO's tenure.[67]

Historically, inside managers dominated a firm's board of directors. A widely accepted view is that a board with a significant percentage of its membership from the firm's top-level managers provides relatively weak monitoring and control of managerial decisions.[68] With weak board monitoring, managers sometimes use their power to select and compensate directors and exploit their personal ties with them. In response to the SEC's proposal to require audit committees to be composed of outside directors, in 1984 the New York Stock Exchange (NYSE) implemented a rule requiring outside directors to head the audit committee. Subsequently, other rules required that independent outsider directors lead important committees such as the audit, compensation, and nomination committees.[69] These other requirements were instituted after SOX was passed, and policies of the NYSE now require companies to maintain boards of directors that are composed of a majority of outside independent directors and to maintain full independent audit committees. Thus, additional scrutiny of corporate governance practices is resulting in a significant amount of attention being devoted to finding ways to recruit quality independent directors and to encourage boards to take actions that fully represent shareholders' best interests.[70]

Critics advocate reforms to ensure that independent outside directors are a significant majority of a board's total membership; research suggests this has been accomplished.[71] However, others argue that having outside directors is not enough to resolve the problems in that CEO power can strongly influence a board's decision. One proposal to reduce the power of the CEO is to separate the chair's role and the CEO's role on the board so

Table 10.1 Classification of Board of Directors' Members

Insiders
• The firm's CEO and other top-level managers
Related outsiders
• Individuals not involved with the firm's day-to-day operations, but who have a relationship with the company
Outsiders
• Individuals who are independent of the firm in terms of day-to-day operations and other relationships

that the same person does not hold both positions.[72] A situation in which an individual holds both the CEO and chair of the board title is called *CEO duality*. As is shown in the CEO duality at JPMorgan Chase with Jamie Dimon, it is often very difficult to separate the CEO and chair positions after they have been given to one person.[73] Unfortunately, having a board that actively monitors top-level managers' decisions and actions does not ensure high performance. The value that the directors bring to the company also influences the outcomes. For example, boards with members having significant relevant experience and knowledge are the most likely to help the firm formulate and implement effective strategies.[74]

Alternatively, having a large number of outside board members can also create some problems. For example, because outsiders typically do not have contact with the firm's day-to-day operations and do not have ready access to detailed information about managers and their skills, they lack the insights required to fully and effectively evaluate their decisions and initiatives.[75] Outsiders can, however, obtain valuable information through frequent interactions with inside board members and during board meetings to enhance their understanding of managers and their decisions.

Because they work with and lead the firm daily, insiders have access to information that facilitates forming and implementing appropriate strategies. Accordingly, some evidence suggests that boards with a critical mass of insiders typically are better informed about intended strategic initiatives, the reasons for the initiatives, and the outcomes expected from pursuing them.[76] Without this type of information, outsider-dominated boards may emphasize financial, as opposed to strategic, controls to gather performance information to evaluate managers' and business units' performances. A virtually exclusive reliance on financial evaluations shifts risk to top-level managers who, in turn, may make decisions to maximize their interests and reduce their employment risk. Reducing investments in R&D, further diversifying the firm, and pursuing higher levels of compensation are some of the results of managers' actions to reach the financial goals set by outsider-dominated boards.[77] Additionally, boards can make mistakes in strategic decisions because of poor decision processes, and in CEO succession decisions because of the lack of important information about candidates as well as the firm's specific needs. Overall, knowledgeable and balanced boards are likely to be the most effective over time.[78]

10-3a Enhancing the Effectiveness of the Board of Directors

Because of the importance of boards of directors in corporate governance and as a result of increased scrutiny from shareholders—in particular, large institutional investors—the performances of individual board members and of entire boards are being evaluated more formally and with greater intensity.[79] The demand for greater accountability and improved performance is stimulating many boards to voluntarily make changes. Among these changes are:

1. increases in the diversity of the backgrounds of board members (e.g., a greater number of directors from public service, academic, and scientific settings; a greater percentage of ethnic minorities and women; and members from different countries on boards of U.S. firms);
2. the strengthening of internal management and accounting control systems;
3. establishing and consistently using formal processes to evaluate board member's performance;
4. modifying the compensation of directors, especially reducing or eliminating stock options as a part of their package; and
5. creating the "lead director" role[80] that has strong powers with regard to the board agenda and oversight of non-management board member activities.

An increase in the board's involvement with a firm's strategic decision-making processes creates the need for effective collaboration between board members and top-level managers. Some argue that improving the processes used by boards to make decisions and monitor managers and firm outcomes is important for board effectiveness.[81] Moreover, because of the increased pressure from owners and the potential conflict among board members, procedures are necessary to help boards function effectively while seeking to discharge their responsibilities.

Increasingly, outside directors are being required to own significant equity stakes as a prerequisite to holding a board seat. In fact, some research suggests that firms perform better if outside directors have such a stake; the trend is toward higher pay for directors with more stock ownership, but with fewer stock options.[82] However, other research suggests that too much ownership can lead to lower independence for board members.[83] In addition, other research suggests that diverse boards help firms make more effective strategic decisions and perform better over time.[84] Although questions remain about whether more independent and diverse boards enhance board effectiveness, the trends for greater independence and increasing diversity among board members are likely to continue.

10-3b Executive Compensation

The compensation of top-level managers, and especially of CEOs, generates a great deal of interest and strongly held opinions. Some believe that top-management team members, and certainly CEOs, have a great deal of responsibility for a firm's performance and that they should be rewarded accordingly.[85] Others conclude that these individuals (and again, especially CEOs) are greatly overpaid and that their compensation is not as strongly related to firm performance as should be the case.[86] One of the three internal governance mechanisms attempts to deal with these issues. Specifically, **executive compensation** is a governance mechanism that seeks to align the interests of managers and owners through salaries, bonuses, and long-term incentives such as stock awards and options.[87]

Long-term incentive plans (typically involving stock options and stock awards) are an increasingly important part of compensation packages for top-level managers, especially those leading U.S. firms. Theoretically, using long-term incentives facilitates the firm's efforts (through the board of directors' pay-related decisions) to avoid potential agency problems by linking managerial compensation to the wealth of common shareholders.[88] Effectively designed long-term incentive plans have the potential to prevent large-block stockholders (e.g., institutional investors) from pressing for changes in the composition of the board of directors and the top-management team because they assume that, when exercised, the plans will ensure that top-level managers will act in shareholders' best interests. Additionally, shareholders typically assume that top-level managers' pay and the firm's performance are more properly aligned when outsiders are the dominant block of a board's membership. Research results suggesting that fraudulent behavior can be associated with stock option incentives, such as earnings manipulation,[89] demonstrate the importance of the firm's board of directors (as a governance mechanism) actively monitoring the use of executive compensation as a governance mechanism.

Effectively using executive compensation as a governance mechanism is particularly challenging for firms implementing international strategies. For example, the interests of the owners of multinational corporations may be best served by less uniformity in the firm's foreign subsidiaries' compensation plans.[90] Developing an array of unique compensation plans requires additional monitoring, potentially increasing the firm's agency costs. Importantly, pay levels vary by regions of the world. For example, managerial pay is highest in the U.S. and much lower in Asia. Historically, compensation for top-level managers has been lower in India partly because many of the largest firms have strong family ownership and control.[91] Also, acquiring firms and participating in joint ventures

Executive compensation
is a governance mechanism that seeks to align the interests of managers and owners through salaries, bonuses, and long-term incentives such as stock awards and options.

in other countries increases the complexity associated with a board of directors' efforts to use executive compensation as an effective internal corporate governance mechanism.[92]

10-3c   The Effectiveness of Executive Compensation

As an internal governance mechanism, executive compensation—especially long-term incentive compensation—is complicated, for several reasons. First, the strategic decisions top-level managers make are complex and nonroutine, meaning that direct supervision (even by the firm's board of directors) is likely to be ineffective as a means of judging the quality of their decisions. The result is a tendency to link top-level managers' compensation to outcomes the board can easily evaluate, such as the firm's financial performance. This leads to a second issue in that, typically, the effects of top-level managers' decisions are stronger on the firm's long-term performance than its short-term performance. This reality makes it difficult to assess the effects of their decisions on a regular basis (e.g., annually). Third, a number of other factors affect a firm's performance besides top-level managerial decisions and behavior. Unpredictable changes in segments (economic, demographic, political/legal, etc.) in the firm's general environment (see Chapter 2) make it difficult to separate the effects of top-level managers' decisions and the effects (both positive and negative) of changes in the firm's external environment on the firm's performance.

Properly designed and used incentive compensation plans for top-level managers may increase the value of a firm in line with shareholder expectations, but such plans are subject to managerial manipulation.[93] Additionally, annual bonuses may provide incentives to pursue short-run objectives at the expense of the firm's long-term interests. Although long-term, performance-based incentives may reduce the temptation to underinvest in the short run, they increase executive exposure to risks associated with uncontrollable events, such as market fluctuations and industry decline. The longer term the focus of incentive compensation, the greater are the long-term risks top-level managers bear. Also, because long-term incentives tie a manager's overall wealth to the firm in a way that is inflexible, such incentives and ownership may not be valued as highly by a manager as by outside investors who have the opportunity to diversify their wealth in a number of other financial investments.[94] Thus, firms may have to overcompensate for managers using long-term incentives.[95] The Strategic Focus provides an examination of some of the issues that confront boards of directors with regard to how much to pay the CEO. The media often focuses on the size of the CEO compensation package, especially if it is exceptionally large and compares it to the pay of the average worker.

Much of the size of CEO pay has been driven by stock options and long-term incentives. Even though some stock option-based compensation plans are well designed with option strike prices substantially higher than current stock prices, some have been developed for the primary purpose of giving executives more compensation. Research of stock option repricing, where the strike price value of the option has been lowered from its original position, suggests that action is taken more frequently in high-risk situations.[96] However, repricing also happens when firm performance is poor, to restore the incentive effect for the option. Evidence also suggests that politics are often involved, which has resulted in "option backdating."[97] While this evidence shows that no internal governance mechanism is perfect, some compensation plans accomplish their purpose. For example, recent research suggests that long-term pay designed to encourage managers to be environmentally friendly has been linked to higher success in preventing pollution.[98]

As the Strategic Focus suggests, this internal governance mechanism is likely to continue receiving a great deal of scrutiny in the years to come. When designed properly and used effectively, each of the three internal governance mechanisms can contribute positively to the firm operating in ways that best serve stakeholders and especially shareholders' interests.

Strategic Focus

Do CEOs Deserve the Large Compensation Packages They Receive?

This question often circulates in the media regarding the large compensation packages that CEOs receive as leaders of large publically traded firms. The negative aspect played up in the media often pertains to the growing inequality between the top executives' pay and the average wages of U.S. workers. In 1983, average pay for leaders of the six largest banks was 40 times the average of all U.S. workers, while the average pay for leaders of the largest Fortune 500 companies was less than 38 times. However, since then large bank CEO compensation has grown exponentially compared to the average worker and now stands at 208 times, while non-bank workers average 224 times. In other words, large industrial companies' top executive compensation has grown even more than the bank executive compensation. Although average worker pay has grown 2.9 times over the last 30 years, bank executives pay has grown 15.4 times, while non-bank executives pay has grown 17.4 times.

Large oversized compensation packages, such as that awarded for 2014 by Discovery Communications CEO, David Zaslav at $156.1 million, add to the media fervor relative to executive compensation. Discovery Communications has primarily focused on developing cable channels, such as Discovery, Animal Planet, and TLC. However, in 2014, while the CEO's pay increased, the adjusted value of Discovery's stock fell 25 percent. The media focused on this discrepancy. However, CEO compensation is more complex than might be explored in the media headlines. Although the stock value was down in 2014, the company's revenue rose 13 percent while its income increased 5.6 percent. Parts of Zaslav's contract were attached to increases in revenue and net income. His package was also facilitated because he has grown market capitalization from $5 billion to $20 billion under his leadership. Some of the awards in the current year were because of value creation in previous years and value associated with future restricted stock option grants. Notwithstanding the complexities, CEO compensation continues to rise although not as much as in the pre-financial crisis period.

Interestingly, among the large diversified financial banks, such as JPMorgan Chase, Citigroup, Morgan Stanley, Goldman Sachs, and Wells Fargo, the CEOs average pay was around $18 million. In 2014, the average pay was 121 times that of the average worker at these large diversified banks, down 55 percent from 273 times in 2006 near the end of the pre-financial crisis period. This is obviously due to closer regulation of these large banks because of legislation such as the Dodd-Frank Act. Furthermore the Securities and Exchange Commission

is working to finalize rules requiring all public companies to report how much the CEO makes more than the firm's typical employee. This will give fodder to media outlets to dampen the oversized pay packages that CEOs have increasingly received over the last 30 years. In part, research from the field of sociology shows that these large pay packages have not always been due to performance increases, but due to the tight networks of managers who sit on executive compensation committees and boards of directors and do comparisons between firms. These inter-board networks have been associated with increases in compensation to help firms keep up with the trends at other firms. Also, because of large mergers and acquisitions such as those that have taken place among the large diversified banks, firms are much larger and executive compensation is associated with size and complexity of the operations top-level executives manage.

Frederick M. Brown/Getty Images

President and CEO of Discovery Communications, David Zaslav, presenting at a conference in this photo, has had his 2014 pay package scrutized heavily by the media.

Research from the finance discipline (versus sociology) finds that the mix of the pay package that most top executives receive has been changing. Instead of an over emphasis on stock options, top executives have been receiving compensation that is based on restricted stock ownership, which cannot be realized unless they meet significant performance targets over time. As such, there is less oversized risk taking that can result in disastrous consequences for these large firms. Accordingly, research finds that managers are taking more measured risks due to the compensation packages that they are receiving.

In summary, executive compensation is a complex issue that cannot be simply determined by the overall size of the package. Although executive compensation has grown dramatically, there are both legitimate and illegitimate reasons for such huge pay packages. Each case needs to be examined closely for possible problems of excess versus appropriateness. However, there is likely to be social problems due to the perception that top management executive compensation relative to the average worker has added to the inequality in our society. As such, care should be taken to manage this issue from a policy point-of-view. Managerial human capital should be rewarded for its capability and the value it creates, but lower levels workers and their human capital should also have opportunities to make progress.

Sources: D. Fitzgerald, 2015, Staples CEO Sargent's pay grew 15% to $12.4 million last year; Chief executive earned $2.6 million in non-equity incentive compensation in 2014, *Wall Street Journal*, www.wsj.com, April 13; K. Hagey, 2015, Discovery Communications CEO gets 2014 compensation of $1.561 million, *Wall Street Journal*, www.wsj.com, April 6; J. W. Kim, B. Kogut, & J.-S. Yang, 2015, Executive compensation, fat cats and best athletes, *American Sociological Review*, 80: 299–328; E. K. Lim, 2015, The role of reference point in CEO restricted stock and its impact on R&D intensity in high-technology firms, *Strategic Management Journal*, 36: 872–889; P. Rudegear, 2015, Wall Street's pay gap slims, *Wall Street Journal*, April 6, A1, A4; E. M. Fich, L. T. Starks, & A. S. Yore, 2014, CEO deal-making activities and compensation, *Journal of Financial Economics*, 114: 471–492; S. Williams, 2014, BG Group draws more heat over CEO compensation; one of the biggest revolts against executive pay in the U.K. in recent years, *Wall Street Journal*, www.wsj.com, November 28; R. Wilmers, 2014, Why excessive CEO pay is bad for the economy, *American Banker*, www.americanbanker.com, March 14.

By the same token, because none of the three mechanisms are perfect in design or execution, the market for corporate control, an external governance mechanism, is sometimes needed.

10-4 Market for Corporate Control

The **market for corporate control** is an external governance mechanism that is active when a firm's internal governance mechanisms fail.[99] The market for corporate control is composed of individuals and firms that buy ownership positions in or purchase all of potentially undervalued corporations typically for the purpose of forming new divisions in established companies or merging two previously separate firms. Because the top-level managers are assumed to be responsible for the undervalued firm's poor performance, they are usually replaced. An effective market for corporate control ensures that ineffective and/or opportunistic top-level managers are disciplined.[100]

Commonly, target firm managers and board members are sensitive about takeover bids emanating from the market for corporate control since being a target suggests that they have been ineffective in fulfilling their responsibilities. For top-level managers, a board's decision to accept an acquiring firm's offer typically finds them losing their jobs because the acquirer usually wants different people to lead the firm. At the same time, rejection of an offer also increases the risk of job loss for top-level managers because the pressure from the board and shareholders for them to improve the firm's performance becomes substantial.[101]

A hedge fund is an investment fund that can pursue many different investment strategies, such as taking long and short positions, using arbitrage, and buying and selling undervalued securities for the purpose of maximizing investors' returns. Growing rapidly, in 2014 hedge fund assets topped $3 trillion and are expected to exceed $5 trillion by 2018. It is expected that up to 65 percent of their funding comes from institutional investors.[102] Given investors' increasing desire to hold underperforming funds and their managers accountable, hedge funds have become increasingly active in the market for corporate control.[103] For example, "Some of the most complex deals in the current market, including Baker Hughes and Halliburton, Allergan and Actavis, Staples and Office Depot, and Time Warner Cable and Comcast, count prominent hedge funds as major stockholders" who are working to close these deals suggesting positive prospects for the combined firms.[104]

The **market for corporate control** is an external governance mechanism that is active when a firm's internal governance mechanisms fail.

In general, activist pension funds (as institutional investors and as an internal governance mechanism) are reactive in nature, taking actions when they conclude that a firm is underperforming. In contrast, activist hedge funds (as part of the market for corporate control) are proactive, "identifying a firm whose performance could be improved and then investing in it."[105] An example is found in the Opening Case with Trian Fund Management, L.P., headed by CEO Nelson Peltz, seeking to change the strategy at DuPont by replacing four board members favorable to Peltz's activist hedge fund. However, the activist fund, Trian, lost the shareholder vote to replace the directors, and DuPont was not forced to breakup into several separate businesses.[106] Interestingly, given the need to search for new opportunities, hedge funds have been pursuing more technology firm deals. In fact, in 2014, 20 percent of such investments were in the technology sector, the highest percentage for any sector. Hedge funds have traditionally avoided technology firms because they change rapidly, and, as such, their future success is difficult to forecast. Overall, activists have been winning more board seats, forcing mergers and divestitures, and winning stock buyback programs, such as the stock buyback program at Apple fostered by Carl Icahn.[107]

However, another possibility is suggested by research results—namely, that as a governance mechanism, investors sometimes use the market for corporate control to take an ownership position in firms that are performing well.[108] A study of active corporate raiders in the 1980s showed that takeover attempts often were focused on above-average performance firms in an industry.[109] This work and other recent research suggest that the market for corporate control is an imperfect governance mechanism.[110] Actually, mergers and acquisitions are highly complex strategic actions with many purposes and potential outcomes. As discussed in Chapter 7, some are successful and many are not—even when they have potential to do well—because implementation challenges when integrating two diverse firms can limit their ability to realize their potential.[111]

In summary, the market for corporate control is a blunt instrument for corporate governance; nonetheless, this governance mechanism does have the potential to represent shareholders' best interests. Accordingly, top-level managers want to lead their firms in ways that make disciplining by activists outside the company unnecessary and/or inappropriate.

There are a number of defense tactics top-level managers can use to fend off a takeover attempt. Managers leading a target firm that is performing well are almost certain to try to thwart the takeover attempt. Even in instances when the target firm is underperforming its peers, managers might use defense tactics to protect their own interests. In general, managers' use of defense tactics is considered to be self-serving in nature.

10-4a Managerial Defense Tactics

In the majority of cases, hostile takeovers are the principal means by which the market for corporate control is activated. A *hostile takeover* is an acquisition of a target company by an acquiring firm that is accomplished "not by coming to an agreement with the target company's management but by going directly to the company's shareholders or fighting to replace management in order to get the acquisition approved."[112]

Firms targeted for a hostile takeover may use multiple defense tactics to fend off the takeover attempt. Increased use of the market for corporate control has enhanced the sophistication and variety of managerial defense tactics that are used in takeovers.

Because the market for corporate control tends to increase risk for managers, managerial pay may be augmented indirectly through golden parachutes (where a CEO can receive up to three years' salary if his or her firm is taken over). Golden parachutes, similar to most other defense tactics, are controversial. Another takeover defense strategy is traditionally known as a "poison pill." This strategy usually allows shareholders (other than the acquirer) to convert "shareholders' rights" into a large number of common shares if an individual or company acquires more than a set amount of the target firm's stock (typically 10 to 20 percent). Increasing the total number of outstanding shares dilutes the potential acquirer's existing stake. This means that, to maintain or expand its ownership position, the potential acquirer must buy additional shares at premium prices. The additional purchases increase the potential acquirer's costs. Some firms amend the corporate charter so board member elections are staggered, resulting in only one third of members being up for reelection each year. Research shows that this results in managerial entrenchment and reduced vulnerability to hostile takeovers.[113] Additional takeover defense strategies are presented in Table 10.2.

Most institutional investors oppose the use of defense tactics. TIAA-CREF and CalPERS have taken actions to have several firms' poison pills eliminated. Many institutional investors also oppose severance packages (golden parachutes), and the opposition is increasing significantly in Europe as well.[114] However, an advantage to severance packages is that they may encourage top-level managers to accept takeover bids with the potential to best serve shareholders' interest.[115] Alternatively, research results show that

Table 10.2 Hostile Takeover Defense Strategies

Defense strategy	Success as a strategy	Effects on shareholder wealth
Capital structure change: Dilution of the target firm's stock, making it more costly for an acquiring firm to continue purchasing the target's shares. Employee stock option plans (ESOPs), recapitalization, issuance of additional debt, and share buybacks are actions associated with this strategy.	Medium	Inconclusive
Corporate charter amendment: An amendment to the target firm's charter for the purpose of staggering the elections of members to its board of directors so that all are not elected during the same year. This change to the firm's charter prevents a potential acquirer from installing a completely new board in a single year.	Very low	Negative
Golden parachute: A lump-sum payment of cash that is given to one or more top-level managers when the firm is acquired in a takeover bid.	Low	Negligible
Greenmail: The repurchase of the target firm's shares of stock that were obtained by the acquiring firm at a premium in exchange for an agreement that the acquirer will no longer target the company for takeover.	Medium	Negative
Litigation Lawsuits that help the target firm stall hostile takeover attempts: Antitrust charges and inadequate disclosure are examples of the grounds on which the target firm could file.	Low	Positive
Poison pill: An action the target firm takes to make its stock less attractive to a potential acquirer.	High	Positive
Standstill agreement: A contract between the target firm and the potential acquirer specifying that the acquirer will not purchase additional shares of the target firm for a specified period of time in exchange for a fee paid by the target firm.	Low	Negative

Sources: L. Guo, P. Lach, & S. Mobbs, 2015, Tradeoffs between internal and external governance: Evidence from exogenous regulatory shocks. *Financial Management*, 44: 81–114; H. Sapra, A. Subramanian, & K. V. Subramanian, 2014, Corporate governance and innovation: Theory and evidence, *Journal of Financial & Quantitative Analysis*, 49: 957–1003; M. Straska & G. Waller, 2014, Antitakeover provisions and shareholder wealth: A survey of the literature, *Journal of Financial & Quantitative Analysis*, 49: 1–32; R. Campbell, C. Ghosh, M. Petrova, & C. F. Sirmans, 2011, Corporate governance and performance in the market for corporate control: The case of REITS, *Journal of Real Estate Finance & Economics*, 42: 451–480; M. Ryngaert & R. Schlten, 2010, Have changing takeover defense rules and strategies entrenched management and damaged shareholders? The case of defeated takeover bids, *Journal of Corporate Finance*, 16: 16–37; N. Ruiz-Mallorqui & D. J. Santana-Martin, 2009, Ultimate institutional owner and takeover defenses in the controlling versus minority shareholders context, *Corporate Governance: An International Review*, 17: 238–254; J. A. Pearce II & R. B. Robinson, Jr., 2004, Hostile takeover defenses that maximize shareholder wealth, *Business Horizons*, 47(5): 15–24.

using takeover defenses reduces the amount of pressure managers feel to seek short-term performance gains, resulting in them concentrating on developing strategies with a longer time horizon and a high probability of serving stakeholders' interests. Such firms are more likely to invest in and develop innovation; when they do so, the firm's market value increases, thereby rewarding shareholders.[116]

An awareness on the part of top-level managers about the existence of external investors in the form of individuals (e.g., Carl Icahn) and groups (e.g., hedge funds) often positively influences them to align their interests with those of the firm's stakeholders, especially the shareholders. Moreover, when active as an external governance mechanism, the market for corporate control has brought about significant changes in many firms' strategies and, when used appropriately, has served shareholders' interests. Of course, the goal is to have the managers develop the psychological ownership of principals.[117] However, such sense of ownership can be taken too far such that narcissistic (i.e., egotistical) top executives can feel that they are personally central to the identity of the firm.[118]

10-5 International Corporate Governance

Corporate governance is an increasingly important issue in economies around the world, including emerging economies. Globalization in trade, investments, and equity markets increases the potential value of firms throughout the world using similar mechanisms to govern corporate activities. Moreover, because of globalization, major companies want to attract foreign investment. For this to happen, foreign investors must be confident that adequate corporate governance mechanisms are in place to protect their investments.

Although globalization is stimulating an increase in the intensity of efforts to improve corporate governance and potentially to reduce the variation in regions and nations' governance systems,[119] the reality remains that different nations do have different governance systems in place. Recognizing and understanding differences in various countries' governance systems, as well as changes taking place within those systems, improves the likelihood a firm will be able to compete successfully in the international markets it chooses to enter. Next, to highlight the general issues of differences and changes taking place in governance systems, we discuss corporate governance practices in two developed economies (Germany and Japan) and in the emerging economy of China.

10-5a Corporate Governance in Germany and Japan

In many private German firms, the owner and manager may be the same individual. In these instances, agency problems are not present.[120] Even in publicly traded German corporations, a single shareholder is often dominant. Thus, the concentration of ownership is an important means of corporate governance in Germany, as it is in the United States.[121]

Historically, banks occupied the center of the German corporate governance system. This is the case in other European countries as well, such as Italy and France. As lenders, banks become major shareholders when companies they financed seek funding on the stock market or default on loans. Although the stakes are usually less than 10 percent, banks can hold a single ownership position up to, but not exceeding 15 percent of the bank's capital. Although shareholders can tell banks how to vote their ownership position, they generally do not do so. The banks monitor and control managers, both as lenders and as shareholders, by electing representatives to supervisory boards.

German firms with more than 2,000 employees are required to have a two-tiered board structure that places the responsibility for monitoring and controlling managerial (or supervisory) decisions and actions in the hands of a separate group.[122] All the functions of strategy and management are the responsibility of the management board (the Vorstand); however, appointment to the Vorstand is the responsibility of the supervisory tier (the Aufsichtsrat). Employees, union members, and shareholders appoint members to the Aufsichtsrat. Proponents of the German structure suggest that it helps prevent corporate wrongdoing and rash decisions by "dictatorial CEOs." However, critics maintain that it slows decision making and often ties a CEO's hands. The corporate governance practices in Germany make it difficult to restructure companies as quickly as can be done in the United States. Because of the role of local government (through the board structure) and the power of banks in Germany's corporate governance structure, private shareholders rarely have major ownership positions in German firms. Additionally, there is a significant amount of cross-shareholdings among firms.[123] However, large institutional investors, such as pension funds (outside of banks and insurance companies), are also relatively insignificant owners of corporate stock. Thus, at least historically, German executives generally have not been dedicated to maximizing shareholder wealth to the degree that is the case for top-level managers in the United States and United Kingdom.[124]

However, corporate governance practices used in Germany have been changing in recent years. A manifestation of these changes is that a number of German firms are gravitating toward U.S. governance mechanisms. Recent research suggests that the traditional system in Germany produced some agency costs because of a lack of external ownership power. Interestingly, German firms with listings on U.S. stock exchanges have increasingly adopted executive stock option compensation as a long-term incentive pay policy.[125] Also, as the Strategic Focus illustrates, activist shareholders are entering Germany and Japan, although the strategy is more engagement with managers rather that confrontation as can be found in the United States and the United Kingdom.

The concepts of obligation, family, and consensus affect attitudes toward corporate governance in Japan. As part of a company family, individuals are members of a unit that envelops their lives; families command the attention and allegiance of parties throughout corporations. In addition, Japanese firms are concerned with a broader set of stakeholders than are firms in the United States, including employees, suppliers, and customers.[126] Moreover, a *keiretsu* (a group of firms tied together by cross-shareholdings) is more than an economic concept—it, too, is a family. Some believe, though, that extensive cross-shareholdings impede the type of structural change that is needed to improve the nation's corporate governance practices. However, recent changes in the governance code in Japan has been fostering better opportunities from improved corporate governance.[127] Consensus, another important influence in Japanese corporate governance, calls for the expenditure of significant amounts of energy to win the hearts and minds of people whenever possible, as opposed to top-level managers issuing edicts.[128] Consensus is highly valued, even when it results in a slow and cumbersome decision-making process.

As in Germany, banks in Japan have an important role in financing and monitoring large public firms.[129] Because the main bank in the keiretsu owns the largest share of stocks and holds the largest amount of debt, it has the closest relationship with a firm's top-level managers. The main bank provides financial advice to the firm and also closely monitors managers. Thus, although it is changing, Japan has traditionally had a bank-based financial and corporate governance structure, whereas the United States has a market-based financial and governance structure.[130] Commercial banks in the United States by regulation are not allowed to own shares of publicly traded firms.

Aside from lending money, a Japanese bank can hold up to 5 percent of a firm's total stock; a group of related financial institutions can hold up to 40 percent. In many cases, main-bank relationships are part of a horizontal keiretsu. A keiretsu firm usually owns less than 2 percent of any other member firm; however, each company typically has a stake of that size in every firm in the keiretsu. As a result, 30 to 90 percent of a firm is owned by other members of the keiretsu. Thus, a keiretsu is a system of relationship investments.

Strategic **Focus**

"Engagement" versus "Activist" Shareholders in Japan, Germany, and China

Activist shareholders and a strong market for corporate control have traditionally been absent in Japan. More recently, shareholders have been more active and the most successful ones have been labeled "engagement" funds. The change is signaled, for example, by the Japanese Government Pension Investment Fund choosing an activist investor, the Taiyo Pacific Partners LP, an U.S. based engagement fund, to manage some of its $1 trillion in assets. The CEO of Taiyo Pacific, Brian Heywood, suggested that "Japanese executives have become more open to outside perspectives as they have developed offshore operations and received more training abroad." Furthermore, the Japanese Financial Services Agency has introduced a "stewardship code" that calls on investors to "press for greater returns." As such, the Japanese environment is becoming more oriented towards "shareholder rights," although the approach is definitely engagement versus activist.

Besides a new brand of activism in Japan, activism is spreading around the globe including Germany. Cevian Capital, an activist fund, is involved in ownership with ThyssenKrupp and Bilfinder. Likewise, Elliott Management, another activist fund, is involved with Celesio and Kabel Deutschland. Although management teams are quite suspicious of activists in Germany and other continental European countries, "Germany is an area where activists may look because of its protections for minority investors in takeover deals."

Although some activism has taken place in mainland China, firms in Hong Kong has been targeted more by activist funds. Hong Kong listed companies have been loosening rules for foreign ownership and thereby companies have been paying more attention to what investors think in regard to governance and transparency. In mainland China, however, often shares are mostly owned by parent business group firms as well as the government or, because they are often younger, they are still owned by the firm's founders. As such, there is less potential influence for investors on company decisions. However the Shanghai-Hong Kong Stock Connect program has accelerated opportunities for activists on the mainland. Through the Connect program, foreign financial institutions can have direct access to mainland China's capital markets. This means that the foreign ownership will have more activist influence because of shareholder voting rights in local mainland China listed firms.

But how do owners from emerging market country and countries with significant government ownership influence the firms they invest in overseas? Interestingly, sovereign wealth funds, many from emerging economies, are playing a dominant role by investing in developed economies as well as other emerging economies. In their own way, they are playing an activist role. For example, since the global financial crisis, many German firms have sought investment from sovereign wealth firms from Gulf States in the Mideast. In particular, many German major automobile firms have recruited Gulf Cooperation Council (GCC) sovereign wealth fund investment during the stresses of financial restructuring spurred by the financial crisis. These sovereign wealth funds are long term investors and reduce the possibility of a hostile takeover which has become a more prominent feature in the German corporate governance landscape.

Sovereign wealth funds are also taking active roles in climate change. For instance, the Norwegian sovereign wealth fund is divesting its assets in coal. Their strategy is to focus their wealth to have an influence on salient sustainability issues, such as climate change.

Courtesy of The Hedgefund Journal.com

(L-R) Lars Förberg, Christer Gardell

Cevian Capital Founders Lars Forberg and Christer Gardell are engaged actively in fostering more shareholder value creation through their fund.

Another example is the acquisition activity of Brazilian multinationals, which have been supported by its sovereign wealth fund, the Brazilian Development Bank (BNDES). BNDES has been "involved in several large-scale operations and helped orchestrate mergers and acquisitions to build large 'national champions' in several industries." For example, "BNDES helped rescue Brazilian meatpacker JBS-Friboi, which aggressively expanded internationally by acquiring large U.S. producers, Swift and Pilgrim's Pride, among others. In summary, shareholder activism has been spreading globally throughout the world, and there are owners in emerging economies participating in the market for corporate control and in restructuring investments, especially sovereign wealth funds that also have influence in developed as well as developing countries by their large ownership positions. These funds often focus to support government strategies, such as in China's energy sector, where the Chinese government is seeking to acquire more energy assets and natural resources to support its economy. Sometimes these sovereign funds also support government positions such as the example provided from Norway fund divesting coal assets in order to increasing its emphasis on sustainability, an important social and political movement.

Sources: B. Alhashel, 2015, Sovereign wealth funds: A literature review, *Journal of Economics & Business*, 78: 1–13; L. Havelock, 2015, New battlegrounds: A global activism update, IR Magazine, www.irmagazine.com, March 10; K. M. Howl, 2015, Norway oil fund sheds more coal assets, *Wall Street Journal*, www.wsj.com, May 5; K. Narioka, 2015, Activist investors in Japan find some doors cracking open, *Wall Street Journal*, www.wsj.com, January 29; M. Goranova & L. V. Ryan, 2014, Shareholder activism: A multidisciplinary review, *Journal of Management*, 40: 1230–1268; D. Haberly, 2014, White knights from the Gulf: Sovereign wealth fund investment and the evolution of German industrial finance, *Economic Geography*, 90: 293–320; S. G. Lazzarini, A. Musacchio, R. Bandeira-de-Mello, & R. Marcon, R. 2015, What do state-owned development banks do? Evidence from BNDES, 2002–09 *World Development*, 66: 237–253; A. Musacchio & S. G. Lazzarini, 2014, *Reinventing State Capitalism: Leviathan in Business, Brazil and Beyond*, Cambridge: Harvard University Press; X. Sun, J. Li, Y. Wang, & W. Clark, 2014, China's sovereign wealth fund investments in overseas energy: the energy security perspective, *Energy Policy*, 65: 654–661.

Japan's corporate governance practices have been changing in recent years. For example, because of Japanese banks' continuing development as economic organizations, their role in the monitoring and control of managerial behavior and firm outcomes is less significant than in the past.[131] Also, deregulation in the financial sector has reduced the cost of mounting hostile takeovers.[132] As such, deregulation facilitated additional activity in Japan's market for corporate control, which was nonexistent in past years. And there are pressures for more changes because of weak performance by many Japanese companies. In fact, there has been significant criticism of the corporate governance practices of the Tokyo Electric Power Company after the severe problems at the Fukushima Daiichi nuclear power plant following the earthquake and tsunami in 2011. Most Japanese firms have boards that are largely composed of internal management, so they reflect the upper echelon of management. However, independent, nonexecutive board members are increasingly important in Japanese firms because they have adopted a new corporate governance code.[133] As the Strategic Focus illustrates, engagement funds are helping to change the landscape as well, given they have become more active in Japan.

10-5b Corporate Governance in China

China has a unique and large, socialist mixed with a market-oriented, economy. Over time, the government has done much to improve the corporate governance of listed companies.[134] These comments suggest that corporate governance practices in China have been changing with increasing privatization of businesses and the development of equity markets. However, the stock markets in China remain young and are continuing to develop. In their early years, these markets were weak because of significant insider trading, but with stronger governance these markets have improved.[135]

There has been a gradual decline in China in the equity held in state-owned enterprises and the number and percentage of private firms have grown, but the state still relies on direct and/or indirect controls to influence the strategies firms use. Even private firms try to develop political ties with the government because of their role in providing access to resources and to the economy.[136] In terms of long-term success, these conditions may affect firms' performance because research shows that firms with higher state ownership tend to have lower market value and more volatility in that value across time. This is because of agency conflicts in the firms and because the executives do not seek to maximize shareholder returns, given that they must also seek to satisfy social goals placed on them by the government.[137] This suggests a potential conflict between the principals, particularly the state owner and the private equity owners of the state-owned enterprises.[138]

Some evidence suggests that corporate governance in China may be tilting toward the Western model. For example, recent research shows that with increasing frequency, the compensation of top-level executives in Chinese companies is closely related to prior and current financial performance of their firm.[139] Research also shows that, due to the weaker institutions, firms with family CEOs experience more positive financial performance than others without the family influence.[140]

Changing a nation's governance systems is a complicated task that will encounter problems as well as successes while seeking progress. Thus, corporate governance in Chinese companies continues to evolve and likely will continue to evolve for some time to come as parties (e.g., the Chinese government and those seeking further movement toward free-market economies) interact to form governance mechanisms that are best for their nation, business firms, and citizens. However, along with changes in the governance systems of specific countries, multinational companies' boards and managers are also evolving. For example, firms that have entered more international markets are likely to have more top executives with greater international experience and to have a larger proportion of foreign owners and foreign directors on their boards.[141]

10-6 Governance Mechanisms and Ethical Behavior

The three internal and one external governance mechanisms are designed to ensure that the agents of the firm's owners—the corporation's top-level managers—make strategic decisions that best serve the interests of all stakeholders. In the United States, shareholders are commonly recognized as the company's most significant stakeholders. Increasingly though, top-level managers are expected to lead their firms in ways that will also serve the needs of product market stakeholders (e.g., customers, suppliers, and host communities) and organizational stakeholders (e.g., managerial and non-managerial employees).[142] Therefore, the firm's actions and the outcomes flowing from them should result in, at least, minimal satisfaction of the interests of all stakeholders. Without at least minimal satisfaction of its interests, a dissatisfied stakeholder will withdraw its support from the firm and provide it to another (e.g., customers will purchase products from a supplier offering an acceptable substitute).

Some believe that the internal corporate governance mechanisms designed and used by ethically responsible leaders and companies increase the likelihood the firm will be able to, at least, minimally satisfy all stakeholders' interests.[143] Scandals at companies such as Enron, WorldCom, HealthSouth, and Satyam (a large information technology company based in India), among others, illustrate the negative effects of poor ethical behavior on a firm's efforts to satisfy stakeholders. The issue of ethical behavior by top-level managers as a foundation for best serving stakeholders' interests is being taken seriously in countries throughout the world.[144]

The decisions and actions of the board of directors can be an effective deterrent to unethical behaviors by top-level managers. Indeed, evidence suggests that the most effective boards set boundaries for their firms' business ethics and values.[145] After the boundaries for ethical behavior are determined, and likely formalized in a code of ethics, the board's ethics-based expectations must be clearly communicated to the firm's top-level managers and to other stakeholders (e.g., customers and suppliers) with whom interactions are necessary for the firm to produce and sell its products. Moreover, as agents of the firm's owners, top-level managers must understand that the board, acting as an internal governance mechanism, will hold them fully accountable for developing and supporting an organizational culture in which only ethical behaviors are permitted. As explained in Chapter 12, CEOs can be positive role models for improved ethical behavior.[146]

A major issue confronted by multinational companies operating in international markets is that of bribery.[147] As a whole, countries with weak institutions that have greater bribery activity tend to have fewer exports as a result. In addition, small- and medium-sized firms are the most harmed by bribery. Thus, bribery tends to limit entrepreneurial activity that can help a country's economy grow. While larger multinational firms tend to experience fewer negative outcomes, their power to exercise more ethical leadership allows them greater flexibility in selecting which markets they will enter and how they will do so.[148]

Through effective governance that results from well-designed governance mechanisms and the appropriate country institutions, top-level managers, working with others, are able to select and use strategies that result in strategic competitiveness and earning above-average returns. While some firms' governance mechanisms are ineffective, other companies are recognized for the quality of their governance activities.

World Finance evaluates the corporate governance practices of companies throughout the world. For 2015, a sampling of this group's "Best Corporate Governance Awards" by country were given to Magna International (Canada), China Communications Services Corporation (China), BASF (Germany), Prosafe (Norway), British Telecom (United Kingdom), and Intel (United States). These awards are determined by analyzing a number of issues concerned with corporate governance, such as board accountability and financial disclosure, executive compensation, shareholder rights, ownership base, takeover provisions, corporate behavior, and overall responsibility exhibited by the company.[149]

SUMMARY

- Corporate governance is a relationship among stakeholders that is used to determine a firm's direction and control its performance. How firms monitor and control top-level managers' decisions and actions affects the implementation of strategies. Effective governance that aligns managers' decisions with shareholders' interests can help produce a competitive advantage for the firm.

- Three internal governance mechanisms are used in the modern corporation:

  - ownership concentration
  - the board of directors
  - executive compensation

  The market for corporate control is an external governance mechanism influencing managers' decisions and the outcomes resulting from them.

- Ownership is separated from control in the modern corporation. Owners (principals) hire managers (agents) to make decisions that maximize the firm's value. As risk-bearing specialists, owners diversify their risk by investing in multiple corporations with different risk profiles. Owners expect their agents (the firm's top-level managers, who are decision-making specialists) to

make decisions that will help to maximize the value of their firm. Thus, modern corporations are characterized by an agency relationship that is created when one party (the firm's owners) hires and pays another party (top-level managers) to use its decision-making skills.

- Separation of ownership and control creates an agency problem when an agent pursues goals that conflict with the principals' goals. Principals establish and use governance mechanisms to control this problem.

- Ownership concentration is based on the number of large-block shareholders and the percentage of shares they own. With significant ownership percentages, such as those held by large mutual funds and pension funds, institutional investors often are able to influence top-level managers' strategic decisions and actions. Thus, unlike diffuse ownership which tends to result in relatively weak monitoring and control of managerial decisions, concentrated ownership produces more active and effective monitoring. Institutional investors are a powerful force in corporate America and actively use their positions of concentrated ownership to force managers and boards of directors to make decisions that best serve shareholders' interests.

■ In the United States and the United Kingdom, a firm's board of directors, composed of insiders, related outsiders, and outsiders, is a governance mechanism expected to represent shareholders' interests. The percentage of outside directors on many boards now exceeds the percentage of inside directors. Through implementation of the SOX Act, outsiders are expected to be more independent of a firm's top-level managers compared with directors selected from inside the firm. Relatively recent rules formulated and implemented by the SEC to allow owners with large stakes to propose new directors are beginning to change the balance even more in favor of outside and independent directors. Additional governance-related regulations have resulted from the Dodd-Frank Act.

■ Executive compensation is a highly visible and often criticized governance mechanism. Salary, bonuses, and long-term incentives are used for the purpose of aligning managers' and shareholders' interests. A firm's board of directors is responsible for determining the effectiveness of the firm's executive compensation system. An effective system results in managerial decisions that are in shareholders' best interests.

■ In general, evidence suggests that shareholders and boards of directors have become more vigilant in controlling managerial decisions. Nonetheless, these mechanisms are imperfect and sometimes insufficient. When the internal mechanisms fail, the market for corporate control—as an external governance mechanism—becomes relevant. Although it, too, is imperfect, the market for corporate control has been effective resulting in corporations reducing inefficient diversification and implementing more effective strategic decisions.

■ Corporate governance structures used in Germany, Japan, and China differ from each other and from the structure used in the United States. Historically, the U.S. governance structure focused on maximizing shareholder value. In Germany, employees, as a stakeholder group, take a more prominent role in governance. By contrast, until recently, Japanese shareholders played virtually no role in monitoring and controlling top-level managers. However, Japanese firms are now being challenged by "activist" shareholders. In China, the central government still plays a major role in corporate governance practices. Internationally, all these systems are becoming increasingly similar, as are many governance systems both in developed countries, such as France and Spain, and in transitional economies, such as Brazil and India.

■ Effective governance mechanisms ensure that the interests of all stakeholders are served. Thus, strategic competitiveness results when firms are governed in ways that permit, at least, minimal satisfaction of capital market stakeholders (e.g., shareholders), product market stakeholders (e.g., customers and suppliers), and organizational stakeholders (e.g., managerial and non-managerial employees; see Chapter 2). Moreover, effective governance produces ethical behavior in the formulation and implementation of strategies.

KEY TERMS

agency costs 316
agency relationship 313
board of directors 319
corporate governance 310
executive compensation 322

institutional owners 318
large-block shareholders 317
managerial opportunism 314
market for corporate control 325
ownership concentration 317

REVIEW QUESTIONS

1. What is corporate governance? What factors account for the considerable amount of attention corporate governance receives from several parties, including shareholder activists, business press writers, and academic scholars? Why is governance necessary to control managers' decisions?

2. What is meant by the statement that ownership is separated from managerial control in the corporation? Why does this separation exist?

3. What is an agency relationship? What is managerial opportunism? What assumptions do owners of corporations make about managers as agents?

4. How is each of the three internal governance mechanisms—ownership concentration, boards of directors, and executive compensation—used to align the interests of managerial agents with those of the firm's owners?

5. What trends exist regarding executive compensation? What is the effect of the increased use of long-term incentives on top-level managers' strategic decisions?

6. What is the market for corporate control? What conditions generally cause this external governance mechanism to become active? How does this mechanism constrain top-level managers' decisions and actions?

7. What is the nature of corporate governance in Germany, Japan, and China?

8. How can corporate governance foster ethical decisions and behaviors on the part of managers as agents?

Mini-Case

The Imperial CEO, JPMorgan Chase's Jamie Dimon

Jamie Dimon, CEO of JPMorgan Chase & Co., is one of the very few top executives at large banks or major financial services firms who was unscathed by the substantial economic recession which began in 2008—a recession largely caused by those firms taking inappropriate risks. He is described as charismatic and an excellent leader. Yet, in 2012, JPMorgan Chase experienced its own scandal caused by exceptional risk taking. Traders in its London operations were allowed to build a huge exposure in credit derivatives that breached the acceptable risk limits of most analytical models. As a result, the bank suffered losses of more than $6 billion. It is referred to as the London Whale trading debacle. In 2013 and 2014, there were large regulatory and legal settlements. Most significant was a $13 billion settlement with regulators over mortgage bond sales in 2013. In addition, to this record settlement, "the bank paid $2.6 billion to resolve allegations that it didn't stop Bernie Madoff's Ponzi scheme and two fines of about $1 billion each stemming from currency rate manipulation and the London Whale trading loss." It may need an additional $20 billion in additional capital to satisfy regulatory bank safety rules. One Democratic Senator from Delaware, Ted Kaufman, noted: "I think Jamie Dimon is Teflon-coated."

Because of the huge loss and concerns about the lack of oversight that led to these fines and settlement, there was a move by shareholder activists to separate the CEO and chair of the board positions, requiring Dimon to hold only the CEO title. Playing key roles were the American Federation of State, County and Municipal Employees (AFSCME) and the Institutional Shareholder Services (ISS). The AFSCME was pushing to separate the holders of the CEO and chair positions at JPMorgan Chase. The ISS was pushing for shareholders to withhold the votes for three directors currently on the Morgan's board policy committee.

Dimon described the London Whale debacle as an anomaly caused by the inappropriate behavior of a few bad employees. However, this debacle plus the huge fines and settlements seems to suggest serious weaknesses in the bank's oversight of activities involving significant risk and compliance with regulatory rules.

Executives and board members of JPMorgan Chase worked hard to thwart these efforts. Lee Raymond, the former CEO of ExxonMobil who has been on the JPMorgan board for 28 years, played a key role in these efforts to support Dimon and avoid a negative vote. This group lobbied major institutional shareholders and even asked (though he declined) former U.S. President Bill Clinton to help work out a compromise with the AFSCME. They even suggested that Dimon would quit if he had to give up one of the roles and it would harm the stock price. In the end, Dimon and the bank won the vote with a two-thirds majority for Dimon to retain both positions.

Several analysts decried the vote and suggested that having a third of the shareholders vote against Dimon is not a major vote of confidence. One even suggested that the vote is not surprising because of the 10 largest institutional owners of the bank's stock, seven have CEOs who also hold the chair position. So, how could they openly argue that this is bad for JPMorgan when they do it in their organizations? Furthermore, these major institutional investors want the banks to engage in high-risk activities with the potential to produce high returns. This is especially true because the downside risk of losses is low as the government cannot afford to allow the big banks to fail.

One analyst suggested that the shareholders voted out of fear (potential loss of Dimon) and for personality instead of good corporate governance. Analysts for the *Financial Times* argued that the outcome of this vote demonstrates how weak shareholder rights are in the United States. Finally, another analyst noted that while splitting the CEO and chair positions does not guarantee good governance, it is a prerequisite for it. Lee Raymond suggested that the board would take action. Several speculate that such actions will not relate to Dimon duel positions, but rather to a reconfiguration of the board members on the risk and audit committees. Some have argued that certain members of these committees have little knowledge of their function and/or have financial ties to the bank, thereby creating a potential conflict of interest. One protection for Dimon is that the JPMorgan Chase continues to perform well, even with poor ratings from governance evaluators.

Sources: E. Bloxham, 2015, J.P. Morgan: Taking on more risk than it can handle?. *Fortune*, www.fortune.com, May 14; S. Gandel, 2015, After complaining about regulations, JPMorgan Chase beats estimates—again. *Fortune*, www.fortune.com, April 29; E. Glazer, 2014, J.P. Morgan's decade of Dimon, *Wall Street Journal*, June 30, C1; J. Eisinger, 2013, Flawed system suits the shareholders just fine, *New York Times DealBook*, http://dealbook.nytimes.com, May 29; J. Plender, 2013, The divine right of the imperial CEO, *Financial Times*, www.ft.com, May 26; J. Sommer, 2013, The CEO triumphant (at least at Apple and Chase), *New York Times*, www.nytimes.com, May 25; H. Moore, 2013, JP Morgan CEO Jamie Dimon remains the Indiana Jones of corporate America, *The Guardian*, www.guardian.com, May 21; J. Silver-Greenberg & S. Craig, 2013, Strong lobbying helps Dimon thwart a shareholder challenge, *New York Times DealBook*, http://dealbook.nytimes.com, May 21; D. Fitzpatrick, J. S. Lublin, & J. Steinberg, 2013, Vote strengthens Dimon's grip, *Wall Street Journal*, www.wsj.com, May 21; A. T. Crane & A. Currie, 2013, Dimon's Pyrrhic victory, *New York Times DealBook*, http://dealbook.nytimes.com, May 21; D. Benoit, 2013, J.P. Morgan's powerful board members, *Wall Street Journal*, www.wsj.com, May 20; M. Egan, 2013, Top J.P. Morgan directors back Dimon as CEO, Chair, *Fox Business*, www.foxbusiness.com, May 10.

Case Discussion Questions

1. How well do you think the governance system of JPMorgan Chase is working in protecting shareholder interests?

2. What particular governance devices are helping or hindering good governance in the JPMorgan Chase situation?

3. What do you recommend to improve the governance system specifically for JPMorgan Chase but also overall relative to the system of governance devices described in Chapter 10?

NOTES

1. G. Subramanian, 2015, Corporate governance 2.0. *Harvard Business Review*, 93(3): 96–105; X. Castaner & N. Kavadis, 2013, Does good governance prevent bad strategy? A study of corporate governance, financial diversification, and value creation by French corporations, 2000–2006, *Strategic Management Journal*, 34: 863–876.

2. I. Filatotchev & C. Nakajima, C. 2014, Corporate governance, responsible managerial behavior, and corporate social responsibility: Organizational efficiency versus organizational legitimacy? *Academy of Management Perspectives*, 28: 289–306; A. P. Cowen & J. J. Marcel, 2011, Damaged goods: Board decisions to dismiss reputationally compromised directors, *Academy of Management Journal*, 54: 509–527.

3. J. Joseph, W. Ocasio, & M. McDonnell, 2014, The structural elaboration of board independence: Executive power, institutional logics, and the adoption of CEO-only board structures in U.S. corporate governance, *Academy of Management Journal*, 57: 1834–1858; P. J. Davis, 2013, Senior executives and their boards: Toward a more involved director, *Journal of Business Strategy*, 34(1): 3–40.

4. S. Ayuso, M. A. Rodríguez, R. García-Castro, & M. A. Ariño, 2014, Maximizing stakeholders' interests: An empirical analysis of the stakeholder approach to corporate governance, *Business & Society*, 53: 414–439; D. R. Dalton, M. A. Hitt, S. T. Certo, & C. M. Dalton, 2008, The fundamental agency problem and its

mitigation: Independence, equity and the market for corporate control, in J. P. Walsh and A. P. Brief (eds.), *The Academy of Management Annals*, NY: Lawrence Erlbaum Associates, 1–64; E. F. Fama & M. C. Jensen, 1983, Separation of ownership and control, *Journal of Law and Economics*, 26: 301–325.

5. H. Zeitoun, M. Osterloh, & B. S. Frey, 2014, Learning from ancient Athens: Demarchy and corporate governance, *Academy of Management Perspectives*, 28: 1–14; J. S. Harrison, D. A. Bosse, & R. A. Phillips, 2010, Managing for stakeholders, stakeholder utility functions, and competitive advantage, *Strategic Management Journal*, 31: 58–74.

6. B. Soltani & C. Maupetit, 2015, Importance of core values of ethics, integrity and accountability in the European corporate governance codes, *Journal of Management & Governance*, 19: 259–284; T. J. Boulton, S. B. Smart, & C. J. Zutter, 2010, IPO underpricing and international corporate governance, *Journal of International Business Studies*, 41: 206–222.

7. A. Capasso, G. Dagnino, & W. Shen, 2014, Special issue on 'corporate governance and strategic management in different contexts: Fostering interchange of a crucial relationship', *Journal of Management & Governance*, 18: 921–927; E. Vaara, R. Sarala, G. K. Stahl, & I. Bjorkman, 2012, The impact of organizational and national cultural differences on social conflict and knowledge transfer in international acquisitions, *Journal of Management*

Studies, 49: 1–27; W. Judge, 2010, Corporate governance mechanisms throughout the world, *Corporate Governance: An International Review*, 18: 159–160.

8. L. S. Tsui-Auch & T. Yoshikawa, 2015, Institutional change versus resilience: A study of incorporation of independent directors in Singapore banks, *Asian Business & Management*, 14: 91–115.

9. G. Bell, I. Filatotchev, & R. Aguilera, 2014, Corporate governance and investors' perceptions of foreign IPO value: An institutional perspective, *Academy of Management Journal*, 57: 301–320; W. Kim, T. Sung, & S.-J. Wei, 2011, Does corporate governance risk at home affect investment choice abroad? *Journal of International Economics*, 85: 25–41.

10. H. Servaes & A. Tamayo, 2014, How do industry peers respond to control threats?. *Management Science*, 60: 380–399; J. Lee, 2013, Dancing with the enemy? Relational hazards and the contingent value of repeat exchanges in M&A markets, *Organization Science*, 24: 1237–1256; M. A. Hitt, R. E. Hoskisson, R. A. Johnson, & D. D. Moesel, 1996, The market for corporate control and firm innovation, *Academy of Management Journal*, 45: 697–716.

11. G. E. Davis & T. A. Thompson, 1994, A social movement perspective on corporate control, *Administrative Science Quarterly*, 39: 141–173.

12. F. Bertoni, M. Meoli, & S. Vismara, 2014, Board Independence, Ownership structure and the valuation of IPOs in Continental Europe, *Corporate Governance:*

An International Review, 22:116–131; V. V. Acharya, S. C. Myers, & R. G. Rajan, 2011, The internal governance of firms, *Journal of Finance*, 66: 689–720; R. Bricker & N. Chandar, 2000, Where Berle and Means went wrong: A reassessment of capital market agency and financial reporting, *Accounting, Organizations, and Society*, 25: 529–554.

13. T. M. Alessandri & A. Seth, 2014, The effects of managerial ownership on international and business diversification: Balancing incentives and risks, *Strategic Management Journal*, 35: 2064–2075; A. M. Colpan, T. Yoshikawa, T. Hikino, & E. G. Del Brio, 2011, Shareholder heterogeneity and conflicting goals: Strategic investments in the Japanese electronics industry, *Journal of Management Studies*, 48: 591–618; R. M. Wiseman & L. R. Gomez-Mejia, 1999, A behavioral agency model of managerial risk taking, *Academy of Management Review*, 23: 133–153.

14. M. Essen, M. Carney, E. R. Gedajlovic, & P. R. Heugens, 2015, How does family control influence firm strategy and performance? A meta-analysis of US publicly listed firms, *Corporate Governance: An International Review*, 23: 3–24; D. L. Deephouse & P. Jaskiewicz, 2013, Do family firms have better reputations than non-family firms? An integration of socioecomotional wealth and social identity theory, *Journal of Management Studies*, 50: 337–360; A. Minichilli, G. Corbetta, & I. C. MacMillan, 2010, Top management teams in family-controlled companies: 'Familiness', 'faultlines', and their impact on financial performance, *Journal of Management Studies*, 47: 205–222.

15. D. Miller, I. Le Breton-Miller, & R. Lester, 2013, Family firm governance, strategic conformity and performance: Institutional vs. strategic perspectives, *Organization Science*, in press; M. W. Peng & Y. Jiang, 2010, Institutions behind family ownership and control in large firms, *Journal of Management Studies*, 47: 253–273.

16. Essen, Carney, Gedajlovic, & Heugens, How does family control influence firm strategy and performance? A. meta-analysis of US publicly listed firms; E. Gedajlovic, M. Carney, J. J. Chrisman, & F. W. Kellermans, 2012, The adolescence of family firm research: Taking stock and planning for the future, *Journal of Management*, 38: 1010–1037; R. C. Anderson & D. M. Reeb, 2004, Board composition: Balancing family influence in S&P 500 firms, *Administrative Science Quarterly*, 49: 209–237.

17. Y. Cheung, I. Haw, W. Tan, & W. Wang, 2014, Board Structure and intragroup propping: Evidence from family business groups in Hong Kong. *Financial* Management, 43: 569–601; E. Lutz & S. Schrami, 2012, Family firms: Should they hire an outside CFO? *Journal of Business Strategy*, 33(1): 39–44; E.-T. Chen & J. Nowland, 2010, Optimal

board monitoring in family-owned companies: Evidence from Asia, *Corporate Governance: An International Review*, 18: 3–17.

18. J. L. Arregle, L. Naldi, M. Nordqvist, & M. A. Hitt, 2012, Internationalization of family controlled firm: A study of the effects of external involvement in governance, *Entrepreneurship Theory and Practice*, 36: 1115–1143; D. G. Sirmon, J.-L. Arregle, M. A. Hitt, & J. W. Webb, 2008, Strategic responses to the threat of imitation, *Entrepreneurship Theory and Practice*, 32: 979–998.

19. R. M. Wiseman, G. Cuevas-Rodriguez, & L. R. Gomez-Mejia, 2012, Towards a social theory of agency, *Journal of Management Studies*, 49: 202–222; G. Dushnitsky & Z. Shapira, 2010, Entrepreneurial finance meets organizational reality: Comparing investment practices and performance of corporate and independent venture capitalists, *Strategic Management Journal*, 31: 990–1017.

20. A. K. Hoenen & T. Kostova, 2014, Utilizing the broader agency perspective for studying headquarters-subsidiary relations in multinational companies, *Journal of International Business Studies*, 46: 104–113; T. J. Quigley & D. C. Hambrick, 2012, When the former CEO stays on as board chair: Effects on successor discretion, strategic change and performance, *Strategic Management Journal*, 33: 834–859.

21. R. Krause, M. Semadeni, & A. A. Cannella, 2013, External COO/presidents as expert directors: A new look at the service role of boards, *Strategic Management Journal*, 34: 1628–1641; A. Mackey, 2008, The effects of CEOs on firm performance, *Strategic Management Journal*, 29: 1357–1367.

22. W. Li & Y. Lu, 2012, CEO dismissal, institutional development and environmental dynamism, *Asia Pacific Journal of Management*, 29: 1007–1026; L. L. Lan & L. Heracleous, 2010, Rethinking agency theory: The view from law, *Academy of Management Review*, 35: 294–314; Dalton, Hitt, Certo, & Dalton, 2008, The fundamental agency problem and its mitigation: Independence, equity and the market for corporate control.

23. B. Kang & R. P Jindal, 2015, Opportunism in buyer-seller relationships: Some unexplored antecedents, *Journal of Business Research*, 68: 735–742; K. Vafai, 2010, Opportunism in organizations, *Journal of Law, Economics, and Organization*, 26: 158–181; O. E. Williamson, 1996, *The Mechanisms of Governance*, NY: Oxford University Press, 6.

24. Y. Luo, Y. Liu, Q. Yang, V. Maksimov, & J. Hou, 2015, Improving performance and reducing cost in buyer-supplier relationships: The role of justice in curtailing opportunism, *Journal of Business Research*, 68: 607–615; F. Lumineau & D. Malhotra, 2011, Shadow of the contract: How contract structure

shapes interfirm dispute resolution, *Strategic Management Journal*, 32: 532–555.

25. B. Balsmeier, A. Buchwald, & J. Stiebale, 2014, Outside directors on the board and innovative firm performance, *Research Policy*, 43: 1800–1815; M. L. McDonald, P. Khanna, & J. D. Westphal, 2008, Getting them to think outside the circle: Corporate governance CEOs' external advice networks, and firm performance, *Academy of Management Journal*, 51: 453–475.

26. Y. Ning, X. Hu, & X. Garza-Gomez, 2015, An empirical analysis of the impact of large changes in institutional ownership on CEO compensation risk, *Journal of Economics & Finance*, 39: 23–47; J. Harris, S. Johnson, & D. Souder, 2013, Model theoretic knowledge accumulation: The case of agency theory and incentive alignment, *Academy of Management Review*, 38: 442–454; L. Weber & K. J. Mayer, 2011, Designing effective contracts: Exploring the influence of framing and expectations, *Academy of Management Review*, 36: 53–75.

27. T. J. Boulton, M. V. Braga-Alves, & F. P. Schlingemann, 2014, Does equity-based compensation make CEOs more acquisitive?, *Journal of Financial Research*, 37: 267–294; T. Hutzschenreuter & J. Horstkotte, 2013, Performance effects of top management team demographic faultlines in the process of product diversification, *Strategic Management Journal*, 34: 704–726; E. Levitas, V. L. Barker, III, & M. Ahsan, 2011, Top manager ownership levels and incentive alignment in inventively active firms, *Journal of Strategy and Management*, 4: 116–135.

28. D. E. Black, S. S. Dikolli, & S. D. Dyreng, 2014, CEO pay-for-complexity and the risk of managerial diversion from multinational diversification, *Contemporary Accounting Research*, 31: 103–135 P. David, J. P. O'Brien, T. Yoshikawa, & A. Delios, 2010, Do shareholders or stakeholders appropriate the rents from corporate diversification? The influence of ownership structure, *Academy of Management Journal*, 53: 636–654; G. P. Baker & B. J. Hall, 2004, CEO incentives and firm size, *Journal of Labor Economics*, 22: 767–798.

29. A. S. Hornstein & Z. Nguyen, 2014, Is more less? Propensity to diversify via M&A and market reaction, *International Review of Financial Analysis*, 34: 76–88; S. W. Geiger & L. H. Cashen, 2007, Organizational size and CEO compensation: The moderating effect of diversification in downscoping organizations, *Journal of Managerial Issues*, 9: 233–252.

30. B. W. Benson, J. C. Park, & W. N. Davidson, 2014, Equity-based incentives, risk aversion, and merger-related risk-taking behavior, *Financial Review*, 49: 117–148; M. Larraza-Kintana, L. R. Gomez-Mejia, & R. M. Wiseman, 2011, Compensation framing and the risk-taking behavior of the CEO: Testing the influence of alternative

reference points, *Management Research: The Journal of the Iberoamerican Academy of Management*, 9: 32–55.

31. 2014, Lockheed Martin, Annual Report, www.lockheedmartin.com, May 20; B. Kowitt, 2013, Lockheed's secret weapon, *Fortune*, May 20, 196–204.

32. M. S. Jensen, 1986, Agency costs of free cash flow, corporate finance, and takeovers, *American Economic Review*, 76: 323–329.

33. J. P. O'Brien, P. David, T. Yoshikawa, & A. Delios, 2014, How capital structure influences diversification performance: A transaction cost perspective, *Strategic Management Journal*, 35: 1013–1031; R. E. Meyer & M. A. Hollerer, 2010, Meaning structures in a contested issue field: A topographic map of shareholder value in Austria, *Academy of Management Journal*, 53: 1241–1262; M. Jensen & E. Zajac, 2004, Corporate elites and corporate strategy: How demographic preferences and structural position shape the scope of the firm, *Strategic Management Journal*, 25: 507–524.

34. T. B. Mackey & J. B. Barney, 2013, Incorporating opportunity costs in strategic management research: The value of diversification and payout as opportunities forgone when reinvesting in the firm. *Strategic Organization*, 11: 347–363; S. F. Matusik & M. A. Fitza, 2012, Diversification in the venture capital industry: Leveraging knowledge under uncertainty, *Strategic Management Journal*, 33: 407–426; G. Kenny, 2012, Diversification: Best practices of the leading companies, *Journal of Business Strategy*, 33(1): 12–20.

35. T. M. Alessandri & A. Seth, 2014, The effects of managerial ownership on international and business diversification: Balancing incentives and risks, *Strategic Management Journal*, 35: 2064–2075; M. V. S. Kumar, 2013, The costs of related diversification: The impact of the core business on the productivity of related segments, *Organization Science*, 24: 1827–1846; F. Neffke & M. Henning, Skill relatedness and firm diversification, *Strategic Management Journal*, 34: 297–316.

36. S. Pathak, R. E. Hoskisson, & R. A. Johnson, 2014, Settling up in CEO compensation: The impact of divestiture intensity and contextual factors in refocusing firms, *Strategic Management Journal*, 35: 1124–1143; D. D. Bergh, R. A. Johnson, & R.-L. Dewitt, 2008, Restructuring through spin-off or sell-off: Transforming information asymmetries into financial gain, *Strategic Management Journal*, 29: 133–148.

37. S. K. Kim, J. D. Arthurs, A. Sahaym, & J. B. Cullen, 2013, Search behavior of the diversified firm: The impact of fit on innovation, *Strategic Management Journal*, 34: 999–1009.

38. J. Kang, 2013, The relationship between corporate diversification and corporate social performance, *Strategic Management Journal*, 34: 94–109.

39. K Kong-Hee & A. A. Rasheed, 2014, board heterogeneity, corporate diversification and firm performance, *Journal of Management Research:* 14: 121–139; E. Rawley, 2010, Diversification, coordination costs, and organizational rigidity: Evidence from microdata, *Strategic Management Journal*, 31: 873–891; T. K. Berry, J. M. Bizjak, M. L. Lemmon, & L. Naveen, 2006, Organizational complexity and CEO labor markets: Evidence from diversified firms, *Journal of Corporate Finance*, 12: 797–817.

40. U. V. Lilienfeld-Toal & S. Ruenzi, 2014, CEO ownership, stock market performance, and managerial discretion, *Journal of Finance*, 69: 1013–1050; R. Krause & M. Semadeni, 2013, Apprentice, departure and demotion: An examination of the three types of CEO-board chair separation, *Academy of Management Journal*, 56: 805–826.

41. W. Rees & T. Rodionova, 2015, The Influence of family ownership on corporate social responsibility: An international analysis of publicly listed companies, *Corporate Governance: An International Review*, 23: 184–202; J. L. Walls, P. Berrone, & P. H. Phan, 2012, Corporate governance and environmental performance: Is there really a link? *Strategic Management Journal*, 33: 885–913; C. J. Kock, J. Santalo, & L. Diestre, 2012, Corporate governance and the environment: What type of governance creates greener companies? *Journal of Management Studies*, 49: 492–514.

42. J. C. Coates & S. Srinivasan, 2014, SOX after ten years: A multidisciplinary review, *Accounting Horizons*, 28: 627–671; M. Hossain, S. Mitra, Z. Rezaee, & B. Sarath, 2011, Corporate governance and earnings management in the pre- and post-Sarbanes-Oxley act regimes: Evidence from implicated option backdating firms, *Journal of Accounting Auditing & Finance*, 28: 279–315; V. Chhaochharia & Y. Grinstein, 2007, Corporate governance and firm value: The impact of the 2002 governance rules, *Journal of Finance*, 62: 1789–1825.

43. S. C. Rice, D. P. Weber, & W. Biyu, 2015, Does SOX 404 have teeth? Consequences of the failure to report existing internal control weaknesses, *Accounting Review*, 90: 1169–1200; Z. Singer & H. You, 2011, The effect of Section 404 of the Sarbanes-Oxley Act on earnings quality, *Journal of Accounting and Finance*, 26: 556–589.

44. 2010, The Dodd-Frank Act: Financial reform update index, Faegre & Benson, www.faegre.com, September 7.

45. B. Appelmaum, 2011, Dodd-Frank supporters clash with currency chief, *New York Times*, www.nytimes.com, July 23.

46. B. J. Bushee, M. E. Carter, & J. Gerakos, 2014, Institutional investor preferences for corporate governance mechanisms, *Journal of Management Accounting Research*, 26: 123–149; M. Goranova, R. Dhanwadkar, & P. Brandes, 2010, Owners on both sides of the deal: Mergers and acquisitions

and overlapping institutional ownership, *Strategic Management Journal*, 31: 1114–1135; F. Navissi & V. Naiker, 2006, Institutional ownership and corporate value, *Managerial Finance*, 32: 247–256.

47. J. C. Hartzell, L Sun, & S. Titman, S. 2014, Institutional investors as monitors of corporate diversification decisions: Evidence from real estate investment trusts, *Journal of Corporate Finance*, 25: 61–72; B. L. Connelly, R. E. Hoskisson, L. Tihanyi, & S. T. Certo, 2010, Ownership as a form of corporate governance, *Journal of Management Studies*, 47: 1561–1589; M. Singh, I. Mathur, & K. C. Gleason, 2004, Governance and performance implications of diversification strategies: Evidence from large U.S. firms, *Financial Review*, 39: 489–526.

48. I. Busta, E. Sinani, & S. Thomsen, 2014, Ownership concentration and market value of European banks, *Journal of Management & Governance*, 18: 159–183; K. A. Desender, R. A. Aguilera, R. Crespi, & M. Garcia-Cestona, 2013, When does ownership matter? Board characteristics and behavior, *Strategic Management Journal*, 34: 823–842; J. Wu, D. Xu, & P. H. Phan, 2011, The effects of ownership concentration and corporate debt on corporate divestitures in Chinese listed firms, *Asia Pacific Journal of Management*, 28: 95–114.

49. M. van Essen, J. van Oosterhout, & P. Heugens, 2013, Competition and cooperation in corporate governance: The effects of labor institutions on blockholder effectiveness in 23 European countries, *Organization Science*, 24: 530–551.

50. C. Inoue, S. Lazzarni, & A. Musacchio, 2013, Leviathan as a minority shareholder: Firm-level implications of equity purchases by the state, *Academy of Management Journal*, 56: 1775–1801.

51. C. Singla, R. Veliyath, & R. George, 2014, Family firms and internationalization-governance relationships: Evidence of secondary agency issues, *Strategic Management Journal*, 35: 606–616; S.-Y. Collin & J. Ahlberg, 2012, Blood in the boardroom: Family relationships influencing the functions of the board, *Journal of Family Business Strategy*, 3: 207–219.

52. A. Zattoni, L. Gnan, & M. Huse, 2015, Does family involvement influence firm performance? Exploring the mediating effects of board processes and tasks, *Journal of Management*, 41: 1214–1243; D. Miller, A. Minichilli, & G. Corbetta, 2013, Is family leadership always beneficial? *Strategic Management Journal*, 34: 553–571; J. J. Chrisman, J. H. Chua, A. W. Pearson, & T. Barnett, 2012, Family involvement, family influence and family-centered non-economic goals in small firms, *Entrepreneurship Theory and Practice*, 36: 1103–1113.

53. L. R. Gomez-Mejia, J. T. Campbell, G. Martin, R. E. Hoskisson, M. Makri, & D. G. Sirmon, 2014, Socioemotional wealth as a mixed gamble: Revisiting family firm R&D investments with the behavioral agency model, *Entrepreneurship: Theory & Practice*, 38: 1351–1374; A. Konig, N. Kammerlander, & A. Enders, 2013, The family innovator's dilemma: How family influence affects the adoption of discontinuous technologies by incumbent firms, *Academy of Management Review*, 38: 418–441; J. J. Chrisman & P. C. Patel, 2012, Variations in R&D investments of family and nonfamily firms: Behavioral agency and myopic loss aversion perspectives, *Academy of Management Journal*, 55: 976–997.

54. A. Berle & G. Means, 1932, *The Modern Corporation and Private Property*, NY: Macmillan.

55. M. Wang, 2014, Which types of institutional investors constrain abnormal accruals?, *Corporate Governance: An International Review*, 22: 43–67; R. A. Johnson, K. Schnatterly, S. G. Johnson, & S.-C. Chiu, 2010, Institutional investors and institutional environment: A comparative analysis and review, *Journal of Management Studies*, 47: 1590–1613; M. Gietzmann, 2006, Disclosure of timely and forward-looking statements and strategic management of major institutional ownership, *Long Range Planning*, 39: 409–427.

56. D. Marchick, 2011, Testimony of David Marchick—The power of pensions: Building a strong middle class and a strong economy, The Carlyle Group homepage, www.carlyle.com, July 12.

57. J. Chou, L. Ng, V. Sibilkov, & Q. Wang, 2011, Product market competition and corporate governance, *Review of Development Finance*, 1: 114–130; S. D. Chowdhury & E. Z. Wang, 2009, Institutional activism types and CEO compensation: A time-series analysis of large Canadian corporations, *Journal of Management*, 35: 5–36.

58. R. Krause, K. A. Whitler, & M. Semadeni, 2014, Power to the principals! An experimental look at shareholder say-on-pay voting, *Academy of Management Journal*, 57: 94–115; Y. Ertimur, F. Ferri, & S. R. Stubben, 2010, Board of directors' responsiveness to shareholders: Evidence from shareholder proposals, *Journal of Corporate Finance*, 16: 53–72.

59. C. Mallin, 2012, Institutional investors: the vote as a tool of governance, *Journal of Management & Governance*, 16: 177–196; D. Brewster, 2009, U.S. investors get to nominate boards, *Financial Times*, www. ft.com, May 20.

60. S. Craig, 2013, The giant of shareholders, quietly stirring, *New York Times*, www. nytimes.com, May 18.

61. 2015, BlackRock's Fink tells S&P 500 firms to think long-term, *Fortune*, www.fortune. com, April 29

62. X. Liu, D. D. van Jaarsveld, R. Batt, & A. C. Frost, 2014, The influence of capital structure on strategic human capital: Evidence from U.S. And Canadian firms. *Journal of Management*, 40: 422–448; M. Hadani, M. Goranova, & R. Khan, 2011, Institutional investors, shareholder activism, and earnings management, *Journal of Business Research*, 64: 1352–1360; L. Tihanyi, R. A. Johnson, R. E. Hoskisson, & M. A. Hitt, 2003, Institutional ownership differences and international diversification: The effects of boards of directors and technological opportunity, *Academy of Management Journal*, 46: 195–211.

63. M. L. Heyden, J. Oehmichen, S. Nichting, & H. W. Volberda, 2015, Board background heterogeneity and exploration-exploitation: The role of the institutionally adopted board model, *Global Strategy Journal*, 5: 154–176; S. Garg, 2013, Venture boards: Differences with public boards and implications for monitoring and firm performance, *Academy of Management Review*, 38: 90–108; O. Faleye, R. Hoitash, & U. Hoitash, 2011, The costs of intense board monitoring, *Journal of Financial Economics*, 101: 160–181.

64. D. Barton & M. Wiseman, 2015, Where boards fall short, *Harvard Business Review*, 93(1/2): 98–104; J. T. Campbell, T. C. Campbell, D. G. Sirmon, L. Bierman, & C. S. Tuggle, 2012, Shareholder influence over director nomination via proxy access: Implications for agency conflict and stakeholder value, *Strategic Management Journal*, 33: 1431–1451; C. M. Dalton & D. R. Dalton, 2010, Corporate governance best practices: The proof is in the process, *Journal of Business Strategy*, 27(4): 5–7.

65. A. Tushke, W. G. Sanders, & E. Hernandez, 2014, Whose experience matters in the boardroom? The effects of experiential and vicarious learning on emerging market entry, *Strategic Management Journal*, 35: 398–418; T. Dalziel, R. J. Gentry, & M. Bowerman, 2011, An integrated agency-resource dependence view of the influence of directors' human and relational capital on firms' R&D spending, *Journal of Management Studies*, 48: 1217–1242.

66. P. Khanna, C. D. Jones, & S. Boivie, 2014, Director human capital, information processing demands, and board effectiveness, *Journal of Management*, 40: 557–585; O. Faleye, 2011, CEO directors, executive incentives, and corporate strategic initiatives, *Journal of Financial Research*, 34: 241–277; C. S. Tuggle, D. G. Sirmon, C. R. Reutzel, & L. Bierman, 2010, Commanding board of director attention: Investigating how organizational performance and CEO duality affect board members' attention to monitoring, *Strategic Management Journal*, 31: 946–968.

67. C. Sundaramurthy, K. Pukthuanthong, & Y. Kor, 2014, Positive and negative synergies between the CEO's and the corporate board's human and social capital: A study of biotechnology firms, *Strategic Management Journal*, 35: 845–868; S. Chahine, I. Filatotchev, & S. A. Zahra, 2011, Building perceived quality of founder-involved IPO firms: Founders' effects on board selection and stock market performance, *Entrepreneurship Theory and Practice*, 35: 319–335; Y. Ertimur, F. Ferri, & S. R. Stubben, 2010, Board of directors' responsiveness to shareholders: Evidence from shareholder proposals, *Journal of Corporate Finance*, 16: 53–72.

68. E. Peni, 2014, CEO and Chairperson characteristics and firm performance, *Journal of Management & Governance*, 18: 185–205; M. A. Valenti, R. Luce, & C. Mayfield, 2011, The effects of firm performance on corporate governance, *Management Research Review*, 34: 266–283; D. Reeb & A. Upadhyay, 2010, Subordinate board structures, *Journal of Corporate Finance*, 16: 469–486.

69. A. D. Upadhyay, R. Bhargava, & S. D. Faircloth, 2014, Board structure and role of monitoring committees, *Journal of Business Research*, 67: 1486–1492; B. Bolton, 2014, Audit committee performance: ownership vs. independence—Did SOX get it wrong?, *Accounting & Finance*, 54: 83–112.

70. D. H. Zhu, W. Shen, & A. J. Hillman, 2014, Recategorization into the in-group: The appointment of demographically different new directors and their subsequent positions on corporate boards, *Administrative Science Quarterly*, 59: 240–270; A. Holehonnur & T. Pollock, 2013, Shoot for the stars? Predicting the recruitment of prestigious directors at newly public firms, *Academy of Management Journal*, 56: 1396–1419; M. McDonald & J. Westphal, 2013, Access denied: Low mentoring of women and minority first-time directors and its negative effects on appointments to additional boards, *Academy of Management Journal*, 56: 1169–1198.

71. Joseph, Ocasio, & McDonnell, The structural elaboration of board independence: Executive power, institutional logics, and the adoption of CEO-only board structures in U.S. corporate governance; R. C. Anderson, D. M. Reeb, A. Upadhyay, & W. Zhao, 2011, The economics of director heterogeneity, *Financial Management*, 40: 5–38; S. K. Lee & L. R. Carlson, 2007, The changing board of directors: Board independence in S&P 500 firms, *Journal of Organizational Culture, Communication and Conflict*, 11: 31–41.

72. R. Krause, M. Semadeni, & A. A. Cannella, 2014, CEO Duality: A review and research agenda, *Journal of Management*, 40: 256–286; S. Crainer, 2011, Changing direction: One person can make a difference, *Business Strategy Review*, 22: 10–16; R. C. Pozen, 2006, Before you split that CEO/chair, *Harvard Business Review* 84(4): 26–28.

73. E. Glazer, 2014, J.P. Morgan's decade of Dimon, *Wall Street Journal*, June 30, C1.

74. Barton & Wiseman, Where boards fall short; M. Huse, R. E. Hoskisson, A. Zattoni, & R. Vigano, 2011, New perspectives on board research: Changing the research agenda, *Journal of Management and Governance*, 15: 5–28; M. Kroll, B. A. Walters, & P. Wright, 2008, Board vigilance, director experience and corporate outcomes, *Strategic Management Journal*, 29: 363–382.

75. J. L. Coles, N. D. Daniel, & L. Naveen, 2014, Co-opted boards, *Review of Financial Studies*, 27: 1751–1796; S. Boivie, S. D. Graffin, & T. G. Pollock, 2012, Time for me to fly: Predicting director exit at large firms, *Academy of Management Journal*, 55: 1334–1359; A. Agrawal & M. A. Chen, 2011, Boardroom brawls: An empirical analysis of disputes involving directors, http://ssrn.com/abstracts=1362143.

76. J. C. Bedard, R. Hoitash, & U. Hoitash, 2014, Chief financial officers as inside directors, *Contemporary Accounting Research*, 31: 787–817; S. Muthusamy, P. A. Bobinski, & D. Jawahar, 2011, Toward a strategic role for employees in corporate governance, *Strategic Change*, 20: 127–138; Y. Zhang & N. Rajagopalan, 2010, Once an outsider, always an outsider? CEO origin, strategic change, and firm performance, *Strategic Management Journal*, 31: 334–346.

77. R. Krause & G. Bruton, 2014, Agency and monitoring clarity on venture boards of directors, *Academy of Management Review*, 39: 111–114; B. Baysinger & R. E. Hoskisson, 1990, The composition of boards of directors and strategic control: Effects on corporate strategy, *Academy of Management Review*, 15: 72–87.

78. B. Balsmeier, A. Buchwald, & J. Stiebale, 2014, Outside directors on the board and innovative firm performance, *Research Policy*, 43: 1800–1815; D. H. Zhu, 2013, Group polarization on corporate boards: Theory and evidence on board decisions about acquisition premiums, *Strategic Management Journal*, 800–822; G. A. Ballinger & J. J. Marcel, 2010, The use of an interim CEO during succession episodes and firm performance, *Strategic Management Journal*, 31: 262–283.

79. 2014, Low director turnover draws investor scrutiny, *Directors & Boards*, 38: 61; Boivie, Graffin, & Pollock, Time for me to fly; C. Shropshire, 2010, The role of the interlocking director and board receptivity in the diffusion of practices, *Academy of Management Review*, 35: 246–264.

80. 2015, Lead director charter, www.franklinresources.com, accessed on June 6; D. Carey, J. J. Keller, & M. Patsalos-Fox, 2010, How to choose the right nonexecutive board leader, *McKinsey Quarterly*, May.

81. A. J. Hillman, 2015, Board diversity: Beginning to unpeel the onion, *Corporate Governance: An International Review*, 23: 104–107; M. K. Bednar, 2012, Watchdog or lapdog? A behavioral role view of the media as a corporate governance mechanism, *Academy of Management Journal*, 55: 131–150; D. Northcott & J. Smith, 2011, Managing performance at the top: A balanced scorecard for boards of directors, *Journal of Accounting & Organizational Change*, 7: 33–56.

82. E. K. Lim & B. T. Mccann, 2013, The influence of relative values of outside director stock options on firm strategic risk from a multiagent perspective, *Strategic Management Journal*, 34: 1568–1590; I. Okhmatovskiy & R. J. David, 2011, Setting your own standards: Internal corporate governance codes as a response to institutional pressure, *Organization Science*, 1–22; J. L. Koors, 2006, Director pay: A work in progress, *The Corporate Governance Advisor*, 14: 14–31.

83. Y. Deutsch & M. Valente, 2013, The trouble with stock compensation, *MIT Sloan Management Review*, 54: 19–20; Y. Deutsch, T. Keil, & T. Laamanen, 2007, Decision making in acquisitions: The effect of outside directors' compensation on acquisition patterns, *Journal of Management*, 33: 30–56.

84. C. Post & K Byron, 2015, Women on boards and firm financial performance: A metaanalysis, *Academy of Management Journal*, in press; D. Cumming, T. Y. Leung, & O. Rui, 2015, Gender diversity and securities fraud, *Academy of Management Journal*, in press; A. J. Hillman, C. Shropshire, & A. A. Cannella, Jr., 2007, Organizational predictors of women on corporate boards, *Academy of Management Journal*, 50: 941–952.

85. E. A. Fong, X. Xing, W. H. Orman, & W. I. Mackenzie, 2015, Consequences of deviating from predicted CEO labor market compensation on long-term firm value, *Journal of Business Research*, 68: 299–305; M. van Essen, P. Heugens, J. Otten, & J. van Oosterhout, 2012, An institution-based view of executive compensation: A multilevel meta-analytic test, *Journal of International Business Studies*, 43: 396–423; M. J. Conyon, J. E. Core, & W. R. Guay, 2011, Are U.S. CEOs paid more than U.K. CEOs? Inferences from risk-adjusted pay, *Review of Financial Studies*, 24: 402–438.

86. M. van Essen, J. Otten, & E. J. Carberry, 2015, Assessing managerial power theory: a meta-analytic approach to understanding the determinants of CEO compensation, *Journal of Management*, 41: 164–202; C. Mangen & M. Magnan, 2012, "Say on pay": A wolf in sheep's clothing? *Academy of Management Perspectives*, 26: 86–104; E. A. Fong, V. F. Misangyi, Jr., & H. L. Tosi, 2010, The effect of CEO pay deviations on CEO withdrawal, firm size, and firm profits, *Strategic Management Journal*, 31: 629–651; J. P. Walsh, 2009, Are U.S. CEOs overpaid? A partial response to Kaplan, *Academy of Management Perspectives*, 23: 73–75.

87. A. Pepper & J. Gore, 2015, Behavioral agency theory: New foundations for theorizing about executive compensation, *Journal of Management*, 41: 1045–1068; G. P. Martin, L. R. Gomez-Mejia, & R. M. Wiseman, 2013, Executive stock options as mixed gambles: Revisiting the behavioral agency model, *Academy of Management Journal*, 56: 451–472; K. Rehbein, 2007, Explaining CEO compensation: How do talent, governance, and markets fit in? *Academy of Management Perspectives*, 21: 75–77.

88. E. Croci & D. Petmezas, 2015, Do risk-taking incentives induce CEOs to invest? Evidence from acquisitions, *Journal of Corporate Finance*, 32: 1–23; T. M. Alessandri, T. W. Tong, & J. J. Reuer, 2012, Firm heterogeneity in growth option value: The role of managerial incentives, *Strategic Management Journal*, 33: 1557–1566; D. H. M. Chng, M. S. Rodgers, E. Shih, & X.-B. Song, 2012, When does incentive compensation motivate managerial behaviors? An experimental investigation of the fit between compensation, executive core self-evaluation, and firm performance, *Strategic Management Journal*, 33: 1343–1362.

89. S. Jayaraman & T. Milbourn, 2015, CEO equity incentives and financial misreporting: The role of auditor expertise, *Accounting Review*, 90: 321–350; E. A. Fong, 2010, Relative CEO underpayment and CEO behavior towards R&D spending, *Journal of Management Studies*, 47: 1095–1122; X. Zhang, K. M. Bartol, K. G. Smith, M. D. Pfarrer, & D. M. Khanin, 2008, CEOs on the edge: Earnings manipulations and stock-based incentive misalignment, *Academy of Management Journal*, 51: 241–258; J. P. O'Connor, R. L. Priem, J. E. Coombs, & K. M. Gilley, 2006, Do CEO stock options prevent or promote fraudulent financial reporting? *Academy of Management Journal*, 49: 483–500.

90. J. J. Gerakos, J. D. Piotroski, & S. Srinivasan, 2013, Which U.S. market interactions affect CEO pay? Evidence from UK companies, *Management Science*, 59: 2413–2434; Y. Du, M. Deloof, & A Jorissen, 2011, Active boards of directors in foreign subsidiaries, *Corporate Governance: An International Review*, 19: 153–168; J. J. Reuer, E. Klijn, F. A. J. van den Bosch, & H. W. Volberda, 2011, Bringing corporate governance to international joint ventures, *Global Strategy Journal*, 1: 54–66.

91. S. Tsao, C. Lin, & V. Y. Chen, V. Y. 2015, Family ownership as a moderator between R&D investments and CEO compensation, *Journal of Business Research*, 68: 599–606; A. Ghosh, 2006, Determination of executive compensation in an emerging economy: Evidence from India, *Emerging Markets, Finance & Trade*, 42: 66–90.

92. J. J. Reuer, E. Klijn, & C. S. Lioukas, 2014, Board involvement in international joint ventures, *Strategic Management Journal*,

35: 1626–1644; M. Ederhof, 2011, Incentive compensation and promotion-based incentives of mid-level managers: Evidence from a multinational corporation, *The Accounting Review*, 86: 131–154; C. L. Staples, 2007, Board globalization in the world's largest TNCs 1993–2005, *Corporate Governance*, 15: 311–332.

93. G. Pandher & R. Currie, 2013, CEO compensation: A resource advantage and stakeholder-bargaining perspective, *Strategic Management Journal*, 34: 22–41; Y. Deutsch, T. Keil, & T. Laamanen, 2011, A dual agency view of board compensation: The joint effects of outside director and CEO stock options on firm risk, *Strategic Management Journal*, 32: 212–227.

94. Krause, Whitler, & Semadeni, Power to the principals! An experimental look at shareholder say-on-pay voting; L. K. Meulbroek, 2001, The efficiency of equity-linked compensation: Understanding the full cost of awarding executive stock options, *Financial Management*, 30: 5–44.

95. L H. Chan, K. W. Chen, C. Tai Yuan, & Y. Yangxin, 2015, Substitution between real and accruals-based earnings management after voluntary adoption of compensation clawback provisions, *Accounting Review*, 90: 147–174; 2013, The experts: Do companies spend too much on 'superstar' CEOs? *Wall Street Journal*, www.wsj.com, March 14.

96. E. K. Lim, 2015, The role of reference point in CEO restricted stock and its impact on R&D intensity in high-technology firms, *Strategic Management Journal*, 36: 872–889; Z. Dong, C. Wang, & F. Xie, 2010, Do executive stock options induce excessive risk taking? *Journal of Banking & Finance*, 34: 2518–2529; C. E. Devers, R. M. Wiseman, & R. M. Holmes, Jr., 2007, The effects of endowment and loss aversion in managerial stock option valuation, *Academy of Management Journal*, 50: 191–208.

97. C. Veld & B. H. Wu, 2014, What drives executive stock option backdating?, *Journal of Business Finance & Accounting*, 41: 1042–1070; T. G. Pollock, H. M. Fischer, & J. B. Wade, 2002, The role of politics in reprising executive options, *Academy of Management Journal*, 45: 1172–1182.

98. P. Berrone & L. R. Gomez-Mejia, 2009, Environmental performance and executive compensation: An integrated agency-institutional perspective, *Academy of Management Journal*, 52: 103–126.

99. R. V. Aguilera, K. Desender, M. K. Bednar, & J. H. Lee, 2015, Connecting the dots: Bringing external corporate governance into the corporate governance puzzle, *Academy of Management Annals*, 9:483–573; V. V. Acharya, S. C. Myers, & R. G. Rajan, 2011, The internal governance of firms, *Journal of Finance*, 66: 689–720; R. Sinha, 2006, Regulation: The market for corporate control and corporate governance, *Global Finance Journal*, 16: 264–282.

100. T. Laamanen, M. Brauer, & O. Junna, 2014, Performance of divested assets: Evidence from the U.S. software industry, *Strategic Management Journal*, 35: 914–925; T. Yoshikawa & A. A. Rasheed, 2010, Family control and ownership monitoring in family-controlled firms in Japan, *Journal of Management Studies*, 47: 274–295; R. W. Masulis, C. Wang, & F. Xie, 2007, Corporate governance and acquirer returns, *Journal of Finance*, 62: 1851–1889.

101. A. Macias & C. Pirinsky, C. 2015, Employees and the market for corporate control, *Journal of Corporate Finance*, 31: 33–53; C. Devers, G. McNamara, J. Haleblian, & M. Yoder, 2013, Do they walk the talk? Gauging acquiring CEO and director confidence in the value-creation potential of announced acquisitions, *Academy of Management Journal*, 56: 1679–1702; P.-X. Meschi & E. Metais, 2013, Do firms forget about their past acquisitions? Evidence from French acquisitions in the United States (1988–2006), *Journal of Management*, 39: 469–495; J. A. Krug & W. Shill, 2008, The big exit: Executive churn in the wake of M&As, *Journal of Business Strategy*, 29(4): 15–21.

102. H. Touryalai, 2014, Everybody loves hedge funds, assets hit record $3 trillion, *Forbes*, www.forbes.com, March 25.

103. M. Hitoshi, 2014, Hedge Fund activism in Japan: The limits of shareholder primacy, *Administrative Science Quarterly*, 59: 366–369; N. M. Boyson & R. M. Mooradian, 2011, Corporate governance and hedge fund activism, *Review of Derivatives Research*, 169–204; L. A. Bebchuk & M. S. Weisbach, 2010, The state of corporate governance research, *Review of Financial Studies*, 23: 939–961.

104. A. Gara, 2015, Breakup artist hedge funds betting billions on corporate marriages, Forbes, February 18, 6.

105. S. Bainbridge, 2011, Hedge funds as activist investors, *ProfessorBainbridge.com*, www.professorbainbridge.com, March 21.

106. D. Benoit & J. Bear, 2015, Goldman Sachs recaptures mojo with DuPont win, *Wall Street Journal*, www.wsj.com, May 22.

107. S. Ovide & D. Clark, 2015, Silicon Valley grits teeth over activist investors, *Wall Street Journal*, May 27, B1.

108. M. Cremers & A. Ferrell, 2014, Thirty years of shareholder rights and firm value, *Journal of Finance*, 69: 1167–1196; M. L. Humphery-Jenner & R. G. Powell, 2011, Firm size, takeover profitability, and the effectiveness of the market for corporate control: Does the absence of anti-takeover provisions make a difference? *Journal of Corporate Finance*, 17: 418–437.

109. J. P. Walsh & R. Kosnik, 1993, Corporate raiders and their disciplinary role in the market for corporate control, *Academy of Management Journal*, 36: 671–700.

110. K. Amess, S. Girma, & M. Wright, 2014, The wage and employment consequences of ownership change, *Managerial & Decision*

Economics, 35: 161–171; M. Schijven & M. A. Hitt, 2012, The vicarious wisdom of crowds: Toward a behavioral perspective on investor reactions to acquisition announcements, *Strategic Management Journal*, 33: 1247–1268; J. Haleblian, C. E. Devers, G. McNamara, M. A. Carpenter, & R. B. Davison, 2009, Taking stock of what we know about mergers and acquisitions: A review and research agenda, *Journal of Management*, 35: 469–502.

111. F. Bauer & K. Matzler, 2014, Antecedents of M&A success: The role of strategic complementarity, cultural fit and degree and speed of integration, *Strategic Management Journal*, 35: 269–291; S. Mingo, 2013, The impact of acquisitions on the performance of existing organizational units In the acquiring firm: The case of the agribusiness company, *Management Science*, 59: 2687–2701; A. Sleptsov, J. Anand, & G. Vasudeva, 2013, Relational configurations with information intermediaries: The effect of firm-investment bank ties on expected acquisition performance, *Strategic Management Journal*, 34: 957–977.

112. 2014, Hostile takeover, *Investopedia*, www.investopedia.com, accessed on June 8.

113. M. Straska & G. Waller, 2014, Antitakeover provisions and shareholder wealth: A survey of the literature, *Journal of Financial & Quantitative Analysis*, 49: 1–32; P. Jiraporn & Y. Liu, 2011, Staggered boards, accounting discretion and firm value, *Applied Financial Economics*, 21: 271–285; O. Faleye, 2007, Classified boards, firm value, and managerial entrenchment, *Journal of Financial Economics*, 83: 501–529.

114. M. Holmén, E. Nivorozhkin, & R. Rana, 2014, Do anti-takeover devices affect the takeover likelihood or the takeover premium? *European Journal of Finance*, 20: 319–340; T. Sokoly, 2011, The effects of antitakeover provisions on acquisition targets, *Journal of Corporate Finance*, 17: 612–627; 2007, Leaders: Pay slips; management in Europe, *Economist*, June 23, 14.

115. J. A. Pearce II & R. B. Robinson, Jr., 2004, Hostile takeover defenses that maximize shareholder wealth, *Business Horizons* 47: 15–24.

116. M. Humphery-Jenner, 2014, Takeover defenses, innovation and value creation: Evidence from acquisition decisions, *Strategic Management Journal*, 35: 668–690; A. Kacperzyk, 2009, With greater power comes greater responsibility? Takeover protection and corporate attention to stakeholders, *Strategic Management Journal*, 30: 261–285.

117. P. Sieger, T. Zellweger, & K. Aquino, 2013, Turning agents into psychological principals: Aligning interests of non-owners through psychological ownership, *Journal of Management Studies*, 50: 361–388.

118. B. M. Galvin, D. Lange, & B. E. Ashforth, 2015, Narcissistic organizational identification: Seeing oneself as central to the organization's identity, *Academy of Management Review*, 40: 163–181.

119. E. Schiehll, C. Ahmadjian, & I. Filatotchev, 2014, National governance bundles perspective: Understanding the diversity of corporate governance practices at the firm and country levels, *Corporate Governance: An International Review*, 22: 179–184; A. Rasheed & T. Yoshikawa, 2012, *The convergence of corporate governance: Promise and prospects*, Basingstoke: Palgrave Macmillan; I. Haxhi & H. Ees, 2010, Explaining diversity in the worldwide diffusion of codes of good governance, *Journal of International Business Studies*, 41: 710–726.

120. M. P. Leitterstorf & S. B. Rau, 2014, Socioemotional wealth and IPO underpricing of family firms, *Strategic Management Journal*, 35: 751–760; P. C. Patel & J. J. Chrisman, 2014, Risk abatement as a strategy for R&D investments in family firms, *Strategic Management Journal*, 35: 617–627.

121. A. Haller, 2013, German corporate governance in international and European context, *International Journal of Accounting*, 48: 420–423; P. Witt, 2004, The competition of international corporate governance systems—a German perspective, *Management International Review*, 44: 309–333; A. Tuschke & W. G. Sanders, 2003, Antecedents and consequences of corporate governance reform: The case of Germany, *Strategic Management Journal*, 24: 631–649.

122. Tuschke, Sanders, & Hernandez, Whose experience matters in the boardroom?; D. Hillier, J. Pinadado, V. de Queiroz, & C. de la Torre, 2010, The impact of country-level corporate governance on research and development, *Journal of International Business Studies*, 42: 76–98.

123. Tuschke, Sanders, & Hernandez, Whose experience matters in the boardroom?

124. T. Duc Hung, 2014, Multiple corporate governance attributes and the cost of capital—Evidence from Germany, *British Accounting Review*, 46: 179–197; J. T. Addison & C. Schnabel, 2011, Worker directors: A German product that did not export? *Industrial Relations: A Journal of Economy and Society*, 50: 354–374; P. C. Fiss & E. J. Zajac, 2004, The diffusion of ideas over contested terrain: The (non)adoption of a shareholder value orientation among German firms, *Administrative Science Quarterly*, 49: 501–534.

125. M. Roth, 2013, Independent directors, shareholder empowerment and long-termism: The transatlantic perspective, *Fordham Journal of Corporate & Financial Law*, 18: 751–820; A. Chizema, 2010, Early and late adoption of American-style executive pay in Germany: Governance and institutions, *Journal of World Business*, 45: 9–18; W. G. Sanders & A. C. Tuschke, 2007, The adoption of the institutionally contested organizational practices: The emergence of stock option pay in Germany, *Academy of Management Journal*, 50: 33–56.

126. J. P. O'Brien & P. David, 2014, Reciprocity and R&D search: Applying the behavioral theory of the firm to a communitarian context, *Strategic Management Journal*, 35: 550–565.

127. N. Kosaku, 2014, Japan seeks to lure investors with improved corporate governance, *Wall Street Journal*, www.wsj.com, June 28.

128. S. Varma, R. Awasthy, K. Narain, & R. Nayyar, 2015, Cultural determinants of alliance management capability—an analysis of Japanese MNCs in India, *Asia Pacific Business Review*, 21: 424–448; D. R. Adhikari & K. Hirasawa, 2010, Emerging scenarios of Japanese corporate management, *Asia-Pacific Journal of Business Administration*, 2: 114–132; M. A. Hitt, H. Lee, & E. Yucel, 2002, The importance of social capital to the management of multinational enterprises: Relational networks among Asian and Western firms, *Asia Pacific Journal of Management*, 19: 353–372.

129. T. Yeh, 2014, Large shareholders, shareholder proposals, and firm performance: Evidence from Japan, *Corporate Governance: An International Review*, 22: 312–329; W. P. Wan, D. W. Yiu, R. E. Hoskisson, & H. Kim, 2008, The performance implications of relationship banking during macroeconomic expansion and contraction: A study of Japanese banks' social relationships and overseas expansion, *Journal of International Business Studies*, 39: 406–427.

130. H. Aslan & P. Kumar, P. 2014, National governance bundles and corporate agency costs: A cross-country analysis, *Corporate Governance: An International Review*, 22: 230–251; P. M. Lee & H. M. O'Neill, 2003, Ownership structures and R&D investments of U.S. and Japanese firms: Agency and stewardship perspectives, *Academy of Management Journal*, 46: 212–225.

131. H. Sakawa, M. Ubukata, & N. Watanabel, 2014, Market liquidity and bank-dominated corporate governance: Evidence from Japan, *International Review of Economics & Finance*, 31: 1–11; X. Wu & J. Yao, 2012, Understanding the rise and decline of the Japanese main bank system: The changing effects of bank rent extraction, *Journal of Banking & Finance*, 36: 36–50.

132. K. Harrigan, 2014, Comparing corporate governance practices and exit decisions between US and Japanese firms, *Journal of Management & Governance*, 18: 975–988; K. Kubo & T. Saito, 2012, The effect of mergers on employment and wages: Evidence from Japan, *Journal of the Japanese and International Economics*, 26: 263–284;

N. Isagawa, 2007, A theory of unwinding of cross-shareholding under managerial entrenchment, *Journal of Financial Research*, 30: 163–179.

133. D. G. Litt, 2015, Japan's new corporate governance code: Outside directors find a role under 'Abenomics,' *Corporate Governance Advisor*, 23: 19–23.

134. F. Jiang & K. A. Kim, 2015, Corporate governance in China: A modern perspective, *Journal of Corporate Finance*, 32: 190–216; J. Yang, J. Chi, & M. Young, 2011, A review of corporate governance in China, *Asian-Pacific Economic Literature*, 25: 15–28.

135. R. Morck & B. Yeung, 2014, Corporate governance in China, *Journal of Applied Corporate Finance*, 26: 20–41; H. Berkman, R. A. Cole, & L. J. Fu, 2010, Political connections and minority-shareholder protection: Evidence from securities-market regulation in China, *Journal of Financial and Quantitative Analysis*, 45: 1391–1417; S. R. Miller, D. Li, E. Eden, & M. A. Hitt, 2008, Insider trading and the valuation of international strategic alliances in emerging stock markets, *Journal of International Business Studies*, 39: 102–117.

136. X. Yu, P. Zhang, & Y. Zheng, 2015, Corporate governance, political connections, and intra-industry effects: Evidence from corporate scandals in China, *Financial Management*, 44: 49–80; W. A. Li & D. T. Yan, 2013, Transition from administrative to economic model of corporate governance, *Nankai Business Review International*, 4: 4–8.

137. T. M. Rooker, 2015, Corporate governance or governance by corporates? Testing governmentality in the context of China's national oil and petrochemical business groups, *Asia Pacific Business Review*, 21: 60–76; J. Chi, Q. Sun, & M. Young, 2011, Performance and characteristics of acquiring firms in the Chinese stock markets, *Emerging Markets Review*, 12: 152–170; Y.-L. Cheung, P. Jiang, P. Limpaphayom, & T. Lu, 2010, Corporate governance in China: A step forward, *European Financial Management*, 16: 94–123.

138. G. Jiang, P. Rao, & H. Yue, 2015, Tunneling through non-operational fund occupancy: An investigation based on officially identified activities, *Journal of Corporate Finance*, 32: 295–311; J. Li & C. Qian, 2013, Principal-principal conflicts under weak institutions: A study of corporate takeovers in China, *Strategic Management Journal*, 34: 498–508; S. Globerman, M. W. Peng, & D. M. Shapiro, 2011, Corporate governance and Asian companies, *Asia Pacific Journal of Management*, 28: 1–14.

139. W. M Peng, S. L. Sun, & L. Markóczy, 2015, Human capital and CEO compensation during institutional transitions, *Journal of Management Studies*, 52: 117–147; P. Adithipyangkul, I. Alon, & T. Zhang, 2011, Executive perks: Compensation and corporate performance in China, *Asia*

Pacific Journal of Management, 28: 401–425; T. Buck, X. Lui, & R. Skovoroda, 2008, Top executives' pay and firm performance in China, *Journal of International Business Studies*, 39: 833–850.

140. R. Amit, Y. Ding, B Villalonga, & H. Zhang, H. 2015, The role of institutional development in the prevalence and performance of entrepreneur and family-controlled firms, *Journal of Corporate Finance*, 31: 284–305; A. Cai, J.-H. Luo, & D.-F. Wan, 2012, Family CEOs: Do they benefit firm governance In China? *Asia Pacific Journal of Management*, 29: 923–947.

141. H. Berkman, R. A. Cole, & L. J. Fu, 2014, Improving corporate governance where the state is the controlling block holder: Evidence from China, *European Journal of Finance*, 20: 752–777; L. Oxelheim, A. Gregoric, T. Randoy, & S. Thomsen, 2013, On the internationalization of corporate boards: The case of Nordic firms, *Journal of International Business Studies*, 44: 173–194.

142. S. Young & V. Thyil, 2014, Corporate social responsibility and corporate governance: Role of context in international settings, *Journal of Business Ethics*, 122: 1–24; S. Muthusamy, P. A. Bobinski, & D. Jawahar, 2011, Toward a strategic role for employees in corporate governance, *Strategic Change*, 20: 127–138; C. Shropshire & A. J. Hillman, 2007, A longitudinal study of significant change in stakeholder management, *Business & Society*, 46: 63–87.

143. G. K. Stahl & M. S. De Luque, 2014, Antecedents of responsible leader behavior: A research synthesis, conceptual framework, and agenda for future research, *Academy of Management Perspectives*, 28: 235–254; J. M. Schaubroeck, S. T. Hannah, B. J. Avolio, S. W. J. Kozlowski, R. G. Lord, L. K. Trevino, N. Dimotakis, & A. C. Peng, 2012, Embedding ethical leadership within and across organizational levels, *Academy of Management Journal*, 55: 1053–1078; R. A. G. Monks & N. Minow, 2011, *Corporate governance*, 5th ed., NY: John Wiley & Sons.

144. A. Soleimani, W. D. Schneper, & W. Newburry, 2014, The impact of stakeholder power on corporate reputation: A cross-country corporate governance perspective, *Organization Science*, 25: 991–1008; J. S. Chun, Y. Shin, J. N. Choi, & M. S. Kim, 2013, How does corporate ethics contribute to firm financial performance? The mediating role of collective organizational commitment and organizational citizenship behavior, *Journal of Management*, 39: 853–877; S. P. Deshpande, J. Joseph, & X. Shu, 2011, Ethical climate and managerial success in China, *Journal of Business Ethics*, 99: 527–534.

145. S. Kaplan, J. Samuels, & J. Cohen, 2015, An examination of the effect of CEO social ties and CEO reputation on nonprofessional investors' say-on-pay judgments, *Journal of Business Ethics*, 126: 103–117; A. P. Cowan &

J. J. Marcel, 2011, Damaged goods: Board decisions to dismiss reputationally compromised directors, *Academy of Management Journal*, 54: 509–527; J. R. Knapp, T. Dalziel, & M. W. Lewis, 2011, Governing top managers: Board control, social categorization, and their unintended influence on discretionary behaviors, *Corporate Governance: An International Review* 19: 295–310.

146. D. Gomulya & W. Boeker, 2014, How firms respond to financial restatement: CEO successors and external reactions, *Academy of Management Journal*, 57: 1579–1785.

147. Y. Li, F. Yao, & D. Ahlstrom, 2015, The social dilemma of bribery in emerging economies: A dynamic model of emotion, social value, and institutional uncertainty, *Asia Pacific Journal of Management*, 32: 311–334; Y. Jeong & R. J. Weiner, 2012, Who bribes? Evidence from the United Nations' oil-for-food program, *Strategic Management Journal*, 33: 1363–1383.

148. S.-H. Lee & D. H. Weng, 2013, Does bribery in the home country promote or dampen firm exports? *Strategic Management Journal*, 34: 1472–1487; J. O. Zhou & M. W. Peng, 2012, Does bribery help or hurt firm growth around the world? *Asia Pacific Journal of Management*, 29: 907–921.

149. 2015, Corporate governance awards 2015, *World Finance*, www.worldfinance.com/awards, March 4.

11

Organizational Structure and Controls

Studying this chapter should provide you with the strategic management knowledge needed to:

11-1   Define organizational structure and controls and discuss the difference between strategic and financial controls.

11-2   Describe the relationship between strategy and structure.

11-3   Discuss the different functional structures used to implement business-level strategies.

11-4   Explain the use of three versions of the multidivisional (M-form) structure to implement different diversification strategies.

11-5   Discuss the organizational structures used to implement three international strategies.

11-6   Define strategic networks and discuss how strategic center firms implement such networks at the business, corporate, and international levels.

LUXOTTICA'S DUAL CEO STRUCTURE: A KEY TO LONG-TERM SUCCESS OR A CAUSE FOR CONCERN?

Founded in Italy in 1961, Luxottica is the world's largest eyewear company, controlling over 80 percent of major eyewear brands. Alain Mikli, Arnette, Oakley, and Persol are some of the company's proprietary brands. Luxottica also makes products under license for a large number of well-known companies such as Armani, Bulgari, Burberry, Coach, Tiffany & Co., Tory Burch, and Versace, to name only a few. Additionally, Luxottica owns and operates a large number of eyewear storefront brands including LensCrafters, Pearle Vision, Laubman & Pank, and Sears Optical. Another measure of the scope of the firm's positions within the eyewear industry is its operations of "one of the largest managed vision care networks in the United States through EyeMed and the second largest lens finishing network, with three central laboratories, over 900 on-site labs at LensCrafters stores, a fully dedicated Oakley lab, and an additional facility based in China dedicated to North America optical retail."

Courtesy of Luxottica

As these product offerings and market positions show, Luxottica dominates all phases of the eyewear industry. One reason for this dominance is that the firm is vertically integrated in that it designs its own products, produces them through manufacturing facilities located throughout the world, and sells them in outlets such as those mentioned above. In the view of those leading the firm, Luxottica's extensive degree of vertical integration is a competitive advantage. The company says that its products are distinguished from competitors' offerings by their excellent design and the quality with which they are manufactured.

Late in 2014, Luxottica changed its organizational structure in a major way, as demonstrated by the fact that co-CEOs were appointed. Long-term Procter & Gamble executive Adil Mehboob-Khan accepted the responsibility for *distribution* in the firm's markets, while long-time Luxottica manager Massimo Vian was appointed as co-CEO with the responsibility for *products and operations*. Wholesale, retail optical, marketing, go-to-market, and e-commerce are examples of the units that comprise the distribution part of the new structure. Style & design, R&D and engineering, quality assurance, and purchasing are some of the units in the products and operations side of the structure. Each co-CEO holds a seat as a member of the firm's board of directors.

A dual CEO structure is unusual; many observers believe that this type of leadership structure cannot lead to long-term firm success. According to an observer of organizational structures, "the adoption of a co-CEO model is often a symptom of weakness. Having two people at the same level shows that the company is undecided about its leadership and it invites too much confusion." Another way of thinking about this some say, is that a ship with two captains is essentially a ship without a captain.

Although used infrequently in many countries, Italy is a nation in which a dual CEO structure is popular, particularly among family controlled/owned firms such as Luxottica. In fact, evidence indicates that more than one-third of "Italian family-owned businesses with annual revenue of more than 50 million euros have at least two bosses."

The critical issue when considering a dual CEO structure is the reason for choosing to use it. If there is a strong strategic rationale for the co-CEO structure, then arguably, a firm for which this is the case should organize itself in such a manner. Luxottica officials claim this is the case, saying that "this new organizational structure will support a new phase of development for

Luxottica that is consistent with its strategic vision and will allow it to take advantage of opportunities in a competitive global market of growing complexity and changing competitive dynamics." A current market opportunity for Luxottica is its collaboration with Google to work on the next version of Google Glass, the firm's futuristic eyewear product. Google's partnership with Luxottica is a result of Google's dissatisfaction with the results of its initial version of the product.

With respect to competitive dynamics, perhaps the co-CEO structure will help Luxottica compete against Warby Parker, the online eyeglass retailer that continues growing and that recently raised a round of capital that valued the firm at roughly $1.2 billion. The low price of Warby Parker's products is thought to be a competitive challenge for Luxottica given the higher costs of its differentiated eyewear.

Although unusual, the co-CEO structure may work for Luxottica. In the final analysis though, Luxottica's board must carefully monitor the firm's performance under a dual CEO structure and be prepared to make a change to that structure if evidence suggests that such an action would be in the firm's best interest.

Sources: 2015, Company profiles, Luxottica Home Page, www.luxottica.com, May 12; 2015, Our business model, Luxottica Home Page, www.luxottica.com, May 12; D. Macmillan, 2015, Eyeglass retailer Warby Parker is valued at $1.2 billion, *Wall Street Journal Online*, www.wsj.com, April 30; M. Mesco, 2015, Luxottica's profit surges as sales rise in North America, *Wall Street Journal Online*, www.wsj.com, May 4; M. Mesco, 2015, Italian eyewear maker Luxottica working on new version of Google Glass, CEO says, *Wall Street Journal Digits*, www.blogs.wsj.com, April 24; M. Mesco, 2015, Luxottica reports profit but looks for areas of growth, *Wall Street Journal Online*, www.wsj.com, March 2; 2014, Luxottica announces the implementation of a new governance structure based on a co-CEO model, Luxottica Home Page, www.luxottica, September 1.

As we explained in Chapter 4, all firms use one or more business-level strategies. Luxottica uses the differentiation strategy for its eyewear that is differentiated on the competitive dimensions of design, manufacturing, and brand name. In Chapters 6 through 9, we discussed other strategies that firms may choose to use (corporate-level, merger and acquisition, international, and cooperative), depending on the decisions made by those leading individual organizations. After being selected, strategies must be implemented effectively for organizations to achieve intended outcomes.

Organizational structure and controls, this chapter's topic, provide the framework within which strategies are implemented and used in both for-profit organizations and not-for-profit agencies.[1] However, as we explain, separate structures and controls are required to successfully implement different strategies. In all organizations, top-level managers have the final responsibility for ensuring that the firm has matched each of its strategies with the appropriate organizational structure and that both change when necessary. The match or degree of fit between strategy and structure influences the firm's attempts to earn above-average returns.[2] Thus, the ability to select an appropriate strategy and match it with the appropriate structure is an important characteristic of effective strategic leadership.[3] In this sense, it will be interesting to see if the co-CEO structure Luxottica recently put into place will prove to be an effective match with the firm's strategies.

This chapter opens with an introduction to organizational structure and controls. We then provide more details about the need for the firm's strategy and structure to be properly matched. The influence of strategy and structure on each other affects firms' efforts to match individual strategies with their appropriate structure.[4] As we discuss, strategy has a more important influence on structure, although once in place, structure influences strategy.[5] Next, we describe the relationship between growth and structural change successful firms experience. We then discuss the different organizational structures firms use to implement separate business-level, corporate-level, international, and cooperative strategies. We present a series of figures to highlight the different structures firms match with different strategies. Across time and based on their experiences, organizations, especially large and complex ones, customize these general structures to meet their unique needs.[6] Typically, firms try to form a structure that is complex enough to facilitate use of their strategies but simple enough for all parties to understand and use.[7]

11-1 Organizational Structure and Controls

Research shows that organizational structure and the controls that are a part of the structure affect firm performance.[8] In particular, evidence suggests that performance declines when the firm's strategy is not matched with the most appropriate structure and controls.[9] Even though mismatches between strategy and structure do occur, research indicates that managers try to act rationally when forming or changing their firm's structure.[10]

In Chapter 2's Opening Case, we talked about problems McDonald's is encountering when trying to cope effectively with changes that are taking place in the external environment. As we noted then, the firm is changing its menu to better accommodate some consumers' preferences for healthier food. Additionally though and more broadly, changes are being made to McDonald's organizational structure with the expectation that doing so will lead to enhanced firm performance. Defined comprehensively below, organizational structure essentially specifies the work that must be completed so the firm can implement its strategy.

McDonald's leaders, including new CEO Steve Easterbrook, believe that changes being made to the firm's structure will increase its efficiency (that is, its daily operations will improve) and its effectiveness (that is, it will better serve customers' needs). We discuss changes that have been made to McDonald's organizational structure in the Strategic Focus.

11-1a Organizational Structure

Organizational structure specifies the firm's formal reporting relationships, procedures, controls, and authority and decision-making processes.[11] A firm's structure determines and specifies the decisions that are to be made and the work that is to be completed by everyone within an organization as a result of those decisions.[12] Organizational routines serve as processes that are used to complete the work required by individual strategies.[13]

Developing an organizational structure that effectively supports the firm's strategy is difficult, especially because of the uncertainty (or unpredictable variation) about cause-effect relationships in the global economy's rapidly changing competitive environments.[14] When a structure's elements (e.g., reporting relationships, procedures, etc.) are properly aligned with one another, the structure increases the likelihood that the firm will operate in ways that allow it to better understand the challenging cause/effect relationships it encounters when competing against its rivals. Thus, helping the firm effectively cope with environmental uncertainty is an important contribution organizational structure makes to a firm as it seeks to successfully implement its strategy or strategies as a means of outperforming competitors.[15]

Appropriately designed organizational structures provide the stability a firm needs to successfully implement its strategies and maintain its current competitive advantages while simultaneously providing the flexibility to develop advantages it will need in the future.[16] More specifically, *structural stability* provides the capacity the firm requires to consistently and predictably manage its daily work routines,[17] while *structural flexibility* makes it possible for the firm to identify opportunities and then allocate resources to pursue them as a way of being prepared to succeed in the future.[18] Thus, an effectively

Organizational structure specifies the firm's formal reporting relationships, procedures, controls, and authority and decision-making processes.

Strategic **Focus**

Changing McDonald's Organizational Structure: A Path to Improved Performance?

Operating close to 37,000 restaurants worldwide and with annual sales closing in on $90 billion, McDonald's is huge. In fact, it is several times larger than Burger King and Wendy's, its closest competitors. In addition to the United States and Canada, McDonald's has a significant presence in France, German, Russia, and the United Kingdom.

But all is not well at McDonald's. Almost immediately upon being appointed as CEO, Steve Easterbrook said that "the reality is our recent performance has been poor. The numbers don't lie." Supporting Easterbrook's position is the fact that 2014 was one of the firm's worst financial performances in its 60-year history. Thus, changes are necessary. In response to this reality, and viewing himself as an internal activist, Easterbrook announced within 33 days of becoming CEO that he wants McDonald's to become a "progressive burger company." Changing the firm's organizational structure is critical to reaching this objective. Saying that he will not shy away "from the urgent need to reset this business" demonstrates the intensity with which Easterbrook is approaching McDonald's challenges.

For a number of years, McDonald's was structured around geographic segments including the United States, Europe, Asia/Pacific, Middle East, and Africa (APMEA). Over time though, this structural configuration became cumbersome, making McDonald's "too slow to effectively respond to the needs of its 69 million daily customers." The way this geography-based structure was being used resulted in "cumbersome" managerial practices and operational inefficiencies. Franchisees were reporting structural problems such as operational inefficiencies to McDonald's officials. In response to the franchisees' complaints, a McDonald's leader said the following: "You've told us that there are too many layers, redundancies in planning and communication, competing priorities, barriers to efficient decision making, and too much talking to ourselves instead of to and about our customers." Overall then, the need for changes to the firm's organizational structure was obvious to virtually everyone associated with the company.

Changes have indeed been made to McDonald's structure. Wanting to simplify, simplify, simplify, at the core of these changes is Easterbrook's desire to strip away the bureaucracy at McDonald's so the firm can anticipate trends as a foundation for moving nimbly and to fully understand and appropriately respond to customers' interests. Additionally, Easterbrook specified that the new structure should be built on "commercial logic" rather than simply geography.

With all of this as a background, a decision was made to restructure McDonald's into "four segments that combine markets with similar needs, challenges, and opportunities for growth." As of July 2015, McDonald's organizational structure found the firm organized into the following market segments:

1. *United States* (the largest market that accounts for over 40 percent of total firm revenue)
2. *International lead markets* (Australia, Canada, France, Germany, and the United Kingdom—markets with similar economic conditions and competitive dynamics that yield similar growth opportunities)
3. *High-growth markets* ("markets with relatively higher restaurant expansion and franchising potential including China, Italy, Poland, Russia, South Korea, Spain, Switzerland, and the Netherlands")
4. *Foundational markets* (all remaining markets in McDonald's system with each market having the potential to operate largely as a franchised model)

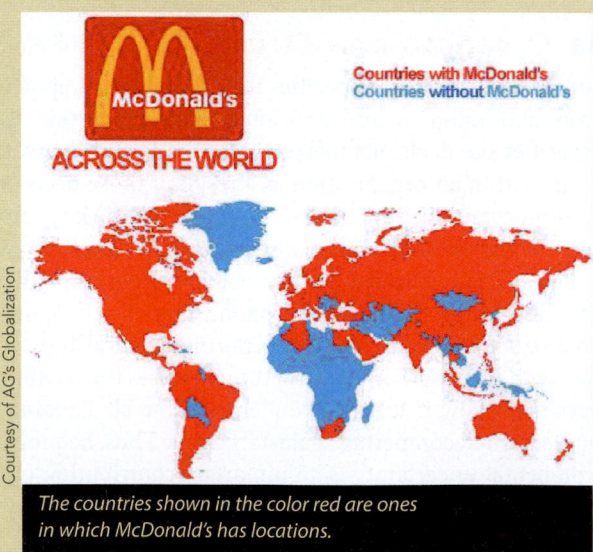

Courtesy of AG's Globalization

The countries shown in the color red are ones in which McDonald's has locations.

Will this new organizational structure contribute to McDonald's effort to increase revenues and profitability? Corporate officials are optimistic that this will prove to be the case. More specifically, the firm's leaders are confident the new structure will enable individual segments to identify and successfully address what are common needs of their markets and customers and that those operating units within each segment will have the flexibility they need to innovate in ways that will create value for customers and, in turn, for the entire corporation.

Sources: 2015, McDonald's announces initial steps in turnaround plan including worldwide business restructuring and financial updates, McDonald's Home Page, www.mcdonalds.com, May 4; 2015, McDonald's challenges: Make it simpler, but add choices, New York Times Online, www.nytimes.com, May 4; L. Baertlein, 2015, McDonald's reset to change structure, cut costs, boost franchises, Reuters, www.reuters.com, May 4; C. Choi, 2015, McDonald's to simplify structure, focus on customers, Spokesman, www.spokesman.com, May 5; A. Gasparro, 2015, McDonald's to speed refranchising, cut costs, Wall Street Journal Online, www.wsj.com, May 4; A. Gasparro, 2015, McDonald's new chief plots counter attack, Wall Street Journal Online, www.wsj.com, Marcy 1; A. Gasparro, 2015, McDonald's shareholder group calls for changes to board of directors, Wall Street Journal Online, www.wsj.com, February 13; R. Neate, 2015, McDonald's plans huge shakeup as CEO admits: 'Our performance has been poor,' The Guardian, www.theguardian.com, May 4.

flexible organizational structure allows the firm to *exploit* current competitive advantages while *developing* new advantages that can be used in the future.[19] Alternatively, an ineffective structure that is inflexible may drive productive employees away because of frustration and an inability to create value while completing their work. Losing productive employees can result in a loss of knowledge within a firm. This is an especially damaging outcome when a departing employee, who may accept employment with a competitor, possesses a significant amount of tacit knowledge.

Modifications to the firm's current strategy or selection of a new strategy call for changes to its organizational structure. However, research shows that once in place, organizational inertia often inhibits efforts to change structure, even when the firm's performance suggests that it is time to do so.[20] In his pioneering work, Alfred Chandler found that organizations change their structures when inefficiencies force them to do so.[21] Chandler's contributions to our understanding of organizational structure and its relationship to strategies and performance are significant. Indeed, some believe that Chandler's emphasis on "organizational structure so transformed the field of business history that some call the period before Chandler's work was published 'B.C.,' meaning 'before Chandler.'"[22]

Firms seem to prefer the structural status quo and its familiar working relationships until their performance declines to the point where change is absolutely necessary.[23] Moreover, top-level managers often hesitate to conclude that the firm's structure or its strategy are the problem because doing so suggests that their previous choices were not the best ones. Because of these inertial tendencies, structural change is often induced instead by actions from stakeholders (e.g., those from the capital market and customers) who are no longer willing to tolerate the firm's performance. For example, this happened at large department store operator J. C. Penney, as the former CEO, Myron Ullman, replaced a relatively new CEO, Ron Johnson, whose turnaround strategy failed.[24] Additionally, some believe that Penney has yet to recover from the effects of the decisions Johnson made during his short 18-month tenure as the retailer's CEO.[25] Evidence shows that appropriate timing of structural change happens when top-level managers recognize that a current organizational structure

The New York times

Pictured here is Alfred Chandler, a scholar whose work enhanced our understanding of organizational structure and strategy.

no longer provides the coordination and direction needed for the firm to successfully implement its strategies.[26] Interestingly, many organizational changes take place in economic downturns because poor performance reveals organizational weaknesses. As we discuss next, effective organizational controls help managers recognize when it is time to adjust the firm's structure.

11-1b Organizational Controls

Organizational controls are an important aspect of structure.[27] **Organizational controls** guide the use of strategy, indicate how to compare actual results with expected results, and suggest corrective actions to take when the difference is unacceptable. It is difficult for a firm to successfully exploit its competitive advantages without effective organizational controls. Properly designed organizational controls provide clear insights regarding behaviors that enhance firm performance.[28] Firms use both strategic controls and financial controls to support implementation of their strategies.

Strategic controls are largely subjective criteria intended to verify that the firm is using appropriate strategies for the conditions in the external environment and the company's competitive advantages. Thus, strategic controls are concerned with examining the fit between what the firm *might do* (as suggested by opportunities in its external environment) and what it *can do* (as indicated by its internal organization in the form of its resources, capabilities, and core competencies). Effective strategic controls help the firm understand what it takes to be successful, especially where significant strategic change is needed.[29] Strategic controls demand rich communications between managers responsible for using them to judge the firm's performance and those with primary responsibility for implementing the firm's strategies (such as middle- and first-level managers). These frequent exchanges between managers are both formal and informal in nature.[30]

Strategic controls are also used to evaluate the degree to which the firm focuses on the requirements to implement its strategies. For a business-level strategy, for example, the strategic controls are used to study value chain activities and support functions (see Figures 3.3, 3.4, and 3.5, in Chapter 3) to verify that the critical activities and functions are being emphasized and properly executed. When implementing related diversification strategies at the corporate level, strategic controls are used to verify the sharing of activities (in the case of the related-constrained strategy) or the transferring of core competencies (in the case of the related-linked strategy) across businesses. To effectively use strategic controls when evaluating either of these related diversification strategies, headquarter executives must have a deep understanding of the business-level strategies being implemented within individual strategic business units.[31]

Financial controls are largely objective criteria used to measure the firm's performance against previously established quantitative standards. When using financial controls, firms evaluate their current performance against previous outcomes as well as against competitors' performance and industry averages. Accounting-based measures, such as return on investment (ROI) and return on assets (ROA), as well as market-based measures, such as economic value added, are examples of financial controls. Partly because strategic controls are difficult to use with extensive diversification,[32] financial controls are emphasized to evaluate the performance of the firm using the unrelated diversification strategy. The unrelated diversification strategy's focus on financial outcomes (see Chapter 6) requires using standardized financial controls to compare performances between business units and those responsible for leading them.[33]

Both strategic and financial controls are important aspects of a firm's structure; as noted previously, any structure's effectiveness is determined using a "balanced" combination of strategic and financial controls. But, determining the most appropriate balance

Organizational controls guide the use of strategy, indicate how to compare actual results with expected results, and suggest corrective actions to take when the difference is unacceptable.

Strategic controls are largely subjective criteria intended to verify that the firm is using appropriate strategies for the conditions in the external environment and the company's competitive advantages.

Financial controls are largely objective criteria used to measure the firm's performance against previously established quantitative standards.

to have in place between strategic and financial controls at specific points in time is challenging, partly because the relative use of controls varies by type of strategy. For example, companies and business units of large diversified firms using the cost leadership strategy emphasize financial controls (such as quantitative cost goals), while companies and business units using the differentiation strategy emphasize strategic controls (such as subjective measures of the effectiveness of product development teams).[34] As previously explained, a corporation-wide emphasis on sharing among business units (as called for by related diversification strategies) results in an emphasis on strategic controls, while financial controls are emphasized for strategies in which activities or capabilities are not shared (e.g., in an unrelated diversification strategy). Those determining how strategies are to be implemented must keep these relative degrees of balance between controls by type of strategy in mind when making implementation-related decisions.

11-2 Relationships between Strategy and Structure

Strategy and structure have a reciprocal relationship, and if aligned properly, performance improves.[35] This relationship highlights the interconnectedness between strategy formulation (Chapters 4, 6–9) and strategy implementation (Chapters 10–13). In general, this reciprocal relationship finds structure flowing from or following selection of the firm's strategy. Once in place though, structure can influence current strategic actions as well as choices about future strategies. The new structure in place at McDonald's that we mentioned earlier has the potential to influence implementation of strategies that are, in part, aimed to better identify and satisfy customers' changing needs.[36] Overall, those involved with a firm's strategic management process should understand that the general nature of the strategy/structure relationship means that changes to the firm's strategy create the need to change how the organization completes its work.

Moreover, because structure can influence strategy by constraining the potential alternatives considered, firms must be vigilant in their efforts to verify how their structure not only affects implementation of chosen strategies, but also the limits the structure placed on possible future strategies. Overall though, the effect of strategy on structure is stronger than is the effect of structure on strategy.

Regardless of the strength of the reciprocal relationships between strategy and structure, those choosing the firm's strategy and structure should be committed to matching each strategy with a structure that provides the stability needed to use current competitive advantages as well as the flexibility required to develop future advantages. Therefore, when changing strategies, the firm should simultaneously consider the structure that will be needed to support use of the new strategy; properly matching strategy and structure can create a competitive advantage. This process can be influenced by outside forces, such as significant media attention, which may either hinder the change or foster it.[37]

11-3 Evolutionary Patterns of Strategy and Organizational Structure

Research suggests that most firms experience a certain pattern of relationships between strategy and structure. Chandler[38] found that firms tend to grow in somewhat predictable patterns: "first by volume, then by geography, then integration (vertical, horizontal), and finally through product/business diversification"[39] (see Figure 11.1). Chandler interpreted his findings as an indication that firms' growth patterns determine their structural form.

Figure 11.1 Strategy and Structure Growth Pattern

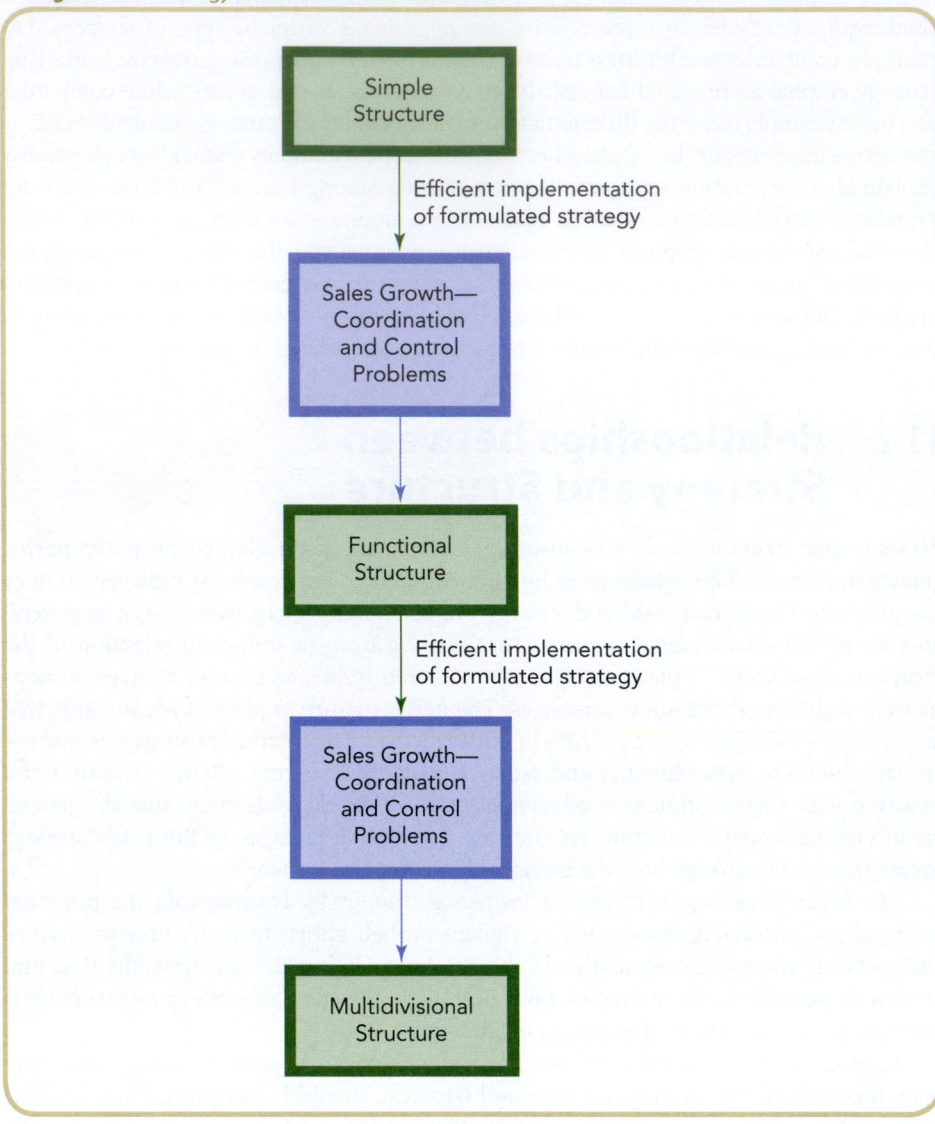

As shown in Figure 11.1, sales growth creates coordination and control problems the existing organizational structure cannot efficiently handle. Organizational growth creates the opportunity for the firm to change its strategy to try to become even more successful. However, the existing structure's formal reporting relationships, procedures, controls, and authority and decision-making processes lack the sophistication required to support using the new strategy,[40] meaning that a new organizational structure is needed.[41]

Firms choose from among three major types of organizational structures—simple, functional, and multidivisional—to implement strategies. Across time, successful firms move from the simple, to the functional, to the multidivisional structure to support changes in their growth strategies.

11-3a Simple Structure

The **simple structure** is a structure in which the owner-manager makes all major decisions and monitors all activities, while the staff serves as an extension of the manager's

The **simple structure** is a structure in which the owner-manager makes all major decisions and monitors all activities, while the staff serves as an extension of the manager's supervisory authority.

supervisory authority.[42] Typically, the owner-manager actively works in the business on a daily basis. Informal relationships, few rules, limited task specialization, and unsophisticated information systems characterize this structure. Frequent and informal communications between the owner-manager and employees make coordinating the work to be completed relatively easy. The simple structure is matched with focus strategies and business-level strategies, as firms implementing these strategies commonly compete by offering a single product line in a single geographic market. Local restaurants, repair businesses, and other specialized enterprises are examples of firms using the simple structure.

As the small firm grows larger and becomes more complex, managerial and structural challenges emerge. For example, the amount of competitively relevant information requiring analysis substantially increases, placing significant pressure on the owner-manager. Additional growth and success may cause the firm to change its strategy. Even if the strategy remains the same, the firm's larger size dictates the need for more sophisticated workflows and integrating mechanisms. At this evolutionary point, firms tend to move from the simple structure to a functional organizational structure.[43]

11-3b Functional Structure

The **functional structure** consists of a chief executive officer and a limited corporate staff, with functional line managers in dominant organizational areas such as production, accounting, marketing, R&D, engineering, and human resources.[44] This structure allows for functional specialization,[45] thereby facilitating active sharing of knowledge within each functional area. Knowledge sharing facilitates career paths as well as professional development of functional specialists. However, a functional orientation can negatively affect communication and coordination among those representing different organizational functions. For this reason, the CEO must verify that the decisions and actions of individual business functions promote the entire firm rather than a single function. The functional structure supports implementing business-level strategies and some corporate-level strategies (e.g., single or dominant business) with low levels of diversification. However, when changing from a simple to a functional structure, firms want to avoid introducing value-destroying bureaucratic procedures since such procedures typically have the potential to damage individuals' efforts to innovate as a means of supporting strategy implementation activities.

11-3c Multidivisional Structure

With continuing growth and success, firms often consider greater levels of diversification. Successfully using a diversification strategy requires analyzing substantially greater amounts of data and information when the firm offers the same products in different markets (market or geographic diversification) or offers different products in several markets (product diversification). In addition, trying to manage high levels of diversification through functional structures creates serious coordination and control problems,[46] a fact that commonly leads to a new structural form.[47]

The **multidivisional (M-form) structure** consists of a corporate office and operating divisions, each operating division representing a separate business or profit center in which the top corporate officer delegates responsibilities for day-to-day operations and business-unit strategy to division managers. Each division represents a distinct, self-contained business with its own functional hierarchy.[48] As initially designed, the M-form was thought to have three major benefits: "(1) it enabled corporate officers to more accurately monitor the performance of each business, which simplified the problem of control; (2) it facilitated comparisons between divisions, which improved the resource allocation process; and (3) it stimulated managers of poorly performing divisions to look for ways of improving performance."[49] Active monitoring of performance through the M-form increases the likelihood that decisions made

The **functional structure** consists of a chief executive officer and a limited corporate staff, with functional line managers in dominant organizational areas such as production, accounting, marketing, R&D, engineering, and human resources.

The **multidivisional (M-form) structure** consists of a corporate office and operating divisions, each operating division representing a separate business or profit center in which the top corporate officer delegates responsibilities for day-to-day operations and business-unit strategy to division managers.

by managers heading individual units will be in stakeholders' best interests. Because diversification is a dominant corporate-level strategy used in the global economy, the M-form is a widely adopted organizational structure.[50]

Used to support implementation of related and unrelated diversification strategies, the M-form helps firms successfully manage diversification's many demands.[51] Chandler viewed the M-form as an innovative response to coordination and control problems that surfaced during the 1920s in the functional structures then used by large firms such as DuPont and General Motors.[52] Research shows that the M-form is appropriate when the firm grows through diversification.[53] Partly because of its value to diversified corporations, some consider the multidivisional structure to be one of the twentieth century's most significant organizational innovations.[54]

No single organizational structure (simple, functional, or multidivisional) is inherently superior to the others. Peter Drucker says the following about this matter:

"There is no one right organization.… Rather the task … is to select the organization for the particular task and mission at hand."[55]

This statement suggests that the firm must select a structure that is "right" for successfully using the chosen strategy. Because no single structure is optimal in all instances, managers concentrate on developing proper matches between strategies and organizational structures rather than searching for an "optimal" structure. We now describe the strategy/ structure matches that contribute positively to firm performance.

11-3d Matches between Business-Level Strategies and the Functional Structure

Firms use different forms of the functional organizational structure to support implementing the cost leadership, differentiation, and integrated cost leadership/differentiation strategies. The differences in these forms are accounted for primarily by different uses of three important structural characteristics: *specialization* (concerned with the type and number of jobs required to complete work[56]), *centralization* (the degree to which decision-making authority is retained at higher managerial levels[57]), and *formalization* (the degree to which formal rules and procedures govern work[58]).

Using the Functional Structure to Implement the Cost Leadership Strategy

Firms using the cost leadership strategy sell large quantities of standardized products to an industry's typical customer. Firms using this strategy need a structure that allows them to achieve efficiencies and produce their products at costs lower than those of competitors.[59] Simple reporting relationships, a few layers in the decision-making and authority structure, a centralized corporate staff, and a strong focus on process improvements through the manufacturing function rather than the development of new products by emphasizing product R&D help to achieve the needed efficiencies and thus characterize the cost leadership form of the functional structure[60] (see Figure 11.2). This structure contributes to the emergence of a low-cost culture—a culture in which employees constantly try to find ways to reduce the costs incurred to complete their work.[61] They can do this through the development of a product design that is simple and easy to manufacture, as well as through the development of efficient processes to produce the goods.[62]

In terms of centralization, decision-making authority is centralized in a staff function to maintain a cost-reducing emphasis within each organizational function (engineering, marketing, etc.). While encouraging continuous cost reductions, the centralized staff also verifies that further cuts in costs in one function won't adversely affect the productivity levels in other functions.[63]

Figure 11.2 Functional Structure for Implementing a Cost Leadership Strategy

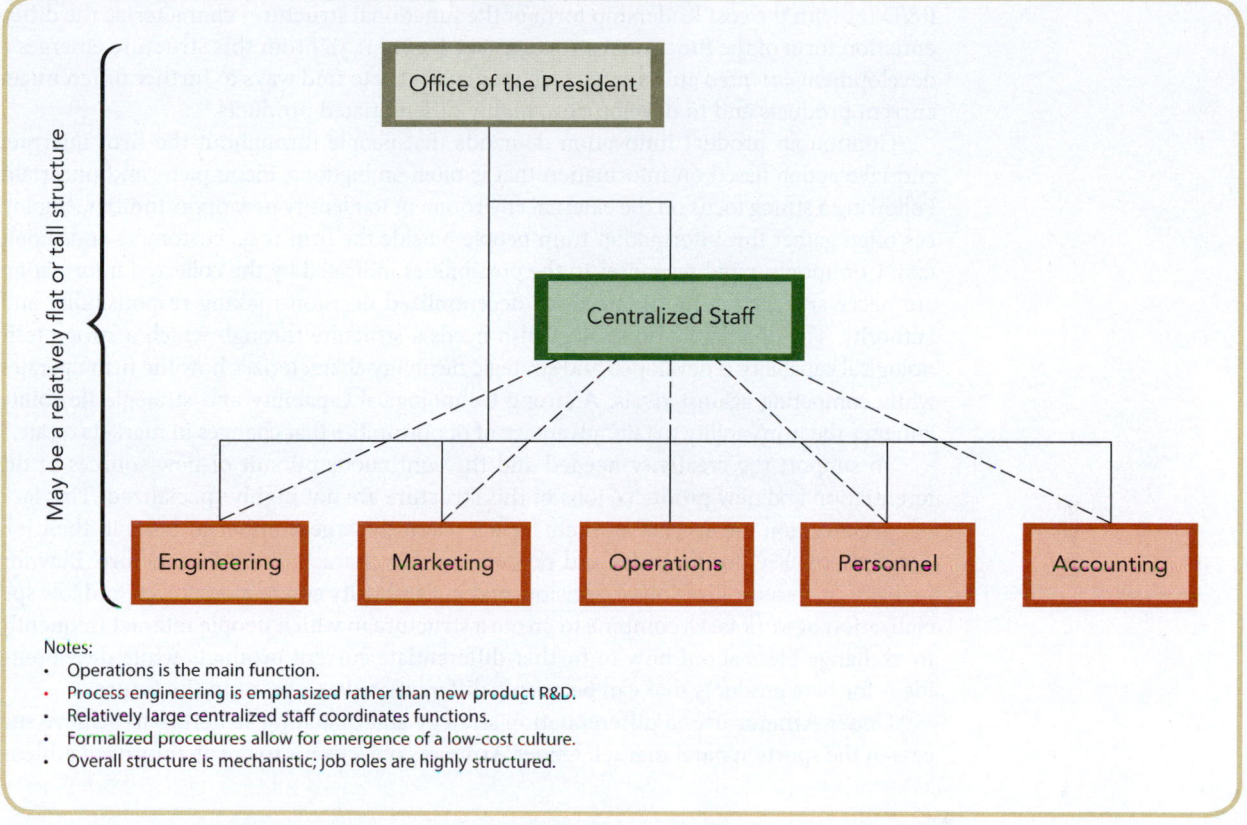

Notes:
- Operations is the main function.
- Process engineering is emphasized rather than new product R&D.
- Relatively large centralized staff coordinates functions.
- Formalized procedures allow for emergence of a low-cost culture.
- Overall structure is mechanistic; job roles are highly structured.

Jobs are highly specialized in the cost leadership functional structure; work is divided into homogeneous subgroups. Organizational functions are the most common subgroup, although work is sometimes batched on the basis of products produced or clients served. Specializing in their work allows employees to increase their efficiency, resulting in reduced costs. Guiding individuals' work in this structure are highly formalized rules and procedures, which often emanate from the centralized staff.

Walmart Stores, Inc. uses the functional structure to implement cost leadership strategies in each of its three operating segments (Walmart U.S., Sam's Clubs, and Walmart International). In the Walmart U.S. segment (which generates the largest share of the firm's total sales), the cost leadership strategy is used in the firm's Supercenter, Discount, Neighborhood Market, and digital retail formats.[64] For the entire corporation, the firm says that it is committed to "saving people money so they can live better."[65] Over the years, competitors' efforts to duplicate the success Walmart has achieved by implementing its cost leadership strategies have generally failed, partly because of the effective strategy/structure matches the firm has formed between the cost leadership strategy and the functional structure that is specific to the mandates of that strategy.

Using the Functional Structure to Implement the Differentiation Strategy

Firms using the differentiation strategy seek to produce products that customers perceive as being different in ways that create value for them. With this strategy, the firm sells non-standardized products to customers with unique needs. Relatively complex and flexible reporting relationships, frequent use of cross-functional product development teams, and a strong focus on marketing and product R&D rather than manufacturing and process R&D (as with the cost leadership form of the functional structure) characterize the differentiation form of the functional structure (see Figure 11.3). From this structure emerges a development-oriented culture in which employees try to find ways to further differentiate current products and to develop new, highly differentiated products.[66]

Continuous product innovation demands that people throughout the firm interpret and take action based on information that is often ambiguous, incomplete, and uncertain. Following a strong focus on the external environment to identify new opportunities, employees often gather this information from people outside the firm (e.g., customers and suppliers). Commonly, rapid responses to the possibilities indicated by the collected information are necessary, suggesting the need for decentralized decision-making responsibility and authority. The differentiation strategy also needs a structure through which a strong technological capability is developed and strategic flexibility characterizes how the firm operates while competing against rivals. A strong technological capability and strategic flexibility enhance the firm's ability to take advantage of opportunities that changes in markets create.[67]

To support the creativity needed and the continuous pursuit of new sources of differentiation and new products, jobs in this structure are not highly specialized. This lack of specialization means that workers have a relatively large number of tasks in their job descriptions. Few formal rules and procedures also characterize this structure. Low formalization, decentralization of decision-making authority and responsibility, and low specialization of work tasks combine to create a structure in which people interact frequently to exchange ideas about how to further differentiate current products while developing ideas for new products that can be crisply differentiated at a point in the future.

Under Armour uses a differentiation strategy and matching structure to achieve success in the sports apparel market. Under Armour's objective is to create improved athletic

Figure 11.3 Functional Structure for Implementing a Differentiation Strategy

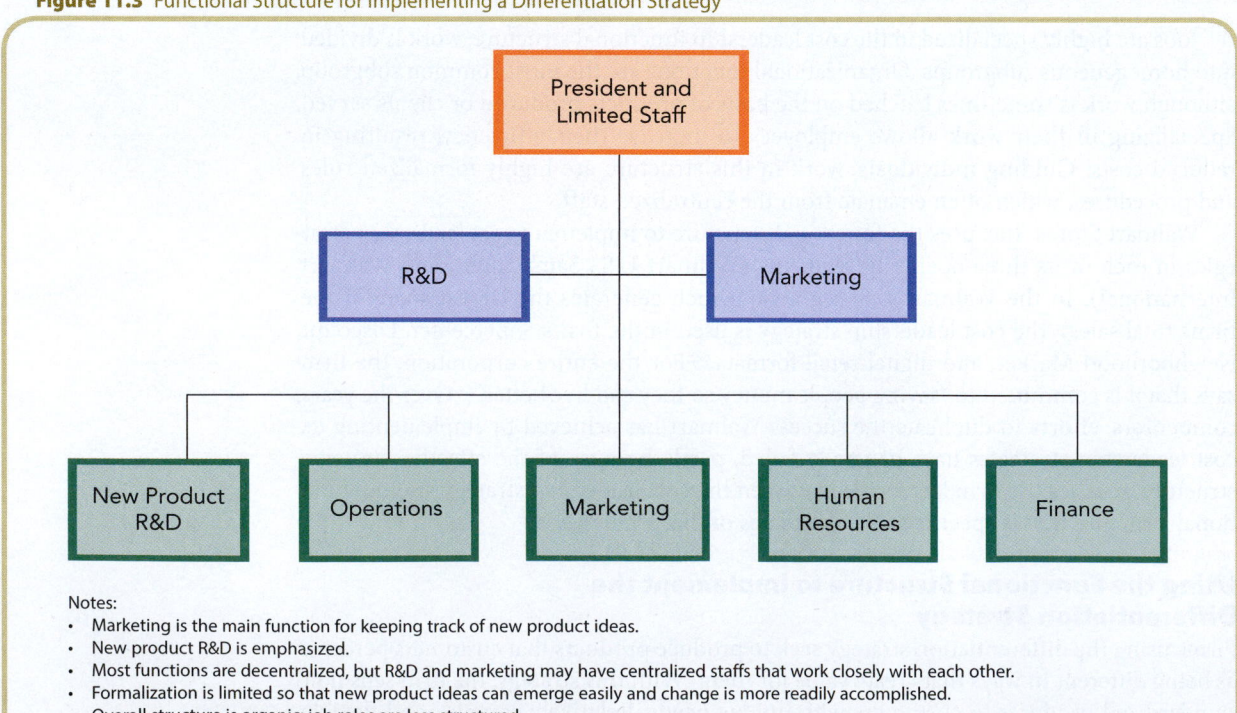

Notes:
- Marketing is the main function for keeping track of new product ideas.
- New product R&D is emphasized.
- Most functions are decentralized, but R&D and marketing may have centralized staffs that work closely with each other.
- Formalization is limited so that new product ideas can emerge easily and change is more readily accomplished.
- Overall structure is organic; job roles are less structured.

performance for customers through innovative design, testing, and marketing. The firm targets its products to athletes at all skill levels, from the novice to the professional. For each customer, the firm intends for its products to help that person improve her/his performance by using Under Armour's products. Calling it a "Universal Guarantee of Performance" (or UGOP), the firm says that its guarantee "means that every Under Armour product is doing something for you: it's making you better."[68]

When exercising, as is the case for this person, individuals wearing Under Armour gear and equipment may believe that the firm's products will "make them better."

Syda Productions/Shutterstock.com

Using the Functional Structure to Implement the Integrated Cost Leadership/Differentiation Strategy

Firms using the integrated cost leadership/differentiation strategy sell products that create value because of their relatively low cost and reasonable sources of differentiation. The cost of these products is low "relative" to the cost leader's prices, while their differentiation is "reasonable" when compared to the clearly unique features of the differentiator's products.

Although challenging to implement, the integrated cost leadership/differentiation strategy is used frequently in the global economy. The challenge of using this strategy is due largely to the fact that different value chain and support activities (see Chapter 3) are emphasized when using the cost leadership and differentiation strategies. To achieve the cost leadership position, production and process engineering need to be emphasized, with infrequent product changes. To achieve a differentiated position, marketing and new product R&D need to be emphasized while production and process engineering are not. Thus, effective use of the integrated strategy depends on the firm's successful combination of activities intended to reduce costs with activities intended to create differentiated features for a product. As a result, the integrated form of the functional structure must have decision-making patterns that are partially centralized and partially decentralized. Additionally, jobs are semispecialized, and rules and procedures call for some formal and some informal job behavior. All of this requires a measure of flexibility to emphasize one or the other set of functions at any given time.[69]

11-3e Matches between Corporate-Level Strategies and the Multidivisional Structure

As explained earlier, Chandler's research shows that the firm's continuing success leads to product or market diversification or both.[70] The firm's level of diversification is a function of decisions about the number and type of businesses in which it will compete as well as how it will manage those businesses (see Chapter 6). Geared to managing individual organizational functions, increasing diversification eventually creates information processing, coordination, and control problems that the functional structure cannot handle. Thus, using a diversification strategy requires the firm to change from the functional structure to the multidivisional structure to form an appropriate strategy/structure match.

As defined in Figure 6.1, corporate-level strategies have different degrees of product and market diversification. The demands created by different levels of diversification highlight the need for a unique organizational structure to effectively implement each

Figure 11.4 Three Variations of the Multidivisional Structure

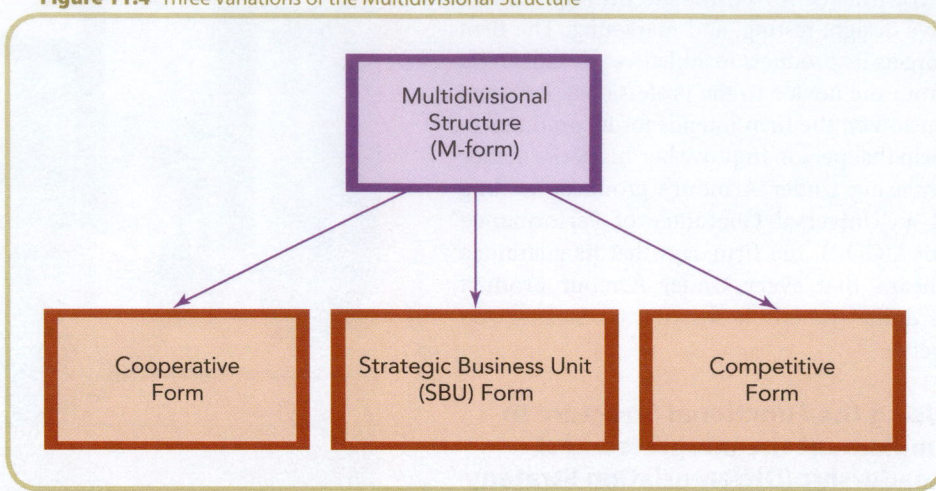

strategy (see Figure 11.4). We discuss the relationships between three diversification strategies and the unique organizational structure that should be matched with each one in the next three sections.

Using the Cooperative Form of the Multidivisional Structure to Implement the Related Constrained Strategy

The **cooperative form** is an M-form structure in which horizontal integration is used to bring about interdivisional cooperation. Divisions in a firm using the related constrained diversification strategy commonly are formed around products, markets, or both. In Figure 11.5, we use product divisions as part of the representation of the cooperative form of the multidivisional structure, although market divisions could be used instead of or in addition to product divisions to develop the figure.

We mentioned in Chapter 6 that Procter & Gamble (P&G) uses a related constrained strategy. We note here that the firm matches the cooperative form of the multidivisional structure to this strategy in order to effectively implement it.

As explained in Chapter 6, the related constrained strategy finds a firm sharing resources and activities across its businesses. Consumer understanding, scale, innovation, go-to-market capabilities, and brand-building are what P&G has identified as its five "core strengths" (or core resources). These strengths are shared across the four industry-based sectors that form the core of P&G's cooperative multidivisional organizational structure. These sectors are Baby, Feminine and Family Care; Beauty, Hair and Personal Care; Fabric and Home Care; and Health and Grooming. The reason P&G shares its five core strengths across the four industry-based sectors is that, according to the firm, these sectors are all "focused on common consumer benefits, share common technologies, and face common competitors."[71] Thus, through its organizational structure, P&G integrates its operations horizontally for the purpose of developing cooperation across the four sectors in which it competes.

Sharing divisional competencies facilitates a firm's efforts to develop economies of scope. As explained in Chapter 6, economies of scope (cost savings resulting from the sharing of competencies developed in one division with another division) are linked with successful use of the related constrained strategy. Interdivisional sharing of competencies, such as takes place within P&G, depends on cooperation, suggesting the use of the cooperative form of the multidivisional structure.[72]

The cooperative structure uses different characteristics of structure (centralization, standardization, and formalization) as integrating mechanisms to facilitate interdivisional cooperation. Frequent, direct contact between division managers, another

The **cooperative form** is an M-form structure in which horizontal integration is used to bring about interdivisional cooperation.

Figure 11.5 Cooperative Form of the Multidivisional Structure for Implementing a Related Constrained Strategy

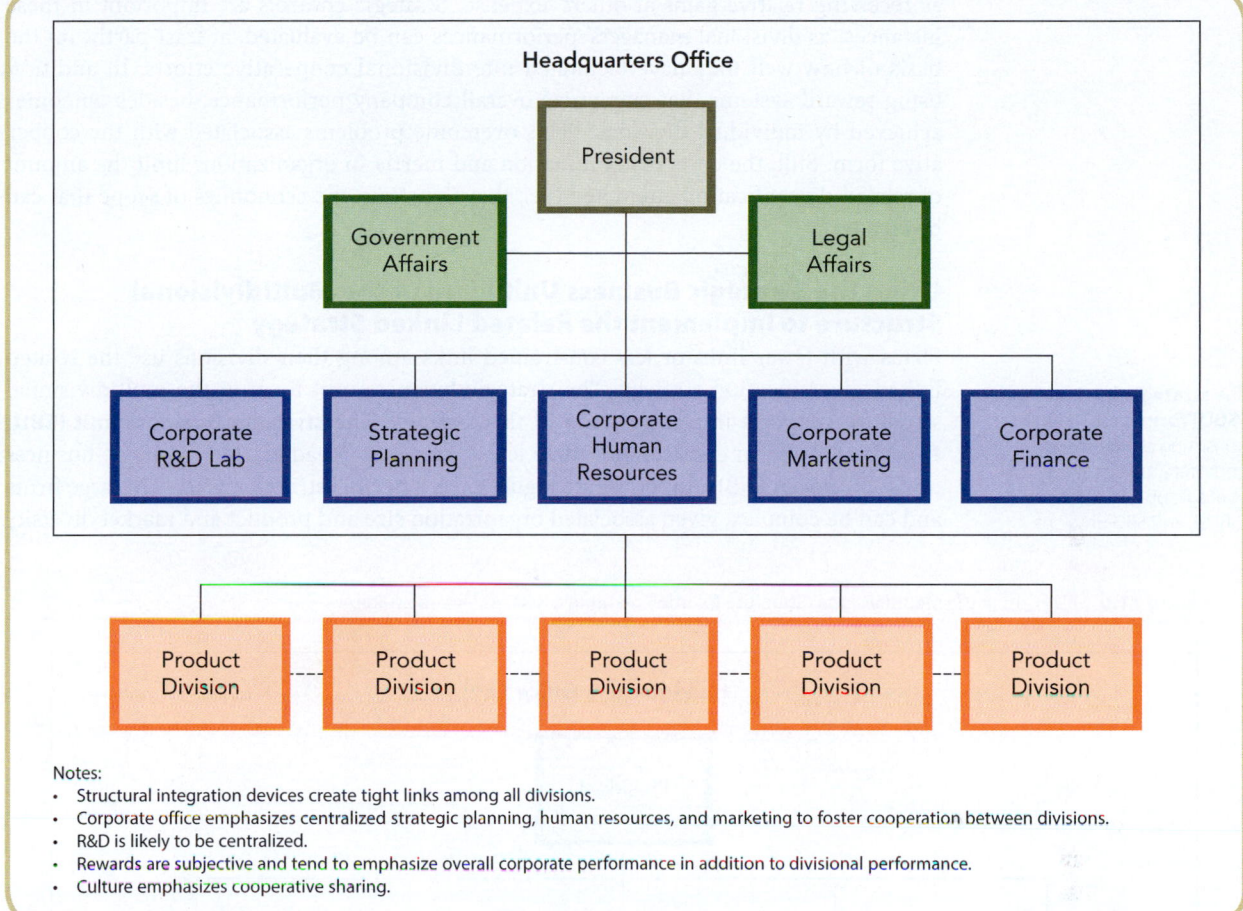

Notes:
- Structural integration devices create tight links among all divisions.
- Corporate office emphasizes centralized strategic planning, human resources, and marketing to foster cooperation between divisions.
- R&D is likely to be centralized.
- Rewards are subjective and tend to emphasize overall corporate performance in addition to divisional performance.
- Culture emphasizes cooperative sharing.

integrating mechanism, encourages and supports cooperation and the sharing of knowledge, capabilities, or other resources that could be used to create new advantages.[73] Sometimes, liaison roles are established in each division to reduce the time division managers spend integrating and coordinating their unit's work with the work occurring in other divisions. Temporary teams or task forces may be formed around projects whose success depends on sharing resources that are embedded within several divisions. Formal integration departments might be established in firms frequently using temporary teams or task forces.

Ultimately, a matrix organization may evolve in firms implementing the related constrained strategy. A *matrix organization* is an organizational structure in which there is a dual structure combining both functional specialization and business product or project specialization.[74] Although complicated, an effective matrix structure can lead to improved coordination among a firm's divisions.[75]

The success of the cooperative multidivisional structure is significantly affected by how well divisions process information. However, because cooperation among divisions implies a loss of managerial autonomy, division managers may not readily commit themselves to the type of integrative information-processing activities that this structure demands. Moreover, coordination among divisions sometimes results in an unequal flow of positive outcomes to divisional managers. In other words, when managerial rewards are based at least in part on the performance of individual divisions, the manager of the division that is able to benefit the most by the sharing of corporate competencies might be viewed as receiving relative gains at others' expense. Strategic controls are important in these instances, as divisional managers' performances can be evaluated, at least partly, on the basis of how well they have facilitated interdivisional cooperative efforts. In addition, using reward systems that emphasize overall company performance, besides outcomes achieved by individual divisions, helps overcome problems associated with the cooperative form. Still, the costs of coordination and inertia in organizations limit the amount of related diversification attempted (i.e., they constrain the economies of scope that can be created).[76]

Using the Strategic Business Unit Form of the Multidivisional Structure to Implement the Related Linked Strategy

The **strategic business unit (SBU) form** is an M-form consisting of three levels: corporate headquarters, strategic business units (SBUs), and SBU divisions.

Firms with fewer links or less constrained links among their divisions use the related linked diversification strategy. The strategic business unit form of the multidivisional structure supports implementation of this strategy. The **strategic business unit (SBU) form** is an M-form consisting of three levels: corporate headquarters, strategic business units (SBUs), and SBU divisions (see Figure 11.6). The SBU structure is used by large firms and can be complex, given associated organization size and product and market diversity.

Figure 11.6 SBU Form of the Multidivisional Structure for Implementing a Related Linked Strategy

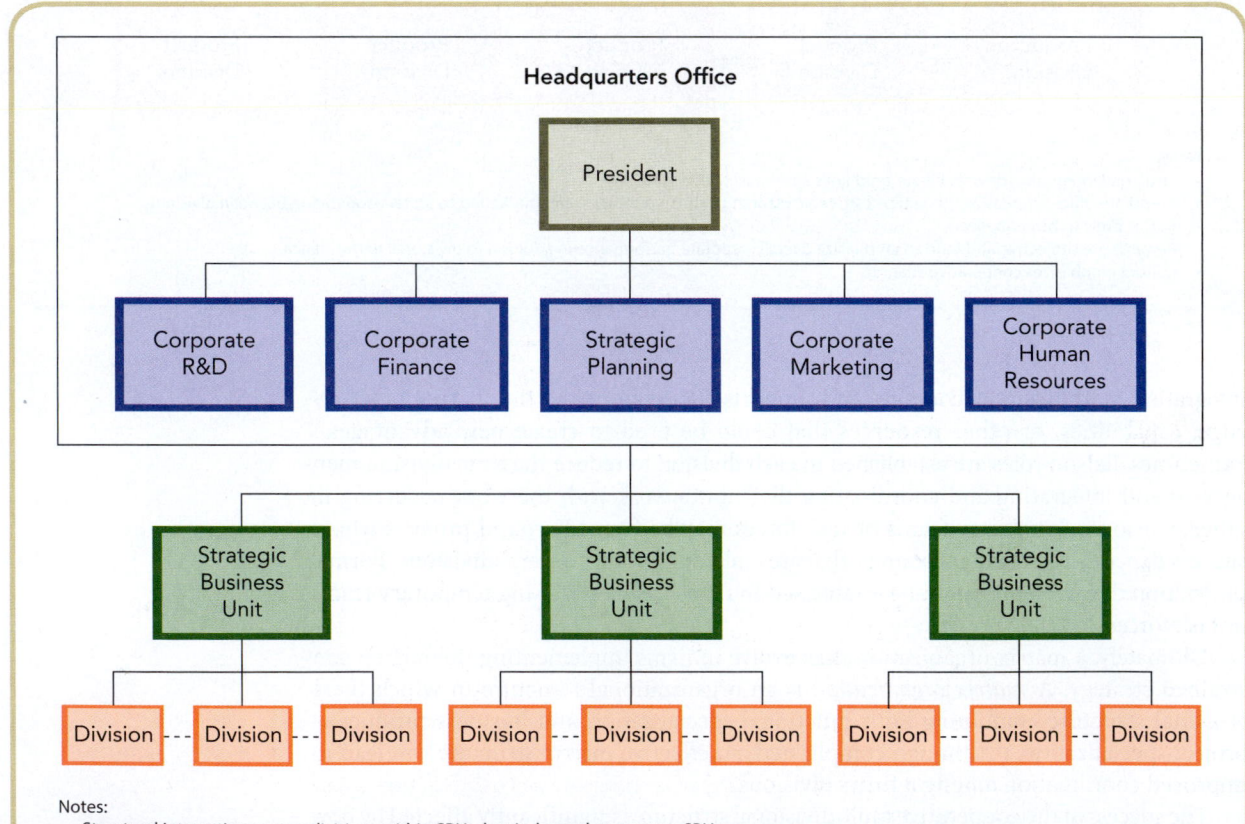

Notes:
- Structural integration among divisions within SBUs, but independence across SBUs.
- Strategic planning may be the most prominent function in headquarters for managing the strategic planning approval process of SBUs for the president.
- Each SBU may have its own budget for staff to foster integration.
- Corporate headquarters staff members serve as consultants to SBUs and divisions, rather than having direct input to product strategy, as in the cooperative form.

The divisions within each SBU are related in terms of shared products or markets or both, but the divisions of one SBU have little in common with the divisions of the other SBUs. Divisions within each SBU share product or market competencies to develop economies of scope and possibly economies of scale. The integrating mechanisms used by the divisions in this structure can be equally well used by the divisions within the individual strategic business units that are part of the SBU form of the multidivisional structure. In this structure, each SBU is a profit center that is controlled and evaluated by the headquarters office. Although both financial and strategic controls are important, on a relative basis, financial controls are vital to headquarters' evaluation of each SBU; strategic controls are critical when the heads of SBUs evaluate their divisions' performances. Strategic controls are also critical to the headquarters' efforts to evaluate the quality of the portfolio of businesses that has been formed and to determine if those businesses are being successfully managed. Sharing competencies among units within individual SBUs is an important characteristic of the SBU form of the multidivisional structure (see the notes to Figure 11.6).

A disadvantage associated with the related linked diversification strategy is that, even when efforts to implement it are being properly supported by use of the SBU form of the multidivisional structure, firms using this strategy and structure combination find it challenging to effectively communicate the value of their operations to shareholders and to other investors.[77] Furthermore, if coordination between SBUs is required, problems can surface because the SBU structure, similar to the competitive form discussed next, does not readily foster cooperation across SBUs. Accordingly, those responsible for implementing the related linked strategy must focus on successfully creating and using the types of integrating mechanisms we discussed earlier.

For many years, Sony Corporation used the related constrained strategy and the cooperative form of the multidivisional structure to implement it. Today though, and in response to declining firm performance, Sony appears to be using the related linked strategy and the SBU form of the multidivisional structure to implement what is a new strategy for the firm. As we discuss in the Strategic Focus, changes to the firm's strategy and organizational structure have occurred recently in order to increase Sony's efficiency (essentially, doing things *right*) and effectiveness (essentially, doing the *right* things).

Using the Competitive Form of the Multidivisional Structure to Implement the Unrelated Diversification Strategy

Firms using the unrelated diversification strategy want to create value through efficient internal capital allocations or by restructuring, buying, and selling businesses.[78] The competitive form of the multidivisional structure supports implementation of this strategy.

The **competitive form** is an M-form structure characterized by complete independence among the firm's divisions that compete for corporate resources (see Figure 11.7). Unlike the divisions included in the cooperative structure, divisions that are part of the competitive structure do not share common corporate strengths. Accordingly, integrating mechanisms are not part of the competitive form of the multidivisional structure.

The efficient internal capital market that is the foundation for using the unrelated diversification strategy requires organizational arrangements emphasizing divisional competition rather than cooperation.[79] Three benefits are expected from the internal competition. First, internal competition creates flexibility (e.g., corporate headquarters can have divisions working on different technologies and projects to identify those with the greatest potential). Resources can then be allocated to the division appearing to have the most potential to drive the entire firm's success. Second, internal competition challenges the status quo and inertia because division heads know that future resource allocations are a product of excellent current performance as well as superior positioning in terms of future performance. Third, internal competition motivates effort in that the challenge of

The **competitive form** is an M-form structure characterized by complete independence among the firm's divisions that compete for corporate resources.

Strategic **Focus**

Sony Corporation's New Organizational Structure: Greater Financial Accountability and Focused Allocations of Resources

Launched in 1946 in Japan, Sony gained a reputation for producing innovative products that were sold throughout the world. In fact, the firm's success was instrumental to Japan's development as a powerful exporter during the 1960s, 1970s, and 1980s. Sony was sometimes "first to market" with an innovative product, while sometimes being able to rapidly enhance a product's capabilities by innovating. Introduced in 1979, the Sony Walkman, which was a personal stereo tape deck, is an example of a "first to market" product from Sony. The transistor radio is a product that Sony innovated in a way that made the product, which was initially developed through a joint venture between Regency Electronics and Texas Instruments, commercially viable. Regardless of the type, innovation has been critical to how Sony competes in multiple product areas.

Realizing the value that could be gained by sharing resources, capabilities, and core competencies across types of businesses, Sony's success for many decades was a product of its commitment to "convergence," which the firm operationalized by linking its activities across businesses such as film, music, and digital electronics. In essence, Sony was successful for many years as a result of being able to effectively implement the related constrained strategy. But as we mentioned earlier when discussing the related constrained strategy and the structure needed to implement it, an inability to efficiently process information and coordinate an array of integrated activities between units are problems that may surface when using the cooperative form of the multidivisional structure. This appears to be the case for Sony. In response to performance problems that have plagued the firm for over a decade, Sony's CEO recently announced significant changes to the company's organizational structure. Put into place in October 2015, these structural changes are thought to be the foundation for improvements to Sony's ability to create value for customers and enhance wealth for shareholders.

At the core of the structural changes are efforts to group the firm's businesses in ways that allow Sony's upper-level leaders to more effectively allocate financial capital. A key objective is to allocate capital to the businesses with the strongest potential not just to grow, but to grow profitably.

Sony is now structured into three core sectors or business units—*growth drivers*, *stable profit generators*, and *volatility management*. In essence, the new structure is an example of the SBU form of the multidivisional structure. According to the CEO, these units have been formed to "emphasize profitability over volume, secure business unit autonomy with a focus on shareholder value, and provide a clearer definition of each business unit's position within Sony's overall business." Devices, Game & Network Services, Pictures, and Music comprise the growth drivers unit. Viewed as potentially profitable areas of growth, Sony intends to invest aggressively to support these businesses. Imaging Products & Solutions and Video and Sound are the business areas forming the stable profit generators unit. These businesses are expected to yield steady profits and positive cash flows. Finally, TV and Mobile Communications formed the volatility management unit. Operating in markets with high volatility and challenging competitive conditions, the intention with this unit is to find ways to generate stable profits. For all three units, Return on Equity (ROE) is the performance criterion being used to judge the success of each business that is included in one of the units. Each business is expected to achieve an annual ROE of 10 percent.

Barone Firenze/Shutterstock.com

Pictured here is Sony's PS Vita as it was introduced during a shown in San Francisco, CA.

Three goals are being sought by using the SBU form of the multidivisional structure. First, Sony's CEO wants the organizational structure to be one that clearly promotes accountability and responsibility for each unit. The second goal "is to foster management policies and direction that place an emphasis on sustainable profit generation and the continuity of each business unit." The third goal revolves around the intention of continuing to eliminate unnecessary managerial layers as a means of enhancing innovation on the part of everyone involved with each business in each unit.

Sony's CEO is confident that the firm's commitment to implementing the SBU form of the multidivisional structure as a foundation for using the related linked strategy will yield positive outcomes. Time will tell if this is the case or not. But, the new organizational structure that has been created at Sony Corporation does appear to be one with the potential to support efforts to successfully use the related linked strategy.

Sources: 2015, Corporate Information, Sony Home Page, www.sony.com, May 17; 2015, Here's Sony's new business strategy, *Business Insider*, www.businessinsider.com, February 21; T. Mochizuki & E. Pfanner, 2015, Sony expects profits to surge this fiscal year, *Wall Street Journal Online*, www.wsj.com, April 30; T. Mochizuki & E. Pfanner, How Sony makes money off Apple's iPhone, *Wall Street Journal Online*, www.wsj.com, April 28; E. Pfanner & T. Mochizuki, 2015, Sony's mobile unit seeks profit, innovation, *Wall Street Journal Online*, www.wsj.com, March 2; M. Schilling, 2015, Sony strategy centers on splitting businesses, not selling—for now, *Variety*, www.variety.com, February 26.

Figure 11.7 Competitive Form of the Multidivisional Structure for Implementing an Unrelated Strategy

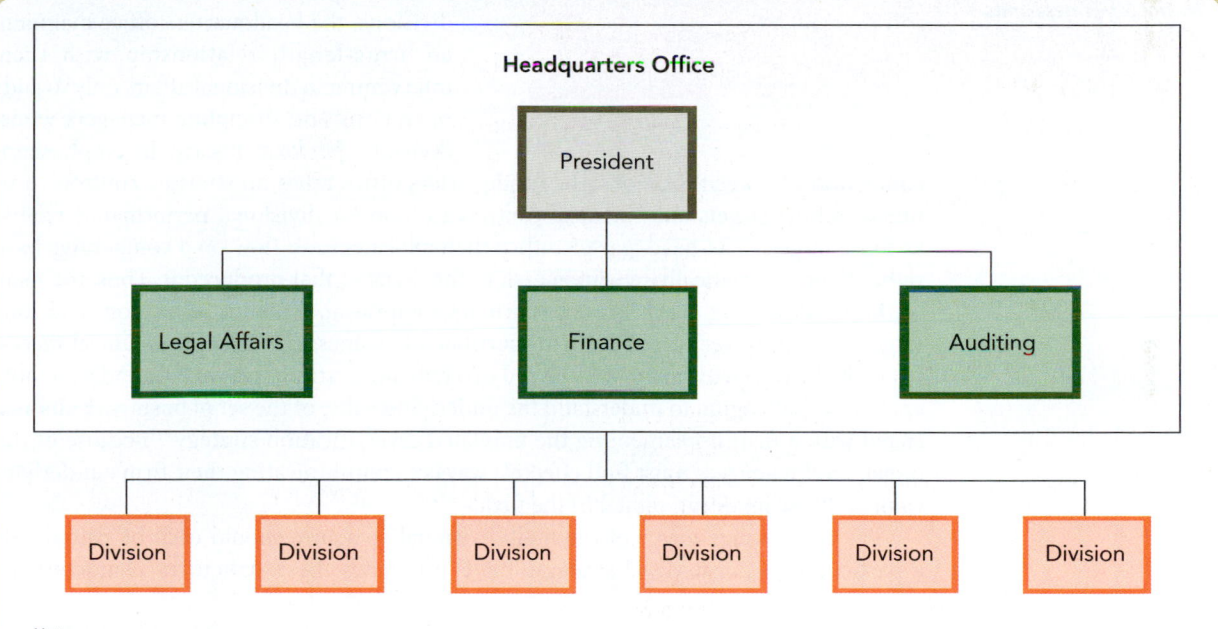

Notes:
- Corporate headquarters has a small staff.
- Finance and auditing are the most prominent functions in the headquarters office to manage cash flow and assure the accuracy of performance data coming from divisions.
- The legal affairs function becomes important when the firm acquires or divests assets.
- Divisions are independent and separate for financial evaluation purposes.
- Divisions retain strategic control, but cash is managed by the corporate office.
- Divisions compete for corporate resources.

competing against internal peers can be as great as the challenge of competing against external rivals.[80] In this structure, organizational controls (primarily financial controls) are used to emphasize and support internal competition among separate divisions and as the basis for allocating corporate capital based on divisions' performances.

Textron Inc., a large "multi-industry" company, seeks to identify, research, select, acquire, and integrate companies and has developed a set of rigorous criteria to guide decision making. Textron continuously looks to enhance and reshape its portfolio by divesting noncore

Pictured here is a Bell Helicopter, a product manufactured by one of Textron's business units.

assets and acquiring branded businesses in attractive industries with substantial long-term growth potential. Textron operates a number of independent businesses including Bell Helicopter, Textron Aviation, Textron Specialized Vehicles, and Textron Finance. Leaders of these businesses are responsible for effectively guiding the day-to-day competitive actions of their units. Consistent with the mandates of the competitive form of the multidivisional structure, "Textron's Corporate Office provides oversight, direction, and assistance to its businesses."[81] The profit earned by individual business units within Textron is an important measure the firm uses to decide future capital allocations.[82]

To emphasize competitiveness among divisions, the headquarters office maintains an arm's-length relationship with them, intervening in divisional affairs only to audit operations and discipline managers whose divisions perform poorly. In emphasizing competition between divisions, the headquarters office relies on strategic controls to set rate-of-return targets and financial controls to monitor divisional performance relative to those targets. The headquarters office then allocates cash flow on a competitive basis, rather than automatically returning cash to the division that produced it. Thus, the focus of the headquarters' work is on performance appraisal, resource allocation, and long-range planning to verify that the firm's portfolio of businesses will lead to financial success.

As is the case with the related linked diversification strategy, investors and shareholders find it challenging to understand the underlying value of the set of business units associated with a firm implementing the unrelated diversification strategy.[83] Because of this, upper-level managers must find effective ways of communicating their firm's underlying value to those investing capital in the firm.

The three major forms of the multidivisional structure should each be paired with a particular corporate-level strategy. Table 11.1 shows these structures' characteristics.

Table 11.1 Characteristics of the Structures Necessary to Implement the Related Constrained, Related Linked, and Unrelated Diversification Strategies

Structural Characteristics	Overall Structural Form		
	Cooperative M-Form (Related Constrained Strategy)	SBU M-Form (Related Linked Strategy)	Competitive M-Form (Unrelated Diversification Strategy)
Centralization of operations	Centralized at corporate office	Partially centralized (in SBUs)	Decentralized to divisions
Use of integration mechanisms	Extensive	Moderate	Nonexistent
Divisional performance evaluation	Emphasizes subjective (strategic) criteria	Uses a mixture of subjective (strategic) and objective (financial) criteria	Emphasizes objective (financial) criteria
Divisional incentive compensation	Linked to overall corporate performance	Mixed linkage to corporate, SBU, and divisional performance	Linked to divisional performance

Differences exist in the degree of centralization, the focus of the performance evaluation, the horizontal structures (integrating mechanisms), and the incentive compensation schemes. The most centralized and most costly structural form is the cooperative structure. The least centralized, with the lowest bureaucratic costs, is the competitive structure. The SBU structure requires partial centralization and involves some of the mechanisms necessary to implement the relatedness between divisions. Also, the divisional incentive compensation awards are allocated according to both SBUs and corporate performance.

11-3f Matches between International Strategies and Worldwide Structure

In Chapter 8 we explained that international strategies are increasingly important for companies' long-term competitive success in what is today virtually a borderless global economy.[84] Among other benefits, firms are able to search for new markets and then form the competencies necessary to serve them when implementing an international strategy.[85]

As with business-level and corporate-level strategies, unique organizational structures are necessary to successfully implement individual international strategies, given the different cultural, institutional, and legal environments around the world.[86] Forming proper matches between international strategies and organizational structures facilitates the firm's efforts to effectively coordinate and control its global operations. More importantly, research findings confirm the validity of the international strategy/structure matches we discuss here.[87]

Using the Worldwide Geographic Area Structure to Implement the Multidomestic Strategy

The *multidomestic strategy* decentralizes the firm's strategic and operating decisions to business units in each country so that product characteristics can be tailored to local preferences. Firms using this strategy try to isolate themselves from global competitive forces by establishing protected market positions or by competing in industry segments that are most affected by differences among local countries. The worldwide geographic area structure is used to implement this strategy. The **worldwide geographic area structure** emphasizes national interests and facilitates the firm's efforts to satisfy local differences (see Figure 11.8).

Using the multidomestic strategy requires little coordination between different country markets, meaning that formal integrating mechanisms among divisions around the world are not needed. Indeed, the coordination among units in a firm's worldwide geographic area structure that does take place is informal in nature.

From a historical perspective, we note that the multidomestic strategy/worldwide geographic area structure match evolved as a natural outgrowth of the multicultural European marketplace. Friends and family members of the main business who were sent as expatriates to foreign countries to develop the independent country subsidiary often adopted the worldwide geographic area structure. The relationship to corporate headquarters by divisions took place through informal communication.

Founded in San Francisco, CA, in 2009, Uber Technologies, Inc. claims that it is "evolving the way the world moves by seamlessly connecting riders to drivers through more possibilities for riders and more business for drivers."[88] Now growing rapidly outside its U.S. home market, Asia is the target of Uber's most recent international growth ambitions. Early evidence from the firm's entry into China, obviously a key market in Asia, is encouraging. In fact, the firm's China expansion manager recently said that "China has exceeded our wildest dreams."[89] Seemingly critical to this success is Uber's decision to "go local" in serving Chinese customers. Technology used to track its services, payment systems in place, and the marketing of its operations were all localized in the first 13 Chinese cities in which Uber chose to operate. Indeed, the firm decided to treat each city

The **worldwide geographic area structure** emphasizes national interests and facilitates the firm's efforts to satisfy local differences.

Figure 11.8 Worldwide Geographic Area Structure for Implementing a Multidomestic Strategy

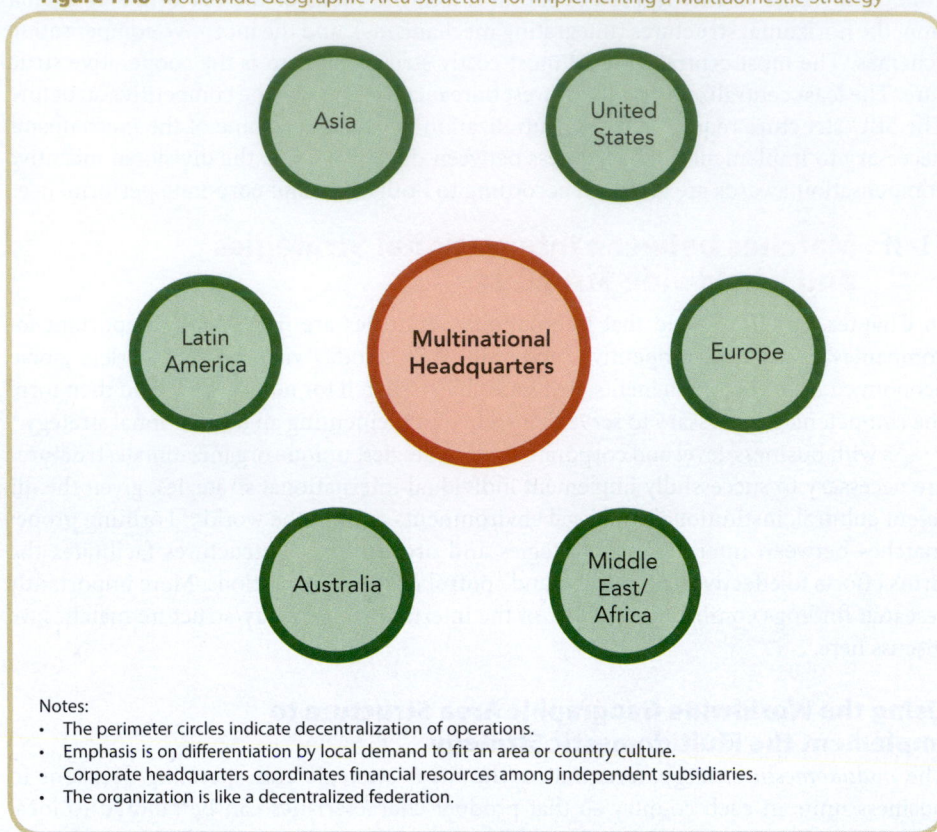

Notes:
- The perimeter circles indicate decentralization of operations.
- Emphasis is on differentiation by local demand to fit an area or country culture.
- Corporate headquarters coordinates financial resources among independent subsidiaries.
- The organization is like a decentralized federation.

as though it was a stand-alone country (facilitating this choice is the fact that each of the 13 cities had a population of 10 million or more).

There is a key challenge associated with effectively using the multidomestic strategy/ worldwide geographic area structure match—namely, the inability to create global efficiencies. This inability is a product of companies' focus on serving unique customer needs particularly well. The inability to create global efficiencies in this match challenges firms to find ways to control costs while trying to serve local customers' unique needs.

Will not being able to create global efficiencies be a problem for Uber? Perhaps. By the same token, as long as the firm can continue to identify and serve the unique needs of customers in different markets in ways that create value for them, being able to develop scale economies will not be a fatal blow to Uber's efforts to succeed in international markets.

In other instances, the nature of products companies seek to sell in international markets and market conditions themselves demand that a firm be able to develop economies of scale on a worldwide basis. This need calls for firms to use the global strategy and its structural match, the worldwide product divisional structure.

Using the Worldwide Product Divisional Structure to Implement the Global Strategy

With the corporation's home office dictating competitive strategy, the *global strategy* is one through which the firm offers standardized products across country markets. The firm's success depends principally on its ability to develop economies of scale while competing on a global basis and while serving customers without specific and unique needs relative to the firm's standardized product.

Figure 11.9 Worldwide Product Divisional Structure for Implementing a Global Strategy

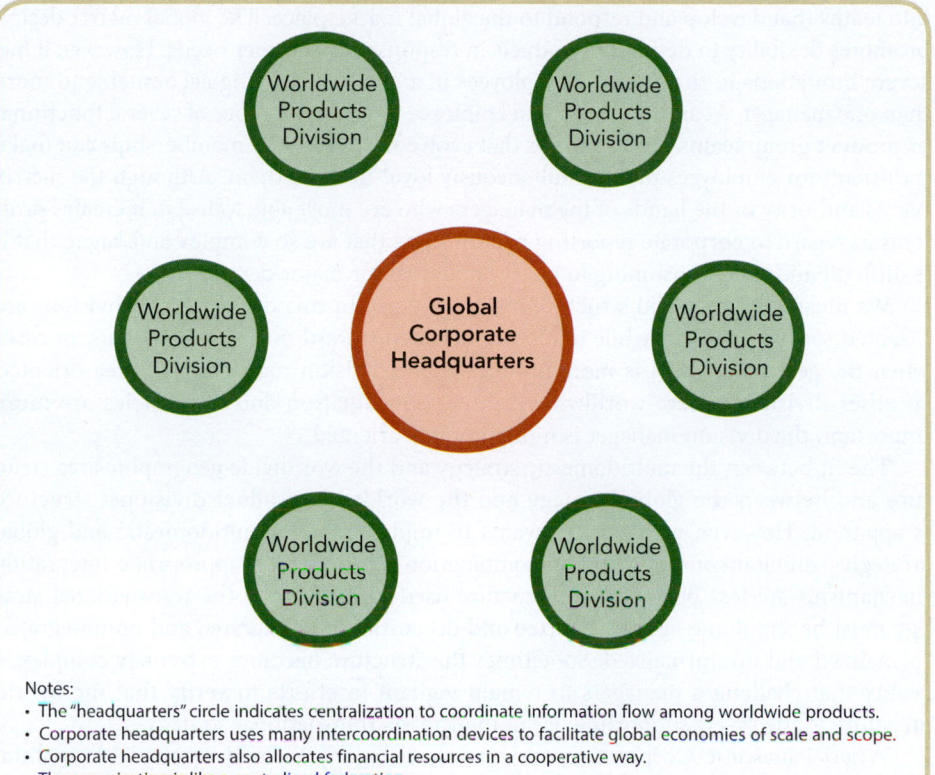

Notes:
• The "headquarters" circle indicates centralization to coordinate information flow among worldwide products.
• Corporate headquarters uses many intercoordination devices to facilitate global economies of scale and scope.
• Corporate headquarters also allocates financial resources in a cooperative way.
• The organization is like a centralized federation.

The worldwide product divisional structure supports use of the global strategy. In the **worldwide product divisional structure**, decision-making authority is centralized in the worldwide division headquarters to coordinate and integrate decisions and actions among divisional business units (see Figure 11.9).

Integrating mechanisms are important to the effective use of the worldwide product divisional structure. Direct contact between managers, liaison roles between departments, and both temporary task forces and permanent teams are examples of these mechanisms. The disadvantages of the global strategy/worldwide structure combination are the difficulties involved with coordinating decisions and actions across country borders and the inability to quickly respond to local needs and preferences. To deal with these types of disadvantages, firms sometimes choose to try to somewhat simultaneously focus on geography and products. This simultaneous focus is similar to the combination structure that we discuss next.

Using the Combination Structure to Implement the Transnational Strategy

The *transnational strategy* calls for the firm to combine the multidomestic strategy's local responsiveness with the global strategy's efficiency. Firms using this strategy are trying to gain the advantages of both local responsiveness and global efficiency.[90] The combination structure is used to implement the transnational strategy. The **combination structure** is a structure drawing characteristics and mechanisms from both the worldwide geographic area structure and the worldwide product divisional structure. The transnational strategy is often implemented through two possible combination structures: a global matrix structure and a hybrid global design.[91]

In the **worldwide product divisional structure**, decision-making authority is centralized in the worldwide division headquarters to coordinate and integrate decisions and actions among divisional business units.

The **combination structure** is a structure drawing characteristics and mechanisms from both the worldwide geographic area structure and the worldwide product divisional structure.

The global matrix design brings together both local market and product expertise into teams that develop and respond to the global marketplace. The global matrix design promotes flexibility in designing products in response to customer needs. However, it has severe limitations in that it places employees in a position of being accountable to more than one manager. At any given time, an employee may be a member of several functional or product group teams. Relationships that evolve from multiple memberships can make it difficult for employees to be simultaneously loyal to all of them. Although the matrix places authority in the hands of the managers who are most able to use it, it creates problems in regard to corporate reporting relationships that are so complex and vague that it is difficult and time-consuming to receive approval for major decisions.

We illustrate the hybrid structure in Figure 11.10. In this design, some divisions are oriented toward products while others are oriented toward market areas. Thus, in cases when the geographic area is more important, the division managers are area-oriented. In other divisions where worldwide product coordination and efficiencies are more important, the division manager is more product-oriented.

The fit between the multidomestic strategy and the worldwide geographic area structure and between the global strategy and the worldwide product divisional structure is apparent. However, when a firm wants to implement the multidomestic and global strategies simultaneously through a combination structure, the appropriate integrating mechanisms are less obvious. The structure used to implement the transnational strategy must be simultaneously centralized and decentralized, integrated and nonintegrated, formalized and nonformalized. Sometimes the structure becomes extremely complex, a reality that challenges managers to remain vigilant in efforts to verify that the hybrid structure is effectively supporting use of their firm's transnational strategy.

When Panasonic Corporation (a Japanese company formally named Matsushita) started selling home appliances in the Chinese market several decades ago, its only attempt at localization was to offer less expensive versions of its developed market standard offerings. Japanese firms often sold standard products across the world, implementing the global strategy using the worldwide product divisional structure. However, they found that local competitors such as Haier were quickly outpacing their appliance sales in China, Haier's home market. Through this experience, Panasonic learned to engage more deeply within a country or regional market to adapt its appliances more closely to the local customer's demands.[92] As a result, the firm is using the transnational strategy and may be using the hybrid form of the combination structure to implement it.[93] (Recently Panasonic's portfolio

Figure 11.10 Hybrid Form of the Combination Structure for Implementing a Transnational Strategy

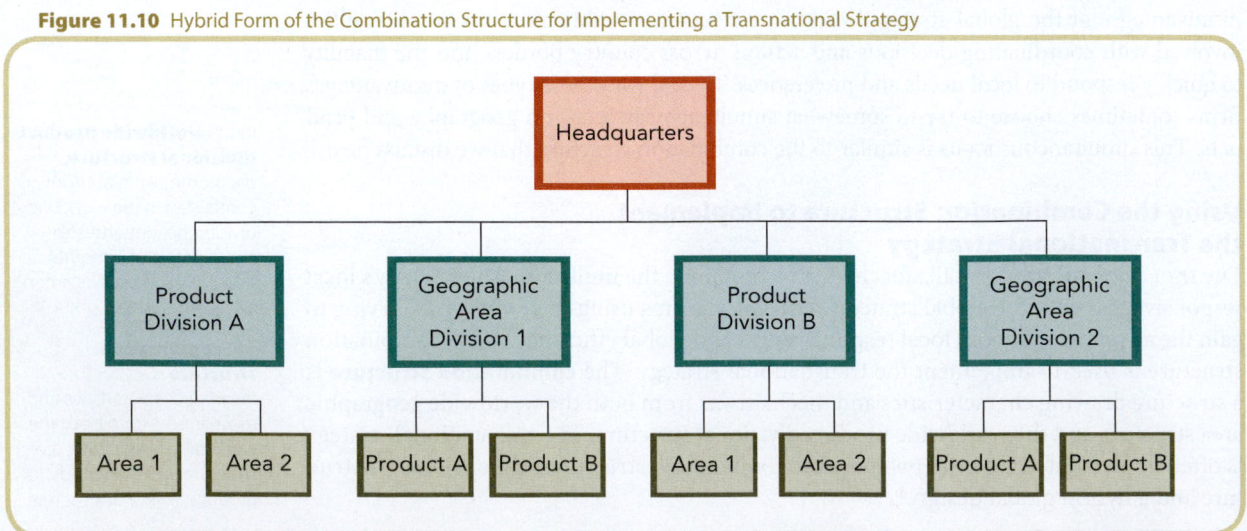

included 473 companies housed in multiple business units. This demonstrates the challenge a firm of this size and complexity faces when determining the optimal structure to match with individual strategies being used as a foundation for hopefully outperform rivals in regions and countries throughout the world.[94])

11-3g Matches between Cooperative Strategies and Network Structures

As discussed in Chapter 9, a network strategy exists when partners form several alliances in order to improve the performance of the alliance network itself through cooperative endeavors.[95] The greater levels of environmental complexity and uncertainty facing companies in today's competitive environment are causing more firms to use cooperative strategies such as strategic alliances.[96] Firms can form cooperative relationships with many of their stakeholders, including customers, suppliers, and competitors. When a firm becomes involved with combinations of cooperative relationships, it is part of a strategic network, or what others call an alliance constellation or portfolio.[97]

A *strategic network* is a group of firms that has been formed to create value by participating in multiple cooperative arrangements. An effective strategic network facilitates discovering opportunities beyond those identified by individual network participants. A strategic network can be a source of competitive advantage for its members when its operations create value that is difficult for competitors to duplicate and that network members can't create by themselves.[98] Strategic networks are used to implement business-level, corporate-level, and international cooperative strategies.

The typical strategic network is a loose federation of partners participating in the network's operations on a flexible basis. At the core or center of the strategic network, the *strategic center firm* is the one around which the network's cooperative relationships revolve (see Figure 11.11).

Figure 11.11 A Strategic Network

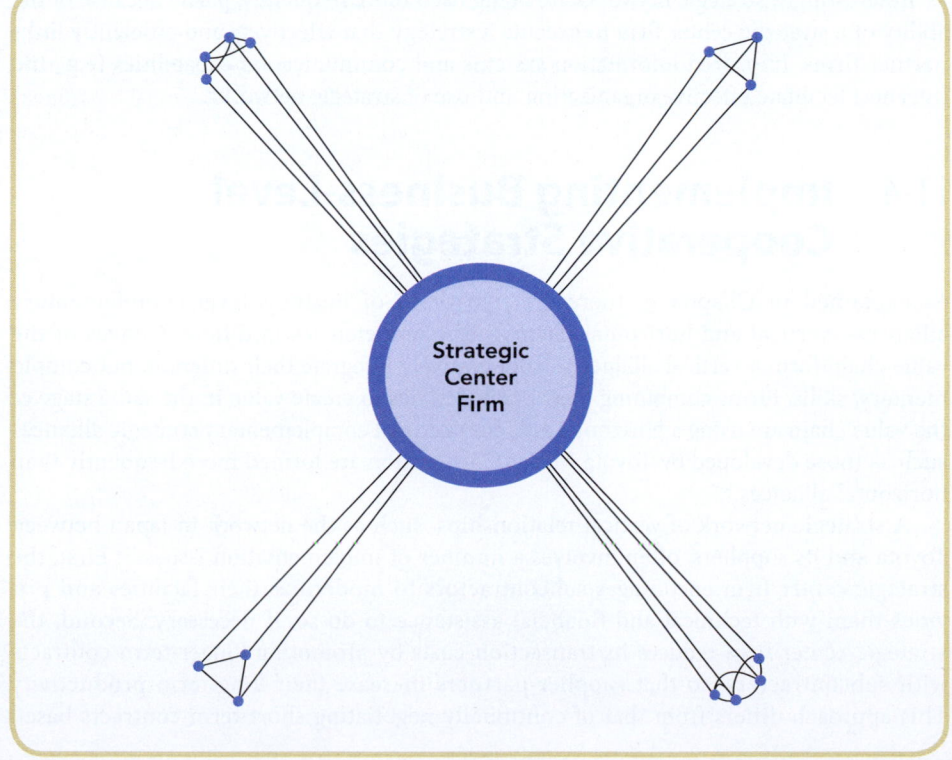

Strategic Center Firm

Because of its central position, the strategic center firm is the foundation for the strategic network's structure. Concerned with various aspects of organizational structure, such as formally reporting relationships and procedures, the strategic center firm manages what are often complex, cooperative interactions among network partners. To perform the tasks discussed next, the strategic center firm must make sure that incentives for participating in the network are aligned so that network firms continue to have a reason to remain connected.[99] The strategic center firm is engaged in four primary tasks as it manages the strategic network and controls its operations:[100]

Strategic Outsourcing.   The strategic center firm outsources and partners with more firms than other network members. At the same time, the strategic center firm requires network partners to be more than contractors. Members are expected to find opportunities for the network to create value through its cooperative work.[101]

Competencies.   To increase network effectiveness, the strategic center firm seeks ways to support each member's efforts to develop core competencies with the potential of benefiting the network.

Technology.   The strategic center firm is responsible for managing the development and sharing of technology-based ideas among network members. The structural requirement that members submit formal reports detailing the technology-oriented outcomes of their efforts to the strategic center firm facilitates this activity.

Race to Learn.   The strategic center firm emphasizes that the principal dimensions of competition are between value chains and between networks of value chains. Because of these interconnections, an individual strategic network is only as strong as its weakest value-chain link. With its centralized decision-making authority and responsibility, the strategic center firm guides participants in efforts to form network-specific competitive advantages. The need for each participant to have capabilities that can be the foundation for the network's competitive advantages encourages friendly rivalry among participants seeking to develop the skills needed to quickly form new capabilities that create value for the network.[102]

Interestingly, strategic networks are being used more frequently, partly because of the ability of a strategic center firm to execute a strategy that effectively and efficiently links partner firms. Improved information systems and communication capabilities (e.g., the Internet) facilitate effective organization and use of strategic networks.

11-4   Implementing Business-Level Cooperative Strategies

As explained in Chapter 9, there are two types of business-level complementary alliances—vertical and horizontal. Firms with competencies in different stages of the value chain form a vertical alliance to cooperatively integrate their different, but complementary, skills. Firms combining their competencies to create value in the same stage of the value chain are using a horizontal alliance. Vertical complementary strategic alliances such as those developed by Toyota Motor Corporation are formed more frequently than horizontal alliances.[103]

A strategic network of vertical relationships, such as the network in Japan between Toyota and its suppliers, often involves a number of implementation issues.[104] First, the strategic center firm encourages subcontractors to modernize their facilities and provides them with technical and financial assistance to do so, if necessary. Second, the strategic center firm reduces its transaction costs by promoting longer-term contracts with subcontractors, so that supplier-partners increase their long-term productivity. This approach differs from that of continually negotiating short-term contracts based on unit pricing. Third, the strategic center firm enables engineers in upstream companies (suppliers) to have better communications with those companies with whom it has contracts for services. As a result, suppliers and the strategic center firm become more interdependent and less independent.

The lean production system (a vertical complementary strategic alliance) pioneered by Toyota and others has been diffused throughout many industries.[105] In vertical complementary strategic alliances, such as the one between Toyota and its suppliers, the strategic center firm is obvious, as is the structure that firm establishes. However, the same is not always true with horizontal complementary strategic alliances where firms try to create value in the same part of the value chain. For example, airline alliances are commonly formed to create value in the marketing and sales primary activity segment of the value chain. Because air carriers commonly participate in multiple horizontal complementary alliances, such as the Oneworld alliance among American Airlines, British Airways, Iberia, Japan Airlines, TAM Airlines, and others, it is difficult to determine the strategic center firm. Moreover, participating in several alliances can cause firms to question partners' true loyalties and intentions. Also, if rivals band together in too many collaborative activities, one or more governments may suspect the possibility of explicit collusion among partnering firms (see Chapter 9). For these reasons, horizontal complementary alliances are used less often and less successfully than their vertical counterpart, although there are examples of success, such as some of the collaborations among automobile and aircraft manufacturers.

11-5 Implementing Corporate-Level Cooperative Strategies

Some corporate-level strategies are used to reduce costs. This was the objective with the collaboration that was formed initially between Walgreens and Swiss-based Alliance Boots, a pharmacy-led health and beauty group. This partnership helped the firms negotiate lower prices with drug suppliers, reducing their overall costs as a result of doing so.[106]

Unilever is partnering with some firms to reach a different objective. Committed to decoupling its growth from negative environmental and social effects from its operations, Unilever formed an alliance with Jacobs Engineering Group Inc. in 2010 to reduce the company's carbon, water, and waste footprint across its manufacturing locations throughout the world. Through a partnership with NGO Rainforest Alliance, Unilever was able to source "100 percent of all tea for its Lipton and PG Tips products from certified growers."[107] (Additional information about Unilever and its commitment to sustainability is provided in this chapter's Mini-Case.) Still other corporate-level cooperative strategies (such as franchising) are used to facilitate product and market diversification. As a cooperative strategy, franchising allows the firm to use its competencies to extend or diversify its product or market reach without completing a merger or acquisition.[108]

The potential to create synergy is a key reason corporate-level cooperative strategies, such as those involving Walgreens, Unilever, and active franchisers including McDonald's, are formed.[109] Historically, McDonald's approach to franchising as a corporate-level cooperative strategy found the firm emphasizing a limited value-priced menu. However, as mentioned in an earlier Strategic Focus, the firm's structure is being changed. One objective of these structural changes is to strip over $300 million from the firm's costs by the end of 2017. Selling 3,500 company-owned restaurants to franchisees by 2018 is an action being taken to help reduce costs. With these sales, global franchise ownership of McDonald's restaurants will reach 90 percent.[110] McDonald's' franchising system is a strategic network. Overall, McDonald's headquarters serves as the strategic center firm for the network's franchisees. The headquarters office uses strategic and financial controls to verify that the franchisees' operations create the greatest value for the entire network.

11-6   Implementing International Cooperative Strategies

Strategic networks formed to implement international cooperative strategies result in firms competing in several countries.[111] Differences among countries' regulatory environments increase the challenge of managing international networks and verifying that, at a minimum, a network's operations comply with all legal requirements.[112]

Distributed strategic networks are the organizational structure used to manage international cooperative strategies. As shown in Figure 11.12, several regional strategic center firms are included in the distributed network to manage partner firms' multiple cooperative arrangements.[113] The structure used to implement the international cooperative strategy is complex and demands careful attention to be used successfully.

Figure 11.12 A Distributed Strategic Network

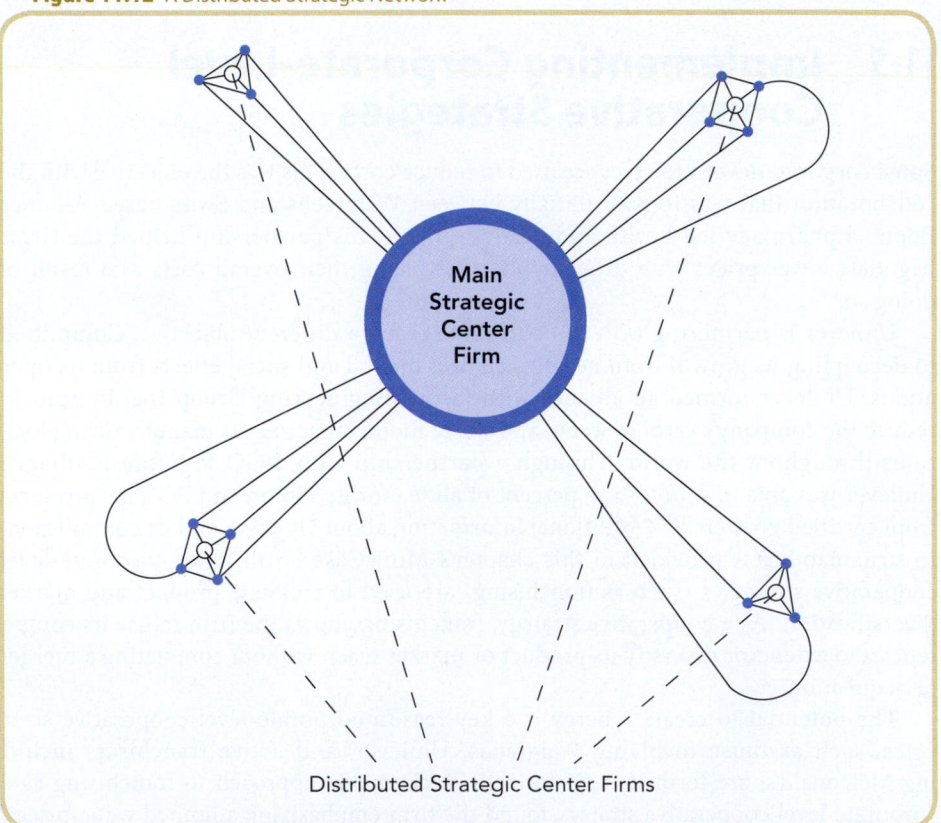

Distributed Strategic Center Firms

SUMMARY

- Organizational structure specifies the firm's formal reporting relationships, procedures, controls, and authority and decision-making processes. Essentially, organizational structure details the work to be done in a firm and how that work is to be accomplished. Organizational controls guide the use of strategy, indicate how to compare actual and expected results, and suggest actions to take to improve performance when it falls below expectations. A proper match between strategy and structure can lead to a competitive advantage.

- Strategic controls (largely subjective criteria) and financial controls (largely objective criteria) are the two types of organizational controls used to support the implementation of a strategy. Both controls are critical, although their degree of emphasis varies based on individual matches between strategy and structure.

- Strategy and structure influence each other; overall though, strategy has a stronger influence on structure. Research indicates that firms tend to change structure when declining performance forces them to do so. Effective managers anticipate the need for structural change and quickly modify structure to better accommodate the firm's strategy when evidence calls for that action.

- The functional structure is used to implement business-level strategies. The cost leadership strategy requires a centralized functional structure—one in which manufacturing efficiency and process engineering are emphasized. The differentiation strategy's functional structure decentralizes implementation-related decisions, especially those concerned with marketing, to those involved with individual organizational functions. Focus strategies, often used in small firms, require a simple structure until such time that the firm diversifies in terms of products and/or markets.

- Unique combinations of different forms of the multidivisional structure are matched with different corporate-level diversification strategies to properly implement these strategies. The cooperative M-form, used to implement the related constrained corporate-level strategy, has a centralized corporate office and extensive integrating mechanisms. Divisional incentives are linked to overall corporate performance to foster cooperation among divisions. The related linked SBU M-form structure establishes separate profit centers within the diversified firm. Each profit center or SBU may have divisions offering similar products, but the SBUs are often unrelated to each other. The competitive M-form structure, used to implement the unrelated diversification strategy, is highly decentralized, lacks integrating mechanisms, and utilizes objective financial criteria to evaluate each unit's performance.

- The multidomestic strategy, implemented through the worldwide geographic area structure, emphasizes decentralization and locates all functional activities in the host country or geographic area. The worldwide product divisional structure is used to implement the global strategy. This structure is centralized in order to coordinate and integrate different functions' activities to gain global economies of scope and economies of scale. Decision-making authority is centralized in the firm's worldwide division headquarters.

- The transnational strategy—a strategy through which the firm seeks the local responsiveness of the multidomestic strategy and the global efficiency of the global strategy—is implemented through the combination structure. Because it must be simultaneously centralized and decentralized, integrated and nonintegrated, and formalized and nonformalized, the combination structure is difficult to organize and successfully manage. Two structures can be used to implement the transnational strategy: the matrix and the hybrid structure with both geographic and product-oriented divisions.

- Increasingly important to competitive success, cooperative strategies are implemented through organizational structures framed around strategic networks. Strategic center firms play a critical role in managing strategic networks. Business-level strategies are often employed in vertical and horizontal alliance networks. Corporate-level cooperative strategies are used to pursue product and market diversification. Franchising is one type of corporate strategy that uses a strategic network to implement this strategy. This is also true for international cooperative strategies, where distributed networks are often used.

KEY TERMS

REVIEW QUESTIONS

1. What is organizational structure and what are organizational controls? What are the differences between strategic controls and financial controls? What is the importance of these differences?

2. What does it mean to say that strategy and structure have a reciprocal relationship?

3. What are the characteristics of the different functional structures used to implement the cost leadership, differentiation, integrated cost leadership/differentiation, and focused business-level strategies?

4. What are the differences among the three versions of the multidivisional (M-form) organizational structures that are used to implement the related constrained, the related linked, and the unrelated corporate-level diversification strategies?

5. What organizational structures are used to implement the multidomestic, global, and transnational international strategies?

6. What is a strategic network? What is a strategic center firm? How is a strategic center firm used in business-level, corporate-level, and international cooperative strategies?

Mini-Case

Unilever Cooperates with Many Firms and Nonprofit Organizations to Implement Its Strategy While Creating a More Sustainable Environment

Unilever, a European-headquartered (in both the Netherlands and the United Kingdom) consumer products company, is committed to using a sustainable environment strategy while manufacturing its large array of food and beverage products. Historically, consumer products companies, especially those from Europe, have pursued the multidomestic strategy, needing to adapt their products to each country or region market. Accordingly, most have implemented their strategy using the worldwide geographic area structure. Many consumer product companies, such as Avon, have begun to use aspects of the worldwide product structure to become more efficient. This is also the case with Unilever. However, Unilever has continued to emphasize geographic areas, but it has done so using the transnational strategy while implementing the combination structure to meet local market responsiveness as well as global efficiency objectives. Moreover, its CEO, Paul Pullman, who took the job in 2009, has also suggested, "our purpose is to have a sustainable business model that is put at the service of the greater good."

Accordingly, Unilever created a manifesto in 2010 called the Sustainable Living Plan. This plan calls for Unilever to double its sales at the same time that it cuts its environmental footprint in half by 2020. One goal embedded in this plan is to source all of the firm's agricultural products in ways that "don't degrade the Earth." Unilver also has a campaign promising to improve the well-being of one billion people by "persuading them to wash their hands or brush their teeth, or by selling them food with less salt or fat." It seeks to realize many of these goals through cooperative strategies with other profit-seeking organizations as well as nonprofit entities.

In 2010, for instance, Unilever signed a contract with Jacobs Engineering Group Inc. forming a global (overall corporate) alliance to facilitate the efficiency of Unilever's capital improvement projects around the world. Unilever has 250 manufacturing sites and is expanding aggressively, especially in developing and emerging economies, to support its ambitious growth goals. Unilever expects emerging economies to drive 75 percent of its growth in the long term. The alliance with Jacobs Engineering will be managed out of Singapore and will provide engineering services for Unilever's manufacturing facilities around the world. Both companies will "work as a team to insure their sustainable growth model," implement cost reductions, and "drive co-innovation and implement the harmonization and cross-category standardization of designs." The alliance will also work with supply chain team members to increase speed to market with designs that "reduce carbon, water, and waste footprints across its manufacturing sites."

In alignment with marketing growth goals, Unilever has initiated the Unilever Nutrition Network. This organization has divided the world into six regions and focused on providing world-class nutrition and health innovation. Its goal is to generate ideas to facilitate sustainable product launches and improve existing products while strengthening their brand value. As part of this overall strategy, Unilever has used Salesforce's Chatter technology in the implementation of its new social marketing platform. This technology allows local markets and distributors of Unilever products to share insights and best practices with the marketing team from Unilever to help drive its "crafting brands for life" strategy.

In a recent Sustainable Living Plan report, Unilver described how it is working with a number of nonprofit, nongovernment organizations (NGOs) to help address real issues, facilitate solutions for suppliers for improving sustainable living, and reach customers in society at large who need information to improve their sustainability approaches to life with better food security and poverty alleviation. Initiatives include partnering with the following NGOs: the Consumer Goods Forum; the World Business Council for Sustainable Development; the World Economic Forum; the Tropical Forest Alliance 2020; Refrigerants, Naturally; the Global Green Foundation Forum; and Zero Hunger Challenge and Scale-Up Nutrition initiatives supported by the United Nations.

Interestingly, Unilever no longer provides quarterly earnings guidance reports and suggests that this has allowed it to focus shareholders on its longer-term goals. Furthermore, since Pullman took over in 2009, Unilever has sustained its positive growth trajectory with better income performance and associated stock market performance. As can be seen, it is accomplishing these things through better organizational design, lofty objectives, but also by using a number of cooperative strategies with many organizations outside the organization, such as Jacobs Engineering and many NGOs.

Sources: 2013, In the green corner: How IBM, Unilever and P&G started winning again: Why big business is wising up to sustainability, *Strategic Direction*, 29(5): 19–22; 2013, Our nutrition network, www.unilever.com, accessed June 17; 2013, Unilever drives efficiency in capital investment program, www.unilever.com, accessed June 17; 2013, Unilever Sustainable Living Plan, www.unilever.com, accessed June 17; 2013, Unilever Annual Report 2012, www.unilever.com, accessed June 17; S. Anand & N. Gopalan, 2013, Consumers in India are an M&A target, *Wall Street Journal Online*, www.wsj.com, May 1; M. Gunther, 2013, Unilever's CEO has a green thumb, *Fortune*, June 10, 124–128; R. Shields, 2013, Unilever boosts international collaboration with social rollout, *Marketing Week*, www.marketingweek.com, May 2; A. Ignatius, 2012, Captain planet, *Harvard Business Review*, 90(6): 112–118.

Case Discussion Questions

1. Why have consumer product companies headquartered in Europe historically used the multidomestic strategy? In your view, is this an effective choice of international strategy for these firms? Why or why not?

2. To implement its "sustainable business model," what types of strategies is Unilever considering for use and why?

3. What organizational structure will Unilever need to use to reach its sustainability objectives?

4. What issues about organizational structure surface as a result of Unilever's proposed strategies and objectives regarding sustainability?

NOTES

1. A. Arora, S. Belenzon, & L. A. Rios, 2014, Make, buy, organize: The interplay between research, external knowledge, and firm structure, *Strategic Management Journal*, 35: 317–337; T. Felin, N. J. Foss, K. H. Heimeriks, & T. L. Madsen, 2012, Microfoundations of routines and capabilities: Individuals, processes, and structure, *Journal of Management Studies*, 49: 1351–1374; K. M. Eisenhardt, N. R. Furr, & C. B. Bingham, 2010, Microfoundations of performance: Balancing efficiency and flexibility in dynamic environments, *Organization Science*, 21: 1263–1273.

2. D. A. Levinthal & A. Marino, 2015, Three facets of organizational adaptation: Selection, variety, and plasticity, *Organization Science*, in press; R. Wilden, S. P. Gudergan, B. Nielsen, & I. Lings, 2013, Dynamic capabilities and performance: Strategy, structure and environment, *Long Range Planning*, 46: 72–96; R. E. Miles & C. C. Snow, 1978, *Organizational Strategy*, *Structure and Process*, NY: McGraw-Hill.

3. C. Heavey & Z. Simsek, 2015, Transactive memory systems and firm performance: An upper echelons perspective, *Organization Science*, in press; M. A. Valentine & A. C. Edmondson, 2015, Team scaffolds: How mesolevel structures enable role-based coordination in temporary groups, *Organization Science*, in press; Y. Y. Kor & A. Mesko, 2013, Dynamic managerial capabilities: Configuration and orchestration of top executives' capabilities and the firm's dominant logic, *Strategic Management Journal*, 34: 233–244; E. M. Olson, S. F. Slater, & G. T. M. Hult, 2007, The importance of structure and process to strategy implementation, *Business Horizons*, 48: 47–54.

4. M. Josefy, S. Kuban, R. D. Ireland, & M. A. Hitt, 2015, All things great and small: Organizational size, boundaries of the firm, and a changing environment, *Academy of Management Annals*, 9: 715–802; P. Boumgarden, J. Nickerson, & T. R. Zenger, 2012, Sailing into the wind: Exploring the relationships among ambidexterity, vacillation, and organizational performance, *Strategic Management Journal*, 33: 587–610; T. Amburgey & T. Dacin, 1994, As the left foot follows the right? The dynamics of strategic and structural change, *Academy of Management Journal*, 37: 1427–1452.

5. M. Menz, S. Kunisch, & D. J. Collis, 2015, The corporate headquarters in the contemporary corporation: Advancing a multimarket firm perspective, *Academy of Management Annals*, 9: 633–714; L. F. Monteiro, N. Arvidsson, & J. Birkinshaw, 2008, Knowledge flows within multinational corporations: Explaining subsidiary isolation and its performance implications, *Organization Science*, 19: 90–107; B. Keats & H. O'Neill, 2001, Organizational structure: Looking through a strategy lens, in M. A. Hitt, R. E. Freeman, & J. S. Harrison (eds.), *Handbook of Strategic Management*, Oxford, U.K.: Blackwell Publishers, 520–542.

6. A. Shipilov, R. Gulati, M. Kilduff, S. Li, & W. Tsai, 2014, Relational pluralism within and between organizations, *Academy of Management Journal*, 57: 449–459; R. E. Hoskisson, C. W. L. Hill, & H. Kim, 1993, The multidivisional structure: Organizational fossil or source of value? *Journal of Management*, 19: 269–298.

7. B. Grøgaard, 2012, Alignment of strategy and structure in international firms: An empirical examination, *International Business Review*, 21: 397–407; E. M. Olson, S. F. Slater, & G. T. M. Hult, 2005, The performance implications of fit among business strategy, marketing organization structure, and strategic behavior, *Journal of Marketing*, 69: 49–65.

8. M. Ahearne, S. K. Lam, & F. Kraus, 2014, Performance impact of middle managers' adaptive strategy implementation: The role of social capital, *Strategic Management Journal*, 35: 68–87; F. A. Csaszar, 2012, Organizational structure as a determinant of performance: Evidence from mutual funds, *Strategic Management Journal*, 33: 611–632; T. Burns & G. M. Stalker, 1961, *The Management of Innovation*, London: Tavistok; P. R. Lawrence & J. W. Lorsch, 1967, *Organization and Environment*, Homewood, IL: Richard D. Irwin; J. Woodward, 1965, *Industrial Organization: Theory and Practice*, London: Oxford University Press.

9. A. K. Hoenen & T. Kostova, 2014, Utilizing the broader agency perspective for studying headquarters-subsidiary relations in multinational companies, *Journal of International Business Studies*, 46: 104–113; A. M. Rugman & A. Verbeke, 2008, A regional solution to the strategy and structure of multinationals, *European Management Journal*, 26: 305–313; H. Kim, R. E. Hoskisson, L. Tihanyi, & J. Hong, 2004, Evolution and restructuring of diversified business groups in emerging markets: The lessons from chaebols in Korea, *Asia Pacific Journal of Management*, 21: 25–48.

10. B. McEvily, G. Soda, & M. Tortoriello, 2014, More formally: Rediscovering the missing link between formal organization and informal social structure, *Academy of Management Annals*, 8: 299–345; M. Reilly, P. Scott, & V. Mangematin, 2012, Alignment or independence? Multinational subsidiaries and parent relations, *Journal of Business Strategy*, 33(2): 4–11.

11. T. Felin, N. J. Foss, & R. E. Ployhart, 2015, The microfoundations movement in strategy and organization theory, *Academy of Management Annals*, 9: 575–632; J. Qiu, L. Donaldson, & B. Luo, 2012, The benefits of persisting with paradigms in organizational research, *Academy of Management Perspectives*, 26: 93–104; R. Greenwood & D. Miller, 2010, Tackling design anew: Getting back to the heart of organization theory, *Academy of Management Perspectives*, 24: 78–88.

12. M. Dobrajska, S. Billinger, & S. Karim, 2015, Delegation within hierarchies: How information processing and knowledge characteristics influence the allocation of formal and real decision authority, *Organization Science*, in press; D. Laureiro-Martinez, 2014, Cognitive control capabilities, routinization propensity, and decision-making authority, *Organization Science*, 25: 1111–1133.

13. M. Loock & G. Hinnen, 2015, Heuristics in organizations: A review and a research agenda, *Journal of Business Research*, in press; S. E. Perkins, 2014, When does prior experience pay? Institutional experience and the multinational corporation, *Administrative Science Quarterly*, 59: 145–181.

14. J. Reuer & S. Devarakonda, 2015, Mechanisms of hybrid governance: Administrative committees in non-equity alliances, *Academy of Management Journal*, in press; C. Cella, A. Ellul, & M. Giannetti, 2013, Investors' horizons and the amplification of market shocks, *Review of Financial Studies*, 26: 1607–1648; T. Yu, M. Sengul, & R. H. Lester, 2008, Misery loves company: The spread of negative impacts resulting from an organizational crisis, *Academy of Management Review*, 33: 452–472; R. L. Priem, L. G. Love, & M. A. Shaffer, 2002, Executives' perceptions of uncertainty sources: A numerical taxonomy and underlying dimensions, *Journal of Management*, 28: 725–746.

15. A. Engelen, H. Kube, S. Schmidt, & T. C. Flatten, 2014, Entrepreneurial orientation in turbulent environments: The moderating role of absorptive capacity, *Research Policy*, 43: 1353–1369; E. Claver-Cortés, E. M. Pertusa-Ortega, & J. F. Molina-Azorín, 2012, Characteristics of organizational structure relating to hybrid competitive strategy: Implications for performance, *Journal of Business Research*, 65: 993–1002.

16. J. B. Craig, C. Dibrell, & R. Garrett, 2014, Examining relationships among family influence, family culture, flexible planning systems, innovativeness and firm performance, *Journal of Family Business Strategy*, 5: 229–238; R. Kapoor & J. Lee, 2013, Coordinating and competing in ecosystems: How organizational forms shape new technology investments, *Strategic Management Journal*, 34: 274–296.

17. H. Merchant, 2014, Configurations of governance structure, generic strategy, and firm size: Opening the black box of value creation in international joint ventures, *Global Strategy Journal*, 4: 292–309; M. S. Feldman & W. J. Orlikowski, 2011, Theorizing practice and practicing theory, *Organization Science*, 22: 1240–1253; J. Rivkin & N. Siggelkow, 2003, Balancing search and stability: Interdependencies among elements of organizational design, *Management Science*, 49: 290–311.

18. A. N. Kiss & P. S. Barr, 2015, New venture strategic adaptation: The interplay of belief structures and industry context, *Strategic Management Journal*, in press; A. J. Bock, T. Opsahl, G. George, & D. M. Gann, 2012, The effects of culture and structure on strategic flexibility during business model innovation, *Journal of Management Studies*, 49: 279–305; S. Nadkarni & V. K. Narayanan, 2007, Strategic schemas, strategic flexibility, and firm performance: The moderating role of industry clockspeed, *Strategic Management Journal*, 28: 243–270.

19. V. Gerasymenko, D. De Clercq, & H. J. Sapienza, 2015, Changing the business model: Effects of venture capital firms and outside CEOs on portfolio company performance, *Strategic Entrepreneurship Journal*, 9: 79–98; S. A. Fernhaber & P. C. Patel, 2012, How do young firms manage product portfolio complexity? The role of absorptive capacity and ambidexterity, *Strategic Management Journal*, 33: 1516–1539; S. Raisch & J. Birkinshaw, 2008, Organizational ambidexterity: Antecedents, outcomes, and moderators, *Journal of Management*, 34: 375–409.

20. C.-A. Chen, 2014, Revisiting organizational age, inertia, and adaptability: Developing and testing a multi-stage model in the nonprofit sector, *Journal of Organizational Change Management*, 27: 251–272; M. Zhao, S. H. Park, & N. Zhour, 2014, MNC strategy and social adaptation in emerging markets, *Journal of International Business Studies*, 45: 842–861; B. W. Keats & M. A. Hitt, 1988, A causal model of linkages among environmental dimensions, macroorganizational characteristics, and

performance, *Academy of Management Journal*, 31: 570–598.

21. A. Chandler, 1962, *Strategy and Structure*, Cambridge, MA: MIT Press.

22. D. Martin, 2007, Alfred D. Chandler, Jr., a business historian, dies at 88, *New York Times*, www.nytimes.com, May 12.

23. D. Albert, M. Kreutzer, & C. Lechner, 2015, Resolving the paradox of interdependency and strategic renewal in activity systems, *Academy of Management Review*, 40: 210–234; B. T. Pentland, M. S. Feldman, M. C. Becker, & P. Liu, 2012, Dynamics of organizational routines: A generative model, *Journal of Management Studies*, 49: 1484–1508; R. E. Hoskisson, R. A. Johnson, L. Tihanyi, & R. E. White, 2005, Diversified business groups and corporate refocusing in emerging economies, *Journal of Management*, 31: 941–965.

24. P. Wahba, 2015, J.C. Penney still blaming Ron Johnson-era for flow profit, growth, *Fortune*, www.fortune.com, February 26; D. Moin & E. Clark, 2013, Ullman returns as Johnson exits, *WWD: Women's Wear Daily*, April 9, 1.

25. M. Townsend, 2015, J.C. Penney marks two years since Johnson nearly ruined it, *Bloomberg*, www.bloombergnews.com, April 8.

26. R. V. D. Jordao, A. A. Souza, & E. A. Avelar, 2014, Organizational culture and post-acquisition changes in management control systems: An analysis of a successful Brazilian case, *Journal of Business Research*, 67: 542–549; S. Sonenshein, 2014, How organizations foster the creative use of resources, *Academy of Management Journal*, 57: 814–848.

27. M. R. Allen, G. K. Adomdza, & M. H. Meyer, 2015, Managing for innovation: Managerial control and employee level outcomes, *Journal of Business Research*, 68: 371–379; G. Valentini, 2015, The impact of M&A on rivals' innovation strategy, *Long Range Planning*, in press; L. Marengo & C. Pasquali, 2012, How to get what you want when you do not know what you want: A model of incentives, organizational structure, and learning, *Organization Science*, 23: 1298–1310;

28. D. F. Kuratko, J. G. Covin, & J. S. Hornsby, 2014, Why implementing corporate innovation is so difficult, *Business Horizons*, 57: 647–655; D. W. Lehman & J. Hahn, 2013, Momentum and organizational risk taking: Evidence from the National Football League, *Management Science*, 59: 852–868; M. A. Hitt, K. T. Haynes, & R. Serpa, 2010, Strategic leadership for the 21st century, *Business Horizons*, 53: 437–444.

29. L. Thomas & V. Ambrosini, 2015, Materializing strategy: The role of comprehensiveness and management controls in strategy formation in volatile environments, *British Journal of Management*, 26: S105–S124; R. MacKay & R. Chia, 2013, Choice, chance, and unintended consequences in strategic change: A process understanding of the rise and fall of Northco Automotive, *Academy of Management Journal*, 56: 208–230; I. Filatotchev, J. Stephan, & B. Jindra, 2008, Ownership structure, strategic controls and export intensity of foreign-invested firms in transition economies, *Journal of International Business Studies*, 39: 1133–1148.

30. S. Groda., A. J. Nelson, & R. M. Slino, 2015, Help-seeking and help-giving as an organizational routine: Continual engagement in innovative work, *Academy of Management Journal*, 58: 136–168; D. Minbaeva, T. Pedersen, I. Bjorkman, C. F. Fey, & H. J. Park, 2014, MNC knowledge transfer, subsidiary absorptive capacity and HRM, *Journal of International Business Studies*, 45: 38–51; D. M. Cable, F. Gino, & B. R. Staats, 2013, Breaking them in or eliciting their best? Reframing socialization around newcomers' authentic self-expression, *Administrative Science Quarterly*, 58: 1–36.

31. M. Menz & C. Scheef, 2014, Chief strategy officers: Contingency analysis of their presence in top management teams, *Strategic Management Journal*, 35: 461–471; K. Favaro, 2013, We're from corporate and we are here to help: Understanding the real value of corporate strategy and the head office, *Strategy+Business Online*, www.strategy-business.com, April 8; M. A. Hitt, R. E. Hoskisson, R. A. Johnson, & D. D. Moesel, 1996, The market for corporate control and firm innovation, *Academy of Management Journal*, 39: 1084–1119.

32. S. Karim & A. Kaul, 2015, Structural recombination and innovation: Unlocking intraorganizational knowledge synergy through structural change, *Organization Science*, 26: 439–455; W. P. Wan, R. E. Hoskisson, J. C. Short, & D. W. Yiu, 2011, Resource-based theory and corporate diversification: Accomplishments and opportunities, *Journal of Management*, 37: 1335–1368; M. A. Hitt, L. Tihanyi, T. Miller, & B. Connelly, 2006, International diversification: Antecedents, outcomes, and moderators, *Journal of Management*, 32: 831–867; R. E. Hoskisson & M. A. Hitt, 1988, Strategic control and relative R&D investment in multiproduct firms, *Strategic Management Journal*, 9: 605–621.

33. W. Su & E. Tsang, 2015, Product diversification and financial performance: The moderating role of secondary stakeholders, *Academy of Management Journal*, In press; I. Clark, 2013, Templates for financial control? Management and employees under the private equity business model, *Human Resource Management Journal*, 23: 144–159; D. Collis, D. Young, & M. Goold, 2007, The size, structure, and performance of corporate headquarters, *Strategic Management Journal*, 28: 383–405.

34. R. Amit & C. Zott, 2015, Crafting business architecture: The antecedents of business model design, *Strategic Entrepreneurship Journal*, in press; X. S. Y. Spencer, T. A. Joiner, & S. Salmon, 2009, Differentiation strategy, performance measurement systems and organizational performance: Evidence from Australia, *International Journal of Business*, 14: 83–103.

35. P. Almodovar & A. M. Rugman, 2014, The M curve and the performance of Spanish international new ventures, *British Journal of Management*, 25: S6–S23; M. Dass & S. Kumar, 2014, Bringing product and consumer ecosystems to the strategic forefront, *Business Horizons*, 57: 225–234; X. Yin & E. J. Zajac, 2004, The strategy/ governance structure fit relationship: Theory and evidence in franchising arrangements, *Strategic Management Journal*, 25: 365–383.

36. A. Gasparro, 2015, McDonald's puts its plan on display, *Morningstar*, www.morningstar.com, May 3.

37. G. Shani & J. Westphal, 2015, Persona non grata? Determinants and consequences of social distancing from journalists who engage in negative coverage of firm leadership, *Academy of Management Journal*, in press; E. Kulchina, 2014, Media coverage and location choice, *Strategic Management Journal*, 35: 596–605; M. K. Bednar, S. Boivie, & N. R. Prince, 2013, Burr under the saddle: How media coverage influences strategic change, *Organization Science*, 24: 910–925.

38. D. C. Mowery, 2010, Alfred Chandler and knowledge management within the firm, *Industrial & Corporate Change*, 19: 483–507; Chandler, *Strategy and Structure*.

39. Keats & O'Neill, Organizational structure, 524.

40. K. Srikanth & P. Puranam, 2014, The firm as a coordination system: Evidence from software services offshoring, *Organization Science*, 25: 1253–1271; E. Rawley, 2010, Diversification, coordination costs and organizational rigidity: Evidence from microdata, *Strategic Management Journal*, 31: 873–891.

41. S. M. Wagner, K. K. R. Ullrich, & S. Transchel, 2014, The game plan for aligning the organization, *Business Horizons*, 57: 189–201; A. Campbell & H. Strikwerda, 2013, The power of one: Towards the new integrated organization, *Journal of Business Strategy*, 34: 4–12.

42. S. Amdouni & S. Boubaker, 2015, Multiple large shareholders and owner-manager compensation: Evidence from French listed firms, *Journal of Applied Business Research*, 31: 1111–1129; C. Levicki, 1999, *The Interactive Strategy Workout*, 2nd ed., London: Prentice Hall.

43. M. Perkmann & A. Spicer, 2014, How emerging organizations take form: The role

of imprinting and values in organizational bricolage, *Organization Science*, 25: 1785–1806; P. L. Drnevich & D. C. Croson, 2013, Information technology and business-level strategy: Toward an integrated theoretical perspective, *MIS Quarterly*, 37: 483–509; H. M. O'Neill, R. W. Pouder, & A. K. Buchholtz, 1998, Patterns in the diffusion of strategies across organizations: Insights from the innovation diffusion literature, *Academy of Management Review*, 23: 98–114.

44. J. Davoren, 2015, Functional structure organization strength & weaknesses, *Small Business*, http://smallbusiness.chron.com, May 10.

45. D. Antons & F. Piller, 2015, Opening the black box of 'not-invented-here': *Academy of Management Perspectives*, in press; P. Leinwand & C. Mainardi, 2013, Beyond functions, *Strategy+Business*, www.strategy-business.com, Spring, 1–5.

46. O. E. Williamson, 1975, *Markets and Hierarchies: Analysis and Anti-Trust Implications*, NY: The Free Press.

47. M. J. Sanchez-Bueno & B. Usero, 2014, How may the nature of family firms explain the decisions concerning international diversification? *Journal of Business Research*, 67: 1311–1320; T. Hutzschenreuter & J. Horstkotte, 2013, Performance effects of top management team demographic faultlines in the process of product diversification, *Strategic Management Journal*, 34: 704–726; Chandler, *Strategy and Structure*.

48. Y. M. Zhou, 2015, Supervising across borders: The case of multinational hierarchies, *Organization Science*, 26: 277–292; J. Joseph & W. Ocasio, 2012, Architecture, attention, and adaptation in the multibusiness firm: General Electric from 1951 to 2001, *Strategic Management Journal*, 33: 633–660; J. Greco, 1999, Alfred P. Sloan, Jr. (1875–1966): The original "organization" man, *Journal of Business Strategy*, 20(5): 30–31.

49. R. E. Hoskisson, C. E. Hill, & H. Kim, 1993, The multidivisional structure: Organizational fossil or source of value? *Journal of Management*, 19: 269–298.

50. A. Zimmermann, S. Raisch, & J. Birkinshaw, 2015, How is ambidexterity initiated? The emergent charter definition process, *Organization Science*, in press; V. Binda, 2012, Strategy and structure in large Italian and Spanish firms, 1950–2002, *Business History Review*, 86: 503–525.

51. J. Hautz, M. Mayer, & C. Stadler, 2014, Macro-competitive context and diversification: The impact of macroeconomic growth and foreign competition, *Long Range Planning*, 47: 337–352; C. E. Helfat & K. M. Eisenhardt, 2004, Inter-temporal economies of scope, organizational modularity, and the dynamics of diversification, *Strategic Management Journal*, 25: 1217–1232; A. D. Chandler, 1994, The functions of

the HQ unit in the multibusiness firm, in R. P. Rumelt, D. E. Schendel, & D. J. Teece (eds.), *Fundamental Issues in Strategy*, Cambridge, MA: Harvard Business School Press, 327.

52. O. E. Williamson, 1994, Strategizing, economizing, and economic organization, in R. P. Rumelt, D. E. Schendel, & D. J. Teece (eds.), *Fundamental Issues in Strategy*, Cambridge, MA: Harvard Business School Press, 361–401.

53. V. A. Aggarwal & B. Wu, 2014, Organizational constraints to adaptation: Intrafirm asymmetry in the locus of coordination, *Organization Science*, 26: 218–238; Hoskisson, Hill, & Kim, The multidivisional structure: Organizational fossil or source of value?

54. D. J. Teece, 2014, A dynamic capabilities-based entrepreneurial theory of the multinational enterprise, *Journal of International Business Studies*, 45: 8–37; R. Duchin & D. Sosyura, 2013, Divisional managers and internal capital markets, *Journal of Finance*, 68: 387–429; O. E. Williamson, 1985, *The Economic Institutions of Capitalism: Firms, Markets, and Relational Contracting*, New York: Macmillan.

55. M. F. Wolff, 1999, In the organization of the future, competitive advantage will lie with inspired employees, *Research Technology Management*, 42(4): 2–4.

56. S. Y. Lee, M. Pitesa, S. Thau, & M. Pillutla, 2015, Discrimination in selection decisions: Integrating stereotype fit and interdependence theories, *Academy of Management Journal*, in press; E. Schulz, S. Chowdhury, & D. Van de Voort, 2013, Firm productivity moderated link between human capital and compensation: The significance of task-specific human capital, *Human Resource Management*, 52: 423–439.

57. N. Malhotra, C. R. (Bob) Hinings, 2015, Unpacking continuity and change as a process of organizational transformation, *Long Range Planning*, 48: 1–22; L. G. Love, R. L. Priem, & G. T. Lumpkin, 2002, Explicitly articulated strategy and firm performance under alternative levels of centralization, *Journal of Management*, 28: 611–627.

58. S. Biancani, D. A. McFarland, & L. Dahlander, 2014, The semiformal organizational, *Organization Science*, 25: 1306–1324; T. F. Gonzalez-Cruz, A. Huguet-Roig, & S. Cruz-Ros, 2012, Organizational technology as a mediating variable in centralization-formalization fit, *Management Decision*, 50: 1527–1548.

59. D. G. Sirmon, M. A. Hitt, R. D. Ireland, & B. A. Gilbert, 2011, Resource orchestration to create competitive advantage: Breadth, depth and life cycle effects, *Journal of Management*, 37: 1390–1412.

60. N. J. Foss, J. Lyngsie, & S. A. Zahra, 2015, Organizational design correlates of entrepreneurship: The roles of decentralization and formalization for

opportunity discovery and realization, *Strategic Organization*, in press. J. B. Barney, 2001, *Gaining and Sustaining Competitive Advantage*, 2nd ed., Upper Saddle River, NJ: Prentice Hall, 257.

61. H. Brea-Solis, R. Casadesus-Masanell, & E. Grifell-Tatje, 2015, Business model evaluation: Unifying Walmart's sources of advantage, *Strategic Entrepreneurship Journal*, 9: 12–33.

62. D. Martinez-Simarro, C. Devece, & C. Liopis-Albert, 2015, How information systems strategy moderates the relationship between business strategy and performance, *Journal of Business Research*, 68: 1592–1594; V. K. Garg, R. L. Priem, & A. A. Rasheed, 2013, A theoretical explanation of the cost advantages of multi-unit franchising, *Journal of Marketing Channels*, 20: 52–72; H. Wang & C. Kimble, 2010, Low-cost strategy through product architecture: Lessons from China, *Journal of Business Strategy*, 31: 12–20.

63. M. Dobrajska, S. Billinger, & S. Karim, 2015, Delegation within hierarchies: How information processing and knowledge characteristics influence the allocation of formal and real decision authority, *Organization Science*, in press.

64. P. Soni, 2015, What investors need to know about Walmart's US segment, *Finance. yahoo*, www.finance.yahoo.com, May 14.

65. 2015, Our story, Walmart Corporate, www.walmartstores.com, May 13.

66. J. Schmidt, R. Makadok, & T. Keil, 2015, Customer-specific synergies and market convergence, *Strategic Management Journal*, in press; A. Ma, Z. Yang, & M. Mourali, 2014, Consumer adoption of new products: Independent versus interdependent self-perspectives, *Journal of Marketing*, 78: 101–117; N. Takagoshi & N. Matsubayashi, 2013, Customization competition between branded firms: Continuous extension of product line from core product, *European Journal of Operational Research*, 225: 337–352.

67. P. C. Patel, S. Thorgren, & J. Wincent, 2015, Leadership, passion, and performance: A study of job creation projects during the recession, *British Journal of Management*, 26: 211–224; D. Singh & J. S. Oberoi, 2014, A rule-based fuzzy-logic approach for evaluating the strategic flexibility in manufacturing organizations, *International Journal of Strategic Change Management*, 5: 281–296; K. Z. Zhou & F. Wu, 2010, Technological capability, strategic flexibility and product innovation, *Strategic Management Journal*, 31: 547–561.

68. 2015, About Under Armour, www.underarmour.com, May 15.

69. J. H. Burgers & J. G. Covin, 2015, The contingent effects of differentiation and integration on corporate entrepreneurship, *Strategic Management Journal*, in press; L. Mirabeau & S. Maguire, 2014, From autonomous strategic behavior to

emergent strategy, *Strategic Management Journal*, 35: 1202–1229; E. Claver-Cortés, E. M. Pertusa-Ortega, & J. F. Molina-Azorín, 2012, Characteristics of organizational structure relating to hybrid competitive strategy: Implications for performance, *Journal of Business Research*, 65: 993–1002.

70. Chandler, *Strategy and Structure*.

71. 2015, Strength in structure, Procter & Gamble Home Page, www.pg.com, May 9.

72. D. Maslach, 2015, Change and persistence with failed technological innovation, *Strategic Management Journal*, in press; S. Wagner, K. Hoisl, & G. Thoma, 2014, Overcoming localization of knowledge—the role of professional service firms, *Strategic Management Journal*, 35: 1671–1688; Y. M. Zhou, 2011, Synergy, coordination costs, and diversification choices, *Strategic Management Journal*, 32: 624–639; C. W. L. Hill, M. A. Hitt, & R. E. Hoskisson, 1992, Cooperative versus competitive structures in related and unrelated diversified firms, *Organization Science*, 3: 501–521.

73. M. Tortoriello, 2015, The social underpinnings of absorptive capacity: The moderating effects of structural holes on innovation generation based on external knowledge, *Strategic Management Journal*, 36: 586–597; M. Makri, M. A. Hitt, & P. J. Lane, 2010, Complementary technologies, knowledge relatedness and invention outcomes in high technology mergers and acquisitions, *Strategic Management Journal*, 31: 602–628.

74. M. Palmie, M. M. Keupp, & O. Gassmann, 2014, Pull the right levers: Creating internationally "useful" subsidiary competence by organizational architecture, *Long Range Planning*, 47: 32–48; J. Wolf & W. G. Egelhoff, 2013, An empirical evaluation of conflict in MNC matrix structure firms, *International Business Review*, 22: 591–601; S. H. Appelbaum, D. Nadeau, & M. Cyr, 2008, Performance evaluation in a matrix organization: A case study (part two), *Industrial and Commercial Training*, 40: 295–299.

75. T. W. Tong, J. J. Reuer, B. B. Tyler, & S. Zhang, 2015, Host country executives' assessments of international joint ventures and divestitures: An experimental approach, *Strategic Management Journal*, 36: 254–275; S. H. Appelbaum, D. Nadeau, & M. Cyr, 2009, Performance evaluation in a matrix organization: A case study (part three), *Industrial and Commercial Training*, 41: 9–14.

76. A. V. Sakhartov & T. B. Folta, 2014, Resource relatedness, redeployability, and firm value, *Strategic Management Journal*, 35: 1781–1797; O. Alexy, G. George, & A. J. Salter, 2013, Cui bono? The selective revealing of knowledge and its implications for innovative activity, *Academy of Management Review*, 38: 270–291; E. Rawley, 2010, Diversification, coordination costs, and organizational rigidity: Evidence from

microdata, *Strategic Management Journal*, 31: 873–891.

77. E. R. Feldman, S. C. Gilson, & B. Villalonga, 2014, Do analysts add value when they most can? Evidence from corporate spin-offs, *Strategic Management Journal*, 35: 1446–1463; M. Kruehler, U. Pidun, & H. Rubner, 2012, How to assess the corporate parenting strategy? A conceptual answer, *Journal of Business Strategy*, 33(4): 4–17; M. M. Schmid & I. Walter, 2009, Do financial conglomerates create or destroy economic value? *Journal of Financial Intermediation*, 18: 193–216.

78. T. M. Alessandri & A. Seth, 2014, The effects of managerial ownership on international and business diversification: Balancing incentives and risks, *Strategic Management Journal*, 35: 2064–2075; N. T. Dorata, 2012, Determinants of the strengths and weaknesses of acquiring firms in mergers and acquisitions: A stakeholder perspective, *International Journal of Management*, 29: 578–590; R. E. Hoskisson & M. A. Hitt, 1990, Antecedents and performance outcomes of diversification: A review and critique of theoretical perspectives, *Journal of Management*, 16: 461–509.

79. Y. Yang, V. K. Narayanan, & D. M. De Carolis, 2014, The relationship between portfolio diversification and firm value: The evidence from corporate venture capital activity, *Strategic Management Journal*, 35: 1993–2011; A. Varmaz, A. Varwig, & T. Poddig, 2013, Centralized resource planning and yardstick competition, *Omega*, 41: 112–118; Hill, Hitt, & Hoskisson, Cooperative versus competitive structures, 512.

80. M. Arrfelt, R. M. Wiseman, G. McNamara, & G. T. M. Hult, 2015, Examining a key corporate role: The influence of capital allocation competency on business unit performance, *Strategic Management Journal*, in press; D. Holod, 2012, Agency and internal capital market inefficiency: Evidence from banking organizations, *Financial Management*, 41: 35–53.

81. 2015, How is Textron organized? Textron Home Page, www.textron.com, May 15.

82. 2015, Our company, Textron Home Page, www.textron.com, May 15

83. C. Custodio, 2014, Mergers and acquisitions accounting and the diversification discount, *Journal of Finance*, 69: 219–240.

84. R. Belderbos, T. W. Tong, & S. Wu, 2014, Multinationality and downside risk: The roles of option portfolio and organization, *Strategic Management Journal*, 35: 88–106; R. M. Holmes, Jr., T. Miller, M. A. Hitt, & M. P. Salmador, 2013, The interrelationships among informal institutions, formal institutions and inward foreign direct investment, *Journal of Management*, 39: 531–566; T. Yu & A. A. Cannella, Jr., 2007, Rivalry between multinational enterprises: An event history approach, *Academy of Management Journal*, 50: 665–686.

85. T. Huang, F. Wu, J. Yu, & B. Zhang, 2015, Political risk and dividend policy: Evidence from international political crises, *Journal of International Business Studies*, in press; A. H. Kirca, G. T. M. Hult, S. Deligonul, M. Z. Perryy, & S. T. Cavusgil, 2012, A multilevel examination of the drivers of firm multinationality: A meta-analysis, *Journal of Management*, 38: 502–530.

86. G. Vasudeva, E. A. Alexander, & S. L. Jones, 2015, Institutional logics and interorganizational learning in technological arenas: Evidence from standard-setting organizations in the mobile handset industry, *Organization Science*, in press; J.-L. Arregle, T. Miller, M. A. Hitt, & P. W. Beamish, 2013, Do regions matter? An integrated institutional and semiglobalization perspective on the internationalization of MNEs, *Strategic Management Journal*, 34: 910–934.

87. L. Li, G. Qian, & Z. Ian, 2014, Inconsistencies in international product strategies and performance of high-tech firms, *Journal of International Marketing*, 22: 94–113; P. Almodóvar, 2012, The international performance of standardizing and customizing Spanish firms: The M curve relationships, *Multinational Business Review*, 20: 306–330; G. R. G. Benito, R. Lunnan, & S. Tomassen, 2011, Distant encounters of the third kind: Multinational companies locating divisional headquarters abroad, *Journal of Management Studies*, 48: 373–394.

88. 2015, Our company, Uber Home Page, www.uber.com, May 15.

89. R. Fannin, 2015, Uber proves going local and partnering works in China, *Forbes*, www.forbes.com, April 30.

90. H. Merchant, 2014, Configurations of governance structure, generic strategy, and firms size: Opening the black box of value creation in international joint ventures, *Global Strategy Journal*, 4: 292–309; B. Brenner & B. Ambos, 2013, A question of legitimacy? A dynamic perspective on multinational firm control, *Organization Science*, 24: 773–795; M. P. Koza, S. Tallman, & A. Ataay, 2011, The strategic assembly of global firms: A microstructural analysis of local learning and global adaptation, *Global Strategy Journal*, 1: 27–46.

91. K. Bondy & K. Starkey, 2014, The dilemmas of internationalization: Corporate social responsibility in the multinational corporation, *British Journal of Management*, 25: 4–22; J. Qiu & L. Donaldson, 2012, Stopford and Wells were right! MNC matrix structures do fit a "high-high" strategy, *Management International Review*, 52: 671–689; B. Connelly, M. A. Hitt, A. DeNisi, & R. D. Ireland, 2007, Expatriates and corporate-level international strategy: Governing with the knowledge contract, *Management Decision*, 45: 564–581.

92. T. Wakayama, J. Shintaku, & A. Tomofumi, 2012, What Panasonic learned in China, *Harvard Business Review*, 90(12): 109–113.

93. Wakayama, Shintaku, & Tomofumi, What Panasonic learned in China.

94. 2015, A better life, a better world, Panasonic Home Page, www.panasonic.com, May 15.

95. Y. Lku & T. Ravichandran, 2015, Alliance experience, IT-enable knowledge integration, and ex-ante value gains, *Organization Science*, 26: 511–530; I. Neyens & D. Faems, 2013, Exploring the impact of alliance portfolio management design on alliance portfolio performance, *Managerial & Decision Economics*, 34: 347–361.

96. D. Filiou & S. Golesorkhi, 2015, Influence of institutional differences on firm innovation from international alliances, *Long Range Planning*, in press; V. A. Aggarwal, N. Siggelkow, & H. Singh, 2011, Governing collaborative activity: Interdependence and the impact of coordination and exploration, *Strategic Management Journal*, 32: 705–730; J. Li, C. Zhou, & E. J. Zajac, 2009, Control, collaboration, and productivity in international joint ventures: Theory and evidence, *Strategic Management Journal*, 30: 865–884.

97. W. (Stone) Shi, S. L. Sun, B. C. Pinkham, & M. W. Peng, 2014, Domestic alliance network to attract foreign partners: Evidence from international joint ventures in China, *Journal of International Business Studies*, 45: 338–362; R. Gulati, P. Puranam, & M. Tushman, 2012, Meta-organization design: Rethinking design in interorganizational and community context, *Strategic Management Journal*, 33: 571–586; J. Wincent, S. Anokhin, D. Örtqvist, & E. Autio, 2010, Quality meets structure: Generalized reciprocity and firm-level advantage in strategic networks, *Journal of Management Studies*, 47: 597–624.

98. P. C. Patel, S. A. Fernhaber, P. P. McDougall-Covin, & R. P. van der Have, 2014, Beating competitors to international markets: The value of geographically balanced networks for innovation, *Strategic Management Journal*, 35: 691–711; V. Van de Vrande, 2013, Balancing your technology-sourcing portfolio: How sourcing mode diversity enhances innovative performance, *Strategic Management Journal*, 34: 610–621; T. P. Moliterno & D. M. Mahony, 2011, Network theory of organization: A multilevel approach, *Journal of Management*, 37: 443–467.

99. F. J. Contractor & J. J. Reuer, 2014, Structuring and governing alliances: New directions for research, *Global Strategy Journal*, 4: 241–256; L. Dooley, D. Kirk, & K. Philpott, 2013, Nurturing life-science knowledge discovery: Managing multi-organisation networks, *Production Planning & Control*, 24: 195–207; A. T. Arikan & M. A. Schilling, 2011, Structure and governance of industrial districts: Implications for competitive advantage, *Journal of Management Studies*, 48: 772–803.

100. C. Bellavitis, I. Filatotchev, & D. S. Kamuriwo, 2014, The effects of intra-industry and extra-industry networks on performance: A case of venture capital portfolio firms, *Managerial and Decision Economics*, 35: 129–144; R. Vandaie & A. Zaheer, 2014, Alliance partners and firm capability: Evidence from the motion picture industry, *Organization Science*, 26: 22–36.

101. M. A. O. Dos Santos, G. Svensson, & C. Padin, 2014, Implementation, monitoring and evaluation of sustainable business practices: Framework and empirical illustration, *Corporate Governance*, 14: 515–530; B. Baudry & V. Chassagnon, 2012, The vertical network organization as a specific governance structure: What are the challenges for incomplete contracts theories and what are the theoretical implications for the boundaries of the (hub-) firm? *Journal of Management & Governance*, 16: 285–303.

102. Z. Kahn, Y. K. Lew, & R. R. Sinkovics, 2015, International joint ventures as boundary spanners: Technological knowledge transfer in an emerging economy, *Global Strategy Journal*, 5: 48–68; R. Gulati, F. Wohlgezogen, & P. Zhelyazkov, 2012, The two facets of collaboration: Cooperation and coordination in strategic alliances, *Academy of Management Annals*, 6: 531–583; M. H. Hansen, R. E. Hoskisson, & J. B. Barney, 2008, Competitive advantage in alliance governance: Resolving the opportunism minimization-gain maximization paradox, *Managerial and Decision Economics*, 29: 191–208; G. Lorenzoni & C. Baden-Fuller, 1995, Creating a strategic center to manage a web of partners, *California Management Review*, 37: 146–163.

103. F. Zambuto, G. L. Nigro, & J. P. O'Brien, 2015, The importance of alliances in firm capital structure decisions: Evidence from biotechnology firms, *Managerial and Decision Economics*, in press; A. C. Inkpen, 2008, Knowledge transfer and international joint ventures: The case of NUMMI and General Motors, *Strategic Management Journal*, 29: 447–453; J. H. Dyer & K. Nobeoka, 2000, Creating and managing a high-performance knowledge-sharing network: The Toyota case, *Strategic Management Journal*, 21: 345–367.

104. A. Lipparini, G. Lorenzoni, & S. Ferriani, 2014, From core to periphery and back: A study on the deliberate shaping of knowledge flows in interfirm dyads and networks, *Strategic Management Journal*, 35: 578–595; N. Lahiri & S. Narayanan, 2013, Vertical integration, innovation and alliance portfolio size: Implications for firm performance, *Strategic Management Journal*, 34: 1042–1064; L. F. Mesquita, J. Anand, & J. H. Brush, 2008, Comparing the resource-based and relational views: Knowledge transfer and spillover in vertical alliances, *Strategic Management Journal*, 29: 913–941; M. Kotabe, X. Martin, & H. Domoto, 2003, Gaining from vertical partnerships: Knowledge transfer, relationship duration and supplier performance improvement in the U.S. and Japanese automotive industries, *Strategic Management Journal*, 24: 293–316.

105. Y. Luo, Y. Liu, Q. Yang, V. Maksimov, & J. Hou, 2015, Improving performance and reducing cost in buyer-supplier relationships: The role of justice in curtailing opportunism, *Journal of Business Research*, 68: 607–615; S. G. Lazzarini, D. P. Claro, & L. F. Mesquita, 2008, Buyer-supplier and supplier-supplier alliances: Do they reinforce or undermine one another? *Journal of Management Studies*, 45: 561–584; P. Dussauge, B. Garrette, & W. Mitchell, 2004, Asymmetric performance: The market share impact of scale and link alliances in the global auto industry, *Strategic Management Journal*, 25: 701–711.

106. Treflis team, 2015, Walgreens reports a strong Q2 driven by growth in holiday sales and Medicare Part D scripts, *Forbes*, www.forbes.com, April 10.

107. 2015, Strategic alliances: Not so niche anymore, *Coherence*, www.coherence360.com, May 10.

108. W. E. Gillis, J. G. Combs, & D. J. Ketchen, Jr., 2014, Using resource-based theory to help explain plural form franchising, *Entrepreneurship Theory and Practice*, 38: 449–472; A. M. Hayashi, 2008, How to replicate success, *MIT Sloan Management Review*, 49: 6–7; M. Tuunanen & F. Hoy, 2007, Franchising: Multifaceted form of entrepreneurship, *International Journal of Entrepreneurship and Small Business*, 4: 52–67.

109. R. Hahn & S. Gold, 2014, Resources and governance in "base of the pyramid"-partnerships: Assessing collaborations between businesses and non-business actors, *Journal of Business Research*, 67: 1321–1333; W. Vanhaverbeke, V. Gilsing, & G. Duysters, 2012, Competence and governance in strategic collaboration: The differential effect of network structure on the creation of core and noncore technology, *Journal of Product Innovation Management*, 29: 784–802; A. Zaheer, R. Gözübüyük, & H. Milanov, 2010, It's the connections: The network perspective in interorganizational research, *Academy of Management Perspectives*, 24: 62–77.

110. L. Baertlein, 2015, McDonald's reset to change structure, cut costs, boost franchises, *Reuters*, www.reuters.com, May 4.

111. C. Lioukas & J. Reuer, 2015, Isolating trust outcomes from exchange relationships: Social exchange and learning benefits of prior ties in alliances, *Academy of Management Journal*, in press; Y. Lew & R. R. Sinkovics, 2013, Crossing borders and industry sectors: Behavioral governance in strategic alliances and product innovation for competitive advantage, *Long Range Planning*, 46: 13–38; T. W. Tong, J. J. Reuer, & M. W. Peng, 2008, International joint

ventures and the value of growth options, *Academy of Management Journal*, 51: 1014–1029.

112. A. Peterman, A. Kourula, & R. Levitt, 2014, Balancing act: Government roles in an energy conservation network, *Research Policy*, 43: 1067–1082; H. Liu, X. Jiang, J. Zhang, & X. Zhao, 2013, Strategic flexibility and international venturing by emerging market firms: The moderating effects of institutional and relational factors, *Journal of International Marketing*, 21(2): 79–98; M. W. Hansen, T. Pedersen, & B. Petersen, 2009, MNC strategies and linkage effects in developing countries, *Journal of World Business*, 44: 121–130; A. Goerzen, 2005, Managing alliance networks: Emerging practices of multinational corporations, *Academy of Management Executive*, 19(2): 94–107.

113. M. de Vaan, 2014, Interfirm networks in periods of technological turbulence and stability, *Research Policy*, 43: 1666–1680; C. C. Phelps, 2010, A longitudinal study of the influence of alliance network structure and composition on firm exploratory innovation, *Academy of Management Journal*, 53: 890–913; L. H. Lin, 2009, Mergers and acquisitions, alliances and technology development: An empirical study of the global auto industry, *International Journal of Technology Management*, 48: 295–307.

Strategic Leadership

Studying this chapter should provide you with the strategic management knowledge needed to:

12-1   Define strategic leadership and describe top-level managers' importance.

12-2   Explain what top management teams are and how they affect firm performance.

12-3   Describe the managerial succession process using internal and external managerial labor markets.

12-4   Discuss the value of strategic leadership in determining the firm's strategic direction.

12-5   Describe the importance of strategic leaders in managing the firm's resources.

12-6   Explain what must be done for a firm to sustain an effective culture.

12-7   Describe what strategic leaders can do to establish and emphasize ethical practices.

12-8   Discuss the importance and use of organizational controls.

CAN YOU FOLLOW AN ICON AND SUCCEED?
APPLE AND TIM COOK AFTER STEVE JOBS

Steve Jobs was Apple's founder and icon CEO. Much of Apple's phenomenal success, especially after 2000, was attributed to Steve Job's "genius" and leadership. Because of this and Tim Cook having a significantly different style from Jobs, he was given little chance for success. Yet, in 2014, several years after Cook assumed the CEO position, Apple had what Tim Cook referred to as an unbelievable year. Apple sold 200 million iPhones and had $200 billion in revenue. Apple's stock price increased by 65 percent, and the company's market value reached more than $700 billion, the largest ever of any U.S. firm. The $700 billion in market value is more than twice as much as either Microsoft or Exxon Mobil. Cook's primary experience has been as manager of operations; he was Apple's COO prior to assuming the CEO role. And, much of Apple's sales are based on products developed and introduced to the market under Job's leadership. So, the jury is still out on Cook, especially with regard to developing new products and making them a success in the marketplace. Steve Jobs was a master at this process.

Cook's style of leadership is much different from the approach used by Jobs. Some considered Jobs to be ruthless and impulsive and almost maniacal in developing new products and ensuring a high quality product desirable in the market. Cook's knowledge and skills do not make him an expert in product development, design, or marketing. So, he delegates those responsibilities but remains as the leader and decision maker. Cook tries to buffer and maintain Apple's corporate culture developed largely by Jobs.

Bloomberg/Getty Images

Thus, the emphasis remains on innovation that is valued in the marketplace. Cook has learned the importance of hiring other top managers with talent but who also fit into Apple's culture. He has made some very good hires, such as Angela Ahrendts who now heads Apple's very important retail stores. Cook takes a much less emotional approach than Jobs. Some refer to it as a "measured emotional approach to leadership." He empowers his team to manage their functional areas and emphasizes the need to take a long-run perspective.

Observers have been able to highlight other differences between Cook's and Job's strategic leadership approaches. Cook shares the limelight with his leadership team, whereas Jobs kept the light on himself. In fact, one analyst suggested that Cook is a good leader who builds an effective team around him. Cook is leading Apple to be more philanthropic than in the past. His strategy has entailed a major acquisition (an audio company for $3 billion) and developing enterprise solutions for corporate IT units, both strategic actions that Jobs eschewed. Apple has formed an alliance with IBM to develop enterprise applications many of which will be designed for the iPad, especially the new and larger versions.

Innovations developed during Cook's leadership include the Apple watch, introduced to the market in April 2015. Many are waiting to learn its rate of success. Initial reports suggest that demand is exceeding supply, causing Apple to increase production. In addition, hints provided by Cook suggest that Apple may be planning to enter the television market. Most importantly, Cook claims that Apple's goal is to change the way people work and will target the development of future products for that purpose.

Sources: T. Loftus, 2015, The morning download: Apple will 'change the way people work,' CEO Tim Cook says, *CIO Journal*, blogs.wsj.com, January 28: 2015, Apple's Tim Cook cites record sales and 'unbelievable' year, *New York Times*, www.nytimes.com, March 10; A. Chang, 2015, Apple CEO Tim Cook is forging an unusual path as a social activist, *Los Angeles Times*, www.latimes.com, March 31, A. Lashinsky, 2015, Becoming *Tim* Cook, *Fortune*, April 1, 60–72; T. Higgins, 2015, Apple iPhones sales in China outsell the U.S. for first time, *BloombergBusiness*, www.bloomberg.com, April 27; J. Lewis, 2015, Tim Cook: A courageous innovator, *Time*, April 27, 26; J. D'Onfro, 2015, Tim Cook dropped a major clue about Apple's next big product, *Yahoo Finance*, finance.yahoo.com, April 28.

As the Opening Case suggests, strategic leaders' work is demanding, challenging, and requires balancing short-term performance outcomes with long-term performance goals. Regardless of how long (or short) they remain in their positions, strategic leaders (and most prominently CEOs) affect a firm's performance.[1] Obviously, Steve Jobs was well known as a highly successful CEO who led Apple to achieve very high performance. There were questions about whether anyone could follow him as CEO and be successful. Those questions dogged Tim Cook, who became Apple's CEO after Jobs passed away. Yet, three and a half years into his tenure as CEO, Apple had an incredibly successful year and became the first company to achieve a market value of $700 billion.

A major message in this chapter is that effective strategic leadership is the foundation for successfully using the strategic management process. As implied in Figure 1.1 in Chapter 1 and through the Analysis-Strategy-Performance model, strategic leaders guide the firm in ways that result in forming a vision and mission. Often, this guidance involves leaders creating goals that stretch everyone in the organization as a foundation for enhancing firm performance. A positive outcome of stretch goals is their ability to provoke breakthrough thinking—thinking that often leads to innovation.[2] Additionally, strategic leaders work with others to verify that the analysis and strategy parts of the A-S-P model are completed effectively in order to increase the likelihood the firm will achieve strategic competitiveness and earn above-average returns. We show how effective strategic leadership makes all of this possible in Figure 12.1.[3]

To begin this chapter, we define strategic leadership and discuss its importance and the possibility of strategic leaders as a source of competitive advantage for a firm. These introductory comments include a brief consideration of different styles strategic leaders may use. We then examine the role of top-level managers and top management teams and their effects on innovation, strategic change, and firm performance. Following this discussion is an analysis of managerial succession, particularly in the context of the internal and external managerial labor markets from which strategic leaders are selected. Closing the chapter are descriptions of five key leadership actions that contribute to effective strategic leadership: determining strategic direction, effectively managing the firm's resource portfolio, sustaining an effective organizational culture, emphasizing ethical practices, and establishing balanced organizational controls.

12-1 Strategic Leadership and Style

Strategic leadership is the ability to anticipate, envision, maintain flexibility, and empower others to create strategic change as necessary. **Strategic change** is change brought about as a result of selecting and implementing a firm's strategies. Multifunctional in nature, strategic leadership involves managing through others, managing an entire organization rather than a functional subunit, and coping with change that continues to increase in the global economy. Because of the global economy's complexity, strategic leaders must learn how to effectively influence human behavior, often in uncertain environments.[4]

Strategic leadership is the ability to anticipate, envision, maintain flexibility, and empower others to create strategic change as necessary.

Strategic change is change brought about as a result of selecting and implementing a firm's strategies.

Figure 12.1 Strategic Leadership and the Strategic Management Process

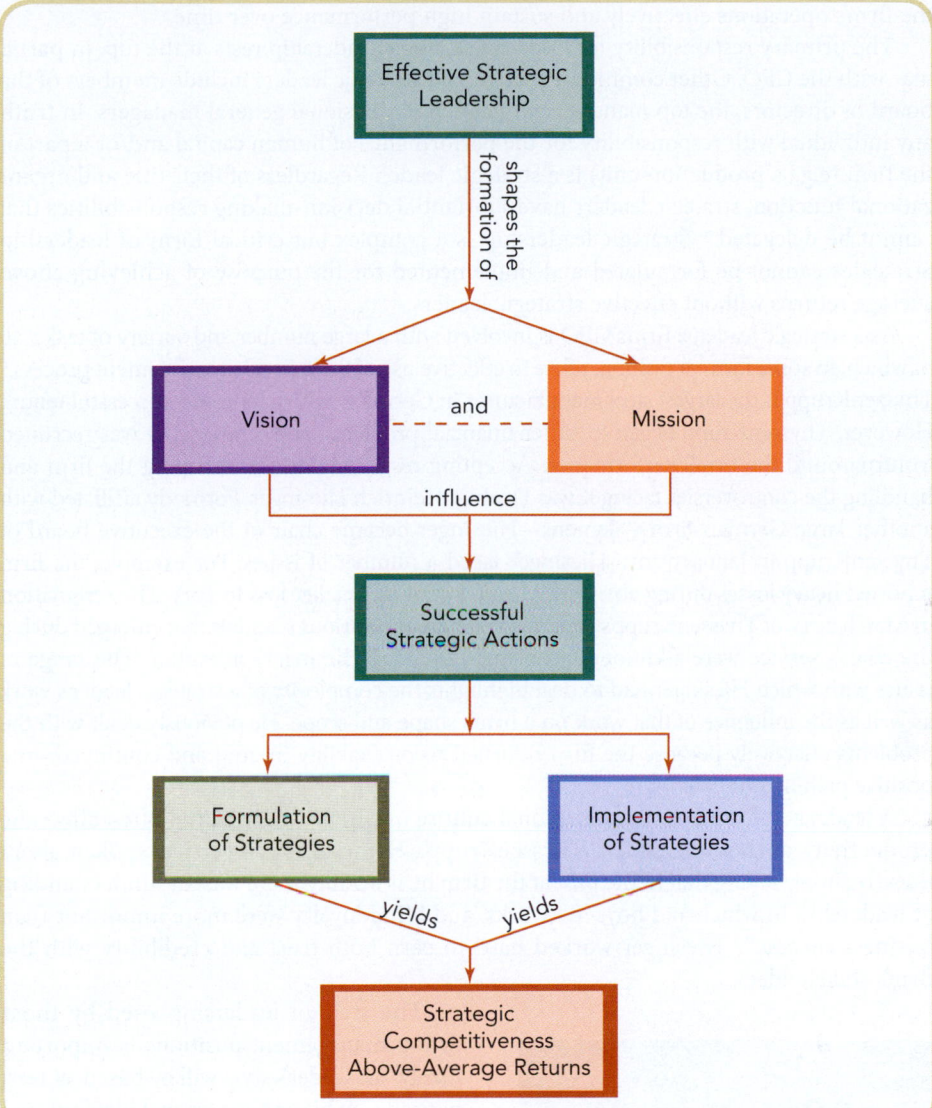

By word or by personal example, and through their ability to envision the future, effective strategic leaders meaningfully influence the behaviors, thoughts, and feelings of those with whom they work.[5]

The ability to attract and then manage human capital may be the most critical of the strategic leader's skills,[6] especially because the lack of talented human capital constrains firm growth. Indeed, in the twenty-first century, intellectual capital that the firm's human capital possesses, including the ability to manage knowledge and produce innovations, affects a strategic leader's success.[7]

Effective strategic leaders also create and then support the context or environment through which stakeholders (such as employees, customers, and suppliers) can perform at peak efficiency.[8] Being able to demonstrate the skills of attracting and managing human capital and establishing and nurturing an appropriate context for that capital to flourish is important, especially given that the crux of strategic leadership is the ability to manage the firm's operations effectively and sustain high performance over time.[9]

The primary responsibility for effective strategic leadership rests at the top, in particular with the CEO. Other commonly recognized strategic leaders include members of the board of directors, the top management team, and divisional general managers. In truth, any individual with responsibility for the performance of human capital and/or a part of the firm (e.g., a production unit) is a strategic leader. Regardless of their title and organizational function, strategic leaders have substantial decision-making responsibilities that cannot be delegated.[10] Strategic leadership is a complex but critical form of leadership. Strategies cannot be formulated and implemented for the purpose of achieving above-average returns without effective strategic leaders.

As a strategic leader, a firm's CEO is involved with a large number and variety of tasks, all of which, in some form or fashion, relate to effective use of the strategic management process.[11] ThyssenKrupp is the largest steel manufacturer in Germany with a long and successful tenure. However, ThyssenKrupp began to suffer financial problems, and a new CEO was recruited to turnaround the firm's performance. Accepting responsibility for reshaping the firm and handling the controversies facing it was Dr.-Ing. Heinrich Hiesinger. Formerly affiliated with another large German firm—Siemens—Hiesinger became chair of the executive board of ThyssenKrupp in January 2011. Hiesinger faced a number of issues. For example, the firm reported heavy losses during 2011 and 2012 and another smaller loss in 2013. The resignation, in March 2013, of ThyssenKrupp's supervisory chair and various scandals that emerged during the chair's service were additional problems requiring Hiesinger's attention. The range of issues with which Hiesinger had to deal highlights the complexity of a strategic leader's work as well as the influence of that work on a firm's shape and scope. He obviously dealt with the problems effectively because the firm returned to profitability in 2014 and continued on a positive path in 2015.[12]

A leader's style and the organizational culture in which it is displayed often affect the productivity of those being led. ThyssenKrupp's Heinrich Hiesinger has spoken about these realities, saying that in the past at the firm he is leading there was an "understanding of leadership in which 'old boys' networks' and blind loyalty were more important than business success."[13] Hiesinger worked hard to earn both trust and credibility with the firm's stakeholders.

PATRIK STOLLARZ/Getty Images

Heinrich Hiesler, Chairman of the Board for ThyssenKrupp, is addressing the shareholders as a part of his effort to maintain their trust.

The style of leadership used by those in top management positions is important. Likely, the leader's style will be based, at least partially, on his or her personal ideology and experience.[14] For example, based on his personal ideology, Tim Cook, CEO of Apple, initiated more philanthropic activities for the firm, and he spoke out on important social issues, such as treating all people equally regardless of ethnicity, gender, or sexual orientation. He also delegated responsibility and authority to other members of the Apple leadership team and empowered them to act. In this way, Cook displayed forms of what are referred to as responsible leadership (demonstrating concern for the firm's stakeholders and society at large).[15] Although Cook has tried to guard the Apple corporate culture, he has obviously made changes in the way people are managed and in the broader corporate focus. Thus, his style has been transformational as well.

Transformational leadership is considered to be one of the most effective strategic leadership styles. This style entails motivating followers to exceed the expectations others have of them, to continuously enrich their capabilities, and to place the interests of the organization above their own.[16] Transformational leaders develop and communicate a vision for the organization and formulate a strategy to achieve that vision. They make followers aware of the need to achieve valued organizational outcomes and encourage them to continuously strive for higher levels of achievement.

Transformational leaders have a high degree of integrity and character. Speaking about character, one CEO said the following:

"Leaders are shaped and defined by character. Leaders inspire and enable others to do excellent work and realize their potential. As a result, they build successful, enduring organizations."[17]

Additionally, transformational leaders have emotional intelligence. Emotionally intelligent leaders understand themselves well, have strong motivation, are empathetic with others, and have effective interpersonal skills.[18] As a result of these characteristics, transformational leaders are especially effective in promoting and nurturing innovation in firms.[19]

12-2 The Role of Top-Level Managers

To exercise the duties of their role, top-level managers make many decisions, such as the strategic actions and responses that are part of the competitive rivalry with which the firm is involved at a point in time (see Chapter 5). More broadly, they are involved with making many decisions associated with first selecting and then implementing the firm's strategies.

When making decisions related to using the strategic management process, managers (certainly top-level ones) often use their discretion (or latitude for action).[20] Managerial discretion differs significantly across industries. The primary factors that determine the amount of decision-making discretion held by a manager (especially a top-level manager) are

1. external environmental sources such as the industry structure, the rate of market growth in the firm's primary industry, and the degree to which products can be differentiated
2. characteristics of the organization, including its size, age, resources, and culture
3. characteristics of the manager, including commitment to the firm and its strategic outcomes, tolerance for ambiguity, skills in working with different people, and aspiration levels (see Figure 12.2)

Because strategic leaders' decisions are intended to help the firm outperform competitors, how managers exercise discretion when making decisions is critical to the firm's success[21] and affects or shapes the firm's culture.

Top-level managers' roles in verifying that their firm effectively uses the strategic management process are complex and challenging. Because of this, top management teams, rather than a single top-level manager, typically make these types of decisions.[22]

12-2a Top Management Teams

The **top management team** is composed of the individuals who are responsible for making certain the firm uses the strategic management process, especially for the purpose of

A **top management team** is composed of the individuals who are responsible for making certain the firm uses the strategic management process, especially for the purpose of selecting and implementing strategies.

Figure 12.2 Factors Affecting Managerial Discretion

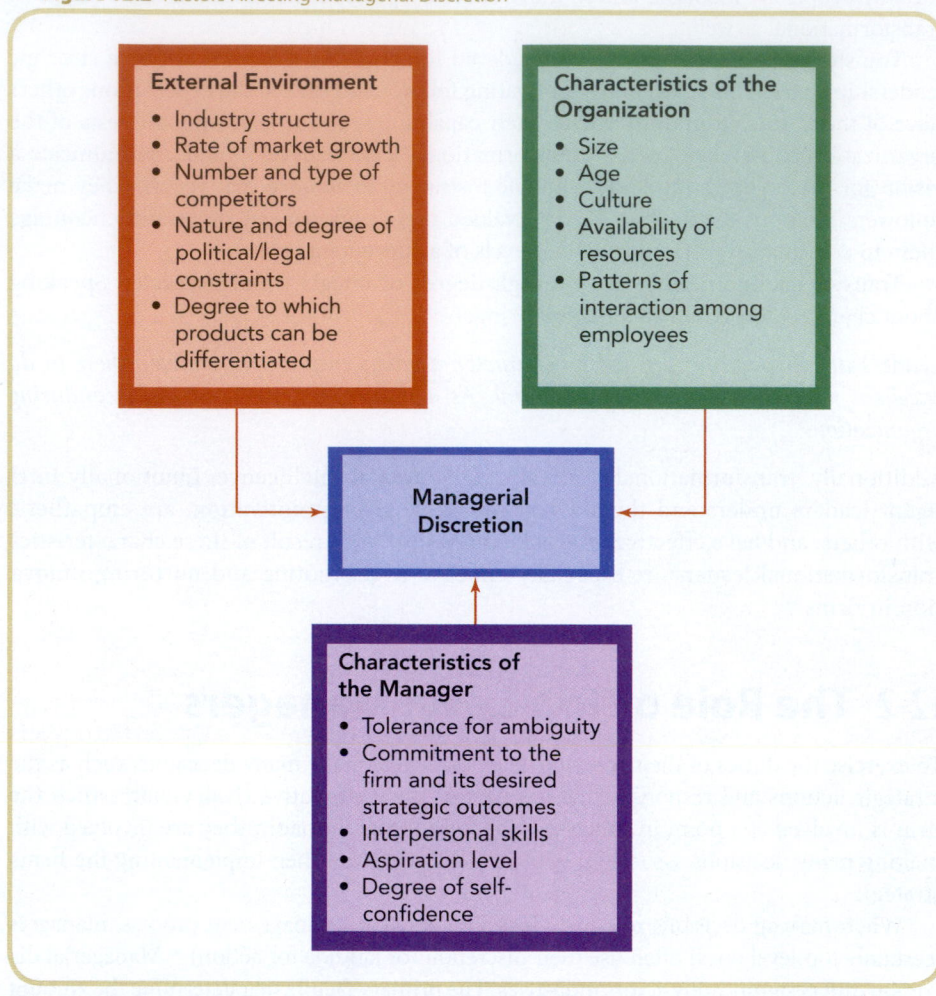

Source: Adapted from S. Finkelstein & D C. Hambrick, 1996, *Strategic Leadership: Top Executives and Their Effects on Organizations*, St. Paul, MN: West Publishing Company.

selecting and implementing strategies. Typically, the top management team includes the officers of the corporation, defined by the title of vice president and above or by service as a member of the board of directors.[23] Among other outcomes, the quality of a top management team's decisions affects the firm's ability to innovate and change in ways that contribute to its efforts to earn above-average returns.[24]

As previously noted, the complex challenges facing most organizations require the exercise of strategic leadership by a team of executives rather than by a single individual. Using a team to make decisions about how the firm will compete also helps to avoid another potential problem when these decisions are made by the CEO alone: managerial hubris. Research shows that when CEOs begin to believe glowing press accounts and to feel that they are unlikely to make errors, the quality of their decisions suffers.[25] Top-level managers need to have self-confidence but must guard against allowing it to become arrogance and a false belief in their own invincibility.[26] To guard against CEO overconfidence and the making of poor decisions, firms often use a top management *team* to make decisions required by the strategic management process.

Top Management Teams, Firm Performance, and Strategic Change

The job of top-level managers is complex and requires a broad knowledge of the firm's internal organization (see Chapter 3) as well as the three key parts of its external environment—the general, industry, and competitor environments (see Chapter 2). Therefore, firms try to form a top management team with the knowledge and expertise needed to operate the internal organization and who can deal with the firm's stakeholders as well as its competitors.[27] Firms also need to structure the top management team in a way to best utilize the members' expertise (e.g., create structural interdependence to make the best decisions).[28] To have these characteristics normally requires a heterogeneous top management team. A **heterogeneous top management team** is composed of individuals with different functional backgrounds, experience, and education. Increasingly, having international experience is a critical aspect of the heterogeneity that is desirable in top management teams, given the globalized nature of the markets in which most firms now compete.[29]

Research evidence indicates that members of a heterogeneous top management team benefit from discussing their different perspectives.[30] In many cases, these discussions, and the debates they often engender, increase the quality of the team's decisions, especially when a synthesis emerges within the team after evaluating different perspectives.[31] In effect, top management team members learn from each other and thereby develop a better decision.[32] In turn, higher-quality decisions lead to stronger firm performance.[33]

In addition to their heterogeneity, the effectiveness of top management teams is also influenced by the value gained when members of these teams work together cohesively. In general, the more heterogeneous and larger the top management team, the more difficult it is for the team to cohesively implement strategies effectively.[34] Noteworthy is the finding that communication difficulties among top-level managers with different backgrounds and cognitive skills can negatively affect strategy implementation efforts.[35] As a result, a group of top executives with diverse backgrounds may inhibit the process of decision making if it is not effectively managed. In these cases, top management teams may fail to comprehensively examine threats and opportunities, leading to suboptimal decisions. Thus, the CEO must attempt to achieve behavioral integration among the team members.[36]

Having members with substantive expertise in the firm's core businesses is also important to a top management team's effectiveness.[37] In a high-technology industry, for example, it may be critical for a firm's top management team members to have R&D expertise, particularly when growth strategies are being implemented. However, their eventual effect on decisions depends not only on their expertise and the way the team is managed but also on the context in which they make the decisions (the governance structure, incentive compensation, etc.).[38]

The characteristics of top management teams, and even the personalities of the CEO and other team members, are related to innovation and strategic change.[39] For example, more heterogeneous top management teams are positively associated with innovation and strategic change, perhaps in part because heterogeneity may influence the team, or at least some of its members, to think more creatively when making decisions and taking actions.[40]

Therefore, firms that could benefit by changing their strategies are more likely to make those changes if they have top management teams with diverse backgrounds and expertise. In this regard, evidence suggests that when a new CEO is hired from outside the industry, the probability of strategic change is greater than if the new CEO is from inside the firm or inside the industry.[41] Although hiring a new CEO from outside the industry adds diversity to the team, such a change can affect the firm's relationships with important stakeholders, especially the customers and employees.[42] Consistent with

A **heterogeneous top management team** is composed of individuals with different functional backgrounds, experience, and education.

earlier comments, we highlight here the value of transformational leadership to strategic change as the CEO helps the firm match environmental opportunities with its strengths, as indicated by its capabilities and core competencies, as a foundation for selecting and/ or implementing new strategies.[43]

The CEO and Top Management Team Power

We noted in Chapter 10 that the board of directors is an important governance mechanism for monitoring a firm's strategic direction and for representing stakeholders' interests, especially shareholders. In fact, higher performance normally is achieved when the board of directors is more directly involved in helping to shape the firm's strategic direction.[44]

Boards of directors, however, may find it difficult to direct the decisions and resulting actions of powerful CEOs and top management teams.[45] Often, a powerful CEO appoints a number of sympathetic outside members to the board or may have inside board members who are also on the top management team and report to her or him.[46] In either case, the CEO may significantly influence actions such as appointments to the board. Thus, the amount of discretion a CEO has in making decisions is related to the board of directors and the decision latitude it provides to the CEO and the remainder of the top management team.[47]

CEOs and top management team members can also achieve power in other ways. For example, a CEO who also holds the position of chair of the board usually has more power than the CEO who does not.[48] Some analysts and corporate "watchdogs" criticize the practice of *CEO duality* (when the positions of CEO and the chair of the board are held by the same person) because it can lead to poor performance and slow responses to change, partly because the board often reduces its efforts to monitor the CEO and other top management team members when CEO duality exists.[49]

Although it varies across industries, CEO duality occurs most commonly in larger firms. Increased shareholder activism has brought CEO duality under scrutiny and attack in both U.S. and European firms. In this regard, we noted in Chapter 10 that a number of analysts, regulators, and corporate directors believe that an independent board leadership structure without CEO duality has a net positive effect on the board's efforts to monitor top-level managers' decisions and actions, particularly with respect to financial performance. However, CEO duality's actual effects on firm performance (and particularly financial performance) remain inconclusive.[50] Moreover, recent evidence suggests that, at least in a sample of firms in European countries, CEO duality can have a positive effect on performance when a firm encounters a crisis.[51] Yet, recent evidence suggests that some firms have begun to separate the CEO and board chair positions. Some of the separations occur because of poor performance but not all. In other cases, the separation is created to allow an experienced board chair to mentor a new CEO (new CEO serves as an apprentice for a period of time).[52] Thus, it seems that nuances or situational conditions must be considered when analyzing the outcomes of CEO duality on firm performance. For example, power differentials can occur among top management team members when a family holds an important ownership position even in large public firms. Typically, top managers who are also members of the family may have a special form of power which can cause conflict unless the power can be balanced across the top management team.[53]

Top management team members and CEOs who have long tenure—on the team and in the organization—have a greater influence on board decisions. In general, long tenure may constrain the breadth of an executive's knowledge base. Some evidence suggests that with the limited perspectives associated with a restricted knowledge base, long-tenured top executives typically develop fewer alternatives to evaluate when making strategic decisions.[54] However, long-tenured managers also may be able to exercise more effective strategic control, thereby obviating the need for board members' involvement because effective strategic control generally leads to higher performance.[55] Intriguingly, it may be that "the liabilities of short tenure … appear to exceed the advantages, while the advantages of long tenure—firm-specific human and social capital, knowledge, and power—seem to outweigh the disadvantages of rigidity and maintaining the status quo."[56] Overall then, the relationship between CEO tenure and firm performance is complex and nuanced,[57] indicating that a board of directors should develop an effective working relationship with the top management team as part of its efforts to enhance firm performance.

Another nuance or situational condition to consider is the case in which a CEO acts as a *steward* of the firm's assets. In this instance, holding the dual roles of CEO and board chair facilitates the making of decisions and the taking of actions that benefit stakeholders. The logic here is that the CEO, desiring to be the best possible steward of the firm's assets, gains efficiency through CEO duality.[58] Additionally, because of this person's positive orientation and actions, extra governance and the coordination costs resulting from an independent board leadership structure become unnecessary.[59]

In summary, the relative degrees of power held by the board and top management team members should be examined in light of an individual firm's situation. For example, the abundance of resources in a firm's external environment and the volatility of that environment may affect the ideal balance of power between the board and the top management team. Moreover, a volatile and uncertain environment may create a situation where a powerful CEO is needed to move quickly. In such an instance, a diverse top management team may create less cohesion among team members, perhaps stalling or even preventing appropriate decisions from being made in a timely manner. In the final analysis, an effective working relationship between the board and the CEO and other top management team members is the foundation through which decisions are made that have the highest probability of best serving stakeholders' interests.[60]

12-3 Managerial Succession

The choice of top-level managers—particularly CEOs—is a critical decision with important implications for the firm's performance.[61] As discussed in Chapter 10, selecting the CEO is one of the boards of directors' most important responsibilities as it seeks to represent the best interests of a firm's stakeholders. Many companies use leadership screening systems to identify individuals with strategic leadership potential as well as to determine the criteria individuals should satisfy to be a candidate for the CEO position.

The most effective of these screening systems assesses people within the firm and gains valuable information about the capabilities of other companies' strategic leaders.[62] Based on the results of these assessments, training and development programs are provided to various individuals in an attempt to preselect and shape the skills of people with strategic leadership potential.

A number of firms have high-quality leadership programs in place, including Procter & Gamble (P&G), GE, IBM, and Dow Chemical. For example, P&G is thought to have talent throughout the organization

© Corepics VOF/Shutterstock.com

Managers participating in a leadership training program.

who are trained to accept the next level of leadership responsibility when the time comes. Managing talent on a global basis, P&G seeks to consistently provide leaders at all levels in the firm with meaningful work and significant responsibilities as a means of simultaneously challenging and developing them. The value created by GE's leadership training programs is suggested by the fact that many companies recruit leadership talent from this firm.[63]

In spite of the value high-quality leadership training programs can create, there are many companies that have not established training and succession plans for their top-level managers or for others holding key leadership positions (e.g., department heads, sections heads). With respect to family-owned firms operating in the United States, a recent survey found that only 41 percent of those surveyed have established leadership contingency plans while 49 percent indicated that they "review succession plans (only) when a change in management requires it."[64] The results are similar for family firms on a global basis as a broader survey of family firms in Asia, Europe, and Latin America found that only the most successful companies have a clear understanding of the party responsible for managing the CEO succession process. In 44 percent of the firms surveyed, the board of directors had that responsibility.[65] On a global scale, recent evidence suggests that "only 45 percent of executives from 34 countries around the world say their companies have a process for conducting CEO succession planning."[66] Unfortunately, the need for continuity in the use of a firm's strategic management process is difficult to attain without an effective succession plan and process in place.

Organizations select managers and strategic leaders from two types of managerial labor markets—internal and external.[67] An **internal managerial labor market** consists of a firm's opportunities for managerial positions and the qualified employees within that firm. An **external managerial labor market** is the collection of managerial career opportunities and the qualified people who are external to the organization in which the opportunities exist.

Employees commonly prefer that the internal managerial labor market be used for selection purposes, particularly when the firm is choosing members for its top management team and a new CEO. Evidence suggests that these preferences are often fulfilled. For example, about 66 percent of new CEOs selected in *Fortune 500* companies were promoted from within. And, the new CEOs chosen had worked at the firm and average of 12.8 years.[68] In the replacement for Steve Jobs at Apple, Tim Cook represents an internal promotion, as discussed in the Opening Case.

With respect to the CEO position, several benefits are thought to accrue to a firm using the internal labor market to select a new CEO, one of which is the continuing commitment to the existing vision, mission, and strategies for the firm. Also, because of their experience with the firm and the industry in which it competes, inside CEOs are familiar with company products, markets, technologies, and operating procedures. Another benefit is that choosing a new CEO from within usually results in lower turnover among existing personnel, many of whom possess valuable firm-specific knowledge and skills. In summary, CEOs selected from inside the firm tend to benefit from their

1. clear understanding of the firm's personnel and their capabilities
2. appreciation of the company's culture and its associated core values
3. deep knowledge of the firm's core competencies as well as abilities to develop new ones as appropriate
4. "feel" for what will and will not "work" in the firm[69]

In spite of the understandable and legitimate reasons to select CEOs from inside the firm, boards of directors sometimes prefer to choose a new CEO from the external

An **internal managerial labor market** consists of a firm's opportunities for managerial positions and the qualified employees within that firm.

An **external managerial labor market** is the collection of managerial career opportunities and the qualified people who are external to the organization in which the opportunities exist.

managerial labor market. Conditions suggesting a potentially appropriate preference to hire from outside include

1. the firm's need to enhance its ability to innovate
2. the firm's need to reverse its recent poor performance
3. the fact that the industry in which the firm competes is experiencing rapid growth
4. the need for strategic change[70]

Overall, the decision to use either the internal or the external managerial labor market to select a firm's new CEO is one that should be based on expectations; in other words, what does the board of directors want the new CEO and top management team to accomplish? We address this issue in Figure 12.3 by showing how the composition of the top management team and the CEO succession source (managerial labor market) interact to affect strategy. For example, when the top management team is homogeneous (its members have similar functional experiences and educational backgrounds) and a new CEO is selected from inside the firm, the firm's current strategy is unlikely to change. If the firm is performing well, absolutely and relative to peers, continuing to implement the current strategy may be precisely what the board of directors wants to happen. Alternatively, when a new CEO is selected from outside the firm and the top management team is heterogeneous, the probability is high that strategy will change. This, of course, would be a board's preference when the firm's performance is declining, both in absolute terms and relative to rivals. When the new CEO is from inside the firm and a heterogeneous top management team is in place, the strategy may not change, but innovation is likely to continue. An external CEO succession with a homogeneous team creates a more ambiguous situation. Furthermore, outside CEOs who lead moderate change often achieve increases in performance, but high strategic change by outsiders frequently leads to declines in performance.[71] In summary, a firm's board of directors should use the insights shown in Figure 12.3 to inform its decision about which of the two managerial labor markets to use when selecting a new CEO.

An interim CEO is commonly appointed when a firm lacks a succession plan or when an emergency occurs requiring an immediate appointment of a new CEO. Companies throughout the world use this approach.[72] Interim CEOs are almost always from inside the firm.

Figure 12.3 Effects of CEO Succession and Top Management Team Composition on Strategy

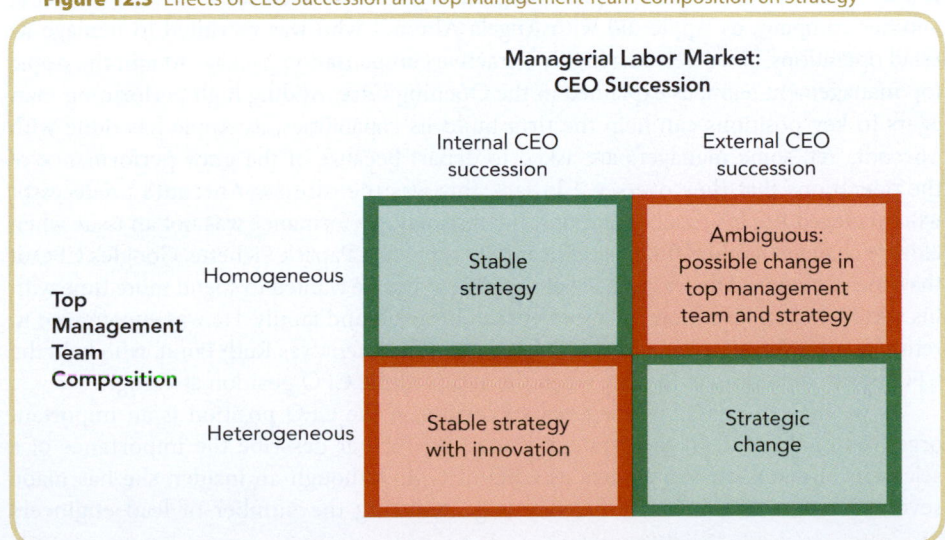

Sir Howard Stringer, the first foreign CEO of Sony in Japan.

Helga Esteb/Shutterstock.com

Their familiarity with the company's operations supports their efforts to "maintain order" for a period of time. Indeed, a primary advantage of appointing an interim CEO is that doing so can generate the amount of time the board of directors requires to conduct a thorough search to find the best candidate from the external and internal markets.

Not all changes in CEOs are successful. For example, some Japanese firms have experimented with foreign CEOs. The intent is to encourage strategic changes, but foreign-born CEOs must have the capability to gain acceptance from other managers and employees in the firm, or their changes are unlikely to be implemented effectively. Thus, most Japanese firms that hire foreign CEOs search for one who has work experience in Japan so that he or she understands the culture and the typical styles used in Japanese firms.[73] Additionally, firms have learned that it is generally important to retain target company executives after the firm is acquired. Without them, integration of the newly acquired firm into the acquiring firm is commonly more difficult. Moreover, the executives often have valuable knowledge and capabilities that are lost to the acquirer if they depart. Thus, turnover among these executives makes the acquisition less valuable to the acquiring firm.[74]

Changes in top management positions other than the CEO are also important. These changes often occur because a promising manager is recruited for a better position at another company, as Apple did with Angela Ahrendt who was recruited to manage its retail operations. She received a highly attractive compensation package to join the Apple top management team, as explained in the Opening Case. Adding high performing managers in key positions can help the firm build its capabilities, as Apple has done with Ahrendt. Yet, some managers are asked to depart because of the poor performance of the operations that they oversee.[75] In fact, this was the case for Ahrendt's predecessor who managed Apple's retail operations. Interestingly, performance was not an issue when Google changed its chief financial officer (CFO) in 2015. Patrick Pichette, Google's CFO at the time, announced he was retiring after seven years. He wanted to spend more time with his family and achieve more balance between his work and family. He was encouraged to retire by his wife and travel more with her. His replacement was Ruth Porat, who held the CFO position at Morgan Stanley when she accepted the CFO position at Google.[76]

As we have discussed, managerial succession in the CEO position is an important organizational event. In the Strategic Focus, we further describe the importance of a selection in choosing Mary Barra as CEO of GM. Although an insider, she has made several changes to increase efficiency (e.g., reducing the number of lead engineers

Strategic **Focus**

Trial by Fire: CEO Succession at General Motors

Late in 2013, Dan Akerson, the CEO of General Motors (GM) during a time of intense scrutiny and criticism of the firm, announced that he was accelerating his retirement. He had planned to retire at the end of 2014, but he learned that his wife had a severe illness, so he decided to retire early. To succeed Akerson, Mary Barra was chosen. She became the first woman CEO of a major automaker in the world. Her selection to become the new CEO for GM was a major celebration for breaking the "glass ceiling" in a formerly male-dominated industry. Her choice represented an inside succession, as she had spent her entire career at GM.

Barra had her hands full trying to create change in an archaic structure and corporate governance system. For example, for years GM used three lead engineers for every new product, requiring more time, extra coordination and often significant inefficiencies. Barra announced changes that resulted in only one lead engineer for every new vehicle. As it turned out the inefficient structure was a minor problem relative to what she soon encountered. She learned about a substantial problem with an ignition switch on GM vehicles that evidently caused wrecks, major injuries, and even death. Worse, the company had known about the problem for years but took no action to fix the problem or to acknowledge it. When she learned of the problem, Barra acted swiftly (although not quick enough for some). GM acknowledged the problem and made compensation offers to families of people who were killed in accidents because of the defective ignition switch. Additionally, GM recalled almost 30 million vehicles to fix the problem. But, this was a public relations disaster, and she was called to testify before Congress about the problem.

Beyond these actions, Barra is trying to change the culture at the company so that such problems do not occur in the future. Her "trial by fire" has been recognized by GM's board of directors because she earned $16.2 million in 2014, which is 80 percent more than her predecessor received. Her challenges continue. Barra is trying to increase capital spending by 20 percent to improve existing product lines and to continue developing an enhanced electric vehicle. However, she also has to deal with declining profits in GM's European and Latin American markets.

Regardless, Barra paid blue collar workers a larger bonus in 2015 than required by the union contract showing her commitment to GM employees. She also announced plans to distribute about $5 billion in dividends to shareholders by the end of 2016. She also hopes to bolster GM's stock price by buying back about $5 billion in stock in the same time period. Thus, Mary Barra made history being named as CEO of GM. She came up through the ranks and knew the firm but still faced substantial challenges during her first year in the position. She has weathered the trial by fire and has a vision for the future.

Mary Barra, CEO of General Motors, introduces the new Chevrolet Volt.

Sources: G. Gardner, 2013, Dan Akerson leaves GM stronger than he found it, *Detroit Free Press*, www.freep.com, December 10; J. Jusko, 2014, CEO Mary Barra is driving culture change at General Motors, *IndustryWeek*, www.industryweek.com; 2014, Mary Barra General Motors, *European CEO*, www.europeanceo.com, November 27; B. Vlasic, 2015, General Motors chief pledges to move beyond recalls, *New York Times*, www.nytimes.com, January 8; C. M. Portillo, 2015, Let's take a peek at Mary Barra's 2015 to-do list at General Motors, *bizwomen*, www.bizjournals.com/bizwomen, January 14; B. Vlasic, 2015, Despite recalls, GM pays workers a big bonus, *New York Times*, www.nytimes.com, February 4; M. Lewis, 2015, GM's Barra bets she can deliver where predecessors fell short, *New York Times*, www.nytimes.com, March 9; R. Wright, 2015, GM disappoints as Europe and South America reverse, *Financial Times*, www.ft.com, April 23; J. D. Stoll, 2015, GM chief executive Mary Barra earned $16.2 million in 2014, *Wall Street Journal*, www.wsj.com, April 24.

on a new product from three to one) trying to change the culture. Changing the culture is very important to avoid future problems similar to the ignition switch malfunction. Barra is trying to resolve the ignition switch problem and increase the company's transparency on such problems. She appears to have been a very good choice as the new CEO of General Motors. Next, we discuss key actions that effective strategic leaders demonstrate while helping their firm use the strategic management process.

12-4 Key Strategic Leadership Actions

Certain actions characterize effective strategic leadership; we present the most important ones in Figure 12.4. Many of the actions interact with each other. For example, managing the firm's resources effectively includes developing human capital and contributes to establishing a strategic direction, fostering an effective culture, exploiting core competencies, using effective and balanced organizational control systems, and establishing ethical practices. The most effective strategic leaders create viable options in making decisions regarding each of the key strategic leadership actions.[77]

12-4a Determining Strategic Direction

Determining strategic direction involves specifying the vision and the strategy or strategies to achieve this vision over time.[78] The strategic direction is framed within the context of the conditions (i.e., opportunities and threats) that strategic leaders expect their firm to face in roughly the next three to five years.

The ideal long-term strategic direction has two parts: a core ideology and an envisioned future. The core ideology motivates employees through the company's heritage while the envisioned future encourages them to stretch beyond their expectations of accomplishment and requires significant change and progress to be realized.[79] The envisioned future serves as a guide to many aspects of a firm's strategy implementation process, including motivation, leadership, employee empowerment, and organizational design.

Determining strategic direction involves specifying the vision and the strategy or strategies to achieve this vision over time.

Figure 12.4 Exercise of Effective Strategic Leadership

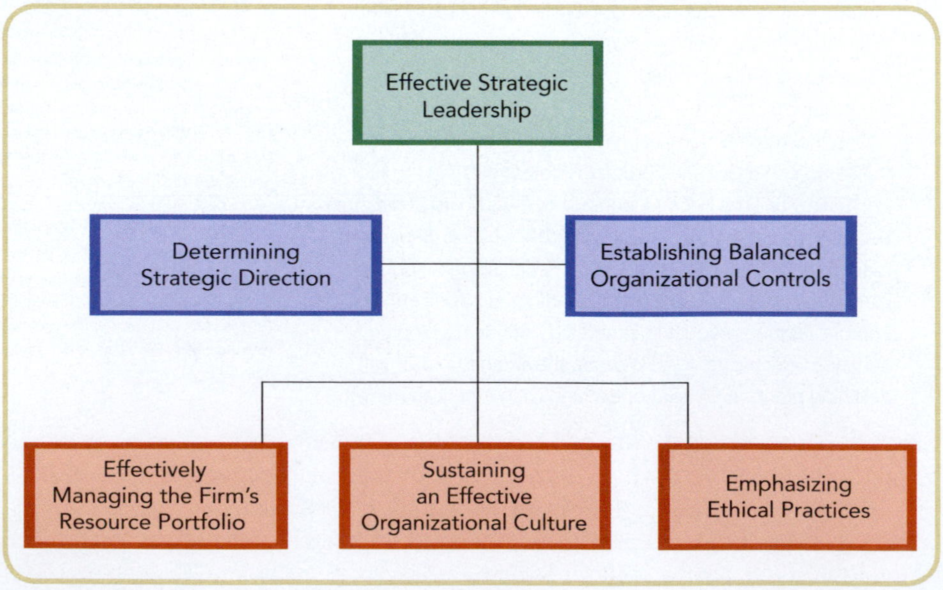

The strategic direction could include a host of actions such as entering new international markets and developing a set of new suppliers to add to the firm's value chain.[80]

Sometimes though, the work of strategic leaders does not result in selecting a strategy that helps a firm reach the vision. This can happen when top management team members and, certainly, the CEO are too committed to the status quo. While the firm's strategic direction remains rather stable across time, actions taken to implement strategies to achieve the vision should be somewhat fluid, largely so the firm can deal with unexpected opportunities and threats that surface in the external environment. An inability to adjust strategies as appropriate is often caused by an aversion to what decision makers conclude are risky actions. An aversion to risky actions is common in firms that have performed well in the past and for CEOs who have been in their jobs for extended periods of time.[81] Research also suggests that some CEOs are erratic or even ambivalent in their choices of strategic direction, especially when their competitive environment is turbulent and it is difficult to identify the best strategy.[82] Of course, these erratic or ambivalent behaviors are unlikely to produce high performance and may lead to CEO turnover. Interestingly, research has found that incentive compensation in the form of stock options encourages talented executives to select the best strategies and thus achieve the highest performance. However, the same incentives used with less talented executives produce lower performance.[83]

In contrast to risk-averse CEOs, charismatic ones may foster stakeholders' commitment to a new vision and strategic direction. Nonetheless, even when being guided by a charismatic CEO, it is important for the firm not to lose sight of its strengths and weaknesses when making changes required by a new strategic direction. The most effective charismatic CEO leads a firm in ways that are consistent with its culture and with the actions permitted by its capabilities and core competencies.[84]

Finally, being ambicultural can facilitate efforts to determine the firm's strategic direction and select and use strategies to reach it. Being ambicultural means that strategic leaders are committed to identifying the best organizational activities to take particularly when implementing strategies, regardless of their cultural origin.[85] Ambicultural actions help the firm succeed in the short term as a foundation for reaching its vision in the longer term.[86]

12-4b Effectively Managing the Firm's Resource Portfolio

Effectively managing the firm's portfolio of resources is another critical strategic leadership action. The firm's resources are categorized as financial capital, human capital, social capital, and organizational capital (including organizational culture).[87]

Clearly, financial capital is critical to organizational success; strategic leaders understand this reality.[88] However, the most effective strategic leaders recognize the equivalent importance of managing each remaining type of resource as well as managing the integration of resources (e.g., using financial capital to provide training opportunities to the firm's human capital). Most importantly, effective strategic leaders manage the firm's resource portfolio by organizing the resources into capabilities, structuring the firm to facilitate using those capabilities, and choosing strategies through which the capabilities can be successfully leveraged to create value for customers.[89] Exploiting and maintaining core competencies and developing and retaining the firm's human and social capital are actions taken to reach these important objectives.

Exploiting and Maintaining Core Competencies

Examined in Chapters 1 and 3, *core competencies* are capabilities that serve as a source of competitive advantage for a firm over its rivals. Typically, core competencies relate to skills within organizational functions, such as manufacturing, finance, marketing, and research and development. Strategic leaders must verify that the firm's core competencies are understood when selecting strategies and then emphasized when implementing those strategies. This suggests, for example, that with respect to their strategies, Apple emphasizes its design competence, while Netflix recognizes and concentrates on its competence of being able to deliver physical, digital, and original content.[90]

Core competencies are developed over time as firms learn from the results of the competitive actions and responses taken during the course of competing with rivals. On the basis of what they learn, firms continuously reshape their capabilities for the purpose of verifying that they are, indeed, the path through which core competencies are being developed and used to establish one or more competitive advantages.

Dan Akerson became CEO of GM in July 2009, a time when the firm required a transformation in order to survive as the foundation for then being able to compete successfully against its global rivals. One of the first decisions Akerson made was to allocate resources for the purpose of building new capabilities in technology development and in marketing, especially in customer service. Akerson helped to turnaround the company, bringing it out of bankruptcy and trying to enrich its core competencies. Now, as explained in the Strategic Focus, Mary Barra is changing the culture and trying to increase the efficiency of GM. In addition, she is trying to gain the trust of human capital (e.g., by paying special bonuses to blue collar workers) thereby building her internal social capital. Strong human capital and social capital are critical for GM to develop and maintain strong core competencies. As we discuss next, human capital and social capital are critical to a firm's success. This is the case for GM as the firm strives to continuously improve its performance. One reason for human capital's importance is that it is the resource through which core competencies are developed and used.

Developing Human Capital and Social Capital

Human capital refers to the knowledge and skills of a firm's entire workforce. From the perspective of human capital, employees are viewed as a capital resource requiring continuous investment.[91]

Bringing talented human capital into the firm and then developing that capital has the potential to yield positive outcomes. A key reason for this is that individuals' knowledge and skills are proving to be critical to the success of many global industries (e.g., automobile manufacturing) as well as industries within countries (e.g., leather and shoe manufacturing in Italy). This fact suggests that "as the dynamics of competition accelerate, people are perhaps the only truly sustainable source of competitive advantage."[92] In all types of organizations—large and small, new and established, and so forth—human capital's increasing importance suggests a significant role for the firm's human resource management function.[93] As one of a firm's support functions on which firms rely to create value (see Chapter 3), human resource management practices facilitate selecting and especially implementing the firm's strategies.[94]

Effective training and development programs increase the probability that some of the firm's human capital will become effective strategic leaders. Increasingly, the link between effective programs and firm success is becoming stronger because the knowledge gained by participating in these programs is integral to forming and then sustaining a firm's competitive advantage.[95] In addition to building human capital's knowledge and skills, these programs inculcate a common set of core values and present a systematic view of the organization, thus promoting its vision and helping form an effective organizational culture.

Effective training and development programs also contribute positively to the firm's efforts to form core competencies.[96] Furthermore, the programs help strategic leaders improve skills that are critical to completing other tasks associated with effective strategic leadership, such as determining the firm's strategic direction, exploiting and maintaining

Human capital refers to the knowledge and skills of a firm's entire workforce. From the perspective of human capital, employees are viewed as a capital resource requiring continuous investment.

the firm's core competencies, and developing an organizational culture that supports ethical practices. Thus, building human capital is vital to the effective execution of strategic leadership.

When investments in human capital (such as providing high-quality training and development programs) are successful, the outcome is a workforce capable of learning continuously. This is an important outcome in that continuous learning and leveraging the firm's expanding knowledge base are linked with strategic success.[97]

Learning also can preclude errors. Strategic leaders may learn more from failure than success because they sometimes make the wrong attributions for the successes.[98] For example, the effectiveness of certain approaches and knowledge can be context specific. Thus, some "best practices" may not work well in all situations. We know that using teams to make decisions can be effective, but sometimes it is better for leaders to make decisions alone, especially when the decisions must be made and implemented quickly (e.g., in crisis situations).[99] As such, effective strategic leaders recognize the importance of learning from success *and* from failure when helping their firm use the strategic management process. To ensure more effective use of the strategic management process, firms have begun to create more diversity among top management team leaders.[100]

When facing challenging conditions, firms may decide to lay off some of their human capital, a decision that can result in a significant loss of knowledge. Research shows that moderate-sized layoffs may improve firm performance primarily in the short run, but large layoffs produce stronger performance downturns in firms because of the loss of human capital.[101] Although it is also not uncommon for restructuring firms to reduce their investments in training and development programs, restructuring may actually be an important time to increase investments in these programs. The reason for this is that restructuring firms have less slack and cannot absorb as many errors; moreover, the employees who remain after layoffs may find themselves in positions without all the skills or knowledge they need to create value through their work.

Viewing employees as a resource to be maximized rather than as a cost to be minimized facilitates successful implementation of a firm's strategies, as does the strategic leader's ability to approach layoffs in a manner that employees believe is fair and equitable. A critical issue for employees is the fairness in the layoffs and how they are treated in their jobs, especially relative to their peers.[102]

Social capital involves relationships inside and outside the firm that help in efforts to accomplish tasks and create value for stakeholders.[103] Social capital is a critical asset given that employees must cooperate with one another and others, including suppliers and customers, in order to complete their work. In multinational organizations, employees often must cooperate across country boundaries on activities such as R&D to achieve performance objectives (e.g., developing new products).[104]

External social capital is increasingly critical to firm success in that few if any companies possess all of the resources needed to successfully compete against their rivals. Firms can use cooperative strategies, such as strategic alliances (see Chapter 9), to develop social capital. Social capital can be built in strategic alliances as firms share complementary resources. Resource sharing must be effectively managed to ensure that the partner trusts the firm and is willing to share its resources.[105] Social capital created this way yields many benefits. For example, firms with strong social capital are able to be more ambidextrous; that is, they can develop or have access to multiple capabilities, providing them with the flexibility to take advantage of opportunities and to respond to threats.[106]

Research evidence suggests that the success of many types of firms may partially depend on social capital. Large multinational firms often must establish alliances in order to enter new foreign markets; entrepreneurial firms often must establish alliances to gain access to resources, venture capital, or other types of resources (e.g., special expertise

Social capital involves relationships inside and outside the firm that help in efforts to accomplish tasks and create value for stakeholders.

Strategic Focus

All the Ways You Can Fail!

NBC News experienced several major problems in 2014. Likely, the biggest problem was the suspension of popular nightly news anchor, Brian Williams, for embellishing his role in several past news stories. When this came to light, concerns about his credibility and thus NBC News credibility caused the top executives to take action. In addition, NBC's former top morning show, the Today Show, fell in the ratings. Because of this, Jamie Horowitz was hired from ESPN to make major changes. However, Horowitz and the staff on the show had major differences of opinion, especially with the manner in which Horowitz dealt with staff. These high profile clashes led top executives to let Horowitz go. As a result, Andrew Lack, former president of NBC News, was hired to replace Patricia Fili-Krushel as chair of the NBC Universal News Group. Time will tell if Lack can restore stability, credibility, and high ratings to NBC.

Nokia is an almost textbook case on how to fail. In 2009, Nokia was the market leader in the global smartphone market, but by 2014 it was not listed as a rival in the market. The Nokia brand had disappeared. Before the launch of the Apple iPhone, Nokia had access to the touch screen technology, and Nokia technology specialists recommended integrating it into its smartphones. But, the top leadership at Nokia rejected this idea because Nokia was doing well and using this technology entailed risk. Of course, rivals Samsung and Apple implemented the technology, and those two firms along with others took the smartphone market from Nokia. Nokia's leaders made absolutely horrible decisions and failed because of it.

The Standard Charter bank's profits declined in 2014 by 37 percent relative to the profit achieved in 2013. Most people attribute the bank's performance problems to its weak capital position and its major exposures to risk in Asian markets. The CEO, Peter Sands, was asked to resign. Investors and others had lost confidence in his ability to manage the bank effectively. Essentially, he made minor changes (e.g., reducing costs) but avoided large changes likely needed to turn around the performance of the bank. To replace Sands as CEO, the bank chose William T. Winters, a former head of JPMorgan Chase's investment bank. Standard Charter has experienced many problems in recent years. For example, it has experienced losses on bad loans in increasing amounts. In 2012, it paid fines of $667 million because of charges that it had transferred billions of dollars to Iran and other such countries in violation of the OFAC sanctions. In 2014, it paid $300 million to settle claims that its computer system failed to identify suspicious transactions with high-risk clients. Winters is said to be a very savvy manager

of risk. Investors at Standard Charter should hope it is true, as they now need that expertise and a leader who makes good decisions.

The problems experienced by each of the firms were due to poor executive decisions. In the case of NBC, top managers failed to provide appropriate oversight to ensure the credibility of its news. Also, poor personnel decisions were made. In the case of Nokia, substantial conservatism led to a very poor product decision. In that case, the company fell from market leader to no longer being in existence. Finally, Standard Charter leaders made poor decisions, failing to manage its risks. Additionally, it made perhaps unethical decisions for which the firm was fined. Finally, inadequate technologies led to additional failures.

Andrew Lack hired to become the chair of the NBC Universal News Group.

Bobby Bank/Getty Images

Sources: J. Bean, 2014, Bye Nokia—A failure of management over leadership, *Jonobean*, jonobean.com, November 12; P. J. Davies, 2015, How to give Standard Chartered breathing room it needs, *Wall Street Journal*, www.wsj.com, February 26; J. Anderson & C. Bray, 2015, Standard Charter overhauls leadership, *New York Times*, www.nytimes.com, February 26; J. Flint, 2015, NBC News bringing in new leadership, after high-profile stumbles, *Wall Street Journal*, www.wsj.com, March 3; C. Bray, 2015, Standard Charter profit fell 37% in 2014, *New York Times*, www.nytimes.com, March 4.

that the entrepreneurial firm cannot afford to maintain in-house).[107] However, a firm's culture affects its ability to retain quality human capital and maintain strong internal social capital.

As explained in the Strategic Focus, NBC News, Nokia, and Standard Charter all experienced failures because of poor top managers' decisions. NBC News made poor decisions in the way it managed its human capital, and because of this, it lost the confidence of its audience (loss of social capital). Nokia was overly conservative. Its top executives made monumental mistakes. Standard Charter was losing the confidence of its investors with very poor decisions (including perhaps some unethical ones).

12-4c Sustaining an Effective Organizational Culture

In Chapter 1, we defined *organizational culture* as the complex set of ideologies, symbols, and core values that are shared throughout the firm and that influence how the firm conducts business. Because organizational culture influences how the firm conducts its business and helps regulate and control employees' behavior, it can be a source of competitive advantage.[108] Given that each firm's culture is unique, it is possible that a vibrant organizational culture is an increasingly important source of differentiation for firms to emphasize when pursuing strategic competitiveness and above-average returns. Thus, shaping the context within which the firm formulates and implements its strategies—that is, shaping the organizational culture—is another key strategic leadership action.[109]

Entrepreneurial Mind-Set

Especially in large organizations, an organizational culture often encourages (or discourages) strategic leaders and those with whom they work from pursuing (or not pursuing) entrepreneurial opportunities. (We define and discuss entrepreneurial opportunities in Chapter 13.) This is the case in both for-profit and not-for-profit organizations.[110] This issue is important because entrepreneurial opportunities are a vital source of growth and innovation.[111] Therefore, a key action for strategic leaders to take is to encourage and promote innovation by pursuing entrepreneurial opportunities.[112]

One way to encourage innovation is to invest in opportunities as real options—that is, invest in an opportunity in order to provide the potential option of taking advantage of the opportunity at some point in the future.[113] For example, a firm might buy a piece of land to have the option to build on it at some time in the future should the company need more space and should that location increase in value to the company. Oil companies acquire land leases with an option to drill for oil. Firms might enter strategic alliances for similar reasons. In this instance, a firm might form an alliance to have the option of acquiring the partner later or of building a stronger relationship with it (e.g., developing a new joint venture).[114]

In Chapter 13, we describe how firms of all sizes use strategic entrepreneurship to pursue entrepreneurial opportunities as a means of earning above-average returns. Companies are more likely to achieve the success they desire by using strategic entrepreneurship when their employees have an entrepreneurial mind-set.[115]

Five dimensions characterize a firm's entrepreneurial mind-set: autonomy, innovativeness, risk taking, proactiveness, and competitive aggressiveness.[116] In combination, these dimensions influence the actions a firm takes to be innovative when using the strategic management process.

Autonomy, the first of an entrepreneurial orientation's five dimensions, allows employees to take actions that are free of organizational constraints and encourages them to do so. The second dimension, *innovativeness*, "reflects a firm's tendency to engage in and support new ideas, novelty, experimentation, and creative processes that may result in new products, services, or technological processes."[117] Cultures with a tendency toward innovativeness encourage employees to think beyond existing knowledge, technologies, and parameters to find creative ways to add value. *Risk taking* reflects a willingness by employees and their firm to accept measured levels of risks when pursuing entrepreneurial opportunities. The fourth dimension of an entrepreneurial orientation, *proactiveness*, describes a firm's ability to be a market leader rather than a follower. Proactive organizational cultures constantly use processes to anticipate future market needs and to satisfy them before competitors learn how to do so. Finally, *competitive aggressiveness* is a firm's propensity to take actions that allow it to consistently and substantially outperform its rivals.[118]

Changing the Organizational Culture and Restructuring

Changing a firm's organizational culture is more difficult than maintaining it; however, effective strategic leaders recognize when change is needed. Incremental changes to the firm's culture typically are used to implement strategies.[119] More significant and sometimes even radical changes to organizational culture support selecting strategies that differ from those the firm has implemented historically. Regardless of the reasons for change, shaping and reinforcing a new culture requires effective communication and problem solving, along with selecting the right people (those who have the values desired for the organization), engaging in effective performance appraisals (establishing goals that support the new core values and measuring individuals' progress toward reaching them), and using appropriate reward systems (rewarding the desired behaviors that reflect the new core values).[120]

Evidence suggests that cultural changes succeed only when the firm's CEO, other key top management team members, and middle-level managers actively support them.[121] To effect change, middle-level managers in particular need to be highly disciplined to energize the culture and foster alignment with the firm's vision and mission.[122] In addition, managers must be sensitive to the effects of other changes on organizational culture. For example, downsizings can negatively affect an organization's culture, especially if they are not implemented in accordance with the dominant organizational values.[123] Mary Barra is trying to change the General Motors corporate culture as explained in the earlier Strategic Focus. In so doing, she appears to be sensitive to having the right people in key managerial positions and in supporting the firm's employees as demonstrated by giving the blue collar employees bonuses even though the firm had to pay for injuries caused by the ignition switch failure and endure the high costs of a large recall of vehicles to fix the problem.

12-4d Emphasizing Ethical Practices

The effectiveness of processes used to implement the firm's strategies increases when they are based on ethical practices. Ethical companies encourage and enable people at all levels to act ethically when taking actions to implement strategies. In turn, ethical practices and the judgment on which they are based create "social capital" in the organization, increasing the "goodwill available to individuals and groups" in the organization.[124] Alternatively, when unethical practices evolve in an organization, they may become acceptable to many managers and employees.[125] Once deemed acceptable, individuals are more likely to engage in unethical practices to meet their goals when current efforts to meet them are insufficient.[126]

To properly influence employees' judgment and behavior, ethical practices must shape the firm's decision-making process and be an integral part of organizational culture. In fact, a values-based culture is the most effective means of ensuring that employees comply with the firm's ethical standards. However, developing such a culture requires constant nurturing and support in corporations located in countries throughout the world.[127]

As explained in Chapter 10, some strategic leaders and managers may occasionally act opportunistically, making decisions that are in their own best interests.

This tends to happen when firms have lax expectations in place for individuals to follow regarding ethical behavior. In other words, individuals acting opportunistically take advantage of their positions, making decisions that benefit themselves to the detriment of the firm's stakeholders.[128] Sometimes executives take such actions due to their own greed and hubris.[129] However, when there is evidence of executive wrongdoing, such as having to restate the financial earnings, stockholders and other investors often react very negatively. In fact, it is not uncommon for new CEOs to be hired when wrongdoing comes to light.[130]

Strategic leaders as well as others in the organization are most likely to integrate ethical values into their decisions when the company has explicit ethics codes, the codes are integrated into the business through extensive ethics training, and shareholders expect ethical behavior.[131] Thus, establishing and enforcing a meaningful code of ethics is an important action to take to encourage ethical decision making as a foundation for using the strategic management process.

Strategic leaders can take several actions to develop and support an ethical organizational culture. Examples of these actions include

1. establishing and communicating specific goals to describe the firm's ethical standards (e.g., developing and disseminating a code of conduct)
2. continuously revising and updating the code of conduct, based on inputs from people throughout the firm and from other stakeholders
3. disseminating the code of conduct to all stakeholders to inform them of the firm's ethical standards and practices
4. developing and implementing methods and procedures to use in achieving the firm's ethical standards (e.g., using internal auditing practices that are consistent with the standards)
5. creating and using explicit reward systems that recognize acts of courage (e.g., rewarding those who use proper channels and procedures to report observed wrongdoings)
6. creating a work environment in which all people are treated with dignity[132]

The effectiveness of these actions increases when they are taken simultaneously and thereby are mutually supportive. When strategic leaders and others throughout the firm fail to take actions such as these—perhaps because an ethical culture has not been created—problems are likely to occur.

12-4e Establishing Balanced Organizational Controls

Organizational controls (discussed in Chapter 11) have long been viewed as an important part of the strategic management process particularly the parts related to implementation (see Figure 1.1). Controls are necessary to help ensure that firms achieve their desired outcomes. Defined as the "formal, information-based … procedures used by managers to maintain or alter patterns in organizational activities," controls help strategic leaders build credibility, demonstrate the value of strategies to the firm's stakeholders, and promote and support strategic change.[133] Most critically, controls provide the parameters for implementing strategies as well as the corrective actions to be taken when implementation-related adjustments are required. For example, in light of an insider-trading scandal, KPMG LLP reviewed its training and monitoring programs. The firm's existing safeguards "include training for employees, a whistleblower system, and monitoring of the personal investments of partners and managers." KPMG also moved to safeguard its reputation, even though it was not implicated in the scandal.[134]

In this chapter, we focus on two organizational controls—strategic and financial—that were introduced in Chapter 11. Strategic leaders are responsible for helping the firm develop and properly use these two types of controls.

As we explained in Chapter 11, financial control focuses on short-term financial outcomes. In contrast, strategic control focuses on the *content* of strategic actions rather than their *outcomes*. Some strategic actions can be correct but still result in poor financial outcomes because of external conditions, such as an economic recession, unexpected domestic or foreign government actions, or natural disasters. Therefore, emphasizing financial controls often produces more short-term and risk-averse decisions because financial outcomes may be caused by events beyond leaders and managers' direct control. Alternatively, strategic control encourages lower-level managers to make decisions that incorporate moderate and acceptable levels of risk because leaders and managers throughout the firm share the responsibility for the outcomes of those decisions and actions resulting from them.

The challenge for strategic leaders is to balance the use of strategic and financial controls for the purpose of supporting efforts to improve the firm's performance. The balanced scorecard is a tool strategic leaders use to achieve the sought after balance.

The Balanced Scorecard

The **balanced scorecard** is a tool firms use to determine if they are achieving an appropriate balance when using strategic and financial controls as a means of positively influencing performance.[135] This tool is most appropriate to use when evaluating business-level strategies; however, it can also be used with the other strategies firms implement (e.g., corporate, international, and cooperative).

The underlying premise of the balanced scorecard is that firms jeopardize their future performance when financial controls are emphasized at the expense of strategic controls.[136] This occurs because financial controls provide feedback about outcomes achieved from past actions but do not communicate the drivers of future performance. Thus, an overemphasis on financial controls may promote behavior that sacrifices the firm's long-term, value-creating potential for short-term performance gains. In effect, managers can make self-serving decisions when they focus on the shortterm. Research shows that decisions balancing short-term goals with long-term goals generally lead to higher performance.[137] An appropriate balance of strategic controls and financial controls, rather than an overemphasis on either, allows firms to achieve higher levels of performance.

Four perspectives are integrated to form the balanced scorecard:

- *financial* (concerned with growth, profitability, and risk from the shareholders' perspective)
- *customer* (concerned with the amount of value customers perceive was created by the firm's products)
- *internal business processes* (with a focus on the priorities for various business processes that create customer and shareholder satisfaction)
- *learning and growth* (concerned with the firm's effort to create a climate that supports change, innovation, and growth)

Thus, using the balanced scorecard finds the firm seeking to understand how it responds to shareholders (financial perspective), how customers view it (customer perspective), what processes to emphasize to successfully use its competitive advantage (internal perspective), and what it can do to improve its performance in order to grow (learning and growth perspective).[138] Generally speaking, firms tend to emphasize strategic controls when assessing their performance relative to the learning and growth perspective, whereas the tendency is to emphasize financial controls when assessing performance in terms of the financial perspective.

Firms use different criteria to measure their standing relative to the balanced scorecard's four perspectives. We show sample criteria in Figure 12.5. The firm should select the

The **balanced scorecard** is a tool firms use to determine if they are achieving an appropriate balance when using strategic and financial controls as a means of positively influencing performance.

Figure 12.5 Strategic Controls and Financial Controls in a Balanced Scorecard Framework

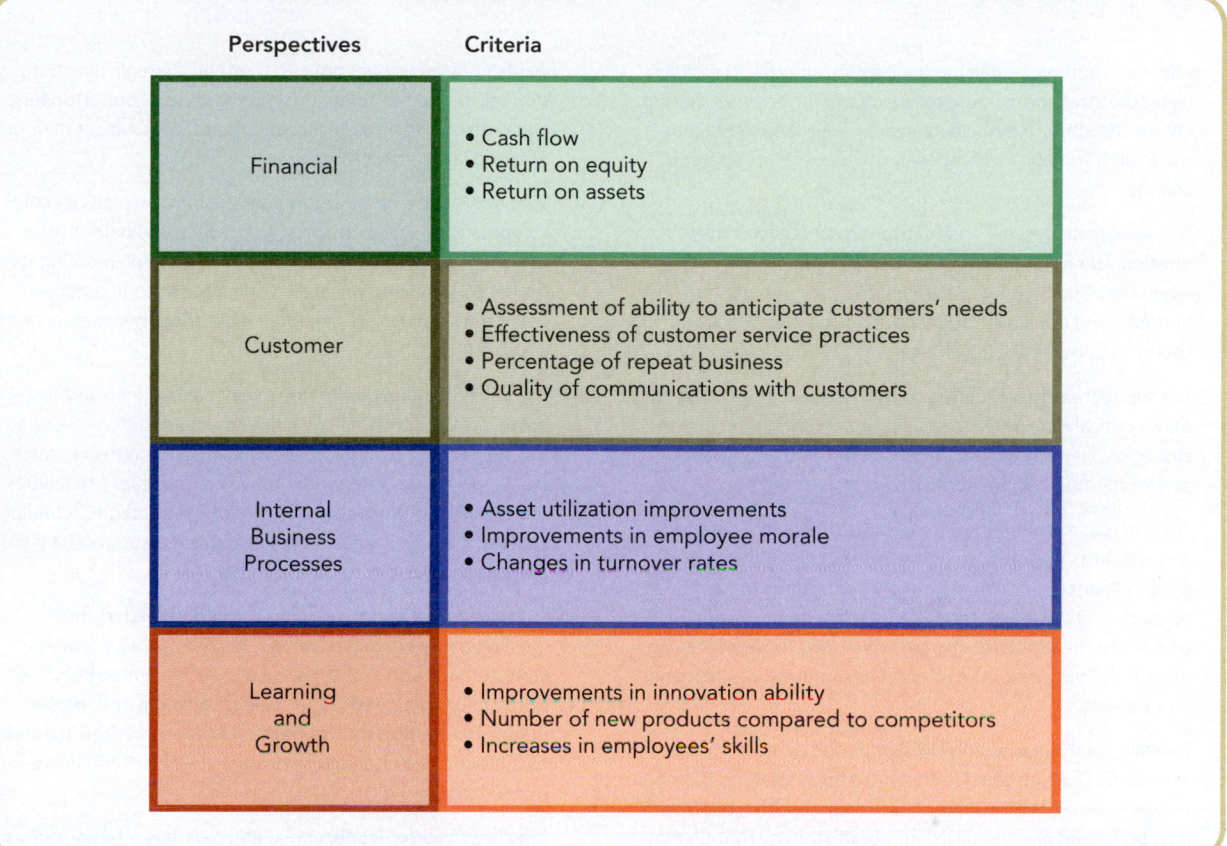

Perspectives	Criteria
Financial	• Cash flow • Return on equity • Return on assets
Customer	• Assessment of ability to anticipate customers' needs • Effectiveness of customer service practices • Percentage of repeat business • Quality of communications with customers
Internal Business Processes	• Asset utilization improvements • Improvements in employee morale • Changes in turnover rates
Learning and Growth	• Improvements in innovation ability • Number of new products compared to competitors • Increases in employees' skills

number of criteria that will allow it to have both a strategic and financial understanding of its performance without becoming immersed in too many details.[139]

Strategic leaders play an important role in determining a proper balance between strategic and financial controls, whether they are in single-business firms or large diversified firms. A proper balance between controls is important, in that "wealth creation for organizations where strategic leadership is exercised is possible because these leaders make appropriate investments for future viability (through strategic control), while maintaining an appropriate level of financial stability in the present (through financial control)."[140] In fact, most corporate restructuring is designed to refocus the firm on its core businesses, thereby allowing top executives to reestablish strategic control of their separate business units.[141]

Successfully using strategic control frequently is integrated with appropriate autonomy for the various subunits so that they can gain a competitive advantage in their respective markets.[142] Strategic control can be used to promote the sharing of both tangible and intangible resources among interdependent businesses within a firm's portfolio. In addition, the autonomy provided allows the flexibility necessary to take advantage of specific marketplace opportunities. As a result, strategic leadership promotes simultaneous use of strategic control and autonomy.

As we have explained in this chapter, strategic leaders are critical to a firm's ability to successfully use all parts of the strategic management process, including strategic entrepreneurship, which is the final topic included in the "strategy" part of this text's Analysis-Strategy-Performance model. We turn our attention to this topic in Chapter 13.

SUMMARY

- Effective strategic leadership is a prerequisite to successfully using the strategic management process. Strategic leadership entails the ability to anticipate events, envision possibilities, maintain flexibility, and empower others to create strategic change.

- Top-level managers are an important resource for firms to develop and exploit competitive advantages. In addition, when they and their work are valuable, rare, imperfectly imitable, and nonsubstitutable, strategic leaders are also a source of competitive advantage.

- The top management team is composed of key managers who play a critical role in selecting and implementing the firm's strategies. Generally, they are officers of the corporation and/or members of the board of directors.

- The top management team's characteristics, a firm's strategies, and the firm's performance are all interrelated. For example, a top management team with significant marketing and research and development (R&D) knowledge positively contributes to the firm's use of a growth strategy. Overall, having diverse skills increases the effectiveness of most top management teams.

- Typically, performance improves when the board of directors and the CEO are involved in shaping a firm's strategic direction. However, when the CEO has a great deal of power, the board may be less involved in decisions about strategy formulation and implementation. By appointing people to the board and simultaneously serving as CEO and chair of the board, CEOs have increased power.

- In managerial succession, strategic leaders are selected from either the internal or the external managerial labor market. Because of their effect on firm performance, the selection of strategic leaders has implications for a firm's effectiveness. There are a variety of reasons that companies select the firm's strategic leaders from either internal or external sources. In most instances, the internal market is used to select the CEO, but the number of outsiders chosen is increasing. Outsiders often are selected to initiate major changes in strategy.

- Effective strategic leadership has five key leadership actions: determining the firm's strategic direction, effectively managing the firm's resource portfolio (including exploiting and maintaining core competencies and managing human capital and social capital), sustaining an effective organizational culture, emphasizing ethical practices, and establishing balanced organizational controls.

- Strategic leaders must develop the firm's strategic direction, typically working with the board of directors to do so. The strategic direction specifies the image and character the firm wants to develop over time. To form the strategic direction, strategic leaders evaluate the conditions (e.g., opportunities and threats in the external environment) they expect their firm to face over the next three to five years.

- Strategic leaders must ensure that their firm exploits its core competencies, which are used to produce and deliver products that create value for customers, when implementing its strategies. In related diversified and large firms in particular, core competencies are exploited by sharing them across units and products.

- The ability to manage the firm's resource portfolio and the processes used to effectively implement its strategy are critical elements of strategic leadership. Managing the resource portfolio includes integrating resources to create capabilities and leveraging those capabilities through strategies to build competitive advantages. Human capital and social capital are perhaps the most important resources.

- As a part of managing resources, strategic leaders must develop a firm's human capital. Effective strategic leaders view human capital as a resource to be maximized—not as a cost to be minimized. Such leaders develop and use programs designed to train current and future strategic leaders to build the skills needed to nurture the rest of the firm's human capital.

- Effective strategic leaders build and maintain internal and external social capital. Internal social capital promotes cooperation and coordination within and across units in the firm. External social capital provides access to resources from external parties that the firm needs to compete effectively.

- Shaping the firm's culture is a central task of effective strategic leadership. An appropriate organizational culture encourages the development of an entrepreneurial mind-set among employees and an ability to change the culture as necessary.

- In ethical organizations, employees are encouraged to exercise ethical judgment and to always act ethically. Improved ethical practices foster social capital. Setting specific goals to meet the firm's ethical standards, using a code of conduct, rewarding ethical behaviors, and creating a work environment where all people are treated with dignity are actions that facilitate and support ethical behavior.

- Developing and using balanced organizational controls is the final key leadership action associated with effective strategic leadership. The balanced scorecard is a tool that measures the effectiveness of the firm's strategic and financial controls. An effective balance between these two controls allows for flexible use of core competencies, but within the parameters of the firm's financial position.

KEY TERMS

balanced scorecard 404
determining strategic direction 396
external managerial labor market 392
heterogeneous top management team 389
human capital 398

internal managerial labor market 392
strategic leadership 384
social capital 399
strategic change 384
top management team 387

REVIEW QUESTIONS

1. What is strategic leadership? Why are top-level managers considered to be important resources for an organization?

2. What is a top management team, and how does it affect a firm's performance and its abilities to innovate and design and bring about effective strategic change?

3. What is the managerial succession process? How important are the internal and external managerial labor markets to this process?

4. What is the effect of strategic leadership on determining the firm's strategic direction?

5. How do strategic leaders effectively manage their firm's resource portfolio to exploit its core competencies and

leverage the human capital and social capital to achieve a competitive advantage?

6. What must strategic leaders do to develop and sustain an effective organizational culture?

7. As a strategic leader, what actions could you take to establish and emphasize ethical practices in your firm?

8. Why are strategic controls and financial controls important aspects of strategic leadership and the firm's strategic management process?

Mini-Case

A Change at the Top at Procter & Gamble: An Indication of How Much the CEO Matters?

A. G. Lafley joined Procter & Gamble (P&G) in 1977 as brand assistant for Joy dishwashing liquid. From this beginning, he worked his way through the firm's laundry division, becoming highly visible due to a number of successes including the launching of liquid Tide. A string of continuing accomplishments throughout the firm resulted in Lafley's appointment as P&G's CEO in June 2000, a post he held until retiring in mid-2009. Bob McDonald, who joined P&G in 1980, was Lafley's handpicked successor. McDonald took the top position at P&G in July 2009, but resigned under pressure in May 2013. Lafley, revered by many, was asked to come out of retirement and return to P&G as president, CEO, and chair of the board of directors. Lafley said that when

contacted to return to P&G, he agreed immediately to do so, committing to remain "as long as needed to improve the company's performance." However, speculation is that Lafley likely would not remain beyond three years.

What went wrong for McDonald, a long-time P&G employee who seemed to know the firm well and who received Lafley's support? Not surprisingly, a number of possibilities have been mentioned in response to this question. Some concluded that, under McDonald's leadership, P&G suffered from "poor execution globally," an outcome created in part by P&G's seemingly ineffective responses to aggressive competition in emerging markets. Other apparent problems were a failure to control the firm's costs and employees' loss of confidence in

McDonald's leadership. Still others argued that McDonald did not fully understand the effects on U.S. consumers of the recession in place when he took over, and that, during that time period, P&G "was selling BMWs when cash-tight consumers were looking for Kias." The net result of these types of problems included P&G "losing a step to rivals like Unilever." In turn, this caused investors to become frustrated by "P&G's inability to consistently keep up with its rivals' sales growth and share price gains."

But why bring Lafley back? In a few words, because of his previous success. Among other achievements during his first stint as P&G's main strategic leader were building up the firm's beauty business, acquiring Gillette, expanding the firm's presence in emerging markets, and launching hit products such as Swiffer and Febreze. An overall measure of P&G's success during Lafley's initial tenure as CEO is the fact that the firm's shares increased 63 percent in value while the S&P fell 37 percent in value. Thus, multiple stakeholders, including investors and employees, may believe that Lafley can return the firm to the "glory days" it experienced from 2000 to 2009.

Product innovations are a core concern and an area receiving a significant amount of attention. Analysts suggest that P&G needs to move beyond incremental innovations, seeking to again create entirely new product categories as it did with Swiffer and Febreze. This will be challenging, at least in the short run, given recent declines in allocations to the firm's research and development programs. These reductions have resulted in a product pipeline focused mainly on "reformulating rather than inventing." Additionally, efforts are underway to continue McDonald's strong, recent commitments to reduce the firm's "bloated" cost structure and reenergize the competitive actions it will take in global markets.

Restructuring P&G's multiple brands and products into four sectors, each of which will be headed by a president, is a major change Lafley is initiating. Currently, the firm has two global business divisions—beauty and grooming and household care. Final decisions about the precise compositions of the four sectors were not announced by mid-2013. Speculation, though, was that each sector would be formed "to reflect synergies between various businesses." For example, one expectation was that paper-based products such as "Bounty paper towels, Charmin toilet paper, Pampers diapers and Always feminine care products" would be combined to form a sector. Moreover, Lafley's replacement was expected to be selected from among the four presidents who would be chosen to lead the new sectors.

Sources: D. Benoit, 2013, Critical P&G analysts still waiting on results, *Wall Street Journal*, www.wsj.com, May 24; D. Benoit, 2013, Procter & Gamble gets an upgrade, *Wall Street Journal*, www.wsj.com, May 24; J. Bogaisky, 2013, Congrats, Bill Ackman: Bob McDonald out at P&G; A. G. Lafley returning as CEO, *Forbes*, www.forbes.com, May 23; E. Byron & J. S. Lublin, 2013, Embattled P&G chief replaced by old boss, *Wall Street Journal*, www.wsj.com, May 23; L. Coleman-Lochner & C. Hymowitz, 2013, Lafley's CEO encore at P&G puts rock star legacy at risk: Retail, *Bloomberg*, www.bloomberg.com, May 28; J. S. Lublin & S. Ng, 2013, P&G lines up executives in race for CEO Lafley's successor, *Wall Street Journal*, www.wsj.com, May 30; J. Ritchie, 2013, P&G's hiring of Lafley may buy time for innovation, *Business Courier*, www.bizjournals.com/cincinnati, May 31.

Case Discussion Questions

1. What makes a CEO's job so complex? Use the mini-case to provide examples that help support your answer.

2. Is it a good practice to rehire a former CEO who has retired? Please explain the potential advantages and disadvantages of doing so.

3. What should P&G do to replace Lafley when he retires for a second time? What actions should they take to prepare for the succession?

NOTES

1.	M. C. Diaz-Fernandez, M. R. Gonzales-Rodriguez, & B. Simonetti, 2015, Top Management team's intellectual capital and firm performance *European Management Journal*, in press; D. C. Hambrick & T. J. Quigley, 2014, Toward more accurate contextualization of the CEO effect on firm performance, *Strategic Management Journal*, 35: 473–491; A. Mackey, 2008, The effect of CEOs on firm performance, *Strategic Management Journal*, 29: 1357–1367.

2.	V. Govindarajan, 2012, The timeless strategic value of unrealistic goals, *HBR Blog Network*, www.hbr.org, October 22.

3.	D. Martin, 2014, Thinking about thinking, *Journal of Business Strategy*, 35(5): 49–54; B.-J. Moon, 2013, Antecedents and outcomes of strategic thinking, *Journal of Business Research*, 66: 1698–1708; M. A. Hitt, K. T. Haynes, & R. Serpa, 2010, Strategic leadership for the 21st century, *Business Horizons*, 53: 437–444; R. D. Ireland & M. A. Hitt, 2005, Achieving and maintaining strategic competitiveness in the 21st century: The role of strategic leadership, *Academy of Management Executive*, 19: 63–77.

4.	D. Cooper, P. C. Patel, & S. M. B, Thatcher, 2014, It depends: Environmental context and the effects of faultlines on top management team performance, *Organization Science*, 25: 633–652.

5.	T. von den Driesch, M. E. S. da Costa, T. C. Flatten, & M. Brettel, 2015, How CEO experience, personality, and network affect firms' dynamic capabilities, *European Management Journal*, in press: M. T. Hansen, H. Ibarra, & U. Peyer, 2013, The best-performing CEOs in the world, *Harvard Business Review*, 91(1): 81–95.

6.	M. A. Hitt, C. Miller, & A. Colella, 2015, *Organizational Behavior*, 4th ed., Hoboken, NJ: John Wiley & Sons; D. Frank & T. Obloj, 2014, Firm-specific human capital, organizational incentives, and agency costs: Evidence from retail banking, *Strategic Management Journal*, 35: 1279–1301; B. A. Campbell, R. Coff, & D. Kryscynski, 2012, Rethinking sustained competitive advantage from human capital, *Academy of Management Review*, 37: 376–395.

7.	M. A. Axtle-Ortiz, 2013, Perceiving the value of intangible assets in context, *Journal of Business Research*, 56: 417–424.

8.	P. J. H. Schoemaker, S. Krupp, & S. Howland, 2013, Strategic leadership: The essential skills, *Harvard Business Review*, 91(1-2): 131–134.

9.	C. Chadwick, J. F. Super, & K. Kwon, 2015, Resource orchestration in Practice: CEO emphasis on shrm, commitment-based hr systems and firm performance, *Strategic Management Journal*, 36: 360–376; J. J. Sosik,

W. A. Gentry, & J. U. Chun, 2012, The value of virtue in the upper echelons: A multisource examination of executive character strengths and performance, *Leadership Quarterly*, 23: 367–382.

10.	D. M. Cable, F. Gino, & B. R. Staats, 2013, Breaking them in or eliciting their best? Reframing socialization and newcomers' authentic self-expression, *Administrative Science Quarterly*, 58: 1–36; T. Hulzschenreuter, I. Kleindienst, & C. Greger, 2012, How new leaders affect strategic change following a succession event: A critical review of the literature, *The Leadership Quarterly*, 23: 729–755.

11.	C. Crossland, J. Zyung, N. J. Hiller, & D. C. Hambrick, 2014, CEO career variety: Effects on firm-level strategic and social novelty, *Academy of Management Journal*, 57: 652–674.

12.	C. Alessi, 2015, ThyssenKrup swings to profit on cost-cutting, weaker euro, *Wall Street Journal*, www.wsj.com, February 13; S. Reed, 2014, ThyssenKrup post first annual profit in 3 years, *New York Times*, www.nytimes.com, November 20; T. Andresen, 2013, Thyssen woes tarnish 99-year-old steel baron's legacy, *Bloomberg*, www.bloomberg.com, May 21; J. Hromadko, 2013, ThyssenKrupp offers workers amnesty to resolve corruption case, *Wall Street Journal*, www.wsj.com, April 16.

13.	J. Ewing, 2012, Embattled German steel maker reports a huge loss, *New York Times*, www.nytimes.com, December 11.

14.	F. Briscoe, M. K. Chin, & D. C. Hambrick, 2014, CEO ideology as an element of the corporate opportunity structure for social activists, *Academy of Management Journal*, 57: 1786–1809.

15.	J. P. Doe & N. R. Quigley, 2014, Responsible leadership and stakeholder management: Influence pathways and organizational outcomes, *Academy of Management Perspectives*, 28: 255–274.

16.	X. Zhang, N. Li, J Ulrich, & R. von Dick, 2015, Getting everyone on board: The effect of differentiated transformational leadership by CEOs on top management team effectiveness and leader-rated firm performance, *Journal of Management*, in press; J. C. Ryan & S. A. A. Tipu, 2013, Leadership effects on innovation propensity: A two-factor full range of leadership model, *Journal of Business Research*, 66: 2116–2129; A. E. Colbert, A. L. Kristof-Brown, B. H. Bradley, & M. R. Barrick, 2008, CEO transformational leadership: The role of goal importance congruence in top management teams, *Academy of Management Journal*, 51: 81–96.

17.	H. S. Givray, 2007, When CEOs aren't leaders, *BusinessWeek*, September 3, 102.

18.	Y. Dong, M.-G. Seo, & K. Bartol, 2014, No pain, no gain: An affect-based model of developmental job experience and the buffering effects of emotional intelligence, *Academy of Management Journal*, 57: 1056–1077; D. Goleman, 2004, What makes a leader? *Harvard Business Review*, 82(1): 82–91.

19.	C. M. Leitch, C. McMullan, & R. T. Harrison, 2013, The development of entrepreneurial leadership: The role of human, social and institutional capital, *British Journal of Management*, 24: 347–366; Y. Ling, Z. Simsek, M. H. Lubatkin, & J. F. Veiga, 2008, Transformational leadership's role in promoting corporate entrepreneurship: Examining the CEO-TMT interface, *Academy of Management Journal*, 51: 557–576.

20.	T. Hutzschenreuter & I. Kleindienst, 2013, (How) does discretion change over time? A contribution toward a dynamic view of managerial discretion, *Scandinavian Journal of Management*, 29: 264–281; T. L. Waldron, S. D. Graffin, J. F. Porac, & J. B. Wade, 2013, Third-party endorsements of CEO quality, managerial discretion, and stakeholder reactions, *Journal of Business Research*, 66: 2592–2599.

21.	B. E. Lewis, J. L. Walls, & G. W. S. Dowell, 2014, Difference in degrees: CEO characteristics and firm environmental disclosure, *Strategic Management Journal*, 35: 712–722; R. Klingebiel, 2012, Options in the implementation plan of entrepreneurial initiatives: Examining firms' attainment of flexibility benefit, *Strategic Entrepreneurship Journal*, 6: 307–334; D. G. Sirmon, J.-L. Arregle, M. A. Hitt, & J. W. Webb, 2008, The role of family influence in firms' strategic responses to threat of imitation, *Entrepreneurship Theory and Practice*, 32: 979–998.

22.	O. R. Mihalache, J. J. P. Jansen, F. A. J. van den Bosch, & H. W. Volberda, 2014, Top management team shared leadership and organizational ambidexterity: A moderated mediation framework, *Strategic Entrepreneurship Journal*, 8: 128–148.

23.	M. Menz, 2012, Functional top management team members: A review, synthesis, and research agenda, *Journal of Management*, 38: 45–80; A. M. L. Raes, U. Glunk, M. G. Heijltjes, & R. A. Roe, 2007, Top management team and middle managers, *Small Group Research*, 38: 360–386.

24.	A. Ganter & A. Hecker, 2014, Configurational paths to organizational innovation: Qualitative comparative analyses of antecedents and contingencies, *Journal of Business Research*, 67:1285–1292; O. R. Mihalach, J. J. P. Jansen,

F. A. J. Van Den Bosch, & H. W. Volberda, 2012, Offshoring and firm innovation: The moderating role of top management team attributes, *Strategic Management Journal*, 33: 1480–1498.

25. K. T. Haynes, M. A. Hitt, & J. T. Campbell, 2015, The dark side of leadership: Toward a mid-range theory of hubris and greed in entrepreneurial contexts, *Journal of Management Studies*, 52: 479–505; J. Li & Y. Tang, 2010, CEO hubris and firm risk taking in China: The moderating role of managerial discretion, *Academy of Management Journal*, 53: 45–68; M. L. A. Hayward, V. P. Rindova, & T. G. Pollock, 2004, Believing one's own press: The causes and consequences of CEO celebrity, *Strategic Management Journal*, 25: 637–653.

26. A. Y. Ou, A. S Tsui, A. J. Kinicki, D. A. Waldman, Z. Xiao, & L. J. Song, 2014, Humble chief executive officers' connections to top management team integration and middle manager response, *Administrative Science Quarterly*, 59: 34–72; P. J. C. Patel & D. Cooper, 2014, The harder they fall, the faster they rise: Approach avoidance focus in Narcissistic CEOs, *Strategic Management Journal*, 35: 1528–1540.

27. A. Carmeli, A. Tishler, & A. C. Edmondson, 2012, CEO relational leadership and strategic decision quality in top management teams: The role of team trust and learning from failure, *Strategic Organization*, 10: 31–54; V. Souitaris & B. M. M. Maestro, 2010, Polychronicity in top management teams: The impact on strategic decision processes and performance in new technology ventures, *Strategic Management Journal*, 31: 652–678.

28. D. C. Hambrick, S. E. Humphrey, & A. Gupta, 2015, Structural interdependence, within top management teams: A key moderator of upper echelon predictions, *Strategic Management Journal*, 36: 449–461.

29. O. Levy, S. Taylor, N. A. Boyacigiller, T. E. Bodner, M. A. Peiperl, & S. Beechler, 2015, Perceived senior leadership opportunities in MNCs: The effect of social hierarchy and capital, *Journal of International Business Studies*, 46: 285–307.

30. R. Olie, A. van Iteraon, & Z. Simsek, 2012–13, When do CEOs versus top management teams matter in explaining strategic decision-making processes? Toward an institutional view of strategic leadership effects, *International Studies of Management and Organization*, 42(4): 86–105; Y. Ling & F. W. Kellermans, 2010, The effects of family firm specific sources of TMT diversity: The moderating role of information exchange frequency, *Journal of Management Studies*, 47: 322–344.

31. R. Klingebiel & A. De Meyer, 2013, Becoming aware of the unknown: Decision making during the implementation of a strategic initiative, *Organization Science*, 24: 133–153;

A. Srivastava, K. M. Bartol, & E. A. Locke, 2006, Empowering leadership in management teams: Effects on knowledge sharing, efficacy, and performance, *Academy of Management Journal*, 49: 1239–1251; D. Knight, C. L. Pearce, K. G. Smith, J. D. Olian, H. P. Sims, K. A. Smith, & P. Flood, 1999, Top management team diversity, group process, and strategic consensus, *Strategic Management Journal*, 20: 446–465.

32. A. Nadolska & H. G. Barkema, 2014, Good learners: How top management teams affect the success and frequency of acquisitions, *Strategic Management Journal*, 35: 1483–1507.

33. T. Buyl, C. Boone, W. Hendricks, & P. Matthyssens, 2011, Top management team functional diversity and firm performance: The moderating role of CEO characteristics, *Journal of Management Studies*, 48: 151–177; B. J. Olson, S. Parayitam, & Y. Bao, 2007, Strategic decision making: The effects of cognitive diversity, conflict, and trust on decision outcomes, *Journal of Management*, 33: 196–222.

34. S. Finkelstein, D. C. Hambrick, & A. A. Cannella, Jr., 2008, *Strategic Leadership: Top Executives and Their Effects on Organizations*, NY: Oxford University Press.

35. A. Minichilli, G. Corbetta, & I. C. Macmillan, 2010, Top management teams in family-controlled companies: 'Familiness', 'faultlines', and their impact on financial performance, *Journal of Management Studies*, 47: 205–222; J. J. Marcel, 2009, Why top management team characteristics matter when employing a chief operating officer: A strategic contingency perspective, *Strategic Management Journal*, 30: 647–658.

36. T. Buyl, C. Boone, & W. Hendriks, 2014, Top management team members' decision influence and cooperative behavior: An empirical study in the information technology industry, *British Journal of Management*, 25: 285–304; Z. Simsek, J. F. Veiga, M. L. Lubatkin, & R. H. Dino, 2005, Modeling the multilevel determinants of top management team behavioral integration, *Academy of Management Journal*, 48: 69–84.

37. A. A. Cannella, J. H. Park, & H. U. Lee, 2008, Top management team functional background diversity and firm performance: Examining the roles of team member collocation and environmental uncertainty, *Academy of Management Journal*, 51: 768–784.

38. J. W. Ridge, F. Aime, & M. A. White, 2015, When much more of a difference makes a difference: Social comparison and tournaments in the CEO's top team, *Strategic Management Journal*, 36: 618–636; A. S. Cui, R. J. Calantone, & D. A. Griffith, 2011, Strategic change and termination of interfirm partnerships, *Strategic Management Journal*, 32: 402–423.

39. P. Herrmann & S. Nadkarni, 2014, Managing strategic change: The duality of CEO personality, *Strategic Management Journal*, 35: 1318–1342; A. E. Colbert, M. R. Barrick, & B. H. Bradley, 2014, Personality and leadership composition in top management teams: Implications for organizational effectiveness, *Personnel Psychology*, 67: 351–387.

40. C. Shalley, M. A. Hitt, & J. Zhou, 2015, Integrating creativity, innovation and entrepreneurship to successfully navigate in the new competitive landscape, in C. Shalley, M. A. Hitt, & J. Zhou (eds.) *Handbook of Creativity, Innovation and Entrepreneurship*, NY: Oxford University Press, pp. 1–14; K. Liu, J. Li, W. Hesterly, & A. A. Cannella, Jr., 2012, Top management team tenure and technological inventions at post-IPO biotechnology firms, *Journal of Business Research*, 65: 1349–1356.

41. J. Tian, J. Haleblian, & N. Rajagopalan, 2011, The effects of board human and social capital on investor reactions to new CEO selection, *Strategic Management Journal*, 32: 731–747; Y. Zhang & N. Rajagopalan, 2003, Explaining the new CEO origin: Firm versus industry antecedents, *Academy of Management Journal*, 46: 327–338.

42. X. Luo, V. K. Kanuri, & M. Andrews, 2014, How does CEO tenure matter? The mediating role of firm-employee and firm-customer relationships, *Strategic Management Journal*, 35: 492–511.

43. P. Y. T. Sun & M. H. Anderson, 2012, Civic capacity: Building on transformational leadership to explain successful integrative public leadership, *The Leadership Quarterly*, 23: 309–323; I. Barreto, 2010, Dynamic capabilities: A review of the past research and an agenda for the future, *Journal of Management*, 36: 256–280.

44. D. H. Zhu & G. Chen, 2015, CEO narcissism and the impact of prior board experience on firm strategy, *Administrative Science Quarterly*, 60: 31–65; M. L. McDonald & J. D. Westphal, 2010, A little help here? Board control, CEO identification with the corporate elite, and strategic help provided to CEOs at other firms, *Academy of Management Journal*, 53: 343–370; L. Tihanyi, R. A. Johnson, R. E. Hoskisson, & M. A. Hitt, 2003, Institutional ownership and international diversification: The effects of boards of directors and technological opportunity, *Academy of Management Journal*, 46: 195–211.

45. K. B. Lewellyn & M. I. Muller-Kahle, 2012, CEO power and risk taking: Evidence from the subprime lending industry, *Corporate Governance: An International Review*, 20: 289–307; S. Wu, X. Quan, & L. Xu, 2011, CEO power, disclosure quality and the variability in firm performance, *Nankai Business Review International*, 2: 79–97.

46. J. Joseph, W. Ocasio, & M.-H. McDonnell, 2014, The structural elaboration of board independence: Executive power,

institutional logics, and the adoption of CEO-only board structures in U.S. corporate governance, *Academy of Management Journal*, 57: 1834–1858; S. Kaczmarek, S. Kimino, & A. Pye, 2012, Antecedents of board composition: The role of nomination committees, *Corporate Governance: An International Review*, 20: 474–489.

47. M. van Essen, P.-J. Engelen, & M. Carney, 2013, Does 'good' corporate governance help in a crisis? The impact of country- and firm-level governance mechanisms in the European financial crisis, *Corporate Governance: An International Review*, 21: 201–224; M. A. Abebe, A. Angriawan, & Y. Lui, 2011, CEO power and organizational turnaround in declining firms: Does environment play a role? *Journal of Leadership and Organizational Studies*, 18: 260–273.

48. C.-H. Liao & A. W.-H. Hsu, 2013, Common membership and effective corporate governance: Evidence from audit and compensation committees, *Corporate Governance: An International Review*, 21: 79–92.

49. P. Cullinan, P. B. Roush, & X. Zheng, 2012, CEO/Chair duality in the Sarbanes-Oxley era; Board independence versus unity of command, *Research on Professional Responsibility and Ethics in Accounting*, 16: 167–183; C. S. Tuggle, D. G. Sirmon, C. R. Reutzel, & L. Bierman, 2010, Commanding board of director attention: Investigating how organizational performance and CEO duality affect board members' attention to monitoring, *Strategic Management Journal*, 32: 640–657; J. Coles & W. Hesterly, 2000, Independence of the chairman and board composition: Firm choices and shareholder value, *Journal of Management*, 26: 195–214.

50. R. Krause & M. Semadeni, 2013, Apprentice, departure, and demotion: An examination of the three types of CEO-board chair separation, *Academy of Management Journal*, 56: 805–826.

51. M. van Essen, P.-J. Engelen, & M. Carney, 2013, Does "good" corporate governance help in a crisis? The impact of country- and firm-level governance mechanisms in the European financial crisis, *Corporate Governance: An International Review*, 21: 201–224.

52. R. Krause & M. Semadeni, 2014, Last dance or second chance? Firm performance, CEO career horizon, and the separation of board leadership roles, *Strategic Management Journal*, 35: 808–825.

53. P. C. Patel & D. Cooper, 2014, Structural power equality between family and non-family TMT members and the performance of family firms, *Academy of Management Journal*, 57: 1624–1649.

54. E. Matta & P. W. Beamish, 2008, The accentuated CEO career horizon problem: Evidence from international acquisitions, *Strategic Management Journal*, 29: 683–700;

N. Rajagopalan & D. Datta, 1996, CEO characteristics: Does industry matter? *Academy of Management Journal*, 39: 197–215.

55. W. Lewis, J. L. Walls, & G. W. S. Dowell, 2014, Difference in degrees: CEO characteristics and firm environmental disclosure, *Strategic Management Journal*, 35: 712–722; R. A. Johnson, R. E. Hoskisson, & M. A. Hitt, 1993, Board involvement in restructuring: The effect of board versus managerial controls and characteristics, *Strategic Management Journal*, 14 (Special Issue): 33–50.

56. Z. Simsek, 2007, CEO tenure and organizational performance: An intervening model, *Strategic Management Journal*, 28: 653–662.

57. M. A. Fitza, 2014, The use of variance decomposition in the investigation of CEO effects: How large must the CEO effect be to rule out chance? *Strategic Management Journal*, 35: 1839–1852; X. Luo, V. K. Kanuri, & M. Andrews, 2014, How does CEO tenure matter? The mediating role of firm-employee and firm-customer relationships, *Strategic Management Journal*, 35: 492–511.

58. M. Hernandez, 2012, Toward an understanding of the psychology of stewardship, *Academy of Management Review*, 37: 172–193.

59. J. W. Ridge & A. Ingram, 2015, Modesty in the top management team: Investor reaction and performance implications, *Journal of Management*, in press; K. Boyd, D. Miller, I. LeBreton-Miller, & B. Scholnick, 2008, Stewardship vs. stagnation: An empirical comparison of small family and non-family businesses, *Journal of Management Studies*, 51: 51–78; J. H. Davis, F. D. Schoorman, & L. Donaldson, 1997, Toward a stewardship theory of management, *Academy of Management Review*, 22: 20–47.

60. M. Menz & C. Scheef, 2014, Chief strategy officers: Contingency analysis of their presence in top management teams, *Strategic Management Journal*, 35: 461–471; A. Holehonnur & T. Pollock, 2013, Shoot for the stars? Predicting the recruitment of prestigious directors at newly public firms, *Academy of Management Journal*, 56: 1396–1419; B. Espedal, O. Kvitastein, & K. Gronhaug, 2012, When cooperation is the norm of appropriateness: How does CEO cooperative behavior affect organizational performance? *British Journal of Management*, 23: 257–271.

61. X. Zhang, N. Li, J. Ullrich, & R. van Dick, 2015, Getting everyone on board: The effect of differentiated transformational leadership by CEOs on top management team effectiveness and leader-related firm performance, *Journal of Management*, in press; J. G. Messersmith, J.-Y. Lee, J P. Guthrie, & Y.-Y Ji, 2014, Turnover at the top: Executive team departures and firm performance, *Organization Science*, 25: 776–793.

62. C. H. Mooney, M. Semadeni, & I. F. Kesner, 2015, The selection of an interim CEO: Boundary conditions and the pursuit of temporary leadership, *Journal of Management*, in press; S. D. Graffin, S. Boivie, & M. A. Carpenter, 2013, Examining CEO succession and the role of heuristics in early-stage CEO evaluation, *Strategic Management Journal*, 34: 383–403.

63. J. P. Donlon, 2013, 40 best companies for leaders 2013, *Chief Executive*, www.chiefexecutive.net, January 12.

64. 2013, Deloitte, Perspectives on family-owned businesses: Governance and succession planning, www.deloitte.com, January.

65. C. Peterson-Withorn, 2015, new survey pinpoints what keeps family businesses going for generations, *Forbes*, www.forbes.com, April 23.

66. 2013, Intersearch survey reveals status of CEO succession plans in companies around the world, Intersearch, www.pendlpiswanger.at/images/content/file/Artikel/CEOsuccession, February.

67. S. Mobbs & C. G. Raheja, 2012, Internal managerial promotions: Insider incentives and CEO succession, *Journal of Corporate Finance*, 18: 1337–1353; S. Rajgopal, D. Taylor, & M. Venkatachalam, 2012, Frictions in the CEO labor market: The role of talent agents in CEO compensation, *Contemporary Accounting Research*, 29: 119–151.

68. 2015, CEO Statistics, Statistic Brain Research Institute, www.statisticbrain.com, March 11.

69. M. Nakauchi & M. F. Wiersema, 2015, Executive succession and strategic change, *Strategic Management Journal*, 36: 298–306; M. Elson & C. K. Ferrere, 2012, When searching for a CEO, there's no place like home, *Wall Street Journal*, www.wsj.com, October 29.

70. W. Li & J. Lu, 2014, Board independence, CEO succession and the scope of strategic change, *Nankai Business Review International*, 5: 309–325.

71. J. J. Marcel, A. P. Cowen, & G. A. Ballinger, 2015, Are disruptive CEO successions viewed as a governance lapse? Evidence from board turnover, *Journal of Management*, in press; Y. Zhang & N. Rajagopalan, 2010, Once an outsider, always an outsider? CEO origin, strategic change and firm performance, *Strategic Management Journal*, 31: 334–346.

72. V. Mehrotra, R. Morck, J. Shim, & Y. Wiwattanakantang, 2013, Adoptive expectations: Rising sons in Japanese family firms, *Journal of Financial Economics*, 108: 840–854; G. A. Ballinger & J. J. Marcel, 2010, The use of an interim CEO during succession episodes and firm performance, *Strategic Management Journal*, 31: 262–283.

73. S. Pandey & S. Rhee, 2015, An inductive study of foreign CEOs of Japanese firms, *Journal of Leadership and Organizational Studies*, 22: 202–216.

74. J. A. Krug, P. Wright, & M. J. Kroll, 2014, Top management turnover following mergers

75. T. Buyl, C. Boone, & J. B. Wade, 2015, non-CEO executive mobility: The impact of poor firm performance and TMT attention, *European Management Review*, in press.

76. J. Baer, 2015, Google hires Morgan Stanley's Porat as finance chief, *Wall Street Journal*, www.wsj.com, March 24; C. Dougherty, 2015, Google CFO is retiring to spend more time with family (No, really), *New York Times*, bits.blogs.nytimes.com, March 10.

77. D. H. Weng & Z. Lin, 2014, Beyond CEO tenure: The effect of CEO newness on strategic changes, *Journal of Management*, 40: 2009–2032; T. Hutzschenreuter, I. Kleindienst, & C. Greger, 2012, How new leaders affect strategic change following a succession event: A critical review of the literature, *The Leadership Quarterly*, 23: 729–755; J. Kotter, 2012, Accelerate! *Harvard Business Review*, 90(11): 45–58.

78. F. F. Jing, G. C. Avery, & H. Bergsteiner, 2014, Enhancing performance in small professional firms through vision communication and sharing, *Asia Pacific Journal of Management*, 31: 599–620; L. Mirabeau & S. Maguire, 2014, From autonomous strategic behavior to emergent strategy, *Strategic Management Journal*, 35: 1202–1229; G. A. Shinkle, A. P. Kriauciunas, & G. Hundley, 2013, Why pure strategies may be wrong for transition economy firms, *Strategic Management Journal*, 34: 1244–1254.

79. Herrmann & Nadkarni, 2014, Managing strategic change; T. Barnett, R. G. Long, & L. E. Marler, 2012, Vision and exchange in intra-family succession: Effects on procedural justice climate among nonfamily managers, *Entrepreneurship Theory and Practice*, 36: 1207–1225.

80. S. Mantere, H. A. Schildt, & J. A. A. Sillince, 2012, Reversal of strategic change, *Academy of Management Journal*, 55: 172–196; S. Sonenshein, 2012, Explaining employee engagement with strategic change implementation: A meaning-making approach, *Organization Science*, 23: 1–23.

81. P. Chaigneau, 2013, Explaining the structure of CEO incentive pay with decreasing relative risk aversion, *Journal of Economics and Business*, 67: 4–23; G. Chen & D. C. Hambrick, 2012, CEO replacement in turnaround situations: Executive (mis) fit and its performance implications, *Organization Science*, 23: 225–243; P. L. McClelland, X. Ling, & V. L. Barker, 2010, CEO commitment to the status quo: Replication and extension using content analysis, *Journal of Management*, 36: 1251–1277.

82. S. Nankarni & J. Chen, 2014, Bridging yesterday, today and tomorrow: CEO temporal focus, environmental dynamism and rate of new product introduction, *Academy of Management Journal*, 57:

1810–1833; J. R. Mitchell, D. A. Shepherd, & M. P. Sharfman, 2011, Erratic strategic decisions: When and why managers are inconsistent in strategic decision making, *Strategic Management Journal*, 32: 683–704.

83. R. Mudambi & T. Swift, 2014, Knowing when to leap: Transitioning between exploitative and explorative R&D, *Strategic Management Journal*, 35: 126–145; J. Wowak & D. C. Hambrick, 2010, A model of person-pay interaction: How executives vary in their response to compensation arrangements, *Strategic Management Journal*, 31: 803–821.

84. G. A. Shinkle & B. T. McCann, 2014, New product deployment: The moderating influence of economic institutional context, *Strategic Management Journal*, 35: 1090–1101; P. M. Wilderom, P. T. van den Berg, & U. J. Wiersma, 2012, A longitudinal study of the effects of charismatic leadership and organizational culture on objective and perceived corporate performance, *The Leadership Quarterly*, 23: 835–848.

85. M.-J. Chen & D. Miller, 2012, West meets east: Toward an ambicultural approach to management, *Academy of Management Perspectives*, 24: 17–24; M.-J. Chen & D. Miller, 2011, The relational perspective as a business mindset: Managerial implications for East and West, *Academy of Management Perspectives*, 25: 6–18.

86. U. Stettner & D. Lavie, 2014, Ambidexterity under scrutiny: Exploration and exploitation via internal organization, alliances and acquisitions, *Strategic Management Journal*, 35: 1903–1925; M. Y. C. Chen, C. Y. Y. Lin, H.-E. Lin, & E. F. McDonough, III, 2012, Does transformational leadership facilitate technological innovation? The moderating roles of innovative culture and incentive compensation, *Asia Pacific Journal of Management*, 29: 239–264.

87. A. Gambardella, C. Panico, & G. Valentini, 2015, Strategic incentives to human capital, *Strategic Management Journal*, 36: 37–52; M. D. Huesch, 2013, Are there always synergies between productive resources and resource deployment capabilities? *Strategic Management Journal*, 34: 1288–1313; J. Kraaijenbrink, J.-C. Spender, & A. J. Groen, 2010, The resource-based view: A review and assessment of its critiques, *Journal of Management*, 36: 349–372.

88. S. D. Julian & J. C. Ofori-dankwa, 2013, Financial resource availability and corporate social responsibility expenditures in a sub-Saharan economy: The institutional difference hypothesis, *Strategic Management Journal*, 34: 1314–1330; T. Vanacker, V. Collewaert, & I. Pacleman, 2013, The relationship between slack resources and the performance of entrepreneurial firms: The role of venture capital and angel investors, *Journal of Management Studies*, 50: 1070–1096.

89. Y. Li, H. Chen, Y. Liu, & M. W. Peng, 2014, Managerial ties, organizational learning, and opportunity capture: A social capital perspective, *Asia Pacific Journal of Management*, 31: 271–291; E. A. Clinton, S. Sciascia, R. Yadav, & F. Roche, 2013, Resource acquisition in family firms: The role of family-influenced human and social capital, *Entrepreneurship Research Journal*, 3: 44–61; H. A. Ndofor, D. G. Sirmon, & X. He, 2011, Firm resources, competitive actions and performance: Investigating a mediated model with evidence from the in-vitro diagnostics industry, *Strategic Management Journal*, 32: 640–657.

90. A. Carr, 2013, Death to core competency: Lessons from Nike, Apple, Netflix, *Fast Company*, www.fastcompany.com, February 14.

91. P. M. Wright, R. Coff, & T. P. Moliterno, 2014, Strategic human capital: Crossing the great divide, *Journal of Management*, 40: 353–370; R. E. Ployhart, C. H. Van Idderkinge, & W. J. MacKenzie, 2011, Acquiring and developing human capital in service contexts: The interconnectedness of human capital resources, *Academy of Management Journal*, 54: 353–368.

92. M. A. Hitt, L. Bierman, K. Uhlenbruck, & K. Shimizu, 2006, The importance of resources in the internationalization of professional service firms: The good, the bad and the ugly, *Academy of Management Journal*, 49: 1137–1157; M. A. Hitt, L. Bierman, K. Shimizu, & R. Kochhar, 2001, Direct and moderating effects of human capital on strategy and performance in professional service firms: A resource-based perspective, *Academy of Management Journal*, 44: 13–28.

93. A. Mackey, J. C. Molloy, & S. S. Morris, 2014, Scarce human capital in managerial labor markets, *Journal of Management*, 40: 399–421; H. Aquinis, H. Joo, & R. K. Gottfredson, 2013, What monetary rewards can and cannot do: How to show employees the money, *Business Horizons*, 56: 241–249.

94. A. Chatterji & A. Patro, 2014, Dynamic capabilities and managing human capital, *Academy of Management Perspectives*, 28: 395–408; R. R. Kehoe & P. M. Wright, 2013, The impact of high-performance human resource practices on employees' attitudes and behaviors, *Journal of Management*, 39: 366–391.

95. Z. J. Zhao & J. Anand, 2013, Beyond boundary spanners: The 'collective bridge' as an efficient interunit structure for transferring collective knowledge, *Strategic Management Journal*, 34: 1513–1530; J. Pfeffer, 2010, Building sustainable organizations: The human factor, *Academy of Management Perspectives*, 24(1): 34–45.

96. K. Z. Zhou & C. B. Li, 2012, How knowledge affects radical innovation: Knowledge base, market knowledge acquisition, and internal knowledge sharing, *Strategic Management Journal*, 33: 1090–1102.

97. J. R. Lecuona & M. Reitzig, 2014, Knowledge worth having in 'excess': The value of tacit and firm-specific human resource slack, *Strategic Management Journal*, 35: 954–973; T. R. Holcomb, R. D. Ireland, R. M. Holmes, & M. A. Hitt, 2009, Architecture of entrepreneurial learning: Exploring the link among heuristics, knowledge, and action, *Entrepreneurship, Theory & Practice*, 33: 173–198.

98. Y. Zheng, A. S. Miner, & G. George, 2013, Does the learning value of individual failure experience depend on group-level success? Insights from a university technology transfer office, *Industrial and Corporate Change*, 22: 1557–1586; R. Hirak, A. C. Peng, A. Carmeli, & J. M. Schaubroeck, 2012, Linking leader inclusiveness to work unit performance: The importance of psychological safety and learning from failure, *The Leadership Quarterly*, 23: 107–117.

99. Hitt, Miller, & Colella, *Organizational Behavior*.

100. A. Cook & C. Glass, 2014, Above the glass ceiling: When are women and racial/ethnic minorities promoted to CEO? *Academy of Management Journal*, 35: 1080–1089.

101. R. Hoskisson, W. Shi, H. Yi, & J. Jin, 2013, The evolution and strategic positioning of private equity firms, *Academy of Management Perspectives*, 27: 22–38; P. M. Norman, F. C. Butler, & A. L. Ranft, 2013, Resources matter: Examining the effects of resources on the state of firms following downsizing, *Journal of Management*, 39: 2009–2038; R. D. Nixon, M. A. Hitt, H. Lee, & E. Jeong, 2004, Market reactions to corporate announcements of downsizing actions and implementation strategies, *Strategic Management Journal*, 25: 1121–1129.

102. R. J. Bies, 2013, The delivery of bad news in organizations: A framework for analysis, *Journal of Management*, 39: 136–162; B. C. Holtz, 2013, Trust primacy: A model of the reciprocal relations between trust and perceived justice, *Journal of Management*, 39: 1891–1923.

103. C. Galunic, G. Krtug, & M. Gargiulo, 2012, The positive externalities of social capital: Benefiting from senior brokers, *Academy of Management Journal*, 55: 1213–1231; P. S. Adler & S. W. Kwon, 2002, Social capital: Prospects for a new concept, *Academy of Management Review*, 27: 17–40.

104. M. Ahearne, S. K. Lam, & F. Krause, 2014, Performance impact of middle managers' adaptive strategy implementation: The role of social capital, *Strategic Management Journal*, 35: 68–87; Y.-Y. Chang, Y. Gong, & M. W. Peng, 2012, Expatriate knowledge transfer, subsidiary absorptive capacity, and subsidiary performance, *Academy of Management Journal*, 55: 927–948; S. Gao, K. Xu, & J. Yang, 2008, Managerial ties, Absorptive capacity & innovation, *Asia Pacific Journal of Management*, 25: 395–412.

105. K. H. Heimeriks, M. Schijven, & S. Gates, 2012, Manifestations of higher-order routines: The underlying mechanisms of deliberate learning in the context of postacquisition integration, *Academy of Management Journal*, 55: 703–726; P. Ozcan & K. M. Eisenhardt, 2009, Origin of alliance portfolios: Entrepreneurs, network strategies, and firm performance, *Academy of Management Journal*, 52: 246–279; W. H. Hoffmann, 2007, Strategies for managing a portfolio of alliances, *Strategic Management Journal*, 28: 827–856.

106. A. M. Kleinbaum & T. E. Stuart, 2014, Inside the black box of the corporate staff: Social networks and the implementation of corporate strategy, *Strategic Management Journal*, 35: 24–47.

107. D. K. Panda, 2014, Managerial networks and strategic orientation in SMEs: Experience from a transition economy, *Journal of Strategy and Management*, 7: 376–397; B. J. Hallen & K. M. Eisenhardt, 2012, Catalyzing strategies and efficient tie formation: How entrepreneurial firms obtain investment ties, *Academy of Management Journal*, 55: 35–70.

108. A. Klein, 2011, Corporate culture: Its value as a resource for competitive advantage, *Journal of Business Strategy*, 32(2): 21–28; J. B. Barney, 1986, Organizational culture: Can it be a source of sustained competitive advantage? *Academy of Management Review*, 11: 656–665.

109. B. Schneider, M. G. Ehrhart, & W. H. Macey, 2013, Organizational climate and culture, *Annual Review of Psychology*, 64: 361–388; E. F. Goldman & A. Casey, 2010, Building a culture that encourages strategic thinking, *Journal of Leadership and Organizational Studies*, 17: 119–128.

110. C. B. Dobni, M. Klassen, & W. T. Nelson, 2015, Innovation strategy in the US: Top executives offer their views, *Journal of Business Strategy*, 36(1): 3–13; P. G. Klein, J. T. Mahoney, A. M. McGahan, & C. N. Pitelis, 2013, Capabilities and strategic entrepreneurship in public organizations, *Strategic Entrepreneurship Journal*, 7: 70–91; R. D. Ireland, J. G. Covin, & D. F. Kuratko, 2009, Conceptualizing corporate entrepreneurship strategy, *Entrepreneurship Theory and Practice*, 33: 19–46.

111. M. S. Wood, A. McKelvie, & J. M. Haynie, 2014, Making it personal: Opportunity individuation and the shaping of opportunity beliefs, *Journal of Business Venturing*, 29: 252–272; R. D. Ireland & J. W. Webb, 2007, Strategic entrepreneurship: Creating competitive advantage through streams of innovation, *Business Horizons*, 50: 49–59.

112. P. L. Schultz, A. Marin, & K. B. Boal, 2014, The impact of media on the legitimacy of new market categories: The case of broadband internet, *Journal of Business Venturing*, 29: 34–54; S. A. Alvarez & J. B. Barney, 2008, Opportunities, organizations and entrepreneurship, *Strategic Entrepreneurship Journal*, 2: 171–174.

113. Y. Tang, J. Li, & H. Yang, 2015, What I see, what I do: How executive hubris affects firm innovation, *Journal of Management*, in press; R. E. Hoskisson, M. A. Hitt, R. D. Ireland, & J. S. Harrison, 2013, *Competing for Advantage*, 3rd ed., Mason, OH: Thomson Publishing.

114. G. Cao, Z. Simsek, & J. J. P. Jansen, 2105, CEO social capital and entrepreneurial orientation of the firm: Bonding and bridging effects, *Journal of Management*, in press; T. W. Tong & S. Li, 2013, The assignment of call option rights between partners in international joint ventures, *Strategic Management Journal*, 34: 1232–1243.

115. C. Bjornskov & N. Foss, 2013, How strategic entrepreneurship and the institutional context drive economic growth, *Strategic Entrepreneurship Journal*, 7: 50–69; M. A. Hitt, R. D. Ireland, D. G. Sirmon, & C. A. Trahms, 2011, Strategic entrepreneurship: Creating value for individuals, organizations and society, *Academy of Management Perspectives*, 25: 57–75; P. G. Kein, 2008, Opportunity discovery, entrepreneurial action and economic organization, *Strategic Entrepreneurship Journal*, 2: 175–190.

116. A. Engelen, C. Neumann, & S. Schmidt, 2015, Should entrepreneurially oriented firms have narcissistic CEOs? *Journal of Management*, in press; G. T. Lumpkin & G. G. Dess, 1996, Clarifying the entrepreneurial orientation construct and linking it to performance, *Academy of Management Review*, 21: 135–172.

117. Lumpkin & Dess, Clarifying the entrepreneurial orientation construct, 142.

118. Ibid., 137.

119. C. L. Wang & M. Rafiq, 2014, Ambidextrous organizational culture, contextual ambidexterity and new product innovation: A comparative study of UK and Chinese high-tech firms, *British Journal of Management*, 25: 58–76; P. Pyoria, 2007, Informal organizational culture: The foundation of knowledge workers' performance, *Journal of Knowledge Management*, 11: 16–30.

120. C. Kane & J. Cunningham, 2014, Turnaround leadership core tensions during the company turnaround process, *European Management Review*, 32: 968–980; W. Langvardt, 2012, Ethical leadership and the dual roles of examples, *Business Horizons*, 55: 373–384.

121. M. N. Kastanakis & B. G. Voyer, 2014, The effect of culture on perception and cognition: A conceptual framework, *Journal of Business Research*, 67: 425–433; J. Kotter, 2011, Corporate culture: Whose job is it? *Forbes*, http://blog.forbes.com/johnkotter, February 17.

122. M. I. Garces & P. Morcillo, 2012, The role of organizational culture in the resource-based view: An empirical study of the Spanish nuclear industry, *International*

Journal of Strategic Change Management, 4: 356–378; E. Mollick, 2012, People and process, suits and innovators: the role of individuals in firm performance, *Strategic Management Journal*, 33: 1001–1015.

123. W. McKinley, S. Latham, & M. Braun, 2014, Organizational decline and innovation: Turnarounds and downward spirals, *Academy of Management Review*, 39: 88–110; R. Fehr & M. J. Gelfand, 2012, The forgiving organization: A multilevel model of forgiveness at work, *Academy of Management Review*, 37: 664–688; E. G. Love & M. Kraatz, 2009, Character, conformity, or the bottom line? How and why downsizing affected corporate reputation, *Academy of Management Journal*, 52: 314–335.

124. Adler & Kwon, Social capital.

125. J. L. Campbell & A. S. Goritz, 2014, Culture corrupts! A qualitative study of organizational culture in corrupt organizations, *Journal of Business Ethics*, 120: 291–311; J. Pinto, C. R. Leana, & F. K. Pil, 2008, Corrupt organizations or organizations of corrupt individuals? Two types of organization-level corruption, *Academy of Management Review*, 33: 685–709.

126. A. Arnaud & M. Schminke, 2012, The ethical climate and context of organizations: A comprehensive model, *Organization Science*, 23: 1767–1780; M. E. Scheitzer, L. Ordonez, & M. Hoegl, 2004, Goal setting as a motivator of unethical behavior, *Academy of Management Journal*, 47: 422–432.

127. J. A. Pearce, 2013, Using social identity theory to predict managers' emphases on ethical and legal values in judging business issues, *Journal of Business Ethics*, 112: 497–514; M. Zhao, 2013, Beyond cops and robbers: The contextual challenge driving the multinational corporation public crisis in China and Russia, *Business Horizons*, 56: 491–501.

128. H. A. Ndofor, C. Wesley, & R. L. Priem, 2015, Providing CEOs with opportunities to cheat: The effects of complexity based information asymmetries on financial reporting fraud, *Journal of Management*, in press; I. Okhmaztovksiy & R. J. David, 2012, Setting your own standards: Internal corporate governance codes as a response to institutional pressure, *Organization Science*, 23: 155–176; X. Zhang, K. M. Bartol, K. G. Smith, M. D. Pfaffer, & D. M. Khanin, 2008, CEOs on the edge: Earnings manipulation and stock-based incentive misalignment, *Academy of Management Journal*, 51: 241–258.

129. K. T. Haynes, J. T. Campbell, & M. A. Hitt, 2015, When more is not enough: Executive greed and its influence on shareholder wealth. *Journal of Management*, in press; Haynes, Hitt, & Campbell, The Dark Side of Leadership; P. M. Picone, G. B. Dagnino, & A. Mina, 2014, The origin of failure: A multidisciplinary appraisal of the hubris hypothesis and proposed research agenda, *Academy of Management Perspectives*, 28(4): 447–468.

130. K. A, Gangloff, B. L. Connelly, & C. L. Shook, 2015, Of scapegoats and signals: Investor reactions to CEO succession in the aftermath of wrongdoing, *Journal of Management*, in press; D. Gomulya & W. Boeker, 2014, How firms respond to financial restatement: CEO successors and external reactions, *Academy of Management Journal*, 57: 1759–1785.

131. M. S. Schwartz, 2013, Developing and sustaining an ethical corporate culture: The core elements, *Business Horizons*, 56: 39–50; J. M. Stevens, H. K. Steensma, D. A. Harrison, & P. L. Cochran, 2005, Symbolic or substantive document? Influence of ethics codes on financial executives' decisions, *Strategic Management Journal*, 26: 181–195.

132. W. H. Bishop, 2013, The role of ethics in 21st century organizations, *Journal of Business Ethics*, 118: 635–637; B. E. Ashforth, D. A. Gioia, S. L. Robinson, & L. K. Trevino, 2008, Re-viewing organizational corruption, *Academy of Management Review*, 33: 670–684.

133. Control (management), 2015, *Wikipedia*, http://en.wikipedia.org/wiki/control, May 18; M. D. Shields, F. J. Deng, & Y. Kato, 2000, The design and effects of control systems: Tests of direct- and indirect-effects models, *Accounting, Organizations and Society*, 25: 185–202.

134. M. Rapoport, 2013, KPMG finds its safeguards 'sound and effective,' *Wall Street Journal*, www.wsj.com, June 4.

135. Balanced scorecard, 2015, *Wikipedia*, en. wikipedia.org/wiki/Balanced_scorecard, May 18; M. Friesl & R. Silberzahn, 2012, Challenges in establishing global collaboration: Temporal, strategic and operational decoupling, *Long Range Planning*, 45: 160–181; R. S. Kaplan & D. P. Norton, 2009, The balanced scorecard: Measures that drive performance (HBR OnPoint Enhanced Edition), *Harvard Business Review*, March.

136. B. E. Becker, M. A. Huselid, & D. Ulrich, 2001, *The HR Scorecard: Linking People, Strategy, and Performance*, Boston, MA: Harvard Business School Press, 21.

137. K. T. Haynes, M. A. Josefy, & M. A. Hitt, 2015, Tipping point: Managers' self-interest, greed, and altruism, *Journal of Leadership & Organizational Studies*, 22: 265–279; R. S. Kaplan & D. P. Norton, 2001, Transforming the balanced scorecard from performance measurement to strategic management: Part I, *Accounting Horizons*, 15 (1): 87–104.

138. R. S. Kaplan, 2012, The balanced scorecard: Comments on balanced scorecard commentaries, *Journal of Accounting and Organizational Change*, 8: 539–545; R. S. Kaplan & D. P. Norton, 1992, The balanced scorecard—measures that drive performance, *Harvard Business Review*, 70(1): 71–79.

139. A. Danaei & A. Hosseini, 2013, Performance measurement using balanced scorecard: A case study of pipe industry, *Management Science Letters*, 3: 1433–1438; M. A. Mische, 2001, *Strategic Renewal: Becoming a High-Performance Organization*, Upper Saddle River, NJ: Prentice Hall, 181.

140. G. Rowe, 2001, Creating wealth in organizations: The role of strategic leadership, *Academy of Management Executive*, 15: 81–94.

141. J. Xia & S. Li, 2013, The divestiture of acquired subunits: A resource dependence approach, *Strategic Management Journal*, 34: 131–148; R. E. Hoskisson, R. A. Johnson, D. Yiu, & W. P. Wan, 2001, Restructuring strategies of diversified business groups: Differences associated with country institutional environments, in M. A. Hitt, R. E. Freeman, & J. S. Harrison (eds.), *Handbook of Strategic Management*, Oxford, UK: Blackwell Publishers, 433–463.

142. J. Wincent, S. Thorgren, & S. Anokhin, 2013, Managing maturing government-supported networks: The shift from monitoring to embeddedness controls, *British Journal of Management*, 24: 480–497.

13

Strategic Entrepreneurship

Studying this chapter should provide you with the strategic management knowledge needed to:

13-1 Define strategic entrepreneurship and corporate entrepreneurship.

13-2 Define entrepreneurship and entrepreneurial opportunities and explain their importance.

13-3 Define invention, innovation, and imitation, and describe the relationship among them.

13-4 Describe entrepreneurs and the entrepreneurial mind-set.

13-5 Explain international entrepreneurship and its importance.

13-6 Describe how firms internally develop innovations.

13-7 Explain how firms use cooperative strategies to innovate.

13-8 Describe how firms use acquisitions as a means of innovation.

13-9 Explain how strategic entrepreneurship helps firms create value.

ENTREPRENEURIAL FERVOR AND INNOVATION DRIVE DISNEY'S SUCCESS

The founder, Walt Disney, once said that as long as there is imagination, Disneyland would never be finished. Likewise, one could say that as long as there is an entrepreneurial spirit and innovation, the Disney Company will never be complete. Sheryl Sandberg, COO of Facebook and a Disney board member suggested that some companies focus on technology and others focus on content, but Disney focuses on and integrates them both. Disney is perhaps best known for its cartoon characters (e.g., Mickey Mouse) and its theme parks (e.g., Disneyland and Disney World). But today, it is much more. For example, during the tenure of the current CEO, Bob Iger, Disney has acquired Pixar (major animation studio), Marvel entertainment (super heroes), Lucasfilm (*Star Wars*) and Magic Bands, among others. And, the company integrates and builds on the innovative capabilities of all of these highly creative operations.

All of these units and others within Disney are being shaped (or strongly influenced) by novel technologies. At one of Disney's five research divisions, Imagineering, new innovations are being developed and previewed by Iger and others to select the ones that are the most economically viable. Interestingly, 84 percent of Disney's active patents have been filed since 2005. The novel technologies are evident in Disney' various divisions but most certainly in its cinematic units (Pixar, Marvel, and Lucasfilm). Disney works to "cross pollinate its films to create a cinematic universe. For example, characters from one film are used to create another film that is related but unique as well. Marvel's cinematic universe includes films which have produced total revenues of $7.2 billion and include two of the top ten all-time highest gross revenue producing films.

Disney is continuing to create. As an example, its Lucasfilm division, which Disney bought in 2012, released its new Star Wars epic, *Star Wars: Episode VII—The Force Awakens* in December 2015. And it has produced *Star Wars Rebels*, an animated series aimed at boys, for Disney's cable network. Long before it was acquired by Disney, Lucasfilm worked hard to build and maintain its 'fan communities.' For example, it had a head of fan relations holding biennial meetings, referred to as the 'Star Wars Celebration,' that drew as many as 45,000 people interested in the *Star Wars* stories and characters. Disney learns from the businesses it acquires. As an example, Disney now has a head of fan relations for the company.

Frazer Harrison/Getty Images

Pixar has developed several animated movies to be released in 2015 and 2016. Among them are *The Good Dinosaur*, *Finding Dory* (a character from *Finding Nemo*), *Zootopia* (an animal tale), and *Moana* (a musical set in Polynesia). Each of these stories is unique, creative, and likely will be highly successful, based on the overwhelmingly successful *Frozen*, the highest grossing animated movie of all time, and the also highly successful *Big Hero 6*. And, Disney not only makes money from box office sales; it also receives returns from consumer products (e.g., based on characters from the movies) and related themes and products will be incorporated in attractions at Disney theme parks.

In 2015, Disney signed a contract with IMAX Corporation to show Disney's animated and live-action movies in the IMAX theaters. The initial agreement runs for three years and provides another and a different outlet for Disney entertainment. In this way, the Disney brand receives greater visibility with the public and continues to increase in value.

Interestingly, Disney's largest profits come from its media division, which includes ABC television network and ESPN. ESPN is a highly valuable unit, with the main ESPN channel being received in 95 million homes. Although it has been primarily sold in packages and on cable, Disney will soon introduce an unbundled subscription to ESPN. Thus, Disney has many ways to create profits, but most of them come from innovations and being creative in the way it deals with and reaches the consuming public.

Sources: M. Lev-Ram, 2015, Empire of Tech, *Fortune*, January 1, 48–56; A. Chen, 2015, Disney, IMAX sign three-year agreement, *Wall Street Journal*, www.wsj.com, April 8; B. Barnes, 2015, For Lucasfilm, the way of its force lies in its 'Star War's fans, *New York Times*, www.nytimes.com, April 17; A. Sakoui & C. Palmeri, 2015, My universe is bigger than your universe, *BloombergBusiness*, www.bloomberg.com, April 23; A. Sakoui, 2015, Disney boosts 'Avengers' U.S. sales total to $191.3 million, *BloombergBusiness*, www.bloomberg.com, May 4; N. Tartaglione, 2015, Disney/Pixar spotlight on 'Finding Dory', 'Good Dinosaur' & more charms Cannes, *Deadline Breaking News*, www.deadline.com, May 20.

In Chapter 6, we explained that Disney had diversified its operations. One of the reasons to diversify is to spread the risk, and it appears that Disney's strategic decisions have been effective. For example, in the second fiscal quarter of 2015, Disney reported that its profits increased by 10 percent, which was well beyond what analysts forecasted. There were declines in profits from the movie and cable businesses, as expected, but Disney had significant increases in profits from its theme parks, cruise line, media and network businesses, and consumer products. Although the movie business was doing well, its revenues did not equal the phenomenal success of its animated movie *Frozen* in the previous year. Income from its other businesses more than offset the decline in movies. Interestingly, Disney's most profitable division focuses on media and networks (ESPN and ABC). However, as explained in the Opening Case, Disney's innovations (creativity and technology) in studio entertainment and interactive businesses are likely to drive future revenues and profits. Of course, successful innovations in its movie entertainment spill over to consumer products and theme parks, suggesting the synergy that Disney creates using its related diversified businesses (see Chapter 6 for more detail).[1] As noted in the Opening Case, Disney is a highly creative company, but its success in innovation has been driven in recent years through acquisitions of innovative businesses such as Pixar, Marvel, and Lucasfilm. These acquisitions have been successful partly because the firm gained access to knowledge that has the potential to meaningfully contribute to enhanced innovative outputs in other operations held by Disney. Disney learned from its acquired businesses. It learned the importance of and how to build and maintain a strong and loyal fan base (as done by Lucasfilm).[2] Building knowledge from external sources by making acquisitions of businesses with valuable knowledge or through networks of relationships contributes to innovation, and helps firms compete both domestically and internationally.[3] Moreover, these sources of information and knowledge help firms identify opportunities to pursue and strategies to implement and exploit today's opportunities while simultaneously trying to find opportunities to exploit in the future.[4]

The focus of this chapter is on strategic entrepreneurship, which is a framework firms use to effectively integrate their entrepreneurial and strategic actions. More formally, **strategic entrepreneurship** involves taking entrepreneurial actions using a strategic perspective. In this process, the firm tries to find opportunities in its external environment that it can exploit through innovations. Identifying opportunities to exploit through innovations is the *entrepreneurship* dimension of strategic entrepreneurship. Determining the best way to competitively manage the firm's innovation efforts is the *strategic* dimension.[5]

Strategic entrepreneurship involves taking entrepreneurial actions using a strategic perspective.

Thus, firms using strategic entrepreneurship integrate their actions to find opportunities, innovate, and then implement strategies for the purpose of appropriating value from the innovations they have developed to pursue identified opportunities.[6]

We consider several topics to explain strategic entrepreneurship. First, we examine entrepreneurship and innovation in a strategic context. Definitions of entrepreneurship, entrepreneurial opportunities, and entrepreneurs (those who engage in entrepreneurship to pursue entrepreneurial opportunities) are presented. We then describe international entrepreneurship, a process through which firms take entrepreneurial actions outside of their home market. After this discussion, the chapter shifts to descriptions of the three ways firms innovate—internally, through cooperative strategies, and by acquiring other companies.[7] We discuss these methods separately. Not surprisingly, most large firms use all three methods to innovate. The chapter closes with summary comments about how firms use strategic entrepreneurship to create value.

Before turning to the chapter's topics, we note that a major portion of the material in this chapter deals with entrepreneurship and innovation that takes place in established organizations. This phenomenon is called **corporate entrepreneurship**, and it is the use or application of entrepreneurship within an established firm.[8] Corporate entrepreneurship is critical to the survival and success of for-profit organizations[9] as well as public agencies.[10] Of course, innovation and entrepreneurship play a critical role in the degree of success achieved by startup entrepreneurial ventures as well. Because of this, a significant portion of the content examined in this chapter is equally important in both entrepreneurial ventures and established organizations.

13-1 Entrepreneurship and Entrepreneurial Opportunities

Entrepreneurship is the process by which individuals, teams, or organizations identify and pursue entrepreneurial opportunities without being immediately constrained by the resources they currently control.[11] **Entrepreneurial opportunities** are conditions in which new goods or services can satisfy a need in the market. These opportunities exist because of competitive imperfections in markets and among the factors of production used to produce them or because they were independently developed by entrepreneurs.[12] Entrepreneurial opportunities come in many forms, such as the chance to develop and sell a new product and the chance to sell an existing product in a new market.[13] Firms should be receptive to pursuing entrepreneurial opportunities whenever and wherever they may surface.

As these two definitions suggest, the essence of entrepreneurship is to identify and exploit entrepreneurial opportunities—that is, opportunities others do not see or for which they do not recognize the commercial potential—and manage risks appropriately as they arise.[14] As a process, entrepreneurship results in the "creative destruction" of existing products (goods or services) or methods of producing them and replaces them with new products and production methods.[15] Thus, firms committed to entrepreneurship place high value on individual innovations as well as the ability to continuously innovate across time.[16]

We study entrepreneurship at the level of the individual firm. However, evidence suggests that entrepreneurship is the economic engine driving many nations' economies in the global competitive landscape.[17] Thus, entrepreneurship and the innovation it spawns are important for companies competing in the global economy and for countries seeking to stimulate economic climates with the potential to enhance the living standard of their citizens.

Corporate entrepreneurship is the use or application of entrepreneurship within an established firm.

Entrepreneurship is the process by which individuals, teams, or organizations identify and pursue entrepreneurial opportunities without being immediately constrained by the resources they currently control.

Entrepreneurial opportunities are conditions in which new goods or services can satisfy a need in the market.

13-2 **Innovation**

In his classic work, *The Theory of Economic Development*, Joseph Schumpeter argued that firms engage in three types of innovative activities.[18] **Invention** is the act of creating or developing a new product or process. **Innovation** is a process used to create a commercial product from an invention. Thus, innovation follows invention[19] in that invention brings something new into being while innovation brings something new into use. Accordingly, technical criteria are used to determine the success of an invention whereas commercial criteria are used to determine the success of an innovation.[20] Finally, **imitation** is the adoption of a similar innovation by different firms. Imitation usually leads to product standardization, and imitative products often are offered at lower prices but without as many features. Entrepreneurship is critical to innovative activity because it acts as the linchpin between invention and innovation.[21]

For most companies, innovation is the most critical of the three types of innovative activities. The reason for this is that while many companies are able to create ideas that lead to inventions, commercializing those inventions sometimes proves to be difficult.[22] Patents are a strategic asset, and the ability to regularly produce them can be an important source of competitive advantage, especially when a firm intends to commercialize an invention and when a firm competes in a knowledge-intensive industry (e.g., pharmaceuticals).[23] In a competitive sense, patents create entry barriers for a firm's potential competitors.[24]

Peter Drucker argued that "innovation is the specific function of entrepreneurship, whether in an existing business, a public service institution, or a new venture started by a lone individual."[25] Moreover, Drucker suggested that innovation is "the means by which the entrepreneur either creates new wealth-producing resources or endows existing resources with enhanced potential for creating wealth."[26] Thus, entrepreneurship and the innovation resulting from it are critically important for all firms seeking strategic competitiveness and above-average returns.

The realities of global competition suggest that, to be market leaders, companies must regularly innovate. This means that innovation should be an intrinsic part of virtually all of a firm's activities. Recent work found that the word 'innovation' appeared 33,000 times in U.S. firms' quarterly and annual reports suggesting the importance of innovation to firms' success.[27] Moreover, firms should recognize the importance of their human capital to efforts to innovate.[28] Thus, as this discussion suggests, innovation is a key outcome firms seek through entrepreneurship, and it is often the source of competitive success, especially for companies competing in highly competitive and turbulent environments.[29]

13-3 **Entrepreneurs**

Entrepreneurs are individuals, acting independently or as part of an organization, who perceive an entrepreneurial opportunity and then take risks to develop an innovation and exploit it. Entrepreneurs can be found throughout different parts of organizations—from top-level managers to those working to produce a firm's products.

Entrepreneurs tend to demonstrate several characteristics: they are highly motivated, willing to take responsibility for their projects, self-confident, and often optimistic.[30] In addition, entrepreneurs tend to be passionate and emotional about the value and importance of their innovation-based ideas.[31] They are able to deal with uncertainty and are more alert to opportunities than others.[32] To be successful, entrepreneurs often need to have good social skills and to plan exceptionally well (e.g., to obtain venture capital).[33] Entrepreneurship entails much hard work if it is to be successful, but it can

---

Invention is the act of creating or developing a new product or process.

Innovation is a process used to create a commercial product from an invention. Thus, innovation follows invention in that invention brings something new into being while innovation brings something new into use.

Imitation is the adoption of a similar innovation by different firms.

Entrepreneurs are individuals, acting independently or as part of an organization, who perceive an entrepreneurial opportunity and then take risks to develop an innovation and exploit it.

also be highly satisfying—particularly when entrepreneurs recognize and follow their passions. According to Jeff Bezos, Amazon.com's founder:

"One of the huge mistakes people make is that they try to force an interest on themselves. You don't choose your passions; your passions choose you."[34]

Evidence suggests that successful entrepreneurs have an entrepreneurial mind-set that includes recognition of the importance of competing internationally as well as domestically.[35] The person with an **entrepreneurial mind-set** values uncertainty in markets and seeks to continuously identify opportunities in those markets that can be pursued through innovation.[36] Those without an entrepreneurial mind-set tend to view opportunities to innovate as threats.

Astrid Stawiarz/Getty Images

Display of Warby Parker's popular eyewear, the product of Fast Company's most innovative company in 2015.

Because it has the potential to lead to continuous innovations, an individual's entrepreneurial mind-set can be a source of competitive advantage for a firm. Entrepreneurial mind-sets are fostered and supported when knowledge is readily available throughout a firm. Indeed, research shows that units within firms are more innovative when people have access to new knowledge.[37] Transferring knowledge, however, can be difficult, often because the receiving party must have adequate absorptive capacity (or the ability) to understand the knowledge and how to productively use it.[38] Learning requires that the new knowledge be linked to the existing knowledge. Thus, managers need to develop the capabilities of their human capital to build on their current knowledge base while incrementally expanding it.[39]

Some companies are known to be highly committed to entrepreneurship, suggesting that many working within them have an entrepreneurial mind-set. In 2015, *Fast Company* identified Warby Parker as the most innovative company, with Apple, Alibaba, Google, and Instagram rounding out the top five most innovative firms.[40] Warby Parker was chosen as the most innovative company in 2015 for developing the first top 'made-on-the-Internet brand of popular eyewear. After only five years, its annual revenue exceeds $100 million. Over time, the cofounders believe that their brand can be used for other products in addition to eyewear.[41].

13-4 **International Entrepreneurship**

International entrepreneurship is a process in which firms creatively discover and exploit opportunities that are outside their domestic markets.[42] Thus, entrepreneurship is a process that many firms exercise at both the domestic and international levels.[43] This is true for entrepreneurial ventures as suggested by the fact that an increasing number of them (perhaps as much as 50 percent) move into international markets early in their life cycle. Large, established companies commonly have significant foreign operations and often start new ventures in international markets, too.[44]

A key reason that firms choose to engage in international entrepreneurship is that, in general, doing so enhances their performance.[45] Nonetheless, those leading firms generally understand that taking entrepreneurial actions in markets outside the firm's home

Entrepreneurial mind-set values uncertainty in markets and seeks to continuously identify opportunities in those markets that can be pursued through innovation.

International entrepreneurship is a process in which firms creatively discover and exploit opportunities that are outside their domestic markets.

setting is challenging and not without risks, including risks of unstable foreign currencies, market inefficiencies, insufficient infrastructures to support businesses, and limitations on market size.[46] Thus, the decision to engage in international entrepreneurship needs to be a product of careful analysis.

Even though entrepreneurship is a global phenomenon, meaning that it is practiced throughout the world, its rate of use differs within individual countries. For example, a new report ranking the most entrepreneurial countries showed that the 10 most entrepreneurial countries in 2014 were (from the most to the least entrepreneurial): India, Turkey, United States, Brazil, China, Iceland, Ireland, Russia, Estonia, and Austria. The report showed that many of the most entrepreneurial countries were emerging economies. It also showed that personal and national wealth experienced the highest rates of growth in the most entrepreneurial countries.[47] Thus, as argued by others, there is a strong positive relationship between the rate of entrepreneurship and economic development within a country.

Culture is one reason for the different rates of entrepreneurship among countries across the globe. Research suggests that a balance between individual initiative and a spirit of cooperation and group ownership of innovation is needed to encourage entrepreneurial behavior. This means that for firms to be entrepreneurial, they must provide appropriate autonomy and incentives for individual initiative to surface while simultaneously promoting cooperation and group ownership of an innovation as a foundation for successfully exploiting it. Thus, international entrepreneurship often requires teams of people with unique skills and resources, especially in cultures that place high value on either individualism or collectivism. In addition to a balance of values for individual initiative and cooperative behaviors, firms engaging in international entrepreneurship must concentrate more than companies engaging in domestic entrepreneurship on building the capabilities needed to innovate and on acquiring the resources needed to make strategic decisions through which innovations can be successfully exploited.[48]

The level of investment outside of the home country made by young ventures is also an important dimension of international entrepreneurship. In fact, with increasing globalization, a larger number of new ventures have been "born global."[49] One reason for this is likely because new ventures that enter international markets increase their learning of new technological knowledge and thereby enhance their performance.[50] They increase their knowledge through the external networks (e.g., suppliers, customers) that they establish in the new foreign markets including strategic alliances in which they participate.[51]

The probability of entering and successfully competing in international markets increases when the firm's strategic leaders, and especially its top-level managers, have international experience.[52] Because of the learning and economies of scale and scope afforded by operating in international markets, both young and established internationally diversified firms often are stronger competitors in their domestic market as well. Additionally, as research has shown, internationally diversified firms are generally more innovative.[53]

The ability of a firm to develop and sustain a competitive advantage may be based partly or largely on its ability to innovate. This is true for firms engaging in international entrepreneurship as well as those that have yet to do so. As we discuss next, firms can follow different paths to innovate internally. Internal innovation is the first of three approaches firms use to innovate.

13-5 **Internal Innovation**

Efforts in firms' research and development (R&D) function are one primary source of internal innovations. Through effective R&D, firms are able to generate patentable processes and goods that are innovative in nature. Increasingly, successful R&D results from integrating the skills available in the global workforce. Thus, the ability to have a competitive advantage based on innovation is more likely to accrue to firms capable of integrating the talent of human capital from countries around the world.[54]

R&D and the new products and processes it can spawn affect a firm's efforts to earn above-average returns while competing in today's global environment. Because of this, firms try to use their R&D labs to create disruptive technologies and products. Although critical to long-term competitive success, the outcomes of R&D investments are uncertain and often not achieved in the short term, meaning that patience is required as firms evaluate the outcomes of their R&D efforts.[55]

As noted earlier, successful R&D programs must have high quality human capital—star scientists. Yet, not all ideas begin in the laboratory. For example, firms have learned that customers are often good sources for new products that will satisfy their needs.[56] They also use external networks such as other scientists, published research, and even alliance partners (discussed later in this chapter).[57] They may even be able to use public knowledge, such as that on a current technology, that can be combined to create an improved technology or perhaps even a new technology.[58]

Companies have created several means of obtaining employees' ideas for new products and other types of innovation. At LinkedIn, employees are encouraged to come up with ideas for innovations, develop a team to work on it and to make a pitch for the innovation to an executive team. Whirlpool uses structured ideation sessions with employees to identify new ideas for innovations. At Ericsson, employees are encouraged to participate in 'ideaboxes.' After employees submit an idea, they are matched with 'idea-to-innovation' managers to develop it further and determine if it is feasible and valuable. Ericsson then has an internal venture funding group that provides startup capital to the best ideas.[59]

13-5a Incremental and Novel Innovation

Firms invest in R&D to produce two types of innovations—incremental and novel. Most innovations are *incremental*—that is, they build on existing knowledge bases and provide small improvements in current products. Incremental innovations are evolutionary and linear in nature.[60] In general, incremental innovations tend to be introduced into established markets where customers understand and accept a product's characteristics. Basically, incremental innovations exploit an existing technology to provide an improvement over a current product. From the firm's perspective, incremental innovations tend to yield lower profit margins compared to those associated with the outcomes of novel or breakthrough innovations, largely because competition among firms offering products to customers that have incremental innovations is primarily on the price variable.[61] Adding a different kind of whitening agent to a soap detergent is an example of an incremental innovation, as are minor improvements in the functionality in televisions (e.g., slightly better picture quality). Companies introduce more incremental than novel innovations to markets, largely because they are cheaper, easier, and faster to produce, and involve less risk. Yet, firms normally cannot rely solely on incremental innovations. If they do so, they move from being market leaders to market laggards.[62] However, incremental innovation can be risky for firms if its frequency of introduction creates more change than can be appropriately absorbed.[63]

In contrast to incremental innovations, *novel* or *breakthrough innovations* usually provide significant technological changes (breakthroughs) and create new knowledge.[64] Revolutionary and nonlinear in nature, novel innovations typically use new technologies to serve newly created markets. The development of the original personal computer was a breakthrough innovation.

Google's new self-driving car is an example of a novel innovation. Under development for several years, Google announced in 2015 that several prototype vehicles were being

Google's self-driving car is an example of a novel innovation.

David Paul Morris/Bloomberg/Getty Images

tested on city streets. The company also noted that the cars are very safe. At present, one of the biggest obstacles to introducing the vehicles to the consumer market is convincing regulators on their safety and ability to adhere to the rules and laws of operating automobiles on public streets and highways.[65] Because they establish new functionalities for users, novel or breakthrough innovations have strong potential to lead to significant growth in revenue and profits. For example, Toyota's innovation, embodied in the Prius, "the first mass-produced hybrid-electric car," changed this segment of the automobile industry.[66] Developing new processes is a critical part of producing novel innovations. Both types of innovations can create value, meaning that firms should determine when it is appropriate to emphasize either incremental or novel innovation. However, novel innovations have the potential to contribute more significantly to a firm's efforts to earn above-average returns, although they also are more risky.

Novel or breakthrough innovations are rare because of the difficulty and risk involved in their development. The value of the technology and the market opportunities are highly uncertain.[67] Because novel innovation creates new knowledge and uses only some or little of a firm's current product or technological knowledge, creativity is required; creativity is as important to efforts to innovate in not-for-profit organizations as it is in for-profit firms.[68] Creativity is an outcome of using one's imagination. In the words of Jay Walker, founder of Priceline.com, "Imagination is the fuel. You're not going to get innovation if you don't have imagination." Imagination finds firms thinking about what customers will want in a changing world. For example, Walker says, those seeking to innovate within a firm could try to imagine "what the customer is going to want in a world where, for instance, their cellphone is in their glasses."[69] Imagination is more critical to novel than incremental innovations.

Creativity alone does not directly lead to innovation. Rather, creativity as generated through imagination discovers, combines, or synthesizes current knowledge, often from diverse areas.[70] Increasingly, when trying to innovate, firms seek knowledge from current users to understand their perspective about what could be beneficial innovations to the firm's products.[71] Collectively, the gathered knowledge is then applied to develop new products that can be used in an entrepreneurial manner to move into new markets, capture new customers, and gain access to new resources.[72] Such innovations are often developed in separate business units that start internal ventures.[73]

Strong, supportive leadership is required for the type of creativity and imagination needed to develop novel innovations. The fact that creativity is "messy, chaotic, sometimes even disgusting, and reeks of failure, experimentation, and disorganization"[74] is one set of reasons why leadership is so critical to its success.

This discussion highlights the fact that internally developed incremental and novel innovations result from deliberate efforts. These deliberate efforts are called *internal corporate venturing*, which is the set of activities firms use to develop internal inventions and especially innovations.[75]

Strategic Focus

Innovation Can Be Quirky

Quirky is a unique new venture founded in 2009 that combines the opportunities provided by the Internet of everything with the more physical world of business (e.g., industrial design, manufacturing, and marketing) to produce innovations. Some have referred to the company as an innovation machine—the mission is to commercialize new product ideas. Ben Kaufman, founder and CEO of the company, suggests that the goal is "to create an engine that accelerates the process of identifying and developing ideas for all kinds of products."

Quirky has built a social network of inventors and others, some of whom submit ideas for new products, who are used to evaluate new product ideas (for marketability and manufacturing feasibility). The approximately one million people involved in this network also offer ideas on how to refine and improve the product ideas. Quirky receives around 4,000 product ideas each week and brought 400 Quirky-generated products to the market by 2015. It has received funding from some large venture capital firms and by one major corporate partner, GE (invested $30 million).

After a product idea is evaluated, refined, and sometimes improved, Quirky uses large 3-D printers to create prototypes. The firm also begins searching for a manufacturer and simultaneously seeking a market for the products through retailers (such as Home Depot, Target, Walmart, etc.). Given the promise of this company to commercialize inventions (create innovation), it raised $185 million in venture capital and grew to 300 employees, opening new offices in California to complement its New York headquarters.

Although there was much excitement, Quirky experienced problems. Some of its products failed to achieve a following in the marketplace (the social network evaluations were not adequate for marketing research), and other products had quality problems (due to inadequate quality control). Quirky tried to move products to the market too quickly. As a result it lost $120 million dollars and had to reduce operations to avoid having a cash shortage. As such, Quirky laid off about 20 percent of its staff and made some other changes to focus its activities.

Quirky decided to focus its efforts to sign up more corporate partners in addition to GE. It is trying to focus more of its efforts on products for the smart home, products that communicate with a smartphone or home Wi-Fi network. Quirky's Wink smartphone and tablet app provides a digital dashboard to link and control smart-home devices (e.g., lights, lawn sprinklers, garage doors, air conditioning, etc.). Quirky now has 15 companies that will offer about 60 Wink-enabled products. Among them are GE, Honeywell, and Philips. The products are sold under the company's own brand but will carry a tagline: "Powered by Quirky."

Courtesy of Innovation excellence

Innovative products developed by Quirky through its partnership with GE.

Sources: S. Lohr, 2014, Quirky to create a smart-home products company, *New York Times*, www.nytimes.com, June 22; G. Karol, 2014, NYC startup Quirky launches platform for Internet of things, *FOXBusiness*, www.foxbusiness.com, June 24; M. Baratz, 2014, Counting down with…Ben Kaufman, *Fortune*, fortune.com, July 21; S. Lohr, 2015, The invention mob, brought to you by Quirky, *New York Times*, www.nytimes.com, February 14; B. Popper, 2015, How the invention factory at Quirky almost imagined its way out of business, The Verge, www.theverge.com, April 24; J. D'Onfro, 2015, How a Quirky 28-year-old plowed through $15 million and almost destroyed his startup, Business Insider, www.businessinsider.com, April 29.

The example of Quirky in the Strategic Focus demonstrates the creative potential of innovation and simultaneously the risk and uncertainty involved in creating and trying to commercialize inventions (particularly novel ones). Quirky is a unique and potentially valuable company that takes new product ideas offered by inventors and evaluates them. For the ones deemed to have potential value, Quirky then develops prototypes, finds a

Figure 13.1 Model of Internal Corporate Venturing

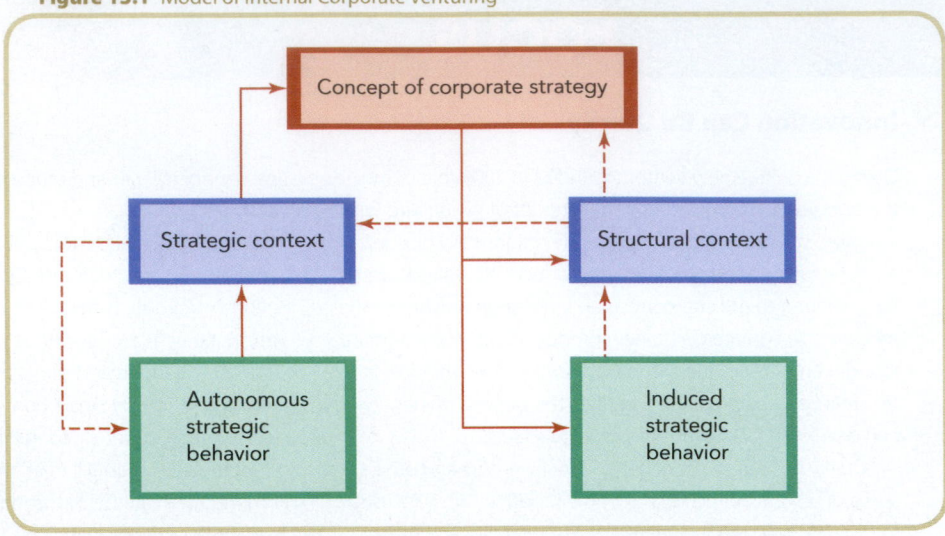

Source: Adapted from R. A. Burgelman, 1983, A model of the interactions of strategic behavior, corporate context, and the concept of strategy, *Academy of Management Review*, 8:65.

manufacturer, and markets the products. In this way, it facilitates many innovations from inventive new ideas that would be unlikely to find a market without such help. Yet, it, too, takes much risk and found that it had to do better market research on the ideas and ensure high quality control of the products produced and marketed. It also has become more focused, which should allow it to be more efficient and to gain some economies of scale, which it badly needed.

As shown in Figure 13.1, autonomous and induced strategic behaviors are the two types of internal corporate venturing. Each venturing type facilitates development of both incremental and novel innovations. However, a larger number of novel innovations spring from autonomous strategic behavior, while a larger number of incremental innovations come from induced strategic behavior.

In essence, autonomous strategic behavior results in influences to change aspects of the firm's strategy and the structure in place to support its implementation. In contrast, induced strategic behavior results from the influences of the strategy and structure the firm currently has in place to support efforts to innovate (see Figure 13.1). These points are emphasized in the discussions below of the two types of internal corporate venturing.

13-5b Autonomous Strategic Behavior

Autonomous strategic behavior is a bottom-up process in which product champions pursue new ideas, often through a political process, by means of which they develop and coordinate the actions required to innovate and to bring the innovation to the market.[76] Actually, the process used by Quirky, as explained in the Strategic Focus, is an example of autonomous strategic behavior. A *product champion* is an individual with an entrepreneurial mind-set who seeks to create support for developing an innovation. Product champions play critical roles in moving innovations forward.[77] Commonly, product champions use their social capital to develop informal networks within the firm. As progress is made, these networks become more formal as a means of pushing an innovation to marketplace success.[78] Quirky plays the role of the product champion outside the bounds of an individual organization. Internal innovations springing from autonomous strategic behavior differ from the firm's current strategy and structure, taking it into new markets and perhaps new ways of creating value.

As a means of innovating, autonomous strategic behavior is more effective when new knowledge, especially tacit knowledge, is diffused continuously throughout the firm.[79]

13-5c Induced Strategic Behavior

Induced strategic behavior, the second form of corporate venturing through which innovations are developed internally, is a top-down process whereby the firm's current strategy and structure foster innovations that are closely associated with that strategy and structure.[80] In this form of venturing, the strategy in place is filtered through a matching structural hierarchy. In essence, induced strategic behavior results in internal innovations that are consistent with the firm's current strategy. Thus, the firm's CEO and its top management team play an active and key role in induced strategic behavior.[81] This is the case at IBM, where CEO Virginia Rometty challenged the firm's employees "to move faster and respond more quickly to customers" as a foundation for developing innovations that will facilitate the firm's efforts to "shift to new computing models."[82]

Induced innovation allows the firm and its managers to determine the type and amount of innovation desired.[83] For example, the firm could develop an intense innovation process in order to be the industry leader by regularly introducing new products even if they cannibalize currently successful products.[84] This has been the approach employed by Intel for many years. An induced approach to innovation is used by a firm to determine if it wishes to create open innovation, where innovation is used to establish industry standards, or closed innovation, which the firm uses to generate returns disallowing others to use it.[85] The majority of innovation is closed innovation, but open innovation has become more common, especially in some industries. Often, firms engage in evolutionary, path dependent R&D, which over time becomes more incremental (because of the path dependence in the knowledge based used).[86]

13-6 Implementing Internal Innovations

An entrepreneurial mind-set is critical to firms' efforts to innovate internally, partly because such a mind-set helps them deal with the environmental and market uncertainty that are associated with efforts taken to commercialize inventions.[87] When facing uncertainty, firms try to continuously identify the most attractive opportunities to pursue strategically. Thus firms use an entrepreneurial mind-set to simultaneously identify opportunities, develop innovations to meet those opportunities, and execute strategies to successfully exploit the opportunities identified in the marketplace.[88] Often, firms provide incentives to individuals to be more entrepreneurial as a foundation for successfully developing internal innovations, sometimes encouraging work teams to specify what they believe are the most appropriate incentives for the firm to use.[89]

Having processes and structures in place through which a firm can successfully exploit developed innovations is critical. In the context of internal corporate ventures, managers must allocate resources, coordinate activities, communicate with many different parties in the organization, and make a series of decisions to convert the innovations resulting from either autonomous or induced strategic behaviors into successful market entries.[90] As we describe in Chapter 11, organizational structures are the sets of formal relationships that support processes managers use to exploit the firm's innovations.

Effective integration of the functions involved in internal innovation efforts—from engineering to manufacturing and distribution—is required to implement the incremental and novel innovations resulting from internal corporate ventures.[91] Increasingly, product development teams are being used to achieve the desired integration across organizational functions. Such integration involves coordinating and applying the knowledge and skills of different functional areas to maximize innovation.[92] Teams must help to make decisions about which projects to continue supporting and which to terminate. Emotional commitments sometimes increase the difficulty of deciding to terminate an innovation-based project.

13-6a Cross-Functional Product Development Teams

Cross-functional product development teams facilitate efforts to integrate activities associated with different organizational functions, such as design, manufacturing, and marketing. Among the team members are research scientists who have the technological content knowledge to bring to the group development decisions.[93] These teams may also include people from major suppliers because they have knowledge that can meaningfully inform a firm's innovation processes.[94] In addition, new product development processes can be completed more quickly and the products can be more easily commercialized when cross-functional teams work collaboratively.[95] Using cross-functional teams, product development stages are grouped into parallel processes so that the firm can tailor its product development efforts to its unique core competencies and to the needs of the market.

Horizontal organizational structures support cross-functional teams in their efforts to integrate innovation-based activities across organizational functions.[96] Therefore, instead of being designed around vertical hierarchical functions or departments, the organization is built around core horizontal processes that are used to produce and manage innovations. Some of the horizontal processes that are critical to innovation efforts are formal and are defined and documented as procedures and practices. More commonly, however, these important processes are informal and are supported properly through horizontal organizational structures—structures that typically find individuals communicating frequently on a face-to-face basis.

Team members' independent frames of reference and organizational politics are two barriers with the potential to prevent effective use of cross-functional teams to integrate the activities of different organizational functions.[97] Team members working within a distinct specialization (e.g., a particular organizational function) may have an independent frame of reference typically based on common backgrounds and experiences. They are likely to use the same decision criteria to evaluate issues, such as product development efforts, when making decisions within their functional units.

Research suggests that functional departments vary along four dimensions: time orientation, interpersonal orientation, goal orientation, and formality of structure.[98] Thus, individuals from different functional departments having different orientations in terms of these dimensions can be expected to perceive innovation-related activities differently. For example, a design engineer may consider the characteristics that make a product functional and workable to be the most important of its characteristics. Alternatively, a person from the marketing function may judge characteristics that satisfy customer needs to be most important. These different orientations can create barriers to effective communication across functions and may even generate intra-team conflict as different parts of the firm try to work together to innovate.[99]

Some organizations experience a considerable amount of political activity (called organizational politics). How resources will be allocated to different functions is a key source of such activity. This means that inter-unit conflict may result from aggressive competition for resources among those representing different organizational functions. This type of conflict between functions creates a barrier to cross-functional integration efforts. Those trying to form effective cross-functional product development teams seek ways to mitigate the damaging effects of organizational politics. Emphasizing the critical role each function plays in the firm's overall efforts to innovate is a method used in many firms to help individuals see the value of inter-unit collaborations.

13-6b Facilitating Integration and Innovation

Shared values and effective leadership are important for achieving cross-functional integration and implementing internal innovations.[100] As part of culture, shared values are framed around the firm's vision and mission and become the glue that promotes integration between functional units.

Strategic leadership is also important to efforts to achieve cross-functional integration and promote internal innovation. Working with others, leaders are responsible for setting goals and allocating resources needed to achieve them. The goals include integrated development and commercialization of new products. Effective strategic leaders also ensure a high-quality communication system to facilitate cross-functional integration. A critical benefit of effective communication is the sharing of knowledge among team members, who in turn are then able to communicate an innovation's existence and importance to others in the organization. Shared values and leadership practices shape the communication routines that make it possible to share innovation-related knowledge throughout the firm.[101]

13-6c Creating Value from Internal Innovation

The model in Figure 13.2 shows how firms seek to create value through internal innovation processes (autonomous strategic behavior and induced strategic behavior). As shown, an entrepreneurial mind-set is foundational to the firm's efforts to consistently identify entrepreneurial opportunities that it can pursue strategically with and through innovations. Cross-functional teams are important for promoting integrated new product design ideas and gaining commitment to their subsequent implementation. Effective leadership and shared values promote integration and vision for innovation and commitment to it. The end result of successful innovations is the creation of value for stakeholders such as customers and shareholders.[102] However, competitive rivalry (see Chapter 5) affects the degree of success a firm achieves through its innovations. Thus, firms must carefully

Figure 13.2 Creating Value through Internal Innovation Processes

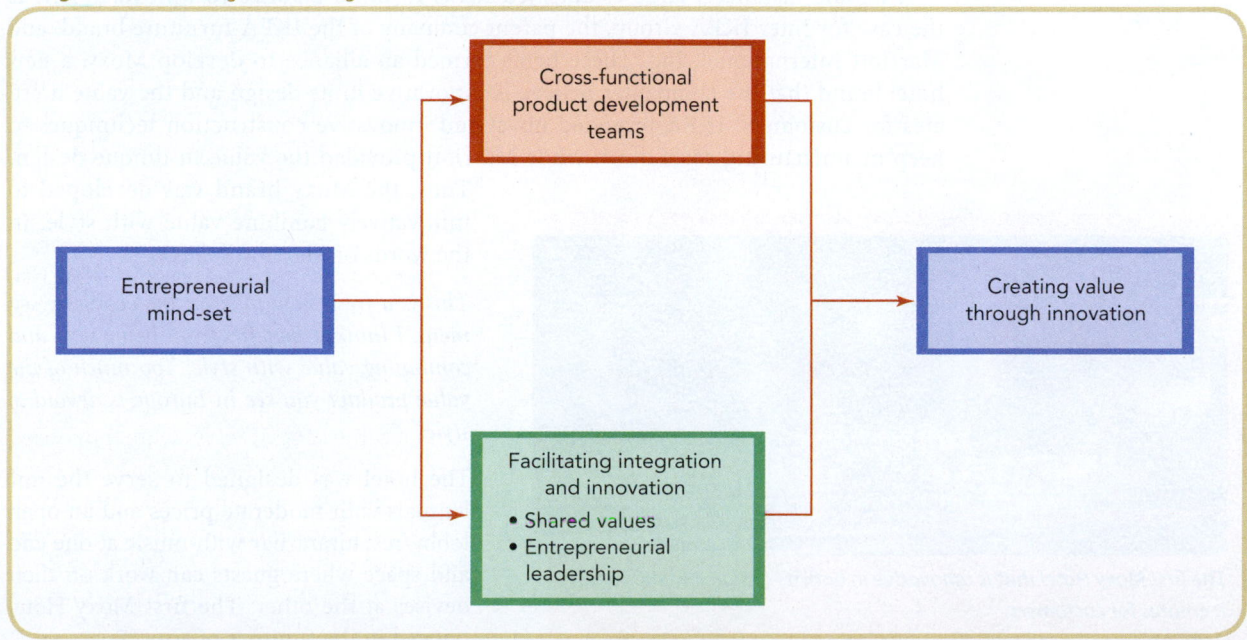

study competitors' responses to their innovations to have the knowledge required to know how to adjust their innovation-based efforts, and even when to abandon those efforts if market conditions indicate the need to do so.[103]

In the next two sections, we discuss the other approaches firms use to innovate—cooperative strategies and acquisitions.

13-7 Innovation through Cooperative Strategies

Alliances with other firms can contribute to innovations in several ways. First, they provide information on new business opportunities and the innovations that might be developed to exploit them.[104] In other instances, firms use cooperative strategies to align what they believe are complementary assets with the potential to lead to future innovations. Compared to other approaches to innovation, combining complementary assets through alliances has the potential to more frequently result in "breakthrough" innovations.[105]

Rapidly changing technologies, globalization, and the need to innovate at world-class levels are primary influences on firms' decisions to innovate by cooperating with other companies. Indeed, some believe that, because of these conditions, firms are becoming increasingly dependent on cooperative strategies as a path to innovation and, ultimately, to competitive success in the global economy.[106] Both entrepreneurial ventures and established firms use cooperative strategies to innovate. An entrepreneurial venture, for example, may seek investment capital as well as established firms' distribution capabilities to successfully introduce one of its innovative products to the market.[107] Alternatively, more-established companies may need new technological knowledge and can gain access to it by forming a cooperative strategy with entrepreneurial ventures.[108] Alliances between large pharmaceutical firms and biotechnology companies increasingly have been formed to integrate the knowledge and resources of both to develop new products and bring them to market.

In some instances, large established firms form an alliance to innovate. This is the case for Inter IKEA Group, the parent company of the IKEA furniture brand, and Marriott International, Inc. These firms formed an alliance to develop Moxy, a new hotel brand that the companies believe is innovative in its design and the value it creates for customers. IKEA provided novel and innovative construction techniques to keep manufacturing costs down while Marriott provided the value in unique design.. Thus, the Moxy brand was developed to innovatively combine value with style. In the words of Marriott's CEO:

"This is a fresh new take on the economy segment. I think it benefits from being new and combining value with style. Too much of the value product you see in Europe is devoid of style."

The hotel was designed to serve the millennials with moderate prices and an open lobby/restaurant/bar with music at one end and space where guests can work on their devises at the other. The first Moxy Hotel opened in the summer of 2014.[109]

The first Moxy Hotel that is innovative in both its design and the value it creates for customers.

Courtesy of Marriott

However, alliances formed to foster innovation are not without risks. In addition to conflict that is natural when firms try to work together to reach a mutual goal, the members of an alliance also take a risk that a partner will appropriate their technology or knowledge and use it for its own benefit.[110] Carefully selecting partner firms mitigates this risk. The ideal partnership is one in which the firms have complementary skills as well as compatible strategic goals.[111] When this is the case, firms encounter fewer challenges and risks as they try to effectively manage the partnership they formed to develop innovations. Companies also want to constrain the number of cooperative arrangements they form to innovate in that becoming involved in too many alliances puts them at risk of losing the ability to successfully manage each of them.[112]

13-8 Innovation through Acquisitions

Firms sometimes acquire companies to gain access to their innovations and to their innovative capabilities.[113] One reason companies do this is that capital markets value growth; acquisitions provide a means to rapidly extend one or more product lines and increase the firm's revenues.[114] In spite of this fact, a firm should have a strategic rationale for a decision to acquire a company. Typically, the rationale is to gain ownership of an acquired company's innovations and access to its innovative capabilities. A number of large technology-based companies have acquired firms largely for these purposes. For example, Microsoft acquired Mojang AB in 2014 to gain access to the technological capabilities of Minecraft. Minecraft is a videogame but different from the norm. It does not provide the context; it allows the players to construct it themselves. So, they get what they want. In other words, they create their own (and desired) innovation. So, Minecraft is a game that is determined by the players not a design team working for the company providing the game. Mojang was highly profitable because of the high demand for Minecraft. In 2013, it made a profit of $115 million on $291 million in sales for a return of almost 40 percent (incredibly high). Microsoft paid about $2.5 billion to acquire Mojang.[115]

Similar to internal corporate venturing and strategic alliances, acquisitions are not a risk free approach to innovation. A key risk of acquisitions is that a firm may substitute an ability to buy innovations for an ability to develop them internally. This may result when a firm concentrates on financial controls to identify, evaluate, and then manage acquisitions. Of course, strategic controls are the ones through which a firm identifies a strategic rationale to acquire another company as a means of developing innovations. Thus, the likelihood a firm will be successful in its efforts to innovate increases by developing an appropriate balance between financial and strategic controls. In spite of the risks though, choosing to acquire companies with complementary capabilities and knowledge sets can support a firm's efforts to innovate successfully when the acquisitions are made for strategic purposes and are then properly integrated into the acquired firm's strategies.[116] Firms that have not been as successful at producing innovation as needed are more likely to acquire firms with technological capabilities, or that have new, potentially valuable innovations, if they have enough financial capital to do so.[117] For example, in recent years some large pharmaceutical firms that have been unsuccessful at producing new blockbuster drugs have resorted to acquisitions in order to gain access to new valuable drugs held by the acquired firm.

The ability to learn new capabilities that can facilitate innovation-related activities from acquired companies is an important benefit that can accrue to an acquiring firm. Additionally, firms that emphasize innovation and carefully select companies to acquire that also emphasize innovation and the technological capabilities on which innovations are often based are likely to remain innovative.[118] Thus, some firms produce innovations internally. Others use external knowledge and external sources for innovations.

Strategic Focus

What Explains the Lack of Innovation at American Express? Is It Hubris, Inertia, or Lack of Capability?

The lack of innovation and entrepreneurial focus at American Express may be becauseof hubris, inertia, *and* lack of capability. American Express (AmEx) had a terrible year in 2014. It lost two major partnerships, and lost a major court case, all of which are likely to have negative effects on its revenues. The executives at AmEx must think so as well because they are cutting costs and plan to layoff as many as 4,000 employees.

AmEx lost its partnership as the exclusive co-branded credit card with the major retailer Costco in 2014. This represents a major problem for AmEx as that business generated approximately eight percent of AmEx's total revenues in 2014. Interestingly, card holders used the AmEx card for many other purchases outside of Costco, as about 70 percent of the revenue generated by the card came from its use in other venues. AmEx also lost its partnership with Jet Blue in the same year.

In addition, AmEx lost a major court case. AmEx charges each merchant higher fees when a customer uses its card to make a purchase than do other major credit card companies such as Visa and MasterCard. AmEx has a contract with each merchant using its card that does not allow the merchant to recommend to the customer to use a different card or to offer discounts favoring other cards. A federal judge ruled that this requirement by AmEx was in 'restraint of trade' and, therefore, violated antitrust laws. This is important because AmEx may have to reduce its fees charged to merchants, and if so, it may have to decrease the rewards paid back to customers. In turn, it could lose some customers if the rewards become equal to or less than competitors' cards.

AmEx has not advanced its purchasing technology in some time, advances such as facilitating customers' car rentals or restaurant reservations. It has been considered to be the "most prestigious" card and thus built a brand image. It also has been respected because it captured and held the most wealthy clientele. However, it has begun to lose some of its wealthiest clients. One such client has been a long-time user of the AmEx card. However, he recently changed because the

"rewards" received with other cards are better. In fact, because he uses the cards for almost all of his purchases, he stands to receive thousands of dollars more in rewards with the other cards.

AmEx recently announced a renewed focus on affluent customers and more benefits for those holding (and using) the 'Gold Card.' It will offer double points for restaurant purchases and a personalized travel service. The annual fee for the 'Premier Gold Card' also increased by a little more than 11 percent. The fee increase for the regular Gold Card was about 28 percent. Although, AmEx executives stated that they continue to target growth goals, most analysts believe that AmEx revenues are likely to fall over the next year or two. Innovation and a new strategy are needed.

The NEW Gold Rewards Card

AMERICAN EXPRESS

3759 876543 21001

95

C F FROST

Realize the potential™

American Express.PNG

Will the new American Express Gold Rewards Card help the firm to regain its competitive position in tthe industry?

Sources: E. Dexheimer, 2015, AmEx is losing its millionaires, *BloombergBusiness*, www. bloomberg.com, February 12; J. Davidson, 2015, Why American Express users should be worried about their rewards, *Money*, www.money.com, February 20; H. Stout, 2015, With revamped gold cards, bruised American Express returns focus to affluent, *New York Times*, www.nytimes.com, February 26; J. Kell, 2015, Visa replaces American Express as Costco's credit card, *Fortune*, www.fortune.com, March 2; H. Tabuchi, 2015, Amex to ask for stay of ruling prohibiting merchants from promoting other cards, *New York Times*, www.nytimes.com, March 25; J. Carney, 2015, American Express struggles to keep up, *Wall Street Journal*, www.wsj.com, April 6; 2015, Stronger dollar drives revenue down at American Express, *New York Times*, www.nytimes.com, April 16.

Both strategies can be successful if implemented effectively.[119] Yet, some mergers can insulate firms, especially large ones with significant market power, because an acquisition may provide an almost monopoly on a particular type of technology. This type of acquisition may focus the firm on path-dependent knowledge development and incremental innovations. It may also discourage new firms from entering the market, thereby reducing entrepreneurial activity in the industry.[120]

American Express has some significant problems, as explained in the Strategic Focus. It has lost two major corporate partners that account for perhaps as much as 10 percent of its annual revenue, In addition, it lost a major court case that may also reduce its revenues or increase its costs. These concerns, when coupled with the fact that the firm has not been innovative (while its rivals have been introducing innovative new services and taking market share), suggest a rather bleak future. It seems that, due to inertia and possibly hubris, AmEx has maintained its strategy and is losing its competitive advantage. AmEx executives need to be entrepreneurial and strategic. In other words, they need to engage in strategic entrepreneurship. To close this chapter, we describe how strategic entrepreneurship helps firms create value for stakeholders.

13-9 Creating Value through Strategic Entrepreneurship

Entrepreneurial ventures and younger firms often are more effective at identifying opportunities than are larger established companies.[121] As a consequence, entrepreneurial ventures often produce more breakthrough innovations than do larger, more established organizations. Entrepreneurial ventures' strategic flexibility and willingness to take risks, at least partially, account for their ability to identify opportunities and then develop breakthrough innovations. Yet, because these innovations are often quite novel, they are also risky. Thus, they sometimes fail which frequently means that the new venture fails because such firms have little slack.[122] Alternatively, larger, well-established firms often have more resources and capabilities to manage their resources for the purpose of exploiting identified opportunities, but these efforts by large firms generally result in more incremental than breakthrough innovations. For example, in recent times, Boeing has focused on developing incremental innovations to build on and improve the successful new aircraft such as the 787 Dreamliner. Currently, Boeing is developing seven new models that will upgrade its existing fleet, largely taking advantage of the technologies already in use.[123]

Thus, younger, entrepreneurial ventures generally excel in the *taking of entrepreneurial actions* part of strategic entrepreneurship, while larger, more established firms generally excel at the *using a strategic perspective* part of strategic entrepreneurship. Another way of thinking about this is to say that entrepreneurial ventures excel at opportunity-seeking (that is, entrepreneurial) behavior, while larger firms excel at advantage-seeking (that is, strategic) behavior. However, competitive success and superior performance relative to competitors accrues to firms that are able to identify and exploit opportunities and establish a competitive advantage as a result of doing so.[124] On a relative basis then, entrepreneurial ventures are challenged to become more strategic, while older, more established firms are challenged to become more entrepreneurial.

Firms trying to learn how to simultaneously be more entrepreneurial and strategic (that is, firms trying to use strategic entrepreneurship) recognize that, after identifying opportunities, entrepreneurs within entrepreneurial ventures and established organizations must develop capabilities that will become the basis of their firm's core competencies and competitive advantages. The process of identifying opportunities is entrepreneurial, but this activity alone is not sufficient to create maximum value, or even to survive over time. In fact, the early goals for entrepreneurial firms are to survive and grow, allowing them to accumulate resources to finance additional innovation and growth.[125] As we learned in Chapter 3, to successfully exploit opportunities, a firm must develop capabilities that are valuable, rare, difficult to imitate, and nonsubstitutable. When capabilities satisfy these four criteria, the firm has one or more competitive advantages to use in efforts to exploit the identified opportunities. Without a competitive advantage, the firm's success will be only temporary (as explained in Chapter 1). An innovation may be valuable and rare early in its life, if a market perspective is used in its development. However, competitive actions must be taken to introduce the new product to the market and protect its position in the market against competitors in order to gain a competitive advantage.[126] In combination, these actions constitute strategic entrepreneurship.

Some large organizations are trying to become more capable of effectively using strategic entrepreneurship. For example, an increasing number of large, widely known firms, including Wendy's International, Gucci Group, Starbucks, and Perry Ellis International, have established a top-level managerial position commonly called president or executive vice president of emerging brands. Other companies such as Coca-Cola, GE, Whirlpool, and Humana have established a position within their top management teams to focus on innovation.[127] These individuals are often known as chief innovation officers.

The essential responsibility of top-level managers focusing on emerging brands or innovation is to verify that their firm is consistently finding entrepreneurial opportunities. They must effectively manage the firm's portfolio of innovation projects, deciding which ones require more investment and which ones should be terminated.[128] These people know that some innovation projects fail but, they also try to learn from those failures to make future ones more successful.[129] The chief innovation officers must then work collaboratively with the firm's chief strategy officer to coordinate the new products with the firm's strategic approach and to implement them. In this sense, those responsible for identifying opportunities the firm might want to pursue and those responsible for selecting and implementing the strategies the company would use to pursue those opportunities share responsibility for verifying that the firm is taking entrepreneurial actions using a strategic perspective. These individuals also help the firm determine the innovations necessary to pursue an opportunity, and if those innovations should be developed internally, through a cooperative strategy, or by completing an acquisition. In the final analysis, the objective of these top-level managers is to help firms identify opportunities and then develop successful incremental and breakthrough innovations and strategies to exploit them.

Firms must carefully analyze their portfolio of innovations and decide which existing products or technologies it should exploit with incremental innovations to improve them and when they need to develop more novel products or technologies. As noted, Boeing invested heavily to develop a new aircraft with breakthrough technologies in the 787 Dreamliner. Now, it is trying to exploit those innovations with incremental innovations. Yet, it must be careful because the emphasis on the innovative technologies can become path-dependent, making it difficult to then break away from them to develop a novel innovation when needed.[130] Interestingly, Honda has recently broken from its conservative innovative tradition to deliver a new personal jet called the HondaJet. It is a seven-passenger jet that is priced at about $4.5 million. In addition to autos, Honda also makes robots, boats, and lawn mowers. With this new product, it enters a new industry. Michimasa Fujino, the CEO of Honda Aircraft Co, suggests that Honda is looking to the future and providing for its longevity.[131]

The Asahi Shimbun/Getty Images

Honda's new focus on the innovative frontier produced its new personal jet, the HondaJet. It carries seven passengers and is priced at $4.5 million.

Many analysts believe that innovation is required to be competitive in global markets over time. Earlier, we listed the top ten countries for entrepreneurial activity. The United States was ranked third, but it was among mostly emerging-economy countries trying to encourage more entrepreneurial activities. The list of the top countries that invest in and produce the most innovation is different, primarily established countries. And the United States is number six in this ranking. The top ten innovative countries are: South Korea, Japan, Germany, Finland, Israel, United States, Sweden, Singapore, France, and United Kingdom.[132] Thus, the competition is significant, requiring even well-known and respected firms such as American Express to be innovative if they wish to compete effectively and survive over time. They must practice strategic entrepreneurship.

SUMMARY

- Strategic entrepreneurship involves taking entrepreneurial actions using a strategic perspective. Firms using strategic entrepreneurship simultaneously engage in opportunity-seeking and advantage-seeking behaviors. The purpose is to continuously find new opportunities and quickly develop innovations and exploit them.

- Entrepreneurship is a process used by individuals, teams, and organizations to identify entrepreneurial opportunities without being immediately constrained by the resources they control. Corporate entrepreneurship is the application of entrepreneurship (including the identification of entrepreneurial opportunities) within ongoing, established organizations. Entrepreneurial opportunities are conditions in which new goods or services can satisfy a need in the market. Entrepreneurship positively contributes to individual firms' performance and stimulates growth in countries' economies.

- Firms engage in three types of innovative activities:

  - invention, which is the act of creating a new good or process

  - innovation, or the process of creating a commercial product from an invention

  - imitation, which is the adoption of similar innovations by different firms.

  Invention brings something new into being while innovation brings something new into use.

- Entrepreneurs see or envision entrepreneurial opportunities and then take actions to develop innovations and exploit them. The most successful entrepreneurs (whether they are establishing their own venture or are working in an established organization) have an entrepreneurial mind-set, which is an orientation that values the potential opportunities available because of marketplace uncertainties.

- International entrepreneurship, or the process of identifying and exploiting entrepreneurial opportunities outside the firm's domestic markets, is important to firms around the globe.

Evidence suggests that firms capable of effectively engaging in international entrepreneurship generally outperform those competing only in their domestic markets.

- Three basic approaches are used to produce innovation:

  - internal innovation, which involves R&D and forming internal corporate ventures

  - cooperative strategies such as strategic alliances

  - acquisitions

Autonomous strategic behavior and induced strategic behavior are the two forms of internal corporate venturing. Autonomous strategic behavior is a bottom-up process through which a product champion facilitates the commercialization of an innovation. Induced strategic behavior is a top-down process in which a firm's current strategy and structure facilitate the development and implementation of product or process innovations. Thus, induced strategic behavior is driven by the organization's current corporate strategy and structure, while autonomous strategic behavior can result in a change to the firm's current strategy and structure arrangements.

- Firms create two types of innovations—incremental and novel—through internal innovation that takes place in the form of autonomous strategic behavior or induced strategic behavior. Overall, firms produce more incremental innovations, but novel innovations have a higher probability of significantly increasing sales revenue and profits. Cross-functional integration is often vital to a firm's efforts to develop and implement internal corporate venturing activities and to commercialize the resulting innovation. Cross-functional teams now commonly include representatives from external organizations, such as suppliers. Additionally, integration and innovation can be facilitated by developing shared values and effectively using strategic leadership.

- To gain access to the specialized knowledge required to innovate in the global economy, firms may form a cooperative relationship, such as a strategic alliance with other companies, some of which may be competitors.

■ Acquisitions are another means firms use to obtain innovation. Innovation can be acquired through direct acquisition, or firms can learn new capabilities from an acquisition, thereby enriching their internal innovation abilities.

■ The practice of strategic entrepreneurship by all types of firms, large and small, new and more established, creates value for all stakeholders, especially for shareholders and customers. Strategic entrepreneurship also contributes to the economic development of countries.

KEY TERMS

corporate entrepreneurship 419
entrepreneurship 419
entrepreneurial opportunities 419
entrepreneurs 420
entrepreneurial mind-set 421

invention 420
innovation 420
imitation 420
international entrepreneurship 421
strategic entrepreneurship 418

REVIEW QUESTIONS

1. What is strategic entrepreneurship? What is corporate entrepreneurship?

2. What is entrepreneurship, and what are entrepreneurial opportunities? Why are they important aspects of the strategic management process?

3. What are invention, innovation, and imitation? How are these concepts interrelated?

4. What is an entrepreneur, and what is an entrepreneurial mind-set?

5. What is international entrepreneurship? Why is it important?

6. How do firms develop innovations internally?

7. How do firms use cooperative strategies to innovate and to have access to innovative capabilities?

8. How does a firm acquire other companies to increase the number of innovations it produces and improve its capability to innovate?

9. How does strategic entrepreneurship help firms create value?

Mini-Case

An Innovation Failure at JCPenney: Its Causes and Consequences

Former CEO Ron Johnson designed and tried to implement a new strategy for JCPenney (JCP). However, the firm's target "middle market" customers did not respond well to the new strategy and the innovations associated with it. In fact, some say that Johnson's innovations and strategy alienated what had historically been the firm's target customers.

Johnson came to JCP after successful stints at Target and Apple. At Apple, he was admired for the major role he played in developing that firm's wildly successful Apple Stores, which a number of analysts say brought about "a new world order in retailing." It was Johnson's ability to establish what some viewed as path-breaking visions and to develop innovations to reach them that appealed to JCP's board when he was hired.

Comparing JCP to the Titanic, Johnson came to the CEO position believing that innovation was the key to

shaking up the firm. Moreover, he reminded analysts, employees, and others that he came to JCP to "transform" the firm, not to marginally improve its performance. Describing what he intended to do at JCP, Johnson said that "in the U.S., the department store has a chance to regain its status as the leader in style, the leader in excitement. It will be a period of true innovation for this company."

The essence of Johnson's vision for JCP was twofold. First, he eliminated the firm's practice of marking up prices on goods and then offering discounts, heavy promotions, and coupons to entice its bargain-hunting target customers. Instead, Johnson introduced a three-tiered pricing structure that focused on what were labelled "everyday low prices." To customers though, the pricing structure was confusing and failed to convince them that the "everyday low prices" were actually "low enough" compared to competitors' prices.

Innovation was at the core of the second part of the new CEO's vision, with one objective being to give JCP a more youthful image. The innovations Johnson implemented to create this image included establishing branded boutiques within JCP stores. To do this, JCP set up branded boutiques "along a wide aisle, or 'street' dotted with places to sit, grab a cup of coffee, or play with Lego blocks." With an initial intention of having 100 branded shops within JCP stores by 2015, Johnson asked people "to envision an entire store of shops with a street and square in the middle representing a new way to interface with the customer." Disney was one of the brands to be included as a shopping destination, as were Caribou Coffee, Dallas-based Paciugo Gelato & Café, and Giggle, a store dedicated to making "it a whole lot easier to become a parent" by offering innovative and stylish "must-have baby items." In addition, and as noted in Chapter 4's Opening Case, Levi's, IZOD, Liz Claiborne, and Martha Stewart branded items were to be included as part of the boutiques.

But, these innovations and the strategy used to exploit them did not work. So what went wrong? Considering the components of the model shown in Figure 13.2 yields a framework to answer this question. While it is true that Johnson had an entrepreneurial mind-set, cross-functional teams were not used to facilitate implementation of the desired innovations such as the boutique stores. In essence, it seems that Johnson himself, without the involvement of others throughout the firm, was instrumental in deciding that the boutiques were to be used as well as how they were to be established and operated within selected JCP stores. In addition, the values associated with efforts to change JCP from its historic roots of being a general merchant in the space between department stores and discounters to becoming a firm with a young, hip image were not shared among the firm's stakeholders. Finally, Johnson's work as an entrepreneurial leader was, seemingly, not as effective as should have been the case. Because of mistakes such as these, the level of success desired at JCP through internally developed innovations was not attained.

Sources: 2013, J.C. Penney ousts CEO Ron Johnson, *Wall Street Journal*, www.wsj.com, April 8; D. Benoit, 2013, J.C. Penney asks customers for second chance, *Wall Street Journal*, www.wsj.com, May 1; D. Benoit, 2013, Ackman thought Johnson could turn around 'Titanic' JCPenney, *Wall Street Journal*, www.wsj.com, April 8; S. Gerfield, 2013, J.C. Penney rehires Myron Ullman to clean up Ron Johnson's mess, *Bloomberg Businessweek*, www.businessweek.com, April 11; S. Clifford, 2013, J.C. Penney's new plan is to reuse its old plans, *New York Times*, www.nytimes.com, May 16; S. Denning, 2013, J.C. Penney: Was Ron Johnson's strategy wrong? *Forbes*, www.forbes.com, April 9; M. Halkias, 2012, J.C. Penney's Ron Johnson shows off his vision of future to 300 analysts, *Dallas News*, www.dallasnews.com, September 19.

Case Discussion Questions

1. The new CEO tried to be innovative. Were the innovations introduced, more incremental or more novel? Please explain.

2. Do the innovations implemented by JCP sound interesting to you? Would you shop at a store with these features? Why or why not?

3. What are the reasons that the innovations implemented by the new CEO failed?

4. What recommendations do you have for turning around the performance of JCP?

NOTES

1. B. Fritz, 2015, Disney unveils details on 'Star Wars: VIII' and 'Frozen' Sequel, *Wall Street Journal*, www.wsj.com, March 12; M. Lev-Ram, 2015, Empire of Tech, *Fortune*, January 1, 48–56.

2. B. Yu, S. Hao, D. Ahlstrom, S. Si, & D Liang, 2014, Entrepreneurial firms' network competence, technological capability, and new product development performance, *Asia Pacific Journal of Management*, 31: 687–704; A. Lipparini, G. Lorenzoni, & S. Ferriani, 2014, From core to periphery and back: A study on the deliberate shaping of knowledge flows in interfirm dyads and networks, *Strategic Management Journal*, 35: 578–595.

3. L. Dai, V. Maksimov, B. A. Gilbert, & S. A. Fernhaber, 2014, Entrepreneurial orientation, and international scope: The differential roles of innovativeness, proactiveness and risk taking, *Journal of Business Venturing*, 29: 511–524; P. C. Patel, S. A. Fernhaber, P. P. McDougall-Covin, & R. P. van der Have, 2014, Beating competitors to international markets: The value of geographically balanced networks for innovation, *Strategic Management Journal*, 35: 691–711.

4. M. Gruber, S. M. Kim, & J. Brinckmann, 2015, What is an attractive business opportunity? An empirical study of opportunity evaluation decisions of technologists, managers and entrepreneurs, *Strategic Entrepreneurship Journal*, in press.

5. M. Wright, B. Clarysse, & S. Mosey, 2012, Strategic entrepreneurship, resource orchestration and growing spin-offs from universities, *Technology Analysis & Strategic Management*, 24: 911–927.

6. T. Felin, S. Kauffman, R. Koppl, & G. Longo, 2014, Economic opportunity and evolution: Beyond landscapes and bounded rationality, *Strategic Entrepreneurship Journal*, 8: 269–282; M. A. Hitt, R. D. Ireland, D. G. Sirmon, & C. A. Trahms, 2011, Strategic entrepreneurship: Creating value for individuals, organizations, and society. *Academy of Management Perspectives*, 25: 57–75.

7. H. Yang, Y. Zheng, & X. Zhao, 2014, Exploration or exploitation? Small firms' alliance strategies with large firms, *Strategic Management Journal*, 35: 146–157; J. Q. Barden, 2012, The influences of being acquired on subsidiary innovation adoption, *Strategic Management Journal*, 33: 1269–1285.

8. D. Kuratko, 2015, Corporate entrepreneurship: Accelerating creativity and innovation in organizations, in C. Shalley, M. A. Hitt, & J. Zhou (eds.), *The Oxford Handbook of Creativity, Innovation and Entrepreneurship*, NY: Oxford University Press, 477–488; D. F. Kuratko & D. B. Audretsch, 2013, Clarifying the domains of corporate entrepreneurship, *International Entrepreneurship and Management Journal*, 9: 323–335; K. Shimizu, 2012, Risks of corporate entrepreneurship: Autonomy and agency issues, *Organization Science*, 23: 194–206.

9. S. L. Sun, X. Yang, & W. Li, 2014, Variance-enhancing corporate entrepreneurship under deregulation: an option portfolio approach, *Asia Pacific Journal of Management*, 31: 733–761; D. Urbano & A. Turro, 2013, Conditioning factors for corporate entrepreneurship: An in(ex)ternal approach, *International Entrepreneurship and Management Journal*, 9: 379–396.

10. V. Hinz & S. Ingerfurth, 2013, Does ownership matter under challenging conditions? *Public Management Review*, 15: 969–991.

11. M. Keyhani, M. Levesque, & A. Madhok, 2015, Toward a theory of entrepreneurial rents: A simulation of the market process, *Strategic Management Journal*, 36: 76–96; P. M. Moroz & K. Hindle, 2012, Entrepreneurship as a process: Toward harmonizing multiple perspectives, *Entrepreneurship Theory and Practice*, 36: 781–818.

12. J. T. Perry, G. N. Chandler, & G. Markova, 2012, Entrepreneurial effectuation: A review and suggestions for future research, *Entrepreneurship Theory and Practice*, 36: 837–861; S. A. Alvarez & J. B. Barney, 2008, Opportunities, organizations and entrepreneurship, *Strategic Entrepreneurship Journal*, 2: 265–267.

13. N. J. Foss, J. Lyngsie, & S. A. Zahra, 2013, The role of external knowledge sources and organizational design in the process of opportunity exploitation, *Strategic Management Journal*, 34: 1453–1471; P. G. Klein, 2008, Opportunity discovery, entrepreneurial action and economic

organization, *Strategic Entrepreneurship Journal*, 2: 175–190.

14. D. A. Shepherd, T. A. Williams, & H. Patselt, 2015, Thinking about entrepreneurial decision making: Review and research agenda, *Journal of Management*, 41: 11–46; J. Tang, K. M. Kacmar, & L. Busenitz, 2012, Entrepreneurial alertness in the pursuit of new opportunities, *Journal of Business Venturing*, 27: 77–94; S. A. Zahra, 2008, The virtuous cycle of discovery and creation of entrepreneurial opportunities, *Strategic Entrepreneurship Journal*, 2: 243–257.

15. J. Schumpeter, 1934, *The Theory of Economic Development*, Cambridge, MA: Harvard University Press.

16. E. E. Powell & T. Baker, 2014, It's what you make of it: Founder identity and enacting strategic responses to adversity, *Academy of Management Journal*, 57: 1406–1433; C. A. Siren, M. Kohtamaki, & A. Kuckertz, 2012, Exploration and exploitation strategies, profit performance, and the mediating role of strategic learning: Escaping the exploitation trap, *Strategic Entrepreneurship Journal*, 6: 18–41; J. H. Dyer, H. B. Gregersen, & C. Christensen, 2008, Entrepreneur behaviors and the origins of innovative ventures, *Strategic Entrepreneurship Journal*, 2: 317–338.

17. C. Bjornskov & N. Foss, 2013, How strategic entrepreneurship and the institutional context drive economic growth, *Strategic Entrepreneurship Journal*, 7: 50–69; W. J. Baumol, R. E. Litan, & C. J. Schramm, 2007, *Good Capitalism, Bad Capitalism, and the Economics of Growth and Prosperity*, New Haven, CT: Yale University Press.

18. Schumpeter, *The Theory of Economic Development*.

19. L. Aarikka-Stenroos & B. Sandberg, 2012, From new-product development to commercialization through networks, *Journal of Business Research*, 65: 198–206.

20. M. I. Leone & T. Reichstein, 2012, Licensing-in fosters rapid invention! The effect of the grant-back clause and technological unfamiliarity, *Strategic Management Journal*, 33: 965–985; R. A. Burgelman & L. R. Sayles, 1986, *Inside Corporate Innovation: Strategy, Structure, and Managerial Skills*, NY: Free Press.

21. K. R. Fabrizio & L. G. Thomas, 2012, The impact of local demand on innovation in a global industry, *Strategic Management Journal*, 33: 42–64; M. W. Johnson, 2011, Making innovation matter. *Bloomberg Businessweek*, www.businessweek.com, March 3.

22. R. Aalbers & W. Dolfsma, 2014, Innovation despite reorganization, *Journal of Business Strategy*, 35(3): 18–25; S. F. Latham & M. Braun, 2009, Managerial risk, innovation and organizational decline, *Journal of Management*, 35: 258–281.

23. L. Marengo, C. Pasquali, M. Valente, & G. Dosi, 2012, Appropriability, patents, and rates of innovation in complex products industries, *Economics of Innovation and*

New Technology, 21: 753–773; S. Moon, 2011, How does the management of research impact the disclosure of knowledge? Evidence from scientific publications and patenting behavior, *Economics of Innovation & New Technology*, 20: 1–32.

24. M. Ridley, 2013, A welcome turn away from patents, *Wall Street Journal*, www.wsj.com, June 21.

25. P. F. Drucker, 1998, The discipline of innovation, *Harvard Business Review*, 76(6): 149–157.

26. Ibid.

27. C. B. Dobni, M. Klassen, & T. Nelson, 2015, Innovation strategy in the U.S.: Top executives share their views, *Journal of Business Strategy*, 36(1): 3–13; B. R. Bhardwaj, Sushil, & K. Momaya, 2011, Drivers and enablers of corporate entrepreneurship: Case of a software giant from India, *Journal of Management Development*, 30: 187–205.

28. J. Brinckmann & S. M. Kim, 2015, Why we plan: The impact of nascent entrepreneurs' cognitive characteristics and human capital on business planning, *Strategic Entrepreneurship Journal*, in press; Y. Yanadori & V. Cui, 2013, Creating incentives for innovation? The relationship between pay dispersion in R&D groups and firm innovation performance, *Strategic Management Journal*, 34: 1502–1511.

29. C. Shalley, M. A. Hitt, & J. Zhou, 2015, Introduction: Integrating creativity, innovation, and entrepreneurship to enhance the organizations capability to navigate in the new competitive landscape, in C. Shalley, M. A. Hitt, & J. Zhou (eds.), *The Oxford Handbook of Creativity, innovation and Entrepreneurship*, NY: Oxford University Press, 1–14; J. Lampel, P. P. Jha, & A. Bhalla, 2012, Test-driving the future: How design competitions are changing innovation, *Academy of Management Perspectives*, 26: 71–85.

30. J. Raffiee & J. Feng, 2014, Should I quit my day job?: A hybrid path to entrepreneurship, *Academy of Management Journal*, 57: 936–963; D. Ucbasaran, P. Westhead, M. Wright, & M. Flores, 2010, The nature of entrepreneurial experience, business failure and comparative optimism, *Journal of Business Venturing*, 25: 541–555; K. M. Hmielski & R. A. Baron, 2009, Entrepreneurs' optimism and new venture performance: A social cognitive perspective, *Academy of Management Journal*, 52: 473–488.

31. Y. Yamakawa, M. W. Peng, & D. L. Deeds, 2015, Rising from the ashes: Cognitive determinants of venture growth after entrepreneurial failure, *Entrepreneurship Theory and Practice*, 39: 209–236; M.-D. Foo, 2011, Emotions and entrepreneurial opportunity evaluation, *Entrepreneurship: Theory & Practice*, 35: 375–393; M. S. Cardon, J. Wincent, J. Singh, & M. Drovsek, 2009, The nature and experience of entrepreneurial passion, *Academy of Management Review*, 34: 511–532.

32. C. Schlaegel & M. Koenig, 2014, Determinants of entrepreneurial intent: A meta-analytic test and integration of competing models, *Entrepreneurship Theory and Practice*, 38: 291–332; M. McCaffrey, 2014, On the theory of entrepreneurial incentives and alertness, *Entrepreneurship Theory and Practice*, 38: 891–911; M. S. Wood, A. McKelvie, & J. M. Haynie, 2014, Making it personal: Opportunity individuation and the shaping of opportunity beliefs, *Journal of Business Venturing*, 29: 252–272.

33. Y. Bammens & V. Collewaert, 2014, Trust between entrepreneurs and angel investors: Exploring the positive and negative implications for venture performance assessments, *Journal of Management*, 40: 1980–2008; S. W. Smith & S. K. Shah, 2013, Do innovative users generate more useful insights? An analysis of corporate venture capital investments in the medical device industry, *Strategic Entrepreneurship Journal*, 7: 151–167; W. Stam, S. Arzlanian, & T. Elfring, 2014, Social capital of entrepreneurs and small firm performance: A meta-analysis of contextual and methodological moderators, *Journal of Business Venturing*, 29: 152–173.

34. T. Prive, 2013, Top 32 quotes every entrepreneur should live by, *Forbes*, www.forbes.com, May 2.

35. J. G. Covin & D. Miller, 2014, International entrepreneurial orientation: Conceptual considerations, research themes, measurement issues, and future research directions, *Entrepreneurship Theory and Practice*, 38: 11–44.

36. J. York, S. Sarasvathy, & A. Wicks, 2013, An entrepreneurial perspective on value creation in public-private ventures, *Academy of Management Review*, 28: 307–309; A. Chwolka & M. G. Raith, 2012, The value of business planning before start-up—A decision-theoretical perspective, *Journal of Business Venturing*, 27: 385–399.

37. W. Drechsler & M. Natter, 2012, Understanding a firm's openness decisions in innovation, *Journal of Business Research*, 65: 438–445; W. Tsai, 2001, Knowledge transfer in intraorganizational networks: Effects of network position and absorptive capacity on business unit innovation and performance, *Academy of Management Journal*, 44: 996–1004.

38. S. Artinger & T. C. Powell, 2015, Entrepreneurial failure: Statistical and psychological explanations, *Strategic Management Journal*, in press; M. Spraggon & V. Bodolica, 2012, A multidimensional taxonomy of intra-firm knowledge transfer processes, *Journal of Business Research*, 65: 1273–1282; S. A. Zahra & G. George, 2002, Absorptive capacity: A review, reconceptualization, and extension, *Academy of Management Review*, 27:185–203.

39. G. Cassar, 2014, Industry and startup experience on entrepreneur forecast performance in new firms, *Journal of Business Venturing*, 29: 137–151.

40. 2015, The world's 50 most innovative companies, *Fast Company*, March, 67–134.

41. M. Chafkin, 2015, #1—Warby Parker, *Fast Company*, March, 68–71.

42. S. Terjesen, J. Hessels, & D. Li, 2015, Comparative international entrepreneurship: A review and research agenda, *Journal of Management*, in press; P. McDougall-Covin, M. V. Jones, & M. G. Serapio, 2014, High-potential concepts, phenomena, and theories for the advancement of international entrepreneurship research, *Entrepreneurship Theory and Practice*, 38: 1–10.

43. A. Al-Aali & D. J. Teece, 2014, International entrepreneurship and the theory of the (long-lived) international firm: A capabilities perspective, *Entrepreneurship Theory and Practice*, 38: 95–116; A. N. Kiss, W. M. Davis, & S. T. Cavusgil, 2012, International entrepreneurship research in emerging economies: A critical review and research agenda, *Journal of Business Venturing*, 27: 266–290.

44. H. Berry, 2014, Global integration and innovation: Multicountry knowledge generation within MNCs, *Strategic Management Journal*, 35: 869–890.

45. L. Sleuwaegen & J. Onkelinx, 2014, International commitment, post-entry growth and survival of international new ventures, *Journal of Business Venturing*, 29: 106–120; P. Almodovar & A. M. Rugman, 2014, The M curve and the performance of Spanish international new ventures, *British Journal of Management*, 25: S6–S23.

46. K. D. Brouthers, G. Nakos, & P. Dimitratos, 2015, SME entrepreneurial orientation, international performance and the moderating role of strategic alliances, *Entrepreneurship Theory and Practice*, in press; T. A. Khoury, A. Cuervo-Cazurra, & L. A. Dau, 2014, Institutional outsiders and insiders: The response of foreign and domestic inventors to the quality of intellectual property rights protection, *Global Strategy Journal*, 4: 200–220; P. Stenholm, Z. J. Acs, & R. Wuebker, 2013, Exploring country-level institutional arrangements on the rate and type of entrepreneurial activity, *Journal of Business Venturing*, 28: 176–193.

47. 2014, New report ranks world's most entrepreneurial countries, Oracle Capital Group, orcap.co.uk, June 23.

48. W. Q. Judge, Y. Liu-Thompkins, J. L. Brown, & C. Pongpatipat, 2015, The impact of home country institutions on corporate technological entrepreneurship via R&D investments and virtual world presence, *Entrepreneurship Theory and Practice*, 39: 237–266; E. Autio, S. Pathak, & K. Wennberg, 2013, Consequences of cultural practices for entrepreneurial behaviors, *Journal of International Business Studies*, 44: 334–362; U. Stephan & L. M. Uhlaner, 2010, Performance-based vs. socially supportive culture: A cross-cultural study of descriptive norms and entrepreneurship, *Journal of International Business Studies*, 41: 1347–1364.

49. J.-F. Hennart, 2014, The accidental internationalists: A theory of born globals, *Entrepreneurship Theory and Practice*, 38: 117–135; T. K. Madsen, 2013, Early and rapidly internationalizing ventures: Similarities and differences between classifications based on the original international new venture and born global literatures, *Journal of International Entrepreneurship*, 11: 65–79.

50. S. T. Cavusgil & G. Knight, 2015, The born global firm: An entrepreneurial and capabilities perspective on early and rapid internationalization, *Journal of International Business Studies*, 46: 3–16; S. A. Fernhaber & D. Li, 2013, International exposure through network relationships: Implications for new venture internationalization, *Journal of Business Venturing*, 28: 316–334; S. A. Zahra, R. D. Ireland, & M. A. Hitt, 2000, International expansion by new venture firms: International diversity, mode of market entry, technological learning and performance, *Academy of Management Journal*, 43: 925–950.

51. M. Musteen, D. K. Datta, & M. M. Butts, 2014, Do international networks and foreign market knowledge facilitate SME internationalization? Evidence from the Czech Republic, *Entrepreneurship Theory and Practice*, 38: 749–774; G. Nakos, K. D. Brouthers, & P. Dimitratos, 2014, International alliances with competitors and non-competitors: The disparate impact on SME international performance, *Strategic Entrepreneurship Journal*, 8: 167–182.

52. D. J. McCarthy, S. M. Puffer, & S. V. Darda, 2010, Convergence in entrepreneurial leadership style: Evidence from Russia, *California Management Review*, 52(4): 48–72; H. U. Lee & J. H. Park, 2008, The influence of top management team international exposure on international alliance formation, *Journal of Management Studies*, 45: 961–981; H. G. Barkema & O. Chvyrkov, 2007, Does top management team diversity promote or hamper foreign expansion? *Strategic Management Journal*, 28: 663–680.

53. R. Belderbos, B. Lokshin, & B. Sadowski, 2015, The returns to foreign R&D, *Journal of International Business Studies*, 46: 491–504; S. Awate, M. M. Larsen, & R. Mudambi, 2015, Accessing vs sourcing knowledge: A comparative study of R&D internationalization between emerging and advanced economy firms, *Journal of International Business Studies*, 46: 63–86.

54. K. Grigoriou & F. T. Rothaermel, 2014, Structural microfoundations of innovation: The role of relational stars, *Journal of Management*, 40: 586–615; A. Teixeira & N. Fortuna, 2010, Human capital, R&D, trade, and long-run productivity: Testing

the technological absorption hypothesis for the Portuguese economy, 1960–2001, *Research Policy*, 39: 335–350.

55. R. J. Genry & W. Shen, 2013, The impacts of performance relative to analyst forecasts and analyst coverage on firm R&D intensity, *Strategic Management Journal*, 34: 121–130; L. A. Bettencourt & S. L. Bettencourt, 2011, Innovating on the cheap, *Harvard Business Review*, 89(6): 88–94.

56. A. K. Chatterji & K. R. Fabrizio, 2014, Using users: When does external knowledge enhance corporate product innovation? *Strategic Management Journal*, 35: 1427–1445.

57. R. Funk, 2014, Making the most of where you are: Geography, networks, and innovation in organizations, *Academy of Management Journal*, 57: 193–222; M. Sytch & A. Tatarynowicz, 2014, Exploring the locus of innovation: The dynamics of network communities and firms' invention productivity, *Academy of Management Journal*, 57: 249–279.

58. E. Operti & G. Carnabuci, 2014, Public knowledge, private gain: The effect of spillover networks on firms' innovation performance, *Journal of Management*, 40: 1042–1074.

59. J. Morgan, 2015, Five examples of companies with internal innovation programs, *Huffington Post*, www.huffingtonpost.com, April 9.

60. R. Mudambi & T. Swift, 2014, Knowing when to leap: Transitioning between exploitative and explorative R&D, *Strategic Management Journal*, 35: 126–145; P. Ritala & P. Hurmelinna-Laukkanen, 2013, Incremental and radical innovation in coopetition—The role of absorptive capacity and appropriability, *Journal of Product Innovation Management*, 30: 154–169; C. B. Bingham & J. P. Davis, 2012, Learning sequences: Their existence, effect, and evolution, *Academy of Management Journal*, 55: 611–641.

61. S. Roy & K. Sivakumar, 2012, Global outsourcing relationships and innovation: A conceptual framework and research propositions, *Journal of Product and Innovation Management*, 29: 513–530.

62. S. W. Smith, 2014, Follow me to the innovation frontier? Leaders, laggards and the differential effects of imports and exports on technological innovation, *Journal of International Business Studies*, 45: 248–274.

63. D. McKendrick & J. Wade, 2010, Frequent incremental change, organizational size, and mortality in high-technology competition, *Industrial and Corporate Change*, 19: 613–639.

64. N. Argyres, L. Bigelow, & J. A. Nickerson, 2015, Dominant designs, innovation shocks and the follower's dilemma, *Strategic Management Journal*, 36: 216–234.

65. B. R. Fitzgerald, 2015, Google taking its self-driving cars to the open road, *Wall Street Journal*, *www.wsj.com*, May 15.

66. T. Magnusson & C. Berggren, 2011, Entering an era of ferment—radical vs incrementalist strategies in automotive power train development, *Technology Analysis & Strategic Management*, 23: 313–330; 2005, Getting an edge on innovation, *BusinessWeek*, March 21, 124.

67. R. Roy & M. B. Sarkar, 2015, Knowledge, firm boundaries, and innovation: Mitigating the incumbent's curse during radical technological change, *Strategic Management Journal*, in press; B. Buisson & P. Silberzahn, 2010, Blue Ocean or fast-second innovation? A four-breakthrough model to explain successful market domination, *International Journal of Innovation Management*, 14: 359–378.

68. R. K. Mitchell, J. B. Smith, J. A. Stamp, & J. Carlson, 2015, Organizing creativity: Lessons from the *Eureka! Ranch* experience, in C. Shalley, M. A. Hitt, & J. Zhou (eds.), *The Oxford Handbook of Creativity, Innovation and Entrepreneurship*, NY: Oxford University Press, 301–337; Z. Lindgardt & B. Shaffer, 2012, Business model innovation in social-sector organizations, *bcg.perspectives*, bcgperspectives.com, November 7.

69. 2013, The power of imagination, *Wall Street Journal*, www.wsj.com, February 25.

70. S. Harvey, 2014, Creative synthesis: Exploring the process of extraordinary group creativity, *Academy of Management Review*, 39: 324–343; D. Lavie & I. Drori, 2012, Collaborating for knowledge creation and application: The case of nanotechnology research programs, *Organization Science*, 23: 704–724.

71. A. K. Chatterji & K. Fabrizio, 2012, How do product users influence corporate invention? *Organization Science*, 23: 971–987.

72. Kuratko, Corporate entrepreneurship; N. R. Furr, F. Cavarretta, & S. Garg, 2012, Who changes course? The role of domain knowledge and novel framing in making technology changes, *Strategic Entrepreneurship Journal*, 6: 236–256; J. M. Oldroyd & R. Gulati, 2010, A learning perspective on intraorganizational knowledge spill-ins, *Strategic Entrepreneurship Journal*, 4: 356–372.

73. M. L. Sosa, 2013, Decoupling market incumbency from organizational prehistory: Locating the real sources of competitive advantage in R&D for radical innovation, *Strategic Management Journal*, 34: 245–255; S. A. Hill, M. V. J. Maula, J. M. Birkinshaw, & G. C. Murray, 2009, Transferability of the venture capital model to the corporate context: Implications for the performance of corporate venture units, *Strategic Entrepreneurship Journal*, 3: 3–27.

74. J. Brady, 2013, Some companies foster creativity, others fake it, *Wall Street Journal*, www.wsj.com, May 21.

75. B. Wu, Z. Wan, & D. A. Levinthal, 2014, Complementary assets as pipes and prisms: Innovation incentives and

trajectory choices, *Strategic Management Journal*, 35: 1257–1278; A. Sahaym, H. K. Steensma, & J. Q. Barden, 2010, The influence of R&D investment on the use of corporate venture capital: An industry-level analysis, *Journal of Business Venturing*, 25: 376–388; R. A. Burgelman, 1995, *Strategic Management of Technology and Innovation*, Boston, MA: Irwin.

76. D. Kandemir & N. Acur, 2012, Examining proactive strategic decision-making flexibility in new product development, *Journal of Product Innovation Management*, 29: 608–622.

77. K. B. Kahn, G. Barczak, J. Nicholas, A. Ledwith, & H. Perks, 2012, An examination of new product development best practice, *Journal of Product Innovation Management*, 29: 180–192.

78. S. S. Durmusoglu, 2013, Merits of task advice during new product development: Network centrality antecedents and new product outcomes of knowledge richness and knowledge quality, *Journal of Product Innovation Management*, 30: 487–499; D. Kelley & H. Lee, 2010, Managing innovation champions: The impact of project characteristics on the direct manager role, *Journal of Product Innovation Management*, 27: 1007–1019.

79. N. Kim, S. Im, & S. F. Slater, 2013, Impact of knowledge type and strategic orientation on new product creativity and advantage in high-technology firms, *Journal of Product Innovation Management*, 30: 136–153; U. de Brentani & S. E. Reid, 2012, The fuzzy front-end of discontinuous innovation: Insights for research and management, *Journal of Product Innovation Management*, 29: 70–87.

80. L. Mirabeau & S. Maguire, 2014, From autonomous strategic behavior to emergent strategy, *Strategic Management Journal*, 35: 1202–1229.

81. N. Anderson, K. Potocnik, & J. Zhou, 2014, Innovation and creativity in organizations: A state-of-the-science review, prospective commentary and guiding framework, *Journal of Management*, 40: 1297–1333; S. Im, M. M. Montoya, & J. P. Workman, Jr., 2013, Antecedents and consequences of creativity in product innovation teams, *Journal of Product Innovation Management*, 30: 170–185; S. Borjesson & M. Elmquist, 2012, Aiming at innovation: A case study of innovation capabilities in the Swedish defence industry, *International Journal of Business Innovation and Research*, 6: 188–201.

82. S. E. Ante, 2013, IBM's chief to employees: Think fast, move faster, *Wall Street Journal*, www.wsj.com, April 24.

83. A. Caldart, R. S. Vassolo, & L. Silvestri, 2014, Induced variation in administrative systems: Experimenting with contexts for innovation, *Management Research*, 12: 123–151.

84. S. B. Choi & C. Williams, 2014, The impact of innovation intensity, scope, and spillovers on sales growth in Chinese firms, *Asia Pacific Journal of Management*, 31: 25–46.

85. P. T. Gianidodis, J. E. Ettlie, & J. J. Urbana, 2014, Open service innovation in the global banking industry: Inside-out versus outside-in strategies, *Academy of Management Perspectives*, 28: 76–91.

86. A. Compagni, V. Mele, & D. Ravasi, 2015, How early implementations influence later adoptions of innovation: Social positioning and skill reproduction in the diffusion of robotic surgery, *Academy of Management Journal*, 58: 242–278; T. Vanacker, S. Manigart, & M. Meuleman, 2014, Path-dependent evolution versus intentional management of investment ties in science-based entrepreneurial firms, *Entrepreneurship Theory and Practice*, 38: 671–690.

87. J. Jia, G. Wang, X. Zhao, & X. Yu, 2014, Exploring the relationship between entrepreneurial orientation and corporate performance: The role of competency of executives in entrepreneurial-oriented corporations, *Nankai, Business Review*, 5: 326–344.

88. T. Kollmann & C. Stockmann, 2014, Filling the entrepreneurial orientation—performance gap: The mediating effects of exploratory and exploitative innovations, *Entrepreneurship Theory and Practice*, 38: 1001–1026.

89. P. Patanakul, J. Chen, & G. S. Lynn, 2012, Autonomous teams and new product development, *Journal of Product Innovation Management*, 29: 734–750.

90. S. Kuester, C. Homburg, & S. C. Hess, 2012, Externally directed and internally directed market launch management: The role of organizational factors in influencing new product success, *Journal of Product Innovation Management*, 29: 38–52.

91. G. Barcjak & K. B. Kah, 2012, Identifying new product development best practice, *Business Horizons*, 56: 291–305; C. Nakata & S. Im, 2010, Spurring cross-functional integration for higher new product performance: A group effectiveness perspective, *Journal of Product Innovation Management*, 27: 554–571.

92. J. P. Eggers, 2012, All experience is not created equal: Learning, adapting, and focusing in product portfolio management, *Strategic Management Journal*, 33: 315–335; R. Slotegraaf & K. Atuahene-Gima, 2011, Product development team stability and new product advantage: The role of decision-making processes, *Journal of Marketing*, 75: 96–108; R. Cowan & N. Jonard, 2009, Knowledge portfolios and the organization of innovation networks, *Academy of Management Review*, 34: 320–342.

93. P. R. Kehoe & D. Tzabbar, 2015, Lighting the way or stealing the shine? An examination of the duality in star scientists' effects on firm innovation performance, *Strategic Management Journal*, 36: 709–727.

94. M. Brettel, F. Heinemann, A. Engelen, & S. Neubauer, 2011, Cross-functional integration of R&D, marketing, and manufacturing in radical and incremental product innovations and its effects on project effectiveness and efficiency, *Journal of Product Innovation Management*, 28: 251–269.

95. D. De Clercq, N. Thongpapanl, & D. Dimov, 2013, Getting more from cross-functional fairness and product innovativeness: Contingency effects of internal resource and conflict management, *Journal of Product Innovation Management*, 30: 56–69; G. Gemser & M. M. Leenders, 2011, Managing cross-functional cooperation for new product development success, *Long Range Planning*, 44: 26–41.

96. F. Aime, S. Humphrey, D. DeRue, & J. Paul, 2014, The riddle of heterarchy: Power transitions in cross-functional teams, *Academy of Management Journal*, 57: 327–352

97. E. L. Anthony, S. G. Green, & S. A. McComb, 2014, Crossing functions above the cross-functional project team: The value of lateral coordination among functional department heads, *Journal of Engineering and Technology Management*, 31: 141–158; V. V. Baunsgaard & S. Clegg, 2013, 'Walls or boxes': The effects of professional identity, power and rationality on strategies for cross-functional integration, *Organization Studies*, 34: 1299–1325.

98. M. Baer, K. T. Dirks, & J. A. Nickerson, 2013, Microfoundations of strategic problem formulation, *Strategic Management Journal*, 34: 197–214; R. Oliva & N. Watson, 2011, Cross-functional alignment in supply chain planning: A case study of sales and operations planning, *Journal of Operations Management*, 29: 434–448; A. C. Amason, 1996, Distinguishing the effects of functional and dysfunctional conflict on strategic decision making: Resolving a paradox for top management teams, *Academy of Management Journal*, 39: 123–148.

99. T. A. De Vries, F. Walter, G. S. van der Vegt, & P. J. M. D. Essens, 2014, Antecedents of individuals' inter-team coordination: Broad functional experiences as a mixed blessing, *Academy of Management Journal*, 57: 1334–1359; H. K. Gardner, 2012, Performance pressure as a double-edged sword: Enhancing team motivation while undermining the use of team knowledge, *Administrative Science Quarterly*, 57: 1–46; D. Clercq, B. Menguc, & S. Auh, 2009, Unpacking the relationship between an innovation strategy and firm performance: The role of task conflict and political activity, *Journal of Business Research*, 62: 1046–1053;.

100. V. Gupta & S. Singh, 2015, Leadership and creative performance behaviors in R&D laboratories: Examining the mediating role of justice perceptions, *Journal of Leadership and Organizational Studies*, 22: 21–36; Y. Chung & S. E. Jackson, 2013, The internal and external networks of knowledge-intensive teams: The role of task routineness, *Journal of Management*, 39: 442–468; J. Daspit, C. J. Tillman, N. G. Boyd, & V. McKee, 2013, Cross-functional team effectiveness: An examination of internal team environment, shared leadership, and cohesion influences, *Team Performance Management*, 19: 34–56.

101. W. Sun, A. Su, & Y. Shang, 2014, Transformational leadership, team climate, and team performance within the NPD team: Evidence from China, *Asia Pacific Journal of Management*, 31: 127–147; H. K. Gardner, F. Gino, & B. R. Staats, 2012, Dynamically integrating knowledge in teams: Transforming resources into performance, *Academy of Management Journal*, 55: 998–1022.

102. Q. Li, P. Maggitti, K. Smith, P. Tesluk, & R. Katila, 2013, Top management attention to innovation: The role of search selection and intensity in new product introductions, *Academy of Management Journal*, 56: 893–916; N. Stieglitz & L. Heine, 2007, Innovations and the role of complementarities in a strategic theory of the firm, *Strategic Management Journal*, 28: 1–15.

103. V. Gaba & S. Bhattacharya, 2012, Aspirations, innovation, and corporate venture capital: A behavioral perspective, *Strategic Entrepreneurship Journal*, 6: 178–199; K. Wennberg, J. Wiklund, D. R. DeTienne, & M. S. Cardon, 2010, Reconceptualizing entrepreneurial exit: Divergent exit routes and their drivers, *Journal of Business Venturing*, 25: 361–375.

104. U. Stettner & D. Lavie, 2014, Ambidexterity under scrutiny: Exploration and exploitation via internal organization, alliances and acquisitions, *Strategic Management Journal*, 35:1903–1929; H. Milanov & S. A. Fernhaber, 2014, When do domestic alliances help ventures abroad? Direct and moderating effects from a learning experience, *Journal of Business Venturing*, 29: 377–391; S. Terjesen, P. C. Patel, & J. G. Covin, 2011, Alliance diversity, environmental context and the value of manufacturing capabilities among new high technology ventures, *Journal of Operations Management*, 29: 105–115.

105. H. Kim, N. K. Park, & J. Lee, 2014, How does the second-order learning process moderate the relationship between innovation inputs and outputs of large Korean firms? *Asia Pacific Journal of Management*, 31: 69–103; S. Zu, F. Wu, & E. Cavusgil, 2013, Complements or substitutes? Internal technological strength, competitors alliance participation, and innovation development, *Journal of Product Innovation Management*, 30: 750–762.

106. J. West & M. Bogers, 2014, Leveraging external sources of innovation: A review of research on open innovation, *Journal of Product Innovation Management*, 31: 814–831; D. Li, 2013, Multilateral R&D alliances by new ventures, *Journal of Business Venturing*,

28: 241–260; D. Li, L. Eden, M. A. Hitt, & R. D. Ireland, 2008, Friends, acquaintances, or strangers? Partner selection in R&D alliances, *Academy of Management Journal*, 51: 315–334.

107. C. Shu, C. Liu, S. Gao, & M. Shanley, 2014, The knowledge spillover theory of entrepreneurship in alliances, *Entrepreneurship Theory and Practice*, 38: 913–940; C. Beckman, K. Eisenhardt, S. Kotha, A. Meyer, & N. Rajagopalan, 2012, Technology entrepreneurship, *Strategic Entrepreneurship Journal*, 6: 89–93.

108. Yang, Zheng & Zhao, Exploration or exploitation?; G. Dushnitsky & D. Lavie, 2010, How alliance formation shapes corporate venture capital investment in the software industry: A resource-based perspective, *Strategic Entrepreneurship Journal*, 4: 22–48.

109. G. Oates, 2014, Marriott wants Moxy to deliver the millennial customer with help from Ikea, *Skift*, skift.com, February 3; A. Berzon & K. Hudson, 2013, IKEA's parent plans a hotel brand, *Wall Street Journal*, www.wsj.com, March 5.

110. H. Van Kranenburg, J. Hagedoorn, & S. Lorenz-Orlean, 2014, *Global Strategy Journal*, 4: 280–291; X. Jiang, M. Li, S. Gao, Y. Bao, & F. Jiang, 2013, Managing knowledge leakage in strategic alliances: The effects of trust and formal contracts, *Industrial Marketing Management*, 42: 983–991; A. Kaul, 2013, Entrepreneurial action, unique assets, and appropriation risk: Firms as a means of appropriating profit from capability creation, *Organization Science*, 24: 1765–1781.

111. J. Partanen, S. K. Chetty, & A. Rajala, 2014, Innovation types and network relationships, *Entrepreneurship Theory and Practice*, 38: 1027–1055; G. Cuevas-Rodriguez, C. Cabello-Medina, & A. Carmona-Lavado, 2014, Internal and external social capital for radical product innovation: Do they always work well together? *British Journal of Management*, 25: 266–284; M. A. Hitt, M. T. Dacin, E. Levitas, J. L. Arregle, & A. Borza, 2000, Partner selection in emerging and developed market contexts: Resource-based and organizational learning perspectives, *Academy of Management Journal*, 43: 449–467.

112. B. B. Tyler & T. Caner, 2015, New product introductions below aspirations, slack and R&D alliances: A behavioral perspective, *Strategic Management Journal*, in press; R. Vandaie & A. Zaheer, 2014, Surviving bear hugs: Firm capability, large partner alliances, and growth, *Strategic Management Journal*, 35: 566–577.

113. J. Sears & G. Hoetker, 2014, Technological overlap, technological capabilities and resource recombinations by technological acquisitions, *Strategic Management Journal*, 35: 48–67; A. Madhok & M. Keyhani, 2012, Acquisitions as entrepreneurship: Asymmetries, opportunities, and the internationalization of multinationals from emerging economies, *Global Strategy Journal*, 2: 26–40;

114. M. A. Hitt, D. King, H. Krishnan, M. Makri, M. Schijven, K. Shimizu, & H. Zhu, 2009, Mergers and acquisitions: Overcoming pitfalls, building synergy and creating value, *Business Horizons*, 52: 523–529; H. G. Barkema & M. Schijven, 2008, Toward unlocking the full potential of acquisitions: The role of organizational restructuring, *Academy of Management Journal*, 51: 696–722.

115. I. Mochari, 2014, Gaming DIY: How Minecraft became an innovation *powerhouse*, *Inc.*, www.inc.com, September 2.

116. C. Grimpe & K. Hussinger, 2014, Resource complementarity and value capture in firm acquisitions: The role of intellectual property rights, *Strategic Management Journal*, 35: 1762–1780; M. Humphrey-Jenner, 2014, Takeover defenses, innovation, and value creation: Evidence from acquisition decisions, *Strategic Management Journal*, 35: 668–690; M. Makri, M. A. Hitt, & P. J. Lane, 2010, Complementary technologies, knowledge relatedness, and invention outcomes in high technology M&As, *Strategic Management Journal*, 31: 602–628.

117. R. Lungeanu, I. Sgtern, & E. J. Zajac, 2015, When do firms change technology-sourcing vehicles? The role of poor innovative performance and financial slack, *Strategic Management Journal*, in press.

118. M. Wagner, 2013, Determinants of acquisition value: The role of target and acquirer characteristics, *International Journal of Technology Management*, 62: 56–74; M. E. Graebner, K. M. Eisenhardt, & P. T. Roundy, 2010, Success and failure in technology acquisitions: Lessons for buyers and sellers, *Academy of Management Perspectives*, 24: 73–92; M. A. Hitt, J. S. Harrison, & R. D. Ireland, 2001, *Mergers and Acquisitions: A Guide to Creating Value for Stakeholders*, NY: Oxford University Press.

119. A. Arora, S. Belenzon, & L. A. Rios, 2014, Make, buy, organize: The interplay between research, external knowledge and firm structure, *Strategic Management Journal*, 35: 317–337.

120. S. K. Majumdar, R. Moussawi, & U. Yaylacicegi, 2014, Do incumbents' mergers influence entrepreneurial entry? An evaluation, *Entrepreneurship Theory and Practice*, 38: 601–633.

121. R. Fini, R. Grimaldi, G. L. Marzocchi, & M. Sobrero, 2012, The determinants of corporate entrepreneurial intention within small and newly established firms, *Entrepreneurship Theory and Practice*, 36: 387–414; D. Elfenbein & B. Hamilton, 2010, The small firm effect and the entrepreneurial spawning of scientists and engineers, *Management Science*, 56: 659–681.

122. A. Hyytinen, M. Pajarinen, & P. Rouvinen, 2014, Does innovativeness reduce startup survival rates?, *Journal of Business Venturing*, 29: 564–581.

123. J. Ostrower, 2015, At Boeing, innovation means small steps, not giant leaps, *Wall Street Journal*, www.wsj.com, April 2.

124. B. Larraneta, S. A. Zahra, & J. L. G. Gonzalez, 2012, Enriching strategic variety in new ventures through external knowledge, *Journal of Business Venturing*, 27: 401–413; H. Greve, 2011, Positional rigidity: Low performance and resource acquisition in large and small firms, *Strategic Management Journal*, 32: 103–114.

125. L. Naldi & P. Davidsson, 2014, Entrepreneurial growth: The role of international knowledge acquisition as moderated by firm age, *Journal of Business Venturing*, 29: 687–703.

126. R, Klingbiel & C. Rammer, 2014, Resource allocation strategy for innovation portfolio management, *Strategic Management Journal*, 35: 246–268; G. Wu, 2012, The effect of going public on innovative productivity and exploratory search, *Organization Science*, 23: 928–950; D. G. Sirmon & M. A. Hitt, 2009, Contingencies within dynamic managerial capabilities: Interdependent effects of resource investment and deployment on firm performance, *Strategic Management Journal*, 30: 1375–1394.

127. R. B. Tucker, 2013, Are chief innovation officers delivering results? *Innovation Excellence*, www.innovationexcellence.com, March 22.

128. J. Behrens & H. Patzelt, 2015, Corporate entrepreneurship managers' project terminations: Integrating portfolio-level, individual-level and firm-level effects, *Entrepreneurship Theory and Practice*, in press; Y. Yang, V. K. Narayanan, & D. M. De Carolis, 2014, The relationship between portfolio diversification and firm value: The evidence from corporate venture capital activity, *Strategic Management Journal*, 35: 1993–2011.

129. J. P. Eggers, 2014, Competing technologies and industry evolution: The benefits of making mistakes in the flat panel display industry, *Strategic Management Journal*, 35: 159–178.

130. H. R. Greve & M.-D. Seidel, 2015, The thin red line between success and failure: Path dependence in the diffusion of innovative production technologies, *Strategic Management Journal*, 36: 475–496.

131. J. Ostrower, 2015, With jet, Honda enters new realm, *Wall Street Journal*, www.wsj.com, May 17.

132. P. Coy, 2015, What's in the innovation sandwich? *Bloomberg BusinessWeek*, January 19, 49–51.

CASE STUDIES

CASE 1
Kindle Fire: Amazon's
Heated Battle for the
Tablet Market

CASE 2
American Express:
Bank 2.0

CASE 3
BP in Russia: Bad Partners
or Bad Partnerships? (A)

CASE 4
Carlsberg in Emerging
Markets

CASE 5
Fisk Alloy Wire, Inc.
and Percon

CASE 6
Business Model and
Competitive Strategy
of IKEA in India

CASE 7
Invitrogen (A)

CASE 8
Keurig: From David to
Goliath: The Challenge of
Gaining and Maintaining
Marketplace Leadership

CASE 9
KIPP Houston
Public Schools

CASE 10
Luck Companies:
Igniting Human
Potential

CASE 11
Corporate Governance
at Martha Stewart
Living Omnimedia:
Not "A Good Thing"

CASE 12
The Movie Exhibition
Industry: 2015

CASE 13
Polaris and Victory:
Entering and Growing
the Motorcycle Business

CASE 14
Safaricom: Innovative
Telecom Solutions to
Empower Kenyans

CASE 15
Siemens: Management
Innovation at the
Corporate Level

CASE 16
Southwest Airlines

CASE 17
Starbucks Corporation:
The New S-Curves

CASE 18
Super Selectos: Winning
the War Against
Multinational Retail Chains

CASE 19
Tim Hortons Inc.

CASE 20
W. L. Gore—Culture
of Innovation

Case Title	Manu-facturing	Service	Consumer Goods	Food/Retail	High Technology	Internet	Transportation/Communication	International Perspective	Social/Ethical Issues	Industry Perspec...
Amazon: Kindle Fire			•		•	•				
American Express		•				•				•
BP in Russia	•							•		•
Carlsberg	•		•					•		•
Fisk Alloy Wire, Inc. and Percon	•								•	
IKEA	•		•	•				•		•
Invitrogen					•				•	•
Keurig	•		•							
Kipp Schools		•								
Luck Companies	•								•	•
Martha Stewart		•	•							
Movie Exhibition Industry: 2015		•	•							•
Polaris and Victory Motorcycles	•		•				•			•
Safaricom		•			•	•	•			
Siemens	•				•					
Southwest Airlines		•					•	•		•
Starbucks			•	•		•			•	
Super Selectos			•	•				•		
Tim Hortons				•				•		•
W.L. Gore	•				•		•			

Case Title	Chapters												
	1	2	3	4	5	6	7	8	9	10	11	12	13
Amazon: Kindle Fire				●	●								●
American Express	●			●	●								●
BP in Russia					●			●	●				
Carlsberg		●			●		●	●	●				
Fisk Alloy Wire, Inc. and Percon		●		●			●						
IKEA		●						●	●				
Invitrogen							●					●	●
Keurig				●	●								●
Kipp Schools		●	●									●	●
Luck Companies		●	●	●		●	●			●		●	
Martha Stewart	●				●	●	●			●			
Movie Exhibition Industry: 2015		●	●	●	●								
Polaris and Victory Motorcycles		●	●	●		●	●						●
Safaricom	●	●		●				●				●	
Siemens			●			●					●	●	●
Southwest Airlines		●		●	●		●					●	
Starbucks						●		●				●	●
Super Selectos		●			●			●			●		
Tim Hortons				●	●		●		●				
W.L. Gore	●									●	●	●	●

Preparing an Effective Case Analysis

What to Expect from In-Class Case Discussions

As you will learn, classroom discussions of cases differ significantly from lectures. The case method calls for your instructor to guide the discussion and to solicit alternative views as a way of encouraging your active participation when analyzing a case. When alternative views are not forthcoming, your instructor might take a position just to challenge you and your peers to respond thoughtfully as a way of generating still additional alternatives. Often, instructors will evaluate your work in terms of both the quantity and the quality of your contributions to in-class case discussions. The in-class discussions are important in that you can derive significant benefit by having your ideas and recommendations examined against those of your peers and by responding to thoughtful challenges by other class members and/or the instructor.

During case discussions, your instructor will likely listen, question, and probe to extend the analysis of case issues. In the course of these actions, your peers and/ or your instructor may challenge an individual's views and the validity of alternative perspectives that have been expressed. These challenges are offered in a constructive manner; their intent is to help all parties involved with analyzing a case develop their analytical and communication skills. Developing these skills is important in that they will serve you well when working for all types of organizations. Commonly, instructors will encourage you and your peers to be innovative and original when developing and presenting ideas. Over the course of an individual discussion, you are likely to form a more complex view of the case as a result of listening to and thinking about the diverse inputs offered by your peers and instructor. Among other benefits, experience with multiple case discussions will increase your knowledge of the advantages and disadvantages of group decision-making processes.

Both your peers and instructor will value comments that contribute to identifying problems as well as solutions to them. To offer relevant contributions, you are encouraged to think independently and, through discussions with your peers outside of class, to refine your thinking. We also encourage you to avoid using "I think," "I believe," and "I feel" to discuss your inputs to a case analysis process. Instead, consider using a less emotion laden phrase, such as "My analysis shows…." This highlights the logical nature of the approach you have taken to analyze a case. When preparing for an in-class case discussion, you should plan to use the case data to explain your assessment of the situation. Assume that your peers and instructor are familiar with the basic facts included in the case. In addition, it is good practice to prepare notes regarding your analysis of case facts before class discussions and use them when explaining your perspectives. Effective notes signal to classmates and the instructor that you are prepared to engage in a thorough discussion of a case. Moreover, comprehensive and detailed notes eliminate the need for you to memorize the facts and figures needed to successfully discuss a case.

The case analysis process described above will help prepare you effectively to discuss a case during class meetings. Using this process results in consideration of the issues required to identify a focal firm's problems and to propose strategic actions through which the firm can increase the probability it will outperform its rivals. In some instances, your instructor may ask you to prepare either an oral or a written analysis of a particular case. Typically, such an assignment demands even more thorough study and analysis of the case contents. At your instructor's discretion, oral and written analyses may be completed by individuals or by groups of three or more people. The information and insights gained by completing the six steps shown in Table 1 often are of value when developing an oral or a written analysis. However, when preparing an oral or written presentation, you must consider the overall framework in which your information and inputs will be presented. Such a framework is the focus of the next section.

Preparing an Oral/Written Case Presentation

Experience shows that two types of thinking (analysis and synthesis) are necessary to develop an effective oral or written presentation (see Exhibit 1). In the analysis stage, you should first analyze the general external environmental issues affecting the firm. Next, your environmental analysis should focus on the particular industry (or industries, in the case of a diversified company) in which a firm operates. Finally, you should examine companies against which the focal firm competes. By studying the three levels of the external environment (general, industry, and competitor), you will be able to identify a firm's opportunities and threats. Following the external environmental analysis is the analysis of the firm's internal organization. This analysis provides the insights needed to identify the firm's strengths and weaknesses.

Table 1 An Effective Case Analysis Process

Step 1: Gaining Familiarity	a. In general—determine who, what, how, where, and when (the critical facts of the case). b. In detail—identify the places, persons, activities, and contexts of the situation. c. Recognize the degree of certainty/uncertainty of acquired information.
Step 2: Recognizing Symptoms	a. List all indicators (including stated "problems") that something is not as expected or as desired. b. Ensure that symptoms are not assumed to be the problem (symptoms should lead to identification of the problem).
Step 3: Identifying Goals	a. Identify critical statements by major parties (for example, people, groups, the work unit, and so on). b. List all goals of the major parties that exist or can be reasonably inferred.
Step 4: Conducting the Analysis	a. Decide which ideas, models, and theories seem useful. b. Apply these conceptual tools to the situation. c. As new information is revealed, cycle back to substeps a and b.
Step 5: Making the Diagnosis	a. Identify predicaments (goal inconsistencies). b. Identify problems (discrepancies between goals and performance). c. Prioritize predicaments/problems regarding timing, importance, and so on.
Step 6: Doing the Action Planning	a. Specify and prioritize the criteria used to choose action alternatives. b. Discover or invent feasible action alternatives. c. Examine the probable consequences of action alternatives. d. Select a course of action. e. Design an implementation plan/schedule. f. Create a plan for assessing the action to be implemented.

Source: C. C. Lundberg and C. Enz, 1993, A framework for student case preparation, *Case Research Journal*, 13 (Summer): 144, NACRA, North American Case Research Association.

As noted in Exhibit 1, you must then change the focus from analysis to synthesis. Specifically, you must synthesize information gained from your analysis of the firm's external environment and internal organization. Synthesizing information allows you to generate alternatives that can resolve the significant problems or challenges facing the focal firm. Once you identify a best alternative, from an evaluation based on predetermined criteria and goals, you must explore implementation actions.

In Table 2, we outline the sections that should be included in either an oral or a written presentation: strategic profile and case analysis purpose, situation analysis, statements of strengths/weaknesses and opportunities/threats, strategy formulation, and strategy implementation. These sections are described in the following discussion. Familiarity with the contents of your book's thirteen chapters is helpful because the general outline for an oral or a written presentation shown in Table 2 is based on an understanding of the strategic management process detailed in those chapters. We follow the discussions of the parts of Table 2 with a few comments about the "process" to use to present the results of your case analysis in either a written or oral format.

Strategic Profile and Case Analysis Purpose

You will use the strategic profile to briefly present the critical facts from the case that have affected the focal firm's historical strategic direction and performance. The case facts should not be restated in the profile; rather, these comments should show how the critical facts lead to a particular focus for your analysis. This primary focus should be emphasized in this section's conclusion. In addition, this section should state important assumptions about case facts on which your analyses are based.

Situation Analysis

As shown in Table 2, a general starting place for completing a situation analysis is the general environment.

General Environmental Analysis. Your analysis of the general environment should focus on trends in the seven segments of the general environment (see Table 3). Many of the segment issues shown in Table 3 for the seven segments are explained more fully in Chapter 2 of your book. The objective you should have in evaluating these trends is to be able to *predict* the segments that you expect

Exhibit 1 Types of Thinking in Case Preparation: Analysis and Synthesis

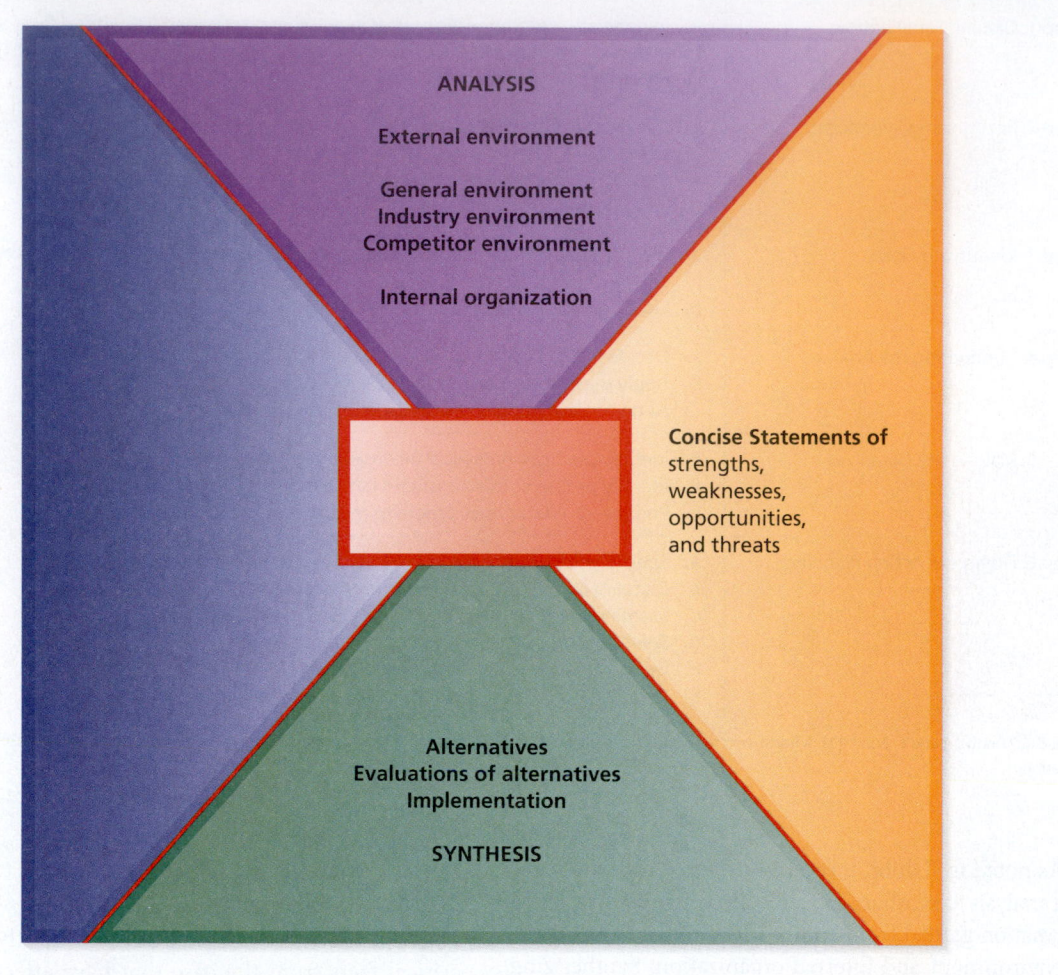

ANALYSIS

External environment

General environment
Industry environment
Competitor environment

Internal organization

Concise Statements of
strengths,
weaknesses,
opportunities,
and threats

Alternatives
Evaluations of alternatives
Implementation

SYNTHESIS

to have the most significant influence on your focal firm over the next several years (say three to five years) and to explain your reasoning for your predictions.

Industry Analysis. Porter's five force model is a useful tool for analyzing the industry (or industries) in which your firm competes. We explain how to use this tool in Chapter 2. In this part of your analysis, you want to determine the attractiveness of an industry (or a segment of an industry) in which your firm is competing. As attractiveness increases, so does the possibility your firm will be able to earn profits by using its chosen strategies. After evaluating the power of the five forces relative to your firm, you should make a judgment as to *how* attractive the industry is in which your firm is competing.

Table 2 General Outline for an Oral or Written Presentation

   I. Strategic Profile and Case Analysis Purpose
  II. Situation Analysis
      A. General environmental analysis
      B. Industry analysis
      C. Competitor analysis
      D. Internal analysis
 III. Identification of Environmental Opportunities and Threats and Firm Strengths and Weaknesses (SWOT Analysis)
 IV. Strategy Formulation
      A. Strategic alternatives
      B. Alternative evaluation
      C. Alternative choice
  v. Strategic Alternative Implementation
      A. Action items
      B. Action plan

Table 3 Sample General Environmental Categories

Technological Trends
- Information technology continues to become cheaper with more practical applications
- Database technology enables organization of complex data and distribution of information
- Telecommunications technology and networks increasingly provide fast transmission of all sources of data, including voice, written communications, and video information
- Computerized design and manufacturing technologies continue to facilitate quality and flexibility

Demographic Trends
- Regional changes in population due to migration
- Changing ethnic composition of the population
- Aging of the population
- Aging of the "baby boom" generation

Economic Trends
- Interest rates
- Inflation rates
- Savings rates
- Exchange rates
- Trade deficits
- Budget deficits

Political/Legal Trends
- Antitrust enforcement
- Tax policy changes
- Environmental protection laws
- Extent of regulation/deregulation
- Privatizing state monopolies
- State-owned industries

Sociocultural Trends
- Women in the workforce
- Awareness of health and fitness issues
- Concern for overcoming poverty
- Concern for customers

Global Trends
- Currency exchange rates
- Free-trade agreements
- Trade deficits

Physical Environment Trends
- Environmental sustainability
- Corporate social responsibility
- Renewable energy
- Goals of zero waste
- Ecosystem impact of food and energy production

Competitor Analysis. Firms also need to *analyze* each of their primary competitors. This analysis should identify competitors' current strategies, strategic intent, strategic mission, capabilities, core competencies, and a competitive response profile (see Chapter 2). This information is useful to the focal firm in formulating an appropriate strategy and in predicting competitors' probable responses. Sources that can be used to gather information about an industry and companies with whom the focal firm competes are listed in Appendix I. Included in this list is a wide range of publications, such as periodicals, newspapers, bibliographies, directories of companies, industry ratios, forecasts, rankings/ratings, and other valuable statistics.

Internal Analysis. Assessing a firm's strengths and weaknesses through a value chain analysis facilitates moving from the external environment to the internal organization. Analysis of the value chain activities and the support functions of the value chain provides opportunities to understand how external environmental trends affect the specific activities of a firm. Such analysis helps highlight strengths and weaknesses (see Chapter 3 for an explanation and use of the value chain).

For purposes of preparing an oral or a written presentation, it is important to note that strengths are internal resources and capabilities that have the potential to be core competencies. Weaknesses, on the other hand, are internal resources and capabilities that have the potential to place a firm at a competitive disadvantage relative to its rivals. Thus, some of a firm's resources and capabilities are strengths; others are weaknesses.

When evaluating the internal characteristics of the firm, your analysis of the functional activities emphasized is critical. For instance, if the strategy of the firm is primarily technology driven, it is important to evaluate the firm's R&D activities. If the strategy is market driven, marketing functional activities are of paramount importance. If a firm has financial difficulties, critical financial ratios would require careful evaluation. In fact, because of the importance of financial health, most cases require financial analyses. Appendix II lists and operationally defines several common financial ratios. Included are tables describing profitability, liquidity, leverage, activity, and shareholders' return ratios. Leadership, organizational culture, structure, and control systems are other characteristics of firms you should examine to fully understand the "internal" part of your firm.

Identification of Environmental Opportunities and Threats and Firm Strengths and Weaknesses (SWOT Analysis)

The outcome of the situation analysis is the identification of a firm's strengths and weaknesses and its environmental threats and opportunities. The next step requires that you *analyze* the strengths and weaknesses and the opportunities and threats for configurations that benefit or do not benefit your firm's efforts to perform well. Case analysts and organizational strategists as well seek to match a firm's strengths with its opportunities. In addition, strengths are chosen to prevent any serious environmental threat from negatively affecting the firm's performance. The key objective of conducting a SWOT analysis

is to determine how to position the firm so it can take advantage of opportunities, while simultaneously avoiding or minimizing environmental threats. Results from a SWOT analysis yield valuable insights into the selection of a firm's strategies. The analysis of a case should not be overemphasized relative to the synthesis of results gained from your analytical efforts. There may be a temptation to spend most of your oral or written case analysis on results from the analysis. It is important, however, that you make an equal effort to develop and evaluate alternatives and to design implementation of the chosen strategy.

Strategy Formulation—Strategic Alternatives, Alternative Evaluation, and Alternative Choice

Developing alternatives is often one of the most difficult steps in preparing an oral or a written presentation. Developing three to four alternative strategies is common (see Chapter 4 for business-level strategy alternatives and Chapter 6 for corporate-level strategy alternatives). Each alternative should be feasible (i.e., it should match the firm's strengths, capabilities, and especially core competencies), and feasibility should be demonstrated. In addition, you should show how each alternative takes advantage of the environmental opportunity or avoids/buffers against environmental threats. Developing carefully thought out alternatives requires synthesis of your analyses' results and creates greater credibility in oral and written case presentations.

Once you develop strong alternatives, you must evaluate the set to choose the best one. Your choice should be defensible and provide benefits over the other alternatives. Thus, it is important that both alternative development and the evaluation of alternatives be thorough. The choice of the best alternative should be explained and defended.

Strategic Alternative Implementation-Action Items and Action Plan

After selecting the most appropriate strategy (that is, the strategy with the highest probability of helping your firm in its efforts to earn profits), implementation issues require attention. Effective synthesis is important to ensure that you have considered and evaluated all critical implementation issues. Issues you might consider include the structural changes necessary to implement the new strategy. In addition, leadership changes and new controls or incentives may be necessary to implement strategic actions. The implementation actions you recommend should be explicit and thoroughly explained. Occasionally, careful evaluation of implementation actions may show the strategy to be less favorable than you thought originally. A strategy is only as good as the firm's ability to implement it.

Process Issues

You should ensure that your presentation (either oral or written) has logical consistency throughout. For example, if your presentation identifies one purpose, but your analysis focuses on issues that differ from the stated purpose, the logical inconsistency will be apparent. Likewise, your alternatives should flow from the configuration of strengths, weaknesses, opportunities, and threats you identified by analyzing your firm's external environment and internal organization.

Thoroughness and clarity also are critical to an effective presentation. Thoroughness is represented by the comprehensiveness of the analysis and alternative generation. Furthermore, clarity in the results of the analyses, selection of the best alternative strategy, and design of implementation actions are important. For example, your statement of the strengths and weaknesses should flow clearly and logically from your analysis of your firm's internal organization.

Presentations (oral or written) that show logical consistency, thoroughness, and clarity of purpose, effective analyses, and feasible recommendations (strategy and implementation) are more effective and are likely to be more positively received by your instructor and peers. Furthermore, developing the skills necessary to make such presentations will enhance your future job performance and career success.

Appendix I Sources for Industry and Competitor Analyses

Abstracts and Indexes	
Periodicals	*ABI/Inform*
	Business Periodicals Index
	InfoTrac Custom Journals
	InfoTrac Custom Newspapers
	InfoTrac OneFile
	EBSCO Business Source Premiere
	Lexis/Nexis Academic
	Public Affairs Information Service Bulletin (PAIS)
	Reader's Guide to Periodical Literature
Newspapers	*NewsBank—Foreign Broadcast Information*
	NewsBank-Global NewsBank
	New York Times Index
	Wall Street Journal Index
	Wall Street Journal/Barron's Index
	Washington Post Index
Bibliographies	*Encyclopedia of Business Information Sources*
Directories	
Companies—General	*America's Corporate Families and International Affiliates*
	Hoover's Online: The Business Network www.hoovers.com/free
	D&B Million Dollar Directory (databases: http://www.dnbmdd.com)
	Standard & Poor's Corporation Records
	Standard & Poor's Register of Corporations, Directors, and Executives
	(http://www.netadvantage.standardandpoors.com for all of *Standard & Poor's*)
	Ward's Business Directory of Largest U.S. Companies
Companies—International	*America's Corporate Families and International Affiliates*
	Business Asia
	Business China
	Business Eastern Europe
	Business Europe
	Business International
	Business International Money Report
	Business Latin America

(Continued)

Appendix I (Continued) Sources for Industry and Competitor Analyses

Abstracts and Indexes	
	Directory of American Firms Operating in Foreign Countries *Directory of Foreign Firms Operating in the United States* *Hoover's Handbook of World Business* *International Directory of Company Histories* *Mergent's International Manual* Mergent Online (http://www.fisonline.com—for "Business and Financial Information Connection to the World") *Who Owns Whom*
Companies—Manufacturers	*Thomas Register of American Manufacturers* U.S. Office of Management and Budget, Executive Office of the President, *Standard Industrial Classification Manual* *U.S. Manufacturer's Directory, Manufacturing & Distribution, USA*
Companies—Private	*D&B Million Dollar Directory* *Ward's Business Directory of Largest U.S. Companies*
Companies—Public	Annual Reports and 10-K Reports *Disclosure* (corporate reports) *Q-File* Securities and Exchange Commission Filings & Forms (EDGAR) http://www.sec.gov/edgar.shtml *Mergent's Manuals:* <ul><li>*Mergent's Bank and Finance Manual*</li><li>*Mergent's Industrial Manual*</li><li>*Mergent's International Manual*</li><li>*Mergent's Municipal and Government Manual*</li><li>*Mergent's OTC Industrial Manual*</li><li>*Mergent's OTC Unlisted Manual*</li><li>*Mergent's Public Utility Manual*</li><li>*Mergent's Transportation Manual*</li></ul>Standard & Poor's Corporation, *Standard Corporation Descriptions:* http://www.netadvantage.standardandpoors.com <ul><li>*Standard & Poor's Analyst Handbook*</li><li>*Standard & Poor's Industry Surveys*</li><li>*Standard & Poor's Statistical Service*</li></ul>
Companies—Subsidiaries and Affiliates	*America's Corporate Families and International Affiliates* *Ward's Directory* *Who Owns Whom* *Mergent's Industry Review* *Standard & Poor's Analyst's Handbook* *Standard & Poor's Industry Surveys* (2 volumes) U.S. Department of Commerce, *U.S. Industrial Outlook*
Industry Ratios	Dun & Bradstreet, *Industry Norms and Key Business Ratios* *RMA's Annual Statement Studies* *Troy Almanac of Business and Industrial Financial Ratios*
Industry Forecasts	International Trade Administration, *U.S. Industry & Trade Outlook*
Rankings & Ratings	Annual Report on American Industry in *Forbes Business Rankings Annual* *Mergent's Industry Review* http://www.worldcatlibraries.org *Standard & Poor's Industry Report Service* http://www.netadvantage.standardandpoors.com *Value Line Investment Survey* *Ward's Business Directory of Largest U.S. Companies*
Statistics	*American Statistics Index (ASI)* Bureau of the Census, U.S. Department of Commerce, *Economic Census Publications* Bureau of the Census, U.S. Department of Commerce, *Statistical Abstract of the United States* Bureau of Economic Analysis, U.S. Department of Commerce, *Survey of Current Business* Internal Revenue Service, U.S. Treasury Department, *Statistics of Income: Corporation Income Tax Returns* *Statistical Reference Index (SRI)*

Appendix II Financial Analysis in Case Studies

Table A-1 Profitability Ratios

Ratio	Formula	What It Shows
1. Return on total assets	$$\frac{\text{Profits after taxes}}{\text{Total assets}}$$ or $$\frac{\text{Profits after taxes} + \text{Interest}}{\text{Total assets}}$$	The net return on total investments of the firm or The return on both creditors' and shareholders' investments
2. Return on stockholders' equity (or return on net worth)	$$\frac{\text{Profits after taxes}}{\text{Total stockholders' equity}}$$	How profitably the company is utilizing shareholders' funds
3. Return on common equity	$$\frac{\text{Profits after taxes} - \text{Preferred stock dividends}}{\text{Total stockholders' equity} - \text{Par value of preferred stock}}$$	The net return to common stockholders
4. Operating profit margin (or return on sales)	$$\frac{\text{Profits before taxes and before interest}}{\text{Sales}}$$	The firm's profitability from regular operations
5. Net profit margin (or net return on sales)	$$\frac{\text{Profits after taxes}}{\text{Sales}}$$	The firm's net profit as a percentage of total sales

Table A-2 Liquidity Ratios

Ratio	Formula	What It Shows
1. Current ratio	$$\frac{\text{Current assets}}{\text{Current liabilities}}$$	The firm's ability to meet its current financial liabilities
2. Quick ratio (or acid-test ratio)	$$\frac{\text{Current assets} - \text{Inventory}}{\text{Current liabilities}}$$	The firm's ability to pay off short-term obligations without relying on sales of inventory
3. Inventory to net working capital	$$\frac{\text{Inventory}}{\text{Current assets} - \text{Current liabilities}}$$	The extent to which the firm's working capital is tied up in inventory

Table A-3 Leverage Ratios

Ratio	Formula	What It Shows
1. Debt-to-assets	$$\frac{\text{Total debt}}{\text{Total assets}}$$	Total borrowed funds as a percentage of total assets
2. Debt-to-equity	$$\frac{\text{Total debt}}{\text{Total shareholders' equity}}$$	Borrowed funds versus the funds provided by shareholders
3. Long-term debt-to-equity	$$\frac{\text{Long-term debt}}{\text{Total shareholders' equity}}$$	Leverage used by the firm
4. Times-interest-earned (or coverage ratio)	$$\frac{\text{Profits before interest and taxes}}{\text{Total interest charges}}$$	The firm's ability to meet all interest payments
5. Fixed charge coverage	$$\frac{\text{Profits before taxes and interest} + \text{Lease obligations}}{\text{Total interest charges} + \text{Lease obligations}}$$	The firm's ability to meet all fixed-charge obligations including lease payments

Table A-4 Activity Ratios

Ratio	Formula	What It Shows
1. Inventory turnover	$\dfrac{\text{Sales}}{\text{Inventory of finished goods}}$	The effectiveness of the firm in employing inventory
2. Fixed-assets turnover	$\dfrac{\text{Sales}}{\text{Fixed assets}}$	The effectiveness of the firm in utilizing plant and equipment
3. Total assets turnover	$\dfrac{\text{Sales}}{\text{Total assets}}$	The effectiveness of the firm in utilizing total assets
4. Accounts receivable turnover	$\dfrac{\text{Annual credit sales}}{\text{Accounts receivable}}$	How many times the total receivables have been collected during the accounting period
5. Average collecting period	$\dfrac{\text{Accounts receivable}}{\text{Average daily sales}}$	The average length of time the firm waits to collect payment after sales

Table A-5 Shareholders' Return Ratios

Ratio	Formula	What It Shows
1. Dividend yield on common stock	$\dfrac{\text{Annual dividend per share}}{\text{Current market price per share}}$	A measure of return to common stockholders in the form of dividends
2. Price-earnings ratio	$\dfrac{\text{Current market price per share}}{\text{After-tax earnings per share}}$	An indication of market perception of the firm; usually, the faster-growing or less risky firms tend to have higher PE ratios than the slower-growing or more risky firms
3. Dividend payout ratio	$\dfrac{\text{Annual dividends per share}}{\text{After-tax earnings per share}}$	An indication of dividends paid out as a percentage of profits
4. Cash flow per share	$\dfrac{\text{After-tax profits + Depreciation}}{\text{Number of common shares outstanding}}$	A measure of total cash per share available for use by the firm

CASE 1

Kindle Fire: Amazon's Heated Battle for the Tablet Market

Mohanbir Sawhney, Joseph R. Owens,
and Pallavi Goodman
Kellogg School of Management, Northwestern university

In January 2012, as Jeff Bezos reflected on the early sales success of Amazon's Kindle Fire device, he was oddly troubled. In a little over three months, Amazon had sold nearly 5 million Kindle Fires and had captured half of the non-Apple tablet market share. Worldwide sales of e-books since the introduction of the Kindle product line had grown from less than 1 percent of all books sold to 15 percent in 2012. But Bezos was not ready to call it a success yet.

As he anticipated Apple's imminent announcement of the third-generation iPad and its entry into the textbook market, Bezos knew he would have to refine his strategy for the Kindle Fire. In addition to Apple, new entrants such as Samsung, Motorola, and Google were beginning to enter the tablet market. Furthermore, Amazon's long-time competitor in the E Ink[1]—based e-readers, Barnes & Noble, was now selling a device nearly identical to the Kindle Fire called the Nook. Bezos had told investors that the Kindle Fire was the key to Amazon's future in the hardware space. The markets seemed to agree. Amazon stock had dropped $40 since the launch of the Kindle Fire. Analysts were concerned about the Kindle product line's economics because Amazon was selling the hardware at cost, betting that content and commerce revenues would make up for the hardware price subsidy.

Bezos was wrestling with several issues with the Kindle Fire strategy. How should Amazon modify the positioning of the device in response to the new entrants in the tablet market since its launch? What was the most promising target market for the Kindle Fire, and how should it be positioned against competing products? How could Amazon turn the sales success of the Kindle Fire into business success? Would revenues and profits from commerce and content justify selling the hardware at cost? What were the likely responses of the competition?

History of Amazon

In 1999 Amazon accomplished its founding mission of becoming the world's largest online bookstore. Two years later it turned its first profit. By 2011, just fifteen years after the company started out of Jeff Bezos's 400-square-foot garage, Amazon had 25 million square feet of warehouse space, reported $50 billion in revenues, and controlled 10 percent of the North American e-commerce market (Exhibit 1 and Exhibit 2). Competitors struggled to transition from brick-and-mortar–based businesses, but Amazon had repeatedly been at the forefront in the e-commerce market. From its pioneering use of user-based reviews for product comparisons to its development of 1-Click® ordering on its website, Amazon had continued to innovate. The company's marketplace for third-party vendors, introduced in 1999, helped grow its selection rapidly.

Bezos's 2010 annual letter to shareholders touted that "invention is in [Amazon's] DNA" and that the long-term interests of its shareholders were perfectly aligned with the needs and wants of its customers. This focus on the long-term, however, with repeated innovation and thrusts into new markets, had created tension with the short-term interests of investors. The $45 fall in stock value between Q3 2011 and mid-Q1 2012 illustrated this tension between Amazon's visionary investments and public market investors (Exhibit 3). Investors were doubtful of the margins Amazon would attain on the new streams of revenue that it was betting would flow through its new devices.

When Amazon began offering its spare server computing power and storage space as a service in 2006, the cloud-based information technology services field was still nascent. Under the rapidly expanding Amazon Web Services (AWS) division, Amazon rolled out its Elastic Compute Cloud (EC2) platform and the Simple Storage Service (S3). AWS was expected to make up just 3 percent of Amazon's revenues by 2012, but AWS revenues were expected to

Exhibit 1 Amazon Financials

	Year Ended December 31		
	2011	**2010**	**2009**
NET SALES ($ in millions)			
North America			
Media	7,959	6,881	5,964
Electronics and other general merchandise	17,315	10,998	6,314
Other[a]	1,431	828	550
Total North America	26,705	18,707	12,828
International			
Media	9,820	8,007	6,810
Electronics and other general merchandise	11,397	7,365	4,768
Other[a]	155	125	103
Total international	21,372	15,497	11,681
Consolidated			
Media	17,779	14,888	12,774
Electronics and other general merchandise	28,712	18,363	11,082
Other[a]	1,586	953	653
Total consolidated	48,077	34,204	24,509
YEAR-OVER-YEAR PERCENTAGE GROWTH (%)			
North America			
Media	16	15	11
Electronics and other general merchandise	57	74	43
Other	73	50	23
Total North America	43	46	25
International			
Media	23	18	19
Electronics and other general merchandise	55	54	53
Other	24	22	9
Total international	38	33	31
Consolidated			
Media	19	17	15
Electronics and other general merchandise	56	66	47
Other	66	46	20
Total consolidated	41	40	28
YEAR-OVER-YEAR PERCENTAGE GROWTH EXCLUDING THE EFFECT OF EXCHANGE RATES (%)			
International			
Media	16	18	20
Electronics and other general merchandise	47	57	56
Other	18	24	19
Total international	31	34	33
Consolidated			
Media	16	16	16
Electronics and other general merchandise	53	67	48
Other	66	46	22
Total consolidated	37	40	29
CONSOLIDATED NET SALES MIX (%)			
Media	37	43	52
Electronics and other general merchandise	60	54	45
Other	3	3	3
Total consolidated	100	100	100

[a]Includes non-retail activities, such as Amazon Web Services, miscellaneous marketing and promotional activities, other seller sites, and Amazon's co-branded credit card agreements.

Exhibit 2 Amazon Earnings Report

AMAZON.COM ANNOUNCES FOURTH QUARTER SALES UP 35% TO $17.43 BILLION; KINDLE DEVICE SALES NEARLY TRIPLE DURING THE HOLIDAYS

SEATTLE—(BUSINESS WIRE)—January 31, 2012—Amazon.com, Inc. (NASDAQ: AMZN) today announced financial results for its fourth quarter ended December 31, 2011.

Operating cash flow increased 12% to $3.90 billion for the trailing twelve months, compared with $3.50 billion for the trailing twelve months ended December 31, 2010. Free cash flow decreased 17% to $2.09 billion for the trailing twelve months, compared with $2.52 billion for the trailing twelve months ended December 31, 2010.

Common shares outstanding plus shares underlying stock-based awards totaled 468 million on December 31, 2011, compared with 465 million a year ago.

Net sales increased 35% to $17.43 billion in the fourth quarter, compared with $12.95 billion in fourth quarter 2010. Excluding the $101 million favorable impact from year-over-year changes in foreign exchange rates throughout the quarter, net sales would have grown 34% compared with fourth quarter 2010.

Operating income was $260 million in the fourth quarter, compared with $474 million in fourth quarter 2010. The favorable impact from year-over-year changes in foreign exchange rates throughout the quarter on operating income was $5 million.

Net income decreased 58% to $177 million in the fourth quarter, or $0.38 per diluted share, compared with net income of $416 million, or $0.91 per diluted share, in fourth quarter 2010.

"We are grateful to the millions of customers who purchased the Kindle Fire and Kindle e-reader devices this holiday season, making Kindle our bestselling product across both the U.S. and Europe," said Jeff Bezos, founder and CEO of Amazon.com. "Our millions of third-party sellers had a tremendous holiday season with 65% unit growth and now represent 36% of total units sold."

Full Year 2011

Net sales increased 41% to $48.08 billion, compared with $34.20 billion in 2010. Excluding the $1.09 billion favorable impact from year-over-year changes in foreign exchange rates throughout the year, net sales would have grown 37% compared with 2010.

Operating income decreased 39% to $862 million, compared with $1.41 billion in 2010. The favorable impact from year-over-year changes in foreign exchange rates throughout the year on operating income was $53 million.

Net income decreased 45% to $631 million in 2011, or $1.37 per diluted share, compared with net income of $1.15 billion, or $2.53 per diluted share, in 2010.

Source: "Amazon.com Announces Fourth Quarter Sales Up 35% to $17.43 Billion; Kindle Device Sales Nearly Triple During the Holidays," Amazon.com press release, December 31, 2011.

almost triple in the following three years. Amazon called its "service-oriented architecture" the "fundamental building abstraction" for all Amazon technologies.[2]

This focus on internal technology development had led to significant benefits for customers. Through the widely popular Amazon Prime express shipping subscription service, the company had built a customer base that was motivated to always shop at Amazon.com first before they went elsewhere. This service, which for an annual fee of $79 provided two-day express shipping on most items sold directly by Amazon, was made possible by the company's logistics innovations. Through its marketplace partners, Amazon had outsourced its long-tail[3] offerings while lowering its overhead. Without the

Exhibit 3 Amazon Stock Price Following the Kindle Fire Announcement

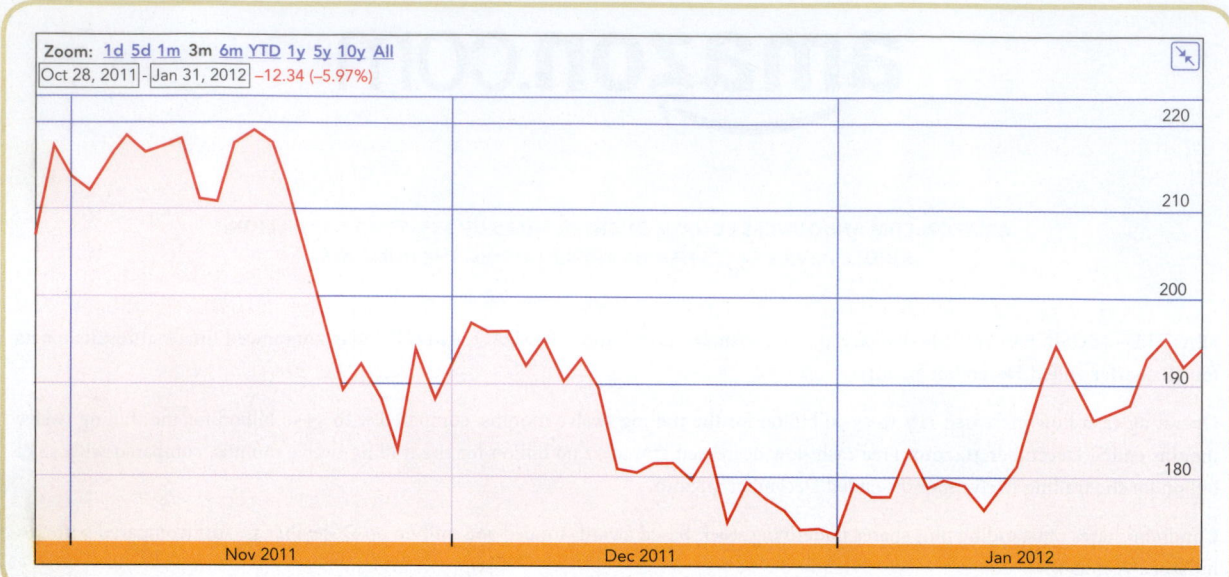

technical advancements that made the logistical infrastructure run smoothly, customers would not have embraced these partners as a seamless extension of the Amazon brand. Additionally, the advanced algorithms driving the popular product recommendations that were integrated into every product page relied on sophisticated management of the underlying data infrastructure.

Amazon, since its founding, had a strong history of investing in emerging opportunities years ahead of revenues or profitability. It took the company six years to become profitable primarily because of its commitment to innovation. It was this commitment to innovation that drove Bezos to found the Lab126 hardware development group, which developed, in extreme secrecy, the future of e-commerce: the first successful e-reader, the Kindle.

The Emergence of E-Readers

Although the attractive prospect of reading long-form texts digitally had led to many e-readers coming to market over the years, e-books had remained a niche curiosity. The original "killer app," the paper book, remained largely unchallenged until the advent of E Ink technology in 1997, which made reading possible in any light condition and with minimal power usage. The new crop of e-readers was born.

In 2007 the market leader was the Sony Reader. It could hold a library of up to one hundred books and was sold for $299–$399, depending on the accessory bundle. More than 10,000 titles were available for purchase

at 75 to 85 percent of the retail price of a physical book. However, the Sony Reader was clunky to use and difficult to load content onto. Even the simple act of page-turning was slow and difficult to manage one-handed.

For more than a decade, various competitors offered iterations on this basic business model, and had sold a combined 400,000 units by the end of 2007. The Iliad by iRex, larger than the Sony Reader, was sold for $799 and could adequately display full-sized PDF files but had similar drawbacks in content acquisition for customers. Many early adopters also used the tiny screens of a variety of personal digital assistant devices such as the Palm III and V, as well as early-generation iPhones, to read e-books. Critics cited the slow and clunky operation and general poor usability of early e-readers as book replacements as well as the inadequate e-book distribution and promotion model as reasons that the e-book had yet to jump the chasm on the innovation curve.

The Amazon Kindle

In a highly successful product launch, Amazon introduced its own e-reader, the Kindle, in November 2007. The Kindle featured a QWERTY keyboard, an onboard dictionary, and access to Wikipedia. It had memory sufficient for two hundred titles, which was expandable via an SD card. Its grayscale, passively lit screen sipped battery and thus could last for more than a week. The stark white, 10.3-ounce device with a 6-inch E Ink screen was, at first glance, similar to competitors' offerings. Under the hood, though, lay Whispernet, an EVDO cellular antenna with prepaid Sprint service that enabled wireless content delivery. At several points during the Kindle's development, Bezos sent engineers back to the drawing board to make Whispernet work seamlessly. Bezos knew the key differentiator for the Kindle would be the capability for customers to discover, purchase, and sync content quickly and easily wherever they happened to be—sans computer.

The first-generation Kindle was priced competitively at $399. In addition to the more than 100,000 e-books offered by Amazon, customers could purchase subscriptions to nineteen newspapers (for $5 to $14 per month), sixteen magazines (for $1.25 to $3.49 per month), and hundreds of blogs (for $0.99 per month) that would self-update wirelessly. Customers were also provided with an e-mail address specific to their device that could be used to load and convert DOC and PDF file formats for viewing on the Kindle. This service cost 15 cents per megabyte.

Prior to the Kindle's release, Amazon sent its representatives to knock on doors and cajole the major book publishers to digitize their offerings for its new e-reader. By bringing the publishers onboard, Amazon hoped to simplify the digital rights management (DRM) issues that were slowing the move toward electronic distribution of books. The company succeeded in convincing all of the "Big Six" publishers to rapidly accelerate their e-book devel-

opment and to offer their content through the Amazon e-bookstore. Amazon subsequently shocked these publishers by subsidizing the price of new titles, many of which were offered at $9.99. This aggressive content pricing model, co-announced with the product launch, helped the first-generation Kindle sell out in the first three hours.

When Amazon started the development of its first-generation Kindle in 2006, the entire e-book market was only $3 million and less than 1 percent of all book sales in the United States. But both e-book reader device sales and revenues for e-book readers were projected to grow substantially in the ensuing years (Exhibit 4). Five years later, Amazon's revenues from e-books were estimated to have topped $1 billion. Amazon had likely (it does not publicly release these metrics) sold a cumulative 30 million Kindle units.

As the Kindle product line evolved, Amazon continued to enhance the user experience, mostly by improving navigational features such as page-turn speed, battery life, and screen resolution, and by reducing the device's weight and width (Exhibit 5). To expand the use cases for the Kindle product line, Amazon developed a larger version of the device. The $549 Kindle DX featured a 10-inch screen, making it the ideal e-reader for displaying figures and tables from textbooks or business documents.

Exhibit 4 E-Book Market Growth and Projection

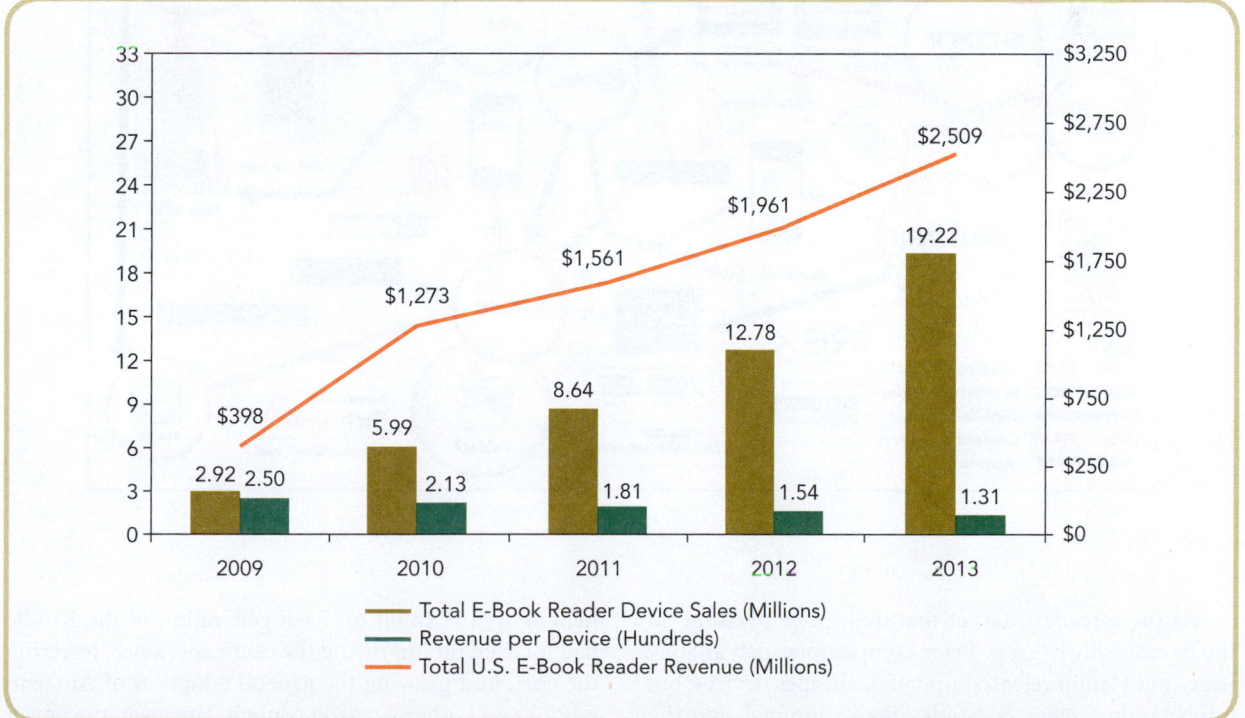

Legend:
- Total E-Book Reader Device Sales (Millions)
- Revenue per Device (Hundreds)
- Total U.S. E-Book Reader Revenue (Millions)

Exhibit 5 The Evolution of Amazon's Kindle Product Line

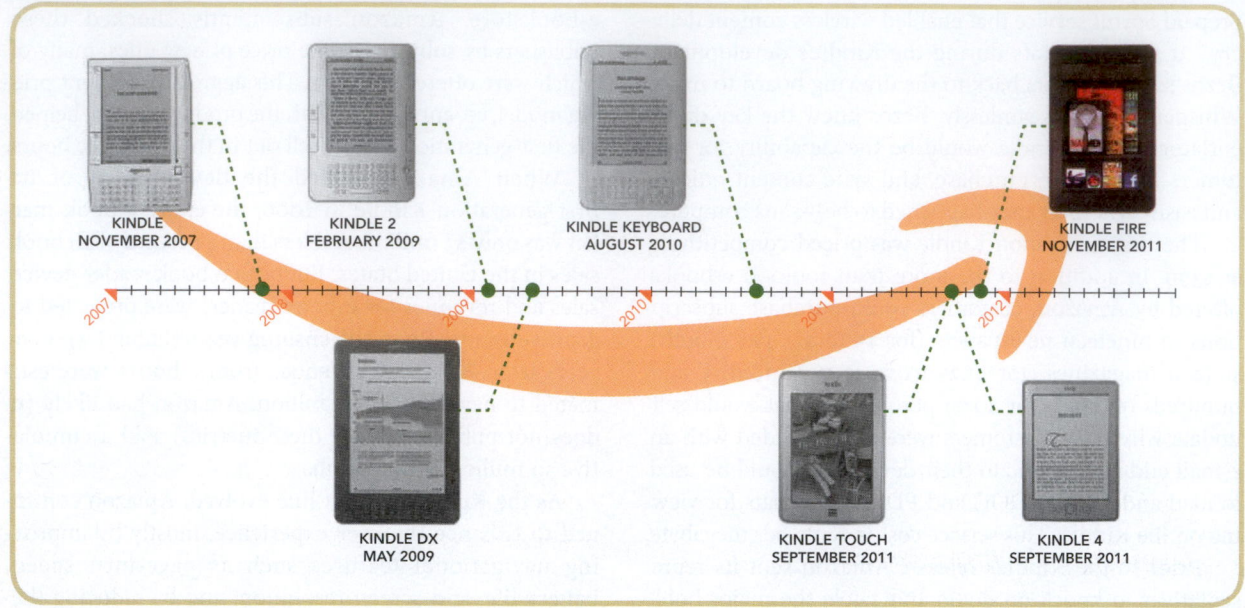

Exhibit 6 E-Book Universe (circa 2009)

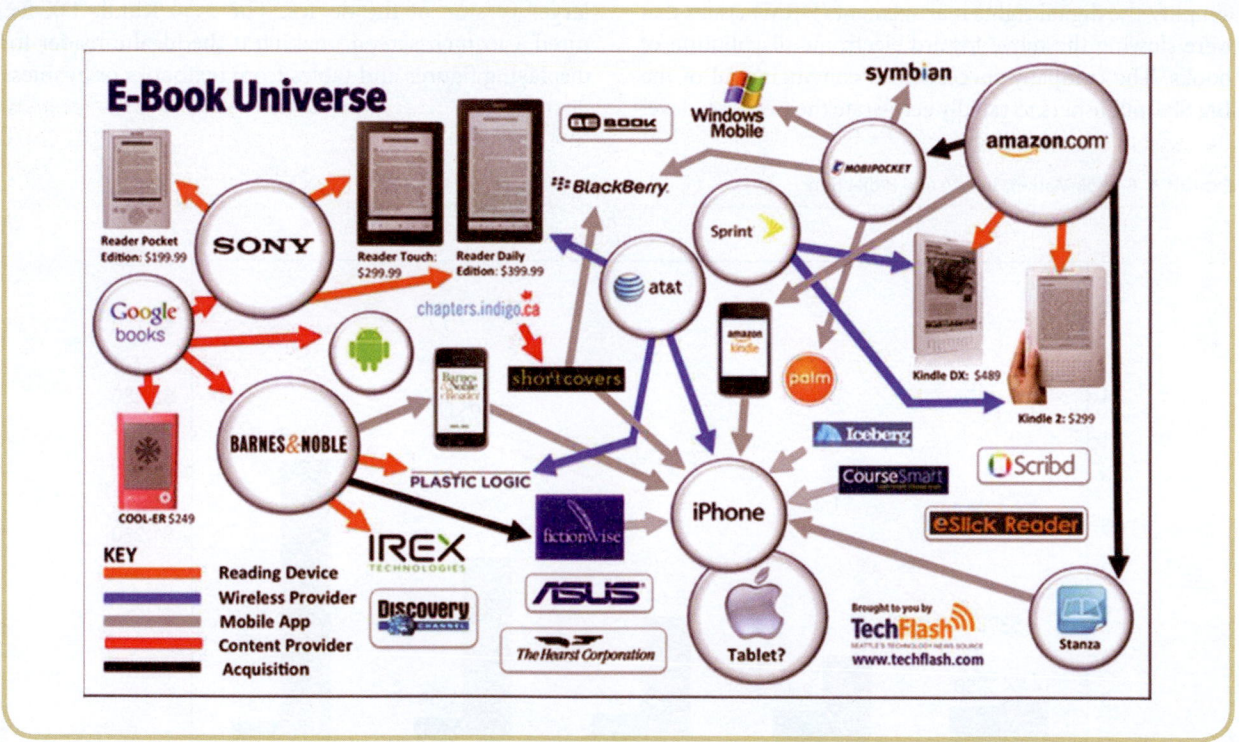

As the e-reader market matured, price pressure on the devices slowly grew. Prior competitors such as Sony, iRex, and Hanlin released updated, cheaper devices, but importantly Barnes & Noble (B&N) jumped into the field as well (Exhibit 6). Each generation of the Kindle had focused on improving the user experience, lowering the cost, and growing the general adoption of Amazon e-books and other Amazon content. However, the newer entrants forced Amazon to begin to discount its devices considerably (Exhibit 7).

Amazon used its installed base[4] of Kindle owners to push higher volumes of e-books, which had significantly lower distribution costs compared to physical books. The company's profit per title fell from $13 for a new-release hardcover to a mere $3, but the increase in volume compensated for this loss. Given that the gross margin on each Kindle device was barely 5 percent and that the margin for each e-book was 20 to 30 percent, the Kindle devices were arguably a tool for getting the Amazon ecosystem of content into the hands of the customer.

With each e-book purchased from Amazon, customers were further committing themselves to the Amazon ecosystem, a completely unheard-of benefit in the traditional print space, where customers had complete independence in choosing a retailer. Bezos shrewdly knew that this lucrative customer base needed to be locked in before a competitor, such as B&N, could do the same.

E-Book Ecosystems

The advent of e-books meant that the traditional methods of book publishing and selling had to adapt to the digital platform. Book distributors began to develop entire ecosystems around the content, publication, and delivery of e-books. E-booksellers had to forge relationships with major publishers to make e-books available and added to their online portfolios. They developed proprietary platforms to adapt to this digital transition, which meant that competing platforms and ecosystems were controlled by the major players—primarily Amazon, followed by Apple and to a lesser extent, Google eBookstore and Barnes & Noble. However, the existence of competing e-book formats meant that digital books did not gain broad popularity until Amazon launched the Kindle e-reader. E-books could be purchased on the Amazon website or directly through the Kindle device via a 3G or Wi-Fi connection for e-book delivery. Amazon's proprietary system was developed initially for its Kindle devices but was later adapted to the world of applications (apps) to encourage a cross-platform reading experience. Not only could books be read on the Kindle but e-books purchased on Amazon could now be read on different platforms, for instance, on iPads and iPhones, personal computers, and Android devices. (By contrast, books purchased from Apple could only be read on Apple devices.) To protect its ecosystem, however, Amazon made it difficult for books purchased outside of Amazon to be accessed on the Kindle device or through Kindle apps.

When Amazon started selling $9.99 e-books in 2007, the major book publishers were not happy to see the erosion of the agency-based pricing model they had enjoyed for more than a century. When approached by B&N in 2008 and Apple in 2009 to develop e-books for their

Exhibit 7 Kindle Price History

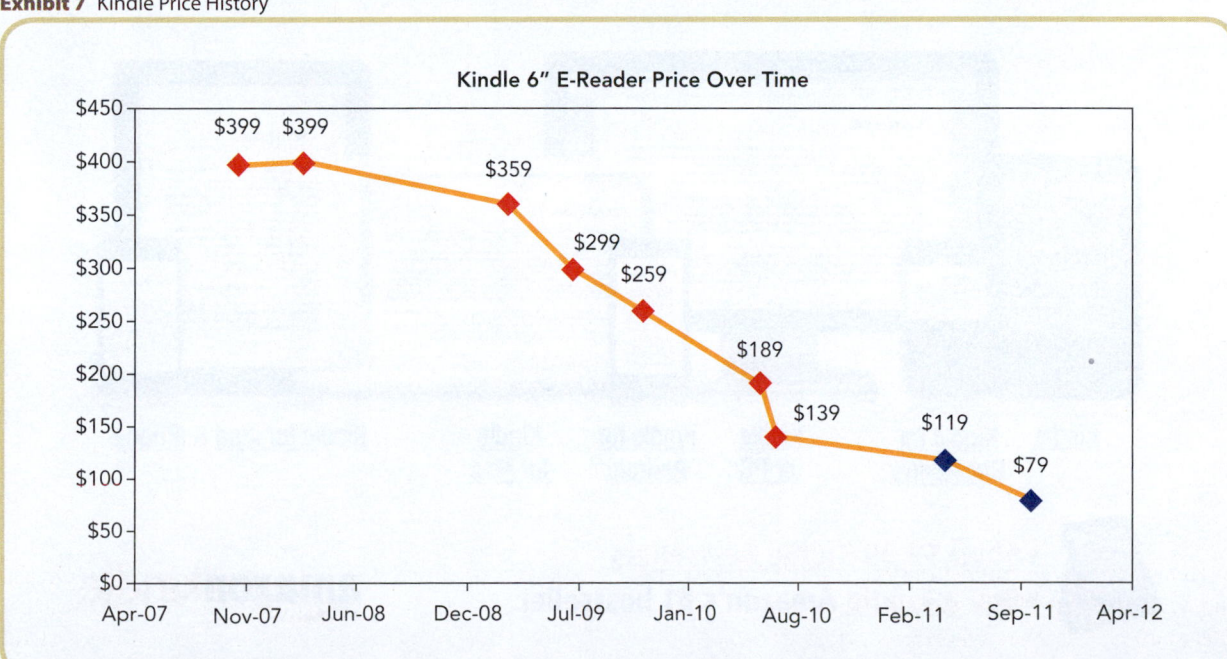

new tablets, book publishers were eager to reassert their favored agency-based pricing model. B&N and Apple, as new entrants into the e-book market, were willing to cede pricing control back to the publishers in order to rapidly gain access to large content libraries for their devices. This move later forced Amazon to follow suit for e-book pricing in late 2009, though these actions launched several anti-trust, price-fixing lawsuits against the publishers and Apple. Consumer expectation of e-book pricing had shifted, however. For most popular titles, e-book prices remained at $9.99 ($13.99 for new releases), a far cry from the old $26 price of a hardcover book.

An area of contention among e-booksellers was competition for content sales through apps on smartphones, third-party e-readers, and computers. Amazon, Sony, Google, and B&N sold e-books through their own branded apps on all the major platforms (Exhibit 8). These apps reduced the switching costs for customers by making the DRM-protected content they purchased from a given retailer available on all their mobile devices and computers.

In July 2011 Apple announced that it would remove all applications from its App Store that did not use Apple's "in-app purchase" platform. Critically, this platform directed a 30 percent cut of all sales to Apple. Apple's change in policy set the stage for its announcement of its cross-platform iBooks App bundled with the iOS 5 release in October 2011. Apple's counter-stroke was an attempt to lock out sales by competitors on its devices and to simultaneously offer its own partners' content in their place.

Barnes & Noble E-Readers

In October 2009 B&N launched its Nook product line. The Nook, an E Ink e-reader similar to the Kindle, was B&N's attempt to capitalize on Amazon's success in e-books. The Nook featured a 6-inch E Ink screen, a

Exhibit 8 Amazon Kindle Cross-Platform Ecosystem

seven-day battery life, Google's Android operating system, native PDF support, and wireless access to the B&N e-bookstore through prepaid AT&T cellular service.

B&N tried to undercut the Amazon Kindle 2 (then priced at $359) by pricing the Nook at $259. A price war ensued. Second-generation Kindles fell from $359 in early 2009 to $259 after the Nook's launch. As the two largest U.S. booksellers vied for the leading position, e-reader prices fell to less than $200 in 2010 and then to less than $100 in 2011 (for the simplest low-end devices from each product line). During this three-year period, sales of e-readers grew from less than 1 million units per year to more than 8 million in the United States. Both B&N and Amazon were focused on getting their customers to build their digital libraries as quickly as possible.

In contrast to Sony and other early Kindle competitors, B&N copied Amazon's entire e-reader/e-book business model. B&N saw the writing on the wall and knew that its traditional book retailer business model was in major decline. It secured e-book deals with its publisher business partners, outsourced the development of the Nook's hardware and firmware, and began a major push to drive Nook sales to the forefront of its physical as well as online stores. Employee retention and compensation metrics were amended to focus on Nook sales per shift, and company profits were divided into two categories: digital (profitable and growing for 2011) and traditional (unprofitable for 2011).

B&N provided one truly unique feature for all Nooks: customers had free Wi-Fi access to read the entire B&N library of e-books in its stores—a popular pastime given the Starbucks coffee shops located in each store. Subsequent versions of the Nook added touch support, more memory, a Wi-Fi–based Internet browser, and a "book-lending" capability compatible with other Nook devices. With the launch of the Nook Color (November 2010) and the follow-on Nook Tablet (November 2011), B&N sought to differentiate itself as the bargain *color* e-reader. These devices featured access to third-party apps in the B&N Marketplace and support for multimedia content.

Apple Introduces the iPad

Apple ported its iPhone operating system (iOS) to the tablet form factor[5] in April 2010 with the iPad. Its beautiful 11-inch touchscreen immediately drew in customers. The iPad was basically a larger version of the popular third-generation iPod Touch, except Apple had painstakingly removed the time lag between a touch and an onscreen response. The responsive, pointer-less operating system allowed for numerous use cases that

far exceeded those offered on the tiny screen of an iPod or iPhone and put the Apple experience comfortably in the lap of the high-end customer.

The iPad immediately became one of the most sought-after devices of 2010. The $499 base model had 16GB of storage, which could be doubled for $100. An optional cellular antenna could be purchased for $139 with an a la carte monthly data service plan from AT&T Wireless. Most Apple stores sold out of all models the first day. Apple sold roughly 1 million units the first week, and users continued to wait in lines for new shipments for weeks after its launch. The iPad broke open the long-underserved tablet market, with 15 million sold by 2010 year-end. Critics were apt to list a litany of features—such as a camera, USB port, and more—that the iPad "lacked," but it became clear from the sales numbers alone that Apple had found the sweet spot for what consumers wanted in a device that sat squarely between smartphone and laptop.

In March 2011 Apple released the iPad 2, which upped the ante on its competitors. The iPad 2 had twice the processor speed (dual-core A5) of the original iPad. It was 15 percent lighter and 33 percent thinner and featured high-resolution front- and back-facing cameras to facilitate Apple's new videoconferencing app, FaceTime. Apple had succeeded in creating a thriving tablet market, selling a total of 55 million iPads since the initial launch.

Tim Cook, Apple's new CEO, became known for his fondness for pushing the idea that Apple's slew of "iDevices" were ushering in the "post-PC era" that the late Steve Jobs had envisioned. Bezos likely knew, as March 2012 approached, that Apple would soon update the iPad product line and further raise the bar on the premium tablet space. What likely most concerned him, though, was whether Apple would release an "iPad mini" device at a lower price point to compete with the Kindle Fire. An iPad for less than $300 would definitely change the market environment for e-readers.

Google Android Tablets

The Open Handset Alliance was founded in 2006 to support the development of a unified mobile operating system experience for smartphones. Original equipment manufacturers (OEMs) Samsung, Motorola, LG, QUALCOMM, Broadcom, and HTC partnered with carriers T-Mobile and Sprint Nextel under Google's leadership to develop the Android OS. These OEMs brought a slew of slick, touchscreen-based smartphones to market.

Apple's success with porting the iPhone user experience (the iOS) to the tablet form factor attracted the

Android OEMs. Android tablets such as Samsung's line of Galaxy tablets and Motorola's Xoom tablets came in several screen sizes (7-inch to 11-inch), packed sophisticated chipsets and graphics, came with high-resolution cameras, and had integrated Wi-Fi and even cellular antennae in some models. These tablets were sold through wireless carriers as well as via traditional electronics outlets at prices ranging from $499 to $799 depending on the feature set.

At the Consumer Electronics Show in January 2011, no less than twenty-one different tablets were introduced. This deluge, along with the release of the iPad 2, led to 2011 being dubbed the "year of the tablet."[6] Android tablet OEMs faced rapid commoditization of their devices, and competition for enhanced hardware specifications quickly led to shortened product life cycles, decreased profitability, and lower-than-predicted sales. Apple's sale of 15 million (67 percent market share) iPads in Q4 2011 alone suggests that 2011 turned out to be the year of the iPad (Exhibit 9).

Introduction of the Kindle Fire

On September 28, 2011, Amazon previewed the Kindle Fire to the technical press in Seattle, Washington. The new tablet came equipped with a 7-inch, color LCD touchscreen, a Wi-Fi radio, a powerful dual-core processor, a fixed 8 GB of internal storage, and free cloud storage for content purchased from Amazon (Exhibit 10). The Kindle Fire came preloaded with a modified version of the Google Android mobile OS.

Bezos, in his announcement, referred to the Kindle Fire as "the culmination of the many things we've been doing for 15 years." He went on to say, "We asked ourselves, 'Is there some way we can bring all of these things together [Amazon Web Services, Prime, Kindle, instant video streaming, and the app store] into a remarkable product offering customers would love?' Yes, the answer is Amazon Kindle Fire."[7] By leveraging its considerable cloud-based resources, Amazon packed numerous unique features and services into its new product. The Kindle Fire featured Amazon Silk, a cloud-accelerated web browser. By handling much of the computation necessary to render webpages in the cloud, Amazon hoped that Amazon Silk would be a differentiator for the Kindle Fire.

The Kindle Fire came with tens of thousands of preapproved apps and games available for purchase and download through the Amazon app market. Amazon provided 18 million movies, TV shows, songs, and magazines available for streaming or download. Amazon Prime subscribers received streaming access to more than 13,000 movies and TV shows for free. All new Kindle Fires came with a free one-month subscription to Amazon Prime to encourage customer integration into the Amazon ecosystem of content, goods, and services.

The $199 Kindle Fire was rumored to have reached 50,000 preorders per day during the two-week preorder period. According to Anthony DiClemente from Barclays, Amazon sold 3–5 million units of the Kindle Fire in Q4 2011, likely generating revenues in excess of $1 billion. The Kindle Fire was widely rumored to be sold at cost or even at a loss, given the relatively sophisticated specifications at such a discounted price. Amazon, true to form, simply stated in the Q4 2011 earnings report that

Exhibit 9 Global Top Five Media Tablet Brands, Q4 2011 (Ranking by Global Unit Shipments)

Q4 '11 Rank	2011 Rank	Brand	Q4 '11 Shipments (in millions)	Q4 '11 Share (%)	Q3 '11 Shipments (in millions)	Q3 '11 Share (%)	Q3–Q4 Change (%)	2011 Shipments (in millions)	2011 Share (%)
1	1	Apple	15,430	57	11,123	64	39	40,493	62
2	3	Amazon	3,885	14	0	0	NA	3,885	6
3	2	Samsung	2,140	8	1,850	11	16	6,110	9
4	4	B&N	1,920	7	750	4	156	3,250	5
5	5	Asus	612	2	801	5	-24	2,063	3
		Others	3,122	12	2,917	17	7	9,389	14
		Total	27,109	100	17,441	100	194	65,190	100

Exhibit 10 Nook, Fire, and iPad Compared

Nook Tablet	Kindle Fire	iPad 2 (Wi-Fi)
By Barnes & Noble	By Amazon	By Apple
• **Height**: 8.1 inches	• **Height**: 7.5 inches	• **Height**: 9.5 inches
• **Width**: 5 inches	• **Width**: 4.7 inches	• **Width**: 7.31 inches
• **Thickness**: 0.48 inches	• **Thickness**: 0.45 inches	• **Thickness**: 0.34 inches
• **Weight**: 0.88 pounds	• **Weight**: 0.91 pounds	• **Weight**: 1.33 pounds
• **Primary orientation**: Portrait	• **Primary orientation**: Portrait	• **Primary orientation**: Portrait
• **Color**: Gray	• **Color**: Black	• **Color**: Silver / White, Silver / Black
• **Speakers**: Mono	• **Speakers**: Stereo	• **Speakers**: Mono
• **Operating system**: Android	• **Operating system**: Android	• **Operating system**: iOS
• **Skin**: Nook Color	• **Skin**: Kindle	• **Launch OS version**: 4.3
• **Launch OS version**: 2.3	• **Launch OS version**: 2.3.3	• **Current OS version**: 5.1
• **Notable apps**: Hulu Plus, Netflix		• **Media streaming**: AirPlay

MEMORY

• **RAM size**: 1 GB	• **RAM size**: 512 MB	• **RAM size**: 512 MB
		• **RAM type**: DDR2

BATTERY

• **Capacity**: 4000 mAh	• **Capacity**: 4400 mAh	• **Capacity**: 25 Wh
• **Removable**: No	• **Removable**: No	• **Removable**: No
• **Quoted use time**: 9 hr	• **Quoted use time**: 7.5 hr	• **Quoted use time**: 10 hr

CONNECTIVITY

• **Wi-Fi**: Yes	• **Wi-Fi**: Yes	• **Wi-Fi**: Yes
• **Wi-Fi support**: 802.11n, 802.11g, 802.11b	• **Wi-Fi support**: 802.11n, 802.11g, 802.11b	• **Wi-Fi support**: 802.11n, 802.11g, 802.11b, 802.11a

the Kindle Fire was the bestselling, most wished for, and most gifted device of the holiday season.

Apple would be responding soon with its update of the iPad product line, and Bezos feared a "mini-iPad" at a competitive price might strike hard at his initial success. The unproven Kindle Fire, despite its strong sales numbers, faced numerous challenges. Initial criticisms of the device focused on its sometimes lagging display, shorter-than-advertised battery life, and a number of smaller feature-set complaints. Although a firmware update would resolve the first two of these problems, the feature-set complaints would have to wait until a new version of the Kindle Fire was released.

Customer Segments for the Kindle Fire

The initial Kindle Fire launch had broad aims in an effort to probe the market and learn which use cases and customer segments would respond most favorably to the new product. Although this "probe-and-learn" process was acceptable at the start, the time had come for Amazon to be more focused in defining its target audience. There were several possible target segments the company could consider.

Media Junkies. Amazon already attracted the most avid consumers of media because of its bargain prices for content and its huge selection. The "media junkie" market had evolved in the digital age to rapidly consume multimedia content from numerous channels, often simultaneously. Indeed, one of the primary use cases for tablets, according to Nielsen, was in front of the TV.[8] As all content transitioned to digital, the case for targeting these most avid of users grew stronger. U.S. consumers were expected to purchase more music digitally than on CD by 2012. Additionally, DVD sales had fallen more than 20 percent in 2011, whereas streaming had risen by 33 percent. Subscription streaming services such as Hulu and Netflix for video and Spotify for audio were attracting millions of customers. Amazon was primed to offer an alternative to these, but only if they could get users to switch.

Media junkies were quite price conscious because of the scale of their purchasing. Amazon fit this niche well because of its extremely competitive pricing on its music, video, and reading content. The Kindle Fire platform was ideally suited for downloading popular content through the Prime Instant streaming feature and for purchasing the more obscure titles that the long tail demanded through the massive Amazon store.

For customers who desired having tens of thousands of books, magazines, music, and movies available in one affordable handheld device, the Kindle Fire would be ideal.

But would the demanding tastes of these customers mean that they would take a pass on the Kindle Fire's smaller screen? For most media junkies, an ideal tablet would need to have a high-resolution screen and a superior graphics chipset. Would these price-sensitive customers gorge on the free content through the Prime Instant service and pass up purchasing Amazon content? Additionally, would Kindle Fire customers increase their content consumption after purchasing a Kindle, or were they at their limit already?

Children and Mobile Gamers. Children were a relatively untapped market for tablets. Handheld gaming devices had been around for decades, but few computers or devices had been created specifically to appeal to children. Although children were not favorable targets for the commerce aspects of Amazon, nor were they able to purchase apps on their own, they did heavily influence the purchasing behavior of their parents. U.S. parents reported that almost 30 percent of the apps on their tablets and smartphones were downloaded for their children. Nielsen reported that in 70 percent of U.S. households that owned tablets, children under the age of 12 used them frequently, and the primary children's use was to play games.[9]

Handheld gaming on tablets and smartphones represented the fastest-growing gaming market for 2009–2011. At more than $20 billion in the United States and $57 billion globally in 2009, the gaming market was a high-value prize and an untapped market for Amazon. By the end of 2011, there were 15 billion apps downloaded from the Apple App Store and 10 billion from the Android Market, later known as Google Play. Games made up more than 25 percent of all available apps and occupied 30 percent of the top one hundred apps in both stores. Many parents, however, still balked at giving children their own $600 iPad or even a low-end $500 Android tablet that they could lose or break.

At less than $200, the Kindle Fire was considerably cheaper than other tablets. The screen was made of Gorilla Glass® and its smaller size made it more rugged than the iPad and some of the larger Android tablets. This combination made it an attractive tablet for children. The addition of a long-lasting battery and a small, hand-friendly, tactile rubberized coating was enough to push the product to the top of many 2011 Christmas lists.

However, the Kindle Fire's slower processor, smaller screen, and limited memory capacity might weaken its perception as a gaming platform. Third-party developers might be hesitant to create special versions of their games expressly for the Kindle Fire. These developers would need to be managed to ensure adequate availability of hit titles in the Amazon App Marketplace.

Higher Education. The higher education industry made an attractive market for transition to digital books. Amazon had served the education market for years through its new and used textbook businesses but had failed to transition these customers to digital. Amazon's first attempt, the 10-inch-screen Kindle DX, had failed to catch on broadly, likely because of its high price point ($459) and its grayscale screen. By 2012, the more than $10 billion new-textbook market had remained relatively untapped by digital alternatives, despite these customers being the largest consumers of Amazon's core service: books.

To succeed in this market, Amazon would need to create a complex set of business-to-business partnerships with colleges, universities, and their bookstores to manage the timely distribution and updating of e-texts. Because students tended to be tech-savvy, adoption of the devices was likely, if adequate content could be made available. And the value proposition of reduced-price textbooks was compelling for students, who craved bargains on their expensive yearly book bills.

Textbooks were exceedingly expensive compared to trade books. Publishers traditionally faced inflated costs as a result of limited-run productions for many texts, and these additional costs were usually passed on to customers. These books also tended to be considerably larger and contained more glossy photos, figures, and equations than the average book. The high costs, in addition to the price sensitivity of students for textbooks, had led to the explosion of the online secondary market, from which Amazon had profited greatly.

College students faced with heavy backpacks and steep prices for their textbooks were very interested in reducing the load both physically and financially. Amazon was the largest online seller of new textbooks and thus had a large customer base to advertise to. This made the textbook market very attractive to Amazon, which could leverage its national brand and partnerships with publishers to bring e-textbooks to the entire U.S. market quickly if the use case could be proven.

By 2011, B&N had partnered with several universities to offer its Nook Color™ e-reader to students through campus bookstores. Titles on the Nook were 30 to 50 percent cheaper than their paper alternatives. These titles were also not transferable, which avoided the growing problem—for publishers, at least—of the secondary used market for textbooks. This limited trial by B&N

represented a considerable threat to Amazon in this emerging market.

However, bringing textbooks to the Kindle Fire would mean updating its file formats significantly. Digital textbooks meant Amazon had to develop the capability to handle large figure and graph display, robust highlighting and annotation features, and complex equation display (which was unavailable in the current MOBI format). The smaller screen was also a significant hindrance to publishers; their offerings would need to be redesigned for the Kindle Fire. Some publishers had shown willingness to do this with the B&N Nook and on the iPad's iTextbook platform, but Amazon had yet to finalize such deals. The iTextbook platform, though still nascent, showed what the premium product in the market might look like. Amazon had yet to figure out how to move a bargain product into this space.

Positioning the Kindle Fire

Multiple new entrants had converged on the tablet and e-reader markets at which the Kindle Fire was targeted. These direct competitors were touted by analysts as direct responses to Kindle's explosive growth in the e-book and periodical market and to the growing reading and web-surfing habits of the U.S. population in general. By Q4 2011, nearly 25 percent of U.S. Internet users were estimated to have some sort of tablet device (Exhibit 11). Analysts wondered if the Kindle Fire could be a credible low-cost entrant into the tablet market. Steven Levy of *Wired* magazine wrote that "the long-awaited Amazon tablet … represents [Bezos's] most ambitious leap into the hearts, minds, and wallets of millions of consumers."[10]

Amazon faced competition on numerous fronts. One of its most promising businesses, selling e-books to Kindle users, was now being attacked head-on by Apple's iBooks and Newsstand apps, in addition to the stiff e-book competition it had received from B&N for the past three years. B&N's Nook tablet was also beginning to push into the education market at universities and colleges in the United States. The mobile gaming market was in renaissance, with gesture- and gravity-based short-play games thriving on tablets and smartphones. And media junkies had a plethora of choices in buying and consuming content. For Amazon content alone, they could now find, purchase, and consume content on nearly three hundred devices.

Positioning The Kindle Fire Versus The iPad. The tablet market was dominated by the first-mover iPad (2010) and subsequent iPad 2 (2011) offerings from

Exhibit 11 U.S. Tablet Sales and Forecast, 2011–2016

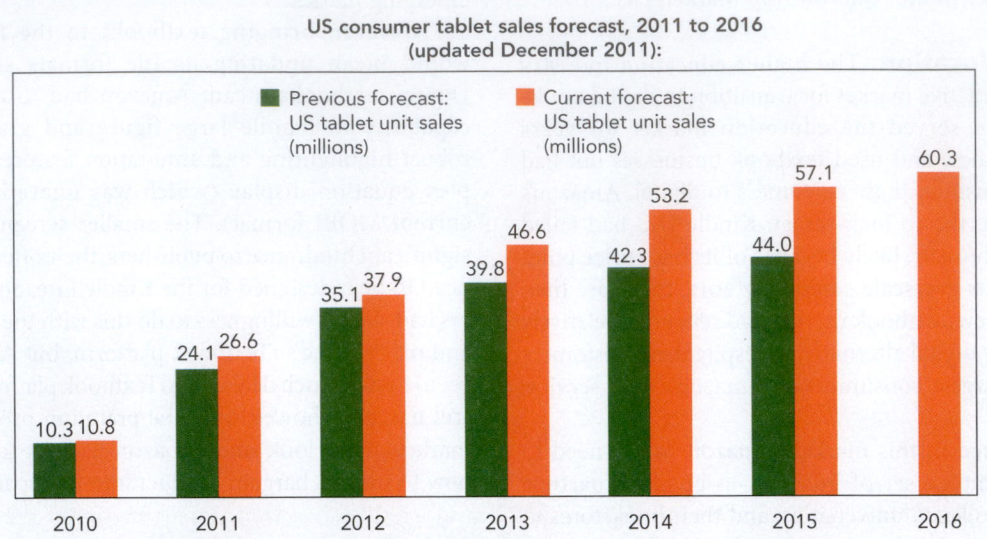

US consumer tablet sales forecast, 2011 to 2016
(updated December 2011):

■ Previous forecast:
US tablet unit sales (millions)

■ Current forecast:
US tablet unit sales (millions)

Year	Previous	Current
2010	10.3	10.8
2011	24.1	26.6
2012	35.1	37.9
2013	39.8	46.6
2014	42.3	53.2
2015	44.0	57.1
2016		60.3

Source: Forrester Research Consumer PC and Tablet Forecast, 2011 To 2016 (US).
Note: Updated forecast includes ipad, Barnes & Noble Nook Color and Nook Tablet, Kindle Fire, other Android tablets, BlackBerry PlayBook, and future Windows 8 and Windows on ARM tablets.

Source: Forrester Research, Inc.

Apple. These feature-rich devices succeeded where other tablets had failed by expertly walking the tight line between smartphone and laptop. Apple's strategy was to teach its customer base to use the iOS on the iPhone and iPod Touch and then graduate them to a larger-screen device that was more fun and convenient to browse and play on. The couch (70 percent) and the bed (57 percent) were the most popular places for tablet use, according to Nielsen Research.[11] Analysts, of course, began comparing the Kindle Fire to the iPad even before it was announced. Would the Kindle Fire be an "iPad killer?" Or, as one headline read, "Help! Santa can't afford the iPad. Will the Kindle Fire do?"[12]

On specifications, the iPad was a multipurpose, Swiss army knife–type device. Importantly, however, it was three to four times as expensive as a Kindle Fire, as well as quite a bit larger and heavier. Amazon had specifically created the Kindle Fire to be an affordable consumption device. Would the minimum viable product[13] beat out the feature-packed iPad? Or would consumers become frustrated by its slower speed, smaller memory, and more limited selection of apps? Both devices were exceptional at consuming streaming video, web surfing, and general reading. So would

customers be satisfied with these uses, or would the Kindle Fire's limitations irk them over time and lead them to opt for the iPad?

A battlefield on which Amazon was better equipped to fight was providing a wide and deep content catalog. Both Apple and Amazon were maneuvering to rapidly cement partnerships with content providers in the hopes of attracting customers by having the largest catalog of media. Early in 2012, Amazon had inked a deal with Viacom to provide a large number of videos through its Prime Instant Video service. This deal, combined with existing partnerships with the major networks, made the Amazon TV offerings significantly richer than those available on competing products.

Positioning The Kindle Fire Versus The Nook Tablet. The Nook and the Kindle Fire were extremely similar (from the hardware point of view) and were following the same pricing strategy as the earlier e-readers. Bezos worried that another price war might ensue. B&N had pursued the additional strategy of offering subsidies for Nooks at the point of sale if subscriptions were purchased with the device. For example, a $19.99 per month subscription to the *New York Times* netted the customer a $100 subsidy on the purchase of any Nook product, which made the Nook tablet only $99. Bezos knew he could make this play as well but remained hesitant to give the appearance that Amazon was willing to "give away" its Kindles. He also knew that while B&N had posted a $6.6 million loss ($0.17 per share) for Q2 2011, it had increased its recently consolidated Nook business revenue 85 percent to $220 million in the same quarter.

Although the devices could not differentiate on hardware specifications, they did offer very different user experiences. Amazon's focus was on its own content and services, whereas B&N focused on providing its own text-based content and allowing third parties to deliver the rest. The Hulu and Netflix apps came preinstalled on the Nook, along with the Google media store, Google Play. However, Amazon differentiated with its Silk web browser, which enhanced the experience of browsing on a limited device. Amazon also had numerous cloud-based services such as the Whispersync® feature, which kept the user's place in a given book or video across all Amazon apps.

Positioning The Kindle Fire Versus Kindle E-Reader.
The traditional Kindle e-reader still maintained strong appeal with avid readers for its ability to wirelessly purchase new books and magazines and its eye-pleasing E Ink screen, as well as its long battery life. But for these same users the Kindle faced stiff competition from newer tablets to be customers' "third device" (the first and second being a laptop and a smartphone). For avid readers, the new Kindle Touch ($99 for the option with advertising "offers" on its lock screen) was an optimum device, but these same users might consider consolidating their devices if a strong reading experience was offered on one of the competing tablets and if they could get the battery life they wanted. The youngest and often most tech-savvy student customers were already reading more and more online, eschewing traditional reference sources in favor of wikis and blogs. A web-enabled tablet offered a strong use case for these customers, as did an electronic medium for their books for class.

Would the Kindle Fire cut into the business of selling Kindles? Bezos believed that customers should want to buy both.[14] His optimism that both the Kindle Fire and the Kindle would find places in his customers' lives seemed to signal that these devices might continue to get cheaper and cheaper. Given the tough competition for e-readers from tablets and larger-screen smartphones, the future profitability of dedicated e-readers was uncertain at best. Bezos was betting that the integration of the Kindle e-book ecosystem via the Kindle family of apps would maintain value for these special-purpose devices.

Pricing and Business Model Decisions
The Kindle Fire was no exception to Amazon's traditional one-two punch of low margins combined with large-scale delivery. This model had succeeded for the company in market after market. Bezos wondered, however, whether the revenue streams from the Kindle Fire would be sufficient to meet the considerable costs of serving up the bevy of content that users desired. Particularly important and difficult to find was the sweet spot between the breadth of content sufficient to attract customers and a bloated library with excessive licensing costs. The success of the Kindle Fire business model would hinge on the demand for digital content, incremental online commerce sales, and price sensitivity for hardware. Bezos was betting that the integration of Amazon content, cloud-based storage, and the convenience of Amazon Prime all at a bargain price would prove to be a compelling proposition and profitable business model.

Hardware Revenues.
At $199, the Kindle Fire was well positioned to undercut the tablets currently on the market. For the first run of production, the components and labor were slated to be near $200. This meant that Amazon was selling the Kindle Fire at cost as a loss leader for content sales. Many analysts wondered if Amazon should have gone even lower with the Kindle Fire's hardware price in order to emphasize the "razor-razorblade" model[15] that Amazon was betting on. They pointed to the cellphone market, in which devices such as the iPhone (which cost more than $600) were subsidized heavily by wireless carriers in return for a long-term subscription contract. Was it possible for Amazon to offer the Kindle Fire for $149, $99, or even free, in return for customers signing up for an enhanced version of its Amazon Prime subscription service that would require them to commit to purchasing a minimum amount of content and products over a two-year period? Other experts felt that Amazon was leaving money on the table because the Kindle Fire was already priced so far below the iPad.

Content Revenues.
As more and more music, movies, and books were consumed in digital form, online content revenues were expected to be a key driver of revenues from Kindle Fire customers.

ABI Research estimated that an average Kindle Fire customer would buy about $10 per month in content (music and movies), which would increase 10 percent annually over the expected two-year life of the Kindle Fire. Amazon netted a gross margin of 30 percent on content sales. An RBC Capital survey of Kindle owners found that the average customer purchased three e-books per quarter, at an average selling price of $10 per book. Amazon's gross margin for e-books was 20 percent. Amazon expected a 10 percent increase in e-book purchases on an annual basis.

Commerce Revenues. Amazon had boasted to its investors that Kindle owners purchased 3.3 times as many e-books than print books once they switched to digital. Bezos hoped that the Kindle Fire would have a similar effect on sales of physical products sold on its website. Customers in the post-PC era would increasingly be making their purchases based on convenience. The Kindle Fire offered a pleasing color video–capable device ideally suited to shopping from the couch. The dedicated Amazon device, combined with the convenience of Amazon Prime, would likely motivate customers to increase the proportion of online purchases they made through Amazon. The average Kindle Fire customer was expected to purchase about $50 per month in incremental products and services from Amazon, at an average gross margin of 20 percent. Amazon estimated that these commerce purchases would increase by 5 percent per year.

Advertising Revenues. Amazon had built advertising for its retail goods and services into the pricing model for the newest generation of Kindle e-readers. The Kindle device became an omnipresent billboard for Amazon to serve ads to its customers. Millennial Media, the second-largest mobile ad network in the United States, reported at the end of 2011 that the Kindle Fire was seeing a daily increase of 19 percent in overall ad impressions on its network. That translated to a monthly rate of about 300 million advertising impressions. Amazon could expect an average CPM (revenue per thousand impressions) of about $10. However, users could pay $30 to permanently dismiss all the ads on the Kindle Fire. An estimated 20 percent of owners were expected to choose this option. Advertising impressions would decrease in subsequent years, but the downward pressure on CPM would offset the increase in installed base so that advertising revenues would essentially remain flat in subsequent years.

Application Marketplace Revenues. The Amazon App Marketplace, a curated version of the Android Market, ensured an optimum experience for its customers. App purchases promised to be a significant source of revenue for Amazon. In a span of just eighteen months, the Amazon AppStore had grown to 50,000 apps after it debuted in March 2011 with just 4,000. Amazon took a 30 percent cut of the sales price (the same percentage Google and Apple took from their own app stores). It was estimated that the Amazon AppStore had logged about 180 million downloads over the first eighteen months. Research also indicated that about 10 percent of apps were paid apps, and the average paid app generated $1.29 in the Amazon AppStore. App revenue was estimated to increase by 20 percent each year.

Conclusion

Amazon was betting that the end-to-end Kindle Fire experience was superior to buying from Amazon on the iPad. Apple, on the other hand, was betting that the Kindle Fire was not quite good enough. As Bezos considered the myriad announcements by competitors likely to come in the following few weeks, he still wondered whether his gamble on the tablet market would be a success. By reaching further into the hardware market, he had exposed Amazon to the grueling product cycles and often-fickle whims of technology customers. Would these customers appreciate the Kindle Fire's value proposition? Who should be the core target for the product? Would the Kindle Fire deliver on the various revenue streams laid out for it? Or would customers just load up on the free content and drain Amazon's servers on subsidized hardware? As the embodiment of the Amazon experience, the Kindle Fire was particularly well-situated to signal to investors the future growth prospects of Amazon's businesses.

NOTES

1. E Ink was a specific proprietary type of electronic paper manufactured by E Ink Corporation and commonly used in mobile devices such as e-readers.

2. Amazon.com, 2010 Letter to Shareholders.

3. Long tail, a term popularized by Chris Anderson in *The Long Tail: Why the Future of Business Is Selling Less of More* (New York: Hyperion, 2006), describes the retail strategy of selling a large number of unique items in relatively small quantities while selling fewer popular items in large quantities. Underpinning this strategy is the belief that the sum of many small markets is worth as much, if not more, than a few large markets.

4. Installed base refers to the total number of operating systems or products actually in use (i.e., that customers have installed), as opposed to market share, which only measures units sold. Analysts view the installed base as a more reliable measure of a platform's popularity. See http://en.wikipedia.org/wiki/Installed_base (accessed January 16, 2014).

5. In computing, "form factor" refers to the specifications of the motherboard (e.g., the dimensions, they type of power supply, the location of mounting holes, etc.).

6. Nicholas Deleon, "Deloitte: 2011 Will Be the Year of the Tablet (Say Goodbye to Your Laptop)," *TechCrunch*, January 20, 2011.

7. Steven Levy, "Jeff Bezos Owns the Web in More Ways Than You Think," *Wired*, November 13, 2011; Shara Tibken, "Amazon Challenges iPad With 'Fire,'" *Wall Street Journal*, September 29, 2011.

8. Nielsen Newswire, "In the U.S., Tablets Are TV Buddies While eReaders Make Great Bedfellows," May 19, 2011, http://www.nielsen.com/us/en/newswire/2011/in-the-u-s-tablets-are-tv-buddies-while-ereaders-make-great-bedfellows.html.

9. Nielsen Newswire, "American Families See Tablets As Playmate, Teacher and Babysitter," February 16, 2012, http://www.nielsen.com/us/en/newswire/2012/american-families-see-tablets-as-playmate-teacher-and-babysitter.html.

10. Levy, "Jeff Bezos Owns the Web in More Ways Than You Think."

11. Nielsen Newswire, "In the U.S., Tablets Are TV Buddies."

12. Marguerite Reardon, "Help! Santa Can't Afford the iPad. Will the Kindle Fire Do?" *CNET*, November 25, 2011.

13. Coined by Frank Robinson and popularized by Eric Reis, a "minimum viable product" refers to an iterative process that allows a product to be launched with basic features.

14. Lance Ulanoff, "Amazon CEO Jeff Bezos: Why Is This Man Smiling?" *Mashable*, September 24, 2013, http://mashable.com/2013/09/25/jeff-bezos-interview.

15. In this model, dependent goods are sold at different prices. One product is sold at a discount, while another is sold at a considerably higher price to make up for the loss.

CASE 2

American Express: Bank 2.0

A New Mission in Enterprise Growth

In June 2011, Kenneth Chenault, CEO of American Express (AXP), announced the formation of a new group within the company, Enterprise Growth (EG), to drive expansion into digital and mobile payments. "New technologies are redefining the payments business and creating opportunities that go beyond our existing businesses," said Chenault in a press release. "The Enterprise Growth group is designed to extend our leadership into the world of alternative payments and create new fee-based revenue streams for the post-recession environment." To lead the group, AXP hired Dan Schulman from Sprint Corporation (where he had headed the Prepaid Group after previously serving as founding CEO of Virgin Mobile USA, as president and CEO of Priceline.com Incorporated, and in other leadership positions).[1] "Technology [is] fundamentally going to change the way you might think about financial services," Schulman said during one of his first meetings with EG, "just as the Internet has redefined one industry after another."[2] EG, he continued, was designed "to challenge existing business models" and "to think about the intersection between software, software platforms, mobile apps, mobile technology in general, and financial services."

For Alpesh Chokshi and Wesley Wright, this was the moment they had been waiting for. Both of them had been at AXP since 2001 and had worked in its prepaid business since 2005. When EG was formed, their group had moved into EG with a mandate to drive expansion beyond AXP's traditional credit and charge business on a global basis. Chokshi was the president and Wright led product development. Before moving into EG, together with their team they had driven the expansion of AXP's prepaid business into gift cards and reloadable cards. Now, with the support of Chenault and Schulman, they saw an opportunity to do something bigger—to move AXP into debit and checking spending, a large sector of payments in which it did not currently play (see Exhibit 1 for AXP consolidated financial performance and Exhibits 2 through 4 for performance metrics of the U.S. cards business). Their team had begun calling the initiative Bank 2.0, indicating the application of technology to usher in a "next iteration" of banking.

As the team focused on this opportunity, Chokshi imagined the concerns some of his colleagues might raise. The team would need good answers to a number of questions. The good news was that the EG team had "gone to school" with regard to the potential opportunity in Bank 2.0. The team was well aware of the magnitude of the potential market that was currently underserved by traditional banking services. In the United States, estimates were that more than one in four households (28.3%) were either unbanked or underbanked[3] and conducting some or all of their financial transactions outside of the mainstream banking system.[4] Even as EG's initial research had gleaned some promising indicators, there was still much that needed to be worked out.

The Closed-Loop Network

AXP cards were accepted at fewer merchants than Visa or MasterCard. One reason was a perception that AXP transactions were more costly to the retailer or merchant due in part to different business models, fees, and pricing structures for processing transactions.

In the Visa and MasterCard business models, external banks and financial institutions owned the relationship with the cardholder (in the vernacular of credit card business models, these were called "issuers"). Issuers provided cards to their customers that bore a Visa or MasterCard logo, and set the interest rate and any fees on the loans the cards would deliver. When the cardholder bought a meal at a restaurant, a transaction network sent the amount of the purchase to the restaurant's

Exhibit 1 Consolidated Financial Highlights

(In millions, except per-share amounts, percentages, and employees)	2011	2010	% INC/DEC
Total Revenues Net of Interest Expense	$29,962	$27,582	9%
Income from Continuing Operations	$4,899	$4,057	21%
Income from Discontinued Operations	$36	—	#
Net Income	$4,935	$4,057	22%
Return on Average Equity	27.7%	27.5%	
Total Assets	$153,337	$146,689	5%
Shareholders/Equity	$18,794	$16,230	16%
Diluted Income from Continuing Operations Attributable to Common Shareholders	$4.09	$3.35	22%
Diluted Income from Discontinued Operations	$0.03	—	#
Diluted Net Income Attributable to Common Shareholders	$4.12	$3.35	23%
Cash Dividends Declared per Share	$0.72	$0.72	—
Book Value per Share	$16.15	$13.56	19%
Average common Shares Outstanding for Diluted Earnings per Common Share	1,184	1,195	−1%
Common Share Cash Dividends Declared	$856	$867	−1%
Common Share Repurchases	48	14	#
Number of Employees	62,500	51,000	2%

 # denotes a variance of more than 100%
Data source: American Express annual report, 2012.

bank for authorization (the restaurant's bank was known as the "acquirer"). After the transaction was approved and cleared, the issuer bank received a percentage of the sale based on the interest on the loan provided to the cardholder at the time. The acquirer received a fee from the restaurant in the form of a discount fee (an industry average of 1.2%).[5] Visa or MasterCard received their revenues for the ownership and management of the transaction-processing services and data management for the entire system. Their business models were based on increasing the number of times that a consumer used a card ("transaction-centric" models). An important distinction in this model was that neither Visa nor MasterCard made any loans to the consumer. Thus they received no interest on the loans made to consumers for their purchases.

AXP's business model, however, had it serving as both the issuer and the lender. Thus the analogous strategy was a "spend-centric" one. In this approach, AXP's cardholders were provided their cards by the company's own banking subsidiaries. AXP received its primary revenues from the discount fees charged to merchants (which were higher than the industry average: an estimated 2.4%).[6] The important distinction in AXP's "closed-loop" network was that the company had the ability to leverage spending data about its customers to create more tailored rewards/offer programs for customers and to share high-level trends and business insights about spending patterns with merchants.

An important performance metric in this model was that customers spent higher amounts per purchase. One study indicated that the average payment volume per transaction for AXP cards was around $150, while Visa's was one-third that amount.[7] This also made AXP members attractive to merchants seeking more affluent customers, and the company used internal data to match merchants with affluent customers that would likely buy their products. Since credit risks were borne internally

Exhibit 2 U.S. Card Services Selected Income Statement Data

Years ended December 31 (millions)	2011	2010	2009
Revenues			
Discount revenue, net card fees, and other	$10,648	$9,884	$9,043
Securitization income, net[1]	—	—	400
Interest income	5,230	5,390	3,216
Interest expense	807	812	568
Net interest income	4,423	4,578	2,648
Total revenues net of interest expense	15,071	14,462	12,091
Provisions for losses	687	1,591	3,769
Total revenues net of interest expense after provisions for losses	14,384	12,871	8,322
Expenses			
Marketing, promotion, rewards and cardmember services	6,593	5,744	4,362
Salaries and employee benefits Operating expenses	3,662	3,623	3,385
Total	10,255	9,367	7,747
Pretax segment income	4,129	3,504	575
Income tax provision	1,449	1,279	171
Segment income	$2,680	$2,225	$404

Data source: American Express annual report, 2012.

1. In accordance with new GAAP governing consolidations and VIEs, the company no longer reports net securitization income in its income statement beginning January 1, 2010.

by AXP's banking subsidiaries, any interest on loans to members was another source of revenue that Visa and MasterCard did not receive.

AXP's business model was supported by a complimentary advertising campaign designed to attract affluent consumers who would tend to spend more per purchase. From 1987 to 1996, the AXP ad campaign tagline was "Membership has its privileges."[8] Ads often featured images of cardmember celebrities, from Elvis Presley in 1958[9] to Robert DeNiro in 2004's "My Life" campaign.[10] The brand became widely associated with affluence and exclusivity, and its average annual spend per cardholder tended to be higher than that of AXP's competitors. The average annual spend per card increased at a double-digit rate from 2009

to 2011, growing from $11,505 to $14,124.[11] Industry analysts were well aware of the differences in approach: "This contrast is evident in the numbers; Visa has more than 2 billion cards in use worldwide and processes more than 60 billion transactions per year, while AmEx has just 107 million cards in force and processes just 6 billion transactions per year. Despite this disparity, American Express has annual gross revenues of $33 billion while Visa earns just $14 billion per year."[12]

Experiencing Exclusion

The EG team recognized that it needed to better understand the Bank 2.0 customer. Rather than simply relying on third-party research about financial inclusion, the team sought to engage directly with the experiences of underbanked people by trying to make payments without accessing credit or checking accounts. Chokshi, for example, stood in line for at least half an hour before attempting to cash a personal check at a check casher. The standard check casher, he found, took between 2% and 5% of the face transactional value. This process, Chokshi discovered, was the first of several instances in which underbanked people lost both money and time relative to affluent customers. Once their checks were cashed—at a substantial price in fees—they had to stand in another line to get a money order to pay their bill. Given the difficulty of finding time to stand in lines— *This is like a part-time job*, Chokshi thought—people often had to contend with late fees.

At a meeting, the team members shared with each other that at least 50% of Americans lived paycheck-to-paycheck. "Most have enough money to cover expenses," one team member explained. "It's a timing issue. It's cash flow. The populations we're talking about can't [take on more debt]. They have no savings, they have no flex." As a result, this segment often resorted to payday loans.

The next task was to develop a specific go-to-market approach. The team had been thinking about an innovative product: a prepaid, reloadable card that could do many of the things one would normally have to go to a bank to do. The physical-branch-based system was increasingly unreliable—not only because of rising fees, but also because branches were closing across the country. In a meeting room, the team wrote on a board: "It's expensive to be poor" and "2,300 bank branches closed last year, 95% in low-income areas. 70 million people in the United States are unbanked or underbanked; they pay 10% of their income on fees and interest to complete everyday transactions." EG thought 10% was about the

Exhibit 3 Selected Statistical Information

As of or for the years ended December 31 *(in billions, except percentages and where indicated)*	2011	2010	2009
Card billed business	$424.3	$378.1	$339.4
Total cards-in-force *(millions)*	40.9	39.9	39.5
Basic cards-in-force *(millions)*	30.4	29.7	29.5
Average basic cardmember spend *(dollars)**	$14,124	$12,795	$10,957
U.S. consumer travel:			
Travel sales *(millions)*	$3,603	$3,116	$2,561
Travel commissions and fees/sales	8.3%	8.2%	8.4%
Total segment assets	$97.8	$91.3	$57.6
Segment capital *(millions)*	$8,804	$7,411	$6,021
Return on average segment capital[a]	33.0%	35.0%	7.9%
Return on average tangible segment capital[a]	34.8%	37.8%	8.6%
Cardmember receivables:			
Total receivables	$20.6	$19.2	$17.8
30 days past due as a % of total	1.9%	$1.1	$16.1
Average receivables	$18.8%	$17.1	$16.1
Net write-off rate—principal only[b]	1.7%	1.6%	3.8%
Net write-off rate—principal and fees[b]	1.9%	1.8%	4.2%
Cardmember loans—GAAP basis portfolio:			
Total loans	$53.7	$51.6	$23.5
30 days past due loans as a % of total	1.4%	2.1%	3.7%
Average loans	$50.3	$449.8	$25.9
Net write-off rate—principal only[b]	2.9%	5.8%	9.1%
Net write-off rate—principal, interest, and fees[b]	3.2%	6.3%	10.4%
Net interest income divided by average loans[c] [d]	8.8%	9.2%	10.2%
Net interest yield on cardmember loans[c]	8.9%	9.4%	9.4%
Cardmember loans—managed basis portfolio:			
Total loans	$53.7	$51.6	$52.6
30 days past due loans as a % of total	1.4%	2.1%	3.7%
Average loans	$50.3	$49.8	$54.9
Net write-off rate—principal only[b]	2.9%	5.8%	8.7%
Net write-off rate—principal, interest, and fees[b]	3.2%	6.3%	9.9%
Net interest yield on card member loans[c]	8.9%	9.4%	10.1%

*Proprietary cards only

(a) Return on average segment capital is calculated by dividing (1) one-year period segment income ($2.7 billion, $2.2 billion and $404 million for 2011, 2010, and 2009 respectively) by (2) one-year average segment capital ($8.1 billion, $6.4 billion and $5.1 billion for 2011, 2010, and 2009, respectively). Return on average tangible segment capital is computed in the same manner as return on average segment capital except the computation of average tangible segment capital, a non-GAAP measure, excludes from average segment capital average goodwill and other intangibles of $425 million, $459 million, and $432 million as of December 31, 2011, 2010, and 2009, respectively. The company believes return on average tangible segment capital is a useful measure of the profitability of its business.

(b) Refer to "Consolidated Results of Operations—Selected Statistical Information".

(c) See table on the following page for the calculation of net interest yield on cardmember loans, a non-GAAP measure, and net interest income divided by average loans, a GAAP measure.

(d) Refer to "Consolidated Results of Operations—Selected Statistical Information."

Data source: American Express annual report, 2012.

Exhibit 4 Calculation of Net Interest Yield on Cardmember Loans

Years ended December 31 (in millions, except percentages and where indicated)	2011	2010	2009
Calculation based on GAAP information:			
Net interest income	$4,423	$4,578	$2,648
Average loans (billions)	$ 50.3	$ 49.8	$ 25.9
Adjusted net interest income	$4,490	$4,684	$2,451
Adjusted average loans (billions)	$ 50.3	$ 49.8	$ 26.0
Net interest income divided by average loans	8.8%	9.2%	10.2%
Net interest yield on cardmember loans	8.9%	9.4%	9.4%
Calculation based on managed information:			
Net interest income	$4,423	$4,578	$5,501
Average loans (billions)	$ 50.3	$ 49.8	$ 54.9
Adjusted net interest income	$4,490	$4,684	$5,558
Adjusted average loans (billions)	$ 50.3	$ 49.8	$ 55.0
Net interest yield on cardmember loans	8.9%	9.4%	10.1%

Data source: American Express annual report, 2012.

amount this portion of the population would spend on food. It troubled the team to think that people spent so much money just to change their income from one form to another (see Exhibit 5 for key indicators of unbanked and underbanked consumers and markets). Through technology, EG believed it could reimagine what it meant to be part of the financial system. Based on this meeting, it was clear that AXP supported the idea.

In 2010, EG had acquired Revolution Money, a payments company.[13] Revolution Money's technology formed the foundation for a beta digital payments product, a prepaid card supported by an online platform.[14] This new product gave customers a way to conduct peer-to-peer transfers and to make payments online; it was reloadable via debit or credit card or checking account. As a beta digital payments product, it was not an outstanding success, but the team believed the platform itself still held plenty of potential.

Wright wondered how much internal resistance he might encounter if he proposed a new product that relied on the same platform as the beta product. Though

the initiative was the result of aggressive innovation, it did not see much traction, and skepticism rose in the company as a result. The digital payments initiative required investment that had far less certainty than AXP credit cards, for which the cost of acquisition and the typical consumer payback were already known. The EG team would be operating in an entirely new market that had uncertain metrics of performance.

Chokshi wondered if EG could use the acquired software platform and knowledge to evolve the AXP mission, moving from an iconic brand for the affluent to an inclusive brand with a much greater reach. "The less money you have, ironically, the more it costs you to manage and move it," he'd written in his notes. AXP could change that by starting to serve a segment that was historically unable to access the company's products. The new concept, Bank 2.0, was a way to increase the consumer base and to develop a new kind of relationship. The more affluent, typical credit and charge customers had access to financial and payment services from a sizable range of institutions and formats. The ideal Bank 2.0 customer would conduct the bulk of his or her financial activity via the platform, including direct deposit of paychecks.

Though AXP's credit and charge businesses were strong, the company saw a chance for growth by offering an alternative to debit, checking, and cash. Global payments amounted to $34 trillion dollars each year; credit and charge constituted $6 trillion of that total.[15] What remained was a market opportunity of $27 trillion in cash, check, and debit that AXP hadn't accessed before. The advent of the Serve platform opened a door to that world. As one member of the EG team put it, "Every company wants to be a growth company [...]. The only way to do that over time is to get new customers."[16]

Bank 2.0 was not actually a bank, but it would enable people to use their mobile phones in ways similar to how they would use a bank branch. Mobile banking transactions were considerably cheaper for financial services firms. William Demchak, president of PNC Bank, estimated that banks saved $3.38 per transaction when a customer deposited a check by snapping a photo of it on a mobile phone versus depositing it at a teller window.[17] The language for such a product was still coming into existence. Defining this category was a challenge AXP would have to face. Other companies had attempted to rebuild the banking sector and had met some challenges: how to achieve scale with the underbanked consumer, technological hurdles to truly enabling mobile and nonbranch delivery, new regulatory requirements of being a banking provider, and getting past the scrutiny of consumer interest groups that

Exhibit 5 Unbanked and Underbanked Consumers in the United States

In 2011, FDIC surveyed 45,000 U.S. households to determine their degree of participation in the banking system. The resulting survey results are projectable to the entire U.S. population.

Definitions and Key Findings:

- ■ **Depository Institutions**. Banks and credit unions that provide insured checking and savings accounts up to $250,000. *There are approximately 90,000 depository branches in the United States.*

- ■ **Alternative Financial Services Providers**. Financial institutions that provide any of the following services: non-bank money orders, nonbank check-cashing services, nonbank remittances, payday loans, rent-to-own services, pawn shops, or tax refund anticipation loans (RALs). *Approximately 25% of households used some form of AFS in the 12 months prior to the survey. Almost 10% used two or more AFS products.*

- ■ **Unbanked Households**. Households in which no individual holds a checking or savings account in an insured depository institution. *8.2% of U.S. households are unbanked, up 0.6% since 2009. An estimated 24.2 million U.S. households are underbanked. An estimated 9.9M households are unbanked.*

- ■ **Underbanked Households**. Households in which an individual has a checking and/or savings account but used AFS providers in the past 12 months to meet financial needs. *20.1% of U.S. households are unbanked, up 1.9% since 2009. An estimated 24.2 million U.S. households are underbanked.*

- ■ **Banked Households**. Households in which all individuals are fully engaged in the financial mainstream, and did not use AFS in the past 12 months. *68.8% of U.S. households are fully banked, down 2.5% since 2009. An estimated 88.2 million U.S. households are banked.*

- ■ **Unbanked Cash Households**. Households in which no individual has a depository account, and have not used AFS in the last 12 months. *29.5% of unbanked households rely purely on cash.*

- ■ **Employment Status.** Not surprisingly, banking status is positively correlated with employment. *64.1% of all underbanked households, however, have members who are employed.*

- ■ **Income.** Having a depository account is positively correlated with income. 40.8% of underbanked households make less than $30,000 in annual income. *17.1% of all underbanked households, however, make between $30,000 and $50,000, and 18.3% of all underbanked households make $75,000 or more.*

- ■ **Home Ownership.** An estimated half of all U.S. homeowners are underbanked (52.1%).

Source: Federal Deposit Insurance Corporation Department of Depositor and Consumer Protection, "2011 FDIC National Survey of Unbanked and Underbanked Households: Executive Summary," September 2012.

were notoriously skeptical of banks' efforts involving moderate-income consumers. (In 2010, the Consumer Financial Protection Bureau [CFPB]was formed, in part, to demystify the agreements consumers made with providers of financial services).[18]

Options in a Competitive Landscape

The EG team wasn't alone in recognizing the opportunities in a changing landscape in financial services. Consumers were gradually changing the way they made transactions, altering the medium they used to make their payments. See Exhibits 6 and 7 for indicators of the movement to a greater reliance on debit and prepaid cards among U.S. consumers. Exhibit 8 provides the purchase volume, market share, and 2010 growth rates of leading U.S. card companies.

Although the Bank 2.0 initiative team was attempting to serve the underbanked, the team knew that the term "underbanked" was in some ways deceiving. First, underbanked consumers regularly engaged in financial transactions—those transactions were simply outside of the traditional banking system. For example, they performed many transactions in cash and used check-cashing centers, payday lenders, and remittance companies (known as alternative financial services [AFS]).[19] The team recognized that all of these were potential services that could be provided by payments companies. Second, in addition to these AFS competitors, a cadre of technology start-ups was already attempting to enter the market with novel solutions.[20] For example, Green Dot was testing the marketplace through a partnership with Wal-Mart, while GoBank and NetSpend had forged relationships with check cashers. Square Cash had also launched, providing an opportunity for consumers to send and receive money to and from one another. Each of these entrepreneurial firms was leveraging mobile and digital technology to offer consumers easier and cheaper alternatives to traditional banks. The largest of these, Green Dot, became a publicly traded company on the NYSE (ticker: GDOT). On July 21, 2010—Green Dot's opening day—the firm was valued at 27 times 2010 profits. Green Dot's owners sold 4.56 million shares at $36. Early shareholders in Green Dot included Wal-Mart and Sequoia Capital.[21] The entry and growth of these firms suggested that there was a market to be served, but which of them would eventually institutionalize and scale?

The team also wondered about the response of traditional depository institutions such as banks and credit unions. According to recent studies by SNL Financial, there were approximately 96,000 bank branches in the United States, but the aggregate number of branches had actually been decreasing in recent decades and the pace of closure had increased since the financial crisis of 2009. In fact, no single U.S. state experienced net bank-branch additions in the cumulative period running from 2010 to 2013.[22]

There were prevailing economic imperatives for this trend: first, structural costs of branch banking were making it difficult to maintain brick-and-mortar presence, especially in lower-income and rural communities. Real estate, maintenance of physical spaces, and labor costs for tellers, branch managers, and security personnel

Exhibit 6 Purchase Volume on U.S. General-Purpose Cards by Type

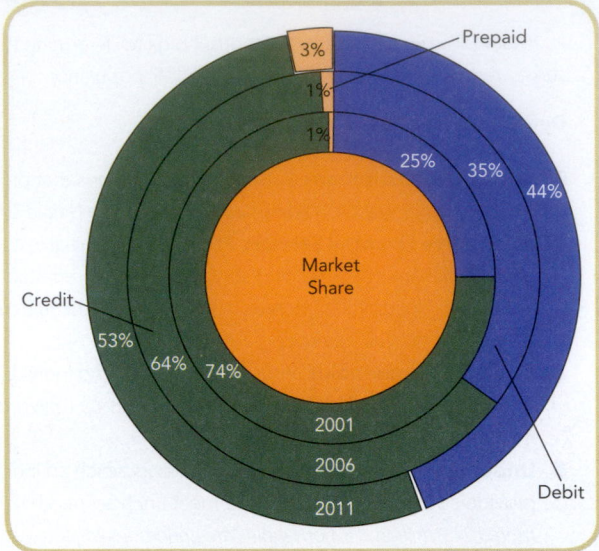

Data source: Case writer adaptation of data from the Nilson Report, 2012.

made paper-thin margins even smaller. Associated Banc-Corp, the largest banking chain in Wisconsin, estimated that it saved $300,000 with each branch closure.[23] A study by consulting firm Simon-Kucher & Partners estimated that two-thirds of existing bank branches were unprofitable, and that an individual branch needed to

Exhibit 7 U.S. Payment Cards by Type (Market Shares) and Manner

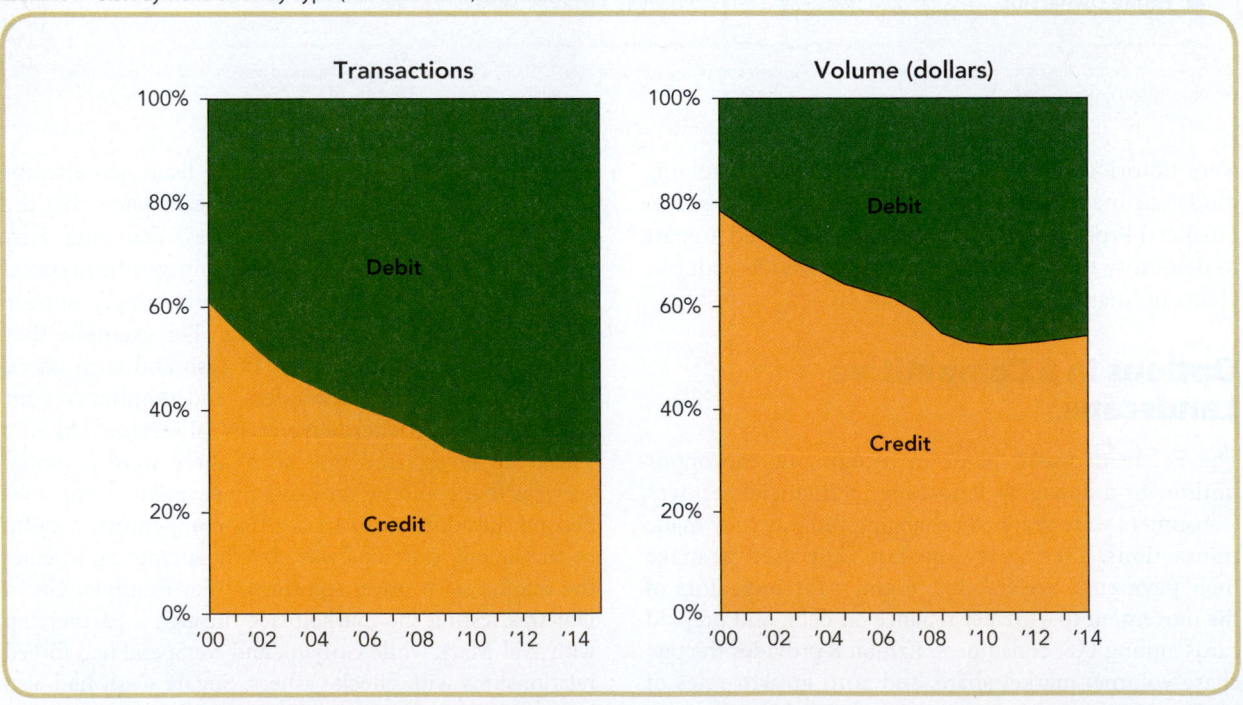

Data source: Case writer adaptation of data from the Nilson Report, 2012.

Exhibit 8 Purchase Volume at U.S. Merchants, Market Size, and Growth, 2011

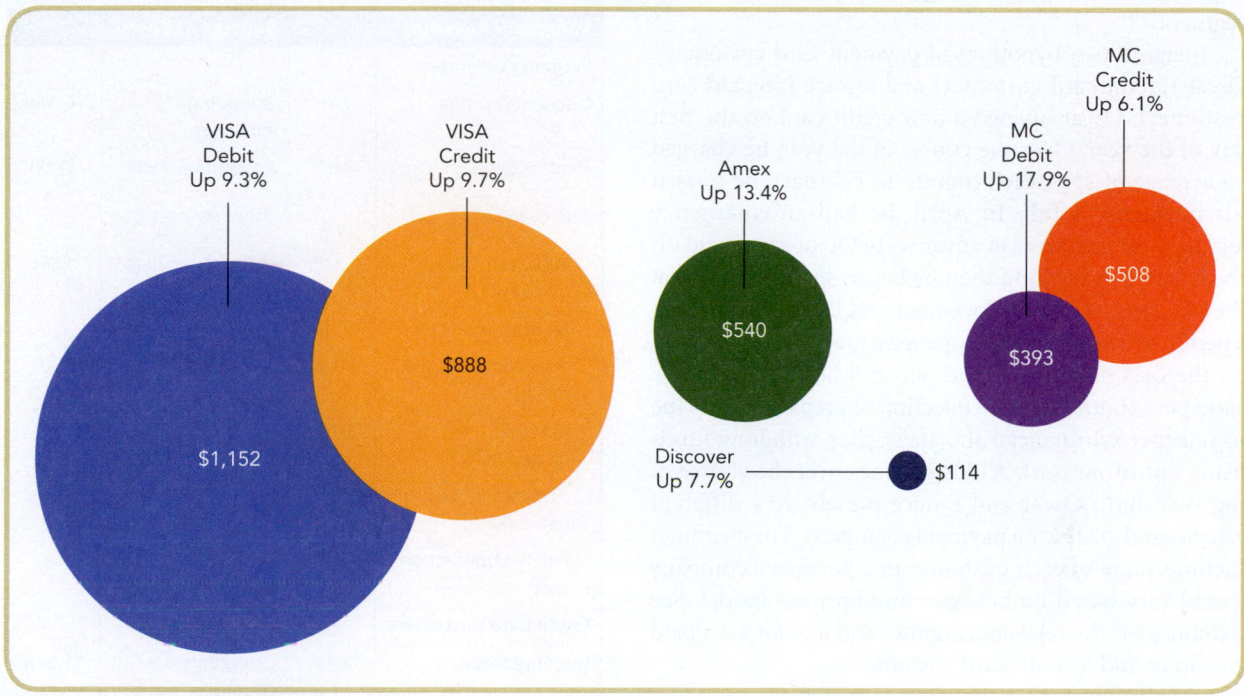

Data source: Case writer adaptation of data from the Nilson Report, 2012.

establish deposits of $30 million to establish break-even profitability.[24] Recognizing that the traditional brick-and-mortar model was becoming difficult to maintain profitably, these banks were also investing in mobile and Internet banking. Traditional depositories might see AXP's entry into depository alternatives as a portentous move into their space.

Another front of competition came from the growing number of traditional merchandise retailers that had begun to enter financial services. Recognizing the advantages of their extensive footprints and interaction with a broad base of consumers, these efforts were structured around the core assumption that retailers' current customers had unserved financial services needs that, if met, could build their spend in stores. "You've got to remember, Wal-Mart is intended to be a one-stop shop," said Charles M. Holley Jr., that company's CFO. "The more kinds of services we can offer our core customer like that, the better for them."[25] Merchandise retailers sensed a second opportunity: general distrust of traditional banks. "A lot of [our] members think their bank fees are too high, or the trust level has gone down over the years, or they're having issues with debit and credit cards," said Jay Smith, Costco's director of business and financial services.[26]

One challenge that merchandise retailers entering financial services faced was that consumer advocates expressed skepticism or outright resistance to these entries. On one hand, they appreciated the general goal of getting a broader range of financial services products into the underbanked. Yet they were also concerned about differences in the level of regulatory scrutiny retailers received relative to traditional depository institutions. "These products can come with high fees and few real protections," said Norma P. Garcia, a senior lawyer for Consumers Union. Wal-Mart sought a banking charter for almost a decade and, after facing considerable opposition from advocacy groups, eventually abandoned the effort in 2007.[27]

Home Depot, Costco, Office Depot, and Sears, among others, had experimented with financial services. But these efforts had shown mixed results. In December 2013, TCF Bank, based in Wayzata, Minnesota, announced it would close 37 branches in Jewel-Osco supermarkets. "Within all of TCF's branches, customer behavior is changing," a TCF executive said. "Clearly, there are fewer visits in all of our branches than there used to be."[28]

AXP had previously entered new markets through cobranded efforts in their credit card business. In recent years, these partnerships had led to the introduction of the Costco TrueEarnings Card and the Delta Air Lines SkyMiles credit card. Both of these were rewards credit cards, however. Bank 2.0 would be an entirely different business model and serve an entirely different customer segment.

Imagine two hypothetical payment card customers: Oscar (credit card customer) and Eunice (prepaid card customer). Oscar opened a new credit card on the first day of the year. Over the course of the year, he charged an average of $700 each month. In February, he missed his payment in full. In April, he had an emergency and took out a $300 cash advance. In October, he paid off the balance in full, and then he began spending again at the old average rate in November and December. Eunice, a parent in a family of four, opened a prepaid card account on the first day of the year. She and her family charge $800 per month on their collection of prepaid cards. Due to unexpected financial shortfalls, they withdraw funds using out-of-network ATMs 17 times over the course of the year. Both Oscar and Eunice present very different returns and costs for a payments company. The customer lifetime value of each customer to a payments company would vary based on behavior and business model. See Exhibit 9 for the relevant revenues and fees for a prepaid customer and a credit card customer.

History of Prepaid Products at American Express

AXP was founded in 1850 as a freight delivery service.[29] Since its most profitable deliveries were to banks, it soon developed financial products and services, including money orders and traveler's checks.[30] Eventually, product lines expanded to include currency exchange, international travel services, military banking ("provid[ing] banking services to U.S. military personnel and their families stationed abroad"), charge cards, and credit cards.[31] As AXP contemplated the Bank 2.0 concept, it reflected on its history of prepaid products. The first prepaid product was the traveler's check, which debuted in 1891; its more recent prepaid products included the American Express Gift Card, launched in 2002, which grew in 2009 by expanding into Canada.[32] The process of launching gift cards in the Canadian market provided experience that managers could draw on during the Bank 2.0 discussions.

Unlike traveler's checks, which could be purchased at financial institutions, prepaid cards demanded a distribution model far more similar to consumer packaged goods than to credit or debit cards (and more similar to what Bank 2.0 would also require). The matter of distribution channels entailed basic retail questions: In what store(s) would the products sell, and how would AXP introduce these products?

Exhibit 9 Value of Prepaid versus Credit Card Customer*

Sources of Revenue		Sources of Costs	
Prepaid Customers			
Discount revenue	2.4%	Operating expense	6.0%
Float revenue	4.8%	Acquisition costs	$7.00
Fee revenue		Other services	
Initial activation/ purchase fee	$3.95	Fraud expense	1.0%
Monthly usage fees	$1.00		
Direct deposit/cash reload	$0.00		
ATM fees (in network)	$0.00		
ATM fees (out of network)	$2.00		
Foreign transaction fees	2.7%		
Credit Card Customers			
Discount revenue	2.4%	Operating expense	11.00%
Annual fee	$75.00	Acquisition costs	$80.00
Rate revenue		Loan loss provision	2.7%
Regular rate on purchases	17.6%	Benefits	
Cash advances	21.0%	Travel insurance	1.25%
Balance transfer rate	15.6%	Credit insurance	1.00%
Fee revenue		Fraud insurance	0.76%
Late payment fees	$35	Rebates	1.00%
Overlimit fees	$25	Miles	1.00%
Cash advance fees	$5.00	Cash back	1.00%
Minimum finance charges	$4.00		
Foreign transaction fees	2.7%		

*These estimated revenues and costs are hypothetical and are not intended to represent actual fees for any credit card or prepaid product, including those of American Express.

Source: Case writer adaptation of company documents.

The business model evolved further when product managers removed the cards' monthly inactivity fees, the result of which seemed to be a positive effect on sales. In 2010, AXP introduced another prepaid product, the PASS card.[33] The company saw that the prepaid industry as a whole was moving beyond gift cards and into reloadable products. PASS was designed for parents and teenagers; effectively, it was an allowance card. Chokshi described it as "driver's ed for the teen's wallet."[34] Parents could reload the card with their AXP credit cards or checking accounts. In theory, PASS could reduce the instances of teenagers asking for money. It was also a response to an increase in online spending; teenagers were more and more likely to make purchases through the web.

Initially, PASS had a monthly fee of between $3.00 and $4.95—"industry practice," according to product managers—which AXP waived during the launch.[35] Reintroducing the fee was difficult. There were clear advantages to choosing a reloadable card over cash: parents could track the money they gave to their children, teens could spend online, and there were protections for lost or stolen cards. But product managers determined that the cash system was not "broken" to such a degree that people were eager to pay for PASS each month.

Galvanized by what it had learned, the executive team sought to turn PASS into a "general purpose reloadable card" that was sold in retail stores and online. From PASS, the team had gained a platform and capabilities that could be leveraged into a new product, the American Express Prepaid Card. The prepared card also removed the monthly fee. Around the same time, the team launched four or five other products, testing to see how they would perform. One product manager described this as an incubation period, during which the team noted changes in the prepaid industry. One trend stood out: prepaid cards were adding the same features people would normally find in a checking account. "That was the real opportunity," one manager said. It was time to "push beyond traditional prepaid."

The team behind PASS wondered if part of the card's limitation was its online distribution model. In discussions about Bank 2.0, EG considered how the process of opening a new financial services product should feel. The team agreed it was more than simply downloading an app. By filling out a brief application with a name, address, and date of birth; activating a physical card; and moving funds into the card's account, one created a "much deeper relationship." Traditional banks, through their retail operations, established personal relationships with their customers. How could EG replicate the service customers appreciated with this business model?

With a technology-based prepaid financial services product, EG was betting that it could form that deep relationship with a new segment of consumer. Like many retail products, the success would rely on scale: the margins might be low, but high volume would compensate. EG's vision for Bank 2.0 enabled the team members to act as "consumer champions," providing underbanked people with financial services that came with fewer fees. With fewer fees, achieving high volume was essential. PASS had demonstrated that online distribution wasn't enough.

Even with a firm grasp of what Bank 2.0 could be—a reloadable prepaid card with direct-deposit capabilities—the EG team surfaced a few options for further research and consideration: provide a technology-based service without the personalization consumers were accustomed to in retail banking; build a brick-and-mortar retail sales operation; or find a partner. The first option seemed to fall short of the consumer promise the team envisioned. The second seemed not only expensive in time, training, resources, and personnel, but would also likely bring AXP under the aegis of an entirely new regulatory regime. The third option was interesting, but how to go about "dating"? The ideal partner would be familiar with the segment AXP wanted to reach. Even if such a partner could easily be found, the company had to consider its traditional customer base. Finally, what would be the effect of any of these major changes on AXP's identity?

An Expansion in Brand Identity and Business Model: "From Exclusive to Inclusive"

The working notion within the EG team was that the brand would make an overture to customers who didn't qualify for charge or credit cards. The company surveyed its traditional customers to get a sense of their reaction to the change. The results conveyed enthusiastic support from credit and charge customers, who seemed to agree with a sentiment Chokshi had expressed in a meeting: "Why wouldn't you want to serve more people?" Chokshi noted that business models based on credit scores necessarily excluded potential customers. Bank 2.0 would not be based on a credit score. A prepaid model, in which AXP took a customer's money, was entirely different from the postpaid dispersal of credit. Such a product could be more accessible than the traditional AXP customer.

As EG conducted early focus groups, it faced the difficulty of describing the product. Technically, Bank 2.0 was neither a bank account nor a traditional prepaid card; what could AXP call it instead? The company's marketing team concluded that the best definition was "a debit and checking alternative." As the team described Bank 2.0's benefits, focus groups responded with disbelief. Bank 2.0 would not charge their customers annual or overdraft fees, and a minimum balance was not required.[36] There were multiple ways to load funds for free, including direct deposit and mobile check capture.[37] Peer-to-peer transfers were possible, as was the formation of subaccounts for family members (with the option of setting spending limits).[38] It simply seemed too good to be true.

As one product manager observed, focus group participants were most concerned about security. "They actually know the banking system better than people that are banked," he said. People with several jobs who managed multiple income deposits often had experience with a range of financial services, and they developed strong preferences. At one focus group, a man explained that he knew what time of day his paycheck was deposited. For AXP to succeed in a market it hadn't explored before, these were the types of concerns Bank 2.0 would need to address.

Chokshi had described the Bank 2.0 initiative as an "aspirational brand." He added that "safety, security, trust is for everyone, not just the affluent." He acknowledged that the new target market might not have an affinity for the brand—even if, as focus groups suggested, people knew they could trust AXP. "Millions of people knock on our door and we have to say no to them on the credit card side because they don't have the right [...] credit scores," Chokshi said. Bank 2.0 was a way of welcoming these same people.

Reaching the Underbanked: How to Distribute the Product?

The team knew that a key success factor would be whether there were concerns among the existing franchise of cardmembers about "diluting the brand" with Bank 2.0. One potential alternative would be to distinguish this franchise through its distribution channel. Perhaps innovations in distribution could help build a bridge between traditional AXP and the underbanked segment.

Schulman had come to EG with start-up experience. He believed that the biggest impediment to a company's future success, ironically, was its past success—a tendency "to become wed to what was and not what could be." He hoped Bank 2.0, and EG in general, could be seen as a complement to AXP's iconic brand.

In a meeting, the team wrote on a board the qualities it sought in a distribution channel for the new product. Effective delivery through novel channels would require investments in systems and expertise that AXP didn't currently have, such as merchandising and CPG. Bank 2.0 was unlike AXP's earlier prepaid products—it was a technology product, not just a card—and it had to stand out on the shelf. As a whole, the prepaid industry presented enormous challenges. Though it was easy for a customer to sign up for a product online, there was

no guarantee that he or she would *use* the product.[39] Since part of Bank 2.0's appeal was its minimal fees, AXP wanted customers to engage fully with the product by signing up for direct deposit. At a bank, customers received a folder (or some kind of documentation) describing the benefits of opening an account; similarly, technology products often came with booklets that described the item's features. Bank 2.0 packaging would need to be heftier than a simple plastic card.

The EG teams saw plenty of reasons to move forward with Bank 2.0: AXP had already spent millions of dollars on the Serve platform, and this was a way to take advantage of the investment. Without losing its traditional affluent customers, the brand could expand into new markets, fulfilling a wish to participate in financial inclusion—to be "consumer champions." If more and more consumers wanted to pay with AXP products, it would become harder and harder for merchants to turn them away. Furthermore, AXP already had 22,000 ATMs that could be made available to the Bank 2.0 customer. On the board, EG posed a question: "Why go into infrastructure when you can replicate it?" Perhaps the team had to shift its point of view: perhaps a familiar infrastructure would be comforting to consumers, who would not have to learn about an entirely new kind of product.

Calling the Question

Chokshi and Wright sketched out a few remaining key questions that would need to be answered in the realization of the EG team's goal of "reimagining banking." They were:

- **Viability of the market?** Was this demographic too much of a financial risk for too little return? The team knew that the company's first reloadable prepaid card, PASS, had not been a great success; did it make sense to try the model again?
- **Build or partner?** Assuming that this new target market was potentially valuable, how would AXP reach those consumers? Should it seek out a recognized partner who already had a strong relationship with the underbanked? Or build on the AXP brand's existing equity in the marketplace?
- **Acquire?** Should the company acquire one of the new entrants, such as Green Dot or Netspend?
- **Competitive response?** How would traditional retail bankers respond to EG's entry? Would partnering with an established retail banker be the best choice for a distribution channel, or should EG innovate and create its own channel?

- **The advocates?** Was it possible that skeptical consumer advocates would wonder why an iconic brand such as AXP was pursuing the underbanked? And if so, how would that skepticism hurt the franchise?

As company veterans, Chokshi and Wright asked: Was AXP ready for this level of innovation—essentially, creating a new financial services category? Was building that category by itself possible or financially prudent? Though they were unsure whether AXP would move forward with Bank 2.0, Chokshi and Wright were certain that the mission of increased financial inclusion would be central to their future at the company.

NOTES

1. "American Express Co., Executive Profile: Daniel Schulman," *Bloomberg Businessweek*, August 26, 2014, http://investing.businessweek.com/research/stocks/people/person.asp?personId=174206&ticker=AXP (accessed Aug. 12, 2014).
2. Case writer interview with Dan Schulman, April 23, 2014; unless otherwise noted, all subsequent quotations by and information about this person derive from this interview.
3. The term "underbanked" indicated households that had at least a single person who held a savings or checking account, but that also had at least one person who had accessed alternative financial services (AFS) providers such as money orders, payday lenders, and check-cashing services. Those who were "unbanked" did not have any household relationship with a mainstream financial services provider. See Exhibit 1 for more details on these consumer groups.
4. Federal Deposit Insurance Corporation Department of Depositor and Consumer Protection, "2011 FDIC National Survey of Unbanked and Underbanked Households: Executive Summary," September 2012.
5. AXP internal data and "How American Express Gains a Competitive Advantage From Its Closed-Loop Network," Trefis, March 13, 2014, http://www.trefis.com/stock/axp/articles/230259/maryhow-american-express-gains-a-competitive-advantage-by-using-a-closed-loop-network/2014-03-13 (accessed Aug. 21, 2014).
6. AXP internal data and http://www.trefis.com/stock/axp/articles/230259/maryhow-american-express-gains-a-competitive-advantage-by-using-a-closed-loop-network/2014-03-13.
7. http://www.trefis.com/stock/axp/articles/230259/maryhow-american-express-gains-a-competitive-advantage-by-using-a-closed-loop-network/2014-03-13.
8. Stuart Elliott, "American Express Gets Specific and Asks, 'Are You a Cardmember?'," *New York Times*, April 6, 2007, http://www.nytimes.com/2007/04/06/business/media/06adco.html?_r=0 (accessed Aug. 12, 2014).
9. "American Express: Our Story," http://secure.cmax.americanexpress.com/Internet/GlobalCareers/Staffing//Files/our_story_3.pdf (accessed Oct. 17, 2014).
10. http://secure.cmax.americanexpress.com/Internet/GlobalCareers/Staffing/Shared/Files/our_story_3.pdf.
11. http://www.trefis.com/stock/axp/articles/230259/maryhow-american-express-gains-a-competitive-advantage-by-using-a-closed-loop-network/2014-03-13.
12. http://www.trefis.com/stock/axp/articles/230259/maryhow-american-express-gains-a-competitive-advantage-by-using-a-closed-loop-network/2014-03-13.
13. http://online.wsj.com/news/articles/SB10001424052970204552304577112611696189378.
14. http://online.wsj.com/news/articles/SB10001424052970204552304577112611696189378.
15. Case writer interview with Alpesh Chokshi, April 23, 2013; unless otherwise noted, all subsequent quotations by and information about this person derives from this interview.
16. Case writer interview with Jon Rosner, April 23, 2013; unless otherwise noted, all subsequent quotations by and information about this person derives from this interview.
17. Robin Sidel, "After Years of Growth, Banks are Pruning Their Branches," *Wall Street Journal*, March 31, 2013. http://online.wsj.com/news/articles/SB10001424127887323699045783268 94146325274 (accessed Aug. 16, 2013).
18. "About Us," Consumer Financial Protection Bureau, http://www.consumerfinance.gov/the-bureau (accessed Aug. 12, 2014).
19. Federal Deposit Insurance Corporation Department of Depositor and Consumer Protection, "2011 FDIC National Survey of Unbanked and Underbanked Households: Executive Summary," September 2012.
20. GoBank was a subsidiary of Green Dot Bank.
21. Lee Spears and Kristin Scholer, "Green Dot Raises $164 Million for Owners in IPO as Investors Pay a Premium," Bloomberg News, July 22, 2010, http://www.bloomberg.com/news/2010-07-21/green-dot-ipo-premium-may-provide-801-return-for-owners-wal-mart-sequoia.html (accessed Aug. 13, 2014).
22. Saabira Chaudhuri, "U.S. Banks Prune More Branches," *Wall Street Journal*, January 27, 2014, http://online.wsj.com/news/articles/SB1000142405270203027770457934722315774 5640 (accessed Aug. 12, 2014).
23. Sidel.
24. Sidel.
25. Stephanie Clifford and Jessica Silver-Greenberg, "On the New Shopping List: Milk, Bread, Eggs and a Mortgage," *New York Times*, November 13, 2012, http://www.nytimes.com/2012/11/14/business/major-retailers-start-selling-financial-products-challenging-banks.html?_r=0 (accessed Aug. 12, 2014).
26. Clifford and Silver-Greenberg.
27. Clifford and Silver-Greenberg.
28. Steve Daniels, "TCF to Close 37 Bank Branches in Chicago Jewel-Osco Stores," *Crain's Chicago Business*, http://www.chicagobusiness.com/article/20131211/NEWS07/131219943/tcf-to-close-37-bank-branches-in-chicago-jewel-osco-stores# (accessed Aug. 12, 2014).
29. http://secure.cmax.americanexpress.com/Internet/GlobalCareers/Staffing/Shared/Files/our_story_3.pdf.
30. http://secure.cmax.americanexpress.com/Internet/GlobalCareers/Staffing/Shared/Files/our_story_3.pdf.
31. http://secure.cmax.americanexpress.com/Internet/GlobalCareers/Staffing/Shared/Files/our_story_3.pdf.
32. http://www.newswire.ca/en/story/477039/american-express-launches-new-gift-card-in-canada (accessed Aug. 12, 2014).
33. http://about.americanexpress.com/news/pr/2010/pass.aspx (accessed Aug. 12, 2014).
34. "American Express Launches PASS from American Express (SM), a Prepaid Reloadable Card Parents Give to Teens and Young Adults," American Express press release, May 3, 2010, http://about.americanexpress.com/news/pr/2010/pass.aspx (accessed Aug. 12, 2014).
35. http://about.americanexpress.com/news/pr/2010/pass.aspx.
36. Bluebird website, https://www.bluebird.com (accessed Aug. 12, 2014).
37. https://www.bluebird.com.
38. https://www.bluebird.com.
39. Case writer interview with Wesley Wright, April 23, 2014; unless otherwise noted, all subsequent quotations by and information about this person derive from this interview.

CASE 3

BP In Russia: Bad Partners or Bad Partnerships? (A)

Since entering the Russian oil market in 1997, BP plc (BP) had two main partners. The first was Rosneft, the Russian state-owned oil company. The second was Alpha Access Renova (AAR), a consortium of Soviet-born oligarchs[1] and one of Russia's largest privately owned financial-industrial conglomerates, with interests in oil, gas, and banking.

In January of 2011, BP and Rosneft announced the formation of a new strategic partnership to develop oil and gas reserves on the continental shelf in the Russian Arctic, covering approximately 125,000 square kilometers in the Kara Sea.[2] Yet within five months, AAR, with whom BP had already formed another partnership, would obtain a series of court injunctions, effectively scuttling the deal with Rosneft.

The failure of the BP-Rosneft alliance could be attributed to a lack of due diligence on BP's part or, perhaps more saliently, to poor alliance management. A key conditional variable of any alliance is the degree of interpartner conflict: Alliance partners' interests can diverge so much that they undermine the initial common goals of the partnership, and "effective cooperation demands a relatively low level of conflict."[3] In the wake of the Deepwater Horizon disaster in the Gulf of Mexico, which cost them tens of billions of U.S. dollars, BP's interest was in expanding its oil assets and revenues. AAR's interest, meanwhile, was in maintaining TNK-BP's position in the Russian oil market, which the BP-Rosneft alliance would have undermined (Table 1).[4]

Russian Oil and BP's Past Investments

Russian privatization

Following the collapse of the Soviet Union in 1992, the Russian government under Premier Boris Yeltsin initiated a series of reforms to end the oil ministry's monopoly over the Russian oil and gas industry. A group of new distinct oil companies was created, including Yukos, Onako, Sibneft, Tyumen (TNK), Lukoil, Sidanko, and Slavneft, and beginning in 1995, stakes in these companies were sold at auction. In 1999, AAR purchased a 51% interest in TNK, with the state retaining 49%.[5]

From 1993 until 1999, Russian oil production was consistently third largest in the world, behind the United States and Saudi Arabia, but following the privatization auctions, Russian production increased steadily, eventually by over 50%. By 2004, Russia had overtaken the United States as the second largest oil producer globally (Exhibit 1).

BP, TNK, and Sidanko

BP entered the Russian oil market in 1997, when it purchased a 10% stake in Sidanko, one of the privatized oil companies, from the Russian banking group UNEXIM-MFK for $571 million USD. Two years later,

Table 1 Ownership of Russian oil firms before and after TNK-BP alliance

Company	AAR pre-alliance share	BP pre-alliance share	TNK-BP share	Share owned by other major
TNK	51%		51%	49% owned by Russian state
Sidanko	56%	25%	81%	
Slavneft	50%		50%	50% owned by Sibneft
Russia Petroleum	29%	33%	52%	
OAO Onako	85%		85%	15% various shareholders

Data sources: *Petroleum Economist* website, November 30, 1999; Laura Board, "BP Boosts Stake in Russia's Sidanko," *Daily Deal* (New York), April 17, 2002; Lachlan Johnston, "BP Adds $1.35bn Slavneft to Russian Joint Venture," *Daily Telegraph* (London), August 20, 2003; "TNK Tosses Slavneft Stake into BP Mix," *Moscow Times*, March 18, 2003; Alla Startseva, "Onako Sale: Better Times Ahead for Investors?," *St. Petersburg Times*, September 22, 2000.

Case 3: BP In Russia: Bad Partners or Bad Partnerships? (A)

C-43

Exhibit 1 Petroleum Production by Country in Millions of Barrels per Day, 1993 to 2010

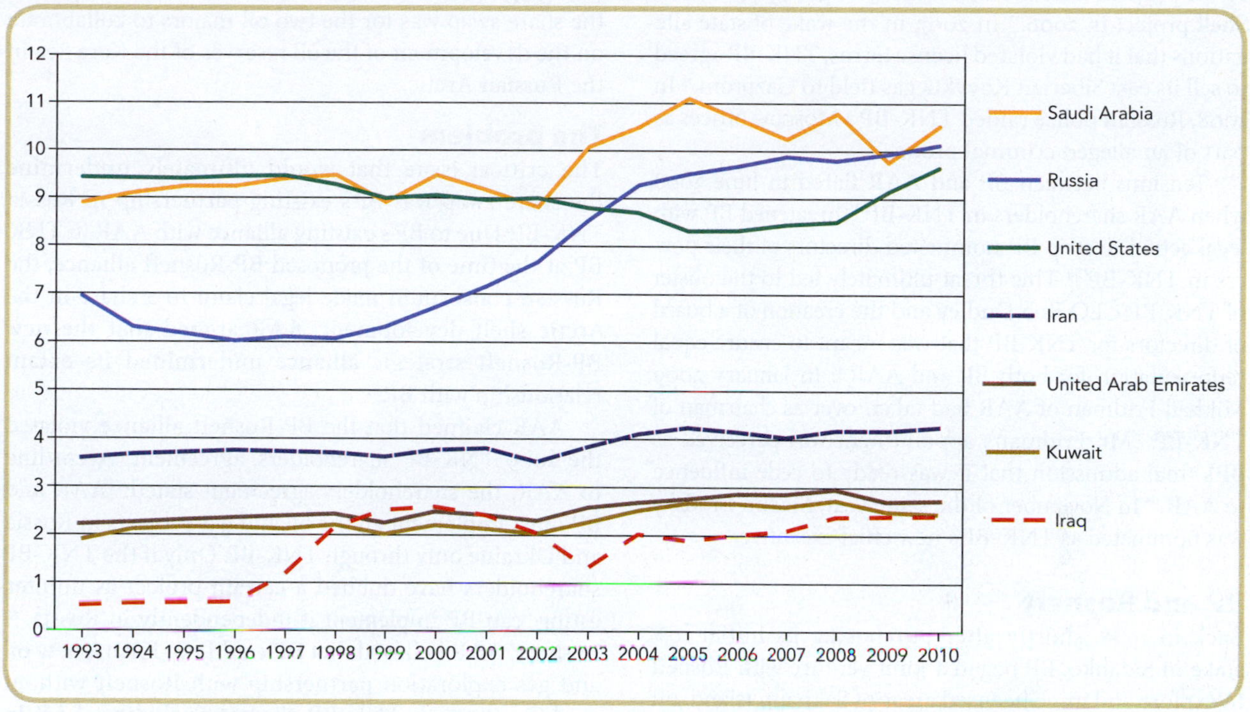

Data source: U.S. Energy Information Administration.

Sidanko filed for bankruptcy, and in an auction of its assets, TNK bought the western Siberian oil field of Chernogorneft—approximately half of Sidanko's asset value—for a fraction of its real value. BP objected, publicly accusing TNK of tampering with the courts to "influence the bankruptcy proceedings and liquidation sales."[6]

In response to the allegations, TNK agreed to return the Chernogorneft oil field to Sidanko in exchange for an equity stake of 25% plus one share (for veto power) in the company. Under the terms of the agreement, BP maintained its 10% stake, but its voting rights were increased to equal to those of TNK (25% plus one share necessary for a blocking vote)[7]. Additionally, BP received managerial authority over Sidanko and its subsidiaries, effectively giving BP control over the highly prized Chernogorneft oil field.[8]

In 2002, BP purchased an additional 15% stake in Sidanko for $375 million USD, increasing its stake to 25%; AAR maintained its 56% stake. The Chernogorneft oil field dispute resolved, BP publicly expressed interest in expanding its involvement in Russian oil and initiated preliminary talks with AAR about buying a stake in TNK.[9]

The next year, BP agreed to invest $6.75 billion USD in a 50/50 joint venture with AAR, to be known as TNK-BP. The venture incorporated both companies' holdings in Sidanko, AAR's controlling interest in TNK and 50% share of Slavneft. The agreement also included the following:

Both companies' interests in Russia Petroleum [the critical component of which was the Kovyotka gas field license], exploration opportunities offshore Sakhalin Island, and a major downstream business that includes interest in five refineries and a retail network of more than 2,100 sites in Russia and Ukraine.[10]

By December 2005, TNK-BP had completed a voluntary share exchange program for the minority shareholders in 14 TNK-BP subsidiaries, thereby facilitating the accession of Sidanko, TNK, and OAO Onako to TNK-BP Holding; the three companies were liquidated, and all their assets and liabilities were consolidated within the holding company.[11]

In the next few years, a series of legal disputes ensued among the Russian government, AAR, and BP. At the time, there was speculation that TNK-BP would be the target of a takeover by Gazprom, the largest state-controlled gas company, which had been taking control of oil projects across Russia, including a Royal Dutch Shell project in 2006.[12] In 2007, in the wake of state allegations that it had violated license terms, TNK-BP agreed to sell its east Siberian Kovykta gas field to Gazprom.[13] In 2008, Russian police raided TNK-BP's Moscow offices as part of an alleged criminal probe.

Tensions between BP and AAR flared in June 2008, when AAR shareholders in TNK-BP "threatened BP with legal action to strip BP-nominated directors of their powers in TNK-BP."[14] This threat ultimately led to the ouster of TNK-BP CEO Bob Dudley and the creation of a board of directors for TNK-BP that was meant to ensure equal representation for both BP and AAR.[15] In January 2009, Mikhail Fridman of AAR had taken over as chairman of TNK-BP. "Mr. Fridman's appointment was perceived as BP's final admission that it was ready to cede influence" to AAR.[16] In November of the same year, Maxim Brodsky was nominated as TNK-BP's new chief executive.

BP and Rosneft

Back in 1998, shortly after purchasing its initial 10% stake in Sidanko, BP began a joint venture with Rosneft to explore and mine licensed areas of Sakhalin Island, off the east coast of Russia, with oil and natural gas reserves estimated at over ten billion tons. In 2002, the two firms announced a joint project to explore and develop an area of the island known as Sakhalin-5. Rosneft took on 51% of the project, while BP would be the minority shareholder at 49%.[17] An additional project to explore another area, Sakhalin-4, followed in 2006.

Both Sakhalin projects were developed under a *carry agreement*, in which BP funded all exploration and Rosneft was only liable for costs if the project was successful. The alliance had cost approximately $80 million USD through 2006; after the second Sakhalin site was added, the cost of the project in its entirety was estimated to be an additional $700 million USD.[18] But according to both companies, continued exploration offered no significant economic value, so the two majors allowed the Sakhalin-4 license to expire in 2008 and the Sakhalin-5 license two years later. The companies continued joint exploration of other sites surrounding the island, with some success.[19]

Proposing a new alliance

In January 2011, following the Deepwater Horizon oil spill in the Gulf of Mexico and the acrimony with its Russian partners in TNK-BP, BP proposed a new strategic alliance with Rosneft, which was still 75% state-owned. BP proposed a share swap worth approximately $16.5 billion USD, in which Rosneft would take on a 5% stake in BP, while BP would secure 9.5% of Rosneft

(bringing its total share of Rosneft to 10.8%). The goal of the share swap was for the two oil majors to collaborate on the development of the oil reserves of the Kara Sea in the Russian Arctic.

The problem

The critical issue that would ultimately undermine the share swap was BP's existing partnership in Russia, TNK-BP. Due to BP's existing alliance with AAR in TNK-BP at the time of the proposed BP-Rosneft alliance, the Russian consortium made legal claim to a share in the Arctic shelf development. AAR argued that the new BP-Rosneft strategic alliance undermined its extant relationship with BP.

AAR claimed that the BP-Rosneft alliance violated the 2009 TNK-BP shareholders' agreement. According to AAR, the shareholders agreement stated: "AAR and BP must implement all the oil and gas projects in Russia and Ukraine only through TNK-BP. Only if the TNK-BP shareholders have dubbed a certain project as uninteresting, can BP implement it independently in Russia."[20] In short, AAR believed that BP could not form a new oil and gas exploration partnership with Rosneft without working through TNK-BP, thereby including AAR in any new strategic alliance.

In order to avoid being excluded from the Kara Sea development, the AAR group sought an interim injunction in an English court to stop the BP-Rosneft alliance.

AAR [believed] the shareholders agreement stipulated that if either side comes up with a new opportunity, it must, 'before any material negotiations commence with a third party,' notify the chief executive of TNK-BP with a view to offering the opportunity for consideration within 45 days by the joint venture's board.[21]

London's High Court granted AAR a temporary injunction against the strategic alliance between BP and Rosneft on February 1, 2011.

In addition to the filing the court injunction, TNK-BP also offered $8.1 billion USD for the 5% stake in BP that Rosneft was due to acquire. "Under the terms of TNK-BP's offer for the 5% of BP, it would buy that stake and then swap it for 10% of Rosneft."[22] The critical component of the TNK-BP offer was that it would own Rosneft, and BP would own only half of the TNK-BP stake in Rosneft, although it would gain $8.1 billion USD in cash.[23]

In response to the TNK-BP offer, Rosneft reaffirmed its plans to complete the Kara Sea alliance with BP:

"TNK-BP has never been considered a potential participant in the alliance due to its lack of required competence," Rosneft said. Deputy Prime Minister Igor Sechin—who

Case 3: BP In Russia: Bad Partners or Bad Partnerships? (A)

C-45

serves as Russia's effective energy tsar—also played down TNK-BP's interest... [saying] "Russia has the right to choose its own partner"... [and calling] plans to explore the Arctic jointly with BP "a matter of Russian energy security and a contribution to the energy security of Europe and the world."[24]

On March 12, 2011, affirming its commitment to work solely with Rosneft, BP blocked a proposal from TNK-BP to join the alliance and share swap. "The four BP-nominated directors on the 11-member TNK-BP board voted against a proposal by TNK-BP management recommending that TNK-BP join Rosneft in the alliance."[25]

Two weeks later, the Stockholm Arbitration Tribunal formally stopped BP's effort to ally with Rosneft for Arctic oil exploration. The tribunal's ruling, which upheld the London court ruling, officially blocked the completion of any share swap and Arctic exploration alliance between BP and Rosneft. This ruling further substantiated the claims made by AAR executives that the BP-Rosneft alliance violated the TNK-BP shareholders agreement.[26]

BP's Past Mergers and Alliances

BP had a history of creating and maintaining successful strategic partnerships and initiating lucrative mergers. BP's past merges and alliances have served critical purposes, as each new partner had diversified BP's business and expanded its share of the global oil market (Table 2).

Alliance Types in the Oil Industry

Any alliance brought with it a set of expectations: to lower costs and gain efficiencies, to gain access to customers or partner technologies, to develop or expand internal competencies, or to respond to actions by competitors.

In the oil and gas industry, there were five basic types of alliances.

The first, and quite prominent, type was a *consolidated joint venture*. Partners might merge all operations, assets, and oil reserves—very similar to an outright merger—or maintain ownership of some reserves, operating licenses, and equipment. "Full consolidation of reserves and other physical assets may offer greater value, but it also presents more hurdles, as valuing reserves, meeting regulatory requirement, and persuading minority shareholders to accept the consolidation can cause difficulties."[27] An example of such an alliance was BP and Tyumen Oil in TNK-BP.

When alliance partners were unwilling or unable to combine assets, a second alliance type arose: *alliances with specialists*. This type of an alliance combined complementary capabilities, for example the oil resources and technology of one firm and the knowledge and business model of the other.[28] The BP alliance with Rosneft on both the Sakhalin-4 and Sakhalin-5 projects, as well as the purposed BP-Rosneft alliance for exploring the Kara Sea, might have been included here.

A third alliance type was a *supplier and contractor* alliance, in which one firm provided money and/ or assistance with exploration in return for a percentage of production. This was the case with Mobil and Halliburton, where the latter invested "$10 million USD to drill five horizontal wells in Mobil's Parks Devonian field in west Texas in return for a percentage of production."[29] Halliburton invested much of the capital and managed the project, providing the drilling, excavation, and site equipment. In exchange, Mobil provided the site knowledge, well supervision, and the construction of the wellbore.[30]

Companies could also serve to "orchestrate a set of alliances and contractual relationships involving suppliers, service providers, and even other operating companies.

Table 2 BP mergers, acquisitions, and partnerships

Year	Company	Amount	Assets acquired
1998	Amoco (purchase)	$48.2 billion USD in stock	Refining and distribution
1999	Atlantic Richfield (ARCO) (merger)	$27.6 billion USD	Prudhoe Bay gas and oil field in Alaska
2000	Burmah Castrol (purchase)	$4.8 billion USD	Worldwide lubricants brand
2002	Veba Oel (Germany) (purchase)	$2.81 billion USD	Aral
2011	Reliance Industries (India) (30% stake and 50-50 joint venture)	$7.2 billion USD	Access to Indian oil reserves, new market for BP expertise in deep water oil exploration and associated technologies

Data source: BP website.

The aim was to reduce the overall system costs and cycle times and to ensure access…to crucial technology and inputs."[31] A useful example of this was the Deepstar alliance led by Texaco, which involved over five dozen suppliers, including other oil majors, in setting standards for well, pipeline, and platform components in oil exploration in waters as deep as 10,000 feet.[32]

A final alliance type was called an *OBO (operated by others) relationship*, a joint venture in which one partner takes on the full responsibility of operating oil explorations while the other solely invests capital.

Moving Forward

In the oil industry, the go-it-alone strategy was cost prohibitive, and access by foreign firms to existing or newly discovered oil sources was less likely without a domestic partner. So managing partnerships was critical, for BP or any other company. Most new oil and gas discoveries would be made in remote areas of the globe, with domestic and state-run oil companies heavily invested in exploration. Short of acquiring these state-owned oil companies, BP would be the minority shareholder in any new strategic partnership. As the demand for these resources increased in large and rapidly growing countries such as China and India, and the value of oil and gas reserves continued to rise, state-owned and domestic oil companies would prefer to remain independent entities to maximize their long-term revenues.

If its behavior in Russia was any indication, BP appeared to lack certain skills necessary for being considered a good partner. What skills would be critical for the company to develop moving forward?

NOTES

1. On AAR see http://www.aar.ru/#. See also Sergey Ilyin, "The Interests of a Small Group are Much More Important Than Those of the State," *What the Papers Say Weekly Review*, April 4, 2011.
2. "BP and Russia in Arctic Oil Deal," *BBC News* website, June 15, 2011, http://www.bbc.co.uk/news/business-12195576 (accessed September 9, 2011).
3. T.K. Das and Bing-Sheng Teng, "The Dynamics of Alliance Conditions in the Alliance Development Process," *Journal of Management Studies* 39, no. 5 (July 2002), 732.
4. Andrew Neff, "Arbitration Tribunal Rules in Favor of AAR, Putting BP-Rosneft Exploration and Share-Swap Deal on Ice," *Global Insight*, March 25, 2011.
5. Petroleum Economist website, November 30, 1999.
6. Neela Banerjee, "BP Reported in Agreement to Regain Important Siberian Oil Field," *New York Times*, December 22, 1999.
7. Eduard Gismatullin, "TNK return Chernogorneft to Sidanko," *St. Petersburg Times*, December 24, 1999.
8. Banerjee.
9. Anna Raff, "BP Buys Sidanko Stake for $375M," *Moscow Times*, April 17, 2002.
10. "BP Plunges Deep into Russia with New Tyumen Production Alliance," *Oil Daily*, February 11, 2003.
11. See Alla Startseva, "Onako Sale: Better Times Ahead for Investors?" *St. Petersburg Times*, September 22, 2000. See also Yulia Bushuyeva and Alexander Tutushkin, "TNK, Sibneft Forge Partnership," *Moscow Times*, October 16, 2002.
12. Catherine Belton and Isabel Gorst, "Police Raid BP's Russian Venture," *Financial Times*, March 19, 2003.
13. The deal collapsed due to disagreements over the price of the sale. See Catherine Belton and Isabel Gorst, "Police Raid BP's Russian Venture" and "BP in Russia: A Timeline," *Telegraph*, May 17, 2011.
14. Belton and Gorst, "BP in Russia: A Timeline."
15. Dudley was the chief executive of BP at the time of the Deepwater Horizon oil spill. See Russel Hotten, "Russians Issue Legal Threat in BP Dispute," *Telegraph*, July 24, 2008, and Neff.
16. Rowena Mason, "Mikhail Fridman to Step Down as TNK-BP Boss," *Telegraph*, November 11, 2009.
17. Anna Ruff, "Rosneft, TNK Eye Sakhalin," *Moscow Times*, July 25, 2002. It should be noted that TNK also made an effort to enter into the Sakhalin oil exploration market with Rosneft as a partner but was rebuffed.
18. Rachel Graham, "Rosneft, BP sign Sakhalin Operating Accords: Agreements over License Blocks at Sakhalin 4 and 5," *Platts Oilgram News*, November 24, 2006.
19. "BP, Rosneft give up on East Schmidt Sakhalin-5," *New Europe*, February 21, 2010.
20. Neff.
21. "BP Faces Court Challenge to Rosneft Pact," *International Oil Daily*, January 28, 2011.
22. Gordon Wilcox, "TNK-BP Makes $8.1B Bid for BP Stake," *Benzinga*, March 1, 2011.
23. "FP Deal Flow: TNK-BP's US $8.16B Stake Offer; Buffett Betrayed," *Financial Post*, March 2, 2011.
24. "Russia's Rosneft Vows to Complete BP Tie-up," *Agence France-Presse* (English), March 11, 2011.
25. Neff, "BP Rejects TNK-BP's Proposal to Join Rosneft Exploration Alliance," *Global Insight* website, March 14, 2011.
26. Neff, "Arbitration Tribunal Rules in Favor of AAR."
27. David Ernst and Andrew M.J. Steinhubl, "Alliances in Upstream Oil and Gas," *McKinsey Quarterly* no. 2 (1997), 149.
28. Ernst and Steinhubl, "Petroleum: After the Megamergers," *McKinsey Quarterly* no. 2 (1999), 48–57.
29. Ernst and Steinhubl, "Alliances in Upstream Oil and Gas," 152.
30. Ernst and Steinhubl.
31. Ernst and Steinhubl, 153.
32. Paul R. Hays and G. Ray Seid "DeepStar Enters Fifth Phase of Deepwater Mission," *WorldOil Online*, May 2000, http://www.worldoil.com/May-2000-DeepStar-enters-fifth-phase-of-deepwater-mission.html (accessed June 20, 2011). See also Ernst and Steinhubl.

CASE 4

IVEY | Publishing

Carlsberg in Emerging Markets

A breeze of optimism blew through the office of Carlsberg A/S's CEO, Jørgen Buhl Rasmussen. After finally gaining 100 percent control over the giant Russian brewery Baltic Beverages Holding (BBH), and with the investments in Western China beginning to bear fruit, the newly appointed CEO was confident that the Danish brewing company's intensified focus on emerging markets would pay off. The company was counting on tapping the massive potential in emerging markets in order to achieve a much-needed reduction in its dependency on the maturing and stagnating Western European beer markets, which accounted for a full 61 percent of the company's revenue in 2007.

Indeed, Carlsberg's emerging market efforts had come a long way. In the Russian market, which was considered to be one of the fastest-growing beer markets in the world, Carlsberg enjoyed market-leader status through its ownership of BBH. In that market, it had a sales volume of approximately 23 million hectoliters of beer in 2007 and revenue of kr 9 billion (US$1.8 billion). As for the highly promising Chinese market, which was regarded as the world's largest beer market in terms of population and size, the Danish company had achieved a 55 percent market share in the western parts of the country, and it operated 20 brewery plants in China with close to 5,000 employees. In fact, as Carlsberg recognized that the European markets would eventually reach a point of saturation, the aim of the Chinese investments was to create a platform for future growth and revenue.

The outlook for Carlsberg had not always been as bright as it appeared by 2008. Carlsberg's emerging market strategy had taken a long and winding road. For instance, Carlsberg's acquisition of the BBH shares was the result of a troubled and expensive partnership with Norwegian Orkla ASA. In addition, before Carlsberg had become successful in the western provinces of China, the company had spent plenty of valuable time and resources trying to enter the rich provinces of southeastern China, a strategy that had failed. Furthermore, in the early 2000s, Carlsberg was on the brink of being reduced to a secondary player in the global beer market—as the consolidation of the industry proceeded, Carlsberg A/S became an obvious takeover target and was also at risk of being cornered as a small regional player. Nonetheless, in 2008 as the first decade of the millennium neared an end, Carlsberg was the fifth-largest brewery in the world in terms of volume produced. Much of this reversal of fortune could be attributed to the company's emerging market focus.

Despite Buhl Rasmussen's optimism about the future, the real question was how Carlsberg A/S could successfully continue to capitalize on its growing engagement in emerging markets. "We don't know how large the Chinese market will be in five years, and I don't know if China can become a new BBH," the CEO explained, "but it is definitely not impossible, as the market is enormous."[1] It was no surprise that competition was becoming increasingly fierce in this booming emerging market, and history had clearly proven that doing business successfully in this market required unconventional approaches.

Introducing Carlsberg A/S

The successful course and strategy which Carlsberg has pursued in recent years will remain basically the same no matter what. The strategy has proved its worth with growth and better results, and it is now strongly rooted in our organisation. Our business is thus to focus on the beer markets in Western Europe, Eastern Europe and Asia.
— Carlsberg A/S CEO, Jørgen Buhl Rasmussen[2]

As the fifth-largest brewing company in the world, Carlsberg A/S's vision was "our brands will be the consumer's first choice, and we will lead our industry in profitability and growth through a culture of quality, innovation and continuous improvement." Moreover, Carlsberg saw itself as "probably the best beer company in the world."[3]

The core businesses of Carlsberg A/S were brewing, marketing and selling beer. In 1847, J.C. Jacobsen opened the doors of Carlsberg A/S's first brewery in Copenhagen, Denmark, and the first foreign brewery was established in Malawi in 1968. In 2007, the company had 33,000

Exhibit 1 Carlsberg A/S Financial Figures

	2003	2004	2005	2006	2007
Sales volume (million hl)					
Beer	81.4	92.0	101.6	100.7	115.2
Soft drinks	21.2	19.4	19.1	20.2	20.8
Profit and loss account (kr million)					
Net revenue	34,626	36,284	38,047	41,083	44,750
Profit before taxation	2,688	1,651	1,892	3,029	3,634
Profit for the year	1,719	1,269	1,371	2,171	2,596
Balance sheet total	46,712	57,698	62,359	58,451	61,220
Equity	11,276	15,084	17,968	17,597	18,621
Net interest-bearing debt	8,929	21,733	20,753	19,229	19,726
Key ratios					
Operating margin, %	10.3	9.4	9.2	9.8	11.8
ROIC, %	12.4	8.1	7.8	9.2	11.7
Equity ratio, %	38.3	29.1	31.3	32.5	32.6
Debt/equity (financial gearing), X	0.50	1.29	1.06	1.01	0.99
Employees	31,531	31,703	30,208	31,680	33,420

Source: Carlsberg Annual Report 2007.

employees, held a portfolio of 75 breweries around the world and sold approximately 115 million hectoliters of beer in more than 150 countries, with net revenue of kr44,750 million (€6,000 million) (see Exhibit 1). Carlsberg's areas of operation focused on the mature beer markets of Western Europe, the growth markets of Eastern Europe and the emerging Asian markets. Behind this strong position of the company was a major reorientation and restructuring of the company in recent years: "Progress in revenue and share prices has been driven by a fundamental revolution of the company," explained former CEO Nils Smedegaard Andersen. "We have purchased and then professionalized the business. At the same time, we have worked with the structure."[4]

Organization

Despite Carlsberg's position as the fifth-largest brewery in the world by 2008 (see Exhibits 2 and 3), at the beginning of the 2000s, it had found itself largely excluded from the league of large international breweries. Carlsberg, it then seemed, was losing ground as one of the strongest brands in the world, and was considered by analysts to be an obvious takeover target for larger breweries. In an attempt to cope with these difficulties, a merger with Norwegian Orkla ASA's brewing activities was executed in 2000 and resulted in the creation of Carlsberg Breweries. Carlsberg A/S owned 60 percent

Exhibit 2 The Global Beer Industry, 2007

Largest breweries	Sales volume (mil. hl)
1 InBev	271.0
2 SABMiller	239.0
3 Anheuser-Busch	128.4
4 Heineken	119.8
5 Carlsberg	115.2

Source: Companies' annual reports.

of the new entity, while Orkla held 40 percent. Among the positive aspects of this merger was Orkla ASA's 50 percent ownership in Baltic Beverages Holdings (BBH), which offered Carlsberg the possibility to strengthen its position in the Eastern European markets. However, after a number of strategic disagreements, Carlsberg bought Orkla out of the merger in 2004. Although this move put Carlsberg into severe debt, former CEO Nils Smedegaard Andersen was content: "We are market leaders in a handful of large countries, we own half of the largest brewery in Eastern Europe and we possess a majority share in a number of European breweries." He also emphasized that "the acquisition of Orkla's Carlsberg shares, as well as Holsten, prove that, during the last five years, we have reached a size and economic capacity that allow us to invest very large sums of money."[5]

Exhibit 3 Carlsberg A/S Global Markets, 2007

	Beer consumption per capita (L/year)	Market Position	Market Share (%)	Employees	Breweries
Western Europe					
Denmark	83	1	64	2,332	2
Norway	59	1	52	1,554	3
Sweden	52	1	38	1,152	1
Finland	87	1	50	1,003	2
United Kingdom	91	4	13	2,060	2
Germany	115	1		1,449	4
Switzerland	59	1	41	1,453	2
Italy	32	3	6	802	1
Portugal	64	1	52	892	2
Eastern Europe (BBH)				8,174	
Russia	75	1	38	n.a.	10
Ukraine	58	3	20	n.a.	3
Baltic states	67–98	1	45	n.a.	4
Kazakhstan	34	1	23	n.a.	1
Uzbekistan	11	2	25	n.a.	2
Eastern Europe (excl. BBH)					
Poland	88	3	13	1,319	3
Southeast Europe	64–84	2–3	15–23	1,336	4
Turkey	11	2	15	564	1
Asia					
Malaysia	5	2	44	596	1
Singapore	19	2	23	67	
Vietnam	17	4	10	570	2
China (Western China)	29 (15)	(1)	(55)	4,754	20
Other countries	n.a.	n.a.	n.a.	n.a.	5

	Invested capital (kr mil.)	Beer Sales Pro Rata (mil. hl)	Revenue (kr mil.)	Operating Profit (kr mil.)	Operating Margin (%)	ROIC (%)
Western Europe	16,152	28.5	27,944	2.738	10.0	16.0
Eastern Europe (BBH)	8,987	29.1	10,435	2.338	22.4	29.1
Eastern Europe (excl. BBH)	4,248	14.8	4,267	477	11.2	11.3
Asia	3,033	9.6	2,535	330	13.0	11.5

Source: Carlsberg Annual Report 2007.

In retrospect, Carlsberg's ownership structure was a main contributor to the difficulties of financing expansion. The largest shareholder of Carlsberg A/S was the Carlsberg Foundation, which was established by J.C. Jacobsen in 1876 with the purpose of funding scientific research and social work. The Foundation was obliged to own at least 51 percent of Carlsberg A/S's shares, which hindered the quick release of capital for acquisitions and blocked potential fusions with large, foreign breweries. This was a serious disadvantage for an international brewery fighting to be among the top players in a rapidly consolidating industry.

Carlsberg A/S appeared unable to secure continuous growth and development, and many feared that the company would become a superfluous player. However, after the buyout of Orkla ASA, Carlsberg's management started to look forward. As Povl Krogsgaard-Larsen, the Carlsberg Foundation's chairman, pointed out, "We then began to prepare ourselves for our next move, namely to change the charter of the Foundation. This would give Carlsberg more freedom to act, as the Foundation was locked in terms of capital after we bought Orkla's shares back."[6] As a result of this process, the Foundation was obligated to own only 25 percent of Carlsberg A/S shares after May 2007, which created more room for new capital.

In May 2008, Carlsberg, in cooperation with Heineken, completed a kr104 billion (US$22 billion) acquisition of the largest British brewer, Scottish & Newcastle. This acquisition gave Heineken control over Scottish & Newcastle's British activities, while Carlsberg obtained the remaining 50 percent of the Russian brewery Baltic Beverages Holding. Naturally, this major acquisition increased Carlsberg's debt, which reached kr58.3 billion in May 2008 (US$12.1 billion).

Towards an Emerging Market Strategy

With global beer brands such as Carlsberg Pilsner ("*Probably the best beer in the world*"), regional brands such as Tuborg, Holsten and Baltika, and a number of leading local brands, Carlsberg's most important markets were in Western Europe, which accounted for 61 percent of revenue in 2007. Furthermore, the company held a strong position in the growth markets of Eastern Europe and in the emerging Asian markets, with Russia and China serving as the most notable examples. The booming Indian market was also regarded as a market of increasing importance. The Eastern European and Asian markets accounted for 33 percent and 6 percent of revenue in 2007, respectively (see Exhibit 3).

The global brewing industry of the mid-2000s was characterized by a process of intense consolidation, in which the number of breweries continuously declined. By 2007, the industry was basically controlled by the four largest breweries in the world (see Exhibit 4). This consolidation process could be ascribed to changes in consumers' beer-drinking habits as well as increasing production costs. In the mature European and American markets, beer consumption had been falling as a result of growing health consciousness and increased competition from wine and spirits, while the Eastern European and Asian beer markets were booming. Given the rising

costs of inputs, such as glass, aluminum and hops, the large breweries were seeking to consolidate and increase their market share as they searched for economies of scale in relation to everything from production to advertising. For the consolidation of foreign markets, acquisitions and joint ventures with local firms were the preferred modes of entry for the largest companies in the beer industry, as they allowed acquiring companies to gain access to local brands, distributional networks and local market knowledge through partnerships with local breweries.

As markets around the world became increasingly consolidated, Carlsberg recognized its inability to become a truly global company. The North and South American markets had been lost to other well-known, established breweries, and the potential offered by the African markets was of limited interest. The Western European markets were already consolidated to a great extent, so Carlsberg decided to focus on Eastern Europe and Asia as a means of achieving future growth. Investments in these emerging markets were financed through revenues from activities in the Western European markets. Carlsberg's activities in Eastern Europe, particularly in Russia, were expected to offer sizeable potential for several years. However, expectations were perhaps even greater for the long-term potential of the Asian markets, especially China, where Carlsberg was making considerable investments. In fact, Carlsberg's emerging market focus was considered vital for the company's ability to remain a major player in the beer industry. "We want to ensure that we have positions with future growth potential, and we will be relatively patient," former CEO Nils Smedegaard Andersen argued in 2005. "We are unable to say anything about how long it will take, but right now we believe that a market-leading position will be interesting in five to 10 years. How interesting will depend on the competition, the economic development and many other conditions."[7] The increase in optimism concerning Carlsberg's future was, therefore, due in large part to the fact that the company had abandoned its strategy of becoming a global player and instead focused on capitalizing on emerging markets.

Central to Carlsberg's business strategy was a focus on value creation and profitable growth. The Western European strategy was to ensure "improved profitability through innovation and streamlining," while "rapid growth and higher earnings" were emphasized in Eastern Europe. The Asian strategy was "long-term growth through building up market positions" (see Exhibit 5).[8]

The beer industry's mantra, according to Heineken CEO Jean-Francois van Boxmeer, was that it was not

Exhibit 4 Carlsberg's Competitors

InBev

	2003	2004	2005	2006	2007
Sales volume (mil. hl)	108	162	224	247	271
Net revenue (mil. €)	7,004	8,568	11,656	13,308	14,430
Net profit (mil. €)	505	719	904	1,411	2,198

Worldwide beer volume 2007, %	
North America	4.6
Latin America North	37.3
Latin America South	11.3
Western Europe	13.3
Central and Eastern Europe	18.2
Asia Pacific	13.4
Global Export and Holding Companies	1.9

Famous brands: Stella Artois, Beck's, Hoegaarden, Leffe, Staropramen, Labatt Blue.

Anheuser-Busch

	2003	2004	2005	2006	2007
Sales volume (mil. hl)	110	117	122	125	128
Net revenue (mil. €)	9,151	9,660	9,726	10,166	10,793
Net profit (mil. €)	1,343	1,449	1,190	1,271	1,368

Worldwide beer volume 2007, %	
United States	81.3
International	18.7

Famous brands: Budweiser, Michelob.

Heineken

	2003	2004	2005	2006	2007
Sales volume (mil. hl)	85	97	101	112	120
Net revenue (mil. €)	9,255	10,062	10,796	11,829	12,654
Net profit (mil. €)	798	642	761	807	1,211

Worldwide beer volume 2007, %	
Western Europe	30.4
Central and Eastern Europe	10.5
Americas	36.8
Africa and the Middle East	6.5
Asia Pacific	15.8

Famous brands: Heineken, Amstel.

Exhibit 4 Carlsberg's Competitors (continued)

SABMiller

	2003	2004	2005	2006	2007
Sales volume (mil. hl)	n.a.	n.a.	n.a.	n.a.	239
Net revenue (mil. €)	8,179	9,407	11,048	13,354	15,412
Net profit (mil. €)	417	984	931	1,067	1,309

Worldwide beer volume 2007, %	
Latin America	25
Europe	20
North America	10
Africa and Asia	12
South Africa	33

Famous brands: Pilsner Urquell, Peroni Nastro Azzurro, Grolsch, Carling's Black Label.

Source: Companies' annual reports.

Exhibit 5 Carlsberg A/S Regional Strategies

	Western Europe	BBH and the Rest of Eastern Europe	Asia
Strategy	Improved profitability through innovation and streamlining	Rapid growth and higher earnings	Long-term growth through build-up of market positions
Group focus	■ Innovation ■ Marketing and brand building ■ Continuous streamlining ■ Corporate culture and management development		
Regional focus	■ Maintaining and developing market positions ■ Marketing ■ Innovation ■ Focus on value ■ Streamlining on every level	■ Strengthening the developing market positions ■ Increased focus on premium segments ■ Investments ■ Optimization	■ Strengthening and product range ■ Improving sales work ■ Strengthening existing market positions through organic growth ■ Establishing new market positions through acquisitions

Source: Carlsberg Annual Report 2007.

worthwhile for a brewing company to be present in a market where it was not the market leader or the runner-up. This philosophy was shared by Carlsberg, as indicated by Carlsberg's press officer, Jens Peter Skaarup: "What is important is the position we have on the markets in which we are present." In relation to the consolidation of the industry, he argued that "competition is something we are happy about. It makes us more 'fit for fight.'"[9]

Carlsberg in Russia

Once Carlsberg gained access to BBH through the Orkla ASA merger, the scene was set for Carlsberg to reap the major benefits of the emerging Eastern European markets. In 2007, when Carlsberg owned 50 percent of BBH's shares, the Russian brewery held a market share of 37.6 percent in Russia and was the market leader. BBH operations in Eastern Europe—Russia, the Ukraine, the Baltic states, Kazakhstan, Uzbekistan and Belarus—accounted for 23 percent of Carlsberg's revenue in 2007. The Russian market was undoubtedly the most important for BBH, as it represented 79 percent of sales volumes and 86 percent of operating profit. From 2006 to 2007, the Russian market grew by 16 percent, while annual beer consumption per capita amounted to 75 liters (the average in the Scandinavian markets was 65 liters).

This positive development was expected to continue in Russia in the coming years, as vodka consumption was declining due to new taxes on liquor, which increased the price of vodka. In fact, the Russian market was considered to be one of the fastest-growing beer markets in the world.

Carlsberg's strategy in terms of BBH and the Russian market was to grow organically by capturing new market share. The company doubted that the Russian state would accept more acquisitions by a company that was the absolute market leader. However, for Christian Ramm-Schmidt, BBH's CEO, organic growth was not a problem: "I cannot see why that should not be possible. BBH is a national company, and it has the best brands, the best distribution and strong management. That should suffice to capture one to two percentage points a year."[10] In order to support this strategy, Carlsberg invested in BBH's production capacity, infrastructure and logistics, as well as in the building of strong brands through product development and advertising.

BBH's best-selling brand was Baltika, "a foamy, golden brew with a delicate flavour of hops and the aroma of first-class malt."[11] It was also Russia's leading brand with a market share of 38 percent in 2007. In order to reduce Carlsberg's dependency on the Russian market, the company had great expectations for Baltika on an international scale, and planned to introduce the brand in Asia and the United States. "I can see possibilities for Baltika in most parts of the world," explained Jørgen Buhl Rasmussen. "Just like you can sell Czech beer almost everywhere today, I believe the same could happen for a brand like Baltika."[12] Furthermore, Buhl Rasmussen did not believe that introducing Baltika in other markets would have negative effects on Carlsberg's other brands: "We do not see any risk at all of cannibalizing our own brands."[13] BBH also distributed the Carlsberg Pilsner and Tuborg brands to the Russian market, where the aim was to capture the premium segments. In fact, the Tuborg brand was BBH's most important international brand, as it represented 11 percent of revenue in 2007. The Carlsberg Pilsner brand accounted for two percent of revenue in the same year.

However, as the Russian market was attractive, Carlsberg was not the only international brewing company interested in capturing market share as the Western European and American markets began to stagnate. Heineken acquired five breweries in Russia in 2005 and was the third-largest beer company in the Russian market in terms of volume by 2007. In addition, Heineken was selling local brands, such as Volga and Ochata. South African/British SABMiller was also active in the Russian market with a six percent market share and was planning to acquire more Russian breweries.

Carlsberg in China

Carlsberg's history in China spanned as far back as the late 1890s when the first barrels of beer were exported from Denmark. It was, however, not until 1981—when Carlsberg Brewery Hong Kong was established—that Carlsberg began to produce beer in China. The Chinese market was considered highly important for Carlsberg, even though the yearly per capita consumption of beer was just 29 liters in 2007. Given its vast size and high population, China was the world's largest market in terms of production and consumption, and the market's estimated growth rate was up to eight percent per year, compared to 0.7 percent in the United States and 2.5 percent in Europe. In other words, the market was not to be underestimated.

The Chinese beer market was immensely fragmented and highly regionalized with no truly national brewery. Local and regional non-premium brands dominated and price was often the determining factor. These types of beer constituted more than 95 percent of total beer sales. In addition, entry barriers were considered to be very high, and the industry was capital intensive in terms of production and distribution. In order to be profitable, it was necessary to be either number one or number two. For that reason, competition had led to a process of consolidation, where the large international breweries mainly competed on buying shares of regional and local breweries.

Following initial setbacks, which led to a complete overhaul of the original strategy, Carlsberg was positioned somewhat differently from its competitors in the competition for the Chinese market. In 2000, Carlsberg had entered into a 50/50 joint venture with the Thai company Chang Beverages Pte Ltd—a leading player in Asian markets for alcoholic beverages—and created Carlsberg Asia Ltd. (CAL) to strengthen Carlsberg's position in the Asian markets. In the important southeastern Chinese market, however, CAL met fierce competition, and earnings and sales did not take off as expected. In 2003, Anheuser-Busch, SABMiller, Interbrew and Heineken together held a substantial proportion of shares in China's four largest breweries, and controlled more than 30 percent of the Chinese beer market in collaboration with their partners. Furthermore, as time passed, disagreements between Carlsberg and Chang Beverages arose, which eventually led to Carlsberg pulling out of the joint venture in 2003. However, as this move was allegedly a violation of the contract between the two partners, Carlsberg was forced to pay compensation of kr734 million. As a result of this episode, Carlsberg not only experienced severe financial losses but also lost three strategically important years in which to establish itself in the Chinese and Asian beer markets. During these years, other international competitors acquired important market share in the southeast Chinese beer market, while Carlsberg, with its assets first tied up in Thailand and later finding itself financially strained from the lawsuit, was unable to muster the financial strength needed to acquire new production facilities and enter the competition.

This significant setback inhibited Carlsberg from taking part in the initial consolidation process in southeast China, which caused the company to revise its strategy for Asia and the Chinese market. The result was a focus on the highly fragmented, poor Western Chinese provinces. "Our strategy is to pursue the provinces in the west, as we can buy cheap and because it is a foundation for growth," explained Carlsberg's information officer, Margrete Skov. She continued, "The good forecasts for growth are a result of China's 'go west' policy with large investments in the provinces in the west. That gives a larger economy and better sale opportunities."[14]

The cornerstone of Carlsberg's new strategy was a focus on achieving leadership and first-mover advantages in Western China, while avoiding the fierce competition in the southeast. Geographically, the Western Chinese region included five provinces, which covered one-third of China and had a population of around 100 million. The Western regions were the poorest parts of China, and the living standards and level of beer consumption were lower than the country averages. In the Western province of Yunnan, for instance, yearly beer consumption per capita only amounted to four liters, in contrast to 70-90 liters in the big eastern cities.

Nevertheless, Carlsberg expected living standards and beer consumption to rise rapidly. According to Michael Fredskov Christiansen, director of the Chinese operations, it was crucial for the company to be present in Western China when growth accelerated. He expected Carlsberg's turnover to rise in line with the general growth in the Chinese beer market.[15] In addition, the Western Chinese market was quite fragmented, and none of the other large players were present, as they all concentrated on the southeast.

Carlsberg's 2007 Annual Report indicated that the company's strategy was "to build up a leading position in these emerging markets through acquisitions and subsequent strong organic growth, so that Asia makes a greater contribution to Carlsberg's overall earnings in the future."[16]

In 2007, Carlsberg had operations in 20 brewery plants and had 4,756 employees in China. Only a handful of the Chinese breweries were fully owned by Carlsberg, while the rest were operated through joint ventures with local partners, the Danish Industrialization Fund for Developing Countries (IFU), and local authorities. These efforts gave Carlsberg an overall market share of approximately 55–60 percent in Western China, making it the only international brewery with a leading position in that region. In addition to selling local brands, Carlsberg experienced increasing success with Carlsberg Chill, a brand designed for the Chinese market. This beer targeted the more exclusive segments and was distributed not only in Western China but also in the east. In this respect, Jørgen Buhl Rasmussen argued, "We are interested in approaching nearby areas by continuously moving from the west towards central China — for instance through acquisitions." However, he also stated, "alone in Western China, the possibilities are enormous. We control approximately 60 percent of [the] Western China [beer market] in an area of a population of approximately 120 million. That is far more than Great Britain and Scandinavia together, and it is a market where the consumers continuously buy better, more expensive beer."[17]

Even though the Asian investments had yet to show their full potential, former CEO Niels Smedegaard Andersen emphasized, "We are in China to create a position. And we are not counting on making money in perhaps five to 10 years. Carlsberg has to establish new markets." He also argued, "We consider Western Europe to be a mature, stagnating market. Russia and Eastern Europe are growth markets, while Asia is a developing market."[18]

Considering Carlsberg's activities in emerging markets, CEO Jørgen Buhl Rasmussen was optimistic. He was convinced that the company's timely and successful emerging market strategy and positioning had ensured that Carlsberg was prepared to successfully capitalize on its investments in the emerging economies. However, Rasmussen was fully aware that the majority of the company's revenue was still generated in the stagnating Western European markets and that new sources of revenue were needed. At the same time, the BBH success story was likely to soon be affected by ever-fiercer competition, and the Russian government was contemplating worrisome taxation proposals for alcohol in general and beer in particular, which could seriously challenge the profitability of Carlsberg's Russian operations. Moreover, despite magnificent forecasts for the Asian markets, the annual consumption per capita was still humble and had yet to take off.

Therefore, Carlsberg's shareholders would need time and patience if they wished to see whether Carlsberg's emerging market strategy would suffice as a response to the operational, competitive and regulatory challenges that these markets posed. In the longer term, the payoff could be significant.

NOTES

1. *Business.dk,* August 18, 2008.
2. Carlsberg Annual Report, 2007.
3. Carlsberg Annual Report, 2007.
4. *Børsen,* May 18, 2007.
5. *Politiken,* April 4, 2004.
6. *Børsen,* February 1, 2008.
7. *Børsen,* October 11, 2005.
8. Carlsberg Annual Report, 2007.
9. *Reuters,* July 14, 2008.
10. *Børsen,* March 19, 2003.
11. www.carlsberggroup.com.
12. *Børsen,* June 12, 2007.
13. Ibid.
14. *Børsen,* July 16, 2004.
15. *Jyllands-Posten,* July 30, 2005.
16. Carlsberg Annual Report, 2007.
17. *Business.dk,* August 18, 2008.
18. *Jyllands-Posten,* October 12, 2005.

CASE 5

Fisk Alloy Wire, Inc. and Percon

Susan F. Sieloff, Raymond M. Kinnunen
Northeastern University

Fully owned by brothers Eric and Brian Fisk, Fisk Alloy Wire, Inc. focused on the development and manufacture of copper alloy wire for electronic components and conductors. By year-end 2008, projected sales were $28 million. Fisk Alloy had developed a copper alloy wire that was cadmium free (cadmium was a known carcinogen affecting both processing and disposal), but also met the characteristics of strength, conductivity, and elongation that defined a high performance wire. The product family was called Percon and was introduced into the market in 2006 around the time the European Union passed the Restriction of Hazardous Substances (RoHS) directive and the related Waste Electrical and Electronic Equipment (WEEE) directives went into effect. By August 2008, the market potential for Percon was still not really known because it had a broad variety of potential applications.[1] Although Fisk Alloy saw Percon as the source of its future growth, because of the unknown timing of the development of potential markets and the related issues of having adequate staff and production capacity to meet demand the Fisks faced a choice: should they grow, slowly and opportunistically, or more aggressively? President Eric Fisk commented:

We want to be the top dog but not necessarily the biggest dog. Companies that manage only for the bottom line often lose sight of the core strengths that got them there. We are a quality house and that's what got us where we are. We also have a core competency in copper alloy wire.

Fisk ran the company to be profitable, but not with the typical short term bottom line mentality that forces growth in many companies. At the same time, he knew there was a critical mass necessary to be sustainable over the long term. He felt there was a huge market potential for Percon, and at some point that market would emerge. He knew that by the summer of 2008, Fisk Alloy was ready to meet that challenge, and he commented on the gatekeepers in the conductor business:

The first gatekeeper is the alloy—if you do not have the alloy, you are not going anywhere. Secondly, you have to
have the equipment, which is as scarce as hen's teeth or far too expensive. Finally, you must have the management and skill set to run the equipment at the required quality levels.

The Company

Fisk Alloy Wire was started in 1973 by John Fisk (father of Eric and Brian) to produce precision square, round, and flat copper alloy wire for electronic connectors and components. At the time he started the business, John Fisk was considered something of maverick in the wire industry for his insistence on product and process quality in wire manufacturing. Although not originally started as a family operation, both brothers (Eric, current CEO and Brian, VP of engineering, respectively) later joined the business. Eric graduated from the University of Washington in forestry and economics and had worked in Alaska in banking. He later took an executive MBA from Columbia University and now handles sales and general administration. When the company was a start-up, Brian took a year off from the engineering program at Purdue University to become the Fisk Alloy's first and only production employee. After graduating and working as an engineer at Alcoa and Boeing, he returned to lead Fisk Alloy's production. By the time John retired late in the 1980s, the wire mill had grown from 8,000 to 125,000 square feet, and had integrated manufacturing operations from initial rolling through finish drawing, annealing, and electroplating, and was expanding its alloy development capability.[2]

Initially, the business focused on the development and manufacture of copper alloy wire for electronic components and conductors. By 2008, projected total sales were $28 million (see Exhibit 1 for financials) and the company had 150 employees in three related divisions. Fisk Alloy Wire, Inc. (FAW) produced the original copper alloy wire in flat, round, square, and specialty shapes. Fisk Alloy Conductor, Inc. (FAC) produced high performance wire that could be stranded or braided. Fisk had also incorporated the Electroplated Wire Corporation, an internal unit that electroplated wire with copper,

Exhibit 1 Electroplated Wire Corporation Fisk Alloy Conductors, Inc. Combined Statements of Operations and Comprehensive Income for the Years Ended December 31, 2007 and 2006

	2007	2006
Net Sales	$28,643,630	$27,659,810
Cost of sales	19,516,161	16,836,644
Engineering expenses	1,057,621	1,142,037
Selling expenses	1,201,502	909,580
General and administrative expenses	4,880,736	4,748,863
Total	26,656,020	23,637,124
Income from Operations	1,987,610	4,022,686
Other Income (and Expenses)		
Interest expense	(194,533)	(55,203)
Interest income	23,740	32,389
(Loss) gain on disposal of assets	(15,094)	53,315
Gain on currency transaction	1,725	1,251
Other income (expense)	75,000	(17,885)
Total Other (Expense) and Income	(109,162)	13,867
Income Before Income Taxes	1,878,448	4,036,553
Income Taxes	32,525	37,000
Net Income	1,845,923	3,999,553
Other Comprehensive Income (Loss)		
Foreign currency translation adjustment	5,779	(8,586)
Comprehensive Income	$1,851,702	$3,990,967
Electroplated Wire Corporation Fisk Alloy Conductors, Inc.		
Combined Balance Sheets December 31, 2007 and 2006		
Assets		
Current Assets		
Cash and cash equivalents	$655,161	$1,068,587
Accounts receivable, net of allowance for doubtful accounts of $75,000 and $75,000 in 2007 and 2006, respectively	4,228,219	3,673,336
Inventories	5,751,113	5,819,601
Prepaid expenses and other	462,860	465,268
Total Current Assets	11,097,353	11,026,783
Property and Equipment, Net	3,762,637	3,485,897
Other Assets		
Deposits	536,483	485,031
Intangible assets, net	42,698	58,249
Total Other Assets	579,181	543,280
Total Assets	$15,439,171	$15,055,960
Liabilities and Equity		
Current Liabilities		
Loans payable, current portion	$1,873,333	$1,441,667
Accounts payable	1,526,134	1,139,203
Accrued expenses	222,378	173,055
Spool deposits—customers	362,250	255,329
Total Current Liabilities	3,984,095	3,009,254
Loan Payable, Net of Current Portion	425,447	673,779
Total Liabilities	4,409,542	3,683,033
Equity		
Common stock	26,000	26,000
Paid-in capital	1,054,401	1,054,401
Retained earnings	9,475,973	9,812,550
Accumulated and other comprehensive loss	(2,807)	(8,586)
Members' equity	476,062	488,562
Total Equity	11,029,629	11,372,927
Total Liabilities and Equity	$15,439,171	$15,055,960

gold, nickel, silver, and tin, a process that other wire manufacturers usually outsourced. The firm had manufacturing operations in Hawthorne, NJ, and Oriskany, NY. The sales managers for both FAW and FAC were in Hawthorne, NJ, as well as an overall marketing manager. There was an independent sales representative in California, and sales offices were located in Bornem, Belgium, and Shanghai, China.

In the early years, locating quality source material required its own development work. As Eric Fisk noted:

The Achilles' heel of this business is raw material. If we can't get good quality cast rod in here, we can't make it better, and a lot of the finished components get gold plating and other finishes, so precision and quality is an acute requirement in the raw material. It has to sustain the finished product requirements.

Solving that problem took years of time working with suppliers. Their casting integrity was good, but their subsequent processing produced a lot of mechanical damage, leading to failure sites on the finished product. The problem ultimately led to our developing what is called heavy gauge processing capability.

The Wire Production Process

Brian Fisk (VP of engineering and head of production) described the process for drawing wire:

The manufacturing process for copper and copper alloy wire starts with molten metal flowing into a chilled mold, solidifying, and then withdrawing as a continuous solid rod. Next, it is normally "cold-rolled," where the large rod is fed between a pair of powered rolls compressing it to a smaller size, making it longer. Throughout this process, the material becomes stronger and harder. Some alloys will become brittle and crack with continued size reduction. Therefore, periodically throughout the reduction process, we heat-treat the wire to "anneal," or soften it.

Further size reduction is done by wire "drawing" using a drawing "die." The die is a very hard material such as tungsten carbide or often synthetic and natural diamonds. A single wire drawing machine will usually have multiple dies in sequence (up to thirty or more) with a capstan on each machine to pull the wire through. Drawing and heat treating will continue until we reach the final size.

When the desired cross-section of wire is something other than round, it is processed as a round wire until it's close to the finish size. Then, it can either be drawn through a series of shaped dies, rolled in a rolling mill with flat or grooved rolls, or rolled using a "turks head." This is a device with four rolls for each pass, which is convenient

for square and rectangular shapes. We use grooved rolls for other shapes. The logo for Fisk Alloy Wire shows the roll configuration for a common style of turks head for rolling square wire. (see Exhibit 2 for diagram of wire drawing process.)

Copper Alloys and High Performance Alloys

Copper has always been known for its high electrical conductivity, which made it the material of choice for wire. Commercially, pure copper was easily processed and readily available as a commodity ore. However, it was hampered in its functionality by its low tensile strength and tendency to soften at relatively low temperatures, whereas many high performance wire and cable applications required higher strength and resistance to softening. To counter the weaknesses of pure copper, the industry alloyed copper with various materials and today can create an engineered set of properties. Each additive provides different advantages and disadvantages to the resulting alloy. The American Society for Testing Materials (ASTM) has set standards for various alloys as electrical conductors such as: cadmium copper, cadmium chromium copper, tin copper, zirconium copper and beryllium copper.

One of Fisk Alloy's strengths was its ability to work with various copper alloys to tailor high performance alloy products. To be defined as high performance, conductor alloys had to incorporate a variety of characteristics: electrical conductivity, reliable strength in service, resistance to softening when exposed to elevated temperatures; flex life to withstand vibration or repeated bending; a surface conducive to soldering; fabrication capability to readily allow economic processing; plating capability (most often nickel, silver or tin) and good price-to-performance value, in order to be cost effective in a finished product.[3] Any new alloys required the development of process technology to assure repeatable quality output in commercial quantities. Fisk Alloy established a working partnership with the Brass Division of Olin Corporation, which had done metallurgical work in creating copper alloys of greater strength. After the alloy (later called Percon) was developed, the technical issue became how to process the high strength alloy into wire. Fisk Alloy recognized that developing the process would increase its alloy offerings and allow it to leverage its investment in production capacity. The two parties discussed a joint venture, but Olin decided not to go forward with it. Eric Fisk commented:

Exhibit 2 Fisk Alloy Wire Production Process (Authors' Diagram)

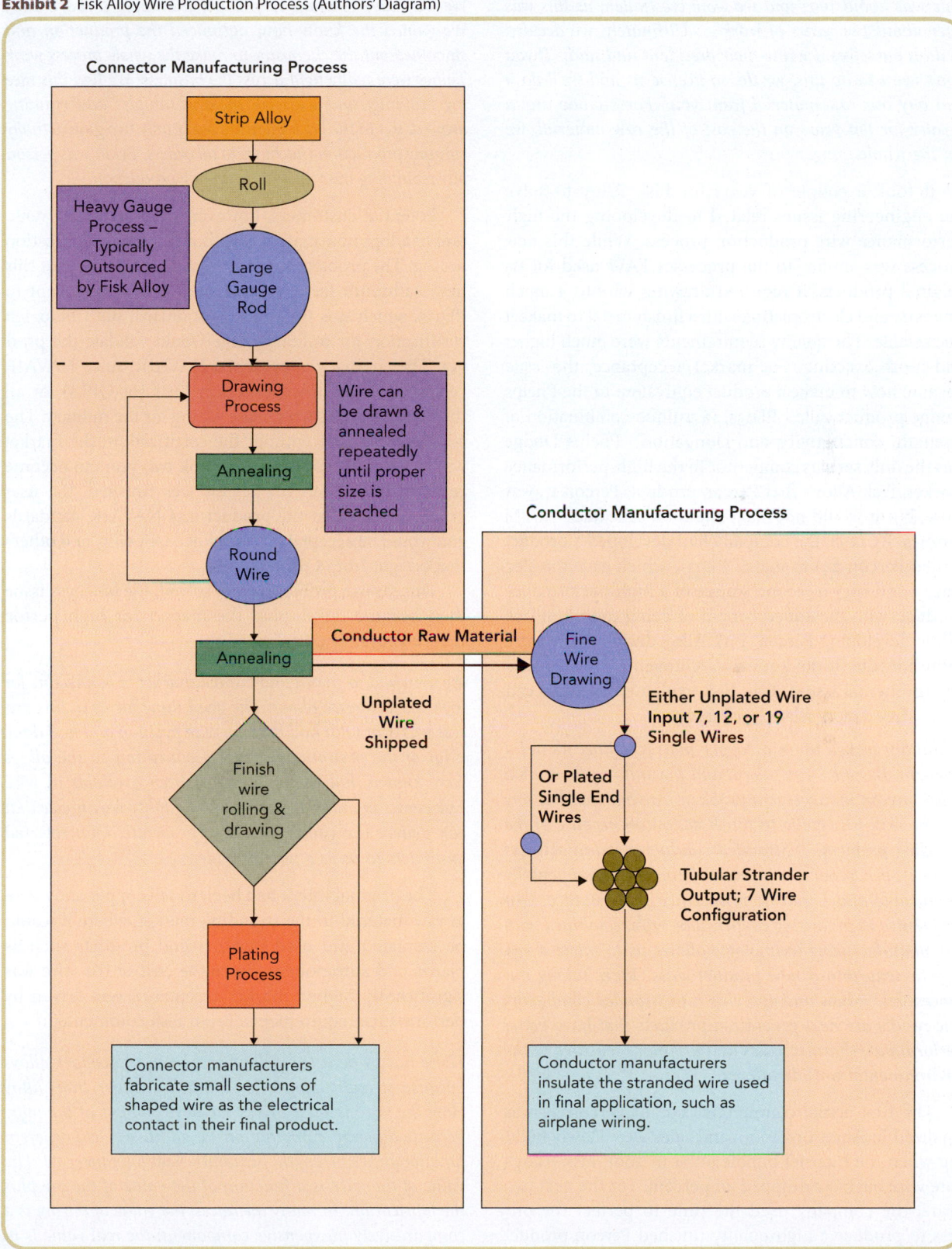

This was about 1992 and we were crestfallen, as this was after about two years of work … Ultimately, we decided to do it ourselves. I wrote their president and said: "If you don't want to do this, we do, so license us and we'll do it and buy our raw material from you." For $10,000 and a royalty for ten years on the cost of the raw material, we got the whole thing.

It took a couple of years for Fisk Alloy to solve the engineering issues related to developing the high-performance wire production process. While this new process was similar to the processes FAW used for its original products, it required drawing wire to a much finer size and electroplating with a finish metal to make it marketable. The quality requirements were much higher and more exacting. For market acceptance, the issue became how to make a product equivalent to the Phelps Dodge product called PD135, (a unique combination of strength, conductivity, and elongation). Phelps Dodge was the only serious competitor in the high-performance market. Fisk Alloy's first Percon product, Percon 17, was close, but it would not make the total scheduled ASTM profiles. By 1998, the company had developed a product (called Percon 24) to match PD135, which gave the electronics industry a second source of a high-performance product, with the added benefit of being cadmium free. While developing Percon, Fisk Alloy decided not to use cadmium due to its known carcinogenic qualities and environmental issues. Eric Fisk explained how the cadmium-free aspect related to Percon:

Cadmium locked up in a copper matrix is fine, it's not a problem. But once you take it and try and recycle it, it's a waste stream management problem. Anyone that has any casting skill isn't going to touch cadmium because of the recycling problem…. Stranded conductor manufacturers haven't been proactive in making more environmentally responsible alloys that don't sacrifice performance. Our experience in producing copper alloy wire, combined with our manufacturing technology, allows us to make a synergistic leap into a new product class. We're taking our process know-how and applying it to stranded conductors. The results are next generation products that have better performance characteristics and are more sensitive to the environmental considerations.[4]

The first actual commercial sale of Percon 24 was finalized in August of 2000, and sales were slowly building when the Internet bubble burst in 2001. Fisk Alloy's core wire business dropped 40 percent. For the next two years, the company used the time to perfect the process to produce a high-quality finished Percon product. Eric Fisk described those years:

We were able to build very slowly from 2001 through 2003. We gained the know-how, optimized the production and smoothed out the chemistry to make the whole process work. Things were really tight across the business. We had this nice big building, and we were making samples and running around, but in the back there are really only two guys actually running production machines to fill orders. Brian was personally rebuilding machines and running production.

Potential customers, however, were extremely reluctant to adopt new materials without lengthy qualification testing. The problem for Fisk Alloy was to show that this new, cadmium-free Percon material was equivalent to PD135, which was the industry standard. Both Fisks felt certification for military usage would validate the product. The company approached NAVAIR, since NAVAIR certified the Qualified Producer Lists (or QPLs) for all the manufacturers who made wiring for the military. The company felt that without the certification, the market would never accept Percon. It took two years to become certified and when the review was finished, the user groups agreed that the product met NAVAIR standards and would be acceptable to Lockheed, Boeing, and others that bought from QPL suppliers.

Once those problems were solved, the business issue then became developing the market for high performance alloys. Eric continued:

We then had to go out and build a market in connectors for high-performance alloys. The good thing for us in this process was that Olin had built an elite position and had done a lot of the preliminary market education so the alloys were known, but they just hadn't been available in wire. Fisk comes in and we're known as a quality wire house that can deliver the goods. Where appropriate, Olin referred customers to us as a wire provider.

The original intent had been to sell copper alloy wire as raw material to the stranding market, where it would be insulated and used in other end products such as planes and automobiles. Since the cost of the wire was significantly higher, market acceptance was driven by performance requirements. Brian Fisk commented:

There has to be a compelling reason to use copper alloys because straight copper is so much cheaper than alloy. How the wire is used drives the development of the alloy because different combinations of additives yield different functionalities, strength, flexibility, heat tolerance, etc. The value of the wire is a function of the value of the ore plus the fabrication. In many instances, the value of the ore is a comparatively inexpensive component; the real value is in the quality of the manufacturing.

Wire was used to bear mechanical loads and to carry electricity, telecommunications, and data signals. Fisk Alloy's focus on product and process improvement in high-performance copper alloy wire has been driven by the demands of the electronics industry, despite the fact that this was a fairly small portion of the total demand for copper. As estimated by Eric Fisk:

… in the copper alloy industry, strip is the big tonnage side of the copper alloy business. To give you a frame of reference, around 2005, 4 billion pounds of copper were sold in the world in strip or wire. 3.5 billion pounds of that was copper wire for power distribution and building wire, and the other 500 million pounds was strip. Maybe 1 percent of that was copper alloy wire, so it is a very, very small market.

Conductor wire was generally anything that was stranded and insulated, with a broad range of complexity. Building wire was a simple copper conductor wire. Light cord was a prosaic copper conductor. The top end of the conductor trade, such as in military, aerospace, electrical and computer applications, consisted of highly engineered products and used copper alloys. Here, the wire was used for circuits, connectors and terminations and in the operation of electrical components, for example, head pins in computer printers or in the headphones and wiring of Bose™ speakers. The miniaturization of components in electrical, biomedical and telecommunications applications, and the service requirements of aerospace applications required stronger materials. The need to carry more current and dissipate more heat in electrical and computer applications required higher conductivity. In addition, the wire had to withstand movement or vibration in the operating environment. Electric blankets and the electrodes and the sensor cables used to attached a patient to an ultrasound machine required flexible copper alloys as raw materials. Wire performance requirements, especially in 'cannot-fail' type situations, required high performance alloys. (see Exhibit 3 for FAC Sales by End Use.)

In February, 2003 the European Union (EU) passed the Restriction of Hazardous Substances (RoHS) directive, to be effective in 2006. It restricted the use of specific contaminants, significantly cadmium (whose threshold limit was ten times lower than other contaminants), making the development of Percon look clairvoyant. Eric Fisk commented:

By the summer of 2004, people were beginning to be aware of the RoHS issue. Six months after that, people were asking us how we knew to get rid of the cadmium. That's literally what happened. They said, "you are brilliant, but how did you know (to get rid of cadmium)?" People wanted samples, people wanted to test it and try the product. This was just in the European market, but it set in motion two things: one, the awareness that cadmium was not a good idea, and two, some of the big corporate names made the corporate decision that it was good business for them to sign onto this ruling early and get cadmium out of their products, particularly those companies that had dual US/ European sales. They chose to support the standard rather than support dual products.

Percon's cadmium-free composition enabled U.S. manufacturers to meet the more stringent environmental standards for applications in Europe and Asia at a price that remained competitive with current cadmium copper alloy products such as PD135 from Phelps Dodge. As a multi-billion dollar corporation and one of the largest copper mining companies in the world with operations in nineteen countries, Phelps Dodge concentrated on copper and aluminum products and was the world's largest producer of molybdenum. It has been a major supplier of wire and cable around the world. It had not tried to come up with any cadmium-free product, since the overall size of the alloy market was very small compared to volume copper wire, Phelps Dodge's primary market.

By 2005, Fisk Alloy had developed and certified Percon as a high performance copper alloy, and the advent of the RoHS legislation might result in significant future sales, but any increased demand could create another problem. To add capacity, FAC needed additional machinery to process stranded wire. Older machines called tubular stranders worked well, but were slow. New equipment ran at two to three times the speed of the older stranders, but cost $250,000 per machine and took a year to custom manufacture. Brian Fisk noted that since stranding machines ran about

Exhibit 3 Fisk Alloy Conductor Total Pounds and Revenue Sold By Sector 1/06–8/08

End Use	Volume (Lbs.)	Revenue ($)
Aerospace	696,695	$20,228,851
Electronics	193,912	5,679,423
Medical	110,566	4,073,513
Military	23,444	1,148,182
Automotive	11,655	695,815
Jewelry	7,527	404,779
Misc.	874	8,129
Total	1,044,673 Lbs.	$32,238,693

twenty-two pounds of wire per production shift, buying a new machine was an economically unfeasible option. Fisk Alloy solved the equipment problem by acquiring Strandflex in Oriskany, NY. This was an older steel wire stranding mill full of tubular stranders in seven-bay, twelve-bay and eighteen-bay configurations. Brian Fisk explained the difference:

Seven-bay machines actually have six bays that strand seven wires. Twelve-bay machines strand thirteen wires and an eighteen-bay machine strands nineteen wires. The seven and twelve are concentric construction, where first, the internal seven-wire core is made in one direction and a twelve-wire closer is made in the opposite direction. This is done because the twist forces are set in opposition and result in a straighter wire. It is a more expensive manufacturing approach because of its step-by-step process. Unilay construction, which is done on the eighteen-bay machines, makes and closes a nineteen-wire construction all at once, before annealing. (The center of the Fisk Alloy Conductor logo [below] shows the 19-wire configuration.)

Brian suggested reconditioning and utilizing any useful machines and selling any they could not use to steel wire producers in India and China. In doing so, Fisk Alloy ultimately recouped 40 percent of the Strandflex purchase price. Brian commented on reconditioning machines:

Oriskany has proven to be the perfect place to build our own eighteen-bay machines. Rather than pay $250,000 for each custom-made new machine, we are literally building a new eighteen-bay machine every eight to ten weeks from old equipment by reconfiguring six and one-bay machines into eighteen-bay machines. We tear them completely apart, weld the frames, re-machine the barrels, and do what it takes, but we wind up with a machine that is better and faster than the original. The original machines ran at 1,600 rpm and the rebuilt machines now run at 2,000 rpm, a 25 percent increase.

In 2008, FAC bought fifty ultrafine tubular stranders, for $800,000 from Medallion Wire and Cable in Houston, TX, to manufacture ultrafine wire (.002 inch down to .0008 inch, finer than a human hair). The acquisition expanded production and product capability. Brian Fisk noted:

When we eventually consolidate all fifty machines in the Hawthorne plant in 2009, we will have the capacity as well as the capability for ultrafine stranded conductors. The ultrafine line will expand our offering for high performance. It will enhance our profile in the conductor

business for both higher volume and specialty products, such as biomedical applications. However, using Percon in biomedical applications will require certification, just like with the military. They see it as a whole new product, especially if it is for an application where the device will be implanted.

Eric summarized the vision of the business segments:

Here's the business model: Oriskany is the volume operation on the high-performance side (FAC), Hawthorne will be the specialty high-performance operation. Hawthorne is a volume operation for the original shaped wire business (FAW) and we need to develop the specialty shaped wire operation.

Market Opportunities

Although the military and aerospace were exempt from the RoHS regulation, equipment recapitalization in the airline industry would eventually increase demand for Percon-type products because under ROHS and the related WEEE statutes, commercial airplane manufacturers were responsible for the ultimate disposal of any toxic component. The Boeing Company noted, "Many manufacturers have a global supply chain, increasing the possibility that suppliers will be affected by diverse chemical bans and use restrictions. More productive, new airplanes will play a greater role, and there will be relentless pursuit of further environmental progress."[5] Suppliers to Boeing were already providing Percon for some applications.

Airbus, the other major airplane manufacturer, had already been informed by a supplier that it had 'gone green' and would no longer supply a cadmium-containing product. It recommended Percon 24 as the certified replacement. Earlier, Airbus had forecasted an average annual delivery rate of new planes at 1,215 from 2007 through 2026, driven by a 4.5 percent annual increase in passenger traffic, fuel and eco-efficiency issues and the replacement of older-generation equipment. (see Exhibit 4 for Airbus Orders and Deliveries 2000–2007).[6]

Based on its commercial airplane forecast 2008–2027, Boeing forecast sales in both new and replacement aircraft, with replacement airplanes taking a greater share of demand. Boeing estimated total fleet size at the end of the twenty-year period at 35,800 airplanes. Long-established airlines were expected to order replacements for the numerous aging airplanes, and leasing companies would order new airplanes.[7] Commercial size airplanes required 632,000 feet[8] of copper wire[9] although Brian Fisk noted that: "We are so far down the component

Exhibit 4 Airbus Orders and Deliveries 2000–2007[10]

Year	Aircraft Ordered	Aircraft Delivered	Order Backlog
2000	520	311	1,626
2001	375	325	1,575
2002	300	303	1,505
2003	284	305	1,454
2004	370	320	1,500
2005	1,111	378	2,177
2006	824	434	2,533
2007	1,458	453	3,538

chain; we're not sure of the total percentage of Percon that a plane contains. We think it's somewhere between 5 and 10 percent."

The older telecommunications applications of Fisk Alloy's shaped connector wire business had declined due to both product change and the shift to offshore manufacturing. The automotive market could replace this sales volume, because automobiles had become increasingly electronic. Current luxury cars contained, on average, 1,500 copper wires totaling about one mile in length. To justify the use of copper alloy wire, shifting to a Percon-type product would likely depend on new models with high performance needs. General Motors was gearing up to produce 30–60,000 Chevy Volt electric cars beginning in 2010.[11] Toyota and Mitsubishi had also announced new electric models. Fisk Alloy was already supplying major automotive component programs with Percon wire.

In 2008, the earlier effort to qualify to supply the military had resulted in Fisk Alloy receiving a DX order. A DX order was an executive order from the White House through the Department of Defense that stipulated a supplier must fill the order on the highest priority basis. Fisk Alloy was required to produce copper alloy wire for the actuators in the electronic door latches for the armored Humvees used in Iraq at the expense of other contracts.

Going Forward

Market potential looked positive for the immediate future. Brian Fisk forecasted that FAC would have forty-nine refurbished stranders on line by 2010 and all would be fully utilized by currently known demand. Eric Fisk estimated the Percon 24 market alone at around 1.2 million pounds, or $30–$40 million dollars based on known applications such as the Volt, the two major aircraft manufacturers Boeing and Airbus, as well as

the military. He felt it was "not big enough for the big competitors, but large enough for the smaller specialty players." Brian noted that FAC was in a unique position:

We have to be careful what we wish for. Right now, we don't sell directly to commercial aerospace, but do we really want to? They aren't yet compelled to become cadmium free, but even if they were, with our current capacity, if we landed the order we might not be able to fill it, and that could actually be worse in the long term.

In addition, we have the attraction of being scarce. Because our product is not readily available, there are buyers who insist they want to buy from us. This sheer lack of availability increases our attractiveness. That's an attractive position. It allows us to pick and choose in the marketplace. No competitor thought it was worthwhile to develop Percon 24, both due to the unknown market size and the technical difficulty. Percon has met or exceeded Phelps Dodge's product and they don't want to invest the time and money to do what we have done. They have bigger fish to fry with volume copper.

Having a cadmium free product available when RoHS hit made us look like boy geniuses, but it was really a case of preparation meeting opportunity. We had ten years of development in place when RoHS hit. And, while some products might be exempt from RoHS, the WEEE directive will drive manufacturing decisions for decades, because the manufacturers will always be responsible for product disposal, even years later, so the component choices now are significant.

Qualified staffing was an issue, because according to Brian, it took a full year for a machine operator to become fully proficient. Finding machine operators with the ability to operate semi-automatic production machinery with a high degree of accuracy was not easy. Fisk Alloy hired machinists at $15 per hour in Oriskany and $20 per hour in Hawthorne. The difference was due to both local employment conditions and the more highly skilled workers available in New Jersey. Another potential problem the company foresaw was the need for knowledgeable hands-on mechanics to rebuild and maintain machines. Recently, Brian Fisk had to extensively rework a custom-ordered, nickel plating machine. Without Brian's knowledge and skill, the equipment would not work at the required level. Finding skilled mechanics was a problem for such a mechanically-oriented, hands-on operation. Eric Fisk saw the biggest issue as not growing the company, but how to grow Percon.

Our biggest problem will be managing growth for the next five years. We've worked hard to create the opportunities and now we need to manage them in accordance with our

Exhibit 5 Reduction of Hazardous Substances and Waste Electrical and Electronic Directives

The Reduction of Hazardous Substances (RoHS) directive was adopted by the European Union in February 2003, to be effective as of July 1, 2006. It was closely allied with the Waste Electrical and Electronic Equipment (WEEE) directive. Each European Union member state was required to adopt its own enforcement and implementation policies using the directives as a guide.

The purpose of the RoHS directive was to establish restrictions of the use of hazardous substances in electrical and electronic equipment, and to contribute to the protection of human health and the environmentally sound recovery and disposal of waste electrical and electronic equipment.[12] RoHS was often referred to as the lead-free directive, but it actually restricted the use of six substances:

1. Lead
2. Mercury
3. Cadmium
4. Hexavalent chromium (Cr6$^+$)
5. Polybrominated biphenyls (PBB)
6. Polybrominated diphenyl ether (PBDE) [PBB and PBDE are flame retardants used in several plastics.]

The WEEE directive's purpose was, as a first priority, the prevention of WEEE, and in addition, to promote the reuse, recycling, and other forms of recovery of such wastes so as to reduce disposal. It also sought to improve the environmental performance of all operators involved in the life cycle of electrical and electronic equipment, e.g. producers, distributors and consumers, and in particular those operators directly involved in the treatment of waste electrical and electronic equipment. The directive imposed the responsibility for the disposal of waste electrical and electronic equipment on the manufacturers of such equipment. Those companies should establish an infrastructure for collecting WEEE, in such a way that, "Users of electrical and electronic equipment from private households should have the possibility of returning WEEE at least free of charge." Also, the companies were compelled to use the collected waste in an ecological-friendly manner, either by ecological disposal or by reuse/refurbishment of the collected WEEE.[13]

The directives were implemented in part to address the global issue of consumer electronics waste. As newer technology arrived at an ever-increasing rate, consumers were discarding their obsolete products sooner than ever and the toxic, hightech trash tended to end up in third world countries.[14] The directives applied to products in the EU, whether they were made in the EU or imported. While there were certain exclusions or exemptions to the RoHS directive, under WEEE, manufacturers remained responsible for product disposal, even years later.

The RoHS directive did not apply to fixed industrial plant and tools, aerospace, or military applications. Compliance was the responsibility of the company that put the product on the market, which in practicality meant that subcontractors and component manufacturers had to convey information to the final producer, since the directive applied at the homogeneous product level. The maximum permitted concentrations of the six substances listed above were 0.1 percent or 1000 ppm (except for cadmium, which was limited to 0.01 percent or 100 ppm) by weight of homogeneous material. This meant that the limits did not apply to the weight of the finished product, or even to a component, but to any single substance that could (theoretically) be separated mechanically—for example, the sheath on a cable or the tinning on a component lead.

As an example, a radio is comprised of a case, screws, washers, a circuit board, speakers, etc. The screws, washers, and case may each be made of homogenous materials, but the other components are comprised of multiple sub-components of many different types of material. For instance, a circuit board is comprised of a bare PCB, ICs, resistors, capacitors, switches, etc. A switch is a combination of a case, a lever, a spring, contacts, pins, etc, each of which may be made of different materials. A contact might be a copper strip with a surface coating. A speaker utilized a permanent magnet, copper wire, paper, etc. Everything identified as a homogeneous material must meet the limit. If it was found that the case was made of plastic with 2,300 ppm (0.23 percent) PBB used as a flame retardant, then the entire radio would fail the requirements of the directive.

China developed a similar directive, which was implemented March 1, 2007, with a key difference: in the EU RoHS, items were included in the ban unless specifically excluded. In the Chinese directive, only the catalogued items were banned. As of 2009, China RoHS has acted primarily as a labeling law. Companies needed to only disclose which hazardous materials are in their EEE.[15] Japan's recycling laws spurred Japanese manufacturers to move to a lead-free process in accordance with RoHS guidelines, although it did not have any direct legislation dealing with the RoHS substances.

California passed the Electronic Waste Recycling Act of 2003 (EWRA), which prevented the sale of a narrow range of electronic devices (mostly those with screens, e.g. televisions, monitors) that were prohibited from being sold under the EU RoHS. Other states and cities were debating similar laws. RoHS-like litigation on the Federal level was not expected in the near or medium term. However, many manufacturers, especially those who shipped internationally, were finding it more cost effective to manufacture and document goods (through their bill of materials) to a single set of specifications, and typically comply with the most stringent regulations.

Exhibit 6 Boeing Company Forecast Deliveries

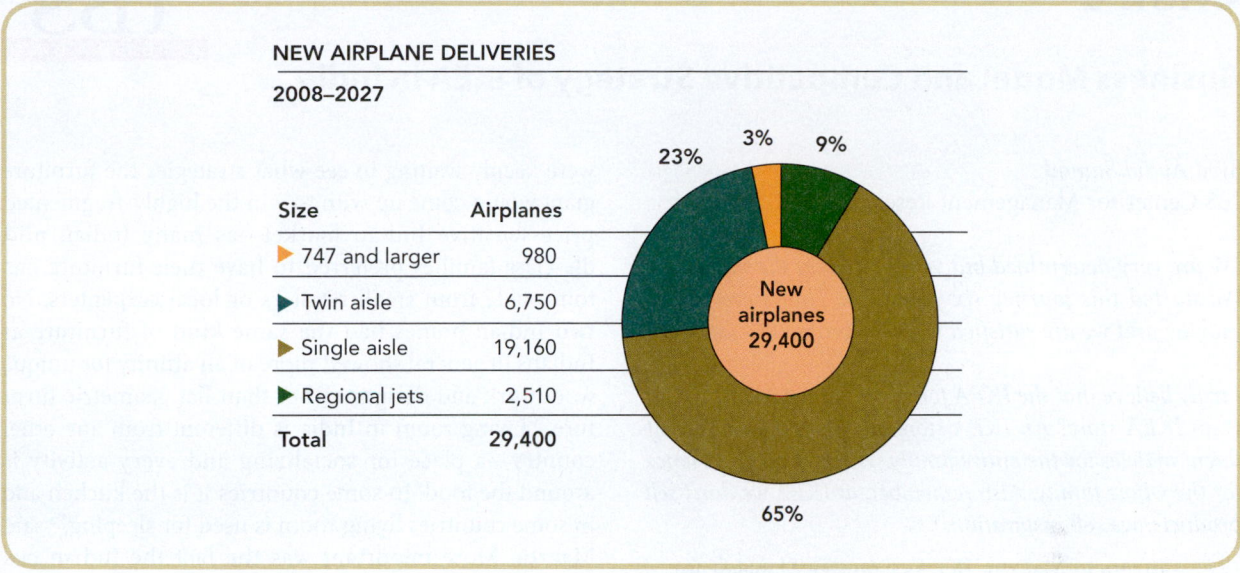

NEW AIRPLANE DELIVERIES

2008–2027

Size	Airplanes
▶ 747 and larger	980
▶ Twin aisle	6,750
▶ Single aisle	19,160
▶ Regional jets	2,510
Total	**29,400**

New airplanes 29,400

3%   9%   23%   65%

lights, not in accordance with the dictates of the industry and without losing our raison d'être, which is quality and maintained value. The metals business has lots of commodity producers who bought into the lure of volume and compromised on the quality side, then resorted to price competition and ultimately ground themselves to pieces. Keeping the quality level up and the innovation up so that you can walk the high road is really our objective.

Growth could come from acquisition, but with purpose, not just for size.

I would like to see us able to acquire some little companies for some strategic structural opportunities and do acquisitions because growth is fun and challenging, but you have to be careful not to do it just because it adds $10, 20, 30 million to the revenue side and everyone says: "Oh, boy, we're a $100 million company and we've got 500 people."

You don't want to get drawn into that. What you want to steer yourself toward is sustaining a position of excellence. As you get bigger that gets harder because the oversight and the detail it takes to effect that excellence gets harder and harder. That's the challenge, to sustain the excellence. That's what turns me on, achieving that type of reputation, not necessarily the kind of size, but that kind of reputation, and that's hard to do. Also, if you have survived from the 1980s on and stayed either #1 or #2 in your business, which we are, and you are technically based, not labor based, you're in a good spot.

We have no intention of being a commodity producer. We make our living only on alloy because that's our specialty. As it turns out, being a specialty is a really good business. The total size of the Percon market is still a mystery. We don't know yet what the ultimate size might be, but we know it's growing. Product characteristics combined with an increasing awareness of processing, product, and disposal waste stream responsibilities, means there will be an increasing demand for environmentally benign alloy conductors wherever they are used.

NOTES

1. www.fiskalloy.com.
2. Wire and Cable Technology International, November 2005.
3. Fisk, Eric S. 2004. Alloy conductor developments in automotive and aerospace wire. EuroWire. September.
4. Manning, William. 2002. Wired for Innovation. Wire and Cable Technology International. November.
5. www.boeing.com/companyoffices/doingbiz/environmental/TechNotes.html.
6. www.airbus.com/en/airbusfor/analysts.
7. www.boeing.com Current Market Forecast
8. Equals approximately 79 lbs/ft of wire.
9. www.copper.org/education/c-facts/c-communications.html.
10. www.airbus.com.
11. www.gm-volt.com.
12. www.conformity.com/artman/publish/printer_25.shtml.
13. http://ec.europa.eu/environment/waste/weee/index_en.ht.
14. 2008. High Tech Trash. National Geographic, September.
15. www.chinarohs.com.

CASE 6

Business Model and Competitive Strategy of IKEA in India

Syed Abdul Samad
IBS Center for Management Research (ICMR)

"We are very determined but very patient at the same time. We started this journey six years ago. Things are finally moving and we are satisfied with the progress so far…

"I truly believe that the IKEA format is going to work. What is an IKEA store? An IKEA store has more than 9000 different articles for the entire family. We offer an experience for the whole family. Also remember, at IKEA we don't sell products, we sell inspiration."[1]

– Juvencio Maeztu, IKEA's Country Manager for India, in 2013

After a year of lobbying and negotiating with and convincing the Indian politicos and bureaucrats, IKEA's €1.5 billion investment proposal to set up its stores in India was finally accepted by the local government on May 2, 2013. However, as of July 2013, Juvencio Maeztu (Maeztu), IKEA's Country Manager for India, found he still had a colossal task ahead of him.

IKEA, the Netherlands-based Swedish company, was the largest furniture retailer in the world with a presence in 44 countries around the globe—in countries like the US, the UK, Russia, the EU region, Japan, China, Australia, etc. However, it did not enter into the Indian market till 2013, though the company had had a presence in the country since the 1980s as a sourcing destination for its global stores. It had even opened its regional procurement office in Gurgaon, India, in 2007. In 2009, IKEA tried to enter the country to establish its stores, but its attempts were thwarted by India's stringent Foreign Direct Investment (FDI) regulations. It again applied for permission for entry in June 2012, after India had made some changes in its FDI rules. However, IKEA had to wait another year, hitting many roadblocks on the way, before it was able to obtain the Indian government's approval to establish its stores. The company also had to tweak its global store model to fit the Indian FDI and sourcing outlines and Indian consumer preferences.

While Maeztu was tasked with tapping the Rs.[*] 925 billion Indian furniture and furnishings market, analysts were keenly waiting to see what strategies the furniture giant would come up with to win the highly-fragmented, price-sensitive Indian market—as many Indian middle-class families preferred to have their furniture custom-made from small retailers or local carpenters. No two Indian homes had the same kind of furniture as Indians in general showed more of an affinity for unique woodwork and designs rather than flat geometric furniture. "Living room in India is different from any other country—a place for socializing and every activity is around the food. In some countries it is the kitchen and in some countries living room is used for sleeping,"[2] said Maeztu. More important was the fact the Indian customer did not prefer the concept of do-it-yourself (where buyers had to assemble different pieces of the product themselves), a key part of IKEA's globally successful business model. Analysts opined that though the company had managed to impress the Indian Government, getting into the homes of Indian consumers would be an entirely different ball game.

About IKEA

IKEA was a privately held company. It designed and sold ready-to-assemble furniture, home appliances, and accessories. From humble beginnings in 1943, the company went on to become the world's largest furniture retailer by the 2000s.[3] In the financial year 2001, the company earned revenue of €10.4 billion (Refer to Exhibit 1 for IKEA's Growth in Revenue). By 2012, the company's revenues increased to €27.6 billion with a net income of €3.202 billion (Refer to Exhibit 2 for IKEA's Income Statement). By August 31, 2012, the IKEA Group had operations in 44 countries, including 30 service trading offices in 25 countries, 33 distribution centers, and 11 customer distribution centers. By August 31, 2012, the IKEA Group had a total of 298 stores in 26 countries and employed 139,000 people.[4] Globally, the company had doubled its sales to €27.6 billion in the past decade and further planned to double them again by 2020 and to open 20-25 stores a year from 2015.

IKEA was founded in Sweden in 1943 by 17-year-old Ingvar Kamprad (Kamprad). IKEA was an acronym of

*Rs. = Indian rupees or INR. As of 2013, US$1 was approximately equal to Rs. 62; €1 was approximately equal to Rs.85.

This case was written by Syed Abdul Samad, under the direction of Debapratim Purkayastha, IBS Hyderabad. It was compiled from published sources, and is intended to be used as a basis for class discussion rather than to illustrate either effective or ineffective handling of a management situation.

Exhibit 1 IKEA's Revenue Growth (2001–2012)

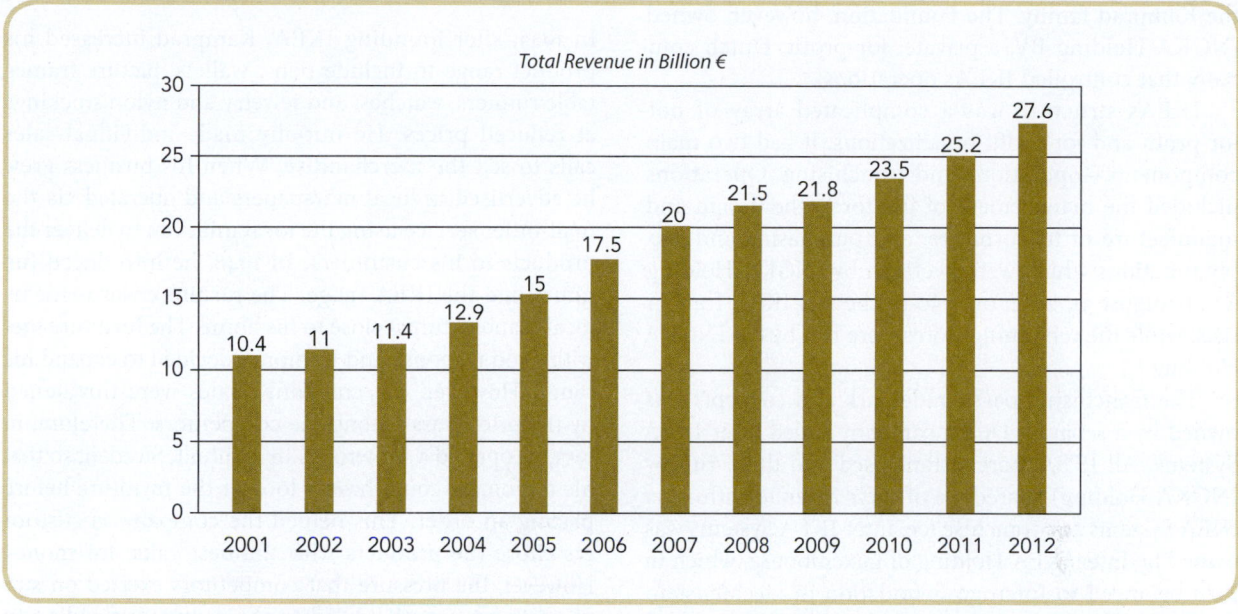

Total Revenue in Billion €

Year	Revenue
2001	10.4
2002	11
2003	11.4
2004	12.9
2005	15
2006	17.5
2007	20
2008	21.5
2009	21.8
2010	23.5
2011	25.2
2012	27.6

Source: Adapted from: "Welcome Inside – IKEA Group Yearly Summary FY12", http://www.ikea.com/ms/en_CA/pdf/yearly_summary/ys_welcome_inside_2012_final.pdf

Exhibit 2 IKEA's Consolidated Income Statement (2008–2012)
In million € (for September 1–August 31 of)

	2012	2011	2010	2009	2008
Revenue	27,628	25,173	23,539	21,846	21,534
Cost of sales	15,723	13,773	12,454	11,878	11,802
Gross profit	11,905	11,400	11,085	9,968	9,732
Operating cost	8,423	7,808	7,888	7,198	7,078
Operating income	3,482	3,592	3,197	2,770	2,654
Total financial income and expense	427	165	76	143	177
Income before minority interest and tax	3,909	3,757	3,273	2,913	2,831
Tax	695	781	577	384	546
Minority interests	12	10	8	–	–
Net income	3,202	2,966	2,688	2,538	2,280

Source: Adapted from www.ikea.com

Ingvar Kamprad, Elmtaryd (the farm where he grew up) and Agunnaryd (his hometown in Småland, South Sweden). The company's products were well known for their modern architecture and eco-friendly designs. In addition, the firm paid attention to cost control, operational details, and continuous product development, which allowed it to lower its prices. Instead of selling pre-assembled products, the company designed furniture that could be self assembled. This helped it cut down on costs and the use of packaging. The company's website featured around 12,000 products which represented its entire range.

Corporate Structure

IKEA was structured in such a way as to prevent any kind of takeover of the company and to protect the Kamprad family from taxes. Though Kamprad was the founder, he did not technically own IKEA. He wanted an ownership structure that stood for independence, long-term approach, and continuity. Therefore in 1982, Kamprad created Stichting INGKA Foundation, a non-profit organization registered in Leiden in the Netherlands. In 1984, Kamprad transferred 100% of IKEA equity as an irrevocable gift to the Foundation. IKEA was privately held by this Foundation. Its purpose was to hold shares, reinvest in the IKEA Group, and to fund charity through it. It also protected IKEA from family squabbling and its inheritance in whole or part by the Kamprad family. Kamprad said, "My family will never have the chance to sell or destroy the company."[5] The Foundation was controlled by a five-member executive committee that was chaired by Kamprad and included his wife and attorney.

The Foundation was only controlled (not owned) by the Kamprad family. The Foundation, however, owned INGKA Holding BV, a private, for-profit, Dutch company that controlled IKEA's operations.

IKEA's structure was a complicated array of not-for-profit and for-profit organizations. It had two main components—operations and franchising. Operations included the management of its stores, the design and manufacture of its furniture, and purchasing and supply functions which were overseen by INGKA Holding. As of August 31, 2012, only 30 of the 298 IKEA franchisees, while the remaining stores were run by the INGKA Holding.[6]

The franchising part (trademark and concept) was owned by a separate Dutch company called Inter IKEA Systems. All IKEA stores (franchised and those run by INGKA Holding) shared 3% of their revenue with Inter IKEA Systems as a franchise fee. Inter IKEA Systems was owned by Inter IKEA Holding of Luxembourg, which in turn belonged to Interogo Foundation in Liechtenstein. This foundation was also controlled by the Kamprad family. Apart from these holdings, the food joints that operated in IKEA stores were directly owned by the Kamprad family and represented a major part of the family income. This corporate structure allowed Kamprad to maintain tight control over the operations of INGKA Holding and IKEA stores (Refer to Exhibit 3 for IKEA's Corporate Structure).

Going Global

In 1943, after founding IKEA, Kamprad increased his product range to include pens, wallets, picture frames, table runners, watches, and jewelry and nylon stockings at reduced prices. He initially made individual sales calls to sell the merchandise. When his business grew, he advertised in local newspapers and operated via the mail-order service using the local milk van to deliver the products to his customers. In 1948, he introduced furniture into the IKEA range. The furniture was made by local manufacturers close to his home. The furniture met with good response and Kamprad decided to expand his range. However, the company's sales were threatened by the price wars among the competitors. Therefore, in 1953, he opened a showroom in Älmhult, Sweden, so that his customers could have a look at the furniture before placing an order. This helped the company as customers chose the products with the best value for money. However, the pressure that competitors exerted on suppliers to boycott IKEA led to the company deciding to design its own furniture. When IKEA began exploring the packaging of its furniture, one of the workers disassembled a table to fit it into a car for transportation. This led to the invention of flat packs and the self assembly concept, which became a huge success.

In 1958, the company opened its first IKEA store 'Möbel-IKÉA' in Älmhult, Småland, Sweden, with 6,700

Exhibit 3 IKEA's Corporate Structure

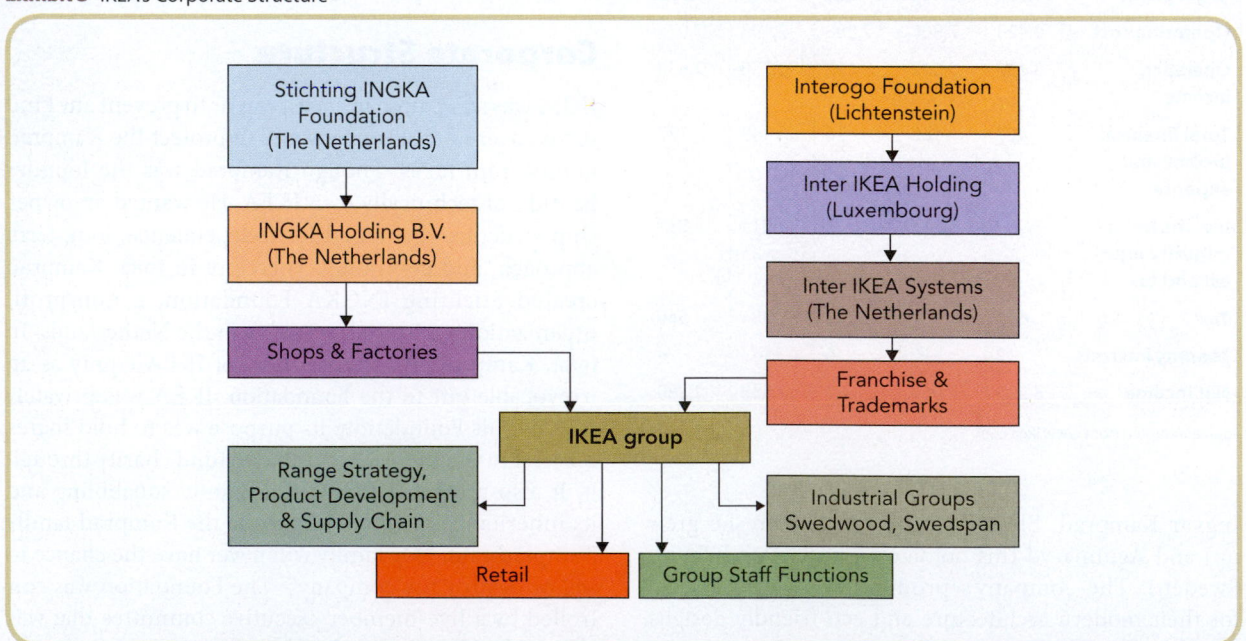

Source: Adapted from "Welcome Inside – Yearly Summary FY09", http://www.ikea.com/ms/en_CN/about_ikea/press/press_releases/Welcome_inside_2010.pdf

square meters of home furnishings—the largest furniture display in the Scandinavia region during those times. In 1960, it added a restaurant to the store, which over a period of time became an integral part of the store concept and layout. However, after this the company began looking at markets other than in its home country. In 1963, the first store outside Sweden was opened in Oslo, Norway. Later in 1969, it entered Denmark with its store at Copenhagen. The company then spread out to other parts of Europe in the 1970s. In 1973, it went outside the Scandinavian region and opened a store in Switzerland followed by a store in Germany in 1974. The global expansion of IKEA stores took place at a rapid pace during the 1970s and 1980s. Stores were soon opened in other parts of the world including Japan (1974), Australia and Hong Kong (1975), Canada (1976), and Singapore (1978). In the 1980s, IKEA further expanded its store network in France and Spain (1981), Belgium (1984), the US (1985), the UK (1987), and Italy (1989) among other areas. It further expanded into more countries in the 1990s and 2000s. In 1998, it entered China by setting up a store in Beijing. In 2010, the company also entered the Latin American region with a store in Santo Domingo, Dominican Republic. However, the company did not have much of a presence in the developing countries.

Germany, with 44 stores, was IKEA's biggest market, followed by the US with 37 stores. The IKEA store at Stockholm Kungens Kurva, Sweden, with an area of 55,200 m2 was the largest in the world, followed by the stores in Shanghai, China (49,400 m2), Shenyang, China (47,000 m2), Tianjin, China (45,736 m2), and Berlin Lichtenberg, Germany (45,000 m2).[7] The IKEA store located in Tempe, Sydney, was the biggest store in the southern hemisphere with an area of 39,000 m2.[8] By the end of 2013, IKEA planned to open its first warehouse in Croatia and its first shopping center in Vilnius, Lithuania, which would be the biggest furniture-selling mall in the Baltic States.

Manufacturing and Other Initiatives

Unlike the traditional retail stores where the customer could directly go to the needed section, IKEA encouraged its customers to go through its store in its entirety. Therefore, its stores were designed in a one-way layout in the anti-clockwise direction. Most of the IKEA stores were very large buildings decorated in blue and yellow patterns. However, the newer stores used more of glass for functional and aesthetic purposes—to give a better impression of the product and a better look to the store,

and to use more of natural light to reduce energy costs. The stores required customers to first go through the display making note of the required items, then proceed to the open shelves to make smaller purchases, and then go to the self serve warehouse to collect the previously noted products. They were then directed to the in-house warehouse or external warehouse to collect the products and make a payment.

All the IKEA products were designed in Sweden but were largely manufactured in developing countries. The company had 50 suppliers mostly in Europe and Asia. China, Poland, Italy, and Sweden formed the top production centers for IKEA. Most of its products were identified by single word names, which were Scandinavian in origin—like names of places, men and women, rivers, lakes, flowers, plants, etc.

"People flock to IKEA stores because of price"[9] said Debashish Mukherjee, partner and vice president at AT Kearney, a global management consulting firm. For instance, in China, the company had cut its prices by 60% since it entered in 1998. The secret lay in its designing, sourcing, and packaging. The company's product developers and designers worked directly with suppliers and the concept of do-it-yourself drastically reduced its cost. Devangshu Dutta (Dutta), chief executive of Third Eyesight, a retail consultancy, explained, "When they sell flat packs, there are no assembling costs, no shipment costs and mostly products are sold on catalogues, which helps them reduce operational costs and lower prices. Those flat packs work well with young consumers whose budgets are normally tight."[10]

Most of the IKEA stores included restaurants serving traditional Swedish food. However, in some countries, a few varieties of the local cuisine and beverages were served besides the Swedish staples. For instance, the IKEA restaurant in Austria offered a free refill policy for soft drinks, a practice that was otherwise unknown in the country. Another important feature of the IKEA stores was Småland (Swedish for Small Lands), where parents dropped off their children at a gate to the playground, and picked them up at another gate after shopping. IKEA also launched a loyalty card called IKEA Family, which was free of charge and could be used to avail of discounts on a special range of IKEA products.

IKEA was involved in various charity and social initiatives. The INGKA Foundation was involved in several international charitable causes like helping the tsunami victims in Indonesia, Sri Lanka, and India; the cyclone affected in Burma; Somali refugees; earthquake victims in Pakistan and China; donating to schools in Liberia, saving and restoring forests;

and reducing pollution. In September 2005, the IKEA Social Initiative was formed to manage the company's social involvements on a global level. The main partners to IKEA's Social Initiative were UNICEF and Save the Children. IKEA also took a proactive stance on environmental issues and developed an Environmental Action Plan in 1990, which was adopted in 1992. The company's environmental measures included elimination of polyvinylchloride (PVC) from its products and packaging and minimizing the usage of formaldehyde, chromium, cadmium, lead, PCB, PCP, and Azo pigments. The company used wood from responsibly managed forests, stopped providing plastic bags to customers, but offered reusable bags. In August 2008, it created IKEA GreenTech, a €50 million venture capital fund, to invest in 8–10 companies with a focus on solar panels, alternative light sources, product materials, energy efficiency, and water saving and purification. In February 2011, IKEA announced its plans for a wind farm in Dalarna County, Sweden, to achieve the goal of running on 100% renewable energy. As of June 2012, IKEA had 17 stores powered by solar panels in the US, with 20 additional installations in progress.

In 2004 and 2005, IKEA was named as one of the 100 Best Companies for Working Mothers by *Working Mothers* magazine. In 2006, it ranked 96 in Fortune's 100 Best Companies to Work For. In 2008, IKEA Canada LP was named one of 'Canada's Top 100 Employers' by Mediacorp Canada Inc., and was featured in Maclean's newsmagazine.[11] In addition to these, the company received many more awards and recognitions.

Global Furniture Industry

The global furniture industry had changed over the years. It was not restricted to the making of chairs, tables and beds, but had expanded into the production of a wide range of furniture, furnishings, and designed interiors which spelt style and elegance. With the world economy developing at a faster rate since the beginning of the new millennium, the furniture industry had witnessed a boom with new markets opening up. While every country had a unique style in its furniture design and usage, the globalization, increasing migration, changing lifestyles, and disposable incomes all contributed to the increased demand for stylish and quality furniture and, in turn, to the growth of the furniture industry.

Because of the long established production capacity, advances in science and technology, greater availability of funds, and management experiences, the traditional furniture making countries in the West took up over 70% of the global market. However, developing countries like China, the Philippines, Indonesia, Malaysia, Singapore, Thailand, Korea, Taiwan, India, Poland, and Mexico, were growing and showing great potential in furniture production. With their newly identified competitive advantages, these countries took up the remaining 30% of the world market. The European region, on the other hand, accounted for about half of the world's furniture production valued at around € 82 billion, with Germany taking the lead with 27% of the total European Union production followed by Italy (21.6%), France (13.5%), and the UK (10.4%).[12] While, the US and Canada were the largest importers at 15% purchase of the global production, China was the world's largest exporter, recording exports of US$38.882 billion in 2011, up by 15.31% year-on-year and accounting for 35.3% of global furniture trade.[13]

By 2015, the global furniture market was expected to reach US$436.5 billion.[14] With a steady improvement in the economy and living standards, Asia was expected to become the center for the long term growth of the global furniture market. According to a study by the World Bank, the organized furniture industry was expected to grow by 20%[15] a year and the demand for luxury furniture was expected to rise in countries such as China, Russia, Brazil, and India.

Furniture Industry in India

India was home to rich traditional handicrafts and artistic work of wood. Indian art and design had earned a worldwide reputation for themselves. The supreme quality, exceptional designs, and luxurious trends lent elegance to the Indian furniture segment. However, with the passage of time, the preferences of the Indian consumer had changed and the furniture industry too had changed to suit the consumer needs. The industry produced a wide range of products related to office, living room, bedroom, kitchen, garden, school furniture, and also mattresses, furnishings, upholstery, parts of furniture, etc., using a wide variety of raw materials like wood, rattan, steel, plastic, and metal and more recently silver.

Based on the raw material used, the furniture market in India was regionally concentrated. According to research by IKON Marketing Consultant, the furniture market in India was estimated at around Rs. 700 billion in 2010.[16] However, it was considered as an unorganized sector, as handicraft production accounted for about 85%–90% of the total furniture production in the country.[17] The market was highly fragmented and production came from small regional firms or individual artisans and only 10%–15% came from the organized sector comprised of leading manufacturers, importers, dealers, and distributors. Within the Indian furniture market, home furniture was the largest segment, accounting for 65% of the industry sales, followed by the office segment with 20%, and the contract segment taking the remaining 15%.[18]

However, Indian imports of furniture were growing at a considerable rate, catering to the need of the urban middle class for stylish homes in compact apartments. Countries like Germany, Italy, Korea, Japan, and recently China and Thailand had been major suppliers of furniture to India. With a promising market potential in place, several international brands like Arredo Classic, Art Design Group, B.T.C. International, Bizzarri, Cantori, Desirée, Girasole, Gold Line, Presotto,

and Reflex were trying to enter the Indian market. Top domestic companies like Godrej, BP Ergo, Featherlite, Hanworth, Style Spa, Zuari, Durian, and Millenium Lifestyles also had a presence in the industry (Refer to Exhibit 4 for The Top 10 Furniture Companies in India). The entry of international brands and changing consumer preference had led to the emergence of furniture retailing in India. IKON Marketing Consultants estimated that with India's robust economy, spurt in real estate and housing activity, burgeoning Information Technology and Services, and the Indian middle-class aspiring for better lifestyles, there would be a further boom in the Indian furniture industry in the near future, the demand mainly coming from the metropolitan cities of the country.

Exhibit 4 Top 10 Furniture Companies in India

	Brand	Company	Head Office	Product Categories	Store Locations
1	Godrej Interio	Godrej & Boyce Mfg. Co. Ltd.	Mumbai	Bedroom, Living Room, Study Room, Dining, Kids, Kitchen, Home accessories, Mattresses, Seating, desks, Storage, Carpet, Healthcare, Lab, Marine	Across India
2	Usha Lexus	Usha Shriram Enterprise s Pvt. ltd.	New Delhi	Bedroom, Living Room, Dining Room, Study Room, Office	Srinagar, Delhi, Jammu, Dehradun, Noida, Lucknow, Muradabad, Jaunpur, Varanasi, Allahabad, Patna, Guwahati
3	Zuari*	KK Birla Group	Chennai	Home Furniture, Soft Furnishing, Home accessories, Lighting, Kitchens	Across India
3	Home Town*	Future Group/ Pantaloon Retail	Mumbai	Home Furniture, Soft Furnishing, Home accessories, Lighting, Kitchens	Across India
4	Durian	Durian Industries Ltd.	Mumbai	Home Furniture, Office furniture, Laminates, Veneers, Turnkey solutions, Plywood, Doors	Across India
5	Damro	Damro Furniture Pvt. Ltd.	Chennai	Bedroom, Living Room, Study Room, Dining, Kids, Seating, storage	Across India
6	Wipro Furniture	Wipro Group	Bengaluru	Home & office furniture and Interior products	Across India
7	Evok	Somany Group/ Hindware (HSIL)	Gurgaon	Home Furniture, Soft Furnishing, Home decor, Flooring, Modular kitchens, Bath, decorative Lighting	Across India
8	@home	Nilkamal Ltd.	Mumbai	Home Furniture, Soft Furnishing, Home accessories, Lighting, Kitchens	Pune, Surat, Vadodara, Mumbai, Kochi, Hyderabad, Ghaziabad, Ahmedabad, Chennai, Coimbatore, Bengaluru
9	Style Spa	Adventz Group of Companie s	Chennai	Home Furniture, Soft Furnishing, Home accessories, Lighting, Kitchens	Across India
10	Housefull	Housefull Furniture Pvt. Ltd.	Mumbai	Bedroom, Living room, Dining & kitchen, office & study, storage, décor	Ahmedabad, Vadodara, Bengaluru, Chennai, Hyderabad, Mumbai, Nashik, Pune, Surat

*Two companies are tied for number 3.

Source: Adapted from Trupti Palhade, "Top 10 Home Furniture Brands in India", http://top10companiesinindia.com, May 27, 2013; "Top 10 Home Furniture Companies in India", http://blogsandyou.com/top-10-home-furniture-companies-in-india/

IKEA's Entry into India

Retailing accounted for 14% of India's GDP. The industry consisted mostly of small shops with organized retail stores accounting for only 4% of the industry. After liberalization in the 1990s, many foreign companies had set their sights on the Indian market. However, till 2011, FDI in multi-brand retail was forbidden by the Indian government and FDI in single-brand retail was permitted only up to 51%. In November 2011, the FDI reforms were announced but due to opposition from different political parties and activists, they were kept on hold. In January 2012, India allowed 100% FDI in single-brand retail on the condition that the retailer should mandatorily source 30% of their goods from India's micro, small, and medium enterprises (MSMEs). And 51% FDI was allowed in multi-brand retailing in December 2012. After the reforms, IKEA, which had been trying for a long time to expand into the Indian market, applied for permission in June 2012 to invest US$1.9 billion (€1.5 billion or Rs 105 billion) and set up 25 retail stores in India in two stages.[19]

However, this was not IKEA's first tryst with India. India had served IKEA as a low-cost sourcing destination since the 1980s. Every year, the company sourced around US$600 million worth of goods (textiles, rugs, lighting, ceramics, and carpets) from 70 suppliers and 1,450 sub-suppliers in India.[20] In August 2003, when the company was on an expansion drive, it set up a raw material trading division in India to ensure better cost management. As the yield of cotton (per hectare) was very low in India (therefore higher priced), IKEA sourced cotton from Australia and China where yields were much higher. This reduced price pressures on its exports from India. The setup in India was its first trading division to offer the service of raw material sourcing.

Later in May 2007, IKEA set up an office in Gurgaon in northern India, to carry out market research and initiate talks with Indian players for an alliance. IKEA was then planning for an Indian debut in 2009. IKEA group president and CEO Anders Dahlvig had said, "We will be there eventually, I'm sure. It is a question of how and when. I think it will mostly depend on things like legislation and infrastructure development."[21] However, there were FDI restrictions and local sourcing conditions prevailing during those times. IKEA tried to persuade the Indian government to ease the FDI rules and seemed hopeful of a breakthrough in 2008, but the company failed. The company anticipated that the opening of the Indian sector would take more time, and abandoned its efforts to set up stores in India with an investment of €300 million. However, IKEA could not ignore the Indian furniture and furnishings market. According to some estimates, the market was Rs. 925 billion[22] of which only 7% belonged to organized retail. IKEA made it clear that it would only enter India when 100% FDI would be allowed.

In the meantime, IKEA continued with its production and sourcing in India. In September 2010, the company's CEO Mikael Ohlsson (Ohlsson), visited India to ensure that its suppliers were not employing young children or forcing people to work in difficult conditions. IKEA had spent millions of dollars to create sustainable audit and transparency networks in India. It also worked in partnership with the United Nations Development Program and UNICEF on grassroots development programs like female empowerment, health awareness, education, water and sanitation, and industry-based programs that benefited 100 million women and children. Ohlsson also proposed doubling production in India. Speaking about the possibility of IKEA setting up its stores in partnership with Indian firms, Ohlsson said, "A joint venture is simply not an option. IKEA has spent years streamlining costs, making investment money go further, and cutting out middlemen. As a result, introducing a foreign partner into the mix now is not something that is under consideration."[23]

In January 2012, India approved reforms to allow 100% FDI in single brand retail. Welcoming the change, an IKEA spokesperson said, "The IKEA Group welcomes the Indian Government's decision to allow 100 percent Foreign Direct Investment for single brand retailers. We will now over the next few days look into the details of the decision and we expect to present more information shortly about our intention to establish retail operations. India is a strong and growing purchase market for IKEA."[24] Industry experts were expecting that IKEA may announce its Indian entry any time soon. Ohlsson too welcomed the change, but stated that India's requirement that 'foreign single-brand retailers' source 30% of goods from local small and medium-sized establishments' came in the way of its proceeding with its investment. IKEA spokeswoman Josefin Thorell (Thorell) said, "India is still a very interesting potential retail market for the IKEA Group, but we need to understand what the guidelines will mean for us. We have found that the conditions applied to local sourcing from [small and midsize enterprises] might be difficult for us to live up to."[25] Some other companies and analysts too voiced the same concern. Abhay Gupta, CEO and founder, Luxury Connect, a retail consultancy, said, "Companies like IKEA and Nike have raised concern on the sourcing clause. Every brand would like to go alone but this is a major bottleneck as it is difficult to find expertise among small vendors. Also, companies will have to go to more suppliers so that they are less than $1 million. This will create supply chain inconsistencies."[26] Arvind Singhal, chairman, Technopak, also supported the concern and said, "This condition (on sourcing) is highly impractical and illogical. Big brands entering India would not like to source from SME players as they cannot match up to the standards of global retailers. We believe that the Government cannot force this condition on brands wishing to scale up in India."[27] But the Indian government ruled out any changes in the local sourcing clause.

On June 22, 2012, Ohlsson met the Indian commerce, industry and textiles minister, Anand Sharma (Sharma), at St. Petersburg in Russia and confirmed its investment and sourcing plans. IKEA filed its application seeking the Indian government's permission to establish 25 stores. The application also sought permission to engage in import, export, distribution, marketing, and warehousing, and to have standard IKEA store features like cafés, restaurants, food mart, nursing homes, children's play area, and publications under its brand name. In the first tranche, the company planned to invest €600 million (Rs 42 billion) in opening 10 stores followed by the remaining €900 million (Rs 63 billion)[28] for setting up 15 more stores later. However, stating its concerns over sourcing norms, the company in its statement said, "We will source at least 30% of the purchase value of products sold in India from our direct and indirect supply chain comprising Indian small industries. In the longer term, however, the mandatory sourcing of 30 percent of the value of goods sold in India from domestic small industries remains a challenge."[29]

IKEA's decision to enter India was met with mixed reactions. While the backers of the reforms opined that this investment would help modernize the country's infrastructure and manufacturing and supply chain, the critics said that the entry of such companies would put millions of small-time shops out of business. In addition, the country's GDP growth was only 5.3% during the first quarter of 2012, and there was a widening trade gap with a current account deficit of 4% of GDP, requiring international capital to overcome the gap. Hence, the pressure on the Indian government to implement the economic reforms announced earlier that year continued, but this move faced opposition from critics. Seema Desai, India analyst for the risk-advisory firm Eurasia Group, said, "It doesn't take the pressure off the government, India's balance-of-payments situation requires some more reforms for foreign-direct-investment flows to strengthen."[30]

However, it was still not clear as to when India would respond to the proposal.

Overcoming Regulatory and Political Roadblocks

In July 2012, IKEA sought a 10-year window (instead of one year) to comply with the sourcing rules. IKEA also expressed concerns that if it procured from MSMEs (firms with a total investment less than US$ 1 million), they would soon grow and become large setups. Then the company would have to find other MSMEs, which would affect its product quality and supply chain setup. There were speculations in the media that the sourcing clause might be relaxed. On the other hand, industry experts opined that India had laid out a welcome mat for single-brand retailing but only theoretically, and opined that a compromise solution had to be found. Saloni Nangia (Nangia), president of retail consultancy Technopak, said, "Keeping in mind IKEA's stature, I'm sure the government will work out something. Meeting the 30% sourcing target will take time—Ikea just wants some latitude."[31]

In September 2012, the Indian government tweaked its sourcing clause. It changed 'mandatory sourcing from MSMEs' to 'preferably from MSMEs' and said that foreign firms expecting a relaxation in the 30% procurement norms would have to set up a manufacturing facility in India. After these reforms, the government asked IKEA to revise and resubmit its application. On October 8, 2012, IKEA submitted its final paperwork to start its retail operations in India. The company, in its application, also gave the assurance that the old furniture collected from Indian customers in exchange for new ones would not be re-sold in the market but donated to needy families or third party small businesses through charitable organizations. Ohlsson said, "Once our application is approved we will develop a solid plan for the establishment of IKEA stores for many years to come, generating investments and new employment. At the same time, we will continue to increase our sourcing in India from both existing and new suppliers building on long-term relations and shared values."[32]

A day after it filed the application, IKEA appointed Juvencio Maeztu (Maeztu) as its Country Manager for India, with a responsibility to find the right real estate and hire talent for its India foray. The outskirts of Indian metropolitan cities such as Delhi, Mumbai, Bangalore, Hyderabad, and Chennai were expected to be its store locations. Maeztu opined that the Indian market was different in terms of the varied tastes and said, "So we have to slightly tweak our model with designs and pricing, keeping in mind the Indian consumers and the dynamics of the retail industry here."[33]

On November 20, 2012, India's Foreign Investment Promotion Board (FIPB) approved IKEA's proposal to start its operations in India. However, it imposed the following conditions—IKEA should not operate food and beverage outlets within the store; it should not sell 18 categories of items (of the 30 initially applied categories) like gift items, home and office products, apparel, leather products, fabrics, textile goods, books, toys, travel and lifestyle items, and consumer electronics; it should not sell any products that it did not brand, including secondhand furniture. Citing the reason for the conditions, a government spokesperson said that according to the norms, a single-brand retailer could not be a marketplace with such a wide range of products and could not sell food items.

Citing the restrictions, some analysts opined that the company might have to change its business model. Ankur Bisen, Vice President (Retail & Consumer Products) at retail consultancy Technopak Advisors, said, "IKEA is known to open 'big-box' stores (above 200,000 sq. ft.) with a standardized design. So far, they have not tweaked the model anywhere in the world. But India is such a strong pull, they will not mind opening stores without food courts."[34] Other industry experts opined that a restriction on so many categories was not a good idea. Harminder Sahni, managing director of Wazir Advisors, said, "Home improvement is still the bread and butter for IKEA. The home furnishing category is all about experience. People do not mind travelling extra to buy IKEA products."[35] The company also opined that all its product categories were sold across stores in 44 countries and it was not demanding anything extra from India. Replying to the government's concerns about in-house cafés, the company opined that as the stores would be located on the outskirts of the city there would not be any displacement of small food retailers. The company wrote to the Department of Industrial Policy and Promotion (DIPP) stating that to keep the 'IKEA experience' intact, the company must be allowed to operate its global model.

On January 22, 2013, FIPB cleared IKEA's business proposal and permitted it to sell non-furniture items and run cafés in India. While FIPB permitted food and beverages to be sold at IKEA's in-store restaurants/cafés, it restricted the retailing of any food item off the shelf in any other part of the store. It also said that IKEA could not use its global procurement of products to satisfy the Indian demand of mandatory sourcing (30%) from the country. However, India had given a five-year window (from the time of the company's initial launch in the country) to fully comply with the sourcing requirements. Other conditions included the restriction of e-commerce sales and used furniture sales. After FIPB's clearance, the proposal was put before the Cabinet Committee on Economic Affairs (CCEA) for final approval as the FIPB had the authority to take a decision only on investments less than Rs. 12 billion. On May 2, 2013, CCEA approved IKEA's investment proposal. Maeztu added, "We feel very welcome in India. This is a big step in our journey to open IKEA stores in India."[36]

Working with Suppliers

After the company got the approval to set up its stores in India, an IKEA spokeswoman Ylva Magnusson said, "It will be another four to five years before Indians can purchase the company's iconic flat-pack furniture."[37] IKEA's planned investment was till then the largest by a foreign retailer in India. IKEA's spokesperson, Josefin Thorell, said, "The Swedish retailer's presence in India will, in a major way, help improve availability of high quality, low-price products, increase sourcing of goods from India and increase the competitiveness of Indian enterprise through access to global designs, technologies, skill development, and global best practices."[38] But the promoter of a Ludhiana-headquartered home furnishing unit (an ex-IKEA supplier) was not too enthusiastic about IKEA's entry and said, "IKEA engages in predatory trade practices. In the first year, they offer excellent margins. In subsequent years, the margins reduce to a level that turns a unit into an unprofitable venture."[39]

After the approval of its application by the CCEA, Ohlsson, said while commenting on the development, "This is a very positive development. IKEA already sources products from the country and will continue to increase our sourcing in India from both existing and new suppliers, building on long-term relations and shared values."[40] India had been IKEA's sourcing destination for textiles and carpets for a long time. However, the company was interested in further tying up with Indian suppliers in the plastics, steel, lighting and natural fiber categories as well. Analysts opined that this investment by IKEA had come at a time when the Indian furniture market lacked big brands and was sure to shake things up for the benefit of the Indian consumer.[41]

IKEA already had 70 suppliers and 1450 sub-suppliers in India. After the company got clearance from the cabinet, it invited all its suppliers to its Gurgaon office and discussed its plans for the future. It focused its discussion on growth and doubling its sourcing from Indian suppliers. In response to these developments, IKEA's Indian suppliers began gearing up to face the sudden surge in order volumes. For instance, V Ashok Ram Kumar, managing director, Asian Fabricx, said, "We certainly need more people when there's a sudden increase in order volumes. To beat labor shortage, automation is being focused on."[42] Some change in the processes was also taken up by the suppliers. For instance, earlier 80% of the yarn was dyed before weaving into fabric; but now, to reduce costs, most of the weaving was done without the yarn being dyed.

Apart from these benefits, analysts expected that IKEA's entry would have a great impact on the industry as a whole. They expected that large box retail formats, which would be located on the outskirts of big cities, would be introduced and gain popularity with other retailers in India. An increase in the competition between large box furniture retailers that had little or no differentiation and a partial or total wipe-out of the low-cost imported furniture market was also expected. However, retailers or brands that maintained sharp differentiation in their products and services were expected to survive the competition. IKEA, since its founding, had played on the price sensitivity of the customer and low cost furniture. The company's website stated, "We design the price tag first and then develop the product to suit that price."[43] According to Thorell, "Product developers and designers work directly with suppliers to ensure that creating the low prices starts on the factory floor."[44]

Challenges

IKEA lobbied hard with the Indian politicos and bureaucrats to overcome the initial hurdles and obtained permission to open its stores in the country with its global model intact. However, this was only one part of the problem; the company was expected to face more challenges after its entry.

A major challenge for the company in establishing its stores was the availability of retail space and its cost. IKEA stores in India were unlikely to be smaller than 350,000 square feet. Some of its biggest stores around the world had an area of 606,000 square feet. The accommodation of such a huge area in any mall in India was highly unlikely. Moreover, any IKEA store had 6-8 unloading bays and 300-400 feet long customer vehicle loading bays, with 20 feet high ceilings.[45] IKEA's 2006 initiative of 100% renewable energy usage required its stores to be supplied with either wind power or energy from solar panels. Its stores in Germany, France, Sweden, and at forty more places used either power from their own wind turbines or from solar panels. The possibility of Indian real estate developers meeting such stringent energy requirements was also doubtful. IKEA planned to open nine stores in seven years—two stores each in the National Capital Region (NCR), Mumbai, and Bangalore, and one store each at Chennai, Hyderabad, and Pune. Therefore, with the existing space constraints, analysts opined that it was more likely for IKEA to opt for standalone suburban stores. "In India, the cost of real estate is high, retail space availability is an issue and overall store efficiency is a big challenge. They can't cut and paste their global model here. They have to develop India-specific strategy,"[46] said Dutta of Third Eyesight. Other industry players opined that though IKEA might opt for suburban locations, it would be difficult to obtain such large chunks of land and the price would also be high. D. K. Jairath (Jairath), deputy managing director of Style Spa, pointed out, "This kind of land tract will only be available on the city outskirts and IKEA will have to join hands with land parcel owners if it is keen to acquire such large land parcels for its use."[47] Experts opined that land acquisition through public auction through government or through individual owners would turn out to be a greater challenge for the company in acquiring such huge chunks of land.

IKEA had started its hiring activities and vendor negotiations to start its operations in India. However, the organized Indian players—including Landmark's Home Centre, Hindware's Evok, Future Group's Home Town, Godrej's Interio, K. K. Birla's Style Spa, and others—claimed that they did not feel threatened by the entry of the ultra big-box retailer IKEA. Anil S. Mathur, COO, Godrej Interio, said, "There will be initial euphoria on IKEA's entry into India. However, they will have to work hard on getting market share in India." Jairath added, "There is no collision course with IKEA. It will definitely add competition to the market as IKEA is an ultra big-box retailer. If it is to survive in India, it will have to play on the volume metrics. Real estate costs are highly prohibitive and they will have to create products suited for the Indian climate and style."[48]

Apart from these two main challenges, IKEA was likely to face many others. As the stores were likely to be located in the suburban areas of big cities and customers had to travel long distances to make purchases from IKEA, AT Kearney's Mukherjee opined that the company might have to face last mile supply chain issues (from IKEA store to home transportation). People in western countries have large cars, houses, and parking lots where folded and packed furniture could be accommodated but Indians have compact cars and homes which would make it difficult for the consumers to stock and transport their products. Moreover, low levels of car ownership and a patchy road network would make it harder for consumers to shop at IKEA and the company might feel the need to locate their stores nearer to urban centers, which in turn would increase its set-up costs and render real estate acquisition more difficult. Apart from that, IKEA's do-it-yourself (DIY) concept might be a hit globally, but people in India prefer readymade furniture or getting it made by their carpenters. Moreover, Indians expect shop assistants to guide them around the store and the lack of such staff would come as a shock to them. Vivek Iyer, a 38-year-old lawyer from south Delhi, said, "I'd go with my driver and he could be doing the loading and carrying I suppose. Then I could get someone in to build it all. But [the] point of a shop is that someone will be doing that for you, isn't it?"[49] Analysts opined that IKEA's DIY model might suffer if faced with such consumer behavior.

It was felt that IKEA's anti-corruption policy might prove to be another hindrance in its growth in India. For instance in Russia, the company could open only 14 stores in 12 years because of this policy. According to the Transparency International's Corruption Perceptions Index, and the World Bank's Ease of Doing Business reports, India ranked 95th and 132nd respectively[50], which indicated that the company might face difficulties with the Indian bureaucratic setup. However, analysts opined that the success or failure of the company lay in the hands of the next generation of customers, whose reception of the company's products was unpredictable.

Looking Ahead

According to retail consultancy, Technopak Advisors, the highly fragmented Indian furniture market was expected to grow from US$10 billion in 2009 to US$15 billion by 2014.[51] But, the working of IKEA's core concept, the DIY model, in India remained a question. However, IKEA still felt that its prospects were bright in the country and that it was ready to tweak its model to win over the Indian consumers. It was tweaking its product range and showrooms and adding services to accommodate a new culture. In places where people lived in smaller rooms, it modeled its showrooms smaller. Ohlsson said, "Most people don't really know and can hardly imagine that we visit thousands of homes round every store in the world every year. We sit down in the kitchen and talk to them … That's the way we try to learn and understand. 'What are you annoyed with? What are your frustrations? What would you like to have? How much can you afford? What are your alternatives?'"[52] In developed markets, IKEA was positioned as a low-priced product, but in emerging markets like India, it planned to target its products at the growing middle class that aspired for an international lifestyle.

In India, the company planned to open 10 stores by 2023 and 15 more in the next phase. The company might also take into consideration the consumers' concerns. As Ridhika Mandavia, a playschool teacher in Mumbai, said, "I'm not sure if I will want to travel to the end of the city to buy their furniture. Plus I have heard about how you are encouraged to pack your furniture up and then take it home and set it up yourself, and that is not something we Indians are used to. So if they can change that model and help pack and deliver furniture at no extra cost, it may work."[53] In India, should IKEA consider building larger stores closer to customers' homes like it did in China? Should it do away with the do-it-yourself (DIY) concept altogether in India?

Country Manager Maeztu also acknowledged the challenge that store locations posed in India. As the whole investment was made from internal accruals, Maeztu said, "An ideal location for us would be 10 acres space (it could be between 5 and 15 acres), close to a highway with good visibility so it is not three kilometers inside and with public transport infrastructure. When I talk of public transport, in India it has to be metro connectivity because you can have a bus stop and if you are struck in the traffic for two hours then you are not properly accessible. We are looking to cater to the real middle class in India. We will never compromise on a good location. So even if it takes five years to locate a place it is no problem. The future is much more important for us than 1-2 years. My job or my salary does not depend on how quickly I open stores. We try to do it right on a long-term basis. We don't depend on banks or on investors and we don't need to show (quick results) to our investors or banks."[54]

As of July 2013, with the approval from the Indian government on opening its stores in India, the company was busy understanding the Indian culture to introduce the best possible and workable IKEA model in the country and had hired a consulting and a market research company to map the demographics and economic parameters of consumers in the top ten cities. Maeztu personally visited about 20 families in the Delhi region, Mumbai, and Bangalore. The question was, could IKEA tweak its globally successful business model to suit the requirements of India without breaking the model?

NOTES

1. "After long wait, IKEA in no rush for quick launch of stores," www.moneycontrol.com, June 2, 2013.

2. Rasul Bailay and Chaitali Chakravarty, "IKEA ready to wait for years for perfect locations: CEO," http://articles.economictimes.indiatimes.com, May 16, 2013.

3. "IKEA mulls joint venture with Bosnia furniture maker," www.reuters.com, January 8, 2008.

4. "Welcome Inside—IKEA Group Yearly Summary FY12," www.ikea.com/ms/en_CA/pdf/yearly_summary/ys_welcome_inside_2012_final.pdf.

5. "IKEA Corporate Structure," www.ikeafans.com/articles/1000-ikea-corporate/330-ikea-corporate- structure-.html.

6. "Welcome Inside—IKEA Group Yearly Summary FY12," www.ikea.com/ms/en_CA/pdf/yearly_summary/ys_welcome_inside_2012_final.pdf.

7. "About IKEA—Facts & Figures," www.ikea.com.

8. "IKEA Tempe Opens for Business," www.dynamicbusiness.com.au, November 3, 2011.

9. Raghavendra Kamath, "What IKEA brings to the table," www.business-standard.com, July 13, 2012.

10. Ibid.

11. "Corporate Awards and Recognition", http://info.ikea-usa.com/centennial/pdfs/9-IKEA%20Awards%20and%20Achievements.pdf.

12. "World Furniture Industry", www.furnituremanufacturers.net/world-furniture-industry.html.

13. "Global Furniture Industry Overview 2013", www.businessvibes.com/blog/global-furniture-industry-overview-2013.

14. "A Review of the World Furniture Summit 2012," www.furniturenews.net, January 11, 2013.

15. "World Furniture Industry", www.furnituremanufacturers.net/world-furniture-industry.html.

16. Taruna Sondarva, " Furniture Market in India: Boom Time Ahead," www.ikonmarket.com, February 2010.

17. "Indian Furniture Industry," www.indianmirror.com/indian-industries/furniture.html.

18. Taruna Sondarva, "Furniture Market in India: Boom Time Ahead," www.ikonmarket.com, February 2010.

19. Arun S., "IKEA to invest € 1.5 b in 2 stages," www.thehindubusinessline.com, June 22, 2012.

20. Manu Kaushik, "Home Run," http://businesstoday.intoday.in, July 22, 2012.

21. "Ikea in JV talks with local cos," http://articles.economictimes.indiatimes.com, May 1, 2007.

22. Amit Bagaria, "Why IKEA will opt for standalone suburban stores in India," www.dnaindia.com, February 8, 2012.

23. Nidhi Dutt, "Ikea makes steps in India's growth market," www.bbc.co.uk, September 21, 2010.

24. Tuhina Anand, "IKEA, Carrefour welcome FDI," www.mxmindia.com/2011/11/ikea-carrefour-welcome-fdi/.

25. Amol Sharma, "IKEA Remains Wary of Entering India," http://online.wsj.com, January 24, 2012.

26. Bindu D Menon, "Govt retains sourcing clause for single brand retailers," www.thehindubusinessline.com, April 10, 2012.

27. Ibid.

28. "IKEA set to enter India with Euro 1.5 billion investment," http://articles.timesofindia.indiatimes.com, June 22, 2012.

29. Arun S., "IKEA to invest € 1.5 b in 2 stages," www.thehindubusinessline.com, June 22, 2012.

30. Amol Sharma and Jens Hansegard, "IKEA Says It Is Ready To Give India a Try," http://online.wsj.com, June 24, 2012.

31. "Ikea's India plans hit snag over sourcing issue," www.thelocal.se, July 8, 2012.

32. "IKEA files fresh application to start retail operations," www.thehindubusinessline.com, October 8, 2012.

33. "IKEA to tweak product design for India," www.thehindubusinessline.com, October 11, 2012.

34. Manu Kaushik, "Ikea to comply with riders on its India investment proposal," http://m.businesstoday.in, December 23, 2012.

35. Ibid.

36. "CCEA paves way for IKEA's Rs 10,500-crore investment plan in India," http://articles.economictimes.indiatimes.com, May 3, 2013.

37. Rajesh Roy, "Indian Clears IKEA's $1.95 Billion Investment Plan," http://online.wsj.com, May 2, 2013.

38. Raghavendra Kamath, "What IKEA brings to the table", http://www.business-standard.com, July 13, 2012.

39. Manu Kaushik, "Home Run", http://businesstoday.intoday.in, July 22, 2012.

40. Rajesh Roy, "Indian Clears IKEA's $1.95 Billion Investment Plan", http://online.wsj.com, May 2, 2013.

41. Bindu D Menon, "IKEA's India foray, a boost for single-brand retail", www.thehindubusinessline.com, June 22, 2012.

42. Nivedita Mookerji, "Asian Fabricx gears up for IKEA's India operations", www.business-standard.com, June 11, 2013.

43. "Our Business Idea", www.ikea.com/ms/en_CA/about_ikea/the_ikea_way/our_business_idea/index.html.

44. Raghavendra Kamath, "What IKEA brings to the table", www.business-standard.com, July 13, 2012.

45. Amit Bagaria, "Why IKEA will opt for standalone suburban stores in India", www.dnaindia.com, February 8, 2012.

46. Raghavendra Kamath, "What IKEA brings to the table", www.business-standard.com, July 13, 2012.

47. Bindu D Menon, "IKEA may have to overcome infrastructure bottlenecks", www.thehindubusinessline.com, November 20, 2012.

48. Ibid.

49. Jason Burke, "Food fight complicates Ikea's entry into India", www.guardian.co.uk, December 28, 2012.

50. Matthew Stych, "IKEA Sets Sights on India", www.stores.org, August 2012.

51. Manu Kaushik, "Home Run", http://businesstoday.intoday.in, July 22, 2012.

52. "One size doesn't fit all: IKEA goes local for India, China", http://in.reuters.com/article/2013/03/07/ikea-expansion-india-china-idINDEE92603L20130307, March 7, 2013.

53. Ibid.

54. Rasul Bailay and Chaitali Chakravarty, "IKEA ready to wait for years for perfect locations: CEO," http://articles.economictimes.indiatimes.com, May 16, 2013.

CASE 7

Invitrogen (A)

Acquisitions will always be a part of our strategy due to the pace of the innovation of our business.

— Greg Lucier, Chairman and CEO of Invitrogen

Mark Gardner, Vice President of Corporate Strategy at Invitrogen, walked briskly up the stairs to his office at the company headquarters in Carlsbad, California at 7 a.m. on a bright, sunny day in January 2008. Invitrogen, a leading consumables company in the life sciences space, had just come off an outstanding year, having grown 11 percent to $1.2 billion in revenue. Invitrogen, however, relied primarily on government-funded research, which could limit growth. CEO Greg Lucier and Gardner had worked together for eight years, both at GE and Invitrogen, and Lucier knew he could trust Gardner to "go big-game hunting" and find the acquisition that would dramatically transform Invitrogen into a major platform company in health care.

Gardner wondered what he should recommend to the CEO. He believed that next-generation sequencing was the "strategic elixir" that could transform Invitrogen. There were three companies that could potentially fit this need. Which company would meet the company's strategic goals?

Invitrogen

Founded in 1987, Invitrogen was one of the largest catalog life science[1] companies in the industry. Its customers came from academic research, biotechnology and pharmaceutical companies and government laboratories. Scientists viewed Invitrogen as a one-stop shop for all major molecular biology, biochemistry and cell culture reagent products, with prices ranging from a hundred dollars to a few thousand dollars.

Invitrogen built its success on an aggressive acquisition strategy combined with merchandising and operational excellence. Since it was founded in 1987, Invitrogen acquired 10 companies under the leadership of Lyle Turner, founder and CEO of Invitrogen. In

2000, Invitrogen made a bold move and acquired Life Technologies, a company four times its size.

In 2003, Lucier was recruited from General Electric to become the CEO of Invitrogen. Upon his arrival, Lucier continued the acquisition strategy. From 2003 to 2005, Invitrogen made an astounding 15 acquisitions (Exhibit 1) so that by 2007, the company had 4,385 employees, 35,000 products,[2] and tens of thousands of customers. Over time, Invitrogen honed its expertise in integrating companies and streamlining costs.

However, not all acquisitions were successful. Bioreliance, a pharmaceutical services business, was acquired for $500 million in 2004, only to be divested for $210 million in 2007. The decision was part of an effort to refocus the company on a "platform of technologies", rather than services.

With nearly a decade of experience acquiring companies, the process of acquiring was embedded into the Invitrogen way of doing business. The process entailed monthly meetings called Growth and Innovation Board Meetings, more commonly referred to as GIBS. At these meetings, there were three levels of discussions/presentations. First, there was a high-level discussion around a market sector, such as animal health, molecular diagnostics, or penetrating China. Discussion could also be around acquisition targets. Occasionally, Lucier would come to the meeting and say "I'd like to acquire Company X" or a business unit leader would come and say, "I need to acquire Company X in order to achieve my growth target" or "because of a key technology that I need." Finally, the team would decide which sector to focus on for a deeper analysis. A team of analysts would then be assembled. In the following month, a team would return with a group of targets that met the criteria laid out during the first discussion. The next "ask" was for resources to do a deep analysis on 5 to 15 companies. Finally, an investment thesis on which company to acquire would be developed. In addition, the company needed to understand whether the acquisition would be accretive or dilutive. Often, acquisition targets were

---

Rosy Lee (Sloan '12), Professor Robert A. Burgelman and Lecturer Robert Siegel prepared this case as the basis for class discussion rather than to illustrate either effective or ineffective handling of an administrative situation.

Exhibit 1 Partial list of Invitrogen Acquisitions from 2003 to 2005

1. 2003: $325M acquisition of Molecular Probes, developer of fluorescent based chemistries.
2. 2003: $95M acquisition of Panvera, developer of high-throughput drug screening products.
3. 2004: Acquisition of Protometrix, privately held developer of protein microarrays.
4. 2004: $500M acquisition of Bioreliance, a pharmaceutical services company.
5. 2004: $65M acquisition of DNA Research Innovations, privately held company that developed DNA purification technology.
6. 2004: $8M acquisition of Bio Asia, leading provider of reagents and services in China.
7. 2005: $381M acquisition of Dynal, developer of molecular separation and purification technologies.
8. 2005: $130M acquisition of Biosource, developer of kinase and cytokine assays.
9. 2005: $60M acquisition of Zymed, developer of antibodies used for research.
10. 2005: Acquisition of Quantum Dot, developer of labeling and detection technologies.
11. 2005: $20M acquisition of Caltag, developer of immunological reagents.
12. 2006: $26M acquisition of Sentigen Biosciences.
13. 2008: $57M acquisition of Cellzdirect, developer of hepatocyte-based cell products.

watched for months or even years. Even entire integration plans were developed: Which sites would remain? Which groups would be eliminated? Or combined? If there were a significant event, such as an acquisition, the plan would be updated with new information.

New product development was fueled both by acquiring technologies and developing technology in-house. Under Lucier's leadership, R&D funding doubled from $55 million in 2003 to $112 million in 2007. Typically, new product development for a consumable would take several months to one year with a budget of $500,000 to $2 million for development. Emphasis was placed on rapid product development with iterative product launches. With this pace of investment and development, Invitrogen was able to support 1,420 product launches in 2007.[3]

Invitrogen's business was highly transactional so the company focused on merchandising excellence. The company launched hundreds of new products every quarter, such as cell culture media used to sustain and feed cells, *Taq* polymerase used for PCR, and enzyme and buffer kits for extracting DNA from tissue (see Glossary of Terms). In addition, the company processed several thousand orders per day. As a result, the company's goal was to drive as much business through the web as possible. Invitrogen invested $83 million in IT,[4] eventually driving 57 percent of North American orders over the web.[5] The e-commerce site won numerous industry awards including, the Life Science Industry Award for "Most Useful Website" in 2007. Invitrogen also pioneered the Supply Center, which consisted of onsite refrigerated kiosks located within the customer laboratories to give scientists immediate access to the most commonly use

molecular biology reagents 24 hours a day, 7 days a week. Bright and colorful, the supply centers became part of nearly every lab. Any graduate student working late at night knew that s/he could get whatever reagent needed at any time with just a signature on a sign-in sheet. Every week, the local sales representative would pick up the sign-in sheet, take stock of the remaining inventory, charge the laboratory for the reagents and order replacement stock.

To supplement the web and over 1,000 supply centers, Invitrogen also relied on a traditional sales force. There were two groups of sales representatives. The account manager was responsible for overall sales of all 35,000 products. Technical sales specialists focused on specific product areas and provided deeper technical expertise for the account managers. Typically, there were two technical sales specialists for every account manager. Within the team, the account manager typically served as the "quarterback" who set the strategy for the account and served as the lead point of contact. All were compensated with base salary and commission.

Invitrogen's Future

With 90 percent[6] of its revenue coming from research, it was clear that Invitrogen would always be at the whim of government funding for the National Institutes of Health (NIH) and National Science Foundation (NSF). The board of directors believed that Invitrogen's core competencies (what are they? RL: leadership position with the basic research market with products, merchandising, sales) could best be leveraged to solve the medical problems of the twenty-first century. This sentiment was particularly acute as the board was made up of former pharmaceutical and clinical executives (Johnson & Johnson, Smithkline Beecham, and St. Jude Medical). With Lucier at the helm, Invitrogen sought to transform itself from a reagent kit company to a healthcare company.

In the CEO letter to the shareholders in the 2004 Annual Report, Lucier wrote:

Over the next several years, we hope to alter the course of our company to more directly serve physicians and patients. The idea that a tools company should remain solely in the laboratory is dated. Due to the pressures facing our clients, and because the value creation is much greater as we move toward the human, we believe that moving towards the patient is the right path for Invitrogen. Our steps will be modest in the beginning. We will continue to explore technologies to both enhance our expanding definition of what constitutes molecular tools and to open up our thinking about how to better treat people with cancer. I am convinced we must continue to drive the business toward a more complete understanding of the human system. As we progress we hope to create new business opportunities in the prediction, diagnosis, treatment, and monitoring of challenges to human health. We're excited by the possibilities of making a bigger difference in the human condition.

In addition, Invitrogen believed that acquiring instrument development and commercialization capability was key to achieving growth and transformation. For example, Invitrogen had the largest portfolio of products in the $6 billion cell biology market and was rated as the number one brand. Yet, Invitrogen had only 12 percent market share because most of the research funding was going toward instrumentation purchases.

Next-Generation Sequencing: Path to Personalized Medicine?

The first human genome was sequenced using Sanger sequencing at a cost of $3 billion[7] and took nearly 10 years to complete. While the project was hailed as a success, scientists believed that the medical and clinical application of the human genome would be limited until full sequencing could be performed routinely for the price of a diagnostic (~$1000).

The arrival of "next-generation sequencing" (NGS) changed all that. NGS referred to a family of new technologies that radically reduced the time and cost of sequencing. What had cost $3 billion was now approaching $100,000. Many believed NGS would lead to personalized medicine, which would enable physicians to

prescribe therapeutics that are tailored to each patient based on his or her genetics.

Initially, three players entered the NGS space. Roche, a $45 billion global healthcare company, was the first to market in 2005 with the 454 System, which promised to sequence a human genome for less than $100,000 in just a few weeks.

In January 2007, Illumina launched the 1G Genome Analyzer, whose throughput was ~50 percent higher than that of the 454 System (1 billion bases per run). In the fall of 2007, Applied Biosystems entered with SOLiD, which generated 1-2 billion bases in one run, and then SOLiD 2.0 in April 2008, which generated 5-6 billion bases in one run (see Exhibit 2). The three players were in an intense race with the goal of delivering a $1,000 genome.

With sequencing becoming faster and cheaper, laboratories around the world rushed to buy a next-generation sequencer. It was projected that NGS would be a $3 billion market by 2015 (Exhibit 2).

Then in 2008, a fourth player emerged. In 2008, Pacific Biosciences announced that it would commercialize a single molecule sequencer (SMS) that would eventually sequence an entire human genome for $100 in just one hour. Dr. Michael Hunkapiller, former president of Applied Biosystems, was an investor and on the board of directors. There was a tremendous amount of excitement about Pacific Biosciences within the investor community, with rumors that the company had raised nearly $200 million.[8]

Invitrogen, whose reagents were a peripheral component of the NGS workflow, believed that NGS was the transformational opportunity that it was looking for. If every individual in the world was sequenced for $1,000 each, this would translate into a $5.5 trillion market.

Strategic Options

Gardner believed that in order to transform Invitrogen, the company needed two things: instrumentation and a "methodological disruption in the space … as change is the strategic elixir." Next-generation sequencing was that "strategic elixir." Initially, acquiring Applied Biosystems seemed to be the best way to achieve Invitrogen's strategic goal. However, there were many skeptics in the company.

Applied Biosystems

Applied Biosystems was viewed as complementary to Invitrogen and therefore an obvious choice for an acquisition. Both were in the life sciences space, although Applied Biosystems was better known as an instrumentation company.

Exhibit 2 Market Growth

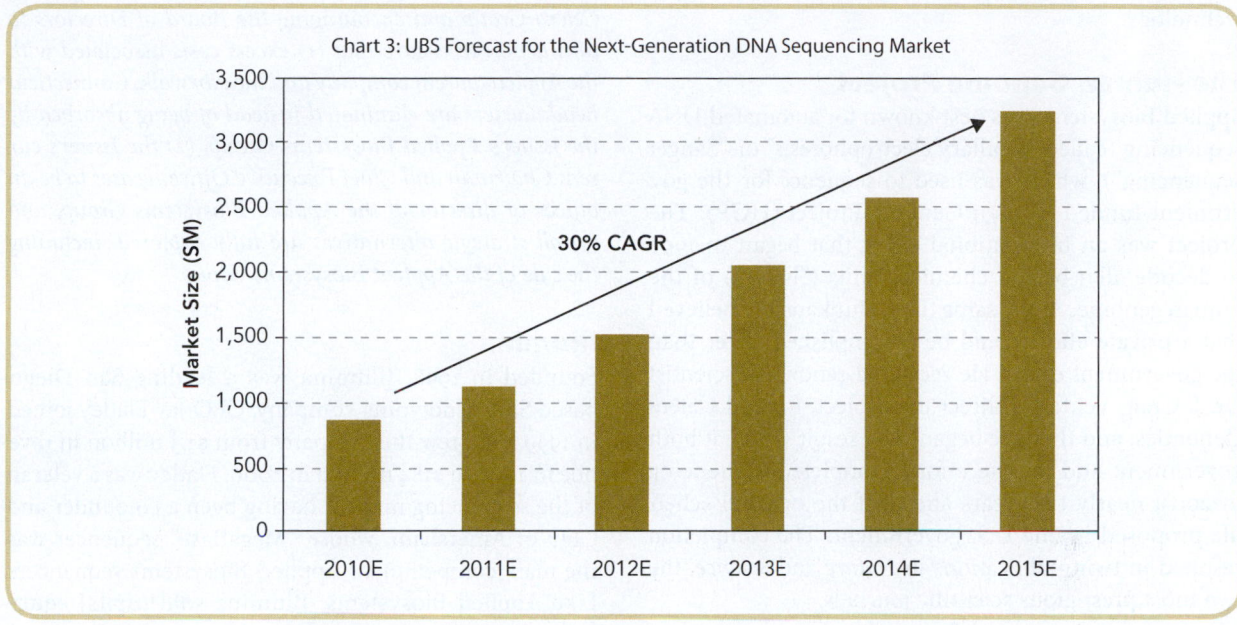

Chart 3: UBS Forecast for the Next-Generation DNA Sequencing Market

30% CAGR

Source: UBS estimates

By 2008, Applied Biosystems was a $2.2 billion instrument and reagent company, with nearly twice Invitrogen's $1.2 billion of annual revenue. Applied Biosystems' focus was developing high-quality scientific analytical systems that included high-priced capital equipment ($5,000 to $500,000) and proprietary reagents that were developed exclusively for use on the Applied Biosystems product (akin to the "razor/razorblade model"). Key product lines included PCR, QPCR, and Sanger sequencing. Development of instrument systems could take several years for $20-$50 million. Therefore, each proposed project underwent thorough due diligence on the market, technical, and financial risks before a project was green-lighted.

The sales cycle could last anywhere from a few months to more than a year, depending on the product and the size of the potential order. The goal was to place an instrument, thereby "plugging the socket," and then rely on the steady stream of reagent revenue and service contract revenue. Applied Biosystems had a highly technical and seasoned field organization. The salespeople used a consultative approach, relying on their technical and scientific expertise and deep relationship with the customer. To support the sales, Applied Biosystems had field application scientists (FAS), who were often PhD scientists who provided technical support and even helped customers design experiments. Applied Biosystems also had a team of field service engineers (FSE) who maintained and repaired the instruments. Often, the three types of employees (sales, FAS and FSE) covered similar

territories and worked collaboratively to get leads, support customers, and secure sales. Of the three, only the salespeople were compensated based on commission.

Applied Biosystems typically had one or two major product launches per year. However, each launch typically included a major piece of capital equipment along with proprietary reagents, service components, software, and service contracts. Most of the products were developed in-house,[9] as Applied Biosystems invested 9-10 percent of revenue in research and development (see Exhibit 3 for Applied Biosystems financials). As a result, Applied Biosystems held 2,400 patents and licenses,[10] approximately twice as many as Invitrogen.

Over the previous 10 years, Applied Biosystems made only two major acquisitions: $273 million for Ambion, a Texas-based company that specialized in RNA reagents in 2005, and $120 million for Agencourt

Exhibit 3 NGS Technology Specifications

	Bases per Read	Price per Run	Time per Run
Sanger Sequencing	100,000		24 hours
Roche 454	70 Million		~1 week
Illumina 1G Genome Analyzer	1 Billion	~$3000 to $5000	~1 week
Applied Biosystems SOLiD	2-3 Billion	~$8000	~2 weeks

Personal Genomics for its "next-generation sequencing" technology.

The Human Genome Project

Applied Biosystems was best known for automated DNA sequencing (called "capillary electrophoresis" or "Sanger sequencing"), which was used to sequence for the government-funded Human Genome Project (HGP). The project was an international effort that began in 1990 to decode all 3 billion chemical units ("bases") of the human genome. At the same time, Hunkapiller[11] believed that a private effort could be accomplished faster than the government effort. He recruited renowned scientist Dr. J. Craig Venter to direct the project, formed Celera Genomics, and the race began. The result was that both government and private efforts completed sequencing in 2003, nearly two years ahead of the original schedule proposed by the U.S. government. The completion resulted in twin publications in *Nature* and *Science*, the two most prestigious scientific journals.

Applied Biosystems in Trouble

In 2000, Applied Biosystems and Celera became subsidiaries of a parent company called Applera (derived from a combination of the names Applied and Celera) with Tony White as the CEO. More importantly, Applied Biosystems and Celera traded as two separate tracking stocks. Applera was headquartered in Norwalk, Connecticut, while Applied Biosystems was headquartered in Foster City, California and Celera was headquartered in Alameda, California. There was historically a great deal of concern on Wall Street about the additional overhead to maintain Norwalk, in addition to the corporate airplane that was available only for White's personal use.[12]

By 2008, Applied Biosystems was at a crossroads. There was a tremendous amount of shareholder unrest. First, revenue growth had stalled. The Human Genome Project had been completed five years earlier, and Wall Street did not see any opportunity for growth. Second, there were significant patents in PCR that were due to expire soon, and with it a significant royalty stream. Sensing volatility in the Applied Biosystems stock, so-called "momentum" or "fast" players had started to take large positions. One such fund was SAC Capital Advisors, whose founder Steve Cohen had a contentious relationship with Tony White, the CEO of Applera. In April 2008, SAC Capital advisors disclosed that it had increased its stake in Applied Biosystems to 5.1 percent (8.6 million shares). In addition, SAC disclosed in a 13D[13] filed with the SEC that it had sent a letter to Applied Biosystems's non-management directors to express

… its continued support for the separation of the Issuer's Celera Group and encouraging the Board of Directors to take action to ensure that (1) excess costs associated with the Applera parent company and the Norwalk, Connecticut headquarters are eliminated instead of being absorbed by the Issuer's Applied Biosystems Group, (2) the Issuer's current Chairman and Chief Executive Officer ceases to be an officer or director of the Applied Biosystems Group, and (3) all strategic alternatives are fully explored, including the sale of the Applied Biosystems Group.

Illumina

Founded in 1998, Illumina was a leading San Diego-based SNP genotyping company. CEO Jay Flatley joined in 1999 and grew the company from $1.3 million in revenue in 2000 to $184 million in 2006. Flatley was a veteran of the sequencing market, having been a cofounder and CEO of Amersham, whose "MegaBase" sequencer was the main competitor of Applied Biosystem's sequencers. Like Applied Biosystems, Illumina sold capital equipment. Its flagship product "BeadStation" listed for several hundred thousand dollars and generated $600,000 in reagent revenue per instrument annually. Illumina had the sales and service infrastructure required to support a global install base of 300 instruments.[14]

In 2006, Illumina jumped into the next-generation sequencing race with the $600 million acquisition of Solexa (based in Hayward, California) and prepared for the launch of its 1G Genome Analyzer. With the acquisition of Solexa, Illumina was poised to enter the next-generation sequencing market with a new technology that could prove to be cheaper and faster than the competition. As John West, CEO of Solexa, stated, "Together we expect to reach and exceed the milestone of the $100,000 genome."[15] However, it was not clear which technology would be the winning one.

Pacific Biosciences

Pacific Biosciences burst onto the scene in 2006, after being in stealth mode since its founding in 2004. The company officially debuted in February 2008 at the annual AGBT (Advances in Genome Biology and Technology) conference and revealed, for the first time, technical details and plans to commercialize a product in 2010. Using a novel technology called "single-molecular sequencing" or "third-generation" sequencing, Pacific Biosciences promised to deliver a $1,000 genome in 15 minutes. Illumina's Solexa technology and Applied Biosystems' SOLiD technology (commonly referred to as second-generation or G2 sequencing) would have required at least 100 or 15 runs, respectively, and cost tens of thousands of dollars.

The sequencing community was tremendously excited by the promise of Pacific Biosciences, and some customers were even holding off on purchases of Illumina or Applied Biosystems for a PacBio, whose instrument was listed at ~$700,000. The investor community was equally excited. Led by CEO Hugh Martin, Pacific Biosciences raised nearly $200 million by the fall of 2008.

Evaluating the Options

In order to ensure that all of the stakeholders were heard, Gardner and his team worked with Deloitte Consulting to implement an explicit process for debating the assumptions of the model, for letting everyone have their say, and for getting buy-in on the synergy targets. The team of 20 met weekly for nearly three months. In this way, there were team-driven milestones that everyone would execute even if they were unsure of the deal. Detailed market-based research, technical diligence and customer interviews ensured that nothing was left to chance. During these meetings, many of the stakeholders expressed concern or support.

Applied Biosystems seemed like a good choice because, as a large instrumentation company, it was a good complement to Invitrogen. Lucier realized that the low cost of sequencing would likely shape the next 10 to 30 years of scientific research. To be successful in this environment, a company required strengths in developing and commercializing instruments. In addition, Applied Biosystems had a large forensics business and strategic alliance with Abbott for molecular diagnostics. Both required development expertise for regulated markets, skills that Invitrogen lacked. Lucier and Gardner believed that capitalizing on Invitrogen's strength in reagent development, the combined companies would be able to achieve product development for cost savings, shorter time-to-market for new products, and secure a larger percentage [of the customer workflow].

From a financial perspective, Applied Biosystems was a sound choice because of its low valuation and large cash reserves. The financial team believed that the acquisition could pay for itself. In addition, activist shareholders had made Tony White vulnerable. Any combined company that emerged was unlikely to have White at the helm. This was a good thing for Lucier, who would want to lead the new company.

However, there were many who did not think Invitrogen should acquire Applied Biosystems.

Members of the R&D community protested that Invitrogen had already invested $20 million[16] in its own third-generation, next-generation sequencing program.

The head of R&D believed that the program would be successful and that there was no need to acquire a technology when one could be developed in-house.

The Invitrogen finance team was concerned that the investment community would look unfavorably on this acquisition. Invitrogen had built a reputation on consistent growth and stable cash flow. Acquiring Applied Biosystems would require an enormous amount of debt that would weigh down the stock.

The various business unit heads pointed out that Invitrogen was best at producing and selling low-priced reagents that were transactional. Instrumentation required a very different approach to R&D, sales, and marketing, all of which Invitrogen had never done. What made Invitrogen think they could do this?

Some skeptics in the company wondered why Applied Biosystems was for sale. Did Applied Biosystems know something that the rest did not? After all, key royalties were expiring and Applied Biosystems was losing its leadership in sequencing.

Finally, the company had gone through 10 acquisitions over the last several years and there had been many challenges acquiring companies far smaller than Applied Biosystems. Some believed that this acquisition was simply too big and too difficult. Given the poor track record, they wondered whether they could take on something so big.

Illumina was also an attractive option. The $400,000 1G Genome Analyzer had launched and was relatively well received, having secured 40 orders within 30 days of the completion of the early access period.[17] In addition, Illumina had the commercial infrastructure to support capital equipment, unlike Pacific Biosciences and Invitrogen. However, it was not clear if Illumina's technology would emerge as the winner. If it did not, then Illumina would be acquiring a microarray company, a technology that many experts claimed would be on the decline with the advent of next-generation sequencing. On the other hand, the Illumina management team included some veterans of the sequencing market and combined with Invitrogen's consumables development team, they would go to market with a strong, integrated solution.

One looming question was the issue of who would lead the combined companies post-merger. In the case of Illumina, Flatley had a strong record, having grown the company from $99 million in 1999 to $367 million by the end of 2007. In addition, the Solexa acquisition was viewed favorably by the stock market (Exhibit 4).

Some skeptics worried about Pacific Biosciences. After all, Invitrogen had its own G3 technology program

Exhibit 4 Illumina Stock Price from 2006 to 2008

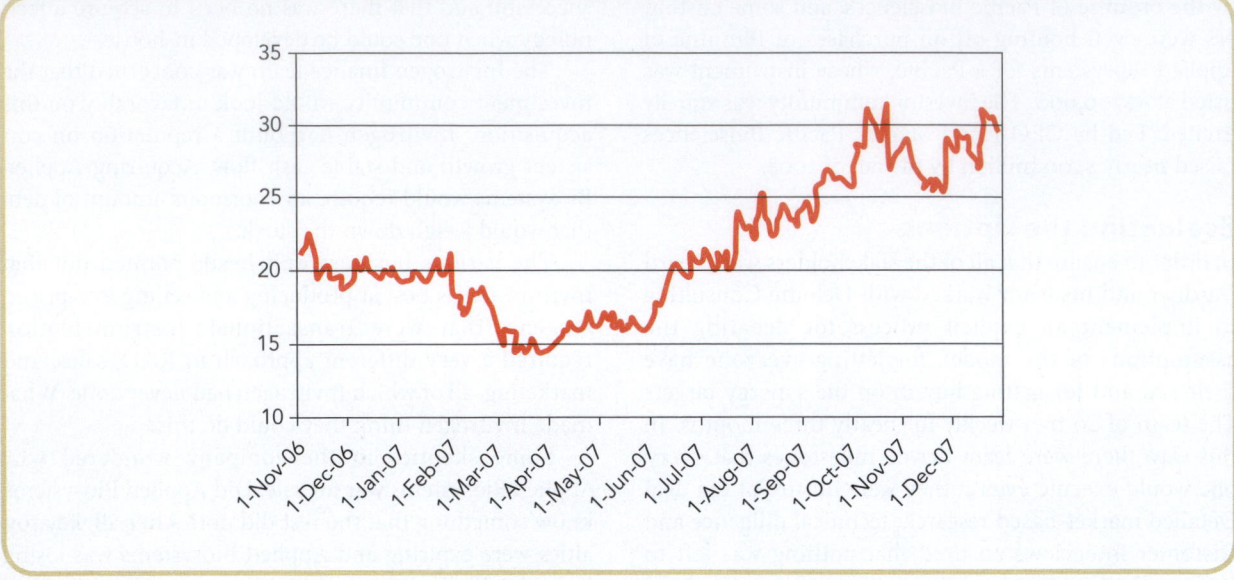

*Includes stock splits.
Key dates: Solexa acquisition announcement in November 2006. Deal closed in January 2007.

Exhibit 5 Biographies (2012)

Greg Lucier, 43, has been the CEO and Chairman of the Board of Invitrogen since 2003. Previously, he was CEO and president of GE Medical Imaging Information System. He earned his BS in engineering from Pennsylvania State University and MBA from Harvard Business School.[18]

Mark Gardner, 43, has held various positions at Invitrogen since 2003, including VP of Corporate Strategy, Chief Marketing Officer, and VP of Product Management/GM of the several business units. Prior to Invitrogen, he was with GE and McKinsey. He served for 10 years in the U.S. Navy with the rank of Lieutenant Commander. He earned his BS in history from the U.S. Naval Academy, MA in National Security Studies at Georgetown University and MBA from University of Pennsylvania Wharton School of Business.[19]

Tony White, 60, is the Chairman, President and CEO of Applied Biosystems, then Applera Corporation since 1995. Previously, he held many senior management positions during his 26-year tenure at Baxter International. He earned a BS from Western Carolina University.[20]

Dr. Mike Hunkapiller, 58, spent 21 years at Applied Biosystems helping to build it into a $2B global life science tools company. He also cofounded Celera Genomics. He is the inventor of the automated DNA sequencer, which was used to sequence the human genome. A renowned scientist, he has more than 100 scientific publications and holds more than two dozen patents. He earned a BS in Chemistry from Oklahoma Baptist University and a PhD in Chemical Biology from the Division of Chemistry and Chemical Engineering at Caltech.[21]

Jay Flatley, 55, has been the President and CEO of Illumina since 1999. Previously, he was the cofounder, President and CEO of Molecular Dynamics, which was acquired by Amersham Pharmacia Biotech and is now part of GE Healthcare. He earned a BA in economics from Claremont McKenna College and BS and MS (summa cum laude) in industrial engineering from Stanford University.[22]

Hugh Martin, 53, has been the CEO, President and Chairman of the Board of Pacific Biosciences since 2004. Prior to joining Pacific Biosciences, he was the chief executive office coach at Kleiner, Perkins, Caulfield and Byers. Martin earned a BS in electrical engineering from Rutgers University.

Source: Compiled by author.

Exhibit 6 Selected Financials for Applied Biosystems (Applera Corporation)

(Thousands USD)	2007	2006	2005	2004	2003
Net revenues	$2,093,467	$1,911,226	$1,787,083	$1,741,098	$1,682,943
Income from continuing operations	$170,875	$275,117	$236,894	$172,253	$199,617
Per Share Information					
Income per share from continuing operations					
Basic	$0.93	$1.47	$1.21	$0.84	$0.96
Diluted	$0.90	$1.43	$1.19	$0.83	$0.95
Dividends	$0.17	$0.17	$0.17	$0.17	$0.17
Cash & Cash equivalents and short-term investments	$494,464	$373,921	$756,236	$504,947	$601,666
Total Assets	$2,386,604	$2,245,772	$2,259,159	$1,921,672	$2,105,179
Long-Term Debt	$0	$0	$0	$0	$0

Source: Applera Annual Report 2007.

Exhibit 7 Selected Invitrogen Financials

(Thousands USD)	2007	2006	2005	2004
Net revenues	$1,282	$1,151	$1,198	$1,024
R&D	$112	$100	$97.0	$73.1
Net Income	$143	–$191	$132	$88.8
Per Share Information				
Income per share from continuing operations				
Basic	$2.79	$1.47	$2.33	$1.57
Diluted	$2.69	$1.44	$2.15	$1.50
Dividends				
Free Cash Flow	$245	$174	$238	$214
Total Assets	$3,330	$3,183	$3,877	$3,614
Long-Term Debt	$1,151	$1,151	$1,152	$1,319

Source: Invitrogen Financial Reports.

and the team understood all of the technical challenges and wondered how much progress Pacific Biosciences could have made. There had to be plenty of development remaining if a product was not going to be available until 2010. Furthermore, Pacific Biosciences had already raised nearly $200 million, so the company was likely to be valued at $1 billion.

On the other hand, many believed that the potential of G3 technology was so great, it would overtake and even obsolete the technologies developed by Applied Biosystems, Illumina and Roche. They wondered if it made more sense to "skip over" next-generation sequencing and acquire Pacific Biosciences to get a head start with G3 technology.

Next Steps

Gardner started to make his way over to Lucier's office for their weekly 1:1. He knew that Lucier would want to know what Gardner would recommend. Which company should Invitrogen acquire? Gardner and his team had been working diligently on the financial models. An acquisition could bring great rewards, but great risks as well. An acquisition would bring painful lay-offs and site closures. "The math part is easy," thought Gardner, "but the real question is: Is it worth it? And are we ready?"

Glossary of Terms

Base: The individual chemical unit that is the basis for DNA sequence. There are four types of bases: adenine, thymine, guanine and cytosine.

Biochemistry: The study of cellular components such as proteins, carbohydrates, lipids, nucleic acids and other biomolecules at a molecular level. The study involves understanding the structure, function and interactions of each cellular component.

Capillary electrophoresis: A process by which molecules are separated based on ionic charges. Automated Sanger sequencing employs capillary electrophoresis to sequence DNA.

Cell culture: A laboratory process by which cells are grown under controlled and sterile conditions.

DNA (Deoxyribonucleic Acid): A long linear polymer made of nucleotides. DNA is located in the nucleus of a cell and is involved with transmitting genetic information.

Enzyme: Biological molecules (or proteins) that catalyze chemical reactions.

Genome: The entire DNA sequence that encodes the complete genetic material for a living thing. The human genome has 3 billion bases.

Molecular biology: The study of biological processes at the molecular (subcellular level).

PCR (polymerase chain reaction): A scientific method by which single or multiple copies of a short piece of DNA are amplified.

QPCR (quantitative polymerase chain reaction): A scientific method based on PCR that quantifies the amount of DNA based on the number of amplification cycles performed.

Reagent: A commonly used term for any generic or specialized chemical used in laboratory experiments.

Sanger sequencing: Sequencing method developed by two-time Nobel laureate Dr. Frederick Sanger. The Sanger method became the preferred method because it is more efficient and uses fewer toxic chemicals than the primary alternative, Maxam-Gilbert sequencing.

Single Molecular Sequencing (SMS): Sequencing method that interrogates single molecules of DNA, avoiding biases found in other methods and increasing speed of sequencing.

SNP (Single nucleotide polymorphism): Variation in DNA sequence in which a base, such as cytosine, is replaced by another base, such as thymine. SNPs represent the most common form of variation amongst human beings. On average, the human genome has 10 million SNPs.[23]

Taq polymerase: *Taq* is a heat-stable bacterial enzyme used to attach the correct base to elongate DNA and proofread its mistakes. *Taq* is used to copy and amplify DNA for research and forensics applications.

Additional References:

William (Bill) Craumer, President, Lavenir, Inc.; former Director of Investor Relations, Applied Biosystems.

Andy Watson, Former Vice President, Invitrogen/Life Technologies.

Michael Hadjisavas, Former Vice President of Corporate Development, Invitrogen/Life Technologies.

NOTES

1. A "catalog life science" company provides a broad range of products that every scientist uses, from purified (or "deionized") water to enzymes. Before the Internet, all of the products were listed in a large catalog, often as thick as a phone book, with every product, part number and price.

2. Invitrogen Q1 2008 Earnings Call.

3. Invitrogen 2007 Annual Report.

4. Invitrogen 2007 Annual Report.

5. Invitrogen 2007 Annual Report.

6. Invitrogen Q4 2007 Earnings Call.

7. National Human Genome Research Institute (http://www.genome.gov/11006943).

8. Pacific Biosciences raised $188 million in 2008-2009 (Source: Pacific Biosciences Raises Additional $68M in Financing, August 12, 2009 press release).

9. Mass spectrometry was one major exception. Applied Biosystems and Sciex had a co-development agreement. Sciex developed the technology and Applied Biosystems provided sales, marketing and service support.

10. Marilyn Chase, "Invitrogen Offers $6.7B for Applied Bio," The Wall Street Journal, June 13, 2008. Marilyn Chase, "Invitrogen Offers $6.7B for Applied Bio," *The Wall Street Journal*, June 13, 2008.

11. Called PE Biosystems at the time.

12. "Pricey Perks let Executives Fly High": http://www.usatoday.com/money/companies/management/2003-08-04-corporatejet_x.htm

13. A 13D must be filed with the SEC any time a person or group acquires more than 5% of a company's shares. The transaction must be reported within 10 days.

14. SNP Genotyping and Analysis Market, June 2008, Kalorama Information.

15. Illumina press release, November 13, 2006.

16. "Invitrogen Discloses $20M Visigen Acquisition," http://www.genomeweb.com/sequencing/invitrogen-discloses-20m-visigen-acquisition-posts-15-percent-q3-revenue-growth.

17. Illumina 2006 Annual Report.

18. Life Technologies website; Forbes.com.

19. Linkedin.com.

20. Forbes.com.

21. Pacific Biosciences website, Wikipedia.

22. Illumina website.

23. "What are Single Nucleotide Polymorphisms (SNPs)?" http://ghr.nlm.nih.gov/handbook/genomicresearch/snp.

CASE 8

Keurig: From David to Goliath: The Challenge of Gaining and Maintaining Marketplace Leadership

Eric T. Anderson

On March 17, 2011, the vice president and general manager of Keurig Incorporated's At Home division, John Whoriskey, sat in his office in Reading, Massachusetts, reminiscing about the changes he had been a part of since joining the company in 2002. At that time Keurig was a privately held company with just over $20 million in revenues and a plan to enter the single serve coffee arena for home consumers, which Whoriskey himself had been hired to head up (see Exhibit 1). Nine years later Keurig was a wholly owned subsidiary of Green Mountain Coffee Roasters, Inc. (GMCR), a publicly traded company with 2010 net revenues of $1.36 billion (see Exhibit 2) and a market capitalization of between $8 and $9 billion.

In 2003 Whoriskey oversaw the introduction of Keurig's first At Home brewer, at the same time convincing the company's board of directors to take the risky approach of launching design and development of a next-generation brewer before the first brewer had reached the marketplace. That decision turned out to be critical to Keurig, providing the basis for a suite of products that secured Keurig the four best-selling coffee makers, in dollars, in Q4 2010.[1] Its strategy had been to offer a wide variety of coffees compatible with its single serve brewing system. Now, the company had just concluded an agreement with Dunkin' Donuts that would make five flavors of its coffee available in K-Cup® portion packs compatible with Keurig brewers. Starbucks, a company synonymous with super-premium gourmet coffee, had also agreed to offer its coffee and Tazo tea for the Keurig® single-cup brewing system.

In the fourth quarter of 2010, approximately 25 percent of all coffee makers sold in the United States were Keurig-branded machines,[2] and Keurig was recognized as among the leaders in the marketplace. Keurig now faced different challenges than in 2003 when it was a small, unknown marketplace entrant. Among them, Whoriskey considered what impact the impending expiration of key technology patents and the perceived environmental impact of the K-Cup® portion packs could have on the company's growth. Whoriskey wondered what Keurig's growth potential was, and how the new arrangements with Starbucks and Dunkin' Donuts could be leveraged to achieve it.

The Company and Its Products

Keurig had been founded to commercialize an innovative technology that allowed coffee lovers to brew one perfect cup of coffee at a time.[3] Beginning with the company's inception in 1992, the word "keurig," derived from the Dutch word for excellence, had been the guiding principle behind the company's products and services. With its patented single serve brewing system, Keurig first entered the office coffee service, or Away From Home (AFH), marketplace in 1998. In 2003 Keurig became one of the first to enter the At Home (AH) marketplace with a single-cup brewer designed for use in the home.

Keurig's single-portion brewer strategy was built on three key product features: a coffee brewer that perfectly controlled the amount, temperature, and pressure of water to provide a consistently superior-tasting cup of coffee; a unique, patented portion-pack system (marketed under the K-Cup® brand) containing ground coffee beans as well as filter paper; and a varied coffee selection to replicate the choices available in a gourmet coffeehouse.

This varied coffee selection was a key differentiator for Keurig and was achieved through licensing arrangements with a variety of gourmet coffee roasters. A selective but nonexclusive relationship with a coffee roaster enabled the roaster to pack its specialty coffees in the K-Cup® portion pack. Coffee roasters controlled the quality of their coffee and the number of varieties available through portion-pack production lines. A production line was owned or leased and operated by the coffee roaster. K-Cup® portion packs were produced by four North American roasters with more than seventy-five

Exhibit 1 Members of Keurig and GMCR Senior Management Teams

Keurig Senior Management Team

- Michelle Stacy, President
- John Whoriskey, Vice President, General Manager At Home Division
- Dave Manly, Vice President, General Manager Away From Home and Consumer Direct Divisions
- Kevin Sullivan, Vice President, Engineering
- Ian Tinkler, Vice President, Brewer Engineering
- Bob McCall, Vice President, Packaging, Equipment, and R&D
- Dick Sweeney, Co-Founder, Vice President, Contract Manufacturing and Quality Assurance
- Basil Karanikos, Vice President, Packaging Special Products
- Chris Stevens, Vice President, Corporate Relations and Customer Development
- Mark Wood, Vice President, New Business Development
- Mike Degnan, Vice President, General Counsel
- John Heller, Vice President, Finance

GMCR Senior Management Team

- Larry Blanford, President and CEO
- Howard Malovany, Vice President, Corporate General Counsel and Secretary
- R. Scott McCreary, President, Specialty Coffee Business Unit
- Frances Rathke, Chief Financial Officer
- Stephen J. Sabol, Vice President, Development
- Michelle Stacy, President, Keurig

Exhibit 2 Green Mountain Coffee Roasters Financial Performance
($ in thousands)

Fiscal Year	Net Sales	Gross Profit	Net Income
2005	161,536	56,975	8,956
2006	225,323	82,034	8,443
2007	341,651	131,121	12,843
2008	492,517	174,040	21,669
2009	786,135	245,391	54,439
2010	1,356,775	425,758	79,506

Note: Net income for 2005 and 2006 is after equity in losses of Keurig, Inc., net of tax benefit. GMCR acquired Keurig in June 2006.
Source: GMCR Annual Reports.

coffee varieties. Roaster partners included GMCR, Diedrich Coffee, Inc., Van Houtte, Inc., and Timothy's Coffee of the World, Inc. The roaster paid Keurig a royalty for each K-Cup sold.[4] Other roaster partners were subsequently added, such as Tully's in 2006.

At the time of Keurig's entrance into the AH marketplace in 2003, the company was privately held, with three significant shareholders. MDT, an investment advisory firm that managed a U.S.-based profit-sharing plan, had served as Keurig's lead venture capital investor since 1995 and led the company's board of directors. GMCR held a 42 percent stake in Keurig, and Van Houtte owned 28 percent. As provided for in separate shareholder agreements with MDT, neither GMCR nor Van Houtte was allowed to have a seat on the board of directors, enabling Keurig to maintain a roaster-neutral company strategy.

At Home Product Introduction

Keurig felt that being one of the first entrants in the product category was critical to its performance. The company's launch of the B100 single-cup brewer in September 2003 coincided with Salton's U.S. launch of the Melitta One:One brewer and Flavia's SB100 brewer. Each brewer differentiated itself by its features, underlying brewing technology, and packaging of the coffee. Both the Keurig and Flavia brewers used a proprietary portion pack, while the Melitta brewer used a 44 mm pod. All three provided the ability to brew a single cup of coffee at a time (see Exhibit 3). The Keurig and Flavia systems (both brewer and coffee) were only available online, whereas the Melitta system was available online and in limited retail outlets.

Exhibit 3 Comparison of Early Single-Cup Brewing Systems

Features	Keurig B100	Melitta One:One	Flavia SB100	Senseo	Home Café HCC100
Manufacturer	Keurig	Salton	Filterfresh	Phillips	Black & Decker
Coffee packaging	Proprietary K-Cup	44 mm pod	Proprietary Filterpack	62 mm pod	62 mm pod
Brewing sizes	8 oz.	5 oz., 8 oz.	5 oz., 8 oz.	4 oz., 8 oz.	7 oz., 9 oz., 14 oz.
Water reservoir	64 oz.	28 oz.	96 oz.	50 oz.	34 oz.
Shortest time to first cup	< 1 min	1 min	< 1 min	2+ min	1 min
Shortest time to second cup	Immediate	45 sec	40–45 sec	30 sec	10 sec
Number of flavors	75+	6	15	4	9
Suggested retail price	$249.99	$49.99	$99.99	$69.99	$59.95

Source: Singleservecoffee.com, company analysis.

A New Business Is Brewing

The AH single serve concept was well received by coffee lovers. Early press and user reviews showed that customers were happy with the ability to brew a single cup of coffee with no mess—no scooping of coffee or dealing with filters—in 60–90 seconds. Feedback among the users of the three initial entrants varied, however, with the selection of coffee varieties a common thread for discussion. Melitta One:One offered only five options and the Flavia system was only slightly better, with a choice of eleven flavors. In addition, both systems' offerings were restricted to a proprietary roaster. Meanwhile Keurig offered a total of more than seventy-five options encompassing a variety of flavors from four different coffee roasters. It quickly became apparent that feedback on a brewing system was often driven by the user's individual coffee preferences, so greater quality and variety of coffee positioned Keurig well in the marketplace. Users complained, however, that all three competitors lacked availability of the proprietary coffee packs in retail stores. Online ordering was the only option and required some advance planning to have a continuous supply of coffee.

Some new, larger players entered the single serve marketplace in 2004. In March of that year, Phillips and Sara Lee International launched the Senseo 7810 in the United States. The pod-based system brewed Sara Lee's Douwe Egberts coffee brand and produced a distinct frothy layer on top of the brewed coffee. The U.S. introduction of the Senseo followed launches in the Netherlands, France, Germany, and Denmark between 2001 and 2003. More than 5 million machines and 2.5 billion pods had already been sold in those countries.[5] The brewer's primarily plastic construction was still viewed as sturdy and overall it received positive reviews for its simplicity and ease of use.

In February 2004 Procter & Gamble announced that it had joined forces with four appliance marketers[6] to launch the Home Café single-cup brewing system in conjunction with a $50 million-plus marketing campaign. The Home Café pod system would brew Folgers and Millstone coffees. Black & Decker produced the first Home Café brewing system in May 2004, but users frequently complained about the machine leaking, the difficulty of properly placing the pod in its holder, and the volume of plastic used in the brewer construction. In late 2004 the Mr. Coffee Home Café brewer was added to the line and received more positive reviews.

Both the Senseo and Black & Decker Home Café systems were available online and in limited retail outlets, an improvement upon the limited distribution of early products. Across all products, however, reviews of the coffee varied from one extreme to the other, highlighting the challenge of being able to meet the taste requirements of a range of coffee drinkers, from the casual one-cup-a-day drinker to the gourmet coffee snob.

Even so, the entrance of P&G marked a turning point for single serve brewing. Extensive ad campaigns, including infomercials and an appearance on the show *Survivor* in September 2004, created awareness of the Home Café product line. In turn, this created spillover recognition for all single serve brewing systems, and the category grew.

Managing Brewer Manufacturing Costs

At the time of Keurig's B100 launch, management knew that its brewer price was very high. Even so, Keurig management felt that it was important to gain experience and consumer exposure in this emerging business. Mark Wood, VP of new business development, explained, "Launching new products stimulates interest in the company and in the category."

When the B100 was introduced in fall 2003, Keurig embarked on an ambitious three-pronged approach to address the brewer's cost structure. The approach consisted of reengineering the existing brewer to reduce cost, evaluating overseas options for brewer manufacturing, and launching a new brewer project in time for the holiday 2004 season, including retail distribution. Kevin Sullivan, VP of engineering, joined Keurig just after the initial launch of the B100 brewer and, after overseeing modest cost reductions on the current design, focused the engineering team's attention on the next-generation brewer, the B50 (see Exhibit 4).

The B50 design effort replicated existing Keurig benefits: time, temperature, and volume (TTV) control, use of the existing K-Cup® portion pack, at least two brew volumes (e.g., 6 oz., 8 oz.), and support of a retail price point of $149. Limiting the variance in the TTV components was key to meeting the taste profile requirements of both the "Cuppers"[7] and Keurig's roaster partners. Engineering evaluated three alternatives in its design process: redesign of the B100 brewer, evaluation of the pod systems in the marketplace to see how they could be modified to achieve the Keurig benefits, and a bottoms-up new design of the brewer. Ultimately Keurig chose to start from scratch when designing the new brewer, balancing the product features with budget and schedule requirements to meet the fourth quarter 2004 deliverable.

In parallel with the B50 design efforts, Dick Sweeney, VP of contract manufacturing and quality assurance, oversaw efforts to select a manufacturer for both the B100 and the new B50 brewers. After narrowing the field down to three companies, Keurig selected a single vendor in late December 2003. Production of the B50 began in September 2004, and in November 2004 the company received the first shipment of brewers via airfreight to meet the goal of holiday distribution.

Keurig's Retail Launch Strategy

Keurig's retail launch strategy included two features central to its success. Whoriskey explained it as follows:

We recognized that retailers were different and competed in different market segments. Selling a single brewer could create conflict among retailers that could limit distribution.

Exhibit 4 Keurig B50 Brewer and K-Cup® Portion Pack

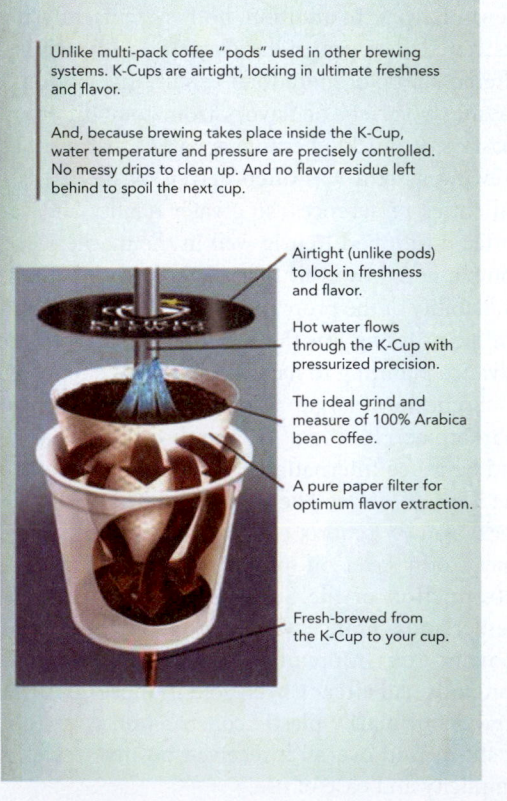

A high-end retailer such as Williams-Sonoma did not typically carry the same product assortment as a mass merchant like Target. We also needed to offer assurance to retailers that their support of a premium brewer would be worth their investment.

As a result, Keurig envisioned producing a suite of brewers—"good, better, best"—that would allow it to offer different products in each retail segment to meet the needs of those retailers' target customers. The products would match varying retail price points and offer a range of product features. The "better" category of product would provide broader appeal for multiple segments. Initially the B50, with its improved cost structure, fit the better category and was designed to meet a price point of around $149. In some cases, a "good, better, best" suite of products also allowed Keurig to meet varying retailer margin requirements. As shown in Exhibit 5, average profit margins varied between mass merchants such as Target and premium retailers such as Williams-Sonoma.

In launching the B50 brewer, Keurig also needed to address retailer concerns that investments in support of Keurig would not be eroded away. That investment included inventory costs to carry the brewer, shelf space, advertising, and training of in-store staff about the product. To address potential retailer concerns, Keurig created a minimum advertised price (MAP) program.

Premium manufacturers in numerous industries, including Bose, Viking, Sub-Zero, HP, and Nintendo, often used MAP programs. These programs minimized intrabrand price competition by providing incentives to retailers who only advertised prices at or above the MAP price; a common incentive was cooperative advertising dollars that could be used to subsidize retailers' advertising expenses. A retailer that chose to advertise in a manner inconsistent with the MAP program could lose out on these financial incentives. A retailer that repeatedly violated these terms could eventually lose the right to distribute a manufacturer's product. From the retailers' perspective, the MAP price provided some comfort that competing retailers would not undercut them on advertised prices.

In the months leading up to the B50 launch, Whoriskey focused on a number of issues associated with moving into the retail environment, including gaining product placements with retailers, identifying a logistics partner that would manage the fulfillment to retail stores, and introducing new, lower-count-size packages of K-Cup® portion packs. By the holiday 2004 season, ten retailers had agreed to distribute the B50 brewer in about a hundred stores. Keurig selected M. Block and Sons as the exclusive retail distribution partner for the brewer and completed repackaging of K-Cup® portion packs to offer quantities of eighteen at a MAP price of $9.95. Whereas Sara Lee and P&G focused their marketing dollars on television and print advertising, Keurig devoted its more limited advertising dollars to in-store demonstrations of the product. The television and print coverage by Keurig's rivals increased consumers' exposure to the single serve concept and sent them to stores with curiosity about the products. Once in the stores, Keurig hoped its demos would get people hooked on the taste, ease, and simplicity of the Keurig system.

The At Home Marketplace Heats Up

With the entry of competitors and heavy advertising spending, interest and awareness of single serve brewing increased and sales of Keurig brewers took off. By the holiday 2005 season, Keurig had grown its retail presence to 3,500 stores. Existing competitors were also adding products, with new entrants joining the fray.

Competitor Activity

Kraft partnered with Braun to introduce the Tassimo Hot Beverage System in the United States in September 2005. Designed by Kraft, the product had been introduced in France, Switzerland, and the United Kingdom in 2004 and was touted as the leading competitor to the Senseo system there. The Tassimo system used a proprietary portion pack, the T-Disc, which included a bar code that provided information to the machine about the appropriate brewing settings (amount of water, brewing time, and temperature). In addition to coffee, the Tassimo offered cappuccino, espresso, café crema, tea, and hot chocolate—a total of about fifteen varieties, featuring Kraft brands such as Gevalia and Maxwell House as well as Kraft-distributed Twinings Tea. The brewer's suggested retail price was $169.99, with a cost of about $0.50 per T-Disc. Like P&G, Kraft used its marketing muscle

Exhibit 5 Retailer Annual Gross Margins (%)

Retailer	2006	2007	2008	2009	2010
Amazon.com	22.9	22.6	22.3	22.6	22.3
Bed Bath & Beyond	42.8	41.5	39.9	41.0	41.4
Kohl's	36.4	36.5	36.9	37.8	38.2
Macy's	39.9	40.4	39.7	40.5	40.7
Target	30.3	30.2	29.8	30.5	30.5
Williams-Sonoma	39.9	38.9	33.8	35.6	39.2

Source: RetailSails data.

to push the Tassimo system and the entire single serve segment of coffee brewing. The system was featured in an episode of *The Apprentice: Martha Stewart*, in which contestants were tasked with creating a retail space for selling the new system. Kraft reportedly invested $75 million in marketing the system's introduction.

Kraft subsequently announced a partnership with Starbucks in December 2007, introducing four Starbucks varieties in time for the holiday season. Starbucks positioned it as a natural fit for the company, a "way to provide an authentic Starbucks coffee experience to our customers, and to do so anywhere and anytime they prefer."[8] This expanded relationship between Kraft and Starbucks (building off a 1998 supply and distribution agreement) came on the heels of a revamped business plan to "spur stronger and more profitable growth"[9] in the Tassimo system. It also expanded Tassimo's beverage offerings to more than sixty worldwide.[10] At the same time, Kraft announced a new brewer alliance with Bosch to replace Braun, which had been acquired by a coffee competitor, P&G.

Additionally, another competitor had appeared on the scene in 2005. Bunn was a manufacturer of drip coffee makers for commercial and AH applications. With the Bunn My Café, the company joined the single serve segment, advertising a patented jet action sprayhead as a differentiator in the brewer's ability to release flavor and aroma. The pod-based brewer used a pour-over method that required the consumer to pour in the desired amount of water, from 4 to 14 ounces, each time a new cup was brewed. The pod drawer was designed to receive a range of pod sizes, enabling the brewer to be used with a variety of different roasters' pods and increasing the variety of coffees available for use with the brewer. The brewer was introduced with a suggested retail price of $199.95.

Not all product introductions were successful, however. P&G experienced slow sales and a smaller adoption of its Home Café line after its initial splash. In June 2006 the company announced it would cut marketing funds for the product, after having spent an estimated $41 million since the launch of the first brewer in 2004. Similarly, after significant success in Europe, Senseo's sales and product innovation in the United States seemed to trail off.

The stumbles and uncertainty of some of its competitors did not slow Keurig down. In fall 2005 Keurig introduced two new AH brewers to its product line: the Keurig Elite B40 and the Keurig Special Edition B60. With variations in the programmability and features, these products helped the company target the "good" and "best" segments of its distribution strategy, respectively. The B40 was generally offered at a retail price of $99.95, while the B60 was generally offered

at $199.95. In fall 2006 the Keurig Platinum B70 was introduced with the most robust set of features and functionality to date, including four cup sizes, a programmable LCD display, and a larger water reservoir. Each brewer provided the same user experience in terms of ease of use and brewing of a great cup of coffee, consistent with Keurig's overall product commitment. By the first quarter of 2007, Keurig had secured a position as one of the market leaders in the small but growing single-cup segment of the broader coffee maker category (see Exhibit 6).

Changes at Keurig

In June 2006 GMCR completed the acquisition of the remaining shares of Keurig, transitioning Keurig from a small, privately held company to a wholly owned subsidiary of a publicly traded company. In doing so, GMCR not only signaled its commitment to single serve brewing but also reaffirmed its support of Keurig's

Exhibit 6 Single Serve Coffee Maker Sales by Brand

Brand	Jan.–Mar. 2005	Jan.–Mar. 2006	Jan.–Mar. 2007
By Dollar Volume ($)			
Keurig	152,730	1,154,135	2,293,802
Braun	0	1,622,884	2,166,536
Phillips	1,379,242	1,120,567	1,172,441
Flavia	0	0	170,719
Mr. Coffee	60,017	249,363	168,508
Krups	0	222,310	152,419
Melitta	1,040,165	525,173	35,214
Bunn	41,408	62,593	24,424
Black & Decker	608,635	645,033	24,168
By Unit Volume			
Keurig	1,022	8,813	17,995
Braun	0	9,925	15,029
Phillips	22,730	18,905	18,881
Flavia	0	0	1,648
Mr. Coffee	1,173	3,471	3,456
Krups	0	1,771	4,109
Melitta	27,252	11,279	634
Bunn	212	337	115
Black & Decker	11,535	11,376	969

Note: Total coffee maker category includes all coffee makers and espresso makers. NPD data does not include all retailers and is estimated to represent 35 to 40 percent of the total marketplace.

Source: NPD data.

multibrand strategy, one of the company's key differentiating features and an important element of its success. This move enabled Keurig to leverage the resources of GMCR to further its growth in the single serve segment. The added financial backing of GMCR was critical to Keurig's ongoing product innovation and also allowed the company to aggressively protect its design and technology investments.

Ownership by GMCR allowed Keurig to pursue a new avenue for expansion of its robust offering of coffee varieties with its single serve brewers. As an example, Keurig and Caribou Coffee announced an agreement in early 2007 that would make eight flavors of Caribou Coffee available in K-Cup® portion packs. This arrangement represented a new model for production and sales of K-Cup® portion packs.

Under the terms of the arrangement, Caribou Coffee will blend and sell its gourmet coffee beans to Keurig. Keurig will be responsible for packaging the coffee into K-Cups in accordance with Caribou Coffee's specifications. Under the license from Caribou Coffee, Keurig will also serve as the wholesale distributor and a direct retailer for all Caribou Coffee K-Cups.[11]

Rather than requiring a roaster partner to operate its own production line, Keurig could benefit from the manufacturing capabilities of its parent to pursue relationships without upfront capital or leasing costs.

At the same time, tension existed between GMCR and the other roasters over the longevity of GMCR's commitment to a multibrand strategy. This tension eased as GMCR embarked on a strategy of acquiring the wholesale businesses, including the K-Cup® portion-pack production lines, of each of the original roaster partners, beginning with Tully's in early 2009, followed by Timothy's in late 2009, and Diedrich's Coffee and Van Houtte in 2010. Driving these acquisitions was GMCR's desire to become a leader in the highly fragmented coffee industry. GMCR added complementary brands to its portfolio while expanding its geographic presence and manufacturing and distribution capabilities.

With GMCR's backing, Keurig's ongoing success enabled it to expand its marketing and distribution presence. In the holiday 2007 season, Keurig launched a $3 million television advertising campaign in sixteen cities, coupling it with in-store demonstrations and cooperative advertising support in retail stores. That investment grew close to $20 million, including a $6 million national advertising campaign, for the holiday 2008 season. In conjunction with that same holiday season, Keurig and GMCR also launched brewer and twelve-count K-Cup®

portion-pack offerings in the grocery channel, adding to the purchase options available to consumers. The total number of retail outlets, including grocery stores, exceeded 16,000 locations by the end of 2008 (see Exhibit 7). Keurig brewer sales continued to grow, and in the fourth quarter of 2008 Keurig had captured close to 20 percent of total coffee maker sales in dollars (see Exhibits 8 and 9). Keurig further expanded the brewer options available to the consumer, introducing the first third-party brewer designed using Keurig's proprietary and patented brewing technology in 2007.[12]

Marketplace Evolution

A question facing Keurig and all manufacturers of single serve brewing systems was the state of the coffee marketplace and the ongoing role of single serve applications. The marketplace for drip coffee makers in the United States was stagnant, with a decline of approximately 3 percent from 2004 to 2010 (see Exhibit 10). Single serve coffee makers, however, had grown to represent about 19 percent of the total sales volume in that same time.

Exhibit 7 Keurig Retail Presence

Year Ending	No. of Retail Stores	No. of Supermarkets	Total Retail Locations
December 2004	200	0	200
December 2005	3,500	0	3,500
December 2006	7,000	200	7,200
December 2007	10,000	1,300	11,300
December 2008	13,800	2,600	16,400
December 2009	17,900	10,000	27,900
December 2010	19,000	14,400	33,400

Source: GMCR earnings releases.

Exhibit 8 Cumulative Keurig Single-Cup System Sales (in thousands)

Year Ending	Keurig-Branded Brewers	K-Cup Portion Packs
September 2004	124	
September 2005	226	312,405
September 2006	474	448,880
September 2007	953	638,298
September 2008	1,936	1,650,654
September 2009	2,342	3,300,532
September 2010	4,543	6,185,532

Source: GMCR earnings releases.

Exhibit 9 Keurig Coffee Maker Sales Share

	2007	2008	2009	2010
Dollar Sales by Quarter				
Q1 (Jan.–March)	2.8	6.7	14.1	24.5
Q2 (Apr.–June)	3.5	7.3	16.9	24.8
Q3 (July–Sept.)	4.1	7.9	17.3	26.5
Q4 (Oct.–Dec.)	8.4	17.8	36.4	45.3
Unit Sales by Quarter				
Q1 (Jan.–March)	0.9	2.3	5.7	10.8
Q2 (Apr.– June)	1.1	2.6	7.4	11.1
Q3 (July–Sept.)	1.3	2.7	6.8	11.3
Q4 (Oct.– Dec.)	3.1	8.1	18.6	25.1

Note: Total coffee maker category includes all coffee makers and espresso makers. Derived from NPD data. NPD data does not include all retailers and is estimated to represent 35 to 40 percent of the total marketplace.
Source: GMCR's NPD data from its earnings releases.

Exhibit 10 Automatic Drip Coffee Maker Sales

	Unit Volume	Single Serve Share (%)	Dollar Sales ($)	Single Serve Share (%)
2004	26,705,000	5.5	804,878,390	8.4
2005	27,250,000	5.7	870,138,800	9.5
2006	27,148,060	5.2	918,040,600	11.2
2007	26,101,870	5.0	903,635,800	11.9
2008	23,281,190	7.0	825,397,700	17.1
2009	25,482,840	12.6	976,260,400	29.6
2010	25,870,160	19.4	1,099,732,000	42.9

Note: Drip coffee makers include automatic drip coffee and pod machines. Restatement of data post-2004. Volumetrics derived from presumed trend 2005 vs. 2004.
Source: NPD Group, Inc./Consumer Tracking Service.

Importantly, about 71 percent of the 115 million households in America owned a coffee maker in 2008. In terms of coffee consumption, research showed that 44 percent of all U.S. consumers had a daily cup of coffee and 75 percent of that consumption was done in the home.[13]

Industry analyst Harry Balzer of the NPD Group commented:

Coffee consumption per capita is fairly stable in the U.S. So for a coffee company to gain share in the marketplace, it needs to shift share or get consumers to pay more for a cup of coffee. Manufacturers of coffee makers have to address one or more of three key components: novelty, time, or money—is it new, does it save time, or does it save money?

Analysis of the foreign marketplace could also provide some insight into the U.S. marketplace's potential. Industry analyst Scott Van Winkle pointed to the success of Nespresso S.A., a business of Nestle Group, in Europe as an indicator of the potential for Keurig in the United States: "I could see Keurig's market share for coffee makers grow close to 50 percent based on the precedent set by Nespresso in Europe, where they have reached the 40 percent range." Initially introduced in Switzerland in 1986, Nespresso's single serve espresso machine experienced a slow start until the mid-1990s, when it entered a period of rapid growth. According to the company, Nespresso achieved organic growth of more than 20 percent in 2010 and estimated "global market share of around 20 percent in the segment of espresso and filter portioned coffee machines."[14]

Choose. Brew. Enjoy.®

Choose

From its initial entry into single serve brewing, Keurig recognized the importance of choice to allow each person to find a coffee that met his individual taste preferences. Keurig continued on this path by entering into relationships with three key coffee brands, each with its own loyal following: Folger's Gourmet Selections in 2010, followed by Dunkin' Donuts and Starbucks in 2011. In February 2011 GMCR entered into a promotion, manufacturing, and distribution agreement with Dunkin' Donuts that would make five flavors available in K-Cup® portion packs, sold exclusively in its restaurants by the second half of 2011. In addition, Keurig brewers occasionally would be sold in the restaurants. GMCR would be responsible for packaging the K-Cup® portion packs using coffee that was sourced and roasted to Dunkin' Donuts specifications.

In March 2011 GMCR entered into a manufacturing, marketing, distribution, and sales relationship with Starbucks that would make Starbucks and Tazo tea K-Cup® portion packs available by fall 2011. Starbucks had previously introduced its own portion pack of instant coffee targeted at single serve consumers, Starbucks VIA Ready Brew, which had achieved $100 million in worldwide sales in under a year.[15] The relationship would enable Keurig to potentially reach the approximately 50 million customers served in Starbucks stores every week, an estimated 80 percent of whom did not have a single serve brewer at home.[16]

The Starbucks relationship presented an exciting opportunity for Keurig to add a super-premium coffee brand to its robust offering of flavors. However, there was some uncertainty concerning the long-term benefit. Starbucks had already announced a strategy to pursue multiple options in single serve brewing.

"The single serve coffee category in the U.S., and much of the world for that matter, is in its beginning stages of development," said Jeff Hansberry, president, Starbucks Consumer Products Group. "At this very early stage, there are numerous contenders and no demonstrated long-term winners related to either format or machines. Following our very successful introduction of Starbucks VIA Ready Brew in the U.S. and into a growing number of international markets, Starbucks will continue to explore the many single serve and on-the-go solutions and options available to us, and to participate in those where we can better and more conveniently serve our customers wherever they may be."[17]

The question remained whether Starbucks's relationship with GMCR and Keurig represented an interim solution or whether it would fulfill a key component in Starbucks's overall single serve offering.

In conjunction with expanding their coffee offerings, Keurig and GMCR also continued to grow the grocery presence to enable consumers to easily obtain K-Cup® portion packs. By the end of 2010, K-Cup® portion packs could be purchased in 98 percent of grocery stores in the Northeast and 61 percent of all grocery stores in the United States.[18]

Brew

Its commitment to technological innovation continued to be a key component of Keurig's success. Where appropriate, Keurig obtained patents covering its innovations and vigorously defended them. In January 2007 Keurig filed a patent infringement lawsuit against Kraft Foods Inc., Kraft Foods Global, Inc., and Tassimo Corporation asserting that Kraft's T-Discs infringed upon a Keurig technology patent filed in August 2003. In October 2008 Kraft agreed to settle out of court with a lump sum of $17 million for a limited, nonexclusive license for applicable Keurig patents related to beverage machines and beverage cartridges.

More recently, Keurig had filed a lawsuit against Sturm Foods:

The Sturm portion packs that we've seen appearing on several retailer shelves contain instant coffee and state they are intended for use in Keurig brewers. As our complaint notes, our lawsuit asserts that Sturm's portion packs infringe two patents, which cover certain technologies relating to the use of brewers and portion packs.[19]

Keurig was looking for similar success in this suit. However, the longevity of some of the existing patents still could pose a problem. Certain patents associated with the current generation of K-Cup® portion packs were set to expire in 2012 and 2017, while brewer patents had expiration dates out to 2023. Pending patent applications associated with the current generation of K-Cup® portion packs, if issued, could extend those expiration dates to 2023 as well. Without patent protection, the door could be opened to competitors such as Sturm Foods, which would look to market a product to compete with the K-Cup® portion pack, thus eroding GMCR's own coffee sales as well as royalties from other roaster coffee sales using the Keurig technology.

Another issue facing Keurig lay in the patented K-Cup® portion pack itself. Key to the quality and freshness of its coffee, the K-Cup® design included materials and a heat-sealing process that made recycling difficult. Keurig had introduced the My K-Cup® reusable filter assembly in 2006, a reusable filter designed to work with the Keurig single-cup brewing system. Although it was initially targeted for use by consumers wanting to use their own gourmet coffee instead of a prepackaged portion pack, it could also provide a solution to environmentally conscious users who were concerned with the disposal of the used K-Cup® portion packs, which contained plastic and other nonrecyclable materials. That solution did not address those consumers interested in the convenience of the traditional K-Cup portion pack, however.

Keurig's competitors were facing the same challenge. In December 2010 Bunn My Café had introduced a new brewer that used pods that could be composted. In Europe, Nespresso had introduced dedicated portion-pack collection points to facilitate capsule recycling, and in 2009 it committed to tripling its recycling capacity by 2013. A similar issue had arisen in the bottled water industry. The convenience of bottled water, together with consumers' desire for a healthier alternative to soda, had resulted in rapid growth in sales of bottled water. But concerns about the volume of empty plastic containers in landfills threatened the industry and caused sales to slow, leaving bottled water manufacturers scrambling to find solutions to their environmental challenge.

Concerns about the environmental impact of the K-Cup portion pack had started to surface in user comments on websites and in newspapers such as the *New York Times*.[20] Estimates of the amount of nonrecyclable material from the K-Cups appearing in landfills had some users contemplating use of another, more environmentally friendly single-cup brewing system. Keurig's own life cycle analysis compared a number of environmental factors of the Keurig single-cup brewing system to traditional drip brewing. The analysis had shown that product-packaging disposal contributed only a fraction of its total environmental impact as compared to the production of the packaging itself.[21] As a result, the company was working with its packaging suppliers to improve the environmental dimensions of the packaging production process. The introduction of nested packaging to reduce the size of a box of K-Cup® portion packs and experimentation with a tea-based K-Cup® portion pack made with paper were additional environmental initiatives undertaken by the company. With the increasing popularity of the Keurig single-cup brewing system, the K-Cup® portion-pack packaging was one of the company's most significant environmental challenges and needed to be addressed to prevent erosion of its position in the marketplace.

Enjoy?

By March 2011, Keurig was in an enviable position. In the fourth quarter of 2010 it had shipped a record number of products, and Keurig models were the four best-selling brewers, in dollar sales, in the United States. The company had also just announced the agreements with Dunkin' Donuts and Starbucks, which would strengthen its multibrand approach and penetrate a new retail outlet.

But Whoriskey and the rest of the senior leadership team at Keurig and GMCR couldn't help but turn their attention to the future. Whoriskey was eager to begin writing the next chapter in Keurig's success story, but questioned the potential size of the single serve opportunity, the impact of expiring technology patents and environmental concerns, and how to maximize the effectiveness of Keurig's relationships with its coffee-roasting partners.

NOTES

1. From company reports, based on NPD data, which does not include all retailers and is estimated to represent 35 to 45 percent of the total marketplace.

2. Ibid.

3. Portions of this overview are excerpted from "Keurig At Home: Managing a New Product Launch," Case #5-105-005 (Kellogg School of Management, 2004).

4. See "Keurig At Home" case. The royalty was estimated to be approximately $0.04 per K-Cup. The royalty was increased by about $0.01 in 2008 to support advertising and market development.

5. Phillips/Sara Lee press release, February 2004.

6. Black & Decker, Krups, Hamilton Beach, and Sunbeam.

7. "Cuppers" were responsible for tasting the finished coffee product to evaluate the flavor profile of a coffee.

8. Kraft press release, September 4, 2007.

9. Ibid.

10. The Kraft-Starbucks relationship was terminated by Starbucks on March 1, 2011.

11. Caribou Coffee, press release, January 8, 2007.

12. Breville was the first third-party manufacturer. Additional relationships with Jarden and Conair were announced in 2009.

13. Harry Balzer, NPD Group, in interview with the author.

14. Nespresso Corporate Backgrounder and Corporate Factsheets, March 2011, http://www.nespresso.com/mediacenter/xml/int/ resources/pdf/CorporateBackgrounder_CorporateFactsheets_EN.pdf.

15. Starbucks press release, August 3, 2010.

16. Starbucks press release, March 10, 2011.

17. Starbucks press release, February 15, 2011.

18. From GMCR first quarter 2011 earnings release based on IRI data for the latest twelve weeks ended December 26, 2010.

19. GMCR, "Prepared Remarks for Fourth Quarter and Year-End Fiscal 2010 Results," December 9, 2010, p. 2.

20. See "A Coffee Conundrum," *New York Times*, August 3, 2010, and "Keurig K-Cups: How Green Is Green Mountain?" *Coffee Amp*, January 27, 2010, http://www.coffeeamp.com/single-cup-coffee/keurig-k-cups/keurig-k-cups-how-green-is-green-mountain.

21. "Reducing Our Environmental Impact: The Keurig® Brewing System," http://www.gmcr.com/csr/ProtectingTheEnvironment/TheKeurigSingleCupBrewingSystem.aspx.

CASE 9

KIPP Houston Public Schools

Dane Roberts
Rice University, Jones Graduate School of Business

Sehba Ali, the recently selected superintendent of KIPP (Knowledge Is Power Program) Houston Public Schools, prefers that people do not refer to KIPP as "a miracle." Yes, it has effectively quadrupled the rate at which its low-income students attend college compared to traditional public schools. Yes, it has created a new model for public education that has spread throughout the United States and beyond. And, yes, visitors to the schools are often astounded by the focus and character shown by its students—often called KIPPsters—in comparison to the chaos that sometimes prevails in other schools serving neighborhoods of high poverty. But Ali believes there is no magic or miracle to it.

Instead she attributes KIPP's success to "a lot of smart people working hard and being nice. It's about innovation. It's about creativity. It's about being as smart as we can and being willing to take risks and make change."[1]

Despite the organization's dedicated staff members and students, who have committed with their signatures to "do whatever it takes" to succeed, there is no guarantee the future will be an unqualified success. KIPP Houston has faced challenges finding enough qualified teachers and leaders to continue its plans for rapid expansion. Securing adequate funding for its programs and facilities is also a perennial challenge. Finally, some lapses in quality among the 21 elementary and secondary schools in the Houston metro area are forcing Ali and other KIPP Houston leaders to grapple with the trade-off between campus autonomy and top-down management.

Setting the Scene

KIPP Houston is a network of charter schools located in Houston, Texas, the fourth largest city in the United States. Charter schools are public, taxpayer funded, and open to all students; however, they operate independently of traditional school districts. The 21 schools KIPP Houston operates are among 125 nationally that use the KIPP name. While all KIPP schools have a high level of autonomy, they share the imprimatur of the KIPP Foundation in San Francisco, California, to whom they pay a licensing fee and which is responsible for the year-long leadership training program that all school principals attend before founding a new KIPP school.

KIPP schools also adhere to a set of common operating principles known as the "Five Pillars," which the KIPP Foundation describes as:

- HIGH EXPECTATIONS—KIPP schools have clearly defined and measurable high expectations for academic achievement and conduct that make no excuses based on the students' backgrounds. Students, parents, teachers, and staff create and reinforce a culture of achievement and support through a range of formal and informal rewards and consequences for academic performance and behavior.
- CHOICE & COMMITMENT—Students, their parents, and the faculty of each KIPP school choose to participate in the program. No one is assigned or forced to attend a KIPP school. Everyone must make and uphold a commitment to the school and to each other to put in the time and effort required to achieve success.
- MORE TIME—KIPP schools know that there are no shortcuts when it comes to success in academics and life. With an extended school day, week, and year, students have more time in the classroom to acquire the academic knowledge and skills that will prepare them for competitive high schools and colleges, as well as more opportunities to engage in diverse extracurricular experiences.
- POWER TO LEAD—The principals of KIPP schools are effective academic and organizational leaders who understand that great schools require great school leaders. They have control over their school budget and personnel. They are free to swiftly move dollars or make staffing changes, allowing them maximum effectiveness in helping students learn.
- FOCUS ON RESULTS—KIPP schools relentlessly focus on high student performance on standardized tests and other objective measures. Just as there are no shortcuts, there are no excuses. Students are expected to achieve a level of academic performance that will enable them to succeed at the nation's best high schools and colleges.[2]

KIPP Houston's mission is to "develop in under-served students the academic skills, intellectual habits, and qualities of character necessary to succeed at all levels of pre-kindergarten through twelfth grade, college, and the competitive world beyond."[3] KIPP Houston takes the college attendance aspect of its mission very seriously. Getting all of its students "to and through college" is a mantra of the organization. They painstakingly track the outcomes of all their students to find out how many attend and matriculate through college. Some KIPP Houston employees work full time to prepare and support students in their college application process.

Within KIPP Houston Public Schools, Ali manages 8 elementary schools (grades pre-kindergarten to grade 4), 10 middle schools (grades 5 through 8), and 3 high schools (grades 9 through 12). In order to establish a strong school culture from the ground up, a school is typically founded with the earliest grade level first, then expands each year into the next grade level. In the 2012–13 school year, KIPP Houston employed 968 people and served about 8,500 students; some schools have not yet added all grade levels. (More student demographic information is found in Exhibit 1.)

Storied Beginnings

The founding of KIPP has become the stuff of legend in education circles. In 1992, Michael Feinberg and David Levin, fresh out of Ivy League colleges, joined Teach for America (TFA), which places top college graduates as teachers in neighborhoods of high poverty for a two-year commitment. After a summer of training, Feinberg and Levin started teaching fifth grade in two poorly performing schools in the Houston Independent School District (HISD).[4]

At first they struggled to control disruptive students and engage their classes in learning activities, but Levin soon discovered a mentor in Harriet Ball, a master teacher down the hall from his classroom. As often as possible he would meet with and observe her teaching. He soon began to adopt some of her unorthodox methods—including singing, chanting, and lots of body movement—which seemed to capture the students' attention, make lessons memorable, and led to higher achievement.

Levin shared these new methods with his roommate, Feinberg. Both teachers also began visiting students in their homes, which strengthened relationships with their families and reinforced their high behavioral expectations. By the end of their first year, Levin and Feinberg

Exhibit 1 KIPP Houston 2013 Enrollment

Total	8584
Eligible for Free or Reduced-Price Meals	**7317**
American Indian/Alaskan	36
Asian	73
Black/African American	3083
Hispanic/Latino	5287
White	55
Hawaiian/Pacific Islander	2
Two or more	48
Limited English Proficiency	**2559**
Pre-Kindergarten	1247
Kindergarten	891
Grade 1	845
Grade 2	696
Grade 3	537
Grade 4	292
Grade 5	719
Grade 6	775
Grade 7	755
Grade 8	668
Grade 9	461
Grade 10	367
Grade 11	206
Grade 12	125
Male	4196
Female	4338

Source: Internal 2013 PEIMS reporting document used with permission.

were succeeding with their improved teaching and determination to reach students.

In their second year, Levin and Feinberg met another legendary teacher named Rafe Esquith. Esquith's inner-city Los Angeles fifth graders would arrive at school as early as 6:30 am and often stayed late into the evening. They performed complete Shakespeare plays, practiced problem-solving and mental math, learned to play musical instruments, and took field trips to Utah's national parks and Washington, D.C. The classroom operated a token economy in which students earned "money" through various efforts and achievements and could spend it on rewards and privileges.

In 1994, at the end of their two-year commitment to Teach for America, feeling confident in the classroom, getting excellent results, and inspired by Esquith's achievements, Levin and Feinberg decided to work together to start a new program for HISD fifth graders called the Knowledge Is Power Program, or KIPP.

After struggling to recruit students and maneuver through the school district bureaucracy to get the program off the ground, Levin and Feinberg launched KIPP, co-teaching about 50 students in one classroom. The students arrived by 7:30 a.m. and stayed until 5 p.m., came for weekend enrichment classes, and were required to attend summer classes. Using a mixture of Ball's engaging teaching practices, Esquith's high expectations and motivational techniques (including the chance to earn a field trip to Washington, D.C., at the end of the school year), a continual emphasis on college attendance, and their own personal innovations, the two teachers succeed in leading 90 percent of their students to pass the state's math and reading tests, after a fourth grade year in which about half had passed.

Nationwide Growth

With the success of KIPP's first year under his belt, Levin moved to New York, his home city, to start another Knowledge Is Power Program in the Bronx. Hoping to continue the gains the KIPP fifth graders had achieved, Levin and Feinberg also decided to expand both programs to become full middle schools, adding grades 6 through 8 as the students moved up through the grades. This expansion brought a new challenge of finding excellent teaching talent to maintain the high academic and behavioral expectations, but both Levin and Feinberg were able to lead their schools to results that far surpassed the neighboring public schools.

The success of the schools began to attract attention. Dozens of Teach for America teachers visited the schools to see the teachers and kids in action. The mayor of Houston and the HISD superintendent and future U.S. Secretary of Education, Rod Paige, dropped in. In the coming years, the two schools broke off from their school districts to become state-sanctioned charter schools, free from some of the constraints of operating in a school district bureaucracy.

In 1999, *60 Minutes* aired a 13-minute segment showcasing the success of the two KIPP middle schools. At the same time, Donald Fisher, who had co-founded the clothing retailer The Gap with his wife Doris, and his family were in the midst of a year-long search for an education-related philanthropic project. Fisher was impressed by what he saw on *60 Minutes* and donated $25 million to help found the KIPP Foundation, which was charged with training principals to start new KIPP schools that would replicate the success of the first two. "Fisher Fellowships" are still awarded each year to those who will train with the foundation before starting new schools.

In its original incarnation, the KIPP Foundation focused on finding the right high-caliber leaders and giving them free rein to start schools anywhere in the United States. In those first years, each individual KIPP school was governed by its own board of directors and operated completely autonomously. Around 2005, when Richard Barth became CEO of the KIPP Foundation, the strategy shifted to a regional model, where KIPP schools in the same city or geographical area were grouped together into regional networks. Today, there are 31 regional KIPP organizations in 20 states and the District of Columbia.

A Region Is Born

Houston got an early start in this regional reorganization effort, creating more middle schools and expanding into elementary and high schools, which made it possible for students to remain with KIPP from pre-kindergarten at age three until high school graduation.

After working for the new KIPP Foundation, Feinberg returned to Houston to serve as superintendent of the growing KIPP Houston district. Feinberg believed the traditional districts, such as the Houston Independent School District, would continue to underperform until they were directly challenged by a competitor capturing a larger share of student enrollment. Using the analogy of the U.S. Postal Service offering overnight mail service only after FedEx had captured a significant share of the market, Feinberg initiated an ambitious growth plan called "KIPP Turbo," which called for 42 KIPP schools in Houston by 2017.[5]

With the economic crisis of 2008, the Great Recession, and a subsequent $5.4 billion cut to education spending in 2011 by the Texas state legislature,[6] KIPP Turbo was scaled back. Instead of the original goal of 42 schools by 2017, KIPP Houston now plans to grow to 50 schools by 2033.[7] The budget shortfalls also led Feinberg to reconsider his role within the district. In 2011, Feinberg announced he would dedicate more of his time to fundraising and political advocacy, on behalf of both KIPP Houston and the KIPP network as a whole. Although he would still play a key role on KIPP Houston's board, Feinberg decided it was time to turn KIPP Houston over to a new leader.

In late 2011, Sehba Ali was announced as the sole finalist for the role of KIPP Houston superintendent, and in July of 2012 she took over the superintendency.[8]

Like Feinberg, Levin, and many other KIPP leaders, Ali started her education career with Teach for America. After her two-year commitment as an English teacher in a low-income Houston middle school, Ali taught for one year at another Houston charter outfit called YES Prep. She then attended Stanford, earning a master's degree in education in 2003. The KIPP Foundation awarded Ali the Fisher Fellowship, and in 2004 she founded KIPP Heartwood Academy, located in a low-income neighborhood near San Jose. The school went on to score among the highest 8 percent of schools in California on standardized achievement tests.[9] When hired, Ali was serving as the chief academic officer of the KIPP Bay Area region.

The "Target Market"

From its founding, KIPP has sought to serve students in high-minority, low-income communities. School leaders actively recruit students from Houston's low-rent apartment complexes and neighborhoods. Of KIPP Houston's roughly 8,500 students, 85 percent are low income (as measured by receiving federal free or reduced-price lunch assistance), 36 percent are African-American, and 62 percent are Latino. Thirty percent are classified as having limited English proficiency.[10]

The Gulfton neighborhood of Houston was among the first areas from which KIPP recruited students and is typical of the areas KIPP schools target. Many of its residents are immigrants, with 58 percent of residents born outside the United States. The median family income is $28,703, with more than half of children under 18 years old living below the poverty level. Of Gulfton residents aged 25 and older, 18 percent have attained a bachelor's degree or higher. Nearly half (47.1 percent) have not graduated from high school. By comparison, in the directly adjacent, affluent neighborhood of Bellaire, 77 percent of residents have attained a bachelor's degree or higher and less than three percent have not graduated high school. The median family income is $184,600; 4 percent of children under 18 live under the poverty level.[11]

Although a bachelor's degree is increasingly necessary to secure a middle-class income in the United States, the socioeconomic realities of KIPP's target neighborhoods can make the attainment of higher education a daunting challenge for students. Many parents have limited education and cannot help their children with homework, let alone navigate the process of preparing for and applying for college admittance. Parents often work in jobs that require long hours or irregular schedules, making it difficult to help their children or hold them accountable for completing school assignments.

Crime is significantly higher in the denser low-income neighborhoods, and some children have to cope with exposure to violence and gang activity. Houston has become an active hub for gangs, with a reported 29 percent increase in the gang presence from 2010 to 2012.[12] Gangs actively recruit young people in neighborhoods of high poverty, primarily in middle school but as early as elementary school, offering camaraderie and protection.[13]

Studies have also found that students from low-income families generally come to school less well-prepared to succeed academically. Due in part to differences in parenting patterns between high-income and low-income parents, poor children have significantly lower vocabularies than the children of the professional classes. Two researchers who observed and quantified the verbal interactions between high-socioeconomic and low-socioeconomic parents found that professional parents directed 2,153 words per hour at their children compared to parents on welfare assistance, who used 616. This substantial gap in exposure to language resulted in a comparable gap in vocabulary when children entered school. Tests of language skill at the ages of 9 and 10 showed the discrepancy persisted, affecting students' readiness for higher-level academic work.[14]

Despite the challenges facing families in poverty, many parents in the target neighborhoods are eager to seize the opportunity KIPP offers to give their children a good education. In a typical recruitment visit, a KIPP teacher will sit in the home of a prospective student and explain exactly what the school requires of parents, students, and teachers. After answering questions, the teacher will ask the parents and student if they are willing to make these promises. If they answer in the affirmative, the student, parents, and teacher will sign the "Commitment to Excellence." The teacher usually takes a photo of the new KIPPster holding a KIPP sign to celebrate his or her decision.

The number of students desiring to "Commit to Excellence" at a KIPP school exceeds the network's current capacity. From those who sign up, KIPP Houston decides which students to enroll through a lottery. The only students not subject to this random selection are those who have siblings who attended or currently attend a KIPP Houston school. Students who are not selected in the lottery are placed on a waiting list. According to KIPP

Houston, there are currently over 8,000 students on the waiting list.[15]

Rules of the Game

Efforts to grow the network to meet excess demand have to meet the regulatory constraints that govern charter schools. The law allowing charter schools in Texas was passed by the state legislature in 1995 and was designed to increase the level of choice for students and teachers, as well as improve student learning by encouraging innovation and performance accountability. The law lays out areas in which charter schools have flexibility and areas in which they must meet the same requirements as other public schools.[16, 17]

Staffing

- Not required to hire certified teachers. The minimum requirement to teach is a high school diploma. In practice, in order to qualify for federal funding, charter schools do require "highly qualified" status (a bachelor's degree and demonstrated competency in the area they teach) for teachers of core academic subjects. These qualifications are still less onerous to obtain than formal state certification.
- Not required to have any minimum qualifications for principals or superintendents
- Not required to establish written employment contracts with teachers
- Not required to follow the minimum salary schedules laid out in the Texas Education Code.

Curriculum and Operations

- Required to teach the learning standards set out in Texas law
- Required to follow regulations in relation to special education, bilingual education, and certain reading instructional programs
- Required to follow graduation standards set out in Texas law
- Required to administer the same yearly achievement tests as other public schools
- Required to follow the same rules for student discipline given in state law
- Required to report daily attendance to the state for the sake of computing average daily attendance (ADA), which determines funding levels
- Required to instruct students for at least four hours during a day in which students are counted for ADA purposes, but are not required to instruct students for at least seven hours like other public schools

- Not required to provide 180 days of instruction as are other public schools (though funding levels depend on days of instruction)
- Not required to follow limitations on student-teacher ratios and class sizes.[18]

The Money Gap

Despite the increased flexibility afforded to charter schools by the state code, KIPP Houston faces other obstacles arising from the way public money is disbursed to schools.

Public schools in the United States are primarily funded through a mix of local, state, and federal sources. Nationally, federal funding accounts for 10 percent of revenues, with the remaining 90 percent coming from a mix of local and state sources.[19] In Texas, most of this money is raised from local property taxes, which can be levied by school districts. Districts use two kinds of property tax: maintenance and operations, or M&O, which is used for staffing and operating costs, and interest and sinking, or I&S, which is used to service debt from bonds issued for facility construction or renovation. These tax revenues, however, are subject to reallocation by the state based on several criteria.

The state determines district M&O funding using formulas that essentially serve three purposes:

- Base funding on actual student attendance. Districts are required to submit attendance reports that are used to calculate the district's ADA, a key input in the funding formula.
- Even out spending across rich and poor districts. A portion of the tax revenue from wealthy districts is reallocated to other districts.
- Weight funding based on how many students in the district have special needs, like special education, bilingual education, and gifted and talented education.

Charter schools, however, do not have taxing authority. Instead of M&O taxes, they depend solely on state reallocations of tax revenues. In the 2010–11 school year, for each student reported as enrolled, they received $7,945.46 in the form of this allocation, which was 77 percent of their government funding.[20, 21] Other state and federal grants amounted to a total of $13,905,811, which yields a total government contribution of $10,269 per enrolled student. (For KIPP Houston's most recent Statement of Financial Position, see Exhibit 2. For a breakdown of government revenues, see Exhibit 3.)

Beyond this funding for operational expenses, charter districts are entitled to none of the revenue from I&S

Exhibit 2 KIPP, Inc. Statements of Financial Position as of June 30, 2012 and 2011

	2012	2011
ASSETS		
Cash and cash equivalents (*Note 2*)	$7,690,223	$12,655,763
Receivables:		
Government agencies	14,688,117	11,556,734
Pledges, net (*Note 3*)	1,504,302	1,692,472
Other	1,032,677	170,908
Prepaid expenses	497,794	551,320
Investments in certificates of deposit	300,000	300,000
Capitalized bond issuance costs	3,205,296	3,322,465
Bond proceeds held in trust (*Note 5*)	12,731,572	21,531,419
Property and equipment, net (*Note 4*)	121,856,439	111,214,248
TOTAL ASSETS	$163,506,420	$162,995,329
LIABILITIES AND NET ASSETS		
Liabilities:		
Accounts payable and accrued expenses	$4,426,361	$2,665,970
Accrued payroll expenses	6,864,303	6,814,000
Due to PHILO Finance Corporation	170,310	2,664,143
Construction payable	1,514,245	4,026,309
Accrued interest	2,607,129	2,629,158
Refundable advances	101,656	75,185
Bonds and notes payable (*Notes 5 and 10*)	125,787,976	125,697,730
Total liabilities	141,471,980	144,572,495
Commitments (*Note 12*)		
Net assets (*Note 8*):		
Unrestricted	17,467,175	14,224,473
Temporarily restricted (*Note 7*)	4,377,265	4,008,361
Permanently restricted for scholarships	190,000	190,000
Total net assets	22,034,440	18,422,834
TOTAL LIABILITIES AND NET ASSETS	$163,506,420	$162,995,329

Source: Financial Statements and Independent Auditors' Report. KIPP, Inc., October 16, 2012. Accessed April 21, 2013. http://kipphouston.org/sites/default/files/file_attach/KHPS_Audit_Report_for_the_Year_Ended_June_30_2012.pdf.

Exhibit 3 2010–2011 Financial Statement – Note on Government Grants

NOTE 9 - GOVERNMENT GRANTS
KIPP is the recipient of government grants from various federal, state and local agencies. Government grants include the following:

	2011	2010
State grants:		
Texas Education Agency Foundation School Program Act	$47,561,540	$37,398,934
Pre-K Expansion Grant	674,260	661,036
Technology Allotment	162,459	127,801
Texas Science, Technology, Engineering, and Math Initiative	160,734	378,097
Intensive Summer Programs	144,770	159,233
Teacher Excellence Awards	117,891	168,164
Above and Beyond Grant	51,001	
SSI Intensive Math Initiative	47,042	96,953
FSP Investment Capital Fund	23,475	52,107
School Lunch Matching	19,469	15,288
Texas Fitness Now	10,297	26,309
APIB Technical Training	3,600	
21st Century Community Learning Centers		194,692
Texas Education Excellence Grant		122,863
Governor's Educator Excellence		21,146
KIPP Coastal Village		11,000
Grants for Student Clubs		7,345
Total state grants	48,976,538	39,440,968
Federal grants:		
U.S. Department of Education	8,267,172	5,389,299
U.S. Department of Agriculture	4,223,641	3,170,398
Total federal grants	12,490,813	8,559,697
Total government grants	$61,467,351	$48,000,665

Source: Financial Statements and Independent Auditors' Report. 2011 Audit Report. KIPP, Inc., October 27, 2011. Accessed April 21, 2013. http://kipphouston.org/sites/default/files/file_attach/KHPS_Audit_Report_for_the_Year_Ended_June_30_2011.pdf.

taxes, which means they receive no state funding for facilities.[22]

KIPP Houston CFO John Murphy says the lack of funding for facilities is without a doubt the biggest financial challenge the district faces.[23] One independent study found that primarily due to this facilities funding discrepancy, in the 2009–10 school year, KIPP Houston received from government sources $966 per pupil less than Houston Independent School District.[24] At KIPP Houston's current enrollment level, that amounts to $8,292,144 per year.

KIPP Houston made up for the deficit through both fundraising and frugality with facilities. Many KIPP Houston schools are housed in low-cost modular buildings, and some have relatively little land and green space compared to other public schools. The facilities KIPP Houston has acquired have come primarily through philanthropy. In the fundraising drive to finance the KIPP Turbo expansion, individuals and foundations committed well over $40 million to KIPP Houston.[25] The KIPP Houston board of directors generally transfers these funds to the PHILO Finance Corporation, an independent nonprofit 501(c)(3), which helps charter schools secure financing by guaranteeing bond issues and issuing grants to repay debt. In 2012, KIPP Houston's total liability for bonds and notes payable was $125,787,976, with most bonds bearing interest rates between 4 and 6.4 percent.[26]

Not surprisingly, KIPP Houston's biggest expense is instruction-related costs, which, over the span of 2008 to 2010, made up about 42 percent of per pupil expenditures.[27] Of this share, the vast majority goes toward teacher salaries. In 2012, the average KIPP Houston teacher earned a salary of $46,883.[28] The next highest cost is school and district administration, which represents 23 percent of per pupil expenditures (2008–10). The district spends about 15 percent on student services (e.g., food services, transportation, and counseling), 9 percent on facilities maintenance and security, and 5 percent on facilities debt service. (For KIPP Houston cost allocations compared to Houston ISD and YES Prep, see Exhibit 4. For the KIPP Houston 2013 expected budget, see Exhibit 5.)

Organization: Bottom Up and Top Down

At the core of KIPP Houston's operations are its teachers. A typical KIPP Houston instructor teaches a single subject in a single grade level of 85 to 110 students. Most schools employ one of the grade-level teachers to be a grade-level chair, leading the culture (behavioral norms)

Exhibit 4 Percentage of Expenditures Per Pupil (ADA), 2007–2010

Cost	Houston ISD	KIPP Houston[1]	YES Prep
Instruction	54.62%	42.31%	53.50%
Administration (Central and School)	10.24%	23.30%	18.49%
Student Services	7.07%	14.99%	14.27%
Plant Maintenance and Security	9.78%	9.88%	10.98%
Facilities and Debt Service	16.05%	5.47%	0.49%
Other	2.22%	4.04%	2.27%

[1] Due to accounting anomalies in 2007–08, KIPP Houston numbers are an average of 2008–09 and 2009–10.

Source: Analysis of McGee, Josh B. "Houston School Finance Report." Arnoldfoundation.org. Laura and John Arnold Foundation, January 18, 2013. Accessed April 20, 2013. www.arnoldfoundation.org/resources/houston-school-finance-report.

Exhibit 5 KIPP, Inc. Consolidated District Final Budget For the Year Ended June 30, 2013

Other Revenues from Local Sources	$9,635,525
State Program Revenues	60,998,666
Federal Revenues	11,149,111
Total Revenue	$81,783,302
Basic Instruction	$33,724,037
Instructional Resources and Media Services	62,510
Curriculum Development and Instructional Staff Development	859,936
Instructional Leadership	1,707,373
School Leadership	9,580,515
Guidance, Counseling & Evaluation Services	2,853,292
Social Work Services	637,097
Health Services	366,415
Student Transportation	4,624,577
Food Services	5,379,537
Extracurricular Activities	728,194
General Administration	6,976,854
Plant Maintenance and Operations	9,880,396
Security & Monitoring Services	1,121,375
Data Processing Services	2,794,611
Community Service	537,479
Debt Service	7,144,023
Fundraising	1,632,532
Total Expenses	$90,610,756
Net Contribution	−$8,827,454

Source: Consolidated District Final Budget. KIPP Houston Public Schools, n.d. Accessed April 21, 2013. http://kipphouston.org/sites/default/files/file_attach/FY13_Functional_Budget_121114.pdf.

and coordinating activities within the grade level in addition to their teaching duties. Some teachers are also given department chair responsibilities, which involves aligning the curriculum and instruction for one content area across the different grade levels.

Given the Power to Lead principle, much of the job descriptions of teachers, how they are trained, and the ongoing professional development they receive is determined at the school level by the principal, who is responsible for the safety and academic performance of the school. Principals have wide discretion in resource allocation, including personnel decisions (teachers are "at-will" employees). This autonomy leads to differences in school organization within KIPP Houston, and the delegation of a school's administrative responsibilities can vary from school to school. Some principals hire a Dean of Students, who heads up student culture and discipline, and a Dean of Instruction, who is responsible primarily for the professional development of teachers. Other principals hire assistant principals, whose job descriptions combine Dean of Student and Dean of Instruction roles but who might be assigned specific grade levels to manage.

The principal reports to a Head of Schools at KIPP Houston's regional office. According to Head of Schools Ken Goedekke, these four heads report to Superintendent Ali and manage a "feeder pattern," which, when fully built out, consists of two elementary schools, two middle schools, and the one high school they feed into. In the last two years, heads of schools have also been in charge of spearheading curriculum alignment, which is the process of ensuring that similar academic standards and performance benchmarks are being used across the region. Curriculum alignment has long been on the radar at KIPP Houston but it has received more emphasis and resources since 2011. Next year, the curriculum alignment responsibilities will be managed by a separate head of schools with the other heads focusing on managing their feeder patterns.[29]

In addition to the line of direct reporting from schools, Ali manages a central office that includes managers of bus transportation, food services, and facilities; HR and finance professionals; and curriculum and student-support specialists. One of Ali's first acts as superintendent was to change the name of this central office from KIPP Inc. to the Regional Services Team (RST) to reflect its role as a support center for the region's campuses.

According to Goedekke, who manages a feeder pattern in Southwest Houston, there has been something of a shift in organizational expectations in the last two or three years. In 2010, most schools were still led by their founding principal. These principals had been given wide latitude to create a school according to the unique visions they had developed during the Fisher Fellowship year. Principals expected to be regionally supported in logistics, such as facilities maintenance, food, and transportation, but did not expect to have curriculum and instructional decisions made at the region level.

"They were given the reins to build a school, and they did," Goedekke says. But in 2013, only one original school founder remains in the principal role, and the new crop of principals expects more regional alignment to take place.[30]

"The new school leaders have seen the benefits of alignment. They asked, 'Why are ten fifth grade math teachers all writing their own lesson plans?' Organizationally, we needed to do something different."[31]

Goedekke says that schools that get excellent results on assessments of student academic progress continue to get wide latitude to make site-based decisions.[32]

Not all schools are performing up to KIPP's high standards. One measure of school performance is the annual state achievement tests that the Texas Education Agency uses to give an "accountability rating" to each school. The ratings measure the percentage of students who meet minimum requirements and are (from highest to lowest): Exemplary, Recognized, Acceptable, and Unacceptable. In the 2010–11 school year (the last year for which ratings are available), of the 10 KIPP Houston middle and high schools that received ratings, two were Exemplary, four were Recognized, three were Acceptable, and one was Unacceptable. By comparison, another Houston charter school network, YES Prep, achieved an Exemplary rating for six of its seven schools, the other school receiving Recognized status.[33]

How does the Power to Lead principle fit with these discrepancies? Goedekke says that for schools not performing well, district leadership needs to delicately intervene by, for example, suggesting exemplary lesson plans that struggling teachers can use.[34]

Sehba Ali believes that the Power to Lead allows for a more entrepreneurial and creative spirit in KIPP schools and can lead to innovation. She does not believe schools should simply try to replicate best practices.

"School leaders have a responsibility to be creative and innovate. We can't just say, 'You're a replication school,'" Ali says. She cites the example of KIPP Courage, a recently founded school that is getting good results using more technology in instruction. Some of their new practices will be adopted by an older, exemplary-rated KIPP school. She believes that when school leaders see compelling evidence of an effective practice, they will make the decision to adopt it without the need for top-down management.

The People Problem

Another of Ali's initiatives as superintendent was to clarify KIPP Houston's niche in the national KIPP landscape. According to Chief People Officer Chuck Fimble (responsible for HR and recruiting), in an early leadership meeting, Ali pointed out that many KIPP regions have a unique emphasis or identity. Some are known for their instructional expertise; others for their academic alignment.

"What is our regional identity?" she asked.

"We couldn't come up anything other than being first and being big," Fimble says.[35]

The answer that was agreed to was that KIPP Houston would become a first-class leadership development organization. This emphasis on leadership development would be important not just for KIPP Houston's identity but, more essentially, for its successful expansion.

Although the brakes were put on KIPP Turbo partly due to the economic downturn, another critical bottleneck was in human capital.

"We're pretty convinced we can find the money and schools [to grow]. The problem is finding the people," Fimble notes.[36]

Ali agrees: "KIPP Turbo assumed an incredible bench depth of talent. It takes more to develop leadership than we thought… [Between funding shortages and the need for talent,] talent is the bigger barrier."[37]

Even though KIPP Turbo has been scaled back, it will still require a large infusion of talent, both in leadership and teaching. Based on growth projections, over the course of the next five school years, KIPP Houston will need to hire about 1,300 new teachers (see Exhibit 6).[38]

Nationally, 32 percent of KIPP teachers are alumni of Teach for America,[39] the same route through which Feinberg and Ali came to the profession, and KIPP Houston depends heavily on former TFA corps members. Other teachers are recruited from the Houston and other surrounding Independent School Districts, some go through Alternative Certification Programs (which are abbreviated routes to certification), and some come to KIPP straight from college education programs.

Whatever their pathway into teaching, all KIPP teachers sign the Commitment to Excellence, which lays out the responsibilities of being a teacher at KIPP:

- We will always teach the best way we know how and do whatever it takes for our students to learn.
- We will always make ourselves available to students and parents for any concerns they might have. [All teachers are issued a cell phone, which students can call in the evenings for help with homework.]
- We will arrive at KIPP by 7:15 a.m. on Monday through Friday.
- We will remain at KIPP until 5:15 p.m. on Monday through Thursday and 4:00 p.m. on Friday.
- We will teach at KIPP during summer school… [2 weeks.][40]

In addition to the 10-hour daily commitment, most teachers work additional hours in the evening and on the weekends to plan lessons and assess student work.

A second-year KIPP teacher reflecting on her first-year reports, "It was difficult. I think the Power to Lead principle trickles down to teachers, too, so you have to find and do everything on your own, especially because as a region our curriculum wasn't aligned. Even if I tried to get help from other teachers, they would be teaching other things, so I couldn't use their resources."[41]

As a second-year teacher, she says things became easier. "I work from 7:00 a.m. to 6:00 p.m., plus about ten hours on the weekend, so about 65 hours per week. It's easier now that I have my curriculum from last year."[42]

Although the challenge of the work and KIPP Houston's social mission are both appealing to many

Exhibit 6 Projected KHPS Instructional Staff Hiring Needs

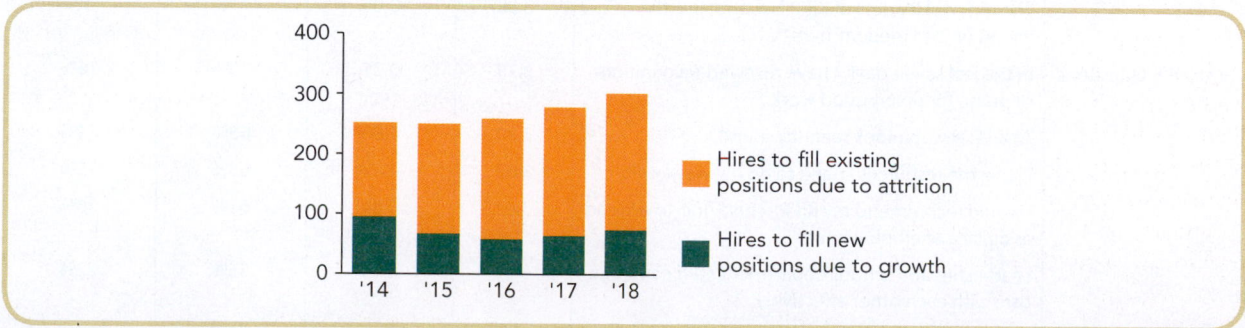

Legend:
- Hires to fill existing positions due to attrition
- Hires to fill new positions due to growth

Source: Internal document used with permission.

young teachers, the heavy workload may be partly responsible for lower-than-average teacher retention rates. In the 2011–12 school year, KIPP Houston had a teacher retention rate of 58 percent, compared with 68 percent for YES Prep charter schools, and 83 percent for Houston Independent School District.[43] Over a longer time span, KIPP Houston reports a 72 percent retention rate, which is 6 percent below what charter management organizations nationally are getting.[44] The high turnover and dependence on Teach for America alumni give KIPP Houston a young teaching force, with a 2012 average of 3.8 years of experience, compared to a statewide average of 11.6 years.[45]

To help the organization better gauge job satisfaction and employee attitudes, KIPP Houston is using a "pulse survey," which KIPP Houston staff respond to twice annually. Many of the responses show high employee commitment. The three statements that employees most strongly agree with are "My team is committed to doing quality work," "The mission of KIPP makes me feel my job is important," and "I know what is expected of me at KIPP." The three statements that get the lowest scores are, "I would recommend my KIPP school/Inc. to a friend as a place of employment," "Leadership and school/department staff communicate with each other effectively," and "I plan to work at KIPP for at least three more years."[46] (See Exhibit 7 for pulse survey results.)

One way KIPP Houston hopes to engender longer-term commitments is through offering pathways to

Exhibit 7

1. Region Snapshot		Current Avt.	Change Year Over Year	Top % (Agree & Strongly Agree)	Bottom % (Disagree & Strongly Disagree)
Updated on Feb 2013. Current through next reporting date of June 2013.					
Top 6 Questions	My team is committed to doing quality work.	4.27	−0.04	88%	3%
	The mission of KIPP makes me feel my job is important.	4.25	−0.07	88%	3%
	I know what is expected of me at KIPP.	4.21	0.06	90%	2%
	I have a trusted, personal friend at KIPP.	4.17	0.07	81%	6%
	My school leader/manager cares about me as a person.	4.16	0.03	83%	6%
	In the last six months my supervisor talked to me about my progress.	4.14	0.10	84%	7%
	There is someone at KIPP who encourages my development.	4.11	0.01	83%	7%
	I have opportunities at KIPP to learn and grow.	4.01	−0.01	78%	9%
	The leaders of my school/department live the values of the Freedom Tree.	3.96	0.03	76%	7%
	At work I have the opportunity to do what I do best every day.	3.89	0.00	75%	10%
	My colleagues live the values of the Freedom Tree.	3.89	0.05	73%	6%
Bottom 6 Questions	The regional leaders of KIPP Houston live the values of the Freedom Tree.	3.88	0.05	71%	5%
	In the last seven days, I have received recognition or praise for doing good work.	3.79	0.01	70%	16%
	At KIPP, my opinions seem to count.	3.70	0.00	66%	14%
	I have the resources I need to do my work well.	3.69	−0.01	68%	15%
	I would recommend my KIPP school/Inc. to a friend as a place of employment.	3.63	0.04	61%	16%
	Leadership and school/department staff communicate with each other effectively.	3.43	0.11	56%	22%
	I plan to work at KIPP for at least three more years.	3.38	0.07	49%	21%

Source: Internal document used with permission.

leadership. In addition to the Fisher Fellowship, KIPP Houston encourages talented teachers to apply for the Miles Fellowship, which is a two-year path to becoming a school founder, the first year spent as a resident leader in an established KIPP school and the second year as a Fisher Fellow (if accepted). Teachers can also remain in the classroom and attend KIPP Foundation—sponsored leadership programs for grade-level chairs and department chairs. In addition, KIPP Houston offers its own leadership classes from central office leaders, which take place after work hours.

Teachers who seek leadership positions are also signing up for a demanding role but one that comes with excellent support and the opportunity for high impact. One former Fisher Fellow who founded a higher-performing KIPP school reports that the Fellowship year prepared him well.

"The Fellowship was extremely flexible. I identified that I needed to learn Spanish, so they sent me to Mexico for a few weeks to learn it. There were a lot of things that I was able to work on—from a framework for evaluating teachers to mapping out curriculum—that set me up for a solid start."[47]

He explained that KIPP Houston was also a good place to found a school because of all the back office logistical support (e.g., in transportation, food services, and facilities) that allowed him to focus on curriculum and instruction.

With the support also came a lot of responsibility: "The workload was fairly intense—an average of eighty hours a week, with some times of the year approaching one hundred and others bottoming out at fifty….I think most school leaders leave because of burn out."[48]

No comprehensive research has been done on the employee attrition problem, so the issue of long hours is just one of many guesses concerning what is driving turnover. KIPP Houston plans to put together a committee to study the issue in the upcoming year.[49]

With the current KIPP Houston expansion plans, the region will need to fill about 40 new administrative positions in five years, but Fimble worries that KIPP Houston has lost its recruiting edge: "The talent exists. The number of teachers and leaders exists in the city as a whole. The problem is getting them to want to come to KIPP. What is our niche in the recruiting war? We used to be new, more entrepreneurial, and have better pay. Now we're not new, not as entrepreneurial, and the pay isn't much better, especially when looked at from a dollar-per-hour-worked perspective."[50]

To fill teaching roles for the upcoming school year the recruitment office has started new initiatives, including a social media campaign, billboards on Houston's highly trafficked freeways, recruitment events around the city, and the offer of a $1,000 referral bonus for anyone who successfully recruits someone to fill an instructional position.[51]

The Curriculum Conundrum

At the heart of the work KIPP Houston does is the curriculum: the learning standards that students are expected to master. In Texas, the elected, 15-member State Board of Education approves the curriculum for each subject in each grade level and schools are required by law to teach it.[52]

However, this process is not straightforward. There are so many learning standards—and many of them are so broad—that teachers have significant flexibility to decide what and how they teach, and most teachers believe it is not possible to teach all of them with any kind of depth and student understanding.

Sixth-grade social studies standard 6.2.B, for example, states that for the subject of history students should "evaluate the social, political, economic, and cultural contributions of individuals and groups from various societies, past and present."[53] One teacher may believe that learning about the Silk Road from China to Europe would be an excellent way to achieve this goal while another may teach it by studying the influence of the Aztec culture on modern Mexico.

This inherent flexibility has led to wide variations in curriculum, even among instructors teaching the same grade level and subject. For example, some KIPP schools used to focus on one section of the science standards each year to create an emphasis on earth science one year and life science the next, etc.; while other schools rotate through all areas of science every year.

In subjects and years that have state achievement tests, there tends to be less variation in curriculum because teachers generally align their classroom goals with the material that appears on the standardized assessment. To help schools and teachers more closely align their curricula and assess student learning, in the 2011–12 school year, KIPP Houston began writing and administering its own Common Assessments. These tests would be administered three times per year in each core academic subject. The effort has been led by both Heads of Schools and "Teacher Leaders" from each grade level and subject. Most subjects now have Common Assessments while other are yet to be developed.

To further complicate the curriculum puzzle, Texas is among the five states in the country that have chosen not to adopt a set of national standards called the

Common Core.[54] The Common Core was developed as a cooperative effort by state governments seeking to clarify and benchmark national learning standards. While education leaders in Texas are free to ignore the Common Core, a study of nationwide state standards showed that what Texas considers "proficient" was the lowest in the nation and well below what national tests deem proficient.[55] While newer versions of the state achievement test are thought to be more rigorous, a school district that ignores the Common Core may risk failing to prepare its students to compete in the national market for college admittance.

"The Common Core standards are really good for preparing kids for college," Sehba Ali says. "We'll find the overlaps. We'll find the holes. We'll align to the Common Core and the TEKS [Texas learning standards]."[56]

One tool that many teachers have used to develop and share curriculum materials is BetterLesson. Adopted by KIPP schools nationwide in the 2010–11 school year, BetterLesson is a Web-based curriculum document storage and retrieval tool developed by a young Boston-based company.[57] Teachers can use the Web site to search for, download, and upload lesson plans, worksheets, PowerPoint presentations, and other curriculum materials. It connects KIPP educators across the country with each other and with teachers from other high-performing schools. With most teachers nationally aligning solely to the Common Core, however, KIPP Houston teachers may have less opportunity to leverage BetterLesson.

The Promise of Technology

Some see Web applications like BetterLesson as the tip of the iceberg when it comes to using information technology (IT) to improve school performance.

Harvard business professor Clayton Christensen predicts that digital learning will be a "disruptive innovation" that revolutionizes education in the coming decade.[58] Proponents of digital learning technologies herald its ability to give students immediate feedback and individualized learning experiences. Some Learning Management Systems (LMS) allow teachers to manage student assignments and track performance on one digital hub, cutting down on routine paper management and data analysis tasks.

Many teachers and schools are experimenting with various combinations of traditional and digital learning. These "blended learning" models can range from classrooms in which students rotate between computers, small group instruction, and independent work, to schools in which students self-manage larger blocks of time for online learning. KIPP first entered the world of blended learning in 2010, with the opening of KIPP Empower Academy in Los Angeles. KIPP Empower, an elementary school that will serve grades K–4 at full enrollment, uses a rotational blended learning model as a way to give students a highly personalized education with a small-group classroom feel.

Inspired by the success of KIPP Empower, educators in other KIPP regions, including KIPP Houston, have begun implementing elements of blended learning. For example, KIPP Courage, founded in Houston in summer 2012, incorporates blended learning in most of its classrooms. In addition to a computer lab where students use software to learn either Spanish or English or engage in individualized math practice problems, almost every classroom has a set of inexpensive netbooks, which students use to do research or access online learning activities. The principal, Eric Schmidt, says he combined the digital learning with practices he picked up from other KIPP schools during his Fisher Fellowship.[59]

Although it is a young experiment, Schmidt says it has helped a high percentage of their students reach their learning goals (see Exhibit 8). "One of the unintended consequences of this model has been our flexibility with human capital," Schmidt says. "We had two teachers call in sick unexpectedly, but we didn't have to request any substitute teachers because teachers or administrators who had planning times could cover the computer lab and still get their work done."[60]

Schmidt says the next step, which he hopes to accomplish before next school year, is to find an online Learning Management System to tie the disparate pieces of digital learning together into one system.

Matt Bradford, the Director of Knowledge Management, works within the IT department for KIPP Houston. Bradford and others in his department help support the back-end management of KIPP Houston IT initiatives; for example, by ensuring that the district's digital student rosters can interface with the various online programs. He sees potential in using IT resources to track student learning but says the big issues are which platform to use and standardization.[61]

"There's a lot of piloting of projects around the district without consistency from school to school. Schools might not agree to use similar systems, which makes it difficult to support," Bradford says.[62] Sehba Ali believes the focus needs to remain on recruiting and developing excellent teachers, noting, "I come from the Bay Area, where the word on the street is that we will put a lot of computers in classrooms and that will solve all our problems. But technology is only good in the hands of

Exhibit 8 Promotional Flyer for the KIPP Courage Blended Learning Model and Initial Results

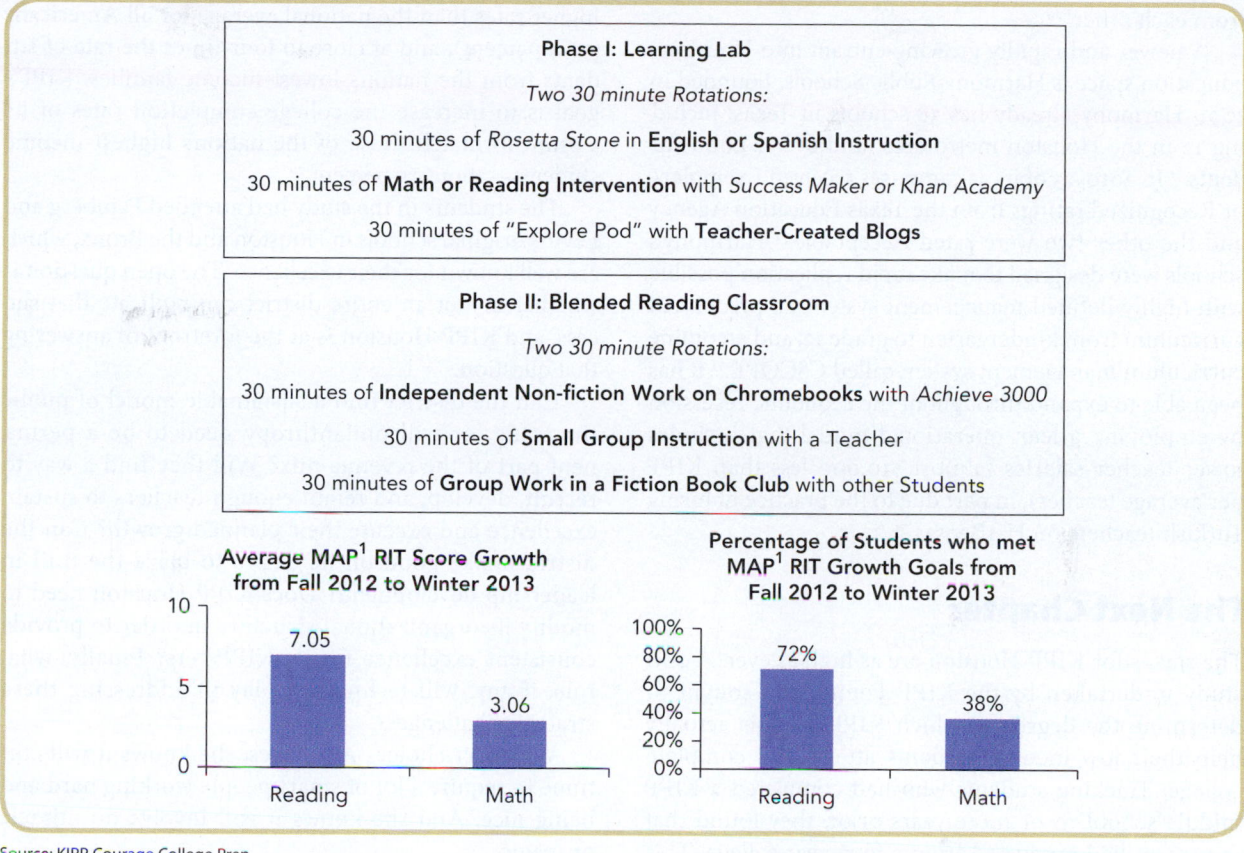

Phase I: Learning Lab

Two 30 minute Rotations:

30 minutes of *Rosetta Stone* in **English or Spanish Instruction**

30 minutes of **Math or Reading Intervention** with *Success Maker or Khan Academy*

30 minutes of "Explore Pod" with **Teacher-Created Blogs**

Phase II: Blended Reading Classroom

Two 30 minute Rotations:

30 minutes of **Independent Non-fiction Work on Chromebooks** with *Achieve 3000*

30 minutes of **Small Group Instruction** with a Teacher

30 minutes of **Group Work in a Fiction Book Club** with other Students

Average MAP[1] RIT Score Growth from Fall 2012 to Winter 2013

Reading 7.05 — Math 3.06

Percentage of Students who met MAP[1] RIT Growth Goals from Fall 2012 to Winter 2013

Reading 72% — Math 38%

Source: KIPP Courage College Prep

great teachers." On the other hand, Ali sees potential for technology to enhance teacher effectiveness by, for example, providing minute-to-minute student performance data. This might indirectly alleviate the retention problem because "teachers who feel good about what they're doing in their classrooms tend to stay."[63]

Competitive Pressures

While KIPP Houston might have been the trailblazer in effective models of public schooling for low-income students, the competition is not sitting on its hands.

The Houston Independent School District has responded to the success of charter schools by attempting to replicate their most effective practices, including a longer school day, a college-bound culture, and one-on-two tutoring, in some of its underperforming schools. The program, called Apollo 20, was launched in the 2010–11 school year.[64] After its first year, HISD reported math "gains [similar] to those seen in charter schools," especially in grades six and nine, in which students had received one-on-two tutoring,[65, 66] HISD has not been

able to fund the program through its regular operating revenues, however, and has depended on philanthropic gifts for funding.[67]

YES Prep, the charter network with consistent "Exemplary" ratings, was founded in 1995 (the same year KIPP established its charter) by another TFA alum and friend of Michael Feinberg.[68] It has long been a friendly competitor but has had a slower growth trajectory and a different management philosophy. From the beginning, YES Prep's focus was less on leadership and more on defining curriculum and teacher expectations. New schools were opened by veteran leaders working side-by-side with less experienced leaders.[69] YES Prep schools aligned assessments of student learning years before KIPP, and they now use a common framework for evaluating, promoting, and compensating teachers.

Sehba Ali feels that KIPP Houston and YES Prep fill different niches in the education landscape:

"We're different. What we bring is innovation and creativity and autonomy for our leaders and teachers. There are people who are better suited for KIPP and people who are better suited for YES, but we have a lot to learn from each other."[70]

A newer and rapidly growing entrant into Houston's education space is Harmony Public Schools. Founded in 2001, Harmony already has 38 schools in Texas, including 12 in the Houston metro area, and over 24,000 students.[71] In 2010, 23 of its 25 campuses received Exemplary or Recognized ratings from the Texas Education Agency and the other two were rated Acceptable.[72] Harmony's schools were designed to make rapid replication possible, with highly defined management systems, a predefined curriculum from kindergarten to grade 12, and an online curriculum management system called CSCOPE.[73] It has been able to expand throughout the economic recession by employing a lean operational model that includes lower teacher salaries (almost $10,000 less than KIPP per average teacher), in part due to the practice of hiring Turkish teachers on H-1B visas.[74, 75]

The Next Chapter

The stakes for KIPP Houston are as high as ever. A 2011 study undertaken by the KIPP Foundation sought to determine the degree to which KIPP schools actually help their low-income students attend and complete college. Tracking students who had completed a KIPP middle school 10 or more years prior, they found that 33 percent had graduated from a four-year college. This means that KIPP's alumni are graduating from college at higher rates than the national average for all Americans (30.4 percent), and at close to four times the rate of students from the nation's lowest-income families. KIPP's goal is to increase the college completion rates of its alumni to match those of the nation's highest-income students—about 75 percent.[76]

The students in the study had attended Feinberg and Levin's original schools in Houston and the Bronx, which are well known for their excellence. The open question is whether or not an entire district can replicate that success, and KIPP Houston is at the forefront of answering that question.

Can the district find a sustainable model of public financing, or will philanthropy need to be a permanent part of the revenue mix? Will they find a way to recruit, develop, and retain enough teachers to sustain excellence and execute their planned growth? Can the district make good on its desire to blaze the trail in leadership development? Does KIPP Houston need to modify its organizational structure in order to provide consistent excellence for its KIPPsters? Finally, what role, if any, will technology play in addressing these strategic challenges?

Whatever choices Ali makes, she knows it will continue to require a lot of smart people working hard and being nice. And she knows it will involve no miracle or magic.

NOTES

1. Ali, Sehba. Personal interview. March 29, 2013.
2. "Five Pillars." *KIPP Public Charter Schools*. KIPP Foundation, n.d. Accessed April 21, 2013. www.kipp.org/our-approach/five-pillars.
3. "KIPP Houston Public Schools." KIPP Houston Public Schools, n.d. Accessed May 1, 2013. http://kipphouston.org.
4. This and the remainder this section and the next is drawn from Mathews, Jay. *Work Hard. Be Nice: How Two Inspired Teachers Created the Most Promising Schools in America*. Chapel Hill, NC: Algonquin of Chapel Hill, 2009.
5. Mathews, Jay. "Growing Up Fast." *Philanthropy* 2008. *Philanthropy roundtable.org*. Accessed April 17, 2013. www.philanthropyroundtable.org/topic/k_12_education/growing_up_fast.
6. Fernandez, Manny. "At Texas Schools, Making Do on a Shoestring." *New York Times*. April 9, 2012. Accessed April 17, 2013. www.nytimes.com/2012/04/09/us/for-texas-schools-a-year-of-doing-without.html?pagewanted=all.
7. Fimble, Chuck. Personal interview. March 29, 2013.
8. KIPP Houston Public Schools. *New Superintendent: Sehba Ali. KIPP Houston Public Schools*. July 2012. Accessed April 17, 2013. http://kipphouston.org/node/227.
9. *KIPPBayArea.org*. KIPP Bay Area Schools, n.d. Accessed April 17, 2013. www.kippbayarea.org/schools/heartwood.
10. KIPP Houston data reported to the Texas Public Education Information Management System (PEIMS). January 15, 2013.
11. Based on 2010 United States Census. ZIP Codes 77081 and 77401. Incomes are in 2011 inflation-adjusted dollars. *American FactFinder*. United States Census Bureau, n.d. Accessed 19 Apr. 2013. http://factfinder2.census.gov/faces/nav/jsf/pages/index.xhtml.
12. Pinkerton, James. "Gangs on Rise, but Idea to Fight Them Raises Eyebrows." Chron.com. *Houston Chronicle*, November 1, 2012. Accessed April 19, 2013. www.chron.com/news/houston-texas/houston/article/Solutions-differ-in-fight-to-curb-increasing-gang-4001924.php>.
13. "Information for Parents, Educators and Community Residents." *Stop Houston Gangs – Report Gang Crime Tips & Violence – Texas Gangs*. Stop Houston Gangs Task Force, n.d. Accessed April 19, 2013. www.stophoustongangs.org/default.aspx?act=frontpage.aspx.
14. Hart, Betty, and Risley, Todd R. "The Early Catastrophe: The 30 Million Word Gap by Age 3." General Services Administration, n.d. Accessed April 20, 2013. www.gsa.gov/graphics/pbs/The_Early_Catastrophe_30_Million_Word_Gap_by_Age_3.pdf.
15. "Past. Present. Future." *KIPP Houston Public Schools*. Accessed April 20, 2013. http://kipphouston.org/past-present-future.
16. "Charter Schools." Texas Education Agency, n.d. Accessed April 20, 2013. www.tea.state.tx.us/Charters.aspx.

17. The law provides for four different classes of charter school. In the following, "charter schools" refers to open-enrollment charters, such as KIPP Houston's schools.

18. "Charter Schools – Frequently Asked Questions." Texas Education Agency, n.d. Accessed April 20, 2013. www.tea.state. tx.us/index2.aspx?id=392.

19. "Revenues and Expenditures for Public Elementary and Secondary Education: School Year 2008–2009 (Fiscal Year 2009)." *National Center for Education Statistics*. Institute of Education Sciences, June 2011. Accessed April 20, 2013. http://nces.ed.gov/ pubs2011/2011329.pdf.

20. 2011 was the most recent year for which total student enrollment data was available. 5986 Students. PEIMS data from State of Texas. Texas Education Agency. *Snapshot 2011.* Accessed April 21, 2013. http://ritter. tea.state.tx.us/perfreport/snapshot/2011/ index.html.

21. Texas Education Agency Foundation School Program funding was $47,561,540 for year ended June 30, 2011. *Financial Statements and Independent Auditors' Report*. 2011 Audit Report. KIPP, Inc., October 27, 2011. Accessed April 21, 2013.

22. *School Finance 101: Funding of Texas Public Schools*. Rep. Texas Education Agency Office of School Finance, Jan. 2013. Accessed April 20, 2013. www.tea.state. tx.us/index2.aspx?id=7022&menu_id=645.

23. Murphy, John. Personal interview. April 17, 2013.

24. McGee, Josh B. "Houston School Finance Report." Laura and John Arnold Foundation, January 18, 2013. Accessed April 20, 2013. www.arnoldfoundation.org/resources/ houston-school-finance-report.

25. Mathews, Jay. "Growing Up Fast."

26. *Financial Statements and Independent Auditors' Report*. Audit Report. KIPP, Inc., October 16, 2012. Accessed April 21, 2013. http://kipphouston.org/sites/default/files/ file_attach/KHPS_Audit_Report_for_the_ Year_Ended_June_30_2012.pdf.

27. McGee, Josh B. "Houston School Finance Report." Laura and John Arnold Foundation, January 18, 2013. Accessed 20 Apr. 2013. www.arnoldfoundation.org/resources/ houston-school-finance-report.

28. Average of 715 teachers employed by KIPP Houston schools in 2012. *2011–12 AEIS Reports*. Rep. Texas Education Agency. Accessed April 21, 2013. http://ritter.tea. state.tx.us/perfreport/aeis/2012/.

29. Goedekke, Ken. Personal interview. April 18, 2013.

30. Ibid.

31. Ibid.

32. Ibid.

33. *2010–11 Academic Excellence Indicator System Campus Reports*. Rep. Texas Education Agency. Accessed April 21, 2013. 2010–11 Academic Excellence Indicator System Campus Reports.

34. Goedekke, Ken. Personal interview. April 18, 2013.

35. Fimble, Chuck. Personal interview. March 29, 2013.

36. Ibid.

37. Ali, Sehba. Personal interview. March 29, 2013.

38. Internal document.

39. Frequently Asked Questions. *KIPP Public Charter Schools*. Accessed April 21, 2013. www.kipp.org/careers/applicant-faqs.

40. Internal document.

41. Personal interview. April 22, 2013.

42. Ibid.

43. *2011–12 AEIS Reports*. Rep. Texas Education Agency. Accessed April 21, 2013. http://ritter. tea.state.tx.us/perfreport/aeis/2012/.

44. Internal documents.

45. *2011–12 AEIS Reports*. Rep. Texas Education Agency. Accessed April 21, 2013. http://ritter. tea.state.tx.us/perfreport/aeis/2012/.

46. Internal documents.

47. Personal interview. April 21, 2013.

48. Ibid.

49. Fimble, Chuck. Personal interview. March 29, 2013.

50. Ibid.

51. Internal documents.

52. "SBOE State Board of Education." Texas Education Agency, April 4, 2013. Accessed April 22, 2013. www.tea.state.tx.us/index3. aspx?id=1156.

53. "19 TAC Chapter 113, Subchapter B." Texas Education Agency. Accessed April 22, 2013. http://ritter.tea.state.tx.us/rules/tac/ chapter113/ch113b.html.

54. "In the States." Common Core State Standards Initiative. Accessed April 22, 2013. www.corestandards.org/in-the-states.

55. Based on 8th grade reading in 2009. "Mapping State Proficiency Standards onto the NAEP Scales: Variation and Change in State Standards for Reading and Mathematics, 2005–2009." Institute of Education Sciences, 2009. Accessed April 22, 2013. http://nces.ed.gov/ nationsreportcard/pdf/studies/2011458. pdf.

56. Ali, Sehba. Personal interview. March 29, 2013.

57. "About BetterLesson." Accessed April 22, 2013. http://betterlesson.com/public/ about.

58. Christensen, Clayton M., Michael B. Horn, and Curtis W. Johnson. *Disrupting Class: How Disruptive Innovation Will Change the Way the World Learns*. New York: McGraw-Hill, 2008.

59. Schmidt, Eric. Personal interview. April 17, 2013.

60. Ibid.

61. Bradford, Matt. Telephone interview. March 27, 2013.

62. Ibid.

63. Ali, Sehba. Personal interview. March 29, 2013.

64. "Apollo 20 Program: A Strong Foundation for Success." Houston Independent School District, n.d. Accessed April 22, 2013. www.houstonisd.org/site/default. aspx?PageType=3.

65. "Study Shows Apollo 20 Academic Achievement Gains Match Top Charters." Houston Independent School District, October 6, 2011. Accessed April 22, 2013. www.houstonisd.org/site/default. aspx?PageType=3.

66. Fryer, Roland G., Jr. "The Impact of Apollo 20 on Student Achievement: Evidence from Year One." Rep. The Education Innovation Laboratory at Harvard University, n.d. Accessed April 30, 2013. www.houstonisd. org/site/handlers/filedownload.ashx? moduleinstanceid=95698&dataid=48186& FileName=ApolloResults.pdf.

67. "Donors Step up to Fund Apollo 20 School Turnaround Effort." Houston Independent School District, December 21, 2012. Accessed April 23, 2013. http:// blogs.houstonisd.org/news/2012/12/21/ donors-step-up-to-fund-apollo-20-school-turnaround-effort/.

68. "About YES" YES Prep Public Schools, n.d. Accessed April 22, 2013. http://yesprep.org/ AboutYES/topic/history/.

69. Phone interview. February 11, 2013

70. Ali, Sehba. Personal interview. March 29, 2013.

71. "Harmony Public Schools: About Us." Accessed April 22, 2013. www.harmonytx. org/AboutUs.aspx.

72. Radcliffe, Jennifer. "Harmony Charter Schools Beat Odds on Rise to the Top in Texas."*Houston Chronicle*. February 27, 2011. Accessed April 23, 2013. www.chron.com/ news/houston-texas/article/Harmony-charter-schools-beat-odds-on-rise-to-the-1585639.php.

73. "Course Descriptions." Harmony Public Schools, n.d. Accessed April 22, 2013. www. harmonytx.org/Portals/0/HPS-Course-Descriptions-2011-12.pdf.

74. "Frequently Asked Questions." *Harmony Science Academy*. Harmony Public Schools, n.d. Accessed Apr 22, 2013. www. hsagarland.org/?page=Category11.

75. *AEIS Reports*. Rep. Texas Education Agency, n.d. Accessed April 21, 2013. http://ritter.tea. state.tx.us/perfreport/aeis/2012/.

76. "The Promise of College Completion: KIPP's Early Successes and Challenges." KIPP Foundation, April 28, 2011. Accessed April 22, 2013. www.kipp.org/files/dmfile/ CollegeCompletionReport.pdf.

CASE 10

Luck Companies: Igniting Human Potential

D. Robley Wood, Jr.
Wallace Stettinius
Robert S. Kelley
Thomas K. Quinton

Early in 2015 Mr. Charlie Luck, IV knew that his leadership skills were soon to be thoroughly tested by all of the activities that needed his attention. In March 2015, he was named Chairman of the National Stone, Sand and Gravel Association where he was tasked with advancing the association's agenda to ensure that the association continued to be the leading voice for the aggregate industry. The agenda is aggressive and includes a new board structure and the execution of the association's Rocks Build America strategic plan.

As third generation CEO of his family owned business, Luck Companies, 2015 was off to a busy start as growth was returning to the aggregate industry in general and Luck Companies in particular. The firm's management had spent years building industry expertise on a foundation of Values Based Leadership. It was now time to use their 800 talented employees to build an even higher performing company. Working with his Chief Growth Officer, Mr. John Pullen, Mr. Charlie Luck had approved a goal of almost doubling the company's size by the year 2020. This stretch goal forced his leaders to think "outside-the-box" about their businesses and this was exactly what he wanted to accomplish. The next five years were going to be fast paced and fun after years of retrenchment and slow growth in the construction aggregate industry.

Mr. Charlie Luck had become President and COO in 1995, and CEO in 1999, succeeding his father. A 1983 graduate of the Virginia Military Institute, Charlie earned a degree in Civil Engineering followed by a three-year career as a professional racecar driver on the NASCAR circuit. At the end of 1986, he put his racing helmet aside and began work as a full-time employee for Luck Companies.

As a teenager, Charlie worked summers at the quarries doing various jobs such as repairing machinery and driving trucks. Growing up around the quarries gave Charlie a good sense of the business from the bottom up, but both he and his father thought it was necessary for him to have extensive experience in all aspects and levels of the business if he was to succeed his father as CEO. Charlie's father tested him by having him work his way through the ranks to the position of CEO. His father not only wanted him to earn the position, but also to earn the respect of the company's associates. Had he not proven capable, his father would not have appointed him CEO.

Thus, in early 1987, he began working full-time in the quarries and other departments; systematically moving through supervisory and mid-management positions for the next eight years. This kind of training had many benefits – among them were learning the various aspects of the business, developing managerial skills, and building relationships. Through this test, Charlie not only learned the importance of having a sound and innovative business strategy but also the role that values and culture played in executing them. The same values and culture that Charlie would later find out were the catalyst to the company's past success.

After eight years of on-the-job training, Charlie's father decided he was ready to run the company. In 1995, he was promoted to President and subsequently became CEO in 1999.

When Charlie was appointed to CEO, the company had a long history of success in the aggregate business in Virginia, driven by the business acumen and values of his father and grandfather. The business had been operated over the years in a very thoughtful, measured manner with little or no debt and a solid but not rapid growth rate.

This case was written by D. Robley Wood Jr., Wallace Stettinius and Robert S. Kelly, School of Business, Virginia Commonwealth University and Thomas K. Quinton, Luck Companies. Unless otherwise noted, all data in this case are based on company documents and field research by the authors. All persons and events are real. Luck Stone Corporation changed its name to Luck Companies in 2011. To avoid confusion in this case, the name "Luck Companies" is used when referring to the corporate enterprise. "Luck Stone" refers solely to the business unit that operates quarries and sells aggregates. Luck Companies is a family owned corporation and releases only limited financial data. This case was written with the full cooperation of management and is solely for the purpose of stimulating student discussion. All rights reserved to the authors.

The company's operations were all in Virginia and, like many small businesses, the management style was "top-down". The industry had experienced little consolidation and was primarily filled with family-owned businesses. Built on a "we care" attitude that emphasized integrity and treating people right, Luck Companies became a leader in customer service. By the late 1990s Luck Stone was known as a technology leader in its industry and was nationally ranked as one of the top 15 crushed-stone producers in the United States. A given was that the culture that had proven so successful would not change, but most everything else was changing.

The new millennium brought with it growing consolidation in the industry and fiercer competition. There was tremendous expansion in the markets, creating faster growth rates, a much larger company, and increased debt to finance the growth. In the mid '90s, Charlie and his leadership team realized that the "top down" management style at Luck Companies was not ideal for meeting the needs of customers or employees. After much deliberation, they determined that there was a need for management decisions to be made closer to the customer. The organizational structure was decentralized and associate duties and responsibilities were changed to enable the company to better handle the growing complexity of sales opportunities.

The company continued to grow under Charlie's leadership, but he understood that he was in a mature industry and therefore needed to diversify. Recognizing the increasing uniqueness of each of the business units, the leadership chose to separate the company into four businesses with distinct brand identities. There was an expectation through the strategic planning process for each to uniquely meet the needs of the marketplace, which resulted in specific strategies, brands and business plans for each business unit.

Thinking back to his father and grandfather's success, Charlie wondered what the future held for Luck Companies. He challenged his management team to operate the company in a manner that not only excelled the company financially but also positively impacted the lives of its customers and associates. He was convinced that the company was well positioned to become even more successful in the future.

Luck Companies and Industry Overview

Luck Stone, founded in 1923 by Charles Luck, Jr., is the largest family owned and operated construction aggregate company in the United States. Over the last century, the Luck family has turned a single quarry in the West End of Richmond, Virginia, into one of the top 20 largest producers of aggregate in the United States. Luck Companies operate under four separate business units or SBU's; Luck Stone, Luck Stone Center, Har-Tru, and Luck Development Partners. Although the Luck Companies business portfolio is divided into four SBUs, each business unit operates under Luck Companies' values-based leadership system. A map of the Luck Stone business locations in 2015 is located below.

Luck Stone

Luck Stone, the largest business unit of Luck Companies, operates fifteen crushed stone plants, one sand and gravel plant, one specialty products operation and four distribution yards in the mid-Atlantic region. Luck Stone supplies a wide range of crushed stone, sand, gravel, and specialty stone; collectively called aggregate. The aggregate industry is further broken down into two main production segments; 1) Crushed Stone and 2) Sand and Gravel. Luck Stone primarily mines and sells crushed stone. Thirteen years ago Luck Stone started producing some sand and gravel. Defined geographically, due to the various sources, weights, sizes, and shipping costs associated with aggregates, the industry is significantly fragmented with about 1,550 companies operating 4,000 quarries in the United States.[1] Luck Stone's operations are located in the Mid-Atlantic Region of the United States, Virginia in particular. In 2014 the production of aggregates in the US totaled 2.17 billion metric tons that had a value of $20.3 billion dollars. Approximately 100,000 people were employed in the US aggregates industry in 2014.[2]

Aggregates are mined from various quarries and serve as inputs for the construction industry. The prosperity of the aggregate industry is directly correlated to the growth and economic stability of the construction industry, consisting of both private and public construction. These segments are further broken down into residential and nonresidential construction segments. Private residential and nonresidential construction spending in the U.S. during 2014 was roughly $349 billion and $337 billion, respectively.[3] Total public construction spending in the U.S. during 2014 was roughly $273 billion.[4] While private construction accounts for the majority of construction spending, historically it has been highly volatile. This volatility has had a crippling impact on the aggregate industry during the recent recession. The public segment, primarily funded by local, state, and federal government organizations, is considerably more stable than the private segment.

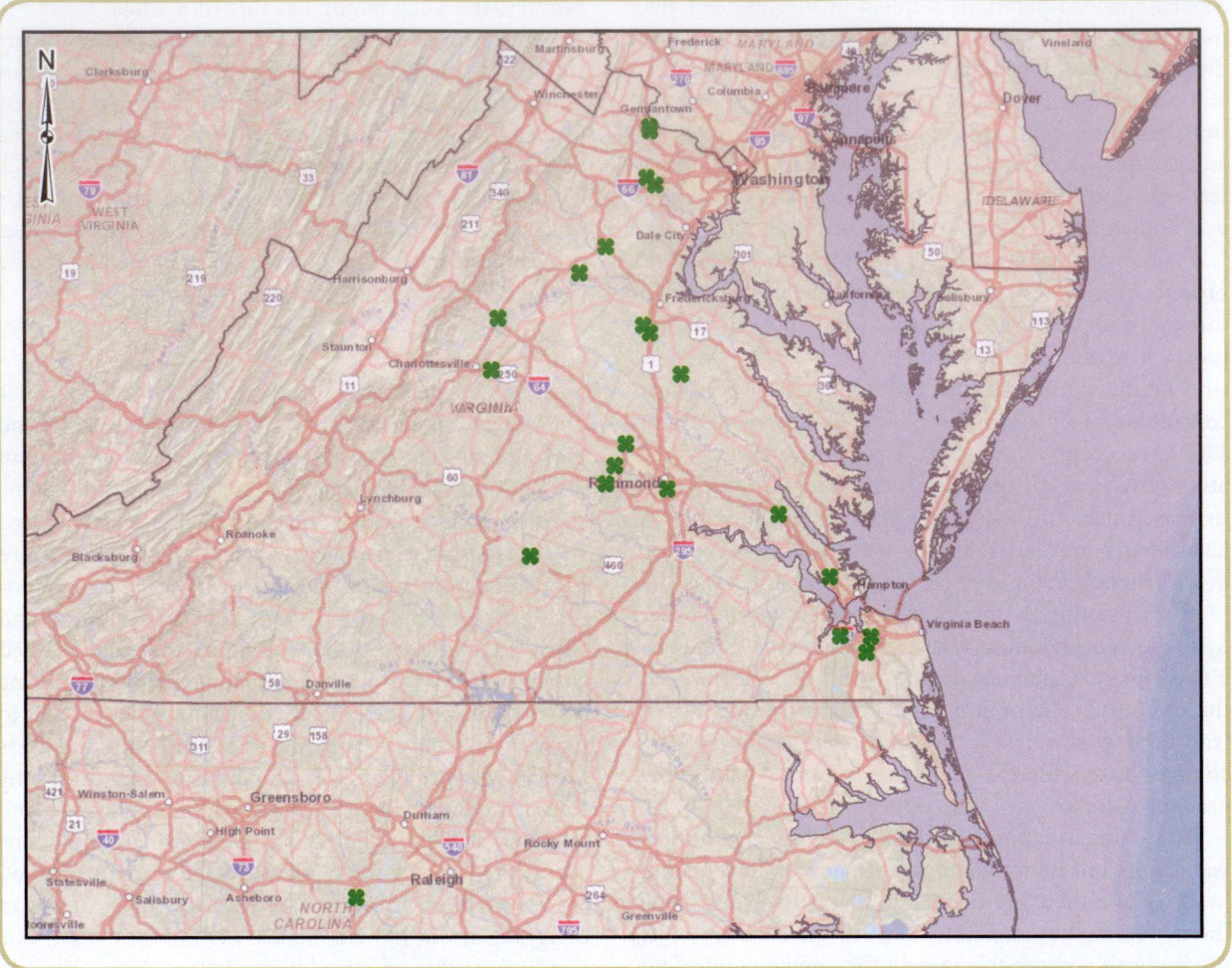

In 2006 Luck Stone sold 27 million tons of aggregate yielding a market share of roughly 30% in Virginia. In 2009 Luck Stone's sales fell to 11.7 million tons of aggregate yielding a market share of roughly 23% in Virginia. The market for aggregate in Virginia has not yet returned to the lofty levels of 2006. In 2014 Luck Stone sold 12.9 million tons of aggregate in Virginia and had a 40% market share in this region. Even with the significant decrease in aggregate sales, Luck Stone remains the most profitable business unit of Luck Companies and contributes more than 80% of total enterprise net sales and profits. In 2014 Luck stone was the 15th largest producer of construction aggregate in the United States. Luck Stone's largest competitors and the largest producers of construction aggregate in the United States are Vulcan Materials and Martin Marietta, respectively. Vulcan Materials and Martin Marietta both operate with an overall cost leadership business strategy, while Luck Stone utilizes a business strategy based on superior customer service and logistical excellence. In 2014 Vulcan Materials produced 11.8 million tons of aggregate in Virginia while Martin Marietta Materials produced 3.2 million tons of aggregate in Virginia that same year.

Luck Stone Center

In 1976, Luck Stone opened its first retail showroom for architectural stone adjacent to its corporate offices. The retail showroom concept was widely praised as being unique in the stone industry. The official name of this business unit was the Architectural Stone Division of Luck Stone. In 1993, Mark Fernandes became V.P. of the Architectural Stone Division. When Charlie Luck was appointed CEO in 1995, he directed Mark Fernandes to develop a five-year strategic plan that focused on expansion. By the end of the 1990s, the Architectural Stone Division was operating six Architectural Stone Centers.

In 2000 a second five-year strategic plan was developed with a strategic focus on product innovation. The Architectural Stone Division sought differentiation through new product offerings and began sourcing stone internationally. During this time period the Architectural Stone Division experienced increasing levels of competition from other contractor stone yards as well as big-box retailers such as Home Depot and Lowes. The management of the Architectural Stone Division knew that further differentiation was necessary to remain profitable.

In 2007 the Architectural Stone Division went through a significant rebranding and name change to Charles Luck Stone Center. The strategic rebranding shifted the brand from a contractor stone yard to an up-scale, design oriented architectural stone center. The new brand focused on a market of design savvy, affluent homebuyers. Unfortunately, over the past ten years, the Charles Luck Stone Center sales were 82% correlated with housing starts. The housing crisis in 2008 significantly reduced Charles Luck Stone Center sales. In 2014, Charles Luck Stone Center shifted strategies to refocus on middle to higher-end consumers and added manufactured products to their product mix. With this new strategy, the business unit was rebranded "Luck Stone Center".

Side Note:

In the early 2000s the Architectural Stone Division supplied granite counter tops and interior surfaces to Home Depot. However, Home Depot became oversaturated with lower-end products and demanded lower prices from the Architectural Stone Division. It was at this point that the division rebranded and shifted their strategy to concentrate only on high-end stone sales and ceased to be one of Home Depot's suppliers. Home Depot contracted a new supplier who was willing to meet their low price demands but unfortunately was unable to deliver on their order promises. Home Depot subsequently fired this new supplier and humbly asked the Architectural Stone Division to come back on as a supplier. The management of the Architectural Stone Division was no longer interested in supplying stone to big-box retailers. However, they agreed to supply Home Depot for 120 days so they had time to find a new supplier. This decision was driven by the values of Luck Companies to always treat each customer right even if it did not fit with their long-term strategies.

Luck Development Partners

Luck Development Partners was founded in 1993 in order to realize the development potential of the real estate held by Luck Companies. Each quarry owned by Luck Companies needs nearly 500 acres to operate efficiently. Location is also vital to the aggregate industry for the aforementioned reasons and serves as one of the largest competitive advantages in this industry. Similarly, the land development industry is highly dependent on location and centrality to population hubs. However, the life of a quarry is limited to the amount of aggregate reserves in the ground. The long-range sustainable use of the land comes in the form of innovative real estate practices. Developing these land assets allows Luck Companies to once again gain revenue from their land holdings. Luck Development Partners creates unique places by integrating and highlighting natural, historical and environmental elements into the design of its projects.

Har-Tru

Har-Tru is a global leader in tennis court surfacing and accessories. Har-Tru was originally branded Lee Tennis Court Products and was founded in the 1950s by engineer Robert Lee. In 1997 Lee Tennis Court Products was acquired by longtime partner and supplier, Luck Companies. Two years after this acquisition, Luck Companies acquired Lee Tennis Court Products' largest competitor, ISP Tennis Products. Shortly after this acquisition Luck Companies acquired the manufacturing assets of the original Har-Tru material provider and, finally, bought the Har-Tru brand name, a surface associated with some of the finest courts in the world.

In 2013 Har-Tru acquired Century Sports, a retailer for tennis court equipment based in Lakewood, New Jersey. Century Sports has been in operation for over 30 years and is the exclusive court equipment licensee of Wilson sports.

Currently Har-Tru maintains between 85% and 90% of the U.S. market share for clay tennis courts. The main competition in the clay tennis court market comes from companies building non-traditional tennis courts with clay substitutes. While they are the leader in their industry, Har-Tru is the smallest business unit of Luck Companies and in 2014 contributed about 6% to the total enterprise net sales.

History

The Founders Years 1923 to 1964

Luck Stone acquired its first quarry, Sunnyside Granite Company, Inc. in Richmond, Virginia, in 1923. First year sales were $22,212 for "chips" and "dust". These sales were fueled by the C. S. Luck and Son, which was owned by

Charles Samuel Luck, the great grandfather of the current CEO. In 1925 the quarry employed 23 men and the first available production records show sales of 94,000 tons of stone at an average price of $1.40/ton for the year 1928.

During the 1930s Luck Stone acquired four more quarries in Virginia. One of the quarries purchased was the Boscobel quarry that is located about 20 miles from the center of Richmond in Manakin-Sabot, Virginia; where the company's headquarters are now located. The Boscobel quarry has been in operation since the 1880s and production records for 1931 show that it produced 130,151 tons of stone with net sales of $138,065. In 1938 Luck Stone purchased Fairfax Quarries Inc. for $17,500. This quarry became one of their most successful quarries because of the growth in Northern Virginia and its proximity to Washington, D.C.

In the 1940s, the U.S. involvement in World War II caused major production problems for Luck Stone. By 1942 there was a freeze on all state road contracts, a slowdown in the construction industry, and labor shortages for nearly all domestic companies. All of Luck Stone's quarries were forced to minimize operations with production coming to a virtual halt in 1943 and 1944. The Boscobel quarry was able to continue operations on a reduced scale selling exclusively to the U.S. government for military base construction in the greater Hampton Roads area. In 1949 the property for a new quarry near Charlottesville, Virginia, was purchased for $43,500 from the Thomas Jefferson Memorial Commission and is still operational.

Expansion, the Charles S. Luck, III, Years, 1965 to 1992

After spending summers working in the quarries, Charles Luck, III, Charlie's father, joined the company in 1957 after his graduation from the Virginia Military Institute and two years of active service in the United States Air Force. He became President of Luck Stone in 1965, succeeding his father, Charles S. Luck Jr., who became Chairman of the Board.

When Charles took over in 1965, sales were approximately two million tons of crushed stone per year. When he passed the baton to his son in 1995, annual tonnage of crushed stone had grown to almost fifteen million tons per year. The company had expanded to 14 crushed stone operations, including one in North Carolina. In Virginia, quarries were purchased or developed and became operational under the Luck Stone name in Goochland County (1965), Loudon County (1971), Green County (land purchased in 1982 and quarry became operational in 1984), Powhatan County (land purchased in 1984 and

quarry became operational in 1985), Fauquier County, land purchased in 1987 and quarry became operational in 1988), Louisa County (land leased in 1989 and limited production started the same year), Loudon County, Leesburg (1993), and King William County (1996).

The oil crisis and recession of 1973 produced skyrocketing energy prices, high inflation, and a major lull in the construction industry. Luck Stone's management used this time to begin an initiative to bring energy savings, cost cutting and efficiency improvements to their operations. Despite the depth of the recession and the need to reduce hours, no employees were laid off.

Following the recession of 1973, corporate management looked for areas into which to diversify in order to lessen the impact of the cyclical nature of the construction industry. As a result, the Architectural Stone Division was started in 1976 and their first stone center opened the next year in Goochland, Virginia.

Under the leadership of Charles, the company established itself as an industry leader in technology and innovation. In 1977 employees of Luck Stone designed and built the industry's first totally automated lime plant in Augusta County, Virginia. The plant was designed to run unattended and had sensors that shutdown the plant if a problem arose. In 1987 Luck Stone's engineering team designed and built segmentation and automation systems that allowed a plant to produce crushed stone 24 hours a day. Through his years as president and CEO of Luck Companies, Charles grew the company significantly, created a culture focused on people, and brought the company to the forefront of innovation.

The Charles Luck IV Years

In 1995, Charles Luck IV (Charlie) was named President of Luck Companies, and his father Charles became Chairman and CEO. At this point the company employed approximately 400 associates, produced over 12 million tons of crushed stone, and was known for their "WE CARE" about our people culture. In addition, Luck Stone established a nationally recognized safety program, which became a model for the industry.

Charlie describes his early years as CEO as follows:

I really did not fully understand the company at first. I knew that decision-making was centralized and we never shared our profit and loss data with our people in the field. I started sharing revenue, cost data, and profitability numbers with our field managers and I also decentralized our management structure. To begin the development of our management team, I sent our officers to executive business programs and we produced our first five-year strategic plan for the years 1995–2000.

Charlie describes his experience for the first five years as:

1. Learning to see the business in totality from a general management perspective. Up until this point he was seeing it from an operational and functional perspective. He found that being CEO required a very different way of thinking about the business.
2. Building his management team while dealing with a generational management succession of his father's team. The existing senior managers were steeped in the quarry business and some found it very challenging to respond to the demanding needs of running a business that was growing so rapidly and thinking about ways to diversify.
3. Restructuring the business to reflect its increasing complexity and size with an emphasis on decentralization of operations.
4. Learning to manage the numbers in terms of growth and profits.
5. Creating a strategic management process with the first 5-year plan.
6. Realizing that in a more decentralized environment there had to be some overall plan with clear goals and objectives to tie the parts into a coherent whole.

Between 1995 and 2006 the company set new profit and volume records every year. In 2003 it employed 830 associates and produced over 21 million tons of crushed stone. It had diversified into tennis courts, land development and stone centers. It nearly tripled sales, associates, and profitability. This was in contrast to the very deliberate and measured growth during Charlie's father and grandfather's time. By 2005, the company had almost 1200 employees. This tripling of associates had led to promoting a lot of people quickly and hiring new talent from outside the company. New people were also gained from numerous acquisitions, which took place during this timeframe.

In spite of the fact that the country was in a mild recession in 2002, the company continued to make progress. The year 2002 was truly remarkable for the company with record sales yet again. Three more Virginia quarries were purchased (Culpeper, Spotsylvania and Bull Run), and work was finished on a new North Carolina based quarry that was to produce roofing granules for a 3M factory in North Carolina. The North Carolina quarry entered 2003 ready to produce almost two million tons of production a year for 3M's facility and for the local market.

Despite record sales and rapid growth over the past eight years, not everyone felt Charlie's enthusiasm. Charlie remembers back to 2000 when George Fox came to him (a key associate who had been with the company for a couple of decades) and said that he felt that Luck Stone was losing its way. He said there were many people making decisions in a way that he did not believe was aligned with the traditional values that the company had held for decades. Charlie goes on to say:

During this same period of time, we had grown our executive leadership group and I was observing that, although we were getting record financial results, we were not working together as effectively as we could or should as a team. Often, there were the "meetings after the meetings" where issues were being discussed that could have, and should have, been resolved and settled in the first meeting.

I felt like we had a team that could be so much more effective in leading our company if we worked together in a high-performing, constructive, but challenging and respectful way where we completed meetings all on the same page. To help us improve, Jay Coffman, VP of Human Resources and I hired a management consultant who was recommended to us by Caterpillar executives in Peoria, Illinois. The management consultant began meeting with us once a quarter for two days. He met with all the leadership team members for about 18 months. During this period, we learned that our values and leadership journey started with ourselves. We realized that we needed to look at our own personal leadership as it pertained to issues in the company.

The Values Journey – Vision 2010 – Phase I: 2003–2007

Beginning in early 2003, the leadership team met to decide what values would define the company. The leadership team did not realize that this endeavor would result in a values-based leadership journey that would dramatically transform the organization.

During this period, officers also began what was coined "Tools Training." Tools Training was built on various forms of insight testing that ultimately taught the officers to understand themselves and others in order to make a difference. In one of these private meetings Charlie came to the realization that the values journey had to start with him:

For two hours I sat in front of the group, while the team filled flip chart pages with comments about what they did and didn't like about my leadership. They then covered the walls with all the pages. At this particular time, I found the negative observations to be painful and I did not see them as gifts but rather as attacks on me. There was a side of me that was extremely upset and mad but I also knew that I had to do something different. Upon returning to Richmond, I talked with my father about this experience. He asked me about the feedback and I told him it was the same thing he had been telling me for the past nine years. He then asked me what I was going to do about it and I promised him that I was not going to quit and that I was going to work as hard as I possibly could to be a better leader for our company and for our people. This was clearly a pivotal point that forced me to look in the mirror and figure out how I could be a better leader at Luck Companies.

After a year of these periodic meetings and Tools Training, other Associates began to notice a difference in the officers. At the end of this 18-month period the values that would lead the company were agreed upon:

- **Commitment**: Take personal responsibility for the success of associates, customers, and communities
- **Integrity**: Earn the trust and respect of others
- **Creativity**: Have a passion for ideas and innovation that add value
- **Leadership**: Ignite Human Potential

These values emphasize the importance of performance, and go beyond that to describe the behaviors required to do the right things. Charlie believed strongly that a values-driven culture was a way to achieve even better outcomes and performance. Examples of outcomes include:

a. Improved customer loyalty and key account retention through integrity and commitment toward anyone that the company came into contact with.
b. Increased product innovation by focusing and embracing creativity throughout the company.
c. Better efficiency and safety through an unwavering commitment to a best-in-class safety program.
d. Acquisition advantages by gaining respect as an industry leader for operating with integrity as a core value in everyday operations.

In 2004, after a year and a half of deciding what values would define Luck Companies, Charlie and the senior team decided it was time to unveil the Values Journey and Vision 2010 to the entire company. A series of departmental meetings were held where Charlie gave the speech that would change the company forever. In his speech, Charlie told the employees that he was no longer worried about just making money but instead how that money was being made. Many associates were shocked at Charlie's newfound Vision 2010, "To be the Model of a Values-Based Organization."

The next task was to embed this newfound vision throughout the company. It was important that these values did not become superficial posters merely hung on a wall to collect dust. Charlie and the senior team knew that in order to truly achieve the vision, the values would have to reach the deepest depths of the company and become ingrained in each and every associate. Every associate would be held accountable to these values and through this accountability the vision would ignite potential in the associates to not only become better employees but better individuals holistically. To assure that the values were adhered to and lived out by every associate, a unique and intense process was developed to make Vision 2010 operational. To ensure the successful implementation of the vision, Luck Companies invested thousands of working hours and millions of dollars to embed it into the organization. Below is an overview of the steps taken to drive the vision:

- *The Monthly Values Program*: A year long program starting with top associates in groups of 40 to undergo the same tools training as the officers.
- *Established the First Ritual*: Any and every meeting would start with 10 – 15 minutes of values stories.
- *Redid the annual associate performance reviews*: The APR's were now built around values and behaviors, and encompassed two sections; 1) what section and 2) how section.
- *Insights Study*: Every employee down to the hourly level took an insights study to learn about themselves.
- *New Values Curriculum*: This new curriculum was built around values, insights, and supporting tools.
- *Introduced Walking the Talk Awards*: Associates submitted people acting out the values (top five received a prize).
- *Hired and embedded sight specific HR Personnel*: Their job was to work out in the fields and teach and train the new values.
- *Quarterly Values Program*: Also was attended by hourly associates.
- *Implemented a Mentoring Program*: Officers began to mentor 5 senior leaders at a time, and once senior leaders went through the program for a year, they turned around and mentored the associates beneath them.

- *Employee Interview Process Overhaul*: Managers began to ask values-based behavior questions to interviewees.
- *New Officer Incentive Plan*: Now 33% of the officers' bonuses were based on self-development (the measures of success were 360 assessments).

In 2005, Mark Barth was appointed as the Director of Values. Others were also appointed as dedicated associates in the Values Journey and Vision 2010. At this point, Luck Companies was allocating between one and two million dollars of resources to Vision 2010 per year. However, institutionalizing the values model as the business grew was no easy feat. A number of managers could not or did not want to adapt to a more values oriented leadership style, preferring to strictly emphasize the importance of performance and/or other variables not aligned with the values. For example, some seasoned Associates working in the Company were unable to see the benefit of incorporating values into their leadership style while some senior leaders' behaviors conflicted with the values in which the Senior Leadership Team believed. Some left, while others were asked to leave.

It took three years, but by 2006, the Values Journey was really gaining traction and people were truly acting differently and adopting these values. Associates were approaching Charlie at company events to tell him how these values not only benefited their work life, but their personal and family life as well.

The Values Journey – Vision 2020 – Phase II: 2007–2008

At this point, Charlie was 46 years old and was thinking even more deeply at a personal level about what life is about. He had been through 15 years of annual financial records, and the Values Journey was working. But, somehow this didn't seem to be enough. He was beginning to think that there had to be a bigger purpose in life. His wife's brother, Kyle Petty, does an annual charity ride across the country with a large group of friends and Charlie joined him. Out in the west, Charlie was riding due east directly into the sunrise. He had been riding for about an hour at 100 miles per hour when he looked over to the right at hundreds of migrant workers picking strawberries. He questioned, "Why wasn't I born into a family of migrant workers?" He thought back to what his mom told him as a young child, "To whom much is given, much is expected."

Charlie returned from his cross-country trip and began seeing his name on trusts and wills, which made him think about his own children. He traveled to a Family Office consultant in Chicago to look into starting a Family Office for the Luck Family. When he arrived, the consultant asked Charlie about his company. He told her about his values journey and his thoughts about a larger purpose in life. They began to talk about this larger purpose and her curiosity grew. She asked about the lives that the company had touched and the progress that the Values Journey had made. He told her stories of associates coming up and telling him how they have a better relationship with their children, with their parents, and with themselves. She stopped him and asked, "How often does a company get the chance to touch the lives of three generations?"

He realized that he and his company had the opportunity and ability to positively impact the lives of more people than he originally thought. Five years of the Values Journey had made a positive impact on the company overall, but there was still more to be done to create a company that could touch the lives of everyone. He came to the realization that the higher purpose he sought was for his company to enrich the lives of the people it touched – from employees to customers to suppliers and the community. He and his top associates began to research literature and others' experiences about doing good as the best path to doing well. They realized that the model would be built based on leadership. Values-Based Leadership would serve as the means to spread these values more effectively throughout the company and in turn the lives of the people the company touches. From here Vision 2020 was created, "To be recognized as one of the top five values based leadership organizations in the world."

The values-based leadership model development process began in the spring of 2007. Another consulting firm was brought in to help facilitate the design and assessment process. A small team of cross-functional leaders from the four business units was selected to build the framework and behavioral components of the model. This team was led internally by two senior leaders, John Pullen, who at the time was VP of Strategy and Real Estate, and Jay Coffman, VP of Human Resources. The development team was given the assignment to align the mission, values, and Charlie's 2010 Vision into a practical inspiring model that would include the essential behaviors required for success as a leader at Luck Companies. The model would also provide a framework for ongoing selection and development of company leaders, content for leadership training, and behavioral standards for performance management. The process used to build the leadership model contained the following steps.

- Step 1: Planning session(s) to understand expectations and deliverables of the project.
- Step 2: The facilitation of design meetings with cross-functional leaders to create the initial draft of the leadership model.
- Step 3: Online content validation with the entire leadership population to generate refinement and Values-Based Leadership acceptance.
- Step 4: Recalibration of the model to include feedback from the content validation process.
- Step 5: Senior leadership team validation and blessing.
- Step 6: Final balancing of the model.
- Step 7: An initial 360 assessment of the top leaders to test out the model.

Steps 1-6 took approximately ten months. The framework of the model was designed to:

- Advance our values-based culture.
- Build Exceptional experiences with our customers and constituencies.
- Drive Differentiated growth.

At the end of 2007, both the Chief Financial Officer and VP of Human Resources announced their retirements in 2008 and 2009 respectively. These pending retirements gave Charlie the opportunity to examine the structure of his senior leadership team to ensure that the proper infrastructure would be in place to drive future growth.

New Strategic Leadership Team

There were several key changes to the senior leadership structure. First, Charlie decided to add a Chief Growth Officer position to the team. John Pullen was appointed to this position and tasked with the responsibility of driving differentiated growth and financial results across the enterprise. Each business unit would report directly to John. The other key change was the creation of a Chief Leadership Officer who would be responsible for the overall strategic and tactical support of the acquisition, development, and retention of high performing talent. This position would have direct accountability for working with other senior leaders to bring the leadership model to life. Mark Fernandes, who had been president of Charles Luck and Har-Tru, was selected as the Chief Leadership Officer. In short, Charlie's intention for these positions was to manage and succeed, in parallel, best in class financial performance and organization wide values alignment.

Another key change to the leadership structure was the addition of a Chief Family Officer. Wanda Ortwine was appointed to this unique position and tasked with the job of developing the leadership and competencies of Charlie's family in preparation for the future, handling family investments, estate planning and serving on the Strategic Leadership Team to transform the organization in alignment with the mission.

After contributing over twenty years of service to the organization, Jim Parker, retired and was replaced by Roy Goodman who was appointed to the position of Chief Financial Officer and Vice President of Finance, Luck Companies. Prior to joining Luck Companies, Roy had been the CFO for RealNetworks, a high growth technology company located in Seattle, Washington.

The organizational changes were announced in the spring of 2008, and an orderly two-year transition plan was put into place. However, three unexpected events

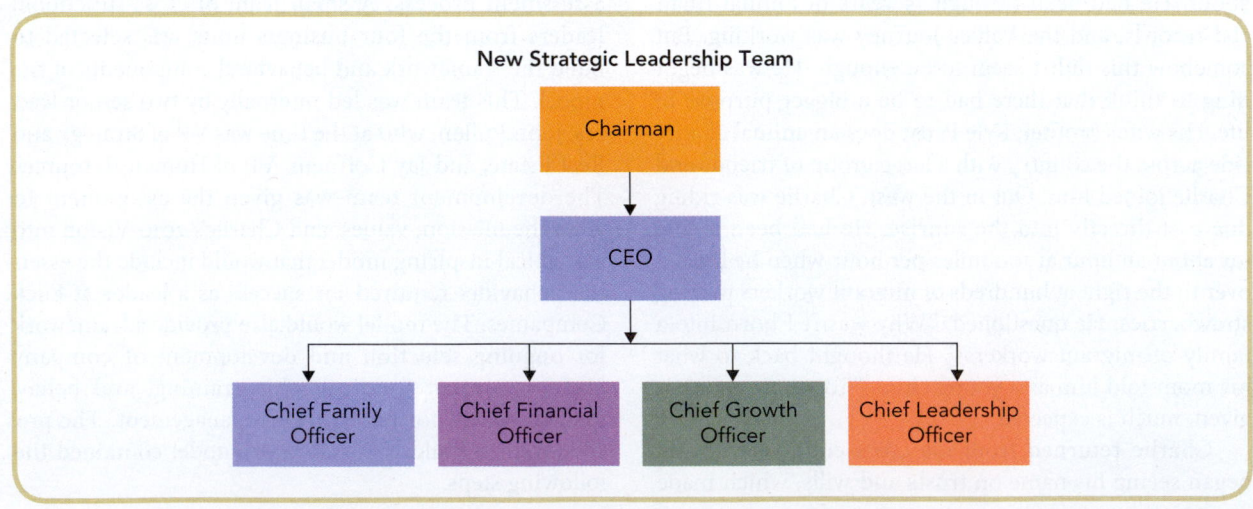

New Strategic Leadership Team

Chairman → CEO → Chief Family Officer, Chief Financial Officer, Chief Growth Officer, Chief Leadership Officer

occurred during the 2008-2009 timeframe. The United States entered into a deep recession, the president of the aggregate division, who had a record of excellent performance, was asked to leave the company due to a misalignment with the organization's values, and Charlie became seriously ill. These events put step 7, the final step of testing the new leadership model, on hold as the company worked to regain traction and overcome the unfortunate events.

Reduction in Force: 2008

Charlie said that in 2008 the "financials fell to pieces". The recession was really hitting all aspects of the stone industry hard and for some of their products demand had been eroding since 2006. The company had expanded to just under 1200 associates in 2008 but it was obvious to the leadership team that the sales were not going to come back anytime soon and that they no longer had the revenue to support such a large workforce.

In September 2008, things got so bad that the federal government had to help save several large US corporations, and Mr. Luck said that "We then knew that 2009 was going to be worse than 2008". Management had already taken the typical expense reduction steps such as a hiring freeze, delaying equipment purchases, and cutting non-essential expenses. However, they now realized that this recession was not like any they had ever experienced before and that they were going to have to take more drastic measures. In the end they came to the conclusion that it would be better to operate with 125 fewer associates who had full pay and benefits than negatively affect everyone. This decision was especially difficult for the managers of a company that had never had a reduction in force in its entire history and was known for treating its employees like family.

In the end they came to the conclusion that it would be better to operate with 125 fewer associates than negatively affect everyone.

Once the decision was made to have the firm's first ever company-wide reduction in force, Charlie and his leadership team discussed the type of company and associates they wanted to have once the recession was over. They decided not to use seniority but instead revisited their core values to guide them in their decisions about who would no longer be an employee of the company. A generous separation package was prepared for each departing employee, which "stretched the company." A video was prepared that explained in great detail why the reduction was necessary and it was shown to every employee on Tuesday, November 11, 2008. The showing of the video ensured that every employee had exactly the same information and hopefully slowed down the inevitable rumor mill. On Wednesday November 12, 2008, and Thursday, November 13, 2008, managers met with the employees that unfortunately had to be let go.

Commenting on the reduction, Charlie had this to say: "We wanted our employees to say, 'It's an awful thing to do, but you did it better than anybody else'". We wanted our people to say, "This is how a values-based company does this."

To aid employees after the RIF, Luck Companies leased a building offsite and turned it into an Employee Relocation Center. They helped the employees write resumes, cover letters, and find new employment. As a testament to the culture and values at Luck Companies, many other companies reached out, eager to accept Luck Companies' ex-employees as new hires.

In March 2009, Charlie fell ill. At first he believed that he had contracted the flu virus and would be back to work soon. However, the illness worsened and Charlie became bed-ridden for nearly 20 hours a day, with disabling fatigue. The doctors were unable to diagnose his illness. During this time Charlie thought a lot about the life he had lived and what else could be done to fulfill his purpose. After two long months he began to improve and returned to work.

The Values Journey Continues – Phase III: 2009 – Present

In the fall of 2009, Charlie returned to an organization that was comprised of businesses that were struggling because of the recession. The past two years of Charlie's life had a significant impact on the way he wanted to continue to run the company. After nearly dying, Charlie decided the Vision 2020 was too far in the future and not significant enough to achieve his goals for the company. He rewrote the vision with an even higher purpose and shortened the time span by five years. The new mission was coined Mission 2015 and states that; "We will ignite human potential around the world and positively impact the lives of others through values based leadership."

He presented the mission to Mark Fernandes, Chief Leadership Officer, and tasked him with making it operational. Mark knew that it would not be an easy job to drive such a lofty mission at a time when the company had fewer financial resources, fewer associates, and operated in markets that were in a recession. Despite these negative circumstances, Mark and rest of the leadership team believed in the mission and worked to develop a new values based leadership model that would make it happen. To guide them in this development, the senior team members relied on the Company's "Core Ideology and Beliefs" as well as the "Values Based Leadership Value Proposition" presented below:

Core Ideology and Beliefs:

"We believe all people are born with the extraordinary potential to make a positive difference in the world. We believe making a difference is a choice, a conscious choice that begins with our own self-awareness and alignment. Values Based Leaders consistently make this choice then insure others do the same, positively impacting the lives of those around them."

Value Proposition:

"At Luck Companies we believe doing good (making a difference) is the best path to doing well (business performance); and Values Based leadership is how we do good and why we do well."

In 2011, Charlie put step 7 into effect and had the senior leadership team collectively go through a robust 360-Assessment process where each leader received feedback on how their behavior was aligned with the model. After the 360-Assesment processes took place, the leaders went through an intense period of values development and behavioral management training.

The years 2012-2014 were very busy for Chief Leadership Officer Mark Fernandes. In an effort to share the Luck Companies' story, mission, and beliefs about Values Based Leadership, Mark and his team traveled locally, nationally and internationally leading speaking engagements on the subject of VBL. During this time period, Mark and his team began to provide consulting services to a variety of organizations on the subject of VBL. The HayGroup was hired to evaluate the Values Based Leadership effort at Luck Companies. Management consultants from the HayGroup constructed a survey that aligned with the Values Based Leadership program at Luck Companies and 98% of the firm's associates completed the survey. The results of this survey were very favorable, placing Luck Companies among the top companies in the world for employee engagement. The results were even more favorable than those from a similar survey that had been conducted in 2011 and management immediately took action on the few problem and

opportunity areas that were identified. For example, a Vacation Donation Policy was created whereby employees could donate unused vacation time to other employees in need. Annual Associate Engagement Surveys have become common practice at Luck Companies and the management team continually challenges themselves to achieve best in class performance year over year.

The Future of the Values Journey

The management team at Luck Companies used the 2012 to 2014 time period to rationalize and reflect on all they had learned about Values Based Leadership. Through all of their engagements and efforts to drive impact on the subject locally and globally, they realized that they needed a platform that would better lend itself to promoting this model on a larger scale. Furthermore, the demand from companies and individuals for information and coaching on VBL began to outpace Luck Companies' capacity. To this end, a decision was made in 2014 to establish a Values Based Leadership Institute in 2015, called InnerWill. Furthermore, Charlie decided that this institute would be established as a 501-(c)(3) not-for-profit organization. Charlie stated that, "My belief from the beginning was to give this, [Values Based Leadership], to the world with nothing in return." The institute will draw on internal leadership talent as well as acclaimed professionals in the leadership field to advance the institute's mission. Luck Companies will ultimately become a "practitioner" of the institute's work. Through InnerWill, management plans to accomplish the following three goals that are part of "Vision 2015". First, to increase the "Number of lives Impacted" through Values Based Leadership; second, to ensure that the "Number of values based leaders developed" is increased; and third, to increase "Our global reputation: Top 5" in the field of Value Based Leadership.

Vision 2020

Over the past ten years, there have been many changes at Luck Companies, from the rebranding of business units to the restructuring of sales teams. However, one constant throughout this time period has been the mission of Luck Companies to Ignite Human Potential through Values Based Leadership and positively impact lives around the world. The dedication to fulfilling this mission has been without question and Luck Companies continues to deepen their impact on people both internally and externally. Internally, Luck Companies' associates are challenged to think about their own purpose and vision and are encouraged and aided in their fulfillment. Externally Luck Companies dedicates a significant amount of effort and resources to initiatives such as the founding of InnerWill, the non-profit founded by Luck Companies to drive Values Based Leadership globally. While Igniting Human Potential has remained unchanged, the "Vision" for 2020 will bring significant change to the company. However, these changes are fueled by one constant, the belief in the mission to Ignite Human Potential.

Three of the four Luck Companies' business units underwent or were in the process of undergoing an intense 5-year strategic planning process in 2014 and 2015. Each strategic plan was developed with a focus on supporting Vision 2020, the most aspirational five-year vision in the company's 93-year history. Vision 2020 is built on the following four strategic objectives and high-level definitions:

- **Financial Performance:** Advance the Mission for future generations by insuring the long-term financial health of the company.
- **Leadership Development and Succession**: Ensure we are developing the environment where each leader has the opportunity to optimize their purpose, passion, and competency in a way that prepares the company for the future.
- **Business Excellence**: Optimize time, energy, and talent in order to build a healthy, profitable, and high performance company.
- **Growth**: Challenge ourselves to intentionally reinvent the growth process in a way that brings value to the company and grow sales from $240M to $450M.

2020 Objectives and Goals by Business Unit

The following objectives and goals were developed in 2014 and 2015 for each individual Luck Companies' business unit:

Luck Stone Center

- Expand builder model to all target markets
- Reestablish account base with countertop strategy
- Increase man-made product sales
- Increase accessory sales
- Focus on operational efficiency and customer service improvements
- Continue culture and training initiatives

Har-Tru
Grow product basket

- Other Sports: Identify and add surfaces, equipment and accessories for other sports that can be sold through our sales channels
- Other Tennis Products: Identify and add other surfaces, equipment and accessories for tennis that can be sold through our sales channels
- Innovation: Develop new products

Broaden and deepen connection to the customer

- Develop new relationships in the markets we serve
- Develop relationships in new markets
- Deepen existing relationships and increase knowledge and awareness to better meet customer needs
- Pilot windscreen measurement and installation service through Century Sports

Luck Development Partners

Luck Development Partners is charged with managing the many land holdings of Luck Companies besides those being used for mining activities. Some of these properties include industrial parks and others are permitted for mixed use including housing and retail. While Luck Development Partners currently manages these holdings, the future of this business unit will be revisited in late 2015.

Luck Stone: The 2015–2020 Growth Engine

The 2015 mantra at Luck Stone was growth. The Chief Growth Officer and Corporate Development Team have been supported with significant resources to deliver the majority of the financial growth for Luck Companies. Management had considered getting into some of the businesses that utilized their aggregate but had concluded that the risks were not worth the rewards. For example, they had an opportunity to pursue business operations in the asphalt industry, similar to the vertical integration of Vulcan Materials with concrete production, but decided that doing so would put them in direct competition with some of their largest and most loyal customers. Therefore, in order to meet their growth goal and nearly double revenue from $240M to $450M by 2020, management decided that growth would be achieved by increasing the sales of aggregate while also expanding the offerings and breadth of the other business units. In establishing this growth goal, Luck Companies will allocate 80% of available capital to growing the Luck Stone business unit, while the remaining 20% of capital will be focused on growing the Luck Stone Center and Har-Tru business units.

Luck Stone accounts for over 80% of the total revenue of Luck Companies, and will continue to lead the firm's growth over the next five years. While Luck Stone's growth plans do not include vertical integration, there are opportunities for innovative new products to help drive these growth efforts. For instance, management has identified a growing demand for engineered soils and bio filtration media. Engineered soils and bio filtration media are used in retention ponds to filter contaminates in water run-off before it is released into streams or large bodies of water. Management believes that new regulations that focus on water quality and eco-friendly systems will make this a viable new opportunity for their Luck Stone business unit. Some of the key inputs to these soils are taken from the top layer of material that covers the stone at quarries, known as over burden. Over burden is typically removed to reach the material below and is stockpiled on site, often taking up valuable real estate. This market has been served through a small division of Luck Stone called Luck Specialty Products. In 2015, Luck Specialty Products was rebranded into Luck EcoSystems and is now aggressively entering the engineered soils market and seeking growth opportunities.

While some new product offerings and innovations in the industry are possible, the almost doubling of revenue for Luck Companies is to be accomplished primarily through a strategy of acquisition and internal growth. Some internal growth is possible given Luck's investment in equipment, processes and people during the past five years. In addition, the volume of aggregate sales in tons is still below peak levels, therefore some capacity in current operations is available.

Side Note:

In the northern region of Virginia, the Luck Stone Fairfax Plant has nearly reached the end of its reserve life. In anticipation of this event, Luck Stone has invested nearly $40 million into their Bull Run Plant, which is only ten minutes from Fairfax, to back fill demand from Fairfax. By 2016, the Bull Run Plant will have the capacity to produce 5 million tons per year, making it the largest of any Luck Stone plant.

Luck Companies devoted considerable effort to identifying acquisition targets. Maps were constructed of all the growth areas from Virginia to Texas and over 600 independent aggregate producers in the targeted markets had been identified. In late 2014 and early 2015 Luck Companies pursued and/or explored potential opportunities in Virginia, North Carolina, Tennessee, Alabama, South Carolina and Maryland. These conversations were typically started with an introduction to Luck Companies' culture and Values Based Leadership model. Many of the quarries that Luck Stone targeted as potential acquisition opportunities were small to medium sized family owned companies. These companies and their owners, similar to Luck, view their employees as an extension of their own family. If and when the various aggregate producers decide to put their companies up for sale, it is the belief of Luck's management team that some will want to sell to Luck Companies because of their reputation of igniting the potential in their associates through values based leadership, thus having a positive impact on all they touch. These owners truly care about their people and therefore do not want to sell to one of the large industry conglomerates. Furthermore, by targeting small to medium sized family owned companies with similar values and beliefs to Luck Companies, it is the belief of management that the integration of these companies into Luck Companies will come with less hardship and burden.

Luck Companies was off to a fast start in 2015 with many "irons in the fire". The largest plant expansion in Luck Stone history was underway at Bull Run. Luck Stone Center was embarking on a new business strategy under a new brand. Luck EcoSystems was developing new products in a relatively new market and growing rapidly. Har-Tru completed their first "turn-key" tennis court installation supplying everything from court material to netting and all other accessories. InnerWill had put a board of directors and strategic development team in place and had submitted an application for 501(c)(3) status. Luck Companies overall was poised for tremendous growth over the next five years. As Charlie reflected back on his time as CEO and thought forward to 2020 and beyond to future generations, he stated, "The firm is in strong financial condition and has many associates who have untapped potential and we need to give them opportunities to realize their wildest dreams. I feel a deep responsibility to handoff this company to the next generation of associates and family who will have significant opportunities for decades into our second century of running a family business."

NOTES

1. U.S. Geological Survey, 2011, Mineral commodity summaries 2011: Reston, VA, U.S. Geological Survey

2. Construction Equipment Guide (2015). Charlie Luck Takes Over as Chairman of the National Stone, Sand, and Gravel Association - National Edition. Pennsylvania. www.constructionequipmentguide.com.

3. U.S. Census Bureau. (2015). Annual Value of Private Construction Put in Place 2008-2014.

Washington, DC: Government Printing Office.

4. U.S. Census Bureau. (2015). Annual Value of Public Construction Put in Place 2008-2014. Washington, DC: Government Printing Office.

CASE 11

Corporate Governance at Martha Stewart Living Omnimedia: Not "A Good Thing"

James B. Shein
Northwestern University

Going to prison usually ends the career of an executive—unless the executive is Martha Stewart.

Stewart's five-month stay in an American prison in 2005 put an unsightly smudge on her highly polished image as doyenne of the domestic arts. She resigned as chairman and CEO of the company she founded and controlled, Martha Stewart Living Omnimedia (MSO), after her 2004 conviction related to an insider-trading[1] investigation, but her personal image was so closely intertwined with her company that revenues and share prices still plummeted.

When she returned to MSO after her release, advertisers and broadcasters were quick to forgive the tall, blonde celebrity; they flocked back to her namesake magazine and even signed her to star in two new TV shows. Under the leadership of a new CEO backed by Stewart and her allies on the board, MSO seemed by 2006 to be headed for a recovery.

But new technology was undermining the company's business model and serious threats loomed from competitors. It would be Stewart herself—a former model and caterer whose devotion to domestic perfection and luxury had made her a brand icon—that would be the central player in the outcome.

A Brief History of Martha Stewart Living Omnimedia

The seeds of Martha Stewart's larger-than-life career were planted in early childhood. Born Martha Kostyra, the second of six children of Polish immigrant parents, she inherited her mother's passion for cooking and sewing and her father's love of gardening. Her father instilled in her "the quest for perfection, with any task," she once told a reporter. "If I was laying a cobblestone path for him in the garden, it had to be lined up straight with a string. The stones had to have the exact same amount of space between them."[2] To her father, and to Martha, perfection in form and detail was synonymous with enduring value.

Stewart worked part-time as a model in high school and college and took a job as a stockbroker after graduation. A former boss said she was "fabulously successful." But when the stock market crashed in 1974, she quit. According to her former boss, she couldn't bear seeing people lose money on her advice.[3] After marrying Andy Stewart (a lawyer and publisher of art books) in 1961, she returned to Barnard College and completed a degree in history and architectural history.

Stewart's talent for decorating became apparent when she and her husband bought and restored an old farmhouse. She also built a successful catering business in her basement with a friend from her modeling days. When she catered a book release party for her husband, Stewart met Alan Mirken, head of Crown Publishing Group, who later contacted her to develop a cookbook. The result was her 1982 book *Entertaining*, a celebration of stylish party giving. Several more books and television appearances followed. Her 1987 book *Weddings* ignited a trend toward lavish wedding ceremonies and receptions in the United States. Mothers of the bride were soon toting the $50 volume around under their arms.

Stewart had caught a wave. As women increasingly made strides in the workplace, yearning for home and hearth was on the rise. With her authoritative, patrician bearing, Stewart was able to elevate domestic skills to an art form. Many fans aspired to adopt her elegant style, and her do-it-yourself ethos provided new outlets for self-expression.

Stewart laid the cornerstones of her media empire in the early 1990s with the launch of her flagship magazine, *Martha Stewart Living*, in partnership with Time Inc., and a syndicated television show by the same name.

©2014 by the Kellogg School of Management at Northwestern University. This case was developed with support from the December 2009 graduates of the Executive MBA Program (EMP-76). This case was prepared by Professor James B. Shein. Early research on this case was provided by Funmi Agbebi '13, Carman Empey '14, Mallory Gregor '14, and Darcy Rutzen '14. Cases are developed solely as the basis for class discussion. Cases are not intended to serve as endorsements, sources of primary data, or illustrations of effective or ineffective management. To order copies or request permission to reproduce materials, call 847.491.5400 or e-mail cases@kellogg.northwestern.edu. No part of this publication may be reproduced, stored in a retrieval system, used in a spreadsheet, or transmitted in any form or by any means—electronic, mechanical, photocopying, recording, or otherwise—without the permission of Kellogg Case Publishing.

She produced and hosted the show, preparing recipes in Julia Child's stand-and-stir style and showing approval with her trademark comment, "It's a good thing." Another magazine, *Martha Stewart Weddings*, followed in 1994. Stewart sought help with operations from Sharon Patrick, a former McKinsey & Co. partner whom she met climbing Mount Kilimanjaro in 1993.

A shrewd negotiator, Patrick helped Stewart acquire control of her business from Time Inc. in 1997 and form Martha Stewart Living Omnimedia. Stewart and Patrick then caught another trend among retailers—a shift away from individual items toward entire categories of goods. Patrick negotiated a ground-breaking deal with Kmart, then the second-largest retailer in the United States, to sell branded Martha Stewart housewares and linens in its stores. The partnership generated big profits for MSO and left an indelible mark on merchandising by bringing tasteful design to low-cost consumer goods. The success of the arrangement paved the way for other low-cost, upscale branding efforts by stores like Target.

Stewart's personal tastes, personality, and lifestyle were the context for everything at MSO. Her TV studio was a replica of her own kitchen. She harvested ingredients from her garden and refinished her lawn furniture on the show. Her maniacal devotion to detail and perfection instilled trust in her brand. "I wash the sheets myself. I count the stitches … We care that we're not disappointing anybody," she told a reporter.[4] By the late 1990s, Stewart had become the nation's preeminent female brand name, inspiring comparisons to Calvin Klein, Tommy Hilfiger, and her personal role model, Ralph Lauren.[5]

As Stewart and Patrick began preparing to take the company public, analysts likened her fans to a cult. Some questioned the wisdom of basing a public company on one person's image. "If you are basing your entire public issue on that one name," one analyst said, "you have to question how you can broaden it so that the whole company does not suffer if the head person gets hit by a bus—or by a scandal."[6] MSO promised in its prospectus to promote "a new generation of Martha Stewart Living experts" and to publicize other members of the creative team.

On the day of the IPO in 1999, it was Stewart herself who stood outside the New York Stock Exchange handing out scones and fresh-squeezed orange juice. Wall Street responded with equal warmth. The stock surged from the $18 initial price to $36, making Stewart America's first self-made female billionaire.[7]

At many companies, the board of directors provided oversight of strategic planning, in some cases by establishing a strategic planning committee to provide stability and continuity during leadership transitions. MSO's bylaws required four committees: audit, compensation, finance, and nominating and corporate governance. The bylaws also made the board responsible for monitoring the "principal risk exposures" of the company, and assigned oversight to the audit committee. Directors received training on risk management during an orientation session that included learning about MSO's officers, auditors, strategic plans, corporate governance, compliance programs, and code of ethics, and were given a corporate headquarters tour. Training beyond that was voluntary; MSO "encouraged directors to participate in education programs" to help them meet their responsibilities.

Because Stewart was not only chairman and CEO but also the controlling shareholder (Exhibit 1), she was able to name Patrick chief operating officer and appoint her as a director. She also invited her old friend Charlotte Beers, former CEO of the ad giant Ogilvy & Mather, onto the board.

Competition

By the 2000s, MSO was facing new competition and changing markets on all fronts. Rivals were taking share in lifestyle-related publishing, the source of 62 percent of MSO revenues. After Stewart cut ties with Time Inc., the Time-Warner unit launched a competing magazine, *Real Simple*, which appealed to a younger, less traditional audience than Stewart's by offering practical, time-saving tips for getting things done. Daytime television diva Oprah Winfrey followed with *O, the Magazine*. Meredith Corp., with a business mix similar to MSO's, including the biggest home-and-garden magazine, *Better Homes and Gardens*, was extending the brand into licensed products, including paint and furniture coverings.

In addition, changing technology was giving rise to a new generation of low-cost competitors. A 1996 Internet startup, TheKnot.com, posted rapid growth in online advertising and content for weddings, a core MSO competency. TheKnot.com soon spun off TheNest.com for newlyweds and TheBump.com for expectant parents. Established competitors, too, were expanding rapidly in e-commerce. Ralph Lauren Corp., also a designer of home and lifestyle products, partnered in 2004 with GSI Commerce, an e-commerce and technology provider, to sell its branded merchandise online, an alliance that generated hundreds of millions of dollars in sales for Lauren.

In broadcasting, the source of 13 percent of MSO's revenues, ad sales were under pressure from online competition and shrinking audiences for daytime TV.

Exhibit 1 Martha Stewart Living Omnimedia Board of Directors, 2003–2012

	2003	2004	2005	2006	2007	2008	2009	2010	2011	2012
Charlotte Beers						■	■	■	■	■
Rick Boyko		■	■	■	■	■				
Frederic Fekkai								■	■	■
Lisa Gersh										■
Michael Goldstein		■	■	■	■	■	■	■	■	■
Jill A. Greenthal				■	■	■	■	■	■	■
Arlen Kantarian							■	■	■	■
Charles Koppelman			■	■	■	■	■	■	■	
Michael Kramer										■
Susan Lyne		■	■	■	■	■				
Arthur C. Martinez	■	■								
Wenda H. Millard		■	■	■	■					
Darla D. Moore	■									
Sharon L. Patrick	■	■						■		
William A. Roskin								■	■	■
Naomi O. Seligman	■									
Thomas Siekman		■	■	■	■	■				
Bradley E. Singer		■	■	■	■					
Claudia Slacik									■	
Todd Slotkin						■	■	■	■	
Margaret Smyth										■
Martha Stewart	■									■
Jeffrey W. Ubben	■	■								
Daniel Walker										■

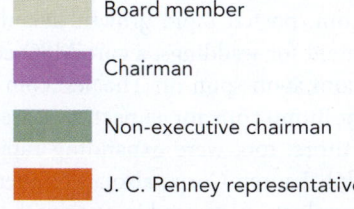

■ Board member

■ Chairman

■ Non-executive chairman

■ J. C. Penney representative

Source: MSO Proxy Statements.

Exhibit 1 (*Continued*)

Director Bios

Charlotte Beers: Former chairman of J. Walter Thompson Worldwide; previously chairman and CEO of Ogilvy & Mather and chairman emeritus of Ogilvy & Mather Worldwide Inc.; Under Secretary for Public Diplomacy and Public Affairs for the George W. Bush Administration from 2001 to 2003. Identified as a candidate for the board by Martha Stewart.

Rick Boyko: Managing director of the VCU Adcenter, a graduate advertising program at Virginia Commonwealth University; formerly co-president and chief creative officer of Ogilvy & Mather, New York. Identified as candidate for the board by Martha Stewart.

Frederic Fekkai: Founder of Fekkai, a luxury hair-care product company with seven hair salons in the United States; founder and brand architect for the Fekkai brand at Procter & Gamble, which purchased the company in 2008. Identified as a candidate for the board by Martha Stewart.

Lisa Gersh: President and chief operating officer of MSO from 2011 to 2013 and CEO of the company from 2012 to 2013. Previously president, strategic initiatives, of NBC Universal and managing director and CEO of The Weather Channel Companies. Previously co-founder of Oxygen Media LLC, serving as president and chief operating officer for nine years.

Michael Goldstein: Chairman of Toys "R" Us Children's Fund Inc., a charitable foundation. Previously chairman of the board, vice chairman, and CEO of Toys "R" Us Inc. Identified as a candidate for the board by Martha Stewart.

Jill A. Greenthal: Senior managing director of the Blackstone Group; previously co-head of the global media group and a member of the executive board of investment banking at Credit Suisse First Boston. Previously co-head of the Boston office of Donaldson, Lufkin and Jenrette and head of the media group at Lehman Bros.

Arlen Kantarian: Former CEO of professional tennis for the United States Tennis Association; previously president and CEO of Radio City Entertainment and vice president, marketing, for the National Football League.

Charles Koppelman: Executive chairman and principal executive officer of MSO from 2009 to 2011. Chairman and CEO of CAK Entertainment Inc., a music and entertainment business. Previously chairman and CEO of EMI Music Publishing; chairman and CEO of EMI Records Group, North America; and chairman of Steve Madden Ltd.

Michael Kramer: Chief operating officer for J. C. Penney Co. Previously president and CEO of Kellwood Co., executive vice president and chief financial officer of Abercrombie & Fitch Co., and former chief financial officer of Apple Inc.'s retail operations.

Susan Lyne: President and CEO of MSO from 2004 to 2008. Previously president of ABC Entertainment and executive vice president of Walt Disney Pictures and Television Inc. Identified as a board candidate by a third-party search firm.

Arthur C. Martinez: Former chairman and CEO of Sears Roebuck and Co.; previously chairman and CEO of Sears Merchandising Group and vice chairman of Saks Fifth Avenue.

Wenda Harris Millard: Co-CEO of MSO from 2008 to 2009; previously chief sales officer at Yahoo! Inc. and chief Internet officer at Ziff Davis Media.

Darla D. Moore: Executive vice president of Rainwater Inc, a private investment firm; previously a managing director of Chase Bank. Chairwoman and founder of The Palmetto Institute, a private policy research group.

Sharon L. Patrick: President and chief operating officer of MSO from 1997 to 2004; CEO from 2003 to 2004; previously president of The Sharon Patrick Company, a strategic consulting firm; president and chief operating officer of Rainbow Programming Holdings, a unit of Cablevision Systems Development, and a principal at McKinsey and Co. leading the media and entertainment practice.

William A. Roskin: Founder of Roskin Consulting, specializing in media-related human relations; previously a senior advisor and senior executive in charge of human resources and administration at Viacom Inc., and senior vice president, human resources, at Coleco Industries Inc.

Naomi O. Seligman: Co-founder of Ostriker von Simson Inc., an e-commerce consultancy; previously co-founder of Research Board Inc., an information technology research group.

Thomas Siekman: Of counsel for Skadden, Arps, Slate, Meagher & Flom LLP; previously senior vice president and general counsel of Compaq Computer Corp. and senior vice president and general counsel of Digital Equipment Corp.

Exhibit 1 (*Continued*)

Bradley E. Singer: Chief financial officer and treasurer of American Tower Corp.; previously an investment banker in the communications, media, and entertainment group at Goldman, Sachs & Co., and chief financial officer at Clyde's Restaurant Group.

Claudia Slacik: CEO, treasury and securities services, Europe, Middle East, and Africa, at JPMorgan Chase; previously chief financial officer for the group; global head of client strategy for Citigroup's $10 billion global transaction services group; global head of trade services and finance at Citigroup; and vice president, strategic planning, at World Color Press, one of KKR's original LBOs.

Todd Slotkin: Portfolio manager of Irving Place Capital, an institutional private equity firm; previously managing director and co-head of Natixis Capital Markets Leveraged Finance business; executive vice president and chief financial officer of MacAndrews & Forbes Holdings Inc.; and chief financial officer of M&F Worldwide Corp.

Margaret Smyth: Former vice president and chief financial officer of Hamilton Sundstrand, a unit of United Technologies Corp.; previously vice president and corporate controller of United Technologies Corp., and vice president and chief accounting officer of 3M Corp.

Martha Stewart: MSO founder and chief editorial, media, and content officer. Previously chairman and CEO from 1996 to 2003; author, creator of *Martha Stewart Living* magazine, television host.

Jeffrey W. Ubben: Founder and managing partner of VA Partners LLC, an investment partnership; previously managing partner of Blum Capital and a portfolio manager for Fidelity Investments.

Daniel Walker: Chief talent officer for J. C. Penney Co.; previously chief talent officer for Apple Inc. and vice president, human resources, for The Gap Inc.

Source: **MSO Proxy Statements.**

Martha Stewart imitators were starting lifestyle cable channels and programs. Oprah Winfrey, MSO's competitor in publishing, helped launch a competing celebrity chef named Rachael Ray, whose "30-minute meals" appealed to time-pressed young consumers.

MSO faced its most formidable competition in an area Wall Street regarded as the company's most promising—merchandising, which accounted for 9 percent of its revenues. Retailing juggernauts Walmart and Target were expanding fast, threatening to crush Kmart, MSO's biggest sales outlet.

A Grand Vision

Management's strategic vision rested on what Stewart, quoting the ancient Greeks in MSO's 2001 annual report, elegantly called *synergia*, or synergy. By uniting publishing, television, merchandising, and Internet businesses under one umbrella, Stewart predicted that results would exceed the sum of the parts as each business generated advertising, sales, or subscriptions for all the others. To make the plan work, Patrick promised to sell more multimedia packages, develop new TV shows, and reduce MSO's heavy dependence on publishing.

A big jump in ad pages for *Martha Stewart Living* drove a 23 percent increase in revenues during 2000, MSO's first full year as a public company. The company's share price surged to within $2 of the 1999 high of $36, more than 45 times earnings.

But signs of softness in revenues and profit margins were emerging. Revenue growth slowed to just 2 percent in 2001 and net income fell 16 percent in 2000 and edged just 3 percent higher in 2001. Ratings faltered at MSO's flagship show, "Martha Stewart Living." Kmart, source of 17 percent of MSO's total revenues, filed for bankruptcy protection in 2002, then sued MSO and won big cuts in guaranteed royalties and advertising. Patrick pledged to find other retail outlets to replace it.

Online, the company was delivering features, recipes, and how-to content on MarthaStewart.com with the intent of generating revenue from advertisers as well as sales of the 2,800 products available there, which ranged from bedding to soap-making kits. However, the website was losing a lot of money. Promising to drive the website to profitability, Patrick hired new management as part of a $7 million company restructuring in 2001. MSO also acquired the Wedding List, a gift registry and retailer operating online and in showrooms.

As MSO's chief talent, Stewart drew total 2000 compensation of $2.8 million (Exhibit 2). That amount was down from $4.7 million the year before the IPO, but analysts said her pay was still out of line with revenues. Stewart also received $2 million a year or more under an "intangible assets licensing agreement"

Exhibit 2 Martha Stewart Living Omnimedia Selected Key Executive Compensation ($)

	2012	2011	2010	2009	2008	2007	2006	2005
Martha Stewart Founding Chairman and CEO	5,460,406[a]	5,501,800	5,907,387	9,784,505[b]	7,018,336	2,061,854	2,096,176	2,226,365[c]
Susan Lyne President and CEO					1,671,633	3,934,693	4,405,782	1,333,622
Charles Koppelman Executive Chairman, Prin Exec Off		3,785,542	2,268,225	2,122,062	8,016,257			
Lisa Gersh President and COO	1,511,625[d]	3,759,903						
Robin Marino President and CEO, Merchandising			1,711,311	1,418,510	2,498,228[e]	1,709,492	1,461,028	2,032,539
Wenda Harris Millard President, Media				734,095	2,325,020[e]	2,718,631		

Notes:
[a]Founder, Chief Creative Officer
[b]Chief Editorial, Media and Content Officer
[c]Founder
[d]Additional title of Chief Executive Officer
[e]Co-Chief Executive Officer
Source: MSO Proxy Statements.

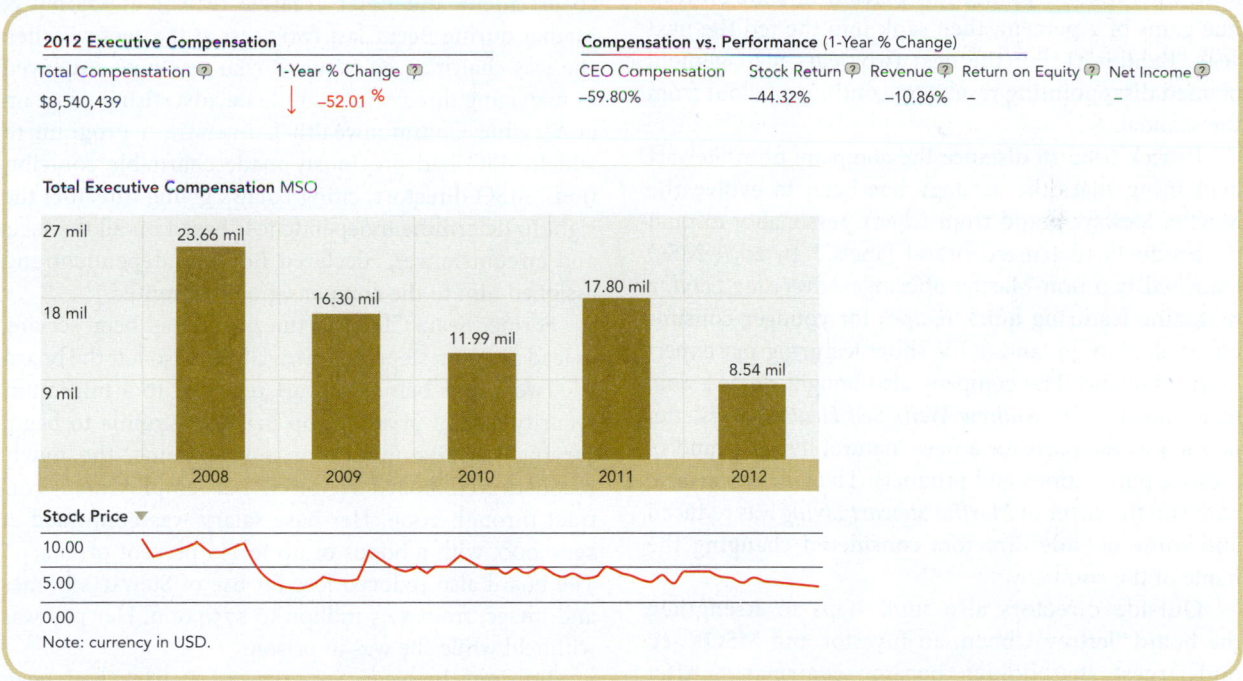

2012 Executive Compensation		Compensation vs. Performance (1-Year % Change)				
Total Compensation ⑦	1-Year % Change ⑦	CEO Compensation	Stock Return ⑦	Revenue ⑦	Return on Equity ⑦	Net Income ⑦
$8,540,439	↓ −52.01 %	−59.80%	−44.32%	−10.86%	–	–

Total Executive Compensation MSO

- 23.66 mil (2008)
- 16.30 mil (2009)
- 11.99 mil (2010)
- 17.80 mil (2011)
- 8.54 mil (2012)

Stock Price ▼

Note: currency in USD.

Source: Morningstar.

that paid her for corporate use of her image and homes in promotions and demos. Stewart expensed many other parts of her life, too, including a weekend driver and a personal trainer. She said all the spending was necessary to maintain the quality for which her brand was known.

There was no question that Stewart and the brand were synonymous. The question on the minds of investors and consumers alike was: Was Stewart creating a powerful brand that would outlive her, like Coco Chanel, or was she more like Laura Ashley, the British fabric designer whose 1985 death thrust her company into a crisis?

A Crippling Blow

In 2002 the media reported that Stewart was the target of an insider-trading investigation in connection with her sale of personal stock in ImClone Systems Inc., in advance of bad news about a key drug. Stewart was indicted in June 2003. The Securities and Exchange Commission also filed civil charges against her, alleging securities law violations. Stewart was convicted in 2004 of conspiracy, obstruction of justice, and making false statements to investigators, and she resigned as chairman and CEO of MSO.

MSO's brand equity took a beating. The *New York Post* ran a photoshopped picture of Stewart in prison stripes on Page One. Cable channels dropped Stewart's show. Publicity about her legal troubles led to a 63 percent drop in ad pages at *Martha Stewart Living*, while competitors' magazine ad sales rose sharply. Meanwhile, MarthaStewart.com was still losing money. Patrick stepped in as CEO, laying off 40 percent of MSO's employees and slashing product offerings by 60 percent. She then shuttered and wrote off the Wedding List acquisition just 15 months after making the deal. MSO's net income plunged 67 percent in 2002 on revenue gains of 2 percent, then sank into the red the next year (Exhibit 3). For the next two years management blamed disappointing results on continued fallout from the scandal.

Patrick tried to distance the company from Stewart, explaining that "the strategy has been to evolve the Martha Stewart brand from expert personality to quality products to trusted brand labels."[8] In 2003 MSO launched two non-Martha offerings—*Everyday Food*, a magazine featuring quick recipes for younger consumers ages 25 to 49, and a TV show featuring pet expert Mark Marrone. The company also bought *Body + Soul* magazine and *Dr. Andrew Weil's Self Healing* newsletter in 2004 as the basis for a new "natural living" brand of lifestyle publications and products. The size of Stewart's name on the cover of *Martha Stewart Living* was reduced, and some outside directors considered changing the name of the company.[9]

Outside directors also took steps to strengthen the board. Jeffrey Ubben, an investor and MSO's second-largest shareholder, became chairman.[10] After complaining that the board lacked enough heavy hitters, Ubben recruited two new independent[11] directors, Thomas Siekman, a former general counsel at Compaq Computer, and Bradley Singer, a former Goldman, Sachs & Co. banker and CFO of American Tower Corp.[12] Former Sears CEO Arthur Martinez, who had joined the board in 2001, was elevated to lead director.

Frustrated over efforts to distance the company from her, Stewart took steps to use her ownership stake, which comprised 94 percent of MSO's voting shares at the time, to regain control. A few months earlier, a friend had introduced her to Charles Koppelman, a former producer and music-industry executive who had served as an advisor to other executives in trouble. He had served as acting chairman of Steven Madden Ltd. from 2000 to 2004 while the shoe retailer's founder and CEO did time for securities fraud and money laundering.[13] Koppelman had also helped entertainer Michael Jackson with his financial problems.

Koppelman advised Stewart to "take control of what you can control—your business."[14] A few days after her sentencing in July 2004, Stewart began remaking the board, adding Koppelman and Susan Lyne, former head of Walt Disney's ABC Entertainment (Exhibit 1). Lyne had a strong television and magazine background and had helped develop programs that would soon become huge hits, including "Desperate Housewives" and "Lost." Three other new directors joined the board, including Wenda Harris Millard, chief sales officer at Yahoo! Inc.

Another new director was Rick Boyko, former co-president and chief creative officer at Ogilvy & Mather during Beers' last two years at the agency, when she was chairman emeritus. Boyko was now employed as managing director of a graduate advertising program at Virginia Commonwealth University, a program to which MSO had previously made charitable contributions. MSO directors, citing bylaws giving directors the right to determine independence "based on all the facts and circumstances," declared Boyko independent and assigned him to the compensation committee.[15]

Former Sears CEO Martinez, who had been serving as lead director, stepped down. Ubben also left the board.

Two weeks before Stewart reported to a minimum-security federal prison camp in West Virginia to begin serving her five-month prison sentence, the newly reconstituted board renewed her employment contract through 2009. Her base salary was continued at $900,000, with a bonus of up to 150 percent of salary.[16] The board also reduced fees for use of Stewart's homes and image, from $2.5 million to $750,000. Her pay was withheld while she was in prison.

Tensions between Stewart and Patrick had been mounting as MSO's losses deepened. Patrick resisted Stewart's urging that she hire a No. 2, saying she could handle the job herself.[17] One week after Patrick reported in October 2004 that MSO's third-quarter net loss had tripled and the fourth-quarter loss would be worse than expected (Exhibit 4), the board fired her. Lyne was named as her replacement, taking over just as the show

Exhibit 3 MSO Financial Statements, 1998–2002 ($ in thousands, except per share data)

	2002	2001	2000	1999	1998
REVENUES					
Publishing	182,600	177,422	175,774	142,993	124,172
Television	26,680	29,522	32,464	30,590	23,351
Merchandising	48,896	35,572	24,345	20,200	15,004
Internet/direct commerce	36,873	46,094	49,739	36,004	14,673
Total revenues	295,049	288,610	282,322	229,787	177,200
Operating income (loss)	19,993	37,064	31,707	22,322	27,385
Income (loss) from continuing operations	13,314	23,615	21,278	25,569	23,806
Loss from discontinued operations	(2,909)	(1,709)			
Cumulative effect of accounting change	(3,137)				
Net income (loss)	7,268	21,906	21,278	25,569	23,806
Pro forma net income (loss)	7,268	21,906	21,278	11,692	12,989
PER SHARE DATA					
Earnings (loss) per share:					
Basic—Income (loss) from continuing operations	$0.27	$0.49	$0.44		
Basic—Loss from discontinued operations	$(0.06)	$(0.04)			
Basic—Cumulative effect of accounting change	$(0.06)				
Basic—Net income (loss)	$0.15	$0.45	$0.44		
Diluted—Income (loss) from continuing operations	$0.27	$0.49	$0.43		
Diluted—Loss from discontinued operations	$(0.06)	$(0.04)			
Diluted—Cumulative effect of accounting change	$(0.06)				
Diluted—Net income (loss)	$0.15	$0.45	$0.43		
Weighted average common shares outstanding:					
Basic	49,250	48,639	48,678		
Diluted	49,343	49,039	49,623		
FINANCIAL POSITION					
Cash and cash equivalents	131,664	68,076	80,320	58,654	24,578
Short-term investments	47,286	73,086	47,105	96,095	
Total assets	324,542	311,621	297,414	281,771	125,372
Long-term debt					27,650
Shareholders' equity	236,635	222,192	196,116	199,402	36,815
OTHER FINANCIAL DATA					
Cash flow provided by (used in) operating activities	38,042	19,389	39,538	28,304	17,524
Cash flow provided by (used in) investing activities	21,493	(34,040)	10,922	(102,393)	(341)
Cash flow provided by (used in) financing activities	4,053	2,407	(28,794)	108,165	(2,576)

Source: MSO 2002 Form 10-K.

she had helped develop at ABC, "Desperate Housewives," became TV's biggest new hit.[18]

Prison rules prevented Stewart from making decisions and conducting business during her incarceration, but Lyne and Koppelman visited her a half-dozen times and were allowed to tell her what was going on at MSO.[19] After she was released, however, she was allowed to work 48 hours a week during her five months of home

Exhibit 4 MSO Financial Statements, 2003–2007 ($ in thousands, except per share data)

	2007	2006	2005	2004	2003
REVENUES					
Publishing	183,727	156,559	125,765	95,960	135,529
Merchandising	84,711	69,504	58,819	53,386	53,395
Internet	19,189	15,775	11,258	27,512	30,813
Broadcasting	40,263	46,503	16,591	10,580	26,111
Total revenues	327,890	288,341	212,433	187,438	245,848
Operating income (loss)	7,714	(2,833)	(78,311)	(60,004)	(6,405)
Income (loss) from continuing operations	10,289	(16,250)	(75,295)	(59,073)	(1,923)
Loss from discontinued operations		(745)	(494)	(526)	(848)
Net income (loss)	10,289	(16,995)	(75,789)	(59,599)	(2,771)
PER SHARE DATA					
Earnings (loss) per share:					
Basic and diluted—Income (loss) from continuing operations	$0.20	$(0.32)	$(1.48)	$(1.19)	$(0.04)
Basic and diluted—Loss from discontinued operations		$(0.01)	$(0.01)	$(0.01)	$(0.02)
Basic and diluted—Net income (loss)	$0.20	$(0.33)	$(1.49)	$(1.20)	$(0.06)
Weighted average common shares outstanding:					
Basic	52,449	51,312	50,991	49,712	49,389
Diluted	52,696	51,312	50,991	49,712	49,389
Dividends per common share		$0.50			
FINANCIAL POSITION					
Cash and cash equivalents	30,536	28,528	20,249	104,647	165,566
Short-term investments	26,745	35,321	83,788	35,309	3,100
Total assets	255,267	228,047	253,828	264,678	309,102
Shareholders' equity	155,529	130,957	160,631	187,628	236,665
OTHER FINANCIAL DATA					
Cash flow provided by (used in) operating activities	11,735	(5,711)	(30,349)	(22,226)	(9,634)
Cash flow provided by (used in) investing activities	(6,606)	40,125	(58,300)	(39,756)	15,956
Cash flow provided by (used in) financing activities	(3,121)	(26,135)	4,251	1,063	404

Source: MSO 2007 Form 10-K.

confinement. Stewart had been barred from serving as a director or officer of the company until August 2011 as part of a settlement with the SEC, so when she returned to work in March 2005 she assumed the title of "founder." At the time of Stewart's return, MSO ad sales already were recovering. Kmart's 2004 purchase of Sears sparked rumors that Martha Stewart products would be sold in Sears stores, driving MSO share price to a new high of $37. A poll commissioned by Lyne found that half of American women still described themselves as "supporters" of Stewart.[20] Lyne later heralded the founder's

return in the annual report as a sign that "our capacity to plan (is) no longer clouded." In June 2005 Koppelman, Stewart's advisor and confidant, became chairman of the board.

Efforts to diversify MSO's brands away from the company's namesake soon lost momentum. Excitement was mounting about "The Apprentice: Martha Stewart," a prime-time reality TV show on NBC from Mark Burnett, the creator of "The Apprentice" with Donald Trump.[21] The original series had turned the irascible Donald Trump into a household name; why could it not do the same—or more—for Stewart? NBC also agreed to broadcast a new syndicated daytime TV show hosted by Stewart.

Although analysts worried that Stewart could become overexposed, she told a reporter for *Fortune* magazine in 2005, "I have learned that I really cannot be destroyed."[22]

Glimmers of Hope

In 2005 the company posted its largest-ever annual loss—$75.8 million. However, in the annual report Lyne and Koppelman chose to focus instead on MSO's 12 percent revenue increase as evidence that the "turn-around is real and the avenues for growth are vast." Lyne, who was well-regarded inside the company and helped restore investor confidence, was praised by Stewart for her "intelligent surehandedness, congeniality, and high-mindedness."[23]

Despite an expanding economy, however, MSO posted another loss in 2006. The shift in publishing toward shorter online content was gaining momentum. Advertisers were dividing their dollars among a growing diversity of media. MSO was losing ground with younger consumers to rising stars such as 37-year-old Rachael Ray, who launched not only a series of cookbooks but also a magazine and her own syndicated daily TV show. MSO targeted younger consumers with the 2006 launch of a new magazine, *Blueprint*, but it flopped within a year.

Reality TV productions pitting celebrity chefs against each other in high-energy cook-offs were making Stewart's stand-and-stir style seem a little passé. Stewart's 2005 foray into reality TV, "The Apprentice: Martha Stewart," featured Koppelman as her cigar-chomping sidekick. Unfortunately, it drew only half as many viewers as Trump's show and was quickly canceled. Stewart's other new show, "Martha," produced 63 percent of MSO's broadcasting revenue but posted losses. Koppelman, who was paid as a deal consultant to the company while also serving as chairman, helped strike other media deals, including one for a Martha Stewart Living satellite radio channel and another with Warner Home Video to produce DVDs from past TV shows.

Competitors were expanding in merchandising as well. In 2007 Meredith Corp. signed a multi-year agreement to sell Better Homes and Gardens products through Walmart. But the looming loss of the partnership with Kmart posed a much greater threat to MSO. Kmart had struggled for years, during which it had closed 600 stores, but it still generated 89 percent of MSO's merchandising revenue. MSO was able to extend its licensing agreement

with Kmart in 2005, but not without additional cuts in guaranteed royalties and advertising.

Lyne's strategy was to capitalize on MSO's high-quality product design by landing more high-margin, low-cost licensing deals in new categories. "Virtually anything having to do with the home … is ours to own," she said.[24] She recruited Robin Marino, former president of the designer-clothing maker Kate Spade Inc., to head merchandising, and the team lined up a pivotal multi-year deal in 2007 with Macy's to sell dinnerware and furniture. Martha Stewart products soon became Macy's biggest sellers in the housewares category, but the contract was less lucrative than Kmart's and gave Stewart less visibility and influence.

MSO signed a food and kitchenware licensing agreement with celebrity chef Emeril Lagasse, an aging Food Network star who had helped pioneer the reality TV format. The company also partnered with a homebuilder to license entire houses—custom versions of Stewart's own homes. Other merchandising deals were planned for products from closet organizers to light fixtures. Analysts said MSO risked diluting its brand, but by 2007, MSO's merchandising revenues were up 22 percent.

Lyne declared the web "a platform we must master," and pledged to make MarthaStewart.com the "go-to lifestyle destination on the web."[25] MSO relaunched the site in 2007 with new blogs and advanced search and community-building tools. Lyne moved more how-to content online and struck deals with 1-800-FLOWERS to sell branded flowers and with Kodak for digital greeting cards. MSO also began sharing content with Yahoo! and the Food Channel, and bought a 40 percent stake in Wedding Wire, an online marketplace and community site.

In 2007 the predicted turnaround seemed within reach. Ad pages in *Martha Stewart Living* were up, aided by growth in the natural-living magazine *Body + Soul*. MSO's revenues rose 54 percent between 2005 and 2007 to a new high of $327.9 million, and in 2007 the company posted a $10.3 million profit, its first since 2002.

The start of a multi-year recession in 2008 hit MSO's markets hard. Home product sales sagged as the housing collapse spiraled out of control. The relaunched website was falling short of expectations. Ad rates softened industry-wide, which reversed the brief recovery in ad pages at *Martha Stewart Living*. Mindful that MSO still depended on publishing for the majority of its revenue, Wall Street drove the stock to new lows near $5 a share.

A dispute over Stewart's compensation reportedly led to major changes in the board. The 2004 contract that reduced annual fees for use of her homes and image was set to expire in 2009, but Stewart began pushing the board in 2008 for "make-whole" payments, or payments that would make up for the reduction. Two respected outside directors—Jill Greenthal, a senior executive at the Blackstone Group and an experienced advisor to media companies, and Ubben's recruit, Bradley Singer—resigned in March 2008.[26] Ubben's second recruit, Thomas Siekman, left the board three months later. Stewart's friend Charlotte Beers, who had left the board in 2001 to become Under Secretary for Public Diplomacy and Public Affairs during the administration of President George W. Bush, came out of retirement to fill one of the slots, and the other two vacancies were filled by William Roskin, a human relations consultant and former Viacom executive, and Todd Slotkin, a portfolio manager for a private equity firm.

Beers took over from Siekman as head of the board's nominating and corporate governance committee, which MSO bylaws charged with overseeing succession planning—a potentially challenging role when Stewart showed little inclination to identify or develop a successor.

The reconstituted board swiftly approved a compensation package that included a $3 million payment to Stewart, which the company alternately labeled a make-whole payment for rights to her homes and image from September 2007 through August 2009, and a "retention" bonus. The package also included a $100,000 "non-accountable expense allowance," $193,066 in "talent fees," and $33,520 to pay people who worked for Stewart.

Amid reports of mounting tensions with Stewart, Lyne's resignation soon followed. The board implemented a complicated setup in her wake, naming two co-CEOs—Robin Marino, the merchandising chief, and Wenda Harris Millard. A former chief sales officer at Yahoo! and a fixture in the advertising business, Millard had joined the board during Stewart's 2004 board shakeup and was later hired to head MSO's media business. The board appointed three more officers—Koppelman, Stewart, and MSO's chief creative officer Gael Towey—to serve in a three-person "office of the chairman." The company said Stewart's position did not violate the terms of her 2006 agreement with the SEC.

Directors continued to wrestle with Stewart's new pay package into 2009. Stewart added two more members to the board, including her former hairdresser, Frederic Fekkai, founder of the eponymous hair-care product company. Known for his skill in formulating fine shampoos and styling spray, Fekkai was seated immediately on the compensation committee responsible for overseeing Stewart's pay, along with two more newcomers, Roskin and Slotkin.

When MSO posted a $14.6 million loss in 2009 (Exhibit 5), Stewart's total compensation hit $9.8 million, including the retention bonus, $2.6 million in intangible-asset fees, a $178,663 "talent fee," $178,352 for security services, $49,440 for a weekend driver, and a $100,000 "non-accountable expense allowance." During the four years ending in 2012, a period when the company's losses totaled $96 million, Stewart collected nearly $27 million.

Koppelman was asked after Lyne's departure if Stewart's elevation to the office of the chairman portended a larger management role for her. He replied that it would be "hard for Martha to be even more involved." He described Stewart and himself as "the glue" that would hold the awkward new management setup together.[27] MSO shares fell 6 percent on the news.

Narrowing Options

The glue did not hold.

Co-CEO Wenda Millard resigned early in 2009 after clashing with Stewart. The remaining co-CEO, Robin Marino, returned to her former role as head of merchandising and was given a seat on the board. Koppelman became executive chairman and principal executive officer and Stewart took a new title: chief editorial, media, and content officer.

MSO shares plummeted to a new low of $1.60 amid renewed criticism that MSO's cost structure was out of line with revenue. The advertising slump had hit MSO's publishing business hard, and subscriptions and newsstand sales fell. The Kmart agreement expired in 2010, reducing total revenue by 10 percent. The company ended its partnership with 1-800-FLOWERS and wrote off its acquisition of the Andrew Weil newsletter.

A flurry of new licensing deals partly offset the losses. These included home-and-garden gear at Home Depot, pet products at PetSmart, branded foods at Costco, Emeril Lagasse cutlery and steaks, and "Martha Stewart Weddings" through Sandals resorts. Merchandising revenue began to recover, causing Koppelman to declare in a 2011 letter to shareholders, "Our strategy is beginning to work."

Stewart's daytime TV show on NBC was canceled due to poor ratings, but Koppelman looked for new ventures in broadcasting. He struck what he called a ground-breaking agreement with Hallmark Channel for shows with pet expert Mark Morrone, chef Emeril Lagasse, and a new personality from within MSO, food director Lucinda Scala Quinn. Stewart began hosting two new TV shows, "Martha Stewart Cooking School" and "Martha Bakes."

Exhibit 5 MSO Financial Statements, 2008–2012 ($ in thousands, except per share data)

	2012	2011	2010	2009	2008
REVENUES					
Publishing	122,540	140,857	145,573	146,100	179,116
Merchandising	57,574	48,614	42,806	52,566	57,866
Broadcasting	17,513	31,962	42,434	46,111	47,328
Total revenues	197,627	221,433	230,813	244,777	284,310
Operating income (loss)	(56,396)	(18,594)	(8,663)	(11,968)	(10,857)
Net loss	(56,085)	(15,519)	(9,596)	(14,578)	(15,665)
PER SHARE DATA					
Earnings (loss) per share:					
Basic and diluted—Net loss	$(0.83)	$(0.28)	$(0.18)	$(0.27)	$(0.29)
Weighted average common shares outstanding:					
Basic and diluted	67,231,463	55,880,896	54,440,490	53,879,785	53,359,538
Dividends per common share		$0.25			
FINANCIAL POSITION					
Cash and cash equivalents	19,925	38,453	23,204	25,384	50,204
Short-term investments	29,182	11,051	10,091	13,085	9,915
Total assets	154,260	216,120	222,314	229,791	261,285
Long-term obligations		7,500	13,500	19,500	
Shareholders' equity	95,516	147,947	139,033	143,820	150,995
OTHER FINANCIAL DATA					
Cash flow provided by (used in) operating activities	239	(2,220)	1,872	(9,273)	39,699
Cash flow provided by (used in) investing activities	(18,918)	6,886	153	(9,617)	(38,856)
Cash flow provided by (used in) financing activities	151	10,583	(4,205)	(5,930)	18,825

NOTES TO SELECTED FINANCIAL DATA:

Loss from continuing operations:

2012 results include a non-cash goodwill impairment charge related to the Publishing segment of approximately $44.3 million and restructuring charges of approximately $4.8 million.

2011 results include restructuring charges of approximately $5.1 million.

2010 results include the recognition of substantially all of the exclusive license fee of approximately $5 million from Hallmark Channel for a significant portion of MSO's library of programming, as well as licensing revenue for other new programming delivered to Hallmark Channel.

2009 results include a net benefit to operating loss of approximately $20 million from certain items, including the revenue from Kmart of $14.5 million, the recognition of previously deferred Kmart royalties of $10 million as non-cash revenue, and an incremental $3.9 million from the conclusion of MSO's relationship with TurboChef Technologies, Inc.

Source: MSO 2012 Form 10-K.

Stewart's and Koppelman's daughters teamed up to host a short-lived satellite-radio talk show and a poorly received cable TV program called "Whatever Martha," in which they made fun of old Martha Stewart shows. Stewart's daughter was paid as much as $407,680 a year as a broadcast talent, and Koppelman's daughter received as much as $350,675 a year. MSO also employed Stewart's sister-in-law as a senior vice president for as much as $200,633 a year; her brother-in-law as property manager for as much as $146,000 a year, and her sister as a blogger for as much as $81,000 a year.

Meanwhile, management cut employee head count by 8 percent in a company-wide reorganization.

A Turning Point

The ban on Stewart's serving as a corporate officer expired in 2011, freeing her to take the CEO slot. The 69-year-old rejoined the board, but decided not to take the CEO job, saying she was too busy with her TV shows, cookbooks, and public appearances.

With MSO shares trading as low as $2.77, management hired investment bankers in 2011 to explore taking the company private. But Stewart rejected the plan, saying the proposed valuation was too low. For Stewart, it was a personal affront: Wall Street failed to appreciate her value and that of her brand. She told a friend she deserved twice her salary and the stock should be trading at $20, declaring, "I am this company."[28]

MSO turned again to the media industry for a new leader, recruiting Lisa Gersh as president and chief operating officer in 2011. A co-founder of Oxygen Media, Gersh had developed content appealing to the younger women who had proven so elusive for MSO. In her new role she reported to Koppelman and was expected to be appointed CEO within 20 months.

The strategic course set by her predecessors had been far from consistent; first Lyne and then Koppelman had veered from diversifying the company's brands to reduce reliance on Stewart, a path set by Sharon Patrick. Instead, each had focused on developing brand extensions and using MSO's unprofitable broadcast operations as a tool to market them.

A flurry of activity followed as Gersh undertook MSO's first real restructuring. She laid off 12 percent of the company's 600 employees, cut $12.5 million in costs by closing MSO's television production studio, terminated Koppelman's programming agreement with the Hallmark Channel, and ended the live audience for "The Martha Stewart Show." Amid declines in advertising and newsstand sales, Gersh axed two non-Martha magazines, *Everyday Food* and *Whole Living*.

The restructuring left MSO in 2011 looking remarkably like the company that had gone public twelve years earlier—dependent on its publishing business for 62 percent of its revenues. Although digital properties accounted for nearly one-fifth of ad revenue, most of the rest came from two print magazines founded in the early 1990s, *Martha Stewart Living* and *Martha Stewart Weddings*. Gersh also redesigned MarthaStewart.com, put more TV programming and how-to content on the site, and built apps for mobile devices. Traffic rose, and the site won awards for content and quality.

Like her predecessors, Gersh chased new merchandising deals. She launched a new line of branded office products and expanded Martha Stewart crafts offerings. She also vowed to expand into the international markets that had proven elusive for MSO; whereas Meredith Corp. had publishing agreements in 40 nations, MSO's overseas expansion had mostly stalled after the failure of a 2001 agreement to publish a magazine and license products in Japan.

Gersh's crowning achievement, it seemed, would be the December 2011 signing of a new licensing deal with department store J. C. Penney to open Martha Stewart boutiques inside Penney stores. Penney paid $38.5 million for a 16.6 percent stake in MSO, strengthening the company's balance sheet, and two Penney executives took seats on MSO's board (see Exhibit 6).

However, the deal raised new questions on Wall Street—the agreement with Penney covered similar products as the 2007 agreement with Penney's archrival, Macy's.[29] Gersh claimed the Penney product lines would be completely different from those sold in Macy's, but two weeks after exercising its option to renew the agreement with MSO, Macy's sued to block the Penney deal.

Macy's CEO Terry Lundgren, who said he had regarded Stewart as a friend, testified during the trial that he was "completely shocked and blown away" when Stewart broke the news to him by phone the day before the Penney deal was announced. When Stewart tried to persuade him that "this was going to be good for Macy's," Lundgren said, he hung up on her.[30] After an embarrassing public trial and a court order to renegotiate the deal, J. C. Penney and MSO reduced the product categories covered, and Penney gave up its MSO ownership stake and seats on the board.

More turmoil erupted in mid-2012 when Stewart dumped her longtime ally and confidant, Charles Koppelman, telling a reporter that "he was not, because of his experience, the right person" to run the company.[31] Upon his departure, Koppelman told a reporter, "It was never my intention or intent to run Martha's company. I just wanted to help Martha regain control of the company that she almost lost. And I believe I accomplished that."[32] The 71-year-old Stewart became non-executive chairman and chief creative officer, blaming the company's poor performance on legal troubles that kept her partly on the sidelines. The board extended her employment contract to 2017. Gersh, president and chief operating officer, assumed the additional title of CEO in July 2012.[33]

Months later, amid reports of tensions with Stewart, Gersh announced she would resign effective February 2013, just seven months after becoming CEO—making her MSO's fifth CEO in a decade. The company said it would look for a CEO who could build the merchandising business.

Despite Gersh's deep cuts, MSO's costs rose 6 percent in 2012, mostly because of costs related to layoffs and severance pay. New licensing agreements increased merchandising revenue by 18 percent, but total revenues

Exhibit 6 Martha Stewart Living Omnimedia Equity Ownership

	2013	2012	2011	2010	2009	2008	2007	2006	2005	2004	2003	1999
Voting Control (%)												
Martha Stewart	86.6	86.7	90.3	90.8	90.9	91.4	91.7	92.1	90.9	93.8	93.9	96.0
J. C. Penney Co.	3.6	3.7										

Source: MSO 10K Reports.

Ownership of MSO Equity	
Market Capitalization	$188 million
Number of Institutional Owners	101
Number of Fund Owners	132
% Owned by Institutions	17.26
% Owned by Funds	9.9
% Owned by Insiders	0.53

Institutional Ownership (%)	
Royce & Associates	2.69
BlackRock Fund Advisors	1.65
Vanguard Group Inc.	1.18
Dimensional Fund Advisors	1.16
Eidelman Virant Capital	0.82
Eagle Asset Management	0.77
State Street Corp.	0.70
Northern Trust Investments	0.59
Renaissance Technologies	0.51
Bryn Mawr Capital Mgmt.	0.35
Top 10 Institutions	10.42

Fund Ownership (%)	
Royce Opportunity Investment	2.23
Fidelity Select Multimedia	0.77
Vanguard Total Stock Market Index	0.58
iShares Russell 2000 Value	0.53
Vanguard Extended Market Index	0.43
Gabelli Small Cap Growth AAA	0.28
DFA US Micro Cap I	0.26
DFA US Small Cap I	0.21
iShares Micro-Cap	0.19
CREF Stock	0.15
Top 10 Funds	5.63

Source: Investors.Morningstar.com (accessed November 16, 2013).

plunged 11 percent to a nine-year low. In a year when MSO's net loss exceeded $56 million, Stewart collected $5.5 million in total compensation. By year's end, MSO shares traded as low as $2.28.

At a Crossroads

At 72, Stewart in 2013 was enjoying a revival of interest among young do-it-yourself consumers and entrepreneurs. MarthaStewart.com traffic from 18- to 34-year-olds rose, and its content was among the most oft-shared among its rivals on the social site Pinterest. MSO's mobile apps also were popular with the same group.[34]

Stewart published her seventy-ninth book in 2013, *Living the Good Long Life*. She landed cameo roles on such TV shows as "2 Broke Girls" and "Law and Order: Special Victims Unit." The hip-hop star Usher had quoted Stewart in interviews and asked her advice on how to build a treehouse.[35] She was frequently sought out by journalists for celebrity roundups.

But at MSO, the CEO job remained open well into 2013. The company's 22-year-old flagship magazine, *Martha Stewart Living*, with circulation of 2.1 million, barely kept pace with rivals *Real Simple*, with 2.1 million, or *O, The Oprah Magazine*, with 2.4 million. The traditional giants, *Better Homes and Gardens*, with 7.6 million readers, and *Good Housekeeping*, with 4.4 million, continued to dominate the field.[36]

Citing a desire to help the company return to profitability, Stewart took a small pay cut in 2013, from $2 million to $1.8 million, plus a $300,000 reduction in the $2 million fee for use of her home and image. She expressed no interest in succession planning. "I'm convinced she'll be carried from her portable kitchen to her coffin," a friend told a reporter.[37]

Critics of MSO said the brand lost its way by wandering into product lines that damaged its image, such as cleaning fluids and dog poop bags. Although there was still "significant life-blood" left in the Martha Stewart brand, according to one of the few analysts still following the company, "we continue to think MSO is a 'show-me' story—and a potential takeover target."[38]

NOTES

1. Insider trading is the purchase or sale of a public company's stock or other securities by anyone with material knowledge about the company that is not publicly available. Insider trading is illegal in the United States because it is unfair to other investors who lack access to the information. Stewart was alleged to have received insider information from her stockbroker.

2. *Wall Street Journal Magazine*, August 22, 2013.

3. Pamela Sebastian, "A Culinary Gilt Trip Is Worth a Fortune to Martha Stewart," *Wall Street Journal*, December 15, 1989.

4. Michael Schrage, "Martha Stewart," *Adweek*, February 14, 2000.

5. Robin Pogrebin, "Master of Her Own Destiny," *New York Times*, February 8, 1998.

6. Diana B. Henriques, "Martha Stewart, the Company, Is Poised to Go Public. But Is It a Good Thing?" *New York Times*, October 12, 1999.

7. Patricia Sellers, "Remodeling Martha," *Fortune*, November 14, 2005.

8. "Martha Stewart, Hot Potato," *BusinessWeek*, March 3, 2003.

9. Sellers, "Remodeling Martha."

10. Matthew Rose, "Martha Stewart Living Names Patrick CEO, Ubben Chairman," *Wall Street Journal*, June 5, 2003.

11. Among other prohibitions, MSO rules barred designating as independent any directors who were current or recent

employees, who had recently received more than $120,000 in compensation from the company, or who had been employed by a company that recently made or received payments of more than $1 million from the company. Directors whose immediate family members met any of the criteria also were barred from being classified as independent.

12. James Bandler, "Martha Stewart's Ubben Resigns Post of Chairman," *Wall Street Journal*, July 28, 2004.

13. Ibid.

14. Sellers, "Remodeling Martha."

15. The New York Stock Exchange required companies to "broadly consider all relevant facts and circumstances" when determining the independence of a director, including "charitable and financial relationships, among others." NYSE Manual, Sec. 3, "Corporate Responsibility," http://nysemanual.nyse.com (accessed December 9, 2013).

16. Sellers, "Remodeling Martha."

17. James Bandler and Kara Scannell, "Martha Stewart Living Names Lyne to Succeed Patrick as CEO," *Wall Street Journal*, November 12, 2004.

18. Sellers, "Remodeling Martha."

19. Ibid.

20. Ibid.

21. Ibid.

22. Ibid.

23. MSO Annual Report 2005, p 7.

24. MSO Annual Report 2005, p. 5.

25. MSO Annual Report 2006, p. 5.

26. James B. Stewart, "A Brand Icon in Need of Some Oversight," *New York Times*, November 10, 2012.

27. Stephanie Rosenbloom, "Chief Executive Resigns at Martha Stewart Living," *New York Times*, June 12, 2008.

28. Stewart, "A Brand Icon in Need of Some Oversight."

29. James B. Stewart, "For Penney and Chief, Houseware Headache," *New York Times*, March 9, 2013.

30. Ibid.

31. Merissa Marr, "Domestic Discord: Martha Stewart Seeks Perfect Touch for Her Empire," *Wall Street Journal*, August 24, 2012.

32. Ibid.

33. Ibid.

34. Christine Haughney, "Martha Stewart Clicks with a Tattooed Crowd," *New York Times*, November 25, 2012.

35. Marr, "Domestic Discord."

36. Alliance for Audited Media, http://auditedmedia.com (accessed October 6, 2013).

37. Stewart, "A Brand Icon in Need of Some Oversight."

38. David Bank, Nicholas Caplan, and Kristina Warmus, "Martha Stewart Living Continues to Transition," RBC Capital Markets, August 5, 2013.

CASE 12

The Movie Exhibition Industry: 2015

Steve Gove,
University of Vermont

Brett P. Matherne,
Georgia State University

While the *Guardians of The Galaxy* were unleashing an infinity stone containing orb to save the universe, the domestic movie exhibition industry was left undefended. Carnage ensued. The *Guardians* $333 million domestic box office gross was a highlight of an otherwise abysmal 2014 for exhibitors. [Exhibit 1] Domestic box office receipts overall declined 5.2% to $10.36 billion as admissions declined to their lowest level since 1995.[1] Much like a well-crafted suspense film, indicators of the fundamental health of the exhibitor market makes an observer question its ability to survive. Consider the following:

- Both revenues and admissions declined in 2014. Revenues peaked in 2013 at $10.9 billion, but have declined in 5 of the prior 10 years; admissions have declined in 7 of the 10 prior years, down 19.5% from the most recent high in 2002. [Exhibit 2]
- At $8.17, the average ticket price has risen 27% since 2005. Yet over the long-term, prices lag inflation, raising questions about the industry's value proposition. [Exhibit 3]
- The long term trend in per-capita admissions is negative. In 2014 the average number of films seen per capita was 3.9.[2] In 1946, the peak of movie going in America, the industry sold 4 billion tickets and the typical American went to the movies 28 times per year.
- Movies are more widely available than ever, creating new substitutes for where, when, and how they are viewed.
- Domestic demographic trends indicate exhibitors' core audience of 12-24 year olds offers limited opportunities for growth. The largest audience for growth consists of those 60 and older, an audience which now goes to the movies the least. [Exhibit 4]
- The industry is increasingly bifurcated along domestic (clear signs of maturity; increasing threat of substitution, difficulty innovating, and signs of consolidation) and international (growth; rapidly expanding theater counts, rising attendance and increasing revenues) lines.

Exhibitors are especially anxious for movie goers to return as they invested an estimated $2.4 billion to convert theaters from film to digital projection since 2005. [Exhibit 5] The promises of the transition to digital projection were to excite audiences with an enhanced viewing experience – primarily 3D – and decrease distribution costs. Yet, the actual benefits of the transition remain elusive given the declining attendance. The potential to increase revenues with the much touted 3D appears fleeting as 3D admissions declining by a third from 21% of domestic revenues in 2010 to just 15% in 2014. [Exhibit 6]

Is there an infinity stone hidden somewhere in the movie exhibition business which can be unleashed? Will any guardians appear to save the movie exhibitor in 2015? Or might the movie theater itself be killed off and any potential sequel cancelled?

The Motion Picture Value Chain

The motion picture industry value chain consists of three stages: studio production, distribution, and exhibition – the theaters that show the films. All stages are undergoing consolidation and technological changes, but the three-stages structure has changed little since the 1920s.

Studio Production

The studios produce the lifeblood of the industry: motion picture content. Studios are highly concentrated with the top 6 responsible for over 81% of box office receipts. [Exhibit 7] Even within the top studios concentration is increasing as the trend among studios is for fewer films with larger budgets and global appeal. In 2014, the top 6 studios produced 99 major pictures, down from 110 in 2000. Yet these films were responsible for an increasingly larger portion of global box office, up from 61% in 2000 to 81% in 2014. This concentration coupled with highly differentiated content gives the studios considerable negotiating and pricing power over exhibitors.

Studios are increasingly managed as profit centers within large corporations. Studios risks are significant as production costs are considerable. [Exhibit 1] Studios invested $3.1 billion for what became 2014's highest grossing 25 film ($123 million per film; range: $12 million to $250 million). Costs have increased faster than inflation.

Exhibit 1 Top 25 Motion Pictures Based on Box Office Receipts During 2014

Movie	2014 Gross	2014 Rank	Studio	Genre	MPAA Rating	Prod. Budg. (mil.)	3D ?	Domestic Gross (mil.)*	Domestic %	Domestic Rank	International Gross (mil.)	International %	International Rank	Total Gross (mil.)	Total Rank	B:P Ratio	% O.W.
Guardians Of The Galaxy	$333	1	Dis	Adv.	PG-13	$170		$333	43%	3	$441	57%	11	$774	4	4.6	28%
Hunger Games: Mockingjay I	$313	2	LG	Thrl / Susp	PG-13	$125		$337	45%	2	$415	55%	13	$752	6	6.0	36%
Captain America: Winter Sold	$260	3	Dis	Act.	PG-13	$170	Yes	$260	36%	4	$455	64%	9	$715	8	4.2	37%
The Lego Movie	$258	4	WB	Adv.	PG	$60	Yes	$258	55%	5	$211	45%	18	$469	17	7.8	27%
Transformers: Age Extinction	$245	5	Para	Sci-F Act	PG-13	$210	Yes	$245	22%	7	$846	78%	2	$1,091	2	5.2	41%
Maleficent	$241	6	Dis	Fant	PG	$180	Yes	$241	32%	8	$517	68%	4	$758	5	4.2	29%
X-Men: Days Of Future Past	$234	7	Fox	Act / Adv	PG-13	$200	Yes	$234	31%	9	$514	69%	5	$748	7	3.7	39%
Dawn Of The Planet Apes	$209	8	Fox	Sci-F Act	PG-13	$170	Yes	$209	29%	11	$500	71%	7	$709	10	4.2	35%
Big Hero 6	$205	9	Dis	Anim	PG	$165	Yes	$222	34%	10	$430	66%	12	$652	12	4.0	25%
The Amazing Spider-Man 2	$203	10	Sony	Act./ Adv	PG-13	$200	Yes	$203	29%	12	$506	71%	6	$709	9	3.5	45%
Godzilla	$201	11	WB	Sci-F Act	PG-13	$160	Yes	$201	38%	13	$328	62%	16	$529	14	3.3	46%
22 Jump Street	$192	12	Sony	Act Com	R	$50		$192	58%	14	$140	42%	21	$331	20	6.6	30%
Teenage Mutant Ninja Turtles	$191	13	Para	Act/Adv	PG-13	$125	Yes	$191	39%	15	$294	61%	17	$485	16	3.9	34%
Hobbit: Battle Five Armies	$190	14	WB	Adv	PG-13	$250	Yes	$255	27%	6	$700	73%	3	$955	3	3.8	21%
Interstellar	$179	15	Para	Sci-F Adv	PG-13	$165		$188	28%	16	$485	72%	8	$673	11	4.1	25%
How To Train Your Dragon 2	$177	16	Fox	Anim	PG	$145	Yes	$177	29%	17	$442	71%	10	$619	13	4.3	28%
Gone Girl	$166	17	Fox	Thrl	R	$61		$168	46%	18	$200	54%	19	$368	19	6.0	22%
Divergent	$151	18	LG	Act/Adv	PG-13	$85		$151	52%	19	$138	48%	22	$289	22	3.4	36%
Neighbors	$150	19	Univ.	Com	R	$18		$150	56%	20	$118	44%	23	$268	23	14.9	33%
Frozen	$138	20	Dis	Anim	PG	$150	Yes	$401	31%	1	$873	69%	1	$1,274	1	8.5	17%
Ride Along	$135	21	Univ.	Com	PG-13	$25		$135	88%	21	$19	12%	25	$154	24	6.2	31%
Rio 2	$132	22	Fox	Anim	G	$103	Yes	$132	26%	22	$369	74%	14	$500	15	4.9	30%
Lucy	$127	23	Univ.	Sci-F Act	R	$40		$127	28%	23	$332	72%	15	$459	18	11.5	35%
The Fault In Our Stars	$125	24	Fox	Drama	PG-13	$12		$125	41%	25	$182	59%	20	$307	21	25.6	38%
Lone Survivor	$125	25	Univ.	Act Drama	R	$40		$125	84%	24	$24	16%	24	$149	25	3.7	30%
Total for Top 25	$4,878					$3,079		$5,259			$9,479			$14,738			
Average for Top 25	$195					$123		$210	41%		$379	59%		$590		6.3	32%

Notes: 2014 Gross includes only domestic revenues in 2014 (January 1 – December 31, 2014); film may have been released in 2013 and/or remained in theaters in 2015. Domestic, international, and total gross encompasses entire theatrical release.

Studios: Dis = Disney, Fox = 20th Century Fox, LG = Lionsgate, Para = Paramount, Univ. = Universal, WB = Warner Bros.,

Genres as follows: Act = Action; Adv. = Adventure, Anim = Animation; Com = Comedy; Drama = Drama; Fant = Fantasy; Hist = Historical; Musc – Musical; Rom = Romance; Sci-F = Sci-Fi; Thrl = Thriller; West = Western. Some production budgets estimated.

B:P Ratio = Total box office (Domestic + International.) to Production Budget.

% O.W. = % of total domestic box office from the opening weekend.

Exhibit 2 Domestic Box Office Receipts & Ticket Sales, 1980–2014

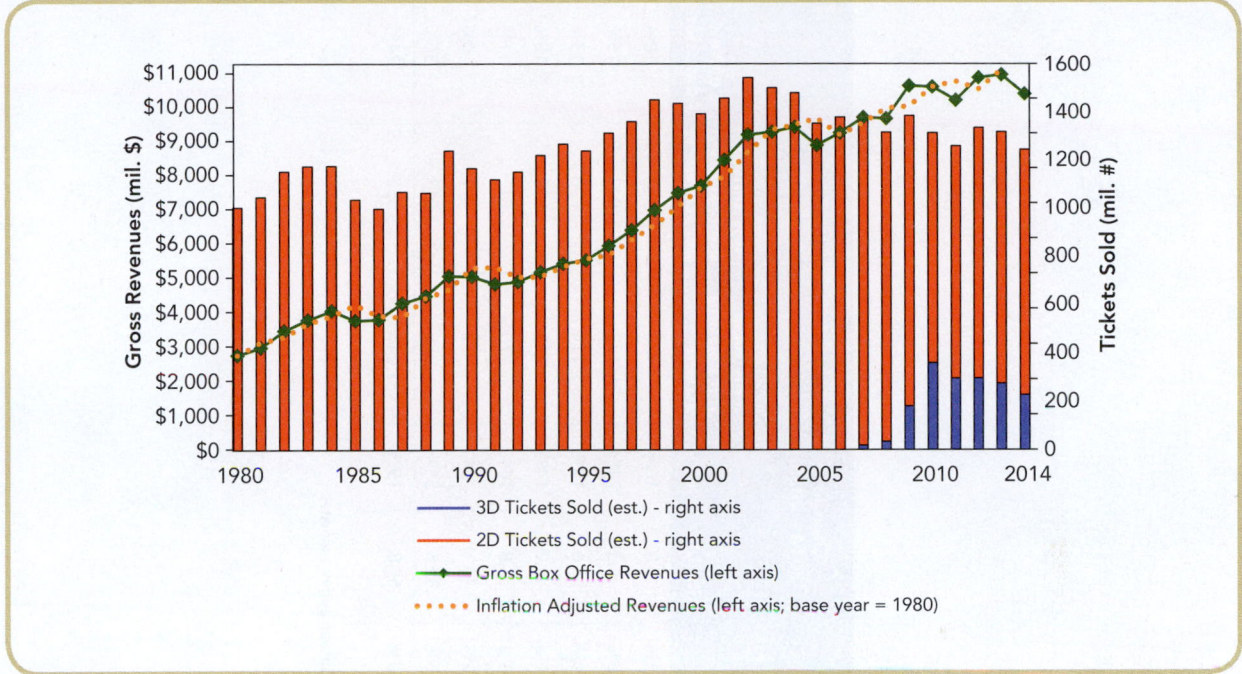

Data Source: Boxofficemojo.com and author estimates. 3D ticket volume estimated based on reported 3D revenues with ticket prices estimated as 30% premium over 2D. Portion of 2012 3D revenue and ticket volume is estimated.

Exhibit 3 Ticket Prices 1980–2014

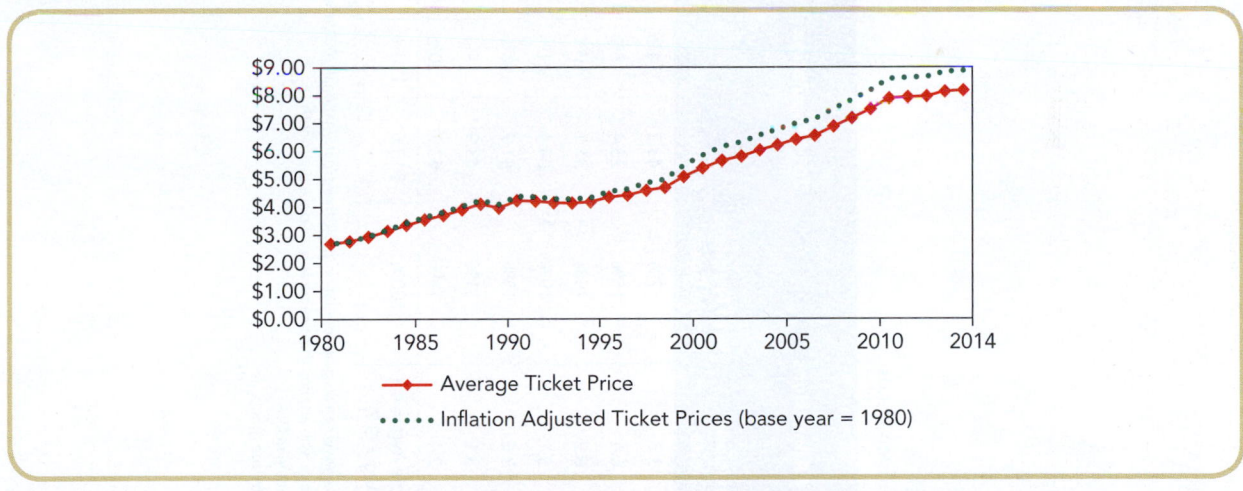

In 1980, the production budget for the highest grossing films averaged just $11 million. In the 1990s, films turned to special effects and costs reached $102 million (up 827%). Today, special effects alone can top $100 million for a major production. These investments are considerable, yet no guarantee for success; a proven formula for success is elusive. Consider the seemingly similar start to two recent animated films.[3] The first, based on a children's toy, was developed at a cost of $60 million and featured the talents of Will Farrell and Chris Pratt. The second was based on an enduring cinema classic for $70 million and featured the talents of Lea Michelle, Kelsey Grammer, and comedy legend Dan Aykroyd. Each went through years of development and investment decisions involving the effort and skill of hundreds of dedicated professionals. Yet, their box office fates differ dramatically. Everything about Warner Bros. *The LEGO Movie* was awesome. The film generated $469 globally at the box office (a 7.8 box office revenue to production cost ratio) while Clarius Entertainment's *Legends of Oz: Dorothy's Return* grossed

Exhibit 4 U.S. Demographic & Admission Trends

| Age Segment | 2014 Admissions | | | 2014 Population | | Est. 2035 Population | | Change 2014 – 2035 | | Projections | | |
	% of Tickets Purchased	Admissions Per Capita	% of Frequent Movie Goers[1]	# (mil.)	%	# (mil.)	%	# (mil.)	%	# Increase per existing screen[2]	New annual admissions per screen[3]	% of New Admissions
2 to 11 yrs	12%	3.3	7%	43.2	14%	50.0	13%	6.8	16%	170	563	10%
12 to 17 yrs	14%	6.4	15%	25.4	8%	30.6	8%	5.3	21%	132	843	15%
18 to 24 yrs	16%	6.2	19%	31.1	10%	35.7	9%	4.6	15%	114	708	13%
25 to 39 yrs	20%	3.7	19%	64.4	21%	73.3	19%	8.9	14%	223	827	15%
40 to 49 yrs	13%	3.6	15%	41.9	13%	48.7	13%	6.8	16%	170	611	11%
50 to 59 yrs	12%	3.1	11%	43.9	14%	43.8	12%	(0.1)	0%	−2	−7	0%
60 yrs+	13%	2.4	14%	63.7	20%	97.3	26%	33.6	53%	839	2,013	36%
	100%	Simple Avg. = 4.1 U.S. Avg. = 3.7	100%	313.6	100%	379.5	100%	65.8	19%	1,646	5,558	14%

Notes: Source: Data: US Census (2008), https://www.census.gov/population/projections/data/national/2008/downloadablefiles.html and author estimates.

[1] Frequent movie goer defined by MPAA as one who attends the cinema at least once per month.

[2] Based on 2014's 40,000 screens, actual # (not in mil.).

[3] Based on 2014 per capita admission rates by age group.

Exhibit 5 U.S. Theaters Screens 2000–2014

Year	Total Screens	Change from Prior Year	Analog Screens #	Change from Prior Year	As % of Total Screens	Digital Screens – Non-3D #	Change from Prior Year	As % of Total Screen	Est. Digital Invest. ($ mil.)	Digital Screens – 3D #	Change from Prior Year	As % of Total Screens	As % of Digital Screens	Est. 3D Invest. ($ mil.)	Total Digital Investment ($ mil.)
2000	37,396		37,396		100.0%										
2001	36,764	−1.7%	36,764	−1.7%	100.0%										
2002	35,280	−4.0%	35,280	−4.0%	100.0%										
2003	36,146	2.5%	36,146	2.5%	100.0%										
2004	36,594	1.2%	36,594	1.2%	100.0%										
2005	38,852	6.2%	38,862	6.2%	100.0%	200		0.5%	$10						$10
2006	38,415	−1.1%	36,412	−6.3%	94.8%	2,003	901.5%	5.2%	$90						$90
2007	38,974	1.5%	34,342	−5.7%	88.1%	3,646	82.0%	9.4%	$82	986		2.5%	21.3%	$74	$156
2008	38,843	−0.3%	33,319	−3.0%	85.8%	4,088	12.1%	10.5%	$22	1,427	44.7%	3.7%	25.9%	$33	$55
2009	39,233	1.0%	31,815	−4.5%	81.1%	4,149	1.5%	10.6%	$3	3,269	129.1%	8.3%	44.1%	$138	$141
2010	39,547	0.8%	23,773	−25.3%	60.1%	7,937	91.3%	20.1%	$189	7,837	139.7%	19.8%	49.7%	$343	$532
2011	39,641	0.2%	14,020	−41.0%	35.4%	12,620	59.0%	31.8%	$234	13,001	65.9%	32.8%	50.7%	$387	$621
2012	42,803	8.0%	6,426	−54.2%	15.0%	21,643	71.5%	50.6%	$451	14,734	13.3%	34.4%	40.5%	$130	$581
2013	42,184	−1.4%	2,990	−53.5%	7.1%	24,042	11.1%	57.0%	$120	15,782	7.1%	37.4%	39.6%	$79	$199
2014	43,265	2.6%	1,747	−41.6%	4.0%	25,372	5.5%	58.6%	$67	16,146	2.3%	37.3%	38.9%	$27	$94
									$1,168					$1,211	$2,379

Notes: Based on author estimates and MPAA reports on # screens. Estimated investments (cumulative) based on estimated cost of digital screen ($50,000 per installation) and digital 3D ($75,000 per installation).

Exhibit 6 Domestic Percentage of Revenue and Tickets from 3D

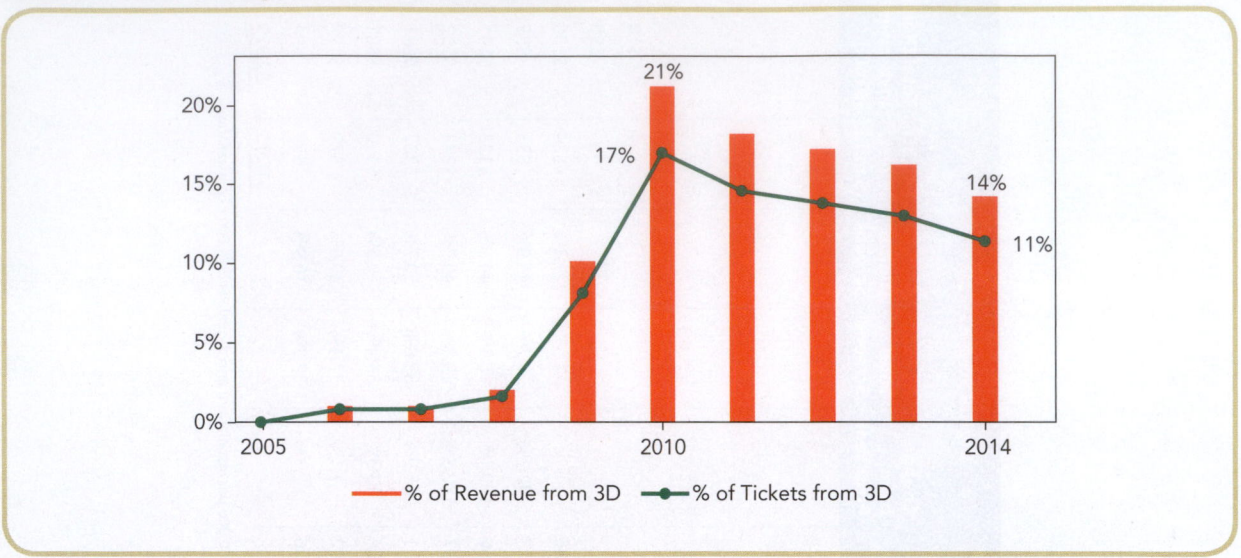

Notes: Data from MPAA 2014 Theatrical Statistics, boxofficemojo, and author estimates.

Exhibit 7 Top 6 Studios/Distributors 2014

Studio / Distributor	2014				2000				% Change 2000–2014	
	Rank	$ Share	Total Gross	# Films	Rank	$ Share	Total Gross	# Films	Total Gross	# Films
20th Century Fox	1	17.3%	$1,791	17	6	9.5%	$723	13	148%	31%
Buena Vista	2	15.6%	$1,618	13	1	15.5%	$1,176	21	38%	−38%
Warner Bros.	3	15.1%	$1,562	22	3	11.9%	$905	22	73%	0%
Sony / Columbia	4	12.2%	$1,262	19	7	9.0%	$682	29	85%	−34%
Universal	5	10.8%	$1,115	14	2	14.1%	$1,069	13	4%	8%
Paramount	6	10.2%	$1,053	14	4	10.4%	$791	12	33%	17%
Total for top 6			$8,400	99			$5,346	110	77%	68%
Industry Total			$10,360	701			$7,661	478	41.4%	66.3%
Top 6 as % of Industry			81.1%	14.1%			61.4%	16.9%	24.3%	

Source: MPAA Theatrical statistics, boxofficemojo.com, and author estimates.

just $18 million globally (box office to production cost ratio of just 0.3). The adage of the industry: Any motion picture can capture the lightning and become a hit; any one can become a flop.

Studios focus on 12-24 year olds, consistently the largest audience for movies. At just 18% of the U.S. population, this group purchases 30% of all tickets – the only segment of the population with a disproportionately high ticket purchases. More narrowly, 10% of the population are "frequent" movie goers who attend more than one movie per month and are responsible for half of all ticket sales. Thirty-four percent of these frequent movie goers are 12-24 year olds.[4] Studios target this audience with PG and PG-13 fare including 19 of 2014's top 25 releases. However, domestic demographic trends within this segment are not favorable. [Exhibit 4] While the U.S. population will increase 19% by 2035, this core audience will increase 18% (9.9 million) or 246 individuals per existing theater screen. The largest growth – in both percentage and number of individuals – is among 60+ year olds. This market currently has the lowest admissions per capita, just 2.4 annually, but represents a potentially lucrative market which will increase by 34 million, up 53%. If per capita viewership rates remain at current levels within age segments, this audience of 60+ year olds represents half of all new movie goers.

Domestic exhibitors were once the sole distribution channel for films. This has changed dramatically. Films must increasingly cross cultural and language boundaries and appeal to a global market. Over 71% of U.S. studio revenues are now international. [Exhibit 8] Studios view this as their primary opportunity for growth as both ticket sales and dollar volume are rising rapidly. From 2000 to 2014, domestic receipts grew at an average annual growth rate of just 2% while international grew 11% annually. The studios are also changing their perspective on ticket prices in large population markets. In India, for example, attendees paid an average of just $0.62 in 2013, but 2.7 billion tickets were sold – more than double U.S. admissions.[5]

This has led studios to internationalize their content. While dramas like *The Fault In Our Stars* and the humor of *Neighbors* require smaller production budgets than science fiction and action and adventure films, they are risky in international markets. Action-packed franchise films with known characters, little dialogue, made in 3D and laden with special effects present the least cross-cultural risk. Yet these films carry their own risk due to large budgets. Among the top 10 highest internationally grossing U.S. studio produced films in 2014, the average production budget was $184 million – 50 percent higher than the average for the top 25 – and only one was below $150 million.

As studios shift their focus to the international market they are less dependent on domestic exhibitors, further increasing their bargaining power over exhibitors. This increases the threat of future disintermediation through alternative distribution channels. Studios increase revenues through product licensing, DVD and digital sales, and international expansion, while domestic exhibitors remain wholly reliant on charging viewers to see a movie.

Distribution

Distributors are the intermediaries between the studios and exhibitors. Distribution entails all steps following a film's artistic completion including marketing, logistics, and administration. Distributors either negotiate a percentage of the gross from the studio for distribution services or purchase rights to films and profit directly from box office receipts. Distributors select and market films to exhibitors' booking agents, handle collections, audits of attendees, and other administrative tasks. There are over 300 distributors, but most is done by a few majors, commonly a division of a studios. Disney Marvel Studios, for example, produced *Guardians of the Galaxy* while distribution was handled by Disney's Buena Vista.

Until 2005, the distribution of all motion pictures in the US entailed the physical shipment of reels of 35mm film, a process largely unchanged since the 1940s. Each theater would receive a shipment of physical canisters containing a "release print" of a film. These prints cost $20,000 – $30,000 up-front plus $1,000 – $1,500 for each print. Print costs for a modern major picture opening on 3,500 screens costs $3.50 – $5.25 million. This was borne by the studios and exhibitors, but paid for by movie attendees.

Exhibit 8 Domestic & International Box Office Receipts ($ bil.)

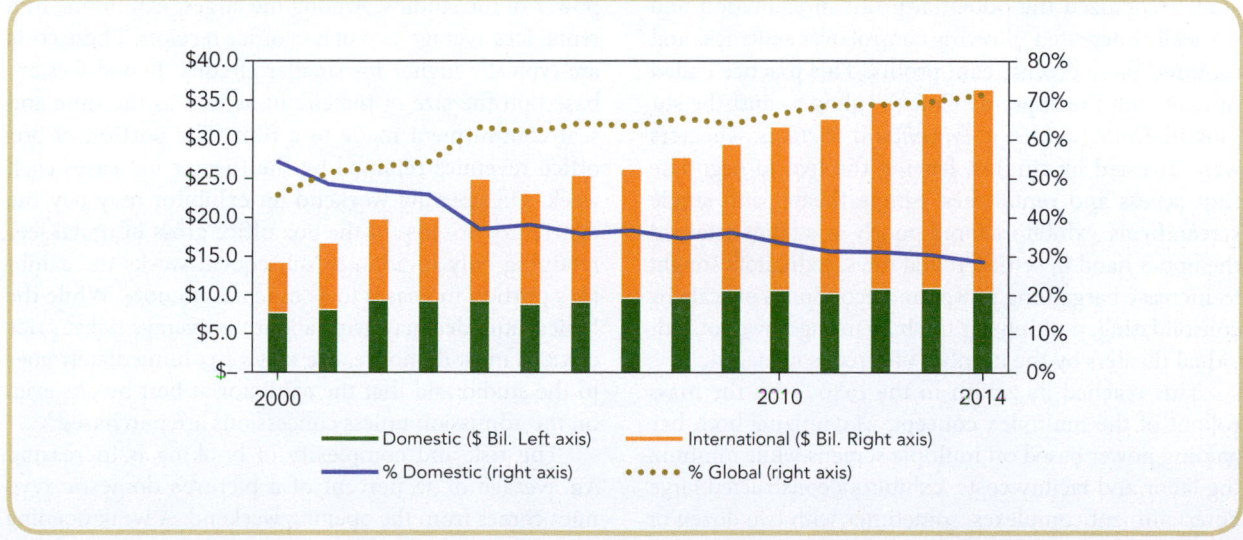

Beginning in 2006, distributors and studios encouraged exhibitors to transition to digital projection technology. The technology works by using high powered LCD projectors to cast the movie onto a specialized screen. In lieu of film, the movies are delivered on reusable hard drives or via satellite or high speed internet. The threat of piracy is a major concern for the industry so all files are encrypted. The cost savings of digital distribution over film are considerable: The cost of each hard drive is $150, just 10% of the cost of physical film. Additionally, digital projection allows for consistently high quality images as there is no physical wear to the film, and enables the exhibition of "alternative content" – images other than motion pictures that are obtained outside of the studio system.

By the end of 2014, more than 95% of U.S. screens had been converted to digital. [Exhibit 5] Each digital projection system serves a single screen and costs $50,000 to $75,000 including the projector, computers and hardware, and a specialized screen. This equates to a capital cumulative investment of approximately $2.3 billion in the U.S. alone. To encourage the transition, distributors offered rebates in the form of virtual print fees (VPFs) for each film received digitally. These fees, as much as 17% of rental costs, expired in 2013.

Exhibition

Exhibitors offer a location where audiences can view a motion picture. The basic business model of exhibitors – using movies as the draw and selling concessions to make a profit – has changed little since the time of touring motion picture shows that would set up in town halls and churches. As the popularity of motion pictures expanded, permanent local theaters were built. Studios soon recognized the potential profit in exhibition and vertically integrated, allowing control over audiences and captured these downstream profits. This practice ended in 1948 with the Supreme Court's ruling against the studios in *United States v. Paramount Pictures*. Theaters were divested by studios, leaving the two to negotiate film access and rental fees. Single theater and single screen firms' exhibitors fared poorly as studios retained the upper hand in setting rental rates. Exhibitors sought to increase bargaining power and economies of scale by consolidating, multiplying the bargaining power of individual theaters by the number of screens managed.

This reached its zenith in the 1980s with the mass rollout of the multiplex concept. Maximizing both bargaining power based off multiple screens while minimizing labor and facility costs, exhibitors constructed large entertainment complexes, sometimes with two dozen or more screens. Most of the original local single screen theaters were doomed as they were unable to compete on cost or viewing experience and unable to gain access to the capital needed to construct multi-screen locations. Today, the typical movie screen in the U.S. is part of a 7-12 screens multiplex likely to be operated by one of four exhibitor "circuits" consisting of Regal, AMC, Cinemark, or Carmike. These four circuits operate 1,528 theaters in the U.S. (just 24% theaters), but control 45.5% of the screens. [Exhibit 9] This market concentration provides the largest exhibitors with greater negotiating power for access to films, prices for films, prices for concessions, and greater access to revenues from national advertisers than smaller circuits. However, the real power continues to remain with the studios due to differentiated content, the ability to play rival exhibitors against each other, and the increasing potential for disintermediation.

The Business of Exhibition

Virtually all revenues for exhibitors come from three sources: box office receipts, concessions, and advertising. [Exhibit 10] Managers have low discretion; their ability to influence revenues and expenses is limited. Exhibitor operating margins average a slim 12%; net income may fluctuate wildly based on the tax benefits of prior losses. Overall, the business of exhibitors is best described as loss leadership on movies, break even on admissions, but make money selling concessions and showing ads to patrons who are drawn by the movie.

Box Office Revenues

Ticket sales constitute two thirds of exhibition business revenues. The return, however, is quite small due to the power of the studios. Among the largest exhibitors, film rental fees average 54% of box office receipts. These costs are typically higher for smaller circuits. Rental fees are based on the size of the circuit as well as the time and seat commitment made to a film. The portion of box office revenues retained by the theater increases each week. On opening weekend an exhibitor may pay the distributor 80-90% of the box office gross in rental fees, retaining only 10-20%. In subsequent weeks the exhibitor's portion increases to as much as 80-90%. While the typical attendee may gripe about the average ticket price of $8.17, most do not realize that $4.33 immediately goes to the studio and that the exhibitor at best breaks even on the admission unless concessions are purchased.

The risk and complexity of booking is increasing. An average of 32 percent of a picture's domestic revenues comes from the opening weekend. A weak opening

Exhibit 9 Leading US Circuits 2014

Company	Theater Brands	U.S. & Canada					Non-U.S. & Canada			Global	
		# Theater Locations	% of U.S. Theaters	# Screens	% of U.S. Screens	Avg. Screens per Theater	# Theater Locations	# Screens	% of Non-U.S. Screens	Screens	% Global Screens
Regal	Regal, United Artists, Edwards	574	9.1%	7,367	17.0%	12.8	0	0	0.0%	7,367	5.2%
AMC*	AMC, Loews, Wanda	345	5.5%	4,931	11.4%	14.3	153	1,344	1.4%	6,275	4.4%
Cinemark**	Cinemark, Century	335	5.3%	4,499	10.4%	13.4	160	1,177	1.2%	5,676	4.0%
Carmike	Carmike	274	4.3%	2,897	6.7%	10.6	0	0	0.0%	2,897	2.0%
	Total for leading four	1,528	24.3%	19,694	45.5%	12.9	313	2,521	2.6%	22,215	15.6%
	Other firms	4,772	75.7%	23,571	54.5%	4.9		96,214	97.4%	119,785	84.4%
	Industry total	6,300	100.0%	43,265	100.0%	6.9		98,735	100.0%	142,000	100.0%

Notes: Data from SEC filings, MPAA, NATO, UNESCO, and author estimates; based on screens at the start of 2015.

* International locations for AMC includes those owned and operated by parent company Wanda Group (includes 150 locations with 1,315 screens in China). AMC in recent years divested operations in Canada, UK, Japan, Hong Kong, Spain, Portugal, France, Argentina, Brazil, Chile, and Uruguay while parent company Wanda expanded rapidly in China.

**Cinemark's international operations includes locations in Brazil (65 theaters: 516 screens), Colombia (28; 144), Argentina (19; 168), Chile (16; 113), Central America (Honduras, El Salvador, Nicaragua, Costa Rica, Panama and Guatemala, 15; 110), Peru (10, 77), Ecuador (6; 36), and Bolivia (1; 13).

Exhibit 10 Typical Revenue & Expenses Per Screen at an 8-Screen Theater

REVENUES		
Box Office ($257,923/$8.59 = 30,037 admissions = 618/week/screen)	$257,923	63%
Concessions ($130,964/30,037 admissions = $4.36/admission)	$130,964	32%
Advertising ($21,117/30,037 admissions = $0.70/admission)	$21,117	5%
Total Revenues ($12.29/admission)	$442,400	100%
EXPENSES		
Fixed		
Facility	$65,942	15%
Labor	$39,565	9%
Utilities	$48,358	11%
Other SG&A	$79,131	18%
Total Fixed Costs	$232,997	53%
Variable		
Film Rental (Percentage of Box Office Admission Revenue)	$139,278	54%
Concession Supplies (Percentage of Concession Revenue)	$17,898	14%
Total Variable Costs	$157,177	36%
Total Expenses	$390,174	88%
OPERATING INCOME	$52,226	12%

Notes: author estimates based on analysis of select large exhibitor SEC filings, MPAA and NATO data; scaled to a single screen within an 8-theater multiplex; values may deviate from industry average and the specifics for the industry and any individual firm.

weekend results in a short run in theaters. In industry terminology the "multiple" (the percentage coming after opening weekend) has been declining steadily, falling 25% since 2002[6] putting exhibitors at increasing risk. Among the top 25 films, the length of theatrical run declined nearly 10 percent from 2004 to 2014. Beyond what movie to show and how many screens to devote to each film, exhibitors must now also make decisions as to how many screens to allocate to 2D and 3D versions. All these factors increasingly make the opening weekend "make or break" and complicate the exhibitor's operations.

Concessions

A frequent movie goer lament is high concession prices. At an average of $4.36 per admission, concessions constitute 30% of exhibitor revenues. Direct costs of under 15% make concessions the primary source of exhibitor profit. These profits are influenced by three factors: attendance, pricing, and material costs. The most important is

attendance: more attendees yields more concession sales. Per patron sales are influenced by prices. The $4.50 and $8.00 price points for the large soda and popcorn are not accidental, but the result of considerable market research and profit maximization calculations. Costs are influenced by purchase volume with larger chains able to negotiation better prices on everything from popcorn and soda pop to cups and napkins.

Audience concession expectations are increasing and theaters are responding. Once consisting of only boxed candy, popcorn, and soft drinks purchased at the counter in the lobby, concessions now include a variety of food, drink, and location options. While concession options such as hamburgers, salads, hot appetizers, and alcoholic beverage sales increase average concession sales per patron, they must be considered in conjunction with higher costs for kitchen facilities, labor, and food costs. A $10 burger has a far lower gross margin than a $8 tub of popcorn due to higher food costs. A variety of location options, such as counter, in-lobby, and in-theater waiter service may also drive revenues, but come with additional costs.

Advertising

The low margins derived from ticket sales cause exhibitors to focus on other sources of revenue. The highest margin, therefore the most attractive, is advertising, including pre-show and lobby advertising and previews. Since 2002, advertising revenues, and the time devoted to them at the start of every feature, increased from $186 to $678 million in 2014.[7] The number of previews increased from 3 or 4 ten years ago to 6 or 7 currently including the two typically provided to the studio as part of the film rental agreement.[8] [Exhibit 11] Though advertising constitutes just 5% of exhibitor revenues, it is highly profitable and growing. Instead of paying for and showing short films prior to the feature, exhibitors show ads which they are paid to show. Advertising revenues for exhibitors averaged $17,221 per screen in 2014, up 100% in the last decade.[9] Yet audiences express dislike for advertising at the theater and, if dissatisfaction increases, may opt to view movies at home. Balancing the lucrative revenues from ads with audience tolerance is an ongoing struggle for exhibitors.

The Major Exhibitor Circuits

Four circuits dominate the domestic exhibition market, serving different geographic markets in different ways.[10] [Exhibit 9] Regal, which operates its namesake Regal Theaters as well as United Artists and Edwards

Exhibit 11 Exhibitor 2015 Advertising Revenue

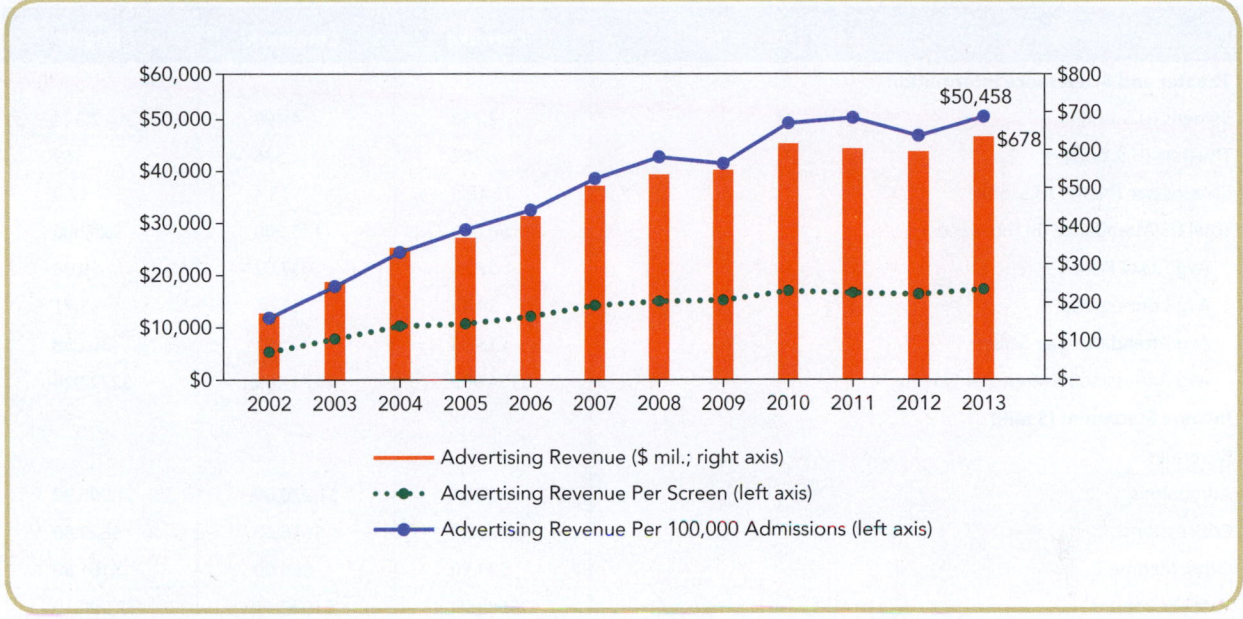

Source: Cinema Advertising Council, 2014

theaters, is the largest with 7,367 screens in 574 domestic theaters. Regal focuses on mid-size markets using multiplex and megaplexes that average nearly 13 screens per location, with an average ticket price of $9.08. AMC, operating under AMC and Loews chains, is the second largest domestic exhibitor with 4,931 screens in 345 theaters. Averaging 14 screens per location, AMC leads the industry in the operation of large multiplexes. They do so by concentrating on urban areas near large population centers such as those in California, Florida, and Texas. By focusing on 3D, IMAX, and other premium viewing experiences, AMC has an average ticket price of $9.43. Cinemark is the 3rd largest player with 4,499 screens in 335 domestic locations under Cinemark and Century brands. Cinemark serves smaller markets, operating as the sole theater in over 92 percent of its markets. Their average ticket price is $7.02. Carmike concentrates on small to midsized markets, targeting populations of less than 100,000 that have few alternative entertainment options. They do so with fewer screens at each location, averaging 106 per location (274 theaters; 2,897 screens). Carmike's ticket price averaged $7.23. [Exhibit 12]

While ticket prices vary, differences in net profit margins are due mostly to differences in utilization and the costs of facilities, labor, and utilities. Despite considerable size differences, the actual cost of content for these circuits varies little among the majors circuits.

Regal's exhibition costs as a percentage of revenue is lowest at 52% of admission revenues, followed by AMC (53%), Carmike (55%) and Cinemark (56%). While the rentals costs for these circuits is similar, it is lower than for smaller circuits.

The circuits ability to efficiently utilize their facilities varies considerably. Cinemark's average of 38,661 attendees per screen is nearly double Carmike's 21,414 per screen. Revenues per screen for both Cinemark ($271,409) and Regal ($272,924) are nearly double that of Carmike ($154,900). The differences in utilization combined with differences in prices, concession sales per person, and facilities, wages and other expenses results in Cinemark having the highest operating income per admission ($2.87), followed by Regal ($1.39), and Carmike ($0.72).

Despite the trend toward internationalization by studios, exhibitors until recently have been exclusively domestic firms. Cinemark has the broadest international presence with 153 theaters (1,344 screens) in Mexico and seven Central and South American countries. In 2012, AMC was acquired by the Chinese conglomerate Dalian Wanda Group Corp for a reported $2.6 billion.[11] Wanda, with interests in property, entertainment, and tourism owns and operates 1,177 screens in 153 theaters in China. Wanda/AMC is the largest global exhibition company based on screen count with 6,575 screens and is expanding rapidly in China.

Exhibit 12 Select 2014 Carmike, Cinemark & Regal Financials

	Carmike	Cinemark†	Regal
Theater and Attendance Information			
Screens (U.S. only)	2,758	4,499	7,324
Theaters (U.S. only)	262	335	569
Screens per Theater (U.S. only)	10.5	13.4	12.9
Total US Attendance (in thousands)	59,056	173,900	220,000
Avg Ticket Price	$7.23	$7.02	$9.08
Avg Concessions	$4.45	$3.65	$3.77
Avg Attendance per Screen	21,414	38,661	30,038
Avg Admission Revenue per Screen	$154,900	$271,409	$272,924
Income Statement ($ mil.)			
Revenues			
Admissions	$427.21	$1,220.80	$1,998.90
Concessions*	$228.21	$635.60	$829.60
Other Income*	$34.50	$66.00	$161.60
Total Revenues	$689.93	$1922.40	$2,990.10
Admissions as % of Revenues	62%	63%	67%
Concessions as % of Revenues	33%	32%	28%
Other as % of Revenues	5%	5%	5%
Expenses			
Exhibition	$235.46	$681.10	$1,047.10
Concessions	$30.31	$86.40	$111.10
Building, Wages, Utilities & Other Operating Costs	$381.39	$828.00	$1,525.50
Total Cost of Operation	$647.16	$1,422.70	$2,683.70
Operating Income	$42.77	$499.70	$306.40
Operating Income per admission	$.72	$2.87	1.39
Operating Income as % total revenue	6%	26%	10%
Exhibition Costs as % of Admission Revenues	55%	56%	52%
Concessions Costs as % of Concession Revenues	12%	16%	13%
Buildings, wages, utilities & other costs as % of Total Revenues	55%	46%	57%
Buildings, wages, utilities & other costs per attendee	$6.46	$6.99	$6.93
Net Income*	$(8.9)	$193.99	$105.20
Net Profit Margin	−891%	7%	3%
Balance Sheet (dollars in millions)			
Total Assets	$898.10	$4,151.98	$2,539.50
Total Debt	$609.56	$3,028.85	$3,436.80
Debt : Assets Ratio	0.68	0.73	1.35

Notes: Data source: SEC filings & author estimates.

† Cinemark per ticket values based on domestic operations; others are based on consolidated domestic and international operations.

* Carmike reports aggregated concession and advertising revenues. Amounts are estimated.

** Theater, screen and revenue, expense data for Carmike's US operations. Net income, assets and debt figures are consolidated (dom. and intl.).

*** Net income may include carryover of substantial tax benefits from losses and interest expense.

Overall, while the major circuits focus on different geographic locations, there is little differentiation in the offerings of exhibitors within individual markets. Prices differ little, the same movies are shown at the same times, and the food and services choices are nearly identical. Competition between theaters within markets often comes down to distance from home, convenience of parking, and proximity to restaurants.

Challenges for Exhibitors

Exhibitors are faced with an increasing number of challenges in their operating environment.

Benefitting From Digital Investments

Exhibitors have made considerable investments in digital projection technology. By the close of 2014, all but 1,747 of the 43,265 screens in the U.S. had been converted from film to digital projection (96% conversion). Those remaining film-based are typically small, one screen local theaters, often operated as not-for-profit organizations. The total investment by exhibitors is approximately $2.4 billion. The benefits of this conversion for exhibitors should manifest themselves in (1) lower exhibitor costs and increased revenues, and (2) opportunities for increased revenues from 3D.

On the cost side, digital distribution dramatically reduces distribution costs when compared to physical film. Digital distribution is expected to save $1 billion annually on print costs and distribution. Yet there is little evidence to date that these savings will accrue to the exhibitors. Film rental fees, which include distribution costs, have held steady despite the transition to digital. Rental fees averaged 54% among Cinemark, Regal, and Carmike in 2014, little changed compared to costs prior to the digital transition.

On the revenue side, exhibitors sought significant additional per ticket movie revenues from surcharges for enhanced viewing experiences, primarily 3D. 3D content requires the cooperation of studios and exhibitors. For studios, 3D adds 15-20% to the cost of production. *Avatar's* planned release in 2009 was used to spur 3D installations, which rose from less than 4% of screen to 8% – an addition of 1,800+ 3D screens in just one year. The film was a box office smash, grossing $750 million domestically with 82% of revenues from 3D viewings.

For exhibitors, 3D requires conversion to digital projection and the added costs for 3D capable equipment. As part of the conversion to digital, exhibitors installed 3D capabilities selectively. 37% of the screens in the U.S. are now 3D capable. Yet, interest in 3D has

waned, accounting for only 14% of box office revenue in 2014, down from 21% in 2010. [Exhibit 6] Some industry observers caution that the future opportunity to capitalize on 3D-driven revenues may be limited. According to industry insider Bob Greenfield, specific movies do well in 3D while others fail as people are getting choosier about which movies they see in 3D versus 2D. Overall, the extent to which the conversion to digital has and will continue to benefit exhibitors through cost reductions and 3D revenue is questionable.

Countering the Declining Allure of the Theater

Traditionally, the draw of the theater may have been far more important than what film was showing. Moviegoers describe attending the theater as an experience, with the appeal based on:[12]

- the giant theater screen
- the experience of watching the movies with a theatrical sound system
- the opportunity to be out of the house
- not having to wait to see a particular movie on home video
- the theater as a location option for a date

The ability of theaters to provide these beyond what audiences can achieve at home is diminishing. Of the reasons why people go to the movies, only the place aspects, the theater as a place to be out of house and as a place for a date, seem immune from substitution within exhibitors current core audience. Few teenagers want movie and popcorn with their date at home with mom and dad.

The overall "experience" offered by theaters falls short for many. Marketing research firm Mintel reports the reasons for not attending the theater more frequently. Specific factors include: the overall cost, at home viewing options, interruptions such as cell phones in the theater, rude patrons, the overall hassle, and ads prior to the show.[13] The movie-going experience is frequently described as one of interruptions caused by cell phones, loud patrons, and noise from adjacent theaters.[14] Add to this an increasing number of pre-movie advertisements and previews and the experience has all the charm of an IRS audit, a delayed flight, and the used-car buying experience.

The time allocated to pre-show ads can be eye opening, even for industry insiders. Toby Emmerich, New Line Cinema's head of production faced a not-so-common choice: attending opening night in a theater or in a private screening room at actor Jim Carrey's home. Seeking the part-of-the-crowd experience, he opted for the latter. After enduring fifteen minutes of ads, he confided to his wife that perhaps it was not the best choice.[15]

The Home Viewing Substitution. Rapid improvements and cost reductions in home viewing technology and the widespread availability of timely and inexpensive content are making home viewing a viable substitute to theater exhibition. The unique value proposition offered by movie theaters' large screens, the audio quality of a theatrical sound system, and avoiding the long wait for DVD release are fading.

The Home Viewing Substitution – Technology. The average home television set is increasingly a large, high definition set coupled with inexpensive yet impressive audio system. Compared to home equipment options of the past, in-home technology increasingly represents a viable visual substitute to the big screen at the theater. Prior to 2009, television transmissions were formatted as 480 interlaced vertical lines (480i) of resolution, the standard since the 1950s. The Federal Communication Commission mandated that all broadcasters convert to digital broadcasting in 2009. Broadcasters often opted to upgrade from 480 to high definition (HD) equipment offering 1080 vertical lines of resolution (1080).[16] This led to consumers upgrading to HD televisions. In 2014, 77% of U.S. households had at least one HD television allowing for very high quality visual images.[17]

While TV picture quality has increased, sets have also gotten larger and cheaper. Wholesale prices for televisions fell 65 percent from the late 1990s to 2007[18] as manufacturing economies from production of LCD screens emerged. TV sets now average $450 retail.[19] This price decrease has occurred at the same time the average TV has increased dramatically in size. In 1997, the average TV set was 23". This increased to 32" in 2010 and to 39" in 2014.[20] As consumers upgrade their sets, they move the 32" set into the bedroom and upgrade to a 40-50" or larger set for the primary TV.[21] Sharp, a leading TV manufacturer predicts the *average* screen will reach 60" in the very near future.[22]

These sets are supported by low cost HD DVD players, and audio and speaker components packaged as low cost home theaters. The average Blu-ray DVD player now costs under $100, often with 3D capability. Bundled home theater systems that include TV, surround sound audio, and a Blu-ray player offer a movie experience that rivals many theaters, all for under $1,500. Mike Gabriel, Sharp's head of marketing and communications, argues that the cinema experience is now possible with

their television. Home screening rooms, once requiring expensive film projection and sound equipment, are now no longer the exclusive domain of the rich and famous.[23] Overall, home TVs are becoming larger and offer high quality images that reduce the differentiated appeal of the "giant" screen offered by exhibitors.

If today's home theaters are a problem for exhibitors, the next generation may be catastrophic. Adoption of the next wave of televisions – "Ultra" HD (UHD) or 4K – has begun. A 4K set has four times the resolution of today's 1080 set. The image quality difference can be striking: On a 480 set a viewer may notice that a football game is being played in the rain. On a 1080 set the same viewer will notice that the field, ball, players and spectators are wet. On a 4K set, individual droplets of water can be seen dripping off players' helmets. No date is set for 4K to become the industry standard, but consumer electronics companies are keen to spur UHD sales as TV sales, overall, have flattened. Sales of 4K sets are the highest growing segment of the TV market, albeit currently aimed at early adopters. Despite an average sales price of $2,400, sales of UHD TVs in the U.S. reached $668 million in 2014, nearly 7 percent of all TV sales revenue.[24] The number of units sold is expected to double in each of the next two years as adoption becomes widespread.[25] Among UHD TVs, 55" sets are the most common (38% of units sold) followed by 65" sets (34% of units sold). Larger sets, 70" and larger, constitute 4% of sales. These sets pose a very direct challenge for theaters differentiation based on screen size and quality as the most common projection standard in theaters – the one exhibitors just invested $2.3 billion in during the conversion to digital – is 4K. The history of technology updates to compete on visual quality is as old as the exhibition business itself. To maintain an advantage in the visual experience provided at the theater, exhibitors must consider moving to the next generation of commercial projection, 8K and 16K, or lose one of a small set of advantages.

The Home Viewing Substitution – Content Availability & Timing. The best hardware offers little value without content. Unfortunately for exhibitors, home content is flourishing and goes well beyond movies. Studios have long relied on a "windowing" model for revenue generation: the sooner a motion picture is viewed following the theatrical release the costlier it is to see it. Currently, studio profits are maximized with the inclusion of a theatrical release which generate an average $4 per admission. This is most often followed by DVD and digital sales which net the studio $12 to $15 per copy and is increasingly made by a consumer who opted to not see the movie in a theater.[26] Studios once relied on these sales to fuel profits but physical DVD sales have declined since peaking in 2006 at $13.7 billion.[27] While digital purchases grew 47% in 20013 to $1.2 billion,[28] studios have seen net declines in total sales from 2011's revenues which totaled $9.5 billion.[29] To spur sales and capitalize on marketing expenditures from the theatrical release, studios have reducing the time between theatrical release and DVD availability. Much to the castigation of exhibitors concerned that the decline cannibalizes theater admissions, this release window has declined from 23.7 weeks in 2000 to 16.6 weeks in 2012.

DVD and digital sales are followed by video on demand (VOD) which generates $3.50 for the studio per purchase,[30] but may include multiple viewers. Later release to the physical rental and streaming market nets studios less revenue. Studios net about $1.25 per DVD sold to a rental company.[31] Once dominated by physical stores, movie rentals expanded into physical DVD channels with subscription (e.g., Netflix, Blockbuster, and Amazon Prime) and one-up (e.g., Redbox and Blockbuster) options as well as subscription streaming (e.g., Netflix, Hulu, HBOGo). These offer very attractive prices for consumers, but have been identified by studios as a contributing factor for declining movie sales. RedBox's kiosk-based rentals are attractive to occasional viewers, costing as little as $1.25 per night.

Streaming is the fastest growing portion of the rental market and among the most cost effective for viewers and providers. Estimates put Netflix's average streaming cost at $0.51 per viewing. Streaming sufficiently cannibalized DVD sales to the point that studios imposed a 28-day delay from DVD sales to the availability of streaming. Exhibitors expressed strong encouragement when several studios expressed a desire for a 56-day delay to increase DVD sales. Both Netflix and Amazon offer SD as well as HD formats and are beginning to offer content in the 4K format.

Streaming services are becoming a direct competitor to both studios and exhibitors as they move into content development. Nextflix, for example, is producing both television series and original movies. In conjunction with movie producer Weinstein Co. and projection and screen technology company IMAX, Netflix has produced a sequel to *Crouching Tiger, Hidden Dragon* for distribution simultaneously on Netflix and on IMAX screens in August, 2015[32]. The announcement resulted in stock price declines for exhibitors including AMC, Regal, and Cinemark.[33] According to Miriam Gottfriend of the *Wall Street Journal*, investors may be fearing that the traditional studio "windowing" system – which makes theaters the only venue for movies upon initial release – may be approaching the end of its life.[34]

It is important to recognize that studios have options beyond the windowed theatrical release model. This includes releasing a film directly to audiences at the same time a film is in the theater, so called "simultaneous release" or to eliminate the theatrical release entirely. Increases in internet technology make disintermediation – the studios redefining their distribution to exclude exhibitors – increasingly possible. Exhibitors threatened a boycott due to Universal's plan for a premium VOD release of *Tower Heist* just three weeks after its theatrical opening. The plan was scrapped due to the threats. While exhibitors won the battle, premium VODs revenue potential – as much as $59.99 per purchase – remains attractive to the studios.

Perhaps the ultimate test of simultaneous release was initiated by North Korea at the end of 2014 when a computer hack of Sony Pictures and fears of violence resulted in exhibitors curtailing the wide theatrical release of the Seth Rogan comedy *The Interview*. The film was instead offered in a limited theatrical release and on demand, generating $30 million. Sony announced that it was their highest grossing online film release.[35] The revenues were, however, well shy of the $60-$70 million forecasted for a wide theatrical release. Arguing against simultaneous release and premium VOD, the North American Theaters Association (NATO), an exhibitor trade group, estimates Sony forfeited $12.5 million in additional box office revenues had the release proceeded.

Overall, the availability of content and the visual and audio experience available in the home is rapidly converging with the offerings available at a movie theater. The separation of movies, television, and other content is creating increased competition for viewers, according to Paul Dergarabedian, president of Hollywood. com's box-office division.[36] While viewing movies on a tablet or other device is common, viewing is returning to the living room television. In 2014 the number of internet enabled televisions rose 70% to 22 million and now exceeds the number of internet connected Blu-ray players.[37] The content being watched goes beyond movies. The leading applications for streaming from a TV are Netflix, YouTube, Amazon Prime & Instant Video, Hulu Plus, and HBOGo.[38] One blogger on the movie fan site Big Picture reports having previously viewed movies in the theater exclusively, then less, and now almost never. The reason? A giant home screen equipped with surround sound, a clean floor and seats, with movies that start on time without ads and no chatty viewers. Best of all: no cell phone interruptions.[39]

Recent Exhibitor Initiatives

Exhibitors are well aware of the increasing number of ways in which to view motion pictures. They have a long tradition of adopting innovations that increase attendance or reduce costs. Exhibitors were among the first commercial adopters of air conditioning, which perhaps drew in as many customers as a refuge from summer heat as for entertainment. Advanced projection systems, screens, and sound systems have been continuously adopted to improve the viewing experience. Other innovations increase experience quality while also lowering costs. Stadium style seating, now ubiquitous, was originally viewed as an experience differentiator, but equally beneficial is a reduction in the square footage needed per seat. This reduces the size and cost of facilities. Exhibitors continue to pursue a number of strategic initiatives aimed at increasing attendance, increasing the viewer's willingness to pay, and lowering costs.

Projection Innovations

The conversion to digital projection and roll-out of 3D are not the only projection innovations being pursued. Some directors are opting to increase image quality by doubling the number of frames per second (fps) of film from the long established standard of 24 to 48. Peter Jackson's 2012 *The Hobbit* was shown in the 48 fps format to a limited number of screens with the required projection technology. The increased frame rate results in an especially crisp image with no blurring that, while jarring to some, is said to create a sense of being part of live action, but requires specialized equipment.

Most large circuits offer some form of extra-large scale screens.[40] Traditionally located only in specially constructed dome-shaped theaters in science museums, the original IMAX format utilized film that was 10 times the size of that used in standard 35mm projectors. IMAX now operates more than 600 screens. These circuit-based IMAX digital screens are far smaller than the original IMAX screens, but can be much larger than the typical theater screen. Located within a Regal or AMC theater complexes, the screens are often booked and operated by IMAX. Action films, usually in 3D, are a staple. To capture more of this differentiated revenue, several circuits have begun creating their own super-size screens and formats. IMAX is typically offered at a premiums of $3 to $7 per ticket.

Sound systems are also being upgraded. In the 1980s, theaters impressed viewers with 7.1 sound systems – two rear channels (left and right), two channels mid screen, two near the screen, one under the screen, and a subwoofer channel for bass. Such systems have long been available for homes. To keep theater sound as a differentiator, Dolby® Laboratories has created Atmos™[41], a full surround system with up to 64 individual channels for speakers in a theater, including multiple ceiling speakers that can truly immerse the audience in sound. Given the number of speakers involved, this may be a technology that is viable in very few homes.

Alternative Content

Exhibitors' transition to digital projection was an enabling technology for alternative content, a broad term encompassing virtually any content that is not a motion picture. This includes live concerts and theater, standup comedy, sporting events, television series premiers and finales, even virtual art gallery tours. Alternative content revenues totaled $112 million in 2010[42] and are growing rapidly, and by some estimates will reach $1 billion annually – 10% of current box office – by 2020.

The current economic logic of alternative content is as a filler of seats during off-peak movie attendance, particularly Monday thru Thursday when only 5% of theater seats are occupied.[43] Bud Mayo, CEO of Digiplex Digital Cinema Destinations, describes the approach: "What happens with those [alternative content] performances is that a single event will out gross certainly the lowest-grossing movie playing that theater that day. The relationship has averaged more than 10 times the lowest-grossing movie for the entire day."[44] In marginal dollar terms, alternative content can be a boon on otherwise slow nights. A recent Wednesday showing of Broadway's *West Side Story* at a Digitech theater had an average ticket price of $12.50 and grossed $2,425. In comparison, screens showing films that night grossed just $56 to $73 each. The alternative content also brought in nearly 200 additional potential customers for concessions.[45]

Distribution is enabled by entities such as Digital Cinema Distribution Coalition (DCDC), which includes all of the major circuits, which owns and operates its own satellite network for distribution. A number of firms have emerged to provide content such as Fathom Events, owned jointly by AMC, Cinemark, and Regal Entertainment with dozens of affiliate exhibitors, provides a single contract point for a variety of music, sports, television, and other alternative content. Having a large scale intermediary as a distributor is essential for exhibitors as the cost of pursuing and licensing content is cost prohibitive for individual exhibitors. The cross-exhibitor cooperation also affords marketing opportunities that are not economically available to an individual exhibitor.

Alternative content can attract repeat visits, such as *Metropolitan Opera Live*, approaching its 10th season, which features 10 live events on Saturday afternoons broadcast by more than 700 domestic theaters. The majority of events are single events, often for one night only, tied to a specific target audience. 2012's *Leonardo Live* broadcast for one night only in 500 US movie theaters.[46] Targeted to art lovers who were also fans of Prince, customers could see the kick-off of his concert series live in theaters for one night only.[47] Identifying the communities can be a challenge and surprising. Dan Diamond, VP of Fathom Events, reports being completely surprised by the firm's most successful event: the November 25, 2013 showing of *Dr. Who: The Day of the Doctor* celebrating the 50th anniversary of the BBC series. At over $17,000 per screen, the showings boasted the highest national per-theater receipts for the night.[48] The challenge for exhibitors, accustom to studio's marketing campaigns promoting that week's box office release, is the development of capabilities in marketing single night events to niche audiences at low cost.

Immersion Experiences: 4D & Beyond

While 3D viewing is in decline in the U.S., it remains a draw in international markets. Additionally, so called 4D theaters are emerging.[49] These theaters are typically seen as occupying niches within the broader theater experience. A 4D theater utilizes 3D technology and draws the viewer further into the action with added elements such as dynamic seating with moving seats synchronized to the onscreen action. The heavy footsteps of a dinosaur, for example, are simultaneously seen on the screen, heard through the sound system, and felt through a motion seat that rumbles as if being shaken by the footsteps; a car chase becomes a drink spilling experience. Some theaters add additional immersive elements such as scents and off-screen light effects which bring the action of the movie off the screen and into theater.

Exhibitors, producers, and equipment companies are working on interaction elements ranging from simple interactions like shooting on-screen targets with lasers to more complex bullet screens where you can text your thoughts about scenes and the movie and they are projected onto the screen in real time.[50] All are seeking to provide a more immersive and interactive experience than passive sitting and movie watching. Some industry observers anticipate that in the coming years these immersion technologies will be expanded to include feedback systems and story forks where the actions and choices of the audience lead to plot twists and different story outcomes with each viewing. Eventually, the line between what constitutes a movie and a video game may blur.

Concession Initiatives

Expanding beyond the standard concession stand offers exhibitors opportunities to capture new revenue streams. Three main formats for concessions have emerged.

Expanded In-Lobby. Many theaters have expanded the concession counter beyond candy, popcorn and soda. This expanded in-lobby dining causes many theater lobbies to resemble mall food courts. In- and off-lobby restaurants operated or licensed by the exhibitor allow for pre-theater dining. Taking a page from restaurants where a primary profit center is often the bar, some theaters now configure the lobby around a bar, with expanded and upscale fare, beer, and alcohol service.

In-Theater Dining. Many theaters have adopted an in-theater dining format where orders are placed from the seat in the theater by a wait staff. Chunky's Cinema Pub, with three New England locations, locates theaters in lower cost underutilized former retail locations. The format combines burger, salad, and sandwich options with beverages, including beer. The format is flat theater with banquet style tables. The seating is unique: Old car seats on castors that allow for easy cleaning. Alamo Drafthouse Cinemas takes a similar approach using a stadium seating configuration. A single bar-style table in front of each row of seats serves as a table for customers' orders. In comparison to traditional theaters, these formats see significant increases in food and beverage sales.

Upscale Within Theater Dining. Several circuits are targeting the high end of the theater market, focusing on the experience of the theater with luxurious settings and upscale food. In addition to their standard theaters, AMC has developed Dine-In Theaters with two theater configurations. Their Fork & Screen theaters are much like the Alamo Drafthouse Cinema with enhanced stadium theater seats and in-theater wait service on an expanded menu. Their Cinema Suite theaters make the experience more intimate. Customers, only 21 and older, purchase tickets for specific seats in smaller theaters with reclining lounge chairs with foot rests and in-theater wait service.

Theater chain iPic offers perhaps the most luxurious theater experience available outside of a private screening room, complete with reclining leather chairs, pillows, and blankets. Lobbies resemble stylish high-end hotels and feature a cocktail lounge and full restaurants. Complete with a membership program, the theaters operate more like social clubs than traditional theaters.

Tickets, $16-$27 per seat, are purchased not from a ticket booth but from a concierge.

Advertising Initiatives

Exhibitors are keen to expand highly profitable advertising, but must do so in ways that does not diminish the theater experience. Revenues are generated from advertisements both on- and off-screen. Off-screen advertising such as promotional videos, lobby events and sponsored concession promotions are 9% of revenues. The majority, 91%, comes from on-screen ads for upcoming releases, companies, and products that play before the feature presentation. Both exhibitors and advertisers seek ways to make on-screen ads more palatable to audiences. Many ads are produced in 3D with production quality rivaling a studio release. Theaters are also incorporating innovative technologies such as crowd gaming into ads where the movement or sound of the audience controls on-screen actions. In October of 2008, audiences attending Disney's *Ratatouille* "drove" an on-screen Volvo XC70 through an obstacle course by waving their arms to steer and scoring points for avoiding obstacles. Results were ranked in real-time to audiences in other theaters.[51] The equipment required? A wireless video camera above the screen, a web-enabled laptop containing the game linked to the developer's website and inexpensive motion-sensing technology all linked to the theater's digital projector.

More interactive approaches are on their way: fans at a formula one race in Singapore played the video game Angry Birds controlling in-game slingshots used to fling birds at the rival pigs based on voice volume. The louder the crowd, the further the birds were launched.[52] Making ads enjoyable rather than loathed may create an opportunity to increase this small but high margin component of exhibitor revenues. The ultimate advertisement initiative may draw from the pages of free software: the ability to pay a premium for an ad free movie experience.

Reserved Seating

Movie theaters are among the minority of entertainment which offers tickets without a commitment to the purchasers' viewing experience. Sports and concert goers, for example, always know where they will be sitting in relation to a performance. Movie theaters have long been the province of a first-come, first-select seating model. However, all of the major exhibition chains have incorporated elements of reserved seating – purchasing a ticket tied to a specific seat during a specific showing – into their theaters. These take a variety of forms,

ranging from theaters consisting entirely of reserved seat screens, to specific screens consisting exclusively of reserved seats, to screens with mixed open and reserved options. For the exhibitor, reserved seating requires a reservation and seat selection system and the ability to enforce seating disputes, but comes with additional revenues. Reserved seating is currently one aspect of luxury formats with prices in the $15 range – about double the industry average.

The argument for widespread reserved seating is perhaps best illustrated in the observations of an India-born ex-patriot currently in the U.S.[53] He observed that the global standard in less developed markets such as India, Singapore, and other countries is to reserve seats in advance and arrive just before the showing starts, assured that the seats will be available. In the developed U.S., by contrast, the standard is to rush to arrive early at the theater so that you can then wait in line for tickets, rush again to get a good seat in the theater, only to then wait more for a movie to start. Trips to the snack bar or restroom need to be coordinated around efforts to keep other patrons out of "your" seats. For this observer, there appears to be no benefit to the viewer for not having reserved seating.[54]

Dynamic Pricing

The technology needed for reserved seating is a gateway to dynamic pricing systems. Most non-movie events have multiple pricing levels based on seating, night versus day, and weekday versus weekend. Movie theaters, partly due to existing exhibition contracts, commonly have limited flexibility. Matinee and youth and seniors discounts are the primary pricing tiers. Ticketmaster, a leader in event ticket sales, is developing a "dynamic pricing" system which incorporates demand into pricing models.[55] This could mean radical changes with lower ticket prices for off-time and poorly attended movies and increased prices for prime seats at peak times on opening weekend. Thus far, no studio or exhibitor will acknowledge investigating the technology.[56]

Multi-Entertainment Venues

Many smaller exhibitors are seeking increased profitability beyond movies by reimagining their theaters as multi-entertainment venues. By adding activities such as game rooms, bowling, even laser tag and at-table trivia, theaters become one stop locations for family-friendly entertainment. At theaters chains like Frank Theaters which combine movies, bowling and games for the whole family with dining it is possible to spend an entertaining evening at the theater without ever seeing a movie.

Is There A *Guardian of the Exhibitors*?

While theaters experiment with a variety of initiatives to draw viewers, the clock is ticking. Prior initiatives, most recently 3D, have failed to live up to their potential as a durable and enduring way to attract audiences. Is one of the initiatives being undertaken by exhibitors an orb hiding a secret infinity stone capable of returning viewer to the theaters? Will a guardian of the exhibitors emerge in 2015? 2016? Or might all future sequels for exhibitors be cancelled?

NOTES

1. All ticket sales and box office data in this section are from: www.boxofficemojo.com.
2. MPAA 2014 Theatrical Statistics.
3. Calculated by author based on data from boxofficemojo.
4. MPAA 2014 Theatrical Statistics.
5. Statista. (2014). Statistics and facts about the film industry in India. http://www.statista.com/topics/2140/film-industry-in-india/.
6. Fritz, B., & Kaufman, A. (2011, December 30, 2011). Solid start, fast fade for movies, *LA Times*. Retrieved from latimes.com/entertainment/news/movies/la-fi-ct-box-office-wrap-20111230,0,2205189.story.
7. Cinema Advertising Council. (2014). Cinema Advertising Revenue [Press release]. URL: http://www.cinemaadcouncil.org/docs/2013_CAC_Revenue_Report_Historical_Data_060114.pdf.
8. Fritz, B. (2014, 1/27/2014). Movie Theaters, Studios in Tiff Over Trailer Lengths. *Wall Street Journal*.
9. Author calculations based on Cinema Advertising Council. (2014) data, SEC filings, NATO press releases, and author estimates.
10. Data on the firms, theaters and screens, location, etc. from web sites and SEC filings.
11. Kung, M., & Back, A. (2012). Chinese conglomerate buys AMC movie chain in U.S. *Wall Street Journal*, p. 2.
12. Mintel Report, Movie Theaters – US – February 2008 – Reasons to go to Movies over Watching a DVD.
13. Mintel Report, Movie Theaters – US – February 2008 – Reasons why Attendance is not Higher.
14. Kelly, K., Orwall, B. & Sanders, P. (2005). The Multiplex Under Siege, Wall Street Journal, December 24, 2005; Page P1.
15. Incident reported in P. Goldstein, 2005, Now playing: A glut of ads, *Los Angeles Times*, July 12, 2005 in print edition E-1; URL: http://articles.latimes.com/2005/jul/12/entertainment/et-goldstein12; accessed December 5, 2008.
16. DuBravac, 2007.
17. Burger, A. (2014, March 7, 2014). LRG: HDTV Penetration In U.S. Households Reaches Nearly 60%, from http://www.telecompetitor.com/lrg-hdtv-penetration-u-s-households-reaches-nearly-60/__

18. DuBravac, 2007.
19. PD Group (2015). 4K/UHD Leads TV Growth Heading into the Holidays, Reports NPD. NPD Group.
20. IHS (2014). LCD TV Shipment Forecast Revised Upward on Strong Consumer Demand for Larger Sizes, DisplaySearch Reports IHS.
21. Hsieh, D. (2012), Average Size of LCD TV Panels Increases by 2 Inches in 12 Months.
22. Source: Average TV size up to 60-inch by 2015 says Sharp, TechDigest, URL: http://www.techdigest.tv/2008/01/average_tv_size.html; Accessed: 2008/12/11.
23. Source: Average TV size up to 60-inch by 2015 says Sharp, TechDigest, URL: http://www.techdigest.tv/2008/01/average_tv_size.html; Accessed: 2008/12/11.
24. NPD Group (2015). 4K/UHD Leads TV Growth Heading into the Holidays, Reports NPD. NPD Group.
25. Ahara-Stubbs, M. (2015). 4K TVs: Much ado about nothing? Retrieved 2015/05/05, 2015, from http://www.cnbc.com/id/102319523.
26. Jannarone, J. (2012, February 6, 2012). As Studios Fight Back, Will Coinstar Box Itself Into a Corner?. *Wall Street Journal*, p. C6.
27. Kung, M. (2012, May 10, 2012). Movie Magic to Leave Home For?, *Wall Street Journal*, pp. D1-D2.
28. Fritz, B. (2014, Jan 7, 2014). Sales of Digital Movies Surge. *Wall Street Journal*.
29. Snider, M. (2012, 1/9/2012). Blu-ray grows, but DVD slide nips home video sales. *USA Today*.
30. Jannarone, J. (2012, February 6, 2012). As Studios Fight Back, Will Coinstar Box Itself Into a Corner?, *Wall Street Journal*, p. C6.
31. Jannarone, J. (2012, February 6, 2012). As Studios Fight Back, Will Coinstar Box Itself Into a Corner?, *Wall Street Journal*, p. C6.
32. Chandran, N. (2014). Netflix to shake up movies with 'Crouching Tiger 2' Retrieved 2014/09/30, 2014, from http://www.cnbc.com/id/102043625.
33. Gottfried, M. (2014, Oct. 3, 2014). Netflix Thickens the Plot for Movie Theaters. *Wall Street Journal*. Retrieved 2014/10/06, from http://online.wsj.com/articles/heard-on-the-street-netflix-thickens-the-plot-for-movie-theaters-1412350570#printMode.

34. Gottfried, M. (2014, Oct. 3, 2014). Netflix Thickens the Plot for Movie Theaters. *Wall Street Journal*. Retrieved 2014/10/06, from http://online.wsj.com/articles/heard-on-the-street-netflix-thickens-the-plot-for-movie-theaters-1412350570#printMode.
35. Han, A. (2015), 'The Interview' Hits Netflix This Weekend; Did the VOD Release Lose Money for Sony? http://www.slashfilm.com/the-interview-netflix-sony-losses/.
36. Verrier, R. (2012, December 30, 2011). U.S. theater owners get lump of coal at box office, *LA Times*. Retrieved from latimes.com/entertainment/news/movies/la-fi-ct-theaters-20111230,0,7228622.story.
37. NPD Group (2015). Connected TVs Surpass Blu-ray Disc Players in App Delivery – Ahead of Forecast, According to NPD.
38. NPD Group (2015). Streaming Media Player Penetration to Reach 40 Percent of U.S. Internet Homes by 2017, According to NPD.
39. The Big Picture | Why is Movie Theatre Revenue Attendance Declining? URL: http://bigpicture.typepad.com/comments/2005/07/declining_movie.htm. Accessed: 12/11/2008.
40. Dodes, R. (2012, April 19, 2012). IMAX Strikes Back. *Wall Street Journal*. Retrieved from http://online.wsj.com/article/SB1000142405270230429930457734794083 2511540.html?KEYWORDS=IMAX+strikes+back.
41. DolbyLaboratories. (2013) Dolby Atmos: Hear The Whole Picture. URL: http://www.dolby.com/us/en/professional/technology/cinema/dolby-atmos.html, Accessed: 1/5/2013.
42. Sony. (2011). Alternative Content for Theatres. *Sony Digital Cinema 4K*, 1.
43. Cinedigm. (2012). Investor Presentation: Jefferies 2012 Global Technology, Media & Telecom Conference. Cinedigm. Retrieved from http://files.shareholder.com/downloads/AIXD/2302444840x0x567367/4a213e2c-11ae-4cdc-8dd1-970919ac80ac/CIDM%20IR%20deck%20050712%20Short.pdf.
44. Ellingson, A. (2012, Oct. 15, 2012). Who's stressed about digital cinema? Not Digiplex's Bud Mayo. *The Business Journal – LA*.

45. Ellingson, A. (2012, Oct. 15, 2012). Who's stressed about digital cinema? Not Digiplex's Bud Mayo. *The Business Journal – LA*.

46. Smith, R. (2012, February 15, 2012). Leonardo's London Blockbuster: The Movie, *NY Times*. Retrieved from Accessed via Factiva.

47. Storm, A. (2014, May, 2014). Alternative content takes center stage: lessons in success from those who've made it work. *Film Journal International*.

48. Storm, A. (2014, May, 2014). Alternative content takes center stage: lessons in success from those who've made it work. *Film Journal International*.

49. Kung, M. (2012, May 10, 2012). Movie Magic to Leave Home For?, *Wall Street Journal*, pp. D1-D2.

50. O'Connor, S. (2015). Chinese cinemas post text messages on-screen during movies. TechDigest.

51. Audience Entertain. (2009, 01/2013/21). AE Case: Volvo XC70 Launch Retrieved from http://www.youtube.com/watch?v=HYVuLGLnyAM.

52. Reuters. (2011, Sept. 22, 2011). Angry Birds to Swoop on Formula One Track, *CNBC*. Retrieved from http://www.reuters.com/article/2011/09/22/us-angrybirds-idUSTRE78L1IY20110922.

53. Jain, M. R. (2013, May 15, 2013). Why do so few US movie theaters offer reserved seating? Retrieved 2015/05/21, 2015, from http://www.quora.com/Why-do-so-few-US-movie-theaters-offer-reserved-seating.

54. Jain, M. R. (2013, May 15, 2013). Why do so few US movie theaters offer reserved seating? Retrieved 2015/05/21, 2015, from http://www.quora.com/Why-do-so-few-US-movie-theaters-offer-reserved-seating.

55. Lazarus, D. (2012, April 26, 2012). Movie tickets: Now how much would you pay?, *LA Times*.

56. Lazarus, D. (2012, April 26, 2012). Movie tickets: Now how much would you pay?, *LA Times*.

CASE 13

Polaris and Victory: Entering and Growing the Motorcycle Business

We will continue to win…, of course, but to take our businesses to a higher level we intend to change how the game is played. Polaris has grown and changed significantly from the little company that Edgar and Allan Hetteen and David Johnson founded 60 years ago in Roseau, Minnesota. But just as they relied on innovation and hard work to satisfy customers, we will strive to do the same in the decades ahead.

Scott Wine, Polaris Chairman and Chief Executive Officer[1]

Steve Menneto, vice president in charge of the Motorcycle Division at Polaris Industries, gazed up at company headquarters in Medina, Minnesota as he pulled his gleaming cruiser into the parking lot. Menneto had been with the company since 1997 and was promoted to head of motorcycles in 2011. He knew his company's Victory bikes had come pretty far since they were first introduced to the riding public in 1998. With the development of new luxury touring bikes and the steady release of aggressively-styled cruisers, along with the acquisition of historic Indian Motorcycles, the motorcycle group had continually innovated throughout its first fifteen years in business. Yet Menneto pondered the recurring questions facing Victory Motorcycles and Polaris. He wondered if the initial decision to diversify into heavyweight motorcycles was the right road to take. He realized Polaris took a big risk by moving into motorcycles and going up against the recognized powerhouses in the industry. Would the Indian brand live up to its tremendous potential and capture market share at the high end of the heavyweight segment? Would Victory continue successfully competing against the Japanese giants, new energetic and innovative motorcycle companies, and their closest rival Harley-Davidson? Could the company continue to produce state-of-the-art motorcycles while maintaining the heritage of some of its iconic brands?

Victory began making motorcycles in 1998. From 1998 to 2006 Polaris had invested over $100 million in motorcycle development and by 2006 the division was profitable for the first time. Victory sales were $113 million, 7 percent of company sales for that year.[2] In 2009 Victory Motorcycles celebrated its first decade in the motorcycle business, but a global recession led to poor sales, corporate restructuring, and company-wide layoffs. In that year Polaris, Victory's parent company, announced a new 'on-road' vehicle division of which Victory would be part. Mike Jonikas was appointed as vice president of the new division and Mark Blackwell as vice president of the motorcycle business.[3] Blackwell, the first Victory Vice President was an accomplished rider himself, winning the national 500cc motocross championship and being inducted into the American Motorcycle Association's Hall of Fame. Both Jonikas and Blackwell reported directly to Polaris Chief Operating officer, Bennett Morgan.

Jonikas and Blackwell organized Victory with the intent of maintaining a high level of quality engineering throughout the production processes. Menneto knew that if Victory was to be a successful brand it needed to be able to meet customer expectations and not fall behind in terms of innovation like its main heavyweight competitor, Harley-Davidson.

Victory could still consider itself a new motorcycle brand. Recent sales were strong but competition was also getting stronger. The challenge now was how to continue to innovate and grow in an increasingly crowded and difficult market segment. The need to examine the motorcycle division's strategy seemed imperative.

Polaris Industries, Inc.

Polaris Industries, Inc., designed, engineered and manufactured snowmobiles, all terrain recreational and utility vehicles (ATVs), motorcycles and personal watercraft (PWC), on and off-road vehicles, and low emission vehicles; and marketed them, together with related replacement parts, garments and accessories (PG&A) through dealers and distributors principally located in the United States, Canada and Europe under the brand names of Victory, Indian, Ranger, Sportsman, RZR, Switchback, and others.[4] The garment and accessory items included helmets, boots, T-shirts, sweat pants, touring luggage and trailers.[5]

This case was written by Dr. Charles B. Shrader, Michelle L. Stotts, and Dr. Samuel M. DeMarie, all of the Department of Management, College of Business, Iowa State University, February 2015. It is intended to be used as a basis for classroom discussion rather than as a demonstration of either effective or ineffective management of a situation. Some of the opening and closing managerial situations included in the case are fictional and are for illustrative purposes only.

The company was widely known as the world's largest manufacturer of snowmobiles and one of the biggest makers of all-terrain vehicles and personal watercrafts in the United States.[6] In 2013, Polaris Industries employed seven thousand people at eleven manufacturing locations and five research and development centers worldwide. The company had over three thousand dealerships and operated in more than one hundred countries.

Polaris produced its first snowmobile in 1954 under co-founder and former CEO Alan Hetteen.[7] Textron, Inc. bought Polaris from its original Roseau, Minnesota ownership group in 1968.[7] Then in 1981, Textron, Inc. sold the Polaris division to a group of private investors led by W. Hall Wendel Jr., a Textron division head.[8]

The snowmobile business kept the Roseau, Minnesota plant busy six months out of the year but company managers wanted to figure out how to fill the other six months, so they extensively surveyed their snowmobiler customer base and decided in 1985 to diversify and produce all terrain vehicles (ATVs).[7] The company once again diversified by manufacturing personal watercrafts (PWC) in 1992, and eventually became a world leader in both ATV and PWC production and sales. In 1987 Polaris became a publicly traded company.[7]

As a result of its diversification strategy, Polaris was able to manufacture products all year. Snowmobile manufacturing took place in the spring through late autumn or early winter and personal watercraft were manufactured during the fall, winter and spring months. Polaris has had the ability to manufacture ATVs year round since May 1993. ATV production starts in late autumn and continues through early autumn of the following year.[5]

Because of the seasonality of the Polaris products and associated production cycles, total employment levels varied throughout the year. Approximately 3,000 individuals were employed by the company. Polaris' employees have not been represented by a union since July 1982. The company announced layoffs in their Osceola, Wisconsin plant in early 2011 due to the recession.[9]

Expansion Into Motorcycles[7,10]

Matt Parks joined Polaris in 1987 as a district sales manager for California, Nevada, and Arizona to develop the dealer network. He was named ATV product manager in 1992 and earned a spot at the company's headquarters. W. Hall Wendel Jr. asked him to do research on prospective acquisitions or expansions. Parks, with the additional title of general manager of new products, considered such things as go-karts, golf carts, lawn-and-garden

products, chain saws, and Hula-Hoops by investigating the various industries in terms of competition, size, level of service, and new trends. Parks and others studied the off-road motorcycle market when two dirt bike companies were put up for sale. Then a European motorcycle company asked to distribute their bikes through Polaris. "That sparked a study of the motorcycle business that uncovered signs of a promising market. Along with the dirt bike research, we did a quick study of the street bike business at that time, and we were kind of interested. We thought, 'You know, this makes some sense,'" recalls Parks.[11]

In 1993, Polaris distributed over 300,000 surveys through the company's Spirit magazine for Polaris vehicle owners to measure the readers' interest in buying a wide variety of products from Polaris. "Motorcycling did really, really well [in the survey]," said Matt Parks.[12] The survey results were personally interesting to Parks since he was a lifetime motorcycle rider and owned several motorcycles, including a '74 Norton, '66 and '91 BMWs, a '77 Harley XLCR and an '81 Ducati. Motorcycles also caught the interest of Wendel who at the time owned a Harley-Davidson.

In pursuing the possibility of motorcycle production, Victory became the project's confidential codename. Parks came up with the name because it was a nonsensical name with positive connotations. "It's 'V' for victory. It's nostalgic; it has World War II connotations."[13]

Parks along with Bob Nygaard, Snowmobile Division General Manager, proceeded with investigating the motorcycle production possibility by hiring two outside firms to assist them in conducting further confidential research on motorcycles. They chose McKinsey and Company, one of the largest and most prestigious consulting firms in the world, and Jerry Stahl, an advertising executive who was very familiar with recreational motorsports and the motorcycle business. Stahl also had experience with Harley-Davidson's advertising campaigns. From May through August of 1993, Parks & Nygaard assessed the Polaris infrastructure, including the company's sales force, dealer network, service and warranty operation, and parts and accessories division. They also looked at Polaris' current customers to see what types of things they were interested in and whether they would buy a motorcycle from Polaris. Polaris analysts and consultants also analyzed statistics from the Motorcycle Industry Council (MIC) in terms of the location, displacement, and types of bikes sold in the industry.

The research showed there was industry capacity for another manufacturer in the cruiser business. The research also revealed that Polaris dealers would like to have on-road motorcycles to sell. Consultants believed that a functionally superior cruiser built in America could find competitive space between Harley-Davidson and the Japanese producers. "We focused in on Harley and the Japanese manufacturers and said to ourselves, 'Is Harley vulnerable from any standpoint?' We thought that their costs were high," Nygaard said. "We thought that, based on re-engineering the Harley bike, we could build it for less money. We felt that customers were waiting too long to take delivery of their Harleys, and they (Harley-Davidson) were vulnerable from that standpoint. We could get to market with a bike that we could make money, and the heavy cruiser end of it was certainly what we wanted to target because that's where the (sales) numbers were, and that's where the (profit) margin was. It was the best fit for us, in that the Japanese were vulnerable there. They really hadn't been able to tackle Harley, because it might look like a Harley, but the real rider knew that it wasn't an American-made bike from an American manufacturer. We were close (at the time) to being in the domestic engine business, and we could build our own U.S. engine, and that gave us a major leg up on the Japanese. We were an American company."[14]

"The result of the study was, believe it or not, yes, there was a tremendous opportunity in the motorcycle market," Parks said. "It's not the off-road motorcycle market; it's the on-road motorcycle market, and the entry point, the best entry point, would be in the cruiser market."[14] Cruisers were defined as stripped-down versions of heavyweight touring bikes that were intended for leisurely travel. Research showed that many cruiser owners immediately replaced many components, such as brakes, seats, wheels, vibration-adsorption devices, frame stiffeners, and intake systems on their brand-new motorcycles. This was interpreted as an opportunity to fulfill demand created by undershot customers in the market.

Polaris had experience producing recreational vehicles for over 44 years. It had the engineering talent and production capabilities to design and produce distinctly different vehicle lines – snowmobiles, ATVs, and personal watercraft – and produce its own engines for many of those vehicles. Parks said the study showed "the manufacturing capabilities and technological know-how required to produce cruisers seemed within Polaris' grasp."[14] "My biggest concern was: Let me sell against price, let me sell against features and benefits, let me sell against more advertising, and I can find ways to do that," Nygaard said. "Help me to sell against the lifestyle, with loyalty that is as passionate as I've ever seen on any

product (Harley-Davidson). To sell against an image is very, very difficult, and that was my biggest concern."[15] In August 1993, the officer group gave the okay to continue with the study to see if it fit with existing manufacturing systems and if it could make money.

Victory Motorcycle Development[7,10]

An early decision was to determine which parts to make or buy. Dapper and Klancher explained that "they bought a Honda Shadow and a Harley-Davidson FXRS, took them completely apart, weighed, measured and estimated the cost of every single part, and determined for each part whether they would make it or buy it."[15] After figuring manufacturer, dealer, profits and sales volumes, the consultants and managers felt there was a good opportunity in the motorcycle business, and in February 1994 the officers group gave the okay to move forward and build a prototype.

A major boost to the motorcycle development occurred in September 1994 when Geoff Burgess agreed to lead the Victory team. His extensive motorcycle industry experiences and his emphasis on thorough analysis and design work set the direction for the Victory development. The Victory team took a very thorough, methodical, and analytical approach to research and development so the program didn't waste time, money, or valuable resources. Extensive computer-aided design was employed in building a prototype. "A lot of up-front thinking has saved us a lot of time on the back end," explained Matt Parks.[16]

The Victory team began an in-depth benchmarking study by obtaining and extensively road-testing a fleet of the competitors' cruisers in Minnesota, Tennessee and Arizona. The Yamaha Royal Star and Virago, Honda Shadow ACE and Valkyrie, Harley-Davidson Road King, Ducati Monster and BMW R1100RS were evaluated, compared, and ranked. The goal was not to copy the competition but to find the benchmarks for building a superior cruiser. The cost of producing the best features was also analyzed to ensure they could produce the motorcycle within their target price range.

The Victory team contacted Dunlop, manufacturer and tire supplier of Polaris ATVs, to obtain information about motorcycle tires. Steve Paulos, a Dunlop test technician with an impressive motorcycle industry background, assisted the Victory team by sharing competitors' development and production process information. He accompanied the Victory team to Arizona and shared valuable insights about the benchmarked bikes.

In the early stages of the motorcycle project, the Victory staff determined the bike must excel in two key performance areas – handling and power. Marketing studies told Matt Parks that the engine had to be a big V-twin, and it had to be U.S.-made; an American company like Polaris couldn't import the engine for a bike whose targeted buyers represented the red, white, and blue image of the cruiser culture. The group felt that the motorcycle needed to have its own signature engine. Talks with consulting firms with power-plant expertise convinced the Polaris team that designing an engine would provide experience curve benefits that would become valuable when Victory Motorcycles broadened its model line to include other classes of bikes in the future. This fit well with Polaris' considerations of starting its own engine manufacturing operation.

Geoff Burgess first laid out the parameters for the Victory V92C engine in November 1994. Victory engineers refined the design, and in February 1995 a concept drawing was created. In March 1995 Polaris engineering department visited England's Lotus, Cosworth and Triumph plant, Italy's Ducati and Aprilia plant, and Germany's BMW operation. The team also benchmarked engines made by Fuji, Kawasaki motorcycles and the Dodge Neon for manufacturing and assembly ideas.

From the Arizona test, the Victory team determined it should build a bigger engine than the competition. This would also give it bragging rights for the biggest cruiser engine with the most horsepower on the market. The Arizona tests helped define handling goals as a top priority, so much so that chassis' and frames were designed as desired, then the engine was reconfigured to fit in the available space in the frame.

The Arizona tests also convinced the team that the Victory engine should be oil-cooled. Since rows of cooling fins are an essential part of the cruiser look, the idea of using liquid cooling was rejected. Instead a system was designed that circulates extra volumes of oil to enhance the fins' cooling effect. Steve Weinzierl, who has deep knowledge of aircraft-engineering history, strapped a Czech-built Velorex sidecar onto a prototype Victory bike and took it to Death Valley, California, for worst-case cooling trials. At temperatures of 121 degrees Fahrenheit, he pulled within ten inches of the Victory going 90 miles per hour, and handed the rider in the sidecar the wires from the thermocouple to test the cooling data. This method was used to test and enhance engine thermal stability.

Once the team had collected and analyzed loads of chassis data, "Francis the Mule," a crude prototype was created in May 1995. It was built with interchangeable clamps and drilled metal brackets so selected components, such as its wheel base, steering-head angle, and rear-suspension geometry, could be mounted in varied positions and adjusted accordingly. The team could test one thing at a time and meticulously evaluate the changes in subsequent test rides. They also used the Mule to focus on the chassis because it was a priority to achieve the Victory ride and handling. After hundreds of hours riding around on Frances and obtaining some assistance from Polaris engineers on the frame and chassis, the team agreed on a chassis design. Their analysis helped reduce the weight of the frame by 20 pounds over the original prototype. In addition, the Victory team sought larger suspension forks to ensure that the chassis would have the desired rigidity and earn bragging rights for the biggest forks on the market.

Some elements of the V92C design were dictated by customer demand. It had to have some traits that are popular with, and familiar to, cruiser enthusiasts. Styling dictated a triangular rear swing-arm that mocked the "hard-tail" look of the unsuspended bikes of the 1940s. A single shock mounted underneath the seat included an aluminum sub-frame supporting the seat and rear fender. They determined that a high-quality Fox shock was to be a standard feature. Polaris still owns several rear suspension patents as a result.

In May 1995, Mark Bader, who was familiar with compact, high-performance engines, was hired to lead the engine design staff. One of the first engine mock-ups was made from paper. Created from CAD drawings using the Victory rapid-prototyping machine, it was made of thousands of precisely cut pieces of paper glued together. These computer-generated mock-ups allow parts to be generated and test-fit without excessive costs. The first engine prototype via computer-aided-design consisted of a tall, 1,507-cc V-twin with a 55-degree angle between its cylinders. This was too big to fit the frame so the angle was narrowed to 50 degrees. After the frame and chassis was developed, the engine had to be shrunk. It seemed backwards to fit the engine to the frame and chassis, but Burgess felt it was appropriate for the V92C in order to deliver the ride and handling they wanted instead of the engine size determining the bike's size and layout. In addition, they decided to solid-mount the engine and utilize it as a stressed member or supportive of the frame and relatively more integral to the bike as a whole. The handling was greatly increased.

To develop the crankshaft, the team also benchmarked the performance of competitors' bikes. The Polaris team also considered using Harley-style cylinder heads with push rods operating the valves, but they decided on a more modern overhead-camshaft design.

The Victory team found that it could eliminate virtually all traces of vibration, but it refused to do so because they felt it was a trademark of a cruiser. They had to determine the proper balance of vibration. Cruisers are supposed to have vibration. As described by Dapper and Klancher, "In the perfect world, there is imperfection. Without it, things just don't seem right. Motorcycles need to have personality; a little rumble here and tingle there lets you know that the machine underneath you is alive and kicking."[18]

The braking system was a concern of the Victory team and they set out to develop braking similar to high-performance sport bikes, rather than what's typically on cruisers. They chose Brembo hardware and worked with Brembo technicians to develop the desired feel and responsiveness. In addition, the Victory team decided to make its own master brake cylinder.

The Victory motorcycle team continued with numerous rigorous tests of the engine, chassis, and other components. The first prototype bikes with Victory engines were known as C bikes and an early prototype cost approximately $250,000 to build. On November 7, 1996, the Victory concept bike C-1 (engine and chassis together for its first test ride) was first ridden at the Osceola, Wisconsin municipal airport. Eighteen people witnessed the event.

Victory Becomes a Reality[7,10]

Finally, on February 19, 1997, Polaris issued a press release announcing that it would be entering the motorcycle market. On June 26, 1997, the Victory was rolled out to the press at Planet Hollywood in the Mall of America in Bloomington, Minnesota. Al Unser Jr. rode a preproduction bike into the restaurant, and Victory team members fielded questions about the new bike. The next day, editors from several motorcycle magazines met the Victory staff in Osceola, Wisconsin to learn more about the new American motorcycle.

Since the announcement the Victory motorcycle has received universally positive reviews in the motorcycle press. It has also received coverage in newspapers such as the Wall Street Journal, New York Times, and USA Today. Matt Parks has appeared on CNN and CNBC television networks promoting the bike. In August 1997, Victory made an appearance at the 57th annual Sturgis Rally & Races in South Dakota. Demonstration rides sponsored by dealers were given for the first time during January 1998 in Palm Springs, California. Over 200 motorcyclists received demo rides on preproduction prototypes of Victory motorcycles during Daytona Bike Week in March 1998. After taking the bikes for a ride, experiencing street speeds, corners and brakes, riders were given a questionnaire and interviewed by the Victory marketing staff. The riders' feedback indicated the bikes delivered outstanding handling and power. The Victory staff also made a few adjustments to the motorcycle based on customer feedback.[19]

The Victory team felt the bike was ready to roll and named the first model the V92C. "V" stood for the V-twin engine, "92" for the engine's 92-cubic inch displacement, and "C" indicated cruiser. The V92C had the stiffest frame of any cruiser on the market (as stiff as some sport bikes), and utilized the engine as a stressed member (fundamental component) of the frame for increased strength and rigidity. Complementing the stiff frame were its large 45mm diameter fork tubes with a rear suspension incorporating a stiff triangulated swingarm controlled by a single shock absorber under the seat. The Victory V92C delivered up to 50% more horsepower than any of its direct competitors. Victory motorcycles were first produced in "Knock-Your-Socks-Off Blue" or "Antares Red."

"The first Victory V92C motorcycles rolled off the assembly line at the Polaris plant in Spirit Lake, Iowa on the Fourth of July, 1998 just over a year after unveiling the prototype."[20] Previously, in May 1998, Cycle World, the largest motorcycle magazine in North America, selected the Victory motorcycle as the "Best Cruiser of 1998" before the first bike was available to consumers.[21]

The Polaris team believed it could successfully produce a motorcycle because of its history of design, manufacturing, and distribution of recreational vehicles along with its engineering talent, business savvy and loyal Polaris customers. Former Polaris CEO W. Hall Wendel Jr. said, "Entering the motorcycle market is a logical extension of our diversification strategy. We have the Polaris name, the engineering and marketing expertise, the manufacturing infrastructure, and the dealer and distributor network worldwide to effectively compete in this marketplace. Our main goal right now is to build the brand name recognition. When somebody says, 'What kind of bike do you have?' we want the answer to be, 'I have a Victory.'"[22]

Today, Victory motorcycles are lighter, have more torque, more storage, better engine performance, and a lower center of gravity than comparable Harley-Davidson bikes. Riders claimed that victory bikes were less tippy, more stable going over bumps, and offered more control while riding than other cruisers and touring bikes. Victory enjoyed a 95 percent owner satisfaction rate in 2010.[23]

Manufacturing and Distribution[7,10]

In addition to developing a new, quality American motorcycle, another challenge was to develop quality manufacturing, distribution and marketing plans. In determining how to best produce their bikes, the Victory team visited three European companies: Triumph Motorcycles in England, a company that made most of its engine parts; Aprilia of Italy, a scooter and small racing-bike builder; and BMW, a well-known German bike producer. As a result of these visits, Polaris decided to combine both outsourcing and original equipment manufacturing. Polaris would manufacture their own parts and components when they felt they could do a superior job, and outsource other components to good suppliers with requisite expertise.

The outsourced components of the Victory come from many sources. Wheels, pre-painted body parts, ignition coils, rear shock absorbers and the lower end of the motor were purchased from reputable U.S. suppliers. Brakes and front forks were supplied by companies in Italy. The electronic fuel-injection system was made by the British firm MBE, and pistons and cylinders were purchased from Mahle, a German company.

Victory motors were assembled at the Polaris plant in Osceola, Wisconsin, alongside lines on which engines for watercraft and all-terrain vehicles are made. Steel tubing for the bike's frames is also formed and fabricated in Osceola.

The engines and frame parts were then shipped to Spirit Lake, Iowa, where robots were used to weld up the frames before they were given a powder-coat treatment. Making the frames in-house was essential, the company believes, because it ensured the consistent geometry required to make each bike behave as the designers intended. Engines and all the other parts came together on an assembly line that consisted of a carrier suspended from an overhead track. The bottom of the carrier is waist high so employees do not have to bend over. The assembly line is staffed by nine two-person teams, who walk from station to station on a padded surface covering the concrete floor, each building an entire motorcycle. At the end of the line each bike is scrutinized by an optical measuring device called a laser theodolite, which checks the chassis for misalignments that could hurt handling. Finally, a few test miles are put on each bike using a "rolling road" dynamometer. The Victory team knows the success of the Victory project depends on the quality of the bike. This philosophy was expressed by Spirit Lake plant manager, Chuck Crone, who said, "The interest is not to make them quick. The interest is to make them right."[24]

The Spirit Lake plant was already producing certain all-terrain vehicles and personal watercraft prior to assembling motorcycles. The Spirit Lake site was chosen because it had production capacity and required Polaris to add only a handful of new jobs. Assembling the Victory motorcycles at the Spirit Lake site allowed approximately 400 employees to change from seasonal workers to year-round workers. This also marked the first time that a motorcycle was manufactured in Iowa for commercial distribution.

Polaris managers planned on keeping the motorcycle break-even point low and to start with conservative numbers to ensure quality, then eventually to expand internationally. Longer term they expected Victory to become a significant part of the company's business. Managers planned initial production to be 2,000-3,000 units.

The first dealer shipments were rolled out in July 1998. To recognize the significance of Victory's entrance into the motorcycle market, Polaris numbered each of the first 1500 bikes with a plate fastened to the handlebar clamp. Victory number 0001 was kept by the company to commemorate its history. Initially, motorcycles were manufactured and assembled in the spring and summer. However, in the long term, manufacturing of motorcycles commenced year round.

Victory motorcycles were sold through the Polaris dealer network. The selection criteria for these dealers were very strict. The intent was to monitor quality. Polaris dealers also sold lawn and garden equipment, marine products, motorcycles, and farm implements. The Victory was designed to eventually help Polaris leverage its existing engineering and manufacturing base, and provide cross-selling opportunities to its entire network of over two thousand dealers.[25]

Matt Parks wanted dealers who were completely committed to the Victory brand. He felt that the company would be very well represented by dealers in all 50 states when the motorcycles became available. All dealers were fully trained in service and sales prior to receiving their motorcycles. The initial Victory rollout involved two hundred dealers, and each dealer received approximately 10 bikes.

Assessing the Market [10]

Polaris managers felt the company's best opportunity for entering the motorcycle industry was the heavyweight segment. Heavyweight motorcycles were utilized as a mode of transportation as well as for recreational purposes. There were four sub-segments including cruisers, touring, sport bikes and standards. Polaris analysts saw that U.S. retail cruiser sales nearly doubled from 1993 to 1997. The company estimated that approximately 128,000 cruiser motorcycles were sold in the U.S. market in 1997. Demand for cruisers at the time was strong. Cruiser sales in the United States increased thirty-one percent between 1994 and 1996. Sales were predicted to jump another nine percent in 1997 just prior to Polaris' entry, to nearly 134,000 bikes. According to industry estimates, the worldwide market for cruiser motorcycles was more than 200,000 units annually in 1997/98.

In their annual report, Polaris predicted an 11-15 percent annual growth for the next five years in U.S. cruiser sales. Polaris started distributing conservative quantities of bikes during the first few years of production. The company estimated that the first sales would be to existing Polaris customers, due to a survey that indicated thirty percent of Polaris ATV and PWC owners also owned motorcycles. Polaris managers felt that re-entry customers were a major potential source of sales for Victory. Longer term, the company expected to expand internationally and broaden the product line to include models in all four motorcycle segments – cruisers, touring, sport bikes and standards. The expectation was for Victory bike sales to become a significant part of the overall company business. The worldwide motorcycle market was larger than that of snowmobiles or PWC, and Victory bikes were priced to sell at about twice the average price of Polaris' other products.[28]

"Our assumption all along has been that our target buyer is also a hard-core Polaris enthusiast," said Matt Parks. "We asked them if they'd be interested in a motorcycle made by us, and they said 'absolutely.' We asked how many of our customers had owned or ridden motorcycles and 100 percent said yes." Parks said they were not aiming at the youth market. "A major source of cruiser business is comeback riders. They've had careers, children and mortgages and got out of bikes. Now they have empty nests, disposable income and more leisure time, and they're getting back into riding." Polaris marketing executives were initially targeting a rising cruiser wave fueled by baby-boomers in their 30s, 40s. One Polaris dealer said his customers had two things in common, "They wanted another choice besides Harley-Davidson for an American cruiser … and people want their money's worth. They don't care what it costs as long as they get their money's worth."[29]

Polaris also intended to build strong owner loyalty through their Preferred Registered Owners (PRO) program, consisting of more than 600,000 members in 1998. Members were eligible for exclusive merchandise, competitive insurance rates for their Polaris vehicles, special group rides, and package tours. In return, these informed, responsible riders served as informal advocates for the Polaris brand. These customer groups provided valuable feedback on their riding habits and product demands. Dealer councils were formed to stay attuned to the market and their retailer needs.

Polaris expected to recoup the money invested in Victory within three years. Victory was expected to break even on 4,000 bike sales a year – about three percent of the market. Managers believed that Victory would help Polaris' overall sales. With an initial retail price of $12,995 nearly all of the 2,000-3,000 bikes made in 1998 were pre-sold. For example, John Gardner at Mt. Hood Polaris sold 10 of his first 15 bikes sight unseen. Gardner said the number of customers was a surprise.

Introducing Victory to the Market[7,10,25,26]

One of the first public appearances of the production version of the Victory motorcycle was during The Rock to Rock Victory Tour. This tour was intended to showcase the quality, performance, and dependability of the Victory motorcycle by riding across America on a Victory motorcycle. "We're doing it to demonstrate the 'rock-solid engineering' of the new Victory V92C," said Mark Klein, owner of Big City Motorcycles in Manhattan, New York.

Mark Klein's father, Joe, started the ride from a historic 'rock' on one coast, the Statue of Liberty, and rode to another one on the opposite coast, Alcatraz, in the San Francisco Bay. The tour started in Manhattan October 2, 1998 and within eight days and over 3,300 miles later, the tour ended in California. At the completion of the tour, Joe Klein said he had no problems with the ride. "I could hop on and ride the bike back home. That's how much confidence I have in the bike. I had a taillight bulb that went out and that was it," Klein said. "The gas mileage increased the further west we went, and the bike just performed flawlessly. It was really great." The only other thing that had to be done to the bike was to adjust the clutch once. They named the support truck driver and mechanic the Maytag repairman because he seemingly was just along for the ride.

A billboard outside Polaris headquarters showed a pair of Victory bikes against the dramatic backdrop of Monument Valley, Arizona—a Harley-Davidson kind of scene. The message on the billboard states, "It's a free country. Act like it." The Victory trailers were also used to market the motorcycles. The graphic on the Victory trailers featured a huge photo of the V92C motorcycle and the image of the American flag provided the background on the truck's sides. The Victory fleet of semi-trailer trucks was honored by Fleet Owner magazine as winner of a 1998 Fleet Owner Vehicle Graphic Award.[27]

Industry Competition[10]

At the beginning of the 20th century there were three big American manufacturers producing large displacement bikes: Harley-Davidson, Indian and Excelsior-Henderson. Harley-Davidson, Indian, and Excelsior accounted for ninety percent of the US market in 1930. The Great Depression devastated the industry, wiping out most of the smaller manufacturers. Starting in 1975 and continuing through the mid-1980s, Japanese companies penetrated the big-bore custom motorcycle market with Harley look-alikes sporting V-twin engines. Harley struggled against Japanese competition in the 1970s, but came back stronger than ever in the eighties. As the twentieth century ended, 1998 marked the first time since 1955 that Americans have had the choice of a large American designed and manufactured motorcycle other than Harley-Davidson.[31] The introduction of the Victory marked the first time in sixty years that a new American motorcycle manufacturer introduced a "significant motorcycle" that will be widely distributed.

The Victory motorcycle was aimed at grabbing market share from both the Japanese manufacturers (Honda, Yamaha, Kawasaki and Suzuki) and Harley-Davidson. Victory's initial assessment of the attractiveness of entry into the motorcycle industry was based on their assessment of Harley's profit margins. When Victory was launched Harley-Davidson had a nearly fifty-four percent share of the U.S. market for heavyweight bikes and held an estimated thirty percent share of the $3 billion worldwide heavyweight market. Victory's goal was to take five percent of that market, or in other words, sales of approximately $150 million.[32] The heavyweight cruiser market had been growing and Harley-Davidson had been unable to satisfy the demand in the United States. By default, the Japanese producers were able to capture increasingly larger shares of the market. Some analysts felt that Victory bikes would take share from the Japanese but not from Harley-Davidson.

Japanese Manufacturers – Honda, Yamaha, Kawasaki and Suzuki[10]

Honda, Yamaha, Kawasaki and Suzuki entered the US market in the seventies at the expense of both Harley-Davidson and the British motorcycle makers, and were now the predominant world industry players. These longtime Japanese motorcycle powerhouses were strong competitors because they enjoyed large overall sales volume and diversified product lines.[33] Polaris had successfully taken on Japanese competitors in the past when it entered the Japanese-dominated market for all-terrain vehicles in 1985 and started selling personal watercraft in 1992. Polaris was now one of the biggest makers of each of those markers and was leading in terms of U.S. market share in snowmobiles. Polaris regarded the Japanese as their significant competitors. At the time of the Victory launch only two manufacturers, Polaris and Yamaha, competed in all four power-sports vehicle markets -snowmobiles, personal watercraft, all-terrain vehicles and motorcycles. Polaris expected their success to continue with motorcycles. The Victory team also felt that US customers could be lured from Yamaha, Suzuki, Kawasaki, and Honda by exploiting the notion that the Japanese-brand bikes were not American-made.

However, by 2009 the Japanese bikes were as popular as ever, and the Japanese companies were showing no sign of retreating from the market. Honda was the world's largest producer of motorcycles and announced its 300-millionth bike in 2014. The Honda motorcycle line included everything from small scooters to the huge 1832cc Valkyrie Rune – one of the largest engines in the market. In 2014 Honda offered an extensive line of cruisers, custom street bikes, racing, and touring bikes. Their Shadow and VTX models were, in effect, Harley look-alikes. The Honda Gold Wing was still considered one of the best touring bikes as well. Honda and the other Japanese manufacturers seemed to be in the heavyweight segment to stay.

Harley-Davidson[10,33]

The Harley-Davidson Motor Company was founded in 1903 in Milwaukee, Wisconsin. During World War I, Harley-Davidson supplied the military with motorcycles and became the largest motorcycle company in the world in 1918. In 1969, AMF (American Machine and Foundry), Inc. purchased Harley and poured money into the company. Some think the strategy used by AMF hurt Harley's quality while others thought AMF actually saved Harley from the Japanese because of its deep pockets. In 1982, a group of Harley managers, led by Vaughn Beals and Jeffrey Bluestein, purchased Harley from AMF and turned around the company in the 1980s. By 1988 Harley was Fortune Magazine's most admired transportation firm and Harley had entrenched itself as a world leader in the heavyweight segment.

Harley-Davidson products included cruisers, factory custom, and touring motorcycles, as well as police and military motorcycles. In 2009, Harley offered over thirty different motorcycle models. Harley-Davidson benefitted from having one of the world's most recognized and respected brand names and their motorcycle models- Sportster, Super Glide, Low Rider, Dyna Glide, Wide Glide, Softail, Road King, Electra Glide and Tour Glide, were among the best-known in the industry. Harley also supplied or licensed motorcycle replacement parts, accessories, riding and fashion apparel and collectibles.

Harley-Davidson formed a riders club in 1983 and by 2006 the Harley Owners Group (HOG) had in excess of 900,000 members worldwide. HOG was the industry's largest company-sponsored enthusiast organization. By comparison, Honda's Gold Wing Road Riders association registered only 75,000 members.[35]

In 1993, Harley-Davidson took an equity stake in the Buell Motorcycle Co. of East Troy, Wisconsin, and began selling Buell cycles through its dealer network.[34] Erik Buell was a former Harley engineer who left the company to start a sport-bike business. Buells were racing bikes powered by modified Harley engines mounted on Harley frames, and were designed to appeal to younger riders. Harley-Davidson acquired one hundred percent of the company in 1998, the same year as the launch of Victory. Approximately, nine thousand bikes were sold at its zenith in 2004. However, Buell sales both in the US and overseas started to decline in 2004.[35] In an attempt to continue to grow its sport bike business, Harley acquired MV Agusta of Italy in 2009. Agusta made sport bikes for both on and off-road enthusiasts.

Harley represented freedom and individuality. Harley viewed competitors as trying to imitate their motorcycles, but unable copy the intangibles that made owning a Harley-Davidson a unique experience. Harley managers felt they were able to determine what was original and authentic in terms of the real riding experience. The quality of their bikes was very good and they were able to charge a price premium in the market. Prices ranged from approximately $8,000 for an entry-level Sportster to $30,000 for a top-of-the line touring bike. They felt that even though competitors were duplicating the Harley design by making look-alike bikes that they could not copy the Harley image. Harley tended to appeal to older riders with relatively more riding experience. In the eighties and nineties Harleys became very popular with higher income groups such as accountants, lawyers and doctors who were attracted by the prestige and image associated with owning a Harley.

In the late nineties Harley commanded forty-eight percent share of the growing North American market for heavy road bikes. Harley's product line was sold through a worldwide network of more than 1,000 dealers. Even though the number of motorcycles produced increased, Harley-Davidson still could not meet the demand for its motorcycles. Customers worldwide who ordered a new Harley sometimes waited at least a year for delivery. For years Harley had been building presold bikes, and some dealers have alienated customers by jacking up prices on scarce models. The wait was sometimes as long as two years for some models. Dealers were upset because they sometimes had no inventory. Customers were upset because they had to wait so long for the product.

Harley was facing a dogfight for the first time since 1983, primarily because of Victory and also because the Japanese were planning to respond to Victory with improvements in their cruisers as well. As Harley's production caught up with the demand, the phenomenal resale value of the bikes would begin to decline. Rival producers saw opportunity in Harley-Davidson's production constraints. Honda, Kawasaki, Suzuki and Yamaha Corp. have all began chipping away at Harley's grip on the high-margin cruiser category. This continued through the nineties into 2014 and beyond.

By 2010 Harley production volume and sales had dropped to 2001 levels.[36] In 2008 the company made over 300,000 motorcycles but planned to cut production in 2009 to around 200,000 units. It also terminated the Buell line of sport bikes, sold the MV Agusta Italian motorcycle business back to the Agusta founder, and forced its labor unions into wage and benefit concessions by threatening to move factories out of Milwaukee. Its bike owners were getting old and not many younger riders were being attracted to Harley products. Harley sales peaked in 2006 at 349,000 units but because the bikes were no longer in short supply, demand hit a wall. As supply met demand Harley became just another industry competitor and in the last quarter of 2009, it experienced its first quarterly loss in sixteen years.[37]

However, in 2014 Harley announced its new electric motorcycle- the Live Wire. The new Live Wire was incredibly fast and quiet. The company also announced a new smaller bike- the Street 750 which was developed to penetrate the Asian market. All in all, Harley was continuing to develop products around its strong brand name and was positioning to compete into the future heavyweight motorcycle segment.

Excelsior-Henderson[10,38]

Brothers Dave and Dan Hanlon attended a 1993 Sturgis bike rally in South Dakota and noticed nearly everyone owned a Harley or a Harley knockoff. As a result they decided to resurrect an American motorcycle manufacturing company, Excelsior-Henderson, and compete in the heavyweight segment. Originally founded in 1876, Excelsior expected to compete with Japanese bikes as well as the new Victory and Harley-Davidson even though they were charging a relatively higher price. Excelsior-Henderson Super X was priced at $17,500 in 1999, which was more than a comparable Harley. The first Super X production bike was shipped to a dealer on January 30, 1999. Excelsior-Henderson appeared to have a strong brand name with historical cachet and a strong management team with some motorcycle-industry experience. Excelsior-Henderson was also an American brand.

The new Excelsior-Henderson Motorcycle Manufacturing Company headquarters and manufacturing plant were both constructed in Belle Plaine, Minnesota, less than 100 miles away from the Victory plant. The original plan was to produce a single heavyweight cruiser- the Super X. Unlike Victory Motorcycles, which drew on the experience and resources of its corporate parent, Excelsior-Henderson booted up design, manufacturing, and marketing operations from scratch. The Hanlons initially signed up dealers, most of whom also sold Harleys. The Excelsior needed to sell 5,000 motorcycles a year to break even. They expected to produce 20,000 bikes per year in the Minnesota plant. However, production facilities never really materialized and sales were not forthcoming. The company went bankrupt in the year 2000.

Other competitors[10]

BMW. In 1997, Germany's Bavarian Motor Works (BMW) unveiled a new heavyweight, low-slung cruiser to take on Harley. Over the years, BMW has continually developed high quality/high performing motorcycles with both comfort and style. BMW had an advantage of engineering that provides excellent handling characteristics. Known for extremely high quality and performance, BMW was able to charge a price premium sometimes up to forty percent over similar bikes. The company announced plans for electric motorcycles in 2014.

Big Dog. Big Dog Motorcycles were custom manufactured in Wichita, Kansas and had a high cost of production and high retail prices.[39] Big Dog produced only five models – the Bulldog, Vintage Sport, ProSport, Vintage Classic, and Pitbull. Their V-Twin motors ranged from 88 to 107 cubic inches. Each bike was painted to customer specifications and is built within 60 days from the time of the order. It had relatively few employees and produced only three hundred bikes in 1997. Sheldon Coleman,

president of Big Dog Motorcycles of Sun Valley, Idaho, built his first bike in 1993 and began the company the following year. Big Dog bikes were cruisers that provided customers with highly customized bikes at a price more competitive with the mass producers.

New markets and emerging technologies

There were many niches in heavyweight motorcycle market segment. Dealernews reported seventy-seven different sellers of new 'big twin' motorcycles, as well as numerous other custom and touring producers and sellers.[40] Companies such as Lifan, a Chinese motorcycle maker, had entered the industry by dominating countries where the Japanese were not present. Lifan marketed initially only in Iran, Nigeria, the Philippines, Vietnam and Indonesia, but was preparing to move into more mature markets in the new millennium. Shanghai Motorcycle Works, another Chinese company, was ready to market its Xing-fu cycle worldwide. Xing-fu meant 'happiness' and was a very practical, energy-efficient small bike targeted at commuters and large city riders.

Traditional Italian bike makers like Bimota, Ducati and Motto Guzzi were continuing to produce super bikes of extremely high quality and style. Bombardier, a Canadian firm, disrupted the market with a remarkably popular three-wheeled roadster. And the British bike companies, Triumph and Norton, were creating very interesting and exciting new motorcycle models as well. Triumph was the fastest growing motorcycle brand, in terms of percentage sales growth, in the world in 2010.[41]

On top of all this, new entrepreneurial companies like Zero Motorcycles were gaining notice in the business press and in the market. Zero produced electric dirt bikes and won praise from both Businessweek and Fortune for their products and business planning.[42] In June of 2010 at the Bonneville Salt Flats in Utah, Mission One, another new company, had a rider set a world speed record of 150 miles per hour on a motorcycle with an electric motor.[43]

By 2014, both Lotus (a car company known for racing) and Catheram (a British company known for excellent track cars) announced new gas-powered motorcycles. Tesla, the leading electric car company, along with LIT motors, BMW, and Daimler announced they were developing electric bikes.

The Indian Acquisition[46]

One major development for Polaris and Victory came on April 19, 2011 when the company announced the acquisition of Indian Motorcycle Company. Indian Motorcycles

(Indian Motorcycle Manufacturing, Inc.) was the most recognizable American brand next to Harley-Davidson. Indian was the first American motorcycle company founded in 1901 and the Indian Chief was a classic heavy cruiser highly desired by motorcycle enthusiasts worldwide. However, the company had been out of business since the British motorcycles knocked it out of the market in the 1950s. There were several attempts to revive the brand in the 1990s although none was very successful in the long term.

The Polaris press release for the acquisition was as follows:

MINNEAPOLIS, Apr 19, 2011 (BUSINESS WIRE) – Polaris Industries Inc. (NYSE: PII) today announced the acquisition of Indian Motorcycle. The business was acquired from Indian Motorcycle Limited ("IML"), a company advised by Stellican Limited and Novator Partners LLP, U.K. Private Equity firms. Terms of the transaction were not disclosed.

"We are excited to be part of the revitalization of a quintessentially American brand," said Scott Wine, CEO of Polaris Industries Inc. "Indian built America's first motorcycle. With our technology and vision, we are confident we will deliver the classic Indian motorcycle, enhanced by the quality and performance for which Polaris and Victory are known."

With this acquisition, Polaris adds one of motorcycling's legendary brands to its strong stable of Victory cruiser and touring bikes. Indian will operate as an autonomous business unit, building upon the potent combination of Polaris' engineering acumen and innovative technology with Indian's premium brand, iconic design and rich American heritage.

"We are delighted to have reached an agreement with Polaris. Polaris will utilize its well-known strengths in engineering, manufacturing, and distribution to complete the mission we undertook upon re-launching the brand in 2006: harness the enormous potential of the Indian brand," said Stephen Julius, chairman of Indian and managing director of Stellican. "Polaris is the most logical owner of Indian Motorcycle. Indian's heritage brand will allow Polaris to aggressively compete across an expanded spectrum of the motorcycle market."

Novator Partners LLP is a London based alternative investment firm founded and led by the investor Mr. Thor Bjorgolfsson. An avid motorcycle enthusiast, Mr. Bjorgolfsson said "After a troubled past, our goal was to bring the legendary Indian bikes back on the roads. The initial phase of that project is done and now our great partners at Polaris will carry on the work to realize the full potential of this classic American brand."

Founded in 1901, Indian was America's first motorcycle company, producing some of the industry's most iconic models and becoming the world's largest motorcycle manufacturer. In recent years, Indian has continued to produce these legendary motorcycles on a smaller scale. The company's instantly recognizable badge is still associated with premium products and strong American heritage by casual consumers and motorcycle enthusiasts alike.

Polaris CEO Scott Wine stated in an April 20, 2011 webcast that the company would incorporate the manufacture of Indian Motorcycles into the current Victory plant in Spirit Lake, Iowa. Wine indicated that Polaris' world-class manufacturing and distribution skill would blend nicely with Indian's rich American heritage and style. He said that Polaris had the corporate resources and strategic strengths to contribute to what Indian needed for success, including a strong dealer network, while Indian provided Polaris and Victory with enhanced brand recognition in the heavy weight segment. He went on to note that the acquisition provided Polaris' motorcycle business access to the 'die hard' component of the heavy weight motorcycle segment.

The amount Polaris paid for Indian was not given in the press release or in the webcast. Scott Wine did say, however, that Polaris had 'plenty on the balance sheet' to support the acquisition. The acquisition of Indian came at a great time for both companies. According to the webcast, Victory sales were up 77 percent for the first quarter of 2011. Sales were up substantially in France and Germany, and were growing internationally in general. Victory revenue was up 59 percent for the 2011 first quarter. Indian, on the other hand, was having financial difficulty and needed help in terms of quality manufacturing.

By 2014, Polaris had moved Indian production to the Iowa Spirit Lake plant and had announced plans to grow the Indian brand. The company indicated they would produce the class Indian Chief model and resurrect the classic smaller Indian Scout motorcycle.

Growing Polaris Motorcycles[46,47]

Additionally, on October 26, 2011, Polaris Industries announced that it had acquired a minority stake in Brammo, an Oregon-based producer of two-wheeled electric vehicles. Brammo, founded in 2002, is an industry leader in electric power-train and battery-pack technologies, and offers the Encite, Empulse, Engage, and Enertia electric motorcycle lines. According to the Polaris press release, Brammo motorcycles are capable of speeds in excess of 60 miles per hour and can travel

Exhibit 1 Victory Sales (dollars in millions)

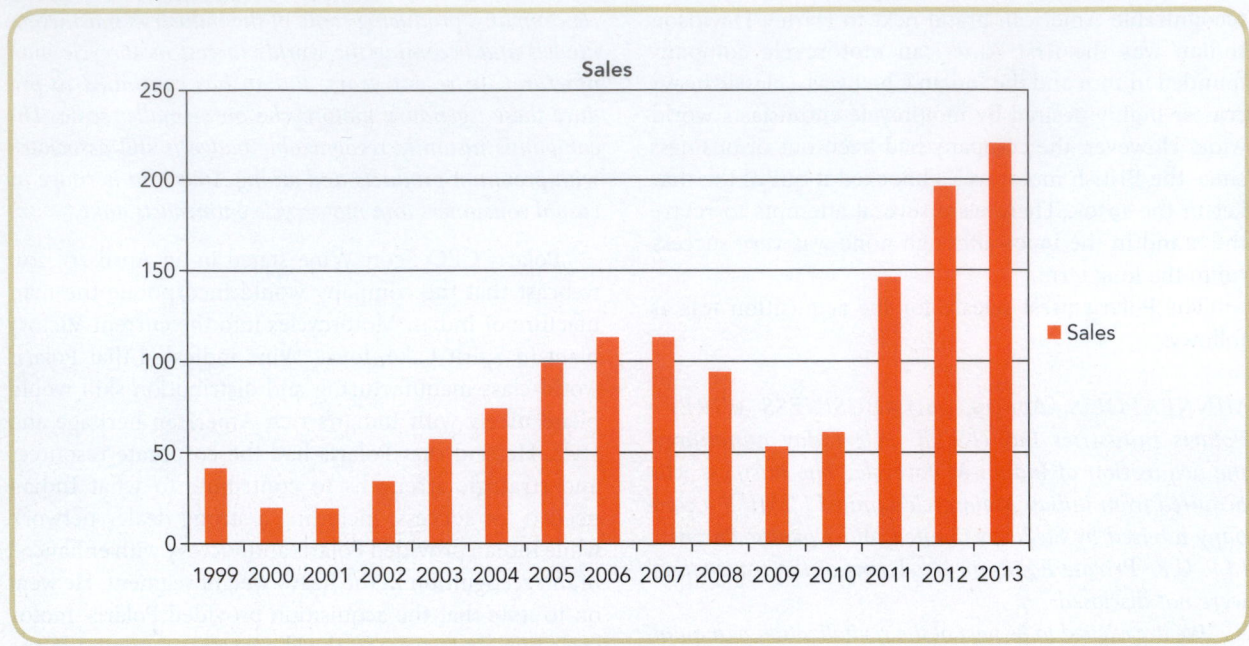

Sources: Polaris Industries 2013, 2009, 2006, 2003 and 2000 annual reports. Polaris Industries 2010 10K Q1, Q2, and Q3, quarterly reports. 2012 and 2013 figures include Indian.

Exhibit 2 Harley-Davidson Sales, Percent increases/decreases, Units Shipped and Sold

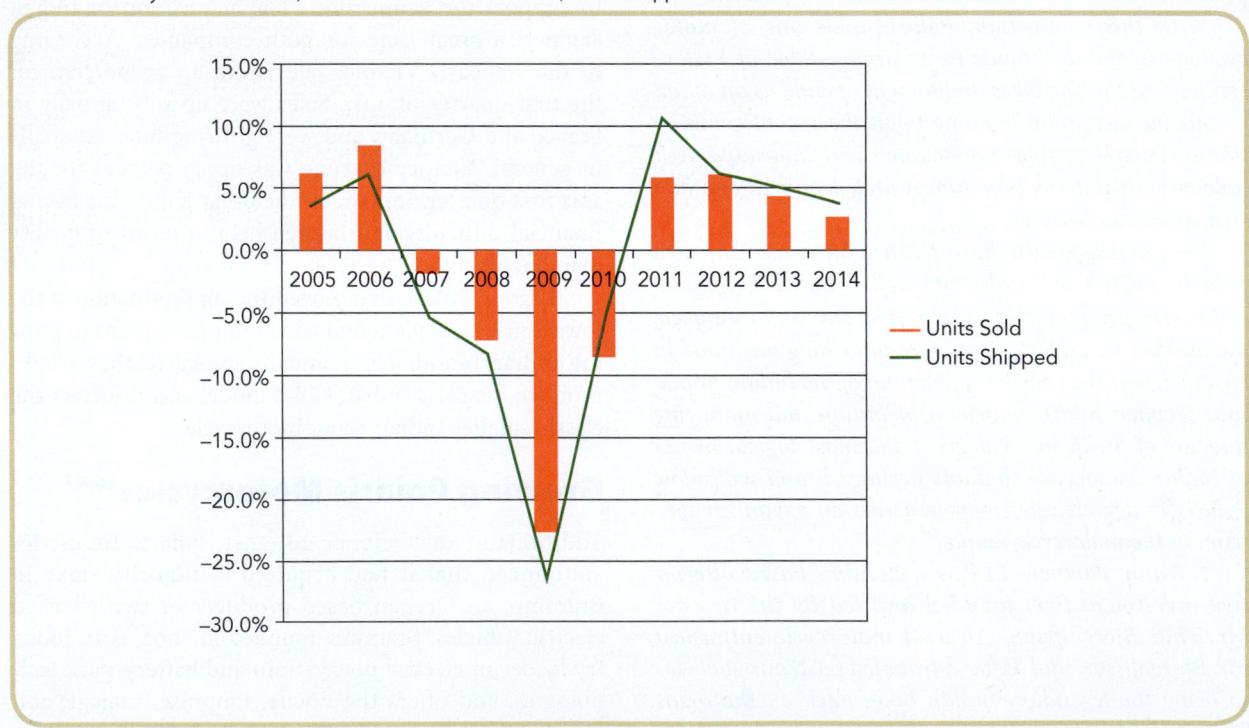

Source: http://www.fool.com/investing/general/2015/02/02/harley-davidson-inc-earnings-the-1-number-that-sho.aspx

more than 100 miles on a single charge. Scott Wine stated that the acquisition positions Polaris well in terms of capitalizing on growth in the electric vehicle market. Wine also noted that Polaris will work with Brammo to grow the core businesses of both companies.

Another strategic move in 2012 further cemented the company's commitment to motorcycles. In July of 2012, Polaris announced a joint venture with Eicher Motors, manufacturer of classic Royal Enfield motorcycles, to market bikes in India. Polaris and Eicher each held fifty percent of the new operation.

On its 60th anniversary in July of 2014, Polaris surprised everyone with another announcement of a new product, the Slingshot. The Slingshot, a three-wheel two-seater roadster, was a head-turning vision of the future of motorcycling. The vehicle featured a 173 horsepower motor and had a five-speed manual transmission. It came in two models- the basic Slingshot at $19,999 and the premium model at $23,999. The Slingshot generated a great deal of media attention drawing more attention to the Polaris Motorcycle Division.

And it didn't take long for the Bammo acquisition to pay dividends. In February of 2015, Polaris and Victory announced the first bike from the partnership- the Victory Charger. Polaris has trade-marked the name of the bike but other details about it are not currently known. However it does appear that having access to Brammo's expertise will allow Polaris to make the Charger available quickly- perhaps even beating the Harley Live Wire to market.

The Future

As Steve Menneto walked into company headquarters, he reflected on all the events surrounding the heavyweight motorcycle industry. His company's motorcycle division had successfully taken on Harley-Davidson, an American icon. Menneto realized his motorcycles had received critical acclaim in the industry. Victorys were perceived as high quality and technologically advanced bikes, especially compared to Harleys, and were offered at a very competitive price. Since 2011 Victory profits constituted over seven percent of Polaris company's bottom line.[44] Victory sales increased by twelve percent from 2012 to 2013[45]. Demand had improved across the

Exhibit 3 Victory Motorcycle Models

Motorcycle category	Suggested retail price	Description
Cruisers		
Vegas 8-Ball	$12,499	basic cruiser
Gunner	$12,999	throwback cruiser
High-Ball	$13,349	custom cruiser
Hammer 8-Ball	$14,499	high end cruiser
Baggers/Touring		
Cross Country 8-Ball	$17,999	basic touring
Magnum	$21,999	performance touring
Cross Country	$18,999	long distance touring
Ness Magnum	$22,999	high end touring
Luxury Touring		
Vision Tour	$20,999	luxury touring bike
Cross Country	$21,999	high storage touring

Source: http://www.victorymotorcycles.com/en-us

Exhibit 4 Indian Motorcycle Models

Motorcycle category	Suggested retail price	Description
Cruiser		
Scout	$10,999	entry-level cruiser
Chief Dark Horse	$16,999	blacked-out crusier
Chief Classic	$18,999	classic cruiser
Chief Vintage	$20,999	custom cruiser
Baggers/Touring		
Chieftain	$22,999	high end touring
Touring		
Roadmaster	$26,999	luxury touring bike

Source: http://www.indianmotorcycle.com/en-us/motorcycles

Exhibit 5 Polaris Products

Side x Side and All-Terrain Vehicles — Ace, Ranger, Sportsman, RZR
Victory Motorcycles
Indian Motorcycles
Slingshot Motorcycles
Electric Motorcycles (announced)
Snowmobiles — Polaris, Indy, RMK, Rush, Switchback
GEM Electric Motorcars — GEM, AIXAM, MEGA
Parts, Apparel & Accessories
Polaris Defense — Dagor
Generators

Source: http://www.polaris.com/en-us/corporate/aboutpolaris/pages/historyheritage.aspx

Exhibit 6 Top Motorcycle Brands, Ranked by Shopper Satisfaction with Dealerships

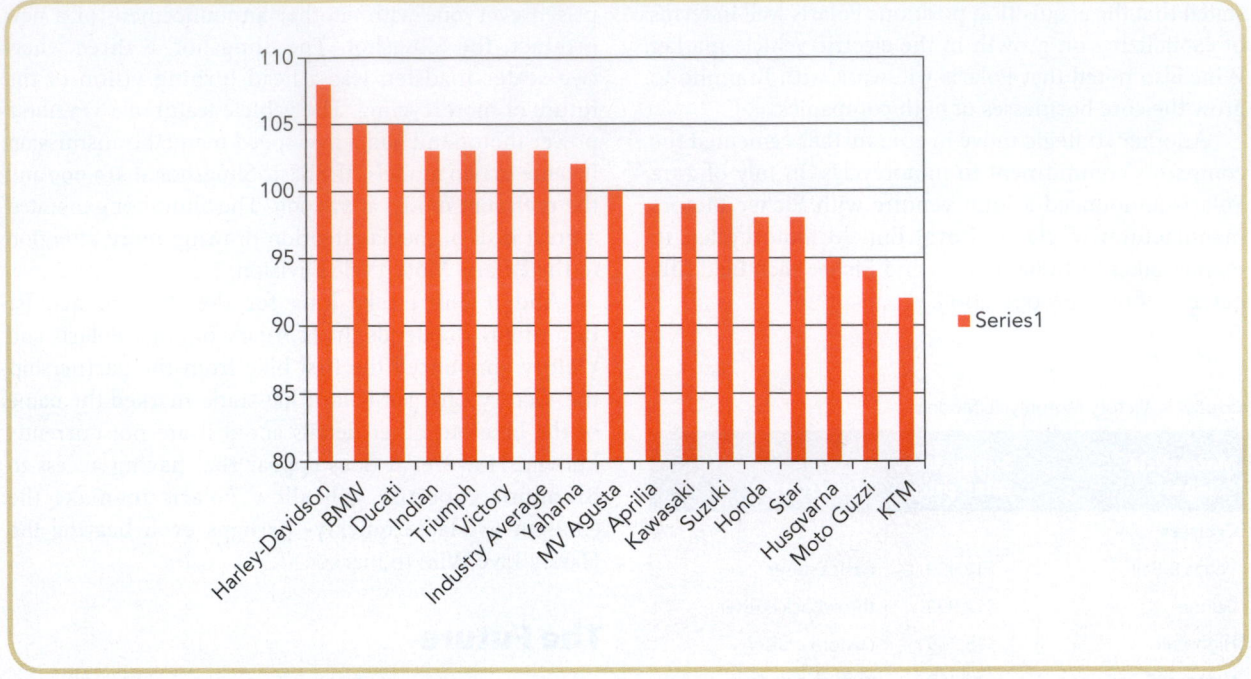

Source: http://www.piedpiperpsi.com/pdf/documents/169.pdf

entire Victory line but particularly for the Cross Roads and Cross Country touring models. Markets outside North America were growing significantly, and sales of accessories, clothing, and parts were also up in 2013. Menneto knew his bikes were good, but had they been marketed and distributed effectively? Was Victory suc-

cessfully capturing the attractive profit-margin potential of the heavyweight segment as they had planned? Menneto also needed to consider whether it was a good decision to limit sales of Victory motorcycles to Polaris dealerships. The goal was to monitor quality through the Polaris dealers – but were they simultaneously losing potential business?

Menneto knew the strategic positioning of the new Polaris on-road vehicle division had tremendous implications for both Victory and Polaris as a whole. He was also aware that current Polaris CEO, Scott Wine, wanted the company to grow into 'adjacent' businesses. Did this mean the company would move into off-road bikes? Did this mean that Victory would engage in some sort of overseas expansion? Or perhaps some sort of energy-efficient scooter would make sense for Polaris? Perhaps the company was thinking of making more acquisitions in order to grow? Would they be in the market for more types of electric motorcycles or other alternative energy-related acquisitions? Victory's future was certainly shaping up to be as challenging and eventful as its recent past.

Exhibit 7 Market Share Rank by Company

Consolidated Market Share (all vehicles) Rank by Company	Motorcycles (Heavyweight/ Cruiser/ Touring only)	Off-Road Vehicles	Snow-mobiles
1- Polaris	1- Harley	1- Polaris	1- Ski-Doo
2- Harley	2- BMW	2- BRP	2- Polaris
3- Honda	3- Victory/Indian	3- Kymco	3- Yamaha
4- Yamaha	4- Triumph	4- Yamaha	4- Arctic Cat
5- Kawasaki	5- Honda	5- CF Moto	
6- Can Am	6- Suzuki	6- Honda	
Others (BMW, Ducati, Triumph, etc.)			

Source: file:///C:/Users/cshrader/Downloads/PII%20Investor%20Pres%20Nov-2014%20(1).pdf (presentation to investors, November 2014)

Exhibit 8 Selected Financial Data

(Dollars in millions, except per-share data)	For the Years Ended December 31,					
	2013	2012	2011	2010	2009	2008
Statement of Operations Data						
Sales Data:						
Total sales	$3,777.1	$3,209.8	$2,656.9	$1,991.1	$1,565.9	$1,948.3
Percent change from prior year	18%	21%	33%	27%	—20%	9%
Sales mix by product:						
Off-road vehicles	67%	69%	69%	69%	65%	67%
Snowmobiles	8%	9%	11%	10%	12%	10%
Motorcycles	6%	6%	5%	4%	3%	5%
Small vehicles	3%	2%	—%	—%	—%	—%
Parts, garments and accessories	16%	14%	15%	17%	20%	18%
Gross Profit Data:						
Total gross profit	$1,120.9	$925.3	$740.6	$530.2	$393.2	$445.7
Percent of sales	29.7%	28.8%	27.9%	26.6%	25.1%	22.9%
Operating Expense Data:						
Total operating expenses	$588.9	$480.8	$414.7	$326.3	$245.3	$284.1
Percent of sales	15.6%	15.0%	15.6%	16.4%	15.7%	14.6%
Operating Income Data:						
Total operating income	$577.9	$478.4	$349.9	$220.7	$165.0	$182.8
Percent of sales	15.3%	14.9%	13.2%	11.1%	10.5%	9.4%
Net Income Data:						
Net income from continuing operations	$381.1	$312.3	$227.6	$147.1	$101.0	$117.4
Percent of sales	10.1%	9.7%	8.6%	7.4%	6.5%	6.0%
Diluted net income per share from continuing operations	$5.40	$4.40	$3.20	$2.14	$1.53	$1.75
Net income	$377.3	$312.3	$227.6	$147.1	$101.0	$117.4
Diluted net income per share	$5.35	$4.40	$3.20	$2.14	$1.53	$1.75
Cash Flow Data:						
Cash flow provided by continuing operations	$499.2	$416.1	$302.5	$297.9	$193.2	$176.2
Purchase of property and equipment for continuing operations	251.4	103.1	84.5	55.7	43.9	76.6
Repurchase and retirement of common stock	530.0	127.5	132.4	27.5	4.6	107.2
Cash dividends to shareholders	113.7	101.5	61.6	53.0	50.2	49.6
Cash dividends per share	$1.68	$1.48	$0.90	$0.80	$0.78	$0.76
Balance Sheet Data (at end of year):						
Cash and cash equivalents	$92.2	$417.0	$325.3	$393.9	$140.2	$27.2
Current assets	865.7	1,017.8	875.0	808.1	491.5	443.6
Total assets	1,685.5	1,488.5	1,228.0	1,061.6	763.7	751.1
Current liabilities	748.1	631.0	586.3	584.2	343.1	404.8
Long-term debt and capital lease obligations	284.3	104.3	104.6	100.0	200.0	200.0
Shareholders' equity	535.6	690.5	500.1	371.0	204.5	137.0

Source: 2013 10K report pp.23-24.

Exhibit 9 Polaris Sales and Selected Financial Ratios

	2009	2010	2011	2012	2013
Sales	$1.6B	$2B	$2.7B	$3.2B	$3.8B
ROA	13%	16%	20%	23%	24%
EPS	$1.53	$2.14	$3.20	$4.40	$5.40

Source: Polaris investor presentation, 2014

Exhibit 10 Polaris Industries – Management Team

Scott W. Wine (age 45)
Chief Executive Officer

Bennett J. Morgan (age 49)
President and Chief Operating Officer

Stacy L. Bogart (age 49)
Vice President – General Counsel and Corporate Secretary

Michael D. Dougherty (age 45)
Vice President – Asia Pacific and Latin America

Stephen L. Eastman (age 48)
Vice President – Parts, Garments and Accessories

William C. Fisher (age 58)
Vice President – Information Systems

Todd-Michael Balan (age 43)
Vice President – Corporate Development

Suresh Krishna (age 44)
Vice President – Global Operations and Integration

Michael W. Malone (age 54)
Vice President – Finance and Chief Financial Officer

James P. Williams (age 50)
Vice President – Human Resources

Matthew J. Homan (age 41)
Vice President – EMEA and Small Vehicles

David C. Longren (age 54)
Vice President – Off-Road Vehicles and ORV Engineering

Michael P. Jonikas (age 52)
Vice President – Snow Mobiles, Slingshot and Corporate Marketing

Steven D. Menneto (age 48)
Vice President – Motorcycles

Source: Polaris Industries 2013 annual and 10K reports.

Exhibit 11 Polaris Board of Directors

Scott W. Wine
CEO and Chairman of the Board
(Technology Committee member)

Annette K Clayton
Chief Supply Chain Officer of Schneider Electric
(Compensation and Technology Committee member)

Brian C. Cornell
Chairman of the Board and Chief Executive
Officer of Target Corporation
(Compensation and Technology Committee member)

Gary E. Hendrickson
Chairman and Chief Executive Officer
of the Valspar Corporation
(Chair of Compensation Committee)
(Nominating and Technology Committee member)

Bernd F. Kessler
Former Chief Executive Officer of SR Technics AG
(Audit, Compensation, and Technology
Committee member)

R. M. Mark Schreck
Academic Program Director
University of Louisville Speed School of Engineering and
Retired Vice President of Technology,
General Electric Company
(Chair of Technology Committee)
(Audit and Nominating Committee member)

Kevin Farr
Executive Vice President and Chief Financial
Officer for Mattel, Inc
(Chair of Audit Committee)
(Technology Committee member)

John P. Wiehoff
Chairman and Chief Executive Officer of
C. H. Robinson Worldwide, Inc.
(Chair Nominating Committee)
(Audit Committee member)

Source: http://phx.corporate-ir.net/phoenix.zhtml?c=108235&p=irol-govboard,
and http://ir.polaris.com/investors/corporate-governance/default.aspx

Exhibit 12 Polaris Mission, Strategy, Objectives, Vision, Creed and Values

Vision

Fuel the passion of riders, workers and outdoor enthusiasts around the world by delivering innovative, high quality vehicles, products, services and experiences that enrich their lives.

Strategy

Polaris will be a highly profitable, customer centric, $8B global enterprise by 2020. We will make the best off-road and on-road vehicles and products for recreation, transportation and work supporting consumer, commercial and military applications. Our winning advantage is our innovative culture, operational speed and flexibility, and passion to make quality products that deliver value to our customers.

Objectives

- Powersports – 5-8% annual growth
- Growth through Adjacencies – $2 billion from acquisitions and new markets
- Global Market Leadership- 33% of Polaris revenue
- Strong Financial Performance – net income of 10%

Creed

At Polaris, making great products is not just a job – it is a way of life. That is why our creed is etched in steel at the entrance at each of our locations. Our employees are not only building and designing our machines, they are also enthusiastic riders. This gives us the competitive edge as we work together to make the riding experience better.

Polaris Values

Polaris is a strong believer that the key to its success is in the ethics and values of its employees. The Polaris values were defined by its employees, and to prove that this is not just lip service, the Polaris Performance Management Program evaluates employee performance not only on delivered results but also on how well they represent company values:

Team Player	Integrity
Innovation	Passion for Excellence
Employee Development	Problem Solver
Customer Focus	Leadership

Source: file:///C:/Users/cshrader/Downloads/PII%20Investor%20Pres%20Nov-2014%20(1).pdf (Presentation to investors, 2014).

NOTES

1. Polaris Industries 2013 annual report (shareholder letter).
2. From Ho Hum Springs a Radical Vision: Victory Motorcycles enters its 10th year with a distinct lineup and a healthy reputation, by Dennis Johnson, Big Twin Dealer, February 2008, pp. 4–6.
3. Dealernews, May 22, 2009.
4. Polaris Industries, Form 10-K, United States Securities and Exchange Commission, December 31, 1997. And http://finance.yahoo.com//pr?s+PII+Profile.
5. Polaris Industries Inc., Corporate Profile, www.polarisindustries.com.
6. Ryberg, William (1998). Polaris Declares 'Victory': A New Motorcycle is Joining the Road – and it's Made in Iowa. Des Moines Sunday Register, August 2. Pp. 1G–2G.
7. Dapper, Michael & Klancher, Lee (1998). The Victory Motorcycle: The Making of a New American Motorcycle. MBI Publishing Company, Osceola, WI.
8. Klebnikov, Paul (1997). Clear the Roads, Here Comes the Victory. Forbes, October 20, 1997, v. 160, n 9, p. 162 (3).
9. http://www.bizjournals.com/milwaukee/news/2010/12/23/polaris-layoffs-in-osceola-begin-march-1.html?ana=yfcpc.
10. Stotts, Micelle, Master's thesis, Iowa State University, 1999.
11. Dapper, Michael & Klancher, Lee (1998). The Victory Motorcycle: The Making of a New American Motorcycle. MBI Publishing Company, Osceola, WI, pg. 12.
12. Ibid, pg. 13.
13. Ibid, pg. 17.
14. Ibid. Pg. 15.
15. Ibid, pg. 16.
16. Ibid, pg. 30.
17. Brown, Stuart F. (1998). Gearing Up For The Cruiser Wars. Fortune, August 3, 1998, p. 128B-L.
18. Dapper, Michael & Klancher, Lee (1998). The Victory Motorcycle: The Making of a New American Motorcycle. MBI Publishing Company, Osceola, WI, pg. 71.
19. Mollet, Kevin. Motorcyclists Impressed by Victory Performance During Demo Rides

at Daytona Bike Week. http://www.victory-usa.com/victory-usa/demo.htm.

20. Polaris Industries' Victory Motorcycles Ready to Roll. July 9, 1998. http://www.victory-usa.com/victory-usa/ready.htm.

21. Polaris Victory Motorcycle Names "Best Cruiser" by Cycle World. May 12, 1998. http://www.victory-usa.com/victory-usa/cyclewld.htm.

22. Murphy, John (1997). Polaris Enters the Motorcycle Market. Dealernews, April 1997, v 33, n 4, p. 36.

23. Victory: the New American Motorcycle, 2010 victory Touring DVD, Polaris Industries, 2009.

24. Ryberg, William (1998). Polaris Declares 'Victory': A New Motorcycle is Joining the Road – and it's Made in Iowa. Des Moines Sunday Register, August 2. Pp. 1G–2G.

25. Miller, James (1998). Polaris Set to Challenge Harley in Motorcycle Market. Wall Street Journal, March 11, 1998, p. B4.

26. Historic Cross-Country Victory Motorcycle Tour – the Rock to RockVictory Tour – Begins with Kick-off at New York Dealership (1998). http://www.victory-usa.com/victory-usa/mtour.htm.

27. Worwa, Susan (1998). Just Like the Motorcycle Itself, Victory Trucks Are Award Winners. http://www.victory-usa.com/victory-usa/victruck.htm.

28. Polaris Industries Inc. 1997 Annual Report.

29. Duchene, Paul (1998). Minneapolis-Based Polaris to Fight Harley-Davidson in Motorcycle Market. Knight-Rider/Tribune Business News, May 13, 1998.

30. Ballon, Marc (1997). Born to Be Wild: Anatomy of a Start-up, Excelsior-Henderson Makes a Bid to Become the Next Harley-Davidson. Inc. Vol. 19, No, 16, November 1997, p. 42–53.

31. Aker, Jean (1998). And Then There Were Three, And Now There are Three. Winding Roads Motorcycle Times, http://members.aol.com/JFA2/three.html.

32. Rose, Robert L. (1997). Polaris is Revving Up to Sell Motorcycles in the U.S. Market. Wall Street Journal, February 20, 1997, p. B2.

33. Shrader, Charles B., David, Fred R., Dannels, Timothy T. (1997). Harley-Davidson 1997.

34. That VROOM! You Hear May Not Be a Harley. Business Week, Oct 20, 1997. p 159–160.

35. Nolan, Richard and Kotha, Suresh, Harley-Davidson: Preparing for the Next Century, Harvard Business School case, April 20, 2006.

36. Harley Shows its Feminine Side, Bloomberg Businessweek, October 4, 2010, pp. 25–26.

37. Taylor, Alex, Fortune, September 17, 2010.

38. The Legend is Back, Excelsior-Henderson Motorcycle Company promotional VHS tape.

39. Big Dog Motorcycles web site www.bigdogmotorcycles.com.

40. Dealernews, December 2008, Vo. 44, No. 12, pg. 177.

41. http://www.forumtriumph.gr/topic2019.html.

42. Zero Motorcycles, by Neal Saiki, Fortune, January 21, 2008, pg. 28.

43. A Motorcycle on a Mission: to get investors to notice its software, a startup built the world's fastest electric bike, by Brian Dumaine, Fortune, June 14, 2010, pg. 30.

44. http://www.motorcyclistcafe.com/forums/showthread.php?8995-Victory-lives-up-to-its-name-for-Polaris-Q3.

45. file:///C:/Users/cshrader/Downloads/PII%20Investor%20Pres%20Nov-2014%20(1).pdf (Investor relations presentation, 2014).

46. Source: Polaris Industries Inc., Marlys Knutson, www.polarisindustries.com/irhome.

47. Source: https://autos.yahoo.com/news/victory-charger-could-first-electric-motorcycle-polaris-183041913.html.

CASE 14

Safaricom: Innovative Telecom Solutions to Empower Kenyans

As the largest mobile provider in Kenya, Safaricom has touched the lives of Kenyans throughout the country, with products and services designed to empower people. Safaricom enjoys a 64.5% market share, 77.5% of voice traffic, and 72.6% of mobile data/internet subscribers.[1] Safaricom facilitates community involvement through various organizations such as the M-PESA foundation, a charitable trust that seeks to advocate programs that improve health, environmental conservation, and education for the financial and social benefit of Kenyans, and the Safaricom Foundation, whose mission is to partner with the community to tackle environmental, economic, and social issues to bring about enduring and progressive change.[2] Safaricom also serves society by sponsoring athletic events through Safaricom Sevens, the biggest rugby event in Kenya, and by sponsoring the music festival Niko na Safaricom Live, an event featuring local music talent and fostering national pride.[3]

Safaricom Ltd. was formed as a private limited liability company (LLC) in 1997 and became a publically traded company in 2002. The original company was 60% owned by the Government of Kenya.[4] In 2000 Vodafone acquired a large stake in the company through Vodafone Kenya Ltd, a locally owned subsidiary.[5] In 2008 the Government of Kenya sold enough shares to the public to lose its majority interest.[6] There are a total of 40 billion shares outstanding, which are owned by 698,863 different investors as of March 31, 2013. Of those shareholders, 61.2% own less than 1,000 shares. The top two shareholders, Vodafone Kenya Limited and Permanent Secretary – The Treasury, now own just over 75% of the company. As of October 18, 2013, 52 institutional investors owned only 2.3 million shares, or 5.86% of the remaining shares.[7]

Safaricom has grown through a variety of strategies, including acqusitions. In 2008, Safaricom purchased a majority stake in One Communications Ltd. in order to gain access to its data services.[8] The company has also made several other small acquisitions to enhance its services and market share.[9]

Operating in Africa

According to KPMG, "Africa is the last great untapped telecommunications market."[10] Market penetration in Africa is only 47%.[11] GDP growth in sub-Saharan Africa remained strong in 2012 at 4.6% despite the global economic slowdown.[12] Kenya is the third largest mobile market in Africa, behind Nigeria and South Africa. Kenya also boasts one of the fasting growing economies in the region. The number of mobile subscribers is expected to grow steadily in the medium to long term with an estimated 13 million new subscribers from 2011 to 2016. There is currently a pricing war going on between the four mobile service providers in Kenya.[13] A graph of market share for each of these firms is shown in Exhibit 1.

Kenya

Kenya is located in East Africa and earned its independence from Great Britain in 1963. Since obtaining independence it has been relatively peaceful. The county is home to over 37 million people and official languages are English and Swahili, although various indigenous languages can be heard throughout Kenya. The currency is the Kenyan shilling (KSh). Its capital is Nairobi, with a population of over 3 million people. There are two heads of state, President Mwai Kibaki and Prime Minister Raila Odinga. In 2010, Kenyan citizens voted to ratify a new constitution, which would decrease the president's power and establish a bicameral parliament. Kenya has a fairly significant but declining trade deficit. Key trading partners for exports are Uganda, Tanzania, Britain and Germany. Kenya exports a lot of legumes. Key trading partners for imports are Britain, Japan, Germany and the United Arab Emirates. The crime rate in Kenya is quite high, especially crimes of petty theft, armed robbery, burglary and fraud. Corruption is also quite common.[14]

The country is fortunate to have one of the most diversified economies in sub-Saharan Africa. Its main economic sectors are agriculture, manufacturing

Written by Laura Beauchesne, Nick Dorion, Nathaniel Griggs, and Jeffrey S. Harrison at the Robins School of Business, University of Richmond. Copyright © Jeffrey S. Harrison. This case was written for the purpose of classroom discussion. It is not to be duplicated or cited in any form without the copyright holder's express permission. For permission to reproduce or cite this case, contact Jeff Harrison at RCNcases@richmond.edu. In your message, state your name, affiliation and the intended use of the case. Permission for classroom use will be granted free of charge. Other cases are available at: http://robins.richmond.edu/centers/case-network.html

Exhibit 1 Kenyan Mobile Operators by Market Share, March 2012

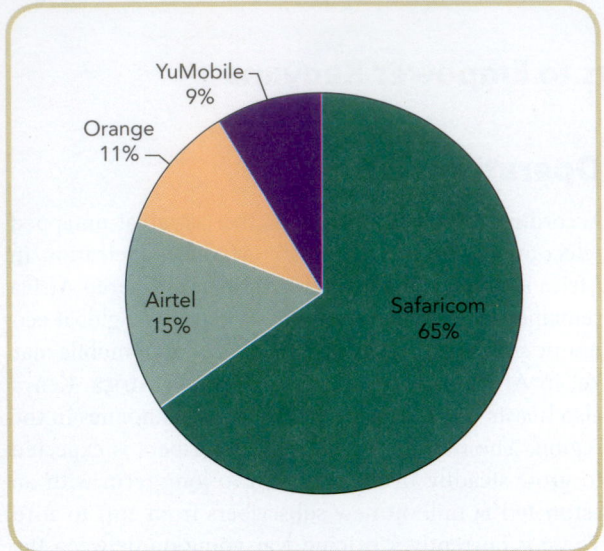

YuMobile 9%
Orange 11%
Airtel 15%
Safaricom 65%

Source: Business Monitor International. 2013. *M&A analysis – Analysis of Essar's Kenya exit plan*. London, England: Business Monitor International.

and services. Tourism and the export of coffee and tea serve as the two chief means for bringing in foreign funds. In addition to coffee and tea, other agricultural products include wheat, corn, sugarcane, fruit, vegetables, dairy products, beef, pork, poultry and eggs. Nominal gross domestic product (GDP) is 3,036 billion Ksh. growing at a rate of 5.7% annually (real) with inflation at 7.5%. The Kenyan government encourages foreign direct investment, and multinational companies make up a significant portion of Kenya's industry. The Nairobi Stock Exchange was established in 1954 and is the fourth largest in sub-Saharan Africa. There are 57 companies listed on the exchange, including Safaricom.[15]

Beginning in 2008, Kenya experienced several events that hurt the economy, including a drought, rising fuel and food prices, and the global economic crisis that slowed growth in the country. Nonetheless, through economic policy changes, the country has curbed inflation and is on the way to cutting interest rates due to better–than-expected economic performance.[16] Despite the challenges in the economy, the country shows vast potential for growth in technology.

Internet use continues to grow in Kenya, partly because of cheap access through mobile phones. Kenya's lack of fixed line internet infrastructure has forced consumers to access the web through mobile devices.[17] The percentage of households with a mobile phone continues to increase.[18] However, continued growth in this industry is somewhat constrained by low household incomes in Kenya.[19]

On the Human Poverty Index, Kenya ranks 64th out of 103 countries, with around 50% of the population living below the poverty line. The unemployment rate for the country is roughly 40%, where 23% of the population lives on less than $1 per day, and 58% of the population lives on less than $2 per day. The average life expectancy at birth is about 57 years. The overall literacy rate is fairly high for Africa at 85.1%; however 90.6% of males can read and write, compared to only 79.7% of females.[20]

While human rights in Kenya have improved, there are still instances of harassment, torture, and extrajudicial murders of citizens by the police. While the government pursues individuals accused of such crimes, often times these people are not convicted. The government has a poor record on issues such as invasion of privacy, freedom of speech, and the right to assemble.[21]

Services

Safaricom has 19.4 million customers, and the company offers prepaid and postpaid mobile, voice, and data services. About 99% of customers are prepaid customers. Safaricom has over 2,900 base stations that provide 2G and 3G cell service to customers, and continues to invest in upgrading and building new base stations through the "Best Network in Kenya" program. 3G coverage is only available in the metropolitan areas of the country. Safaricom's growth in cell phone and wireless internet base stations is shown in Exhibit 2.

In the voice segment, the largest revenue segment for the company, Safaricom offers a wide range of pricing plans, which are often bundled with other services such as data. Services include: *Okoa Jahazi*, an emergency credit based top-up service; *Bonga*, a customer loyalty rewards program; *Skiza*, a call ring-back service; Contacts, a backup service; and premium services including ring tones, wall paper, music, and games.

Within the data segment, Safaricom offers high-speed data for access to email and internet through fixed and mobile broadband. It also offers *Sambaza Internet*, which allows customers to transfer data airtime to another subscriber. Another program, *Night Shift*, gives customers cheaper data bundles at night. This incentivized better network utilization during off-peak hours.

Through the Enterprise Business Unit Safaricom provides businesses with data service and dedicated solutions for data storage, hosting, and security problems. In the messaging segment, Safaricom offers customers a wide variety of bundles for SMS, MMS, and video messaging.

Exhibit 2 Safaricom Base Stations

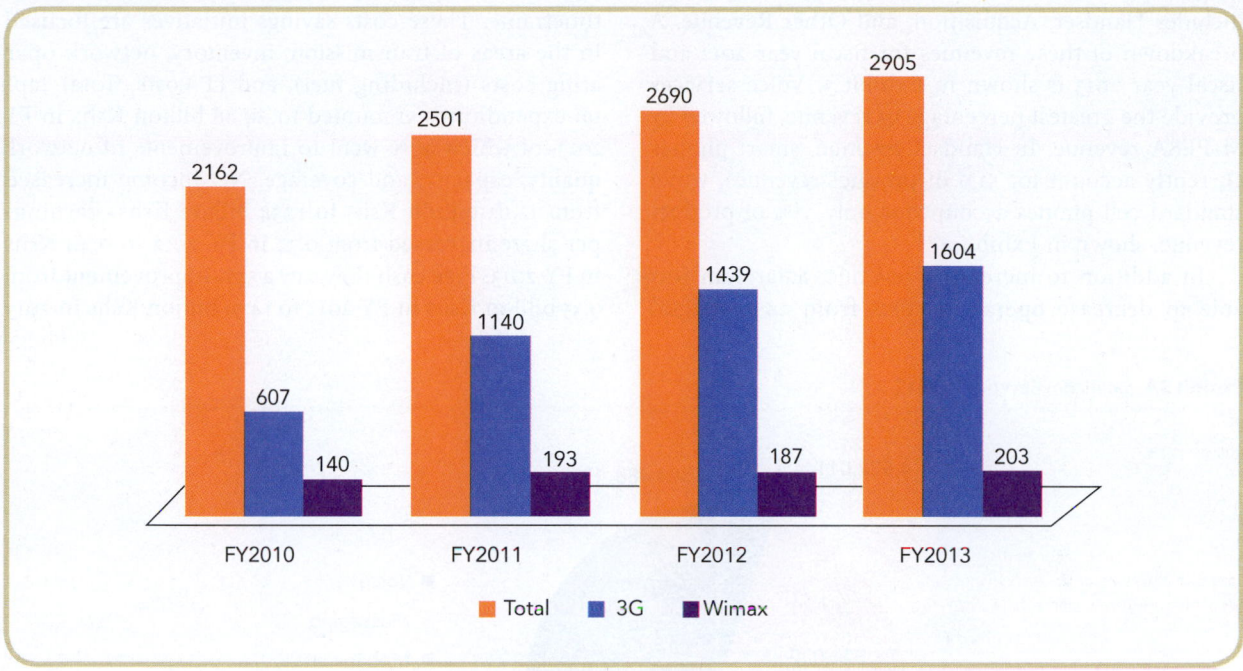

Source: Safaricom Limited. 2013. *Annual report*. Nairobi, Kenya: Safaricom Limited

Safaricom provides a competitive platform called AppStar for application developers to showcase and be recognized for new mobile applications. The company also introduced new services such as m-agriculture, which gives tips to farmers, m-health, which connects Safaricom customers to medical professionals via SMS to give advice on health issues, and e-learning, which allows mobile access to educational resources for Safaricom customers.[22]

M-PESA, Safaricom's money transfer service, has over 17 million customers and is available in over 65,000 agent outlets, which include supermarkets, gas stations, selected banks, and other authorized Safaricom retailers, and over 2,000 payment partners which include registered businesses that accept M-PESA payments.[23] M-PESA is a fast and affordable way to send and receive money via mobile devices. The service provides many Kenyans access to financial services that they would not normally have. In 2013, Safaricom launched M-Shwari through a partnership with the Commercial Bank of Africa. Customers can transfer funds from M-PESA to M-Shwari, allowing them to save money, earn interest, and even borrow small amounts of money through a "microloans" program. Customers can save as little as 1 Ksh ($0.012 USD) and borrow as little as Ksh 100 ($ 1.22 USD). There are no application forms, no ledger limits,

no limits on the frequency of withdrawal, no minimum operating balances, and no charges for moving funds from M-PESA to M-Shwari and vice versa.[24]

Safaricom has partnered with the Commercial Bank of Africa in order to add innovative solutions to the M-PESA service with M-Shwari. The Commercial Bank of Africa is the largest privately-owned bank in Kenya. It is one of 43 licensed commercial banks operating in the country.[25] The Commercial Bank of Africa has operations in both Kenya and Tanzania, where the bank was originally founded. It has only been during the last few years that Safaricom's competition has followed suit by providing mobile banking services in Kenya.[26] Safaricom will also continue to expand its M-PESA service and increase financial inclusion for Kenyans by expanding the distribution network, reducing system downtime, and ensuring geographic redundancy.[27]

Financial Performance

Financially, the firm is performing quite well. Total revenue increased from 107 billion Kshs in fiscal year 2012 to 124.28 billion Kshs in fiscal year 2013. Revenue within the firm is broken into seven categories in two major segments, service revenue and other revenues. Service revenue includes Voice, Messaging, Mobile

Data, Fixed Service, and M-PESA. Other revenue includes Handset, Acquisition, and Other Revenue. A breakdown of these revenues for fiscal year 2012 and fiscal year 2013 is shown in Exhibit 3. Voice services provide the greatest percentage of revenue, followed by M-PESA revenue. In Handset revenue, smart phones currently account for 51% of product revenues, while standard cell phones account for only 32% of product revenue, shown in Exhibit 4.[28]

In addition to increasing revenue, Safaricom was able to decrease operating costs from 24% of total revenue to only 23% of total revenue during that same timeframe. These costs savings initiatives are focused in the areas of transmission, inventory, network operating costs (including fuel), and IT costs. Total capital expenditures amounted to 24.88 billion Kshs in FY 2013, of which 90% went to improvements in network quality, capacity, and coverage. Net income increased from 12.63 billion Kshs to 17.54 billion Kshs. Earnings per share increased from 0.32 in FY 2012 to 0.44 Kshs in FY 2013. Free cash flow saw a 55% improvement from 9.35 billion Kshs in FY 2012 to 14.51 billion Kshs in 2013.

Exhibit 3A Safaricom Revenue in 2013

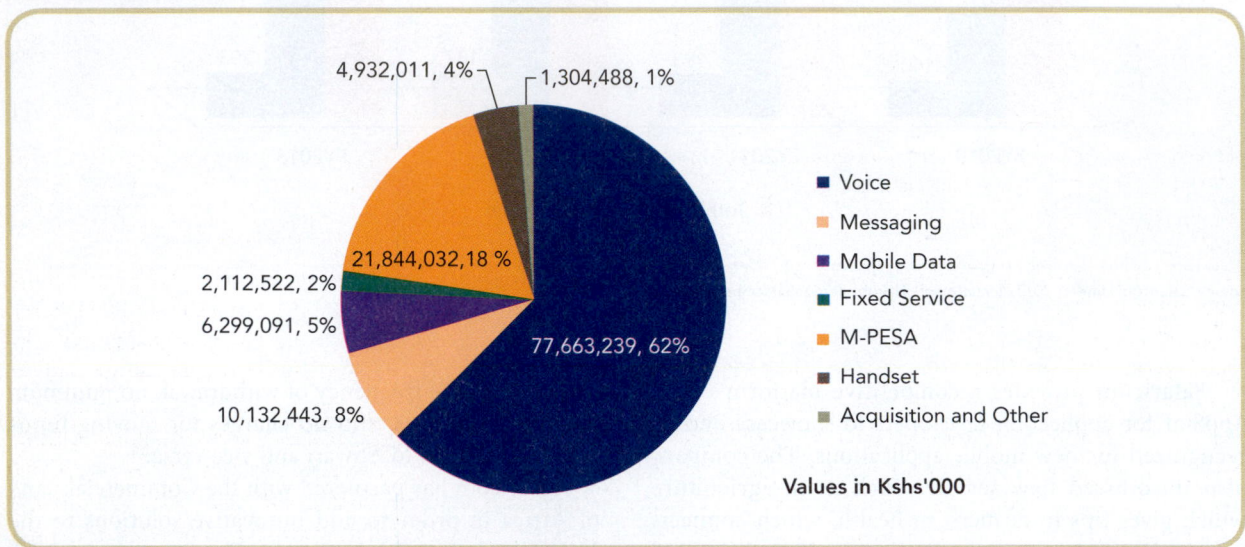

Source: Safaricom Limited. 2013. *Annual report*. Nairobi, Kenya: Safaricom Limited.

Exhibit 3B Safaricom Revenue in 2012

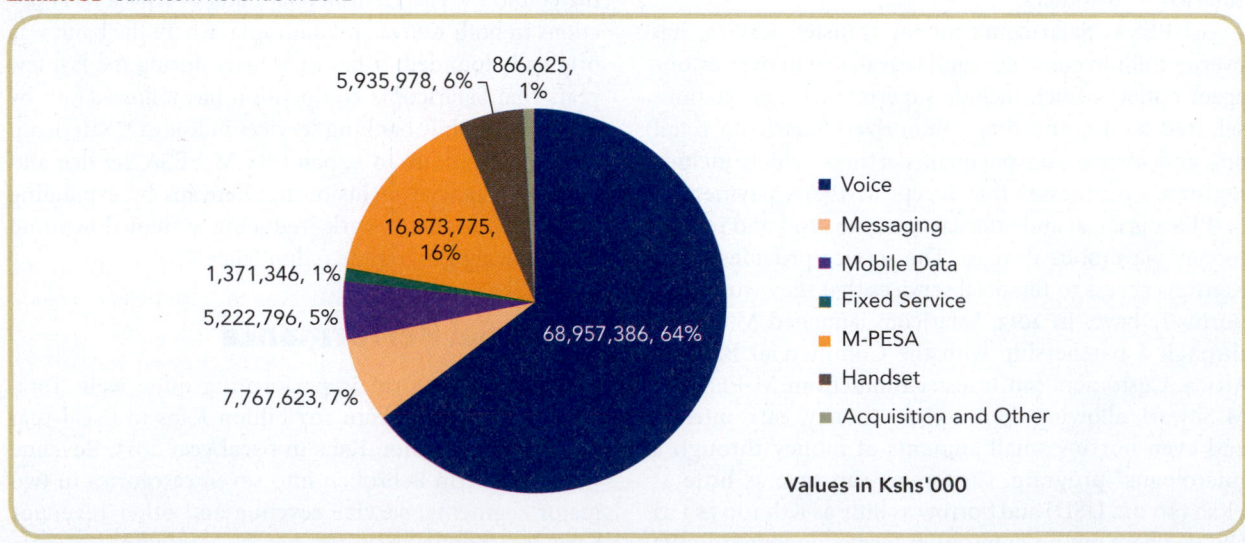

Source: Safaricom Limited. 2013. *Annual report*. Nairobi, Kenya: Safaricom Limited.

Exhibit 4 Product Revenue Contribution

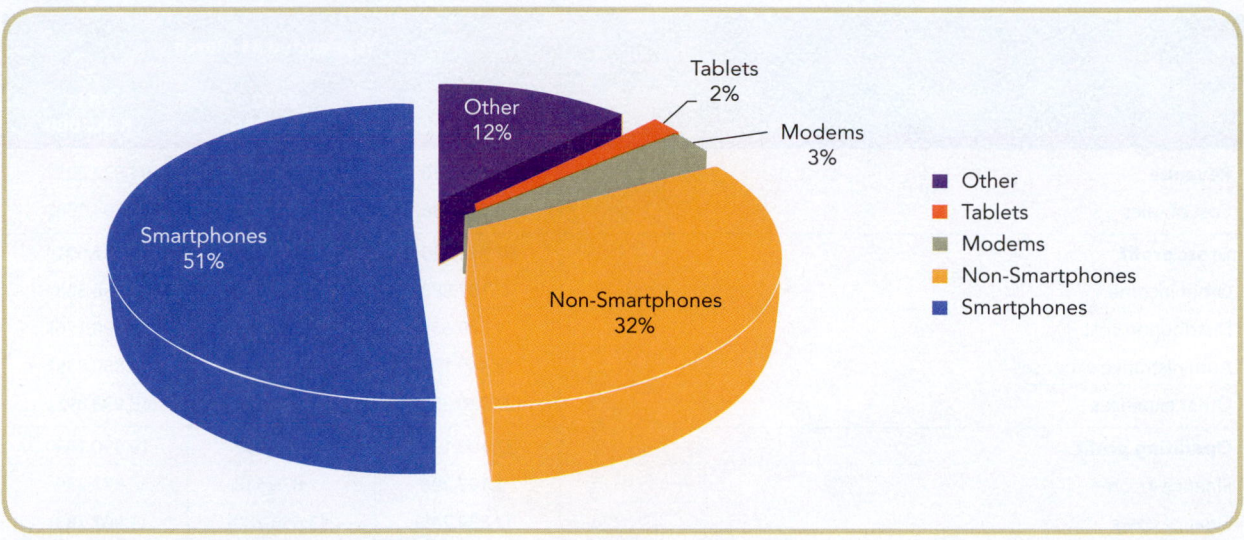

Source: Safaricom Limited. 2013. *Annual report*. Nairobi, Kenya: Safaricom Limited.

Safaricom's dividend policy pays out 85.5% of free cash flow in dividends. Pending shareholder approval, the total dividend for FY 2013 will be 12.4 billion Kshs, the largest dividend in Kenyan corporate history.[29] Financial statements are prepared according to the International Financial Reporting Standards and are shown in Exhibits 5 through 7.

Inside Safaricom

Management

Most of Safaricom's senior management team has vast experience in telecommunications. Leading the team is Robert (Bob) Collymore, who took on the responsibilities of CEO in November of 2010. Bob Collymore replaced Michael Joseph, who had held the position since 2000.[30] The transition was amicable as Michael Joseph was heading to retirement and wanted to wait until "a successor is in place".[31] Collymore is also the Executive Director on Safaricom's board of directors, leading with twenty-five years of commercial work experience in the telecommunications sector. Collymore is supported by CFO John Tombleson, who joined the company in November 2011 and has a strong background in financing growth. Prior to Tombleson's arrival at Safaricom, he held executive positions at Vodafone Qatar, which captured 48% market share within two years of its founding. Biographic information for the senior management team and top members of the board of directors is shown in Exhibits 8 and 9.

Training

Safaricom's experienced management team has worked to share its expertise with the entire organization. The Subject Matter Expert Program has been set up with 50 staff members in various disciplines who teach technology, finance, team building, and soft skills to other members in the organization. The goal is to ensure a high customer experience at all points of contact with the customer by providing employees with world-class programs and exposure to new technologies, professional development, and service offerings. In addition to internal training and professional growth opportunities, Safaricom expanded their Graduate Management Program in the second quarter of 2013. This program takes employees with high potential through a university program that equips them with functional and business skills. This year 25 employees are expected to complete this program.[32]

Human Resources

Safaricom directly employs 3,254 people in the ranks of management and strives to promote from within the organization. Some of its key hiring practices include filling open positions 50% of the time with internal employees and hiring equal numbers of men and women. Safaricom has achieved female representation in 30% of G4 management level positions and above. A breakdown of the company's employment and headcount statistics is shown in Exhibit 10. A survey was recently completed to measure overall employee satisfaction and manager engagement. Both metrics have improved by over 10%

Exhibit 5 Consolidated Statement of Comprehensive Income

	Year ended 31 March		
	2013 Kshs'000	2012 Kshs'000	2011 Kshs'000
Revenue	124,287,856	106,995,529	94,832,227
Cost of sales	(56,544,436)	(54,139,219)	(45,794,536)
Gross profit	67,743,420	52,856,310	49,037,691
Other income	197,888	487,881	36,368
Distribution cost	(4,680,665)	(3,544,561)	(3,896,176)
Administrative expenses	(8,440,194)	(7,652,870)	(6,850,839)
Other expenses	(27,720,255)	(21,995,403)	(18,936,895)
Operating profit	27,100,194	20,151,357	19,390,149
Finance income	1,199,298	873,518	871,249
Finance costs	(2,839,249)	(3,656,280)	(1,907,783)
Share of (loss) / profit of Associate	(9,678)	805	7,748
Profit before income tax	25,450,565	17,369,400	18,361,363
Income tax expense	(7,910,755)	(4,741,793)	(5,202,390)
Profit for the year (of which Kshs 17,320,185,000 (2012: Kshs 12,873,482,000) has been dealt with in the accounts of the Company)	**17,539,810**	**12,627,607**	**13,158,973**
Other comprehensive income for the year, net of tax	–	–	–
Total comprehensive income for the year	**17,539,810**	**12,627,607**	**13,158,973**
Attributable to:			
Owners of the Company	17,539,810	12,737,837	13,311,587
Non-controlling interest	–	(110,230)	(152,614)
	17,539,810	**12,627,607**	**13,158,973**
Earnings per share for profit attributable to the equity holders of the Company			
Basic and diluted (Kshs per share)	0.44	0.32	0.33

Source: Safaricom Limited. 2013. *Annual report*. Nairobi, Kenya: Safaricom Limited.

since the inception of the program, which shows management's commitment to improving the working environment within the organization.[33]

Distribution Channel

Safaricom manages a direct dealership network of 2,600 locations, which directly or indirectly employs over 22,000 people. Furthermore, there are over 250,000 retail outlets in Kenya that offer Safaricom products. To help stimulate the growth of these dealers, Safaricom has rolled out several initiatives to incentivize increased sales. These include training on data and data related products, offering short-term credit to ensure airtime can be sold at peak times (holidays or special events),

introduction of an 8% commission on data used on lines sold by the specific dealer, and financial support on distribution tools such as motorbikes, used for advertising and promotion.

Sales and Advertising

In 2010 Safaricom sacrificed some operating profits by increasing sales and advertising expenses by 16.3% from fiscal year 2009 levels. This was a conscious decision made by the senior management team as they sought to reach and educate their diverse market. In 2011, to expand their marketing efforts, Safaricom focused on understanding the voice of the customer, improving the way the company communicates its messages, and

Exhibit 6 Consolidated Statement of Financial Position

	Year ended 31 March		
	2013 Kshs'000	2012 Kshs'000	2011 Kshs'000
Capital and reserves attributable to the Company's equity holders			
Share capital	2,000,000	2,000,000	2,000,000
Share premium	1,850,000	1,850,000	1,850,000
Retained earnings	64,015,128	59,940,584	56,002,747
Proposed dividend	12,400,000	8,800,000	8,000,000
Attributable to owners of the Company	80,265,128	72,590,584	67,852,747
Non-controling interest	–	(508,886)	(398,656)
Total equity	80,265,128	72,081,698	67,454,091
Non-current liabilities			
Borrowings	12,000,000	12,104,554	12,104,932
Payables and acctued expenses	–	97,525	178,013
Total non-current liabilities	12,000,000	12,202,079	12,282,945
Total equity and non-current liabilities	92,265,128	84,283,777	79,737,036
Non-current assets			
Property, plant, and equipment	95,296,398	91,659,218	83,022,590
Intangible assets – Licences	1,422,011	2,094,951	2,722,706
Intangible assets – Goodwill	219,151	219,151	219,151
Investment in associate	–	9,678	8,873
Indefeasible right of use	4,006,681	4,240,400	3,756,343
Deferred income tax	2,553,665	2,480,063	2,421,142
Prepaid operating lease rentals	2,227	2,021	2,661
	103,500,133	100,705,482	92,153,466
Current assets			
Inventories	2,234,294	2,653,125	5,880,837
Receivables and prepayments	8,124,808	8,190,298	9,440,461
Derivative financial instruments	–	–	111,382
Current income tax	–	1,542,714	1,009,581
Cash and cash equivalents	14,996,922	8,808,058	5,259,035
	25,356,024	21,194,195	21,701,296
Current liabilities			
Payables and accrued expenses	27,825,322	30,463,358	31,101,667
Current income tax	537,749	–	–
Derivative financial instruments	–	147,000	–
Borrowings	8,227,958	7,005,542	3,016,059
	36,591,029	37,615,900	34,117,726
Net current liabilities	(11,235,005)	(16,421,705)	(12,416,430)
	92,265,128	84,283,777	79,737,036

Note: These numbers may vary slightly from company-reported numbers due to differences in accounting conventions
Source: Safaricom Limited. 2013. *Annual report*. Nairobi, Kenya: Safaricom Limited.

Exhibit 7 Consolidated Statement of Cash Flows

	Year ended 31 March		
	2013 Kshs'000	2012 Kshs'000	2011 Kshs'000
Cash flows from operating activities			
Cash generated from operations	46,486,321	40,038,720	38,268,803
Interest received	740,395	427,402	293,516
Interest paid	(2,192,078)	(1,896,201)	(1,363,200)
Income tax paid	(5,903,893)	(5,333,847)	(6,197,250)
Net cash generated from operating activities	39,130,745	33,236,074	31,001,872
Cash flows from investing activities			
Acquisition of IGO Wireless Limited, net of cash acquired	–	–	(494,094)
Acquisition of Instaconnect Limited, net of cash acquired	–	–	(2,095)
Purchase of property, plant and equipment	(24,875,965)	(25,278,428)	(25,482,597)
Acquisition of One Communications Limited	(556,380)	–	–
Additions of property, plant, and equipment - IGO Wireless Limited	–	–	(11,608)
Purchase of intangible assets	–	–	(1,600)
Investment in indefeasible rights of use	–	(419,158)	(913,214)
Proceeds from disposal of property, plant and equipment	71,041	16,048	17,590
Net cash used in investing activities	(25,361,304)	(25,681,538)	(26,847,618)
Cash flows from financing activities			
Proceeds from long-term borrowings	4,227,958	6,392,231	7,496,030
Repayments on long-term borrowings	(3,008,535)	(2,399,755)	(9,112,653)
Dividends paid	(8,800,000)	(8,000,000)	(8,000,000)
Net cash used in financing activities	(7,580,577)	(4,007,524)	(9,616,623)
Net increase in cash and cash equivalents	6,188,864	3,547,012	(5,462,369)
Movement in cash and cash equivalents			
At start of year	8,808,058	5,261,046	10,723,415
Increase	6,188,864	3,547,012	(5,462,369)
At end of year	14,996,922	8,808,058	5,261,046

Source: Safaricom Limited. 2013. *Annual report*. Nairobi, Kenya: Safaricom Limited.

aiming to become more intimately involved within the community. The "Niko na Safaricom" campaign was launched in November 2010 and gained traction in 2011. The campaign's goal is to stimulate customer loyalty and to reduce customer turnover. This campaign fortified the Safaricom brand by communicating a commitment to Kenya and its people, reminding the public they are a successful Kenyan company built and made up of the people of Kenya. Motivation segmentation took center stage as Safaricom strived to understand differing segments of their target market in hopes to align product development, communication, resources, and distribution strategies to meet diverse needs. In 2012, Safaricom was voted the most valuable brand in Kenya. As marketing activities continued to expand, 2013 saw the consolidation of all marketing functions across Safaricom, centralized into a single division led by Rita Okuthe, who was appointed Marketing Director in May 2013. Under her leadership the "Naweza" campaign was launched. This campaign was to further weave the Safaricom brand into the Kenyan culture. Safaricom now sponsors the largest sporting event in Kenya (seven-a-side rugby)

Exhibit 8 Safaricom Senior Management Team

Robert Collymore – Chief Executive Officer and Executive Director

Robert (Bob) Collymore, who took on the responsibilities of CEO in November of 2010. He is also the Executive Director on Safaricom's board of directors leading with 25 years of commercial work experience in the telecommunications sector. Collymore is also a trustee for M-PESA in both Kenya and Tanzania.

John Tombleson – CFO

John Tombleson joined Safaricom as CFO in November 2011 from Vodafone Qatar and has a background in financing growth. Tombleson first joined Vodafone in New Zealand in 2003. After two years of being founded they captured 48% market share. Tombleson also resides on the board of directors as the CFO.

Joseph Ogutu – Director Strategy & Innovation

Starting in October 2012 Joseph Ogutu was appointed as the Director, Strategy & innovation. In his role Ogutu develops Safaricom's position in the industry by formulating strategic direction and driving innovation in their products and services. Mr. Ogutu also has 25 years of experience in telecommunications and severs as the chairman of Safaricom Foundation.

Rita Okuthe – Director, Marketing

Rita Okuthe joined Safaricom in August 2009 as the Head of Consumer Segments and then was appointed as the Director, Marketing in May 2013. Okuthe has a Master's degree in Marketing and is known to drive revenues by having a great understanding of consumer behaviors.

Sylvia Mulinge – General Manager Enterprise Business Unit

With over a decade of marketing experience, half of which was in the telecommunications industry, Sylvia Mulinge joined Safaricom as the General Manager Enterprise Business Unit in February of 2006. Coming from Unilever she and has a honed skill in consumer marketing and brand activation.

Betty Mwangi – General Manager, Financial Services

Betty Mwangi-Thuo was appointed General Manager of Financial Services in March 2011. She has over 13 years of experience in the telecommunications industry and manages the business unit that includes M-PESA. Mwangi was recognized by MCI in June 2010 as one of the top 10 women in mobile globally.

called Safaricom Sevens, and launched Niko Na Safaricom Live to give local music talent the chance to perform on a world class platform.[34]

Strategic Priorities

Safaricom has identified its intent to transform the lives of its customers, shareholders, business partners, staff, and the communities Safaricom serves. The company has defined the following strategic priorities:

1. Deliver the 'Best Network in Kenya'
2. Grow mobile and fixed data
3. Deepen financial inclusion
4. Retain and reward the loyal customer base
5. Encourage further innovation.[35]

Under its "Best Network in Kenya" initiative, Safaricom has worked to increase 2G and 3G coverage, modernize the network in six key cities, roll-out fiber in 40% of sites

in Nairobi, increase speeds, deliver value-based pricing, lower the pricing of 3G smartphones, and improve customer services. Other actions include: upgrading old cell sites, reducing the number of dropped calls, decreasing network downtime, and broadening the reach of their telecom services. Although improvements in network quality are a tremendous opportunity, there is some risk, including the risk of vandalism leading to service disruption, general security, especially in northeastern Kenya, energy availability and reliability, and M-PESA service delays. The instability of the Kenyan national energy grid and lack of energy grid availability in some rural or isolated parts of the country limits growth.[36]

The Safaricom Foundation

The Safaricom Foundation was founded in 2003 and disbursed 416.8 Ksh million to 119 projects in 2012. The foundation is divided into ten areas, including Education,

Exhibit 9 Safaricom Board of Directors

Nicholas Nganga – Chairman

Nicholas Nganga joined Safaricom's board of directors in May 2004 and was elected the chairman January 2007. Mr. Nganga also holds positions at G4S Security (chairman) and the University of Nairobi (Vice-chair of the Council).

Michael Joseph – Non-Executive Director

Michael Joseph was the previous CEO of Safaricom and has extensive international experience in the implementation and operation of large wireless and wire line networks. Mr. Joseph was elected to the board in September 2008, and has been a recipient of the CEO of the Year award.

Robert Collymore – Executive Director

Bob Collymore is the current CEO of Safaricom and has more than 25 years of commercial experience working in the telecommunications sector. Collymore is also a trustee for M-PESA in both Kenya and Tanzania.

John Tombleson - CFO

John Tombleson joined Safaricom as CFO in November 2011 from Vodafone Qatar and has a background in financing growth. Tombleson first joined Vodafone in New Zealand in 2003.

Susan Mudhune – Non-Executive Director

Susan Mudhune is the former chairman of Kenya Commercial Bank and joined the Safaricom board in May 2009. She also holds the position of Director at Kenya Commercial Bank.

Nicholas Jonathan Read – Non-Executive Director

Nick Read joined Vodafone in 2001 and is responsible for operations in Africa, Middle East, and Asia Pacific. Read joined the Safaricom board in January 2010.

Ahmed Essam – Non Executive Director

Ahmed Essam joined Vodafone Egypt in 1999 and now is responsible for the commercial operations in Africa, Middle East and Asia Pacific. Essam joined the board in September 2012.

Sunil Sood – Non Executive Director

Sunil Sood is the COO for Vodafone India and joined the Safaricom board in September 2012. Sood has a diverse background and was originally the CEO of Pepsi in Bangladesh, until building 12 years of telecom experience with Vodafone.

Health Education, Disaster Relief, Water, Economic Empowerment, Sport, Environment, World of Difference, M-PESA Foundation, and Other.[37] Safaricom recognizes "the continued need to invest in maternal and child health; as well as the important role that mobile communications technology plays in transforming lives in areas such as health, education, and economic empowerment."[38] The Safaricom Foundation's "World of Difference" program is a multi-phase initiative that empowers the citizens of Kenya to make a difference in the areas of health, education, economics, access to clean water, disaster relief, environmental conservation, arts, culture, and sports.[39]

Vodafone Group PLC

Vodafone Kenya Ltd., whose parent corporation is Vodafone Group Plc, is the largest shareholder in Safaricom Limited.[40] Vodafone has over 404 million customers, with 68% of these customers located in emerging markets.[41] The company has operations in every continent except Antarctica. In Africa and the Middle East, Vodafone operates in nine countries including: Qatar, Egypt, Kenya, Democratic Republic of the Congo, Ghana, Tanzania, Mozambique, Lesotho, and South Africa.[42] According a study by the World Bank, a 10% increase in mobile penetration can add 1.2% to the annual economic growth in a developing nation. The company's vision is for Vodafone mobile services to further improve people's livelihoods and the quality of life.

Vodafone licenses (although Safaricom operates) the M-PESA service in Kenya.[43] M-PESA is currently also in place in Tanzania, South Africa, Afghanistan, Qatar, and Fiji. Moreover, Vodafone launched M-PESA on a small scale in Rajasthan, India, in preparation for launch across Indias in 2013.[44] Safaricom has roaming agreements in place with several Vodafone subsidiaries

Exhibit 10 Headcount Statistics

Job Level	Total Staff '12[i]	Women '12[i]	Total Staff '13[ii]	Women '13[ii]	% Women '12[i]	% Women '13[ii]
1	1	0	1	0	0.00%	0.00%
2	10	3	11	4	30.00%	36.36%
3	34	14	36	15	41.18%	41.67%
4	126	33	142	41	26.19%	28.87%
5	220	66	259	67	30.00%	25.87%
6	516	181	548	210	35.08%	38.32%
7	545	238	572	249	43.67%	43.53%
8	1247	623	1095	560	49.96%	51.14%
9	2	0	2	0	0.00%	0.00%
Temp	n/a	n/a	588	364	n/a	61.90%
Total	2701	1158	3254	1510	42.87%	46.40%

[i]Source: Safaricom Limited. 2012. *Annual report*. Nairobi, Kenya: Safaricom Limited.
[ii]Source: Safaricom Limited. 2013. *Annual report*. Nairobi, Kenya: Safaricom Limited.

in other countries, which benefits Safaricom customers when they travel. There is an additional agreement in place that gives Safaricom access to Vodafone's global price book and supply chain resources for the purposes of procurement, terminals management, technical expertise, best practices, business knowledge, business assurance, consumer products, and marketing support. This agreement also stipulates a participation fee, fixed at six million Euros annually.[45]

Industry Competition

Safaricom currently has three direct competitors in Kenya – Bharti airtel, Telkom Kenya, and YuMobile.[46] There are also several other potential competitors, defined as firms that operate in Africa but not in Kenya, including Millicom, Etisalat Emirate Telecommunications Company, and MTN Group.

Bharti airtel

Bharti Airtel Limited is a leading global telecommunications firm with operations in Africa and Asia. The company is headquartered in New Delhi, India and has 190 million mobile subscribers in India alone, with an additional 72 million mobile customers internationally.[47] The firm describes itself as a multi-platform service firm operating in telecom, enterprise, and digital television, unified under the "airtel" brand.[48] In terms of subscribers, it ranks in the top four for global mobile service providers. Under IFRS standards, the firm's revenue was Rs. 202,995 million and EBITDA was Rs. 65,449 million.[49] This amounts to revenue of $14.7 billion USD

and EBITDA of $4.3 billion USD. Of this revenue, 49% can be attributed to Indian and South Asian wireless services and 27% comes from African wireless services. Bharti airtel has the greatest market share in India, holding 22% of the wireless subscriber market. Vodafone is in second place with a 17% market share. In 2011, Bharti airtel acquired Zain Africa B.V., gaining entry to the continent. The firm now operates in 20 countries with the objectives of growing the brand, diversifying to reduce its India risk, and replicating its effective operations model. Bharti believes it has achieved a global stature with a focus on emerging markets, significant synergies and a strong platform for future expansion.[50]

Bharti airtel operates under its unique business model known as the "Minutes Factory", which focuses on producing the lowest cost minutes while maintaining/growing margins. This strategy focuses on driving affordability to gain more users and thus more usage, which leads to improved economies of scale and an increase in profitability, thereby also allowing the firm to make the product more affordable.[51]

Telkom Kenya (Orange)

Telkom Kenya was established in 1999 as Kenya's original telecommunications operator.[52] The firm's mission states, "We will connect every Kenyan through integrated communication solutions that simplify and enrich their lives. We are a social and business catalyst, liberating and inspiring people with ideas and services to connect, collaborate, and co-create in new and exciting ways".[53] Their values are: friendly, straightforward, honest, refreshing and dynamic.[54] Telkom Kenya provides integrated communications solutions in Kenya with a wide range of voice and data services as well as network facilities for residential and business customers. The company has 2.8 million subscribers on various wireless platforms throughout Kenya.[55] Furthermore, the firm reinvests profits to promote corporate social responsibility, which includes a commitment to sustainable development achieved through Telkom Kenya's three chief focus areas: health, environment, and digital solidarity, spreading the benefits of mobile technology and the internet to enable more people to communicate, learn, and share knowledge.[56]

In 2008, Telkom Kenya formed a partnership with Orange Group (formerly France Telecom) to launch the Orange brand in Kenya.[57] Telkom Kenya operates prepaid and postpaid mobile services through the Orange Brand, provides Internet through 3G services, and offers fixed landline voice and internet services for homes and business. The company also offers Orange Money, which competes directly with Safaricom's M-PESA.[58] The firm is not publically traded; no financial information is available.

Essar Telekom Kenya (yuMobile)

The Essar Group is a multinational firm based in India, with operations in a variety of industries including steel, oil and gas, power, telecom services, shipping, ports, and other projects. Essar Group employs 75,000 people, operates in 25 countries and has revenues of over $27 billion USD. Essar Telekom Kenya operates in Kenya under the brand "yuMobile", which launched in December 2008. The company was able to achieve countrywide coverage in only ten months, and currently has three million subscribers.[59] In August 2012 Essar Group confirmed its plans to exit the mobile market in Kenya by selling its 72% stake in yuMobile due to a tough operating environment and a negative earnings trend. This move may be linked to Essar's strategic move to hedge risk in the increasingly competitive telecom sector.[60] So far no one has acquired the yuMobile brand from Essar. yuMobile provides value added services such as yuRadio, yuRoaming, yuCredo, an emergency airtime credit service, various bundles available for SMS, MMS, Data, and yuCash, a mobile money transfer service.[61] The firm is not publically traded.

Millicom

Millicom offers digital products and services to emerging markets in Latin America and Africa through its brand "Tigo"[62]. The origins of the firm began in 1979, but it was in 1990 that the organization Millicom International Cellular was formed from the merger of Kinnevik and Millicom Inc. The company ran into financial trouble in 2002 and it had to restructure its balance sheet. The Tigo brand was launched in Latin America in 2004, followed shortly by the brand's launch in Africa.[63] Revenue in 2012 was $4,814 million USD, with net profit of $508 million USD. The firm is fueled by an ethos of "demand more", stating that "the markets we are creating are themselves demanding more of us and we must respond." Additionally, Millicom wants to "transform Tigo from a telecommunications operator to a digital lifestyle brand by becoming an integral part of our customers' everyday lives."[64] Millicom operates in four core areas: mobile, cable, mobile financial services, and commerce and services. Of particular interest is Millicom's mobile financial service, which operates in Latin America and Africa, where the vast majority of the population lacks access to banking services. The firm has 47 million mobile customers across three regions. Operations in Africa account for $974 million USD in revenue, $359 USD in EBITDA, and 18.9 million customers. The company operates in the Democratic Republic of Congo, Tanzania, Chad, Mauritius, Rwanda, Senegal, and Ghana.[65]

Etisalat Emirate Telecommunications Company

Etisalat Emirate Telecommunications Company (Etisalat) is a leading telecommunications operator in the Middle East and Africa, with global headquarters located in the United Arab Emirates. The firm has operations in 15 different countries, including five countries in Africa: Tanzania, Sudan, West Africa, Egypt, and Nigeria. In Tanzania, the firm operates under the brand name Zantel, an abbreviation for Zanzibar Telecom Limited. In Sudan, the firm operates as Canar and commands a 61.5% market share. Atlantique Telecom is a subsidiary of Etisalat in Western Africa, operating under the brand name MOOV, with operations in the Ivory Coast, Benin, Gabon, Togo, and Central Africa. In Egypt, the company operates as Etisalat Misr and covers 98% of the country. Finally, Etisalat Nigeria, launched in 2007, has over two million subscribers already.[66] Nigeria is the continent's biggest mobile market with over 90 million subscribers. The company operates a service called Easy Wallet, which allows customers to transfer money using their mobile devices. Overall, the company has 139 million subscribers, and in 2012 generated 32.9 billion United Arab Emirate Dirham (AED) in revenue and 6.7 billion AED in profit.[67]

MTN Group

MTN Group Ltd. was formed in South Africa in 1994 and maintains its headquarters in Johannesburg. The group now does business in 21 countries in Africa and the Middle East including: Afghanistan, Benin, Botswana,

Cameroon, Congo Brazzaville, Cote D'Ivoire, Cyprus, Ghana, Guinea-Bissau, Guinea Conakry, Iran, Liberia, Nigeria, Rwanda, South Africa, Sudan, Swaziland, Syria, Uganda, Yemen, and Zambia. In 2013, the company had 201 million subscribers. MTN Group has over 34,000 employees who speak five different languages and represent 55 nationalities. Services include 2G and 3G voice networks, including prepaid and postpaid airtime, international roaming, SMS, MMS, and internet access via various platforms, including MTN MobileMoney.[68] In 2011, MTN launched the first 4G (LTE) network pilot in South Africa. In 2012, MTN became the first African brand represented in the BrandZ Top 100.[69] The firm's vision is to be the "leading telecommunications provider in emerging markets".[70] In 2012, the company had revenues of R135.1 billion and net income of R10.498 billion.[71]

Next Moves

With the turnaround in the Kenyan economy, Safaricom is poised to continue to grow in both revenues and profits. How should Safaricom maximize growth, increase profitability, and maintain or expand their market share? Is the firm's recent announcement to start providing television services a good move, or will this diversification outside of its core business hurt Safaricom in the long-run? Should Safaricom differentiate its banking services from those of its competitors? Safaricom originally differentiated its service by providing access to banking functions through its mobile platform; however, the company's top competitors have started services that mimic Safaricom's mobile banking services such as YuCash and Airtel Money.[72] How can it stay ahead of the competition? Should Safaricom look to grow through acquisitions? Is geographic expansion outside of Kenya the best way to grow? If so, to which nations should they expand and how? The internet is a wonderful tool for linking people together. Is investment in 4G LTE technologies a good option for Safaricom? How can Safaricom take maximum advantage of its relationship with Vodafone? These are difficult questions to answer, but questions the board of directors will need to carefully consider if they want Safaricom to continue to prosper in the growing and dynamic telecommunications market in Africa.

NOTES

1. Communications Commission of Kenya. 2012. *Quarterly Sector Statistics Report (Oct-Dec 2012)*. Nairobi, Kenya: Communications Commission of Kenya.

2. Safaricom Foundation, 2013. The Safaricom Foundation's Purpose: Who We Are. http://www.safaricom.co.ke/foundation/index.php?id=27, Accessed October 14, 2013; Safaricom Limited. 2013. *Annual report*. Nairobi, Kenya: Safaricom Limited.

3. Safaricom Limited. 2013. *Annual report*. Nairobi, Kenya: Safaricom Limited.

4. Safaricom Limited, 2013. Our Heritage. http://www.safaricom.co.ke/about-us/about-safaricom/our-history-heritage, Accessed October 20, 2013.

5. Balancing Act – Telecoms, Internet and Broadcast in Africa, 2013. Safaricom IPO Confirmed for Next Week. Issue no. 397. http://www.balancingact-africa.com/news/en/issue-no-397/money/safaricom-ipo-confir/en, Accessed October 20, 2013.

6. Safaricom Limited, 2013. Our Heritage. http://www.safaricom.co.ke/about-us/about-safaricom/our-history-heritage, Accessed October 20, 2013.

7. Financials: Safaricom Ltd (SCOM. NR). *Reuters (Online)*. http://www.reuters.com/finance/stocks/financialHighlights?symbol=SCOM.NR). Accessed October 5, 2013.

8. Shanna. 2008. Safaricom acquires 51% stake in One Communications Ltd. *Africaninvestor*. August 21. http://www.ainewswire.com/?p=277. Accessed November 15, 2013.

9. Obulutsa, G. 2010. Update 1- Safaricom plans to buy two ICT firms. *Reuters*. June 24. http://www.reuters.com/article/2010/06/24/kenya-safaricom-idUSLDE65N08V20100624. Accessed November 15, 2013.

10. Smith, J. 2013. Africa: Industries: Telecommunications. *KPMG Africa Telecoms Group*. http://www.kpmg.com/Africa/en/industry/Telecommunications/Pages/default.aspx, Accessed November 17, 2013.

11. Smith, J. 2013. Africa: Industries: Telecommunications. *KPMG Africa Telecoms Group*. http://www.kpmg.com/Africa/en/industry/Telecommunications/Pages/default.aspx, Accessed November 17, 2013.

12. Millicom, 2012. *Millicom The Digital Lifestyle: 2012 annual report*. Luxembourg, Grand Duchy of Luxembourg: Millicom International Cellular SA.

13. Business Monitor International. 2013. *M&A analysis – Analysis of Essar's Kenya exit plan*. London, England: Business Monitor International.

14. Youngblood Coleman, D. 2013. *Countrywatch Review: Kenya*. Houston, Texas: CountryWatch, Inc.

15. Youngblood Coleman, D. 2013. *Countrywatch Review: Kenya*. Houston, Texas: CountryWatch, Inc.

16. Youngblood Coleman, D. 2013. *Countrywatch Review: Kenya*. Houston, Texas: CountryWatch, Inc.

17. "Kenya's Internet Market Shows Rapid Growth." Mar 2012. Passport Euromonitor International. Retrieved from Euromonitor Passport database.

18. "Technology, Communications and Media: Kenya." Sep 2013. Passport Euromonitor International. Retrieved from Euromonitor Passport database.

19. "Kenya's Internet Market Shows Rapid Growth." Mar 2012. Passport Euromonitor International. Retrieved from Euromonitor Passport database.

20. Youngblood Coleman, D. 2013. *Countrywatch Review: Kenya*. Houston, Texas: CountryWatch, Inc.

21. Youngblood Coleman, D. 2013. *Countrywatch Review: Kenya*. Houston, Texas: CountryWatch, Inc.

22. Safaricom Limited. 2013. *Annual report*. Nairobi, Kenya: Safaricom Limited; United Nations Foundation, 2012. Commitments to Every Woman Every Child: Safaricom. http://www.everywomaneverychild.org/commitments/all-commitments/entry/1/180, Accessed, November 15, 2013.

23. Safaricom Limited, 2013. Pay Bill. http://www.safaricom.co.ke/personal/m-pesa/m-pesa-services-tariffs/corporate-services/pay-bill, Accessed November 17, 2013.

24. Safaricom Limited. 2013. *Annual report*. Nairobi, Kenya: Safaricom Limited.

25. Central Bank of Kenya, 2011. Directory of Commercial Banks and Mortgage Finance Companies. http://www.centralbank.go.ke/images/docs/Bank%20Supervision%20Reports/Commercial%20Banks%20Directrory%20-%2013%20December%202011.pdf, Accessed November 15, 2013.

26. Di Castri, S. and Gidvani, L. 2013. *The Kenyan Journey to Digital Financial Inclusion*. Mobile Money for the Unbanked. http://www.gsma.com/mobilefordevelopment/wp-content/uploads/2013/07/MMU-Infographic-The-Kenyan-journey-to-digital-financial-inclusion.pdf, Accessed November 15, 2013.

27. Safaricom Limited. 2013. *Annual report*. Nairobi, Kenya: Safaricom Limited.

28. Safaricom Limited. 2013. *Annual report*. Nairobi, Kenya: Safaricom Limited.

29. Safaricom Limited. 2013. *Annual report*. Nairobi, Kenya: Safaricom Limited.

30. Senior Management Team. Safaricom Website. http://www.safaricom.co.ke/about-us/about-safaricom/senior-management. Accessed October 16, 2013.

31. Ombok, Eric. July 22, 2010. Kenya's Safaricom Appoints Bob Collymore as CEO, Replacing Michael Joseph. *Bloomberg (Online)*. http://www.bloomberg.com/news/2010-07-22/kenya-s-safaricom-appoints-bob-collymore-as-ceo-replacing-michael-joseph.html. Accessed October 16, 2013.

32. Safaricom Limited. 2013. *Annual report*. Nairobi, Kenya: Safaricom Limited.

33. Safaricom Limited. 2013. *Annual report*. Nairobi, Kenya: Safaricom Limited.

34. Safaricom Limited. 2013. *Annual report*. Nairobi, Kenya: Safaricom Limited.

35. Safaricom Limited. 2013. *Annual report*. Nairobi, Kenya: Safaricom Limited: 14.

36. Safaricom Limited. 2013. *Annual report*. Nairobi, Kenya: Safaricom Limited.

37. Safaricom Limited. 2013. *Annual report*. Nairobi, Kenya: Safaricom Limited.

38. Safaricom Limited. 2013. *Annual report*. Nairobi, Kenya: Safaricom Limited: 46.

39. Safaricom Foundation, 2013. Safaricom Foundation. http://safaricomfoundation.org/home, Accessed November 15, 2013.

40. Safaricom Limited. 2013. *Annual report*. Nairobi, Kenya: Safaricom Limited.

41. Vodafone, 2013. About Vodafone: Sustainability: Our Vision. http://www.vodafone.com/content/index/about/sustainability/our_vision.html, Accessed November 17, 2013.

42. Vodafone, 2013. About Vodafone: Where We Are. http://www.vodafone.com/content/index/about/about-us/where.html, Accessed November 17, 2013.

43. Vodafone, 2013. About Vodafone: Sustainability: Our Vision. http://www.vodafone.com/content/index/about/sustainability/our_vision.html, Accessed November 17, 2013.

44. Vodafone Group Plc. 2012. *Annual report*. London, United Kingdom: Vodafone Group Plc.

45. Safaricom Limited. 2013. *Annual report*. Nairobi, Kenya: Safaricom Limited.

46. Business Monitor International. 2013. *M&A analysis – Analysis of Essar's Kenya exit plan*. London, England: Business Monitor International.

47. Bharti airtel, 2013. Investor Relations: Company Profile: Fact Sheet. http://www.airtel.in/about-bharti/investor-relations/company-profile/fact-sheet/, Accessed November 17, 2013.

48. Bharti Airtel Limited, 2013. *Management Presentation*. New Delhi, India: Bharti Airtel Limited.

49. Bharti airtel, 2013. Investor Relations: Company Profile: Fact Sheet. http://www.airtel.in/about-bharti/investor-relations/company-profile/fact-sheet/, Accessed November 17, 2013.

50. Bharti Airtel Limited, 2013. *Management Presentation*. New Delhi, India: Bharti Airtel Limited.

51. Bharti Airtel Limited, 2013. *Management Presentation*. New Delhi, India: Bharti Airtel Limited

52. Essar Telecom Kenya Limited, 2013. History of Telkom Kenya. http://telkom.co.ke/index.php?option=com_content&view=article&id=60&Itemid=1, Accessed November 17, 2013.

53. Essar Telecom Kenya Limited, 2013. About Us: Mission, Vision and Values. http://telkom.co.ke/index.php?option=com_content&view=article&id=170&Itemid=94, Accessed November 17, 2013.

54. Essar Telecom Kenya Limited, 2013. About Us: Mission, Vision and Values. http://telkom.co.ke/index.php?option=com_content&view=article&id=170&Itemid=94, Accessed November 17, 2013.

55. Essar Telecom Kenya Limited, 2013. History of Telkom Kenya. http://telkom.co.ke/index.php?option=com_content&view=article&id=60&Itemid=1, Accessed November 17, 2013.

56. Essar Telecom Kenya Limited, 2013. Corporate Social Responsibility: Our Philosophy. http://telkom.co.ke/index.php?option=com_content&view=category&layout=blog&id=43&Itemid=109, Accessed November 17, 2013.

57. Essar Telecom Kenya Limited, 2013. History of Telkom Kenya. http://telkom.co.ke/index.php?option=com_content&view=article&id=60&Itemid=1, Accessed November 17, 2013.

58. Essar Telecom Kenya Limited, 2011. Home: Services: Residential Services. http://www.telkom.co.ke/index.php?option=com_content&view=article&id=72&Itemid=97, Accessed November 18, 2013.

59. Essar Telecom Kenya Limited, 2013. Company Profile: About Essar Telecom Kenya Limited. http://yu.co.ke/about-us/company-profile, Accessed November 17, 2013.

60. Business Monitor International. 2013. *M&A analysis – Analysis of Essar's Kenya exit plan*. London, England: Business Monitor International.

61. Essar Telecom Kenya Limited, 2013. Value Added Services. http://yu.co.ke/value-added-services?start=12, Accessed November 18, 2013.

62. Millicom, 2013. About Us. http://www.millicom.com/about-us, Accessed November 17, 2013.

63. Millicom, 2013. About Us: Our History. http://www.millicom.com/about-us/our-history, Accessed November 17, 2013.

64. Millicom, 2012. *Millicom The Digital Lifestyle: 2012 annual report*. Luxembourg, Grand Duchy of Luxembourg: Millicom International Cellular SA: 5.

65. Millicom, 2012. *Millicom The Digital Lifestyle: 2012 annual report*. Luxembourg, Grand Duchy of Luxembourg: Millicom International Cellular SA.

66. Etisalat, 2013. About Us: Company Profile. http://www.etisalat.com/en/about/profile/company-profile.jsp, Accessed November 17, 2013.

67. Etisalat Group, 2012. *Annual report 2012*. Abu Dhabi, United Arab Emirates: Emirates Telecommunications Corporation.

68. MTN Group, 2013. MTN Home: MTN Group: Company Profile. http://www.mtn.com/MTNGROUP/Pages/CompanyProfile.aspx, Accessed November 17, 2013.

69. MTN Group, 2013. MTN Home: MTN Group: Leadership: History. http://www.mtn.com/MTNGROUP/About/Pages/History.aspx, Accessed November 17, 2013.

70. MTN Group, 2013. MTN Home: MTN Group: Company Profile. http://www.mtn.com/MTNGROUP/Pages/CompanyProfile.aspx, Accessed November 17, 2013.

71. MTN Group, 2013. *Welcome to the new world: MTN Group Limited integrated report for the year ended 31 December 2012: Annual report*. Johannesburg, Republic of South Africa: MTN Group Limited.

72. Kopo Kopo Inc, 2010. The Kenyan Mobile Money Ecosystem. http://www.kopokopo.com/the-kenyan-mobile-money-ecosystem/, Accessed November 15, 2013.

CASE 15

Siemens: Management Innovation at the Corporate Level

Markus Menz
Günter Müller-Stewens
Institute of Management, University of St. Gallen

Introduction

At the Annual Shareholders' Meeting in February 1998, Siemens announced disappointing overall results for fiscal 1997. While the firm's sales growth met shareholder expectations, net income remained largely stable. During the following weeks and months, Siemens' top management not only faced increased pressure from its shareholders, but also higher environmental uncertainty and stronger global competition than during the early and mid-1990s. The challenge for the top management team was to optimize the business portfolio in a way that promised to add substantial shareholder value over the next years. Hence, the need was to develop and implement a revised and more coherent corporate strategy.

In response to the developments in 1997 and early 1998 and to facilitate the implementation of the corporate strategy, Siemens launched its first comprehensive corporate program in July 1998. A critical part of the so-called Ten-Point Program was the *top+* program, which exclusively addressed issues of business excellence and management innovation. How did Siemens design and implement the *top+* program and its management innovations? To what extent and how did Siemens benefit from these efforts? These and other related issues will be illustrated in the following.

Company Profile of Siemens

Founded in 1847, Siemens developed into one of the leading global electrical engineering and electronics firms over the past 160 years. At the end of fiscal 2007 (September 30, 2007), Siemens employed nearly 400,000 people at 1,698 locations all over the world. From 1998 to 2007, firm revenues and profits increased almost every year, resulting in revenues of 72.448 billion EUR and net income of 4.038 billion EUR. Headquartered in Munich, Germany, Siemens is publicly listed in Germany at the Frankfurt Stock Exchange and in the US at the New York Stock Exchange (NYSE). By the end of fiscal 2007, Siemens' market capitalization had reached 88.147 billion EUR.[1]

During the period from 1998 to 2007, the business *portfolio* was frequently adjusted (see Exhibits 1 and 2). Examples include the spin-off of the semiconductor business under the name Infineon Technologies by an initial public offering (IPO) in 1999. At the end of 2007, the firm's portfolio consisted of the following operating groups: Automation & Drives (A&D), Industrial Solutions and Services (I&S), Siemens Building Technologies (SBT), Osram, Transportation Systems (TS), Power Generation (PG), Power Transmission and Distribution (PTD), Medical Solutions (Med), and Siemens IT Solutions and Services (SIS). In addition, Siemens Financial Services (SFS) and Siemens Real Estate Services (SRE) were part of the portfolio.

Together with about 180 regional companies in five regions (Germany, Europe other than Germany, Americas, Asia-Pacific, and Africa, Near and Middle and Commonwealth of Independent States), the operating groups were part of a matrix *organizational structure* (see Exhibit 2). Although the operating groups had profit-and-loss responsibility and were largely autonomous regarding their operative business activities, some influence from the central top management and central organizational functions existed. First, the group presidents were frequently also members of the overall firm's managing board. Second, although the central entity primarily exercised financial control over the operating groups, some strategic measures that affected the way the businesses operate also existed. For example, the centrally controlled operational excellence initiatives were mandatory for all operating groups.

This case was prepared by Dr. Markus Menz and Professor Dr. Günter Müller-Stewens, Institute of Management, University of St. Gallen, Switzerland. Its objective is to illustrate a corporate-level management innovation program. It is intended to be used as the basis for class discussion rather than to illustrate either effective or ineffective handling of a management situation. Our information sources included interviews with Siemens management as well as publicly available corporate information (annual reports 1993-2008, presentations, press releases, websites of Siemens AG and its subsidiaries) and press articles. We would like to thank Siemens AG for the support. This case was written with the support of a Philip Law Scholarship by the European Case Clearing House (ECCH).

Exhibit 1 Siemens Corporate Structure 1998

CORPORATE STRUCTURE

Managing Board

Heinrich v. Pierer, Dr. jur. Dr.-Ing. E. h.
President and
Chief Executive Officer
Planning and Development
Special responsibilities:
UK, WPA

Volker Jung, Dr. Eng. h. c.
Special responsibilities: EC, HL, ICN, ICP, PR, SBS
Africa, Middle East, C.I.S.

Edward G. Krubasik, Dr. rer. nat.
Special responsibilities: A&D, ATD, AT, PL,
SBT, VT, ZT

Heinz-Joachim Neubürger
(from 11/5/97)
Finance
Special responsibilities: SFS, SIM

Peter Pribilla, Prof.
Human Resources
Special responsibilities: IK
the Americas

Jürgen Radomski
Special responsibilities: EL, Med, Osram
Europe

Günter Wilhelm, Dr.-Ing. E. h.
Special responsibilities: EV, KWU
Asia, Australia

Adolf Hüttl KWU
Roland Koch ICN
Ulrich Schumacher, Dr.-Ing. HL
Claus Weyrich, Prof. Dr. phil. ZT

until 12/31/97:
Werner Maly, Dr. h. c.

until 2/19/98:
Karl-Hermann Baumann, Dr. rer. oec.
Finance
Special responsibilities: SFS, SIM

until 9/30/98:
Horst Langer, Dr.-Ing.
Special responsibilities: Med, VT, Osram, the Americas

Wolfram O. Martinsen, Dr.-Ing. E. h.
VT

Corporate departments*

Groups*

Energy

Power Generation
(KWU)
Adolf Hüttl
Andreas Kley
Norbert König
Randy H. Zwirn

Power Transmission and Distribution (EV)
Uriel J. Sharef, Dr. rer. pol.
Klaus Voges

Communications
(until 9/30/98)

Public Communication Networks (OEN)
Roland Koch
Hans-Walter Bernsau
Helmuth von Deimling
Anthony Maher

Private Communication Systems (PN)
Rudi Lamprecht
Adrian v. Hammerstein, Dr. phil.
Werner Schmücking

Information (until 9/30/98)

Siemens Nixdorf Informationssysteme AG (SNI)
Gerhard Schulmeyer
Friedrich Fröschl, Dr. rer. nat.
Reinhard Grasse
Rudi Lamprecht
Alfred Nowosad

Industry

Automation and Drives (A&D)
Klaus Wucherer
Günther Fritsch
Hans M. Strehle

Industrial Projects and Technical Services (ATD)
Konrad Pernstich
John Schubert
Udo N. Wagner, Dr. rer. oec.

Production and Logistics Systems (PL)
Manfred v. Raven
Alfred Frank

Siemens Building Technologies AG (SBT)**
Oskar K. Ronner
Paul E. Otth

Transportation

Transportation Systems (VT)
Herbert H. Steffen
Hans-Dieter Bott
Karl-Heinz Sämann, Dr.-Ing.

Automotive Systems (AT)
Franz Wressnigg, Dr.-Ing.
Jürgen Mache

Information and Communications (from 10/1/98)

Information and Communication Networks (ICN)
Roland Koch
Hans-Walter Bernsau
Anthony Maher
Werner Schmücking

Information and Communication Products (ICP)
Rudi Lamprecht
Helmuth von Deimling
Adrian v. Hammerstein, Dr. phil.

Siemens Business Services GmbH & Co OHG (SBS)**
Friedrich Fröschl, Dr. rer. nat.
Alfred Nowosad

Health Care

Medical Engineering (Med)
Erich R. Reinhardt, Prof. Dr.-Ing.
Robert Kugler, Dr. techn.
Götz Steinhardt

Components

Semiconductors (HL)
Ulrich Schumacher, Dr.-Ing.
Peter Fischl

Passive Components and Electron Tubes (PR)
Klaus Ziegler
Bodo Lüttge, Dr. oec. publ.

Electromechanical Components (EC)
Volkhart P. Matthäus
Helmut Brauneis

Lighting

Osram GmbH**
Wolf-Dieter Bopst, Dr. oec. publ.
Heinz-Peter Mohr (until 11/30/98)
Jörg Schaefer, Dr.-Ing.
Thomas Seeberg, Dr. rer. pol.
(from 12/1/98)

Financial Services

Siemens Financial Services (SFS)
Gerhard Kluth, Dr. rer. pol. (until 11/30/98)
Herbert Lohneiß, Dr. rer. nat.
(from 12/1/98)

Finance (ZF)
Heinz-Joachim Neubürger
Charles Herlinger
Gerhard Kluth, Dr. rer. pol. (until 11/30/98)
Herbert Lohneiß, Dr. rer. nat.
(from 12/1/98)
Karl Heinz Midunsky
Albrecht Schäfer, Dr. jur.

Human Resources (ZP)
Peter Pribilla, Prof.
Günther G. Goth

Technology (ZT)
Claus Weyrich, Prof. Dr. phil.
Horst Fischer, Dr. rer. nat.

Planning and Development (ZU)
Heinrich v. Pierer, Dr. jur. Dr.-Ing. E. h.
Reinhart Bubendorfer
Hansjörg Franzius, Dr.-Ing.
Michael Mirow, Prof. Dr. rer. pol.

Corporate Purchasing and Logistics (EL)
Erich Hautz, Dr. rer. comm.

Information and Communication Structures (IK)
Chittur Ramakrishnan

Siemens Real Estate Management (SIM)
Peter Niehaus, Prof.

Corporate Communications (UK)
Eberhard Posner, Dr. rer. oec.

Economics and Corporate Relations (WPA)
Bernd Stecher, Dr. sc. pol.

* The first named is Group president or corporate department head
** Separate legal unit

Regional organization Regional offices, regional companies, representative offices, agencies

as of January 1, 1999

Source: Siemens Annual Report 1998.

Exhibit 2 Siemens Corporate Structure 2007

Managing Board of Siemens AG[1]

Corporate Executive Committee

Peter Löscher
President and Chief Executive Officer
Head of CD
Special responsibility: CC

Joe Kaeser
Head of CF
Special responsibilities: SFS, SRE

Jürgen Radomski
Head of CP
Special responsibilities: Med, OSRAM, MCP

Heinrich Hiesinger
Special responsibilities: SBT, SIS, COO, CSP, GSS, Europe including RO

Rudi Lamprecht
Special responsibilities: SEL[2] SHC[4] Africa, Middle East, C.I.S.

Hermann Requardt
Head of CT
Special responsibilities: SV, Japan

Uriel J. Sharef
Special responsibilities: PG, PTD, Americas

Peter Y. Solmssen
Head of CL

Klaus Wucherer
Special responsibilities: A&D, IBS, TS, Asia, Australia

Eduardo Montes
Special responsibility: SEN[5a]

Erich R. Reinhardt
Head of Med

Corporate Departments

Corporate Development (CD)
Peter Löscher
Herbert Figge
Thomas Frischmuth
Horst-J. Kayser

Corporate Finance (CF)
Joe Kaeser
Karl-Heinz Seibert
Ralf P. Thomas
Hans Winters

Corporate Legal and Compliance (CL)
Peter Y. Solmssen
Paul Hobeck
Andreas Pohlmann

Corporate Personnel (CP)
Jürgen Radomski
Walter Huber

Corporate Technology (CT)
Hermann Requardt
Reinhold Achatz
Winfried Büttner

Corporate Centers

Corporate Communications and Government Affairs (CC)
Stephan Heimbach

Corporate Information Office (CIO)
Norbert Kleinjohann

Corporate Supply Chain and Procurement (CSP)
Bernd Regendantz

Global Shared Services (GSS)
Denice Konau

Management Consulting Personnel (MCP)
Hans-Jürgen Schloß

Operations

Industry

Automation and Drives (A&D)
Helmut Gierse
Hannes Apitzsch
Peter Drexel
Anton S. Huber

Industrial Solutions and Services (I&S)
Joergen Ole Haslestad
Bernd Euler
Hans-Jörg Grundmann
Joachim Möller

Transportation Systems (TS)
Hans M. Schabert
Alfred Frank
Jörn F. Sens
Friedrich Smaxwil

Siemens Building Technologies (SBT)[3]
Johannes Milde
Rolf Renz

OSRAM GmbH
Martin Goetzeler
Kurt Gerl
Johannes Närger
Claus Regitz

Energy

Power Generation (PG)
Klaus Voges
Ralf Guntermann
Michael Süß
Randy H. Zwirn

Power Transmission and Distribution (PTD)
Udo Niehage
Pamela Knapp
Christian Urbanke

Healthcare

Medical Solutions (Me-S)
Erich R. Reinhardt
Thomas Miller
Siegfried Russwurm
Klaus Stegemann

Financing and Real Estate

Siemens Financial Services GmbH (SFS)
Dominik Asam
Peter Moritz
Johannes Schmidt

Siemens IT Solutions and Services (SIS)
Christoph Kollatz
Jürgen Frischmuth
Michael Schulz-Drost
Rolf Unterberger

Siemens VDO Automotive (SV)[6]
Wolfgang Dehen
Klaus Egger
Helmut Matschi
Reinhard Pinzer

Siemens Real Estate (SRE)
Zsolt Sluitner

Regional organization
Regional Organization Germany (RD), Regional Companies, Representative Offices, Agencies[1]

Source: Siemens Annual Report 2007.

The influence on some of the strategic decisions of the firm's businesses was indeed part of Siemens' *corporate strategy*, aiming at superior value creation for the overall firm. During the period from 1998 to 2007, the firm's corporate strategy developed towards a concept of simultaneous vertical and horizontal optimization. First, vertical optimization included active portfolio management and operational excellence in the areas of innovation, customer focus, and global competitiveness. Vertical optimization was designed to lead to synergy by leveraging corporate capabilities and tools to individual operating groups. Second, horizontal optimization concerned the exploitation of synergies across the operating groups facilitated by initiatives such as Siemens One. As illustrated in this case study, the firm's corporate strategy was executed with the help of several corporate programs.

The firm's *corporate center* was supposed to contribute to the overall corporate development, including the corporate programs, and to support the operating groups. It consisted of so-called corporate departments, including corporate development, corporate finance, corporate legal and compliance, corporate personnel, and corporate technology. Further, the corporate center comprised five sub-centers: corporate communications and government affairs, corporate information office, corporate supply chain and procurement, global shared services, and management consulting personnel. During the period from 1998 to 2007, the corporate center of Siemens was itself subject to extensive restructuring activities. For example, in 2001 the firm planned to cut corporate center costs by 15 percent in each of the following two years.[2] In addition to the corporate center functions, Siemens founded the in-house consultancy Siemens Management Consulting (SMC) in 1996. This internal top management consultancy not only contributed to the implementation of a variety of different corporate projects but also served as talent pool for future management positions at Siemens.

Management Innovation Activity at Siemens

According to Johannes Feldmayer, a former managing board member of Siemens, management innovation means changing the management system of the firm, which involves the principles and rules of structuring and managing the organization. Concerning a change in the "how" rather than in the "what" of management, it has a systemic and sustainable character and is supposed to lead to significant improvements of the firm's competitive position.[3] While Siemens frequently had

introduced single management innovations during the past decades, the electrical engineering giant started a more structured and systematic approach to management innovation and business excellence during the early 1990s. In 1993, then CEO von Pierer and his top management team initiated the *top* (time-optimized processes) program. Because of its importance for the overall firm, Siemens management decided to continue the program under the slightly revised name *top*[+] from 1998 onwards. As we will illustrate in the following for the ten-year period from 1998 to 2007, what started as a productivity improvement initiative developed into a comprehensive management innovation program. Overall, its objective was to improve firm performance by a guided approach to business excellence. Broadly speaking, the main issues of the initiative were innovation, customer focus, and global competitiveness.

Context and Evolution of the *top*[+] Program

Initiated by von Pierer in 1993, the *top/top*[+] program was directly supervised by a member of the managing board (see Exhibit 3 for an overview on the program's names, responsible managing boards members, and corporate programs from 1993 until 2007). The Siemens operational excellence program *top*[+] was characterized by a high degree of continuity concerning its supervision by the firm's top management team. Until September 2000, Günter Wilhelm, Siemens' head of the Automation and Drives (A&D) and Industrial Solutions and Services (I&S) Groups as well as of the overall Asian and Australian business activities, was responsible for launching and establishing the program. In the following years, Klaus Wucherer was in charge of the firm's business excellence initiatives. Finally, Erich Reinhardt, then CEO of the Siemens Healthcare Sector, succeeded Wucherer, who resigned from the Siemens managing board by the end of 2007.

Since the program was primarily aiming at a similarly high level of operational excellence across the business portfolio, the program was structured on the firm and group levels. In 2007, *top*[+] was coordinated in the Siemens corporate center by a team of seven people (excluding the customer focus program Siemens One). The team head was responsible for the firm-wide *top*[+] efforts and reported directly to the Siemens managing board member overseeing the program. The role of this team was coordinating the *top*[+] initiatives of the different groups, further development of the overall program and single initiatives, and monitoring the progress of its implementation in the firm's groups.[4] For example, each of the three pillars of *top*[+], innovation, customer focus,

Exhibit 3 Context and Development of Siemens *top*⁺

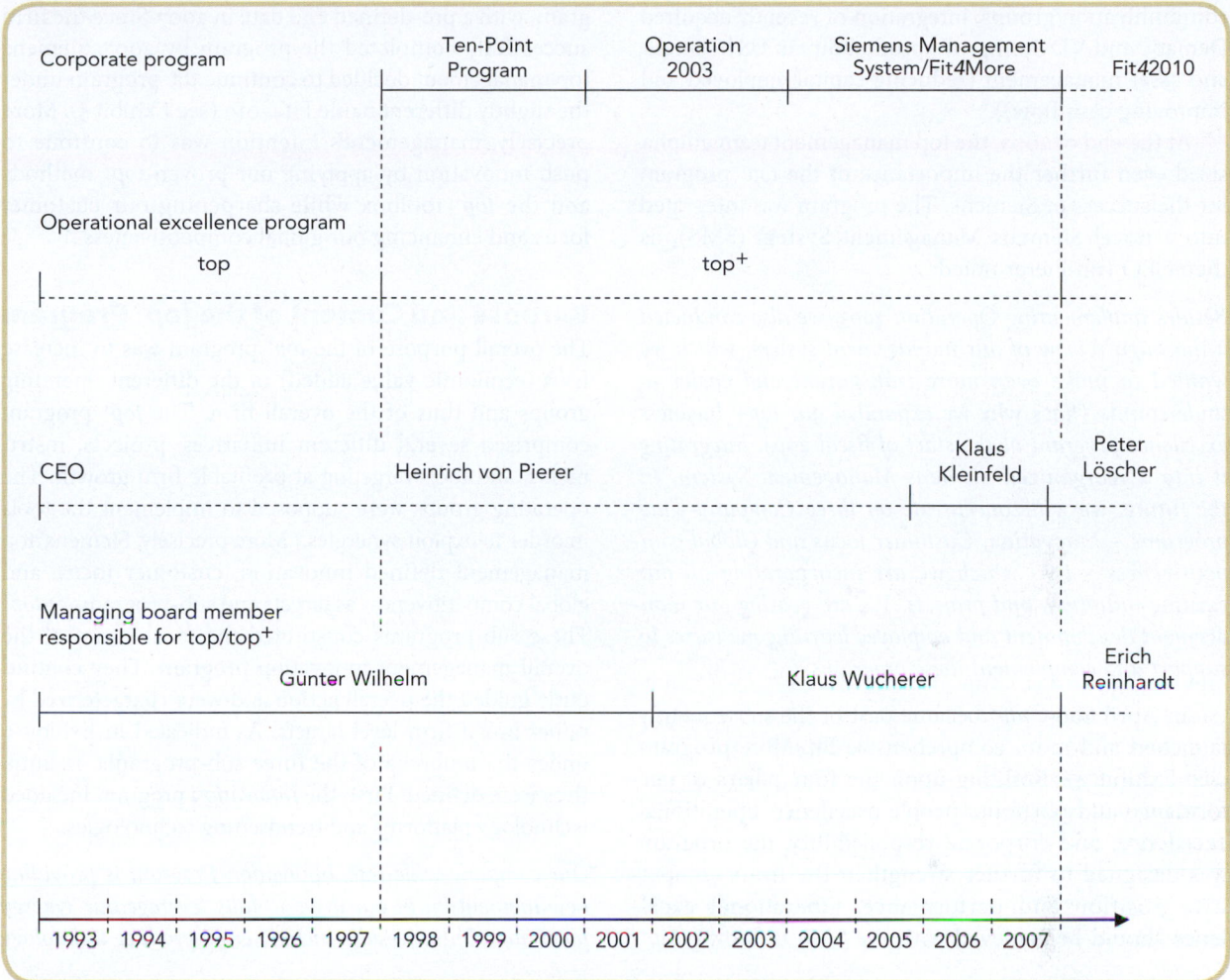

Source: Siemens Annual Reports, www.siemens.com.

and global competitiveness, was coordinated by one person. In addition to this central unit, several other organizational units were involved in the implementation of *top*⁺. First, the central *top*⁺ team was supported by the Siemens in-house consultancy, SMC, which employed about 160 consultants at the end of 2007. Involved in *top*⁺ issues from the beginning of the program, typically teams of two to six SMC consultants were assigned to single implementation efforts. Second, in each of the firm's divisions and regional companies, one manager was responsible for *top*⁺. Third, for Siemens One as part of the *top*⁺ customer focus program, a dedicated corporate-level unit within the central corporate development department was created.

In the beginning, the *top* program was largely independent from other corporate-level programs. Over the course of its development, however, it became an integral part of the firm's management system and more and more intertwined with other firm programs or initiatives. From July 1998 until the IPO of Siemens at the NYSE in March 2001, *top*⁺ was part of the *Ten-Point Program* aiming at sustainable performance improvements. Besides fostering the firm's business excellence efforts, the Ten-Point Program included activities such as the restructuring of the semiconductor business, reorganizing the business segments, and optimizing the business portfolio.[5]

Because of its prior success and the permanent need for methods of business excellence, Siemens top management decided to continue the *top*⁺ initiative following the IPO. Therefore, in December 2000, the firm's top management team defined margin targets for each group that were to be reached by fiscal 2003. Called *Operation 2003*, the new program was supposed to direct firm-wide attention to five important actions for enhancing firm performance (increase profitability in information and communication groups; integration of recently acquired Dematic and VDO; improve profitability in US business; and asset management (reducing capital employed and improving cash flow)).[6]

At the end of 2003, the top management team emphasized even further the importance of the *top*[+] program for the success of Siemens. The program was integrated into a novel Siemens Management System (SMS), as then CEO von Pierer noted:

"Besides implementing Operation 2003, we also conducted a thorough review of our management system, which we wanted to make even more transparent and easier to understand. That's why we expanded our top+ business excellence program at the start of fiscal 2004, integrating it into a reorganized Siemens Management System. In the future, we will concentrate on three Company-wide programs – Innovation, Customer focus and Global competitiveness – into which we are incorporating all our existing initiatives and projects. We are gearing our management development and employee learning measures to support and complement these programs."[7]

In April 2005, *top*[+] became part of the subsequently launched and more comprehensive Fit4More program (see Exhibit 4). Building upon the four pillars of performance and portfolio, people excellence, operational excellence, and corporate responsibility, the program was designed to further strengthen the firm's competitive position and performance. Operational excellence should be achieved with the SMS including *top*[+].

The Fit4More program was planned as a mid-term program, with a pre-defined end date in 2007. Since the firm successfully completed the program by 2007, Siemens' top management decided to continue the program under the slightly different name Fit42010 (see Exhibit 5). More precisely, management's intention was to continue to "push innovation by applying our proven *top*[+] methods and the *top*[+] toolbox while sharpening our customer focus and enhancing our global competitiveness".[8]

Purpose and Content of the *top*[+] Program

The overall purpose of the *top*[+] program was to increase EVA (economic value added) of the different operating groups and thus of the overall firm. The *top*[+] program comprised several different initiatives, projects, instruments, and tools targeting at profitable firm growth. The operating groups were supposed to implement the tools in order to exploit synergies.[9] More precisely, Siemens' top management defined innovation, customer focus, and global competitiveness as targets and sub-programs of *top*[+]. These sub-programs constituted the focal issues of the overall management innovation program. They continuously guided the overall action and were characterized by rather broad firm-level targets. As indicated in Exhibit 6, under the umbrella of the three sub-programs, 11 initiatives were defined. First, the *innovation* program included technology platforms and trendsetting technologies:

"Our company-wide top[+] *Innovation Program is providing new momentum in our drive to fully leverage our synergy potentials. Initial results include cross-product technology*

Exhibit 4 Elements of Fit4More

Fit 4 More: Profit & Growth - Program			
Performance and Portfolio	**Operational Excellence**	**People Excellence**	**Corporate Responsibility**
■ Solve Mobile Devices ■ Finalize strategic reorientation of I&C i.e.,Com and SBS ■ Reach target margins at all Groups ■ Build portfolio for 2x GDP growth	■ Execute Siemens Management System (powered by *top*[+]) with focus on – Innovation – Customer Focus – Global Competitiveness	■ Achieve high performance culture ■ Establish Leadership Excellence Program ■ Increase global talent pool ■ Strengthen expert careers	■ Best in Class – Corporate Governance – Business Practices ■ Continue focus on – Sustainability – Corporate Citizenship

Source: Presentation of Klaus Kleinfeld at EPG Conference, May 2005.

Exhibit 5 Elements of Fit42010

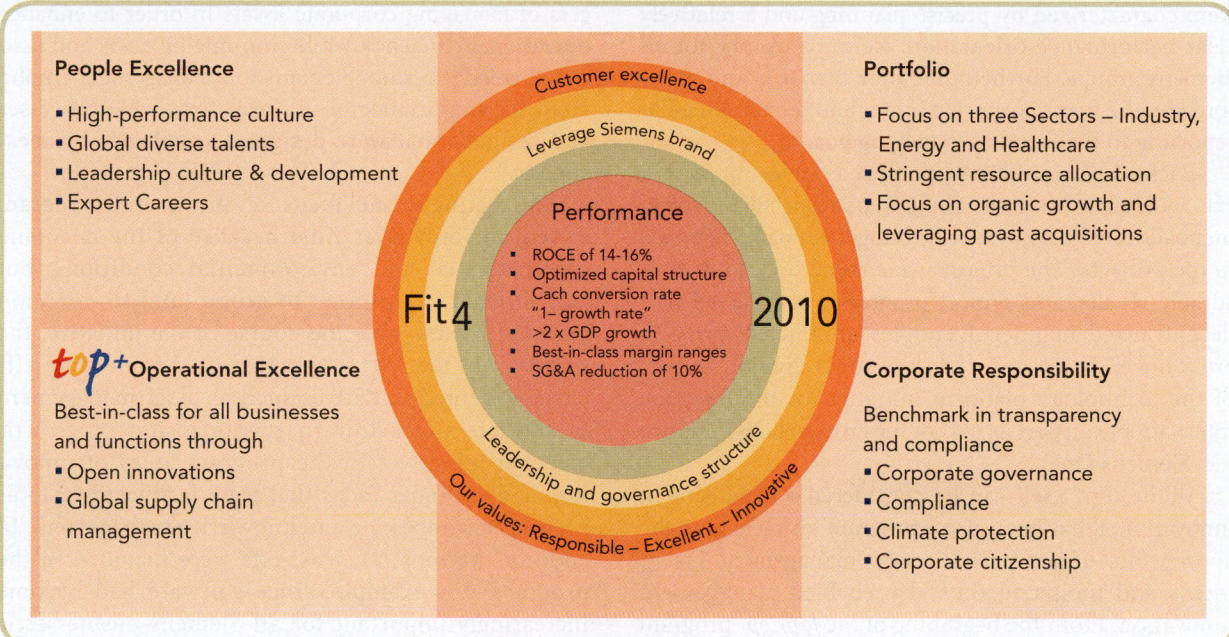

Source: Siemens Annual Report 2008.

Exhibit 6 Sub-Programs and Initiatives of Siemens *top⁺*

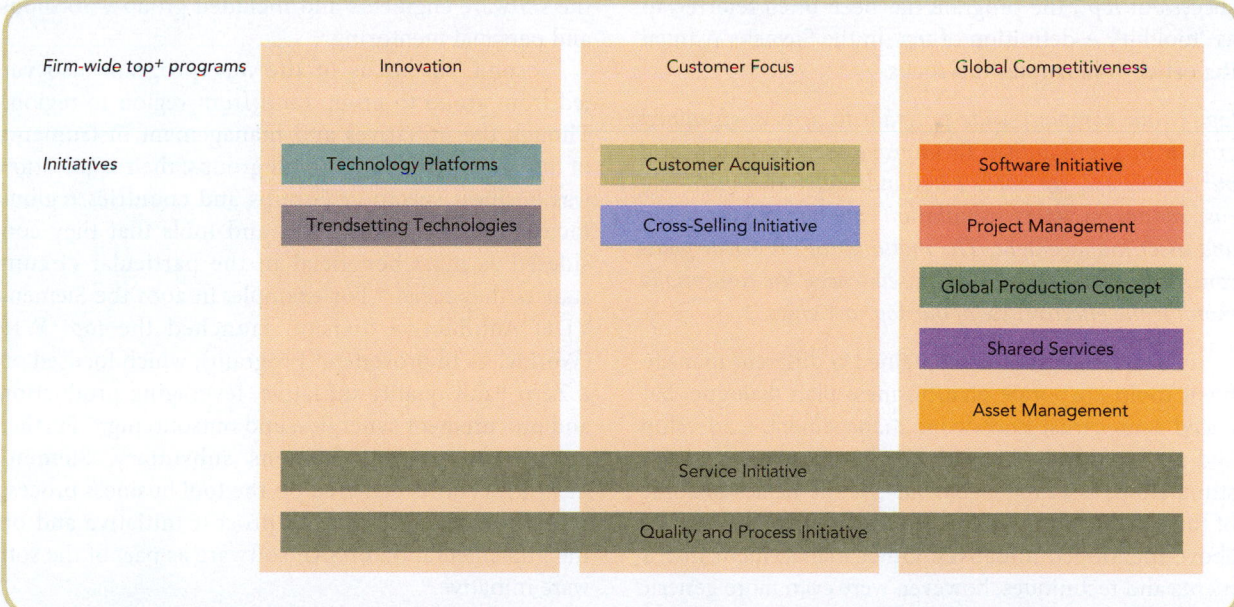

Source: Feldmayer 2006.

platforms for remote services; a uniform controls architecture for applications ranging from power plants and railway systems to industrial controls and communications networks; and systematic best practice sharing of the kind that has long characterized our software initiative. By moving toward technological leadership in all our businesses, we are also strengthening our customer focus and global competitiveness."[10]

Second, *customer focus* was comprised of the customer acquisition and the cross-selling initiative. Third, *global competitiveness* encompassed the software initiative, project management, a global production concept, shared services, and asset management. In addition to the initiatives relating exclusively to one of the sub-programs, the service and the quality initiative concerned all sub-programs. The 11 initiatives, which were characterized by precise planning and a relatively clear performance orientation, were mandatory for all Siemens groups. Further, they were managed and monitored by the firm's corporate center and required regular reporting to the Siemens managing board.[11]

Each of the initiatives comprised one or more projects with a precise task. The group's respective management allocated resources (e.g., budget, human resources) to the projects. The projects were meant to lead to measurable results, and project progress was reported in a decentralized manner. Examples of concrete projects are a novel drive concept in the A&D division as part of the technology platform initiative, or the Bangkok international airport as part of the cross-selling initiative (i.e. Siemens One).[12]

While top+ itself can be considered a management innovation, it has been also a program for managing the appropriate use of partially new management instruments and tools and thus also enabled management innovation. From the beginning of the top/top+ program onward, management tools have been an integral part to achieve business excellence. Because management frequently emphasized the importance of tools for the success of top+, the program has been often referred to as "tool kit". A definition of top+ in the Siemens Annual Report 2001 illustrates this focus:

"top+ is our company-wide program to achieve sustained growth in profitability. To improve the performance of our businesses, we apply tried and tested methods – e.g. cost reduction, sales stimulation, quality enhancement and asset management. The motto of top+ is: Clear goals, concrete measures, rigorous consequences. We continually monitor the effectiveness of our top+ activities."[13]

In 2002, the program contained 11 different management tools: corporate plan/business plan dialogue; balanced scorecards; knowledge management; leadership and co-operation; innovation; cost effectiveness; sales stimulation; asset management.[14] As the names of some of the tools indicate, they were partly identical with the above-mentioned initiatives. Other management instruments and techniques, however, were even more generic and similarly applicable for several initiatives. An example of the latter was the introduction of knowledge management with corresponding tools such as databases, etc. It was used in most of the initiatives, for example, in the project management and the service initiative. On the other hand, the asset management initiative consisted almost exclusively of a new and standardized approach to asset management and thus of a single management

innovation. This initiative was concerned with "the process of managing corporate assets in order to enhance operational efficiency while minimizing costs and associated risks".[15] In sum, Siemens top management emphasized the importance of uniform firm-wide processes and methods that were designed to enhance business success.[16]

Interestingly, the focus of the overall program varied not only over time because of the changing organizational and environmental conditions, but also differed from group to group (and from region to region). First, over the course of the initiative, the priorities of the top+ program shifted from more efficiency-oriented initiatives such as asset management in the late 1990s toward the inclusion of growth-oriented initiatives in the program areas of innovation and customer focus that were facilitated by tools such as benchmarking and knowledge management. In addition, various other aspects were included in the program. For example, since software had become increasingly important for all Siemens businesses, a systematic qualification improvement program for the firm's software engineers was launched as a new element of top+. This program enhanced the abilities of the software engineers and included group workshops and personal mentoring.[17]

Second, the focus of the top+ program also varied from group to group (and from region to region). Though the initiatives and management instruments of top+ were mandatory for all groups, their application was business specific.[18] Groups and countries/regions focused on those initiatives and tools that they considered as most beneficial in the particular circumstances they faced.[19] For example, in 2001 the Siemens VDO Automotive division launched the top+ WIP (Worldclass Improvement Program), which focused on a Zero Fault quality initiative, leveraging production and procurement synergies, and outsourcing.[20] Further, as a wholly-owned Siemens subsidiary, Siemens Australia's efforts centered on the tool business process reengineering (BPR) in the process initiative and on the implementation of SAP software as part of the software initiative.[21]

Besides considering aspects of the organizational and environmental context, decisions on which instruments or tools to include in the top+ program depended on extensive internal and external benchmarking. An important requirement was that the tools that became part of top+ be "generic" enough to be applicable across a diverse business portfolio but also be proven with concrete examples within Siemens. Therefore, the process of including certain tools started in most cases with a pilot project in one of the groups, often a consulting project of SMC. Contingent upon the successful adoption or development of a tool in the pilot project, they became part of the *top*[+] program and were implemented throughout the firm. Hence, a positive track record of a tool in at least one Siemens group was required:

"All the tools we use have already demonstrated their effectiveness for our business. Firmly anchored in all of our activities around the world, this proven approach is driving successful top[+] programs at every level of the Company."[22]

Further, external benchmarking with direct competitors as well as with best-in-class competitors in certain areas was very important. Hereby, the operating businesses compared their value chains regarding different dimensions (processes, people, organization) and identified a cost-cap. The measures to close a potential gap compared to competitors included learnings derived from the benchmarking and the respective adaptation to Siemens. *Top*[+] made benchmarking a mandatory step for all operating businesses. Because of the substantial differences between the operating businesses, the benchmarking cycle was based on the product lifecycle of the respective operating business.

In addition, two other mechanisms led to the inclusion of new management tools. First, sometimes new management tools were developed "from scratch" by SMC, facilitated by SMC's extensive consulting experience. Second, business groups and regions also developed their own business- or country-specific tools without the involvement of the corporate center. If the tools substantially improved the business group or regional company in a particular area, the corporate center analyzed whether they could also be implemented in other business groups and regional companies. An example is "low cost benchmarking", which was developed by Siemens China and subsequently implemented in other firm businesses. Similarly, solutions for problems in single business groups led to changes for the overall firm, as von Pierer described in 2004:

"In response to the problems at our Transportation Systems Group, quality management has been reorganized throughout the entire Company. In every Group and every Region, we have established quality managers who are authorized to intervene and halt projects and processes if quality problems arise. In such cases, improvements that would entail high costs after project completion can be defined and implemented at an early stage."[23]

Implementation of the *top*[+] Program

From its launch in 1993 until 2007, Siemens top management considered *top/top*[+] as a firm-wide program that was obligatory for all groups and regions of Siemens. Many groups and regions, however, initially only implemented parts of the overall program. While management tools were meant to guide the implementation of the *top*[+] program's goals, groups and regions were ultimately responsible for assessing their specific situations and for choosing the appropriate measures. This led to varying implementation rates in different groups and regions.[24]

In the beginning, the implementation of *top* appeared difficult, mainly because of the autonomy and power of the different group presidents and their management teams. Although the implementation was mandatory for all groups, only some groups applied all instruments and tools provided. The main reason for the partial implementation of *top* was the still prevalent Siemens culture in the early and mid-1990s, which was characterized by a lack of firm-wide transparency and a lack of consequences for the management of low-performing groups. In the following years, however, von Pierer was able to change the culture by obliging every single group president to implement the program. This was also facilitated by introducing more transparent and standardized performance measures and clear consequences for managers who did not fulfill the agreed performance targets. Despite these changes, even during the subsequent years, the implementation varied across groups and regions. In 2002, then CFO Heinz-Joachim Neubürger noted:

"The instruments of top/top[+] itself are good. Yet, we recognize again and again that they are not applied with the necessary consequence and persistence."[25]

Indeed, the *top/top*[+] program was criticized for being too broad instead of focusing on different or even conflicting targets such as innovation or productivity. This breadth hampered commitment to the program by the firm's groups, particularly in the first years following the launch of *top*.[26] To foster the implementation of the *top*[+] program throughout the firm, two measures were taken. First, management required all groups to undertake extensive external benchmarking every two to three years. If a business failed to achieve its targets, the management team had to propose how it would close the performance gap. Since the standardized tools of the *top*[+] program already existed, the businesses frequently opted to apply them in order to enhance performance. Hence, although most of the tools of the *top*[+] program were not mandatory, business groups were indirectly required to apply them. Second, Siemens initiated the *top*[+] award in 1999.

It became the firm's most important award and was given to the best performing teams, divisions, units and subsidiaries. Award criteria included an increase in EVA and the successful implementation of the *top*[+] philosophy within a certain period of time.[27] An SMC project manager described the implementation of the overall program as a "mixture of push and pull efforts".[28]

Numerous examples of the (successful) implementation of single aspects of *top*[+] in groups or regions exist. Since 2000, Siemens used *top*[+] as a framework for achieving performance improvements in their US business. The measures not only targeted the businesses independently, but also included initiatives for synergy realization across businesses. The latter included aspects such as "one face to key customer groups" and "shared services for corporate functions".[29] As early as in 2002, the results of implementing elements of the *top*[+] initiative appeared promising. Interestingly, at that time, Klaus Kleinfeld, one of the initiators of *top*[+] and SMC and later Siemens President and CEO, served as CEO of the US business. Siemens' CEO von Pierer noted:

"Launched two years ago, our top[+] U.S. Business Initiative has begun to show results. Earnings at our American companies have increased significantly."[30]

A further example is the strategic reorganization of the group Information and Communication Networks (ICN) in 2001. Following the changing strategic focus, tools of the *top*[+] program were applied. The group defined concrete measures that were monitored monthly and, if necessary, adjusted. This included "reducing the number of production sites by half, optimizing sales channels and accelerating development activities in promising innovation fields".[31] A variety of other businesses implemented elements of *top*[+] in 2001 (e.g., A&D and Siemens Real Estate). For example, A&D in the Automation and Control (A&C) group applied tools such as asset management, quality, and cost reduction.[32]

An example of a particular implementation aspect of *top*[+] and of the challenges firms such as Siemens face when dealing with a diverse business portfolio is the "business excellence leadership training" in the Power Generation division. In 2000, the division's management team decided to implement the *top*[+] quality initiative, mainly aiming at improvements of the process quality. The power generation business is characterized by large customized orders for single customers. Compared to businesses with large-scale production facilities, relatively small series and individual customer demands lead to a typical project duration of 18 to 24 months. Process improvements by quality management tools such as Six

Sigma are difficult to (statistically) measure since the different projects are only partly comparable. Nevertheless, process quality and customer satisfaction needed to be improved. Therefore, management decided to develop a distinct competence aiming at continuous improvement that builds upon elements of Six Sigma.[33]

As the in-house consultancy SMC notes, today the *top*[+] program is implemented in all groups and regions.[34] Though *top*[+] has become the "standard" for operational excellence in many divisions and regions, the implementation rigor and scope, however, still varies. To successfully implement the *top*[+] program requires the commitment of the firm's group managers. Familiarizing them with three sub-programs innovation, customer focus, and global competitiveness, and their respective contents appears critical.[35] Indeed, Siemens management identified two success factors of the *top*[+] program. First, top management team commitment is decisive for implementation efforts. Second, communication across all firm levels is key. Both factors are strongly interrelated. For example, the annual winners of the *top*[+] award are invited to an awards ceremony in Berlin, where they are awarded a prize by the CEO. Further, there are management training programs reflecting the *top*[+] program and methods. These training programs are targeted at different management levels, ranging from members of the top management to team managers.

Capability Development and the *top*[+] Program

As indicated above, enabling the development of competences, for example, in quality or process management was a critical aspect of *top*[+]. Indeed, Siemens top management acknowledged the importance of capabilities as well as its fit with the environment for the firm's long-term success. In 2007, then Chief Strategy Officer Horst Kayser remarked:

"Management Capabilities are decisive for sustainable competitive advantage. We regard a portfolio of experiences and competences and its consistency with the external environment as critical for success."[36]

In particular, the *top*[+] program emphasized different aspects of organizational learning such as experiential learning, knowledge management, and best-practice transfer. First, the program aimed at using accumulated management experience in multiple areas. For example, in 2001, Siemens Dematic and Siemens VDO Automotive launched restructuring and integration programs that explicitly built upon prior experiences with *top*[+] and were expected to result in productivity gains of about 1 billion EUR for each group.[37] Second, knowledge management was a central aspect of *top+* and an integral part of several different initiatives such as the project management initiative and the quality initiative. Third, Siemens top management emphasized the importance of best-practice transfer for the success of the *top+* program. From the relaunch of *top+* in 1998 onwards, *top+* reflected Siemens' corporate principles and built upon best-practice sharing and learning. For example, in 1998 von Pierer remarked:

"The associated best-practice campaign stresses learning from outstanding models of efficiency both within and beyond the Company. top+ is driven by the new corporate principles, which were formulated last year."[38]

Knowledge management and best-practice transfer both were facilitated by dedicated initiatives, which were also part of *top+*. These initiatives aimed at issues such as providing the infrastructure and assistance necessary to effectively store individual experiences via databases, etc. Further, they included a communication strategy for exchanging both experiences and stored knowledge (Davenport & Probst, 2002). Although the application of the *top+* tools was supposed to result in value creation, the sharing of best practices across group boundaries was considered important. As von Pierer noted, the complementary function of knowledge transfer also demanded significant cultural changes within the firm:

"These tools are complemented by the systematic sharing of best practices: each Siemens business learns from the others. We are also continuing to reshape our corporate culture, particularly in the areas of management and cooperation."[39]

Siemens' *top+* program not only comprised initiatives and tools to build distinct managerial competences, but also was itself intended to lead to a business excellence or management innovation competence. Several aspects facilitated the development of such a corporate-level capability, particularly through experience accumulation. First, from the beginning of the initiative, the firm's top management created a dedicated function in the corporate center for centrally coordinating and managing the *top+* program. Second, *top+* was characterized by a high degree of management continuity. For example, from 1993 until the beginning of 2007, only two members of the managing board were responsible for the program. In addition, the manager heading the initiative until the end of the investigated period in 2007 held this position for more than five years. Further, *top+* managers were frequently recruited from the in-house

consultancy SMC and thus often had prior experience with the program.

Besides accumulating experience, more deliberate learning also occurred. Knowledge management tools such as databases, directories, and manuals were used for storing the knowledge acquired.[40] Communication of the knowledge acquired was another central element of the *top+* program. For example, from the beginning of the *top+* initiative onward, Siemens centered its efforts on the development of a common language. Facilitated by internal publications such as magazines, intranets, and even a "*top+* book", a common understanding of the *top+* program and its key learnings was considered critical for the success of the program.

Performance (Measurement) of the *top+* Program

From the (re)launch of the program in 1998 until 2007, increasing firm performance was the primary objective of *top+* (and is still today). Therefore, the firm's top management team considered performance measurement at all levels as a highly critical task. The *top+* program was not only supposed to result in major improvements, but was also meant to enable common performance measures:

"When it comes to performance, our proven top+ processes and procedures ensure that we all speak the same language. We set clear and measurable goals and define and rigorously implement the concrete measures required to achieve them."[41]

As indicated in Exhibit 7, Siemens management assessed the performance at the firm, operating group, and program levels. First, the overall priority was to achieve an increase in EVA.[42] Further measures included the growth rate (which should be twice the global gross domestic product (GDP)), return on capital employed (ROCE), the cash conversion rate (CCR) minus the revenue growth rate, and the ratio of adjusted industrial net debt to (adjusted) earnings before interest, taxes, depreciation, and amortization (EBITDA)). Second, operating group-level performance was also assessed with financial measures. Specific target margins ranges were defined individually for each group and periodically revised. For example, management adjusted the margin ranges with the transition from the Fit4More to Fit42010 SMS. Third, the *top+* program management assessed performance with non-financial measures on the program- and sub-program level. The different measures were customized for the specific targets of three sub-programs – innovation, customer focus, and global competitiveness.

Exhibit 7 Siemens Performance Measures in 2007

Level of Performance Analysis	Type of Performance Measure	Performance Measure(s)	Description/Details/Targets
Overall Firm	Financial	EVA	EVA equals net operating profit after taxes (NOPAT) less a charge for capital employed in the business (cost of capital).
		Growth	Sales Growth of 2x GDP
		ROCE (return on capital employed)	"Appropriate" ROCE (return on capital employed)
		CCR (cash conversion rate)-revenue growth rate	CCR (cash conversion rate) of 1 minus the revenue growth rate
		Adjusted industrial net debt to (adjusted) EBITDA	Defined ratio of adjusted industrial net debt to (adjusted) EBITDA (see Outlook)
Operating Groups	Financial	Margin ranges	Individual margin ranges for all operating groups
top[+] Innovation	Non-financial	Benchmarking	Comparison of the products, services, processes and financials within an organization, in relation to "best of practice" in other similar organizations.
		Lead customer feedback	Collection of feedback from key accounts concerning state and improvement of innovation
		"New Generation Business"	Identification and promotion of disruptive innovation topics of significant relevance to our future business
		"Siemens Top Innovators"	Development and expansion of network of top innovators, and intensively applying their experience throughout Siemens
		"Innovator Image"	Expansion of the corporate image as a leader in innovation
top[+] Customer Focus	Non-financial	Market transparency	Involves setting goals on what percentage of the overall market must be secured in terms of individual customers and specific projects
		Customer relationship management	Systematically collecting and making available sales information from a central source; firm-wide introduction of the "Net promoter score" (a key indicator to measure the willingness of customers to recommend our products and services)
top[+] Global Competitiveness	Non-financial	Lean production system	Developing lean production system, accelerating its expansion through the reference configuration of a "Siemens Production System (SPS)"

Source: Siemens Annual Report 2007: 160, 194–197; descriptions partly from Siemens Annual Report 2001.

To assess the performance of the *top[+]* customer focus program, for example, the quality of the customer relationships in operating businesses was measured by the "Net Promoter Score" (likelihood that customers recommend products/services).[43]

Overall, the performance impact of *top[+]* appeared to be very significant. During the period of investigation from 1998 to 2007, Siemens was able to increase sales by 28.7 percent, earnings by 197.3 percent and market capitalization by 213.9 percent (see Exhibit 8). A project manager of SMC, for example, noted:

"From my perspective, top[+] is the major reason why Siemens AG as a diversified entity with different unrelated businesses makes sense and exists to date. top[+] is the primary lever of corporate-level value creation and to achieve the goal of an integrated technology company."[44]

Different operating groups of Siemens also confirmed the positive influence of the successful *top[+]* implementation on performance. At Siemens Building Technologies in the Automation and Control Group, *top[+]* was considered to substantially contribute to productivity. Indeed, the improved productivity was credited to the application of *top[+]* tools for enhancing production processes and outsourcing certain areas.[45] Here, the introduction of a new production-optimization system at a facility resulted in a 20 percent productivity increase.

Exhibit 8 Selected Siemens Financial Data 1998–2007

In EUR million	CAGR	Y2007	Y2006	Y2005	Y2004	Y2003	Y2002	Y2001	Y2000	Y1999	Y1998
Sales	1.87%	72,448	87,325	75,445	75,167	74,233	84,016	87,000	78,396	68,582	60,177
Total Operating Expenses	1.34%	67,827	83,520	71,998	72,152	71,951	82,702	88,662	74,855	67,964	59,365
Selling, General, and Admin. Expenses	0.12%	15,502	20,494	18,839	18,630	18,601	21,274	23,422	19,354	17,663	15,321
Cost Of Goods Sold	1.95%	48,563	60,099	50,213	50,701	50,177	57,873	60,011	51,075	46,071	40,024
EBITD	2.45%	8,901	7,903	7,642	7,504	7,089	7,773	8,737	14,658	6,940	6,988
EBIT	6.61%	5,998	4,976	4,696	4,683	3,916	4,218	3,631	10,377	3,648	3,163
Net Income	11.69%	3,710	3,087	3,058	3,405	2,409	2,597	2,088	7,549	1,615	1,228
Total Assets	2.87%	88,961	85,990	79,884	74,707	73,246	74,253	86,434	93,366	72,741	67,048
Total Current Assets	1.97%	47,932	51,611	46,803	45,946	43,489	44,062	51,013	58,076	41,371	39,436
Total Liabilities	1.41%	59,334	55,982	52,111	47,323	48,897	50,191	58,602	67,728	55,541	51,560
Total Current Liabilities	5.94%	43,894	38,957	39,833	33,372	32,028	34,712	44,524	34,602	28,113	24,643
Total Debt	7.66%	15,497	15,574	12,435	11,219	13,178	12,346	12,610	9,134	7,262	7,406
Total Common Equity	7.09%	28,996	29,306	27,117	26,855	23,715	23,521	23,812	23,226	16,229	14,614
Year End Market Capitalization	12.10%	87,992	61,316	57,163	52,573	45,434	30,227	36,773	85,789	46,126	28,069
Capital Expenditures	0.10%	3,751	3,970	3,544	2,764	2,852	3,894	7,048	5,189	3,816	3,714
Free Cash Flow	N/A	1,116	−190	−1,535	1,338	1,964	782	−1,444	2,372	1,443	−2,116
ROA	N/A	4.17%	3.59%	3.83%	4.56%	3.29%	3.50%	2.42%	8.09%	2.22%	1.83%
ROE	N/A	12.79%	10.53%	11.28%	12.68%	10.16%	11.04%	8.77%	32.50%	9.95%	8.40%
Employees	−0.74%	386,200	475,000	460,800	430,000	417,000	426,000	484,000	446,800	440,200	416,000

Source: Thomson Financial.

A similar effect was present in other groups. For example, Wolfgang Dehen, then Group President of Siemens VDO Automotive, remarked in 2002:

"The rapid implementation of our top⁺ World Class Improvement Program has been decisive for our success. This initiative has helped us more closely align our development, production and administrative processes to customer needs. We have also increased our efficiency by reorganizing our production capacities worldwide."[46]

Interestingly, Siemens' top management categorized the business portfolio according to what extent the predefined margin ranges were met by the operating groups. By the end of fiscal 2004, Automation and Drives, Medical Solutions, Power Generation, Osram, Siemens VDO Automotive, Siemens Financial Services, and Power Transmission and Distribution "met or exceeded the margin targets agreed upon with the Managing Board, proving that sustainable success can be achieved by utilizing all the tools of our top⁺ management system".[47] Unlike the operating groups in the first category, Transportation Systems, the Communications Group, and Siemens Business Services had failed to reach their margin targets by 2004. Siemens top management demanded from them a more rigorous application of the SMS facilitated by the top⁺ program. Since the firm's corporate strategy partly built upon synergy from vertically optimizing the portfolio, Siemens' management regarded the top⁺ program as critical for operational excellence and thus for superior firm performance. As von Pierer noted in 2002, those businesses in which the top⁺ program did not lead to substantial future improvements (i.e., reach margin target ranges), would be restructured and potentially divested:

"We remain committed to continuously improving our profitability – even beyond the margin targets we have defined. Where we cannot achieve this with our top⁺ business excellence tools alone, we will further adjust our portfolio."[48]

A further benefit of the top⁺ program was that it strongly facilitated the integration of acquired businesses. As top⁺ also provided a platform on how Siemens understands "doing business", the acquired businesses had the

Exhibit 9 Profiles of Selected Top Management Team Members

Name	Position	Profile
Heinrich von Pierer	President & CEO (1992-2005)	Dr. Heinrich von Pierer studied law and economics at the Friedrich-Alexander University in Erlangen-Nuremberg, Germany. He joined Siemens in 1969 and began his career working in the company's legal department. In 1977, he moved to the company's power generation subsidiary Kraftwerk Union AG (KWU), where he was involved with major power plant projects throughout the world. Pierer took over as head of business administration at KWU in 1988 and was appointed to the board. The following year, he was named President of KWU and, at the same time, a member of the Managing Board of Siemens AG. He was appointed to the Corporate Executive Committee in 1990, and the next year was named Deputy Chairman of the Managing Board of Siemens AG. Pierer served as President and CEO from October 1992 to January 2005. Pierer was elected to the Supervisory Board at the Annual Shareholders' Meeting on January 2005, and subsequently held the post of Chairman until April 2007.
Klaus Kleinfeld	President & CEO (2005-2007)	Dr. Klaus Kleinfeld held the post of CEO of Siemens AG from January 2005 to June 2007. Kleinfeld worked at Siemens for about 20 years and transformed, among other things, Siemens Management Consulting into an effective partner for the global businesses. Furthermore, he was a member of the Group Executive Management of the Medical Solutions Group. As CEO of Siemens' regional business in the U.S., he contributed significantly to the profitable turnaround of the business there within two years. Kleinfeld started his business career in a consulting firm in Germany. Prior to joining Siemens, he was a strategic product manager at the CIBA-GEIGY Pharmaceuticals Division in Basel, Switzerland. He earned a Master's degree in Business Administration/Economics from the University of Göttingen (Germany) in 1982, followed by a Ph.D. in Strategic Management from the University of Würzburg (Germany) in 1992.
Peter Löscher	President & CEO (2007-present)	Peter H. Löscher has been CEO and President of Siemens AG at Siemens Healthcare since July 2007. He served as President and CEO of GE Healthcare Bio-Sciences since April 2004. He served as President of Global Human Health for Merck & Co. Inc. from May 2006 to July 2007. He served as COO of Amersham PLC since January 2004. He joined Amersham PLC in December 2002 as President of Amersham Health. Prior to Amersham Plc, Mr. Löscher served more than 16 years in senior management roles in the pharmaceutical industry, including a position as Chairman of Aventis Pharma Japan and also as its President and CEO from 1999 to 2002. Mr. Löscher served as Managing Director of Hoechst Roussel Veterinaria A.I.E., Spain, U.S. Vice President, Hoechst Roussel Agri-Vet Company; Head of Corporate Planning, Hoechst AG, Germany and Project Leader for NYSE Listing, Hoechst AG, Germany since 1988. He served as CEO of Hoechst Marion Roussell Limited in the UK since 1997. He served as Senior Management Consultant of Kienbaum Consulting Group since 1985. He is MBA graduate of the Vienna University School of Economics and he also has studied at the Chinese University of Hong Kong and at Harvard Business School.
Günter Wilhelm	Member of the Managing Board; responsible for *top/top⁺* 1993-2001	Dr. Günter Wilhelm served as a Member of the Managing Board of Siemens AG from 1992 to 2001. He studied mechanical engineering at the University of Applied Sciences Friedberg, Germany. Following his studies, he joined Siemens-Schuckert-Werke AG in 1958 as a project engineer. In 1974, he became head of a department in the energy division of Siemens AG. In 1978, he was promoted to area head in the same division. In 1988, he became deputy head of the division "E-Industry" and in 1989 was promoted to chair the managing board of the division "Automation".
Klaus Wucherer	Member of the Managing Board; responsible for *top⁺* 2001-2007	Prof. Dr-Ing. Wucherer served as an Executive Vice President of Siemens AG and its Member of the Managing Board from October 2000 to December 2007. Wucherer started his career with Siemens AG in the Bremen Regional Office, Germany, in 1970 and has held the following positions Technical Office, Osnabrück, Germany, since 1973, he served as Head of Controlled Three-phase and DC Drives SIMATIC Department, Bremen Regional Office, since 1978, Head of Drives at SIMATIC, Process Control Computers Department, Bremen Regional Office, since 1983, Head of Systems Sales and Marketing Department at Siemens S.A., São Paulo, Brazil, from 1986 to 1996, Head of various Subdivisions and Divisions of the Energy and Automation Group in Nuremberg, Germany and Erlangen, Germany: Industrial Communications, Software House, Automation Systems for Machine Tools and Industrial Automation Systems SIMATIC, since 1996, Member of the Group Executive Management at Automation Group, Nuremberg, since 1998, President Automation and Drives Group since January 2003. Wucherer holds Honorary Professorships includes Technical University of Chemnitz (engineering) University of Applied Sciences.
Erich Reinhardt	Member of the Managing Board; responsible for *top⁺* 2007-2008	Prof. Dr. Erich R. Reinhardt was a Member of the Managing Board of Siemens AG since December 2001. He served as the Head of Medical Solutions (Med). Prior to joining Siemens, he served as a Researcher of University of Stuttgart, Institute for Physical Electrical Engineering. In 1983, Reinhardt joined Siemens AG, Medical Engineering Group and his other positions at Siemens are Applications Development in Magnetic Resonance Tomography, Head of Department; since 1986, Magnetic Resonance Tomography Division's Head; since 1990, Siemens Ltd. Bombay, India's Managing Director; since 1994, Member of the Group Executive Management of the Medical Engineering Group; since April 1994, and President of the Medical Engineering Group. Reinhardt holds a degree in Electrical Engineering, a Doctorate, and Honorary Professorship from the University of Stuttgart.

Source: www.siemens.com, www.businessweek.com.

opportunity to openly and continuously reflect its *top*[+] offered Siemens the opportunity to assess the processes, tools etc. of the acquired businesses and to adopt suitable best practices from them within the overall firm.[49]

While the implementation of entire sub-programs of *top*[+] enhanced overall firm performance, the contributions of applying single management tools of the *top*[+] "tool-kit" were also substantial. For example, in the firm's 2004 annual report, von Pierer stated the following in reference to the tool asset management:

"Cash flow development, which has been positive in each of the past four years, was again very gratifying. Net cash from operating and investing activities totaled €3.3 billion. Our managers have learned the art of professional asset management. Strong cash flow is giving us the entrepreneurial leeway we need for targeted strategic moves."[50]

The Future of Management Innovation At Siemens

While technological and product innovation have always played central roles at Siemens, management innovation appears to be critical for future success, too. As this case study illustrates, a distinct form of vertical optimization is management innovation performed with support by the corporate level. Synergy may result not only from leveraging tools to individual operating groups, but also from the development of superior capabilities. Although the firm's corporate center was repeatedly restructured during the period from 1998 to 2007, the case suggests that corporate development and corporate-level programs aiming at management innovation will always remain important for the firm's overall value creation. In 2007, Siemens top management team decided to continue the efforts of the *top*[+] program as part of the updated corporate program Fit42010. Because of its past contribution to operational excellence and thus firm performance and because of the increasing present and future importance of innovative management, *top*[+] is likely to constitute an integral part of future corporate programs, even beyond 2010. Indeed, current CEO Peter Löscher, an executive with extensive management experience at GE, wants to strengthen the efforts of Siemens in management innovation and operational excellence with the *top*[+] program.

NOTES

1. Siemens Annual Report 2007; Siemens Company History, Document from the Siemens History Online Archives, www.siemens.com.
2. Siemens Annual Report 2001: 18.
3. Johannes Feldmayer, Presentation "Management-Innovationen" at Fachkonferenz Innovation@Siemens, Berlin, July 10, 2006.
4. Interview with head of Siemens top[+] program, April 2008.
5. Siemens Annual Report 1998.
6. Siemens Annual Report 2000: 14; Siemens Annual Report 2001: 16.
7. Heinrich von Pierer, Siemens Annual Report 2003: 7.
8. Siemens Annual Report 2007: 33.
9. Siemens Annual Report 2007: 41
10. Siemens Annual Report 2004: 15.
11. Siemens Annual Report 2004.
12. Johannes Feldmayer, Presentation "Management-Innovationen" at Fachkonferenz Innovation@Siemens, Berlin, July 10, 2006.
13. Siemens Annual Report 2004: 123.
14. Zhao, F. 2004. Siemens' business excellence model and sustainable development. Measuring Business Excellence, 8(2): 55–64.
15. Siemens Annual Report 2001: 122.
16. Klaus Wucherer, Siemens Annual Report 2006: 23.

17. Siemens Annual Report 2007: 41.
18. Siemens Annual Report 1999.
19. Siemens Annual Report 2001: 5.
20. Siemens Annual Report 2003: 31.
21. Zhao, F. 2004. Siemens' business excellence model and sustainable development. Measuring Business Excellence, 8(2): 55–64.
22. Siemens Annual Report 2005: 19.
23. Heinrich von Pierer, Siemens Annual Report 2004: 7.
24. Zhao, F. 2004. Siemens' business excellence model and sustainable development. Measuring Business Excellence, 8(2): 55–64.
25. Heinz-Joachim Neubürger, found in and translated from Preissner, A. 2002. Zwei Männer unter Strom. Manager Magazin 06/2002: 68–78.
26. Preissner, A. 2002. Zwei Männer unter Strom. Manager Magazin 06/2002: 68–78.
27. www.siemens.com.
28. Interview with project manager of SMC, March 2009.
29. Siemens Annual Report 2001: 17-18.
30. Siemens Annual Report 2002: 16.
31. Siemens Annual Report 2001: 17.
32. Siemens Annual Report 2001: 29.
33. Kleemann, B., Seitz, N., & Wio, H.-J. 2007. Das Führungskräftetraining für top[+] Qualität und Six Sigma bei Siemens Power Generation. In A. Töpfer (Ed.), Six Sigma - Konzeption und Erfolgsbeispiele für

praktizierte Null-Fehler-Qualität, 4th ed.: 278–288. Berlin: Springer.
34. Siemens Management Consulting (SMC), www.smc.siemens.com.
35. Siemens Annual Report 2003: 7.
36. Presentation of Horst Kayser at the University of St. Gallen, June 2007.
37. Siemens Annual Report 2001: 17.
38. Heinrich von Pierer, Siemens Annual Report 1998: 6.
39. Heinrich von Pierer, Siemens Annual Report 1999: 9.
40. Interview with head of Siemens top[+] program, April 2008.
41. Siemens Annual Report 2007: 41.
42. Siemens Annual Report 1998: 6.
43. Siemens Annual Report 2007: 160.
44. Interview with project manager of SMC, March 2009.
45. Siemens Annual Report 2003: 27.
46. Wolfgang Dehen, Siemens Annual Report 2002: 27-28.
47. Heinrich von Pierer, Siemens Annual Report 2004: 6.
48. Heinrich von Pierer, Siemens Annual Report 2002: 16.
49. Correspondence with project manager of SMC, April 2010.
50. Heinrich von Pierer, Siemens Annual Report 2004: 5.

CASE 16

Southwest Airlines

Andrew Inkpen

You are now free to move about the country.™

In 2013, Southwest Airlines (Southwest), the once scrappy underdog in the U.S. airline industry, was one of the largest U.S. airlines and, based on number of passengers, one of the largest in the world. The company, unlike all of its major competitors, had been consistently profitable for decades and had weathered energy crises, the September 11 terrorist attacks, and the 2008-09 recession. An insight into Southwest's operating philosophy can be found in the company's 2001 annual report:

Southwest was well poised, financially, to withstand the potentially devastating hammer blow of September 11. Why? Because for several decades our leadership philosophy has been: we manage in good times so that our Company and our People can be job secure and prosper through bad times….Once again, after September 11, our philosophy of managing in good times so as to do well in bad times proved a marvelous prophylactic for our Employees and our Shareholders.

As Southwest entered its 42nd year of service, the company was facing some major challenges. Legacy carriers in the United States had become more efficient, and the recent mega-mergers involving Delta/Northwest, Continental/United, and American/US Airways were shaking up the industry. Smaller companies like JetBlue, Alaska, and Spirit were pressuring Southwest's cost advantage and low-fare focus. A major internal challenge for Southwest would be managing its acquisition of AirTran, a deal completed in 2011. To make the acquisition a success, the company would have to integrate a workforce of more than 8,000 (about 25% the size of Southwest) and manage a fleet of aircraft different from the Boeing 737s used by Southwest.

The U.S. Airline Industry

The U.S. commercial airline industry was permanently altered in October 1978 when President Carter signed the Airline Deregulation Act. Before deregulation, the Civil Aeronautics Board regulated airline route entry and exit, passenger fares, mergers and acquisitions, and airline rates of return. Typically, two or three carriers provided service in a given market, although there were routes covered by only one carrier. Cost increases were passed along to customers, and price competition was almost nonexistent. The airlines operated as if there were only two market segments: those who could afford to fly, and those who couldn't.

Deregulation sent airline fares tumbling and allowed many new firms to enter the market. The financial impact on both established and new airlines was enormous. The fuel crisis of 1979 and the air traffic controllers' strike in 1981 contributed to the industry's difficulties, as did the severe recession that hit the United States during the early 1980s. During the first decade of deregulation, more than 150 carriers, many of them start-up airlines, collapsed into bankruptcy. Eight of the 11 major airlines dominating the industry in 1978 ended up filing for bankruptcy, merging with other carriers, or simply disappearing from the radar screen. Collectively, the industry made enough money during this period to buy two Boeing 747s.[1] The three major carriers that survived intact—Delta, United, and American—ended up with 80% of all domestic U.S. air traffic and 67% of trans-Atlantic business.[2] Exhibits 1A and 1B provide summary financial data for the major airlines. The rapid growth of Southwest was in stark contrast to the much slower growth of its major competitors.

Competition and lower fares led to greatly expanded demand for airline travel. Controlling for inflation, the average price to fly one domestic mile dropped by more than 50% since deregulation. By the mid-1990s, the airlines were having trouble meeting this demand. Travel increased from 200 million travelers in 1974 to 700 million in 2007 in the U.S. Demand fell significantly during the recession and then started to grow again in 2010. Despite the overall growth in demand, from 2001 through 2011 total financial losses for the U.S. airline industry exceeded $50 billion.

The financial performance notwithstanding, new firms continued to enter the airline industry. For example, during the period 1994 to 2004, 66 new airlines were

Exhibit 1A Revenue Passenger-Miles (RPM)* 1989–2011 (in 000s) for Major U.S. Airlines, All Airports

Year	American	America West	Continental	Delta	Northwest	Southwest	Trans World	United	US Airways
2011	126.4			164.2		83.9		97.8	60.7
2010	125.4			164.1		78.1		100.4	58.9
2009	122.4		77.8	100.7	62.9	74.6		100.5	57.9
2008	131.7		80.5	105.7	71.6	73.7		110.0	60.6
2007	138.4	17.7	81.4	103.3	72.9	72.3		117.4	43.5
2006	139.4	23.5	76.3	98.8	72.6	67.7		117.2	37.4
2005	138.4	24.3	68.4	103.7	75.9	60.3		114.3	40.2
2004	130.2	23.3	63.4	98.3	73.4	53.5		115.2	40.5
2003	120.3	21.3	57.6	89.4	68.8	48		104.4	37.8
2002	121.7	19.9	57.3	95.3	72.1	45.5		109.4	40
2001	106.2	19.1	58.8	97.7	73.3	44.7	20.8	116.6	46
2000	116.6	19.1	62.4	107.8	79.2	42.4	27.3	126.9	46.9
1999	110.2	17.7	58	104.8	74.2	36.8	26.1	125.5	41.5
1998	108.9	16.4	51	102	66.8	31.6	24.5	124.6	41.4
1997	107	16.2	44.3	99.7	72.1	26.4	25.2	121.4	41.7
1996	104.6	15.3	37.6	93.9	68.7	27.3	27.3	116.7	39.2
1995	102.7	13.3	35.8	85.2	62.6	23.5	25.1	111.8	38.1
1994	98.8	12.2	38.1	86.4	58.5	19.9	24.8	108.2	38.4
1993	97.1	11.2	40.1	82.9	58.7	16.9	22.8	101.3	35.5
1992	97.1	11.8	43.5	80.6	58.7	13.9	29.2	92.7	35.4

*Revenue Passenger-Miles, or RPM, is a measure of the volume of air passenger transportation. A revenue passenger-mile is equal to one paying passenger carried one mile.
Source: Bureau of Transportation Statistics Table T1: U.S. Air Carrier Traffic and Capacity Summary by Service Class.

certified by the FAA. By 2004, 43 had shut down. Most of the new airlines competed with limited route structures and lower fares than the major airlines. The new airlines created a second tier of service providers that saved consumers billions of dollars annually and provided service in markets abandoned or ignored by major carriers.

Although deregulation fostered competition and the growth of new airlines, it also created a regional disparity in ticket prices and adversely affected service to small and remote communities. Airline workers generally suffered, with inflation-adjusted average employee wages falling from $42,928 in 1978 to much lower levels over the subsequent decades. About 20,000 airline industry employees were laid off in the early 1980s, while productivity of the remaining employees rose 43% during the same period. In a variety of cases, bankruptcy filings were used to diminish the role of unions and reduce unionized wages. Between 2000 and 2011, 51 U.S. passenger and cargo airlines filed for bankruptcy—13 of them in 2008.[3] In the most recent round of bankruptcies,

airline workers at American, Delta, and other airlines were forced to accept pay cuts of up to 35%.

Industry Economics

About 80% of airline operating costs are fixed or semi-variable. The few variable costs per passenger included travel agency commissions, food costs, and ticketing fees. The operating costs of an airline flight depended primarily on the distance traveled, not the number of passengers on board. For example, the crew and ground staff sizes were determined by the type of aircraft, not the passenger load. Therefore, once an airline established its route structure, most of its operating costs were fixed.

Because of this high fixed-cost structure, the airlines developed sophisticated software tools to maximize capacity utilization, known as load factor. Load factor was calculated by dividing RPM (revenue passenger miles—the number of passengers carried multiplied by the distance flown) by ASM (available seat miles—the

Exhibit 1B Operating Revenues (in millions of dollars) 1992–2011 for Major U.S. Airlines, All Regions

Year	American	America West	Continental	Delta	Northwest	Southwest	Trans World	United	US Airways
2011	23,958			35,271		13,655		21,155	13,340
2010	22,150			31,894		12,103		19,682	12,195
2009	19,898		10,635	18,046		10,350		16,359	10,781
2008	21,210		11,382	20,973	10903	11,023		20,237	12,459
2007	22,833	2,737	10,615	19,238	9,545	7,369		20.049	9.317
2006	22,493	3,770	13,010	17,339	12,555	9,086		19,334	8.076
2005	20,657	3,397	11,108	16,112	12,316	7,584		17,304	7,212
2004	18,608	2,482	9,851	15,154	11,266	6,530		15,701	7,073
2003	17,403	2,223	7,333	14,203	9,184	5,937		13,398	6,762
2002	15,871	2,021	7,353	12,410	9,152	5,522		13,916	6,915
2001	15,639	2,035	7,972	13,211	9,592	5,555	2,633	16,087	8,253
2000	18,117	2,309	9,129	15,321	10,957	5,650	3,585	19,331	9,181
1999	16,090	2,164	8,027	14,901	9,868	4,736	3,309	17,967	8,460
1998	16,299	1,983	7,299	14,630	8,707	4,164	3,259	17,518	8,556
1997	15,856	1,887	6,361	14,204	9,984	3,817	3,330	17,335	8,501
1996	15,136	1,752	5,487	13,318	9,751	3,407	3,554	16,317	7,704
1995	15,610	1,562	4,919	12,557	8,909	2,873	3,281	14,895	6,985
1994	14,951	1,414	4,734	12,346	8,929	2,417	3,350	13,887	6,579
1993	14,737	1,332	5,086	12,376	8,448	2,067	3,094	14,354	6,623
1992	13,581	1,303	5,210	11,639	7,964	1,685	3,570	12,725	6,236

Source: Bureau of Transportation Statistics, Air Carrier Financial Reports Table P-12.

number of seats available for sale multiplied by the distance flown).

On each flight by one of the major airlines (excluding Southwest and a few other carriers), there were typically a dozen categories of fares. The airlines analyzed historical travel patterns on individual routes to determine how many seats to sell at each fare level. All of the major airlines used this type of analysis and flexible pricing practice, known as a "yield management" system. These systems enabled the airlines to manage their seat inventories and the prices paid for those seats. The objective was to sell more seats on each flight at higher yields (total passenger yield was passenger revenue from scheduled operations divided by scheduled RPMs). The higher the ticket price, the better the yield.

Although reducing operating costs was a high priority for the airlines, the nature of the cost structure limited cost reduction opportunities. Fuel costs (17% of total operating costs at Southwest in 2004; 37% in 2012) were largely beyond the control of the airlines, and many of the larger airlines' restrictive union agreements limited labor

flexibility. The airline industry's extremely high fixed costs made it one of the worst net operating margin performers when measured against other industries. Airlines were far outpaced in profitability by industries such as banks, health care, consumer products, and oil and gas.

In recent years, a la carte or ancillary revenues such as baggage fees and change fees had become increasingly important for most airlines. Some low-cost airlines, such as Spirit and Allegiant, generated more than 25% of total revenue from ancillary fees. In contrast to most of its competitors, Southwest did not charge for checked bags.

To manage their route structures, the major airlines (except Southwest) maintained their operations around a "hub-and-spoke" network. The spokes fed passengers from outlying points into a central airport—the hub—where passengers could travel to additional hubs or their final destination. For example, to fly from Phoenix to Boston on Northwest Airlines, a typical route would involve a flight from Phoenix to Northwest's Detroit hub. The passenger would then take a second flight from Detroit to Boston.

Establishing a major hub in a city like Chicago or Atlanta required a huge investment for gate acquisition and terminal construction. JetBlue's new facility at JFK in New York opened in 2009 and cost about $800 million. Although hubs created inconveniences for travelers, hub systems were an efficient means of distributing services across a wide network. The major airlines were very protective of their so-called "fortress" hubs and used the hubs to control various local markets. For example, Northwest (now Delta) handled about 80% of Detroit's passengers and occupied nearly the entire new Detroit terminal that opened in 2002. And, Northwest's deal with the local government assured that it would be the only airline that could have a hub in Detroit. When Southwest entered the Detroit market, the only available gates were already leased by Northwest. Northwest subleased gates to Southwest at rates 18 times higher than Northwest's costs. Southwest eventually withdrew from Detroit, and then re-entered, one of only three markets Southwest had abandoned in its history (Denver and Beaumont, Texas, were the other two; Southwest re-entered Denver in 2006).

Recent U.S. Airline Industry Performance

Despite steadily growing customer demand, the airline industry always seemed to be one recession away from crisis. In 2013, the major airlines were on track to be profitable, a marked contrast to the heavy losses of just a few years earlier (with the exception of Southwest). The continuing consolidation in the industry was expected to lead to lower operating costs and higher ticket prices.

After the September 11, 2001, terrorist attacks, domestic airlines lost about $30 billion. The continuing specter of terrorism cast a long shadow on the global airline industry. In the United States, passengers were frustrated by increasingly more-invasive security procedures. Volatile fuel costs were a constant uncertainty, and new entrants continued to put pressure on the incumbents.

Other pressures on the industry included:

1. **Customer Dissatisfaction with Airline Service**. Service problems were leading to calls for new regulation of airline competitive practices.
2. **Aircraft Safety Maintenance**. The ageing of the general aircraft population meant higher maintenance costs and eventual aircraft replacement. The introduction of stricter government regulations for older planes placed new burdens on operators of older aircraft.
3. **Debt Servicing**. The airline industry's debt load exceeded U.S. industry averages.
4. **Air-Traffic Delays**. Increased air-traffic control delays caused by higher travel demand and related airport congestion were expected to negatively influence customer satisfaction.
5. **Environmental Regulation**. Following actions in Europe, various U.S. groups were advocating new standards and taxes on airline emissions.
6. **Open Skies Agreement**. Legislation allowing greater access to U.S. markets by non-U.S. carriers was expected to increase competitive pressure.

Southwest Airlines Background

In 1966, Herb Kelleher was practicing law in San Antonio when a client named Rollin King proposed starting a short-haul airline similar to California-based Pacific Southwest Airlines. The airline would fly the Golden Triangle of Houston, Dallas, and San Antonio and, by staying within Texas, avoid federal regulations. Kelleher and King incorporated a company, raised initial capital, and filed for regulatory approval from the Texas Aeronautics Commission. Unfortunately, the other Texas-based airlines, namely Braniff, Continental, and Trans Texas (later called Texas International), opposed the idea and waged a battle to prohibit Southwest from flying. Kelleher argued the company's case before the Texas Supreme Court, which ruled in Southwest's favor. The U.S. Supreme Court refused to hear an appeal filed by the other airlines. In late 1970, it looked as if the company could begin flying.

Southwest began building a management team, and the purchase of three surplus Boeing 737s was negotiated. Meanwhile, Braniff and Texas International continued their efforts to prevent Southwest from flying. The underwriters of Southwest's initial public stock offering withdrew and a restraining order against the company was obtained two days before its scheduled inaugural flight. Kelleher again argued his company's case before the Texas Supreme Court, which ruled in Southwest's favor a second time, lifting the restraining order. Southwest Airlines began flying the next day, June 18, 1971.[4]

When Southwest began flying to three Texas cities, the firm had three aircraft and 25 employees. Initial flights were out of Dallas' older Love Field airport and Houston's Hobby Airport, both of which were closer to downtown than the major international airports. Flamboyant from the beginning, original flights were staffed by flight attendants in hot pants. By 1996, the flight attendant uniform had evolved to khakis and polo shirts. The *Luv* theme was a staple of the airline from the outset and became the company's ticker symbol on Wall Street.

Southwest management quickly discovered that there were two types of travelers: convenience, time-oriented business travelers, and price-sensitive leisure travelers. To cater to both groups, Southwest developed a two-tiered pricing structure. In 1972, Southwest was charging $20 to fly between Houston, Dallas, and San Antonio, undercutting the $28 fares of the other carriers. After an experiment with $10 fares, Southwest decided to sell seats on weekdays until 7:00 p.m. for $26, and after 7:00 p.m. and on weekends for $13.[5] In response, in January 1973, Braniff Airlines began charging $13 for its Dallas-Houston Hobby flights. This resulted in one of Southwest's most famous ads, which had the caption, "Nobody's going to shoot Southwest out of the sky for a lousy $13." Southwest offered travelers the opportunity to pay $13 or $26 and receive a free bottle of liquor. More than 75% of the passengers chose the $26 fare and Southwest became the largest distributor of Chivas Regal scotch whiskey in Texas. In 1975, Braniff abandoned the Dallas-Houston Hobby route. When Southwest entered the Cleveland market, the unrestricted one-way fare between Cleveland and Chicago was $310 on other carriers; Southwest's fare was $59.[6] One of Southwest's problems was convincing passengers that its low fares were not just introductory promotions but regular fares.

Southwest's Operations

Although Southwest became one of the largest airlines in the United States, the firm did not deviate from its initial focus: primarily short-haul (less than 500 miles), point-to-point flights, a fleet consisting only of Boeing 737s, high-frequency flights, low fares, and no international flights (excluding the AirTran route system, which included flights to various international locations). In 2012, the average Southwest one-way fare was $147.17.

Southwest was the only large airline to operate without major hubs, although cities such as Phoenix, Houston, Chicago, Dallas, Denver, and Las Vegas were increasingly becoming important transit points for Southwest trips. For example, there were 198 daily departures from Chicago, Southwest's busiest airport. Point-to-point service provided maximum convenience for passengers who wanted to fly between two cities, but insufficient demand could make such nonstop flights economically unfeasible. For that reason, the hub-and-spoke approach was generally assumed to generate cost

savings for airlines through operational efficiencies. However, Southwest saw it another way: hub-and-spoke arrangements resulted in planes spending more time on the ground waiting for customers to arrive from connecting points.

Turnaround time—the time it takes to unload a waiting plane and load it for the next flight—was about 15 minutes for Southwest, compared with the industry average of 45 minutes. This time savings was accomplished with a gate crew 50% smaller than other airlines. Pilots sometimes helped unload bags when schedules were tight. Flight attendants regularly assisted in the cleanup of airplanes between flights.

Relative to the other major airlines, Southwest had a no-frills approach to services: no reserved seating or meals were offered. Seating was first come, first served. As to why the airline did not have assigned seating, Kelleher explained: "It used to be we only had about four people on the whole plane, so the idea of assigned seats just made people laugh. Now the reason is you can turn the airplanes quicker at the gate. And if you can turn an airplane quicker, you can have it fly more routes each day. That generates more revenue, so you can offer lower fares."[7]

Unlike some of the major carriers, Southwest rarely offered delayed customers a hotel room or long distance telephone calls. Southwest had only a limited participation in computerized reservation systems, preferring to have travel agents and customers book flights through its reservation center. Southwest was the first national carrier to sell seats from an Internet site and was the first airline to create a home page on the Internet. In the 4th quarter of 2012, 81% of passenger revenues were booked via southwest.com. The company estimated that the online ticketing cost was $1 per booking and $6-8 with a travel agent. Southwest was also one of the first airlines to use ticketless travel, offering the service first in 1995. Southwest was the only major airline with a frequent flyer program based on dollars spent by a passenger, not miles flown.

Over the years, Southwest's choice of markets resulted in significant growth in air travel at those locations. In Texas, traffic between the Rio Grande Valley (Harlingen) and the Golden Triangle grew from 123,000 to 325,000 within 11 months of Southwest entering the market.[8] Within a year of Southwest's arrival, the Oakland-Burbank route became the 25th largest passenger market, up from 179th. The Chicago-Louisville market tripled in size 30 days after Southwest began flying that route. Table 1 shows a comparison of Southwest across several years from 1971 to 2012.

Table 1 Southwest Across the Years

	1971	1999	2007	2012
Size of Fleet (End of Year)	4	306	515	694
Number of Employees	195	29,005	34,378	46,000
Number of Passengers Carried	108,554	52,600,000	101,947,800	109,000,00
Number of Cities Served	3	55	64	97
Number of Trips Flown	6,051	602,578	1,160,699	>1,284,800
Total Operating Revenues (Millions $)	2.33	4,736	7,369	17,100
Net Income (Millions $)	−3.8	433	645	421

Sources: Company press releases and Southwest Airlines Fact Sheet at http://www.southwest.com/about_swa/press/factsheet.html.

Recent Service Changes

In 2007, Southwest made various changes to its service offerings, including:

- Three new fare categories, including higher-tier fares for business travelers.
- New boarding processes; for example, travelers could pay extra to board first.
- Allowing customers with high status in the frequent flier program to board first.
- Increased emphasis on corporate sales.
- Promoted the "two-bags-fly-free campaign" aggressively.

The rationale for the 2007 changes was explained by CEO Gary Kelly:

We've always been a business traveler's airline. At the same time, over 37 years we hadn't done much to try to customize the travel experience for the varieties of customer needs that we had. It was one-size-fits-all, and in today's competitive environment we felt that was not the best way to remain on top. We had the desire to improve our overall customer experience for the business traveler.[9]

In 2011, Southwest launched its new Rapid Rewards frequent flyer program. Under the new program, members earned points for every dollar spent, whereas under the prior program customers earned credits for flight segments flown. The new frequent flyer program was designed to increase revenue by (a) bringing in new customers, including new Rapid Rewards members, as well as new holders of Southwest's co-branded Chase Visa credit card; (b) increasing business from existing customers; and (c) strengthening Rapid Rewards hotel, rental car, credit card, and retail partnerships.

Southwest's Performance

Southwest bucked the airline industry trend by earning a profit for 40 consecutive years. Among the major airlines, Southwest consistently ranked first in fewest overall customer complaints as published in the Department of Transportation's Air Travel Consumer Report. For example, in December 2012, there were 18 complaints reported against Southwest and 140 against United. In Zagat's 2010 airline survey, Southwest won awards for top website; best consumer on-time estimates—domestic; best check-in experience; best value—domestic; and best luggage policy—domestic.[10]

The average Southwest flight had a duration of about one hour and 55 minutes and a length of 694 miles. This was up from 462 miles in 1999 and 394 in 1996. Each plane flew about seven flights daily, almost twice the industry average. Planes were used an average of 13 hours a day, about 40% more than major carriers like Delta and United. Table 2 shows that Southwest's cost per available seat mile was lower than the legacy

Table 2 Operating Data

	Alaska	Southwest	American	Delta	JetBlue	United	US Airways
Load Factor	86.6%	80.4%	84.1%	85.7%	84.3%	85.1%	85.7%
Operating cost per ASM (cents)	14.52	14.18	16.79	16.71	11.34	17.07	17.79
Revenue per ASM (cents)[1]	16.49	14.82	16.30	18.22	12.45	17.26	18.89
On-time departure rank	#2	#11	#14	#5	#13	15	#3
On-time arrival rank	#2	#8	#15	#4	#12	14	#5

[1]Calculated by dividing operating revenue by available seat miles.
Source: U.S. Department of Transportation (US DOT).

Exhibit 2 Operating Margins for Major U.S. Airlines

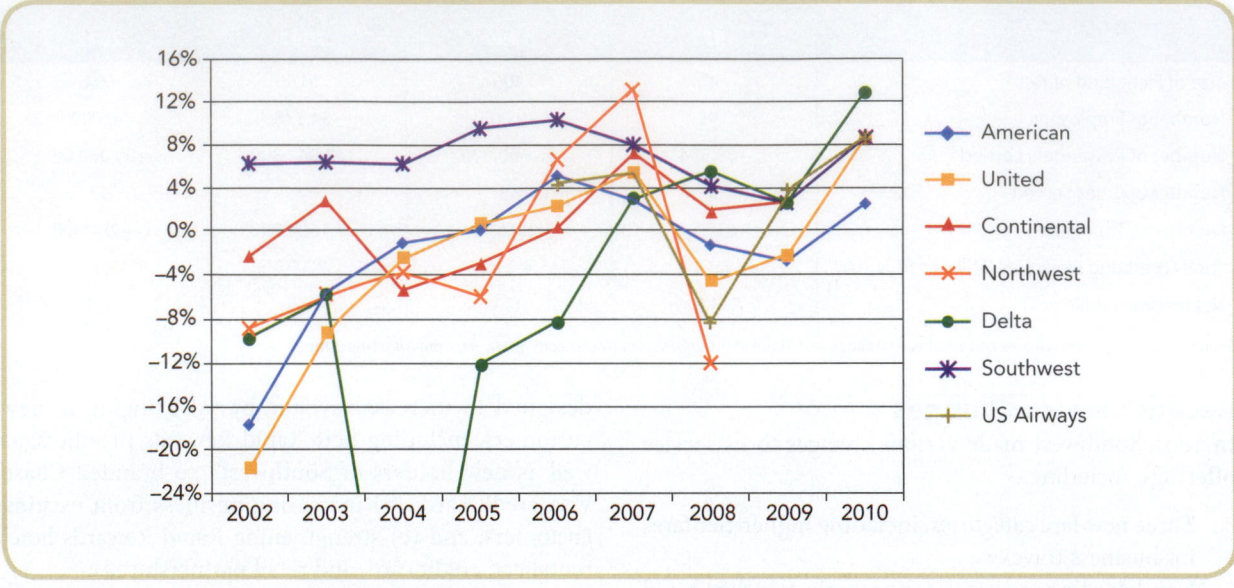

Source: Airline Data and Analysis Largest Airlines 2002-2010 by AirlineFinancials.com.

carriers (American, Delta, US Airways, United) but not lower than some of the newer and smaller carriers such as JetBlue (one of the reasons for JetBlue's lower cost per ASM was its longer average flight length—1,085 miles at JetBlue). Southwest's on-time arrival and departure record, for many years near the top in the industry, had declined in recent years.

The average age of the Southwest fleet was 11 years, the lowest for the major carriers. Employee cost per available seat mile was lower than major competitors (but not lower than some smaller carriers like Spirit and Allegiant).

Exhibits 2-10 provide data on the major U.S. competitors for the period:

- Exhibit 2—Operating margins: Southwest had the highest margin position until 2007.
- Exhibit 3—Average revenue passenger miles (RPM) per passenger: Southwest has the lowest in all years.
- Exhibit 4—Passenger yield (passenger revenue per RPM): Southwest is the highest
- Exhibit 5—Load factor: Southwest is the lowest in all years.
- Exhibit 6—Costs per available seat mile: Southwest is the lowest in all years.
- Exhibit 7—Unit costs per available seat mile excluding labor cost: Southwest is the lowest in all years.

- Exhibit 8—Labor cost per available seat mile: Southwest cost moved from the lowest in 2003 to the second highest in 2007, where it has remained. Southwest also has the highest wage/salary per employee.
- Exhibit 9—Employees per aircraft: Southwest is the lowest in all years. This is a function of both labor productivity and aircraft size; Southwest has, on average, smaller aircraft than the legacy carriers.
- Exhibit 10—Net debt: Southwest is the lowest in all years.

Southwest accomplished its strong record by challenging accepted norms and setting competitive thresholds for other airlines to emulate. The company established numerous new industry standards. Southwest flew more passengers per employee than any other major airline, while at the same time had the fewest number of employees per aircraft. Southwest maintained a debt-to-equity ratio much lower than the industry average and was one of the few airlines in the world with an investment grade credit rating. The company had never curtailed service because of a union strike and no passenger had ever died because of a safety incident.

Southwest had a fleet of 606 Boeing 737s, up from 417 in 2005, 106 in 1990, and 75 in 1987. Southwest also had 88 Boeing 717s from the AirTran deal, which were to be sold. Of the total 737 fleet, 497 aircraft were owned and the remainder leased.

Exhibit 3 Average RPM's Per Passenger (Average Mileage Per Passenger Flight) for Major U.S. Airlines

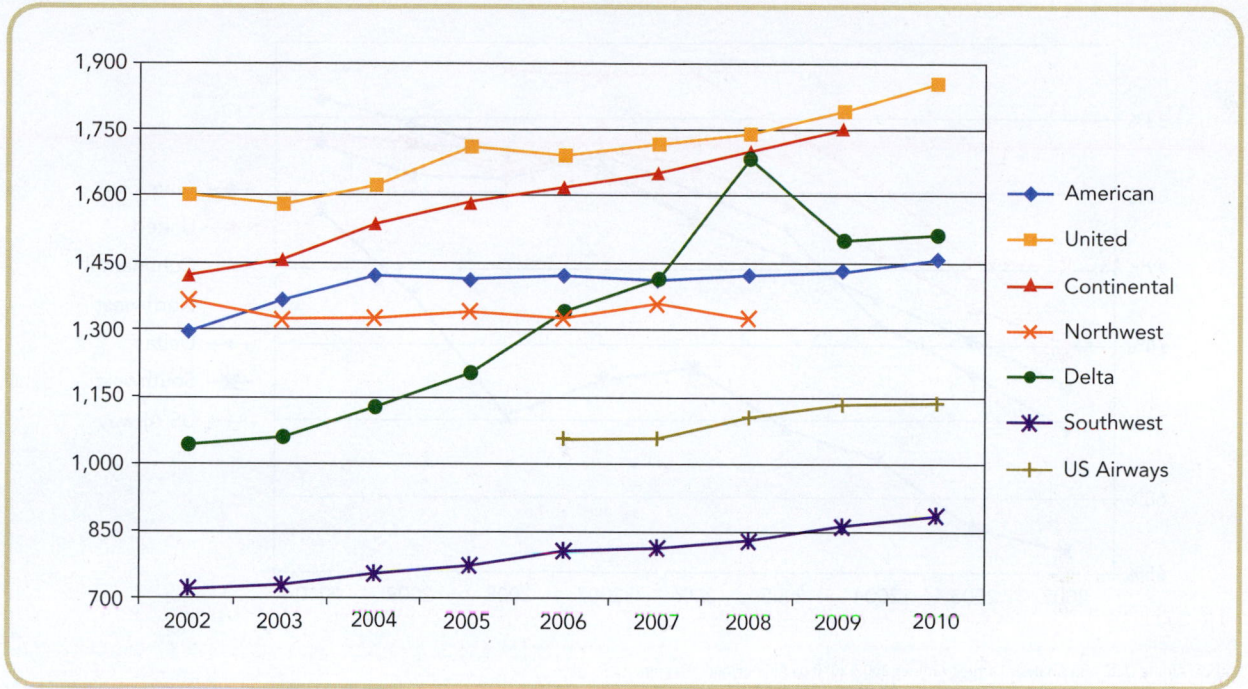

Source: Airline Data and Analysis Largest Airlines 2002-2010 by AirlineFinancials.com.

Exhibit 4 Passenger Revenue Per RPM* 2002-2010 (in cents) for Major U.S. Airlines

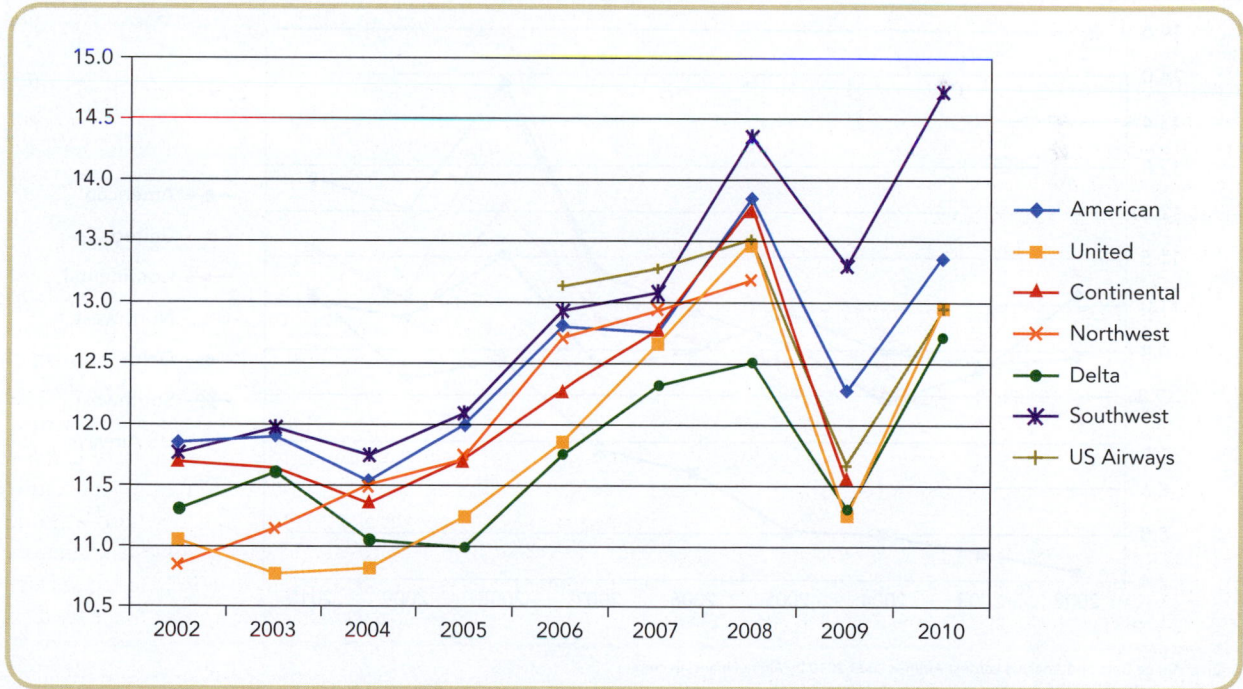

* Passenger Revenue Per Revenue Passenger Mile, also known as Passenger Yield, is computed by dividing passenger revenues by revenue passenger-miles.
Source: Airline Data and Analysis Largest Airlines 2002-2009 by AirlineFinancials.com.

Exhibit 5 Load Factors 2002-2010 for Major U.S. Airlines

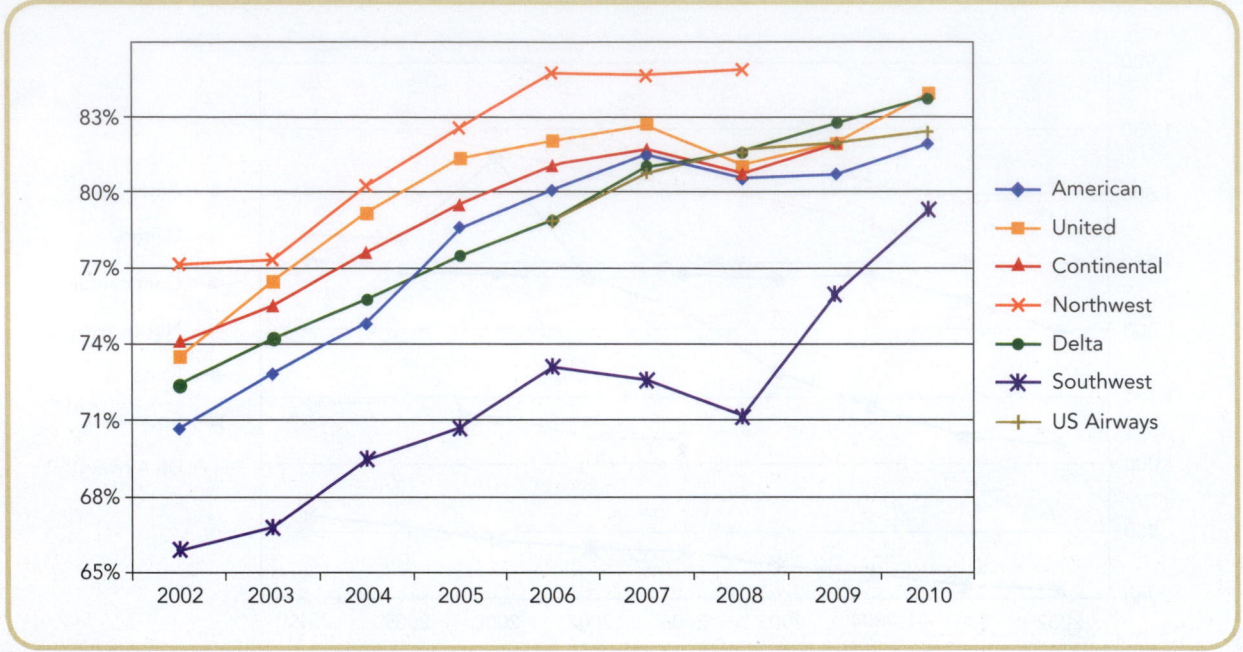

Source: Airline Data and Analysis Largest Airlines 2002-2010 by AirlineFinancials.com.

Exhibit 6 Unit Cost (CASM) (cents/ASM) for Major U.S. Airlines

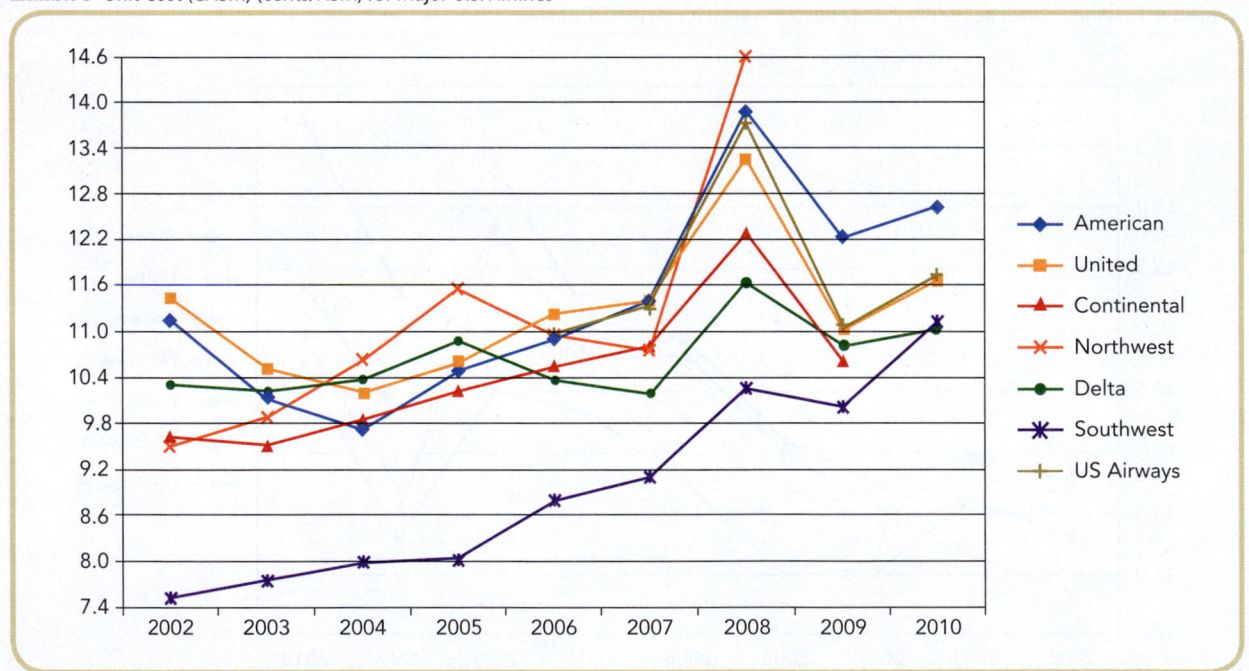

Source: Airline Data and Analysis Largest Airlines 2002-2010 by AirlineFinancials.com.

Exhibit 7 Unit Costs Without Labor (cents/ASM) for Major U.S. Airlines

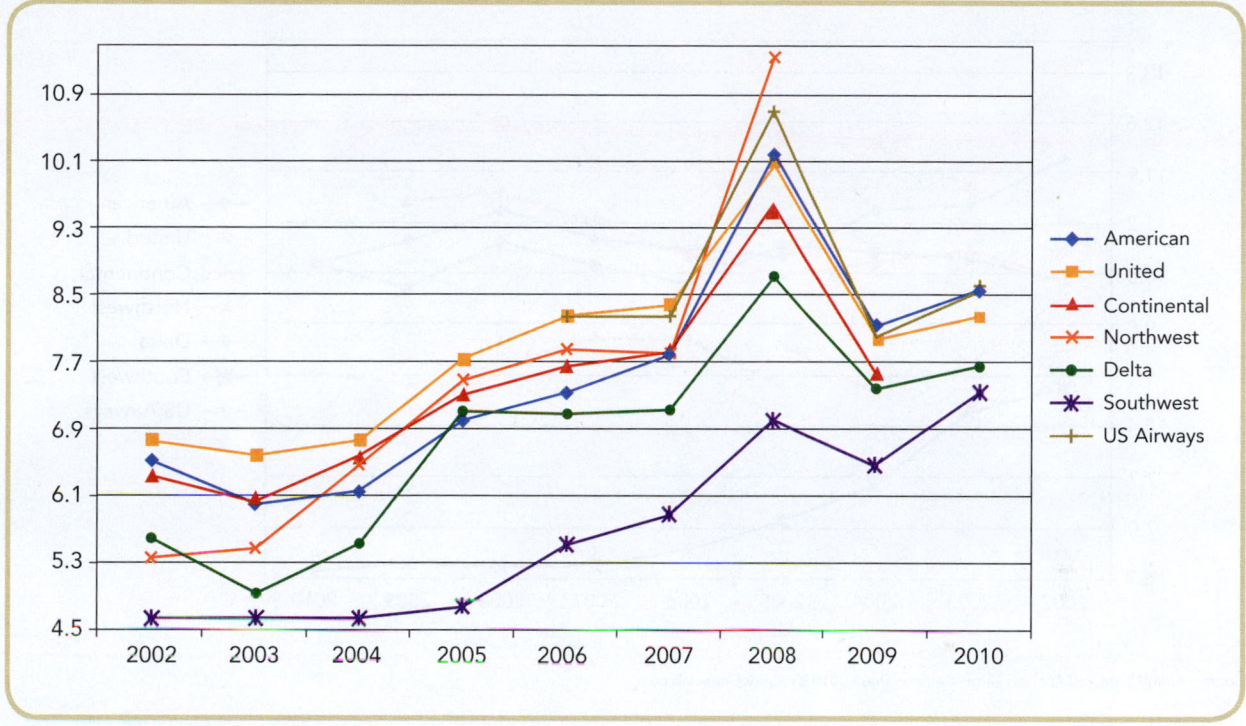

Source: Airline Data and Analysis Largest Airlines 2002-2010 by AirlineFinancials.com.

Exhibit 8 Total Labor Cost Per ASM (Cents/ASM) for Major U.S. Airlines

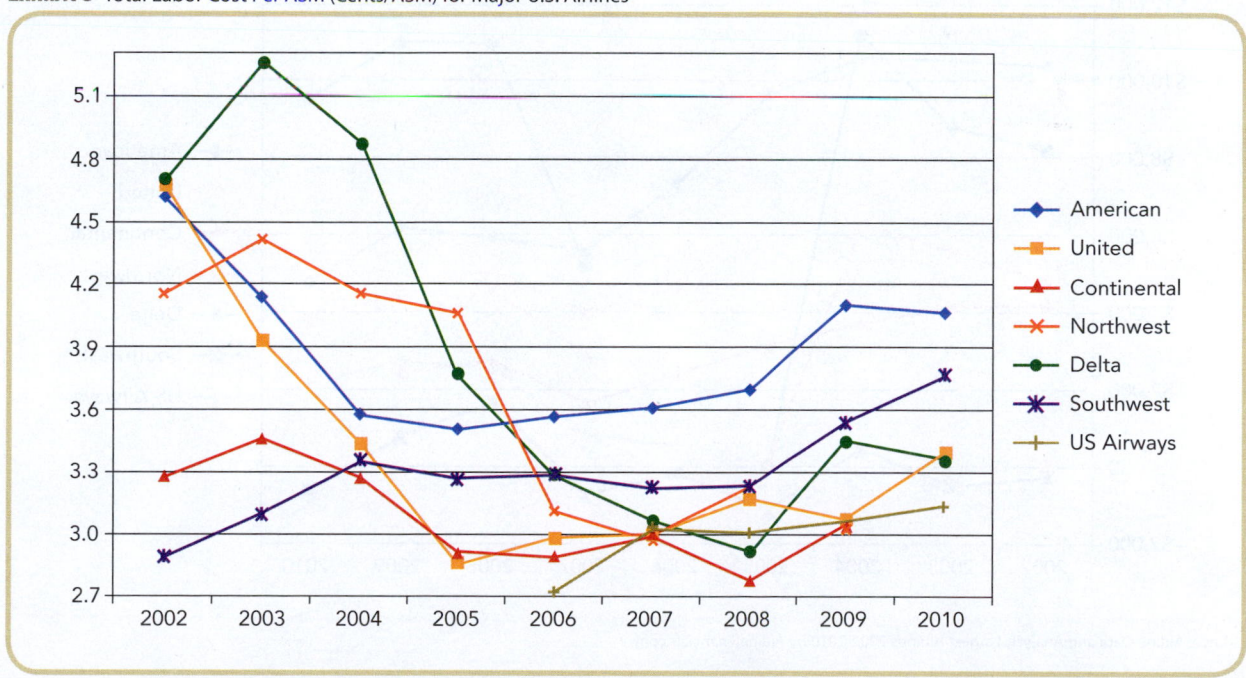

Source: Airline Data and Analysis Largest Airlines 2002-2010 by AirlineFinancials.com.

Exhibit 9 Average Employees Per Aircraft (x 10) for Major U.S. Airlines

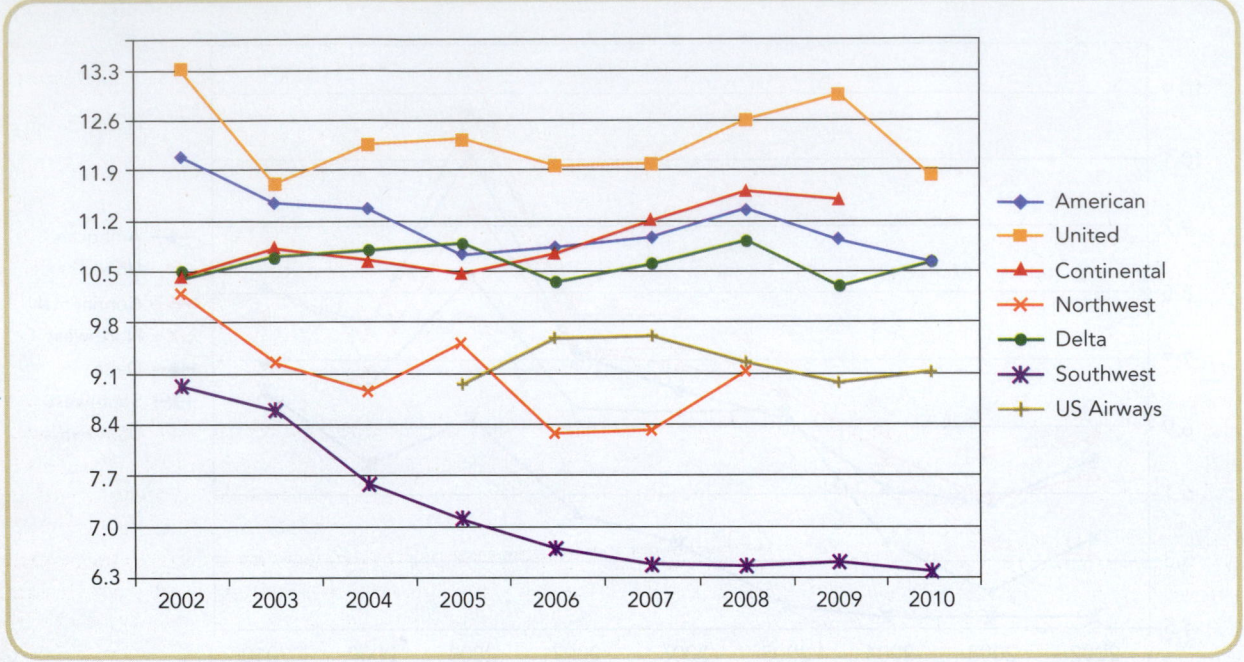

Source: Airline Data and Analysis Largest Airlines 2002-2010 by AirlineFinancials.com.

Exhibit 10 Net Debt for Major U.S. Airlines

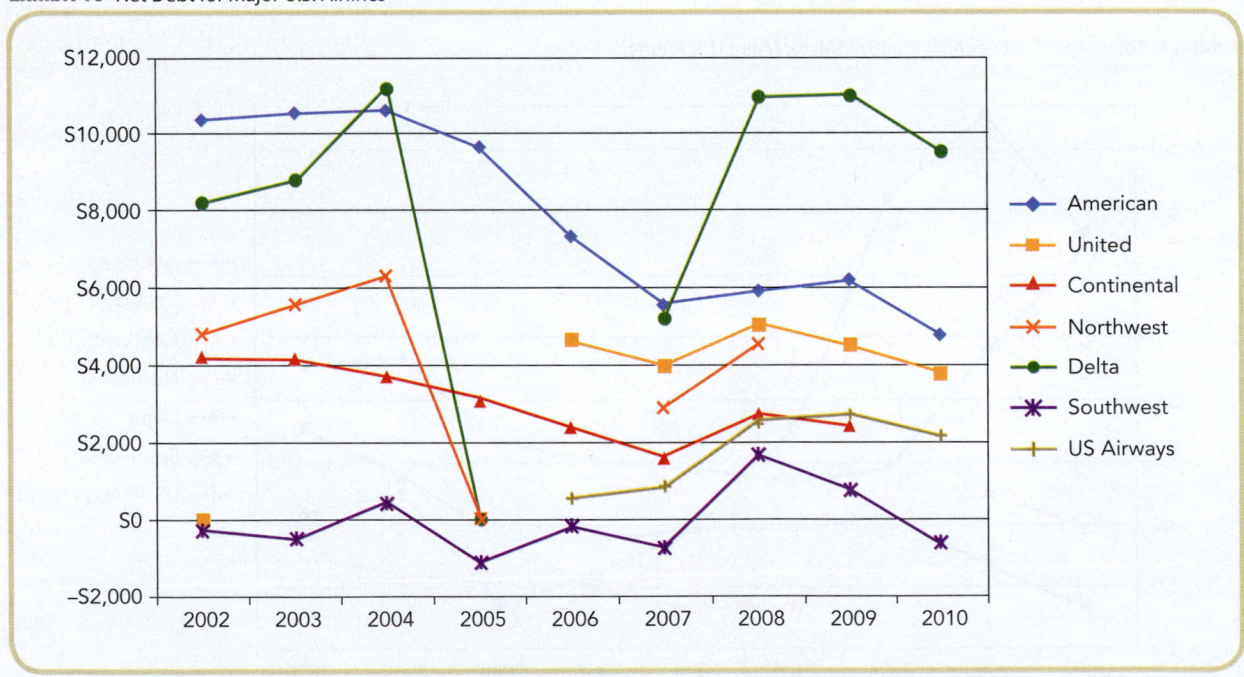

Source: Airline Data and Analysis Largest Airlines 2002-2010 by AirlineFinancials.com.

Herb Kelleher

Herb Kelleher was CEO of Southwest from 1981 to 2001. In 2001, at age 71, Kelleher stepped down as CEO but remained Chairman until 2008 when he resigned from the Board of Directors. Kelleher's leadership style combined flamboyance, fun, and a fresh, unique perspective. Kelleher played Big Daddy-O in one of the company videos, appeared as Elvis Presley in in-flight magazine advertisements, and earned the nickname "High Priest of Ha-Ha" from Fortune.[11] Although Kelleher was unconventional and a maverick in his field, he led his company to consistently new standards for itself and for the industry. Sincerely committed to his employees, Kelleher generated intense loyalty to himself and the company. His ability to remember employees' names and to ask after their families was just one way he earned respect and trust. At one point, Kelleher froze his salary for five years in response to the pilots agreeing to do the same. Often when he flew, Kelleher would help the ground crew unload bags or help the flight crew serve drinks. His humor was legendary and served as an example for his employees to join in the fun of working for Southwest. He was called "a visionary who leads by example—you have to work harder than anybody else to show them you are devoted to the business."[12]

Although Kelleher tried to downplay his personal significance to the company, especially when he gave up the CEO position in 2001, many analysts following Southwest credited the airline's success to Kelleher's unorthodox personality and engaging management style. As one analyst wrote, "The old-fashioned bond of loyalty between employees and company may have vanished elsewhere in corporate America, but it is stronger than ever at Southwest."[13] From October 1 to December 2001, Kelleher, CEO James Parker, and COO Colleen Barrett voluntarily relinquished their salaries. Gary Kelly, Southwest's former CFO, became CEO in 2004.

The Southwest Spirit

Customer service far beyond the norm in the airline industry was not unexpected at Southwest and had its own name—Positively Outrageous Service. Some examples of this service included: a gate agent volunteering to watch a dog (a Chihuahua) for two weeks when an Acapulco-bound passenger showed up at the last minute without the required dog crate; an Austin passenger who missed a connection to Houston, where he was to have a kidney transplant operation, was flown there by a Southwest pilot in his private plane. Another passenger, an elderly woman flying to Phoenix for cancer treatment, began crying because she had no family or friends at her destination. The ticket agent invited her into her home and escorted her around Phoenix for two weeks.[14]

Southwest Airlines customers were often surprised by Southwest's Spirit. On some flights, magazine pictures of gourmet meals were offered for dinner on an evening flight. Flight attendants were encouraged to have fun; songs, jokes, and humorous flight announcements were common. One flight attendant had a habit of popping out of overhead luggage compartments as passengers attempted to stow their belongings, until the day she frightened an elderly passenger who called for oxygen.[15] Herb Kelleher once served in-flight snacks dressed as the Easter Bunny.

Intense company communication and camaraderie was highly valued and essential to maintaining the esprit de corps found throughout the firm. The Southwest Spirit, as exhibited by enthusiasm and extroverted personalities, was an important element in employee screening conducted by Southwest's People Department. Employment at Southwest was highly desired. In 2012, Southwest received 114,845 job applications. Once landed, a job was secure. The airline had not laid off an employee since 1971 (the company had used some voluntary employee buyouts). Historically, employee turnover hovered around 7%, the lowest rate in the industry. In 2012, Southwest had about 46,000 employees; in 1990, Southwest had 8,600 employees and less than 6,000 in 1987.

During initial training periods, efforts were made to share and instill Southwest's unique culture. New employee orientation, known as the new-hire celebration, has in the past included Southwest's version of the Wheel of Fortune game show, scavenger hunts, and company videos, including the "Southwest Airlines Shuffle," in which each department introduced itself, rap style, and in which Kelleher appeared as Big Daddy-O. To join the People Department (i.e., Human Resources), employees required frontline customer experience.

Advanced employee training regularly occurred at the University of People at Love Field in Dallas. Various classes were offered, including team building, leadership, and cultural diversity. Newly promoted supervisors and managers attended a three-day class called "Leading with Integrity." Each department also had its own training division, focusing on technical aspects of the work. "Walk-a-Mile Day" encouraged employees from different departments to experience firsthand the day-to-day activities of their co-workers. The goal of this program was to promote respect for fellow workers while increasing awareness of the company.[16]

Employee initiative was supported by management and encouraged at all levels. For example, pilots looked for ways to conserve fuel during flights, employees proposed designs for ice storage equipment that reduced time and costs, and baggage handlers learned to place luggage with the handles facing outward to reduce unloading time.

Red hearts and Luv were central parts of the internal corporate culture, appearing throughout company literature. A mentoring program for new hires was called CoHearts. "Heroes of the Heart Awards" were given annually to one behind-the-scenes group of workers, whose department name was painted on a specially designed plane for a year. Other awards honored an employee's big mistake through the "Boner of the Year Award." When employees had a story about exceptional service to share, they were encouraged to fill out a "LUV Report."

Southwest placed great emphasis on maintaining cooperative labor relations: 82% of all employees were unionized and represented by 11 different unions. Southwest pilots belonged to an independent union and not the Airline Pilots Association, the union that represented more than 60,000 pilots. The company encouraged the unions and their negotiators to conduct employee surveys and to research their most important issues prior to each contract negotiation. At its 1994 contract discussion, the pilots proposed a 10-year contract with stock options in lieu of guaranteed pay increases over the first five years of the contract. In 1974, Southwest was the first airline to introduce employee profit sharing. Through the plan, employees owned about 10% of the company's stock.

Herb Kelleher summed up the Southwest culture and commitment to employees:

We don't use things like TQM. It's just a lot of people taking pride in what they're doing… You have to recognize that people are still the most important. How you treat them determines how they treat people on the outside… I give people the license to be themselves and motivate others in that way. We give people the opportunity to be a maverick. You don't have to fit in a constraining mold at work—you can have a good time. People respond to that.[17]

Southwest Imitators

Southwest's strategy spawned numerous imitators, most of which failed. Two of the more successful start-up firms, Midwest Express and America West, both went through Chapter 11 bankruptcy proceedings. ValuJet was grounded after its May 1996 crash in the Florida Everglades, reemerging a year later as AirTran.

The major airlines tried to compete directly with Southwest. The Shuttle by United, a so-called airline within an airline, was started in October 1994. United's objective was to create a new airline owned by United with many of the same operational elements as Southwest: a fleet of 737s, low fares, short-haul flights, and less-restrictive union rules. United saturated the West Coast corridor with short-haul flights on routes such as Oakland-Seattle, San Francisco-San Diego, and Sacramento-San Diego. The Shuttle was unable to achieve the same level of productivity as Southwest, and in 2001 United discontinued Shuttle service and folded the remaining flights into its regular service. US Airways did the same with its Metrojet discount service. In 2003, United started a new discount carrier called TED.

Some of the attempts to imitate Southwest were almost comical. Continental Lite (CALite) was an effort by Continental Airlines to develop a low-cost service and revive the company's fortunes after coming out of bankruptcy in April 1993. In March 1994, Continental increased CALite service to 875 daily flights. Continental soon encountered major operational problems with its new strategy.[18] With its fleet of 16 different planes, mechanical delays disrupted turnaround times. Various pricing strategies were unsuccessful. The company was ranked last among the major carriers for on-time service, and complaints soared by 40%. In January 1995, Continental announced that it would reduce its capacity by 10% and eliminate 4,000 jobs. By mid-1995, Continental's CALite service had been largely discontinued. In October 1995, Continental's CEO was ousted.

In East Asia in 2013, the airline-within-an-airline strategy was being used by many of the large carriers such as Singapore Airlines and Thai Airways as a means of competing against the many new start-ups in that region.

A Successful Start-Up: JetBlue Airways

Morris Air, patterned after Southwest, was the only airline Southwest had acquired. Prior to the acquisition, Morris Air flew Boeing 737s on point-to-point routes, operated in a different part of the U.S. than Southwest, and was profitable. When Morris Air was acquired by Southwest in December 1993, seven new markets were added to Southwest's system. In 1999, Morris Air's former president, David Neeleman, announced plans for JetBlue Airways, a new airline based at New York's JFK Airport. JetBlue had a successful IPO in April 2002, with the stock rising 70% on the first day of trading. JetBlue had a geographically diversified flight schedule that included both short-haul and long-haul routes. Although JetBlue was viewed as a low fare carrier, the airline emphasized various service attributes, such as leather seats, free LiveTV (a 24-channel satellite TV service with programming provided by DirecTV) and preassigned seating.

In 2013, JetBlue served more than 75 cities in the United States, Mexico, the Caribbean, and South America with more than 15,000 employees. Jet Blue had a fleet of 127 Airbus A320 aircraft and 54 Embraer 190 regional jet aircraft. JetBlue revenue in 2012 was $5.0 billion, about one third that of Southwest. The company was profitable in the three years 2010 through 2012.

Southwest Expansion

Southwest grew steadily over the years but the growth was highly controlled. New airports were carefully selected and only a few new cities were added each year. As Kelleher wrote to his employees in 1993, "Southwest has had more opportunities for growth than it has airplanes. Yet, unlike other airlines, it has avoided the trap of growing beyond its means. Whether you are talking with an officer or a ramp agent, employees just don't seem to be enamored of the idea that bigger is better."[19]

In October 1996, with the initiation of flights to Providence, Rhode Island, Southwest entered the northeast market. The entry into the northeast region of the U.S. was, in many respects, a logical move for Southwest. The northeast was the most densely populated area of the country and the only major region where Southwest did not compete. New England could provide a valuable source of passengers to Florida's warmer winter climates. Southwest's entry into Florida was exceeding initial estimates.

Despite the large potential market, the northeast offered a new set of challenges for Southwest. Airport congestion and air-traffic-control delays could prevent efficient operations, lengthening turnaround time at airport gates and wreaking havoc on frequent flight scheduling. Inclement weather posed additional challenges for both air service and car travel to airports. Nevertheless, Southwest continued to add new northeast cities. A few years later, Southwest was flying to various northeast airports, including Long Island, New Hampshire, and Hartford. In 2004, Southwest began flying to Philadelphia, which was the first major northeast market entry.

In 2013, the company planned to add two new states (Maine and Kansas) and seven new U.S. cities to its network. Excluding AirTran service, Southwest had not entered any markets outside the domestic United States, but CEO Gary Kelly publicly stated that "opportunities for growth now lie beyond U.S. borders."[20]

The AirTran Deal

In September 2010, Southwest announced that it would buy AirTran Airways for $1.4 billion. The acquisition would give Southwest access to more than 30 new markets, including Atlanta and several tourist destinations in Mexico and the Caribbean. The deal strengthened Southwest's position in the Southeast and on the East Coast. AirTran had a lower cost structure than Southwest, and integrating AirTran into Southwest's operations and culture could prove challenging. Most of AirTran's fleets were Boeing 717s, whereas Southwest only flew 737s. AirTran had international routes and offered first-class seats. Complicating the integration would be Southwest's limited experience with acquisitions.

Perhaps the most difficult challenge would be ensuring that the acquisition did not change or weaken the Southwest culture. According to Southwest's pilots' union president, "The Achilles' heel of this transaction is how our company will be able to maintain our culture, and keep it alive for the next 40 years."[21] In 2013, the integration was well under way and Southwest forecasted pre-tax annual synergies from the deal of $400 million in the current fiscal year.

Future Challenges

Although Southwest was profitable and had a strong financial position, competition was stiff. The newly merged legacy carriers were expected to become more efficient, and smaller players like JetBlue and Alegiant had lower costs than Southwest. While Southwest's employee productivity remained high, its operating costs were rising. The company had the highest salaries for pilots of narrow-body jets, and salaries for mechanics and flight attendants were among the highest in the industry.

Clearly, the future promised dramatic changes to airline industry structure. Would Southwest be able to maintain its position as America's most prosperous airline? Could Southwest complete the AirTran acquisition and still ensure that customer service and company performance were satisfactory? Could Southwest grow profitably in international markets? Would the major airlines finally learn how to compete on cost with companies like Southwest and JetBlue?

According to CEO Gary Kelly, "We still have an underdog mentality. It's not a comfortable country-club environment for us… We're still a maverick."[22]

NOTES

1. P. S. Dempsey, "Transportation Deregulation: On a Collision Course," *Transportation Law Journal*, 13, 1984, p. 329.

2. W. Goralski, "Deregulation Deja Vu," *Telephony*, June 17, 1996, pp. 32–36.

3. Office of Inspector General, *Aviation Industry Performance: A Review of the Airline Industry, 2008-2011*, September 24, 2011.

4. K. Freiberg and J. Freiberg, *Nuts: Southwest Airlines' Crazy Recipe for Business and Personal Success* (Austin, TX: Bard Press, 1996), pp. 14–21.

5. Ibid., p. 31.

6. Ibid., p. 55.

7. Herb Kelleher, @ www.iflyswa.com/cgi-bin/imagemap/swagate 530.85.

8. Freiberg and Freiberg, p. 29.

9. "The 25 Most Influential Executives of 2007," *Business Travel News*, February 4, 2008.

10. http://www.zagat.com/airlines.

11. K. Labich, "Is Herb Kelleher America's Best CEO?" *Fortune*, May 2, 1994, p. 45.

12. "24th Annual CEO Survey: Herb Kelleher, Flying His Own Course," *IW*, November 20, 1995, p. 23.

13. Labich, p. 46.

14. *IW*, p. 23.

15. B. O'Brian, "Flying on the Cheap," *Wall Street Journal*, October 26, 1992, p. A1.

16. A. Malloy, "Counting the Intangibles," *Computerworld*, June 1996, pp. 32–33.

17. H. Lancaster, "Herb Kelleher Has One Main Strategy: Treat Employees Well," *Wall Street Journal*, August 31, 1999, p. B1.

18. B. O'Brian, "Heavy Going: Continental's CALite Hits Some Turbulence in Battling Southwest," *Wall Street Journal*, January 10, 1995, pp. A1, A16.

19. Freiberg and Freiberg, p. 61.

20. http://www.southwest.com/assets/pdfs/about-southwest/garys-greeting.pdf.

21. Jad Mouawad, "Pushing 40, Southwest Is Still Playing the Rebel," *New York Times*, Nov. 20, 2010.

22. Ibid.

CASE 17

Starbucks Corporation: The New S-Curves

Despite being a public company for 20 years, Starbucks is in the early days of its growth and development.[1]

—Howard Schultz, chairman and CEO of Starbucks

By the end of fiscal year (FY) 2010, Starbucks' painful, three-year transformation agenda, which included closing more than 900 stores, terminating 18,700 jobs, replacing the senior leadership team, and implementing new Lean store practices to achieve operational excellence, was essentially complete. Starting with the return in 2008 of Starbucks founder and board chairman Howard Schultz as its president and CEO, Starbucks had pulled itself back from the brink of "destruction" after an unsustainable store expansion strategy coupled with a global economic recession had the company's future looking uncertain and its stock losing half its value. Finishing FY2010 with a record $10.7 billion in revenue and a first-ever shareholder dividend, Starbucks began FY2011 poised to celebrate its 40th anniversary by focusing on a new blueprint for growth described by Schultz: "Sourcing, roasting, and serving high-quality coffee will remain our core, but we are also pursuing sustainable, profitable growth with a more diversified, multichannel and multibrand business model."[2]

That growth would be enabled by a new organizational and leadership system supported by lessons the company learned during the transformation. Schultz outlined those lessons at the end of his second book:

Grow with discipline. Balance intuition with rigor. Innovate around the core. Don't embrace the status quo. Find new ways to see. Never expect a silver bullet. Get your hands dirty. Listen with empathy and over communicate with transparency. Tell your story, refusing to let others define you. Use authentic experiences to inspire. Stick to your values, they are your foundation. Hold people accountable but give them the tools to succeed. Make the tough choices; it's how you execute that counts. Be decisive in times of crisis. Be nimble. Find truth in trials and lessons in mistakes. Be responsible for what you see, hear, and do. Believe.[3]

By the end of FY2013, it looked as if the new growth strategy and system were paying off. In the United States, comparable-store sales had risen by 7% or greater in 15 consecutive quarters on the strength of a number of new products and customer service–enhancing innovations such as mobile payments integrated with the company's longstanding gift and loyalty card programs. The evolving Starbucks channel development segment had grown to $1.4 billion, and to boost its business both inside and outside its cafés, the company had acquired three new brands: a premium fresh juice company, a bakery, and a purveyor of premium loose-leaf tea.

Starbucks shares surged by 46% in FY2013, while the Standard & Poor's 500 Index advanced 30% during that time. By Q1 2014, Starbucks stock had reached an all-time high of just over $80—a more than 800% increase over a low of just over $8 during the company's downturn in 2009.

Still the question remained whether the company could consistently maintain this phase of rapid growth in a more disciplined manner than it had pursued during its previous phase of rapid growth, which had ended in financial crisis and a souring of the brand that destroyed material shareholder value. What were the potential risks of another aggressive growth implosion? Could the company pursue so many diverse products and channels without damaging its core coffee business? Had the company created an internal growth system and organizational environment to support this new surge and preserve the differentiating essence of Starbucks?

New Products and Categories

To signal this new era of multichannel, multibrand growth, Starbucks dropped the words "Starbucks Coffee" from its green mermaid logo in 2011. Although single sales of premium coffee and coffee drinks in U.S. bricks-and-mortar retail shops continued to drive the majority of its revenue between 2010 and 2013, the company focused on diversifying its product offerings to appeal to changing preferences, enhancing the customer experience, and expanding internationally. Because approximately half of all sales at Starbucks stores occurred before 11:00 a.m., the company also set its sights on maximizing its global storefronts and stretching its goal to be the third-most-common place to frequent (after work and home) in the morning and during the lunch and evening hours as well.

Super-Premium Juice

One of the company's first moves toward leveraging its core retail competencies with new products and new categories was to go after the $50 billion health and wellness industry. For those consumers looking for options beyond high-calorie lattes, Frappuccinos, and blueberry muffins, Starbucks first began focusing on healthier packaged fare by offering Naked Juice beverages and Kind all-natural snack bars in its coffee stores. Then, in 2011, the company laid out $30 million in cash for Evolution Fresh, Inc., a California-based juicery started by one of the original founders of Naked Juice. It was one of the few remaining juiceries that still cracked, peeled, squeezed, and pressed its own raw fruits and vegetables using an innovative pasteurization process that preserved more nutrients while enabling production scaling.

At the time of the acquisition, many in the media questioned the move into premium juice and wondered whether Starbucks was moving too far from its core business. In one such article, Schultz responded to the skepticism:

Well, you have to ask: What is the core?...We have 40-plus years of acquiring real estate and designing and operating stores all over the world. We understand how to elevate and romanticize an experience built around a beverage. And we think we can do that again on a platform of health and wellness and elevate the nutritious value of what fresh fruit and vegetables can be in a world that is longing for educational tools to eat and live healthier.[4]

Starbucks moved quickly to ramp up the new brand. By the end of FY2012, Starbucks had opened four Evolution Fresh stores, which sold vegan and vegetarian dishes as well as premium fresh juice. It also was selling ready-to-drink Evolution Fresh juice in 2,200 of its Starbucks cafés—replacing the Naked Juice previously sold—as well as in 1,500 supermarkets and other convenience stores. By the end of FY2013, the locations numbered 8,000, and the company had built a new, state-of-the-art juicery in California to quadruple production.

Better food

Pairing food items with its high-quality beverages had long been the bane of Starbucks. Inconsistent quality from outside suppliers did little to boost sales or attract additional customers, and unpleasant aromas often annoyed the coffee purists. Generally, only one in three Starbucks transactions involved food. Food sales improved somewhat during the transformation as a result of efforts by the company to improve quality and offer healthier and more savory fare such as the Starbucks bistro box, which contained such items as hard-boiled eggs, cheese, crackers, vegetables, and fruit. Food items accounted for 19% of revenue in 2010—up from 13% during the downturn.

But food sales remained flat for 2011 and 2012 and only comprised 30% of store transactions during that time, which was why many industry analysts were skeptical to dubious about the company's decision to shell out $100 million in cash in 2012 to acquire Bay Bread, LLC, and its 19-store La Boulange Café & Bakery chain, located in San Francisco. By the end of FY2013, however, La Boulange croissants, sweet and savory pastries, breads, and muffins, all served warm, occupied bakery display cases in 3,500 U.S. Starbucks stores, and overall food sales had increased to 20% of the retail product mix at company-operated stores.

During the earnings call for Q1 2014, Starbucks CFO Troy Alstead stated that food had become a "disproportionate driver" of same-store sales and that the sale of croissants alone had doubled since the La Boulange upgrade. The company planned for the full La Boulange rollout in all U.S. company-operated stores by the end of 2014.[5]

Starbucks was looking for ways to not only improve quality and thus drive sales, but also to reduce costs and continue to boost profits by cutting out the middleman for its packaged food items. According to Daniel Lubetzky, founder of Kind Healthy Snacks, which made the Kind snack bars first sold in Starbucks coffee shops, Starbucks had long been trying to acquire his company or negotiate a deal for a private-label snack bar.[6] Either option would have reduced Starbucks's costs and increased its margins, but Lubetzky refused. As a result, in late summer 2013, Starbucks nixed its relationship with Kind Healthy Snacks and rolled out its own Evolution Harvest fruit-and-nut bars for sale at its cafés as well as nationally at Whole Foods Market.

Also in 2013, Starbucks announced that it had entered into a multiyear strategic agreement with Danone to develop an exclusive line of Evolution Fresh, Inspired by Danone, fresh dairy products, starting with a Greek yogurt parfait to be sold exclusively in Starbucks stores in 2014 and expanded to grocery store distribution in 2015.

While clearly working to boost same-store sales by increasing its offerings, Starbucks maintained focus on its core morning crowd, so as not to cede market share to other quick-service chains such as McDonald's and Burger King, which were striving to increase breakfast-hour sales. In March 2014, Starbucks launched four new and improved breakfast sandwiches: ham and swiss on a croissant; spinach, sun-dried tomatoes, and cheese on ciabatta; egg and cheddar on toast; and a lower-calorie egg white, bacon, and cheese on an English muffin. To industry analysts, the improved low-calorie breakfast sandwich was a direct response to McDonald's recently launched Egg White Delight McMuffin.[7] Starbucks planned to test similar upgrades to café lunch sandwiches during the summer of 2014.[8]

Shortly after the La Boulange rollout, Starbucks again proved its commitment and responsiveness to its core customer base when, after numerous complaints, it brought back the popular pumpkin and lemon loaves that had been pushed out by the new La Boulange menu.

Another wrinkle of the rollout—long lines and wait times—appeared more ominous, however. Many observers thought the delay was due to the new requirement of having the baristas heat the baked goods before serving, but it may have been the coincidental implementation of a new cost-cutting store management process that was to blame. The process, called Playbook, was based on Lean assembly-line production practices designed to maximize efficiency and speed, and it required store employees to maintain rigid schedules and stay on singular tasks. For example, a store employee might be tasked with cleaning tables at specific times, thus affecting the employee's flexibility to help on the second register during rush times. Many baristas complained on the Internet that Playbook prevented customer engagement, destroyed employee morale, and actually compromised and delayed service.[9]

The national media began taking notice of Playbook in 2010, when customer backlash regarding Starbucks's more mechanical, posttransformation focus on operational excellence first started. *The Wall Street Journal* reported that in an attempt to bring back the perception of an artisanal coffee shop, corporate headquarters was telling baristas to actually slow down their drink-making pace by preparing no more than two drinks at a time and steaming milk separately for each drink, which further exacerbated delays.[10]

The question remained whether these hiccups in the company's new system to support its growth strategy would prove to be temporary growing pains or early indications of more systemic future problems.

Tea

Starbucks made its first major move into branded tea in 1999, when it acquired the Tazo brand of bagged tea to be sold in Starbucks stores as well as through grocery stores and related channels. It also developed Starbucks- and Tazo-branded single-serve products, but it wasn't until 2012 that the company made another major move into the estimated $90 billion tea industry, and this one was meant to be a game changer. In its biggest acquisition to date, Starbucks paid a whopping $620 million in cash for Teavana Holdings, Inc., a purveyor of high-end loose-leaf teas and tea-making products that had 300 shopping mall locations. The company said it planned to expand Teavana's mall-based shops worldwide as well as develop stand-alone neighborhood tea shops with retail components, tea bars, and food menus. Schultz said: "We believe the tea category is ripe for reinvention and rapid growth. The Teavana acquisition now positions us to disrupt and lead, just as we did with espresso starting three decades ago."[11]

Schultz also explained that in much the same way that the company's Seattle's Best Coffee brand provided a lower price counterpoint to the higher-end Starbucks brand as a means of expanding the company's customer base, together with the Tazo brand, the Teavana acquisition would enable a two-tier approach to the immense and rapidly growing tea category. While Tazo would continue its pursuit of the less expensive bagged-tea market in grocery stores, Teavana would attract customers of premium loose-leaf tea.[12] As further proof of its dual strategy and commitment to both brands, in January 2014, Starbucks launched three new organic Tazo teas—Organic Earl Grey Blanc, Organic Earl Grey Noir, and Organic Sultry Strawberry—for sale exclusively at Whole Foods.

In 2013, Starbucks unveiled its design concept for the new stand-alone Teavana shops in two stores, including a flagship Teavana Fine Teas + Tea Bar in New York City and one in Seattle. The company said it would also debut Teavana-branded teas at Starbucks stores in 2014. To further illustrate his commitment and confidence in Starbucks's tea strategy, Schultz welcomed a surprise guest at the end of the company's 2014 annual shareholders meeting—celebrity talk-show host and philanthropist Oprah Winfrey, who announced her endorsement of Teavana. Winfrey and Starbucks had collaborated on a new tea blend called Teavana Oprah Chai Tea that debuted at Starbucks and Teavana stores later that spring. In another dose of goodwill for the Starbucks brand, Winfrey announced that her proceeds would be donated to three youth-education charities she supported.

Never before had Winfrey agreed to endorse a commercial product in this manner, although she'd been pursued relentlessly for years. She told Starbucks shareholders it was because both tea and Starbucks "nurture the human spirit" that she took the plunge. Undoubtedly, it also helped that Winfrey and Schultz had become good friends since he had appeared on Winfrey's "Super Soul Sunday" show to discuss, in part, his social agenda for Starbucks.

During the spring and summer of 2014, the company expanded its Teavana-branded offerings with new shaken iced teas and new chai flavors at Starbucks stores and the opening of a new Teavana Fine Teas + Tea Bar location with new menu items in Los Angeles.

Starbucks Evenings

In 2010, Starbucks began an experiment to offer beer and wine after 4:00 p.m. in one nonbranded Seattle location. By the end of 2013, the company had expanded the project into a branded program called Starbucks Evenings in other cities such as Atlanta, Chicago, Los Angeles, Portland, other Seattle areas, and in the terminals at the Los Angeles and Washington Dulles International Airports. The company added the savory and sweet evening menu items bacon-wrapped dates and truffle macaroni and cheese to accompany the alcoholic beverages, which, by the end of FY2013, were sold in 23 select stores. With the help of a certified sommelier added to the ranks at Starbucks headquarters, the company devised individual wine and beer lists for the Starbucks Evenings in different regions.

Many industry analysts announced their skepticism about the potential success of the Starbucks Evenings concept, citing the complex web of differing state and local alcohol regulations as one reason why the expansion would prove more trouble than it was worth.[13] In contrast to the company's other aggressive steps to expand its food and drink offerings, however, Starbucks's strategy on this front remained relatively limited. Although Starbucks stated that additional stores would offer Starbucks Evenings "soon," the company also announced that it had no plans to add the adult beverages and evening menu beyond a "small selection of stores."[14]

Carbonated beverages

During the summer of 2013, Starbucks began testing its own carbonated, handcrafted, caffeine-free cold beverage called Fizzio, in select U.S. and Chinese markets. Based on the success of the experiment, Starbucks planned to roll out three flavors of Fizzio—Golden Ginger Ale, Spiced Root Beer, and Lemon Ale—in June 2014 in more than one-third of its U.S. company-operated locations. The company planned to debut more regionally derived flavors of Fizzio in locations in Singapore, Korea, and several Chinese cities as the 2014 summer progressed.[15]

Keeping Up with Coffee and the Core Business

In addition to attacking all the new strategies to expand product and menu offerings during this period, Starbucks continued to invest in its core business and strived to attract more customers and changing tastes. In 2012, Starbucks introduced Blonde Roast to appeal to the estimated 40% of U.S. consumers who preferred a lighter roast, many of whom had criticized Starbucks for its traditionally darker roasts by referring to it as "Charbucks."[16]

In the same year, Starbucks tapped into the $8 billion energy-drink market and the base of consumers who preferred a cold, fruity jolt to a warm coffee buzz by launching Starbucks Refreshers in two flavors: Cool Lime and Very Berry Hibiscus. The drinks derived their "energy" (i.e., caffeine) from flavorless green coffee extract made from unroasted beans. Julie Felss Masino, Starbucks's vice president of global beverage, said that this use of green coffee extract, which already was being used in cosmetics and pharmaceuticals, amounted to a "breakthrough innovation" for Starbucks.[17]

In addition to handcrafted versions prepared over ice in Starbucks stores, the company began marketing Refreshers in a ready-to-make powdered form (alongside its Starbucks VIA Ready Brew instant coffee brand) as a carbonated version in cans in three new flavors: Strawberry Lemonade, Raspberry Pomegranate, and Orange Melon.

For the traditional Starbucks consumer, the company also added more seasonal coffee beverages, expanded the line of its signature Macchiato to include a vanilla version (to join the original caramel and recently added hazelnut versions), and in 2010 started its Starbucks Reserve coffees—exotic and limited blends available at select stores by the half-pound or cup using the patented single-cup Clover brewing system, which Starbucks had acquired in 2008. Approximately 500 coffeehouse locations in 25 U.S. markets and 10 international markets offered the Clover brewing system technology in 2013.[18] The company announced plans to double its Clover locations by the end of 2014 and to introduce 14 different reserve coffees per year to its growing base of customers interested in unique, personalized coffee options.[19] The company also planned to continue innovating with the

Clover system as part of its Internet-of-Things strategy by developing a process for keeping track of customers' preferences and settings.[20]

Additional investments to its core coffee business during this time included developing support centers for coffee farmers in Manizales, Columbia, and Yunnan, China, in 2012, and a new coffee-farming research and development center in Costa Rica.

Seattle's Best Coffee

Another chapter in the Starbucks posttransformation growth story involved the Seattle's Best Coffee brand, which the company had acquired in 2003 and then essentially ignored while the former rival remained in approximately 500 now-defunct Borders bookstores. Leading the charge on a new branding strategy was Michelle Gass, a veteran of the company who had been Schultz's chief strategist during the transformation agenda and had had major success both with marketing the Frappuccino in 1996 and introducing the Starbucks VIA Ready Brew instant coffee in 2009. After turning what was once a taboo practice in Starbucks circles (instant coffee) into $100 million in sales within 10 months of VIA's national launch, Gass said that Schultz called her into his office and stated, "I want you to turn [Seattle's Best] into a $1 billion business. You can do whatever you want."[21]

As president of Seattle's Best, Gass's approach was to take the brand to market through partnerships with Delta, Subway, Burger King, Royal Caribbean cruise line, AMC Theaters, Rubi Coffee Kiosks, and numerous other hotels, restaurants, airlines, convenience shops, college campuses, and grocery stores. Within a year, the brand expanded from 3,000 distribution points to more than 50,000. Starbucks decreased the Seattle's Best packaged line to five core offerings and revamped the packaging with new, brighter colors to replace the brown bags.

Although Starbucks never publicly admitted that reinvigorating the Seattle's Best Coffee brand at its lower price point and partnering with fast-casual retailers such as Burger King was a direct counter to McDonald's roll-out of its McCafé brand of coffee drinks the previous year, it seemed to others that Starbucks' newest coffee rival was at least part of the story.[22]

After barely two years, the Seattle's Best Coffee transformation was deemed, by the company at least, to be a success, and Schultz again reassigned Gass to rescue another business line—the company's EMEA (Europe, the Middle East, and Africa) business division headquartered in London; however, by the end of FY2013, the Seattle's Best Coffee brand had not reached $1 billion in revenue. For financial reporting purposes, the brand was included along with Teavana, Evolution Fresh, and Digital Ventures under All Other Segments in the company's 2013 annual report. As a group, the segment generated $393.7 million, a $185 million increase over the previous year, which the company attributed to incremental revenues from the Teavana acquisition during Q2 of that year.

Starbucks's continued commitment to growing the business was illustrated during Q2 FY2014, when it announced new Seattle's Best Coffee's "house" and "breakfast blend" packaged varieties as well as a new bag design that represented a return to the more subdued colors of its old packaging. In an interview with Bloomberg, Jennifer Dimaris, the vice president of brand management for Seattle's Best Coffee, explained that the new varieties were replacing the previous varieties (labeled "one" and "two") because the lighter roasts, number-ranking system, and neon packaging weren't resonating enough with all customers.[23]

Dimaris also explained that these latest pushes into the grocery aisles for Seattle's Best Coffee were part of the company's "investing heavily" in the supermarket and retail store side of the business.[24] The same was true for nearly all the new products previously described. Yet Starbucks maintained a focus on shoring up its core retail coffee shop presence and customer experience, as well on expanding its storefronts internationally.

Store Improvement, Development, and Expansion

Starbucks' earlier, destructive growth strategy aimed at global domination was an attempt to commoditize the premium coffee shop—to combine ubiquity with higher-quality, pricier product offerings. As the company's dramatic, pretransformation growth implosion showed, that plan proved too elusive. By 2013, the company still aimed to be "the leading retailer and brand of coffee" in its target markets but this time in a "disciplined manner by selectively opening additional stores in new and existing markets, as well as increasing sales in existing stores."[25] By mid-2014, the company had expanded to 20,000 stores in 64 countries and was serving more than 70 million customers per week,[26] and yet the company claimed that by still only accounting for a small share of the total "global coffee occasions," it remained "significantly under-stored" and ripe for expansion in several markets, including North America, China, Brazil, and India.[27]

As evidence that the company had further honed its best-in-class store development and construction expertise, company executives pointed to a sales-to-investment ratio of more than 2:1, a return on investment in excess of 50%, and first-year average unit volumes of more than 1.2 million, all while Starbucks continued to deliver an "enhanced" customer experience.[28] After rolling out new Lean store techniques to cut costs during the transformation, now the company was highly focused on boosting its brand and generating customer loyalty by enhancing customer service and convenience, particularly with digital innovations such as free high-speed Wi-Fi and mobile payments. The company also wanted to dazzle with high-minded design and a new nod to regional and cultural differentiation, both domestically and internationally. The company divided its core coffee retail business into global divisions—Americas, China/Asia-Pacific (CAP), and EMEA—and developed 18 design studios with 200 designers around the world to better customize its stores and source locally.

Rather than locating a Starbucks on every corner (sometimes two), now the company focused on authenticity and a neighborhood feel. Building on its nonbranded neighborhood shop experiments in Seattle during the transformation, the design team focused on adding unique and local aesthetic touches (e.g., a chandelier made from old brass instruments at a New Orleans shop). The company even designed its seating arrangements to fit cultural norms, placing long communal tables in urban U.S. areas where strangers think nothing of sitting together and using more single stools for the impromptu group gatherings common in China and Mexico.[29]

Although massive customization still wasn't scalable and truly customized designs were limited to select, high-earning flagship locations such as Downtown Disney and Dazaifu, Japan, the company experimented with scaling regional designs—for example, using lighter flooring in sunny locales. In a 2011 interview with the *McKinsey Quarterly*, Schultz said:

What we're trying to do is create a balance between this being a Starbucks store with all the trappings and, at the same time, a very deep level of sensitivity to local relevancy. That's hard to do when you're all over the world in 55 countries. The reason it's working is that we're decentralizing and, for the first time, trusting that the people in the marketplace know better than the people in Seattle.[30]

In 2011, Starbucks rolled out a new prototype drive-through-only retail store with a walk-up window made from refurbished shipping containers in Tukwila, Washington. By early 2014, there were several such locations in the United States. In its Q1 FY2013 earnings call, the company announced that more than half of the 1,500 new U.S. stores the company planned to open during the

next five years would have a drive-through component,[31] and in its Q2 FY14 earnings call, Schultz said the company's new class of "highly profitable drive-thrus represents a significant growth opportunity for us and continues to remain a focal point of our store development efforts."[32]

The Americas and Digital Ventures

The Americas remained the company's largest segment during this period, comprising 74% of revenue in 2013. A Seattle-based blogger estimated in 2012 that more than 80% of the U.S. population lived within 20 miles of a Starbucks location.[33] A total of 680 net new stores were opened in the United States in 2013.[34] Although that didn't exactly cover every street corner in America, it did illustrate that market saturation seemed closer than ever and that the company's prospect for growing through the addition of more brick-and-mortar storefronts was limited. Still, the company announced plans to increase net U.S. store openings by 13% by 2017.[35]

Comparable-store sales rose over this same period, but average ticket increases from such things as additional food items only accounted for one-third of that growth, meaning that increased traffic was the major driver. Part of that traffic increase resulted from steps to appeal to consumers during the lunch and evening hours with additional product offerings (Table 1).

The increase in traffic was likely due to improvements in customer service as well, or what Starbucks described in its 2013 annual report as the "Starbucks Experience." Boosting that experience were a robust loyalty program and major investments in its Digital Ventures business, including the addition of free and unlimited Wi-Fi in 2010 and mobile payments in 2011.

Yet by the end of Q1 FY14, analysts were already starting to downgrade their "strong buy" ratings of the company's stock because of a slowdown in the growth of U.S. comparable-store sales to the midsingle digits—down from 7% in 2013 and 8% in 2012 and 2011, respectively. The company attributed the slight drop in growth to increasing

Table 1 Percentage Change in Comparable-Store Sales for the Americas Segment*

Fiscal Year Ended	2013	2012	2011	2010	2009
Sales growth	7%	8%	8%	7%	(6%)
Change in transaction	5%	6%	5%	3%	(4)%
Change in ticket	2%	2%	2%	3%	(2)%

* Includes Starbucks company-operated stores open 13 months or longer.
Data source: Starbucks annual report, 2013.

e-commerce and less foot traffic in brick-and-mortar retail shops during the 2013 holiday season. During the company's earnings call for that quarter, Schultz said: "No longer are many retailers only required to compete with stores on the other side of the street. They are now required to compete with stores on the other side of the country. Navigating the seismic shift will continue to be very, very difficult for me."[36]

Schultz also described how the unique Starbucks Experience, robust My Starbucks Rewards loyalty program, and ongoing digital investments would offset expected ongoing losses in traditional retail traffic.[37]

One of those investments was a new partnership with Google in 2013 to increase the speed of the Wi-Fi offered in Starbucks cafés to 10 times faster than the previous service powered by AT&T. In announcing plans to roll out the new Google service in all of its U.S. locations over the next 18 months, Starbucks's chief digital officer (CDO), Adam Brotman, said, "We're moving to much more of a streaming world across all media types."[38]

Increasing bandwidth to offer better web downloading and streaming for store customers was just one of many initiatives of the Digital Ventures group spearheaded by Brotman, who had joined Starbucks in 2009 to help form the group. The group's other initiatives during this period included creating mobile payment applications for iOS and Android; developing an in-house e-commerce platform and a branded Wi-Fi strategy featuring the Starbucks Digital Network (a page of original news and entertainment content to which users were directed when accessing the Wi-Fi at Starbucks); developing a social media engagement platform; and building the My Starbucks loyalty programs globally.

The group launched the mobile payment application in the United States in 2011. Then in 2012, Starbucks entered into a partnership agreement with mobile payments start-up Square to cover all the company's U.S. debit and credit card transactions. The agreement also gave Starbucks customers the option to use Square's mobile app, which through GPS technology allowed a customer to pay simply by saying his or her name. By the end of FY2013, Starbucks was processing 4 million mobile transactions per week, for a total of 14% of all U.S. store sales.[39] Rather than offering a mere convenience for customers, Brotman said the purpose of the app was to "enhanc[e] the experience and the relationship with the customer."[40] The application also enabled Starbucks to leverage its customer loyalty program by offering discounts, coupons, and an easy way for customers to reload their My Starbucks cards and rack up additional digital rewards called Stars, all of which made

the loyalty program even stickier. During the 2013 holiday season alone, 1.5 million new members registered their Starbucks gift cards and joined the My Starbucks Rewards loyalty program for the first time.[41] The mobile application also provided a direct marketing link to customers. In 2014, analysts predicted that the mobile payments would be a game changer for Starbucks.[42]

Organizational shifts during this period reflected the company's investment in digital innovation as a new source of both growth and operational excellence. During the transformation, Schultz had given technology a seat at the executives' table for the first time when he hired former CNET VP of IT Stephen Gillett to the position of CIO, reporting directly to him on the senior leadership team. Prior to the transformation, the CIO had reported to the CFO. Gillett, who was 31 at the time, said he was intimidated by the level of responsibility and knew nothing about retail, but "[I]t was an exciting time in that Howard gave us a lot of leeway to reinvent the roles we were taking on and to develop some really creative ideas…Howard offered the permission to be curious and creative, and the rest took over."[43]

It was under Gillett that the company's IT department became a major source of cost leverage and efficiency. After Gillett departed Starbucks for a COO position at Symantec, new CIO Curtis Garner explained how the company's focus on technology had become customer- and employee-facing ("partner" in Starbucks parlance) as well:

We replaced the point-of-sale system in our stores, a fairly routine thing that a retailer would do. After spending a bunch of time videotaping and talking to partners, we made a couple of changes to the point-of-sale system to make it easier to ring transactions and decrease the time it takes to do an electronic transaction. We were able to save 10 seconds a swipe for any kind of Starbucks card, mobile payment, credit card, or debit card transaction. That ended up saving us 900,000 hours of line time a year.[44]

It was also in March 2012 that Schulz promoted Brotman to the newly created post of CDO, putting Starbucks on the forefront of companies investing in a top digital position. The company again illustrated its focus on the growth potential of its Digital Ventures business when it announced another organizational shift during Q2 2014. CFO Troy Alstead was promoted to the newly created position of COO to take over day-to-day operations management from CEO Schultz, which, the company explained, freed up Schultz to work more closely with Brotman and Chief Security Officer

Matt Ryan on next-generation retailing and payments initiatives.[45] One such new initiative the company planned to launch by the end of 2014 was mobile ordering.[46]

In its FY2014 second-quarter earnings conference call, Schultz stated that as the retail industry's "unquestioned" leader in mobile payment and mobile loyalty, Starbucks was uniquely positioned to develop and monetize its digital leadership into new platforms, revenue streams, and growth.[47] As an example, Schultz revealed that Starbucks had been approached by major tech companies and retailers about licensing its mobile technology and platforms and said the company was taking a very "thoughtful and disciplined" approach to analyzing these overtures.[48]

Starbucks also invested heavily in social media during this time, including the Starbucks Digital Network, as well as Facebook, Twitter, Instagram, Pinterest, YouTube, Google+, and a successful crowdsourcing platform called My Starbucks Idea, which served not only to generate ideas, but also as a tool for marketing and customer engagement. The company's Twitter presence became even more lucrative when it started a Tweet-a-Coffee campaign in October 2013. Through the campaign, customers could send friends a $5 Starbucks gift card via Twitter by first linking their Starbucks accounts and credit cards to the social media platform. By December of that year, Starbucks had linked 54,000 users' Twitter IDs to their mobile phones and customer IDs—a boon that far overshadowed the $180,000 in purchases that were made through the program in its first two months. With more than 33 million fans, Starbucks was one of the most "liked" consumer brands on Facebook,[49] and its My Starbucks Idea online community had generated more than 80,000 ideas. One of the most popular customer-generated ideas was digital tipping, which Starbucks added as a feature to its mobile payment app in 2014.

To advertise its focus on both operational excellence and growth through innovation, Starbucks also announced plans to leverage the Internet of Things by turning its store refrigerators and coffee makers into smart machines that could alert store employees when the milk was about to spoil, for example. The company also planned to experiment with coffee cup sensors to monitor coffee quality and collect data on such customer preferences as cream and sugar.[50]

The company clearly saw Digital Ventures as a major driver of new growth, customer loyalty, and shareholder value; however, Starbucks continued to bet heavily on international expansion by planning for almost 900 new global stores in 2014.

EMEA

The company's EMEA business segment continued to struggle toward profitability during this period. Comprising 8% of total revenues, comparable-store sales remained flat in 2012 and 2013. Due to cost-management efforts and a major shift in ownership structure away from company-operated stores in favor of licensed and franchised stores, however, EMEA operating margins improved to 5.5% in fiscal 2013, and a 2% growth in total revenue for 2013 came from licensed-store revenue growth.[51]

Under a store licensing model, previously shunned by the company before the transformation but now making up a large and growing percentage of its international revenue, Starbucks received a reduced share of store revenues but also a disproportionately reduced share of expenses borne mostly by the licensee. At the end of FY2013, the region had 853 company-operated stores and 1,116 licensed stores, down from 911 and up from 707 respectively in 2009.[52]

By Q2 FY14, same stores for EMEA were up 6%.[53]

CAP

In contrast to EMEA, the relatively young CAP segment increased revenues by 27% in 2013. Although it only comprised 6% of the company's total revenues, it was the fastest-growing business segment and had the highest profit margin. During 2013, the company added 600 net new stores, including 317 in China and its first stores in Vietnam and India.[54] Starbucks clearly saw the region as one of the major sources of growth and said it planned to have 1,500 stores in China by the end of 2015.[55] But it was India that earned the title of fastest-growing market in Starbucks history during this period. Through a 50-50 joint venture with Tata Global Beverages Limited, the first Starbucks store opened in October 2012, and India had a total of 40 stores only 17 months later.[56]

"The biggest opportunity we have is clearly in Asia," Schultz told the *Wall Street Journal* in September 2013. "We've been in China now for over a decade. The most gratifying thing is, when we first got there, most of our customers were tourists and expats, and now they're Chinese nationals."[57]

Channel Development

Probably the most interesting part of Starbucks' post-transformation growth story occurred outside the iconic Starbucks coffee shop. What had started with the sale of packaged Starbucks and Seattle's Best Coffee beans and ground coffee at supermarkets grew during this period into an aggressive, multifaceted strategy to turn the coffee giant into a diverse consumer packaged goods (CPG) company. By the beginning of 2014, Starbucks' CPG business included sales of whole-bean and ground coffees, premium Tazo teas, Starbucks- and Tazo-branded single-serve products, ready-to-drink beverages such as Starbucks Refreshers and Evolution Fresh juices, Evolution Harvest snack bars, and other branded products sold worldwide through grocery stores, warehouse clubs, specialty retailers, convenience stores, and foodservice accounts.

In 2012, this segment, which Starbucks called its channel development business, experienced a whopping 50% net revenue increase (due in part to taking all distribution activities back from Kraft) before landing at a more sustainable pace of 10% growth, or $1.4 billion in revenue in 2013 (9% of total company revenue). It is important to note that those numbers did not include the relatively new CPG business from the Evolution Fresh brand, which Starbucks still accounted for under All Other Segments in its 2013 annual report. A consolidated look at the mix of net revenues for all of CPG and other segments as a percentage of total revenues and against net revenues from company-operated stores and licensed stores is provided in Table 2. According to Schultz:

There hasn't been one company I can identify that has been able to build complementary channels of distribution by integrating the retail footprint and the ubiquitous channels of distribution—in our case, grocery stores and drug stores. So the model is, Starbucks can seed and introduce new products and new brands inside our stores.[58]

Notably, it was in 2013 that Starbucks finally settled a legal dispute with Kraft Foods that stemmed from Starbucks's 2011 termination of a contract with Kraft to distribute Starbucks and Seattle's Best Coffee. In a binding decision, an arbitrator ordered Starbucks to pay Kraft $2.7 billion in damages, interest, and legal fees for terminating the contract three years prematurely. Although Starbucks issued a statement saying it fully disagreed with the arbitrator's decision, Schultz stated that ending the relationship was the right call at the time:

We are literally in [the] very nascent stages of building a multibillion-dollar global consumer packaged business… Having gained full operating control, we now have the flexibility and the freedom to control our own destiny and, most importantly, preserve and enhance the Starbucks Global business and brand around the world.[59]

It wasn't only packaged coffee that the break with Kraft affected. It was also in 2011 that Starbucks entered the single-serve coffee-pod market through a partnership with Keurig Green Mountain (formerly Green Mountain Roasters), which manufactured Keurig K-Cup coffee brewing systems for home and commercial use. Keurig was the U.S. leader among systems that with the push of a button forced a high-speed jet of water to pierce a small coffee capsule and filtered a single-serve cup of coffee within 30 seconds. As part of the Kraft deal, Starbucks had been limited to producing single-serve coffee exclusively for Kraft's much less popular Tassimo system.

The Keurig system required a patented K-Cup capsule for its machines, and the partnership agreement with Keurig made Starbucks the producer of the exclusive, licensed super-premium coffee brand used in the K-Cup pods; however, by 2012, Keurig's patents had expired and generic K-Cup pods began flooding the market, which was growing at a rapid pace. Starbucks continued its aggressive pursuit of single-serve that year by launching its own branded system, the Verisimo, for brewing not only coffee but also espresso drinks and lattes. Then, in 2013, the company expanded the Keurig partnership to triple the number of Starbucks K-Cup products and brands covered, including Seattle's Best Coffee, Torrefazione Italian Coffee, Teavana, and Starbucks cocoa. By 2014, Starbucks had 15% of the single-serve market and had agreed to amend the Keurig agreement to terminate its exclusive position for supplying premium coffee in exchange for better business terms.

Rather than cannibalizing coffee store sales and, in the case of the Verisimo, its successful Keurig partnership, Starbucks saw the single-serve market as fitting into its customers' daily routine, and with the espresso- and latte-brewing Verisimo, attracting an entirely different customer segment from Keurig.[60] Because U.S. consumers purchased $3.1 billion worth of coffee pods in 2013 versus $132 million in 2008, it clearly was an area Starbucks couldn't afford to ignore. In a conference call to discuss Q1 FY2014 earnings results, Troy Alstead said the company's premium single-cup platform would be a significant driver of the company's long-term growth.

Table 2 Net Revenues by Segment as a Percentage of Total Net Revenues

Net Revenues	FY13	FY12	FY11	FY10	FY09
Company-operated stores	79.2%	79.2%	82.3%	83.7%	83.7%
Licensed stores	9.1%	9.1%	8.6%	8.2%	8.1%
CPG, food service, and other	11.7%	11.7%	9.1%	8.1%	8.2%
Total net revenues	100%	100%	100%	100%	100%

Data sources: Starbucks annual reports, 2011–13.

Starbucks also continued to experience success and growth in channel sales of its ready-to-drink beverages through its North American Coffee Partnership with PepsiCo, which manufactured and distributed Starbucks bottled energy drinks, Frappuccinos, Refreshers, iced coffee, and Tazo teas.

In other developments during this time, Starbucks introduced Evolution Fresh products in grocery stores and unveiled that exclusive organic line of Tazo-bagged teas for Whole Foods. Despite a May 2013 price reduction on packaged coffee to reflect the lower cost of coffee beans, the company continued to achieve revenue growth and increased operating margins. During the Q2 FY2014 earnings call, Alstead said the company continued to see packaged coffee as a growth driver that would sustain channel development's expected double-digit revenue growth. The company had increased from about 50 employees running the segment in 2010 to about 500.[61]

In summer 2013, Starbucks also began a cross-channel program to link its My Starbucks Rewards to grocery store purchases of Starbucks packaged coffee. As of Q2 FY2014, the company had issued 5 million Stars to grocery customers.[62]

Schultz said that he believed sales in this segment, which as of FY2013 were worth about $2 million per year, could reach $10 billion per year in the United States alone.[63] Schultz claimed this was possible because of the "flywheel effect":[64] "We can introduce a product in our stores and then use social media and mobile payments to draft off that unique asset. That reduces the cost of customer acquisition and creates value," he said.[65]

Shortly after Starbucks began testing its Fizzio carbonated beverages in select cafés during the 2013 summer, it was this flywheel notion that helped generate rumors that Starbucks might acquire a stake in the Israeli at-home soda machine manufacturer SodaStream. In fact, Coca-Cola had recently acquired a stake in rival Keurig and finalized a deal to collaborate on a Keurig at-home cold beverage system, making the SodaStream strategy seem plausible at the time; however, both Starbucks and SodaStream declined to comment on the speculation.[66]

Leadership, Culture, and Employee Engagement

We are a performance-driven company through the lens of humanity.[67]

—Howard Schultz

During this same period of rapid growth, Starbucks also invested heavily in its organizational brand, which internally was focused on culture and employee engagement and externally Schultz saw as "redefining the role and responsibility of a for-profit, public company."[68]

"I recognize we are not a perfect company," Schultz said at the 2014 annual meeting of shareholders, "but we have a responsibility to use our scale for good. The currency of leadership is truth and transparency. What we need now more than ever before is citizenship over partisanship."[69]

More than mere rhetoric, the company used the turnaround to not only share the wealth with its shareholders in the form of dividends and with its employees in the form of compensation and benefits, but also with the community at large through several social initiatives. Starting with the transformation, the company also implemented new internal policies that eliminated the kind of leadership hubris that likely contributed to its previous growth implosion and focused on cultivating the kind of organizational system whereby the structure, culture, and leadership behaviors fostered innovation, experimentation, and employee engagement.

Implementing these policies was a humbled but invigorated leadership team. Eight of ten senior leaders had departed the company in the wake of the transformation, and a majority of the senior leadership as of 2013 had either joined the company or the team since Schultz returned as CEO. But loyalty was a factor too. As of 2013, four of the five highest-paid executive officers under Schultz had been promoted from within the company and had tenures dating back from 1992 to 2002—well before the turnaround. Schultz hired the other top executive, Jeff Hansberry, president of Starbucks China and Asia-Pacific, in 2010 to grow the CPG business globally. Hansberry came with prior experience from E. & J. Gallo Winery and 17 years with Procter & Gamble.

In 2010, Schultz had high praise for his new senior leadership team, stating, "Our team meets weekly as well as monthly, and as a group we are open to building consensus; we welcome creative tension, and we always try to learn from our past."[70]

By all accounts, Schultz himself set the tone for this new, more humble form of leadership by "walking the talk." Whereas he'd previously been perceived by the media as headstrong, egoistic, and overly ambitious, Schultz now took pains to publicly admit his mistakes and tried to change his ways by embracing focus groups and taking more controlled, smaller risks with new products and initiatives. Alstead told *The New York Times* in 2011, "There's been more arguing, challenging, and debate in the last two to three years than there's ever been," and Michelle Gass said Schultz had become more disciplined and a better listener.[71]

Loyalty and employee engagement were factors in this new growth period not only at the top but also throughout the organization. Despite its cost-cutting during the transformation and rising health insurance premiums in the wake of the Affordable Care Act (causing many other public companies to slash employee coverage), Starbucks maintained its medical, dental, life, and disability insurance benefits for eligible full- and part-time (more than 20 hours per week) employees and continued to give them a free pound of coffee per week. Starbucks also kept up its Bean Stock program—an employee stock-purchase plan for both full- and part-time employees that Starbucks started in 1988. Starbucks remained one of the only retailers to offer a stock program to part-timers. In 2013, the company spent $250 million insuring its full- and part-time employees. That same year, it shared $234 million in pretax stock gains with employees and matched $50 million in 401(k) contributions.[72]

One Wall Street blogger called the level of satisfaction among Starbucks employees the company's "magic bullet" that contributed to its success during this period of rapid growth.[73] The blogger claimed that the company's generous benefits motivated employees to provide the superior customer service that justified Starbucks' higher prices.[74] Some evidence of this perceived employee satisfaction was the positive feedback given on the employee rating site Glassdoor.com—a 3.7 out of 5 overall rating and an 88% CEO approval rating in Q2 2014.

Perhaps what contributed at least as much as the generous benefits program to employee satisfaction and engagement during this time was the fact that Starbucks had become "cool" again. In February 2014, Nitrogram 50, a website that calculated the top 50 brands on Instagram, listed Starbucks as number two, thanks to its 2,398,226 followers and 11,345,441 comprehensive posts on hashtag, (i.e., photos of Starbucks coffee cups, morning lattes, and café scenes posted by Instagram users).[75]

During its downturn, Starbucks became a poster child for growth run amok—the popular satirical newspaper the *Onion* once published an article titled "New Starbucks Opens in Rest Room of Existing Starbucks."[76] Now, however, the company's more artisanal and disciplined retail footprint, savvy social media presence, and declared focus on both high quality and the environmentally sustainable and ethical sourcing of its products[77] restored its cachet and earned admiration. Having been absent from everyone's "best" lists for years, in 2011, Schultz was named *Fortune*'s Business Person of the Year, and Starbucks placed 16th on *Fortune*'s list of the Top 50 Most Admired Companies in 2011. By 2013, the company was 5th on the list.

Community Service

It was also in 2011 that Schultz began taking very public stands on political and social issues. He incited a media frenzy by publicly announcing his disgust regarding the dysfunction in the U.S. Congress and then working to fix it. In an open letter, Schultz urged fellow CEOs of public companies to join him in boycotting all campaign contributions in order to send a message to politicians who had "chosen to put partisan and ideological purity over the well-being of the people."[78] CEOs from 140 companies joined the boycott.

During the October 2013 federal government shutdown, Starbucks led a nationwide petition through its company-operated U.S. stores and digital channels to reopen the government.[79] Within a week, the company collected nearly 2 million signatures, which Starbucks employees personally delivered to the U.S. Congress and the White House. The month prior, Schultz had sent an open letter to customers asking them to refrain from bringing firearms into Starbucks stores.[80] Earlier that year, Schultz told an outspoken shareholder at the 2013 annual meeting that he was free to sell his shares when the shareholder complained about a dip in the stock price after the National Organization for Marriage launched a "Dump Starbucks" boycott the previous year. In defending the company's support of marriage equality, Shultz responded, "It is not an economic decision. The lens in which we are making that decision is through the lens of our people. We employ over 200,000 people in this company, and we want to embrace diversity."[81]

Schultz received high praise from other shareholders inside the meeting room as well as later in the media for his response to the disgruntled shareholder. No doubt, the fact that Starbucks stock had earned a 38% return in 2012 helped most investors accept Starbucks'—or, more appropriately, Schultz's—more aggressive political profile.

In addition to the ethical sourcing and environmental sustainability initiatives undertaken by Starbucks during this time, the company also used its brand and coffers to address the growing wealth gap. Starbucks created a nonprofit funding model called a community store. In five such U.S. stores and one in Thailand, a Starbucks café partnered with a local nonprofit to help revitalize a struggling neighborhood by providing jobs as well as a source of funding for the nonprofit. Starbucks also helped launch the Create Jobs for U.S.A. program with the Opportunity Finance Network to provide loans to small businesses. Starbucks also pledged to hire 10,000 veterans and military spouses by 2018 and to open five new community stores to help support veterans entering the civilian work force and the spouses of active-duty military personnel. In doing so, Starbucks not only raised its brand's profile in the eyes of socially minded customers but also increased goodwill among its employees.

Conclusion

"If Starbucks was a 20-chapter book, we are only in chapter 4 or 5 and heading toward a $100 billion market cap," Schultz told shareholders at the company's 2014 annual meeting.[82] "Our ability to grow income at a pace that exceeds revenue growth clearly demonstrates the strategic synergies we generate across our global footprint, which combined with the diversity of our portfolio, enables consistent delivery of excellent results," said Troy Alstead in the Q3 FY2013 earnings release.[83]

By Q2 2014, it certainly seemed that Starbucks had found a winning synergistic strategy. From the coffee snobs to the health-conscious, and from the millennials who embraced a more digital third place to the world's estimated millions of tea drinkers who'd never stepped into a coffee shop, Starbucks seemed poised to attract continued growth.

But several questions about its strategy loomed as well. Would Starbucks' diverse bets on digital assets, global expansion, consumer packaged goods, and tea counteract an inevitable slowing of its core U.S. coffee shop business? Could it really do for tea what it had done for coffee? Would Starbucks hold off its growing list of competitors—from the cheaper quick-service restaurants such as McDonald's and Dunkin' Donuts; more experienced casual food purveyors such as Panera Bread; and single-serve beverage companies such as Keurig?

Considering its diverse and growing portfolio, new focus on technology and innovation, and reinvigorated organizational system aligned with its growth strategy, was Starbucks armed to combat another economic recession? And even more important, would Starbucks be able to manage its appetite for growth to avoid its previous mistakes? Was the Starbucks multiple-stakeholder model firmly entrenched enough to avoid dilution from future leadership successions?

NOTES

1. Remarks before the 2014 Annual Meeting of Shareholders.
2. Starbucks annual report, 2010.
3. Howard Schultz, *Onward: How Starbucks Fought for Its Life without Losing Its Soul* (New York, NY: Rodale, 2011), 309.
4. Jon Gertner, "Most Innovative Companies 2012: No. 24 Starbucks for Infusing a Steady Stream of New Ideas to Revive Its Business," *Fast Company* online, February 7, 2012, http://www.fastcompany.com/3017375/most-innovative-companies-2012/24starbucks (accessed Jun. 1, 2014).
5. Starbucks annual report, 2013.
6. Patrick Clark, "Why a Snack Bar Maker Turned Down a Deal with Starbucks," *Bloomberg Businessweek*, September 18, 2013, http://www.businessweek.com/articles/2013-09-18/why-a-snack-bar-maker-turned-down-a-deal-with-starbucks (accessed Jun. 1, 2014).
7. Venessa Wong, "Starbucks Revamps Sandwiches in a Bid to Defend Its Breakfast Turf," *Bloomberg Businessweek*, March 4, 2014, http://www.businessweek.com/articles/2014-03-04/starbucks-revamps-sandwiches-in-a-bid-to-defend-its-breakfast-turf (accessed Jun. 1, 2014).
8. Jessica Chou, "Starbucks to Revamp Breakfast Sandwiches, Lunch Offerings,"

The Daily Meal, September 17, 2013, http://www.thedailymeal.com/starbucks-revamp-breakfast-sandwiches-lunch-offerings (accessed Jun. 1, 2014).
9. Marty Frantz, "Will Starbucks Assembly-Line Coffee System Hurt Investors?," Seeking Alpha, December 2, 2013, http://seekingalpha.com/article/1870751-will-starbucks-assembly-line-coffee-system-hurt-investors (accessed Jun. 1, 2014); Ashley Lutz, "Starbucks' New Bakery Has Had a Demoralizing Effect on Baristas," *Business Insider*, December 12, 2013, http://www.businessinsider.com/how-workers-feel-about-starbucks-bakery-2013-12 (accessed Jun. 1, 2014).
10. Julie Jargon, "At Starbucks, Baristas Told No More Than Two Drinks," *Wall Street Journal* online, October 13, 2010, http://online.wsj.com/news/articles/SB10001424052748704164004575548403514060736 (accessed Jun. 1, 2014).
11. "Starbucks Announces Agreement to Acquire Teavana to Globally Transform Tea Industry," Starbucks press release, November 14, 2012, http://news.starbucks.com/news/starbucks-announces-agreement-to-acquire-teavana-to-globally-transform-tea- (accessed Jun. 1, 2014).

12. Candice Choi and Sarah Skidmore, "Starbucks Buys Teavana Holdings for $620 Million," *Huffington Post*, November 14, 2012, http://www.huffingtonpost.com/2012/11/15/starbucks-buys-teavana-holdings_n_2136048.html (accessed Jun. 1, 2014).
13. Lisa Baertlein, "Starbucks Alcohol: Beer & Wine Coming to Stores in Atlanta, Southern Calif.," Reuters, January 23, 2012, http://www.huffingtonpost.com/2012/01/23/starbucks-alcohol_n_1224097.html (accessed Jun. 1, 2014).
14. "Starbucks Evenings," Starbucks website, http://www.starbucks.com/coffeehouse/starbucks-stores/starbucks-evenings (accessed Jun. 1, 2014).
15. "Starbucks CEO Discusses F2Q2014 Results: Earnings Call Transcript," Seeking Alpha, April 25, 2014 http://seekingalpha.com/article/2164683-starbucks-ceo-discusses-f2q2014-results-earnings-call-transcript (accessed Jun. 1, 2014).
16. Starbucks annual report, 2012.
17. Rachel Tepper, "Starbucks Refreshers: Energy Drink Line Expanding With VIA, Handcrafted Varieties," *Huffington Post*, July 9, 2012, http://www.huffingtonpost.com/2012/07/09/starbucks-refreshers_n_1658852.html (accessed Jun. 1, 2014).

18. Lisa Jennings, "Starbucks to Expand Clover Brewing System," Nation's Restaurant News, August 14, 2013, http://nrn.com/technology/starbucks-expand-clover-brewing-system (accessed Jun. 1, 2014).

19. "Starbucks Expands Clover Brewing to 500th U.S. Location, Aims to Double the Number of Stores Featuring the Clover System in 2014," Starbucks press release, August 13, 2013, http://news.starbucks.com/news/starbucks-expands-clover-brewing-to-500th-u.s.-location-aims-to-double-the- (accessed Jun. 1, 2014).

20. Mike Elgan, "FAIL! Why You Should Experiment Like Amazon and Starbucks Do," Forbes online, December 5, 2013, http://www.forbes.com/sites/netapp/2013/12/05/fail-experiment-amazon-starbucks/ (accessed Jun. 1, 2014).

21. Jenna Goudreau, "Starbucks' Secret Weapon," Forbes online, November 2, 2011, http://www.forbes.com/sites/jennagoudreau/2011/11/02/starbucks-secret-weapon-michelle-gass/ (accessed Jan. 6, 2015).

22. Michael Brush, "McDonald's or Starbucks: Who Wins?," MSN Money, July 5, 2011, http://money.msn.com/investment-advice/mcdonalds-or-starbucks-who-wins-brush.aspx (accessed Jun. 1, 2014); Lisa Baertlein and Andre Grenon, "Burger King to Sell Starbucks' Seattle's Best Brew," Reuters, February 16, 2010, http://www.reuters.com/article/2010/02/16/us-burgerking-starbucks-idUSTRE61F56820100216 (accessed Jun. 1, 2014).

23. Leslie Patton, "Starbucks Pushes Further into Grocery with Seattle's Best," Bloomberg, January 15, 2014, http://www.bloomberg.com/news/2014-01-15/starbucks-pushes-further-into-grocery-with-seattle-s-best.html (accessed Jun. 1, 2014).

24. http://www.bloomberg.com/news/2014-01-15/starbucks-pushes-further-into-grocery-with-seattle-s-best.html.

25. Starbucks annual report, 2013.

26. "Starbucks Annual Shareholders Meeting Spotlights Record Performance Driven through the Lens of Humanity," Starbucks press release, March 19, 2014, http://investor.starbucks.com/mobile.view?c=99518&v=203&d=1&id=1910182 (accessed Jun. 1, 2014).

27. http://seekingalpha.com/article/2164683-starbucks-ceo-discusses-f2q2014-results-earnings-call-transcript.

28. http://seekingalpha.com/article/2164683-starbucks-ceo-discusses-f2q2014-results-earnings-call-transcript.

29. Liz Stinson, "With Stunning New Stores, Starbucks Has a New Design Strategy: Act Local," Wired online, January 8, 2014, http://www.wired.com/2014/01/starbucks-big-plan-to-be-your-cozy-neighborhood-coffee-shop/ (accessed Jun. 1, 2014).

30. Allen Webb, "Starbucks' Quest for Healthy Growth: An Interview with Howard Schultz," McKinsey Quarterly, March 2011.

31. "Starbucks' CEO Discusses F1Q2013 Results: Earnings Call Transcript," Seeking Alpha, January 24, 2013, http://seekingalpha.com/article/1132671-starbucks-ceo-discusses-f1q13-results-earnings-call-transcript (accessed Jun. 1, 2014).

32. http://seekingalpha.com/article/2164683-starbucks-ceo-discusses-f2q2014-results-earnings-call-transcript.

33. James R. A. Davenport, "The United States of Starbucks," If We Assume (blog), October 4, 2012, http://www.ifweassume.com/2012/10/the-united-states-of-starbucks.html (accessed Jun. 1, 2014).

34. Starbucks annual report, 2013.

35. "Starbucks Unveils Accelerated Global Growth Plans," Starbucks press release, December 5, 2012, http://investor.starbucks.com/phoenix.zhtml?c=99518&p=irol-newsArticle&ID=1764541&highlight (accessed Jun. 1, 2014).

36. "Starbucks CEO Discusses F1Q2014 Results: Earnings Call Transcript," Seeking Alpha, January 23, 2014, http://seekingalpha.com/article/1964831-starbucks-ceo-discusses-f1q-2014-results-earnings-call-transcript (accessed Jun. 1, 2014).

37. http://seekingalpha.com/article/1964831-starbucks-ceo-discusses-f1q-2014-results-earnings-call-transcript.

38. Shara Tibken, "At Starbucks, AT&T Is Out and Google Is In for Wi-Fi," CNET, July 31, 2013, http://www.cnet.com/news/at-starbucks-at-t-is-out-and-google-is-in-for-wi-fi/ (accessed Jun. 1, 2014).

39. Starbucks annual report, 2013.

40. Steven Bertoni, "How Do You Win The Mobile Wallet War? Be Like Starbucks," Forbes online, February 21, 2014, http://www.forbes.com/sites/stevenbertoni/2014/02/21/how-do-you-win-the-mobile-wallet-war-be-like-starbucks (accessed Jun. 1, 2014).

41. http://investor.starbucks.com/phoenix.zhtml?c=99518&p=irol-newsArticle&ID=1910182.

42. http://www.forbes.com/sites/stevenbertoni/2014/02/21/how-do-you-win-the-mobile-wallet-war-be-like-starbucks.

43. Peter High, "Stephen Gillett's Rise from CIO of Starbucks to COO of Symantec," Forbes online, July 15, 2013, http://www.forbes.com/sites/peterhigh/2013/07/15/stephen-gilletts-rise-from-cio-of-starbucks-to-coo-of-symantec/ (accessed Jun. 1, 2014).

44. Michael Fitzgerald, "How Starbucks Has Gone Digital," MIT Sloan Management Review online, April 4, 2013, http://sloanreview.mit.edu/article/how-starbucks-has-gone-digital/ (accessed Jun. 1, 2014).

45. "Starbucks Promotes Chief Financial Officer Troy Alstead to CFO and Group President," Starbucks press release, September 20 2013, http://news.starbucks.com/news/starbucks-promotes-chief-financial-officer-troy-alstead-to-chief-financial (accessed Jun. 1, 2014).

46. Leslie Patton and Brian Womack, "Starbucks Plans to Test Mobile Ordering This Year," Bloomberg, March 12, 2014, http://www.bloomberg.com/news/2014-03-12/starbucks-plans-to-test-mobile-ordering-this-year.html (accessed Jun. 1, 2014).

47. http://seekingalpha.com/article/2164683-starbucks-ceo-discusses-f2q2014-results-earnings-call-transcript.

48. http://seekingalpha.com/article/2164683-starbucks-ceo-discusses-f2q2014-results-earnings-call-transcript.

49. David Moth, "How Starbucks Uses Pinterest, Facebook, Twitter, and Google+," Econsultancy, March 6, 2014, https://econsultancy.com/blog/62281-how-starbucks-uses-pinterest-facebook-twitter-and-google#i.1lloxyk8xocwht (accessed Jun. 1, 2014).

50. http://www.forbes.com/sites/netapp/2013/12/05/fail-experiment-amazon-starbucks/.

51. Starbucks annual report, 2013.

52. Starbucks annual reports, 2010 and 2013.

53. "Starbucks Reports Record Q2 Results and Reaffirms FY14 Growth Targets," Starbucks press release, April 24, 2014, http://investor.starbucks.com/phoenix.zhtml?c=99518&p=irol-newsArticle&ID=1922140&highlight (accessed Jun. 1, 2014).

54. Starbucks annual report, 2013.

55. Starbucks annual report, 2013.

56. "Starbucks Says India Operations Fastest Growing in History," Press Trust of India, March 21, 2014, http://profit.ndtv.com/news/corporates/article-starbucks-says-india-operations-fastest-growing-in-history-383449 (accessed Jun. 1, 2014).

57. Alexandra Wolfe, "Howard Schultz: What Next Starbucks?," Wall Street Journal online, September 27, 2013, http://online.wsj.com/news/articles/SB10001424052702304213904579093583249134984 (accessed Jun. 1, 2014).

58. Webb.

59. Venessa Wong, "Starbucks's $2.7 Billion Decision to Control Its Own Destiny," Bloomberg Businessweek, November 13, 2013, http://www.businessweek.com/articles/2013-11-13/starbucks-2-dot-7-billion-decision-to-control-its-own-destiny (accessed Jun. 1, 2014).

60. Angel Gonzales, "Single-Serve Coffee Revolution Brews Industry Change," Seattle Times online, February 15, 2014, http://seattletimes.com/html/businesstechnology/2022910303_singleservexml.html (accessed Jun. 1, 2014).

61. Leslie Helm, "Howard Schultz's Master Plan Extends Well beyond the Bean," Seattle Business, April 2014.

62. http://seekingalpha.com/article/2164683-starbucks-ceo-discusses-f2q2014-results-earnings-call-transcript.

63. Beth Kowitt, "Starbucks' Grocery Gambit," Fortune, December 5, 2013, http://fortune.com/2013/12/05/starbucks-grocery-gambit/ (accessed Jun. 1, 2014).

64. Helm.

65. Helm.

66. Matt Egan, "Starbucks Might Buy a Stake in SodaStream," CNN Money, April 23, 2014, http://money.cnn.com/2014/04/23/investing/sodastream-starbucks/ (accessed Jun. 1, 2014).

67. Leslie Brodie, "Starbucks CEO: We're In Early Stages of Growth," CNBC, June 27, 2013, http://www.cnbc.com/id/100850266 (accessed Jun. 1, 2014).

68. Starbucks, 2014 Annual Meeting of Shareholders, http://news.starbucks.com/2014annualmeeting/howard-schultz-2014-shareholders-speech (accessed Jun. 1, 2014).

69. http://news.starbucks.com/2014annualmeeting/howard-schultz-2014-shareholders-speech.

70. Schultz, 326.

71. Clair Cain Miller, "A Changed Starbucks. A Changed CEO," New York Times online, March 12, 2011, http://www.nytimes.com/2011/03/13/business/13coffee.html?pagewanted=all&_r=0 (accessed Jun. 1, 2014).

72. Starbucks annual report, 2013.

73. Ted Cooper, "Wall Street Won't Tell You About the Starbucks Magic Bullet," The Motley Fool, March 5, 2014, http://www.fool.com/investing/general/2014/03/05/starbucks-magic-bullet.aspx (accessed Jun. 1, 2014).

74. http://www.fool.com/investing/general/2014/03/05/starbucks-magic-bullet.aspx.

75. Clare O'Connor, "Starbucks and Nike Are Winning Instagram (and Your Photos Are Helping)," Forbes online, February 13, 2014, http://www.forbes.com/sites/clareoconnor/2014/02/13/starbucks-and-nike-are-winning-instagram-and-your-photos-are-helping/ (accessed Jun. 1, 2014).

76. "New Starbucks Opens in Rest Room of Existing Starbucks," The Onion, June 27, 1998, http://www.theonion.com/articles/new-starbucks-opens-in-rest-room-of-existing-starb,560/ (accessed Jun. 1, 2014).

77. Starbucks, "Global Responsibility Report Goals & Progress 2013," http://www.starbucks.com/responsibility/report (accessed Jun. 1, 2014).

78. Leslie Patton, "Starbucks Schultz Urges Fellow CEOs to Halt Campaign Giving," Bloomberg, August 15, 2011, http://www.bloomberg.com/news/2011-08-15/starbucks-schultz-urges-fellow-ceos-to-boycott-campaign-giving.html (accessed Jun. 1, 2014).

79. Howard Schultz, "If We Come Together Our Voices Will Be Heard," October 10, 2013, http://news.starbucks.com/views/if-we-come-together-our-voices-will-be-heard (accessed Jun. 1, 2014).

80. Howard Schultz, "An Open Letter from Howard Schultz, CEO of Starbucks Coffee Company," September 17, 2013, http://www.starbucks.com/blog/an-open-letter-from-howard-schultz/1268 (accessed Jun. 1, 2014).

81. Kim Bhasin, "Starbucks CEO Howard Schultz Slaps Down Anti-Gay Marriage Activist at Shareholder Meeting," Business Insider, March 22, 2013, http://www.businessinsider.com/starbucks-ceo-howard-schultz-slams-anti-gay-marriage-shareholder-2013-3 (accessed Jun. 1, 2014).

82. http://news.starbucks.com/2014annualmeeting/howard-schultz-2014-shareholders-speech.

83. "The Starbucks EPS Jumps 28% to a Q3 Record $0.55 Per Share," Starbucks Corporation press release, July 25, 2013, http://investor.starbucks.com/mobile.view?c=99518&v=203&d=1&id=1841346 (accessed Jun. 1, 2014).

CASE 18

Super Selectos: Winning the War Against Multinational Retail Chains

Esteban R. Brenes [a], Luciano Ciravegna [a,b], Daniel Montoya [a]

Abstract

This case describes how Super Selectos, a local food retail chain from El Salvador, succeeds in competing against Walmart, the number one food retailer in the world. The case's structure facilitates a discussion of competitive strategy and positioning in the food retail industry in emerging markets. The case provides enough information for the reader to understand the differentiation strategy that allowed Super Selectos to increase its market share even after Walmart entered its domestic market. The goal of the case is to illustrate how a well formed and executed strategy allows a firm to succeed even against the most resourceful rivals. Discussing the case provides insights into the development of the food retail industry and consumer segmentation in developing economies. The case provides the basis for discussing the strategic options that Walmart has in the Salvadorian market and illustrating the challenges that large multinational corporations face when they are entering new emerging markets.

1. Introduction

The morning of March 3, 2011, after listening to a radio announcement promoting the Super Selectos stores, Carlos Calleja, senior vicepresident of this Salvadorian supermarket chain, met with his management team to discuss a latent threat: Walmart. Walmart Central America, a division of the world's largest retailer, had just announced plans to implement its global strategy in the region: to brand its stores as Walmart and offer everyday low prices to its clients. By then Walmart was the dominant player in each country of Central America with the exception of El Salvador. It was only a question of time before the largest company in the world leveraged its expertise to capture the Salvadorian market. Despite the fact that Super Selectos owned 84 retail stores, 51%

of the market and close to US$600 million in annual income, continuing as El Salvador's number one supermarket would be a very tough challenge. After analyzing the situation, Carlos and his team asked themselves what measures they should take to continue winning the battle in the local market, as they had done up until that point.

2. Economic, Political and Social Situation

In the year 2010 the Central American region grew by 4.4% with Guatemala, Honduras, El Salvador, Nicaragua, Costa Rica and Panamá experiencing growth rates of respectively 2.9%, 3.7%, 1.4%, 3.6%, 4.7% and 7.5% (see Table 1) (International Monetary Fund, 2011).

El Salvador is the fourth largest economy in the Central America (CA) region, after Guatemala, Costa Rica, and Panama. In 2010 its GDP reached US$21.2 billion, approximately US$3400 per inhabitant. According to the Central Bank, one of the country's main sources of income was family remittances from the US that reached US$3.5 billion in 2010, a 2.2% growth over 2009.

America's average inflation rate in 2010 was 6.5%. Most countries faced increased inflation from 2009 due in large part to an increase in food and beverage prices. El Salvador's inflation equaled 2.1%, one of the lowest rates in the region. However, consumers had to deal with an almost 7.9% increase in the price of food (corn and beans) and a 3.4% increase in the cost of transportation, due to higher international fuel prices (Ramírez, 2011).

Improvements in the country's economic and social areas were backed by an anti-crisis plan proposed by President Mauricio Funes in 2009, when he announced the creation of 100,000 jobs by 2011. In 2010, he proposed a law to increase public employee lowest salaries and pensions 45% and 44% and the rest 6% and 8% respectively. In addition, he established the National

[a]INCAE Business School, Strategy, Corporate Strategy/ Entrepreneurship, Steve Aronson Chair of Strategy and Agribusiness, 2 km west of Procesa Nursery #1, La Garita, Alajuela, PO Box 960-4050, Costa Rica
[b]King's College, University of London, United Kingdom

Table 1 Economic Context

	2000	2001	2002	2003	2004	2005	2006	2007	2008	2009	2010	2011
Latin America and the Caribbean	3.9%	0.4%	0.4%	2.1%	6.0%	4.7%	5.7%	5.8%	4.2%	− 1.5%	6.1%	4.6%
Central America	2.2%	1.4%	2.9%	5.7%	4.4%	5.6%	8.1%	7.6%	3.0%	− 1.0%	4.4%	4.3%
Costa Rica	1.8%	1.1%	2.9%	6.4%	4.3%	5.9%	8.8%	7.9%	2.7%	− 1.0%	4.7%	4.2%
El Salvador	2.2%	1.7%	2.3%	2.3%	1.9%	3.6%	3.9%	3.8%	1.3%	− 3.1%	1.4%	2.0%
Guatemala	2.5%	2.4%	3.9%	2.5%	3.2%	3.3%	5.4%	6.3%	3.3%	0.5%	2.9%	4.1%
Honduras	5.7%	2.7%	3.8%	4.5%	6.2%	6.1%	6.6%	6.2%	4.2%	− 2.4%	3.7%	3.7%
Nicaragua	4.1%	3.0%	0.8%	2.5%	5.3%	4.3%	4.2%	5.0%	4.0%	− 2.2%	3.6%	5.4%
Panamá	2.7%	0.6%	2.2%	4.2%	7.5%	7.2%	8.5%	12.1%	10.1%	3.9%	7.5%	10.8%

Source: International Monetary Fund, 2011.

Consumer Protection Policy to be enacted by the National Consumer Protection System, which, among other objectives, enforced warranties for purchased products and the right to be reimbursed in cash when a product was defective.

3. Retail Industry

Since the 1990s retail business began to experience rapid change. One such change was an increase in the size of commercial establishments, which allowed businesses to offer a greater variety of products in larger volumes (Dobson & Waterson, 1997). The adoption of information technology in logistics and operations management allowed retailers to lower their costs and become more efficient, for example by optimizing inventory management. Walmart was at the forefront of these innovations, which allowed retailers to be profitable in spite of lowering their average selling prices (Foster, Haltiwanger, & Krizan, 2002; Holmes, 2001).

New layouts, such as hypermarkets became popular as they offered food and traditional products, and other categories, such as appliances, electronics, books, garden products, clothing, shoes, toys and decorations. These categories represented 35% of the floor space which usually totaled more than 2500 m² and included the traditional supermarkets.

Global retail industry sales were US$3.3 trillion by 2005 and US $4.3 trillion in 2009 with an annual growth rate of 6.9%. The industry was characterized by its high concentration of players, since the largest 15 retailers accounted for 30% of sales (USDA, 2009). Globally in 2010, hypermarkets and supermarkets represented 46.4% of the market, followed by convenience stores with 30.7%; specialized food and beverage stores with 15.1%;

pharmacies and beauty stores with 1.7%; wholesale stores with membership clubs with 1.6%; other stores represented 4.5% (Datamonitor, 2010). In El Salvador, supermarkets, hypermarkets and convenience stores accounted for 38% of the market, neighborhood stores accounted for 60% and pharmacies 2% (ACNielsen, 2011). Some consumers wanted to reduce the time spent shopping and their costs, being able to buy most items at the same time and place—known as "one-stop shopping" (see Table 2). However, other customers do not always see large supermarkets as the best place to shop, since they only needed some products and shopped quickly—known as "on-the-run".

For customers, switching among supermarkets and other retail outlets does not entail costs. Hence, the industry is characterized by high rivalry, where efficiency and customer service are important tools for competitiveness.

Another characteristic of the industry is that the largest players have acquired dominant positions in different regions. Walmart is the dominant player in North, Central and Latin America while Carrefour and Tesco are, for example, stronger in Europe.

4. Strategies of Global Retailers

In the year 2010, the average revenue per customer per visit to a store in the US was US$26.80 therefore, volume was important to retailers. To attract consumers, retails deploy different strategies. Walmart, by far the dominant player in the US market, adopted a "low prices everyday" strategy (ELDP), positioning itself as the chain capable to offer prices that were lower than competitors on the vast majority of products, every day. EDLP retailers charge a constant low price every

Table 2 Costs Associated with Purchasing vs. Retail Services

Costs associated with purchasing	Retail services
Time spent buying;	Variety of products to reduce consumer's time spent buying;
Distance between consumer and store;	Accessibility to locale, decreasing the distance between consumer and store;
Change that the consumer has to make if he or she cannot find the exact brand and size of what he or she is looking for;	Ambience at locale to lower psychological costs of purchasing;
Information costs in terms of products to be purchased;	Availability of information and probability of getting the desired product at the right time, which lowers costs of change that consumers have to make if they cannot find the exact brand and size they want.
Storage of bought products;	
Psychological costs of buying, issues with noise, cleanliness, etc.	

Source: Lira (2005).

day and do not use promotions with temporary discounts creating price consistency and reducing customers' uncertainty (Hoch, Drèze, & Purk, 1994). Other retailers use a variety of commercial strategies, some offer promotions—known as Hi-Low or promo pricing which emphasizes deep and frequent discounts on a smaller set of goods during a determined period of time (Ellickson & Misra, 2008). The Hi-Low strategy is characterized by average daily prices higher than those offered by firms deploying EDLP, coupled with frequent promotions which reduce temporarily the price of a limited range of products to the same or below that offered by EDLP retailers. Other retailers positioned themselves as niche players, for example Whole Foods, and others focused on providing superior consumer service. Most retailers strengthened their negotiating position by establishing their own brands know as private label (Datamonitor, 2010) (Fig. 1).

4.1. Suppliers

Large global retailers, such as Walmart and Carrefour, have today much more bargaining power with suppliers than the supermarket chains of the 1970s because they account for a large share of the total volume of food sales (Deloitte, 2011). Suppliers had to adapt, improving their delivery times and accepting discounted prices, which translated into savings for the end consumer, and hence competitiveness for retailers. To avoid stocking problems retailers prefer establishing long term relationships with trusted suppliers. Small retailers, such as specialty or organic shops and neighborhood stores do not have the same negotiation advantage.

Figure 1 Value of Global Food Retail Industry, Period 2005–2009

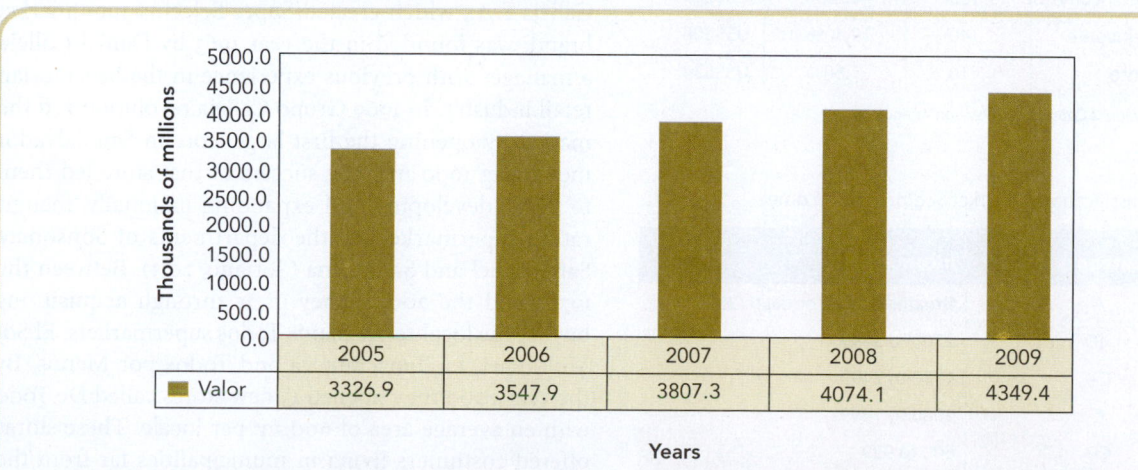

	2005	2006	2007	2008	2009
Valor	3326.9	3547.9	3807.3	4074.1	4349.4

Years

Source: Elaborated by the author with data from the Global Food Retail Report (Datamonitor, 2010).

4.2. Consumers

Another trend that characterized the industry was the increasing sophistication of consumers: through the use of internet websites, price comparator websites, and mobile devices, consumers have gained accessed to an increasing wealth of information about products, prices and the offerings of competing retail chains.

El Salvador's Consumer Protection Agency grouped consumers into three levels; "low-income markets", including 100 municipalities with extreme poverty rates of 40.2% and household incomes averaging US $201; "moderate-income markets", including 146 municipalities with extreme poverty rates of 19.4% and household incomes averaging US $308; and "high-income markets", including 16 municipalities with extreme poverty rates of 7.6% and household income averaging US$534 (Defensoría del consumidor, 2008). The agency found that in urban areas, 63.6% of the population bought fresh and processed food, while 35.7% only bought fresh food and a small proportion (0.7%) only bought processed food. In rural areas, around 55.4% of the population bought both types, while more bought only fresh (44.3%), and fewer bought only processed (0.4%) (see Tables 3 and 4).

5. Food Retailers in Central America

CA's retail market was worth $44 billion. Informal neighborhood stores and municipal farmers markets represented between 40 and 50% of the total market (CBS News, 2011). Neighborhood stores are used mainly by low- and middle-income customers, who tend to buy on a daily or weekly basis, prefer small packages, a personalized service and no-interest loans to be paid back on the payday and simply controlled by an informal notebook.

Guatemala had approximately 100,000 neighborhood stores, with an average area of 3 m² and US$500 in inventory. El Salvador had 70,000 stores and only 14% managed inventory over US$500. Nicaragua had around 85,000 of these stores. "Farmer markets" or "city markets" in which farmers or local intermediaries offered fresh produce were also common. With locales measuring 3 × 3 m, these markets opened seven days a week, or just on fair days and weekends. Honduras had 16 markets in Tegucigalpa and 17 in San Pedro Sula. San Salvador had seven markets and at least one in each town (Salinas, 2008; USDA, 2009).

In El Salvador the largest retail chain belonged to Grupo Calleja, which had 84 supermarkets under two brands, Super Selectos and Selectos Market. It competed face-to-face with Walmart, which owned 78 stores under the name Despensa Familiar (53) and Despensa de Don Juan (25), as well as two hypermarkets called Hiper Paiz. The third largest supermarket chain belonged to Saca Group and had four supermarkets and one hypermarket under the name Europa; Saca Group had 4% of the market. PriceSmart a membership club had two stores and approximately 8% of the market. Finally, there were around 140 convenience stores, mostly located at gas stations.

6. Calleja Group

Calleja S.A., which created Super Selectos supermarket brand, was founded in the year 1963 by Daniel Calleja, a manager with previous experience in the Salvadorian retail industry. In 1969 Grupo Calleja revolutionized the market by opening the first large store in San Salvador, measuring 1600 m². The success of that store led them to begin developing and expanding nationally, inaugurating supermarkets in the departments of Sonsonate, San Miguel and Santa Ana (Soriano, 2011). Between the 1970s and the 2000s, they grew through acquisitions, buying the local retail chains Todos supermarkets, El Sol, Multimart, La Tapachulteca and Todos por Menos. By the year 2000 they opened 13 new stores called De Todo with an average area of 600 m² per locale. These stores offered costumers living in municipalities far from the capital refrigerated and perishable products, such as meat, fruit and vegetables, dairy products, juices and

Table 3 Income segments in El Salvador

Segments	# Munici-palities	Poverty rate	Average household income
Low market income	100	40.20%	US$201
Moderate-income	146	19.40%	US$308
High-income	16	7.60%	US$534

Source: El Salvador's Consumer Protection Agency.

Table 4 Classification of Market Segment by Income

Category	Income US$
A	Greater than or equal to 3500
B	2500 to 3499
C+	1500 to 2499
C	1000 to 1499
C−	600 to 999
D	250 to 599

Source: Grupo Calleja.

other food products, as well as clothes, cosmetics, toys and some appliances.

Francisco said: "The idea behind De Todo was to get closer to customers, especially those that had a hard time getting to larger cities to make purchases to satisfy their basic needs. The idea we had was for us to go to the customer, not make the customer come to us. Our mission is "to serve customers where they live"" (Menjívar, 2011). The CEO of Selectos pointed to the strategic reasons for its success in the Salvadoran market, including being a flexible and locally focused organization: "In order to implement the company's strategy, we employed a day-to-day sales strategy, making tactical decisions quickly and at the right time after rapid analysis. That had allowed us to retain a certain competitive advantage over our main competitors who many times had to wait for approval from their headquarters in order to make a decision and implement it."

By 2000 Grupo Calleja had 69 stores throughout most of the country, except Chalatenango and Morazan regions. With 44 Super Selectos, 13 La Tapa supermarkets, 12 De Todo supermarkets and more than 5000 employees, they were positioned as the country's leading supermarket chain. In 2003, Walmart made its intentions to enter the Salvadorian market very clear by showing its interest in buying the Group Calleja, this was the first challenging decision for Calleja's management team: should they sell or compete with one of the largest and most resourceful companies in the world?

They decide to compete with Walmart. They invested in new stores with better layouts, continuing their organic growth in the Salvadorian market (Barrera, 2004). In 2005, Walmart formally entered the Salvadorian market. Calleja Group knew that investing in infrastructure was not enough. They still had logistics problems, such as theft of merchandise at warehouses and stores, inappropriate inventory controls, launched sales that did not satisfy the needs of consumers and did not know which products were most demanded at each store. By 2006, they set up

an Integrated Business Management System (IBMS), a Point of Sale (POS) Information System in order to obtain real time data on merchandise sold and a HR scheduling system with an investment of US$3 million. With a total investment of US$9 million, they closed the year 2006 with 76 stores and over 55% of the market (Barrera, 2006).

In February 2009 they announced the opening of five new stores despite the fact they had experienced a 7% reduction in sales that month, with respect to the previous year. Carlos Calleja believed they had to continue investing, and he also said that part of their sales strategy was to reduce the price of 400 basic need products (El Diario de Hoy, 2009).

In 2010 the group maintained their long time Hi-Low pricing strategy, offering a limited variety of products at much more competitive prices for a certain period of time representing savings for customers. "We did follow our pricing strategy during the economic crisis of 2009, even though it meant a temporary drop in our profit margin. We're a Salvadorian supermarket, so we had to respond to their needs," stated Carlos Calleja. At that time they had 82 stores and had restructured spaces taking advantage of their specialization in supermarkets; they also decided to change the name of their stores to Super Selectos (67) and create a new space called Selectos Market (15) (El Diario de Hoy, 2010). They differentiated the spaces based on the market served. Super Selectos is focused on urban populations: 20% of their stores served upper and upper–middle classes (AB), 40% the middle-class (C), and the other 40% the middle and lower classes (CD) (see Table 5). Selectos Market served smaller towns with low- to middle-income; prices were 5 to 7% lower than at Super Selectos.

The selection at Super Selectos was much better (35,000 SKU) than Selectos Market (15,000 SKU) which offered only leading brands and the company's own brand and did not have as much of a variety in perishable foods, such as fruits, vegetables and meats, among

Table 5 Types of Super Selectos

Type	Logo	Observations
Super selectos Complete selection, personalized service, serves urban areas with middle to high purchasing power, open 14 hours.	SUPER SELECTOS El Súper de El Salvador	69 stores national 81% of sales in 2010
Super selectos Limited selection, personalized service, experience, serves smaller populations with low to middle consumption, open 12 hours, on average	SELECTOS Market	15 stores 19% of sales in 2010

Source: Grupo Calleja, Commercial Presentation, 2011.

others. Super Selectos averaged 1250 m², while Selectos Market averaged 600 m². However, their personalized customer service was similar and both had air conditioning, provided grocery bags and following their long time Hi-Low pricing strategy but now advertising more than 800 promotions per month (see Fig. 2A and B). These similarities made customers perceive both types of stores as "Selectos". This perception had allowed the company to win over new customers quickly when they had entered in informal markets (in other words, where no other supermarkets already existed) and those that had been recently formalized by the competition, especially in small cities. The Selectos brand was considered the number one supermarket by 63% of the population,

Figure 2 A) Promotions from Super Selectos and Selectos Market. B) Promotions from Super Selectos and Selectos Market

while Despensa de Don Juan and Despensa Familiar reported only 17% and 13%, respectively.

At the beginning of 2011 the company continued to offer competitive prices and a large number of promotions and sales and opened two more Super Selectos. They had a total of 84 stores and close to 52% of the market. In general, their prices were slightly lower than Despensa de Don Juan, but Despensa Familiar was cheaper, offering prices 8 to 10% less than those of Selectos. Between 2004 and 2010 sales had grown 8% to reach US$551 million. Most of this growth results from large purchases by captive customers, new customers and an increase in the remittances business. They estimated that on average, Salvadorians spent US$120 per month (see Table 6). Their operational cash flow (EBITDA) over sales was above the 6% average for CA. The best companies in the region had an EBITDA to sales ratio between 8.5 and 10%. As a reference, the New York Stock Exchange's EBITDA for US supermarkets, Whole Foods and Kroger, showed 8% and 3%, respectively.

Selectos wanted to maintain and even increase its market presence, so the company decided to invest more than US$40 million in two large projects: the first was to build a center to manufacture food products and manage logistics for perishable products; and the second was to open 12 new stores (López, 2011). They set aside US$13 million to build an agro-industrial meat and poultry processing plant, fruit and vegetable packaging plant and bakery. They projected productivity would increase by 15% in meat processing, while in baked goods, they would be able to bake for the entire chain with in-store bakeries. In addition, they would centralize 20 fruit and vegetable suppliers and 20 meat suppliers. Little by little, this would allow them to work with new suppliers, as long as they complied with the company's quality standards and delivery conditions (López, 2011).

This investment would allow them to strengthen their own brands, such as La Rioja cold meats, Dany (groceries), Brisa (toilet paper, paper towels and napkins) and Casablanca (cleaning products). These brands included more than 120 products that had represented between

3% and 4% of sales in 2010. Carlos Calleja stated: "Our brand plays an important role in the country's economy, since we offer customers an excellent quality product at a competitive price" (Azucena, 2009).

Selectos had followed this strategy in 2010 with producers from the northern part of the country. The company bought their products directly, substituting a large part of the US$24 million that they imported in fruit and vegetables with 100% Salvadorian products. The company is therefore contributing with the development of the country (Choto, 2010). Ricardo Velasquez commented: "Different from other supermarket chains, we are concerned with building a relationship that also benefits suppliers, even if that relationship temporarily affects our company's profit margin."

6.1. Organizational Structure

In 2011 the company finished its organizational strengthening process that it had begun implementing five years earlier. This process consisted of restructuring personnel in central offices and at the supermarkets. Francisco Calleja remained as President. He delegated the administrative and operational management to a Management Committee that was informally staffed by the Vice-president (Carlos Calleja), CEO (Herbert Tobar) and Deputy CEO (Ricardo Velasquez). These men were in charge of evaluating different decision-making issues and defining guidelines for implementation. The President authorized this committee to approve and finalize investments and define the group's strategy. However, Francisco continued to be involved in the company. His vast experience was useful, providing advice to the committee when he thought fit, especially when they were making large investments or major strategic decisions. A new organizational structure was defined (see Fig. 3).

In addition to the management committee, they had also created an executive committee that included the management committee members plus the sales, purchasing, financial and systems directors. This committee held weekly meetings and analyzed each department's work and performance. Despite the committee and organizational restructuring, the company still lacked a formal Board of Directors; they had a board, but it operated informally.

7. Walmart and Walmart Mexico and Central America

Walmart was founded in 1962 in Rogers, Arkansas, by Sam Walton, who, under the philosophy of "buy it low, stack it high and sell it cheap," started an adventure into the world of retail initially mostly in small towns.

Table 6 Annual Sales of Super Selectos

Year	Net sales (million US$)
2006	403
2007	440
2008	446
2009	514
2010	551

Source: Grupo Calleja.

Figure 3 Organizational Structure

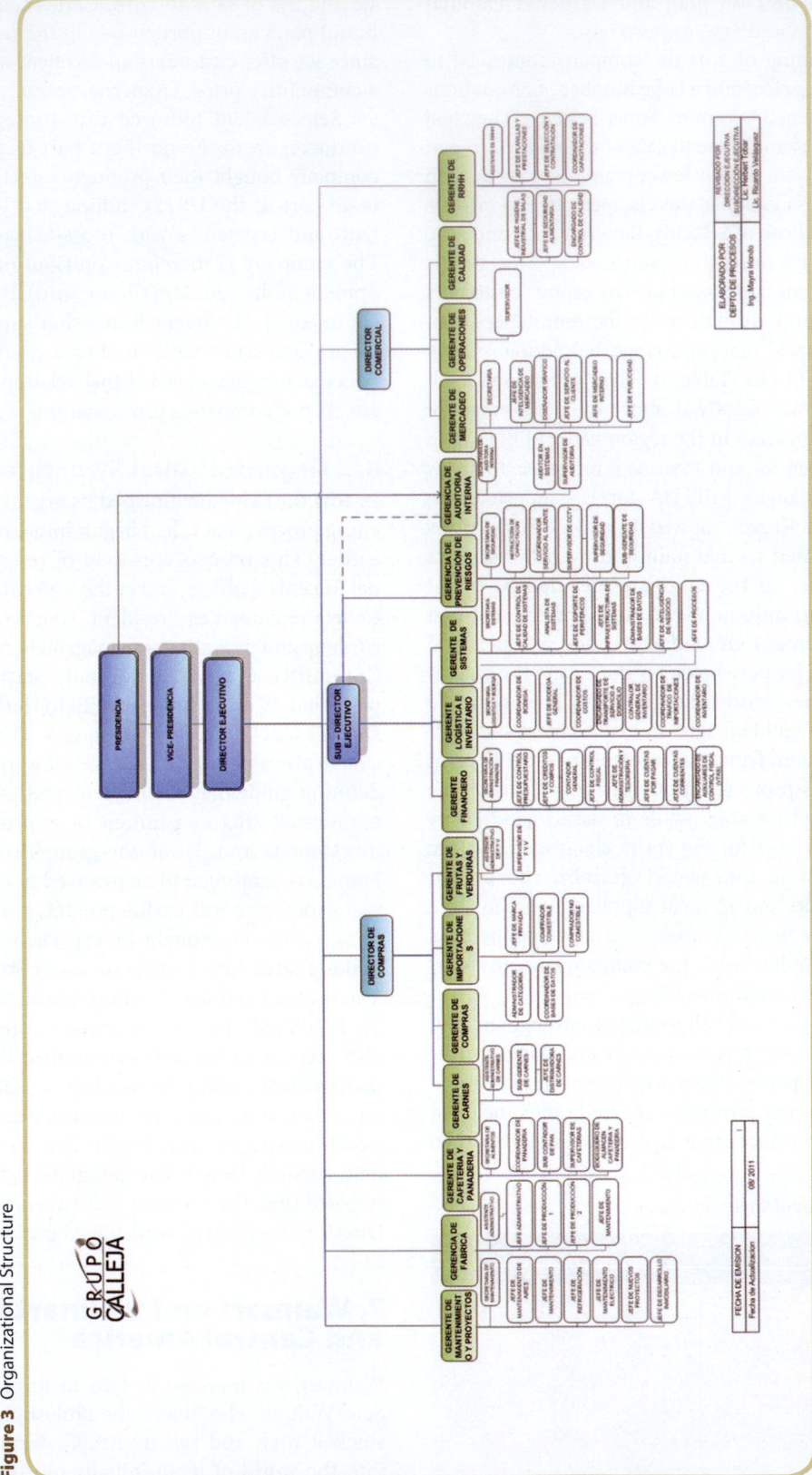

Offering EDLP, the main strategy of Walmart, was not an easy task. This strategy entailed improving its efficiency to ensure that its operational costs were consistently lower than its competitors. This was achieved through substantial investments in logistics and information technology.

By 2010 Walmart had 129 distribution centers each serving more than 75 stores. The IT system allowed the company to have real time information on sales, stock, deliveries by store, to manage the size and mix of the products by store based on specific customer characteristics and more. Information was shared with some suppliers to help them plan their deliveries. Walmart paid industry salaries plus an interesting profit sharing system and bonuses that make employees work the extra mile.

In the 1990s, Walmart began to move little-by-little up the supply chain and negotiate directly with manufacturers saving between 3 and 4% of the cost of the goods. It also expanded its private label business with third parties, getting involved in marketing and plant supervision roles. The price of Sam's American Choice detergent was 50% lower than Procter and Gamble's Tide. Walmart's private label products represented around 40% of sales in the US and 10% in CA.

Walmart was also a hard negotiator. In 2002 the company decided to start making direct purchase. Suppliers were limited to accept conditions and prices that Walmart offered. Different from other retailers, the price negotiated included additional costs for suppliers, such as commissions to manage returns, publicity and promotional expenses and the cost of merchandizing which runs from 5% to 15% of the value of the product, and included people to demonstrate the product and give samples in the stores, among other promotions. The company was always looking for new suppliers and became the largest importer of products from China in the 1990s.

Walmart's internationalization began in 1991 when the company entered Mexico and opened a Sam's Club in partnership with a domestic Mexican retailer, CIFRA, later acquired by Walmart. In 1994 Walmart expanded to Canada and then the large emerging markets in South America and Asia.

In 2005 Walmart acquired one-third of the Central American Retail Holding Company (CARHCO). CARHCO had been created as a commercial alliance among Grupo La Fragua (Guatemala), Royal Ahold (Holland) and Corporación Supermercados Unidos (Costa Rica) with one third each. CARHCO owned 254 stores in the five countries, of which 191 were discount stores, 55 were supermarkets, seven were hypermarkets and one was a membership store with an estimated regional market share of 60%. This alliance

was expected to generate sales upward of US$3 billion throughout Central America (El Diario de Hoy, 2011). Eduardo Solorzano, President of the Board of Directors of Walmart Mexico and Central America and General Manager of Walmart Latin America said, "I am pleased to end this year with a historic operation. The acquisition of Walmart Central America makes Walmart Mexico an international company, with 1929 stores operating in six countries, generating annual sales of more than US$25 billion. It also gives our shareholders additional opportunities for growth in five countries, in addition to the opportunities that exist here in our country." (Table 7).

In 2006 Walmart became the owner of 51% of the alliance and changed the name from CARHCO to Walmart Central America. In January 2010 Walmart Mexico with 1410 stores and sales of US$22 billion announced its merger with Walmart Central America paying US$2.7 billion and acquiring a total of 519 stores, in different formats, but all of which were market leaders in their socio-economic segment; 11 distribution centers; agribusiness operations that provided its stores with perishable goods; and total annual sales of US$3.3 billion (see Table 8) (Walmart México, 2009).

At the end of 2010 operations in CA were promising, profits were growing faster than sales, sales reached 3.6 billion, production capacity grew 3.7%, the use of private labels increased 5.2% and market shares were 75% in Guatemala, 70% in Costa Rica and approximately 50% in Nicaragua and Honduras. Walmart was not present in Panama yet (see Table 9). Scot Rank, President and CEO of Walmart Mexico and CA, together with his team, made an effort to align synergies between operations in Mexico and CA in order to function as just one company. The company's 2011 strategy had to be implemented based on operations both in Mexico and CA (Rank & Solórzano, 2011).

In El Salvador, since its entrance in 2005, Walmart competed following the same Hi-Low pricing strategy used by Selectos. By 2011 managers had committed to growing regional sales from 9.7% annually in 2010 to 12% annually in 2011 and 15% in 2012. To achieve this

Table 7 Purchase Price to Acquire Walmart Central America

Type of payment	Thousands of US$
Stock payments	2,146,643.78
Cash payments	110,835.81
Contingent liability	439,671.07
Total purchase price	2,697,150.66

Source: Walmart México (2011).

Table 8 Financial Statements of Walmart Mexico and Central America

		Mexico			Central America			Consolidated		
		2010	2009	% var.	2010	2009	% var.	2010	2009	% var.
Net sales (millions of US$)		23,458.3	21,380.7	9.7	3648.9	3414.8	6.9	26,548.5	21,380.7	24.2
% of income	Gross margin	22.0	21.7	11.6	22.2	22.1	7.4	22.1	21.7	26.4
	General expenses	13.5	13.4	9.9	17.4	17.3	7.5	14.0	13.4	29.4
	Profit	8.6	8.2	14.3	4.8	4.8	7.2	8.1	8.2	21.4
	Operational cash flow (EBITDA)	10.4	10.0	14.2	6.5	6.5	7.5	9.9	10.0	23.0

Source: Walmart México (2010) "Información Anual Financiera".

Table 9 Types of Stores Walmart Mexico and Central America

Type	Logo	Observations
Warehouses and discount stores Inexpensive stores that offer basic merchandise, food and household goods. Value proposal: price.		718 stores 457 cities 38.6% of sales in 2010
Hypermarkets Hypermarkets that offer wider selection of merchandise, from groceries and perishable items to clothing and general merchandise. Value proposal: price and selection.		230 stores 84 cities 27.0% of sales in 2010
Price club Wholesale price clubs with membership, focused on businesses and consumers who buy the best price. Value proposal: price leader, volume, new and different merchandise.		128 stores 75 cities 22.7% of sales in 2010
Supermarkets Supermarkets located in residential areas. Value proposal: quality, convenience and service.		184 stores 44 cities 7.0% of sales in 2010
Department Clothing stores that offer the best fashion for the whole family at the best price. Value proposal: fashion with value, price and quality.		94 stores 34 cities 3.0% of sales in 2010
Restaurants Restaurant chain, leader in cafeteria-restaurant industry. Includes Mexican food with El Portón restaurants. Value proposal: convenience, flavor and quality.		365 stores 65 cities 1.7% of sales in 2010
Bank Commercial bank for clients of Walmart Mexico stores, basic products and financial services. Value proposal: convenience, simple and price.		263 stores 31 cities 910,000 account holders in Mexico

Source: Walmart Mexico and Central America.

goal, they had decided to go back to the global EDLP strategy, based on headquarters' operations and culture, and deploy it in all of the markets of Central America, including El Salvador (see Fig. 4).

Walmart's management believed that promotions and discounts and merchandizing were no longer necessary when using EDLP. They asked suppliers to incorporate the cost of merchandizing as an additional discount (between 5% and 15%) to the price. According to the company's 2011 expansion plan, Walmart expected to open 80 new stores equaling over 43,000 m² in CA.

Strategy execution in CA was a challenge. First, they had to change the way they grew, and the redefinition of space was essential because of the need for larger retail spaces. Alberto Ebrard, Executive Vice-president and COO for CA mentioned: "The first strategic change to prepare the region for accelerated growth will be the redefinition of a multi-format strategy. The first thing was to redefine the correct customer that each store targeted and redirect business strategies based on those customers. For example, even though the Maxi Bodega format is a warehouse, it had much higher prices than discount store formats. We are re-launching the Bodega, lowering prices, improving selection and changing the name to Maxi Palí or Maxi Despensa to put it under our umbrella of discount stores" (Walmart México, 2011) (see Table 9).

In addition, Walmart's brand will be incorporated, starting by changing the names of the hypermarkets to Walmart Supercenters. According to Scot Rank and Alberto Edbrard, aligning the regional strategy based on store type, rather than using the previous structure that had been to align by country, allowed them to focus on the specific needs of the customers targeted by each type of store, while permitting operational efficiencies and reduced expenses in order to offer EDLP (Rank & Solórzano, 2011).

7.1. SUCAP

Walmart reached US$3 billion in sales for 2008. Its management and investment capacity terrorized domestic chains who fought to retain a portion of the Central American market, which included more than 35 million customers. That same year, the owners/founders/CEOs of the leading domestic supermarket chains in Central America responded by forming a strategic alliance called SUCAP—Supermercados de Central America y Panamá. It includes nine companies, owning 16 supermarket chains. In 2008 SUCAP owned 278 supermarkets in six countries with US$2.2 billion in annual sales and close to 24,000 employees (see Exhibit 1). The alliance started as a broad agreement to cooperate to face competition from foreign retailers. It gradually evolved acquiring a

Figure 4 Walmart Everyday Low Prices

structured organizational form, and a Board of Directors led by President Francisco Calleja of Selectos.

The first step was sharing information and ideas about what could be done. Secondly, the retailers began sharing best practices in the areas of logistics, operations and information systems, which they deem essential for their competitiveness (Retana, 2008). Thirdly, they began deploying a joint purchases strategy. Unlike multinational firms, local retailers purchase products for a limited number of stores, and thus have lower bargaining power with suppliers. Through join purchases the members of SUCAP can achieve better economies of scale, matching, at least at the regional level, the strategy of Walmart. Another related strategy of SUCAP is to support a small group of domestic suppliers with high capabilities providing them with long term contracts at a regional as opposed to national level, and helping them improve their products and fine tune their offerings to each specific market through advisory services. SUCAP is thus working as a mechanism to pursue joint strategies that allow each member to reach a higher scale. Through SUCAP Selectos and the other domestic retailers are sharing their knowledge of their respective markets so that it becomes shared regional knowledge. SUCAP members are adjusting their strategies to exploit the best regional knowledge and additional economies of scale to face larger, and more resourceful multinational competitors. By 2011 SUCAP membership has not changed dramatically but has grown in terms of the number of supermarkets (Table 10).

8. Closing

Super Selectos' management team was evaluating what strategy to follow in order to continue as El Salvador's number one supermarket chain. In the last few months their promotional war with Walmart had been the strongest yet. "They're killing us," said Carlos Calleja. However, now Walmart decided to go for EDLP. Carlos and the executive committee were asking themselves what should be the next steps in this never ending war.

9. Exhibit 1

9.1. Hypermarkets and Supermarkets in Central America by 2011

In Guatemala Walmart had seven hypermarkets, 166 supermarkets under different names and two membership club stores. The second chain was Unisuper, with 44 supermarkets and one discount warehouse.

PriceSmart had three stores. There were also over 70 convenience stores that were mostly located at gas stations.

In Honduras, Walmart had seven hypermarkets and 49 supermarkets under different names. The next largest retailer was La Colonia supermarket with 17 stores. PriceSmart had two stores. Also, there were different local competitors in each department and there were around 400 convenience stores, mostly located at gas stations.

In Nicaragua Walmart owned seven supermarkets under La Unión brand focused in the high and middle-high income segments and 53 supermarkets under Palí brand for lower and middle income segments. La Colonia owned by the Mantica family, which was not related to the Honduran chain, had 15 supermarkets and, discount warehouses and one hypermarket. PriceSmart had one store, and there were many convenience stores operated in the country.

Costa Rica had 333 supermarkets in 2010. Walmart had 180 stores including supermarkets and hypermarkets under the names Mas x Menos, Maxi Bodega, Palí and Hipermas. Corporacion Megasuper owned 82 stores. Grupo Gessa owned 59 with several brands and had acquired small locales or chains in rural parts of the country since 2004 as part of its expansion strategy. Automercado competed with 12 stores focused on the middle to upper segments and PriceSmart had five stores. AM-PM supermarkets had 20 stores and nine

Table 10 SUCAP Membership by Country in 2011 and Number of Stores

Country	Name of supermarket chain	Number of stores
Costa Rica	Turribasicos	3
	Peri	19
	Auto Mercado	14
	Jumbo	6
	Super Compro	32
El Salvador	Super Selectos	68
	Selectos Market	16
	Dollar market	2
Guatemala	La Torre	27
	Econo Super	18
Honduras	La Colonia	20
Nicaragua	La Colonia	16
Panama	Mega Depot	2
	El Machetazo	12
	Super 99	34

Source: Elaborated by the author with data from SUMMA (2012).

convenience stores. Finally, there were also convenience stores located at gas stations.

In Panama, Super 99 had 33 stores owned by the Martinelli family. Grupo Rey owned the second largest chain and had a total of 18 supermarkets by 2010. PriceSmart had four stores. Convenience stores were opened at 17 Esso gas stations, but planned to open more stores in their 45 gas stations. Shell had a total of nine stores under the name Select and Texaco had 15 years of experience managing the StarMart convenience stores.

Appendix A. Supplementary Data

Supplementary data to this article can be found online at http://dx. doi.org/10.1016/j.jbusres.2014.09.030.

ENDNOTES

ACNielsen (2011). *Censo de Establecimientos Detallistas 2011*. El Salvador: ACNielsen.

Azucena, M. (2009, Jul. 6). *Marcas Propias Cobran Auge*. El Salvador.com (Retrieved from http://www.elsalvador.com/mwedh/nota/nota_completa.asp?idCat=6374&idArt= 3799888).

Barrera, J.A. (2004, Dec. 10). *Selectos Ancla de Multiplaza*. El Diario de hoy (Retrieved from http://www.elsalvador.com/noticias/2004/12/10/negocios/neg12.asp).

Barrera, J.A. (2006, Mar. 22). *Selectos invertirá $9 millones en cinco salas*. El Diario de Hoy (Retrieved from http://www.elsalvador.com/noticias/2006/03/22/negocios/neg9.asp).

CBS News (2011, Mar. 21). *Goal is to increase growth rate*. CBS News (Retrieved from http://findarticles.com/p/articles/mi_hb3235/is_6_28/ai_n57259340).

Choto, D. (2010, Sep. 28). *Súper selectos firma alianza estratégica con los productores*. El Salvador.com (Retrieved from http://www.elsalvador.com/mwedh/nota/nota_completa.asp?idCat=6374&idArt=5182963).

Datamonitor (2010). *Global food retail*. Retrieved from: www.datamonitor.com Defensoría del consumidor (2008). *Perfil del consumidor salvadoreño en el siglo. XXI*, PNUD.

Deloitte (2011). *Global powers of retailing 2011*. Retrieved from: http://www.deloitte.com/assets/Dcom-Australia/Local%20Assets/Documents/Industries/Consumer%20business/Deloitte_Global_Powers_of_Retail_2011.pdf.

Dobson, P., & Waterson, M. (1997). *Countervailing power and consumer prices. The Economic Journal, 107*(441), 418–430.

El Diario de Hoy (2009, Mar. 2). *Selectos abrirá cinco salas en 2009*. El Diario de Hoy (http://www.elsalvador.com/mwedh/nota/nota_completa.asp?idCat=6374&idArt= 3404132).

El Diario de Hoy (2010, Apr. 13). *Selectos abrirá dos sucursales en 2010*. El Diario de Hoy (Retrieved from http://www.revistasumma.com/negocios/2740-grupo-callejasabrira-dos-supermercados-mas-en-el-salvador.html).

El Diario de Hoy (2011, Nov. 7). *Grupo Paiz busca alianzas en el país*. El Diario de Hoy (Retrieved from http://www.elsalvador.com/noticias/2001/11/7/NEGOCIOS/negoc2. html).

Ellickson, P.B., & Misra, S. (2008). *Supermarket pricing strategies. Journal of Marketing Science, 27*(5), 811–828.

Foster, L., Haltiwanger, J., & Krizan, C.J. (2002). *The link between aggregate and microproductivity growth: Evidence from retail trade*. Working paper no. 9120. National Bureau of Economic Research (Retrieved from, website: http://www.nber.org).

Hoch, S., Drèze, X., & Purk, M.E. (1994). *EDLP, Hi-Lo, and margin arithmetic. The Journal of Marketing, 58*(4), 16–27.

Holmes, T. (2001). *Bar codes lead to frequent deliveries and superstores. Rand Journal of Economics, 32*(4), 708–725.

International Monetary Fund (2011). World economic outlook database. Retrieved from: http://www.imf.org/external/pubs/ft/weo/2011/01/weodata/index.aspx.

Lira, L. (2005). *Cambios en la industria de los supermercados concentración, hipermercados, relaciones con proveedores y marcas propias*. Estudios Públicos, 135–160 (No.97).

López, K. (2011, Sep. 16). *Grupo Calleja invertirá $13 mil en centro de acopio*. La Prensa Gráfica (Retrieved from http://www.laprensagrafica.com/economia/nacional/ 218052-grupo-calleja-invertira-13-mill-en-centro-de-acopio.html).

Menjívar, C. (2011, Aug. 11). *Calleja, S.A. va a la caza del consumidor del interior del país*. El Diario de Hoy (Retrieved from http://www.elsalvador.com/noticias/ EDICIONESANTERIORES/2000/AGOSTO/agosto11/NEGOCIOS/negoc3.html).

Ramírez, S. (2011, Jan. 14). *El Salvador cerró 2010 con 2.13% de inflación*. La Prensa Gráfica (Retrieved from http://www.laprensagrafica.com/economia/nacional/164503-elsalvador-cerro-2010-con-213-de-inflacion.html).

Rank, S., & Solórzano, E. (2011). *Séptima reunión con analistas [Power point slides]*.

Presentation to shareholders Walmart Mexico and Central America.

Retana, K. (2008, Feb. 8). *Supermercados centroamericanos retan a Walmart*. La Republica (Retrieved from http://www.larepublica.net/app/cms/cms_periodico_showpdf.php? id_menu=50&pk_articulo=10760&codigo_locale=es-CR).

Salinas, C. (2008, Dec. 14). *Comprar al fiado en las pulperías*. El País (Retrieved from http://elpais.com/diario/2008/12/14/negocio/1229262746_850215.html).

Soriano, M. (2011). Logística y cadena de abastecimiento [PowerPoint slides]. Retrieved from. http://katiadianaanakeren.files.wordpress.com/2011/05/grupo-callejas.pdf

SUMMA (2012, Mar.). *La unión hace la fuerza*. SUMMA, 24.

USDA (2009). *Global food markets: Global food industry structure*. Economic Research Service (Retrieved from: http://www.ers.usda.gov/Briefing/GlobalFoodMarkets/ Industry.htm).

Walmart México (2009, Dec. 6). *Walmart De México Adquiere Operación De. Walmart En Centroamérica*. (Retrieved in May 2012 from http://www.walmex.mx/assets/ files/Informacion%20financiera/BMV/BMV/Esp/2009/12062009%20-Adquiere%20Operacion%20De%20Walmart%20En%20CA.pdf).

Walmart México (2010). *Informe Anual*. (Retrieve from http://www.walmex.mx/assets/files/Informacion%20financiera/Anual/Esp/Financiero/financiero2010esp.pdf).

Walmart México (2011). Resultados del Tercer Trimestre 2011 [Video Webcast]. http://www.walmex.mx/ (Retrieved from).

CASE 19

⛨ **IVEY** | Publishing

Tim Hortons Inc.[1]

It would be a year of dramatic change for Tim Hortons Inc. On August 26, 2014, the company's board of directors had agreed to be acquired by G3 Capital, the investment firm that owned Burger King. The new company would become the third largest fast food restaurant chain in the world with 18,000 locations in 98 countries and combined international sales of $23 billion dollars.[2] The new company would be headquartered in Oakville, Ontario, Canada and largely operate as two separate entities.

The deal still had to be approved by Tim Hortons' shareholders and potentially by Canadian and American regulatory authorities. It was believed that this deal would help Tim Hortons with its plans for international expansion. 2013 had been an ambitious year. Tim Hortons had opened 261 new locations and refreshed more than 300 existing locations in Canada and the United States. While Tim Hortons was almost synonymous with the Canadian identity, its brand and products were far less known outside of Canada's borders; to hit ambitious growth targets, international expansion was a must, and Burger King's global experience could provide expert advice. Marc Caira, Tim Hortons' president and chief executive officer (CEO), commented, "We are very, very confident that we can grow much quicker in this must-win battle called the United States with our partners than we would have otherwise done on our own."[3]

Even with the acquisition, Tim Hortons would need to make clear strategic choices to achieve its aggressive growth and financial goals. Inconsistent economic growth was fostering increased competition and consumer tastes were evolving, making menu innovation an important priority. Achieving the returns shareholders expected would be challenging. 2014 would be the 50th year of operations for Tim Hortons. Even with Burger King's help the company would need to have clear competitive advantages and make smart strategic choices for the next 50 years to be as successful as its first half century.

The Restaurant Industry

With over 900,000 locations, the restaurant industry in the United States was projected to reach US$683.4 billion in 2014, up 3.6 percent from 2013.[4] While this would be the fifth consecutive year of real growth, it was lower than expected for post-recession recovery.[5] The restaurant industry's share of the overall food dollar was up to 47 percent, almost double the 25 percent it held in 1995.[6] It was expected to employ 13.5 million people in 2014. The industry was highly fragmented, with the 50 largest companies accounting for only 20 percent of the revenue.[7]

In Canada, revenues from commercial food service were projected to be $57.5 billion in 2014, an increase of 4.7 percent over 2013. Growth was expected to come from higher average bills rather than from additional food traffic in restaurants.[8] In 2012, there were approximately 1.1 million employees in the Canadian restaurant industry at more than 81,000 restaurants, bars and catering businesses.[9]

The restaurant industry in North America was divided into two categories: full service and limited service. Full service included family, casual and fine dining where patrons would be seated and food was ordered at the table. Customers paid after eating, and the average bill was the highest for any of the segments at $13.66 in 2013.[10] Full service dining restaurants incorporated all types of cuisines and included Boston Pizza, Red Lobster, and Ruth Chris' Steak House, among others. However, the majority of restaurants in this segment continued to be individual or family-owned establishments.

The limited service restaurant sector differed from full service dining in that consumers were not waited on at the table. Instead, customers went to a central counter where they ordered, paid before receiving their food and either ate in the restaurant or had it "to go." The limited service restaurant sector in the United States was expected to post total revenues of US$195.4 billion in 2014, a 4.4 percent increase over 2013.[11] Customers in this category looked for good service, good value, convenience to their home or work place, favourite types of food and healthy menu items.[12] Limited service restaurants were divided into fast casual restaurants and quick service restaurants. While limited service restaurants felt that competition was most intense within their category, fast casual restaurants also competed with full service restaurants and quick service restaurants competed with grocery and convenience stores.[13]

Fast casual was a growing segment in the overall restaurant market, accounting for about 5 percent of the limited service category;[14] in 2013, it saw an 11 percent increase in sales[15] and was the only category to experience an increase in customer visits.[16] Fast casual was differentiated from quick service restaurants in that menu items were higher priced based on a perceived value by consumers (e.g., higher quality, customizability, handmade and/or locally sourced); as a result, average bills were higher than quick service restaurants at $7.40 compared to $5.30 respectively.[17] Ninety-five percent of the fast casual segment was made up of chains including Panera Bread, Chipotle Mexican Grill and Five Guys Burgers.

Restaurants such as Tim Hortons and McDonald's fell into the quick service category—often called "fast food." Their menu items were fast to prepare, offered at a low cost to the consumer and easy to consume. The average bill at quick service restaurants was the lowest of all of the categories; as such, the quick service sector was largely recession proof. There was also customer loyalty as 39 percent of quick service restaurant customers visited more than once a week compared to 19 percent for fast casual restaurants.[18] In Canada, the quick service restaurant market represented 64.7 percent of all meals and snacks sold in the food service industry and generated $22.6 billion in sales in 2013.[19]

The restaurant industry overall was facing challenges. The number of visits to restaurants was stagnant in the United States and Canada in the year ending June 2014.[20] Future forecasts predicted that food service industry traffic would grow at less than 1 percent for the next few years. In addition, in the 12 months prior to July 2014, wholesale food prices rose 7.1 percent while menu prices rose only 2.4 percent.[21] Food and labour costs were typically the largest general cost categories for restaurants, with each accounting for approximately one-third of every sales dollar.[22] Occupancy costs were generally 5 percent and net profits after tax from 3 percent to 6 percent.

Consumer Trends

There were a number of consumer-related trends in the food industry. From a food perspective, this included consumer preferences for locally sourced meats, seafood and produce as well as natural ingredients. Restaurants, both quick serve and full serve, were increasingly looking to ethnic menu items and flavours to differentiate their product offerings as consumers became more aware of ethnic cuisines. There was a desire for more gluten-free cuisine and non-wheat noodles and pasta. Finally, more attention was being placed on children's meals with a focus on catering to children's healthy nutritional needs.[23]

Behavioural and demographic shifts were changing restaurant trends. In North America, the aging population was growing and consisted of individuals who were healthier and wealthier than any generation before them. They did not eat out more frequently than younger generations, but they were more likely to visit full service restaurants. Younger generations (in particular millennials who were 18 to 34 years old) were gaining increased purchasing power and, given their busy lifestyle, were more likely to grab food at quick service restaurants. In particular, the morning snack, afternoon snack and evening snack were the fastest growing day segments.[24] According to Robert Carter, the executive director of food service at The NPD Group, "the overarching trend … is that Canadians of all ages are having more sitdown meals at home and grabbing quick bites from fast food restaurants while on the go."[25] Mobile and digital technologies were driving consumers' desire for information and offering companies new ways to attract consumer engagement. Consumers, particularly in quick service restaurants, wanted the convenience of paying for purchases or accessing rewards through their mobile devices.[26]

Tim Hortons: A History

Tim Hortons' restaurants, commonly called "Tims or Timmy's" by devoted customers, had become part of the Canadian identity. Internationally, the stores had been branded as Tim Hortons Cafe and Bake Shop. The chain was first opened in Hamilton, Canada in 1964 by hockey legend Miles G. "Tim" Horton. Ron Joyce was the franchisee of Restaurant #1, also located in Hamilton. By 1967, he and Horton had become full partners in the company. After Horton's tragic death in a car accident in 1974, Joyce purchased Hortons' shares from his wife for $1 million, becoming the chain's sole owner. At the time, there were 40 stores, and an independent audit had appraised the business at $1.7 million.[27]

Using a franchisee model (99.5 percent of the stores were franchised owned), Tim Hortons became the largest quick service restaurant chain in Canada, specializing in coffee, baked goods, breakfasts and homestyle lunches. Its commitment to maintaining a close relationship with franchisees and the communities where it operated generated immense guest loyalty and built the company into one of the most widely recognized consumer brands in Canada. The company was originally incorporated as Tim Donut Ltd. Then, in 1990 it changed its name to

The TLD Group Ltd. In 1995, it merged with Wendy's International Inc.; however, on September 28, 2006, it was spun off as a separate public company incorporated in Delaware, trading on the Toronto Stock Exchange and the New York Stock Exchange under TSI. Three years later, in September 2009, the company reorganized its corporate structure and became a Canadian public company named Tim Hortons Inc., effectively repatriating itself to Canada.

Tim Hortons was the fourth largest publicly traded quick service restaurant chain in North America based on market capitalization and the largest in Canada. It had more than 100,000 employees, the majority of whom worked in franchised locations. The head office was in Oakville with smaller regional offices located across Canada and in the United States.

Organizational Structure

Tim Hortons' head office in Oakville employed more than 1,800 people who performed corporate functions in the main and regional offices, distribution centres and manufacturing facilities. The head office buildings included Tim Hortons University (a training centre for franchisees), corporate restaurants and an innovation centre. There were five regional offices in Canada and two in the United States.

The central team supported all facets of the business including operations, finance, human resources, information technology, legal services, research and development, training, real estate acquisitions, franchising, purchasing and marketing. Marc Caira became President and CEO in July, 2013. Caira had extensive food experience, having been the CEO of Nestlé Professional and the president and CEO of Parmalat North America. Caira led an executive team of nine individuals. Tim Hortons also had a Franchisee Advisory Board made up of 16 restaurant owners from across the chain and management. This board met quarterly to discuss issues impacting on the industry or the chain.[28]

Mission and Vision

Tim Hortons' guiding mission was "to deliver superior quality products and services for [its] guests and communities through leadership, innovation and partnerships."[29] Its vision was "to be the quality leader in everything [it] did."[30]

Foundation

Created in 1974, the Tim Hortons Children's Foundation (the Foundation) supported several charitable events, but its main focus was a summer camp program for under-privileged children. Since 1975, more than 150,000 children and youth had attended one of six summer camps at no cost to them or their families. While donations were collected year-round through counter and drive-thru coin boxes located at Tim Hortons' stores, once a year on "Camp Day" the proceeds from coffee sales and related activities at the majority of Tim Hortons' locations were given to support the summer camp program.

Store Locations

As of the end of August 2014, there were 3,588 Tim Hortons' restaurants in Canada, 859 in the United States and 38 in the Gulf Cooperation Council (GCC).[31] With a few locations in Europe, this resulted in a total of 4,546 restaurants globally. In Canada, operations originally were focused in Ontario and Atlantic Canada. This expanded over time to include Quebec and western Canada.

The most unique Tim Hortons' location was the Canadian Forces (CF) operations base in Kandahar, Afghanistan. It opened on Canada Day in 2006 and served four million cups of coffee, three million donuts and half a million iced cappuccinos and bagels to over 2.5 million customers from more than 37 countries. More than 230 Canadians travelled overseas to work at this Tim Hortons and served approximately 30,000 CF members over 11 rotations. The Kandahar Tim Hortons was operated by the Canadian Forces Personnel and Family Support Services with proceeds benefitting military community and family support programs. Tim Hortons waived all fees and operating costs typically associated with a franchise and the Kandahar operation ended in November 2011 when all CF troops left Afghanistan.

Some analysts believed that Tim Hortons had reached its saturation point in Canada.[32] In 1984, the company opened its first international store in Tonawanda, New York. During the 1990s, it expanded into other states including Ohio, Kentucky, West Virginia and Michigan. By 2004, the acquisition of 42 Bess Eaton restaurants allowed the company to gain a foothold in New England, the traditional stronghold of Dunkin' Donuts. Tim Hortons' locations in this area did not perform well, leading to the closing of 36 stores in the northeastern United States in 2010.[33] U.S. locations close to the Canadian border seemed to perform the best, due to brand awareness. In 2014, Tim Hortons' locations continued to be focused in the northeastern United States with 859 stores in Michigan, Maine, Connecticut, Ohio,

West Virginia, Kentucky, Pennsylvania, Rhode Island, Massachusetts and New York.[34]

Tim Hortons had also expanded into the GCC. By August 2014, there were 38 stores in the United Arab Emirates, Oman, Qatar and Kuwait.[35] There were further plans for expansion into Bahrain with a goal of opening an additional 120 locations in the GCC region by 2018.[36] Tim Hortons had a small number of European locations as a result of a partnership with the Spar convenience store chain in 2007. By the end of 2013, Tim Hortons' coffee and donuts were available at approximately 255 locations in Ireland and the United Kingdom; the majority of these locations (252) were self-service kiosks.[37]

Products

Tim Hortons' biggest drawing card was its legendary coffee. It was so popular that the company constantly battled rumours that it added nicotine to make it addictive.[38] The coffee was a blend of 100 percent Arabica beans grown in the world's coffee producing regions. To ensure the coffee was always fresh, Tim Hortons served it within 20 minutes of being brewed; after 20 minutes, it was thrown away. The premium blend was sold in tins at most Tim Hortons' locations and at supermarkets. Its coffee was also available in pods compatible with at-home single-cup coffee brewing systems such as Tassimo and Keurig. A number of Tim Hortons' locations sold branded mugs and seasonal merchandise.

The chain focused on continuous product innovation—as consumer tastes grew, so did choices. The original menu included coffee and donuts but expanded to include tea, a small selection of cold beverages and baked goods (e.g., donuts, "timbits" and pastries). Originally, the baked goods were produced in-store. In 2003, the company switched from in-store preparation to preparing them centrally in Brantford, Ontario and then shipping them frozen to franchised stores to be baked and finished with fillings or glazes. This was initially controversial with franchisees and consumers but the outrage dissipated quickly.

During the 1980s, the baked goods offering expanded to include muffins, cakes, pies and cookies. This was followed by more substantial items including soups, chili and sandwiches. In 2006, Tim Hortons introduced breakfast options including breakfast sandwiches on biscuits, bagels and English muffins, as well as oatmeal. These items became wildly popular with Canadian customers. According to NPD research, by May 2011, Tim Hortons held 57 percent of the hot breakfast sandwich market in Canada compared to McDonald's 29 percent domestic

share.[39] To gain more of the lunch and dinner crowd, Tim Hortons aggressively expanded its food choices. It heavily promoted its soups, chili and cold sandwiches by offering combos, which included a traditional baked good and a coffee. It further expanded to include more hot offerings such as paninis, crispy chicken sandwiches and wraps. The company continued to invest in product innovation to keep the menu fresh and responsive to consumer trends.

Consumer tastes were also shifting as almost half of all Canadians and Americans surveyed stated that their last coffee was a dark roast.[40] In order to compete with other retail outlets such as Starbucks, which offered a bolder base coffee taste, Tim Hortons officially launched a dark roast coffee in its North American stores in August 2014.[41] This was the first time in the company's history that it had offered a coffee flavour other than its original premium blend. Caira commented on the launch, saying:

Tim Hortons prides itself on serving best-in-class coffee and responding to the evolving tastes of our guests, and our new Dark Roast blend speaks to that commitment. We know that our guests want choice when consuming their daily coffee and we applied our passion for coffee and brewing expertise to develop a superior tasting Dark Roast blend our guests will love.[42]

In recent years, it had expanded its hot and cold beverage offerings to compete with McDonald's McCafé menu; this included lattes, cappuccinos, iced teas and coffees, smoothies and iced lemonades, which were offered at a price point similar or lower than McDonald's and much less than Starbucks.

Franchise System

The cost to acquire a Tim Hortons' franchise was approximately $500,000. This included all furniture, equipment and signage; a seven-week training program; staff assistance opening the store; the right to use trademarks and trade names; and support from the corporate office. The corporate office assumed all of the costs associated with the development of the land and the building. Given the demands of running a franchise, Tim Hortons required franchise locations to have two partners, both of whom had to be permanent residents of Canada. Individuals granted a Tim Hortons' franchise were not allowed to operate any other business without the written approval of the company.

Licences were usually provided for 10 years with the option of extending for an additional 10 years. For the term of the licence, franchisees were obligated to provide a weekly royalty fee of 4.5 percent of gross sales and a monthly advertising levy of 4 percent of gross sales. They also had a monthly rental fee, which was the greater of a fixed minimum rent or 8.5 percent of gross monthly sales.[43] Even with these stipulations, there was a high demand for Tim Hortons' franchises in Canada. While almost all of Tim Hortons' restaurants in Canada and the United States were franchised, corporately owned and operated restaurants were used for the purposes of training and product/market development.

Store Operations

Most standard Tim Hortons' locations were open 24 hours. Guests could eat in the dining areas, take the food out or use the drive-thrus, which catered to consumers on the go. Additionally, the company's "we fit anywhere" strategy led to a number of non-traditional locations in gas stations, convenience stores, universities, hospitals, office buildings and airports. A number of the locations were unionized.[44]

Tim Hortons also co-located with other franchise restaurants. In Canada, there were a number of combo unit locations, which housed both a Tim Hortons and a Wendy's. In 2007, Tim Hortons partnered with Cold Stone Creamery, a franchise that sold customizable, single-serve ice cream, jointly locating stores in selected Canadian locations. This partnership ended in 2014, and Cold Stone Creamery counters were removed from Tim Hortons' locations. 2014 also saw the closure of a number of underperforming locations in the United States.[45]

Sourcing

Tim Hortons sourced coffee from the world's coffee producing regions. In 2005, it created the Tim Hortons Coffee Partnership in Brazil, Guatemala, Honduras and Columbia to help local coffee farmers improve their lives economically, socially and environmentally. The program had assisted 3,400 farmers. This approach was different from Starbucks that had aggressive targets for responsibly grown and ethically sourced coffee through its Coffee and Farmer Equity (C.A.F.E.) practices.

Production and Distribution

Three manufacturing facilities, six warehouse distribution centres and one warehouse serviced Tim Hortons' restaurants across Canada and the United States (see Exhibit 1); corporate-owned trucks delivered food and supplies from the distribution centres to the restaurants.[46] It was a highly sophisticated operation; over 50,000 to 60,000 cartons of baked goods per week were shipped worldwide from the Guelph Distribution Centre alone.[47]

Marketing

On a chainwide basis, Tim Hortons advertised on television, radio, outdoor (billboards, transit shelters) and in some print vehicles (magazines). On a regional or restaurant basis, Tim Hortons also utilized newspaper advertising.[48] Commercials in Canada were used to introduce new products, but a number also reinforced the connection between Tim Hortons and Canadian culture. Its wildly successful "Roll up the Rim to Win"

Exhibit 1 Tim Hortons' Production/Distribution Facilities

Type	Location	Ownership	Approximate Square Footage
Manufacturing (U.S. coffee roasting facility)	Rochester, New York	Leased	38,000
Manufacturing (Fondant and Fills Facility)	Oakville, Ontario	Owned	36,650
Manufacturing (Canadian coffee roasting facility)	Hamilton, Ontario	Owned	76,000
Distribution/Office	Guelph, Ontario	Owned	191,679
Distribution/Office	Calgary, Alberta	Owned	35,500
Distribution/Office	Debert, Nova Scotia	Owned	28,000
Distribution/Office	Langley, British Columbia	Owned	27.500
Distribution/Office	Kingston, Ontario	Owned	135,080
Distribution/Office	Montreal, Quebec	Leased	30,270
Warehouse	Oakville, Ontario	Owned	37,000

Source: Adapted from Tim Hortons Inc., "2013 Annual Report," www.timhortons.com/ca/en/pdf/Tim_Hortons_2013_AR_full.pdf, p. 33, accessed August 22, 2014.

promotion, which started in 1986, gave away millions of prizes including cars, gift cards and Tim Hortons' products and was eagerly anticipated by its customer base.

Goals

Tim Hortons had strong short- and long-term goals. As stated in the company's 2013 Annual Report:

Our number one imperative is to deliver profitable growth, measured by same-store sales, operating profit improvement and sustainable earnings per share [EPS] growth. In 2014, while continuing our growth agenda, we plan to make transitional investments and further position our business for success.[49]

From 2015 to 2018, Tim Hortons had goals of an 11 to 13 percent compounded annual growth rate, cumulative free cash flows of approximately $2 billion, operating income generated through the U.S. segment of up to $50 million, and opening 800 or more new locations in North America and the GCC.[50]

Financial Performance

From a financial perspective, Tim Hortons grew overall revenues by 4.7 percent to $3.3 billion and operating income by 4.5 percent to $621 million in 2013. It had an operating margin of 19.1 percent and a net profit margin of 13.0 percent. Finally, the company's dividend per share had increased for the seventh year in a row from $0.24 to $0.32.[51] However, on the balance sheet were a number of issues, including a current ratio of 1.0, a quick ratio of 0.4 and a debt to equity ratio of 132.9 percent.[52]

Even though the company experienced its 22nd consecutive year of same-store sales growth in Canada and 23rd year in the United States, the growth in 2013 was very modest at 1.1 percent in Canada and 1.8 percent in the United States.[53] This was below the 2013 target of 2 to 4 percent in Canada and 3 to 5 percent in the United States.[54] While the company's EPS rose from $2.59 in 2012 to $2.82 in 2013 (an 8.9 percent increase), it was below the targeted EPS of $2.87 to $2.97.[55] As of its second quarter in June 2014, Tim Hortons was tracking well on a number of key financial indicators.[56] It had a return on assets of 20.5 percent, a return on equity of 53.0 percent and a return on invested capital of 24.9 percent. The debt to equity ratio had also improved to 3.7 percent. Exhibits 2 and 3 provide additional details.

The Competition

In Canada, Tim Hortons led its competition with 27 percent share of dollars and 42 percent share of traffic in the quick service industry; this was more than the next 15 chains combined.[57] However, competition was heating up in all categories, particularly at breakfast, as noted by Canaccord Genuity analyst Derek Dley who stated, "Now you've got a number of chains in the breakfast category all looking to capture more market share. Where is that going to come from? Well, it's going to be Tims."[58]

Tim Hortons had traditionally competed with the typical coffee and baked goods chains. However, with its stronger presence in the breakfast and lunch market, it faced increasing competition with restaurants in the broader quick service category (e.g., hamburgers, submarine sandwiches, pizzas and tacos). Its main competition in Canada and the United States came from Starbucks, McDonald's and Dunkin' Donuts.

McDonald's

McDonald's was founded in 1955 in Des Plaines, Illinois by Ray Kroc. The company went public in 1965 with 700 restaurants. In 1967, the first international location opened in Richmond, British Columbia. McDonald's quickly became the world's leading quick service retailer with more than 35,000 local restaurants in over 119 countries. At the end of 2013, 80 percent of these stores were franchise-owned. There were approximately 1,400 McDonald's restaurants in Canada; 80 percent were franchise stores. Franchise/licence agreements were generally for a 20-year term.

McDonald's products included distinct breakfast and lunch/dinner options. Menu items included egg-based sandwiches, muffins, hamburgers, French fries, salads, wraps and ice-cream based desserts along with beverages such as soda, milkshakes, fruit-based smoothies and coffee. McDonald's was very aware of the competition in the coffee category. In 2011, it launched McCafé, an espresso-based beverage to compete with Starbucks. McCafé was offered at a much lower price than Starbucks beverages, but they were not as customizable. From a strategy perspective, McDonald's was focused on balancing core menu items with new product innovation, improving customer service and strengthening its value platform.

In 2013, McDonald's globally increased its revenues by 3 percent in constant currencies to US$28.1 billion and experienced a 0.4 percent growth in comparable store sales. It also increased operating income by 3 percent in constant currencies and its EPS by 4 percent.[59] The company's financial performance in 2013 just met its

Exhibit 2 Tim Hortons' Income Statements (2009 to 2013)
(in thousands of Canadian dollars, except for weighted average number of shares)

Fiscal Years	2013	2012	2011	2010	2009
Sales	$2,265,884	$2,225,659	$2,012,170	$1,755,244	$1,704,065
Franchise revenues:					
Rents & royalties	$821,221	$780,992	$733,217	$687,039	$644,755
Franchise fees	$168,428	$113,853	$107,579	$94,212	$90,033
Total revenues	$3,255,533	$3,120,504	$2,852,966	$2,536,495	$2,438,853
Corporate reorganization expenses	$11,761	$18,874	–	–	–
Debranding costs	$19,016	–	–	–	–
Asset impairment and related closure costs	$2,889	$(372)	$372	$28,298	–
Other costs and expenses	$2,600,772	$2,507,477	$2,283,119	$1,997,034	$1,913,251
Total Costs and Expenses	$2,634,438	$2,525,979	$2,283,491	$2,025,332	$1,913,251
Gain on sale of interest in Maidstone Bakeries	–	–	–	$(361,075)	–
Operating Income	$621,095	$594,525	$569,475	$872,238	$525,602
Interest expense, net	$35,466	$30,413	$25,873	$24,180	$19,184
Income before income taxes	$585,629	$564,112	$543,602	$848,058	$506,418
Income taxes	$156,980	$156,346	$157,854	$200,940	$186,606
Net income after income taxes	$428,649	$407,766	$385,748	$647,118	$319,812
Net income attributable to non-controlling interests	$4,280	$4,881	$2,936	$23,159	$23,445
Net income attributable to Tim Hortons Inc	$424,369	$402,885	$382,812	$623,959	296,367
Diluted Earnings per Share	$2.82	$2.59	$2.35	$3.58	$1.64
Weighted average number of shares	150,622	150,676	162,597	174,215	180,609
Dividends per common share	$1.04	$0.84	$0.68	$0.52	$0.40

Source: Tim Hortons Inc., "2013 Annual Report," www.timhortons.com/ca/en/pdf/Tim_Hortons_2013_AR_full.pdf," p. 38, accessed August 22, 2014.

system-wide sales growth target of 3 percent to 5 percent but did not meet its operating income growth target of 6 percent to 7 percent.[60] In addition, its return on incremental invested capital (ROIIC) of 11.4 percent in 2013 did not meet its target of achieving a ROIIC in the high teens. The U.S. market had revenues of US$8.8 billion in 2013, roughly the same as the year previously.

Starbucks

Starbucks was founded in 1971 with a single location at Seattle's Pike Place Market. It incorporated in 1985 and went public in 1992. By June 2014, there were approximately 23,305 locations in 62 countries. This included 13,493 stores in the Americas (United States, Canada and Latin America) of which 8,078 were company-owned and 5,415 were licensed. Worldwide, Starbucks employed approximately 182,000 people in 2013, with 13,000 of the employees working in the United States.[61] The majority

of Starbucks' employees were not represented by a union. The company owned its own roasting facilities and leased the majority of its warehouse and distribution centres.

Starbucks' products included more than 30 blends and single-origin coffees; blended, customizable beverages; fresh food (sandwiches, pastries, salads, oatmeal, yogurt and fresh fruit); consumer products including ready-to-drink coffees, teas and juices; and merchandise including mugs, music, books and seasonal products. Starbucks was committed to ethical sourcing, environmental stewardship and community involvement. It offered generous compensation packages and supplementary benefits to its employees and invested in ongoing employee training.

In 2013, Starbucks had global revenues of US$14.9 billion, a 12 percent increase over 2012 revenues. This was driven by a 7 percent increase in global comparable store sales; the 7 percent increase was also achieved in

Exhibit 3 Tim Hortons Inc. and Subsidiaries — Consolidated Balance Sheet
(in thousands of Canadian dollars)

	Dec. 29, 2013	Dec. 30, 2012
ASSETS		
Current assets		
Cash and cash equivalents	$50,414	$120,139
Restricted cash and cash equivalents	155,006	150,574
Accounts receivable, net	210,664	171,605
Notes receivable, net	4,631	7,531
Deferred income taxes	10,165	7,142
Inventories and other, net	104,326	107,000
Advertising fund restricted assets	39,783	45,337
Total current assets	574,989	609,328
Long-term Assets	1,858,834	1,674,851
Total assets	$2,433,823	$2,284,179
LIABILITIES AND EQUITY		
Current liabilities		
Accounts payable	$204,514	$169,762
Accrued liabilities	274,008	227,739
Deferred income taxes	–	197
Advertising fund liabilities	59,912	44,893
Short-term borrowings	30,000	–
Current portion of long-term obligations	17,782	20,781
Total current liabilities	586,216	463,372
Long-term obligations		
Long-term debt	843,020	406,320
Capital leases	121,049	104,383
Deferred income taxes	9,929	10,399
Other long-term liabilities	112,090	109,614
Total long-term obligations	1,086,088	630,716
Equity		
Equity of Tim Hortons Inc. Common shares $2.84 stated value per share, Authorized: unlimited shares, Issued: 141,329,010 and 153,404,839 shares, respectively	400,738	435,033
Common shares held in Trust, at cost: 293,816 and 316,923 shares, respectively	(12,924)	(13,356)
Contributed surplus	11,033	10,970
Retained earnings	474,409	893,619
Accumulated other comprehensive loss	(112,102)	(139,028)
Total equity of Tim Hortons Inc.	761,154	1,187,238
Non-controlling interests	365	2,853
Total equity	761,519	1,190,091
Total liabilities and equity	$2,433,823	$2,284,179

Source: http://annualreport.timhortons.com/downloads/Balance-Sheet.xls, accessed August 21, 2014.

Exhibit 4 Comparables of Quick Service Restaurants

Company	Global Revenues (2013)	Number of Locations (Total)	Number of Locations (United States)	Number of Locations (Canada)
Tim Hortons	Cdn$3.3 billion	4,546	859	3,588
McDonald's	US$29.1 billion	35,429	14,278	1,400
Starbucks	US$14.9 billion	23,305	13,049	1,555
Dunkin' Donuts	US$7.4 billion	10,083	7,015	4

Source: Compiled by case authors.

the U.S. market.[62] It was believed that this increase was due to a 5 percent increase in the number of transactions and a 2 percent increase in the average bill. Globally, Starbucks achieved a non-GAAP operating margin of 16.5 percent based on a non-GAAP operating income of US$2.5 billion. However, due to the conclusion of litigation with Kraft Foods Global, Inc., Starbucks globally ended fiscal 2013 with an operating margin of −2.2 percent as compared to 15 percent in 2012.

Dunkin' Donuts

Founded in 1951 in Quincy, Massachusetts, Dunkin' Donuts franchises were established across the United States by 1955. By 2012, it had 10,083 in 32 countries worldwide, including 7,015 franchised restaurants in the United States and over 3,100 stores in international locations. The typical franchise agreement in the United States had a 20-year term, and initial franchise fees ranged from US$25,000 to $100,000 depending on the location.[63] From a product perspective, it offered 52 varieties of donuts as well as coffee, baked goods and breakfast sandwiches. The majority of stores were franchisee-owned, predominately located in the northeastern United States. It had expanded into Canada, but by the early 2000s, it had largely exited the Canadian market except for four locations in Quebec.

Dunkin' Donuts was a wholly owned subsidiary of Dunkin' Brands, which also included Baskin Robbins. For the full year 2013, Dunkin' Donuts' restaurants had global franchisee-reported sales of approximately US$7.4 billion.[64] This was driven by revenues in the United States of US$6.7 billion.[65] Dunkin' Donuts United States experienced a 3.4 percent comparable store sales growth in 2013, down from 4.3 percent in 2012. Dunkin' Donuts International experienced a comparable store sales decline of 0.4 percent in 2013. It planned to aggressively expand in the western United States, targeting California, and in Europe (in particular, Germany and the United Kingdom), the Middle East and Southeast Asia. Exhibits 4 and 5

Exhibit 5 Average Cost Comparison of Select Menu Items (in Canadian dollars before tax as of August 28, 2014)

	Tim Hortons	McDonald's	Starbucks
Coffee (Medium)	$1.52	$1.54	$1.85
Latte (Medium)	$2.69	$2.99	$3.45
Muffin	$1.29	$1.19	$2.00
Breakfast Sandwich	$2.99	$3.19	$3.95

Source: Compiled by case authors.

provide a comparison of Tim Hortons, McDonald's, Starbucks and Dunkin' Donuts.

Tim Hortons' Strategic Plan 2014 to 2018

Tim Hortons was facing tough competition domestically and internationally. In 2014, the company had unveiled a five-year strategic plan called "Winning in the New Era." Caira stated:

We envision a rejuvenated Canadian business that is the growth engine during our Strategic Plan time period. By 2018, we are working to have a profitable U.S. business that is ready to be aggressively scaled. We are looking to build on our established, growing international presence. We are building new capabilities and talent to execute flawlessly against our plans, and we are working to create above-market-average total shareholder returns.[66]

The plan focused on four core ideas: (i) driving same-store sales by targeting specific segments of the day category and marketing opportunities, (ii) investing to build scale and brand in new and existing markets, (iii) growing in new ways, and (iv) leveraging the firm's core business strengths and franchise system.

i. Same-store growth was not performing as well as had been forecasted. There was a desire to grow the hot and cold beverage category and market share, as well as to take advantage of the growing trend of snacking between meals. In addition, Tim Hortons was branded differently in the United States than in Canada; there was an opportunity to use product innovation to further differentiate the company in the U.S. market. This could involve new advertising and marketing campaigns.

ii. While Tim Hortons was primarily located in Canada, there were still growth opportunities in western Canada, Quebec and major urban markets. Strategically, the U.S. market was considered to be a must win battle which would require aggressive and rapid expansion.

iii. Tim Hortons had been considering changing the standard design of its restaurants to increase capacity and throughput. This could involve different interior and exterior features, equipment and menu items. The goal was to maximize throughput, not have patrons linger in the store. This was different than the Starbucks model of creating a third living space for customers outside of their homes and offices.

iv. The franchise system worked very well for Tim Hortons, and there was an opportunity to build on the success of the system. Over the next five years, the company could pursue additional vertical integration and supply-chain opportunities to maintain control over more facets of the business.

Acquisition

The strategic plan was now linked to the likely acquisition of Tim Hortons by 3G Capital, a Brazilian private equity firm that was Burger King's majority owner. The deal, announced in August 2014, would pay current Tim Hortons' shareholders approximately $94 a share, structured as $65.50 cash for each existing Tim Hortons' share in addition to 0.8025 shares in the new company for each Tim Hortons' share.[67] Shareholders had the flexibility to select an all-share or all-cash option. The $94 share price was 39 percent higher than the average price Tim Hortons' shares had traded at in the month prior to the announcement of the merger. 3G Capital would own 51 percent of the combined company in the $12.5 billion merger, which would create the world's third largest quick service restaurant company; $3 billion of preferred equity financing for the deal was to come from Warren Buffet's Berkshire Hathaway.

3G Capital owned two-thirds of Burger King and the deal had already been approved by its board and had unanimously accepted by the Tim Hortons' board. However, it still had to be approved by Tim Hortons'

shareholders and likely Canadian and U.S. regulators. The new company would be headquartered in Oakville, Ontario along with the Tim Hortons' corporate office. Burger King's head offices would continue to be in Miami, Florida. It was expected that Tim Hortons and Burger King would continue to operate as separate organizations and that the franchisee relationships would be managed independently by the separate brands.[68] Financial analysts felt this move benefitted both parties in that the location of the company headquarters in Canada allowed the new company to take advantage of Canada's lower corporate tax rates while Tim Hortons would benefit from Burger King's global expansion experience. Caira was very positive about the growth potential this merger offered for Tim Hortons stating: "As an independent brand within the new company, this transaction will enable us to move more quickly and efficiently to bring Tim Hortons' iconic Canadian brand to a new global customer base."[69]

Path Forward: Strategic Choices

While the merger talks were exciting, Tim Hortons had to continue implementing its strategic plan. There were important options to consider. Its recent crispy chicken sandwich was beginning to resemble products found at McDonald's. Menu innovations to target the dinner market could include more complex items. This would change the food operation of the kitchen and the length of time required to prepare the food. Were there other menu innovations Tim Hortons should consider to drive customer traffic to stores?

Geographic expansion opportunities seemed limitless. Canadian and U.S. expansion were a priority, but where should it occur and in what order? All of Tim Hortons' competitors were either already present or were expanding into Europe; should this market share just be ceded to them? Tim Hortons had a different brand presence in each of its three existing jurisdictions—Canada, the United States and the GCC. Should the company be positioned the same way in each area with the same marketing, menu and pricing? And how could the partnership with Burger King help with this expansion?

Finally, how could Tim Hortons take advantage of food trends? Food trucks were becoming popular, and Starbucks was experimenting with coffee trucks on university and college campuses. Tim Hortons had experience using semi-mobile retail space while stores were undergoing renovations. Was this type of alternative store format something it should try, recognizing that it was outside the franchise model?

To have an international presence, Tim Hortons would need financial resources, organizational capabilities, store saturation, product innovation and brand recognition to compete with some of the world's largest and best known quick service companies. The potential merger with Burger King would help, but would it be enough to create a competitive advantage on a global scale?

NOTES

1. This case has been written on the basis of published sources only. Consequently, the interpretation and perspectives presented in this case are not necessarily those of Tim Hortons Inc. or any of its employees.

2. All dollars in the case are stated in Canadian dollars unless otherwise noted.

3. David Hains, "Six Things You Need to Know About the Tim Hortons Deal," August 26, 2014, www.theglobeandmail.com/report-on-business/six-things-you-need-to-know-about-the-tim-hortons-deal/article20208297/, accessed August 28, 2014.

4. National Restaurant Association, "2014 Restaurant Industry Forecast," www.restaurant.org/Downloads/PDFs/News-Research/research/2014Forecast-ExecSummary.pdf, accessed August 10, 2014.

5. Ibid.

6. National Restaurant Association, "2014 Restaurant Industry Pocket Factbook," www.restaurant.org/Downloads/PDFs/News-Research/research/Factbook2014_LetterSize.pdf, accessed August 20, 2014.

7. First Research, "Restaurant Industry Profile," www.firstresearch.com/industry-research/Restaurants.htm, accessed August 20, 2014.

8. Jeff Dover, "11 Trends and Factors Affecting Canada's Food Service Industry," May 1, 2014, www.restaurantcentral.ca/trendsfactorsCanadasfoodserviceindustry.aspx, accessed August 20, 2014.

9. Restaurant Central, "Canada's Restaurant Labour Force: 16 Employment Facts and Figures," www.restaurantcentral.ca/Canadasrestaurantlabourforce.aspx, accessed August 20, 2014.

10. NPD Group, "Fast Casual Is Only Restaurant Segment to See Traffic Growth in 2013, Reports NPD," www.npd.com/wps/portal/npd/us/news/press-releases/fast-casual-is-only-restaurant-segment-to-see-traffic-growth-in-2013-reports-npd/, accessed August 21, 2014.

11. National Restaurant Association, "Restaurant Industry 2014: Limited-Service Trends," www.Restaurant.org, accessed August 10, 2014.

12. Ibid.

13. Alicia Kelso, "Report: Limited Service Restaurants Fighting Harder for Customers," June 17, 2013, www.qsrweb.com/articles/report-limited-service-restaurants-fighting-harder-for-customers/, accessed August 21, 2014.

14. NPD Group, "Fast Casual Report," www.npd.com/latest-reports/fast-casual-restaurants-foodservice-report/, accessed August 21, 2014.

15. Daniel Campbell, "How QSRs and Fast Casuals are Fighting for Market Share," July 29, 2014, www.qsrweb.com/articles/how-qsrs-and-fast-casuals-are-fighting-for-market-share/, accessed August 21, 2014.

16. NPD Group, "Fast Casual Is Only Restaurant Segment to See Traffic Growth in 2013, Reports NPD," op.cit.

17. Ibid.

18. Campbell, op.cit.

19. A&W, "A&W Revenue Royalties Income Fund," www.awincomefund.ca/aboutfund/indicators.asp, accessed August 22, 2014.

20. QSR Web, "Consumer Traffic, Unit Growth Low in 2014," www.qsrweb.com/news/consumer-traffic-unit-growth-low-in-2014/, accessed August 21, 2014.

21. National Restaurant Association, "Economist's Notebook: Restaurant Indicators a Mixed Bag in 2014," www.restaurant.org/News-Research/News/Economist-s-Notebook-Restaurant-indicators-a-mixed, accessed August 21, 2014.

22. National Restaurant Association, "Restaurant Operations Report," www.restaurant.org/News-Research/Research/Operations-Report, accessed August 20, 2014.

23. National Restaurant Association, "2014 Culinary Trends: Top 10 Trends," www.restaurant.org/Restaurant/media/Restaurant/SiteImages/News%20and%20Research/Whats%20Hot/What-s-Hot-Top-Ten.jpg, accessed August 22, 2014.

24. Dover, op.cit.

25. NPD Group, www.npdgroup.ca/wps/portal/npd/ca/news/press-releases/fast-food-still-king-in-canada/, accessed August 22, 2014.

26. Tim Hortons Inc., "2013 Annual Report," http://annualreport.timhortons.com/winning.html, accessed August 22, 2014.

27. CBC Digital Archives, "Tim Hortons: Ron Joyce Has a Story to Tell," www.cbc.ca/archives/categories/economy-business/consumer-goods/tim-hortons-coffee-crullers-and-canadiana/ron-joyce-has-a-story-to-tell.html, accessed August 26, 2014.

28. Tim Hortons Inc., "Company Facts," www.timhortons.com/ca/en/about/media-company-facts.html, accessed August 21, 2014.

29. Ibid.

30. Ibid.

31. Tim Hortons and Burger King, "Creating a Global QSR Leader," Investor Call Presentation. August 26, 2014.

32. Jeff Beer, "Fresh Trouble for the Double Double?," January 16, 2013, www.canadianbusiness.com/companies-and-industries/tim-hortons-sales-slow/, accessed August 20, 2014.

33. James Cowan, "Why Tim Hortons Can't RRRoll into the United States," February 19, 2013, www.canadianbusiness.com/blogs-and-comment/tim-hortons-american-expansion-failure/, accessed August 21, 2014.

34. Tim Hortons Inc., "About Us: The Story of Tim Hortons," http://shopus.timhortons.com/info/about, accessed August 20, 2014.

35. Tim Hortons and Burger King, op.cit.

36. Madhavi Acharya-Tom Yew, "Tim Hortons Opens in Oman," November 12, 2012, www.thestar.com/business/2012/11/12/tim_hortons_opens_in_oman.html, accessed August 19, 2014.

37. Tim Hortons Inc., "2013 Annual Report," op.cit.

38. Tim Hortons Inc., "Frequently Asked Questions," www.timhortons.com/ca/en/about/faq.php, accessed August 21, 2014.

39. Jason Buckland, "Tim Hortons' Greatest Success Stories," November 17, 2011, http://money.ca.msn.com/savings-debt/gallery/tim-hortons%e2%80%99-greatest-successes?cp-documentid=31401616&page=5, accessed August 21, 2014.

40. Tim Hortons Inc., "Tim Hortons Goes Dark Across North America," August 14, 2014, www.timhortons.com/ca/en/corporate/tim-hortons-goes-dark-across-north-america.php, accessed August 24, 2014.

41. Ibid.

42. Ibid.

43. Tim Hortons Inc., "Frequently Asked Questions," op.cit.

44. CBC News, "First Quebec Union at Tim Hortons Approved," December 4, 2003, www.cbc.ca/news/business/first-quebec-union-at-tim-hortons-approved-1.380806, accessed August 21, 2014.

45. Tim Hortons Inc., "2013 Fourth Quarter and Year-End Conference Call," http://files.shareholder.com/downloads/ABEA-333FKS/3412937430x0x727310/46189b5c-fbb3-4dcb-8de8-6aa6bf55f681/THI%20Q4-2013%20Conference%20Call%20Slides%20(FINAL-FINAL).pdf, accessed August 21, 2014.

46. Tim Hortons Inc., "About Us: Company Facts," op.cit.

47. Guy Broderick, "Tim Hortons' Trucking Recipe," June 12, 2012, www.todaystrucking.com/tim-hortons-trucking-recipe, accessed August 26, 2014.

48. Tim Hortons Inc., "Frequently Asked Questions," op.cit.

49. Tim Hortons Inc., "Winning in the New Era: Tim Hortons 2014-2018 Strategic Plan," http://annu alreport.timhortons.com/winning.html, accessed August 22, 2014.

50. Ibid.

51. Tim Hortons Inc., "Dividend History," www.timhortons.com/us/en/corporate/dividend.php, accessed August 20, 2014.

52. Tim Hortons Inc., "2013 Annual Report: Financial Highlights," http://annualreport.timhortons.com/2013-highlights.html, accessed August 21, 2014.

53. Tim Hortons Inc., "2013 Annual Report," op.cit.

54. Tim Hortons Inc., "2013 Fourth Quarter and Year-End Conference Call," op.cit.

55. Ibid.

56. Tim Hortons Inc., "Q2 2014: Investor Fact Sheet," www.timhortons.com/ca/en/pdf/THI_Q2_2014_Investor_Fact_Sheet.pdf, accessed August 21, 2014.

57. Tim Hortons Inc., "2013 Annual Report," op.cit.

58. Canadian Business, "Fresh Trouble for the Double Double," January 16, 2013, www.canadianbusiness.com/companies-and-industries/tim-hortons-sales-slow/, accessed August 21, 2014.

59. McDonald's Corporation, "2013 Annual Report," www.aboutmcdonalds.com/content/dam/AboutMcDonalds/Investors/McDs2013AnnualReport.pdf, accessed August 21, 2014.

60. Ibid.

61. Starbucks Coffee, "Starbucks 2013 Annual Report," http://investor.starbucks.com/phoenix.zhtml?c=99518&p=irol-irhome, accessed August 21, 2014.

62. Ibid.

63. Dunkin' Donuts, "2013 Annual Report," http://files.shareholder.com/downloads/ABEA-68SCR9/3419859776x0x737142/968D8A70-6911-43A5-AE59-791BF8FD6504/DNKN_Annual_Report_Final_.pdf, accessed August 21, 2014.

64. Dunkin' Donuts, "About Dunkin' Donuts," http://news.dunkinbrands.com/Content/Detail.aspx?ReleaseID=190&NewsAreaID=29&ClientID=3, accessed August 21, 2014.

65. Dunkin' Donuts, "2013 Annual Report," op.cit.

66. Tim Hortons Inc., "2013 Annual Report," op.cit.

67. CBC.ca, "Tim Hortons Agrees to Burger King Offer for $94 a Share," http://news.ca.msn.com/top-stories/tim-hortons-agrees-to-burger-king-offer-for-dollar94-a-share/?ocid=binganswers, accessed August 26, 2014.

68. Tim Hortons and Burger King, op.cit.

69. Eric Atkins and Jacqueline Nelson, "Burger King, Tim Hortons Ink Merger Deal for $12.5 billion," August 26, 2014, www.theglobeandmail.com/report-on-business/burger-king-tim-hortons-ink-merger-deal-for-125-billion/article20203522/, accessed August 26, 2014.

CASE 20

W. L. Gore—Culture of Innovation

"Why … couldn't an entire company be designed as a bureaucracy-free zone?"[1]

This was the thought that enthralled Wilbert ("Bill") L. Gore, a chemical engineer at E. I. du Pont de Nemours and Company (DuPont). This thought led him to break out of the traditional management practices and create a company that would cherish human imagination and freedom.

W. L. Gore & Associates, Inc. (referred to as W. L. Gore, or just Gore, in what follows) was founded in 1958. It was a privately held company headquartered in the suburbs of Newark, Delaware. In 2011, it was ranked for the 14th consecutive year among the "100 Best Companies to Work For" by *Fortune* magazine. Also, for several years in a row, it was named one of the best workplaces in the United Kingdom, Germany, France, and Italy. In recent years, it had appeared in the Sweden and Spain lists as well.[2]

The voluntary turnover rate at Gore was around 5%—one-third the average rate in its industry (durable goods) and one-fifth that for private firms of similar size.[3] In 2012, it had "more than 9,500 employees, called associates, located in 30 countries worldwide, with manufacturing facilities in the United States, Germany, Scotland, Japan, and China, and sales offices around the world."[4]

Though the company did not publish its financials, it had reportedly been profitable every year since its inception, and its revenues were approximately $3 billion.[5]

When Bill Gore embarked on his dream to create an innovative enterprise over a half century ago, he had a lot of questions:

Could you build a company with no hierarchy—where everyone was free to talk with everyone else? How about a company where there were no bosses, no supervisors, and no vice presidents? Could you let people choose what they wanted to work on, rather than assigning them tasks? Could you create a company with no "core" business, where people would put as much energy into finding the next big thing as they did into milking the last big thing? And could you do all of this while still delivering consistent growth and profitability?[6]

Background and Brief History

In April 1938, Dr. Roy J. Plunkett, a research chemist at DuPont, discovered PTFE (polytetrafluoroethylene resin), which was trademarked under the brand name Teflon.[7] Bill Gore, during his 17-year career at DuPont, was assigned several times to small R&D task forces, the last one of which was responsible for finding a meaningful commercial use for Teflon. While they were working on this assignment, another group at DuPont came up with a way to make thermoplastics out of Teflon. Hence, DuPont felt no need for Gore's group to continue. Gore observed, "Du Pont felt that [the thermoplastic version of Teflon] was good enough, and our group was dissolved."[8]

Gore believed that DuPont was largely underestimating the potential of this "slick, waxy fluoropolymer,"[9] so he continued to work on it in his spare time. Gore knew Teflon's unique properties as an electrical insulator and was trying to coat wire with it. Finally, in the fall of 1957, with help from his son Bob, he succeeded in producing a good ribbon cable by sandwiching wire between Teflon tapes. DuPont, with its traditional business of supplying raw materials, didn't want to enter the wire business. Nonetheless, it granted Bill Gore permission to start his own company and agreed to provide the required supply of Teflon.[10]

In 1958, Bill and his wife, Genevieve ("Vieve"), both 45 years old, invested their life savings to form W. L. Gore & Associates, which operated from the basement of their home in the suburbs outside of Newark, Delaware. The company's first product was the Multi-Tet insulated wire and cable. In 1960, Gore received its first major order for 7.5 miles of insulated ribbon cabling from the Denver Water Company. This required increased manufacturing capacity and prompted the company's move from the family basement into its first manufacturing plant nearby.[11]

In 1969, Bob Gore discovered that rapidly stretching PTFE did not break the material but made it strong, highly porous, and extremely versatile. This new polymer, expanded polytetrafluoroethylene (ePTFE), was the

Exhibit 1 A Few Notable Events in W. L. Gore's History

Year	Event
1958	The enterprise's first product was Multi-Tet insulated wire and cable. Early associates were paid in part with awards of Gore stock, establishing a tradition of associate ownership through shareholding.
1960	The company issued its first profit share to associates.
1963	The company earned its first patent. U.S. Patent 3,082,292 was issued to Bob Gore for the "Multiconductor Wiring Strip" known as Multi-Tet cable.
1972	Gore's annual sales reached $10 million.
1981	Gore fibers were used in space suits in the inaugural space shuttle mission.
1986	Bill Gore died while hiking in Wyoming at age 74. Bob Gore became CEO.
1992	Glide dental floss was introduced nationally.
1997	Elixir guitar strings were introduced.
2000	Chuck Carroll became president and CEO.
2005	Vieve Gore passed away at age 91. Terri Kelly succeeded Chuck Carroll as president and CEO.
2007	Gore hit the $2 billion sales mark.

Source: Casewriter's extracts from "50 Years of Gore History Online," W. L. Gore & Associates Web site, http://www.gore.com/timeline/, accessed March 11, 2012.

first step towards Gore-Tex, the waterproof and breathable fabric that made the company famous. This polymer found its way into shoes, gloves, head gear, and other outdoor adventure wear that was used in expeditions to the North and South poles and Mount Everest.[12] In 1981, the spacesuits worn by NASA astronauts on the space shuttle *Columbia* were made with Gore-Tex fabric.[13]

By 2011, Gore held more than 2,000 patents worldwide in fields ranging from fabrics, electronics, medical devices (implant biomaterials), consumer products, pharmaceuticals and polymer processing.[14] More than 25 million people around the world had Gore's medical implants. Gore also supplied the most technologically advanced portfolio of Membrane Electrode Assemblies

(MEA products) for the fuel cell industry.[15] Refer to Exhibit 1 for some other notable events in the history of the company.

Lattice Enterprise; No Hierarchies

"I spend a significant amount of time focusing on the environment at Gore. I'm a firm believer that if you get the environment right, the business stuff is easy."
—Terri Kelly, CEO, Gore[16]

Gore's mission statement put the culture of the firm ahead of its employees and its products (Exhibit 2).

While at DuPont, although Bill Gore was part of a much bigger organization, the small, focused teams that

Exhibit 2 The Mission

Nurture a vibrant **Culture** that engages talented **Associates** who deliver innovative **Products** that create extraordinary value for all of our stakeholders

Culture
- Believes in individuals and the power of small teams
- Encourages the entrepreneurial spirit
- Instills ownership for the success of the Enterprise
- Takes a global, long term view

Associates
- Live the culture
- Act with the utmost integrity
- Offer diverse perspectives
- Are passionate about what they do

Products
- We are proud of
- Build upon our deep knowledge
- Leverage core technology and other competencies
- Do what we say they will do

Source: Casewriter, adapted from Terri Kelly, "Nurturing a Vibrant Culture to Drive Innovation," talk given on December 9, 2008 at Wong Auditorium, MIT Sloan School of Management, Cambridge, MA, available from MIT World video collection, http://mitworld.mit.edu/video/643.

he used to work in had innate passion, initiative, and courage. The freewheeling spirit and operational autonomy that drove these small teams energized Gore, and he knew they invigorated his colleagues, too.[17] Further, Bill Gore's philosophy of management was deeply inspired by two sets of management theory: Abraham Maslow's Hierarchy of Needs, published in 1943, and Douglas McGregor's 1960 bestseller, *The Human Side of Enterprise*.[18]

Maslow suggested that there are five human needs—physiological, safety, belonging, esteem, and self-actualization—and these needs are in a hierarchical order in the shape of a pyramid. At the base of the pyramid are the most basic physiological needs—food, water, shelter, and clothing. At the next level of the need pyramid is safety, i.e., security in one's person, finances, and health. At the next level is belonging, which is about friendship, intimacy, and family. Esteem needs include achievement, confidence, and respect. Finally, at the top of the pyramid is self-actualization, which includes creativity, morality, and problem solving.[19]

McGregor challenged the prevailing management beliefs of his time, which he labeled Theory X. According to him, Theory X assumes that the average human being has an inherent dislike of work and will avoid it if possible. Most people need to be forced to put in effort adequate to attain organizational success. By contrast, Theory Y assumes that the average human being finds work a source of satisfaction and will exercise self-direction and self-control in achieving the objectives he or she is committed to.[20]

These beliefs have been at the core of Gore's culture since its founding (Exhibit 3). Bill Gore deliberately set up his fledgling firm with the notion that an entire company can be designed to be bureaucracy-free:

The simplicity and order of an authoritarian organization make it an almost irresistible temptation. Yet it is counter to the principles of individual freedom and smothers the creative growth of man. Freedom requires orderly restraint. The restraints imposed by the need for cooperation are minimized with a lattice organization.[21]

A lattice organization is one that involves direct transactions, self-commitment, natural leadership, and lacks assigned or assumed authority. Every successful organization has a lattice organization that underlies the façade

Exhibit 3 Gore Culture

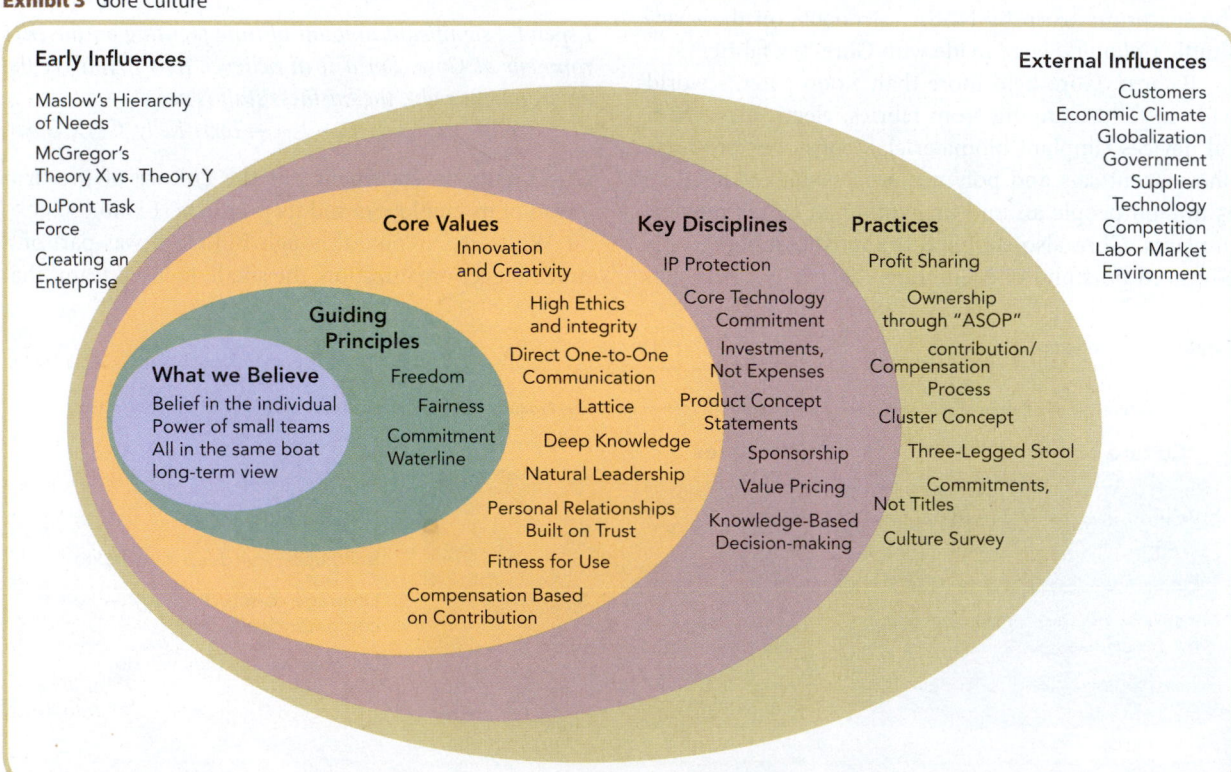

Source: Casewriter, adapted from Kelly.

of authoritarian hierarchy. It is through these lattice organizations that things get done, and most of us delight in going around the formal procedures and doing things the straightforward and easy way.[22]

While W. L. Gore & Associates seemingly had a divisional structure, underneath it was a very flat lattice organization: "no traditional organizational charts, no chains of command, nor pre-determined channels of communication."[23] Each person in the lattice could interact with every other person without an intermediary. All employees were known by the same title, "Associate." There was no hierarchy of communication. Associates were free to go directly to whoever they believed had an answer.

The lack of a formal organizational chart meant that the associates had to build their own network through personal relationships. It was their personal responsibility to connect and build their own lattice on their own initiative. This heavy emphasis on relationships extended beyond associates to customers, vendors, and surrounding communities. Direct face-to-face communication and phone calls were found to work best in collaborating, building, and maintaining long-term relationships.[24] So co-location of facilities and plants was very important for Gore. For instance, there were 15 sites clustered around their headquarters, in Delaware, and 10 plants around Flagstaff, Arizona. This density enhanced both cross-functional and cross-team communication and collaboration.[25] Further, most of Gore's buildings were very un-corporate-like: unassuming, bland, boring, and unimpressive.[26]

The company had four major divisions: fabrics, electronic products, medical products, and industrial products. It had small, product-focused business units, with all the company-wide support functions to ensure smooth day-to-day operation. No business unit was allowed to grow beyond a certain size and, with only a few exceptions, facility and manufacturing sites were limited to no more than 250 associates. Bill Gore believed that the firm had "to divide so that you can multiply."[27] A cluster of small plants in proximity allowed for everyone to know everyone else, have a sense of "ownership and identity,"[28] as well as accountability for their decisions. This closeness also helped associates to move easily between projects.

Bill Gore was not in favor of manuals or bureaucratic rules for prescribing a fixed solution in any given situation. So, according to Terri Kelly, president and CEO, policy manuals were quite useless, since every situation was different, and they took judgment away from individuals.[29] Gore's associates had the freedom to analyze and come up with their own conclusion as to the best way to deal with different situations. Rather than providing a playbook, the firm used a set of four guiding principles, originally articulated by Bill Gore, to help associates with their decisions and behaviors:

- **Freedom**: The company was designed to be an organization in which associates can achieve their own goals best by directing their efforts toward the success of the corporation; action is prized; ideas are encouraged; and making mistakes is viewed as part of the creative process. We define freedom as being empowered to encourage each other to grow in knowledge, skill, scope of responsibility, and range of activities. We believe that associates will exceed expectations when given the freedom to do so.
- **Fairness**: Everyone at Gore sincerely tries to be fair with each other, our suppliers, our customers, and anyone else with whom we do business.
- **Commitment**: We are not assigned tasks; rather, we each make our own commitments and keep them.
- **Waterline**: Everyone at Gore consults with other associates before taking actions that might be "below the waterline"—causing serious damage to the company.[30]

At Gore, a governing metaphor was "the Gore Ship": every ship has a "waterline." If you make one bad decision, and that makes a hole in the ship above the waterline, the ship may be damaged, but it will survive and not sink. You can learn from that experience and move on. But if you make a hole below the waterline, the ship could sink.

At most firms, guiding principles tended to be nice displays in entrances and in hallways or brochures. At Gore, the associates had to live them every day, since there were no job descriptions or direct reports.

Leaders, Sponsors, and Associates; No Titles or Bosses

"[Gore] is a tough place to lead."[31]

There were no fixed or assigned authorities at Gore. Even the CEO did not have direct reports.[32] Leaders at Gore focused on decentralization, made working groups cross-functional, and allocated resources. Leaders could not make commitments for others. Extreme freedom and autonomy meant that all associates had to understand their own capabilities and limits, set their own agendas, and make commitments to deliver results. Results were evaluated by their peers.

Hiring was considered a "waterline" decision, so candidates were interviewed by a broad and diverse team.

The hiring process was heavily weighted towards a candidate's fit with the values and the culture, rather than merely a technical fit. Gore hired fiercely motivated people who were able to take initiative, felt free to pursue ideas on their own, communicated effectively, built their own networks, and collaborated to create innovative products. Gore cherished the notion of "natural leadership."[33]

Natural leadership was defined by followership. It was not possible to be a leader at Gore unless you had followers. No one started as a leader at Gore. Leadership was earned over time. Most often, leaders emerged naturally by demonstrating special knowledge, skill, or experience that advanced business objectives. A leader had to keep re-earning the respect at every step, because teams had the liberty to fire their chief at any time. "We vote with our feet," [said] Rich Buckingham, a manufacturing leader in Gore's technical fabrics group. "If you call a meeting, and people show up, you're a leader."[34] A leader who had repeatedly earned such a label was free to use the word "leader" on his or her business card.[35]

Leadership was defined by one's ability to influence followers: leadership without authority. Influence was cultivated by building credibility. This required a great deal of preparation, validation, and people skills to marshal the resources, rather than dictation based on authority. This lack of authority also meant that leaders were often required to explain their decisions and actions. As Steve Young, a consumer-marketing expert hired from Vlasic Foods, quickly discovered, "If you tell anybody what to do here, they'll never work for you again."[36]

Kelly's path to becoming CEO, one of the very few titles at Gore, reflects the company's overall approach to leadership.[37] In 1983, Kelly joined Gore as a process engineer. During her early years at Gore, she focused on gaining experience as a product specialist with the then-small military fabrics business unit. She later led the unit and helped it grow into a leading producer of protective products for the armed forces globally. In 1998, Kelly gained recognition as part of the leadership team for the global Fabrics Division and helped establish Gore's first Asian fabrics manufacturing plant, in Shenzhen, China. Concurrently serving on the Enterprise Operations Committee, she also contributed to guiding the company's strategic direction.[38] In 2005, when Chuck Carroll retired as CEO, the management asked associates to choose someone they would be willing to follow. They weren't given a pre-defined list of names and were free to choose anyone. As Kelly recalled, "To my surprise, it was me."[39]

Every associate had a personal sponsor, someone who had voluntarily made a commitment to the associate's development, maximizing his or her contribution to the organization.[40] All understood that their job was to make everyone else successful.[41] The sponsors helped newcomers with their commitments and in fulfilling what it would take to deliver on them. They guided new recruits in finding a good fit between their skills and the needs of a particular team. During the first few months, a new associate was likely to experience different teams and be audited for a role. As the associates' commitments and needs changed, they or their sponsors were free to determine whether changes were needed, or even a new sponsor. Similarly, teams could choose whether they wanted to adopt a new member.[42] So, if an associate had difficulties finding a sponsor or a team, it was a strong indication that the associate would not be a good fit at Gore.[43]

One of the primary responsibilities of a sponsor, as a positive advocate, was to collect 360-degree information and feedback regarding the associate's personal development. This information, gathered from peers and leaders, was then shared with the appropriate compensation committee. Most sponsors were responsible for about five to seven associates. Leaders at Gore had four overarching requirements, centered on "living the culture" (see also Exhibit 4).

Leading Self—Be introspective, determine your capabilities, how your actions could impact the enterprise.

Getting it done—Be capable of doing the work, influencing others to get the necessary work done in an appropriate amount of time.

Shaping the vision—This differentiates a "Leader" and "Associate," the ability to shape or define the vision.

Leading others—One cannot go it alone and then have the ability to influence others to complete the tasks.

Exhibit 4 Leadership Expectations

Source: Casewriter, adapted from Kelly.

Living the culture—Did the leader uphold the values of culture in the process of getting their work done?[44]

While these requirements described what was expected, certain behaviors did not fit with the culture. Self-promotion, being a "know-it-all," declaring, "I am an expert," and displaying a Lone Ranger[45] type of behavior were disdained at Gore. It would be evident when an associate did not exhibit the behaviors consistent with the culture. When this happened, the associate's sponsors and mentors would try to work with the individual to create an action plan to correct these behaviors; otherwise, the parties would look at other options—including voluntary or involuntary termination.

Only Commitments; No Assignments

Associates were responsible to managing their own workload and would be accountable to others on their team. Only the associate could make a commitment to do something—a task, a project, or a new role. Once the commitment was made, the associate was expected to meet it. New associates were regularly cautioned against overextending themselves, and associates could reject any request. But once someone said, "I will do this," it was considered a near-sacred oath.

Projects and teams were not formed by assignment; rather, a product or project concept was usually formed by an individual, who garnered support to move forward. As the project progressed, project founders—not managers—had to sell their idea to other associates who they felt had the necessary technical, market, and organizational skills to advance the project.

Objectives were set by those who made them happen. This strategy was based on the belief that associates who were allowed to choose which projects to sponsor—by committing their resources—would more likely be motivated, because they would choose projects they believed in and felt they had an ownership stake in their success. Further, small teams with highly motivated associates supporting a project or product concept were more likely to succeed, because they believed in what they were doing. Exhibit 5 highlights this link between associate engagement, autonomous teams, and business success.

Teams were usually quite diverse, consisting of mathematicians, engineers, accountants, machinists,

Exhibit 5 Setup for Success

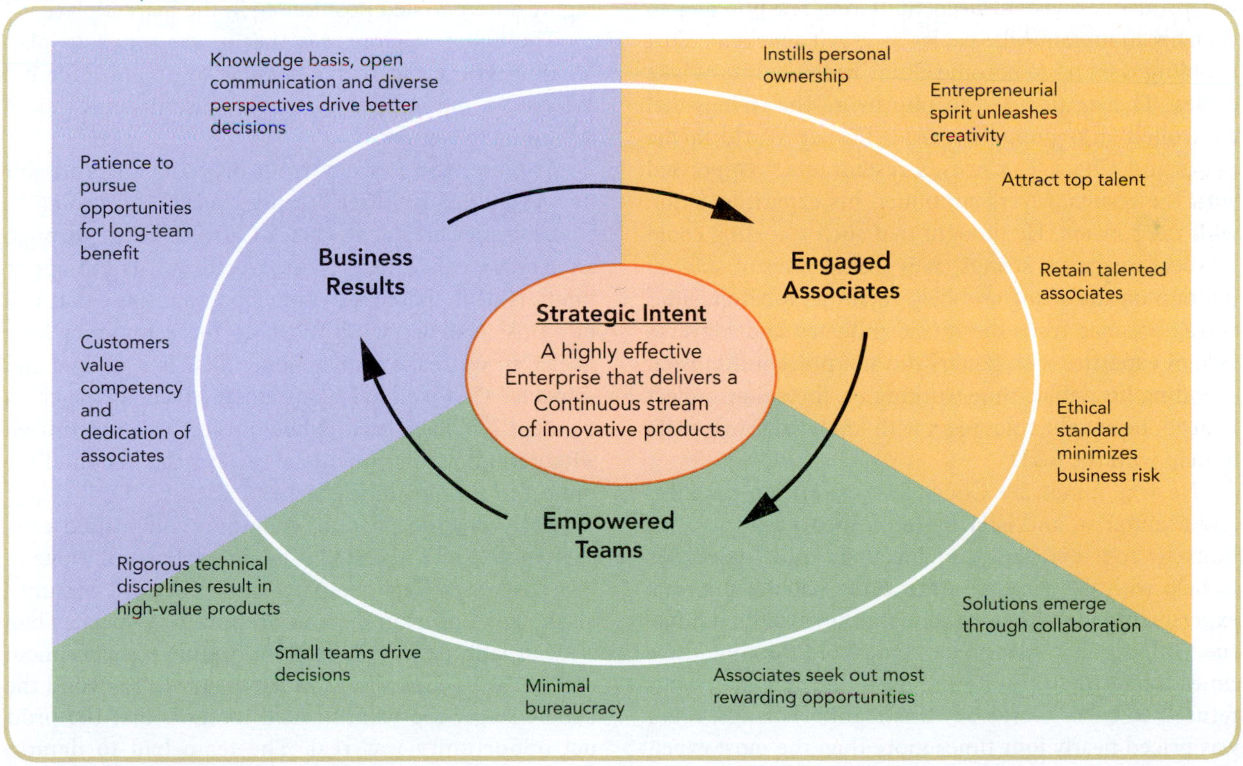

Source: Casewriter, adapted from Kelly.

and chemists. All these small, multi-disciplinary and boundary-crossing teams were freewheeling R&D groups who shared two common goals: to make money and have fun. Project teams were usually one-of-a-kind teams. They did not regroup over and over for subsequent projects. The composition of teams was opportunity driven—each one required different types of people with different kinds of expertise.

Anyone Can Be an Innovator; Nerds Are Mavericks

All associates were given free dabble time. They could spend up to 10% of their work hours in pursuing their own purpose.[46] When associates joined Gore they wouldn't have endless freedom; rather, the dabble time had to be earned.[47] Associates competed for the discretionary time of other talented individuals who were keen to work on something new and exciting and be part of promising projects. Assembling a self-motivated team to work on a new idea was, according to Kelly, "a process of giving away ownership of the idea to people who want to contribute. The project won't go anywhere if you don't let people run with it."[48]

As an instance, Dave Myers, an engineer who was principally developing cardiac implants for Gore's medical products division, used the Gore-Tex polymer to coat his mountain-bike cables as a grit repellent. That dabbling went on to become Gore's Ride-On line of bike cables. That in turn led to improving the strings that controlled large puppets at Walt Disney World theme parks and Chuck E. Cheese's restaurants.[49] Impressed with the results, Myers continued his experimentation with the concept. He thought that such a coating could be ideal for guitar strings, as it would prevent skin oil buildup on the string and help retain its tonal qualities. Gore's absence from the music industry and Meyers's lack of expertise with guitars did not prevent him from spending his dabble time working on the guitar project. Instead, he sought volunteers with knowledge of guitars to help with the R&D.[50]

He was joined by Chuck Hebestreit, an engineer and a guitarist, and later by John Spencer, a musician himself. Together, they convinced six other associates to help with the project.[51] After three years of informal experimentation, the team thought they had hit a home run with a guitar string that could hold the tone three times longer than traditional ones did. But merchants refused to carry Gore's $15 Elixir guitar strings. Elixir was priced nearly four times more than the most expensive string on the market in 1996. So Gore went directly to the backstage—the shows and subscriber lists of guitar magazines—and gave away 20,000 samples in the first year.[52] The artists were hooked and Elixir quickly became the leading brand of acoustic guitar strings in the United States.[53]

At any given time, Gore had hundreds of projects at various stages of development.[54] While this proliferation could be perceived as chaotic, there was discipline behind it. First, most of the opportunities were clearly rooted in Gore's deep knowledge and mastery in ePTFE. Applications and adjacencies were explored and filtered using this technology boundary. Almost all of Gore's thousands of products were based on just that one very versatile polymer (Exhibit 6). Second, ideas died if associates didn't sign up for projects. Product champions gave the gift of a new opportunity, and in return other associates donated their talent, experience, and commitment. So Gore could be considered as a "gift economy."[55] Associates had to "gift" their dabble time and get involved in their colleagues' projects.

"Real, Win, Worth"[56]

Gore did not care for me-too products. They pursued opportunities that were "unique and valuable."[57] Gore aimed for quantum improvements that gave them a highly differentiated positioning in the market place.

The belief at Gore was that it was tough to plan for innovation, but it was possible to organize for it.[58] "We have a methodical way of how we do innovation," according to Kelly.[59]

At Gore, the journey from dabbling to profitability was guided by three "reality checks." According to Gore's former president, Chuck Carroll, "We go through an exercise called Real, Win, Worth. . . . Is the opportunity real? Is there really somebody out there that will buy this? Can we win? What do the economics look like? Can we make money doing this? Is it unique and valuable? Can we have a sustained advantage [such as a patent]?"[60] Each post-dabble project was scrutinized with periodic cross-functional reviews that required the project to survive these checks.[61]

Early on, the product champions identified critical hypotheses and tested fundamental assumptions in low-cost ways. The company never invested big until all the key uncertainties were resolved. Associates had a lot of latitude and discretionary time to experiment and test their ideas. But to take the project beyond the dabble stage, the team needed to show that the product opportunity was real. The team had to demonstrate that the opportunity solved a genuine customer

Exhibit 6 Product Mix: Core Technology as a Common Link

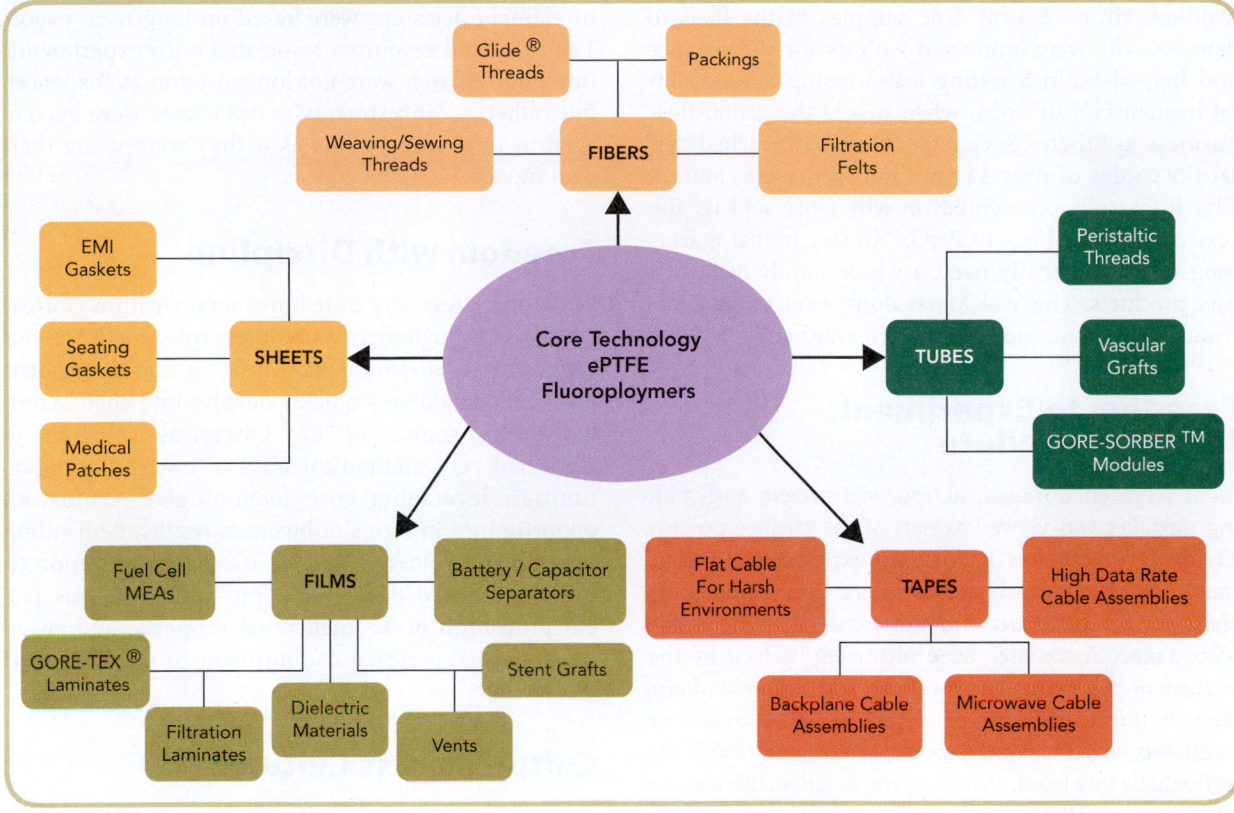

Source: Casewriter, adapted from Kelly.

problem for which the customer would be willing to pay—usually a premium. This step was crucial in order to attract resources to the project.[62] "It starts with the consumer. If we have a new technology but if it is not matching a consumer need, then it won't go far," [said] Christy Haywood [product manager from Gore's fabric division].[63]

As a project evolved from dabble-time experiment to one that sought formal support, the team prepared to participate in a series of peer reviews in which they were pressed on the fitness of the project. First, did the opportunity create a unique and differentiated product? Did the company get a technological advantage that it could defend? And did Gore have the resources and capabilities to make sure the product would do what the team said it would do?

Purpose, Passion, Persistence, Patience

"Gore has immense patience about the time it takes to get it right and get it to market," says Bob Doak, who leads a

Gore plant in Dundee, Scotland. "If there's a glimmer of hope, you're encouraged to keep a project going and see if it could become a big thing."[64]

Project teams self-organized or coalesced around passionate champions. Promising projects got nurtured for as long as they continued to pique the interest of a few associates and were not "burning through too much cash."[65] Concepts were given ample time, sometimes even years, to take form, and there were no cut-throat timelines or calendar marks. However, the company often knew when to pull the plug on a project, whether it was a new initiative or a successful business.

For instance, the origin of Glide dental floss dated back to 1971, when Bill Gore tried to use a Gore-Tex fabric ribbon to floss his teeth. For about twenty years, the company wasn't able to take the product to market, as it could not get health care product companies to adopt its technology or local drug stores to put the product on its shelves. In 1991, John Spencer came up with the idea of promoting the floss as a medical technology product instead of a normal consumer product. He gave away free samples of the floss to dentists, who were impressed with its shred resistance and helped build a strong followership among dental hygienists.[66] By 2003, when it sold the dental floss business to Procter & Gamble, Gore had reached dental floss sales of over $45 million in the U.S. market. Chuck Carroll commented on why Gore sold its successful Glide business to P&G: "To stay in that market long-term, you really need a whole family of healthcare products. The Wal-Marts don't want to buy floss from one guy and toothpaste from another."[67]

Freedom to Experiment; No Fear of Failure

Ideas were encouraged, action was prized, and making mistakes was viewed as part of the creative process. There were very low barriers to experimentation, as there was always ready access to equipment and materials. A project failure did not necessarily mean the team failed. Associates were ultimately judged by the success of the entire organization, and the individual's contribution to the enterprise was evaluated by a thorough 360-degree review process to score and rank the individuals in a team. When a project failed, there was a post-mortem: Was the concept flawed? Were there poor decisions made along the way? Was it a flawed approach to the solution, or was it simply poorly executed? The goal of this post-mortem was to learn from the experiment and to leverage it in other parts of the enterprise. When an initiative was killed, they "celebrated" with beer and Champagne.[68]

Compensation for associates was based on contribution. It was determined by a committee of leaders with expertise in the functional area. The committee reviewed and rank-ordered the associates on the basis of input from the leaders as well as the associate's peer group regarding his or her impact and effectiveness.[69] Even if projects failed or couldn't hit targets, contribution was judged on the basis of the associate's overall impact on the enterprise. For instance, coaching new hires was considered as a significant contribution. To ensure fairness and competitiveness externally, Gore continually compared compensation packages with similar firms and rewarded associates accordingly. They were also compensated through stock and profit-sharing programs.[70] "We are all in the same boat."[71]

After one year of employment, all associates were eligible to be owners in the firm. Employees owned nearly 25% of the firm.[72] Both risks and rewards were shared, with a commitment to long-term success. Investment decisions were based on long-term payoff. The costs and resources associated with experimentation and research were not looked upon as "expenses" but rather as "investments."[73] Associates were encouraged to treat investments as if they were using their own money.

Freedom with Discipline

While there was very little bureaucracy within Gore, it was not as though there was endless freedom. It was not a free-for-all environment. Knowing that distributed leadership could very quickly devolve into chaos, Gore had several sources of "Key Disciplines" (Exhibit 3). Gore had very methodical ways of describing opportunities, leveraging core technologies, evaluating opportunities in terms of business results, demanding peer-review processes, giving associates discretion to explore (earned over time), pursuing rigorous patent protection of its intellectual property, and ensuring sponsors' personal commitment to the success of associates.[74]

Culture across Cultures

In 2012, Gore was operating in 30 countries. One would have expected that a strong culture like Gore's would be quite a challenge to implement in certain countries, especially in Asia. Gore had made sure that there was room for adaptation. For instance, in Korea it was inconceivable not to have business cards with clearly labeled titles. It was critical for communication with customers and business partners, as well as for the associates' families. So Korean associates had all kinds of fancy titles on their business cards. Yet they very well knew that these titles didn't mean anything internally, and having them didn't mean they could behave differently.[75]

While sub-cultures existed within Gore around the world with subtle differences, some of the fundamental beliefs of Gore were held sacrosanct. According to Kelly, "The values are the same in Asia. Who doesn't want to be believed in? Who doesn't want to feel they can make a huge contribution? Most people want to be part of a team."[76]

Fifty years after its founding, a majority of the core tenets of Bill Gore's management philosophy were still thriving at W. L. Gore & Associates—not just in the U.S. operations, but in several of its divisions around the world.

NOTES

1. Gary Hamel with Bill Breen, *The Future of Management* (Boston: Harvard Business School Press, 2007), p. 85.

2. W. L. Gore & Associates, Inc., "Working in Our Unique Culture," W. L. Gore & Associates Web site, http://www.gore.com/en_xx/careers/whoweare/ourculture/gore-company-culture.html, accessed March 10, 2012.

3. Rebecca Serwer, "Creating Competitive Advantage in Today's Labor Market: Lessons Learned from Three Model Companies" (Master of Professional Studies thesis, University of Denver University College, 2008), p. 54.

4. W. L. Gore & Associates, Inc., "Gore Locations Worldwide," W. L. Gore & Associates Web site, http://www.gore.com/en_xx/aboutus/locations/index.html, accessed March 19, 2012.

5. W. L. Gore & Associates, Inc., "About Gore," W. L. Gore & Associates Web site, http://www.gore.com/en_xx/aboutus/index.html, accessed March 9, 2012.

6. Hamel, p. 86.

7. "Dr. Roy J. Plunkett, Discoverer of Fluoropolymers," obituary, *The Fluoropolymers Division Newsletter*, Summer 1994, p. 1, available at http://www.fluoropolymers.org/news/PlunkArt94.pdf, accessed March 10, 2012.

8. Alan G. Robinson and Sam Stern, *Corporate Creativity: How Innovation and Improvement Actually Happen* (San Francisco: Berrett-Koehler, 1998), p. 177.

9. Hamel, p. 85.

10. Robinson and Stern, pp. 177–178.

11. W. L. Gore & Associates, Inc., "Our History," W. L. Gore & Associates Web site, http://www.gore.com/timeline/, accessed March 10, 2012.

12. Hamel, p. 85.

13. W. L. Gore & Associates, Inc., "Our History," W. L. Gore & Associates Web site, http://www.gore.com/timeline/, accessed March 10, 2012.

14. Ibid.

15. W. L. Gore & Associates, Inc., "About Gore," W. L. Gore & Associates Web site, http://www.gore.com/en_xx/aboutus/index.html, accessed March 10, 2012.

16. Terri Kelly, "Nurturing a Vibrant Culture to Drive Innovation," talk given on December 9, 2008 at Wong Auditorium, MIT Sloan School of Management, Cambridge, MA, available from MIT World video collection, http://mitworld.mit.edu/video/643, accessed March 9, 2012.

17. Hamel, p. 85.

18. Ibid., p. 86.

19. Abraham Maslow, "A Theory of Human Motivation," *Psychological Review, 50*: 376–390.

20. Douglas McGregor, *The Human Side of Enterprise* (New York: McGraw-Hill, 1960).

21. "The Lattice Organization" (slide presentation), (Newark, DE: W. L. Gore & Associates, Inc., n.d.), p. 13, available at http://www.boozersclass.org/Gore_lattice.pdf, accessed April 10, 2011.

22. Ibid., p. 2.

23. W. L. Gore & Associates, Inc., "Our Culture," W. L. Gore & Associates Web site, http://www.gore.com/en_xx/aboutus/culture/index.html, accessed March 10, 2012.

24. W. L. Gore & Associates, Inc., "Working in Our Unique Culture," W. L. Gore & Associates Web site, http://www.gore.com/en_xx/careers/whoweare/ourculture/gore-company-culture.html, accessed March 19, 2012.

25. Hamel, p. 93.

26. Alan Deutschman, "The Fabric of Creativity," *Fast Company*, December 19, 2007, http://www.fastcompany.com/magazine/89/open_gore.html?page=0%2C1, accessed March 12, 2012.

27. Simon Caulkin, "Gore-Tex Gets Made Without Managers," *The Observer*, November 2, 2008, http://www.guardian.co.uk/business/2008/nov/02/gore-tex-textiles-terri-kelly, accessed March 10, 2012.

28. Ibid.

29. Kelly, "Nurturing a Vibrant Culture."

30. W. L. Gore & Associates, Inc., "What We Believe," W. L. Gore & Associates Web site, http://www.gore.com/en_xx/careers/whoweare/whatwebelieve/gore-culture.html, accessed March 10, 2012.

31. Kelly, "Nurturing a Vibrant Culture."

32. Jeffrey Hollender, "Inventing the Future of Management: Part IV," JeffreyHollenderPartners: The Next Generation of Business, http://www.jeffreyhollender.com/?p=309, accessed March 10, 2012.

33. Deutschman, "The Fabric of Creativity," p. C2.

34. Hamel, p. 88.

35. Ibid.

36. Ibid., p. 92.

37. Hamel, p. 88.

38. Kelly, "Nurturing a Vibrant Culture."

39. Hamel, p. 89.

40. Ibid.

41. Kelly, "Nurturing a Vibrant Culture."

42. Hamel, p. 89.

43. Kelly, "Nurturing a Vibrant Culture."

44. Paraphrased by casewriter from Kelly, "Nurturing a Vibrant Culture."

45. Business jargon for going it alone on decisions rather than consulting and including others in setting priorities and objectives. Based on a fictional character of radio and television shows, although the business connotation is a reductionist version of the character's ethic. See http://en.wikipedia.org/wiki/Lone_Ranger.

46. Deutschman, p. C2.

47. Kelly, "Nurturing a Vibrant Culture."

48. Hamel, p. 91.

49. Deutschman, p. C2.

50. Hamel, p. 90.

51. Deutschman, p. C2.

52. Deutschman, p. C3.

53. Ann Harrington, "Who's Afraid of a New Product? Not W. L. Gore. It Has Mastered the Art of Storming Completely Different Businesses," *Fortune*, November 10, 2003, available at http://money.cnn.com/magazines/fortune/fortune_archive/2003/11/10/352851/index.htm, accessed March 18, 2012.

54. Ibid.

55. Hamel, p. 91.

56. Harrington.

57. Ibid.

58. Hamel, p. 96.

59. Kelly, "Nurturing a Vibrant Culture."

60. Harrington.

61. Ibid.

62. Hamel, p. 95.

63. Emily Walzer, "Ingredients for Innovation," *Textile Insight*, May/June 2010, p. 18, available at http://www.gore.com/MungoBlobs/861/698/TextileInsightW_L_Gore.pdf, accessed March 18, 2012.

64. Deutschman, p. C4.

65. Hamel, p. 95.

66. Lindsay Hunt, "W. L. Gore, MarketBuster," p. 2, available at http://www.marketbusting.com/casestudies/WL%20Gore.pdf, accessed March 18, 2012.

67. Harrington.

68. Deutschman, p. C3.

69. Hamel, p. 92.

70. Dawn Anfuso, "1999 Optimas Award Profile W. L. Gore and Associates Inc.," *Workforce*, March 1, 1999, available at http://www.workforce.com/article/19990301/NEWS02/303019952, accessed March 18, 2012.

71. Kelly, "Nurturing a Vibrant Culture."

72. Anfuso.

73. Kelly, "Nurturing a Vibrant Culture."

74. Ibid.

75. Kelly, "Nurturing a Vibrant Culture."

76. Tina Nielsen, "WL Gore (Company Profile)," *Director*, February 2, 2010, http://www.director.co.uk/magazine/2010/2_Feb/WLGore_63_06.html, accessed April 4, 2012.

NAME INDEX

Fitzsimmons, J., 31
Fjeldstad, O.D., 35, 138
Flammer, C., 169
Flannery, R., 4, 127, 197
Flatten, T.C., 376, 409
Fleury, A., 170
Fleury, M., 170
Flint, D.J., 137
Flint, J., 400
Flores, M., 438
Flores, R.G., 72
Florou, G., 140
Flynn, A., 273
Folta, T.B., 31, 199, 201, 379
Fong, E.A., 340
Fonseca, M.A., 304
Foo, M.-D., 438
Foo, S., 71
Forberg, L., 330
Forbes, D.P., 102, 169
Ford, J.D., 103
Ford, L.W., 103
Ford, R.C., 170
Forest, S.A., 201
Fornes, G., 273
Foroohr, R., 11
Foroudi, P., 104
Fortuna, N., 439
Fortune, A., 234
Fosfuri, A., 73
Foss, N.J., 34, 71, 268, 375–376, 378, 413, 438
Foster, R.N., 101
Fourne, S.L., 137, 169, 268
Fracassi, C., 200
Francis, B., 233
Francis, J., 269
Francoeur, C., 105
Frank, D.H., 200
Franklin, J., 209
Frankly, A., 168
Frattini, M., 271
Frazer, L., 304
Frazier, G., 199
Freeman, K., 104
Freeman, R.E., 168, 198, 376, 414
Freer, M., 21
Freitas, E., 32, 270
Frey, B.S., 336
Friedman, T., 31
Friesl, M., 414
Fritz, B., 437
Froese, F.J., 72, 268
Frost, A.C., 339
Frow, P., 105
Frown, P.E., 137
Fry, E., 270
Fry, L.W., 34
Fu, L.J., 342, 343
Fu, W., 305
Fu, X., 137, 273
Fuentelsaz, L., 72, 199

Fujino, Michimasas, 434
Fukase, A., 206
Fukui, E.T., 73
Fulmer, I.S., 202
Funk, C.A., 137
Funk, R., 440
Furchtgott-Roth, H., 230
Furlan, A., 72, 140
Furr, N.R., 32, 34, 72, 106, 137, 139, 168–169, 171, 375, 440
Futterman, M., 261

G

Gaba, V., 441
Gabrielsson, M., 271
Gabrielsson, P., 271
Gaddis Rose, D., 31
Gaffney, N., 36
Gage, D., 78
Galan, J.L., 169, 305
Galan Gonzalez, J.L., 34
Galbreath, J., 73
Gallagher, D., 21, 137
Gallo, C., 18, 34
Galunic, D.C., 200
Galvin, B.M., 342
Galvin, P., 73
Gamache, D., 233
Gambardella, A., 101, 268, 306, 412
Gandel, S., 310, 336
Gangloff, K.A., 414
Gann, D.M., 31, 137, 376
Gannon, M.J., 170
Ganotakis, P., 270, 271
Ganter, A., 70, 409
Gantumur, T., 231
Gao, S., 442
Gara, A., 310, 341
Garces, M.I., 413
Garces-Ayerbe, C., 35
Garcia-Canal, E., 106, 139
Garcia-Castro, R., 34, 105, 336
Garcia-Cestona, M., 338
Garcia-Prieto, P., 105, 269
Garcia-Quevedo, J., 230
Garcia-Sanchez, J., 31, 33, 136
Gardell, Christer, 330
Gardner, G., 395
Gardner, H.K., 441
Garg, S., 32, 70, 71, 339, 440
Garg, V.K., 71, 73, 304, 378
Garner, J.L., 200
Garrett, R., 376
Garrette, B., 304, 380
Garrido, E., 72
Gary, M., 102–103
Garza, A.S., 36
Garza-Gomex, X., 337
Gasparro, A., 40, 110, 137, 139, 199, 272, 349, 377
Gassman, O., 379
Gates, S., 104, 233, 303

Gaur, A., 198, 230, 268, 272
Gavetti, G., 169
Gedajlovic, E.R., 268, 337
Geier, B., 191
Gelabert, L., 73
Gelb, B.D., 35, 201
Geldes, C., 305
Gelfand, M.J., 414
Gelhard, C., 33
Gemser, G., 441
Gentry, R.J., 104, 339, 440
Gentry, W.A., 409
George, G., 31, 105, 139, 168, 302, 305, 376, 379, 439
George, R., 338
Geppert, M., 303
Gerakos, J.J., 338, 340
Gerasymenko, V., 376
Gerfield, S., 437
Gergaud, O., 73
Gerhard Dijkstra, S., 170
Gerhart, B., 202
Germain, R.N., 305
Germano, S., 139, 266
Geron, T., 229
Gerschewski, S., 270
Geyskens, I., 106
Ghauri, P.N., 268
Ghemawat, P., 270
Ghobadian, A., 233, 270, 272
Ghosh, A., 340
Ghosh, C., 327
Ghoshal, S., 271
Giachetti, C., 74, 167
Giacomin, J., 139
Gianidodis, P.T., 441
Giannetti, M., 376
Giarratana, M.S., 33, 139, 198, 268, 271
Giddings, J., 304
Giersch, C., 272, 273
Gietzmann, M., 140, 339
Gigerenzer, G., 103
Gilad, B., 70
Gilbert, B.A., 30, 102, 114, 119, 124, 198, 201, 306, 378, 437
Gilbert, C., 101
Gilley, K.M., 340
Gillis, W.E., 304, 380
Gilsing, V., 380
Gilson, S.C., 379
Gimeno, J., 31, 102, 138, 169, 170, 199, 200
Gino, F., 377, 409, 441
Gioia, D.A., 34, 414
Girma, S., 341
Girod, S., 270
Givray, H.S., 409
Glaister, K.W., 105
Glazer, E., 336, 340
Gleason, K.C., 338
Glick, W.H., 31

Globerman, S., 273
Glunk, U., 409
Glusac, E., 30
Gnan, L., 338
Goddard, C.R., 273
Goel, V., 104
Goergen, M., 235
Goerzen, A., 74, 381
Gold, S., 380
Goldstein, S.M., 34
Goleman, D., 409
Golesorkhi, S., 380
Goll, I., 74
Golovko, E., 170, 270
Gomes, E., 233
Gomez, J., 102, 103, 199
Gomez-Mejia, L.R., 73, 198, 337, 339, 340, 341
Gomulya, D., 343, 414
Gong, Y., 32, 269
Gonzalez, J.L.G., 171, 442
Gonzalez-Benito, J., 138
Gonzalez-Cruz, T.F., 378
Gonzalez-Rodriguez, M.R., 409
Goold, M., 198, 200, 377
Gopalan, N., 375
Goranova, M., 35, 331, 338–339
Gordon-Bloomfield, N., 288
Gore, J., 340
Goritz, A.S., 414
Gorovaia, N., 305
Goswami, G.G., 272
Goteman, I., 139
Goto, M., 71
Gotsopoulos, A., 137
Gottfredson, M., 33
Gottfredson, R.K., 412
Gottfried, M., 174, 198, 200
Gottschalg, O., 234
Goudreau, J., 71
Gouillart, F.J., 137
Gove, S., 102, 137, 168, 201, 231
Govindarajan, V., 127, 409
Gozubuyuk, R., 71, 380
Grace, D., 304
Graebner, M.E., 199, 232, 233, 442
Graefe, A., 71
Graffin, S.D., 233, 340, 409, 411
Grant, C., 186
Gray, D., 140, 268
Greckhamer, T., 73
Greco, J., 378
Green, H., 137
Green, S.G., 441
Greene, K., 71
Greengard, S., 31
Greenwood, R., 269, 376
Greger, C., 409, 412
Gregersen, H.B., 438
Gregoire, D.A., 274
Gregoric, A., 343
Grenness, T., 72

COMPANY INDEX

SUBJECT INDEX